THE TEACHER'S COMMENTARY

The TEACHER'S COMMENTARY

LAWRENCE O. RICHARDS

VICTOR BOOKS®
A DIVISION OF SCRIPTURE PRESS PUBLICATIONS INC.
USA CANADA ENGLAND

9 10 Printing/Year 94 93

Unless otherwise noted, Scripture quotations are from the *Holy Bible, New International Version,* © 1973, 1978, 1984, International Bible Society. Used by permission of Zondervan Bible Publishers; other quotations are from the *New American Standard Bible* (NASB), © the Lockman Foundation 1960, 1962, 1963, 1968, 1971, 1972, 1973, 1975, 1977; *The Living Bible* (TLB), © 1971, Tyndale House Publishers, Wheaton, IL 60189. Used by permission; J.B. Phillips: *The New Testament in Modern English,* Revised Edition (PH), © J.B. Phillips, 1958, 1960, 1972, permission of Macmillian Publishing Co. and Collins Publishers; the *King James Version* (KJV).

Recommended Dewey Decimal Classification: 220.7

Suggested Subject Headings: BIBLE, COMMENTARY

Library of Congress Catalog Card Number: 87-81010

ISBN: 0-89693-810-7

The charts, maps, and diagrams in this book are intended for use by the teacher. They may be copied and used by teachers in a classroom setting.

VICTOR BOOKS
A division of Scripture Press Publications, Inc.
Wheaton, Illinois 60187

Contents

Preface

The Bible is an exciting and enriching Book. It is a privilege to study, and an even greater privilege to teach.

For years now I've felt a need for a commentary just for teachers. A commentary that will guide a teacher to understand the broader meaning of any passage or story he or she might teach, and that will also contain ideas to help that teacher communicate life-changing truth to learners of every age. It has been a joy to work with Victor Books and its fine editorial staff to create just such a commentary.

I have had the privilege over the years of teaching every passage covered in this commentary—to graduate students at Wheaton College, to adult classes and home Bible studies in several churches, and often to boys and girls directly and through Sunday School curriculum.

If this commentary enriches your study as you prepare to teach, stimulates your creativity, and helps you experience the joy to be found in sharing God's Word with others, it will fulfill my greatest desires.

Lawrence O. Richards
Florida, 1987

Explanation of Symbols

Because this commentary is written for teachers, it has special features that are included for those who are using it to teach a class. The ▶ symbol indicates a word or phrase that is defined to help you better understand the lesson. The ■ symbol points to the pages in the Victor *Bible Knowledge Commentary* (2 vols.) where you can turn to get a more detailed, verse-by-verse commentary of the passage you are teaching. The ♥ symbol indicates teaching tips for either children or youth and adults that will be helpful in teaching the passage to the age-group you work with.

Old Testament Overview

One series of Sunday School lessons for older children tells them to look at parts of the Bible as a myth, a "story made up to explain something mysterious in days when people knew no science, and did not know the cause of things like thunder or mountains." According to this view, much of the Old Testament is legendary or mythical, particularly Genesis. The same writer dismisses the Flood story and explains the rainbow "myth" by saying, "We now know what causes rainbows and we do not think of God as a warrior with a great war bow. But this story shows us how the Jews, a very long time ago, tried to explain this mysterious thing they saw at times in the sky."

To that lesson writer, the difficult elements in the Old Testament are to be dismissed as myth or legend, or as true-to-life, but made-up stories.

Man's Word, or God's?

Such a view of the Bible is not unusual. Many people start from the assumption that Scripture is best viewed as human groping after God, or even as the best insights of truly religious people. But those who hold this view must also hold open the possibility that the writers of Scripture were wrong, that their ideas might be false, and their stories fiction. If the Bible merely represents man's best efforts to understand the universe, there is no real reason why the Scriptures have any authority now.

But are the Scriptures simply human documents? Certainly the authors of Bible books did not think of Old or New Testament writings as merely the thoughts of men. Over 2,600 times in the Old Testament alone the writers claim to be speaking or writing not their words, but God's! "The word of the Lord came to Jeremiah. . . . Thus saith the Lord. . . . Hear the word of the Lord." These men had no doubts about what they were reporting. They firmly believed that they recorded messages from God to man.

This is the view of the New Testament as well. One passage says it plainly. In 1 Corinthians 2:9-13 we're told that God has communicated to us what we could never discover for ourselves, or even imagine. God has revealed His very thoughts through His Holy Spirit.

This certainly was Jesus' view. He spoke of Creation and the Flood, of Jonah, and of the destruction of Sodom and Gomorrah. And He viewed them as historic events, not as myths. What's more, He saw events reported in the Old Testament as having a living, vital message for persons of every era, every age.

There's another striking thing that sets the Scriptures apart from the myths and legends that make up the folklore of other peoples. Not only are the sacred writings of the Jews historically accurate and factual, not only are these documents which trace Israel's heritage understood as divine revelation rather than human speculation, but these sacred writings are a *living* heritage. Through the Scriptures the God who spoke to men then speaks to believers today.

In a very special sense, our heritage in God's Word is contemporary as well as historical. To understand the Word of God and to be enriched by it, we have to come to the Bible as truth to be understood, and as a living Word from God addressed to us now.

The Old Testament is a vital part of our Christian heritage. It is the very root of our faith and our understanding of God as He reveals Himself to men. The Old Testament is a vital part of our living heritage. It is designed by God to speak to you and me, to transform our lives as we respond to Him.

This is the emphasis of the Apostle Paul, as he looked back at one Hebrew generation and said, "These things happened to them as examples and were written down as warnings for us, on whom the fulfillment of the ages has come" (10:11). God ministered directly to that Old Testament generation. Now, in the record of those events, God ministers to us too.

In all that God said and did, in all that men of old experienced, we mine our own rich heritage. The Old Testament record was made and preserved across the millennia, for us.

Not Myth, Message

This, then, is the conviction we share as we prepare to teach the Old Testament. Each book is a message to us. Each book, including Genesis, is historical, reporting accurately events which actually happened in space and time, in the reality of our own universe. It is at the same time a focused revelation. The events recorded have been purposefully selected. The details included—and those left out—have been carefully chosen. The reasons behind the choice, the criteria of selection which gives the Old Testament its focus and which guides us as we plan to teach it, is the criteria of its message. God through His Word speaks carefully and clearly to you and me.

What the Bible records is history, but it is more than history. The events recorded, God's mighty acts as He intervened in the world, show us who He is and tell us of His ways. The Scriptures even go beyond reporting events: they explain in words the intentions and purposes, the emotions and concerns, which moved God to His acts. In this way the Bible is an important blend; it shows us God in action, then reveals His very thoughts and intentions.

When we realize this, we come face-to-face with a great wonder. The Bible involves both *propositional revelation* (objective statements of truth expressed in words) and *personal revelation* (contact with God Himself, not merely with ideas about Him). When we read or teach about what God has done in history, and when we learn His thoughts and motives, God Himself meets with us. We are introduced to Him; He speaks to us. Through His Word faith draws us into personal relationship with Him. As we respond in obedience, our relationship grows and deepens even more.

So the message of Scripture involves communication of truth about God and revelation of God Himself as a Person. As you and I trace God's dealings with His people across the centuries, we come to know Him better. And we can come to know Him well.

Because of the nature of God's Word our approach to both study and teaching is dramatically affected. As we teach we remember that:

**The Old Testament is to be approached as the very Word of God.* It is not a record of human speculation, but is a divine, verbal (in words) revelation.

**The Old Testament is to be approached as living history.* The events recorded are historical. But the record speaks to you and to me today.

**The Old Testament is to be approached as God's message.* Everything here is focused, selected to tell us about God and His intentions. We are to look for the message in recorded events.

**The Old Testament is to be approached as God's personal self-revelation.* We not only find truth about God; we meet God face-to-face in His Word. We are to open our hearts to Him, eager to see His face, ready to respond as He speaks to us.

**The Old Testament is to be approached from the vantage point provided by Christ.* The New Testament is a divine commentary on the Old. We need to see the Old Testament as true, yet not complete. It is Jesus and the New Testament which bring the Old Testament into perspective.

What happens when we take the stand of faith and adopt these perspectives in studying and teaching the Old Testament?

What happens is that we discover our heritage. We find identity in the faith we share with all who have trusted God. We sink our roots deep into the realization of who God is. And, knowing God better, we are strengthened to live each day with joy. All this is our heritage. All this is our ministry, as we teach the Old Testament to children, to youth, and to adults.

The Old Testament in Brief
Genesis, the first book of the Old Testament, is extremely rich. In a sense, Genesis provides an overview of the whole Old Testament.

In its message, Genesis presents two strong and distinct themes. The first, the emphasis of chapters 1–11, affirms that we live in a *personal universe*. The physical universe is the creation and design of a Person. Human beings are distinct from the rest of animate and inanimate creation, shaped to fit within the framework of both physical and spiritual reality. There is no hint in Genesis or the rest of the Old Testament of the pagan ideas that personify the inanimate. Sun and moon are not "gods" who made the earth, or from whose substance animal life sprang. There is the strongest denial of the similar modern fiction that life somehow generated spontaneously from nonliving matter and gradually evolved from simple, single cells into the complex and many forms of life we know today.

No, a personal God is introduced in Genesis, and it is He who reveals Himself in the whole Old Testament. He is the ultimate reality, distinct from and yet the ground of being of all that exists. Everything in our lives must be understood in the light of His personality and His purposes.

Hearing the message in Genesis, and seeing it developed in the entire Old Testament, we come to understand ourselves and to sense our destinies. We learn to value ourselves as special to God, not merely another of the animals. As the objects of God's love, we take our place as heirs of all He has made.

God has made a personal universe. And He has placed us as persons in it; the objects of His love, and the center of His purposes.

There is another message, an emphasis found in chapters 12–50. The second message is that we live in a *purposive universe*. The personal God who shaped all that exists remains involved. He gives His creation direction and purpose. God has a plan that gives shape and meaning to all of history, a plan that helps us understand ourselves and the human condition. Understanding that plan gives us security, even when wars and crime and tragedy mar our contemporary world. Starting with this second message of the Book of Genesis, all Bible history begins to take shape and form.

Genesis 1–11 focuses our attention on God's *personal universe*. The basic issues of life are summarized here. God creates humanity in His image (chaps. 1–2). Sin brings death and suffering (chaps. 3–4). God demonstrates that He must judge sin (chaps. 6–9), yet is willing to deliver those who like Noah trust in Him. Each of these themes is woven again and again through the Old Testament, giving us a biblical perspective on reality.

Overview of the Old Testament

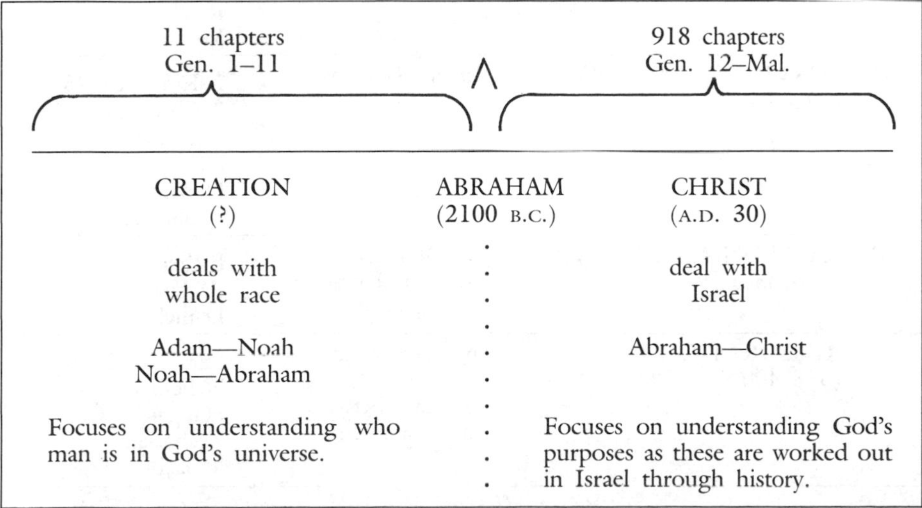

I. PRIMEVAL PERIOD	CREATION Creation to Abraham	Genesis 1–11 Job
II. PATRIARCHAL PERIOD (2166–1446)	COVENANT Abraham to Moses	Genesis 12–50
III. EXODUS PERIOD (1446–1406)	LAW Moses' Leadership	Exodus Numbers Leviticus Deuteronomy
IV. CONQUEST OF CANAAN (1406–1390)	CONQUEST Joshua's Leadership	Joshua
V. TIME OF JUDGES (1367–1050)	JUDGES No Leadership	Judges Ruth 1 Samuel 1–7
VI. UNITED KINGDOM (1050–931)	KINGDOM Monarchy Established	1 Samuel 8–30 2 Samuel 1 Kings 1–11 1 Chronicles 2 Chronicles 1–9
	Establishment (David)	Psalms
	Decline (Solomon)	Ecclesiastes Proverbs Song of Solomon
VII. DIVIDED KINGDOM (931–722) Israel Elijah Elisha Judah	PROPHETIC MOVEMENT Two Kingdoms	1 Kings 12–22 2 Kings 1–17 2 Chronicles 10–29 Isaiah Hosea Joel Amos Obadiah Jonah Micah
VIII. SURVIVING KINGDOM (722–586)	Judah Remains	2 Kings 18–25 2 Chronicles 30–36 Jeremiah Nahum Habakkuk Zephaniah
IX. BABYLONIAN CAPTIVITY (586–538)	JUDGMENT Torn from Palestine	Esther Ezekiel Daniel
X. RESTORATION (538–400)	The Jews Return 400 Years between the Testaments	Ezra Nehemiah Haggai Zechariah Malachi

Bible History Periods

Genesis 12–Malachi shifts from consideration of the whole human race to trace the development of God's purposes as these are expressed in God's covenant-promises to Abraham. We are launched in Genesis on an adventure that lasts through the centuries, always moving toward fulfillment in Christ.

It's clear, as the bulk of the Old Testament is given to exploring God's purposes, that the Lord wants us to understand what He has done and what He intends to do. In fact, as we look through the Old Testament we will find at least three overarching purposes of God. God has:

**A redemptive purpose.* Abraham's family is set aside as God's special people. Israel was in a sense a womb; a womb in which Jesus was formed. And Jesus is the Source of our salvation.

**A regal purpose.* The Old Testament prophets looked forward to a time when God will establish His sovereign rule and personal authority over our world. This purpose too will be fulfilled in Jesus, who as Israel's promised Messiah will one day rule over all the earth.

**A revelatory purpose.* God revealed Himself through the Old Testament writings given to Abraham's family, and through Israel to the world. In the written Word God continues to reveal Himself to us. So the knowledge of God was also given to us through Abraham's family.

As we study the Old Testament we will often see the outworking of these three dominating purposes of God, and will be drawn closer to Him as we sense in each purpose His great and wonderful love.

An Outline of Old Testament History

Our study of the Old Testament is broken down into units which help us to trace the unfolding of God's purposes through history. The 929 chapters of the Old Testament span some thousand years of history. That history can be divided into 10 historic periods. Each period reflects a step in the unfolding of God's purposes. Each is associated with specific books of the Old Testament. The chart on page 16 outlines these historic time periods, and identifies the emphasis of each. You can use the chart for your reading and teaching of the Old Testament. By seeing where each Old Testament passage fits into the sacred history you can immediately relate that passage to God's unfolding purpose and to His message to humankind.

Studying and teaching the Old Testament can be tremendously exciting. Every story has its message, not only in itself, but in the grand scope of God's revealed purposes. Each event shows us more about the Lord, and teaches us how to respond to Him. In studying the Old Testament together we will come to understand God's purposes more clearly. We will come to know God in a deeper, more personal way. And we will grow in our awareness of what it means to be Christian in every aspect of our lives.

Using This Commentary in Your Teaching

The Teacher's Commentary is designed specifically for those who teach the Word of God, to children, to youth, and to adults. It will help you in several specific ways.

**It provides vital background.* This commentary takes a "survey" rather than a "verse-by-verse" approach. Survey deals with the "big picture" rather than with details: it tries to help you see the forest as well as individual trees. You may be teaching a Bible story that takes up just a few paragraphs in the Old Testament. What survey does is place that story in the vital context of God's purposes and of the basic message of the Bible book or historical period. You'll find that this commentary gives you a sense of confidence in teaching, for it gives you a broad understanding of the deeper significance of the specific story or passage you must teach.

**It provides spiritual enrichment.* Your own spiritual growth is important if you are to have a spiritual impact on those you teach. This commentary is designed to enrich you spiritually by helping you apply God's truth to your own life. It goes beyond giving you facts about the Old Testament and helps you sense the personal meaning of God's Word for your own as well as your students' lives.

**It explains key words and events.* Special features give succinct definition of key theological terms and the meaning of historic events. You'll understand more about the real meaning of

Bible words as those words were used in the historical context.

**It provides teaching ideas.* Link-to-life ideas show you how to communicate the Bible's message to children, to youth, and to adults. These are not intended to replace Sunday School curriculum, but to supplement what you'll find in your lesson material, and to give you fresh, creative ideas for making God's Word clear and relevant.

**It can be taught as Bible survey.* Each of the 174 units in this commentary is concluded with a lesson plan, suggesting ways to teach the material to a youth or adult class. You can use this commentary as a resource for teaching a short course on any Old or New Testament book, a full quarter course on a theme like the minor prophets or Matthew's Gospel, or even as a three-and-one-half-year survey of the entire Bible! You can use it as a guide for teaching in Sunday School, or in a weekday Bible Study group.

In all these ways *The Teacher's Commentary* is different from the typical commentary. As you prepare to teach from the Old Testament or from the New you'll want to turn first to this commentary that has been designed just for you, the teacher. You'll teach with confidence and with enthusiasm, for you will have a better understanding of the Word of God, and a deeper sense of its personal meaning for you and for your class.

STUDY GUIDE 1

Genesis 1

HE MADE OUR WORLD TO BE LIVED IN

Overview

Genesis 1–11 affirms that you and I live in a *personal universe*. The material and moral world were designed by a Person, who made mankind distinct from the rest of Creation. There is no hint here of the pagan notion that objects (like the sun or moon) are "gods." There is no hint of the modern fiction that life was generated spontaneously from nonliving matter, to gradually evolve from single cells into the complex forms we know today. Genesis sets forth a personal God as the ultimate reality. He is the root and source of all that exists.

Genesis 12–50 emphasizes another message. We live in a *purposive universe*. These chapters tell the story of God's call of Abraham, and God's unveiling in the Abrahamic Covenant of a divine plan and purpose to history. We can outline Genesis by these two themes:

I. A Personal Universe (Gen. 1–11)
II. A Purposive Universe (Gen. 12–50)

▶ ***Create.*** The Hebrew word *bara'* is used only of *God's activity in initiating a thing or project*. The Bible teaches that God initiated (created) the universe, humanity, forgiveness, and new life for sinners.

■ See the *Bible Knowledge Commentary* (Victor) pages 15-26 for a thorough discussion of the date, authorship, and nonmythical nature of Genesis.

Commentary

Genesis 1 isn't the only source of our conviction that God is Creator. Both Old and New Testaments teach the essential integrity of all we read in Genesis. Both help us explore the meaning of Genesis' towering affirmations about God and the world which we meet first in this initial chapter of our Bible.

One of the most striking additions is in Isaiah: "For Jehovah created the heavens and earth and put everything in place, and He made the world to be lived in, not to be an empty chaos" (Isa. 45:18, TLB). The universe was shaped for a purpose: to be the home of humankind. However vast our expanding universe may be, God cares most about living beings, not inanimate matter. Psalm 104 reviews God's creative act and praises Him for forming our world as a habitation for "living things both great and small." The psalmist's heart fills with wonder as he realizes:

> These all look to You to give them their food at the proper time. When You give it to them, they gather it up; when You open Your hand, they are satisfied with good things. When You hide Your face, they are terrified; when You take away their breath, they die and return to the dust. When You send Your Spirit, they are created; and You renew the face of the earth.
>
> Psalm 104:27-30

The psalmist concludes, "Praise God forever! How He must rejoice in all His works!" (v. 31, TLB)

♥ ***Link to Life: Youth / Adult***
God's people have been captivated from earliest times by the witness of the universe to our Lord. How have they responded? Look in Job 38; Psalms 104; 148; and Isaiah 40. Meditate on God as Creator, then express your own heart response to Him as did these authors of Scripture.

The Personal Touch

When we teach the familiar Creation story, it's important for us to adopt the attitude of the psalmist. The psalmist acknowledges God as Creator. He knows the story of the seven days. But as the psalmist meditates, his thoughts are not drawn off to speculations about, "How?" Instead, the psalmist moves quickly beyond the "scientific" questions that so attract us to focus on the central message: All that exists is the work of a Person. Everything around us has been carefully and thoughtfully designed. Creation is a mirror, placed to reflect our thoughts and our worship back to the Person whose image Creation enables us to see.

This is the central message of Genesis 1. Our attention is directed not to the world, but to its Maker. The psalmist, recognizing this, exults, "I will sing to the Lord as long as I live. I will praise God to my last breath! May He be pleased by all these thoughts about Him, for He is the source of all my joy" (Ps. 104:33-34, TLB).

♥ ***Link to Life: Children***
You can help children respond to God with praise for His creation. Begin with a nature walk, asking the boys and girls to look for things that are beautiful, and things they especially like. On return teach them the hymn "For the Beauty of the Earth" (in most church hymnals). After learning the first two verses, work as a class to construct a third verse, featuring the things your children liked and thought of as beautiful.

Old and New Testaments agree that Creation gives a compelling witness to God. Psalm 19 points out that the universe itself is a wordless message about God which anyone, whatever his language, can hear.

> The heavens declare the glory of God; the skies proclaim the work of His hands. Day after day they pour forth speech; night after night they display knowledge. There is no speech or language where their voice is not heard. Their voice goes out into all the earth, their words to the ends of the world.
> Psalm 19:1-4

Paul made this same point in Romans 1. But there Paul saw Creation as evidence to be used against those who do not believe. Paul argued that man's wickedness is revealed in the human struggle to suppress the knowledge of God available to all in creation. "What may be known about God is plain to them," the New Testament affirms, "because God has made it plain to them. For since the Creation of the world God's invisible qualities—His eternal power and divine nature—have been clearly seen, being understood from what has been made, so that men are without excuse" (vv. 19-20). Creation is such compelling proof of God's existence, and such a clear reflection of His character, that any explanation of beginnings which rules God out serves only to underline human perversity.

It is striking to trace attempts to explain the material universe apart from God. In the culture from which Abraham sprang, the ancients imagined that the material universe was rooted in a great waste of waters, sweet water and salt water, personified in myth as two gods, male and female. Creation began as intercourse between this pair. Then war arose between the parents and their children, viewed as secondary gods. One of these lesser gods killed the original father, but the original female was a much greater threat. However, the hero god, Marduk, was elected leader and overthrew her, ultimately shaping earth and sky from her dead body. The epic poem, "Enuma Elish," telling this story reports:

> Then the lord paused to view her dead body.
> That he might divide the monster and do artful works
> He split her like a shellfish into two parts;
> Half of her he set up and called it sky.

For decades liberal scholars have noted slight similarities between this Babylonian myth and the Genesis Creation story. They suggested that the stories sprang from a common origin and share a common character. Yet Henry Frankfort, in *Before Philosophy* (Penguin Books), observed that fundamental pagan assumptions about the world were "in fact universally accepted by the peoples of the ancient world *with the single exception of the Hebrews.*"

In reality there are so many fundamental differences between ancient concepts of Creation and the Scripture, which insists that God be understood as the One who made the material universe from nothing and who remains distinct from it, that Genesis can hardly be explained by appeal to some supposed common cultural heritage! The Bible's teaching about God and Creation is explained only by the fact that, in His Word, God speaks. God has cut through the distorted notions of fallen humanity about this world and about Him, to show us a totally different vision of reality.

Even today, men continue their attempts to explain God away and to find a different face in the mirror of Creation. These attempts are a striking reversal of the Babylonian myths. While the ancients saw the material universe as the remains of once-living gods, moderns suggest that life sprang from dead and inert matter!

How could it have happened? Somehow in the great shallow seas life, it is said, was spawned. Over the eons, life forms grew more complex. The single cell multiplied, differentiating into eye and lung and brain and blood and bone. Never mind the fact that biologists "know of no other way than random mutation by which new hereditary variation comes into being" (C.H. Waddington, *The Nature of Life*, Athenium). Ignore the fact that "there is a delicate balance between an organism and its environment which a mutation can easily upset" so that "one could as well expect that altering the position of the brake or gas pedal at random would improve the operation of an automobile" (Frederick S. Hulse, *The Human Species*, Random House). Today, as in the ancient world, the urge persists to find some explanation for man and the universe, but an explanation which leaves out God.

Yet reason and revelation both bear witness. You and I live in *God's* universe. As we teach this wonderful passage we do so with the attitude of the psalmist, who acknowledged God, and who worshiped and praised the Lord for His wonderful creative works.

♥ ***Link to Life: Youth / Adult***
What difference does it really make if the universe has its origin in God, or if lifeless matter is the source of our existence? Jot down the following two lists of words: (1) cold, dead, lifeless, uncaring, and (2) warm, vital, loving, alive. Suppose that you or your group exist in a universe described by the first set of words. How will you feel about yourselves, about others, about your future, about what has value? Then suppose you exist in a universe characterized by the second set of words. Now how will you feel about yourself, others, about your future, about what has value? Compare conclusions. How wonderful that God has revealed to us the true nature of His universe, that we might have comfort and hope.

God of the Universe

Even the first few words of Genesis 1 convey concepts that are vast in their sweep and power.

"In the beginning." The Greeks had a cosmology of endless cycle. They thought that the universe was born in fire, cooled to shape the world they knew, but was destined to soon flare up again and then repeat the same cycle endlessly every 10,000 years. The life they knew was just another rerun of what had always been, and what would be again.

But God affirms a beginning. Genesis teaches a point in time at which an irreversible process began. We must go back to this origin if we are ever to grasp the nature of the world we live in, and the meaning of our individual lives.

"In the beginning God." This too is a powerful concept. Unlike men who struggle to find the meaning of life within the limits of the physical universe, we seek meaning by looking beyond material things to the Person of the Creator.

Others can attempt to explain themselves as the result of random surgings in a lifeless sea billions of years ago. But those who do so surrender the possibility of purpose and meaning for themselves as individuals. What meaning can be found in chance happenings in an impersonal universe? What meaning, when not only our individual lives flicker out after sparking briefly in the endless dark, but when mankind itself must look back to a mindless past and ahead to the certain dimming of our sun and the settling mantle of an eternal chill?

But Genesis 1 affirms *God.* God, a Person with mind and emotion and the power of choice, existed before the beginning. With the discovery of God the very character of the universe shifts and changes before our eyes. The ultimate reality is not random motion in dead, impersonal matter. The ultimate reality is a living, vital, personal Being. Life, not death, is the eternal ground of all that is.

You and I can find no meaning in a life

which has roots in the chance interplay of mindless atoms. But we can find meaning when we realize that our lives were given us by another living personality. If God exists, and God is the cause of the material world, then we can look for meaning in His purposes in creating.

"In the beginning God created." Here we find a special sense of comfort and joy. God did act, freely and from His own choice, to create. There *is* meaning to the universe, and a purpose to human life.

This is a particularly important thought. The Deists of eighteenth-century England, like the Aucas of modern South American jungles, had the notion of a "watchmaker God." They saw God as someone who wound up the universe like a clock, and then left it ticking, to run down, as he wandered off on other business, unconcerned about the toy he'd formed. But the Genesis portrait of Creation implies something far different. The complexity of what is made, the care God takes in shaping it, the purpose and design revealed, all show that God acted with a sense of purpose, making our world more meaningful than an abandoned toy.

"In the beginning God created the heavens and the earth." God stands behind it all. The God of Genesis is no platonic demiurge who, like a potter, merely shaped an already existing clay. The living God does not share His eternity with rock, or even with the billion stars that span our sky. The Source of all, the only and the ultimate reality, is God.

♥ ***Link to Life: Children***
Have your boys and girls make reminders of the love of God that shines through His creation. Let them make multiple pinpricks in black construction paper. This can be used to cover a small lampshade in a child's room. With the light on, dots of "starlight" will shine through the dark paper. With this project teach Psalm 148:1-6:

> *Praise the Lord from the heavens, praise Him in the heights above. Praise Him, all His angels, praise Him, all His heavenly hosts. Praise Him, sun and moon, praise Him, all you shining stars. Praise Him, you highest heavens and you waters above the skies. Let them praise the name of the Lord, for He commanded and they were created. He set them in place forever and ever; He gave a decree that will never pass away.*

I've shared these few thoughts, not because I intend to comment on each verse and phrase in Genesis 1, but to show how important it is not to pass on too quickly. We've read or heard these words a hundred times. Our very familiarity with them may blind us to the fact that this chapter, from its first words, expresses truths as powerful as any we might imagine.

We're not dealing here with "primitive myth." We're listening to the thoughts, the revelations, of God. We are invited into His heart and mind to find a clear expression of the deepest issues with which men can be concerned. And so we need to read and to listen—and to teach—well.

I suggested earlier that we might view the biblical story of Creation as a mirror; a mirror that reflects the person of God. How true this is of the first verses of this powerful Genesis chapter. In just a few short words God wiped away the mists that cloud the mirror and commands us to look at *Him*. "In the beginning God created the heavens and the earth."

What will you see as you read through this chapter, looking closely into the mirror to glimpse our God's features? You'll see many things that reveal what God is like.

You'll see, for instance, that God is a God of *order*. Isaiah said, "He made the world to be lived in, not to be an empty chaos" (Isa. 45:18, TLB).

Many have noted patterns within the days of Creation. Joseph Free (*Archeology and Bible History*, Scripture Press) notes the orderly progression of the process through each day:

1st, light	4th, light-bearers
2nd, firmament	5th, marine and aerial life
3rd, dry land	6th, land animals and man

Charles Pfeiffer (*The Biblical World*, Baker) suggests this pattern:

Work of Division	Works of Adorning
1st: light	4th: sun, moon, stars
2nd: air and sea	5th: birds, fish
3rd: land, plants	6th: animals and man

However we wish to express it, it's clear that in the Creation account there are distinct sequences and order. Chaos and randomness are rejected.

Several patterns you will find in Genesis 1 are tremendously revealing of who God is and what He is like.

Differentiation. Often our text says, "And God separated," as in, "He separated the light from the darkness" (v. 4). The Hebrew word here means "to make a distinction between." Light is distinguished from dark, earth from sea, day from night—as God sets up a stable pattern for His universe.

Dominion. Priority is also found in Creation. Genesis 1 speaks of rule and dominion. There is a difference in function, and some functions have a higher value or priority.

Diversity. The vast complexity and multiple forms of inanimate matter and of life are also revealing. From the uniqueness of each snowflake to the individuality shown in the animal world, God's delight in creative expression and His concern for individuals are shown.

Dependability. Through it all, in the alternation and pulse between night and day, season and season, God's consistency is clearly revealed.

Delight. And then we hear God's judgment: "It was good." In the pattern of the universe which God created we discover a God who we can trust because He clearly *cares.* He is not changeable or capricious, for He designed the world to be stable and orderly. We discover a God who values and, in valuing, chooses always to do that which is, in every way, good.

♥ ***Link to Life: Youth / Adult***
Explore Genesis 1 to discover these and other traits of God. Make a list of all you believe you can learn about Him from the actions reported here. Then see how many "because . . ." statements you can generate. For instance, "Because God is a Person who chooses to do what is good, I can trust myself and my life to Him." Or, "Because God is a Person who values individuals, I can be assured that I am special to Him."

Finally, Genesis 1 has a climax. Creation has a purpose beyond the pleasure expressing His character might give to the Lord. Creation is also an expression of love, for God designed the world as a gift to be given to the highest of His creations: humankind. And so the text tells us that God created man in His own image (a teaching we'll look at in the next study guide). And God determined to give man dominion over all He had made.

Thus the words repeated to Adam, "I give you . . ." stand as a benediction to the wonders revealed in Genesis 1. "I give you" is a benediction which marks God as One who cares for others; a benediction which is the Bible's first indication that the God of Creation is a God of love.

But, God

I suppose that it isn't strange, but when we read the first chapter of Genesis we sometimes find it hard to recapture the mood of the psalmist. We see the problems, the questions we want answered. We ignore God's great affirmation about Himself and our universe to pose the query, "But God, what about those 24-hour days? And, when did Creation really take place?"

The days. There have been many speculations offered which try to relate Genesis 1 to what we think we know about the origins of the universe. Suggestions about how to understand the "days" include:

1. The gap theory. This supposes an original Creation of order and beauty, ruined by Satan's fall. Genesis 1 describes a reconstruction. The name comes from the proposal of an ages-long gap between Genesis 1:1 (God created) and verse 2 (the earth was in chaos).

2. The indefinite age theory. This supposes that the term "day" is figurative; that, in fact, the creative activity of each day covers geologic eras. The "day" in which man appeared has not yet ended.

3. The Creation *in situ* theory. This suggests a Creation in 24-hour days, a short few thousand years ago. Coal, petroleum, and fossils were all created in place. The history in the fossil record is only "apparent."

4. The revelatory day theory. This supposes that God revealed His work to Moses in seven literal days. The evenings and the mornings mentioned in Genesis 1 were days in Moses' life, not actual days of Creation.

5. The literary device theory. This sug-

gests that the human author simply used "days" to organize his material. The facts are true, but not the framework.

6. The myth theory. This, the first theory not advanced by orthodox believers, suggests that the passage is not historical in any sense, but is symbolic. It contains only "theological" truths, not history.

There are many books and articles that argue for one or another of these theories. But the fact is, the text of Genesis and the doctrine of revelation do not seem to demand that we reject any of them except the last. Which is right? Our curiosity is not satisfied. God seems to care only that we look beyond the "how" to Him.

Dating. Dating the Creation has also generated endless speculation. Some 300 years ago an Irish bishop, Ussher, computed the date of Creation by studying the genealogies of Genesis. His conclusion? Creation took place in 4004 B.C. But by 1738 there had been over 200 known attempts to compute the date, with proposed times ranging from 3483 B.C. to 6984 B.C.

These attempts at dating assumed that the genealogies of the Bible were complete, and overlooked the Hebrew way of compressing genealogical records. For instance, compare Exodus 6:16-20 where there are only 4 links between Levi and Moses mentioned with 1 Chronicles 7:20-27 where 17 links are listed between a nephew of Levi (Ephraim) and Joshua. Clearly, the terms "son of" and "beget" are used in Hebrew literature in the sense of "descendant" and "progenitor" rather than of "child" and "parent."

Modern approaches to dating also fall short. For instance, we can accept Carbon-14 dating for antiquities of 7,000 to 10,000 B.C. in the Middle East. But this tells us nothing about the cosmic time scale, nor does it suggest when Creation might have taken place.

Somehow, Genesis does not seem concerned with the kind of questions we like to raise. It is enough for the writer of Genesis to affirm God. It is enough for the writer to show us that we human beings live today in a universe that can only be understood when we too affirm God.

Perhaps that should be enough for you and me too. Perhaps we should adopt the focus of Genesis 1, and the attitude of the psalmist. We are to look not to our instruments but to the clear witness of God which is provided by the vast and orderly universe in which we live.

We are to study and teach not to satisfy curiosity, but to enrich our own and others' wonder at and love for the God who gives us such a bright vision of Himself in this beautiful chapter of His trustworthy Word.

TEACHING GUIDE

Prepare

Prepare for study of Genesis 1 by reading Psalm 104:1-5, 33-34. Read these verses aloud; then silently as a prayer.

Explore

1. The study guide suggests that indications of what God is like are found in the Genesis report of Creation (such indications as evidence of His dependability, of His valuing, etc.). Locate these and as many other indications of God's character as you can find in the Old Testament text. The key to this inductive study activity is to look at the verbs which describe God's acts, and then reason back to what His actions suggest about the Lord.
2. Christian bookstores and church libraries often carry books that compare the biblical and modern "scientific" views of origins. When we study the evidence, we discover that Scripture's account better explains that evidence than does the secular, evolutionary view. If this is a concern of yours, or of group members, check out such books to read or to make available to your group.

Expand

1. The New Testament teaches that Jesus was the active Agent in Creation (cf. John 1:1-5; Col. 1:15-20). Read Genesis 1, substituting Jesus' name for "God." Does this help you sense Creation as a personal and loving act?
2. Make the two lists suggested in the "link-to-life" feature on page 21. Compare the lists, to sense how wonderful and how important God's revelation of Himself as Cre-

ator is to you and me today.
3. Write down as many "Because God is" statements as you can to express the difference that living in God's personal universe makes to human beings. See the "link-to-life" feature on page 23.

Apply

How we respond to God's revelation of Himself as Creator is an issue emphasized throughout the Bible. The unbeliever tries to suppress the evidence of God found in Creation, refusing to glorify God or give thanks to Him (cf. Rom. 1:21). We who believe joyfully acknowledge Him, glorifying Him with our praise and thanksgiving.

You can respond in these ways: in prayer, in music, by writing your own psalm, or by combining verses from Genesis 1 with psalms to build a worship liturgy to share in your church or group.

STUDY GUIDE 2

Genesis 2

IN THE IMAGE OF GOD

Overview

Genesis 2 answers a basic question. What is the origin and nature of human beings? The answer is that we human beings are the special creation of God, made in His image and likeness. Our special creation gives each human being individual worth and value. Because God made us, and made us like Himself, you and I are precious beings.

Genesis 2, then, lays the foundation for our understanding of ourselves and for our view of others. If human beings are special to God, we must learn to love others, and can love ourselves as well.

The rest of the Bible demonstrates how important human beings truly are to God. Despite man's fall into sin, God continues to love. The Bible is the history of redemption, of God reaching out to humankind to rescue and to save.

▶ ***Image and Likeness.*** When found together, as in Genesis 1:26; 5:1, 3, *selem* and *demut* make a theological statement about human nature, affirming that we bear a "likeness-image" to God. Like God we are persons, with an emotional, moral, and intellectual resemblance to our Creator.

▶ ***Rule.*** The Hebrew word in 1:28 is found 25 times in the Old Testament and is used of the rule of human beings rather than of God. It does suggest authority, but also implies responsibility. We are to care for God's earth, which He entrusted to humankind.

■ See the *Bible Knowledge Commentary,* pages 29-31 for a verse-by-verse discussion of the creation of human beings.

Commentary

Some time ago a book entitled *The Naked Ape* (Desmond Morris, Random House) received considerable attention. It was an attempt to explain human actions by comparing similarities between man and simian, and the author suggested that modern man's ills come from culture, the rejection of primitive reaction for socially programmed response. This was quickly followed by a book by a feminist who resented the ape transition in anthropology because it made man the hunter and woman the servant. She solved that problem by arguing that humanity evolved from a dolphinlike progenitor; in the setting of the seas, male and female roles would have been the same!

These books introduced nothing new in the long history of speculation about man's origins. The Greek philosopher Thales, who lived centuries before Christ, had already propounded the dolphin theory. He suggested that man had evolved from these intelligent mammals of the sea. And the supposed descent from simian ancestors has provided psychologists with a rich field for speculation. Particularly this supposed heritage was viewed as the source of a "vast, subconscious will, that acts out of a monstrous irrationality—an irrationality that has made it evolve its own enemy, rational consciousness" (Colin Wilson, *New Pathways in Psychology*, Taplinger, p. 95). This picture of the untamed animal in man lurking beneath the thin and weak veneer of civilization is a desperate one, but one accepted by evolutionists. It seems to them to explain the tragic ways in which human beings so often behave. The hatred, the brutality, the crime, the strange selfishness and propensity to hurt even those we love, make sense to those who find the identity of man in some distant, mindless brute.

What About Good?

It's fascinating to realize that man's search for origins is organized around probing the reason for human evil. Few seem compelled to explain the good! Yet the good is far more difficult to explain. If the roots of our behavior are imbedded deeply in some "great invisible octopus writhing in the depths of the mind" then what is the source of love? The source of appreciation for truth and beauty? Of a sense of responsibility for others? Of altruism, and willingness to sacrifice? Where is the source of man's curiosity and creativity? Where is the spring of thought and reason, of the ability and the desire to value? And how do we explain that universal awareness that there is something beyond, an awareness that expresses itself even in the most isolated cultures in some kind of worship? How do we explain serving—or placating—the supernatural?

It's strange that the believer has been cast as hung up on sin. In fact, it is the man who rejects God whose every attempt to understand himself seems to draw him inexorably to struggle with the awesome gap between what man feels he ought to be—and what he is.

Scripture is different. Yes, it recognizes the fact of sin. But the Bible insists that you and I see our origin and explain our essential nature as springing from an earlier source. In fact, the Bible insists that you and I begin our search for identity by affirming, with God, that we bear the image of the Lord and not the image of the ape.

This teaching, which we meet first in Genesis 1 and 2, is not isolated to these passages. After the Fall, God instituted capital punishment for murder as the ultimate crime. For murder is the taking of the life of a person made in God's image (9:5-6). James pointed out the inconsistency involved in blessing God and, with the same voice, cursing men "who have been made in the likeness of God" (James 3:9).

Even more striking is the meditation of David in Psalm 8:

> When I consider Your heavens, the work of Your fingers, the moon and the stars which You have set in place; what is man that You are mindful of him, and the son of man that You care for him? You made him a little lower than the heavenly beings and crowned him with glory and honor. You made him ruler over the works of Your hands; You put everything under his feet.
>
> Psalm 8:3-6

Hebrews 2 comments on this psalm: "In putting everything under him [man], God left nothing that is not subject to him. Yet at present we do not see everything subject to him" (v. 8). What we do see, Hebrews goes on to say, is Jesus. Jesus, who died, who is now crowned with glory and honor. Through His death Jesus has succeeded in "bringing many sons to glory" (v. 10).

In this great New Testament passage God recognizes the gap between man's intended destiny and his experience, and God affirms man's value. Even as sinners you and I are still so important to God that He sent His Son to share our humanity (see v. 14). You and I are still so important that Jesus died to free us from slavery and to restore the glory and the dominion our heritage demands.

As J.B. Phillips paraphrases it, "It is plain that for this purpose He [Christ] did not become an angel; He became a man" (v. 16). Man was, at the Creation, special. And each human being remains just as special today.

♥ ***Link to Life: Children***

Even young children can grasp the concept of "image and likeness." Show a picture of parents and their children. How is the picture like, and how different from, the real people? How are the children like, and different from, their moms and dads? In each case the pictures, the children, are like the real person in some ways, not like in others. Human beings too are like God in some ways, not like Him in others.

Help the children sense the wonder of this likeness. Show pictures of boys and girls playing, studying, making something, hugging another person, etc. Ask: "What are the boys and girls doing here that God does too?" Afterward thank God for giving us minds to think with, emotions so we can feel love, and a will to make right choices.

The Image

The Genesis 1 portrait of man's creation and the days before the Fall provides the foundation for our self-understanding.

Dominion. There are many things in verses 26-31 that are exciting. For instance, the interplay in God's words about Himself is fascinating. "Let Us make man in Our image," God said, and so "in the image of

God . . . He created them." Here is the first hint of Trinity, the first faint indication that God is One, yet somehow plural in His unity. In these verses too are the roots of the Christian's concern for ecology. The earth and all its creatures were given into man's keeping. To us then came both the gift and the responsibility.

In these verses too is the first affirmation of the essential rightness of sex. Far from supporting the old notion that the original sin was intercourse between Adam and Eve, God before the Fall commanded them to "be fruitful and increase in number; fill the earth and subdue it" (v. 28). It was God who created us "male and female" (v. 27). It was God who designed human sexuality and, looking at "all He had made," pronounced it "very good" (v. 31).

As significant as these things are, it's clear that the Genesis 1 account of man's creation stresses two messages. One of them is this: Man was created to have dominion. God shared His authority with man and, in the sharing, God gave man the privilege of responsibility.

This mantle of dominion settles over us as a dynamic reversal of all we have thought ourselves to be. Too often you and I feel a helplessness and impotence that drain us of the will to act. All too commonly we are overwhelmed by the vast impersonality of circumstance, overcome by the feeling that we are unable to struggle upstream against events we cannot control. With modern apostles of despair, we feel like bits of flotsam tossed on surging seas. But the Bible insists that you and I have a different heritage! A heritage in Creation that restores our confidence to meet and master circumstance. Only God is our Master. And in His plan we have been shaped to have dominion over all.

Certainly sin has robbed us of the full experience of dominion. Sin enslaves us. But Hebrews 2 cries out that through Jesus' death you and I have been freed! (v. 15) Freed to taste again, in our personal experience, the meaning of dominion. Freed to live beyond circumstances, we are once again in relationship with God and once again in control.

♥ ***Link to Life: Youth / Adult***
Do young people and adults feel in control today? Have your group brainstorm (throw out suggestions without pausing to discuss or to evaluate them): What is most likely to make people like you feel helpless, or that things are beyond your control? When at least a dozen ideas have been suggested, ask: "Which of these is hardest for you personally? Why do you find it hard?" After the sharing, look at the Genesis passage, and then at Hebrews 2. God will keep the promise of Creation, and in Christ will give us dominion and victory over all that frustrates us.

Imago Dei. The other message of the Creation story, *imago dei* (God's image), explains our dominion. God could give man this gift because God shaped man to be like Him.

There is a long history of debate concerning the nature of the "image of God." In what respect did God make man like Himself? Some have felt the key to likeness was an original holiness. But even after the Fall, the image persists (Gen. 9:6; James 3:9). And the New Testament makes it plain that the holiness Adam had was lost, and only now is being renewed in us by Christ (Eph. 4:24; Col. 3:9-11). So most commentators have agreed that the uniqueness of man is the key to understanding image. Mankind and mankind alone shares with God all the attributes of personhood.

We know from the Bible that God has emotions, values, chooses, appreciates beauty, demonstrates creativity, makes distinctions between right and wrong, loves and even sacrifices Himself for the sake of others. We know from the Bible that God is a Person, with identity and individuality.

These attributes constituting personhood mark humanity from the rest of creation. In fact, all those elements of good which are found in man must have their source in likeness to the Divine. How utterly foolish men are to imagine that the root of evil can be seen in a heritage from beasts, and never to realize that the explanation for good must be found in our heritage from God.

But this is the message of God's Word. Man comes from God. All the things on which we pride ourselves are ours because of this original heritage all human beings share.

"So God created man in His own image; in the image of God He created him; male and female He created them" (Gen. 1:27).

As a reflection of the Creator, each person is precious to God. As a bearer of God's image, each person is worth even the price of redemption. You and I can never again look at others or ourselves as valueless or base. We bear the image of God. And we are important to Him.

♥ ***Link to Life: Youth / Adult***
Many Christians have poor self-images. These may be reflections of parental criticism, or of personal failures and past bad choices. But a poor self-image is not in harmony with the high value God places on each individual. We are special; to grasp the meaning of Genesis 1–2 we need to sense our specialness.

You might go around the room and ask each group member: "What is one thing you really like in yourself?" When all have shared, think together about how the traits shared are expressed in God's own character. We are special because of our likeness to Him: we should never dismiss ourselves as without worth or value.

Or have members jot down three successes in life, from age three to the present. Share these, and then discuss how each success shows the use of some ability given by God, but found first in Him.

When we realize that we are made in God's image, we will worship and praise Him, and sense more deeply the reality of His great love.

Genesis 2

It's popular in some circles to think of Genesis 2 as a second, somewhat contradictory account of human creation. In fact, Genesis 2 employs a common literary device. Background is sketched first, and then one feature is highlighted with additional details. A chorus sings, then one singer steps forward into the spotlight. A guide exposes the panorama of a giant mural and then leads his tour closer to examine the detail.

There is every indication that this is what we have in Genesis 2. The phrase in verse 4, "This is the account of," sets off the introduction of each new section in Genesis (5:1; 6:9; 10:1; 11:10, 27; 25:12, 19; 36:1, 9; 37:2). The Creation scenery is set in place in Genesis 1; now the writer invites us to take our seats and observe the play.

Special. Looking closely at chapter 2, we see many evidences that man truly is special to God. These are found primarily in the record of how God planned Eden to meet the various needs of Adam's personality.

Remember that God's own personality was mirrored in Adam. With God, Adam shared a capacity to appreciate. So the plantings of Eden included all trees "that were pleasing to the eye" (v. 9). God knew that man would be dissatisfied without work, so in the Garden God let Adam "work it and take care of it" (v. 15). God knew man's need for opportunity to use his intellectual capacities, so God brought all the animals to the man "to see what he would name them; and whatever the man called each living creature, that was its name" (v. 19). God knew man's need for freedom to choose, so He placed a forbidden tree in the Garden and commanded man not to eat fruit from it. This action once for all set man apart from programmed robots and demanded that he use his capacity to value and to choose. God knew man's need for intimacy with others of his kind, so God gave Adam and Eve to each other. And, finally, God knew man's need for fellowship with Him. So God gave Adam and Eve His own presence as evenings fell (3:8).

Each of these actions shows how deeply concerned God was that man's needs be met, and how special man, this being who was "in His own image" (1:27), was to Him. In the design of Eden, God continued to reveal the fact that His own nature is one of love.

♥ ***Link to Life: Youth / Adult***
Share the point made above: the design of Eden reveals many ways that human beings reflect God's image. Have your group engage in direct Bible study, to examine Genesis 2:4-25 for insights into God's nature as well as evidence of His love expressed in planning Eden to meet our human needs.

There are many ways in which we might respond to this witness to the special place man has in God's heart. For one, we might worship, echoing the wonder of the psalmist, "What is man, that You are mindful of him?" (Ps. 8:4)

For another, we might take comfort. The God whose care we see exhibited here still cares for you and me today. "In all things God works for the good of those who love

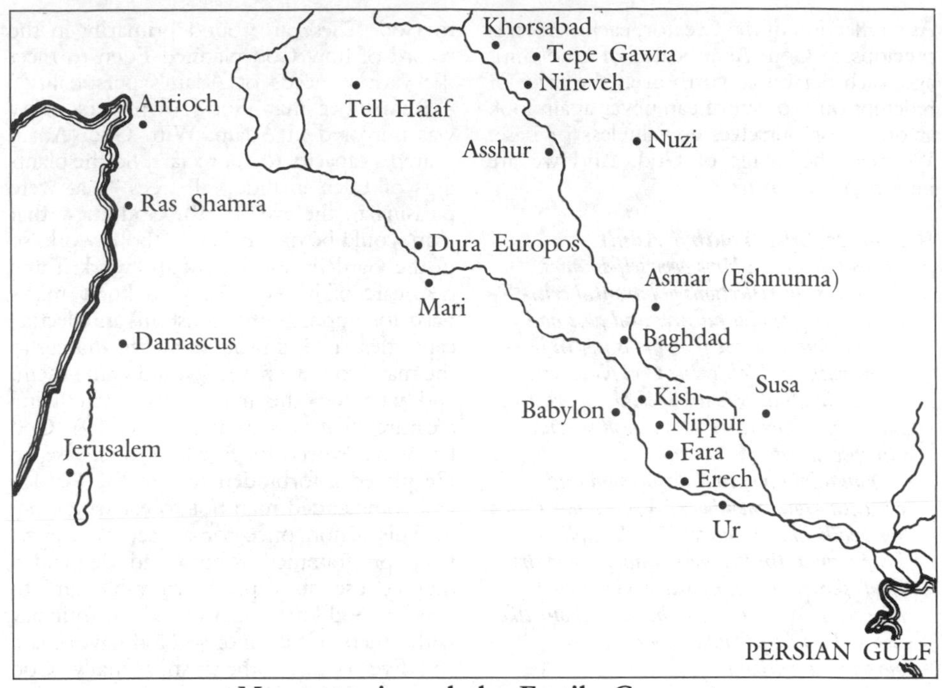

Mesopotamia and the Fertile Crescent

Him" (Rom. 8:28). God still designs experiences as loving gifts to those whom He holds dear.

For another response, we might take heart. "If God be for us, who can be against us?" (v. 31, KJV) When God has affirmed us as His own concern, no circumstance can overcome us. Dominion, still a gift from Him, is ours.

New life. The Genesis account makes it plain that man is a special creation, not a being whose flesh was formed from brutes, with the spark of likeness added as an afterthought. The picture in Genesis 2 shows God kneeling in tenderness to mold fresh clay. Then God breathed His own breath into that shape, and "man became a living being" (v. 7). Both the material and immaterial dimensions of the human personality come from God, combined in a unique blend. And that blend will persist through all eternity, as ultimately you and I share both the shape and the character of Christ, who unites God with man in His own Person.

Eden. What is important about Eden is the care God took in its design and what this tells us about ourselves and about Him. What we usually ask about Eden is, "Where was it?"

Two of the rivers mentioned in the biblical text are well known, so this has led scholars to suggest the narrowing above Babylon, or further south near the Persian Gulf, as likely sites.

While archeologists have agreed that the Fertile Crescent area is the focus of the most ancient and advanced civilizations on earth, there is no way today to pinpoint the location of Eden.

Woman. When we turn again to Scripture, the focus remains on Genesis 2 and its messages.

One of the most important messages has to do with the identity of women. This is something we are all concerned about these days, and with good reason. In church and society, women's identity has been clouded with a variety of myths. Popular notions often project girls as more suggestible than boys, as having less self-esteem, as lacking motivation to achieve, as less aggressive, and certainly as less analytic. Tragic misunderstandings of Scripture have led some to affirm an actual inferiority of women on supposed religious grounds. Not only does this violate the spirit of Ephesians 5, in which man's headship is associated not with the right to command but with the responsibility to love as Jesus loved, but it totally misses the implications of the Genesis Creation account.

What do we see in Genesis? We see first a deep need for woman as someone designed to fit the emptiness in a man's life ("a helper suitable for him," Gen. 2:18). To fill the need, God did not turn again to clay. If He had, man might later have imagined that woman, as a second creation, was somehow inferior to him. No, God put Adam to sleep and, while he rested, took a rib from him. Working His great wonders, from that rib God shaped Eve. When God brought Eve to Adam, the man recognized her, and the words of verse 23 stand as a witness to the essential identity of woman with man:

> This is now bone of my bones and flesh of my flesh; she shall be called "woman," for she was taken out of man.
>
> Genesis 2:23

When God sought fellowship, He created man in His own image. But when this person God had made knew a similar need for intimacy, God gave an even greater gift. Woman, taken from the living flesh of man, is far more than a reflection of man's image. Woman, taken from the living flesh of man, shares fully in man's identity. In a testimony echoed by the New Testament, the Word of God lifts man and woman and places them, side by side, at the pinnacle of God's creation. There, together, each shares fully as a fellow heir of the dominion God proclaims, each of us a choice and precious object of His love.

TEACHING GUIDE

Prepare
Read and meditate on Psalm 8, letting verse 9 be your concluding word of praise.

Explore
1. Have your group share "one thing I really like about myself" ("link-to-life," p. 29). After sharing, ask: "Is it all right for us to like the good things in ourselves? Why?" Then explore *imago dei* in the Old Testament text.
2. Or, make a T/F quiz with which to begin your group time that touches on concepts covered in Genesis 2. For instance, "Man's true identity is found in Creation rather than the Fall." Or, "It makes little practical difference if a person holds a creationist or evolutionist view of human origins."

Expand
1. Define "image and likeness" and "dominion" for your group (see *overview*.) Give a minilecture on the origin of good in mankind. Discuss: "How does the Bible answer questions that the evolutionist has no answer for? How does this Bible truth help believers accept and value themselves as well as other people?"
2. Or, pose two questions and have your group work in fours to find Bible answers in Genesis 1:12–2:22.
(1) How did God's design of Eden show ways that humans are like Him? (see p. 29 *Special* and "link-to-life")
(2) How does Genesis 2:20-23 affect a Christian view of women? When done, have teams report to the whole group.

Apply
1. Review *explore* 1. It is all right for us to recognize the good in ourselves, for we realize its source is God. Ask each group member to share something else he or she likes about himself. Then conclude with sentence prayers, asking each to thank God for the gift of His image, which is the source of the good in humankind and gives each human being worth and value.
2. Or review the three ways the author suggests Christians might respond to the Genesis teaching on *imago dei*. Describe each, then ask group members to share how they feel when they realize God has shared His own image-likeness with them, and that they are special to the Lord. After sharing, close in prayer, letting each who wishes respond to the Lord with praise.

STUDY GUIDE 3

Genesis 3–4

DEATH REIGNS

Overview
With Genesis 3 there comes a shattering of the idyllic picture of man in Eden. With a sudden jolt the harmony of original Creation is torn with discord; a wild cacophony of sounds among which we can hear notes of anger, jealousy, pride, disobedience, murder, and the accompanying inner agonies of pain and shame and guilt. God's creation of man as a person stands as the source of good in us; now we face the source of evil.

Genesis 3 describes the Fall; Genesis 4 is included to help us realize the consequences of the Fall and the implications of the spiritual death that grips humanity.

Yet even this dark message is brightened by the promise contained in God's continued love, and in history's first sacrifice.

▶ ***Sin.*** There are three primary words for "sin" in the Hebrew language. Each of them implies the existence of a standard of righteousness established by God. One of the three, *hata'*, means to "miss the mark," or to "fall short of the divine standard." *Pesa'* is usually rendered by "rebellion" or "transgression," and indicates revolt against the standard. *'Awon*, translated by "iniquity" or "guilt," is a "twisting of the standard or deviation from it." Psalm 51 is the Old Testament's greatest statement on the nature of sin, and uses all three of these Hebrew words to express David's great prayer of confession of his own failures.

■ See pages 32-35 of the *Bible Knowledge Commentary* for a verse-by-verse commentary on Genesis 3 through 4.

Commentary
We meet the specter early, in Genesis 2. In order to give man freedom to be a responsible moral being, God placed a certain tree in the center of the Garden and commanded man not to eat. With the command came warning of the consequences: "When you eat of it you will surely die" (v. 17).

This opportunity to eat was no trap, or even a test. Given the intention of God that man should be in His own image, that tree was a necessity! There is no moral dimension to the existence of a robot; it can only respond to the program imposed by its maker. Robots have no capacity to value, no ability to choose between good and bad, or good and better. To be truly like God, man must have the freedom to make moral choices and the opportunity to choose, however great the risk such freedom may involve.

Daily Adam and Eve may have passed that tree, gladly obeying a God they knew and trusted. Until finally a third being stepped in.

Satan
Scripture portrays a host of living, intelligent beings with individuality and personality called angels: "messengers." Some of these rebelled against God, and it is from this cosmic rebellion that evil has its origin, and from this source that the demons we read of in both Testaments have come.

At the top of the hierarchy of the rebellious angels is Satan. One interpretation equates Satan with the Lucifer of Isaiah 14:12 (KJV), whose rebellion is so graphically portrayed:

> I will ascend to heaven; I will raise my throne above the stars of God; I will sit enthroned on the mount of assembly. . . . I will make myself like the Most High.
>
> Isaiah 14:13-14

This rebellion against established order brought divine judgment and Lucifer, with a great number of angelic beings who followed him, was judged in a titanic fall. Lucifer's name was changed to Satan, and from his arrogance was born an unending hatred of God.

It was this being, this great adversary of God and His people, who came in the dawning of the world in the guise of a serpent, to tempt Eve.

The temptation (Gen. 3:1-7). It is fascinating to note the strategies of the tempter. First he isolated Eve from Adam. He gave the pair no opportunity to strengthen each other in a resolve to choose the good (cf. Heb. 10:24-25). Then he cast doubt on God's motives. Did God possibly have a selfish motive for the restriction? (Gen. 3:4) Satan went on to contradict God. God had warned of death; Satan cried, "That's a lie!" Now two opposing views stood in sharp contrast, and a choice had to be made.

Satan also focused Eve's attention on desirable ends, a common device of what has been called "situation ethics." Never mind the fact that the means to an end involves disobedience to God. Act only on examination of the supposed results.

Satan also proposed a mixed good as the end: "You will become like Him, for your eyes will be opened—you will be able to distinguish good from evil!" (v. 5, TLB) How could becoming more like God be wrong?

Finally, Satan relied on the appeal of the senses. The fruit was "lovely and fresh looking" (v. 6, TLB). How could anything that looked and smelled so pleasant be bad?

Led along by the tempter, Eve made her choice. She rejected trust in God and confidence in His wisdom and, as Satan himself had before her, Eve determined to follow her own will and reject God's. Then she offered the fruit to Adam, and he too ate.

♥ ***Link to Life: Youth / Adult***

Ask your group members to think of a time when they felt tempted. Get the incident clearly in mind, and then answer these questions about it: Was I alone, or with other Christians? Did what I was tempted by seem desirable? Did what I was tempted by seem to lead to something good? Did what I was tempted by not seem so bad, even though I knew it was not God's will?

Talk about these issues linked with personal temptations. After sharing experiences, work together as a group to develop Five Principles for Overcoming Temptation.

After Adam and Eve had made their choice and had eaten the forbidden fruit, they suddenly realized what they had done. They *did* know good and evil! But, unlike God, their knowledge came from a personal experience of the wrong. With wide open eyes they looked at each other and, for the first time, looked away in shame.

Death. When God set that single tree to stand as a testimony to man's freedom, He warned, "When you eat of it you will surely die" (2:17). That day had now come. Now death began its reign.

It is important to realize that much more than the end of physical life is involved in the biblical concept of death. Death in Scripture involves not only a return of the body to dust, but also a terrible distortion of the divine order. Death involves a warping of the human personality, a twisting of relationships, and alienation from God and from God's ways. Ephesians describes men's state apart from Christ as "dead in your transgressions and sins, in which you used to live when you followed the ways of this world and of the ruler of the kingdom of the air, the spirit [Satan] who is now at work in those who are disobedient. All of us also lived among them at one time, gratifying the cravings of our sinful nature and following its desires and thoughts" (Eph. 2:1-3). Romans portrays the universal reign of death and sin, and insists, "There is no one righteous, not even one" (Rom. 3:10, cf. vv. 9-18).

The implications of the first man's sin are traced in Bible passages like Romans 5:12-21. Adam had been created in God's image. Then came the choice and, with it, death. The human personality was warped and marred. The image of God, dimmed and twisted now, did remain. But man was ruled by death and all that death implies. What heritage had Adam to pass on to humanity? Only what he was. He fathered a son in his image: a son who, like Adam, had worth and value because of his correspondence to the Divine, but who, like Adam, lived in chains. "Therefore just as sin entered the world through one man, and death through sin, and in this way death came to all men, because all sinned" (v. 12). The history of humankind is the dark record of the rule of death, and stands as a grim testimony to the truth of God. What God warned Adam would happen, did happen. And what God says to us today, in warning or in invitation, will just as certainly prove true.

♥ ***Link to Life: Youth / Adult***
Bring several newspapers to your group's meeting. Suggest that a friend has asked you to prove that the Bible's view of sin as spiritual death is true. Give your members papers, and give teams of two or three about five minutes to locate in today's news evidence of the impact of sin on human beings.

After teams have shared, have one member read aloud Romans 5:12-21, and another read aloud Ephesians 2:1-3. Then let them suggest how a Christian might defend and explain a biblical view of sin to a skeptic.

Demonstration of death. In looking at the message of Genesis 3 and 4 it is important to see that each detail is purposefully included. The principle of selection in these chapters seems clear: God is concerned that you and I understand the seriousness of sin and the reality of spiritual death. The series of events included provides an unmistakable demonstration of the death principle operating in human experience.

*We see death in the sudden flush of shame that spread as Adam and Eve recognized their nakedness (Gen. 3:7). Today the more "mature" defend public nakedness as morally neutral. "Evil is in the eye of the beholder," is the phrase they often use to attack anyone who objects, never realizing how condemning that excuse is. Evil *is* in the eye of the beholder, not in the creation of God. But since the Fall, the eye *is* evil!

*We see death demonstrated in the first pair's flight from God. They had known His love, yet awareness of guilt alienated them from Him, and they tried to hide (vv. 8-9).

*We see death in Adam's refusal to accept responsibility for his choice. He tried to shift the blame, first to Eve, and then ultimately to God Himself. "It was the woman You gave me who brought me some" (v. 12, TLB).

*We see death in the judgment on earth for man's sake (vv. 17-19).

*Most of all, we see death in the anger of Cain, whose bitterness led him to murder his own brother, Abel (4:8). How deeply that tragedy must have driven home to Adam and Eve the implications of their choice. Father and mother must have stood in tears, gazing at the fallen body of one son, knowing only too well that the hand of their older boy was crimson with his blood.

*We see death in the civilization that sprang up as the family of man multiplied. Lamech broke the pattern of man/woman relationship which God had ordained: "The two shall become one flesh" (2:24). Not only did Lamech commit bigamy, but he boldly justified the murder of another man who had in some way injured him.

Actually, we hardly need repeated proofs. Each day's headlines bring us new testimony. The wrong we choose, the guilt and shame we bear, the way we strike out to hurt and to harm, are ever-present internal witnesses to Eden's loss.

Yes, how well man knows good and evil now!

With that first choice the power to experience the truly good was lost. We know the good, but only as an ideal, a yearning desire. We know the meaning of evil far more intimately. And we join with Paul in the lament, "What I want to do I do not do, but what I hate I do" (Rom. 7:15).

The longer we live, the stronger the realization grows: Paradise is lost.

The Recovery of Hope

While Genesis 3 and 4 are among the most poignant chapters in the Bible, they do not leave us without hope. We find hope in God's action as He clothes the naked pair in animal skins, the first intimation that for redemption, blood must be shed. That first blood speaks of sacrifice, and sacrifice speaks of Christ.

We find hope in God's action in seeking out the sinning pair. Sin will distort our idea of God, erecting a grim barrier that we are unwilling to approach. But God came into the Garden seeking Adam, just as later Jesus came into the world to seek and to save those who were lost.

We find hope in the promise of God that an Offspring of the woman would destroy the serpent. Here too we see a glimmering prospect of the Incarnation, and the Saviour's victory over death.

We also find hope as we trace through

Scripture some of the theological concepts introduced in chapters 3 and 4. In fact, these chapters stand almost unmatched as seedbeds for basic truths about ourselves in God's universe—a universe we too have shaped, through sin.

Sin. One of the themes introduced here is human sin. The concept will continue to be developed through the revelation of the Old Testament and the New. Many different words will be used to describe the perverse twist that sin has introduced into human experience.

One set of Bible words portrays sin as missing the mark, as "falling short."

Another set of Bible words portrays sin as willful action, the conscious choosing of known wrongs. Here we find words like transgress, trespass, go astray, and rebellion. Both ideas are seen here in Genesis 3. Adam and Eve fell short of God's requirements. They did so by obeying rationalized desire rather than obeying the command of God.

And so Genesis 3 and 4 sum up the human predicament. And with it, they sum up mankind's dilemma. Sin not only blinds us and leaves the good beyond our grasp, but sin also twists our will, moving us to desire and to choose what we know is wrong. Lost in impotence, men do not even desire to be truly free!

♥ ***Link to Life: Children***
Use a simple chalkboard visual to help boys and girls sense both aspects of sin. Draw a straight line that intersects the top of a hill. This represents what God tells us to do. Draw some stick figures trying to get up the hill, but short of the top. Draw others running down the hill. Explain that sometimes we try to do what's right, but aren't quite able to. Other times we don't want to do what is right, and purposefully go the wrong way. Let the children suggest times they try to do right ("I was going to pick up my room, but forgot.") and times they consciously choose wrong ("Dad told me to come home, but I was having too much fun.").

Disobedience is sin, whether the reason we disobey is that we just fell short or whether the reason is that we rebel.

How is this revelation of sin a word of hope? In this: by sketching for us how complete our ruin is, God calls us to look away from ourselves, to Him.

Have you ever thought how striking the portrait of Cainitic culture is? (4:19-22) This is no subsistence-level economy, struggling in primitive poverty to scratch a meager living from the earth. The text portrays division of labor and the taming of animals to man's use. We see culture. There is time for leisure, music, and the arts. There is a technical competence that involves the smelting of ores and the development of metallurgy in bronze and iron. There is no suggestion here that the Fall limited the ability of man to function effectively in his world.

Instead, what we see is that no matter what progress man makes technologically, the underlying moral fault is unrepaired! Men can master the environment. But men cannot master themselves. We are competent to deal with our physical needs, but not to deal with the deepest needs of the human heart. Sin has warped the moral fabric of our universe, and only by looking to God to cover and transform can man be saved.

Ultimate salvation. It's good to trace the story of sin through Scripture because in so doing we find the ultimate solution. For acts of willful sin, Christ's blood has won forgiveness. For our impotence, the Holy Spirit's presence brings wisdom and new power. For our final destiny, resurrection promises removal of the last vestiges of sin. Even the earth, which shares the curse (3:17), will know renewal. In a poetic passage the New Testament reveals that the very "creation waits in eager expectation for the sons of God to be revealed. For the creation was subjected to frustration, not by its own choice, but by the will of the one who subjected it, in hope that the creation itself will be liberated from its bondage to decay and brought into the glorious freedom of the children of God" (Rom. 8:19-21). The groaning world itself will know a liberation day when you and I are at last freed by God's great sacrifice from all that death and sin involve.

This is our destiny, and this is our hope. One day the fullness of the image of God will be restored.

Avenues to Explore

So far we've looked only at the central message of Genesis 3 and 4. Sin *is* real; death is the common experience of the human race;

only God's intervention offers hope.

But there are many additional riches in these chapters. Just a few of the areas of interest are:

The forbidden tree (Gen. 2:9). The importance of the tree was not in the nature of its fruit, but in the choice of man to listen to God's word or to disobey. Paul asserts, "Nothing is intrinsically unholy" (Rom. 14:14, PH). What was important was allegiance to God and to His will.

The serpent (Gen. 3:1). Satan used the snake. It seems there was correspondence between its shrewd ("crafty") character and his. Certainly the continued identification of Satan as "that old serpent" is significant (cf. John 8:44; Rom. 16:20; 2 Cor. 11:3; 1 Tim. 2:14; Rev. 12:9; 20:2), as is the fact that the serpent who was used suffered judgment, apparently for his cooperation in the confrontation between Satan and Eve. If there is a deeper meaning in the scene, it is obscure.

Authority (Gen. 3:16). Along with added difficulty in childbirth, the woman was told that her husband "shall rule over you." Here the theme of authority and subjection is introduced, but only after the Fall. As long as Adam and Eve lived in harmony with God, harmony with one another was assured. But with sin the harmony of the natural order was shattered. Each of us now must live under the rule of others. Only when patterns of authority exist can societies or families lead healthy lives.

Work (Gen. 3:17-29). The added curse of toil placed on Adam was not the introduction of work, to replace an early state of blissful idleness. Meaningful work is one of God's good gifts (cf. 2:15). What is spoken of here is work as toil: work as a never-ending struggle to make a living from resisting soil. Toil replaced the creative and joyous labors in fruit-filled Eden.

The tree of life (Gen. 3:22-25). The first pair's expulsion from the Garden is best seen as a good gift. Only tragedy could be in store for those who now knew the living death sin brought. How awful if Adam and Eve had been doomed to live on, forever to witness death's despairing impact on each new generation of their descendants. For Adam and for Eve—and for us as well—death comes as gain, a welcome pause before resurrection launches us into the full experience of eternal life in a world at last set right.

Cain's offering (Gen. 4:2-5). Hebrews 11:4 points out that "by faith" Abel's sacrifice was "better." In the Scripture, faith involves response to God's revelation. Certainly the principle of sacrifice had been demonstrated to Adam and Eve in their clothing made of skins. It's likely the boys were so instructed by their parents or by God. Yet only Abel brought lambs. Cain brought farm produce. It may have been the best he had, but redemption knows no acceptable sacrifice except blood. Cain's underlying attitude toward God is shown by his reaction. He was very angry. Even God's gentle urgings (Gen. 4:6-7) left Cain untouched.

Cain's wife (Gen. 4:17). The question is mocking and ages old. Where did Cain get his wife? A little reading gives the answer: Adam and Eve had many sons and many daughters (5:4).

Marked for life (Gen. 4:15). Cain's punishment involved expulsion from his agricultural life and from God's own society (apparently the boys had known God and been instructed by Him, v. 14). A mark identified Cain, and his continued existence served as a vivid reminder to that generation of the result of rejecting God.

And so the brief report concludes with an onward glance toward future generations (vv. 18-26). The seed of sin planted by Adam and Eve had sprouted in their sons, and each succeeding generation would bear bitter fruit.

As well we know.

For you and I recognize the taste of that fruit in our mouths to this very day.

TEACHING GUIDE

Prepare
Read and meditate on Psalm 51. Make David's prayer your own, as you seek to become sensitive to sin and to God's great remedy in Christ.

Explore
1. The Greek philosopher Plato argued that if only human beings knew "the Good," they would do it. Ask your group to discuss this idea. Then ask them to review their own personal experiences. Have their own moral struggles been over knowing what is right? What other issues are involved in moral choice? You want to help them realize that our problem is not usually in knowing what is right, but in choosing what is right!
2. Or, ask the group to think of a recent time when they felt tempted to make a choice they felt was wrong. Without telling what the choice was, have them work together to list what made them *want* to do wrong. What made the wrong so attractive or seem so desirable?

Expand
1. Have teams of three study the temptation of Eve (Gen. 3:1-7). Each team is to (1) list strategies that Satan used in trying to get Eve to disobey God, and (2) come up with at least one illustration of how that strategy is still used in our personal temptations.

When this direct Bible study is completed, use the "link-to-life" idea on page 33 to guide your group to develop their own *Five Principles for Overcoming Temptation.*
2. Or, cover the temptation and Fall in a minilecture. Then focus your group's attention on the impact of sin in human experience. Use two teaching approaches, the first to see sin in general (in society), and then to personalize the impact of sin.

Bring in and distribute daily newspapers as described on page 34. When your group has found and listed evidences of sin in society, return to the biblical text.

You can use three study teams, each to look at one of these three passages: Sin in Adam and Eve (3:7-17), sin in Cain (4:1-12), and sin in Lamech (vv. 19-24). Each team is to find evidence of the way sin is expressed in human experience in its passage. Be sure the teams see the blaming, the shame, the guilt, the anger, the pride, and the self-justification as sin as well as see the sinful actions.

As each group reports, list its findings on the chalkboard in parallel columns. Then add a fourth column: "Us." Have your group talk about ways sin shows up in their own personal experiences and inner lives, even when it may not be expressed in the acts of a Cain or Lamech.

Apply
1. Conclude with a minilecture on Romans 5:12-21. Sin came into the world through Adam. But God has brought redemption to us through Christ. How much we, and others, need the gift Jesus brings us to counteract the terrible heritage that all men have received from Adam's Fall.
2. Conclude with a brief minilecture on "death." For a complete discussion see the author's *Expository Dictionary of Bible Words.* Or simply read Ephesians 2:1-3, then move on to emphasize the gift of life that God's grace has brought to us despite our deaths in trespasses and sins.

STUDY GUIDE 4

Genesis 5–11

THE GENESIS FLOOD

Overview

The first meaning of "moral" listed in the massive *Random House Dictionary of the English Language* is: "Pertaining to, or concerned with right conduct or the distinction between right and wrong." To many it seems presumptuous or even ridiculous to suggest that we live in a moral universe. How can the universe be concerned with right and wrong?

But we saw in the first chapter of Genesis that the foundation of our universe is not laid on inert and nonliving matter. Dead rocks have no concern with right conduct. But God, the personal source of our universe, does!

In the creation of man (Gen. 2) there is a reflection of God's image, giving us ability to distinguish between good and evil, and extending to us the freedom to choose. In Genesis 3 and 4 we've seen the terrible consequences of Adam's and Eve's choice of disobedience. In seeing this we have learned that, in God's universe, there are basic realities with which all must come to grips. Life. Death. Sin.

Now, in the story of the Genesis Flood, we meet two new themes, and face two new realities. We meet judgment. And we find the good news of salvation.

In these chapters we have the proof that ours truly is a moral universe. God, who created and who even now sustains all, truly is concerned with right and wrong.

■ See the *Bible Knowledge Commentary*, pages 40-45 for helpful discussions of the curse on Canaan, the Tower of Babel, and the archeologically significant "table of nations" in Genesis 10.

Commentary

Genesis 5 sets the scene. The genealogies do not tell us the years between Adam and the Flood. Remembering the characteristics of Hebrew genealogies (which typically compressed generations), we can be sure only that centuries passed, and Adam's children did begin to "multiply and fill the earth and subdue it" (1:28). But the taint of sin and its deadly stamp on the human personality remained all too clear. "The Lord saw how great man's wickedness on the earth had become, and that every inclination of the thoughts of his heart was only evil all the time" (6:5). The lifestyle incipient in Cain, and seen in later generations in Lamech (4:19-24), now had permeated the race. Perhaps in the New Testament Book of Romans, in a passage that summarized a decline we can trace in every civilization, we have a picture of the days of Noah as well.

> Although they knew God, they neither glorified Him as God nor gave thanks to Him, but their thinking became futile and their foolish hearts were darkened. Although they claimed to be wise, they became fools and exchanged the glory of the immortal God for images made to look like mortal man and birds and animals and reptiles.
>
> Therefore God gave them over in the sinful desires of their hearts to sexual impurity for the degrading of their bodies with one another. They exchanged the truth of God for a lie, and worshiped and served created things rather than the Creator—who is forever praised. . . .
>
> Furthermore, since they did not think it worthwhile to retain the knowledge of God, He gave them over to a depraved mind, to do what ought not to be done. They have become filled with every kind of wickedness, evil, greed, and depravity. They are full of envy, murder, strife, deceit, and malice. They are gossips, slanderers, God-haters, insolent, arrogant, and boastful; they invent ways of doing evil; they disobey their parents; they are

> senseless, faithless, heartless, ruthless. Although they know God's righteous decree that those who do such things deserve death, they not only continue to do these very things, but also approve of those who practice them.
>
> Romans 1:21-25, 28-32

Every inclination of the thoughts of their hearts, Genesis records, was only evil continually.

The Living Bible notes that "When the Lord God saw the extent of human wickedness . . . He was sorry He had made them. It broke His heart" (Gen. 6:5-6). God was not unmoved. God is always concerned with righteousness. But He is also concerned with humankind.

The text goes on to tell how one man in this corrupt society, Noah, walked with God. God warned Noah of coming judgment and instructed him to build a great ark: a boat in which his family and animal life might be preserved. Noah and his sons labored 120 years to complete the task (Gen. 6:3), finally caulking the mighty hull with bitumen and storing fodder for the animals.

♥ ***Link to Life: Children***

How large was the ark? And how can we help children sense its vast dimensions? Based on the biblical specifications, you can take them to the top of a five story building, and have them look down. The ark was about that height. You can take them to a football field, and see how long it takes the fastest to run 50 yards. The ark was three times this long. You can take them to a six lane superhighway and have them look across. The ark was about this wide. No wonder it took Noah and his sons some 120 years to build this great boat God commanded them to construct (cf. 6:3).

When Noah and his sons completed the ark, they waited. The Bible tells us how representatives from the animal world "according to their kinds" found their way to the ark. When they and the human family were safe inside, the Lord Himself sealed the door (7:16).

The Genesis account says that in the Flood every person and animal on earth "in whose nostrils was the breath of life" died (v. 22). The New Testament puts it even stronger: "The world of that time was deluged and destroyed" (2 Peter 3:6). Certainly the Genesis account indicates that more than a generation of mankind perished. A world that differed in significant ways from ours was also washed away. When Noah landed and finally left the ark on Mount Ararat, it was to enter a new, fresh world, a world in which the pattern of man's life and also his responsibilities would change.

Long life for men before a great flood (Gen. 5) is a common element in many ancient legends. The Sumerian king list from around 2300 B.C. gives the length of reign of one pre-flood ruler as 43,200 years! This reflects traditions both of a great flood, and of extended life span before its deluge. Also, before the biblical flood, men were apparently vegetarian. Afterward, God gave Noah flesh to eat. Human government was instituted as the responsibility of man to govern man (9:4-6). Capital punishment was commanded for murder because murder is the ultimate denial of the worth and value of human life. So Noah was set down in a new world where he was to learn a new way of life.

As Noah was deposited in a new world to learn a new lifestyle, so the believer is brought into a totally new experience in Christ, not to live the rest of his earthly life for evil human desires, but rather for the will of God (cf. 1 Peter 3:20–4:11). Judgment does strike down man because of sin, yet with the judgment, escape is provided for those who look to God in faith.

♥ ***Link to Life: Children***

Children may be concerned about the fairness of God's judgment in the Flood. Yet the people of Noah's day had adequate warning! For 120 years the great structure rising on the plain foretold the coming Flood. How the crowds must have come to watch, to listen to Noah explain, and then to ridicule.

To help younger boys and girls sense this, let them make and color cardboard "STOP" signs. Tell the ark story, describing the building step-by-step (keel, ribs, etc.). Tell how tall the ark was, so it could be seen for miles and miles, and of the thousands of trees that needed to be cut. Tell how the animals gradually gathered, ready to go aboard, and how Noah's sons grew or bought feed to store in the ark for them. Invite the children to hold up their STOP signs every time you describe something that the people of Noah's day might see or hear that would warn them about God's coming judgment.

Afterward, talk about how God loves even people who do wrong, and does give them warnings about any punishment to come, so they can turn to Him and be saved.

In the waters of the Flood, then, we see God speak out in powerful affirmation and in warning. This *is* a moral universe. God *is* concerned about right and wrong, and God will act to punish wrongdoers. Peter sums up the message of the Flood in these words:

> In the last days scoffers will come, scoffing and following their own evil desires. They will say, "Where is this 'coming' He promised? Ever since our fathers died, everything goes on as it has since the beginning of Creation." But they deliberately forget that long ago by God's word the heavens existed and the earth was formed out of water and with water. By water also the world of that time was deluged and destroyed. By the same word the present heavens and earth are reserved for fire, being kept for the day of judgment and destruction of ungodly men. . . . But the Day of the Lord will come like a thief. The heavens will disappear with a roar; the elements will be destroyed by fire, and the earth and everything in it will be laid bare.
>
> 2 Peter 3:3-7, 10

In the destruction of that future day, when what is solid now dissolves, and things now unseen remain, the moral nature of the universe will be fully known. God, who in the Flood etched His moral message indelibly on our world, will expose even those who now cover their eyes to the final moral reality.

Did the Flood Happen?

Many are willing to accept the Genesis Flood story as a myth revealing essential religious truth. But they draw back from any claim of historicity. And many conservatives who believe that a flood really did happen argue for a limited flood—a flood of local rather than worldwide extent. They point out that God's purpose was to judge the race of man, suggesting that probably humankind had not as yet spread beyond the Fertile Crescent Valley.

Behind this line of argument lies the almost universally accepted view of scientific uniformitarianism. This is the theory that all we find in our world, biologically and particularly geologically, can be explained by processes which presently operate in the physical universe. Geologic uniformitarianism, which suggests that millenniums of erosion and repeated ice ages sculptured earth's topography, is accepted and taught in many Christian colleges. While these Christian scientists unhesitatingly accept the creationist view of life and the special creative act by which God made man, they do not take seriously the view that once our earth knew a universal flood.

Uniformitarianism, the view that "everything goes on as it has since the beginning of Creation" (2 Peter 3:4), maintains its sway.

Universal? The term "universal" presents two distinct questions to the believer. Does the biblical account of the Flood necessarily teach that it was worldwide? And, if the Bible does indicate a universal flood, is the geologic record so sure that we must question the accuracy of Genesis?

Many have argued that Genesis must be understood to describe a universal flood. They point to the following evidence:

*Every living thing was to be destroyed in the floodwaters (7:4). This assumes that man and animal life had spread far beyond the Mesopotamian Plain in the centuries or the millennia since the Fall.

*After the Flood God specifically stated that "every living thing" was in fact destroyed (v. 23).

*The text states clearly that "all the high mountains under the entire heaven were covered" to a depth of at least 23 feet [15 cubits] (v. 19).

*Finally the ark is said to have come to rest "on the mountains of Ararat," a range that reaches some 10,000 feet in height (8:4). A local flood might have brought them to the foothills. But "on" the mountains?

This textual argument has been answered by suggesting that "all the high mountains" refers simply to all the heights in the inhabited area. And that "the whole heaven" is phenomenological language; that is, it refers to the visible heavens so far as Noah and his culture were concerned, or to the horizon. To support this view, Driver and others computed the amount of water required to cover the mountains, and argued that not nearly enough exists within our seas and atmosphere. But this in turn rests on the uniformitarian assumption! Was the pre-Flood world essentially like ours geologically and geographically? Or is it possible that the mountain heights and the sea depths we know are in fact caused by the watery cataclysm of the Flood?

Cataclysm. Recently Christians and non-Christians have suggested that geologic features of our earth must be explained in terms of one or more past cataclysms. Detailed scientific arguments have been advanced, pointing out data not readily explained on the uniformitarian hypothesis. As Donald W. Patten, a popularizing layman has asked (*Creation*, Baker):

> Why were dinosaurs quickly drowned and buried in sediments? Why were mammoths quickly drowned in North America, and quick-frozen or flash-frozen in Siberia, even with subtropical vegetation in their mouths and stomachs? Why were petrified forests found 100 miles from the South Pole by Admiral Byrd? Why were land animals found fossilized in locations below sea level, and why were sea animals found fossilized at high elevations?

The same author tells of a tree found in an English quarry "about 100 feet long, and at a forty-degree angle. It went down through strata after strata, each supposedly laid down millions of years apart. At the top the tree was about one foot in diameter. At the bottom it was five feet in one radius and two feet in the other radius, as if it had come under immense pressure."

In a controversial 1961 book, *The Genesis Flood* (Presbyterian and Reformed), Dr. Henry M. Morris, a hydrolics engineer, and Dr. John C. Whitcomb, an Old Testament professor, thoroughly explored the geologic and fossil evidence and attempted to show that a Flood geology better explains the physical data. Their picture suggests a pre-Flood world insulated by great concentrations of water vapor in the atmosphere (partially explaining the lengthened life as due to a blockage of cosmic radiation, which has been shown to be associated with aging). The Flood itself involved not only the release of this mass to fall on earth, but also the breaking up of "springs of the great deep" (7:11), subterranean waters beneath a flat and shallow single continent. This unimaginable hydrologic power and weight broke up the land mass, causing what science now recognizes as the puzzling "continental drift," and also causing the depression of the ocean beds and the upthrust of the mountain ranges that mark the earth of our time.

A later, similar cataclysmic view postulates the approach to earth of a giant comet or another planet. This celestial catastrophe, with the fantastic gravitational interactions involved, would cause tides of subcontinental dimensions, with the earth's lava itself flowing and heaving and land masses jolted out of shape. Many of the unexplainable features of fossil and rock records would find a ready explanation.

The point of all this, of course, is not that evidence exists to compel us to accept the universal flood theory. The point is simply this: There is no necessary reason to base interpretation of the Scriptures on current geological theory. The Flood may have been local. On the other hand, the Flood may have been the greatest single shaper of the features of the world we now live in. But whichever happened in the past, we can be confident that as we read the Genesis text we are revisiting history, and that in the account of these events we do meet God and hear His message.

We do live in a moral universe.

Sin brings judgment, for the God behind it all cares about right and wrong.

Yet we see that He still cares for us as well. The surging waters of judgment may swirl around you and me. But God has prepared His ark. Through faith in His Son you and I, like Noah, can be carried safely through to Christ's new world.

♥ ***Link to Life: Youth / Adult***
Earlier I noted that the early chapters of Genesis demonstrate the principle of selection. *Each event reported is carefully chosen to communicate a clear, basic message. If your group has been studying the Book of Genesis together, they should be able to identify the key message of each unit of*

thought. So list the Genesis chapter divisions on the chalkboard (1, 2, 3, 4, 6–9). Ask individuals to jot down the message of each as a review. Their responses may run something like this:

Chapter 1	*It's a personal universe.*
Chapter 2	*Man is made in God's image, or, man is valuable to God.*
Chapter 3	*Sin is a tragic reality.*
Chapter 4	*Sin is demonstrated in our attitudes and actions.*
Chapters 6–9	*It's a moral universe, or God does judge sin.*

Such a simple activity will help your group sense the continuity of Scripture, and help them develop the ability to think through the Bible.

Observations on the Text

As in other early Genesis chapters, many things here draw our attention and stimulate our curiosity. Most of them we can only speculate about. Yet it is fascinating to observe them.

The sons of God (Gen. 6:2). Were these fallen angels (cf. Job 1:6) who somehow had impregnated human women and fathered the Nephilim? (giants, as it says in the KJV) Were these the sons of princes, as rabbinic tradition holds? Or was there an intermingling of the "godly" line of Seth with that of Cain?

The word "Nephilim" is used in only two places in the Bible, and it is not at all certain it means "giant." A different word is used when giants like Goliath are referred to. If this problem arouses your curiosity, use an analytical concordance and several commentaries on Genesis to examine the different interpretations.

Change of heart (Gen. 6:7). Does God's sorrow at man's descent into deeper expression of sin show regret for Creation? Is this His confession of a mistake? Or are we to understand this phrase as nothing more than a deeply emotional way of expressing anguished hurt at the state of sinning mankind?

The ark's size (Gen. 6:15). Using the smallest known size for the cubit (18 inches rather than 22 inches), the ark was built with three decks, about 450 feet long, 75 feet wide, and 45 feet in height. It would displace some 43,000 tons. Thus it had the proportion and size of some modern oceangoing vessels!

The animal "kinds" (Gen. 6:20). In the past, "kinds" sometimes has been translated "species," a term now used in many different senses in biology. It is likely that the many breeds of dogs, for instance, were represented in a single pair. Also, note that seven pairs of "clean" animals (that is, sacrificial and food animals) were taken into the ark, and probably so used after the waters receded.

Length of the Flood. The following chart traces the events of the Flood.

Events of the Flood

Month	Day	Events	Number of Days
2	10	Noah enters ark; God shuts door.	7
2	17	Rains fall; waters rush from seas. Ark floats.	40
3	27	Rain stops. Flood rushing in and water still rising.	110
7	17	Ark touches bottom on high mountains. Water stops rising; stationary.	40
8	27	Waters settle 15 cubits.	34
10	1	Ark on dry ground. Noah waits.	40
11	11	Noah sends raven; waits.	7
11	18	Noah sends dove; it returns with olive leaf.	7
11	25	Noah sends dove; it does not return. Noah waits.	22
12	17	Water recedes.	14
1	1	Noah sees dry land; waits.	56
2	27	Noah commands all to abandon the ark. Total time on ark.	377

Promise (Gen. 8:21-22). The uniformitarian principle is introduced here, after the Flood, as a promise. God will not again interrupt the regular flow of seasons or break into the orderly actions of natural law in order to judge the race.

Rainbow (Gen. 9:12-17). Why was the rainbow selected as the sign of the covenant promise between God and humankind? Could it have been because the rainbow appeared only after the Flood, due to drastically changed atmospheric conditions caused by dropping of the water canopy? It's fascinating to suppose that when Noah left the ark he saw the beauty of a rainbow for the first time in his 600 years of life!

Canaan's curse (Gen. 9:18-28). The meaning of "saw his father's nakedness" (v. 22) is obscure. But the clear implications of the picture of the drunkenness of Noah and the moral fault of Ham make one thing clear. The world may have been significantly changed. But man's heritage from Adam—his sin nature—remained!

Many have noted that the "curse" on Canaan is in fact a prophetic utterance by Noah. His words are not the cause of what would happen later, but do foretell it. It is important to note that only Canaan of the Hamitic family was selected out. The peoples involved are not Negroid, but rather the people who later inhabited the land of Canaan (Palestine) before the Israelites.

The table of nations (Gen. 10). Of the 70 names selected for inclusion in this list, some are well known to Bible scholars and students of ancient history (as "Mizraim," Egypt). Others are lost in antiquity. And still other peoples, like the Sumerians, are not included at all.

Babel (Gen. 11). The "fresh start" given Noah's clan soon settled into sin's stagnation. Told to go out and replenish the earth (9:1), Noah's descendants remained on a single plain, "Lest we be scattered abroad over the face of the whole earth" (11:4, NASB). They built a tower, which probably resembled the Babylonian ziggurat, possibly for astrological divination or perhaps even in the hope that its top in "the heavens" would provide a place of refuge should another flood come.

In any case, this disobedience led the Lord to act in a fresh judgment. He confused the languages. If you ever doubt God's sense of humor, picture sometime the next morning when one of the workers asked another for a brick!

These peoples refused to go out and fulfill God's plan. So now He acted to "scatter them over the face of the whole earth" (v. 8).

And so we come to the end of the first act of the cosmic drama. Up to this time God has dealt with the whole human race. And mankind has demonstrated in each situation sin's distortion of the original image God planted in man.

Yet, in it all, there are glimmerings of hope. God speaks, and some do respond with faith. And those who respond are delivered from the impending doom.

Now the Scriptures are about to focus on the men who do believe. We meet some of them in the genealogy of chapter 11. In meeting them, we are prepared for our introduction to a towering figure in Old Testament history. We are ready to meet Abram, a pagan on whose discovery of faith the future of the race of man depends.

TEACHING GUIDE

Prepare

Read and meditate on 2 Peter 3:3-18. How are you and I—and the group you lead—to apply the Flood story to our own lives?

Explore

1. If your group is interested, plan a Flood debate. Ask four to prepare beforehand, with two taking the side of a local, two a universal Flood. Limit time to 18-20 minutes.

Remember, one's view of the Flood is not a test of orthodoxy. Nor is the view of the Flood the critical teaching of this passage! The true message of Genesis 6–9 is that we do live in a moral universe. God is a moral judge, and He will punish sin!

2. Sum up the events reported in Genesis 6–9 in a minilecture. Highlight (1) society's sinful condition, (2) the faith-response of Noah, (3) the witness of the ark to that generation during its 120 years of building,

and (4) the assurance that God does judge sin. Use your minilecture to launch your group on a verse-by-verse study of 2 Peter 3:3-18.

3. Do a group study of 2 Peter 3:3-18. Do this by reading a verse, then having your group agree on a title, or a summary statement of the verse. For instance, verse 3, "Evil people will laugh at judgment"; verse 4, "They argue that nothing has changed from the beginning of the world," etc. By the time you have worked through each verse in this way, your group will have a very complete picture of what this key passage teaches.

Apply

1. From 2 Peter 3:14-18, have your class develop a list of statements about "How the Genesis Flood can affect the Christian life today." When the list is completed, pray that knowledge of divine judgment past and coming truly may be a purifying reality in your lives.

2. Or focus on the witness that Noah's faithfulness was to his generation. They did not respond. But in Noah Christ warned them, giving them a chance to be saved (cf. 1 Peter 3:19-20). How do we witness to others today? How important is the vision of coming judgment for Christians who need to share Jesus with those who might otherwise be lost?

STUDY GUIDE 5

Genesis 12

ABRAHAM: HIS CALL AND TIMES

Overview
Abraham stands as the greatest figure to be found in the ancient world. Three world religions—Islam, Judaism, and Christianity—revere him as the father of their faiths. Archeologists have explored the city of his origin, traced his journeys, probed the ruins of towns mentioned in Genesis, and have reconstructed a striking portrait of life 2,000 years before Christ that in detail after detail confirms the accuracy of the Old Testament account.

But what makes Abraham important to the Bible student is not the reverence in which he is held. It is not even the belief *The National Geographic* once expressed, that "Abraham the patriarch conceived a great and simple idea: the idea of a single Almighty God" (Dec. 1966, p. 740). Abraham's importance is not even found in the fact that he is today a prime model of saving faith. No, the importance of Abraham in Genesis is that through Abraham God reveals His purpose and His goal for the universe. In promises to Abram God revealed that He had a plan!

To Abraham were given wonderful covenant promises that show us history's direction, and reassure us that our personal universe is a purposive universe as well.

▶ ***Covenant.*** In Old Testament times the *berit* was at the foundation of social relationships. It might represent a treaty between nations, or a business contract, or a national constitution. In each case it represented a binding agreement, and expressed a firm commitment which was to be faithfully honored by all.

Commentary
Genesis 11:10-32 traces the genealogy of the man who was to become such a key to understanding the Old Testament. We read of his birthplace. He began a journey when God first spoke to him and instructed him to leave Mesopotamia to go to a land God would show him (Acts 7:2). Abraham left. While pausing in Haran along the way, God spoke again, repeating His command (Gen. 12:1), and adding words of promise. In a series of great "I wills," God stated an unshakable purpose which has remained constant through the millennia, and which is the foundation on which our grasp of Old and New Testament revelation must rest today. All the Old Testament and the New can be understood as a progressive unfolding of the purpose God first announced to Abraham some 4,000 years ago!

Yet, glancing at the words in Genesis 12, we're apt to miss this significance. It is only as we note the restatement of the promises, which come periodically throughout the Old Testament, that we begin to see their implications. As we hear the words of promise developed by the prophets, we see how completely central this revelation of purpose is. As we take these promises as a literal and changeless expression of God's purpose, the relationship between the Old and New Testaments becomes clear. And the history of our own day, as we await the return of Christ, is filled with fresh meaning.

The Genesis promises stand. They are at the root of the Jewish identity through the millenniums. They are the key to understanding the Old Testament. They are a window on current events.

I will. These words introduce the covenant promise as expressed in Genesis 12:2-3. The details are unclear at this point. But the general shape of God's purpose is taking form.

I will make you a great nation. From Abraham, Arab and Jew alike trace their origin. More than one nation now calls Abraham "father."

I will bless you and make your name great.

The reverence of millions in the three great monotheistic faiths has more than fulfilled this promise.

I will make you a blessing. From Abraham came the people of Israel. From Israel came both our Scriptures and our Saviour. What blessings indeed!

I will bless those who bless you, and curse those who curse you. In striking ways, the rise and fall of empires bears out the stated intention of God to deal with men and nations as they deal with His chosen people.

In you will all the families of the earth be blessed. God's choice of Abraham and his children was not designed to exclude others. From the very beginning God's choice of Israel was intended for the benefit of mankind. And on the return of Christ, the King, the fullness of blessing will be extended to all.

There is a final promise, one added after Abraham had responded in faith and left Haran, finally entering the land of Canaan. The Lord appeared and said:

To your descendants I will give THIS land. The purposes of God, and the future of Israel, are focused on a particular place: a land, Palestine, where in our own day we've seen the planting once again of a Jewish state.

Tracing the Promise

The statement of promise found in Genesis 12 is only a first, faint outline of that divine purpose which gives shape to the Old Testament and to the history of the world. As we read on in the Bible we realize that these first promises give the Jewish people their sense of identity. Then these first promises are developed. At critical times in the history of Israel, various dimensions of God's basic purpose are amplified and revealed.

♥ ***Link to Life: Children***

Children may not be old enough to explore God's early covenant promises. But they can understand the idea of promise, and claim many of the promises that God has given to believers.

To help boys and girls claim God's promises, play a game with them. Let them stand in front of you, and promise to catch them if they fall backward. After doing this with a few volunteers all will want to play. But then pretend with them that different people are behind them. You are one of them, and you promise to catch them. Another is God, and He promises to catch them. But another is the "meanest boy in town." Will he keep his promise to catch you?

This fun activity will help your boys and girls realize that promises are only as good as the people who make them. Because we can trust God completely, we can be sure He will keep every promise He makes.

God made basic promises to Abraham which are expanded as the Old Testament develops. It's helpful to look ahead briefly, and to see some of the dimensions of the promise, and the development of the purpose first expressed in Genesis 12.

Genesis 15. The promises given to Abraham must have placed a strain on his faith, for Abraham and Sarah were childless. How could he become a great nation? As was common in that culture, Abraham had designated Eliezer of Damascus (who probably had the status of an adopted son) to be his heir, and to care for his wife should he die. In Genesis 15 the question is raised by Abraham: How could the announced purpose of God be fulfilled since he had no child?

In verse 4 is God's response: Your own son shall be your heir. God's promises would be passed on to Abraham's physical seed, and that seed would be as impossible for man to number as the stars of the heaven are to count (v. 5).

Here too God defined the extent of the land to be given Abraham's children: "From the river of Egypt to the great river, the Euphrates" (v. 18). The land was further defined for Abraham by listing the peoples who then lived within it.

Genesis 17. Years have now passed since Abraham had been given the initial promises; years during which he and his wife Sarah had no children. Finally, some 12 years before the scene sketched in this Bible chapter, Abraham, following established custom of this time, had fathered a son by Hagar, his wife's servant. The child, Ishmael (progenitor of the Arabs), was rejected as the heir of the covenant promises. Instead God changed Abram's name (which meant "father") to Abraham (which meant "father of a multitude"). This 99-year-old man was told that he and Sarah, who was then 90

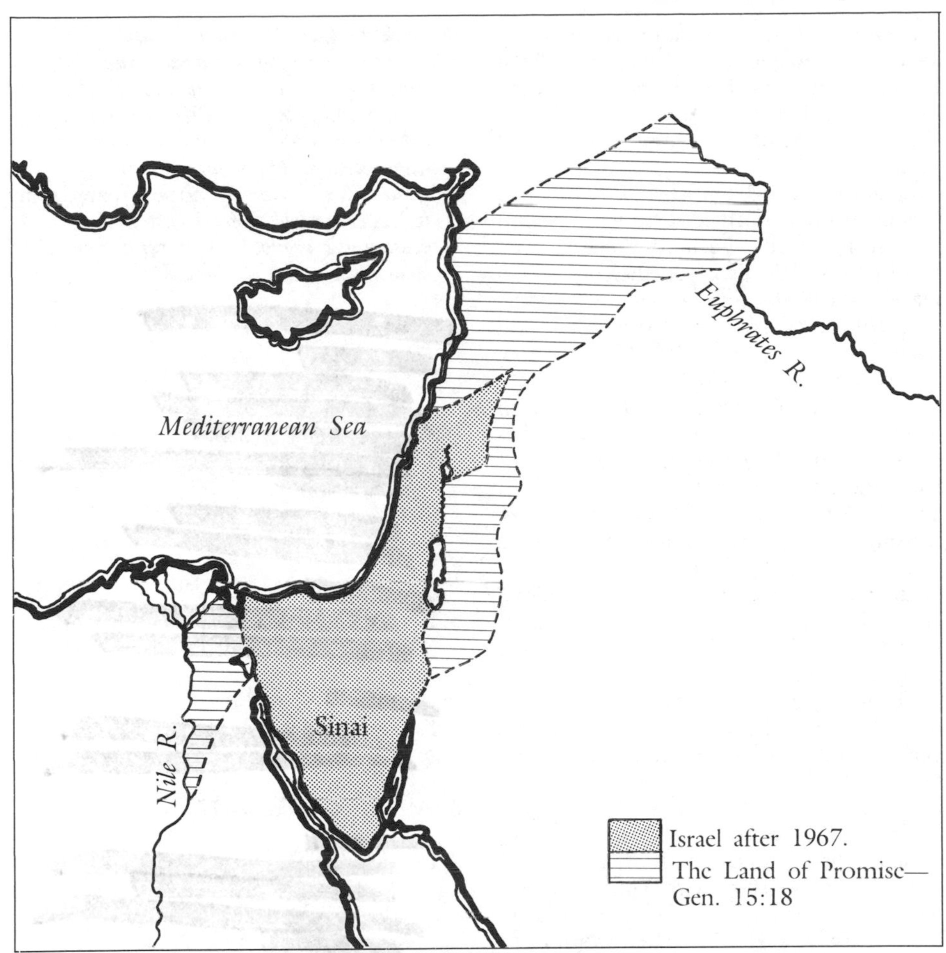

The Promised Land

and beyond childbearing years, would have a son of their own. This child of miracle was to be named Isaac, and he was to inherit the promises.

In this statement of the covenant promise, two new dimensions are added. First, God's special relationship with Abraham's descendants is to last forever, "for the generations to come" (v. 7). Second, the title deed to Palestine is given the same "everlasting" status. As history has demonstrated, sin might cause Israel to be expelled from her land. But the title is retained. The promises made to Abraham, and the purposes they express, are to be viewed as changeless.

2 Samuel 7. Centuries passed before another significant amplification of the original covenant promise. In the early days of Israel's organization as a monarchy, David was selected to be king and special promises were given to him. His line was to be established as a royal line, and from his descendants was to come an Offspring whose kingdom would be established forever (vv. 12-13). A Davidic ruler might not always sit on a throne in Jerusalem. But there would always be a rightful heir to the throne, until finally the promised King would ascend the throne to rule over an endless kingdom.

From the perspective given by the New Testament, the promise becomes strikingly clear. Matthew carefully traced the line of David to Jesus. Even today Jesus, the rightful Heir, lives! And one day soon He, Jesus of Nazareth, will take the throne. The eternal purposes of God in Israel will be fulfilled, and the promises kept through Jesus' endless reign.

Jeremiah 30–31. Still more centuries followed. The people of God were torn from the Promised Land and dragged into Captivity. Then Jeremiah was used by God to reveal yet another dimension to the purpose.

In the Book of Jeremiah, the Abrahamic Covenant is reconfirmed. God would bring the captive people back to the Promised Land (30:3). What's more, the promise to David is reconfirmed as well. A Davidic king will be raised up as Israel's ruler and relate God to man (vv. 9, 21). And now comes the new revelation!

Long after Abraham, God had given Abraham's descendants a Law to keep. Obedience to the Law provided evidence of faith, and obedience was the basis on which a particular generation of Jews might expect blessing or judgment. To obey meant that a generation would have a present experience of the blessings promised to Israel at history's end. Disobedience meant a generation would suffer judgment, though the basic promises remained sure.

Through Jeremiah now comes word that the fulfillment of God's covenant promise deals not only with the external life of men, but with the inner man as well! The promise is not simply one of a day of peace and plenty. The promise of God involves conversion: the gift of a new heart and a new personal relationship with God that will mend the ravages of sin upon the human personality (31:31-35). The promise to Abraham is ultimately related to the undoing of the curse! The very sin that mars the image of God in man will be dealt with, iniquity will be forgiven and washed away, and a new heart implanted that is in full harmony with God and godliness.

Through Abraham's race God intends to purify humankind!

It is here that the line of promise spills over into New Testament revelation. In the second coming of Christ we see the appearance of the promised King. But in the Cross we see the reconciliation of mankind! Thus in this one Person, God is working out all His purpose and all His plan. In this one Person, Jesus, God will act "to bring all things in heaven and on earth together under one Head, even Christ" (Eph. 1:10). This total purpose of God, which the later millennia have revealed, lies latent in the seed of promise planted in Genesis 12.

♥ ***Link to Life: Youth / Adult***
It's best to help youth or adults trace the unfolding of God's purpose through His covenant promises in direct Bible study. Put the following chart on the chalkboard, or duplicate it as a handout sheet. But include only the numbers, not the material in italics. *Then look through each Bible passage as a group, listing covenant promise elements as each is discovered.*

ABRAHAMIC COVENANT

Genesis 12
1. *make a great nation*
2. *bless you and your name*
3. *make you a blessing*
4. *bless those who bless you, curse those who curse you*
5. *in you bless all families*
6. *give this land to your seed*

Genesis 15
1. *covenant to Abraham's physical seed*
2. *land defined: Euphrates to Nile*

Genesis 17
1. *covenant with physical seed, forever*
2. *land of Canaan everlasting possession*

DAVIDIC COVENANT

2 Samuel 7
1. *David's line a royal family forever*
2. *David's kingdom to be forever*
3. *Chastisement provided for, but kingdom to last forever*

NEW COVENANT

Jeremiah 30–31
1. *Abrahamic promises reconfirmed*
2. *Davidic promises reconfirmed*
3. *Summary of elements*
   - *physical seed of Abraham in view*
   - *Davidic line through which covenant fulfillment is realized*
   - *land of Canaan in view*
   - *New Covenant made with Israel*
   - *involves individual and national conversion*
   - *looks to time of universal knowledge of the Lord*

A Covenant

Our understanding of the significance of these promises is heightened when we realize that they were given specific expression as *covenants.*

The covenant was a contract in the ancient world. Agreements between parties were given binding status by the "cutting" or making of a covenant. While there were several forms for making a covenant, the most binding of all was the "covenant of blood." Animals were killed and divided (hence the term "cutting" a covenant), and both parties to the treaty passed between the pieces, binding themselves to its provisions. It is such a solemnizing of God's promise to Abraham we read of in Genesis 15. Keil and Delitzsch note, "Thus God condescended to follow the custom of the Chaldeans, that He might in the most solemn manner confirm His oath to Abram the Chaldean."

What is so significant about the Genesis 15 scene is not so much its conformity with ancient practice as its one-party nature. In the normal covenant relationship two parties entered into a conditional relationship. If one failed to perform as required, the other was freed from his responsibility as well. But the Bible tells us that God caused a deep sleep to come on Abraham, and only the Lord passed between the sacrifices.

God had announced a purpose that no act of man can alter. Now God confirmed by promise that His purpose would surely be fulfilled through Abraham's seed.

There were no conditions laid on Abraham or his descendants. God, and God alone, pressed His seal on the contract made and witnessed that day. Looking back, the New Testament comments:

> When God made His promise to Abraham, since there was no one greater for Him to swear by, He swore by Himself, saying, "I will surely bless you and give you many descendants." Men swear by someone greater than themselves, and the oath confirms what is said and puts an end to all argument. Because God wanted to make the unchanging nature of His purpose very clear to the heirs of what was promised, He confirmed it with an oath. God did this so that, by two unchangeable things in which it is impossible for God to lie, we who have fled to take hold of the hope offered to us may be greatly encouraged.
>
> Hebrews 6:13-14, 16-18

The promise *is* clear. Confirmed with an oath, the purpose of God as it began to take shape in the promise to Abraham is unchangeable and sure.

♥ ***Link to Life: Youth / Adult***

Some who hear the Gospel find it hard to grasp that accepting Christ brings them into a saving relationship with God. They believe, but they doubt their salvation, and may be anxious or worried. This Hebrews passage about the nature of God's promise as an unshakable oath can help such folks find fresh assurance in Christ.

Work through the passage with your group, noting together the strongest words and phrases: oath, swear by, unchanging purpose, not possible for God to lie, etc. Then lead your adults to look at several salvation promises such as John 3:16; 5:24; 10:28; etc. These are promises to all who trust themselves to Jesus. Do you believe in Him? Then according to God's Word—His promise, His oath, His unchangeable nature—what has He given you? What is actually yours, now?

Unchangeable. Across the years Bible students have argued concerning various elements of God's purpose as expressed in these Genesis chapters. Some have felt that the promises have been fulfilled in a "spiritual" way in the Christian church, for we are the "spiritual seed" of Abraham, whose faith in God we share.

But it is difficult to explain away that which God takes so much care to define.

Who are descendants of Abraham as far as the covenant promise is concerned? Not Eliezer, no matter how deeply he may have shared the faith of Abraham (cf. Gen. 24). Not Ishmael, though Abraham was his physical father. But Isaac, a child of Abraham in both senses—physical and spiritual.

And the land is not mountaintop experiences, or milk and honey spiritual provision. It is the actual land of Palestine, marked out carefully by geographical boundaries and defined by the names of tribes and cities that are still reflected in the place-names of our own day.

On what basis might God break the ancient promises? None, for the contract God drew with Abraham was unconditional. God bound Himself, and Himself alone, "to make the unchanging nature of His purpose very clear" (Heb. 6:17).

After that contract was ratified, Scripture continues to give witness to its unbreakable character. In Genesis 17:7 God calls the promise "everlasting." After a long age of apostasy, the covenant is confirmed and David is given the promise of a throne "forever." At the very moment of Israel's expulsion from the land for apostasy and idolatry, the covenants are confirmed again, and even greater promises added through Jeremiah. Here too the unconditional character of the covenant promise is emphasized (Jer. 31:35-38).

No, the purpose once expressed has not been changed. God does have a direction for history, a direction tied up in the experience of a chosen race, a race chosen to be a channel through which God will bless the world.

The Dominant Theme

Why have we spent so much time looking at the promise here in Genesis? Because the concept of this covenant, the idea that God chose Israel and made certain promises to her that reveal His eternal purposes, dominates the Old Testament. And because God's purposes as expressed in the promise are unchangeable, it is to the Old Testament we must look for a key to understand many of our day's current events.

The concept of this covenant also helps us in the study of the rest of Genesis. The stories of two of the patriarchs, Isaac and Jacob, are not told simply because they were "interesting" men. Or even because they were believers, through whose experiences we can learn about walking with God. No, Isaac and Jacob are significant in Genesis because these men are inheritors of the divine promise. In them we see the preservation of the promise, and to them Israel traces the title deed to Palestine and its identity as the people of God.

Later, as a mob of millions struggled out of Egyptian slavery, Moses would remind Israel of her origin and destiny. The children of Abraham, of Isaac, of Jacob/Israel, would become a nation: a nation called to reveal God to a world that lived without understanding, and without hope.

TEACHING GUIDE

Prepare

Read and meditate on Hebrews 6:13-18. Consider God's oath and the impossibility that He might lie. How wonderful that we have a faithful God, who can be trusted to keep His promises always.

Explore

1. Develop a simple quiz to launch your group session. Ask members to check "always," "sometimes," or "never" in response to items like these: *I have doubts about God really accepting me. *I worry when I do something wrong that God will reject me. Etc. Survey results by a simple show of hands. Promise that in this study you will see things about God that will quiet all fears.

2. Or ask your group to brainstorm. What elements of God's plan do they know from Scripture? Have them find Scriptures that reveal God's plan. List things they suggest. (Later, you can see how these elements relate to the purposes revealed in God's covenant promises.)

Expand

1. In a minilecture explain the nature of a covenant. Then you might work as a group in direct Bible study to complete the covenants chart (see "link-to-life," p. 48).

2. Cover all the covenant material in a lecture, having your group fill in handout charts (p. 48) as you talk. Be sure to explain the importance of the covenant promises, to Israel, to our understanding of the Old Testament, and as links between the two Testaments.

Apply

1. How did God's faithfulness help His people build their image of the Lord? Two psalms express something of Israel's praise, and sense of confidence in God's covenant-keeping character. Let teams of three or four read one of the psalms, and from it develop a series of "God is . . ." statements. Each statement is to reflect something the psalmist knew about God, and learned about from His commitment to His covenant promises.

The psalms are 111 and 136.
2. Focus attention on the great Hebrews 6 affirmation of God as an oath-keeping, faithful God. If your initial quiz showed that some in your group are uncertain in their own relationships with God, use the "link-to-life" activity suggested on page 49.

If not, follow the procedure suggested on page 49 for study of the passage, but conclude with a "go around." After the study, go around the group and let each person complete this statement: "Because God is completely trustworthy, I. . . ."
3. Or conclude by having your group write its own praise psalm, thanking God for His great faithfulness to all His promises to us.

STUDY GUIDE 6

Genesis 13–24

BY FAITH

Overview

In the New Testament, God looks back on Abraham, and reminisces. There the Lord focuses on Abraham's positive traits, and especially on Abraham's faith. For it is faith that Abraham exemplifies.

But Abraham was not without faults. He failed all too often, and showed many of the weaknesses that plague believers today. So we are to learn from Abraham's one great strength, but also to learn from his many weaknesses. In fact, we are to discover that faith is the one principle that lifts any person beyond his inadequacies; the one quality that wins approval from God.

▶ ***Faith.*** In the Old Testament faith is a personal, trusting response to God, who speaks words of promise. This same basic meaning is carried over into the New Testament as well. In different ages the word of promise has been different: to Abraham, it was God's promise of a son to be born from his and Sarah's dead flesh. To us, the word of promise is Jesus Himself. When we respond, as Abraham did, with a simple trust in God, we receive the same gift he was given—righteousness, and a personal relationship with God.

▶ ***Loving-kindness.*** This term in new versions, and "grace" in older ones, translates *hesed.* The Hebrew word means "covenant love" or "covenant faithfulness." God loves us because He is committed to us by His oath.

■ For a verse-by-verse study of each event reported in Genesis 13–24, see pages 50-67 of the *Bible Knowledge Commentary.*

Commentary

What does the New Testament emphasize as the central message of Abraham's life? What it emphasizes is not that he, like us, was a lost sinner, but that Abraham was lifted beyond himself by faith.

Hebrews 11:8-19 focuses on three events in Abraham's life that God fondly remembers:

> By faith, Abraham, when called to go to a place he would later receive as his inheritance, obeyed and went, even though he did not know where he was going. By faith he made his home in the Promised Land like a stranger in a foreign country; he lived in tents, as did Isaac and Jacob, who were heirs with him of the same promise. For he was looking forward to the city with foundations, whose architect and builder is God.
>
> By faith Abraham, even though he was past age—and Sarah herself was barren—was enabled to become a father because he considered Him faithful who had made the promise. And so from this one man, and he as good as dead, came descendants as numerous as the stars in the sky and as countless as the sand of the seashore. . . .
>
> By faith Abraham, when God tested him, offered Isaac as a sacrifice. He who had received the promises was about to sacrifice his one and only son, even though God had said to him, "It is through Isaac that your offspring will be reckoned." Abraham reasoned that God could raise the dead, and figuratively speaking, he did receive Isaac back from death.

These three times when reason might well have challenged the spoken word of God, Abraham responded with faith.

It is here, in Abraham's faith-response to God, that we find this basic Bible theme brought into clear focus.

Earlier God had affirmed His existence

and His care for men. God had spoken to individuals before, like Noah and Cain. But it is in Abraham that we discover a clear illustration of what has always separated mankind's Noahs from its Cains. It isn't that Cain was intrinsically "worse." Both were men of mixed character. Both did good things, yet found reflected in their actions the taint of sin.

No, what sets men apart as far as relationship with God is concerned has always been a simple thing: faith. Noah trusted God and built an ark in which he and his family were saved. Cain refused to trust God. This led directly to his final bondage to sin, a servitude whose full expression is found in the murder of his brother.

Faith divides man from man. The way you and I respond to God as He speaks His message to us is the critical issue of our lives. This is the message we hear in the story of Abraham. From Abraham we learn much of the nature of that faith which pleases God and frees Him to act in our lives today.

♥ ***Link to Life: Children***

Boys and girls can understand faith and respond to God trustingly. A simple illustration may help. Hold out a small gift to a child in your classroom. "Bobby, this is for you." If Bobby takes the gift, say, "Good! I told you it was for you. You believed me, didn't you, and came and took it." If Bobby does not take the gift, say, "Bobby, I promise you can have this. Will you come and take it?" Again give praise when Bobby comes.

Tell your boys and girls that Jesus has a gift for us too. It is the gift of forgiveness for all our sins. Jesus promises us this gift in the Bible. All we need to do is what Bobby just did: take the gift that was offered to him.

Boys and girls can bow their heads and talk to Jesus, telling Jesus they take His forgiveness-gift right now.

Abraham's Failures

Sometimes we tend to idealize Bible people. We forget that, while they were giants in many ways, they were also all too human. In fact, before we look at the faith of a man like Abraham, we need to realize that he was, like all believers, far from perfect!

We have an early indication of Abram's flaws in Genesis 12. Abram had been called by God to go to a land which the Lord Himself chose. He had obeyed in an act that required real faith. But once in the land, Abram's faith was shaken by a famine. Rather than trust God or wait for further direction, he went to Egypt. There he continued to show lack of trust by getting Sarah to tell a half-truth about their relationship, to deny she was his wife. Fear that he might be killed outweighed his commitment to his wife! Even when she was taken in Pharaoh's household, Abram did not reveal their relationship. Instead he profited in silence from the favor extended to the supposed brother!

Abraham's tendency to rely on his wits rather than on God also is shown in the events leading up to the birth of Ishmael. Some 10 years passed while Abraham waited for God to send the son He had promised. Finally Sarah began urging him to take her maid as a secondary wife. Even though this was a custom of the land, it took Sarah's nagging to make him take action. He "hearkened to [obeyed] the voice of Sarai" (16:2, KJV). Perhaps Abram thought he would "help" God keep His promises! Perhaps he felt that 86 was just too old to wait any longer. In any case, Abram did not consult God. He simply went ahead, without direction, relying on his own plan to fulfill God's purposes. Self-reliance and self-effort took the place of trust in God.

And then, how stunning. Abraham repeated the sin he did in Egypt! Again Abraham misrepresented Sarah as only his sister, and she was placed in the harem of a king named Abimelech. God protected Sarah even though her husband was not willing to, and before Abimelech came to her God spoke to him in a vision. Abimelech, fearful at the divine visit, complained to Abraham that he might have led the king into unknowing sin! Abram's reply was weak (20:11-12). Abraham was worried, afraid that the people of the foreign land they visited might not fear God, and thus might kill him for Sarah. Abraham feared for his life—but not for his wife!

Abraham apparently had not stopped to think that though a particular people might not know God, God knew them! There was no place that Abraham could go to be beyond the protection of the Lord. Yet, even after an earlier rebuke in Egypt, Abraham

Abraham's Character

	ACTIONS	CHARACTER TRAIT INFERRED
"GOOD ACTS"	leave Ur	trusting, adventurous
"BAD ACTS"	go to Egypt lie about Sarah	lack of trust, fearfulness selfishness, materialism

repeated the same sin and let fear and selfishness control his choices.

No, the Abraham we meet on the pages of the Bible is no idealized man. He is a man we need to see both as weak, and as a willful sinner.

♥ ***Link to Life: Youth / Adult***
To help your group members get a clear picture of Abraham the man, display the following chart. Work together as a group to list Abram's actions, and to suggest traits they may imply. More than one trait can be implied by a single event.
You can personalize this study by giving each group member a sheet of paper on which this chart has been reproduced. Ask each to do a similar, but private, analysis of his own life and character.

Not good? The normal reaction at this point is to object. We want to point out some of the many good qualities that Abram exhibits, to balance the portrait of the sinner. We want to stress Abraham's initial trust in God, his generosity to Lot, his refusal to risk God's glory when offered the loot of Sodom.

We can find many things to praise in Abraham. In this too Abraham is like each of us. We're not totally bad—not totally good. We are a strange mixture of admirable traits, and traits that in all honesty must be labeled despicable. Abraham was a man whose best traits are flawed by the mark of Adam's sin. In him as well as in all believers lie weakness and willfulness. God's image is there, but so is the unmistakable stamp of Adam's Fall.

It is just this fact that makes Abram such an important illustration of Bible truth. No, he cannot be held up as an illustration of the goodness of man. He is, instead, an example of the fact that God cares for, and gives His salvation to, the unworthy!

In later centuries Abraham's children would miss this message. The men of Israel would look back and claim God's favor as their birthright on the basis of their descent from Abraham and on the basis of their possession of the Law. They would not, as Abraham did, admit sin and need, and come to God with no empty boast of ability to earn His favor. They would not be willing, as Abraham was, to bow as a sinner before God and to trust God alone, in order that faith might be counted for righteousness.

This is Paul's point:

> What then shall we say that Abraham, our forefather, discovered in this matter? If, in fact, Abraham was justified by works, he had something to boast about—but not before God. What does the Scripture say? "Abraham believed God, and it was credited to him as righteousness." Now when a man works, his wages are not credited to him as a gift, but as an obligation. However, to the man who does not work but trusts God who justifies the wicked, his faith is credited as righteousness.
>
> Romans 4:1-5

God, who justifies the wicked. It is in this way that you and I need first to see Abraham. We need to look at him as the Bible shows him to be in order to explain so many of his failures and sins. Yet it is in his failures that you and I can find comfort!

For our failures and our sins are just as real as his were. Like Abraham, we need to turn away from our own works to rely on God alone. "This is why 'it was credited to him [Abraham] as righteousness.' The words 'it was credited to him' were written not for him alone, but also for us, to whom God will credit righteousness—for us who believe in Him who raised Jesus our Lord from the dead" (vv. 22-24).

And so in Abraham we have a mirror—of ourselves. And we have a message from God. As Abraham did, we need to turn away from any confidence in our own goodness and find in God's promise in Jesus our own way of faith's escape.

Abraham's Faith

The three incidents recalled in Hebrews 11 now become the focus of our study of Abraham as well as the key to understanding how his experience ministers God's message to us today.

Abraham obeyed and went (Gen. 12). It would be wrong to picture Abraham as an adventurous man eager to travel. It would also be a mistake to see him as a crusader, a man gripped with the vision of one God which he was determined to transplant to another land. The Bible says that when the family lived "beyond the river . . . [they] worshiped other gods" (Josh. 24:2). During the first 75 years of his life, Abraham lived in a pagan world—and prospered. There's no reason to suppose that when God spoke to him Abraham was other than a successful businessman who enjoyed considerable wealth and a comfortable life in a center of world civilization.

Even today, when people move so often, it's difficult for a person to be uprooted. God's call to Abraham demanded total restructuring of his lifestyle. He left his own civilization for a foreign land. He left a place of culture to move to the backward home of wanderers. He left his home to take up residence in a tent. He left stability for the uncertainty of travel and everchanging circumstances. He left the security of an established code of laws to wander, afraid, from land to land (cf. Gen. 20:11). He left a long tradition of worship of Nanna, the moon god, for the God who had spoken to him, but whom he did not yet really know.

Leaving Ur was an act of faith. In making this difficult decision Abraham exhibited a unique trust.

In some ways each of us makes this kind of decision when we first trust Christ as Saviour. Our lives have developed a pattern, sometimes one that is well established. We don't really know what the Christian experience may bring, or where God is leading. So we take a risk. We give up the familiar for the strange. We too leave our past for a "land we know not of." The beginning of Abraham's pilgrimage is a picture of the beginning of each man's pilgrimage into Christ.

♥ ***Link to Life: Children***

Faith is expressed as obedience in Abraham, and in children too. When we obey we show that we trust God enough to do what He says.

Help the children see faith as obedience. Draw three pictures, each to represent an adult speaking to a child: (1) Come in. The dog won't bite. (2) Go along to school. I won't let the big boys hurt you. (3) You go and ask Mrs. Brown if you can come in. I'm too busy to phone just now.

Talk about the pictures and why the child shown might not want to do what he or she is told to do. What bad thing might happen? What do you suppose he or she is worried about?

Talk about the adult's promises. What will the child do if he or she believes the adult? (Real trust will lead to obedience.) Point out that we can obey God, because we can trust Him always. People who have faith in God obey Him, just as Abraham left his home when God told him to go.

Abraham considered God faithful (Gen. 15). We see the next great act of faith in Genesis 15. God had given Abraham great promises which hinged on the founding of a family line. But Abraham had no child. When Abraham raised this issue with God, the Lord promised, "A son from your own body shall be your heir" (v. 4). God then went on to promise Abraham uncountable descendants. "Abram believed the Lord; and He credited it to him as righteousness" (v. 6).

The New Testament emphasizes the great trust this act of faith required. "Without weakening in his faith, he faced the fact that his body was as good as dead—since he was about a hundred years old—and that Sarah's womb was also dead. Yet he did not waver through unbelief regarding the promise of God, but was strengthened in his faith and gave glory to God, being fully persuaded that God had power to do what He had promised" (Rom. 4:19-21).

In this event we gain deep insight into saving faith. Faith faces the facts. Abraham had no illusions about his own ability to father a son, or Sarah's to become a mother. Physically speaking this was impossible. The two were, as far as parenthood was concerned, "as good as dead." Yet Abraham's kind of faith also faced the fact of God. And God changes every equation!

Abraham stands here as evidence that God *can* be trusted to keep His word, and that such trust is never disappointed.

Several factors need to be noted to grasp the message God is communicating.

**The promises*. Abraham did not exercise blind faith. Instead, he responded to a word spoken by the Lord. It is the concrete, objective expression of God's promise that calls out response.

"Faith" in what we *imagine* to be God's will is not Abraham's kind of faith. Abraham's faith is a response to divine revelation.

**The Person*. Abraham's confidence was in God as a Person who is both able and committed to do what He promises. At times we think of "faith" as subjective; as something *we* do. Abraham's kind of faith does not rely on its own intensity or sincerity. Abraham's kind of faith puts reliance on the object of faith: God Himself. It is God's trustworthiness and not our trusting that is critical.

**The perspective*. Abraham boldly faced the fact of his and Sarah's ages. He realistically looked at the situation, and just as realistically ignored the circumstances! Realism understands that physical and other limitations do not apply to God, for God is the underlying reality; and whatever the circumstances, God can bring to pass what He promises.

Abraham might very well have cried out, "I can't!" And he would have been right. Instead Abraham cried, "God can!" This perspective, which sees God as the touchstone of reality, is to characterize our faith as well.

**The product*. God announced it: "It was credited to him as righteousness" (Rom. 4:22). Like you and I, Abraham was not a righteous person. There was no basis on which God and Abraham could fellowship until God revealed that He would accept faith and, because of it, credit Abram's account with righteousness.

More is involved here than a divine bookkeeping transaction. Through faith God works to produce actual righteousness in us. As we learn to live by Abraham's kind of faith, facing each test and trial with our eyes on God and His trustworthiness, God the Holy Spirit produces in our lives the fruit of a righteousness which we ourselves do not possess (cf. Gal. 5:18-23). God counts faith as holiness, and then through faith produces in us the very holiness He has promised is—and will be—ours.

Abraham reasoned (Gen. 22). This is one of the most unusual and, at the same time, most exciting stories in the Bible. Isaac, the promised heir, had been born. The old man had grown to dearly love this child for whom he had waited so long with such eager expectation. Suddenly, as if to shatter the old man's world, God spoke to him again. "Take your son, your only son Isaac, whom you love, and go to the region of Moriah. Sacrifice him there as a burnt offering on one of the mountains I will tell you about" (v. 2).

Then the Bible tells us an amazing thing: "Early the next morning Abraham got up and saddled his donkey. He took with him two of his servants and his son Isaac. When he had cut enough wood for the burnt offering, he set out for the place God had told him about" (v. 3).

There was no hesitation.

Abraham obeyed.

We can't know how Abraham felt on the three-day journey, or the doubts and fears that may have filled his heart and mind. But we do know that before he arrived, Abraham had worked the problem through. "Abraham reasoned that God could raise the dead" (Heb. 11:19). Abraham knew that God had promised, "through Isaac . . . your offspring will be reckoned" (v. 18). God would not go back on His stated word. If God chose to accept Isaac as a sacrifice, Abraham would give him, sure that the Lord would give the child back again.

And so the Genesis text reveals, in a Hebrew plural: "Stay here," Abraham told the servants who accompanied them. "I and the boy [will] go over there. We will worship, and then we will come back to you" (Gen. 22:5). Abraham did not know the means. But he did know that God would provide.

God did. As Abraham was about to plunge the knife into the bound body of his son, the Lord stopped him and pointed out a ram whose horns had been caught in a thicket. The ram was slain; the boy was freed. God Himself had provided a substitute.

And then God spoke again. The test was complete. God's promises to Abraham were reconfirmed and Abraham, his trust also confirmed by the events, returned with Isaac to their tents.

What is there in this story for us? Much!

Faith's life. The life of faith that God calls us to is not an easy one. Like Abraham you and I may well be called to make some heartrending decisions. But also like Abraham, we can fix our confidence securely in God.

A reasoned faith. Faith is not opposed to reason. The man who relies on God simply takes more into account than the man who does not believe. Often an appeal to "reason" means no more than an insistence we consider only what a person can see and touch and feel.

We all face this danger. In the decisions you and I make, do we look only at factors we can see? Or do we reason that God is able to alter circumstances to fit His will? Abraham reasoned that God's will is the ultimate reality and that His expressed purposes are sure. It was this kind of reasoning—that takes God into account—that was part of Abraham's faith. And must become a part of ours.

An unhesitant faith. Abraham did not wait. He rose up early to obey God. An overt response to God's Word is still an integral part of what it means to have "faith." Often our feelings and desires struggle against our intention to respond to God. But trust in God as a Person not only frees us to respond; our actions give evidence of the reality of our trust.

Abraham's journey to Mount Moriah is portrayed in Scripture as a test. It was a test that Abraham passed, and in passing demonstrated to God, to himself, to Isaac—and to us—the reality of his trust in God.

♥ ***Link to Life: Youth / Adult***
Have your group develop a definition of faith from Genesis 22; Hebrews 11; and Romans 4. Let each member write down a 20-word "faith is" statement. Then divide into study teams. Each team is to take one *of the three faith incidents, to (1) study it in its Old Testament context, (2) to study the Hebrews 11 commentary on it, and (3) to think of it in light of Romans 4. Then each team is to make a* list of elements *that must be included in a biblical definition of "faith."*

Have the teams come together to report, and work as a group to see if you can come up with an adequate definition of faith.

Observations on the Text

Even today a visit to a foreign land may introduce us to customs and folkways that are easily misunderstood. Imagine a visit to the lands of Abraham, some 4,000 years and half a world away!

But the science of archeology has provided many insights into Abraham's time. Through the discovery of codes of law and customs, of business contracts and letters, etc., we can understand many otherwise hard to understand events of Abraham's life. Here are a few discoveries which will enrich your grasp of Genesis.

Genesis 11:31–12:9. Abraham's journey was taken along well-established trade routes that connected Ur with Haran, Palestine, the Mediterranean coast, and Egypt. Even the towns that Abraham visited lie in rainfall zones, with annual inches of rain sufficient to support the sheep and herds he brought along.

Genesis 12:10-20. Abraham's fear that Pharaoh might kill him to obtain Sarah had some precedent. There is a record of a Pharaoh doing just this in the case of a visitor from the north!

Genesis 13. Lot went against custom when he failed to give Abraham, his elder, first choice, even though Abraham offered it to him. Lot chose the more prosperous and populated valley areas; Abraham had less-populated hill country.

Genesis 14. Until recent years the story of the invasion of the five kings reported here was questioned by liberal scholars. Archeol-

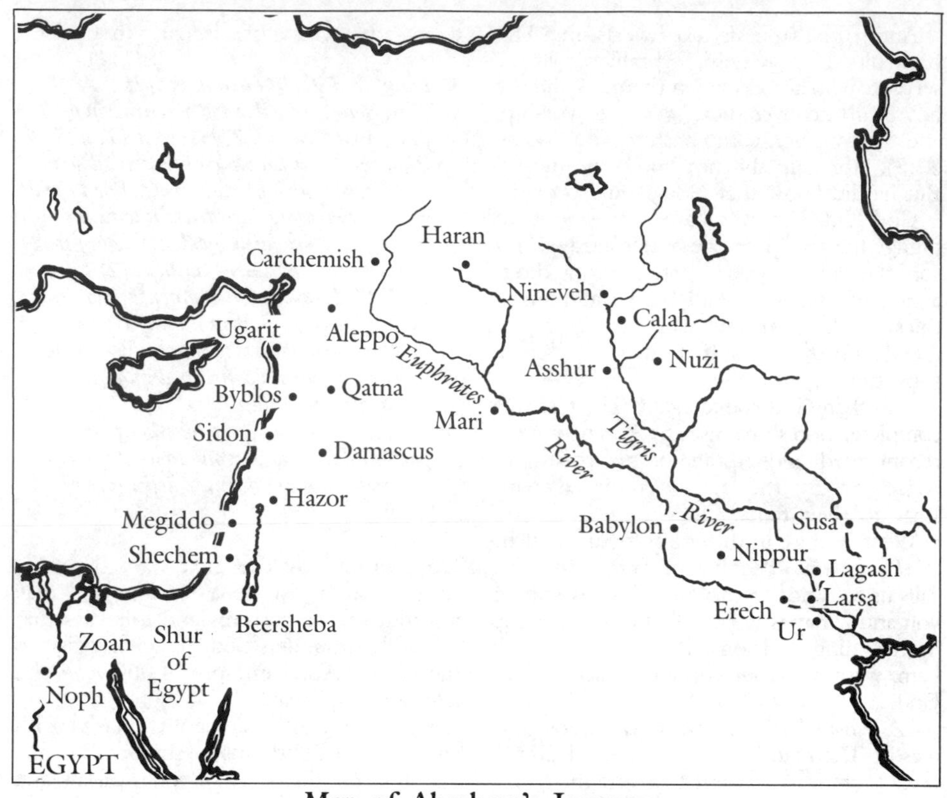

Map of Abraham's Journey

ogy has now shown that kings from as far away as lower Mesopotamia (see map of Abraham's Journey) did make such incursions, and both people and place-names fit what we know of Abraham's time. Even the reason for such invasions is now known: copper, asphalt, and manganese were valuable natural resources of the region.

Genesis 15. The Nuzi tablets, about 20,000 documents written on hardened clay discovered in 1925-41, date within 400 or 500 years of the patriarchs. They show customs like those mentioned in Scripture. One custom involves adoption of a slave or freeman who in return for serving his benefactor becomes his heir. The contract of adoption also contained provisions stating that if the patron later had a son, the son would be the heir. This is reflected in verses 1-4, with Eliezer designated as "the one who will inherit [Abraham's] estate."

Genesis 16. Ten years after the promise of a son to be Abraham's heir, Sarah suggested that Abraham take her maid, Hagar, as a secondary wife. This was by custom a moral action, and may have seemed to Abraham the way God would keep His promise. But it was not God's plan.

Sarah's bitterness and her insistence that Hagar and Ishmael be expelled went *against* custom (21:10). God had to personally intervene to move Abraham to do what the patriarch felt was a wrong action.

Abraham's statement in 16:6, "Your servant is in your hands," was not, however, permission to mistreat Hagar. Instead it recognized the existing legal right of Sarah to "deal harshly" with a slave.

Genesis 18. The picture of Abraham and Sarah themselves preparing a meal for the three strangers reflects a strong cultural emphasis on hospitality.

Genesis 19. The city gate, where Lot met the two angels who came to search out the righteous in Sodom, was a place where men of the ancient world gathered to talk, conduct business, and settle disputes. It was the focus of city life.

The heavy doors on Lot's own house (v. 9) are also interesting. Archeologists have found that homes of a later date were not hung with heavy doors. But homes in Palestine in Abraham's day were so protected.

Leon Wood describes the destruction of Sodom and Gomorrah and shows how the biblical description fits geological and other data:

> The destruction of Sodom was effected by a rain of "brimstone and fire." In examining the meaning of the phrase, scholars have ruled out volcanic action on the basis of geological indications. Many believe that it refers to an earthquake resulting in an enormous explosion. Several factors are pointed out as favoring this view. The idea of brimstone and fire suggests incendiary materials raining down upon the city as the result of an explosion. Another descriptive word used is "overthrew" (Gen. 19:29), and this fits the thought of an earthquake. That Abraham saw smoke rising in the direction of the city indicates that there was a fire. Inflammable asphalt has long been known in the area. Records from ancient writers speak of strong sulfuric odors, which suggest that quantities of sulfur were there in past time. Further, the whole Jordan Valley constitutes an enormous fault in the earth's surface, given to earthquake conditions. It's possible, then, that God did see fit to miraculously time an earthquake at this precise moment, which would have released great quantities of gas, mixed sulfur with various salts found in abundance, and measurably increased the flow of asphalt seepage. Lightning could have ignited all, and the entire country have been consumed as indicated (*A Survey of Israel's History*, Zondervan).

The action of Lot's daughters after the destruction finds no justification in custom or ancient culture.

Genesis 21. Even though Sarah was upset by the 15-year-old Ishmael teasing her 2-year-old (v. 9, TLB), there was no excuse in custom for her insistence that Ishmael and his mother be sent away with no part of Abraham's wealth. In fact, custom dictated that Ishmael be provided for. No wonder it "distressed Abraham greatly" (v. 11). God intervened to promise Abraham that He would care for Ishmael and make him a nation too. Only then was Abraham willing to expel the two.

TEACHING GUIDE

Prepare

Think for a moment about the impact of faith in your own life. How have your choices and actions in the past few years shown that you trust God?

Explore

1. Begin by working on each group member's personal definition of "faith." Compare, and then do the study activity suggested in the "link-to-life" feature on page 57.

2. Or, you may begin with a look at Abraham the "all too human." Share the material on pages 53-55 on Abraham's Failures. Then use the chart suggested on page 54 to list his weaknesses.

When that chart is complete, ask: "How does seeing Abraham's weaknesses make you feel? Why? Why do you suppose they are so clearly spelled out in the Bible?"

You might then turn with your group to Romans 4, and see Paul's emphasis there. The justification of Abraham by faith offers hope to us all, for each of us is, like Abraham, an imperfect person.

Expand

1. A minilecture on the promises, person, perspective, and product of faith might be appropriate. Or, on what we can learn about living by faith, drawn from Abraham's willingness to sacrifice his son Isaac.

Keep the focus on faith as an intelligent (not blind) response to God, which leads to a transformed life. Show too that faith must be expressed in obedient action, or else it is a pseudo rather than real thing.

2. Complete the chart of Abraham's weaknesses by working together from his three great tests of faith to fill in the top cells. We want to avoid Abraham's mistakes. But what positive lessons for living can we learn from him?

After completing the chart, work in teams to develop a list of at least five "steps of faith" the believer is likely to take if he or she has a settled confidence in God.

Apply

1. Go around the circle and ask your group members to share one difference that having faith in Christ has made in their lives.
2. Or, go around the circle and ask your group members to share one way that they express their faith in God in their choices and actions.

Close in prayer, thanking God that we can trust Him as Abraham did, and asking Him to deepen our faith in Jesus.

STUDY GUIDE 7

Genesis 25–36

ISAAC AND JACOB

Overview

Isaac and Jacob, Abraham's son and grandson, are significant men. This is not so much because of any contribution their lives make to us, but because they are links in the line through which the covenant promises of God are passed on. The genealogical record proves the right of Israel to special relationship with God and to the land promised to Abraham.

▶ ***Birthright.*** The birthright was the extra portion of a father's goods which ancient custom dictated must go to the eldest son. In these chapters of Genesis, the birthright which Esau despised and Jacob valued was the covenant promise of God.

Commentary

These chapters are almost a rest, or a pause, in the dramatic stories told in Genesis. They report the lives of the son and the grandson of Abraham, men to whom the covenant promises were confirmed, and through whom the line is traced. But their lives mark a pause in the development of the divine purpose. No great and single message shines through these chapters, as it did through early Genesis. In Abraham God introduced the covenant theme which dominates the Old Testament. And in the man Abraham God illustrates the nature of faith, and the role faith will always play in man's relationship with God.

But Isaac and Jacob are lesser men, and consequently play less significant roles. Yet, like all "less significant" people, they are easy for you and me to identify with. In God's dealings with them, we can find much to enrich our own lives.

Studying the Old Testament

There are many approaches to take in studying Scripture. Each has its role and function. Each is appropriate; each gives us insight into the meaning and the message of the sacred text.

Among the ways we might study Genesis 25–36 are these: the archeological, the theological, and the devotional, and what we might call the comparative; looking at the rest of Scripture to see what God seeks to emphasize.

The archeological. This approach involves examining the customs and folkways of Bible times to help us understand actions reported in the Bible.

This method is helpful on two counts. First, we're kept from reading motives and causes into the actions of Bible characters which really are not there. For instance, in Genesis 31 we read that Rachel, Jacob's wife, stole her father's household gods (idols). The immediate reaction might be, "Ah ha! The family is involved in pagan worship, and Rachel wants to hold on to her religion. The family may go back to Palestine, but Rachel will keep on being pagan." I'm sure sermons must even have been preached on this text, on the danger of bringing along our old "gods" when we turn to Jesus and journey toward our own "promised land."

There's only one thing wrong with such an application. The interpretation of Rachel's action is in error. In those days the household gods were a symbol of family headship. The heir was the one to possess the household gods. When Jacob fled with his family, Rachel's theft was her way of laying claim for her husband and children to all her father had. It's possible this theft and the claim it implies were major factors leading Laban and his sons to pursue Jacob so far.

Archeology also gives us insight into Jacob's "gift" to Esau when he sent herds of animals on ahead to his brother (Gen. 32–33). When the two brothers met, Esau

The Covenant Line in Genesis

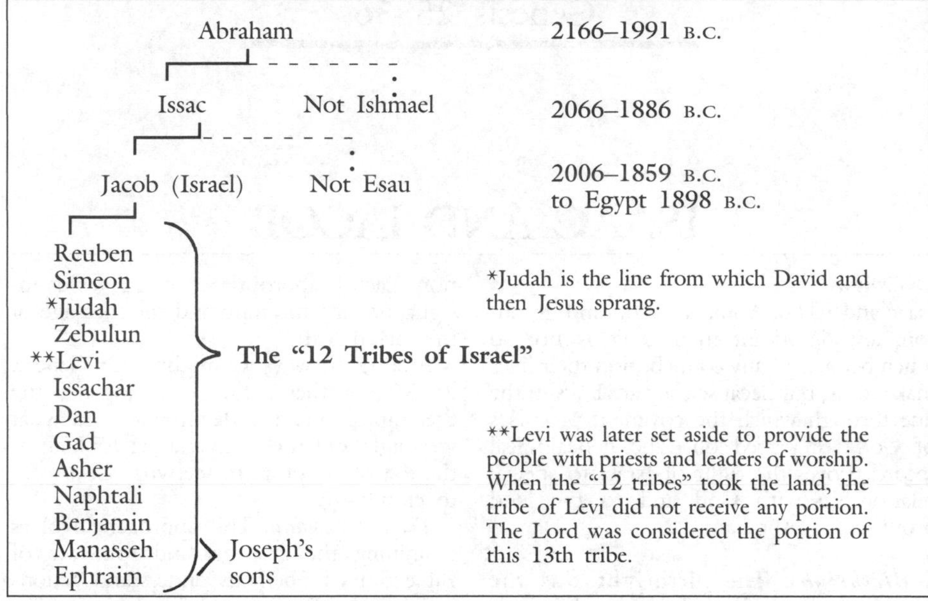

at first politely protested that he had plenty and did not need the gifts. Jacob urged him to accept. This urging was not from mere politeness, nor even a salve to a guilty conscience. In Jacob's time, to refuse such a gift would have meant that Esau was declaring himself to still be an enemy. Acceptance of the gift bound Esau to friendship. It was a visible sign to all that the rift between the two brothers was healed.

Without some knowledge of the customs of Bible times, it is dangerous to make hasty judgments about the meaning or application of such incidents. We're too inclined to read into them meanings that are not there.

The second value of the archeological approach to the study of a passage is found in the way the biblical record is confirmed. The customs are those of Palestine or Egypt, or wherever the location is, and at just the time when the events were supposed to take place. We are compelled to believe that, whatever else the Bible may be, it is an accurate record. It is a historical document in which we can have full confidence.

The theological. When we look at a portion of Scripture from a theological perspective, we're concerned about what it reveals of God and/or of His ways.

If we look at Genesis 25–36 this way, our attention is drawn at once to the centrality of the covenant. After Abraham died, God spoke to Isaac. He told Isaac to stay in Palestine and promised to fulfill the oath which He swore to Isaac's father (26:3). The obedience of faith had kept Abraham in the place of blessing; now Isaac was exhorted to trust and obey, and assured that through his line the original promise would be kept.

An express personal promise is communicated as well. God promised to be with this man, Isaac, to bless him (v. 3). God was not making a new covenant. The covenant had already been established with Abraham. Abraham's descendants were simply invited to participate in it; there was no need to constantly renew a promise once given.

It's the same with Jacob. Isaac, Jacob's father, blessed him as inheritor of the covenant. (Note: Archeological discoveries indicate that a father's deathbed blessing had the force of a will in patriarchal times.) Then God appeared to Jacob, identifying Himself as "the God of your father Abraham and the God of Isaac" (28:13). In this appearance God told Jacob that the promises were now given to him; he was the heir and inheritor. Then, while returning to the Promised Land after being away 20 years, Jacob called on God as the covenant-keeping God (32:9-13), and God appeared to him, reconfirming again the promises.

These repeated affirmations of the covenant promise to Isaac and Jacob make it clear that the announced purpose of God will be fulfilled through the family line, a line that has its source in Abraham both as its physical progenitor and as an example of faith.

In these passages we see that God is working out His promises. The purpose is sure, restated to each generation of patriarchs. The land, the special relationship with God, the blessing, and being a blessing are the very root of each generation's sense of identity. These are a people chosen "for the sake of My servant [your father] Abraham" (26:24).

The theological approach, then, allows us to keep the main emphasis of a section of Scripture in view. It lets us trace what God is doing and what He views as important by noting the repeated concepts and the personal interventions of God, which give us our clues.

The comparative. In this approach to studying a section of Scripture, we look at other parts of the Bible to find some divine commentary. What application has the Holy Spirit made of incidents recorded here?

Both direct and indirect application are made in the Old and New Testaments of earlier incidents. The main theme of a passage may be directly commented on, as in Romans 4 where Paul examines the meaning of Abraham's experience with God, exploring what it is that makes him the father of all who believe. At times, incidents may be pointed out simply as illustrations of principles which are not themselves the central message of the earlier passage. This is an indirect application.

For instance, in Romans 9 Paul looks back to the patriarchs to demonstrate a point he is arguing. It seems that some Jewish people in Paul's time had looked at Christianity as an implicit rejection of the covenant and the covenant people. They could not believe that God would abandon His promises, and so they rejected this new faith in Jesus as the long-awaited Messiah.

In answer, Paul pointed out that not every Hebrew is a spiritual descendant of Abraham, even though he may be able to trace his physical descent to him. Isaac and Ishmael were both Abraham's children, but God said the covenant promise applied only to Isaac's seed. A reader may object at this point. Ishmael was also the son of a slave! But Paul goes on to point out that Isaac fathered and Rebekah bore twins: Jacob and Esau. Yet God chose Jacob and rejected Esau, even before the boys were born.

The point is made. God has freedom to choose some as recipients of the covenant blessings while rejecting others. And this choice does not in any way indicate a repudiation of the covenant. Nor does God's decision to extend the benefits of the covenant to Gentiles repudiate the promise to Abraham. The Gentiles who believe in God find a relationship with God through faith just as Abraham did, thus fulfilling the intention of God that in Abraham all the nations of the earth should share in the blessings.

This then is an indirect use of the Old Testament. The main message of the Genesis record is not that God is free to choose those who will benefit under the covenant. But the historical events do demonstrate that God makes just this kind of choice, and that the covenant itself is not violated by the selection of some but not all of Abraham's descendants as benefactors.

The covenant was made with *Abraham*. Those who, like Abraham, have faith are invited to share its blessings. Even an entire generation's unbelief could never invalidate the promise and the purpose of the Lord.

Devotional Study

This is a very important and helpful approach to Bible study, one we all need to learn. In a way, it builds on the comparative approach we've just seen.

In Romans 9 Paul goes back to Genesis and focuses on two incidents that illustrate how God deals with people. In devotional study we do something very similar. We fix on an incident, and think about it. We ask, "What can I learn here about God's ways of working in my life?"

This is what sets the devotional approach apart from others. Our primary concern is personal application. We want to enter into the experiences of men and women of the past, to see mirrored in their experiences with the Lord God's ways with us. We hear warnings in their faults, encouragement in their faith, and hope in God's faithfulness to them. As all of these experiences are applied to our daily lives, our own lives are enriched and our confidence in God grows.

♥ ***Link to Life: Youth / Adult***
Your group can quickly learn the devotional method for their own Bible study. Duplicate for each person the following guide. Then select several incidents from these Genesis chapters. Have teams do 20-minute devotional studies, following the guide step by step. Then let each group share applications with the rest of the group.

Devotional Study Guide

I. *Observation*
Look for significant features. What's the background of the incident? Who is involved? What are the relationships between people? What is happening? Why are particular choices made or actions taken?

II. *Interpretation*
Why did these events happen? What are the cause-effect relationships? What were the results? What does this passage reveal about God and His ways? What is the primary message of the passage?

III. *Application*
How am I like the people here? What experiences of mine are parallel? When do I have similar feelings, face similar situations? How can I profit from or be guided by what is recorded?

Let's look then at several incidents in these chapters to see how they might be approached devotionally.

Esau's hunger (Gen. 25:29-34). Esau was the oldest son of Isaac and, according to law and custom, was in line to inherit a double portion of Isaac's possessions, including the covenant promise of God. This was his birthright: his right by birth.

But one day after a hunting trip Esau came home hungry. Jacob was boiling a stew of lentils, and Esau asked for some. Seeing his chance, and knowing his brother well, Jacob demanded Esau's birthright in return. The Bible tells us that Esau "despised" his birthright and swore it to Jacob as the price of the pottage.

What a picture! Esau weighed the promise of God's continual presence and blessing against a bowl of soup—and valued the soup more highly. What a revelation of Esau's character. He was a man who valued the present rather than the future, the material rather than the invisible. The momentary satisfaction of physical desires seemed more important to him than the approval of God. The body, not the spirit, dominated his scale of values.

I can look at Esau's act and be amazed by it. But what I need to realize is that this act of selling the birthright was an action that is in character, not out of character. It was the result of a long process of character formation, a long history of choice after choice which shaped Esau's personality.

Right now I may look at Esau with wonder and say, "I'd never do that." Instead I ought to look at the action as an expression of character, and wonder: In what direction are my daily choices leading me? Do I so value my present experiences that I fail to discipline myself to wait when waiting is best? Do I have to have the pleasures of eating despite the fact that I'm overweight? Is God high enough on my priority list to cause me to spend time with Him, or do other things push Him out of my thoughts?

I can shake my head in wonder at Esau, but I had better realize that unless I make a daily habit of rejecting Esau's values, I might someday be faced with a similar choice—and make the wrong one!

The stolen blessing (Gen. 27). Rebekah, and Jacob her son, plotted to deceive Isaac and get the blessing for Jacob that Isaac wanted to go to his oldest son, Esau. Disguised to fool the now-blind Isaac, Jacob stood before his father and lied, "I am Esau your firstborn" (v. 19).

How completely unnecessary! At the brothers' births God had told Rebekah that the older would serve the younger (25:23). Yet as the critical time drew closer and closer, mother and son felt impelled to "help God out."

What was the result? Jacob did receive the blessing—which he would have received anyway. Bitterness was heightened between the brothers, and Esau's hatred became so intense that he planned to kill Jacob after their father died. Rebekah, who had plotted to help her favorite son, was forced to send him away for 20 years, and did not live to see him return.

True, it worked out in the end. But the anger, the fear, the separation—all these might have been avoided had Jacob and

Rebekah simply trusted God and rejected deceit.

♥ ***Link to Life: Youth / Adult***

Play a game of "Might Have Been" with your group. Let teams of three imagine how God might have given the promise to Jacob as He intended, but without the stress and pain that lying and deceit brought. Let your imaginations soar on this one—be creative and have fun.

Afterward, sum up by noting that though Rebekah and Jacob made bad choices, God worked despite their mistrust and blessed Jacob, giving him a large family, riches, and the new name Israel. How clearly the story illustrates the reality of Romans 8:28!

Then play the game again, using personal experiences. Tell of a time when you made a bad choice (or ask a volunteer to share). Let the group brainstorm. What might you or the volunteer have done differently? When the brainstorming is over, share how God has used even your mistakes to teach, correct, or enrich you.

The purpose of this exercise is not to assure people that they can do wrong, and good will come. The purpose is to help each member realize that God intends good for us. How much better to simply obey His will, and receive the good without all the pain that actions like those of Jacob bring.

There are two important lessons in the story of Jacob and Esau. I don't have to take Jacob's road to blessing. Instead, I can trust God and commit myself to do the right thing at all times. Truth, not lies, will serve me far better. God's will still will be done, and I'll be able to live in harmony with those around me. How great it is to shrug off all sense of pressure and to commit my way to God, confident that as I daily do His will, His good purposes will be performed.

Jacob at Bethel (Gen. 28:10-15). Afraid that his brother would kill him, Jacob fled to his mother's relatives in Haran. On the way, alone and at night, he lay down in the dirt with only a stone for a pillow. How Jacob must have missed his family then. How alone and frightened he must have felt. But there God appeared to him, and confirmed the transmission of the covenant promises. And God added a personal word for Jacob: "I am with you and will watch over you wherever you go."

♥ ***Link to Life: Children***

This is a wonderful story for children. They can identify with the feelings of Jacob as he is alone in the dark, worried, and afraid. But they may need help in their own times of anxiety and fear to remember God's presence.

After telling this Bible story and talking about God's promise to be with us too (cf. Heb. 13:5), do what Jacob did. Make a pile of smaller rocks to bring to class. Give each child a "with you" rock to carry in his or her pocket, or put by the bed at night. Encourage your children when they feel afraid or lonely to grip the rock tight, and repeat the promise God gives to all His children: "I am with you and will watch over you."

Jacob's prayer (Gen. 32:9-12). After 20 years with his father-in-law, Laban, Jacob took his wives and children and flocks to return to the Promised Land. God told him to return, but Jacob was frightened. The remembrance of the wrong he'd done Esau 20 years before as well as of Esau's hatred combined to produce guilt and terror.

Now Jacob was about to meet his brother. Driven to the Lord, he prayed the longest recorded prayer up to this time. It's fascinating to see what Jacob said. He reminded God of His covenant promise (v. 9). Then he denied any personal merit as a possible basis for God's favor and reminded God (and himself) of the blessings from God he had enjoyed (v. 10). Then he honestly admitted his fear of Esau and begged God's help (v. 11). Finally Jacob reminded God of His personal promise to him that his descendants would be the chosen people (v. 12).

In many ways this prayer of Jacob's is a model for us. We have to give up all notion of personal merit as a basis for claiming God's favor. We can and must rely on the character of God as a covenant-keeping God, one who keeps all His promises to His people. We need to be honest in expressing our fears and doubts and uncertainties to God, to face our own deep need of Him and Him alone for strength and provision. Also we need to remember God's personal promises as one of the "whosoever" for whom

Christ died. Because in Jesus God has freely given all things, we can know that He seeks only to do us good. Because of who God is, we can abandon everything to Him, and rest.

The wound of grace (Gen. 32:24-32). On the night Jacob prayed, he went out to plan his own way to gain Esau's favor. He prepared a number of gifts for his brother and sent them on ahead. He trusted God—and then took out insurance.

That night a "Man" whom Jacob assumed to be an angel or theophany (a preincarnate appearance of God in human form, v. 30) wrestled with him. In the struggle the Man touched the back of Jacob's thigh. Some commentators feel the ball and socket there were thrown out of joint. Others say that a ligament (sinew, or tendon) was torn. Jacob was left with a permanent limp.

Sometimes a wound is a very special act of God's grace. Jacob struggled to hold onto the man, for after suffering the wound he must have realized how much more powerful this Visitor was than he himself, and he wanted His blessing.

How often we need to be wounded for the same reason! It's easy for us to trust our own skills and abilities. But sometimes a wound (physically, or in a broken relationship, or in the failure of a much-loved plan) will remind us to cling to God again, totally dependent on Him for blessing. How good it is that God doesn't hold back from hurting us—for our own good.

In this experience Jacob received a new name: Israel, "he who strives with God." Jacob had struggled with God, refusing to give up until God blessed him. That name may well represent the transformation of character that had begun in Jacob. But now the wound remained, a constant reminder of Jacob's need for God. A Jacob wholly dependent on God can become an Israel. What can we become if we let each wound draw us closer to the Lord and make us more dependent on Him?

TEACHING GUIDE

Prepare

Select an incident from Genesis 25–26, and use the devotional method outlined on pages 63-64 to study and apply it to your own life.

Explore

1. Give a minilecture on the four methods of studying the Old Testament discussed in this unit. Illustrate each as the text does.
2. Select four or five incidents from these chapters. Tell each story briefly, and ask every group member to write down one lesson he or she can apply to his personal experience.

Expand

1. Give out Devotional Study Guide sheets. Let each group member pick one of the stories you told in *explore (2)* to study more carefully. Those who pick a particular story can meet together as a study team. Follow the process outlined in "link-to-life," page 64.
2. Try the "might have been" game approach with your group. See "link-to-life," page 65.

Apply

Sometimes physical reminders of spiritual truths are valuable to adults as well as to children. So why not pass around "with you" rocks to each member of your group, to carry that week as reminders of the promise of God's presence.

STUDY GUIDE 8
Genesis 37–50

JOSEPH IN EGYPT

Overview
God had told Abraham, "Know for certain that your descendants will be strangers in a country not their own, and they will be enslaved and mistreated 400 years. But I will punish the nation they serve as slaves, and afterward they will come out with great possessions" (Gen. 15:13-14). The story of Joseph relates how Israel came to Egypt, where the little family multiplied to the mil lions needed to establish a nation.

▶ ***Egypt.*** During the Middle Kingdom Age when Joseph went to Egypt, it was a powerful and unified land; a land of peace, effective government, and general prosperity. Massive mud forts guarded frontiers and Egypt's trade and gold mining interests. Documents of the day reveal trade with western Asia, and that Canaan was divided into tribal areas and city states, just as the Bible describes. This classical age of the Egyptian language produced exciting short stories, and even a treatise on the *Pleasures of Fishing and Fowling*. It was a confident, powerful people who welcomed the little Hebrew family to Egypt, their haven of safety.

▶ ***Dreams.*** The Old Testament distinguishes between ordinary and revelatory dreams, through which God communicated information. Numbers 12:6 seems to suggest that dreams were the primary way that God spoke to His prophets, and here to Egypt's king.

■ Pages 86 to 100 of the *Bible Knowledge Commentary* give verse-by-verse exposition of Genesis 37–50.

Commentary
The story of Joseph has fascinated laymen and scholars for centuries. As a man Joseph is one of the Bible's most commendable characters. And his experiences remind us in many ways of Jesus. As a historical record, the portrait given in Genesis of life in Egypt has been demonstrated to be amazingly accurate—amazing at least to those who used to argue that Joseph's story was written a millennium or so after the supposed events. Leon Wood *(Survey of Israel's History*, Zondervan) summarizes some of the details in the Genesis account that ring so true.

> Corroboration of details in this overall story with contemporary Egyptian practices and customs illustrates the accuracy of the biblical record. The titles, "chief of the butlers," and "chief of the bakers," occur both in Genesis (40:2) and extant Egyptian texts. Famines were known in Egypt and the idea of persons being assigned to dispense food during these famines is borne out in tomb inscriptions. One inscription even speaks of a seven-year famine at the time of the Third Dynasty (2700 B.C.). Indication is made on the Rosetta Stone that the Pharaoh had a custom of releasing prisoners on his birthday, as he did the butler (40:20). Joseph shaved before seeing Pharaoh (41:14), and shaving was a distinctive practice of Egypt. Pharaoh gave Joseph a signet ring, linen clothing, and a gold chain (41:42), all three of which are mentioned in Egyptian texts for similar use. Some scholars have objected to the idea of Joseph, a Semite, being elevated to such a high position in Egypt; but a letter dating from the Amarna period has been found written to a person in similar position having the Semitic name Dudu (David). It fits too that the Twelfth Dynasty, ruling at this time, had now moved the capital back from Thebes to the northern site of Memphis. Joseph was thus more accessi-

ble to his brothers coming down from Canaan, as the continuing story indicates, and also to them living later in Goshen after Jacob's arrival.

Joseph and His Mission

Joseph, the son of Rachel, his father Jacob's favorite wife, was younger than the sons of the other wives. The Bible says that Jacob loved Joseph more than his brothers, and showed open favoritism (37:2-4). As a result the brothers hated Joseph, and were constantly critical and cutting in speaking to him.

At 17 Joseph had dreams which indicated he was to have authority over his brothers and his parents. He foolishly told the dreams, and while his father took them seriously, the brothers became more jealous. A short time later Joseph was sent to make sure that all was well with his brothers, who were herding the family flocks on a distant range. Seeing Joseph approach, the brothers conspired to kill him but were restrained by Reuben. When a trade caravan of Midianites passed near, they decided to sell Joseph as a slave.

♥ ***Link to Life: Children***

Children can identify with the story of Joseph and his unkind brothers. They can even understand the brothers' jealousy. This story can be used to help boys and girls explore their own sibling relations, and think of how to act in more loving ways.

Begin by exploring feelings. Why were the brothers angry? How did Joseph make things worse? What makes us angry sometimes at our brothers and sisters? When they are angry at us, what do we do that makes things worse?

Then introduce stick puppets. (Simply draw faces on popsicle sticks.) Ask children to pretend these are Joseph and his brothers and act out several scenes from the story: Joseph getting his special coat, Joseph telling his dream, Joseph visiting his brothers in the field. First act out what did happen. Then ask the children to act differently, to help the brothers not become so angry.

Give the children freedom to invent their own ideas—they will prove more creative than you might expect!

To apply, let the stick puppets now represent a modern family. What do brothers and sisters do that may upset each other? Act it out. How can we act toward each other to help a brother or sister not be jealous or angry? Act this out too.

In the biblical story, God used the anger and jealousy of Joseph's brothers to work His good plan. How good that in our own families He is most likely to use love and sensitivity for our children's good.

It's hard to imagine Joseph's feelings at the time his brothers sold him. His own family had rejected him, plotted to kill him, and in fact had sold him into a life of slavery in a foreign land. We could hardly blame this teenager if he had simply given up and surrendered to despair.

But when Joseph was sold in Egypt to Potiphar, a high Egyptian official, he actively applied himself to serving. He became so successful that he was advanced to oversee all of Potiphar's affairs. And "the Lord blessed the household of the Egyptian because of Joseph" (39:5).

But Joseph had attracted the passion of Potiphar's wife, who tried many times to seduce him. Joseph resisted, unwilling to sin against his master and against God (vv. 7-9). One day when Joseph entered the house alone Potiphar's wife literally tore his cloak from him. Joseph fled. Convinced she would never have Joseph, the scorned wife lied to her husband. Joseph was stripped of his position and thrown into political prison "where the king's prisoners were confined" (39:20).

Again Joseph might have lost heart. But again he approached the situation with perseverance, and his capabilities won him quick advancement. In time Joseph became supervisor of the prison under the head jailer, and again the Lord prospered his activities.

In each of these positions Joseph gained administrative experience—which would serve him well later as a ruler in Egypt!

In prison Joseph met two high court officials, the chief butler and chief baker. He interpreted dreams for them. One was to be restored to favor, the other executed by Pharaoh. Joseph's God-given interpretation came true. Two years later when Pharaoh had puzzling dreams, his chief butler remembered Joseph. He was brought to the palace to interpret. Joseph explained that the dreams of Pharaoh were a divine warning of a great famine to follow a time of great plenty. Joseph also proposed a solution: someone should be appointed to gather food during the time of plenty, and administer distribution during the famine. The impressed Pharaoh responded, "Since God has made all this known to you, there is no one so discerning and wise as you. You shall be in charge of my palace and all my people are to submit to your orders" (41:39-40).

God had brought Joseph to Egypt as a teenage slave: now, at 30, he was exalted to the second place in the mighty kingdom.

♥ ***Link to Life: Youth / Adult***

"Good News, Bad News" is a familiar comedy ploy. "Good news," the comedian says, "Mother-in-law is leaving town. Bad news, it's only because my house burned down."

The story of Joseph illustrates the fact that God often works in His people's lives in a reverse sort of way. "Bad news, Joseph is sold as a slave. Good news, he's sold to Potiphar and rises to a position of trust. Bad news, Joseph is falsely accused and thrown into prison. Good news, it's the king's prison and he meets powerful people there. These and other experiences of Joseph seem to have a pattern—a bad thing happens which God uses for good.

Let your group identify all the "bad news" experiences in Joseph's early life story, and then list ways that each was really God's "good news." List on the board.

When completed, give each group member paper and pencil to list five "bad news" experiences of his or her own. Then divide into small teams of four or five. Share the "bad news" items one at a time, but then think together about how God has transformed them into "good news" in each life. We can usually see the good in bad experiences that are long past. But your team members may need to help each other think of possible good outcomes for difficulties being experienced now.

The rest of the Joseph story traces the trips of his brothers to Egypt during the famine years to buy grain. They confronted Joseph several times but did not recognize him. After several visits Joseph revealed himself to his brothers, urging them not to be afraid. Joseph had come to realize that "God sent me ahead of you to preserve for you a remnant on earth and to save your lives by a great deliverance" (45:7). Looking beyond the brothers' sinful motives, Joseph realized that it was God, not they, who had ordained his sojourn in Egypt. This realization had removed all bitterness from Joseph's heart.

Joseph then had his entire family, some 76 persons, come to live in Egypt, and he set aside a fertile area for them. After the death of Jacob, whose body was returned to Palestine for burial, the brothers still feared Joseph and expected revenge. They could not understand this man whose willingness to do the will of God had given him joy even in suffering. Again Joseph reassured them: "You intended to harm me but God intended it for good to accomplish what is now being done, the saving of many lives" (50:20-21).

And with this explanation Joseph promised to provide for them and their little ones.

The last paragraph of Genesis reveals even more of Joseph's faith. He relied on the covenant of God. Someday God would visit this family and take them again to the land sworn to Abraham and Isaac and Jacob. At that time, Joseph decreed that his people should carry his coffin with them on their return journey. Joseph's life had been lived in a land that, for all its power, was a land of exile. But his body would lie, awaiting the final fulfillment of the covenant, in the dust of the Promised Land.

There are many riches to explore in these chapters. It is particularly fascinating to study Joseph's character. No matter how discouraged he must have become at the many reversals he experienced, we never see Joseph doing less than his best. In moments of crisis we see him choosing to do what is right. Rather than being eaten up with bitterness against his brothers, or returning hatred for hatred, Joseph looks beyond them to see the hand of God. And he remains sure that God's hand is on him "for good."

How often we look at our tragedies as injustice, or as punishment for some unknown fault. We need more of Joseph's trust in the loving goodness of God. God does sometimes lead His children into suffering. But it is always done in order that He might bring through the suffering some greater good.

♥ ***Link to Life: Children***
Play "Future Fishing" with boys and girls to help them realize that even bad things can lead to good. Have a screen labeled "today" on one side, "tomorrow" on the other. Have a pole, with a paper clip "hook" tied to a string "line."

Also have 3 x 5 cards prepared. On one set write the bad things in Joseph's life. On another have the matching good things God brought from them.

Let a child stand on the "today" side of the screen and draw a card. Read it aloud, and talk about how sad the experience must have made Joseph feel. Say, "But that was Joseph's today. What good thing do you supposed that will lead to tomorrow?" Let the child who drew "fish" over the screen on the tomorrow side, as a helper slips the matching card on the paper clip.

Read it, and talk about how God's plan for Joseph's tomorrow was good, even though his today was full of pain.

You can then play this game with experiences children face. A friend moves away. They get sick. As you write the children's ideas of bad things on cards, your helper behind the screen can write possible good results on corresponding cards. One friend moved . . . but a family with someone who will become your very best friend might buy their house.

As the children draw "bad" today cards and then fish in "tomorrow" for a corresponding "good," remind them that God knows tomorrow, and is planning our lives for good just as He loved Joseph and planned his life for good.

Typology
In the unit on Isaac and Jacob, we saw four ways to study the Old Testament. The story of Joseph lends itself to yet another study approach: the typological.

A *type* is an event, character, or institution which has a place and purpose in Bible history, but which also, by divine design, foreshadows the future.

For instance, Christ is sometimes called the "second Adam," and in Romans 5:14 Adam is spoken of as a "pattern of the One to come." There is no exact correspondence here. Yet Christ and Adam are alike in that each is the head of a race: Adam of sinful man; Christ of redeemed humanity. In regard to headship, Adam as the source of humankind does foreshadow Jesus, the source of mankind's transformed brotherhood.

Another type is seen in the Passover lamb, the animal whose blood was sprinkled over the door of Jewish households at the time of Exodus. When the angel of death saw the blood on the doorposts, he passed over the blood-protected home. So 1 Corinthians says, "Christ, our Passover Lamb, has been sacrificed" (5:7). The helpless lamb, whose blood bought safety for an Old Testament generation, speaks to us of Jesus' blood as well.

A type, then, bears some resemblance in function or meaning in the original historical setting, to something or to someone yet to come.

Some Bible teachers have gone too far in seeking types of Christ or of Christian doctrines in the Old Testament. So we want to be careful in seeking typical significances. We never, for instance, build doctrine on types. What we do is to study carefully a historical setting for a basis of typical meaning. At times we'll find areas of strong resemblance between Old Testament events or persons and features of the New Testament. And these correspondences will help us appreciate the meaning of truths which stand constant throughout the sweep of history as central elements in God's plan.

But why speak of types and typology here? Because many Bible students have seen in Joseph's life and mission many parallels to Christ. Rejected by his brothers, sold for silver, suffering in a foreign land for the good of those who betrayed him, Joseph does bear a striking resemblance to the Saviour. And Joseph's forgiving spirit also foreshadows the attitude of Jesus, who one day would cry from a cross, "Father, forgive them; for they do not know what they are doing" (Luke 23:34).

♥ ***Link to Life: Youth / Adult***
Do a typological study comparing Joseph to Jesus. Use a chart to record similarities between the two. Several similarities have been noted. Begin with these, and then add others as you discover them in Genesis 37–50.

To Egypt?
The story of Joseph does more than give us

JOSEPH	CHRIST

Comparison of Joseph and Christ

a portrait of a man of great faith and admirable character. It also marks a major turning point in the history of God's chosen people. Israel moved from the Promised Land to the land of Egypt, where, after a time, Joseph was forgotten and the people enslaved.

Why was Egypt part of God's plan for His people? We'll learn more about this in coming studies in Moses' first five Old Testament books. But even now we can sense several reasons why the Hebrews needed to leave Palestine, and spend centuries in Egypt. Leon Wood (*Survey*) summarizes:

> Egypt was a country in which Jacob's descendants would have to remain a separate people, for Jacob and his sons were shepherds, and shepherds were an abomination to the Egyptians (Gen. 43:32; 46:34). The fact would remain a natural barrier to intermarriage. In Canaan there had already been some intermarriage with the inhabitants and continued living there would have brought more. This could only have led to serious amalgamation with these Canaanites, rather than distinctiveness as a nation. Further, Egypt afforded excellent living conditions for the necessary rapid growth in numbers. The land of Goshen was fertile and regularly watered by the flooding Nile for adequate food supply.

We might also point out that Canaan, during the centuries that the Jews were in Egypt, was a highway for the armies of nations to the north and south. The Hebrews could hardly have grown in such numbers as they did in the protected environment of Egypt. In a very real sense, Egypt was a womb in which the seed of Israel grew and multiplied until in God's own time a nation was born.

A glimpse of God's purpose in bringing Israel into Egypt helps us to focus on the primary message of these Genesis chapters. Joseph himself summed it up as he reassured his brothers: "God sent me ahead of you to preserve for you a remnant on earth, and to save your lives by a great deliverance. So then it was not you who sent me here, but God" (45:7-8). What is the message? God is a Person who is in control of circumstances, who works providentially to accomplish His good purposes.

It's important that we grasp this truth about God as firmly as Joseph did. In Genesis we've seen God act in direct interventions. He created Adam and Eve. He set aside the orderly processes of nature to bring on earth a cataclysmic flood. He spoke to Abraham directly. He acted in a clearly supernatural way to overthrow Sodom and Gomorrah. But there is no record that God spoke directly to Joseph. Joseph had heard stories of the covenant from his father. Joseph had dreamed dreams. But God did not meet with Joseph or confront him.

There is no record of God acting to set aside natural processes on Joseph's account. God blessed Joseph's efforts in Potiphar's house, in prison, and in his position as a ruler of Egypt. But it was through Joseph's own honesty and efforts that the Lord worked. In the unfolding of circumstances, Joseph saw the hand of God. But certainly others would have seen only luck—both good and bad.

But Joseph's view is the true one.

As we trace through the rest of the Old Testament, we'll see that God does sometimes intervene directly. But in most cases God works through the ordering of circumstances: through the natural progress of events whose sequence nonetheless is patterned to shape history according to God's plan and will.

It is important for us to see that this same will is active in our own circumstances. Each child of God is as important to Him as Joseph. Not because we have a task as great as Joseph's, but because we are just as precious to the Lord. Thus we have that great New Testament affirmation of God's control of circumstance for our benefit: "We know that in all things God works for the good of those who love Him, who have been called according to His purpose" (Rom. 8:28). Even tragedies such as Joseph experienced are meant for good. True, they may not lead us to a place of blessing in some earthly Egypt. But one day we will find our place as kings and priests to reign with the triumphant Christ.

In that day the pattern of our individual lives will be seen, woven into the great tapestry of the overall plan of our God: a plan that has in sharp focus the preservation of human beings for a life that extends far beyond the short span allotted you and me on earth. A plan that involves, with eternity, the full restoration in our personalities of the purified image of our God.

Chapters	*Key Word*	*Theme and Message*
Gen. 1	Creation	The universe is *personal*
2	Man	Men are made in God's image
3–4	Sin	Sin introduces death's reign
6–9	Judgment	The universe has moral order
12; 15	Covenant	God's promise reveals purpose in the universe
12–21	Sinful	Abraham and all men fall short
22–24	Faith	Faith in God is "counted . . . for righteousness"
25–36	Transmission	The covenant promise was transmitted through Issac and Jacob
37–50	Egypt	God providentially orders events to work out His purposes

Chart of the Primeval and Patriarchal Periods

TEACHING GUIDE

Prepare

What traits of Joseph do you want to see in your own life and the lives of your group members? Pray that God will use this study to that end.

Explore

1. Go around your group and ask each member to finish the following sentence: "The quality of Joseph that I would most like to see in my own life is ________."

2. Or begin with a review of the Book of Genesis. Use the chart of the primeval and patriarchal periods to help your group members think through Genesis and its vital messages to us. You may want to put the

chart framework on the board, and have your group fill it in together. Or leave just a few of the sections empty as a pop "quiz."

Expand

1. Give a minilecture on typology. Then put the suggested chart on the board and work on it together, as explained in the "link-to-life" activity on pages 70-71.
2. Or, give a longer lecture on the significance of Egypt in God's plan for Abraham's family. A good Bible dictionary or encyclopedia will give you information on that land during the Middle Kingdom Era. Also more information is developed in the next unit in this study.

Apply

1. You may want to focus here on how the evidence that God can and does work good through tragedy and suffering affects our own outlook on our hard times.

The "link-to-life" suggestion on studying Joseph with a "bad news, good news" approach—and then looking at our personal experiences in the same way—can help here. See page 69.

2. Or use the chart on the contents of Genesis for a helpful review/application activity. Ask each group member to look at the chart and pick the one message that has been most meaningful to him or her personally. Then go around the group, asking each to identify the "most meaningful" message and to share why that message was important in his or her own life.

STUDY GUIDE 9

Exodus 1–4

MOSES, GOD'S MAN

Overview

The lash flicked; the pain came. For a moment the Hebrew slave's muscles corded in rebellion. But then he bent again to the task of mixing stubble with the slimy clay.

"I didn't want to. . . ." It sounded almost like someone else's voice. "I don't know why I went along with them. I guess, well, I guess I was afraid."

Slavery is not just surrender of control of one's body. There is a worse bondage, a worse slavery, to indwelling sin. The history of Israel's redemption mirrors and instructs us in the freedom from slavery to sin that we are invited to know in Christ.

Outline

I. Story of Deliverance	1–19
A. Moses, Man of God	1–4
B. God's Mighty Power	5–12
1. The Ten Plagues	5–11
2. The Passover	12
C. Journey to Sinai	13–18
1. The Red Sea	13–15
2. The Wilderness	15–18
D. Law Covenant Made	19
II. Design for Holy Community	20–40
A. The Ten Commandments	20
B. Illustrations	21–24
C. Tabernacle Design	25–27
D. Priesthood	28–31
E. The Golden Calf	32–34
F. Tabernacle Built	35–40

▶ ***Yahweh.*** The personal name of God is revealed now to Moses. It means "the One who is always present," and emphasizes God's commitment to be with His people. It is rendered LORD in our English versions.

Commentary

The Hebrew people, the family of Abraham and Isaac and Jacob, had come to Egypt in the days of Joseph. They had settled on the west of the Nile's delta, an area called Goshen, on the southern end of which Cairo stands today. Even after Joseph's death, probably during the rule of Amenemhet III (about 1805 B.C.), the Israelites experienced good years. Then, about 1730 B.C., a new people began a gradual conquest of Egypt. The country was ruled by a foreign aristocracy, the Hyksos, Semites from Asia. Goshen was one of the first areas conquered, and slavery was imposed on Israel.

Later, when the Hyksos were driven out, Israel's lot was no easier. The people had grown numerous. And they were more closely related to the Asiatic Hyksos than to the Egyptians. By the time of Thutmose I, Egypt's great empire builder, the presence of this foreign population was threatening. Thutmose's concern over a potential enemy at home while his armies were away seeking new conquests led to severe measures. He commanded Egypt's midwives to kill newborn Hebrew boys. When this failed, he directed all Egyptians to seize the male children that were born to the Hebrews and fling them into the Nile to drown. Israel's plight was desperate.

And then God acted.

This is why a study of Bible history can sometimes be so exciting for us. At times our plight too becomes desperate. We too feel helpless, and can only call on God to act.

But what does God do? How does He work in our lives to lift us out of our bondage, and set us on the way to freedom? In the New Testament, looking back on the days that Exodus reports, God tells us that the things that happened to Israel were "examples." The word "example" literally means "type"—a model or pattern. Israel's experiences were written down as signposts for us . . . signposts along a common road to freedom that we too are invited to travel (cf. 1 Cor. 10:11). Simply put, our own personal experience with God closely parallels the experience of Israel as recorded in the Old Testament story of redemption. These Old Testament books show us how Israel was led from slavery to freedom. They tell the story of redemption, and help us understand what God intends to do in our lives as well.

Why Egypt?

It seems strange, but God did lead the people He loved into slavery.

God had appeared to Abraham, and had given him great covenant promises. Abraham was to become a great nation. Through his offspring the entire race of man was to be blessed. And the chosen people were to enjoy God's favor and His protection. What's more, the family of Abraham was to inherit a land that, at that time, was particularly rich. Canaan was to be a Jewish homeland, a perpetual possession set aside for them.

But after just three generations, God led the 70 people of that family out of Canaan into Egypt. There, as God knew, they would rest and multiply—but would also become enslaved. God's leading of the people of Israel into Egypt was unquestionably leading them into bondage.

Yet there were reasons for the detour into Egypt. During the years that the Children of Israel lived there, the Promised Land was a battlefield. Invaders from the north, Hurrians and Hittites, had surged south. During the decades when Egypt's power was great, Egyptian armies had flowed north. Palestine, a bridge between the two areas, knew the continual march of foreign armies, and often the devastation that war brings.

The Jewish people could hardly have multiplied or have developed national strength in such a land.

But in Egypt the people grew. The Bible tells us they "multiplied greatly and became exceedingly numerous, so that the land was filled with them" (Ex. 1:7). Exodus 12:37 reports that when the Jewish people left Egypt, there were some 600,000 men, plus women and children; a total of at least 2 million people. Strikingly, when Israel left Egypt, both northern and southern world powers were weak. A power vacuum existed, which permitted time for the Jews to become established as a nation.

The geography of Palestine gives us another reason why the captivity was in God's plan for Israel. The land was divided by ranges of mountains and hills. In a similar land the Greeks developed a structure of independent and warring city-states. The Greeks had a common heritage. But they lived divided lives. This could not be allowed to happen to God's people. Tribal distinctions could be retained, but the people must see themselves as one nation, linked forever by their common heritage in Abraham's God.

A third and striking reason for the time spent in Egypt is found in Genesis 15:16. In making the promise to Abraham, God told him that his descendants would be enslaved and oppressed in Egypt for some 400 years. Following that experience of slavery, they would return. And then this puzzling note is added: "For the sin of the Amorites has not yet reached its full measure."

The Amorites were the people who lived then in the land God had promised to Abraham and to Israel. Archeological research tells us much about them—particularly about their depravity. They were a people whose moral and religious decline was marked by cult prostitution, and even involved the sacrifice of babies, who were burned alive to their nature gods.

For 400 years God, in grace, held back His judgment and permitted His own people to suffer. Only when the iniquity of the Amorites was complete—when they had reached a point of no return—did God use Israel to judge and to destroy this depraved civilization.

And so for centuries Israel waited in Egypt. For centuries their suffering deepened. Only now, looking back, can we sense some of the reasons. Even in their agony God was at work, to do them—and to do others—good.

The Experience of Suffering

The reasons we've seen for Israel's time of suffering in Egypt may fall short of a full explanation. Perhaps Exodus 2:23 suggests another reason. "The Israelites groaned in their slavery and cried out, and their cry for help because of their slavery went up to God." It took the experience of suffering to lead Israel to cry out to God for help.

It's peculiar, but it's true of most of us. When things are going well, we lose awareness of our need for God. Somehow we feel capable in ourselves to meet the challenges of life and eternity. But a sense of need, of helplessness, leads us to trust ourselves afresh to God. When we lose our sense of need, we may lose touch with spiritual reality.

♥ ***Link to Life: Youth / Adult***
Psalm 73 illustrates how troubles draw our thoughts to God. Asaph had become jealous of the prosperity of the wicked (vv. 1-12). He felt his own commitment to God was useless, as he was still "plagued" all the day long (vv. 13-16). He struggled to understand, and finally realized that his trials were a blessing, and the ease of the wicked was actually "slippery ground" (vv. 17-20). Seeing at last, he realized his troubles had helped to keep his eyes and his hope fixed on the Lord, and he was satisfied with God as his "portion forever" (vv. 21-28).

Duplicate this psalm for your group. Have each person individually jot down the feelings and attitudes Asaph described—his own, and those of the wicked. The believer may know trials, but in being forced back to God we find all that is truly important in life.

Why was Egypt in Israel's experience? Why so many little Egypts for you and me? Perhaps so that God's people might never be deceived about our constant need for the Lord. The sense of helplessness that comes from suffering can be a first step down freedom's road. We can never find spiritual freedom by looking within ourselves. We, like Israel, need to look away, to God.

Moses, the Man

Scripture gives us an unmatched picture of the formative decades of the life of Moses, the man God selected to lead Israel from slavery to freedom. We all know the familiar details of his infancy. But we can learn much by looking ahead, at the full scope of his ministry.

Formation (Ex. 2–5). Moses, placed in a floating basket of reeds, was found by the daughter of Thutmose I, Hatshepsut. Captivated by the infant, she adopted him as her own. Later, when a youth, Hatshepsut seized power from a nephew who had been crowned Thutmose III, and she ruled impressively for 22 years. Moses, secure in the affections of this powerful and brilliant woman ruler, was well trained: "Educated in all the wisdom of the Egyptians" (Acts 7:22).

When about 40, Moses was forced to make a choice. The burdens on his people Israel had grown greater during his lifetime. Finally Moses actually stepped in and killed an Egyptian who was beating an Israelite slave. When he discovered the killing had been observed, and when Thutmose III tried to kill him, Moses fled. No doubt this Pharaoh, who resumed the throne after his aunt's death (and immediately ordered the defacing of all her monuments and the destruction of all records of her rule!) was glad to find an excuse to remove his aunt's favorite.

Moses fled to Midian, a desert country far from Egypt, probably east of the present-day Gulf of Aqaba. There he lived for 40 years, his culture and his pride worn away by the harsh, simple life of a shepherd. Moses abandoned his vision of himself as Israel's deliverer (cf. Ex. 2:11-15). Now, meek at last, Moses was finally a usable man.

What lessons can we learn from Moses as we meet him in Exodus 2–5? Several.

**Use opportunities.* God placed Moses, of slave heritage, in the palace of his people's oppressors. There he was "educated in all the wisdom of the Egyptians and was powerful in speech and action" (Acts 7:22). We too need to take opportunities to grow, and to develop within our own culture.

**Dream dreams.* Moses had a vision of himself as his people's deliverer. When he killed the Egyptian taskmaster he supposed "that his own people would realize that God was using him to rescue them, but they did not" (Acts 7:25). Not all of us are called to fulfill our early dreams. But the desire to do great things for God, and to dare great things to help those for whom He cares, is admirable in us as well as in Moses.

**Accept discipline.* The Jews didn't share Moses' vision of himself as a hero. Pharaoh heard what he had done, and Moses fled. For 40 years he lived as a simple shepherd in a backward land. The image of the hero faded under the stress of repetitious toil. Finally Moses learned to accept himself as a "nobody." We too need this kind of discipline. God does not want to break our spirits. But He cannot use pride. When we accept ourselves as nobodies, only then can we become somebodies whom God can use.

**Face limitations.* At the burning bush Moses carried his "nobodyness" too far. At 80 God spoke to him, and announced that the youthful dream would be fulfilled. Now Moses hesitated. He saw so many reasons why he could not do what he had once planned to do.

"What if they do not believe me?"

"Lord, I have never been eloquent."

"Lord, please send someone else."

Each of these objections indicates clearly that Moses now was all too aware of his inadequacy. From "I can" he had swung to "I can't."

It's important that we face our own limitations, and reject trust in our natural abilities. But we can be too overwhelmed by our weaknesses. We need to remember God, and shift our gaze from ourselves to Him.

**Accept God's commission.* In the call to Moses, God had announced His purpose. "I am sending you . . . to bring My people the Israelites out of Egypt" (Ex. 3:10). For each objection, God had a promise:

"The elders of Israel will listen to you."

"Go, and I will help you speak and will teach you what to say."

God is well able to do in us what He intends. With the commission of God comes the presence and power of God that enables us to fulfill it.

**Expect disappointments.* Moses did go as God commanded. And the Hebrews did welcome him. But, as God had also warned, Pharaoh did not listen. The burdens of the slave race were now increased. The people of Israel turned on Moses, and Moses turned to God. "Why have You brought trouble upon this people? Is this why You sent me?"

Every ministry knows disappointments. No path God asks us to follow will always be smooth. Learning to accept the disappointments and yet to always turn back to God is an important aspect of preparation for ministry.

Faithful service (Ex. 15–40). The events immediately following the Lord's exhilarating victory over Pharaoh thrust Moses into burdensome spiritual leadership.

Moses' basic problem was with the people he had been called to lead. Their character was all too quickly revealed. When Pharaoh's army followed Israel to the sea, the people begged in terror to return to slavery (14:11-12). Even after the parting of the Red Sea, the people "grumbled against Moses" within three days because of a lack of water! As the journey toward Sinai continued, the attitude of the people became more and more sour. The "whole community murmured" (16:2), and finally expressed their rebelliousness in an anger so fierce they were ready to stone Moses himself! (17:4)

As we look at Moses the man, we need to see him as a person under pressure. Being a leader means carrying very real and very heavy burdens. Yet this stage of Moses' life also has helpful lessons for us.

**Don't try to do it alone (Ex. 17–18).* Exodus 17:4 shows Moses crying out in frustration. "What am I to do with these people?"

What a fascinating question. What shall *I* do? Moses was about to learn a vital lesson. He had begun to look at himself as the only one God uses, the one who had to provide all the solutions. He was alone, and indispensable. "What shall *I* do?"

All too often this is the cry of the ordained in our churches. Somehow the pastor and people alike come to feel that the ministry is one person's task, and his or her responsibility alone. No wonder it seems impossible. It is!

God's instructions to Moses give us insights. "Walk on ahead of the people. Take with you some of the elders of Israel" (v. 5). Then God told Moses to strike a rock: "I will stand there before you," God told him, "and water shall come out of it."

Here are two ways that Moses was not alone. God was there before him. And some of the elders of Israel were there with him.

The lesson was immediately reinforced. As Israel traveled on, they met an enemy force. Joshua led Israel against the Amalekite army, and whenever Moses held up his arms, stretching them out toward the battlefield, Israel won! But soon Moses' arms became tired. He couldn't hold them up alone. And when he lowered his arms, Israel lost. There was only one solution. Moses sat on a rock, and allowed Aaron and Hur to stand beside him and hold up his arms.

What a message for Moses. Moses couldn't do it alone. He had to have others' help.

In chapter 18 we see the culmination. Moses, the lonely leader, was still trying to do it all himself. All day long he sat and settled disputes that arose among the people. Finally his visiting father-in-law, Jethro, broke in. "Why do you alone sit as judge, while all these people stand around you from morning till evening?" (v. 14) Moses explained: "Because the people come to me to seek God's will." Jethro's comment was as potent today as it was then. "What you are doing is not good. You and these people who come to you will only wear yourselves out. . . . You cannot handle it alone."

At last Moses heard! Moses chose capable men, and delegated authority to them (vv. 24-27). Hard cases were still brought to Moses. But the others were solved within the community.

Ministry in the Christian church is a shared responsibility. Even when members of a congregation are not yet spiritually mature, no leader is to bear the burden alone. The people of God are dependent on God, but interdependent on each other.

♥ ***Link to Life: Children***
Play games that call for boys and girls to cooperate. Have a three-legged race. Run a relay. Hold a tug-of-war. Play "Red Rover." Afterward talk about how in God's family too we need to help each other. We can help by praying. We can help a friend by explaining a school assignment he or she missed. Loving and helping each other, with each of us willing to help, is one way God's people live together in love.

♥ ***Link to Life: Youth / Adult***
Christians are given spiritual gifts which enable each of us to make some contribution to the common good (1 Cor. 12:7). Each of us is to be involved in ministry.

Why not invite a pastor or other church staff member to share with your group about a typical day of his or her ministry. How do members of the congregation serve and help to lighten that ministry?

Ask him or her to share also about needs seen within your own congregation or community. How are typical Christians working to meet those needs, either through some organized group or in personal contact with individuals? Your goal should be to help your group get a clearer vision of the kinds of needs that exist, and the ways they might respond to meet one or more of them.

Moses couldn't do it alone. Nor can church staff today. Ministry is the privilege of the whole people of God, and we can each contribute.

**Don't neglect prayer (Ex. 32).* When Moses was on Mount Sinai receiving instruction from God, Israel was busy down in the valley. Under pressure from the people, Aaron had weakly given in, and actually made a golden calf for them to worship!

God told Moses what had happened, and invited intercession with these words: "Now leave Me alone, so that My anger may burn against them. . . . Then I will make you into a great nation" (v. 10). God expressed His commitment to judge sin, and offered Moses an even greater place in history than he now fills! What did Moses do?

Moses prayed.

The striking prayer is recorded in verses 11-14. Moses called on God to glorify Himself by remembering His covenant promises to Abraham. Moses was looking to God and seeking His glory. He wanted to see God glorified in His people, and to this end he prayed for them.

God did respond to Moses' prayer. The guilty individuals would die, but the nation would live.

Yet when Moses returned to camp, and saw for himself what the people were doing, his "anger burned and he threw the tablets out of his hands, breaking them to pieces" (v. 19). When Moses saw what God had seen he reacted just as God did, with anger!

An angry Moses could never have prayed with the same concern as had Moses on that Mount.

This too teaches us. In our lives we will see much which might appropriately anger or disgust us. Yet on the mountain, when Moses' eyes were fixed on God, he prayed. We too are to keep our eyes on God and to pray, and not to keep our eyes on the sins of others. The New Testament says it. "For man's anger does not bring about the righteous life that God desires" (James 1:20). Keeping close to the Lord, we will be protected, as Moses was, from an anger which might keep us from helping others. By keeping close to the Lord, we will also rely on Him, and express our concern for others in intercessory prayer.

A faithful life (Num.—Deut.). Moses led Israel for 40 years. And 38 of those years were spent leading a doomed generation through the wilderness—waiting. Two incidents selected from Exodus have helped us sense something of the lesson Moses learned of ministry's burdens. The Book of Numbers helps us realize that leaders bear limited responsibility.

In many ways, Moses seems to have been a failure. He failed to bring Israel into the land. He saw the generation that left Egypt wander aimlessly in the desert and, one by one, die. In all that time Moses saw little change in their responsiveness to God or to himself. Was Moses to blame?

In Numbers 13 and 14 we read of Moses and the people hearing the report of spies about the strength of the Canaanites. In terror the people refused to obey God's command to enter the land. The Bible tells us that "Moses and Aaron fell facedown in front of the whole Israelite assembly gathered there." In horror they, with Joshua and Caleb, begged the people to listen to God.

But the people would not.

In Deuteronomy we read of Moses leading a new generation to a similar point of decision. Moses did not choose for this new generation. He could not. The people had to choose for themselves. And this time they chose to trust and to obey.

There are limits to the responsibility of leaders. These limits are imposed by the very freedom God Himself gives all men—to turn to Him, or to turn away. Moses' ministry could bring Israel to the point of decision. Moses performed this ministry well. But Moses could not decide for them. One generation turned from God. And one generation turned to God. It was their own choice.

It was not through Moses' failure that the first generation turned away. Nor was it by Moses' skill and success that the second turned to the Lord.

The point, of course, is simple. Moses was called to be faithful to God and to fulfill his commission. He was not called to "succeed" or to "fail." And so the New Testament commendation of Moses focuses not on what Moses accomplished, but on his faithfulness. "Moses . . . faithfully discharged his duty in the household of God" (Heb. 3:2, PH). It was Moses' faithfulness to his task which counted with God all along.

It's the same for us today. Where there is faithfulness, failure does not bring blame. And it should not bring a sense of guilt! Where faithfulness is, success does not bring glory. Our responsibility is limited. We are called merely to bring others to the place where they can freely choose.

Exodus, a Great Adventure

The Book of Exodus truly does launch us on a great adventure. We trace the wonders worked by God as He delivered Israel and led them, via Sinai, toward the Promised Land. And we travel with Moses, a man from whose life we can learn so much.

In this book, and in the other early books of the Bible that tell the story of redemption, we meet our God. And we learn more of what it is like to travel from spiritual slavery to the freedom that is ours as sons of God.

TEACHING GUIDE

Prepare

Read the prayer of Moses found in Exodus 32:9-14. Meditate on how you might pray for members of your own study group. Pray for your group daily.

Explore

1. Give a minilecture on Israel in Egypt. Cover the present situation, and highlight the reasons God permitted this suffering of His people.

Scholars differ about the time Moses lived, and who was ruler in Egypt then. The dating system adopted here is one suggested by Leon Wood in *A Survey of Israel's History* (Zondervan).

2. Or begin your time with "first impressions" of Moses. Have your group skim Exodus 3–4 and develop quick impressions of what Moses was like. Was he decisive? Indecisive? Confident? Weak? Strong?

Let class members suggest one or two word descriptions, and write them on a chalkboard.

Moses' Lifeline

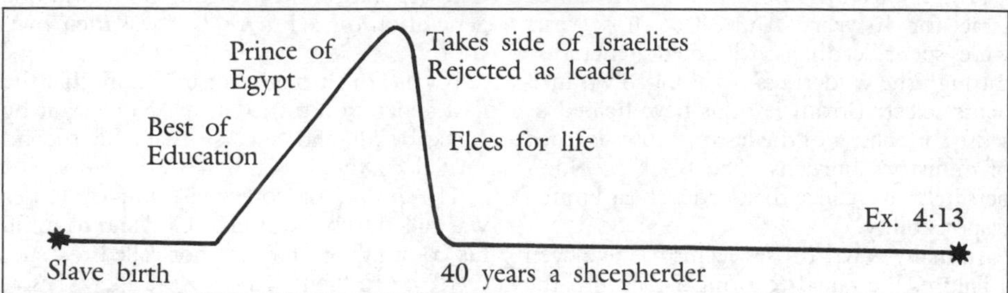

Expand

1. Give a minilecture on the life of Moses, stressing some of the points made in the commentary. Often the usable person may not fit our image of the strong, confident, successful individual of today.
2. Draw a graph of Moses' early life, showing its ups and downs through Exodus 1–4. Discuss: "What were the values of each peak and valley experience? How did they affect Moses, or shape him?" Your chart might look something like the one above.

Apply

1. Following a discussion of the role of the ups and downs in shaping Moses' character, divide your group into teams of four or five. Have each person draw his or her own lifeline chart, also showing ups and downs.

Then share, having each tell the others about experiences he or she has graphed, and talking about how they have influenced his or her life. During the sharing, others are to be free to ask questions and make comments. In the process your group members will come to know each other better, and individuals will gain insights into how God has been at work in each life.

2. Or focus on lessons we learn from Moses' life in Exodus 2–5 (see commentary, pp. 76-79). List each italicized lesson on the chalkboard and have your group see how it is drawn from the text. Be ready to add what they do not discover.

When each lesson is understood, divide into pairs. Each is to tell his or her partner which of these lessons is most important to him, and to share why.

Close with prayer in the pairs, as each individual prays for his or her partner.

STUDY GUIDE 10

Exodus 5–12

GOD'S MIGHTY POWER

Overview

These best known of Old Testament chapters tell the story of God's personal intervention in history. By acts of power God forced Egypt to release the Israelite slaves, who were His covenant people.

The events reported here are important for their major contribution to a biblical concept of God. God is the One who made covenant promises to Abraham (Gen.). God is the One who is able to act powerfully in our world of space and time—and who will act to deliver His people (Ex.). In addition, the concepts of miracle and of redemption have their roots in these significant Exodus chapters.

▶ ***Miracle.*** The Hebrew words that are associated with miracles are: *pala'*, "to be marvelous, wonderful"; *mopet*, "wonder, sign"; and *'ot,* "sign." As used in the Old Testament they suggest miracles are acts of God intended to create awe and wonder in the observer; a sense that God is real and present. In addition they contain a message of God to humankind, not only about Him but also about their beliefs or situations. We'll see how the 10 plagues on Egypt fit this well.

▶ ***Redemption.*** Each of the Hebrew words linked with redemption finds human beings helpless, captive to powers or forces they cannot fight. Only the action of a third party can break the bonds that hold the captives, and set them free.

■ An excellent chart on page 120 of the *Bible Knowledge Commentary* shows the link between the plagues and the gods of Egypt.

Commentary

God is a great dramatist. Now, in a series of striking confrontations, God acted out on history's stage a play which communicated, as words alone could not, the reality of His power and personal concern for Israel. It is helpful for us to read these chapters with the drama of these confrontations in view: to discover, with the men and women of that time, the identity of God and the identity of those on whom God set His love.

Moses vs. Pharaoh

Moses' old enemy, Thutmose III, was dead. The new Pharaoh, Amenhotep II, was probably about 22 when confronted by the 80-year-old Moses. More than age contrasted when these two men met. There was a confrontation between lifestyles and attitudes as well: a confrontation between meekness and pride. Moses had been 40 years in Egypt, nurtured to be a somebody. For 40 years in the desert he had learned that he was a nobody. Now God would show what He could do with a somebody who was willing to be a nobody.

Not so the young Pharaoh. In Egypt, society was structured around religion: a religion in which secular and sacred distinctions were lost, and the Pharaoh was himself considered a god. In official monuments the Pharaoh was often called *neter nefer*, the perfect god. We even have records in which a courtier describes Amenhotep II, this young man confronting Moses, as *neter aa*, the great god! Imagine the pride of Amenhotep. Imagine Moses speaking in the name of the Lord God of Israel (e.g., "God of slaves!"). How easy it is to visualize the haughty pride that moved Amenhotep to respond, "Who is the Lord that I should obey Him and let Israel go? I do not know the Lord, and I will not let Israel go" (Ex. 5:2).

Through the succeeding judgments we watch the Pharaoh coming to know the Lord . . . and struggling against Him. At first judgments fail to move Pharaoh. Then, under the pressure of the supernatural, Pharaoh promised to yield . . . only to return to his pride and obstinacy when a miraculous plague was removed. Even after the ultimate judgment, striking against his son and the firstborn of every Egyptian, Pharaoh changed his mind and sent an army to pursue freed Israel.

In the confrontations between these two men we see in stark contrast the patience and steadfastness of faith against the backdrop of a self-exalting pride. It is this kind of pride which will not permit men to bow to God, even when it is clearly for their own good.

Israel vs. Egypt.

One of the purposes expressed in the design of the plagues which the Lord brought on Egypt was so that "you will know that the Lord makes a distinction between Egypt and Israel" (Ex. 11:7). Anyone looking at the two peoples would have made a distinction between them. But not the distinction the Lord made!

The Israelites themselves were conditioned to evaluate . . . and to bow in shame, before the culture and power of Egypt. Everything that men tend to value . . . the evidences of accomplishment, all the wealth, the education . . . were there in a high degree in Egypt. Archeologists still wonder at the mechanical feats of that people. Mathematicians and astronomers are amazed at the precise measurements that allowed great pyramids to mark with various architectural features the exact time of summer and winter solstices.

The Israelites were slaves. Mere tools to be used by the master race, then tossed aside when they had served their purpose. Worthless. Poor. Subhuman. The Jews were beneath the notice of men.

But God made His own distinction between Egyptian and Jew! And God's value system is different than man's! God affirmed the worth and value of the slave people. In doing so, God not only kept the covenant He had made with Abraham, but God also shouted out for all to hear that no man is "nothing" to Him.

We value what men *do*.

God values what men *are*.

The Prophet Hosea beautifully revealed God's attitude and helps us see that the distinction God drew between Egypt and Israel was no mere legal act, performed to honor a previous contract. It was that. But God also acted in compassion, expressing deep love and concern for the suffering.

> When Israel was a child, I loved him, and out of Egypt I called My son. . . . It was I who taught Ephraim to walk, taking them by the arms; but they did not realize it was I who healed them. I led them with cords of human kindness, with ties of love, I lifted the yoke from their neck and bent down to feed them.
>
> Hosea 11:1, 3-4

The confrontation between these two peoples is important for us to see. We too are forced to choose between the value system each represents. We too are challenged to have compassion on the downtrodden of this world . . . and in compassion to reflect the character and the values of our God.

Yahweh vs. the Gods of Egypt

This is the third, and greatest, confrontation. We need to see these chapters of Exodus as a mighty struggle staged for our special benefit. In these chapters the God who *is* confronts all which men call "gods" but which are not. Dramatically, convincingly, God shows that He is Victor over all.

Religion played a central role in the life of Egypt. Each of the many gods was seen as having control over vital aspects of Egyptian existence. Together, the structure focused on insuring a safe passage beyond this life into the next. Now, in a series of 10 judgments, the gods of the pagan pantheon were challenged by the Lord and defeated. The Pharaoh had asked, "Who is the Lord, that I should obey Him?" Through the subsequent judgments, God announced, "The Egyptians will know that I am the Lord" (Ex. 7:5). They would see His power, and His fame would spread throughout the earth (9:16). What's more, the Jews would come to "know that I am the Lord your God" (6:7).

In the plagues God would reveal Himself, and He announced, "I will bring judgment on all the gods of Egypt" (12:12).

The first plague, the turning to blood of the floodwaters of the Nile, set the pattern for the others. To the Egyptians, the Nile itself was sacred. In its annual flood the river enriched Egypt's farmlands. The water from the Nile irrigated those narrow strips of fertile land on each bank which held and fed Egypt's population. No wonder this people of many gods dedicated hymns like this one, from the Middle Kingdom Period, to the Nile:

> Hail to thee, O Nile that issues from the earth and comes to keep Egypt alive. He that waters the meadows which recreate, in order to keep the kid alive. He that makes to drink the desert and places distant, that is his dew coming down from heaven.

This Nile, that re-created life each spring, God at Moses' word turned rotten . . . polluted and stinking as spilled blood (7:14-24). The source of Egypt's life died, and brought death. The gods of Egypt were powerless before the God of Egypt's slaves.

And so it went. The frog god of fertility, *Heka*, was represented in rotting piles of dead frogs. The god of the earth, *Seth*, was infested with lice, speaking to the Egyptians of ceremonial pollution. *Isis* and *Serapis*, gods of fire and water, were unable to protect Egypt from hail or locusts. *Ra*, the sun god, lost all power to overcome the blanket of darkness God threw over the land.

In each encounter, the gods of Egypt were judged, and found wanting. They went down in defeat before Yahweh, the Creator.

Bernard Ramm suggests that the confrontation of Yahweh and the gods of Egypt has even deeper significance. In God's judgments on Egypt, Ramm sees pictured a confrontation "with all gods, power, authorities, principalities, and ideologies, visible or invisible, that oppose God and His truth and that enslave and oppress men." Whatever enslaves you, God can conquer, even as He conquered the empty gods of Egypt! (*His Way Out,* Zondervan)

This is important to grasp. There is no power but God's power. *He* is the one underlying reality. As you and I come to know Him, the powers that enslave us will assuredly meet a similar defeat at His hand. The God who visited judgment on the gods of Egypt has the power to visit judgment on our captors too. And, because He is a God who has compassion, as we come to know and to trust Him, He will!

♥ ***Link to Life: Children***

"I can't swallow a pill," the eight-year-old cries. "I can't win the race, so I won't try." There are many things that look overwhelmingly big to some children. How good for them to realize that our God of miracles has the power to help them even as He helped the Israelites. Have your class think of some things that are "impossible" for them to do. Something they are worried about, something that may be a temptation, something they are supposed to do but seems too hard.

After the list is made, tell the story of the 10 plagues on Egypt. Emphasize God's power, and His willingness to help the helpless Israelite slaves.

If they had been there watching, how powerful would they have thought God is? Powerful enough to help? (here mention items on chalkboard list) Assure your boys and girls that God is with them and able to help them do "impossible" things. If you wish give each a Bible verse on a card to take home as a reminder of God's power. Appropriate verses are Isaiah 40:29; Ephesians 3:16; 2 Thessalonians 3:3; 2 Timothy 1:7; 1 Peter 1:5; Jude 24-25.

♥ ***Link to Life: Youth / Adult***

Youth and adults also need a strong sense of who God is, and what He is able to do. Ask your group to read through the miracle section in Exodus 7:14–11:10. Have them imagine they were there, as slaves, observing. What would they have thought and felt?

This can be done as a role play, with your class a group of slaves sitting together at night. Or simply by discussion. Your goal is to help your class sense what it was like to be eyewitnesses to the exercise of God's power—for them.

Then move on. "Do we have a sense today of how powerful God is? Do we see Him as Someone involved in our lives? What can help us remember that His power is still available to us? In what area do you most need to trust God's power and step out in faith today?"

The Message

Many have poured over these chapters of Scripture, and have noted exciting truths. These chapters are so full it's all too easy to be distracted from the primary thrust.

The Pharaoh's hard heart. This question has been a favorite one for speculation. In some verses the Bible says God hardened Pharaoh's heart. In others Pharaoh hardened his heart. Do these phrases mean that God moved the Pharaoh to sin against his will? Was God the source of Pharaoh's evil?

Exodus 3:19 reports that God told Moses that He knew Pharaoh would not let Israel go unless compelled. Certainly Pharaoh's first reaction to Moses (Ex. 5) is a spontaneous one . . . one that gives us solid evidence that Pharaoh by nature was not responsive to God. And yet in 7:3-4 God told Moses that He would "harden Pharaoh's heart, and though I multiply My miraculous signs and wonders in Egypt, he will not listen to you." What is this hardening? And what does it all mean?

Explanations have varied. Some point to the Hebrew view of causation, which tends to trace responsibility back to God, ignoring intervening acts or choices by men. Others have suggested that God refers to the natural result of revelation: when God speaks to responsive hearts, they melt before Him. When God speaks to unresponsive hearts, they harden. Thus the same sun's growing heat will melt wax, yet harden clay.

The Hebrew word most frequently used in this setting means "to be or become strong." Thus the derivation "to strengthen, to harden." We might paraphrase, "God strengthened Pharaoh's resolve to resist." This paraphrase would have one advantage. It would make very clear the fact that God did not force Pharaoh to act against his own conscience or against his will.

But even this would not resolve the problem. God does say to Pharaoh, "I have raised you up for this very purpose, that I might show you My power and that My name might be proclaimed in all the earth" (9:16). God could have acted differently than He did. Yet He let Pharaoh, whose rebellion and mistreatment of Israel merited death, live. He let the Pharaoh live that he might be used by God for His own glory.

But this is just the fear that strikes many of us when we read these chapters. It's not the theological debate between free will and God's sovereignty that troubles us. It's a far more personal issue. It's the doubt and the uncertainty that lead us to ask, "Will God use me? Am I a pawn to Him, or does He care?"

The continual response of Scripture to this question is reassuring. Yes, God does care. He reached down in compassion to deliver Israel. He Himself stepped into our world—and was jerked upward on a wooden cross—because He does care. To all who respond with faith to His message, God commits Himself, even as He committed Himself to Abraham in a covenant oath. I can know, I do know, that I am not a pawn to God. He loves me for myself. He cares, and because God cares He has lifted me to freedom in Jesus Christ.

♥ ***Link to Life: Children***

Young children can appreciate the fact that God cared for the people of Israel, and helped them. Tell the story, emphasizing the pains of slavery, and the fact that in the plagues on Egypt God was at work to help His people be free.

God cares for boys and girls today. God is with them everywhere, as He was with the slaves in faraway Egypt.

Give the children a large sheet of paper, with crayons or markers. On half the sheet have them draw a picture of slaves in Egypt. (Perhaps drawing a triangle for a pyramid will help the younger children get started.) On the other half each child is to draw a place he goes where he is glad God is with him or her.

Let the children explain their pictures to each other. Pray and thank God that He cares for us, and is with us as He was with ancient Israel.

The miracles. Over a nine-month span God brought a series of miraculous judgments on Egypt. These were recognized by Egyptian and Jew alike as God's special intervention . . . as "wonders" done by God's hand. Later speculation has grown about the nature of the miracles. Some have associated them with a volcanic cataclysm in the Mediterranean that destroyed what we have come to call "Atlantis." The *Reader's Digest* even published serious articles explaining the supposed relationship between Atlantis and the Exodus. Others have tried to explain away the miraculous elements by insisting these were merely normal occurrences, expanded by the storyteller. After all, locusts often infested that part of the world. The "bloody" Nile might be explained away as some unexpected infestation of algae.

Even the death of Egypt's youths has been considered a sudden, but not unusual, childhood epidemic.

It is certainly probable that God did use natural events in the course of His judgments on Egypt. But the extent and the timing of these events made it very clear that they came by God's hand. On Moses' word judgments began; at his prayer they ended. Hail struck the Egyptians, but the Hebrew territories were free. The "childhood epidemic" struck only the firstborn sons of Egyptian families, and hit the entire land in a single night. And Hebrew children were strangely "immune"! No, to think that by suggesting "natural" elements the miraculous can be removed is to miss the point entirely.

Whatever means God chose to use, Egyptian and Jew alike knew that it was God who acted.

God known anew. As fascinating as it is to speculate about Pharaoh's hardening and about the nature of the plagues, to focus on these issues is to miss the message of these vital chapters of our Bible. That message, what God was saying through these events to Israel and to us, is made strikingly clear.

God said to Moses:

> I am the Lord. I appeared to Abraham, to Isaac, and to Jacob, as God Almighty, but by My name the Lord I did not make Myself known to them. . . . Therefore, say to the Israelites: "I am the Lord, and I will bring you out from under the yoke of the Egyptians. I will free you from being slaves to them and will redeem you with an outstretched arm and with mighty acts of judgment. I will take you as My own people, and I will be your God. Then you will know that I am the Lord your God who brought you out from the yoke of the Egyptians. And I will bring you to the land I swore with uplifted hand to give to Abraham, to Isaac, and to Jacob. I will give it to you as a possession. I am the Lord."
>
> Exodus 6:2-3, 6-8

It is important for us to realize what God was saying here. He was not saying that the name "the Lord" or "Yahweh" had never been applied to Him before. It had. He was saying instead, "You have not *known* Me as Yahweh." This is a vital distinction. For the Hebrew, the word "know" spoke not only of casual information, but of intense and intimate personal experience. God told His people, "You have heard the name Yahweh; now you will experience Me as Yahweh."

What then does Yahweh mean, and why is it so special? The name itself is a form of the verb "to be," and is a proper name rather than a descriptive name. In descriptive names the Lord is spoken of as "God of battles" or as "God our refuge." But He is never called "Yahweh of" anything. "God" is a description. "Yahweh" is a personal name. In God's revelation of Himself to us as Yahweh we have a disclosure of His central character and being.

What, then, does Yahweh imply? Simply that we are to see God as One who *is*. In fact, we might expand the idea expressed in this form of the verb "to be" and say that we are to know the Lord as the "*God who is always here!*"

In this character, as a God of the present, the Hebrew people had not known the Lord. They thought of Him as a God of the past, who long ago spoke to their forefathers. Or they thought of Him as a God of the future, who might one day keep His covenant promises. But the Hebrew slaves simply had not thought of God as a God of their present, who would act in their world of here and now!

But God did act.

And Israel came to know their God as Yahweh, *The One Who Is Always Present,* always with us, always able to act.

Today to truly understand God you and I must see Him as Someone who is with us now. What a revelation! How it can revolutionize our spiritual lives! When we know God as One who is present with us now, willing and able to act for us, we are freed to live our present lives by faith. We are free to obey God, knowing He walks beside us. Knowing His power is available to enable us to do whatever He asks, no matter how far it may be beyond our own weak powers.

The Passover

The final stroke against Egypt was the death of each firstborn. Following God's instructions, Moses moved the Israelites to hurried preparation. They were told to ask gold and jewels from the Egyptians. The Lord would move their masters to give. The Israelites were to pack and prepare for a sudden journey. Bread must not be mixed with yeast—there might not be time to let it rise. Also, a young, unblemished lamb was to be taken into each household. It was to be kept for four days, and then on the 14th day of the month the lamb was to be killed and its blood sprinkled on the doorposts of the home. The family within that structure was to eat the lamb, taking care not to break a single bone.

But why should this ceremony be called "Passover"? Because on the night the lamb was slain, God's death angel would move through the land of Egypt. The firstborn in every family, from Pharaoh's own home to the home of the lowest peasant, would die. Yet the death angel would pass over homes protected by the blood of the lamb.

God distinguished between Egyptian and Jew. The lamb of sacrifice, the sign of the blood on the door, marked off God's people from all others. They alone were exempt from the decree of death.

The full significance of this event waited the coming of Christ. His death on Calvary took place as the Lamb of God, slain for the sins of the world. Yet the Old Testament believer could learn vital lessons.

**Relationship with God is a life or death issue.* Only identification with the people of God as one of His own exempted one from death.

**Redemption brings freedom at the cost of death.* Breaking the bondage of Egypt was not accomplished until the death penalty had been imposed. Israel's freedom was costly.

**Release from the death penalty is accomplished by sacrifice.* Somehow the blood of the sacrificial lamb covered and protected the household of the believing Jew. Later God would explain to this same generation, "The life of a creature is in the blood; and I have given it to you to make atonement for yourselves on the altar; it is the blood that makes atonement" (Lev. 17:11). Much later, the writer of the New Testament Book of Hebrews would see in *sacrifice* the necessity for Jesus' death. "Without the shedding of blood there is no forgiveness" (Heb. 9:22). Sacrifice and forgiveness, the death of a substitute and spiritual freedom, would be forever linked.

**Remember.* The importance of this first Passover is underlined by the divine demand that every year, without fail, the Passover experience be reenacted. Each year for seven days God's people were to commemorate their deliverance, "as a lasting ordinance for the generations to come" (Ex. 12:17). From the 14th through the 21st of Abib (Nisan, the modern Jewish equivalent of Abib, falls during March-April) the Jews were to eat no leaven. On the last night of the feast they were to take a lamb, kill and eat it. They were to eat the Passover meal standing, with their traveling clothing on, and their walking staffs in their hands. And each year when the children asked, "What do you mean by this service?" the father was to respond, "It is the Passover sacrifice to the Lord, who passed over the houses of the Israelites in Egypt and spared our homes when He struck down the Egyptians" (v. 27).

Israel was never to forget her origin.

Israel was never to forget she was a people delivered from slavery, exempted from death. Israel was to remember, and yearly make the sacrifices which looked back to Egypt—and forward to the suffering Messiah.

♥ ***Link to Life: Youth / Adult***

Today the Christian Communion service has a similar function in our faith. The Jewish people were to see Passover as a reenactment of history; as an experience in which each Jewish family actually would participate. When we take the cup and the bread of Communion we too remember history. We remember the Cross of Christ, and we participate by faith in His death.

A study of the Passover and the call of each Israelite generation to participate in the historic deliverance each year can help you communicate the significance of the Communion service to Christians. So after studying the Passover, why not hold Communion with your group. Do it gravely, asking each person to close his or her eyes and imagine as he tastes each element that he is there, with Jesus, at the cross.

Forgotten. It's fascinating to trace through the Old Testament and note what happened to the Passover remembrance.

*Numbers 9 tells us of the first anniversary experience, and of the special relaxation of ritual rules that made it possible for all of God's people to keep this unique feast.

*Deuteronomy 16 repeats the command to keep Passover, and adds that when Israel comes into the Promised Land, Passover is to be kept at the place where God's temple will be established. All the families of Israel are to come there and, if necessary, live in tents Passover week.

*Second Kings 23 tells of a revival under King Josiah, some 800 years after the Exodus, during which the Passover is reinstituted. After a 400-year lapse! Israel had forgotten redemption. In neglecting their beginning, the Hebrews had strayed from God into a series of deep spiritual and moral declines.

*In New Testament times Passover was carefully kept. In fact, Passover week is the focal point of each of the four Gospels. Matthew 21–28 report the events of Passover week culminating in Good Friday and Easter. Mark 11–16; Luke 19–24; and John 12–20 (a good half of that Gospel!) all focus on that same Passover week. Why? Because it is here that the shadow cast by the first Passover is replaced by the solid reality it foretold. During this week, Christ our Passover Lamb was sacrificed, for us (1 Cor. 5:7).

It is here that our freedom, and our new life, must begin. Redemption's work is done. By the blood of Jesus Christ you and I are set free forever.

TEACHING GUIDE

Prepare
Read the Passover remembrance instructions (Ex. 12:24-27). Which of God's acts for you would you want to celebrate annually?

Explore
1. You may wish to cover the large amount of material in this unit by a lecture. Why not prepare your group by giving a "quiz." Then use the questions on it as an outline for your talk. Use such questions as: (1) List 5 of the 10 plagues. (2) Give two reasons why Israel needed to see God's power exhibited at this point in history. (3) What is the significance of the name Yahweh? (4) How do we know that Passover is a very significant event? (5) What relationship exists between the Passover and Jesus?
2. Ask your group members to look up how the judgments on Egypt affected various peoples. They should read Deuteronomy 4:34; 7:19; Joshua 24:5; 1 Samuel 4:8; Psalms 78:43-51; 135:8-9; Jeremiah 32:21. After reading and reporting, discuss: "Why did these events have such an impact? What impact does God intend them to have on our lives?"

Expand
1. Read in class Exodus 6:2-3, 6-8. Ask each person to quietly imagine that God is speaking to him or her personally. Then say, "God was speaking to Israel about deliverance from slavery. What would God be speaking about in your life? Where do you need to know deliverance?"
2. Or, discuss how looking back on the Exodus and reliving it each year at the Passover service helped to keep Israel's vision of God as One Who Is Always Present fresh and new. What personal spiritual experiences with God could your group members commemorate that would remind them of this truth? After all have had the chance to share, go around the circle and let each tell something he or she might do as an annual reminder. Perhaps it's revisiting a place. Or reading a special passage of Scripture. Or calling a friend who shared the experience. How important that we remember the wonders God does for us!

Apply
Why not hold a group Communion service, as suggested in the "link-to-life" activity on page 86.

Enjoy the sense of Jesus Christ's presence with you as you remember Him at Calvary—and by faith participate in His great sacrifice.

STUDY GUIDE 11

Exodus 13–19

THE NEED FOR LAW

Overview

Redemption from slavery was to be the beginning of Israel's new relationship with God as One Who Is Always Present. That relationship, as our own relationship with the Lord, has a goal: transformation. People with whom God shares Himself are expected to share the Lord's qualities, and especially His holiness!

The events we read of in Exodus 13–19 demonstrate all too clearly that Israel was not yet a holy people, and not yet ready to respond to God. These events demonstrate to us why the introduction of Mosaic Law was a historic necessity.

▶ ***Law.*** The Hebrew word *torah* means "teaching" or "instruction." It is instruction focused on how to live, not on abstract or academic issues.

The idea expressed by *torah* or *law* is broad and has different shades of meaning. The first five books of Moses are called the *torah*. The total way of life these books lay out for Israel are also called *torah*. And of course the Ten Commandments are *torah*. Thus biblically, law includes all the instruction God gave to guide the nation Israel, including ceremonial or ritual instruction as well as civil and moral guidelines. In this part of Exodus, however, "law" is used in its narrower sense of a specific rule of life; a standard God's people are to live by. Law in this sense was never intended as a permanent feature of faith's life. But the righteousness that is expressed in the Law is to find living expression in the life of everyone who walks with God.

Commentary

Passover night was an end to slavery, but a beginning of life with God. While the people of Israel were always to remember that "the Lord brought [them] out of it" (Ex. 13:3), they were *not to remember Egypt!* They were not to look back, but to move out immediately on their journey to the Promised Land.

The route of Exodus (Ex. 13:17-22). The most direct route to Palestine was along the coast. But this would have thrown Israel into immediate conflict with powerful enemies. The people needed time to learn to trust God, time to become organized. So God led them by a roundabout route, paralleling the Red Sea for about 100 miles southward down the Sinai Peninsula. Their journey brought them to the shore of a great body of water, in Hebrew called *yam suph*. This means literally, "sea of reeds," and probably is best identified as the Bitter Lakes (see map, p. 89). It was at this point, trapped against the waters and a dry wilderness, that Israel realized the Egyptian army was pursuing them!

Deliverance: Exodus 14

Pharaoh and the Egyptian people (v. 5) recovered quickly. Perhaps the wealth that Israel took with them motivated pursuit. At any rate, Pharaoh set out to recapture his slaves, sending a 600-chariot army on ahead. The Israelites were overtaken at the seaside.

Pharaoh had forgotten God. But so had the Israelites! The people cried out bitterly against Moses, begging him to let them return and serve the Egyptians rather than die in the wilderness. Moses' response makes a good watchword for us today: "Do not be afraid. Stand firm and see the deliverance the Lord will bring you today" (v. 13).

Redemption had been God's work. Now deliverance of His people from each new peril must be His work as well.

We all know the familiar story of the crossing. God opened and dried a path for His people. When the Egyptians tried to follow, He brought the walls of water swirl-

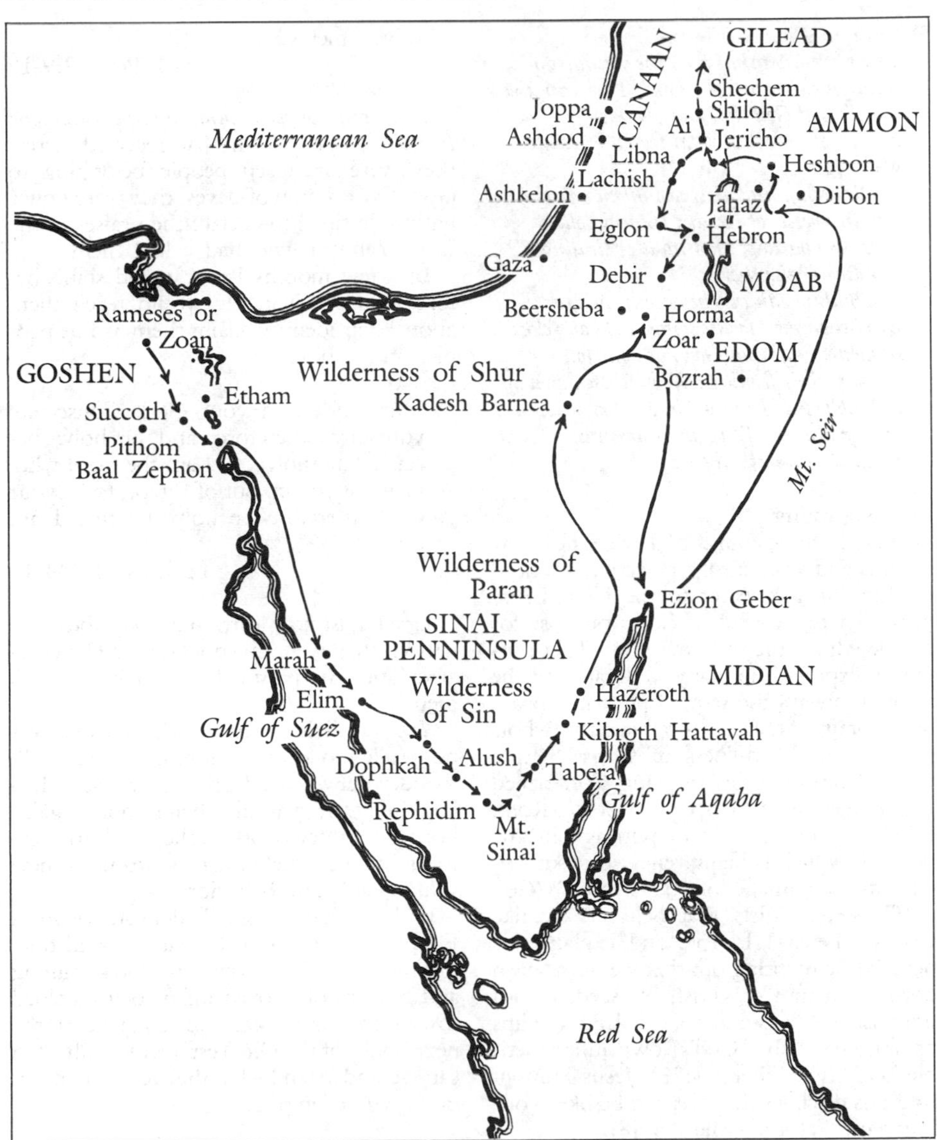

Route of the Exodus

ing back to destroy them. Perhaps we can even imagine ourselves there, and realize what it must have meant to God's people to see their oppressors' dead bodies along the seashore (v. 30). We can sense the great feeling of release from fear, the joy of that moment. The people believed God and sang.

The Song: Exodus 15
Exodus 15 concludes with a record of the song the people of Israel sang.

Like our own worship and praise, the song lifts up the person of God. It reviews what God had done. And it lifts up for all to see the fact that God truly is "One Present With Us."

> I will sing to the Lord, for He is highly exalted. The horse and its rider He has hurled into the sea. The Lord is my strength and my song; He has become my salvation.
>
> Exodus 15:1-2

♥ ***Link to Life: Children***

There are ways that even the youngest of children can praise the Lord. They can give thanks, tell God they love Him, sing praises, even talk of what they appreciate about Him.

Older boys and girls can memorize the first two verses of Exodus 15 and hold a classroom parade, quoting it or singing a familiar praise chorus.

Children can also be encouraged to write their own praise songs. Let your class suggest things that God has done for them or their families. Write these down on a chalkboard. Then work together to express praise and fit them to the music of a familiar children's song.

Just Beginning

To put the happenings of Israel's next few months and years into perspective, we need to shift for a moment to the New Testament. There we read of God's purpose for people who come to know Him. That purpose is expressed in many ways, and yet the thrust is always the same. Ephesians speaks of becoming "mature, attaining the whole measure of the fullness of Christ" (Eph. 4:13). Romans speaks of being "conformed to the likeness of His [God's] Son" (Rom. 8:29). Colossians talks of putting on "the new self, which is being renewed in knowledge in the image of its Creator" (Col. 3:10). Peter insists that believers be like God (1 Peter 1:14-15), and explains his demand by pointing out that we have "been born again, not of perishable seed, but of imperishable." We have, as J.B. Phillips paraphrases, "His [God's] own indestructible heredity" (1 Peter 1:23). Jesus Himself told His disciples they were to be like "your Heavenly Father" (Matt. 5:48).

The thrust of this line of teaching is clear. For the believer, salvation is the beginning of a process in which the individual is to grow up into the likeness of Jesus Christ. Peter sums it up beautifully:

> But you are a chosen people, a royal priesthood, a holy nation, a people belonging to God, that you may declare the praises of Him who called you out of darkness into His wonderful light. Once you were not a people, but now you are the people of God; once you had not received mercy, but now you have received mercy.
>
> 1 Peter 2:9-10

This same purpose sums up the calling of Israel! As a people who had received mercy, they were a chosen people belonging to God. Once a mob of slaves, they were now a nation destined to declare the praises of the Lord Yahweh who had called them.

In a few months Israel would stand before God at Sinai. He would teach them about their identity, claim them as His people, and announce:

> I am the Lord your God. Consecrate yourselves therefore, and be holy; because I am holy. . . . I am the Lord who brought you up out of Egypt, to be your God; therefore be holy, because I am holy.
>
> Leviticus 11:44-45

Israel must now learn to be like God! As a nation, they were called to reflect His character and His personality as a light to all men.

Yet the divine lifestyle which Israel was now called to learn was foreign to them. No wonder deliverance from Egypt was only a beginning. It was like being born again: born into a new world, called to learn new thoughts, new feelings, new attitudes, new values, and new behaviors.

Only by seeing Israel's deliverance from Egypt as the birth of the nation—and tracing the subsequent events as God's training and nurture of a loved infant being helped toward maturity—can we understand the next books of the Old Testament. Only then can we understand what they teach us about our own redemption.

♥ ***Link to Life: Youth / Adult***

Conversion for some has little outward change associated with it. Some of us were brought up in the home of Christians, and taught Christian values. For others, though, conversion means a radical change in lifestyle.

Go around your group and ask each to reflect aloud on the most difficult change he or she had to face in learning to live as a real Christian. Afterward, talk about how the new life pattern was learned. From books? Sermons? The Bible? From friends? Explain that God needed to teach redeemed

Israel a new lifestyle, when the pattern of their life had simply left God out for decades!

The Child
Events reported in Exodus 15:22 through 17:7 show us how like a child Israel was. Looking back the Prophet Hosea used that image:

> When Israel was a child, I loved him, and out of Egypt I called My son. But the more I called Israel, the further they went from Me. They sacrificed to the Baals and they burned incense to images. It was I who taught Ephraim to walk, I took them up in My arms; but they did not know I healed them.
>
> Hosea 11:1-3

Squalling and willful, toddling off to grasp at forbidden "pretties," infant Israel soon forgot the great acts of God through which she was delivered, and lapsed into complaint and a childish, willful bitterness.

Three days after crossing the Red Sea, the people were in a waterless wilderness, led there by God Himself by the agency of a cloudy, fiery pillar which was always visible to them (Ex. 13:21). When they did find water, it was undrinkable, and the people "grumbled against Moses." The Lord purified the water, and promised that if the people would be responsive and listen to His voice, He would continually be a "healer" to them (15:22-26). Immediately after, God led them to Elim, an oasis with 12 springs and 70 palm trees, where they could rest from the desert journey and refresh themselves.

When they journeyed on, the people murmured against Moses again, complaining of hunger. The supplies they brought from Egypt had dwindled. God responded by bringing quail to the camp that evening, and in the morning produced the first of the *manna* which would feed Israel all the time they were in the wilderness (16:1-15). This manna was a waferlike substance that appeared on the ground with the dew. It tasted like honey and nuts. Only as much as a person could eat in a single day was gathered, except the day before the Sabbath, when two days' supply could be collected. On weekdays any extra manna spoiled; on the Sabbath it did not.

In spite of Moses' warning that their murmuring was against the Lord, and His command not to gather more manna than they needed, the people "paid no attention to Moses" (v. 20).

Moving on in easy stages, Israel was again led to a place where there was no water. Panicked, they accused Moses of bringing them out of Egypt to kill them with thirst. In their anger, they were about ready to stone Moses. But again God acted in grace to supply water, this time from a rock (17:1-8).

What then is the picture we have of infant Israel? It is a picture of people too immature to respond to grace; too willful to respond to guidance. God constantly demonstrated both His love and His ability to meet their every need. Yet in each crisis the people panicked and were unable to trust Him. Their response to pressure was more violent each time: they "grumbled against Moses" (15:24); then "the whole community grumbled against Moses" (16:2); then "they quarreled with Moses" and were "almost ready to stone" him (17:2, 4). These people were not learning the divine lifestyle. They in fact rejected the first and most basic lesson: the lesson of trust. God had proven Himself faithful over and over again. Yet there was no awakening of response in the hearts or the minds of His chosen people.

Israel proved herself to be a child.

♥ ***Link to Life: Youth / Adult***
Make a chart diagramming God's acts and Israel's responses on the journey to Sinai (Ex. 15–18).

Then ask your group to share ideas of Israel's "personality" at that time. What were the people really like? What words describe them, or their relationship with God? Why would such a people need discipline, or clear "do" and "don't" guidelines?

Introduction of the Law: Exodus 19
We cannot understand the Mosaic Law and the Ten Commandments without realizing that they were given to Israel as a child. It was the infancy of Israel that made it necessary for God to introduce the Law.

Put in modern terms, we can look at the journey to Mount Sinai as a time when God dealt with Israel permissively. He let them respond "naturally." He acted in love to

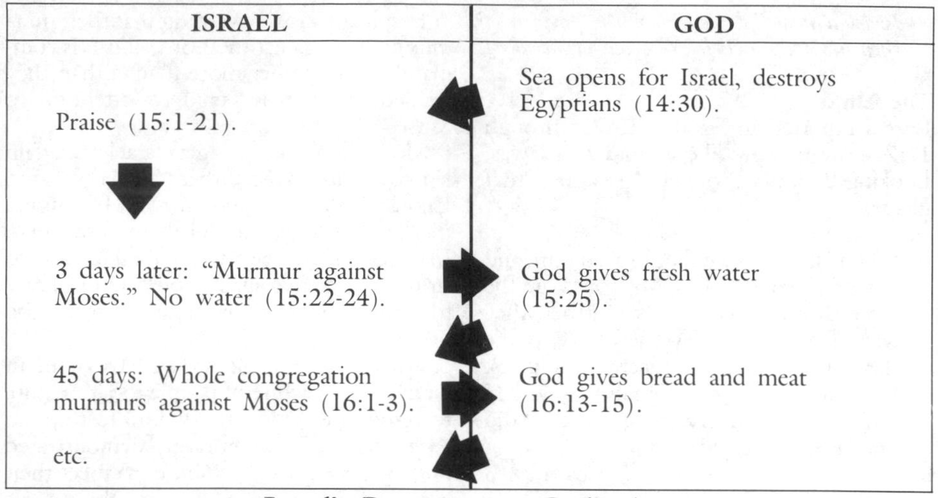

ISRAEL
GOD
Sea opens for Israel, destroys Egyptians (14:30).
Praise (15:1-21).
3 days later: "Murmur against Moses." No water (15:22-24).
God gives fresh water (15:25).
45 days: Whole congregation murmurs against Moses (16:1-3).
God gives bread and meat (16:13-15).
etc.

Israel's Responses to God's Acts

meet their needs. He did not correct or punish. And the result showed the outcome common to all permissive approaches to child-rearing. The people failed to develop inner discipline. They did not mature. They did not respond to God as a Person, or delight in His purposes.

The Bible makes it very clear that God is not a permissive parent. And this section of Scripture shows us why.

Scripture tells us "the Lord disciplines those He loves, and He punishes everyone He accepts as a son" (Heb. 12:6; see also Prov. 3:11-12). What's more, Scripture tells us the purpose of God's discipline. "God disciplines us for our good, that we may share His holiness" (Heb. 12:10). It takes discipline to develop holiness, and God will not shrink back from giving His children any good gift—no matter how painful that gift may initially seem!

It was because of love, then, and for the introduction of a discipline through which Israel might come to share God's holiness that the Lord led His people to Mount Sinai. Love, and Israel's desperate need for discipline, led to giving of the Law. In later years the Law would be tragically misunderstood by God's people. Its purpose and meaning would be distorted, and its true role clouded. But the Law was nevertheless necessary—for Israel.

A voluntary covenant. As we study the Law we'll see a striking difference between the Law Covenant made at Sinai and the covenant God made earlier with Abraham (Gen. 12; 15; 17). Each makes clear what God is committed to do. But how God acts under Law is linked to the response of each generation and individual to His revealed Word. God said "I will . . . " to Moses, and gave him unshakable promises. God said, "If you obey Me fully," to Israel at Sinai (Ex. 19:5).

Under Law, obedience would bring blessing; through obedience the people would become "a kingdom of priests and a holy nation" (v. 6). But if a generation would not respond to God, and continued in childish rebellion, they would not be blessed. Instead they would know the chastising hand of God.

Fear of the Lord. The events at Sinai now take on a striking appearance. The God who brought vast judgments on Egypt now thundered at Israel! Boundaries were set around the mountain, and no living thing was permitted to approach its slopes. A thick cloud covered the mountaintop; thunder and lightning constantly played above the camp. Then, dramatically, a voice that stunned Israel's senses spoke. The Bible tells us that the people "trembled with fear. They stayed at a distance and said to Moses, 'Speak to us yourself and we will listen. But do not have God speak to us or we will die' " (20:18-19).

Awed and fearful, the willful people of Israel, for a time at least, were cowed. Psalm 111:10 says it: "The fear of the Lord is the beginning of wisdom." And Proverbs 1:7 echoes the thought: "The fear of the Lord is the beginning of knowledge." The child must learn respect for the parent before he will respond to love.

"The Law." Often in Scripture "the Law" speaks of these first uttered commandments of God to Israel. But the word Law (*torah*) does not always refer to the Ten Words of Sinai. It also refers at times to the whole system of life expressed by the continuing Old Testament revelation; a system containing many positive statutes and ordinances as well as the apparent negatives of the Ten. Also, the believing Jew thought of the Books of Moses (Gen. through Deut.) as *torah*, "the Law."

But here it is the Ten Commandments and their explanation in Exodus that will soon draw our attention. For these stand today as the epitome of the moral revelation of the Old Testament. Looking at them, remembering that Israel is a people who need discipline and training in holiness, we need to ask, "Why these? What was God's purpose in giving Israel this Law, now?"

The Law

This first revelation of Law to Israel performed two clear functions. First of all, it *revealed the character of God.* If Israel was to reflect God's character, and thus bring Him praise, they must understand His character. The Ten Commandments are our first sharp revelation of the moral character and the deepest values of our God.

Oh, we can infer much from earlier revelation: for instance, we know that God is faithful to His promises. But His moral character still remained something of a mystery. But no more. The Ten Words from Sinai reveal the moral nature of this God who had taken it on Himself to redeem a people to become like Him.

A second important function of the Law is that it *defines God's expectations.* In objective, clear, and well-defined standards, the people of God are told how He expects them to behave.

There is a tremendous value in any relationship in having expectations revealed. Some of us grew up in homes where we simply did not know how to please our parents. Nothing we did seemed to meet with their approval, and their commands to us would change from day to day. There was to be no such uncertainty for Israel in its relationship with God. God defined clearly the way He expected them to go; so clearly that even a child could not miss his way.

With the limits established, and with God's expectations clearly expressed, the people would now have a standard by which to measure their own responses and behavior.

In modern terms this might be called an "immediate feedback system"—something very important when anyone is being trained. For example, imagine a golfer practicing daily to eliminate a slice from his drive. He stands on the tee, swings, and watches the ball . . . adjusts, and tries again. He gauges each effort by watching that ball in flight, and, when he begins to straighten out the drive, he continues to practice to make sure that he has mastered the correct swing. Now, how much chance would the golfer have to improve if a screen were placed so he could tee up and hit, but not watch the ball's flight?

Obviously, without the feedback of seeing how he is doing, he simply could not correct his problem. In the same way, the Law provided an objective standard and served as a background against which the Israelites would obtain immediate feedback on their behavior. They could measure their plans, their goals, their values, and their actions against the divine revelation of morality.

There are other functions of the Law as well, but these two help us see its tremendous value to Israel at this point in history. The Law would be for Israel a dual revelation. In it they would see the moral character of God. And in it they would also see themselves.

♥ ***Link to Life: Children***

Children can understand that rules are good for them. To help them sense this in a special way, invite them to play several games.

Begin with a hopping game. "Let's everybody hop." After they hop a bit, stop and say, "Who won?" There is no answer, of course. No one knows the object or the rules of the game. Then set two goals, line up even teams, and have them do a relay hopping race, with the next person on a team to be touched by the one hopping before he or she can begin.

Do this with several games, and after-

ward talk with the children: "How did knowing the rules help? Was it better playing with rules or without?"

When God gives us rules to live by He is doing it to help us, not to harm us. God's rules help us live a happy, successful life, just as rules for games help us have a happy, successful time together.

TEACHING GUIDE

Prepare
Read and meditate on Psalm 119:97-104. How does David see God's Law? Why is it so precious to him?

Explore
1. Put on the board, "Children do not need rules. They should be allowed to do what comes naturally." Let group members agree or disagree with this statement. Discuss: "When do children need rules? What kind of rules do they need?"
2. Ask your group to think of feelings they associate with the word "Law." (The feelings will range from "restricted" and "guilty" to "secure" and "free.") When the feeling words have been listed on the board, ask group members to explain why a word they suggested is associated for them with "Law."

Expand
1. Do the chart study of Israel's responses to God during the journey to Sinai (see "link-to-life," p. 91). How does the description of the character of Israel which they discover help provide a background for the introduction of Law?
2. Give a minilecture covering God's goal for His people, and explaining how giving the Law to Israel at this point in history fits in with His purpose.

Apply
1. Examine Hebrews 12:5-13 and note the commitment God has to discipline those He loves. Talk about the relationship of this text to Exodus. But then encourage group members to share about times they have experienced God's discipline. Are there parallels between their experiences and those of Israel?
2. First Timothy 1:9 says that the Law is not made for good persons, but "lawbreakers and rebels." How is this illustrated in Israel? What does this suggest about the Christian who loves and follows Jesus closely?

How good to know that when we live close to the Lord, law is unnecessary, for we will love and act as Jesus wants us to without its external discipline.

STUDY GUIDE 12

Exodus 20–24

THE TEN COMMANDMENTS

Overview

Law is one of the most important biblical concepts. But its nature and purpose must be clearly grasped. Law reveals the character and the standards of God, and marks the way in which human beings can express love for God and for each other. But Law also condemns, for no human being except Jesus Christ has ever kept its requirements.

The Law reveals something of the righ teousness of God. But Law has never been able to produce righteousness in human beings.

In Exodus 20 God's moral Law is crystallized into Ten great Commandments. Nine of these are expressed as life principles in the New Testament. The Ten are followed by several pages of "case law"—illustrations of the principles as they are to be applied in specific cases (chaps. 21–23). We will survey the Ten and glance at the case law. And then give our attention to understanding the unique nature of Law and the role it played in Old Testament times, as well as the role it plays today.

▶ ***Kill.*** The Hebrew word in this commandment is more properly "murder." Old Testament Law makes distinctions between justifiable homicides and unjustifiable murder.

▶ ***Righteousness.*** Hebrew terms emphasize conforming to a norm. A person is "righteous" in a limited sense when his or her personal and interpersonal behavior is in harmony with an established moral/ ethical standard.

■ See *Bible Knowledge Commentary*, pages 139-140, for discussion of each individual commandment.

Commentary

For many people "Law" seems terribly restricting. And standards designed to apply to everyone seem cold and impersonal. So some years ago the idea emerged that rules were unnecessary: all an ethical person needed to do was, in any situation, simply determine the "loving thing to do."

It's an attractive notion. But just how does a person tell what is "loving"? How can we, fallible as we are, look ahead and determine the results of our possible choices, and select the course which will lead to our own and others' good?

Still, these folks do have a point. The Bible itself says that love sums up the whole Law (Rom. 13:8-10). Love is at the very foundation of Law. Love is at the root of its restrictions, just as love is at the root of the rules a good parent imposes on a toddler too young to know what is best for him.

The difference is that rather than you and me looking ahead to determine the loving thing to do, God has looked ahead for us! And in the Law He has expressed principles of morality that lead us to what is good.

For instance, Deuteronomy 15:4 promises that if Israel will only obey the Law "there will be no poor among you." The Law God gave Israel was to produce a just society and eliminate poverty!

Yes, God does know "the loving thing to do." And we can never separate His Law from His love.

Ten Commandments

Exodus 20 contains the 10 basic moral laws God revealed to Moses for Israel. The laws on the first tablet of the Law focus on human relationship with God. The laws on the second tablet focus on our relationships with each other. We can glance through them, and see the purpose in each.

Relationship with God	*Relationship with others*
1. No gods before Me	5. Honor father and mother
2. No idols	6. Do not murder
3. Do not take My name in vain	7. Do not commit adultery
	8. Do not steal
4. Keep Sabbath holy	9. Do not give false testimony
	10. Do not covet

Each of these deserves comment, for they lay the moral foundation for a holy community and help us grasp the importance of personal relationships in biblical thought.

1. *No other gods (Ex. 20:3)*. God has exclusive claim to our allegiance. No rival is to exist for the believer.

2. *No idols (Ex. 20:4-6)*. We are to respond to the Word and Spirit of an invisible God (cf. Deut. 5:8-10; Isa. 40:18-20).

3. *Do not take name in vain (Ex. 20:7)*. Yahweh means the One Who Is Ever Present. To take His "name in vain" means to consider the name empty or meaningless: to deny or doubt His presence and power.

4. *Keep Sabbath holy (Ex. 20:8-11)*. The day of rest honors God (cf. 16:23) and is to benefit God's Old Testament people (v. 29). To keep the Sabbath involved remembering God. This is the only commandment not repeated in the New Testament.

5. *Honor father and mother (Ex 20:12)*. Respect of parents leads to knowing God.

6. *Do not murder (Ex. 20:13)*. The right of every person to life is protected. Any act which might rob another of life is included in the prohibition.

7. *Do not commit adultery (Ex. 20:14)*. The value of faithfulness in personal commitments is stressed. Sex is not an "animal function," but an expression of deep, personal commitment between one man and one woman.

8. *Do not steal (Ex. 20:15)*. Respect for persons extends to their property. We do not "use" people for gain.

9. *Do not give false testimony (Ex. 20:16)*. An individual's reputation is to be guarded with his life and property.

10. *Do not covet (Ex. 20:17)*. We are to care for persons, not property. God's value system is to be our own.

Someone has suggested that we might visualize the Ten Commandments in terms of protection: protection of health in man's relationship with God, and the protection of health in man's relationship with other men.

How do the Ten Commandments protect relationships with God? First, we're taught that He alone is to be recognized as God, and that He is to be worshiped in ways that are appropriate to His nature as Spirit. What's more, we are to forever affirm the meaningfulness of Yahweh's name as the One Who Is Always Present, never taking it as an empty symbol. Finally, we are to build into our lives a weekly reminder of God: a day of rest on which God's works of Creation, rest, and redemption can be recalled.

"Protection" is also a theme of the commands dealing with interpersonal relationships. The parents' role, the sanctity of life, the institution of marriage, the right of property, and to expect fair treatment from others, all provide protection for man in society. The final commandment, however, goes beyond all comparable law codes, and implies protection of the individual from himself! The prohibition against coveting strikes at the root of what motivates us to violate the rights of others. It warns us to look within, and deal immediately with stirring motives which might lead us to sin.

As for external standards, then, the Ten Commandments excellently perform the function for which they were designed. Looking to this Law, an Israelite could come to know more about his God, and see in the words of the Law the divine heart of love. For God has expressed in the Law His concern for the rights and the integrity of each individual.

At the same time an Israelite could receive immediate feedback on himself. He could know, from the first stirrings within to their expression in action, any thought or behavior which was wrong.

For Israel, the fear of the Lord and the commands of the Lord truly were vital as a beginning to obedience.

Case Law: Exodus 21–23

In our culture we're used to dealing with abstract ideas and concepts. "Love," for instance, is a term we like. Yet for all our familiarity with the abstract, we are likely to misunderstand the real meaning of such terms. If God had only said, "Love," we might have been hard put to know what to do!

The Bible is practical. And so in Scripture God is careful to take abstract ideas and cast them in ordinary situations. Essentially, God provides in the Law multiple illustrations.

This is the best way to understand the "case law" we find in Exodus 21–23, which follows immediately after the Ten Commandments are stated in Exodus 20. The great "thou shalt nots" thundered from Mount Sinai provide the framework for a moral lifestyle in Israel. They set boundaries, showing clear limits. But now in the multiplied cases that follow, God gives insight into the freedom provided *within* those limitations.

What freedom?

Why, the freedom this people was to have to love. The freedom to grow. The freedom to live in harmony with God and with each other.

This is what we all want when we ask for "freedom." We want room to expand. We want freedom to become all we can be, and to achieve it without harming others or being harmed by them. This freedom, true freedom, is exactly what God provided for Israel within the framework of the limits established by the divine Law.

A positive lifestyle. The Ten Commandments provided a framework within which a positive lifestyle could be developed. Case law describes and illustrates that lifestyle, so no one can miss the practical implications of the Ten. What is the positive lifestyle like? Here are some examples.

*21:2. A Hebrew forced to sell himself as a slave shall be freed in six years.

*21:18-19. A man injured in a quarrel is to be paid for the loss of his time and for required medical treatment.

*21:33-34. A man leaving an open pit shall pay for another's animal that falls into it.

*22:1-4. A thief will repay what he has stolen—and repay at least double!

*22:16. A man seducing a virgin will marry her if the family of the girl is willing.

*22:21. A Jew shall not wrong an alien: the Law's protection extended to strangers.

*22:26-27. A man taking another's garment as a pledge for a loan shall let him have it nights; he may need to sleep in it for warmth.

*23:3. In court, judges are not to be partial to the poor, but to consider only justice.

These are just a few examples in the Old Testament describing the freedom God intended to bring to His people through the Law. It was freedom too, because under this Law each person was protected from wrongs others might commit against him, and then was charged with a responsibility for others' welfare.

The Old Testament Law was given to Israel by a loving God. Its very provisions constantly reveal God's love in action.

♥ ***Link to Life: Youth / Adult***
Have your group members read through either Exodus 21–23 or Leviticus 19, both of which contain examples of case law. Remember, these cases illustrate how the Law principles expressed in the 10 are to be applied. From that reading, each should select two or three items and note (a) how they express love, and (b) how they apply 1 of the basic 10 to a specific situation.

Have your group members form teams of five or six persons, to share what each has found, and to develop a group list of at least 10 items.

Cultural relevance. In reading the Old Testament, some have missed the spirit of love that infuses the Law. They have instead noted the fact that "slavery" was still permitted to God's people. They have been upset that the murderer is to be executed rather than "corrected." They have felt it unfair that women do not seem to stand here as "equals."

How, they ask, can such a primitive moral code as these passages reveal be considered a divine revelation—and how can the laws ever be understood as loving?

There are several answers to this kind of question; answers we need to consider carefully.

(1) *Whose standards do we accept?* Capital punishment is a good issue to illustrate this problem. It's popular to decry capital punishment as "cruel and unusual" treatment, and something which brings the state down to the level of the murderer. "Forgiveness," we hear, "is a Christian virtue that super-

sedes the archaic vengeance motive of the Old Testament."

It's appropriate, before we accept such arguments, to ask, "Who has the best and most accurate understanding of what is moral? Modern man—or God?" I certainly would hesitate to affirm that my own moral judgment is more sensitive than His. If we do not take seriously the notion that God might have moral insight beyond our own, it then seems appropriate to ask why capital punishment was instituted, and is stressed in the Law. Is it really from some "primitive vengeance motive"?

Without belaboring the point, it seems that far more than vengeance is involved. The prohibition against murder and the command to execute the murderer are first stated in Genesis 9:6. They are associated with the affirmation that man is made in God's image. Capital punishment is ordained not for vengeance, but as necessary affirmation of the value and worth of human life. Where life is cheap in people's eyes, justice is impossible. There is no adequate response to murder but the death penalty, for there is no other way to affirm the ultimate value of each human individual.

(2) *What world do we live in?* This question raises the issue of culture. The Jews of the Old Testament lived in their own culture and time—not in ours. In that culture slavery was a way of life. So Old Testament Law guided the Israelites to live God's way in the world that existed then—not in the world of today.

There is no doubt that freedom for all men under God's rule is the divine ideal. But that ideal did not exist in the ancient world. The divine Law thus showed Israel how to express God's love *in the real world.* Strikingly, the Law demonstrates unusual compassion for slaves—and for women—foreign to the laws of other contemporary cultures. In both these areas, disenfranchised people by the culture were lifted up and given rights that reflect more of their worth and value as human beings.

We might note a modern parallel. You and I would probably agree that Communism is "less Christian" than our free-enterprise system. Does that mean, if we were living under Communism, that we believers should commit ourselves to the overthrow of that way of life? Or does it mean that we should commit ourselves to live as Christians within the system? I think the answer, in Romans 13, is clear. We all live within our cultures. In our own here and now, each of us is to live a life marked out by love. A life that reflects the humane and good principles expressed in the Ten Commandments of our God.

The Mosaic System

We've seen some of the uniqueness of the Law given at Sinai. That Law was spoken to a nation in its infancy; to a people whose every response to God was childish and harmful.

What the Law did for Israel was, first of all, to reveal something of the moral character of God. Second, it laid out clearly what God expected from Israel. The Jewish people now had a standard against which to measure their thoughts and their actions.

But Israel had even more! In the Law Israel had been given a framework for freedom and for blessing. The way of life that Law describes would bring the growth and the joy which human beings long for. Law was to guide Israel into joy, by defining clearly those responses to God and to others that would make for a fulfilling life.

A conditional covenant. Yet, for all its benefits, the Law was a distinctly different kind of covenant than that made earlier with Abraham. And different from the later covenants, the one made with David and the New Covenant announced by Jeremiah. The Covenant of Law announced what God would do—*conditioned on the behavior of Israel.* At the first God had said, "If you will obey My voice and keep My covenant" (Ex. 19:5). The blessings the Law offered to Israel would depend on the people obeying that Law.

Israel had accepted the condition. The generation that stood before Mount Sinai heard, and responded: "We will do everything the Lord has said" (v. 8). This was repeated after the 10 had been communicated, and case-law descriptions of their meaning provided. Again the people said, "Everything the Lord has said we will do" (24:3).

A mutually binding pact had been made. A pact in which, for the first time, God's commitment to act in the life of a particular generation of Abraham's descendants was to be conditioned by the people's response to Him.

A basis for discipline. For God, this willing entry of His people into the Law Covenant provided a basis on which He could exercise necessary discipline. Before the Law wrong actions did not receive punishment, for punishment would have no corrective value. But when Israel knew what was right, and then rejected God's guidance, punishment might teach the importance of return to His ways. Hebrews tells us God's chastisement is always purposive, always geared to stimulate growth in holiness (Heb. 12:10).

♥ ***Link to Life: Youth / Adult***

Tell your group the story of eight-year-old Matthew, who kept running outside to play in his stocking feet. His mom and dad repeatedly told him not to go outside without shoes, but it did no good. Finally Dad told Matt that he would be fined $1, to be taken from his savings, every time he ran out to play without his shoes. From that time on, Matt never "forgot" again!

Ask: "How do we explain the change in Matt's behavior? Why wasn't just knowing what was right enough to help him change? Why did the threat of a $1 fine make such a difference?"

Then look back into Israel's history. Law provided a basis by which God could justly discipline His people. Compare how God reacted to the same acts before *and* after *the Law was given. Compare Exodus 32:25-35 and Numbers 11:1-21, 31-33 with Exodus 16:1-12; Numbers 15:32-36 with Exodus 16:23-30. What do we learn about Law from these comparisons? About God? About Israel?*

An existential covenant. There is one more important thing to realize about the Mosaic or Law Covenant. Its focus is entirely on the present experience of a living generation of Israelites. In this too it stands in contrast with the other biblical covenants. The promises given to Abraham, to David, and in the New Covenant look ahead to the distant future for their fulfillment. Thus these tell what God will do at history's end, when His purposes will be finally fulfilled. But the Law Covenant said to living Jews, "If *you* obey Me and keep My Law, then *you* will experience blessings, now."

Covenant renewal. The fact that the Law's purpose was to guide the present experience of living generations, and that its blessings and punishments were to be experienced by them, is reflected in the way new generations of Jews were invited to "enter" that covenant relationship. One of Moses' last acts as a leader was to call a new generation before the Lord and, setting out the blessings and the curses associated with Law, to invite them to "enter into a covenant with the Lord your God, a covenant the Lord is making with you this day" (Deut. 29:12). Still later, Joshua called yet another generation to him and demanded, "Choose for yourselves this day whom you will serve" (Josh. 24:15). And the people responded. They committed themselves to serve the Lord and obey His voice (v. 24). That generation too entered the covenant.

Even to this day individual Jews agree to accept and abide by the relationship with God defined by the Mosaic Covenant. The infant is circumcised on the eighth day, indicating that his parents choose to bring him under the covenant with Abraham, and to affirm his identity as a Jew. But then, at 13, each Jewish boy makes a personal decision. At his *bar mitzvah* (Aramaic for "son of the commandment") he repeats ancient words, accepts the obligations the Law spells out, and by his own choice commits himself to live under the rule of God's Law.

What the Law Is . . . Not

If we miss the unique nature of the Mosaic Law we are all too likely to fall into the same errors which plagued later generations of Jews, and have warped the lives of many Christians. If we miss the uniqueness of the Law, we're likely to misunderstand the nature of our redemption and the role of faith, both in salvation and in our subsequent Christian life.

In the Law, Israel had a sharp and clear portrait of the moral character of her God. In the Law, men could see love and righteousness blend, and could understand God's commitment to do right by all persons. The Law's revelation of morality also served as a standard by which men could measure themselves. God had announced, "Be holy, because I am holy" (Lev. 11:44). The Law's careful delineation of holy behavior let people match their deeds to the standards which God presented as right and good.

But when God's people did measure themselves against the Law, a striking mes-

THREE KEY CONTRASTS

Other Covenants	*Law Covenant*
1. God only Maker	1. Each generation/individuals enter it with Him
2. Future in view	2. Present experience in view
3. Unconditional promise	3. Conditional, with promises and warnings

Law's Functions

1. To reveal God's character
2. To reveal individuals to themselves in contrast to the pure standards of God
3. To guide the believer's faith-response to God by specifying His expectations
4. To provide a basis on which God can discipline His people

Old Testament Law Summary

sage was heard! The men and women who had experienced redemption from Egypt discovered that they were not holy. Law demonstrated their sin.

The Law, even when first given, did not produce righteousness. Instead it revealed human unrighteousness. Through the Law men had the opportunity to discover their true state; to become conscious of the reality of their sin and need. This role of the Law continues today. It is stressed often in the New Testament. "We know," says Paul, "that whatever the Law says, it says to those who are under the Law, so that every mouth may be silenced and the whole world held accountable to God. Therefore no one will be declared righteous in His sight by observing the Law; rather, through the Law we become conscious of sin" (Rom. 3:19-20).

Law, then, was never intended to produce righteousness. It was instead designed to help us see our need of forgiveness, and lead us to search out a righteousness that comes through faith.

But this message has often been missed. People come to the Law, but fail to see in it either God's heart—or their own. They miss the heartbeat of love that the Law reveals, and they treat it as a mere rule book. They treat the divine revelation as though it were a set of do's and don'ts through which a person might gain God's favor, and earn His approval.

Isaiah cried out against such a distortion of Law's message, and against reducing righteousness to rule-keeping. In the Law, Isaiah reminded Israel, God had spoken and had said:

> "This is the resting place, let the weary rest"; and "This is the place of repose"—but they would not listen. So then, the Word of the Lord to them will become:
> Do and do, do and do,
> rule on rule, rule on rule;
> a little here, a little there—
> so that they will go and fall backward,
> be injured and snared and captured.
> Isaiah 28:12-23

Men ripped the commandment from its context, and tried to build from God's revelation of righteousness a system of regulations by which they might feel themselves to be righteous. Missing the heart of the Law, and missing its function, they fell backward. They were broken, snared, and taken.

In the Letter to Titus, Paul writes of God, "He saved us, not because of righteous things we had done, but because of His mercy" (Titus 3:5). The apostle here adds nothing to our knowledge of God. Salvation has always been a gift, flowing from

God's heart of mercy. Salvation was never based on "righteous things we had done."

Even father Abraham was acceptable only because his faith was credited to him as righteousness (Gen. 15:6; Rom. 4). As Paul argued so strongly, and as every Jew knew, "it was not through law that Abraham and his offspring received the promise that he would be heir of the world, but through the righteousness that comes by faith" (v. 13).

No one who knew the history of Israel and the Old Testament revelation should have misunderstood this basic point.

Righteousness comes through faith—not by Law. And yet many did misunderstand. Generation after generation of the Jewish people tried to reduce the Law to a rule book, and righteousness to do's and don'ts. By their own efforts they struggled to develop (or to pretend) a righteousness which they simply did not possess. They refused to let the Law condemn them, that forgiveness might make them alive. And this mistake was fatal.

"All who rely on observing the Law are under a curse, for it is written: 'Cursed is everyone who does not continue to do everything written in the Book of the Law.' Clearly no one is justified before God by the Law, because 'the righteous will live by faith' " (Gal. 3:10-11).

How clear it all seems. If you and I want to be righteous, we must look away from ourselves to God. God's perfect standards have shown us how imperfect and how at fault we are. If we admit our sin, we are free to surrender to God and to throw ourselves on His mercy. If we are to become righteous, it must be through the work of God Himself in our lives, as we abandon ourselves and learn to live by faith.

TEACHING GUIDE

Prepare

If you have questions about the relationship between Law, faith, grace, and righteousness, see the units on Romans and Galatians before teaching this lesson.

Explore

1. Discuss: "In what ways do people today try to make Christianity into a 'legal' system? Have you experienced any effects of this effort?"
2. Or write Leviticus 19:9-10 on the chalkboard: "When you reap the harvest of your land, do not reap to the very edges of your field or gather the gleanings of your harvest. Do not go over your vineyard a second time or pick up the grapes that have fallen. Leave them for the poor and the alien."

How does this show love? How does it provide for freedom? How does it show sensitivity to the poor and to the wealthy as well?

Expand

1. In a minilecture discuss the specific role and the uniqueness of the Mosaic Law. Summarize the Ten Commandments, but also show the special and limited function Law was to have for Israel. You may want to use the chart on page 100 as a visual.
2. To look at the Law as a basis for God's discipline of Israel, do the study suggested in "link-to-life," page 99.
3. Or involve your whole group in direct Bible study, discovering how biblical case law illustrates basic principles in the Ten Commandments. Use the approach suggested in "link-to-life," page 97.

Apply

1. The Law did not provide a way of salvation. It did not make a person righteous. Instead, a person who was made righteous by faith would express his love for God by keeping the Law. How did the true believer view the Law? Read aloud Psalm 19:7-10 or 119:33-48. How does the attitude of David reflect the attitude of the Christian today to God's Word?
2. Read and meditate together on Christ's words in John 14:23-24: "If anyone loves Me, he will obey My teaching. . . . He who does not love Me will not obey My teaching."

STUDY GUIDE 13

Exodus 25–40

ACCESS FOR SINNERS

Overview

The sequence of events at Sinai shows that the Law was never viewed as a way of salvation. The Law was given first to bring Israel awareness of sin. Immediately afterward a sacrificial system, with a priesthood and worship center, was established. The system permitted the approach of a sinful human being to a holy God, providing access through sacrifice.

God then spoke to a cleansed people, to carefully define the way of holy living. A forgiven people are to grow in their relationship with the Lord.

Finally the camp was organized. A disciplined people will be able to live successfully in a hostile world.

The Sequence of Events

Law given	*Ex. 19–24*
Tabernacle established	*Ex. 25–40*
Instructions for holy life	*Lev. 1–27*
Camp organized	*Num. 1–10*

▶ ***Tabernacle.*** This "tent of meeting" symbolized God's presence with His people. It was the place where He met with Israel's leaders, and was the visible worship center. The tabernacle also prefigures the work of Jesus for us. Hebrews calls its worship and furnishings "an illustration for the present time" (see Heb. 9:1-10).

■ The *Bible Knowledge Commentary* contains a thorough discussion of the tabernacle, of its role in history, and of its theological/typical significance. See pages 146-162 for verse-by-verse comment.

Commentary

The events reported in Exodus through Deuteronomy tell of Israel's redemption from Egypt. And they give us a portrait of our own redemption from sin. In the early chapters of the Book of Exodus, we've seen several key truths.

We have a deep need for redemption. As Israel was in slavery, so all men are lost and powerless under the sway of sin.

Only God's action can deliver. God had to intervene in acts of power to break the authority of Pharaoh over Israel. God Himself had to intervene, in Jesus Christ, to save us.

New life emerges from death: the Lamb must die. The Passover lamb's blood on the door protected Israel from the death angel. It is the blood of Christ, shed for the sins of the world, which provides our salvation.

Our new life is to be marked by a holiness we do not have. Israel's response to God after deliverance demonstrated her need for standards and for a clear revelation of God's expectations. God is concerned about our righteousness as well: we are called to bear the image of His Son. The standard revealed in words in the Law has been unveiled in person by Jesus.

We fall short of the goal to which God calls us. The Law defined the pathway of love for Israel. At the same time it demonstrated conclusively that Israel fell short. The New Testament also defines, in terms of principles rather than rules, the pathway of love. A look into the New Testament shows that we, like Israel, fall short of being all that God calls us to be.

These are central messages that God gave Israel in the events we've read about. Today the record of those events speaks the same messages to you and to me that were spoken to Israel. The last of these messages—the revelation that even after redemption we stand in need—launches us into an exciting segment of Scripture. God reminds us that we are a needy people. But He also gives us insight into the way He plans to meet that very need!

♥ ***Link to Life: Youth / Adult***

It's important to use review to help people

Scripture	Events	Message	Key Word(s)	Key Verse
Ex. 1–5	Enslaved in Egypt	Man needs redemption	Helplessness	Ex. 2:23b
Ex. 6–11	Plagues on Egypt	God acts to redeem	Yahweh	
Ex. 12–15	The journey begun	Redemption comes through death	Passover/ sacrifice	
Ex. 15–20	Murmurings on the way to Sinai	Redeemed people are to be holy	Law/God's character	
Ex. 20–24	Commandment and case law given	Holiness involves love for God and for men	Law/God's expectations	
Ex. 25–40	Sacrificial, tabernacle systems instituted	Redeemed people need cleansing and enablement	Tabernacle	

Summary of Exodus

maintain awareness of the major teachings of a passage of Scripture. Use the summary chart of Exodus to structure a review of the Book of Exodus.

You may want to place just the outline on a chalkboard, and fill in cells together. Or leave a few of the cells blank, and let your group members recall events, messages, and key words.

A good concluding activity for such a review is to ask group members to select one topic and pick a key verse *that expresses the message of the section.*

The Days After

Some who become Christians experience an almost immediate glow. Somehow life seems different! For some this glow persists for days or weeks. But, sooner or later, most find life itself brings a sudden jolt. The first flush of love fades. We become irritated again at our coworkers. We get angry at someone close.

An alcoholic may feel free from dependence on drink—and then find the urge returns with overwhelming intensity as he passes a favorite bar.

You think that salvation has freed you from an old temptation—and then find your thoughts and desires returning to it with nagging intensity.

Often when such things happen new believers may be confused. Sometimes a young Christian will wonder about the reality of his conversion. Very often a believer blames himself, feeling deeply the shame of falling into old patterns of life after being so sure that everything was new.

It's helpful for us, when we are captured by such feelings, to learn the lesson that God taught Israel in the events that followed the giving of the Law. Israel had known redemption from Egypt. But Israel had a continued and continual need for God. Only divine provision could lift individuals and the nation beyond themselves, to become the person and the people that God had redeemed them to be.

Exodus 25–31

God knows the need of believers for continual cleansing and enablement. Israel had not yet seen herself as a still-needy people. Yet God began to meet the need before it was understood. His provision was in the tabernacle—a tent of worship which became the only place where Israelites might approach God. (Later it was replaced by a temple, erected in the Promised Land.)

Looking back, the writer of the New Testament Book of Hebrews focuses on Exodus 25:9. The tabernacle was to be made "exactly like the pattern I will show you." The New Testament points to this as evidence that the tabernacle is a kind of mirror of reality. Its design reflects truth

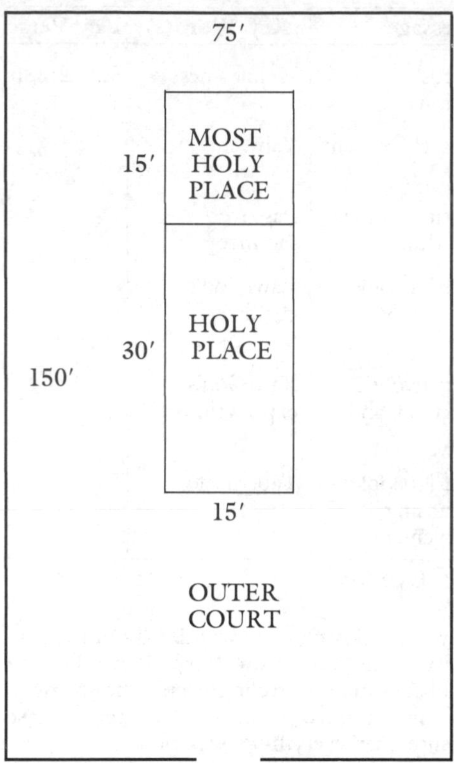

The Court and Tabernacle

about our relationship with God and the special provision God has made for us. In the New Testament the tabernacle is called "a copy and shadow of what is in heaven" (Heb. 8:5). Looking at it, we can discover much about the reality you and I experience in Christ.

The tabernacle plan. The tabernacle is a "type" (an Old Testament character, event, or institution which has a place and purpose in Bible history, but which also, by divine design, foreshadows something future). In every aspect the tabernacle pictures the relationship between God and a redeemed people. In every aspect the tabernacle shows how God's presence with us not only sets us apart from all others, but meets our need for daily deliverance from sin's power.

What, then, was the tabernacle like—and what does it tell us about our own need to experience freedom?

The tabernacle was a large tent, surrounded by an outer court—a long, rectangular enclosure 150 by 75 feet. It was portable, the walls of the court and the tent itself being made of curtains. The tabernacle was a sanctuary, a dwelling place for God. It consisted of an outer "holy place" and an inner "most holy place" into which the high priest alone could enter, and then only once a year.

During the time in the wilderness, God's presence was a visible thing, marked by a cloudy, fiery pillar which always stood over the tabernacle. When erected, the tabernacle always stood in the middle of the camp, with the people ranged around it on every side.

God chooses to dwell in the center of His people. He is to be the center of our lives. Never just on the periphery.

The tabernacle furnishings. It is, however, in the furnishings of the tabernacle that we gain insight into what God's presence in our lives provides. Each of the furnishings speaks clearly of a ministry of God through which the believer is protected from himself and enabled to become all God intends.

(1) *The bronze altar.* There was only one door to this "tent of meeting." Any person who wanted to come into God's presence had to come through the one door which the plan of God provided. At the door, placed so that no one who entered could avoid it, stood the bronze altar. This was the altar of sacrifice; the place on which daily the prescribed offerings for Israel would be laid. As Leviticus would later make clear, "The life of a creature is in the blood, and I have given it to you to make atonement for yourselves on the altar; it is the blood that makes atonement for one's life" (Lev. 17:11). No one could approach God or receive the benefits of His presence without entering by the door of sacrifice and atonement.

Later Jesus would use this same picture in speaking of Himself. "I am the gate," He announced. "Whoever enters through Me will be saved. I am the Good Shepherd. The Good Shepherd lays down His life for the sheep" (John 10:9, 11). The message is clear. Access to the benefits God has provided for us is ours only as we come to God in the single way He has planned.

(2) *The bronze laver.* The laver, a large container for water, was made of the same bronze metal as the altar. It stood at the entrance of the tabernacle itself, and was for the cleansing of those who entered the Presence. Jesus used a similar symbolism at the time of the Last Supper when He washed

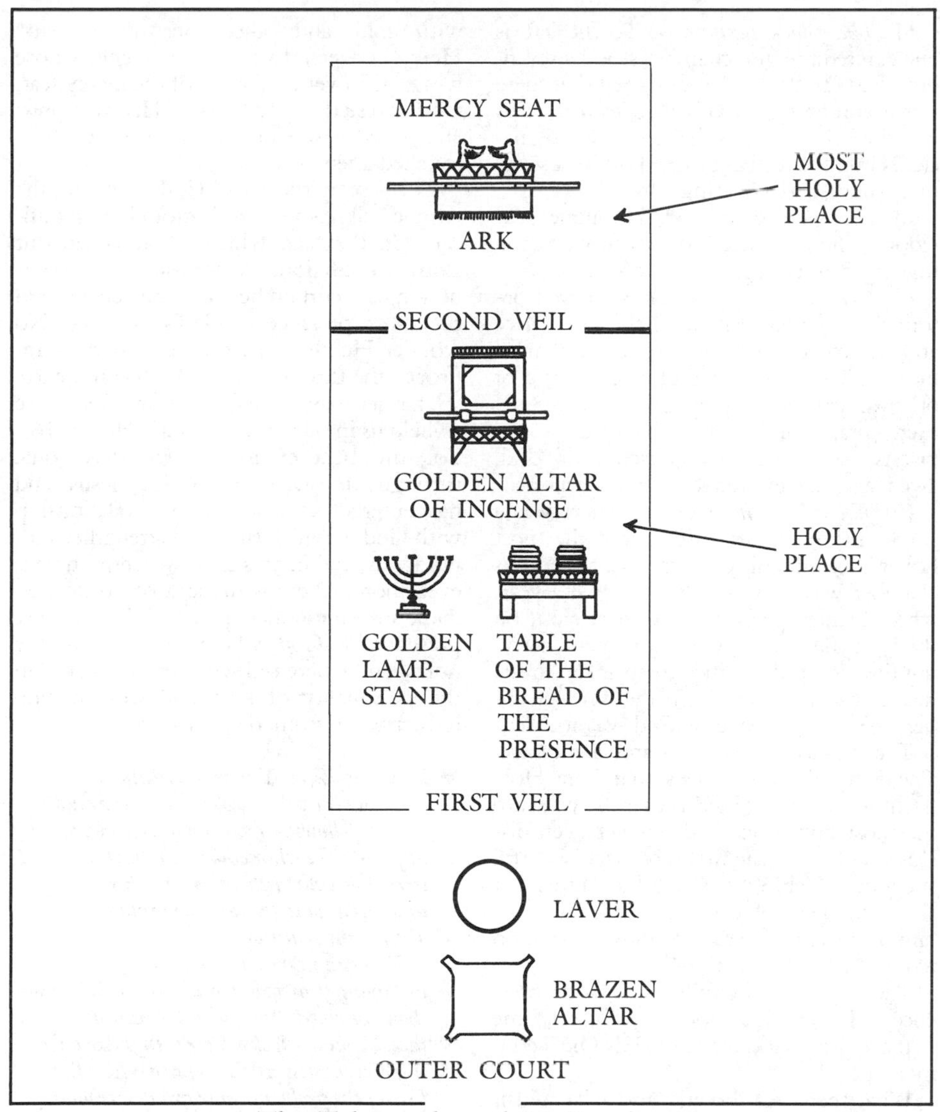

The Tabernacle and Its Furniture

the disciples' feet. They have been cleansed, He told them, so they did not need another "bath." But as they had walked the dusty roads after the bathing, their feet needed to be washed again and again (John 13:2-12).

Believers have been cleansed by the blood of Christ. Yet daily we need to turn to God for cleansing. The provision of cleansing is clearly ours: "If we confess our sins [those daily failures that mar the lives even of those who have experienced salvation], He is faithful and just and will forgive us our sins and purify us from all unrighteousness" (1 John 1:9).

The continual cleansing each of us needs is provided in Christ, and pictured in the laver before the tabernacle entrance. Purified, we can freely enter the presence of our God.

(3) *The table of the bread of the Presence.* Immediately inside the first veil a table was set. On this table, placed to the right in the chamber, was kept a constant supply of fresh food and drink. All that the believer needs to strengthen and sustain him is found in God's presence.

(4) *The golden lampstand.* To the left as one entered the first chamber stood a seven-branched candlestick, so designed that there was a constant flow of oil to feed it. This was the sole source of light in the tabernacle. Natural light was blocked off by a series of curtains and coverings.

In the presence of God, He alone provides the light we need to see our way. And that light is enough.

(5) *Golden altar of incense.* Centered before the veil that separated the holy place and the most holy place stood an altar of incense. This altar spoke of worship and of other dimensions of prayer (cf. Rev. 8:3-4). Here praise and prayer blended as the priests approached the presence of God, awed and yet exalted by His closeness.

(6) *The ark of the covenant.* There was a single article of furniture within the most holy place. The thick veil that separated this chamber was moved only one time a year, when the high priest entered there alone on the high and holy Day of Atonement, carrying the blood of sacrifice to sprinkle on the mercy seat. It was here, in the inner chamber, that the presence of God was focused.

The veil itself communicates a message. The New Testament says that "the Holy Spirit was showing by this that the way into the most holy place had not yet been disclosed as long as the first tabernacle was still standing" (Heb. 9:8). The Bible tells us that at the moment of Christ's death, "the curtain of the temple was torn in two from top to bottom" (Matt. 27:51).

There is for us the fullness of God's presence, a fullness that goes beyond even the rich provision God made for His Old Testament people.

What then was the ark, and what did it speak of? The ark itself was a gold-covered chest, containing special reminders of God's work for His people. There was a container of manna, speaking of complete and miraculous provision. There were the tablets on which the Ten Commandments were written, speaking of the righteousness God alone can produce. Later there was added Aaron's rod, which miraculously budded and bore fruit, speaking of God's power to bring life from the dead.

The ark itself was named "of the covenant," a reminder of God's commitment to fulfill all His promises.

On the ark rested a special cover, overlaid with gold, and called the "mercy seat." Here, between two carved angels whose wings met over the center of the mercy seat, God invested the fullness of His own presence—and it was here alone that God fully touched men.

This is why the act of God in tearing the temple veil from top to bottom is so significant. In that act, which accompanied our Lord's crucifixion, we are told that there is no longer a curtain between the believer and the full experience of God's presence! No wonder Hebrews invites, "Let us then approach the throne of grace with confidence, so that we may receive mercy and find grace to help us in our time of need" (Heb. 4:16). For the believer today, who has come through the one door to God, Jesus, and has entered, cleansed, into a relationship with God in which the Lord strengthens us, guides us, and invites us to worship, there is even more. There is full and complete welcome into the holiest place of all—the very presence of God where miracles are the norm, and where righteousness is worked in the personality of men and women who have passed from death to life.

♥ ***Link to Life: Youth / Adult***

To study the tabernacle with your group, put the following chart on a chalkboard, or duplicate so each member can have a copy. The chart lists tabernacle furnishings and has a space for corresponding New Testament realities.

You can make this study very practical by having your group brainstorm, before you show the chart, "problems Christians face." You are looking for things like a feeling of weakness when tempted, etc. After listing the problems your group members suggest, and working through the chart, try to relate the provision symbolized in the tabernacle to present-day needs. For instance, a vision of Christ as strengthener and sustainer, symbolized in the bread of the Presence, reminds us that we have His power in which to meet our temptations.

Exodus 32–34

While Moses was receiving instructions on the construction of the tabernacle, an event was taking place at the base of the mountain which clearly revealed Israel's need for its provision.

Moses had been on the mount for days.

The Tabernacle

FURNISHING	SYMBOLISM	N.T. REALITY
Brazen Altar	Entrance demands sacrifice	Christ died to win us access
Brazen Laver	Those within need cleansing	
Bread of the Presence	All needed to strengthen and supply provided daily	
Golden Lampstand	Light by which to see provided	
Golden Altar of Incense	Praise and prayer	
Ark of the Covenant	Presence of God	
Veil	Way into God's presence not open	

All this time thunder and lightning gave constant testimony to the presence of God. Yet as the days passed, and Moses did not return, Israel became restless. A number of the people went to Aaron, Moses' brother, and insisted that he make an idol. He took their gold and melted it to shape a golden calf, and then proclaimed a "feast to the Lord." The molten calf was presented to the people with the announcement, "These are your gods, O Israel, who brought you up out of Egypt" (Ex. 32:4).

When Moses returned, those who had sinned were severely judged. Yet even those who had not actually been involved bore their share of the responsibility. How could God identify Himself with such a sinful people?

Yet it was just this, the presence of God, that made Israel distinct. As Moses prayed, "How will anyone know that You are pleased with me and with Your people unless You go with us? What else will distinguish me and Your people from all the other people on the face of the earth?" (33:16) God's presence distinguished His people from all others.

In the presence of God there must be found a remedy for the constant outbreak of sin which so threatened Israel—and which threatens you and me today.

Exodus 35–40

The failure of Israel at Sinai demonstrated graphically that even a redeemed people constantly need God. The failure of the people prepared them to sense that need and to see the importance of the tabernacle. In each detail, the tabernacle spoke of God's provision for His people. In each detail the people could discover another dimension of what God's presence with them would mean.

The chapters here may seem to be merely a repetition of what has already been written in Exodus 25–27. But they are more than that. The story of the building of the tabernacle points up the fact that what God has provided for us must be appropriated. We must build into the very fabric of our lives all that God says He has given us in Christ.

For Us
It is doubtful if Israel understood all that the tabernacle and furnishings promised. Only in the light of God's full revelation in Christ do we begin to see.

But while the tabernacle pictures for us the realities we can experience in Christ, the tabernacle also had a practical message for Israel.

Israel had sinned, and failed to meet the standard God's holiness imposed. Aware of failure, the people of God must have finally crouched in shame, wondering how they could ever be restored again to relationship with their God. And wondering too how they could ever find strength to live as a people whose holiness must in some sense approach the Lord's.

At this point in time, when the people of Israel stripped themselves of their ornaments in mourning for their sin (33:6), God had His remedy ready. Again the commandments were repeated (chap. 34), and then all Israel was invited to bring their offerings, to construct a tabernacle in which God might dwell.

The presence of God within Israel's camp, and the promise of that presence—reflected in every aspect of the tabernacle and its furnishings—was the divine answer to man's need. A redeemed Israel would continue to be in daily need of God. But God would be there, available, and able.

This is, of course, the great message of God to you and me today. We too continually need God. We too fail and fall short. That first moment of salvation is but the beginning of a long process of transformation. For our daily walk along that way there is only one possible source of help: God, present within us.

He alone can meet our every need.

TEACHING GUIDE

Prepare
Meditate on how much you have needed God's presence with you as you have lived your Christian life. Pray that your group members may sense that reality for themselves.

Explore
1. Ask, "What has your life been like since you became a Christian?" Have each person draw a continuous single line that visualizes his or her experience. Then share and compare. How are your lines alike? Different?
2. Brainstorm "needs Christians have." That is, try to quickly make a list of problems Christians face in daily life. Discuss: "Why isn't everything smooth or uphill after conversion?"

Expand
1. Do a historical review of the events at Sinai. Highlight the giving of the Law, the golden-calf incident, and the building of the tabernacle. Show the spiritual significance of the sequence. The Law made Israel guilty when she sinned, cutting her off from her holy God. But the tabernacle symbolized God's provision through sacrifice of forgiveness, and the furnishings speak of strengthening to live a holy life.
2. Do a study of the tabernacle and its furnishings. See the "link-to-life" idea and chart on pages 106-107.
3. Review the Book of Exodus, using the overview chart on page 103.

Apply
1. Discuss: "What one article of furniture in the tabernacle signifies something that is most important to me in my Christian life, and why?"
2. Read Hebrews 9 aloud, and take time then to thank God that the reality pictured in the tabernacle is ours at last.

STUDY GUIDE 14
Leviticus 1–17

SACRIFICE AND OFFERINGS

Overview
The Book of Leviticus is often viewed as God's instruction to Israel on holy living. Earlier God spoke from the mountaintop; now, with the tabernacle erected, God's presence was among the people. The people were in unique fellowship with God, and it was His "going with" them that set Israel apart from all others (Ex. 33:16).

But how might they live so close to the holy God? Only by continual cleansing and commitment to a holy lifestyle. J. Sidlow Baxter (*Explore the Book*, vol. 1, Zondervan) notes this dual need and divides Leviticus into two parts:

Outline

I. Sacrifice: Ground of Fellowship
   A. Offerings—absolution 1–7
   B. Priesthood—mediation 8–10
   C. People—purification 11–16
   D. Altar—reconciliation 17
II. Separation: Way of Fellowship
   A. Rules for people 18–20
   B. Rules for priests 21–22
   C. Rules concerning feasts 23–24
   D. Rules concerning Canaan 25–27

We'll follow this outline as we explore this book that teaches us so much about our own relationship with the Lord. Here too we discover basic truths about sacrifice, atonement, and priesthood.

▶ ***Fellowship.*** *Selem* is the word in the Old Testament for fellowship, most often used for the fellowship or peace offering. This freewill offering speaks of peace and harmony in our relationships with God.

■ The *Bible Knowledge Commentary* offers excellent charts and a complete discussion of each of the many different offerings and sacrifices detailed in Leviticus 1–7.

Commentary
The Book of Leviticus is a book of detailed regulations. It may seem dull to many. But imbedded in the instructions of this book are many principles which have relevance to us today.

Sacrifice: Leviticus 1–7
The Bible Knowledge Commentary makes these points about the role of sacrifice in the Old Testament system. First, under the Law sacrifice was given as the only sufficient means for Israelites to remain in fellowship with the Lord. But second, with one possible exception, the sacrifices were limited in scope, dealing only with certain kinds of personal sins. They were "mainly concerned with sins of ignorance, accident, carelessness, and omission" and included sins of ritual and social nature. There was no individual sacrifice provided for willful violation of God's commands. Such sins could be forgiven—as David's experience and psalms testify (cf. Pss. 32; 51)—on the basis of a grace response to faith and repentance. But *the sacrificial system was not in itself a way of salvation.* Yet, sacrifice in the Old Testament has continually been associated with forgiveness and with fellowship with God.

A historic overview. In other cultures, sacrifice was viewed usually as food for the gods, and the priests often used the entrails of sacrificial beasts for occult divination. In Israel the sacrifice was not divine food (cf. Ex. 29:38-41; Ps. 50:8-15). And in Israel it was the blood of the sacrificed animal that was significant. In fact, the blood was crucial, for God said, "I have given it [the lifeblood of the sacrificial animal] to you to make atonement for yourselves on the altar; it is the blood that makes atonement for one's life" (Lev. 17:11). The worshiper was taught that sin calls for the surrender of life, and that God will accept a substitute.

The practice of sacrifice precedes the Mosaic Law. Some see God's killing of an animal to cover Adam and Eve with skins as the first sacrifice. The story of Cain and Abel certainly suggests that the first family was taught this way to approach God. Cain "brought some of the fruits of the soil as an offering to the Lord" (Gen. 4:3), while Abel "brought fat portions from some of the firstborn of his flock" (v. 4). God rebuked Cain. "If you do what is right," God said (v. 7), implying clearly that Cain's offering was in willful violation of God's known will.

Animal sacrifices continued to be the norm. They were offered by Noah (8:20-21). Job, who may have been a contemporary of Abraham, offered sacrifices for sins (Job 1:5; 42:7-9). Genesis shows that the patriarchs built altars when they called on the name of the Lord (Gen. 12:8; 13:4; 26:25). The Passover lamb was a family sacrifice, rich in powerful imagery.

Now, before Sinai, God gave Israel in His Law a carefully designed, detailed system of offerings and sacrifices.

As noted earlier, however, these sacrifices were for personal sins of a limited nature. They were to be offered for *unintentional* sins (cf. Lev. 4:13, 22, 27; 5:14; etc.). In such cases a common ritual was followed. The one who sinned unintentionally was guilty. The guilty sinner brought an animal to the priests, who offered it in sacrifice. "In this way the priest will make atonement for the man's sin, and he will be forgiven" (4:26).

But forgiveness was not really won through the ritual itself. That is, the ritual was not sufficient in itself. The later prophets made more clear the implications of forgiveness offered for the *unintentional* sins. The individual who chose to dishonor God by refusing to live the just and merciful life the Lord commanded had no real recourse to sacrifice, even though generations of Israelites failed to grasp this reality. Thus Isaiah thundered against the sinful of his days who enjoyed both sin and "worship":

> Stop bringing meaningless offerings! Your incense is detestable to Me. . . . Your New Moon festivals and your appointed feasts My soul hates. They have become a burden to Me; I am weary of bearing them. When you spread out your hands in prayer, I will hide My eyes from you; even if you offer many prayers, I will not listen. Your hands are full of blood; wash and make yourselves clean. Take your evil deeds out of My sight! Stop doing wrong, learn to do right. Seek justice, encourage the oppressed. Defend the cause of the fatherless, plead the case of the widow.
> Isaiah 1:13-17 (See also Jer. 7:20-23; Amos 5:21-27; Micah 6:6-8.)

The message of sacrifice was never that one could sin impudently, and then come to God for an easy remedy. Sacrifice was for those whose hearts were already turned to the Lord.

♥ ***Link to Life: Youth / Adult***
Tell the story of an imaginary Israelite, Basar. He is wealthy, but holds back wages from workers. He lends to the poor, but at high interest. And he's quick to take possessions or sell another into servitude if he or she can't pay. He has many fields, but never leaves anything unharvested for the poor, as the Law commands. Yet Basar seems to be pious. He sacrifices regularly and makes additional offerings. How does God view this man and his sacrifices?

Divide into teams to try to find answers to this question. For team 1, assign Leviticus 4. For team 2, Isaiah 1:13-17; Jeremiah 7:20-23. For team 3, Psalm 51.

Share reports. Then discuss: "What do we learn from these passages that we can apply to our own walk with God?"

Day of Atonement: Leviticus 16
The Old Testament says that the blood of the sacrifice is given to make atonement. What does "atonement" mean? The Hebrew words translated atonement in English versions are *kippur* (noun) and *kapar* (verb). The root occurs about 150 times in the Old Testament, and is intimately linked with forgiveness of sin and with reconciliation to God.

Many believe the root idea is "to cover" or "to conceal." If so, atonement suggests a covering that conceals a person's sin and makes it possible for him to approach God. Certainly this is the role that atonement played in the Old Testament system. A person who sinned unintentionally would discover his failing, and as an act of confession, bring an animal offering to the priest. The sacrifice would be made, the blood shed, and "in this way the priest will make atonement for the man's sin, and he will be forgiven" (4:26).

But what about intentional, willful sins? While there was no individual offering for such sins, provision was made for them in the Day of Atonement.

Leviticus 16 gives detailed instructions for a special sacrifice to be offered once a year, on the tenth day of the seventh month. On that day the whole community of Israel was to gather at the tabernacle (and later, the temple) to fast and to pray. The high priest followed carefully prescribed steps and entered the inner room of the tabernacle, bringing the blood of a sacrificed animal. There he sprinkled the blood on the cover of the ark, called the mercy seat. This animal was a "sin offering for the people" (16:15). It is specifically said to have been required "because of the uncleanness and rebellion of the Israelites, whatever their sins have been" (v. 16, cf. v. 21). That sacrifice was an "atonement . . . to be made once a year for *all the sins* of the Israelites" (v. 34, italics mine). Following that sacrifice, Israel was told, "You will be clean from all your sins" (v. 30).

So the sacrificial system did make provision for intentional as well as unintentional sins. This was the only way the holy God could continue to dwell among a sinful and sinning community.

The message of sacrifice. It is important in looking at the Old Testament to realize that in it we see realities *acted out* that would be unveiled later. It's not hard to grasp why.

When a young child is about to go into a hospital for a tonsillectomy, parents are often told to play "hospital" with him beforehand. For several days or weeks Mom and Dad rehearse the upcoming trip: they pack his bags, pretend to check in, look at pictures of hospital beds, take each other's temperatures. In every way the young child is prepared, so that when he actually does enter the hospital, it will all seem familiar. He will not be as fearful, because the reality is so much like the pretend.

Should we be surprised, then, that God took the same kind of care? That God planned for continuous enactments of reality, so that when Jesus finally came to lay down His life for us, we would realize just what He was doing? Should we be surprised at the centuries of animal sacrifice, and the stress on the shedding of blood as necessary for forgiveness? No. In the repeated sacrifices of the Old Testament we are led to understand that, to God, death has always been the price of life for sinful men.

What should surprise us is that God would give His Son for us. What should amaze us is that the blood spilled on history's ultimate altar would be His own. But we should never be surprised that only the sacrifice of another life can exempt one from the death penalty that sin and guilt deserve. Sacrifice has always been central in the history of God's gracious dealings with men. Over and over again the picture is presented to us. Over and over again we see the blood. Over and over—till with awed amazement we look at Calvary and suddenly the pictures from the past merge into one. And we bow, stunned by the reality.

He died.

He died for me.

Isaiah 53. Even in Old Testament times God lifted the veil to let us peek beyond the shadows at the reality. Isaiah 53 was long understood by the Jews to speak of the coming Messiah—the Deliverer to be sent to them by God. In this passage we have a clear picture of Jesus, and of sacrifice.

"He was led like a lamb to the slaughter" (v. 7).

"The Lord makes His life a guilt offering" (v. 10).

"He poured out His life unto death" (v. 12).

"He bore the sin of many" (v. 12).

We cannot read these words today without realizing that they contain God's explanation for Jesus' life—and for His death.

Hebrews 10. This New Testament chapter looks back on the Old Testament sacrifices from the perspective of the Cross. The sacrifices of that day were "only a shadow of the good things that [were] coming—not the realities themselves" (v. 1). The blood of bulls and goats could not take away sins (v. 4). The sacrifices only covered and concealed sin, thus permitting God to overlook His people's sins until Jesus could come to actually *take away sins* by the sacrifice of Himself (Rom. 3:25-26). What the ancient sacrifices foreshadowed, Christ accomplished! "By one sacrifice He has made perfect forever those who are being made holy" (Heb. 10:14). In Jesus our sins and lawless acts have been forgiven fully, and we have been cleansed. Thus "there is no longer any sacrifice for sins" (v. 18).

Today you and I look back on Calvary and mark it, as Israel did the first Passover, as the beginning of our lives as a freed people. We remember, as did the Jews, but with our own ritual. For us the reminder is bread and wine. And what a message in this! The Old Testament animal sacrifices had to be repeated again and again.

Their repetition was a continual reminder to Israel that sin, while temporarily covered, must still be dealt with. The repeated sacrifices served to demonstrate that no animal's life could ever satisfy the righteousness of God. What a different message the bread and wine of Communion! No longer is fresh blood required. Jesus has died, offering "for all time one sacrifice for sins" (v. 12).

It is enough.

Redemption's work is done.

By the blood of Christ, you and I have been set forever free.

♥ ***Link to Life: Children***

Sacrifice and atonement are very difficult concepts for young boys and girls. But the repetition that led to the cross, and makes Calvary so meaningful to any who grasp the implications of Old Testament sacrifice, can help prepare children for later understanding.

Cut out one-fourth of a paper plate, leaving room to put a brad through its center. On another paper plate draw four pictures, placed so they will be seen in sequence when the cut-out plate is fastened to it and rotated.

Picture 1: sad-faced person saying, "I've sinned." 2: same person carrying lamb, still looking sad. 3: priest with arms raised, lamb on fiery altar. 4: person going away with a smiling, happy face. When completed, let the boys and girls turn through the cycle again and again, as you tell how a person had to come to make a sacrifice for each and every sin he found he'd committed.

On the other side of the bottom plate have the children draw a cross. Tell how Jesus came to be the sacrifice for our sins, so that we could be forgiven forever.

The Priesthood: Leviticus 8–10

There are three reasons why we need to pay particular attention to the priesthood which is introduced in these Leviticus chapters.

First, the priesthood is a basic Old Testament institution. We cannot really understand the Old Testament without some grasp of its nature and function.

Second, Christ is called our High Priest in the New Testament. An understanding of the Old Testament priesthood helps us to grasp more of His present ministry for us today.

Third, we believers today are "being built into a spiritual house to be a holy priesthood, offering spiritual sacrifices acceptable to God through Jesus Christ" (1 Peter 2:5). Since we are "a chosen people, a royal priesthood" (v. 9), we need to see the meaning of priesthood if we are to understand our own calling as Christians.

We hear little of priesthood today. In fact, the priestly system is foreign to Protestantism, and to our culture. But if we are to learn to live as ministers of the New Covenant (2 Cor. 3:6), and break out of the tragically passive role laymen have in our society, we need to rediscover our identities as believer-priests, called to minister for and before God.

Mediators. We begin a survey of the priest's role by noting that priests served as mediators between God and man. The priest "is selected from among men and is appointed to represent them in matters related to God, to offer gifts and sacrifices for sins" (Heb. 5:1).

The individual in Israel who wished to approach God brought his offering to the priest. That offering may have been an offering of obligation (one which had to be made because of guilt for sin), or a freewill offering of thanks or praise.

But either kind of offering had to be brought to God through the priest. The priest, who served the altar, was the doorkeeper. His ministry kept the approach to God open.

At the same time, the priest taught and interpreted God's revelation. "You must distinguish between the holy and the profane, between the unclean and the clean," Aaron and his sons were told. "And you must teach the Israelites all the decrees the Lord has given them through Moses" (Lev. 10:10-11).

Thus the mediating priest was not only a person through whom an individual might approach God—he was a person who understood and interpreted God's words to the people. Communication between God and man in early Israel was focused in the person of the priest.

Aaron and his descendants were set aside for this doorkeeping ministry. In the land, the priests and the Levites (the other descendants of Levi) were not given territory with the other families of Israel. They were instead dedicated to care for the things of God. Special cities were set aside for them to live in throughout the territories of the other tribes. But there was no land this tribe could call its own. God was to be their portion, and they were supported by an offering of a tenth of all that was produced by the other tribes. Their ministry was so important that it required total dedication.

What do other basic Old Testament passages tell us about this class of mediators whose ministry foreshadows both the work of Christ, and our own?

Exodus 28–29. With the tabernacle pattern revealed, God instructed Moses to set Aaron and his sons aside from the people of Israel to serve Him as priests. They, and especially Aaron the high priest, were given holy garments "for dignity and honor" (28:2). One striking feature: the names of the 12 tribes were engraved on precious stones and attached to the shoulder clasps of Aaron's garment, and on the breastplate. Thus whenever he entered the holy place, Aaron was to "bear the names of the sons of Israel on the breastpiece of decision as a continuing memorial before the Lord" (v. 29).

In the breastpiece too were the Urim and Thummim, which some believe were three polished stones, on which yes and no and nothing were engraved. When Israel sought God's will, God guided the hand of the high priest to select His answer as the priest reached blindly inside the breastpiece pocket. Thus the judgment of the people of Israel was also borne "over his heart before the Lord" (v. 30). The priest carried the people by name before the Lord, and God's will was carried on his heart back to them.

The Exodus passage also speaks of the priests' ordination, and points out that, for Aaron and his sons, sacrifice must also be made. All associated with their ministry was set aside for service by the sprinkling of sacrificial blood. To maintain the blood-won point of contact with God, a continual burnt offering was made daily "at the entrance of the tent of meeting before the Lord," where God said, "I will meet you, and speak to you. There also I will meet with the Israelites, and the place will be consecrated by My glory" (29:42-43).

Leviticus 10. Following ordination of the priests (reported in chaps. 8–9) an incident occurred which emphasized the critical role the priest was to play. Nadab and Abihu, two of Aaron's sons, broke the ordained pattern of ministry to offer "unauthorized fire before the Lord" (10:1). God acted immediately; the pair died there before the Lord.

Verses 8-10 of this chapter explain one possible reason for their deaths. No priest was to drink alcoholic beverages when ministering: a priest must be fully aware. The priest was called to "distinguish between the holy and the profane" and to "teach the Israelites all the decrees" which the Lord had spoken. One who taught holiness must himself be holy.

Leviticus 13–14. The ministry of the priest in evaluating and judging is seen in a task assigned here. The priest was to examine diseased individuals and places. Leprosy, one of many skin conditions that separated the diseased person from society as unclean, was diagnosed by the priest on the basis of clear descriptions in Scripture.

When a person recovered, the priest also was to examine him and pronounce him cleansed, and to officially restore him to fellowship.

The priest did not cure. But the priest did make a distinction between the clean and unclean, the sick and the well.

Leviticus 21–22. This passage emphasizes the holiness that was to characterize the priests. "They must be holy to their God. . . . Because they present the offerings by fire to the Lord." Thus the priest was under special restrictions. Priests were restricted as to whom they could marry, and in other ways. Baxter (*Explore the Book*) comments:

> *All* the sons of Aaron, whether young or old, defective or normal, were priests to Yahweh, by virtue of their birth and life-relationship with Aaron; and nothing

could break that relationship. Yet those among them who were physically defective were not allowed to officiate at the altar or enter within the veil of the sanctuary (21:21-23). And those who were in any way defiled were not allowed even to eat of the priests' portion (22:6-7). Even so, every true believer is a priest by virtue of life-giving union with the Lord Jesus, and nothing can break that union. But all Christians do not enjoy the same intimacy of fellowship, or exercise the same ministry within the veil! Union is one thing; communion is another.

Christ's High Priesthood: Hebrews 4:14–10:25

This extended section of the New Testament discusses the high priesthood of Jesus. It compares Him to the Aaronic priests of the Old Testament, and contrasts His ministry to theirs.

Chapters 4 and 5 of Hebrews emphasize the necessity for the priest to be identified with those he serves. A mediator must have contact with those who need his ministry.

Hebrews 7 emphasizes the primacy of Christ's priesthood, stressing its superiority over the Aaronic. The passage also points out a crucial concept: perfection could not come through the old priesthood. By a continual and repetitive ministry the Aaronic priests held the door to God open. But only a permanent priest could save completely and guarantee us access. As believers, we no longer need human priests to meet us at the door and then to turn within, while we stand outside and wait. Christ, in His death and resurrection, has thrown the door wide open, and has invited us to enter freely. Christ Himself, living forever, is God's eternal guarantee that the door to eternal life will never be closed to you and me.

Chapter 8 of Hebrews elaborates on this. Christ is a Priest of an entirely new system, a system which reaches within men's hearts to transform them. According to Hebrews 9 this required that Christ as High Priest present a perfect offering—one able to clear the conscience of the worshiper. Chapter 10 goes on to show the efficacy of Christ's sacrifice. Through His sacrifice we have been made holy once for all. We are now able to confidently enter into the very presence of God. "Let us then approach the throne of grace with confidence, so that we may receive mercy and find grace to help us in our time of need" (4:16). Our ever-living High Priest, who has made a single sacrifice and by it perfected us, has thrown open wide the door by which the Old Testament priest once stood—and has commanded us to enter boldly.

Our Priesthood

This brief survey of some of the aspects of priesthood helps us understand our present standing with God. Because of Christ, the old need of a doorkeeper is gone. We have direct, personal access to God's throne through Jesus.

But what about *our* priesthood? How do we serve?

Partly in worship. The offerings made on the altar were not all for sin. Many were offerings of thanksgiving and praise, expressing the joy of communion with the Lord. The Book of Revelation speaks of the prayers of God's saints, rising up to God as a pleasant incense. This worship is something that we can offer to God as part of our present priestly service.

In part, we serve as priests by serving our brothers and sisters. As Aaron bore the names of Israel before the Lord, and as Jesus bears our names on His heart, so we are to carry the names and the needs of our brothers before the Lord. There are fellow priests of ours who experience needs. There are fellow believers who experience needs. They have a relationship with God, but do not experience communion. These too we can serve in prayer, and also by reaching out to them to teach and encourage.

And there is another class of people; those who have never met Christ or come to know Him in a saving way. The concept of priesthood is very important here, in helping us understand ourselves. The priest was "chosen from among men." He established a point of contact with other human beings, based on his likeness to them. The New Testament stresses the fact that Jesus too became fully human. He did this that He might sympathize with our weaknesses. He never sinned, and yet He knew fully all that it means to be a human being, subject to human weaknesses.

Because of Jesus' identification with humanity, Christ is able to reach out to grasp the hand of the sinner and lead him to God.

Our priestly ministry carries the same demand, the demand that we reach out to people, confessing our common identity with them, and together drawing near to and serving God.

♥ ***Link to Life: Youth / Adult***
Set up a three-column chart on priesthood. Above the first column write Old Testament Priesthood; *above the second write* Christ's High Priesthood; *above the third write* Our Priesthood. *Because of the amount of data needed to fill in these charts, it's probably best to cover content with a lecture on material drawn from this unit and from the Bible chapters discussed.*

Then work from the chart as a group to list: "What needs were to be met by the priesthood?" You can do this with each column (e.g., each priesthood). Your purpose in taking this approach is to help your group members sense that their own priesthood should be seen in terms of ministry rather than as a role.

If your group members are new Christians, or not yet believers, focus on the priestly ministry of Jesus. If your group members are mature Christians, focus on the believer's priestly ministry—to God in worship, and to others by sharing Jesus effectively with them.

The People: Leviticus 11–15

Priests and people in Israel were to make distinctions between clean and unclean in Israel (cf. Lev. 11:47). The regulations that covered diet and certain ritual requirements are discussed in this context.

Some have gone to great lengths to invent "logical" reasons for some of the commands that God gave here. Even today, the proscription against pork has led to the imaginative notion that pork is "bad" meat. I recently talked with a person who argued that a pig's digestive system is incomplete, and that consequently waste materials are stored in the body rather than eliminated as by other animals. Thus pork is supposed to be intrinsically dirty—and thus God is justified in telling the Jews not to eat pork.

It's a little more difficult to find similar explanations for other dietary laws, such as, "You shall not boil a kid in its mother's milk."

In fact, such explanations miss the point. To teach Peter that the Old Testament economy was passing and that Jew and Gentile were no longer to be viewed as distinct, different races, God caused a great sheet to be lowered from heaven full of "unclean" animals. And Peter was commanded to kill and eat! Peter, a pious Jew, objected. But then the word of God came: "Do not call anything impure that God has made clean" (Acts 10:9-15).

Later Paul wrote in Romans, "I am fully convinced that no food is unclean in itself. But if anyone regards something as unclean, then for him it is unclean" (Rom. 14:14-15).

The point is simply this. Some things are immoral and unclean in themselves for all persons at all times. Adultery, for instance, is never right. Such things are rooted in the very nature of man as God has created him, and reflect something of God's own moral character and His righteousness. But many things that we read of here in Leviticus have no intrinsic rightness or wrongness. These things were "unclean" simply because God said they were to be so regarded by Israel.

Why did God create this whole set of unclean things? In answering, we do not need to give a logical excuse for each item, as some attempt with the dietary laws. Instead, we need to realize that God was acting to train and to discipline His people. He was working with them, to give them a sense of their own unique identity as His people: to help them realize constantly the privilege—and responsibility—of fellowship with Him.

There was a tremendous danger that this people would forget their God. Sinai demonstrated how quickly and easily they forgot! Now, however, the very pattern of daily life in Israel was so structured that it was almost impossible to forget God. Each meal served was a reminder. The specialness of the offerings served as a reminder. The presence of the priests, scattered throughout the other tribes in their cities and supported by yearly tithes, were reminders. The Sabbath was a weekly reminder and, as we will see in the next unit, a system of annual festivals also helped to keep God in focus.

Everything in the customs God gave to Israel was designed to constantly remind the people that they had a special relationship with God, and were called to walk in fellowship with Him.

Many of these customs in Israel are irrelevant to us today. Others have some deep typical significance, and speak of Christ. Still others reflect God's own character and are rooted in righteousness. But all of them serve as unique reminders of how special it is to live in fellowship with God.

TEACHING GUIDE

Prepare
Read and meditate on the Hebrews passages which deal with the high priesthood of Jesus: Hebrews 4:14–5:10; 7:11-28; 9:11-28.

Explore
1. Describe the role of sacrifices under Old Testament Law. Then brainstorm with your group for lessons which Old Testament believers might have learned from the Law. (You may want to use the analogy of the child going to the hospital suggested on p. 111.)
2. Set up the three-column chart described in the "link-to-life" activity on page 115, and work through the process described there.

Expand
1. Compare the efficacy of Old Testament sacrifices and the sacrifice of Jesus. Do this by describing the limitations of Old Testament sacrifices as shown in Leviticus 4 and 16. Then have your group look together at Hebrews 10:1-25. Work through this vital passage verse by verse, letting your group members discover and list key points.
2. Or explore the meaning of Jesus' death as a sacrifice by looking at three passages: Leviticus 16; Isaiah 53; and Hebrews 10:1-25. Let one team take each passage, and look for what the passage can teach us of the meaning of Jesus' death for us.
3. Or plan an inductive study of 2 Corinthians 3:1-18, which speaks of believers as "ministers of a New Covenant." This passage contrasts the priest who ministered under the Old Covenant and the believer-priest who ministers under the New.

Some contrasts they will find: God now writes on hearts, not stone. His new law is "read" by all: we communicate Christ by who we are. We "judge," but only as God leads through the Spirit. (The O.T. priest had to judge on the basis of externals.) The priests' clothing was their "beauty and glory"; we remove veils for, while still vulnerable and human, we are being "transformed into His likeness." We accept identification with frail and imperfect humanity, yet show God's work in our lives.

Apply
1. If there are several non-Christians in your group, ask members to volunteer how accepting Christ as Saviour has changed their lives. Do they experience the freedom from guilt and fear that forgiveness is to bring?
2. If most of your group members are believers, focus on how they can fulfill a personal ministry as a believer-priest. Go around the group and ask each to complete: "As a believer-priest today, what I learn from this study is that I. . . ."

STUDY GUIDE 15

Leviticus 18–27

WALKING IN FELLOWSHIP

Overview

The people of Israel were to be wholly separated unto the Lord. In all features of their individual and corporate lives, this people who bore God's name was to be holy.

Many of the features of Old Testament Law, particularly those having to do with dietary and other elements, had no underlying moral basis. The people were given those laws to help establish a distinction between them and all the other peoples of the world. Such laws reminded Israel that she was a people of God, and because of that relationship, was to be different from others.

In the latter part of Leviticus we discover regulations that do have deep moral roots: regulations that are designed to create a just and moral society.

How vital to note that included are regulations concerning the feasts and festivals at which one is to worship God. It is impossible to have a truly just society without a deep faith in and a commitment to the Lord God.

II. Separation: Way of Fellowship

A.	Rules for people	18–20
B.	Rules for priests	21–22
C.	Rules concerning feasts	23–24
D.	Rules concerning Canaan	25–27

▶ ***Separation.*** The key Hebrew term is *badal.* It means to remove from something, and thus to make a distinction between them. In Genesis 1 God separated light from dark, land from sea. Now God separated Israel from all other nations of the world to be His own covenant people. A separation to God linked everything in Jewish life to her Lord.

Commentary

We noted in the last unit that many of the regulations under the Mosaic Law had no "logical" purpose. We cannot try to explain the dietary laws, for instance, by arguing that flesh Israel was forbidden as food is somehow intrinsically "dirty." These and a number of other Old Testament regulations that structured the lifestyle of Israel were designed to underline this people's separation from all other people. Israel was in covenant relationship with Almighty God, and the life lived in the nation was to be different from life as it was lived in other lands.

The Holy

To understand the importance of some of the regulations that we are about to look at in Leviticus, we need an understanding of the Old Testament concept of holiness. The following discussion of the Old Testament concept of holiness is quoted from the author's *Expository Dictionary of Bible Words* (Zondervan).

> The root of the words translated "holy" and "holiness" is *qadas.* The verb means "to be consecrated," "to be dedicated," "to be holy." Anything that is holy is set apart. It is removed from the realm of the common and moved to the sphere of the sacred.
>
> The focus of the sacred realm is God Himself, Israel's Holy One (2 Kings 19:22; Job 6:10; Pss. 16:10; 22:3; 71:22, etc.). "Holy" becomes a technical religious term used of persons, places, times, and things that were considered sacred because they were associated with and consecrated to God. The seventh day was holy, to be reserved for worship and rest (Gen. 2:3; Ex. 20:8-11; Deut. 5:12). Mount Sinai was holy, for God appeared there in fire to give the Ten Commandments (Ex. 19:23). The priests of Israel were holy (Lev. 21:7), and everything associated with worship

and sacrifice was to be considered holy. In a very significant sense Israel itself was considered holy, for this people was chosen by God to be His own special possession (Deut. 7:6; 14:2, 21).

It is important to realize that great stress is placed in the Old Testament on maintaining the distinction between what is sacred and what is secular. The holy must never be used in a common or profane way. That which was consecrated to God must be for His use alone—forever.

Ritual holiness. The religion of Israel was both cultic and moral. The cultic element established religious ritual and many aspects of the lifestyle of God's people. A person was in a state of holiness when he observed cultic restrictions. It was a responsibility of the priests to "distinguish between the holy and the profane, between the unclean and the clean, and [they were required to] teach the Israelites all the decrees the Lord [had] given them through Moses" (Lev. 10:10-11). Both essential and nonmoral practices, such as not cooking a young goat in its mother's milk (Ex. 34:26), and religious ceremonies were aspects of ritual uncleanness.

Moral holiness. Two aspects of God's nature are associated with holiness in the Old Testament. One is His essential power and splendor. When two of Aaron's sons violated the ritual regulations governing worship, God, as quoted by Moses, announced: "Among those who approach Me I will show Myself holy; in the sight of all the people I will be honored" (Lev. 10:3). Fire flared from the Lord on that occasion and consumed the men who had treated Him with contempt by ignoring His commands. God's holiness was displayed in this exercise of awesome power.

Leviticus 19:2 displays a moral dimension to God's holiness. "Speak to the entire assembly of Israel," the Lord told Moses, "and say to them: 'Be holy because I, the Lord your God, am holy.' "

The commands that follow this statement are not cultic but are moral in character. They deal with theft, idolatry, lying, fraud, slander, revenge, etc., and include the command to love one's neighbor. These commands are punctuated regularly by the reminder, "I am the Lord."

In this Old Testament passage and many others, God's holiness is directly linked with His own moral character. That holiness is displayed in His moral perfection and His faithful commitment to good and in His judgment on those who desert the way of goodness for sin. "The Lord Almighty will be exalted by His justice, and the Holy God will show Himself holy by His righteousness" (Isa. 5:16). When Israel was set apart to God by God's sovereign choice, both the ritual and the moral aspects of obedience to God were essential in their life of holiness.

Because God is a holy God, those who are associated with Him are to be holy in all they do.

Regulations for Holiness in the People: Leviticus 18–20

Sexual regulation (Lev. 18). Sex is God's invention. It is He who created human beings male and female; He who told the first pair to be fruitful and to multiply. The New Testament even calls teaching that believers are to refrain from marriage, "which God created to be received with thanksgiving by those who believe and who know the truth," the teachings of "demons" and "deceiving spirits" (1 Tim. 4:1-5).

But sex has a specific and wonderful function in human experience. While pleasurable and exciting, sex is designed as a bonding experience: an expression of union and oneness to be known by a man and woman who commit themselves to each other for life. Outside of this context of lifelong union, and outside the context of intimate self-giving, sexual activity will be destructive rather than constructive.

Leviticus 18 reflects this and even goes beyond it. It identifies certain sexual liaisons as "detestable things" which defile not only individuals but the society ("the land," v. 27). Included are sexual relations with blood relations and in-laws, sexual relations with animals, and homosexuality (vv. 7-23).

This last practice, which the Old Testament text calls "detestable," is an issue today as gay men and women demand not just civil rights but to be recognized by society as persons who practice an acceptable "alternative lifestyle." There are even openly homosexual clergy, who demand that their denominations affirm them as ministers of God and give congregations into their care.

The prohibition against homosexuality is not found solely in this one passage. Leviticus 20 expands on the sin and decrees the death penalty "if a man lies with a man as one lies with a woman" for "both of them have done what is detestable" (v. 13).

The New Testament Book of Romans speaks of homosexual acts as a "degrading of their bodies with one another" and calls such passions "shameful lusts" that lead to "indecent acts" (Rom. 1:24-27). Whatever moderns say about homosexuality, the Bible clearly identifies this sexual practice as sin.

As Christians, living in a secular society rather than in Israel's "society under God," we can take a moral stand on what is right. But probably we will not be able to criminalize homosexuality. As for those outside the Christian community who practice it, their real spiritual need is for Jesus Christ. With them, we need to keep the focus not so much on this sin as on the message of forgiveness for all sins that comes with personal faith in the Saviour.

But those who claim to be Christians and still demand a right to be homosexual must be challenged with a vision of our Holy God, who insists that all who have a relationship with Him depart from their iniquity, to live a holy and godly life.

♥ ***Link to Life: Youth / Adult***
Because homosexuality is such an issue today, you may want to spend group time discussing it, particularly if any in the group have homosexual relatives, friends, or are unclear on the Bible's teaching.

Have your group brainstorm a list of "statements people might make about homosexuality." (This will give everyone an opportunity to raise any questions they may have in a "safe" way.)

Read together and discuss Leviticus 18:22; 20:13; and Romans 1:24-27. Go through and evaluate the listed statements based on these passages.

Then discuss: "How are we to relate to homosexual persons?" After opinions have been expressed, look in 1 Corinthians 5 for guidelines. This passage teaches that immorality outside the church is not to be judged, but that immoral people within the church are to be judged, and if they do not repent are to be expelled from fellowship.

Various responsibilities (Lev. 19). Many of the regulations in this chapter expand on the basic Ten Commandments. Not only is a person not to kill, but also "not do anything that endangers your neighbor's life" (v. 16). Respect is to be shown for the elderly (v. 32), and aliens who live in the land are to be given the same consideration as those native-born.

But mixed with these regulations which show deep moral responsibility to others are also cultic rules: do not mate different kinds of animals, do not plant two kinds of seed in the same field (v. 19), do not "cut the hair at the sides of your head or clip off the edges of your beard" (v. 27).

In the Old Testament the cultic regulations which were designed simply to mark Israel as different, and the moral regulations which guard the value of every individual, are mixed together. When we move to the New Testament, the cultic is set aside. But the moral obligations that are expressed in Old Testament laws are repeated as life-principles for believers of every day and age.

Punishments (Lev. 20). This chapter established the death penalty for a number of different sins, with lesser penalties indicated by "he will be held responsible." Does the death penalty here suggest a harsher society? No, for that penalty is imposed not for a private kind of criminal act like theft, but only for sins which threaten the whole community.

Sins which would shatter the integrity of the family as the basic unit of society are particularly in view here, as is spiritism, which draws the hearts of the people away from the Lord.

Regulations for Priests: Leviticus 21–22

The priesthood, set aside for service to God, was regarded as specially holy. Priests lived under more restrictions than the rest of the people. This was particularly true of whom a priest was allowed to marry: "The woman he marries must be a virgin. He must not marry a widow, a divorced woman, or a woman defiled by prostitution, but only a virgin from his own people" (21:13-14).

♥ ***Link to Life: Youth / Adult***
This feature of priestly life may stimulate a thought-provoking debate. Divide your group into pro and con teams to study Leviticus 21. Each team is to suggest arguments for or against: "Ministers should live by higher standards than ordinary Christians." After discussion, have each research team choose two members to debate. When the debate is finished have general discussion. But then introduce this thought: in the church all are believer-priests. Because we have been called into this unique relationship with God, we are all—every one of us—to live most holy lives.

Regulations concerning Festivals: Leviticus 23–24

God established a religious year for Israel, broken into patterned celebrations which permitted Israel to relive its heritage annually.

Three of the annual feasts were "pilgrim festivals," during which families were to journey to a central place of worship, later established in Jerusalem. These were times of special joy and celebration, linked with the agricultural seasons, but intended to help Israel relive salvation history and reaffirm commitment to God.

The three pilgrim festivals were Passover, including the week-long Feasts of Unleavened Bread (Ex. 13:3-10; Lev. 23:4-8; Deut. 16:1-8), Firstfruits (also called the Feast of Weeks and Pentecost) (Lev. 23:9-21; Deut. 16:9-11), and Tabernacles (also called the Feast of Booths) (Ex. 23:16; Lev. 23:33-43; Deut. 16:13). During this last festival the people lived outside in rough shelters, commemorating the years of travel from Sinai to the Promised Land.

A vital principle underlying this religious system helps us understand how we can better communicate our own faith.

The principle is expressed in a Hebrew term, *zikkaron,* which is often translated as "memorial" and means "a reminder" or "a remembrance." It is used of objects or actions that help Israel identify with some particular religious truth. For instance, the pile of stones beside the River Jordan that commemorated Israel passing through on dry ground is one such memorial (Josh. 4:7).

What was the *zikkaron* intended to do? It was intended to help individuals who saw or participated in it sense his or her identity with what God had done in the past. In essence the festivals of Israel were designed to help each new generation *relive God's great and wonderful acts for His people.* In the festivals that annually reminded Israel of what God had done for them, the people were intended to sense their own identity with their forefathers, and to realize that God had worked His wonders for each one of them!

♥ ***Link to Life: Children***
The Christian year, featuring Christmas, Good Friday, and Easter, are annual reminders to you and me of all God has done for us in Christ. We can help boys and girls appreciate the significance of these occasions best by using them as God used the festivals in Israel, as opportunities for individuals to relive, to participate in, the sacred events.

In class and at home we can let children act out different roles: let them be Mary or Joseph or a shepherd or be a disciple of Jesus when He is crucified, or one of the women who finds the empty tomb.

After telling and playing the story, be sure to talk about the feelings of the people they played. How did the shepherd feel when he saw the Baby Jesus? How did the disciple feel when Jesus was dying? The opportunity to relive these wondrous events each year, associated with songs, celebration, and joyful church services, lets us build into the lives of growing children a sense of the reality of the great events of Christian faith.

Regulations concerning Canaan: Leviticus 25–27

The rest of Leviticus focuses on the way that God's people were to live when He brought them out of the wilderness and settled them in the Promised Land.

This section too is linked with God's holiness, but in a distinctive way. We move here to God's design for a just, moral community: a holy social order.

That order is expressed in part in the establishment of a Sabbatical year and a Year of Jubilee, and even in regulations concerning slavery!

To understand the significance of these striking laws, we need to understand the total system God's Law sets up for the care

Festival System

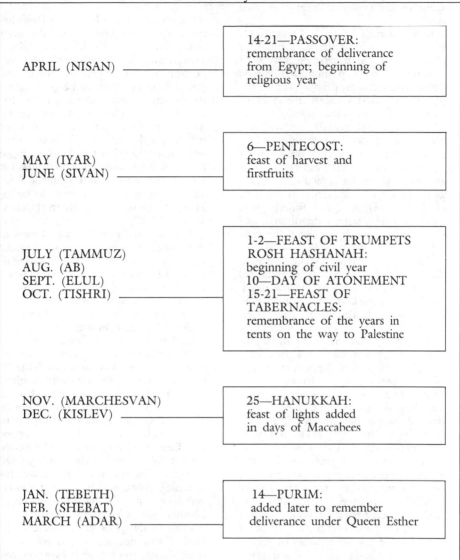

APRIL (NISAN)	14-21—PASSOVER: remembrance of deliverance from Egypt; beginning of religious year
MAY (IYAR) JUNE (SIVAN)	6—PENTECOST: feast of harvest and firstfruits
JULY (TAMMUZ) AUG. (AB) SEPT. (ELUL) OCT. (TISHRI)	1-2—FEAST OF TRUMPETS ROSH HASHANAH: beginning of civil year 10—DAY OF ATONEMENT 15-21—FEAST OF TABERNACLES: remembrance of the years in tents on the way to Palestine
NOV. (MARCHESVAN) DEC. (KISLEV)	25—HANUKKAH: feast of lights added in days of Maccabees
JAN. (TEBETH) FEB. (SHEBAT) MARCH (ADAR)	14—PURIM: added later to remember deliverance under Queen Esther

of the poor and needy. This system is summarized in the *Expository Dictionary of Bible Words.*

Preservation of capital. This is one of the most significant of Old Testament social mechanisms. Israel was an agrarian society: originally wealth was based on land and what the land could produce. Old Testament Law decreed that the land was to remain perpetually in the family of the first settlers. "The land must not be sold permanently. . . . Throughout the country that you hold as a possession, you must provide for the redemption of the land" (Lev. 25:23-24).

What the Old Testament Law did permit was sale of the *use* of the land. The value of a property was to be computed by the projected value of crops between the time of sale and the Year of Jubilee. Every fiftieth year was a Year of Jubilee. In that year, people were not to work the land but to enjoy a year of rest; and in that year everyone was to take possession again of his family heritage—his own land.

In addition, if a person needed funds and sold the use of his land and later prospered or found a rich relative who was willing to help him, that person could reclaim his property by recomputing its projected value to the Year of Jubilee and paying that sum.

The potential significance of this mechanism cannot be overestimated. A person might make bad decisions or squander his wealth, but there was always provision for capital for the next generation, to be reclaimed in the Year of Jubilee. Thus, every fiftieth year, wealth was in a sense redistributed, and the poor were given the means for making a fresh start.

Voluntary servitude. Another option that the poor in Israel had was to sell their personal services to a fellow Israelite. This relationship was carefully governed by Old Testament Law (Lev. 25:39-54; Deut. 15:12-18). Such a sale of services was paid for in an initial purchase price, but it was not a permanent sale of the individual. Rather, at the end of his seventh year, a Hebrew servant was to be released. "And when you release him, do not send him away empty-handed. Supply him liberally from your flock, your threshing floor and your winepress" (vv. 13-14).

In a sense we can perhaps look at this as an apprenticeship program. A poor person who could not meet his financial obligations was given a sum of money to pay off his creditors. He bound himself to serve the person who had purchased him. During the seven years of service the servant should have learned skills, both for working and for managing his own finances, so that when he was released, he would be able to make it on his own. At the time of his release his former master supplied him "liberally" with the resources he needed for a fresh start.

While these two features of God's design of a just, moral community are presented here, there are other mechanisms imbedded in Old Testament Law we need to grasp if we are to understand the whole picture. The *Expository Dictionary* continues:

Access to necessities. Two social mechanisms were designed to give the poor immediate access to life's necessities. First, during the seventh Sabbatical year no crops were to be planted. Instead, the poor of the land were to be given access to any crops that had grown up (Ex. 23:10-11). In addition, during regular harvests in other years, the landowner was to go through the fields one time only. Everything that had been missed and all that fell to the ground or was left on the vine or tree was to be made available to the poor. They were to be allowed to glean such fields freely (Lev. 19:10; 23:22).

Interest-free, forgivable loans. Loans to other Israelites were to be made without charging interest (25:35-37; Deut. 23:19-20) and were to be canceled when the Sabbatical (seventh) year came (15:1-3). Of course a person was to try to repay a loan he made, but if this was impossible, that debt was not to be permitted to weigh him down forever.

The proper and loving attitude toward a brother is indicated in verses 7-11: "If there is a poor man among your brothers in any of the towns of the land that the Lord your God is giving you, do not be hard-hearted or tightfisted toward your poor brother. Rather be openhanded and freely lend him whatever he needs. Be careful not to harbor this wicked thought: 'The seventh year, the year for canceling debts, is near,' so that you do not show ill will toward your needy brother and give him nothing. . . . There will always be poor people in the land. Therefore I command you to be openhanded toward your brothers and toward the poor and needy in your land."

Organized collections. A number of tithes were to be collected from the people of Israel. One such collection described in 14:28-29, was to be undertaken every three years, and what was collected was to be stored in each locality. This was to supply the Levites and also "the aliens, the fatherless, and the widows."

Taken individually, or together, these social mechanisms are extremely striking.

They make provision for the immediate needs of individuals, for training of the ineffective, for the preservation of capital, and for the preservation of the respect of the poor as well as of the wealthy.

♥ ***Link to Life: Youth / Adult***
It's fascinating to speculate on the relevance of some of these social mechanisms for our society today. You can profitably build a group session around this issue. Have your members study the passages referred to in this section. Then give a lecture summary, drawing from the above discussion. Then assign your group the task of redesigning our social welfare system. What laws might be drawn? How could a modern businessman participate? What might individuals and local communities do?

While Israel was to be a unique community that expressed God's holiness in its law and way of life, many of the principles seen in the Old Testament are superior to those on which our country's treatment of the poor and needy is based. And who knows? One of your group might become involved in the political process and make a difference in our own country's future.

Obedience (Lev. 26). God's regulations are not intended to be burdensome. Instead they are intended to bring blessing. Now God reaffirmed His personal commitment to bless if His people would be obedient. "I will grant peace in the land, and you will lie down and no one will make you afraid" (v. 6). Only if Israel disobeyed and violated God's covenant would life hold disappointment and tragedy. As God warned, "If you remain hostile toward Me and refuse to listen to Me, I will multiply your afflictions seven times over, as your sins deserve" (v. 21).

TEACHING GUIDE

Prepare
Consider the makeup and needs of your group. Which of the emphases in these chapters would best minister to, or challenge, your members?

Explore and Expand
Select one of the following emphases for your group study of this section and, except perhaps for a brief lecture overview, give your entire time to it.
1. How do we respond to homosexuality and homosexuals? Follow the process outlined in the "link-to-life" suggestion on page 119.
2. Should Christian ministers be expected to live by higher standards than lay Christians? Follow the process outlined in the "link-to-life" suggestion on page 120.
3. How can we make Christian holidays meaningful to our children? Explore the meaning of Israel's festivals as *zikkaron,* and plan meaningful family holiday activities. See page 120.
4. How can our society become more just in its treatment of the poor and needy? Follow the process outlined on page 123.

Apply
Conclude each study with the assignment to list: What will I do?

STUDY GUIDE 16

Numbers 1–20

RESPONSIBLE CHOICE

Overview

With the Law given, the priests ordained, and the sacrificial system which provided for forgiveness of sin instituted, it was time for God's people to move on.

Israel had come to Sinai exactly three months after leaving Egypt. On the twentieth day of the second month of the second year out of Egypt they would set out again (Num. 10:11).

From this point on, Israel would be responsible to God for the choices individuals, groups, and the whole community made. Despite punishments for disobedience along the way, this generation did not learn the vital lesson of obedience. When the time came to make life's most significant choice, these people would hear God's voice, and turn away.

Outline

I.	At Sinai	1–9
	A. Organizing the people	1–4
	B. Culminating worship	5–9
II.	The Lost Generation	10–20
	A. The journey	10–12
	B. Israel's disobedience	13–14
	C. Years of wandering	15–19
III.	Prelude to Victory	20–36
	A. Warfare	20–21
	B. Baalam	22–25
	C. The new generation	26–31
	D. Victory preview	32–36

A most significant statement about God is found in this section of Scripture: "The Lord is slow to anger, abounding in love and forgiving sin and rebellion. Yet He does not leave the guilty unpunished" (Num. 14:18). God is love. But persons are responsible to Him for their choices.

Commentary

I remember Laura as she sobbed in my office. She'd just become a Christian, and life was hard. As a teen she was fighting against the pull of her past and her conflicts with her parents. And she felt a good deal of guilt as well as frustration.

It was good to remind her that God had forgiven her, so she could forgive herself too. And to point out that everyone makes mistakes. It's part of growing. The exciting thing is that God promises we *will* grow in Him, grow beyond ourselves and our limitations.

But for the pain of her present, Laura didn't really need either sympathy or pity. She needed only help to face the problems that her circumstances created. In the face of her difficulties, in the conflict with her family, the help she needed was help to make responsible choices.

Responsible

This was the issue confronting Israel at the beginning of the Book of Numbers. This people had been redeemed from slavery by God's great power. The people had been taught God's will in a Law that revealed much of His character. And provision had been made to cleanse the Israelites from the sins that would inevitably come. The door to God was held open, guaranteed by the tabernacle, sacrifice, and the priesthood. The forgiven people had been instructed how to live in fellowship with their God.

The message that came then to Israel was simply this: "You have been provided with everything you need to live a holy life. Now you are responsible."

The people of Israel were about to face difficult and challenging circumstances. But there could be no excuses for failing to respond to God. In each situation Israel was now responsible for the choices the people made—and also responsible for the results of those choices. What happened now would inevitably be a direct consequence of

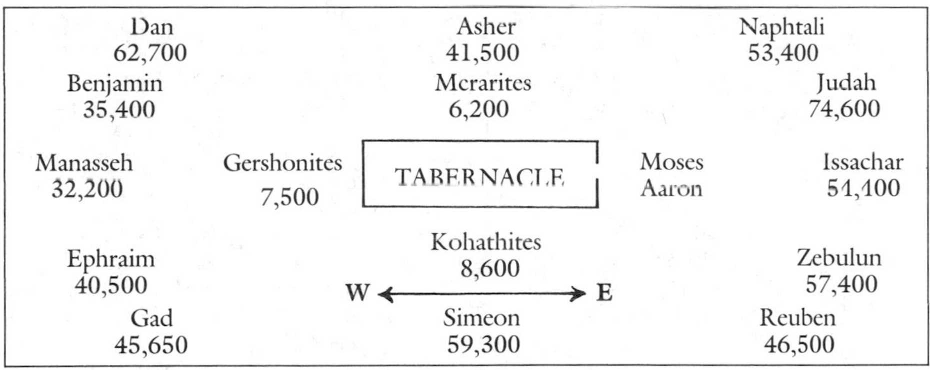

Organization of the Camp

Israel's decision to follow—or to reject—the leading of God.

My friend Laura was young, both as a person and as a Christian. Learning to be responsible was hard for her. It's hard at any age. Some of us learn the lesson of responsibility only after a great deal of pain, as wrong choices work out their results in our lives. Some of us learn quickly, from others.

In this section of Scripture we have lessons on responsibility that we can learn from others, and thus avoid the pain of learning the hard way. First Corinthians 10:11-12 tells us that "these things happened to them as examples and were written down as warnings for us. . . . So if you think you are standing firm, be careful that you don't fall!"

It's comforting to understand our position in Christ as forgiven people. But it is important to realize that, however exalted our position, as we live our daily lives we must accept responsibility for all our choices and act as redeemed people—lest we fall.

A Nation: Numbers 1–10

Here is where we see the first indication that the great mob of people who swarmed out of Egypt are now to be treated as a responsible nation. A census was taken, with the men of military age numbering 603,550. This figure is given in several different texts, though in some it is rounded off (Ex. 12:37; 38:26; Num. 1:46; 2:32; 11:21). The later census of Numbers 26:51 shows similarity, but also some change over the 38-year period. The total population of Israel now ready to leave Sinai probably ranged between 2 and 2½ million people.

Tribal marching and camping positions were set. The duties of the Levites were defined, and a system of trumpet calls was set to signal assembly, the order of departure, alarms, etc.

As the people of Israel marched they were to respond to the direct leading of God. The pillar of cloud and fire which had appeared as Israel left Egypt (Ex. 13:21) now rested over the tabernacle. When the cloud rested, the people remained in camp. But when in the morning the cloud lifted up, the people set out and followed it as God led them where He chose. As the Bible says, "At the Lord's command they encamped, and at the Lord's command they set out. They obeyed the Lord's order in accordance with His command through Moses" (Num. 9:23).

Even in this, the people were being taught to respond to God. God's people must always look to Him for guidance, and go or wait at His command.

♥ ***Link to Life: Children***

The story of the cloudy-fiery pillar is attractive to boys and girls. It can be used to build into their thoughts the same thing God intended to build into Israel's thinking: we must go where God leads us.

Make a "cloudy-fiery pillar" from red construction paper, shaded with black crayon, rolled into a tube. After telling the Bible story play a variation of "May I." Tell the children to sit down, stand up, take three steps, etc., only when you give the command and *move the "pillar" in the appropriate way. A person who doesn't follow pillar-led directions is out. The last person left is the winner.*

Children can also take turns being the leader.

Give the children construction paper and crayons to make or draw their own

Judah
Issachar
Zebulun
Gershon and Merari*
Reuben
Simeon
Gad
Kohath*
Ephraim
Manasseh
Benjamin
Dan
Asher
Naphtali

*The Levites were divided into two companies (see Num. 10:14-27). The sons of Gershon and Merari carried the tabernacle itself, while the Kohathites carried the holy articles from the tabernacle. With the order of march arranged as it was, the carriers of the tabernacle had time to set it up before the holy things arrived.

Israel Marching

cloudy-fiery pillar. A Bible verse that guides behavior might be printed or glued to this Primary take-home project.

♥ ***Link to Life: Youth / Adult***
The cloudy-fiery pillar is a historic illustration of God's guidance of His people. God continues to guide His people today, but seldom in such an unmistakable, visible way. Have group members think back to one or more times when each was aware of God's personal guidance in his or her life.
When each has identified one or more experiences, have everyone share. What did the guidance concern? How did the guidance come? How did you recognize it?

Sharing will help each person in your group broaden his or her awareness and understanding of God's leading in the Christian life.

Three Lessons: Numbers 11:1–12:15
When Israel moved away from Sinai after having been camped there so long, three incidents occurred which were truly "examples" for Israel (1 Cor. 10:11). Each involved a rejection of God, and each was the occasion of immediate judgment. Israel was being taught the difficult lesson of responsibility. As God's people they had to respond to Him with trusting obedience. Any failure to respond led to tragic consequences.

In these three experiences Israel was being graciously prepared for a coming choice that would establish the destiny of the entire generation.

Rejection of God's guidance (*Num. 11:1-3*). It took only three days of journeying in desert country for the Israelites to revert to a pattern they had established before they arrived at Sinai. Forgetting all that God had done for them, they let discomfort dominate their thinking. They "complained about their hardships in the hearing of the Lord" (v. 1). This was an explicit rejection of God as the One who guided them, and who had guided them from the beginning. In their murmuring they denied His wisdom, and ignored the supernatural provision of the cloudy-fiery pillar that directed their every move.

God immediately acted—in judgment. Fire destroyed some outlying parts of the camp. In panic the people turned to Moses, who prayed, and the fire was controlled.

Rejection of God's provision (Num. 11:4-35). Shortly afterward the people began to complain about something else. They became dissatisfied with their diet, and were ready to trade their freedom for the meat and vegetables they had lived on in Egypt. The manna that God provided was despised, and every man at the door of his tent complained and plotted because of a craving for meat.

This rejection of God's provision was a last straw to Moses, who had long felt the burden of leading a people who behaved like squalling infants (v. 12). God responded to Moses' need by distributing his leadership responsibility and gift to 70 of the elders. And God responded to the people too. God had Moses inform the people that the next day they would have meat. Meat enough for a whole month, "until it comes out of your nostrils and you loathe it" (v. 20). "You have rejected the Lord who is among you" (v. 20), is the divine comment on their behavior and its meaning.

God provided meat by bringing a great flock of quail (perhaps like the giant flocks of carrier pigeons which in the early days of our continent darkened the sky for days).

The quail flew about three feet off the ground (v. 31), and for two days were gathered by the bushel. Meat for the millions had been provided.

But when the people began to eat, a great plague struck the camp. Thousands and thousands of the murmurers died (vv. 33-34). The people who had rejected God and His provision bore the dreadful consequences of their choice.

♥ ***Link to Life: Youth / Adult***
The story in Numbers 11:4-35 illustrates a basic principle: God knows what is best for us. When we insist on begging for something that is not best, He may give it to us. But the consequences show that what we wanted was not really best.

Ask your group members if they have had experiences that illustrate this point. Such sharing can help motivate your group members to willingly submit to God in the future.

Rejection of God's appointed (Num. 12). Shortly afterward another incident of rebellion occurred. This time Miriam and Aaron, Moses' sister and brother, resented the special role Moses was given by God. They were aware that God had used them as well as Moses. So they challenged Moses' authority.

God responded angrily, pointing out the special relationship that He Himself had chosen to have with Moses. "He is faithful in all My house[hold]" (v. 7). In judgment, Miriam was stricken with leprosy, and put out of the camp for seven days. Afterward she was healed in answer to Moses' prayer. (Aaron, who served as high priest, would have been disqualified from his office if he had been similarly judged.) The entire nation was intended to learn by this experience. Everyone was forced to wait for Miriam for those seven days, and did not set out again until she was brought in healed.

Why did God deal so harshly and so decisively with the people at fault in these three incidents? These things happened to them as examples. Israel was about to make a vitally important decision—one that would affect her future drastically. On the journey to the place of decision, God permitted these three incidents so that Israel might learn the lesson of responsibility. Notice the parallel in each situation:

- Circumstances, rather than God's presence, were given priority by the people.
- God's revealed will and purposes were rejected.
- The rejecting attitude was expressed in actions.
- Israel's wrong choices led to judgment and to suffering.

In unmistakable and dramatic ways Israel was shown that they were now responsible for their own choices. Whenever they chose to turn away from God, tragic results would inevitably follow.

The Choice: Numbers 13–14

Israel had been given instruction in responsibility on the way to the Promised Land. When they arrived at the borders of Palestine, Moses sent 12 men out in pairs to spy out the land. The 12 were to evaluate the strength of the peoples, their numbers, and whether the land was rich or poor. God was giving Israel information, that the dangers might be known and weighed against their confidence in God.

Ten of the 12 spies were overawed by the strength of the enemy and by the fortified towns they found in the land. Two of the spies, Caleb and Joshua, encouraged the people to trust in God. "We should go up and take possession of the land, for we can certainly do it" (13:30). But the fears of the others prevailed. Crying in fright and anguish, the whole congregation was ready to choose other leaders to guide them back to Egypt!

Stunned by the choice Israel was making, Moses and Aaron "fell face down in front of the whole Israelite assembly gathered there" and Caleb and Joshua tore their clothing (an action indicating great depth of feeling). They urged Israel, "Do not rebel against the Lord. . . . Their protection is gone but Lord is with us" (14:9).

This affirmation of faith showed vividly the response that Israel should have made when faced with their choice. Instead, "the whole assembly talked about stoning them."

The choice had been made.

Now, as a responsible people, Israel had to accept the full consequences of her decision.

God appears. At this point the Lord visibly intervened. His "glory" suddenly flashed from the tabernacle. The action of Israel justified their total destruction. . . . God could make of Moses alone a greater people than Israel. But Moses again prayed for the people, and they were pardoned.

Yet even with the pardon, the people of Israel would bear the consequences of their decision.

"Not one of the men who saw My glory and the miraculous signs I performed in Egypt and in the desert but who disobeyed Me and tested Me 10 times—not one of them will ever see the land I promised on oath to their forefathers. No one who has treated Me with contempt will ever see it" (vv. 22-23).

Only Caleb and Joshua were exempted, because they had responded to God with trust. The rest would be led out again into the wilderness, to wander there for 38 years.

"Your bodies will fall—every one of you 20 years old or more who was counted in the census and who has grumbled against Me. Not one of you will enter the land I swore with uplifted hand to make your home except Caleb . . . and Joshua" (vv. 29-30).

When the children of the next generation had learned to accept responsibility and to trust God, then they would come again to the Promised Land. A people who refused to trust could never experience the Promised Land's rest.

Unfair? Lest we think this judgment was too severe, we need to look at the aftermath. When Moses told the people the judgment of God, they "mourned greatly." And the next morning they jumped up—and mounted an attack on the land they had been unwilling to approach. But this was after God had expressly commanded them to turn back to the wilderness!

Moses cried out, "Why are you disobeying the Lord's command? This will not succeed!" (v. 41) But the people stumbled on to meet the enemy, though God's ark and His presence remained in the camp.

They were defeated and pursued.

The people had once again demonstrated that they simply would not listen to God or respond to Him. Over and over the failure of Israel to be obedient led them into disaster. Yet they refused to be responsible.

The lesson still had to be learned. Until it was learned, the people would know only the tragic consequences of disobedience with each wrong choice.

The Lost Rest: Hebrews 3:7-11

This New Testament passage is a divine commentary on the event we have just reviewed. Hebrews 3 also contains one of the clearest explanations of our personal responsibility to God today.

The writer of this passage quotes from Psalm 95:7-11, which focuses on the attitude of the Israelites who came out of Egypt. Their hearts were hardened against God, and they were "always going astray." But for us:

> Today, if you hear His voice, do not harden your hearts as you did in the rebellion, during the time of testing in the desert, where your fathers tested and tried Me and for 40 years saw what I did. That is why I was angry with that generation, and I said, "Their hearts are always going astray, and they have not known My ways." So I declared on oath in My anger, "They shall never enter My rest."
>
> Hebrews 3:7-11

Hebrews 4 goes on to apply this incident directly to you and me. "Today if you hear His voice," the Scripture warns, "do not harden your hearts" (v. 7). Because distrust kept Israel from obeying God, the people were unable to enter the Promised Land. They never knew rest from their wanderings in desolate wilderness. And they died there.

But how does this apply to us? The Bible says "There remains, then, a Sabbath-rest for the people of God" (v. 9). There remains the promise of experiencing life and meeting its challenges with peace in our hearts, and confidence that God's good will is being worked out in every circumstance. We can miss the experience of peace if we follow the Israelites' "example of disobedience."

All this helps us see more clearly the nature of Christian responsibility. We are to listen for God's voice today. And when the Holy Spirit makes us aware of God's will, we are to trust God completely—and express that trust in obedience.

Like Joshua and Caleb, we are to see our enemies clearly, but are also to have such a clear vision of the Lord that we remember we are well able to overcome them. With this kind of confidence in God, we will obey Him, and find the peace and joy that only obedience can provide.

ISRAEL	US TODAY
HEAR GOD'S WORD	HEAR GOD'S WORD
ATTITUDE: UNBELIEF	ATTITUDE:
ACTION: DISOBEY	ACTION:
RESULT: WILDERNESS EXPERIENCE ("Not enter His Rest")	RESULT:

Believer's Responsibility

This responsibility of the believer remains the same across the centuries. It is the same, under Law or under grace. Redemption's story is one—a story replayed at different times on different stages, but with unifying themes. Redemption brings men and women to God, frees and cleanses them, and provides a choice.

Wilderness—or Promised Land?

Disobedience—or obedience to God's voice?

Unbelief—or a complete and childlike trust in the God who has broken our chains and who promises to enrich our forgiveness with an experience of His rest?

Will we find that rest? The choice, and the responsibility, is ours and ours alone.

♥ ***Link to Life: Youth / Adult***
Use the chart above to organize a study of Israel's choice and God's commentary on it in Hebrews 3:7–4:11.

The Lost Generation: Numbers 15–20

The generation that had stood at the entrance to Canaan had thrown away the Promised Land. How striking that the first words of Numbers 15 are these: "The Lord said to Moses, 'Speak to the Israelites and say to them, "After you enter the land." ' " One generation had lost its opportunity to know rest, but their children would make a different choice. One generation had violated the Law Covenant, but God's commitment to His own covenant promises remained firm.

The years that followed were years of continuing rebellion. Korah, a Levite, led a rebellion, and on Moses' word the ground opened to swallow up Korah and all his followers (chap. 16). The congregation challenged this judgment, and a plague struck 14,700 (vv. 41-50). The strain of being the link between God and sinful man was fully recognized now by Moses and by Aaron. To Aaron God said—and now the old man understood—"You, your sons, and your father's family are to bear the responsibility for sins against the sanctuary" (18:1). Those close to God know a constant tension and struggle with those who draw back from Him and His Word.

But the dreary years passed. The old spirit of complaint continued to mark this generation of Israelites until the end (20:2-9). But the end did come.

In the fortieth year of deliverance from Egypt, in the thirty-eighth year of wilderness wandering, Aaron died and the role of high priest passed to one of his sons. The old generation was dying, soon to pass away in final outbreaks of rebellion and quick judgment. Then a new generation would come.

That new generation would accept the responsibility that comes with redemption. That generation would choose obedience—and would come to know God's rest.

TEACHING GUIDE

Prepare
Read and meditate on Hebrews 3:7–4:11. How can you best help your group members commit themselves to obey the Lord?

Explore
1. Tell the story of Laura that introduces this unit. Are we right to confront young people and older Christians with personal responsibility? Or do they need a more comforting, sympathetic message?
2. Share experiences when you may have failed to choose God's will even when you sensed it. What happened? How have the consequences of any wrong choices you have made helped you become a more responsible person?

Expand
1. Examine the three lessons taught Israel by the experiences reported in Numbers 11:1–12:15. How did these events prepare Israel for the national choice the people would soon face? After examining the incidents, share: "Has God ever prepared you for a significant decision in a similar way?"
2. As a group read Numbers 13 and 14, and suggest lessons which we can learn from Israel's experience. List these lessons on a chalkboard.

Then turn to Hebrews 3:7–4:11 and give a minilecture on God's commentary on this Old Testament event. What is the basic or primary lesson of this passage? How do we apply it to ourselves today? You may want to use the "Believer's Responsibility" chart for this purpose.

Apply
Have your group members share experiences of God's guidance, as suggested in the "link-to-life" idea on page 126. We are to do the will of God. Can we really come to know it? This sharing will help members to discern ways that God continues to make His voice heard by believers today.

STUDY GUIDE 17

Numbers 21–36

NO ENCHANTMENT AGAINST ISRAEL

Overview

With Numbers 21 we begin a new and positive chapter in the history of redemption.

God's people are not suddenly perfect. They still fail. But a new generation takes over from the old. The generation that would not trust or obey is dying out. In Numbers 26 we read about "those numbered by Moses and Aaron . . . in the wilderness of Sinai. For the Lord had said of them, 'They shall die in the wilderness.' There was not a man left of them, except Caleb the son of Jephunneh and Joshua the son of Nun" (vv. 64-65).

The new generation began to respond to God's voice. And they made a great discovery. When God's people live in right relationship with Him, they are fully protected!

▶ ***Hope.*** There are two Hebrew words translated "hope" in the Old Testament. Each invites us to look ahead eagerly, with confident expectation. Each also calls for patience; the fulfillment of hope lies in the future. "Hope" in the Old Testament is based on relationship. It affirms trust in God. We are confident, not because we know the future, but because we know God is wholly trustworthy. The new generation we meet now in Numbers is confident, expecting victory, for this is a people with trust in the Lord.

▶ ***The Story of Redemption.*** The last four books of Moses tell a single story: the story of redemption. In this unit you'll find a chart tracing the story of redemption, and summarizing its vital messages to you and to me.

Commentary

There is a definite unity to the story of redemption related in the events of the Exodus. The experiences of God's Old Testament people, in fact, parallel our individual experiences with God. The redemption they knew is ours too. And just as the new generation of Israel that we meet in Numbers 26 learned to anchor its faith in redemption history, we too need to anchor our faith in an understanding of what God has done for us.

So before we move on to look carefully at Numbers 21–36, we can profit from an overview of the four Old Testament books that tell redemption's story, and an overview of their messages to you and to me. That overview, and a summary of their messages, is incorporated in the chart, "Understanding Redemption." Use it now to look back over the experience of the old, disobedient generation of Israelites. Use it to look ahead to the challenge God gives to the new, fresh generation that would trust Him and through faith would take the Promised Land.

Transition: Numbers 21–25

Lessons from the recent history of Israel provided a firm foundation for the new generation's view of God. Yet there were still struggles. The old, untrusting generation was still with the new. In these transition chapters we see struggle: a struggle in which the tendency to reject God's ways is matched against a tendency to respond. Sometimes the nation sins, sometimes it obeys. In the outcome of each course of action, the new generation is taught the results of sin—and given a taste of the fruit of obedience.

Numbers 21 shows the uncertainty and the fluctuations. First Israel vows to do battle "if You will deliver these people into our hands." Confidently they go into battle—and win (vv. 1-3).

Yet shortly after that the people became impatient and returned to their old habit of

Understanding Redemption

Scripture	Events	Message	Key Words
Ex. 1–4	Enslaved in Egypt	Man needs redemption	Helpless
Ex. 5–12	Plagues on Egypt Passover	God acts to redeem Redemption comes through death	Yahweh Passover
Ex. 13–19	Red Sea crossed Murmuring on way to Sinai	Redeemed people must be godly	Rebelliousness
Ex. 20–24	Ten Commandments and case law	Redeemed people must be holy, in relationship with God, other persons	Law/God's character
Ex. 25–40	Tabernacle built	Redeemed people need cleansing	Tabernacle
Lev. 1–17	Sacrificial system Priesthood system instituted	Redeemed people are to worship, draw near to God	Sacrifice Priesthood
Lev. 18–27	Regulations given	Redeemed people are to live holy lives	Fellowship
Num. 1–20	Camp organized People disobey God's voice	Redeemed people are responsible to obey God	Responsibility
Num. 21–36	New generation wins victories	Redeemed people who obey are under God's protection	Protection
Deut. 1–4	Moses reviews history	Redeemed people are reminded of God's faithfulness	Remembrance
Deut. 5–11	Moses teaches the meaning of Law to the new generation	Redeemed people are loved—and are to be loving	Love
Deut. 12–26	Godly practices are taught the new generation	Redeemed people are to live to please God	Law/holiness
Deut. 27–34	Moses calls the new generation to personal decision	Redeemed people are to be fully committed to God	Commitment

murmuring against Moses. In discipline God sent poisonous snakes among them. Many died. Then the Lord told Moses to erect an image of a serpent and lift it high up on a pole. Moses was to announce to all that anyone bitten could look at the bronze serpent and live (vv. 4-9).

There was no healing power in the image. Clearly the healing was from God—and any individual who trusted God enough to seek out what must have seemed a ridiculous remedy actually was healed. Individuals as well as the nation had the power to choose.

The new generation was being taught that they had to take their destiny into their own hands!

♥ ***Link to Life: Youth / Adult***
Jesus looked back on this Old Testament incident and said, "Just as Moses lifted up the snake in the desert, so the Son of man must be lifted up, that everyone who believes in Him may have eternal life" (John 3:14-15).

Brainstorm with your group. How is this incident, in which deliverance from the serpent's deadly bite came through faith's look at a bronze serpent lifted up on a pole, like Christ's death on Calvary?

The final incident in Numbers 21 again shows Israel in battle, and again victorious (vv. 33-35). God's promise ("Do not be afraid of him, for I have handed him over to you, with his whole army and his land.") was now enough.

Protected from enemies without (Num. 22–24). As fear of Israel struck the region, the peoples there began to look desperately for weapons to use against them. The king of Moab, Balak, frightened at the "horde" which seemed to him to "cover the face of the land," attempted to call in spiritual powers to defeat Israel. He sent for a man named Balaam, saying, "I know that those you bless are blessed, and those you curse are cursed" (22:6). Balak wanted to use Balaam to lay a curse on Israel, and thus drain their strength.

There is no reason to doubt that Balaam had some spiritual powers. Israel was warned that when they entered the land they were to destroy all those who were spiritualists, possessed by evil spirits, and necromancers (cf. Deut. 18:1). Though Balaam clearly used omens, as did pagan seers, in his divinations (cf. Num. 24:1), it is possible that Balaam was a channel for God to speak to a pagan people. But it is more likely that the roots of Balaam's spiritual power were in the demonic than the divine. Throughout the Bible Balaam is spoken of in a negative way, and held up as a negative example. His ways and his motives are condemned in the New Testament, and his death is recounted in chapter 31 as a divine judgment.

At any rate, Balak called on Balaam to curse Israel for him. The word translated "curse" here is *qabab*, which suggests the idea of binding, to reduce ability, or to render powerless. Peoples in the ancient world considered curses magic tools to be used to gain power over enemies. Balak was attempting to mount a supernatural attack on this people against whom natural resources seemed inadequate.

But Balak was ignorant of the fact that the source of Israel's power was itself supernatural: Israel's strength came from the presence of Yahweh Himself in their camp.

God spoke to Balaam and told him not to go with Balak's messengers. Yet greed moved Balaam to ask God's permission again. This time God did permit Balaam to go, but warned him sternly that he must speak only the words God would give him.

We can picture Balaam's arrival. Balak had been waiting anxiously. Angrily he insisted that Balaam hurry and curse his enemy.

Balak took Balaam to a range of hills that looked down over Israel's encampment. There the Moabite offered the sacrifices that Balaam called for—and waited. Balaam finally spoke. But rather than speaking a curse, Balaam was forced by God to pronounce a blessing!

> From the rocky peaks I see them, from the heights I view them. I see a people who live apart and do not consider themselves one of the nations. Who can count the dust of Jacob or number the fourth part of Israel? Let me die the death of the righteous, and may my end be like theirs!
>
> Numbers 23:9-10

Three times the sequence was repeated. Balak took Balaam to a different height, hoping that from a different viewpoint Israel might be cursed. Yet no matter from where the attack was launched, it returned not as a curse but as a blessing on this people that God has chosen and whom He protects. God has dealt with Israel's sins in sacrifice and forgiveness. Thus:

> No misfortune is seen in Jacob; no misery observed in Israel. The Lord their God is with them; the shout of the King is among them. God brought them out of Egypt; they have the strength of a wild ox. There is no sorcery against Jacob, no divination against Israel. It will now be said of Jacob and of Israel, "See what God has done!"
>
> Numbers 23:21-23

It is God who is at work in His people. We are His workmanship. Protected by His very presence, there is no enchantment against us now.

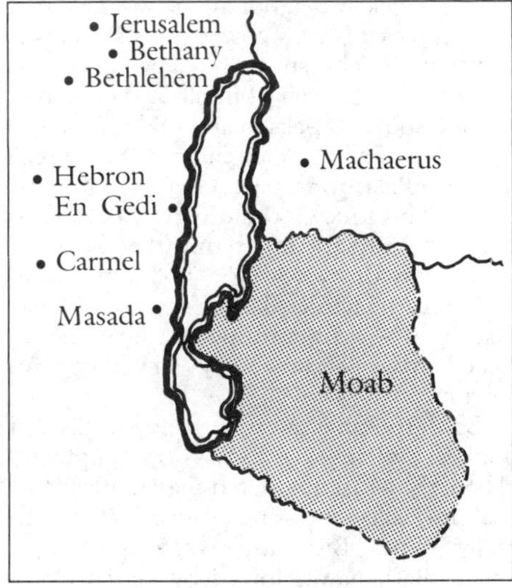

Location of Moab

The attack from without had failed. But Balaam made an effort to earn his fee. He suggested a strategy which he felt might force God to curse Israel against His will! Balaam reasoned that God could not bless a sinning people—and so he recommended to Balak that his women attempt to corrupt Israel and lead them into idolatry!

♥ ***Link to Life: Youth / Adult***
The New Testament makes three references to Balaam, identifying his "way" (2 Peter 2:15), his "error" (Jude 11), and his "teaching" (Rev. 2:14).

Turn your group members into detectives. Assign teams to look for clues to the meaning of each of these terms by comparing the Old Testament story and each New Testament context.

Your group members will conclude that Balaam's "way" is taken by false teachers who see religion as a way to make money. Balaam's "error" is also characteristic of false teachers, who are so dominated by greed that they view obedience to God as irrelevant. And Balaam's "teaching" involves any religious sanctioning of immorality, for whatever reasons.

After the teams report, discuss: "How can we guard ourselves against the way, error, and teaching of Balam?"

Protected from enemies within (Num. 25). This chapter begins, "While Israel was staying in Shittim, the men began to indulge in sexual immorality with Moabite women, who invited them to the sacrifices to their gods. The people ate and bowed down before these gods" (vv. 1-2). As in most religions of Canaan, ritual prostitution and sexual excess was an intrinsic part of the religion of Moab.

In this the Moabites followed the strategy suggested by "Balaam's advice" (31:16).

As in the past, God's anger now flared against His people. But at this time the sin was dealt with in a way which indicated a distinct change in the character of the people of Israel.

A plague began among the people, but Moses was told that the people themselves must "put to death those of your men who have joined in worshiping the Baal of Peor" (v. 5). (*Baal* is a Semitic word meaning "lord" that designated pagan deities in Canaan.) At that moment an Israelite man was openly leading a Midianite woman to his family. A priest, Phinehas, followed the two into the tent and drove a spear through them both. The plague was stopped, and Phinehas was rewarded by God "because he was zealous for the honor of his God" (v. 13).

The incident is important, because for the first time Israel is dealing with sin by self-discipline! The new generation is demonstrating its difference from the old. The choice to follow God completely was being made now—and the price of self-discipline was being paid.

Protected from enemies without, and cleansed by self-discipline within, the people of Israel were nearly ready to enter the land of rest.

♥ ***Link to Life: Youth / Adult***
Not long ago a church was sued by a member whom it attempted to expel for openly living with a man to whom she was not married.

Ask your group: "If you were a member of that church board, would you vote to expel her, or not?" After the votes are counted, let each person express his or her reasons. Then study the incident reported in Numbers 25, first putting it in historical perspective with a minilecture.

Then together also look at 1 Corinthians 5:1-12, a parallel incident in the New Testament.

Go back now to the original situation and evaluate. What should the church board do? What are the reasons why they should take that action?

In what areas should Christians exercise church discipline today? When should and when should we not discipline?

Expectation: Numbers 26–36

The old generation was gone now, the last of them carried away in the plague of Baal Peor. Some 600,000 men are numbered: the new generation matched in number the numbers of their fathers, who by now had fallen in the wilderness (26:64-66).

With the old generation gone, a new spirit infused Israel. In fellowship with God, sure of divine protection, and confident that they would choose what was right, the new generation looked forward to victory with optimism and hope.

This is shown strikingly in Numbers 27. Before a single battle had been fought in Palestine, five women approached Moses. Their father had died in the wilderness, and they had no brothers. They felt it would be unfair for their family to have no possession in the land, even though no son was alive to inherit.

What a striking faith! They never doubted the ultimate victory of Israel. They looked beyond the warfare to the time when the land would be divided among God's people, and believed so confidently that they treated inheritance as a present possession.

God's protected people had a right to this kind of confidence.

We too can look forward with complete assurance to victories that will surely be ours.

The census (Num. 26). All the first generation was now dead, their bodies scattered in the wilderness Israel had wandered for 38 years (vv. 64-65). The census established the number of Israel's fighting men at 601,730 (not counting the 23,000 Levites who were set aside to serve the Lord).

The census was important. On the journey, if the deaths were averaged across the years, there would have been some 200 funerals a day! The new census established the fact that there was no loss of strength. The new generation numbered within a few thousand of the generation that had left Egypt!

How faithful God is, even in the years that we must wait for Him to act.

Zelophehad's daughters (Num. 27). The five daughters of Zelophehad not only demonstrated faith, but they helped to establish the rights of women in Israel. The command that "if a man dies and leaves no son, turn his inheritance over to his daughter" (v. 8), is not reflected in the law codes of other peoples of that era.

Offerings (Num. 28–29). The offerings to be made on Israel's special feast and festival days are reviewed. For the significance of the religious year, see Study Guide 15.

Vows (Num. 30). In both Testaments a "vow" is a pledge or a promise that is made to God, never to other persons. Vows were, as in this chapter, expressions of special devotion or commitment, and were usually voluntary.

There was a limitation placed on women, whose vow could be overruled by a husband or father. This is because in the Old Testament era the men were legally responsible for their wives and their children.

One special vow described in Numbers 6 is that of the Nazirite, which was a vow of separation.

The Old Testament views faithfulness in keeping vows as an indication of the piety and faithfulness of God's people (cf. Pss. 50:14; 56:12; 76:11; Isa. 19:21; Jer. 44:25; Jonah 2:9; Nahum 1:15).

Transjordan tribes (Num. 32). Two of the Israelite tribes, who had very large herds and flocks, noted that the lands east of the

Jordan were suitable for livestock. So they requested permission to settle in those lands, which had been taken in battle.

Permission was granted on the condition that the men fit for war go with their brothers to battle for the Promised Land, which lay beyond the Jordan River.

What faith the men of these tribes exhibited! They were willing to build cities for their families and flocks, and then leave them unprotected as they traveled across the river to fight! God would take care of their families while they were away. They would do their duties, and trust Him.

Cities of refuge (Num. 35). This chapter establishes a very important feature in Israel's legal justice system. To sense their significance, we need to understand how criminal justice was to be handled under Old Testament Law. The *Expository Dictionary of Bible Words* gives this summary:

> The Mosaic Law established a system in which responsibility to deal with criminal matters was distributed throughout the society. Each community was to have its own panel of elders who would serve as judges in civil and criminal matters. The Old Testament emphatically enjoins the judges to show no partiality and to accept no bribes (Deut. 16:18-20). Rules of evidence were established for serious cases (17:1-7; 19:15) and a "supreme court" of priests was established to inquire of the Lord in cases "too difficult" for the judges. Later, when the monarchy was established, the king became the chief judicial officer. In biblical times, all governing functions were considered to be located in the king as the head of the nation. But the king, like the lower courts, was to be subject to God. The law itself established the standards according to which the ruler must judge.
>
> How were criminal matters dealt with? The Old Testament justice system, unlike our own, did not rely heavily on imprisonment to punish criminals. The Old Testament does report a number of cases of imprisonment—many of them under foreign jurisdiction (Gen. 39:20-22; 40:3, 5, 14; 42:16, 19; Jud. 16:21, 25; 2 Kings 17:4; 25:27, 29; Jer. 52:11, 31, 33; Ezek. 19:9) and some under rulers in Israel and Judah (1 Kings 22:27; 2 Chron. 16:10; 18:26). Confinement could involve simply restriction to one's residence or city (1 Kings 2:36), but in other instances it seems to have been in a room or pit in some official's residence (Jer. 20:2; 32:2; 37:4, 15, 18; 38:6).
>
> The Old Testament justice system relied more on restitution than on imprisonment. A person who was responsible for another's loss was to reimburse the value of the property destroyed (Ex. 22:1-15). Property that was stolen or obtained illegally had to be returned, and a penalty of one to four times its value was added. Murder and accidental homicide were special cases with a distinct code to govern how they were to be judged.
>
> Other penalties were prescribed for various personal injury and civil violations, including provisions for covering a person's loss of income if an injury prevented work.
>
> With many such guiding principles provided in the Mosaic Law, local judging elders were to call on witnesses within the community to establish the facts of a case and to supervise payment of the appropriate restitution or penalty.
>
> The Old Testament justice system relied heavily on the existence of a community in which individuals were responsive to God and to His laws. History shows that, with few exceptions, God's kind of justice was not administered during the Old Testament era.

The Numbers chapter dealing with homicide and establishing the cities of refuge must be understood in the context of the total system found in Old Testament Law.

The family "avenger of the blood" in this chapter is neither a vigilante nor an ancient Hatfield setting out to rid the world of a McCoy. Justice in Israel was a community responsibility, and there was no police force. Thus the one with primary responsibility to execute a murderer was the one in the community most affected by that crime: a member of the murdered person's family. Should such a person kill a murderer, he did not murder him but rather served as the executioner appointed by the Law to purify the holy community.

At the same time, this passage makes a distinction between *intentional, hostile kill-*

ing, which is murder, and what we would call *accidental homicide*. The cities of refuge were established for the protection of a person who killed another accidentally. These were cities scattered throughout the land where such a person could flee an overzealous relative whose motives might involve a desire for revenge, even if the death was an accident.

The elders of the home city of the killer were to hear the arguments of the accused and the avenger, and to "judge between" the one accused of murder and the "avenger of blood" according to rules established in this chapter. If the accused was judged to have killed accidentally, "the assembly must protect" him, and see him safely to one of the cities of refuge where he would live in safety until the high priest died, and he could return home. By then the anger of the avenger might have died, and the accidental killer would receive the full protection of law. Should he then be attacked by a family avenger, the avenger himself is to be put to death.

♥ ***Link to Life: Youth / Adult***

This Numbers chapter draws us deeply into the Old Testament concept of legal justice. While not all features of that system could be reproduced in modern society, there are many elements which might guide reform of our own criminal justice system. Have group members read Numbers 35 to themselves. Then ask: "Does this system seem fair and right?" Let everyone express his or her opinion. Then give a minilecture on the Old Testament legal justice system, as summarized. Show how the Numbers 35 instructions fit into and reflect that system.

Break into teams to discuss the following questions. Should all lawbreakers be put in jail? How do we protect the rights of victims? What distinction should we make between crimes of violence and those which do not involve violence? What are the responsibilities of individuals for criminal justice?

When you have finished team discussions, come together and see if you can outline a framework for improving our own criminal justice system.

TEACHING GUIDE

Prepare

Read and meditate on Ephesians 1:1-14. How well protected Jesus' people are, from enemies within and without.

Explore

1. Focus on Israel's protection from external and internal enemies. In a minilecture review Balaam's attempt to curse Israel. Then let your group members explore the attempt to destroy Israel by inner corruption.

Have your members read and react to Numbers 25.

2. If you have non-Christians in your group you may wish to look at the parallels between Moses' bronze serpent and Christ at Calvary.

3. How important is discipline in the church? Tell the story of the woman who sued the congregation that expelled her for openly living with a man to whom she was not married, and follow the process outlined in "link-to-life," page 135.

Expand

1. Look together at Balaam and his tragic approach to religion. Explore his way, his error, and his teaching. How can we avoid these perversions in our own spiritual lives?

2. You may want to take the entire hour to look at the Old Testament legal justice system, suggesting ways we might be guided to reform our own justice system.

Apply

1. How can Christians today display the kind of confidence in God shown by the new generation of Israelites?

2. Examine the chart on page 132. What seem to be the most important lessons that Christians today can learn from Israel's history?

STUDY GUIDE 18

Deuteronomy 1–4

THE CHALLENGE

Overview
The Book of Deuteronomy is one of the most significant in the Old Testament. Jesus often quoted Deuteronomy. When tempted by Satan in His own wilderness (Matt. 4), Jesus quoted this great book three times!

"Deutero-nomy" means "second law." But the book is far more than a restatement of the Law given at Sinai. This book is also a commentary on the Law's deeper meanings. As we study Deuteronomy we sense the deep love that underlies God's gift of Law—and the love for God that is necessary if any person is to be obedient to Him.

Outline

I.	Moses' First Sermon	1:1–4:43
II.	Moses' Second Sermon	4:44–28:68
III.	Moses' Third Sermon	29:1–30:20
IV.	Moses' Last Days	31:1–34:12

▶ ***"You."*** In this first sermon Moses reviewed what God had done for Israel. But in looking back on what happened to the first, now-dead generation, Moses talked of what God did for "you" and of how "you" responded to God. In the Old Testament there is a strong sense of *corporate responsibility* for the acts not only of the present community but also of past generations. God's mighty acts of deliverance were performed not just for the Exodus generation, but for "you" the living. In the same way, the living are to identify with and to learn from the sins and failures of past generations.

Commentary
The Book of Deuteronomy is both important and fascinating. It's a book that puts new stress on personal relationship with God. Here the phrase "Yahweh *our* God" (The LORD our God) is not only introduced, it is repeated. The Law is not some rigid set of impersonal rules. It is a vital expression of the love relationship that flows from God to His people, and is expressed by the people in obedient response.

This book does have many passages that are parallel to teaching already given in Exodus. For instance:

Ex. 21:1-11	matches	Deut. 15:12-18
Ex. 21:12-14	matches	Deut. 19:1-13
Ex. 22:21-24	matches	Deut. 24:17-22
Ex. 22:29	matches	Deut. 15:19-23
Ex. 23:2-8	matches	Deut. 16:18-20
Ex. 23:10-13	matches	Deut. 15:1-11
Ex. 23:14-17	matches	Deut. 16:1-17
Ex. 23:19a	matches	Deut. 26:2-10

Still, some 50 percent of the content of Deuteronomy is new. And what is repeated is often expanded by exhortations or by explanation of the deeper meaning of the duplicated laws.

Many have pointed out that Deuteronomy has great historical significance. It is written in a well-known contemporary form. It has the structure of a national constitution: a treaty between a ruler and his subjects.

This form is important because of the message it contained for Israel. God's redeemed people had a faith relationship with the Lord. Now God established the fact that in this relationship He is the Ruler, they the subjects. He is ready to bind Himself by solemn treaty to fulfill His obligations as their Ruler. But they must also bind themselves by the same treaty to fulfill their obligations as His subjects.

In essence, this kind of treaty spelled out the obligations of Ruler and ruled, and set the pattern for a harmonious relationship between the two.

The well-known form of this treaty, followed in the structure of Deuteronomy, included:

Historical Prologue	Reviewing the relationship which the Ruler has with His subjects.
Basic Stipulations	Specifying the general principles that are to guide behavior.
Detailed Stipulations	Expanding on certain rules that are to be followed.
Document Clause	Calling for ratification by the subjects themselves.
Blessings	Explaining the benefits the Ruler provides for good subjects.
Cursings	Explaining the punishments due subjects who violate treaty stipulations.
Recapitulation	Summarizing the treaty.

How is this form seen in Deuteronomy? Here are the passages that fit this treaty format. Prologue: 1:6–3:29. Basic Stipulations: 5:1–11:32. Detailed Stipulations: 12:1–26:19. Document Clause: 27:1-26. Blessings: 28:1-14. Cursings: 28:15-68. Recapitulation: 29:1–30:10.

So the very form of Deuteronomy held an important message for Israel. This nation had as its ruler not some human tyrant, but God Himself! There was no need for a human king in Israel, for God Himself was King. There was no need for a human military leader, for God Himself would lead, protect, and bless.

If only Israel would live according to the covenant regulations God gave, the Lord was committed to do His people good.

Moses' first sermon then was particularly fitting. In it, Moses revealed what God had done for "us," His special people. And in that review of the relationship between God and His people, there are many lessons for you and me, and for those whom we are called to teach!

Lessons in Relationship: Deuteronomy 1:6–4:40

God's promises are sure (Deut. 1:6-8). It's striking to note the way that the Lord talks about His promises in this passage. He speaks of them not as that which He will do, but as something He has already done.

"Go in and take possession of the land," the Lord told Israel. "See, I *have given* [italics mine] you this land."

What a striking statement. God's promises are so sure that God can speak of what He intends as already complete.

We can apply this in our own lives. When we find God's promises in the Bible, we can claim them with confidence. They do not simply express what God will do for us: they are so sure, they express what He has already accomplished.

♥ ***Link to Life: Youth / Adult***

We need to help youth and adults see God's promises in their "has done" and not "will do" character. Why not list a number of Bible promises on a chalkboard. (You can find promises for all situations in Zondervan's inexpensive, pocket-size Believer's Promise Book.*)*

Ask each person in your group to select a promise which is important to him or her because it seems to speak to a present personal need.

Go around the circle and have each person tell what promise he or she selected, and why it seems important.

Then read Deuteronomy 1:8, and point out how sure God is of His promises. Lead your group to pray, thanking God now for what He has given *(not will give!) to them.*

Be fearless and fair (Deut. 1:9-18). When the burden of leadership was too great for Moses to carry alone, he appointed "wise and respected men" (v. 15) in the community to share his ministry. These leaders, with authority over as few as 10 and as many as thousands, were responsible to "hear disputes" and to "judge fairly."

Moses laid down basic principles which apply in any leadership role. "Do not show partiality in judging; hear both small and great alike. Do not be afraid of any man, for judgment belongs to God" (v. 17).

Leaders are not to be influenced by fear of what others will think, or by the position held by any woman or man. Each person is to be valued alike; each is to be heard. God's will is to be the ultimate consideration in how the leader leads and what he does, for God is the ultimate Judge.

Face reality (Deut. 1:19-25). Here Moses

explained something of his motives for sending spies into the Promised Land. His original impulse had been to simply point to the land, and command the people to "charge!"

"See," Moses said, "the Lord your God has given you the land. Go up and take possession of it as the Lord, the God of your fathers, told you. Do not be afraid, do not be discouraged" (v. 21).

But the people wanted to send spies ahead, "to bring back a report about the route we are to take and the towns we will come to."

Moses did not stop to inquire of God what he should do. He simply liked the people's idea, and acted on it.

Was Moses wrong? Not necessarily. It's never wrong to find out as much as we can ahead of time about decisions we need to make. As long as when we do we are not overcome by the problems we foresee. After all, God is the ultimate reality, so whatever the difficulties that seem to lie ahead as we follow God's leading we need not be afraid or discouraged.

In fact, these two warnings uttered by Moses ("do not be afraid; do not be discouraged"), are warnings for us today. It is not facing realities in our lives that gives us problems. It's how we react to what we see. Because God truly is with us, and we live by His promises to us, we can remain confident and calm. We can enter our own promised lands, unfrightened by difficulties and undiscouraged by setbacks.

♥ ***Link to Life: Youth / Adult***

You might want to hold a debate over this passage. Resolved: "Moses made a tragic mistake when he listened to the people and sent spies ahead into the Promised Land."

There are good arguments for the negative as well as the positive of this resolution. For instance, it wasn't having information about Canaan that created the problem—it was how the people reacted to what they discovered (see Rom. 4:18-21).

After the debate, have a general discussion. How should you and I go about making decisions? Should we try to look ahead and determine difficulties? Should we move on blindly? How large a role should circumstances have in our making of decisions? Should we really take circumstances as indicators of God's will?

Fear is an enemy of faith (Deut. 1:26-46). The people of Israel had been terrified when the spies reported how strong the peoples of Canaan were militarily. Their fear led them to even doubt God: "The Lord hates us," they cried (v. 27).

Moses simply called on the people to remember all that God had done for them, and to let thoughts of His faithfulness bring back their confidence. Moses' words to Israel are wonderful words for us too.

"Do not be terrified; do not be afraid of them. The Lord your God, who is going before you, will fight for you, as He did for you in Egypt, before your very eyes, and in the desert. There you saw how the Lord your God carried you, as a father carries his son, all the way you went until you reached this place" (vv. 29-31).

The problem with Israel was that despite all the evidence of God's care, they still would not trust in Him (v. 32). Their rebellion was a direct result of a fear that flared up into a terror so great that they could no longer see God as He truly is.

This passage speaks to you and me too. When fears come—and they will—we are to look away from what causes us terror to remember who God is, and what wonderful things He has done for us. The memory of God's work in our lives is to quiet our fears, and restore our trust.

♥ ***Link to Life: Youth / Adult***

One of the ways that Christians can encourage each other to trust the Lord is to share personal experiences we have had of His faithfulness.

Read Deuteronomy 1:26-31 aloud. Then ask each person to rewrite *verses 29-31, as if Moses were speaking to him or her about something he has personally experienced in his walk with God.*

When the new paragraphs are written, go around the circle and ask each person to share what he or she has written. Talk about the experiences mentioned in each of their paragraphs, trying to help each other sense those ways that God has demonstrated His faithfulness to each of you.

God shares our wildernesses (Deut. 2:1-13). When the people of Israel had rebelled and refused to enter the Promised Land, God turned them toward the wilderness. There they would wander until the entire generation of rebels died.

But looking back on those wilderness years Moses said, "The Lord your God has blessed you in all the work of your hands. He has watched over your journey through this vast desert. These 40 years the Lord your God has been with you, and you have not lacked anything" (v. 7). Later Moses would add, "Your clothes did not wear out and your feet did not swell during these 40 years" (8:4).

There is no question that the years in the wilderness were harsh and painful. They were years of discipline, marked by daily deaths of those who had rebelled against God.

How stunning to realize that God "watched over [their] journey" and that in all those 40 years "the Lord [their] God [had] been with [them]."

God doesn't abandon us even when He is angry with us and forced to discipline. Even in the darkest of times there is evidence of His continuing love.

The evidence in Israel was in the smaller things. Their feet did not swell. Their clothing, which could not have been replaced in the desert's hot, empty lands, did not wear out. It was in such little things, as well as in the manna God supplied daily and in the presence of the cloudy-fiery pillar over the tabernacle, that God showed His presence and His love.

♥ ***Link to Life: Youth / Adult***

Ask your group members to think back on a dry and empty time in their lives. How did they feel then about God? Near—or distant? Loved—or abandoned?

Let those who wish share about those experiences.

Then read Deuteronomy 2:7 and 8:4. Point out that even in the wilderness God stayed close to His people, tenderly caring for them, even when they did not sense His closeness.

Talk then about the little ways that God may have communicated His love and presence to your group members in their desert experiences.

Helping your group be aware of and sensitive to little evidences of God's love can make a vital difference in how they may handle the difficult times in life in the future.

Remembering victories (Deut. 2:14–3:20). In this review of history Moses honestly examined Israel's failures and time of discipline. But there are more verses given to the recall of victories than to defeats. It was in the victories that the clearest evidence of God's love and presence are found.

He is present at all times. But how we enjoy Him when the good days come!

Moses' sin (Deut. 3:21-29). In most of this passage Moses speaks of "you," setting himself apart from the people that he led.

But Moses too had failed. The incident is reported in Numbers 20. The company came to a waterless area, and again murmured and quarreled with Moses. God told Moses to gather the people, and to speak to a great rock there, and "it [would] pour out its water."

But Moses instead shouted out, "Listen, you rebels, must we bring you water out of this rock?" Then Moses struck the rock with his staff, twice.

The waters came. But God rebuked Moses. "Because you did not trust in Me enough to honor Me as holy in the sight of the Israelites, you will not bring this community into the land I give them" (Num. 20:12).

Many have debated the cause of God's displeasure. Some suggest that the explanation is found in the fact that the rock was a type of Christ (cf. 1 Cor. 10:4). Moses had struck a rock once before (cf. Ex. 17). This seems to them to represent Christ being stricken on the cross for our sins. To strike the rock twice violated the type, for Jesus' one sacrifice was sufficient. On the basis of that one sacrifice, healing waters flow whenever we call on Him in faith.

Others see the cause of God's anger with Moses in his words, "*We* bring you water." Moses here seems to take the credit for the miracle for himself and Aaron, and not give the credit to God.

Whatever the explanation, God was angered. Moses had been told to speak, and Moses disobeyed. He struck it rather than spoke to it.

A person who expects to lead others to trust God enough to obey Him must himself trust enough to obey—completely.

Deuteronomy 3 tells us how much the

punishment hurt Moses. He pleaded with God. "O Sovereign Lord, You have begun to show Your servant Your greatness and Your strong hand. . . . Let me go over and see the good land beyond the Jordan" (3:24-25). Moses yearned to see *all* that God would do for His people.

But it was not to be.

Moses was allowed to climb a height across the Jordan River and look out on the land. But God told him, "You are not going to cross this Jordan."

Moses finally accepted what must be. And he had one of his greatest fears relieved. God would appoint another leader who would lead the people across the river, and cause them to inherit the land (v. 28).

How good to know that you and I are not the only ones who can carry out what God intends for His people, or even for our own families. God is able to work with us as long as we trust Him. But even if we are set aside, as Moses was, God's work will not be hindered or destroyed.

Continue to obey (Deut. 4:1-14). As Moses concluded his review of the past, he looked ahead to the future. The men and women who heard Moses speaking that day were those who "held fast to the Lord [their] God." They were alive; the generation that turned its hold on God loose and surrendered to fear had rebelled, and their bodies all lay in the wilderness.

Moses was about to teach again the laws and decrees of God. If the new generation would follow the laws and decrees, they would continue to be blessed with success.

The passage points out two purposes which God had in giving Israel His Law. First, obedience would bring the people blessing. But second, an obedient Israel was intended to be a witness to the world.

If Israel observed the laws of God carefully, Moses declared, "This will show your wisdom and understanding to the nations, who will hear about all these decrees and say, 'Surely this great nation is a wise and understanding people.' What other nation is so great as to have their gods near them the way the Lord our God is near us whenever we pray to Him? And what other nation is so great as to have such righteous decrees and laws as this body of laws I am setting before you today?" (4:6-8)

As long as Israel did not let God's Law slip from their hearts, but obeyed it, they would be a beacon to a lost humanity. In Israel God intended to display His beauty to the entire world.

But Israel would never respond fully to God. There might be flashing moments of greatness—in this second Exodus generation, in David and his kingdom—but history records a great darkness as the people of God again and again turned away from God's Word.

Their witness was not only lost, but their misunderstanding of the meaning of God's call and His Law became so great that Paul was forced to say, as had the earlier prophets, "God's name is blasphemed among the Gentiles because of you" (Rom. 2:24; cf. also Isa. 52:5; Ezek. 36:22).

♥ ***Link to Life: Youth / Adult***

How important is a Christian's life to his or her witness? This passage suggests that the ancient world was to be convinced of the greatness of God not by Israel's preaching, but by her commitment to living out His Law. The evidence of such a national and personal life would compel admiration for God.

Is it the same today? What is the most compelling witness that Christians can give to Jesus?

To help your group grapple with this question, you might:

- *Read and talk about this Old Testament passage.*
- *Share conversion experiences. What influenced each of your group members to accept Jesus? Was it something impersonal? A relationship with a friend or relative? How important was that person's life and character? Can it be expressed in percentages—70 percent of his or her life, 30 percent of his or her words?*
- *Look at John 13:34-35. What does Jesus suggest will compel the world to acknowledge His reality and presence among His people?*

In fact, both a verbal witness and a life-witness are important in sharing Jesus with others. What is important is that our lives back up and demonstrate all that we say about Jesus. Showing people Jesus, and telling them about Him, are inseparable parts of effective evangelism.

No Idols—God: Deuteronomy 4:15-40 From the time of the Exodus on through the final Captivity and destruction of the kingdom of Judah in 586 B.C.—a span of some 850 years—the people of God would be plagued by idolatry.

Again and again they would desert the worship of God to follow pagan practices, entranced by the open sensuality of such religions and insensitive to the reality of a God who could not be touched or seen.

In this Deuteronomy passage Moses warned against making "an idol, an image of any shape, whether formed like a man or woman, or like any animal" (vv. 16-17). Moses looked ahead here, to foretell both Israel's failure and her punishments. But he also infused his warning with promise. When "all these things have happened to you, then in later days you will return to the Lord your God and obey Him" (v. 30). Even though the people would be unfaithful, God would remain true (v. 31).

Idolatry (Deut. 4:15-31). The *Expository Dictionary of Bible Words* has this to say about idolatry:

> The idol, or image, is anything that one may shape for use as an object of worship. The basic reason for this prohibition is that idols necessarily distort one's concept of God, who is Spirit (John 4:24) and who must be worshiped in harmony with His nature. Human beings who worship idols are led from dependence on God to reliance on something that expresses their own religious thoughts and motivations. In Isaiah 2:8-22 the prophet asserts that idolatry is an expression of human pride and arrogance. He insists, "Stop trusting in man, who has but a breath in his nostrils. Of what account is he?" (v. 22)
>
> Though idolatry is essentially a spiritual sin, representing rejection of the true God, it is a sin that has moral implications. This is seen clearly in Romans 1:18-32. Here Paul clearly rejects the theory that idolatry is a "primitive" religion, which in time must naturally develop into higher forms. Paul portrayed mankind as having a knowledge of God but suppressing the truth by their wickedness (v. 18). People reject creation's testimony to the Creator and, instead of worshiping and thanking Him, create images to worship. This rejection of God cuts human beings off from a knowledge of their own moral character and denies them a standard against which to measure choices. Consequently humans turn to all forms of immorality (vv. 26-27) and sin (vv. 28-31). Deep within these God-rejectors is a sense of sin, but rejection of a knowledge of God renders them unable and unwilling to sense Him.
>
> This process of alienation had its culminating expression in Canaan, and in Canaanite religion. Yet it was in Canaan that God led the Israelites to settle. The stern warnings against idolatry and the original inhabitants' practices linked with idolatry are found throughout the Old Testament. These passages, which use some 10 different Hebrew words for "idol" and "image," are found in nearly every book in the Bible up to the time of Captivity.
>
> The Exile purged Israel: after the Exile, idolatry held no attraction to Israel. For a powerful satire on the futility of idolatry, see Isaiah 44:6-23.
>
> Idolatry was widespread in the world of the first century. Paul warned believers to stay away from events featuring idol worship (1 Cor. 10:14). Though the idol has no real existence (v. 19; 12:2; Gal. 4:8; 1 Thes. 1:9) and idol worship accomplishes nothing (1 Cor. 10:19), demonic beings are involved in pagan worship (vv. 10-22), and immorality was often interwoven (vv. 6-13).

The remedy (Deut. 4:32-40). What is the remedy for idolatry in all its forms? This last chapter of Deuteronomy's prelude informs us.

We are to look back into history, and realize all God has done for us in this world of space and time. "Has anything so great as this ever happened?" Has any other God ever spoken? Or created a nation out of slaves by miracles and power?

All this, Moses explained, was "because He [God] loved your forefathers and chose their descendants after them" (v. 37). God had acted because of His ever-faithful covenant love.

In view of all this, Israel, and you and I, are to "acknowledge and take to heart this day that the Lord is God in heaven above and on earth below. There is no other."

Because we have a living God, we trust Him alone and keep His commandments.

TEACHING GUIDE

Prepare
Memorize Deuteronomy 4:39: "Acknowledge and take to heart this day that the Lord is God in heaven above and on the earth below. There is no other."

Explore
Give a minilecture overview of Deuteronomy, drawing on material in this guide. You can find additional helpful material in the Scripture Press *Bible Knowledge Commentary,* pages 259-323.

Expand
This introductory Deuteronomy passage touches on many different themes. Any or several might be developed as an effective group study. So consider the makeup of your own group, and their needs as you know them. Then pick one or two of the following activities to use when you meet.

1. How do we claim God's promises? Help your group learn and do with the "link-to-life" process outlined on page 139.
2. What is the role of circumstance in Christian decision-making? Young adults are often concerned about discerning God's will and making choices that will affect their futures. The study suggested on page 140 gives an extremely practical study of Deuteronomy 1:19-25.
3. How can we encourage each other to press on? Everyone faces moments of decision. How can we help each other respond to God when we sense His will? Let Moses' encouragement of Israel teach your group how to help each other to a deeper trust in the Lord. The process to follow is outlined in "link-to-life," page 140.
4. Can we still sense God when everything goes wrong? Help your group members look back to their wilderness times, and discover the little things that showed Jesus still loved them, and still was with them. See page 141.
5. How do we witness most effectively? By word, or by life? To help your group members learn how to share Christ effectively and to evaluate their own conversions, follow the "link-to-life" ideas on page 142.

Apply
Moses concludes this preamble to the constitution of Israel with a call to reject all idols in favor of the living God.

Like him we are to "acknowledge and take to heart this day that the Lord is God in heaven above and on the earth below" (Deut. 4:39).

Write this verse on a chalkboard and have your group members repeat it. Then remove it by erasing a word at a time, but each time have the group repeat the whole verse. By the time it is erased, they will have memorized this key Bible affirmation.

Close with prayer, asking God to help each of you take to heart in your todays the reality of the God who is Lord—above, and on the earth below as well.

STUDY GUIDE 19

Deuteronomy 5–11

THE FOUNDATION IS LOVE

Overview
Following the form of ancient treaties, Moses now introduced the *basic stipulations* which explained how persons were to live in relationship with God under Law.

To this expression of underlying principle, the Old Testament brings one dominant theme: the theme of love. We cannot understand the Old Testament or its Law without seeing it in love's perspective, as a way of working out our relationships with God and with other human beings.

▶ ***Jealous.*** Here we meet the idea of God as a jealous person. What does this term mean? The Hebrew root portrays a very strong emotion, even a passionate desire. In a negative sense the emotion is directed against another person, or when directed to an object, is *envy*. There is a positive aspect when the Old Testament speaks of God's jealousy. In this case jealousy is intense love: a high level of commitment that demands expression in a relationship which excludes all others.

No wonder God said to Israel, "I, the Lord your God, am a jealous God" (Ex. 20:5). God loved Israel as He loves us, totally and completely. And He asks that we love Him in this same, intense way.

To memorize: "Hear, O Israel: The Lord our God, the Lord is one. Love the Lord your God with all your heart and with all your soul and with all your strength" (Deut. 6:4-5).

■ See the *Bible Knowledge Commentary*, pages 272-283 for a verse-by-verse commentary on this section.

Commentary
The other day one of the neighborhood children went to court. The judge warned him: "Once more, and you'll be locked up." That very afternoon, that same 13-year-old stole money from our car to buy a birthday present. And that evening he insisted, "Mom doesn't really love me."

Young Nat needs love. But he is constantly testing the limits: constantly pushing to see how far he can go before the inevitable rejection. Sure that he's not loved, Nat is driven to prove over and over that he is right about his unloveliness. When he is rejected or disciplined because of his actions, he confirms what he has decided his identity to be.

I have another friend who was brought up in a home without love. Married now, she is unable to express love for her husband, or to sense his love for her. The cause has been traced and understood. But the void that lovelessness has left in her personality has scarred her and, against her will, has hurt others as well.

The effects of lack of love have been noted and traced by generations of psychologists—and myriads of sufferers. Some substitute food for affection, and grow fat. Others feel worthless, unable to value a personality that their parents rejected. Still others are driven to prove themselves and try to earn love by accomplishments that stretch their nerves and energies to the breaking point. No wonder social psychologist Abraham Maslow places a need for "love and belongingness" as a basic need of the human personality; a need which must be met if a person is to grow toward becoming his potential self.

"Do I belong [acceptance]?" and "Am I loved?" are perhaps two of the most basic questions that can be asked in thinking about *any* relationship. It's not surprising, then, to realize that these basic questions are answered for Israel in an unmistakable way. Moses, speaking to a new generation of Hebrews about to cross into the Promised Land, brought into clearest focus God's great assurance, "You are loved!" (Deut. 7:7-8) The heritage of the Jews was a living heritage—God Himself, walking in personal relationship with them.

Sometimes you feel unloved and unaccepted. So do I. But something both of us need to do is to learn that we *are* loved: "When my father and my mother forsake me, then the Lord will take me up" (Ps. 27:10, KJV).

As we teach these vital chapters of Deuteronomy, let's remember that these same affirmations of love are made to you and to me. We too have a heritage in our personal relationship with God through Jesus Christ. In Him we are accepted and loved.

♥ ***Link to Life: Youth / Adult***

Go around the group and ask each person to think of one time he or she felt loved. When each person has identified a time, break into teams of four or five, letting each person share.

Back in the whole group, go around the circle asking each to talk briefly about how love or lack of love in his childhood home affects him now.

This simple activity will help your group members come to know each other on a deeper level, and will also help them realize the importance of love in each human being's life. What important preparation for study of this vital Deuteronomy passage that focuses on God's love!

Loved and Loving: Deuteronomy 5–6

In Deuteronomy 4, Moses explained God's deliverance of this generation's parents from Egypt this way: "Because He loved your forefathers [referring to Abraham, Isaac, and Jacob] and chose their descendants after them, He brought you out of Egypt by His presence, and His great strength" (4:37). The love God had for these men, who lived on in their descendants, led to a deep commitment on God's part that extended across the centuries.

But in chapter 5 we see a new and striking emphasis. Moses moved from history to Israel's *now.* He insisted that God sought relationship "not with our fathers" with whom the Law covenant was made, "but with us, with all of us who are alive here today" (v. 3). It is this relationship that these next chapters of Scripture help us understand.

The nature of the relationship (Deut. 5). Several elements of relationship with God are defined.

(1) *Love is personal (5:1-3).* The relationship is between "us, who are . . . alive here," and Yahweh, who is also here and living. Often a person grows up in a home where the Lord is God of his parents. His relationship with God is through Mom and Dad; he goes to church because they do. This falls short of a love relationship. One who cares for us wants to reach out and touch us personally, not through others. God wants to know and to love us personally, warmly, intimately—with nothing and no one between.

(2) *Love is urgent (5:4-14).* The urgency of the relationship is emphasized in the first four of the Ten Commandments, all of which are repeated here from Exodus 20. God wants our eyes fixed on Him. As any lover, God is unwilling to share our affection with competitors.

It's hard to imagine a husband who truly loves his wife unaffected by her unfaithfulness, or encouraging her to date around. Truly intimate love is to be exclusive. God wants and helps us to love other people (even as a good husband/wife relationship enriches the context of the home for their children). But God will not share us with other gods—whether they be idols of the ancient world or the financial success of the modern.

(3) *Love is demonstrated (5:15).* Love that lets us feel our belongingness must be demonstrated. How clearly God had demonstrated to this generation His personal and practical involvement with them: "God brought you out of there with a mighty hand and an outstretched arm."

Christ is the ultimate demonstration of God's love for us. But each of us can find many other special ways in which God has acted in our lives to show His love.

♥ ***Link to Life: Youth / Adult***

Your group may have shared how they have experienced love from others or their parents. Why not share what has communicated a sense of God's love?

(4) *Love is expressive (5:16-20).* It is hard to feel loved when we don't really know what is going on inside a person who claims to love us. In this restatement of the Ten

Commandments, we see God's willingness to communicate His expectations. This communication was first heard at Sinai with fear, but also with a certain responsiveness that pleased the Lord. "All that the Lord our God will speak to you," the people told Moses, "we will hear and do" (Deut. 5:27).

Love communicates and expresses; love desires a response. What is even more significant for us in our relationship with God is this: God wants to help us grow in our own capacity to love. As we saw earlier, these manward commandments are rooted in God's own concern for men. As we listen to Him and respond to His Law, we grow in our ability to love others.

This is an important thing to see. A person who loves another desires to see him grow. We can be utterly sure that God loves us because His every word to us is designed to help us grow to our full potentials.

(5) *Love is unselfish (5:21-33)*. This last element of real love is affirmed in these verses. God enters into relationship with us, and speaks to us "that it might go well with" us. As verse 33 summarizes, you shall "walk in all the way that the Lord your God has commanded you, so that you may live and prosper and prolong your days in the land that you will possess."

People who come into personal relationship with God are not pawns in some cosmic game. We are not His playthings. No, God's love for us is unselfish. He honestly has our best interests at heart.

All this helped Israel realize that it did have a personal relationship with the Lord, and that God truly did care. This people was loved. And so are we.

Perhaps your parents, or your spouse, have never let you know how deeply you are loved. Perhaps they haven't truly cared. But through Christ you can have a personal relationship with God Himself, in which you are loved and do belong. Personally, urgently, practically, expressively, unselfishly, God Himself says to you and to me today: "You are loved."

The communication of relationship (Deut. 6). The people of Israel who stood on the plains across the Jordan and heard Moses' words knew they were true. They knew from personal experience.

Many of them had as children seen God's acts of judgment on Egypt. They had all eaten the manna, all followed the fiery cloud, all participated in the victory over Moab. Every one had evidence of God's presence and of His concern.

But when this generation crossed the River Jordan, many things would change. The manna would cease, and they would begin to eat the corn of that land. The cloud that guided them would be gone. There would be victories, but the daily evidence of God's supernatural presence would be removed. This generation knew from direct, personal experience, that they truly were special to God. But how could they communicate to the generation to come the specialness of their relationship with God? How do we, who know God now, share His reality with others, and help them to experience Him as real?

(1) *We give God priority (6:1-9)*. The reality of God's love can only be communicated by those who give Him priority. The central command here is, "Love the Lord your God with all your heart" (v. 5). All flows from this, for such a love leads to a unique lifestyle.

This passage is a crucial one:

> Love the Lord your God with all your heart and with all your soul and with all your strength. These commandments that I give you today are to be upon your hearts. Impress them on your children. Talk about them when you sit at home and when you walk along the road, when you lie down and when you get up.
>
> Deuteronomy 6:5-8

First, the lover of God responds to Him. This means that we take the words He speaks to us in our today, and write them "on our hearts." Memorization isn't in view here. Instead the verse calls on us to make God's words a part of our lives: to let His teachings reshape our values and our attitudes and our ways.

Second, we share that which has taken root in our lives with persons we are close to. *You* shall teach them (God's words) diligently to *your* children.

This speaks not only of a parent's responsibility in nurture, but of the nature of the relationship in which God's reality can be shared. It is in a you/your relationship—a very personal relationship between human beings—that the personal nature of God comes through.

Third, the context in which the reality of God is shared is that of daily life and activity. God's words are the touchstone which guide us in life, and we refer to them to explain our actions, our attitudes, and all our ways.

(2) *We assume God's presence (6:10-19).* Here we read of promises and instructions which are to comfort and reassure Israel in the land. The whole tone is one of expectation. God will be with them, even though the miracles have ceased. In this context verse 16 is especially significant: "Do not test the Lord your God, as you did at Massah."

In that incident, recorded in Exodus, the people had rejected the many signs of God's presence and had challenged, "Is the Lord among us, or not?"

The instruction is clear. Believers may not see supernatural evidence of God's presence. But He truly is here. We are to assume His presence, knowing that He has promised never to leave or forsake us.

Sometimes you and I must take God's love on faith. When others see us rejoicing in God's love in spite of circumstances, they too will perceive that He is real.

(3) *We rely on God's provision (6:20-25).* In such a relationship with the Lord, there can be only one answer when "in time to come" sons ask their fathers, "What is the meaning. . . ?" (v. 20) Then the parents are to remind the children of God's action in delivering Israel from Egypt. God is to be glorified as the One who not only provided the land of promise, but who, in that land continues to provide Israel with all she needs.

In the context, then, of a personal relationship with God, adults who have themselves given God priority, trusted Him to be present, and experienced His provision, can communicate the reality of God's love to others.

Ultimately, this is the only way. We can tell others about God. We can even lead them to agree with God's Word. But to bring them to know the Lord as a God who loves and who will welcome them into a personal relationship too, we need more. We need the foundation of our own personal relationship with God. And on that foundation we need to identify ourselves with others and to love them as God Himself loves them.

How thrilling to know that we are loved by God.

How thrilling to be freed by His love to love others. Our heritage is love.

God's Love: Deuteronomy 7–11

Reading through these next chapters is an enriching and freeing experience, for God continually affirms His love for us. There is no better way to sense the affection God pours out than to let His Word speak for itself.

Deuteronomy 7. Once in the land, Israel was to destroy the pagans and their images, lest they draw God's people away from Him. Every alternative to a life of godliness was to be rejected. Why?

> The Lord your God has chosen you out of all the peoples on the face of the earth to be His people, His treasured possession. The Lord did not set His affection on you and choose you because you were more numerous than other peoples, for you were the fewest of all peoples. But it was because the Lord loved you and kept the oath He swore to your forefathers. . . . Know therefore that the Lord your God is God, He is the faithful God, keeping His covenant of love to a thousand generations of those who love Him and keep His commands.
>
> Deuteronomy 7:6-9

Deuteronomy 8. Here God reviewed His discipline of the unresponsive generation. What a purpose that discipline had—and how accompanied it was by love! Why did God discipline? "That He might make you understand that man does not live by bread alone, but man lives by everything that proceeds out of the mouth of the Lord. Your clothing did not wear out on you, nor did your foot swell these 40 years. Thus you are to know in your heart that the Lord your God was disciplining you" (vv. 3-5, NASB). Every stroke of suffering was administered in love.

Deuteronomy 9–10. Israel was again promised full possession of the land. But with the promise came a warning: "Do not say in your heart, when the Lord your God has driven them out before you, 'Because of my righteousness the Lord has brought me in to possess this land' " (9:4, NASB).

Israel was then reminded of its history of

unresponsiveness, and warned. Then, in touching words, God again showed how deeply He loved this people, even though they had been rebellious. In an extended and touching section, the place of love in God's actions, and the role love is to play in Israel's lifestyle under Law, is reaffirmed.

> And now, Israel, what does the Lord your God require from you, but to fear the Lord your God, to walk in all His ways and love Him, and to serve the Lord your God with all your heart and with all your soul, and to keep the Lord's commandments and His statutes which I am commanding you today for your good? Behold, to the Lord your God belong heaven and the highest heavens, the earth and all that is in it. Yet on your fathers did the Lord set His affection to love them, and He chose their descendants after them, even you above all peoples, as it is this day. Circumcise then your heart, and stiffen your neck no more. For the Lord your God is the God of gods and the Lord of lords, the great, the mighty, and the awesome God who does not show partiality, nor take a bribe. He executes justice for the orphan and the widow, and shows His love for the alien by giving him food and clothing. So show your love for the alien, for you were aliens in the land of Egypt. You shall fear the Lord your God; you shall serve Him and cling to Him, and you shall swear by His name. He is your praise and He is your God, who has done these great and awesome things for you which your eyes have seen. Your fathers went down to Egypt 70 persons in all, and now the Lord your God has made you as numerous as the stars of heaven.
>
> Deuteronomy 10:12-22, NASB

Chapter 11 states the conclusion: "You shall therefore love the Lord your God" (11:1, NASB).

Love, because you are loved.

Respond, because God has acted for you.

Lay up God's words in your heart—because God has laid you on His heart.

Believers are loved, and are to be loving.

This too is part of the redemption message to humankind. Out of slavery into freedom. Growing through discipline to finally understand. God loves us. God accepts us. God has chosen us as His own. You and I stand secure, surrounded by the love of God.

TEACHING GUIDE

Prepare
Read and meditate on Deuteronomy 10:14-22.

Explore
1. Begin your group study by thinking together about your own experiences of love. Use the "link-to-life" activity on page 146 or simply ask, "How has love or the lack of love affected your life?"
2. Give a minilecture on the need of human beings for love. You can use the illustration of Nat with which the chapter begins. You can also explain psychologist Abraham Maslow's, "hierarchy of human motivations." The theory is outlined on the chart on page 150.

Maslow suggests that lower order needs must be satisfied before a person will respond to higher motivations. For example, if physical needs are not being met, there will be little motivation to achieve or to be creative. All energy will be focused on finding food and shelter.

The need for love is expressed in each of the next two levels. To be loved adds to our security. To feel accepted, to know that we belong, frees us to reach out to others and to contribute to others' lives. But if a person does not experience love, rather than being able to reach out or achieve, he or she will necessarily focus energy on his or her own needs.

This theory is, of course, not necessarily "truth." But it does point up something we all know—that we need to love and be loved.

How wonderful that God, moved by love, showed Israel by His actions how much He loved this people, and showed Israel in the Law how they could love Him.

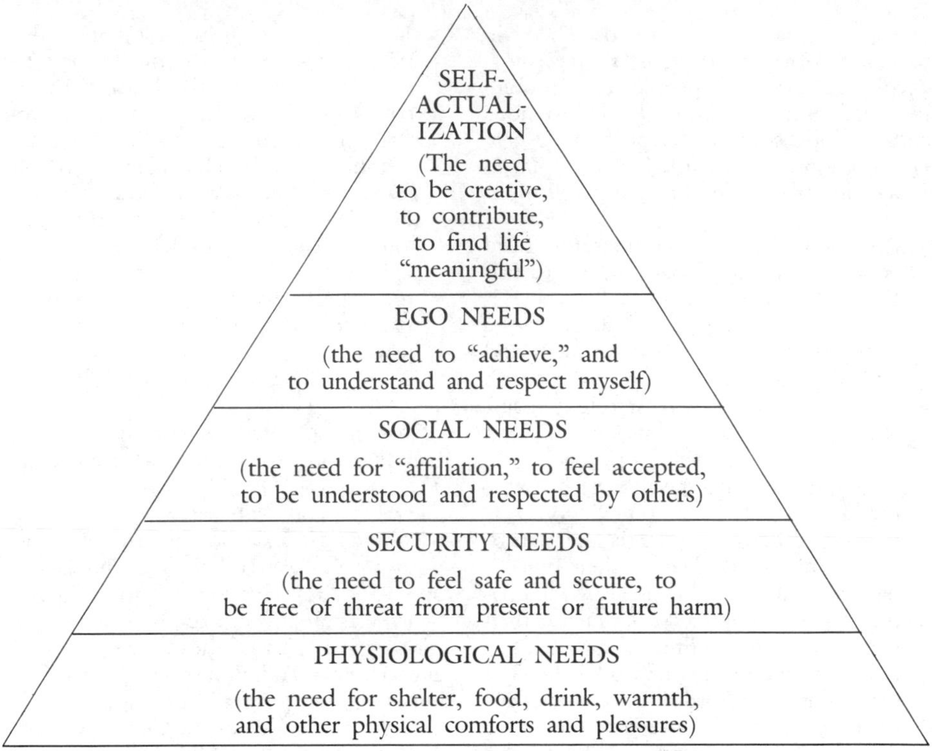

Maslow's Hierarchy of Human Motivations

Expand

1. Let your group members choose whether to focus on *being loved* or *loving*. Use the categories marked off in the text by numbers (e.g., [1], [2], etc.) as an outline. Assign those who want to look at *being loved* Deuteronomy 5, and those who want to look at *loving* Deuteronomy 6.

After they study the text have the teams report to each other what they learned, and suggest two ways in which what they learned can be applied.

2. Have your group imagine they are members of Moses' audience as this sermon is preached to them. Read aloud Deuteronomy 7, asking your members to listen as if hearing for the first time. Then discuss: "How would these words lead you to feel about your relationship with God? How would they lead you to feel about yourself as a worthwhile person?"

Apply

Give each person in class a copy of Deuteronomy 10:12-22. Have each person read the text carefully, and *underline* any statements which they believe God is saying to them now, as well as to Israel.

In conclusion, go around the group and ask each person to share one such statement, and express what that word from God means to him or her.

Close in prayer, thanking God for His certain love.

STUDY GUIDE 20

Deuteronomy 12–26

WAYS OF WORSHIP

Overview

This section of Deuteronomy contains the *detailed stipulations* of the covenant which governed the relationship between God and His Old Testament people.

Chapters 5–11 of Deuteronomy affirmed the basic principle of love which God's gift of Law expresses. Then Moses reviewed the Law given earlier at Sinai, and highlighted specific ways in which God's people could express their love for Him. In essence this chapter explores a variety of ways of worship: ways in which God's people can honor, glorify, and love the Lord their God.

Ways of Worship

One place	chapters 12; 16
One God	chapters 13; 17–18
Tithes	chapters 12; 14
Clean and Unclean	chapters 14; 23
Compassion	chapters 15; 24–25
Justice	chapter 19
War	chapter 20

▶ ***Worship.*** In the Old Testament, "worship" is usually *sahah,* "to bow down" or "to prostrate oneself out of respect." *'Asab,* "to serve," is also translated "worship." The underlying idea is to show respect and reverence, not only in a worship service where God is praised, but in every aspect of one's life.

Our lives are to be expressions of worship of God.

▶ ***Tithe.*** Ten percent of all that the Prom ised Land produced was to be set aside by Israelites as "holy to the Lord" and to be used as He commanded.

Commentary

The people of Israel, who were so deeply loved by God, were to return that love in worship–by showing respect and reverence for God in every way.

In these chapters of Deuteronomy we find a number of mixed themes—special instructions about tithes, about ritual cleanness, about war, justice, and compassion. At first glance they seem unrelated. But what ties them together is the fact that every action commanded describes another aspect of a life so intimately linked to God that all the godly Israelite said and did could be considered an act of worship.

As you plan to teach from this section, it's possible to survey these themes, or to focus on any one of them which seems to suggest ways in which Christians can show loving respect for our God today.

One Place: Deuteronomy 12; 16

Many of the ritual elements of Israel's worship are explained by a simple phrase we find repeated in Deuteronomy 12. "You must not worship the Lord your God in their way" (vv. 4, 31). The worship of God must be as distinct from the worship of pagan idols as God Himself is from dead wood and stone.

A basic feature of pagan worship was its localization. The peoples of Canaan called their gods *Baals,* a word which means "master" or "owner." The baals were thought of as owners of their area—a hillside, a valley, a plot of land, or a larger section of territory. One worshiped the local Baal as an act of respect, for it was thought to control the fruitfulness of the land.

Because of this localized concept of a deity's rights and powers, Canaan under the pagans was filled with "high places"—spots on the tops of hills or groves of trees set aside for worship of the local deity.

Many years later, when the Assyrians resettled the Northern Kingdom of Israel after deporting most of its Jewish inhabitants, the people resettled there took up the worship of Yahweh along with worship of their old gods. They did not do this because they respected Yahweh as Lord God Almighty. They did it because He was viewed as the God of that land, and it was wise to show respect for One who controlled the fertility of the fields they plowed!

But God is God of the whole earth. His sovereign power extends over all! To truly worship God, His overarching sovereignty must be acknowledged and He must be worshiped for who He truly is. God is no local diety—and it would be totally inappropriate for Him to be worshiped as if He were nothing more than God of these few trees, that plot of land.

So God commanded Israel that, when they entered the land of Canaan, they were to "destroy completely all the places on the high mountains and on the hills and under every spreading tree where the nations you are dispossessing worship their gods" (v. 2). In place of these localized places of worship, God promised to choose one place where He would put His name. "To that place you must go; there bring your burnt offerings and sacrifices" (vv. 5-6). This command is repeated and underlined (vv. 11-14). Israel was to worship "only at the place the Lord will chose in one of your tribes."

When the people first entered the land they worshiped wherever the tabernacle was located. That was the one place where God met with His people, and where the sacrifices the Law ordained could be made. Some 400 years would pass before David established Jerusalem as his capital city, and set aside a mount on which his son Solomon would build the promised temple of God.

Deuteronomy 16 reviews again the three pilgrim festivals, religious feasts which were to be held annually at the central place of worship. Here again the "one place" theme is repeated. "You must not sacrifice the Passover in any town the Lord your God gives you except in the place He will choose as a dwelling for His name" (vv. 5-6).

What is the significance for us of these crystal clear instructions to Israel? Primarily they serve as a reminder of the wonders that are now ours as Jesus' people.

Corporate worship in Israel was to be focused in the one place on earth where God's presence was established. But where is God present today? God is present in His people—God has come in the person of the Holy Spirit and taken up residence in you and me!

No wonder Jesus taught, "Where two or three come together in My name, there am I with them" (Matt. 18:20).

For many today, "worship" is an experience generated by the stately music and quiet surroundings of some beautiful sanctuary. The church is just a building, and worship is a Sunday kind of thing. But we Christians do not worship God in their way!

Instead we gather together, realizing that we ourselves are the church and that Jesus, living in each one, is the living focus of our praise.

In Old Testament times God's special presence was in one place. Today His special presence is felt whenever we who love Jesus come together to worship and honor our Lord.

One God: Deuteronomy 13; 17–18

Again and again Moses emphasized the total commitment to God that personal relationship with Him demands. "If your very own brother, or your son or daughter, or the wife you love, or your closest friend secretly entices you, saying, 'Let us go and worship other gods' . . . do not yield to him or listen to him. Show him no pity. Do not spare him or shield him. You must certainly put him to death. Your hand must be the first in putting him to death" (13:6-9).

It was absolutely essential for the spiritual future of Israel to maintain a complete and total commitment to God.

However, God carefully protected His people against the kind of thing that marked the Spanish Inquisition—false and anonymous accusation. Deuteronomy 17 repeats the command that a person who traffics with other gods should be put to death, but specifies "on the testimony of two or three witnesses a man shall be put to death, but no one shall be put to death on the testimony of only one witness." And then "the hands of the witnesses must be the first in putting him to death" (vv. 6-7).

What might be so attractive as to turn the hearts of the Israelites to pagan gods? One answer of course is found in the immorality which was associated with Canaanite religious rites. But another is located in man's sense of helplessness in a universe too big for control. One aspect of pagan religions was their suggestion that through magical means a person might gain control over his or her environment and other persons. Through the seers and diviners of paganism people were offered some insight into the future, and some hope of controlling or guarding themselves from future events.

Twice in these chapters Moses dealt with the question of those who seemed to have some supernatural powers that offered supernatural help and guidance.

The key passage is found in Deuteronomy 18, and is the background against which we must understand the role of the prophet in Israel.

> When you enter the land the Lord your God is giving you, do not learn to imitate the detestable ways of the nations there. Let no one be found among you who sacrifices his son or daughter in the fire, who practices divination or sorcery, interprets omens, engages in witchcraft, or casts spells, or who is a medium or spiritist or consults the dead. Anyone who does these things is detestable to the Lord, and because of these detestable practices the Lord your God will drive out those nations before you. You must be blameless before the Lord.
>
> Deuteronomy 18:9-13

While God's people were forbidden to consult pagan or occult sources for information, God knew that there would be times when the written Law did not provide enough guidance to know God's will in a specific situation.

So Moses promised that the Lord would raise up for them a prophet like him from among their own brothers. They must listen to him (v. 18).

The prophet, then, would be God's own spokesman, giving Israel the guidance required to live in a given situation in the will of God. As God said, "I will put My words in his mouth, and he will tell them everything I command him" (v. 18).

There was no reason, ever, to turn to pagan gods. God was ready and able to meet every need of His dearly loved people.

These chapters also tell the Israelites how to distinguish a true prophet from a false prophet. These tests are:

- The prophet must be an Israelite "from among your own brothers" (v. 18).
- He will "speak in My name," and anyone who prophesied in the name of other gods was to be put to death (v. 20).
- What he says will happen will actually take place, for "if what a prophet proclaims in the name of the Lord does not take place or come true, that is a message the Lord has not spoken." Such pseudoprophets are not to be feared, for the words of a true prophet will always come true (v. 22).
- Anyone who encourages the following of other gods, even if he works miracles, is to be rejected and put to death. The Word of God stands as an objective test of the prophet's message.

God does meet all the needs of His people. To look elsewhere for guidance or aid is to treat Him with contempt. We are to count on God to meet our every need, for He truly is committed to us.

♥ ***Link to Life: Youth / Adult***

Why do some turn to the occult today? Bring to your group meeting the astrology column from several newspapers. Break into teams of five or six to compare the "advice" in several columns. What do group members observe about the advice? How do items for their "sign" relate to their actual experience?

In the whole group again, share observations. Then discuss: "Why do people turn to the occult for advice? Why are spiritists, palm readers, astrologers, and others so popular? How should Christians, who do believe in a spiritual world, view the occult?"

Then study together Deuteronomy 18:9-22, in the context of the message of chapters 13; 17–18.

How wonderful that God commits Himself to guide us Himself! And how important that we look to Him alone to lead.

Tithes: Deuteronomy 12; 14

The Old Testament speaks of tithes and freewill offerings in its discussion of how God's people can worship the Lord with their possessions. The *Expository Dictionary of Bible Words* summarizes the teaching of this and other Old Testament passages as follows:

At first glance, the concept of tithing seems simple. Leviticus 27:30-33 says: "A tithe of everything from the land, whether grain from the soil or fruit from the trees, belongs to the Lord; it is holy to the Lord. If a man redeems any of his tithe, he must add a fifth of the value to it. The entire tithe of the herd and flock—every tenth animal that passes under the shepherd's rod—will be holy to the Lord. He must not pick out the good from the bad or make any substitution." Ten percent of everything the land produced was to be set aside, to be used as God commanded.

Other passages expand our knowledge of Old Testament tithing. Numbers 18:21-32 instructs that tithes were to be used to maintain the Levites. That tribe was set apart to serve God, and its members were not given a district when Israel possessed the Promised Land. Deuteronomy 12:5-14 and 14:22-29 introduce another tithe, to be collected every third year for local distribution to the needy. Some argue for as many as three separate tithes designated in these passages. It is likely that there were at least two: the annual 10 percent taken for the support of those who served the Lord, and the third-year tithe taken to sustain the widow and orphan.

These tithes were not to be viewed as a burden. They were to express both love and trust for God, as the Lord promised to bless the works of His people's hands (v. 29). Giving was thus no threat to security. In fact, it showed confidence that God would make the land produce. As Malachi announced later to a then struggling generation that withheld the payment of the tithe. " 'Test Me in this,' says the Lord Almighty, 'and see if I will not throw open the floodgates of heaven and pour out so much blessing that you will not have room enough for it' " (Mal. 3:10).

The Old Testament reports giving that goes beyond the tithe. This is most clearly expressed in the *nedabah,* or voluntary contribution. The emphasis here is on a giving that flows spontaneously, expressing devotion to the Lord. It is not a gift given out of a sense of duty, nor to win promised blessings. The voluntary contributions are most often associated with the construction of the tabernacle (Ex. 36) or the temple (1 Chron. 29; Ezra 1:4). Psalm 119:108 speaks of prayer as a voluntary offering, and God is praised for His own generous voluntary offerings to man (68:9), even when His people had not been faithful to their covenant commitments (Hosea 14:4).

The Lord has always been concerned with the heart attitude of worshipers. The grateful believer who did not find the required tithes enough to express his or her devotion was invited to bring freewill offerings as well.

Giving in the Old Testament then was an expression of trust and reliance on the Lord as well as a loving response to Him. The funds collected were used to support Israel's worship, and particularly the priests and Levites who served the temple, and also as a "safety net" for care of the widowed and the poor.

♥ ***Link to Life: Youth / Adult***
How does the tithe in the Old Testament compare and differ from our contemporary concepts of giving?

Begin by asking your group to brainstorm a list of statements about Christian giving. They'll want to include statements on amount to give, motivations, use of money, etc. When a relatively complete picture of giving as your groups understands it has been developed, break up into teams to study the key passages mentioned in the previous quote (Lev. 27:30-33; Num. 18:21-32; Deut. 12:5-14; 14:22-29; 26:12-15).

Each team is to compare and to contrast what they find in the Old Testament with the statements on their list.

Come together and share what each team has found. Then discuss: "What can we learn about giving from the Old Testament? What principles might apply to us today?"

NOTE: The practice of tithing is not taught in the New Testament. The basic passage on giving in the New Testament is 2 Corinthians 8–9.

Clean and Unclean: Deuteronomy 14; 23
The concept of "clean" and "unclean" in these early books of the Old Testament is primarily ritual in nature. That is, ceremoni-

al uncleanness is in mind, which is a state or condition that has an impact on one's relationship with God.

A person who was ceremonially unclean could not take part in the worship ceremonies of Israel.

Later the prophets pick up the concept of uncleanness and apply it to Israel's moral condition (Neh. 7:64; Isa. 59:3; 63:3; Lam. 4:14; Dan. 1:8; Zeph. 3:1; Mal. 1:7, 12). Sin, not ritual, is the thing which ultimately separates human beings from God.

Why was this ritual aspect of cleanness and uncleanness built into the worship of Israel? In part as a teaching aid, to indicate that no one can approach God presumptuously. And in part as another element in a system of laws that was designed to make Israel different from all other nations. Only a people who are separated to God from every competing influence can live out the commitment that covenant life requires.

Compassion: Deuteronomy 15; 24–25

Strikingly, the laws of interpersonal relationship that are emphasized in the Book of Deuteronomy are uniquely compassionate. They stress the care of the poor (15:1-11) and of servants (vv. 12-18).

Just a few samples demonstrate the great sensitivity expressed in these statutes, which help us see that our respect for the Lord is to find expression in our loving care of others.

- "If a man has recently married, he must not be sent to war or have any other duty laid on him. For one year he is to be free to stay at home and bring happiness to the wife he has married" (24:5).
- "Do not take a pair of millstones—not even the upper one—as security for a debt, because that would be taking a man's livelihood as security" (v. 6).
- "Do not take advantage of a hired man who is poor and needy, whether he is a brother Israelite or an alien living in one of your towns. Pay him his wages each day before sunset, because he is poor and is counting on it" (vv. 14-15).
- "When you are harvesting in your field and you overlook a sheaf, do not go back to get it. Leave it for the alien, the fatherless, and the widow" (v. 19).

Chapter 25 introduces the practice of "levirate marriage." A near relative of a man who died childless was to take his widow as a secondary wife. The first child of that union "shall carry on the name of the dead brother so that his name will not be blotted out from Israel" (25:6).

Justice for All: Deuteronomy 19

Instructions concerning cities of refuge are included here too (see the discussion on Num. 35).

Important justice principles are repeated in this chapter. First, in criminal cases, testimony of at least two witnesses is required (Deut. 19:15). Second, in criminal cases a person who brings false charges against another is to be himself punished with whatever penalty is prescribed for the crime (vv. 16-19).

How fascinating if this were applied to civil suits in our own day. A person who filed a false or malicious suit would be liable to pay the person charged the amount he tried to gain.

War: Deuteronomy 20

It's particularly difficult for us to place war in the context of worship. Yet even this feature of Israel's experience was governed by God's loving laws. War is always tragic. Yet in this world, wars come. How good to see that even in the conduct of war God teaches His people to act in a responsible and compassionate way.

What are the unique features of war as it was to be conducted by God's people?

First, when war began a priest was to encourage God's people not to fear: "The Lord your God is the One who goes with you to fight for you against your enemies to give you victory" (20:4). Israel was to rely not on military superiority or advanced weaponry, but on God.

Second, after the exhortation, army officers were to excuse persons who had just married, or built a new home, or planted a new vineyard. In addition "any man afraid or fainthearted" was also excused. Only those with a strong trust in God were invited to battle. The fearful were to go home "so that his brothers will not become disheartened too" (v. 8).

Third, when the army marched to an enemy city, the army was to "make its people an offer of peace" (v. 10). The people of a city that surrendered were not to be harmed, but would become subject to Israel. If the city resisted, the men were to be killed but the women and children spared.

Fourth, when a city was under siege the Israelites were told, "Do not destroy its trees by putting an ax to them, because you can eat their fruit. Do not cut them down. Are the trees of the field people, that you should besiege them?" (vv. 19-20) The land and its productivity were not to be destroyed in battle rage.

Finally, one regulation here has troubled many who find it hard to reconcile with their understanding of God. That is the regulation which says,

> However, in the cities of the nations the Lord your God is giving you as an inheritance, do not leave alive anything that breathes. Completely destroy them—the Hittites, Amorites, Canaanites, Perizzites, Hivites, and Jebusites—as the Lord your God has commanded you.
>
> Deuteronomy 20:16-17

But God went on to explain. These nations so corrupted by paganism and immorality were deserving of divine punishment, even as Sodom and Gomorrah had been. But now God would use Israel as His instrument, not fire that falls from heaven.

Also, complete destruction was a necessity. As the text explains, these peoples must be totally wiped out, "otherwise, they will teach you to follow all the detestable things they do in worshiping their gods, and you will sin against the Lord your God" (v. 18).

The centuries that followed demonstrated the wisdom of the Lord. Israel did not completely destroy the inhabitants of Canaan. And generation after generation was led into idolatry and away from God by the peoples whom Israel allowed to survive.

At heart, worship is not just what happens on a Sunday morning. Worship is that heart reverence for God that finds expression in every aspect of our lives. We do worship God by coming together as His people. But we also worship by turning to Him for guidance rather than to any other source. We worship Him with our possessions. We worship in the compassionate love we show others, and in the totally honest way we deal with disputes. We can even worship in the way we conduct war, showing trust and fearlessness, seeking to save the lives of our enemies, and being careful not to destroy the land from which they must derive a living.

TEACHING GUIDE

Prepare
Read and meditate on what Jesus said about worship recorded in John 4:23-24.

Explore
1. Put the following definition of worship on the chalkboard: *Worship is any way that we honor, love, and show respect for God.*

Ask your group to react to this definition. Do they agree or not? Is the definition specific enough? How do group members think of worship?
2. Introduce the definition of worship given in the *overview* of this lesson, and outline the issues identified there that are covered in Deuteronomy 12–26.

Expand
1. Let group members select from the topics covered in this chapter any areas that interest them. Form teams by interest groups, to examine relevant Old Testament chapters. After 30 minutes let teams report. Supplement their insights from the commentary in the text and verse-by-verse information pages 283-309 of the *Bible Knowledge Commentary*.
2. Or focus on either Old Testament giving or on the occult. Follow the process outlined in "link-to-life" on pages 154 and 153.

Apply
Go around the circle asking each other to complete this sentence: "This week I will worship God by. . . ."

Close in prayer, thanking God for letting us respond to His love and for so many different ways to express our praise.

STUDY GUIDE 21

Deuteronomy 27–34

DESTINY

Overview

Thirty years ago a traveler taking a train across dry and dusty Palestine remarked, "And the Bible calls this a land of milk and honey!"

A man overheard, tapped him on the shoulder, and showed him these words:

> Your children who follow you in later generations and foreigners who come from distant lands will see the calamities that have fallen on the land and the diseases with which the Lord hath afflicted it.
>
> The whole land will be a burning waste of salt and sulfur—nothing planted, nothing sprouting, no vegetation growing on it. It will be like the destruction of Sodom and Gomorrah, Admah and Zeboiim, which the Lord overthrew in fierce anger.
>
> All the nations will ask: "Why has the Lord done this to this land? Why this fierce burning anger?"
>
> Deuteronomy 29:22-24

God had spelled out the principle of love which underlay the Law, and had detailed the specific stipulations of the contract He made with each generation of Israelites. Now the new generation ratified that covenant (Deut. 27), and God spelled out the blessings of obedience (28:1-14). But God also spelled out the tragedies which would surely come if Israel went back on her commitment (vv. 15-68). The treaty was then summarized (chaps. 29–30), and this great Old Testament book concludes with the personal words, and the story of the death of Moses. The message? It is one of commitment. Commitment determines destiny.

Commitment

Earlier, when Israel stood poised at Paran and sent spies to examine Canaan, the people reached a time of decision. God spoke and told them, "Go." And they refused.

On this decision the destiny of that entire generation hinged. Because of their lack of trust in God, their decision was to disobey.

We know how that single act of disobedience—though representative of a basic attitude and lifestyle—forced that generation away from the Promised Land out into the wilderness to die.

But now we're dealing with a new generation, a generation that did "hold fast" to the Lord. This generation was ready and eager to respond to the command to cross the Jordan and to battle for their heritage, Palestine. This new generation had a different heart attitude toward God, and was marked by a different lifestyle. They were a people who trusted God and who were willing to obey. But they too faced an important decision. This decision would express itself not in a single act of obedience or disobedience, but in a continuing pattern of life.

The decision now facing Israel had to do with commitment.

New Testament parallel. We can find a similar point of decision reflected in the Gospels. Jesus had spent a long time with His disciples, and a similar length of time in ministry to the crowds. Then one day He asked the Twelve, "Who do people say the Son of man is?"

He received many apparently flattering answers. John the Baptist. Elijah. Another of the ancient prophets.

Then our Lord asked the Twelve, "Who do you say I am?"

And He received the right, the only adequate, response. "You are the Christ, the Son of the living God."

The disciples knew who Jesus is, and trusted themselves to Him. They had made that initial, critical decision to respond to God's Word about His Son, even as this new, believing Israel was ready to respond to God's Word and to go up into Canaan. But that initial decision, vital as it is, had to be followed up. Jesus said to His disciples:

> If anyone would come after Me, he must deny himself and take up his cross daily and follow Me. For whoever wants to save his life will lose it, but whoever loses his life for Me will save it. What good is it for a man to gain the whole world, and yet lose or forfeit his very self?
>
> Luke 9:23-24

In these words, Jesus sets before believers the second choice: the choice of commitment.

Jesus was spelling out the ultimate impact of that choice on the human personality. If we choose to follow Jesus in daily commitment, we will "save" our lives. We will become the self we potentially are through the presence of God within us.

Or we can make the wrong choice. We can live for ourselves rather than in commitment to Christ. An inevitable result of that choice will be that we lose ourselves. The person we might have been because of intimate relationship with God—our "very self"—will be forfeited.

Commitment determines the destiny ahead in this world for each one of us.

♥ ***Link to Life: Youth / Adult***
Divide your group into several teams. Have each work together to list words and phrases that describe "the kind of people we really want to be." The only criteria for the list is that each of the several team members agree that the item represents something that he or she wants to be or be like personally. When the teams have had 10 or so minutes to work on their lists, come together and compare. You'll find that most items on the lists agree.

Then give individuals 2 minutes to list privately present personal characteristics that they do not *like; that fall short of their ideal self. These will* not *be shared.*

Read the Luke passage, and point out that the bridge between our two selves—the self we are, and the self we want to be—is daily commitment to Jesus. As we surrender our lives and our wills to Jesus, and are obedient to Him, our gain is the new self that each of us wants so badly to be.

For Israel too. As we trace the culminating events in Deuteronomy, we see over and over again how the commitment decision determines the experience of Israel. Ultimately the promised Messiah will come, and all of God's promises to Abraham will be fulfilled. But until then, each generation's choice will determine its own destiny.

Commentary

Blessing or Curse: Deuteronomy 27–29

Covenant entered (Deut. 27). It seems strange to read words like these in this section of Deuteronomy: "You have now become the people of the Lord your God" (v. 9).

Weren't these descendants of Abraham automatically the people of the Lord?

Yes, in one sense.

But in another sense the Hebrews, as a people and as individuals, chose to enter into the relationship with God that was defined by Law. The promise made to Abraham held firm, no matter what a given generation did. But each generation's own experience of God's blessing, and its own relationship with the Lord, was defined by the Mosaic Law Covenant, and that covenant was entered into by personal choice and commitment. Thus the Deuteronomy passage we're studying picks up this critical point, and explains for living Israel for all time the meaning of this commitment decision.

"All of you are standing today in the presence of the Lord your God. . . . In order to enter into a covenant with the Lord your God, a covenant the Lord is making with you this day and sealing with an oath" (29:10, 12).

The Lord is "the Lord *your* God." But only by entering voluntarily into the covenant of Law would an individual or given generation experience the blessings of being "His people."

To mark off this day as special, an appropriate ceremony was determined. Israel was told to act out her commitment in an unmistakable way. When she was over Jordan, the commandments were to be written plainly on large, whitewashed stones. Half the tribes were to stand on Mount Ebal, and shout out "Amen" to the curses pronounced by the Levites for disobedience (cf. 27:15-26). The other half of the tribes were to stand on Mount Gerizim to bless. And an altar was to be built—on the mount of cursing.

Thus commitment was to be marked formally. It was to be a distinct experience, this entering of the covenant, and was to be remembered by the Israelites.

Definition and outcome of commitment (Deut. 28). The definition of commitment given here is extremely simple.

Daily obedience.

We see it over and over. "If you fully obey the Lord your God, and carefully follow all His commands I give you today" (28:1).

It is just as simple to define lack of commitment, or uncommitment.

Daily disobedience.

"If you do not carefully follow all the words of this Law, which are written in this Book, and do not revere this glorious and awesome name" (v. 58).

The decision the believer makes is to live out his commitment to God as daily obedience—or not to do so.

♥ ***Link to Life: Youth / Adult***
As your group members enter ask them to each write down a brief definition of "commitment." Share these and let them talk for a few minutes of the basic nature of commitment. Then put Deuteronomy 28:1, 58 on the chalkboard, side by side.

If you wish, have teams work with concordances to find "obey" and "disobey" in the New Testament. Can they find parallels to these Deuteronomy verses that suggest commitment still is a choice between daily obedience and daily disobedience?

What is the outcome of commitment, for the nation and for the individual? We see it clearly in this chapter.

Obedience brings blessing. For Israel there would be an increase of cattle and crops in the land. Israel's undertakings would prosper. They would be victorious in warfare. God promised, "The Lord will establish you as His holy people, as He promised you on oath, if you keep the commands of the Lord your God, and walk in His ways. Then all the peoples on earth will see that you are called by the name of the Lord" (vv. 9-10).

In serving the Lord "joyfully and gladly" (v. 47), Israel would find her fulfillment.

The men and women Moses spoke to that day beyond the Jordan River did move on. They lived a life of commitment. And their generation received all the blessings that God had promised. Theirs was an experience of true fulfillment.

But their descendants, to whom Moses also spoke through the written Word, did not.

The descendants of this generation turned from serving God, and the very experiences so graphically described in Moses' warnings are inscribed on the record of history. In Deuteronomy 28:15-68 the destiny ahead of Israel is described, and the pivot on which sacred history turns defined. At every point in Israel's history—and in our own personal destiny—the issue is one and the same.

Commitment.

What was the future against which Israel was futilely warned?

> The Lord will send fearful plagues on you and your descendants, harsh and prolonged disasters, and severe and lingering illnesses. He will bring upon you all the diseases of Egypt that you dreaded, and they will cling to you. The Lord will also bring on you every kind of sickness and disaster not recorded in this Book of the Law until you are destroyed. You who were as numerous as the stars in the sky will be left but few in number; because you did not obey the Lord your God. Just as it pleased the Lord to make you prosper and increase in number, so it will please Him to ruin and destroy you. You will be uprooted from the land you are entering to possess.
>
> Then the Lord will scatter you among all nations, from one end of the earth to the other. There you will worship other gods—gods of wood and stone, which neither you nor your fathers have known. Among those nations you will find no repose, no resting place for the sole of your foot. There the Lord will give you an anxious mind, eyes weary with longing, and a despairing heart. You will live in constant suspense, filled with dread both night and day, never sure of your life.
>
> Deuteronomy 28:59-66

The land of milk and honey, of fulfillment and promise, would also bear the judgment, to become a "burnt-out waste."

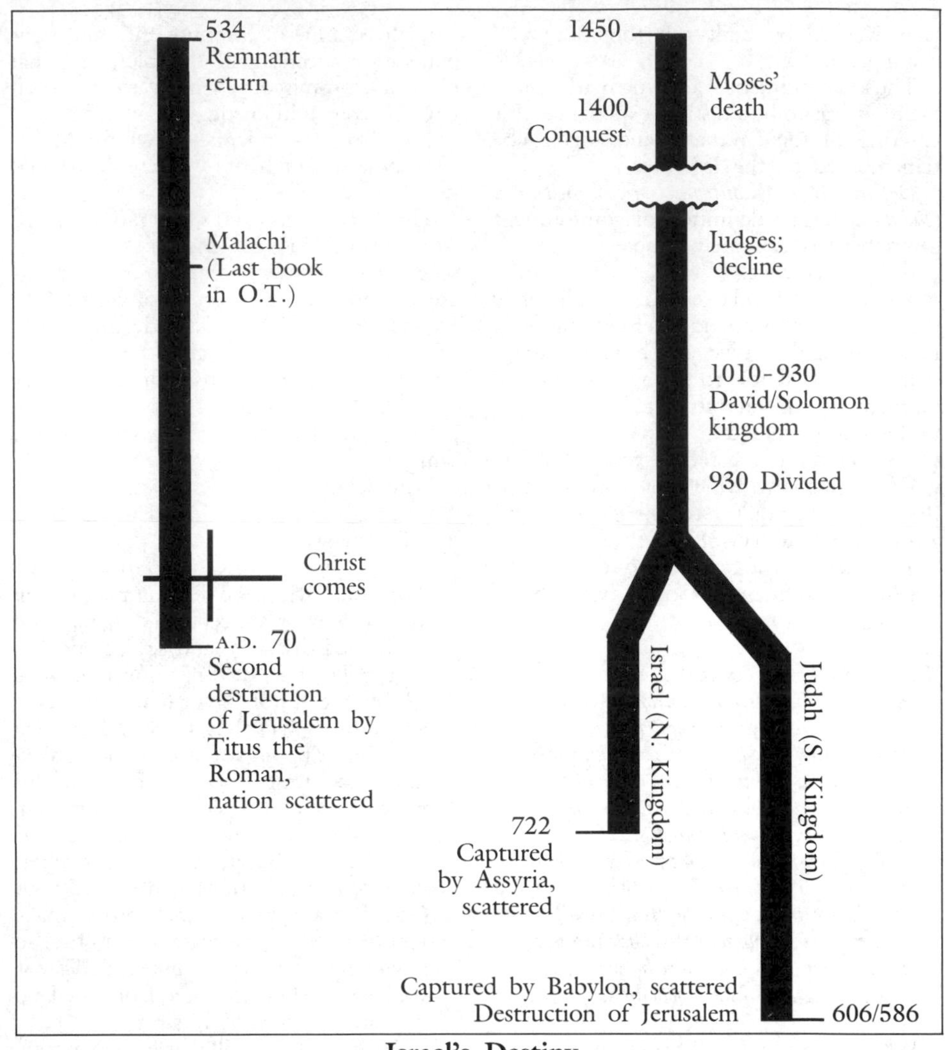

Israel's Destiny

And just this has happened.

The destiny written as a warning so long ago has become history. The word was true. The danger inherent in rejection of commitment is very, very real.

♥ ***Link to Life: Youth / Adult***

A German emperor of the last century is said to have asked his court pastor to prove to him that the Bible is true. The minister replied, "I can prove the Bible is God's Book in just two words."

The Emperor looked amazed. "What are they?"

And the pastor answered, "The Jew."

Tell your group this story, and have them read Deuteronomy 28:59-66.

Then discuss: "What did this pastor mean?"

NOTE: If your group is not familiar with the Bible and what happened to Israel, use the chart, "Israel's Destiny," to review the history of Israel from the Conquest to deporting from Israel in 722 B.C. and Judah in 586 B.C.

Return: Deuteronomy 30

Along with the warning, God gave Israel promises. Even in the middle of judgment, if the blessings and the cursings would be called to mind and God's people would "return to the Lord your God and obey Him with all your heart and with all your soul according to everything I command you today, then the Lord your God will restore your fortunes and have compassion on you and gather you again from all the nations where He scattered you" (30:2-3).

This too we have seen in history, in the return from Babylon. And many Christians believe that the establishment of Israel in 1948 is the precursor of an even more wonderful regathering that will be associated with the return of Christ.

But what is important for us here is a bright and wonderful message:

The invitation to commitment is an open one!

It is never too late for the believer to return to God. The door remains open to the people of God. All the Lord asks is that we respond to Him. "I set before you today," God says to every generation, "life and prosperity, death and destruction. For I command you today to love the Lord your God, to walk in His ways, and to keep His commands, decrees, and laws: then you will live and increase. . . . But if your heart turns away, and you are not obedient" (vv. 15-17).

If you will not hear, then destiny becomes history. Again.

So Jesus' words to His disciples in Luke really echo an age-old story. The person who will not follow his Lord may gain the whole world, but he will forfeit himself. What he could have become he will not be, even as Israel's tragic choices would lead her to forfeit the blessings of the Promised Land.

Observations on the Text: Deuteronomy 31–34

Moses' life work was now done. He had been marvelously used by the Lord. His confrontation with Pharaoh, the plagues God brought at Moses' word, the parting of the Red Sea, the Ten Commandments, all these will be forever linked with the name of Moses, Israel's Law-Giver.

But now that Moses was about to die, he left a last heritage to the new generation.

Moses left a new leader (Deut. 31:1-8). Joshua, who with Caleb remained faithful to God when the first generation rebelled, and who had served as Israel's military chief, would guide the people in the Promised Land.

Moses left a written Law (Deut. 31:9-13). The contents of our first five books of the Old Testament were traditionally, and conservative scholars are sure actually, written by Moses or at his direction. This written Law was entrusted to the priests, to be carried in the ark of the covenant, and to be read to all the people every seventh year at the Feast of Tabernacles. This Word was for all the people—"men, women and children, and the aliens living in your towns." And while it was read to all only the seventh year, the priests and Levites were to teach it to all, and the elders to administer communities by it.

Moses left a song to memorize (Deut. 31:30–32:47). Copies of Scripture were not available to the people of Israel. How would they remember the central teachings of Moses, and retain their commitment to the Lord? Moses wove promise and blessing together in a song or poem that affirms the greatness of Israel's God. This was written down to be taught to the people, so that memorized and sung, it would always remind them of the necessity of personal commitment to Yahweh. Like the final chapters of the covenant, it contains an open invitation to commitment and to blessing.

> See now that I myself am He! There is no god besides Me. I put to death and I bring to life, I have wounded, and I will heal, and no one can deliver from My hand.
>
> Deuteronomy 32:39

In commitment to this God is safety and joy. They can only be found in Him.

Moses left his blessing on each tribe (Deut. 33). "Bless" and "blessing" occur some 415 times in the Hebrew Old Testament, showing the importance of this concept in biblical times. Essentially, to bless means "to endue with power for success, prosperity, fecundity, longevity, etc." The person who is "blessed" is giving some gift which will lead to a rich and abundant life.

It was common for superiors to bless children or subordinates, as Moses here spoke God's blessing on the tribes of Israel. For a verse-by-verse commentary, see the *Bible Knowledge Commentary,* pages 320-322.

Moses left an example (Deut. 34). The book closes with the death of Moses. The Lord took His faithful servant to the top of the mountains across from Jericho. There, Moses could look out over then-green slopes and purpled mountain ranges. "This is the land," God told Moses. And there Moses, the servant of the Lord, died.

And a scribe added an epitaph which stands erect over the unknown grave, marking Moses forever in the eyes of God's people.

> Since then no prophet has risen in Israel like Moses, whom the Lord knew face-to-face, who did all those miraculous signs and wonders the Lord sent him to do in Egypt—to Pharaoh and to all his officials and to his whole land. For no one has ever shown the mighty power or performed the awesome deeds that Moses did in the sight of all Israel.
>
> Deuteronomy 34:10-12

TEACHING GUIDE

Prepare

Meditate for a time on Moses, and on what Hebrews 3:2-5 tells you about him. Pray that you and your group members will grow to be as faithful in your commitment to God as Moses was.

Explore

1. Have group members individually define, and then briefly discuss *commitment*. How might a committed Christian be or act differently than an uncommitted Christian?
2. Or begin by having your group members define "the person I want to be" from the activity suggested in the "link-to-life" activity on page 158.

Expand

1. Have your class members read aloud together, Deuteronomy 28:59-66. Then use the chart on page 160 to give a summary of Israel's future history. Show how the decision not to make a full commitment to God led to tragedy.
2. Introduce verses 16 and 58 as Keys to Commitment. Follow the suggestions in the "link-to life" activity outlined on page 159.

Apply

1. Moses developed a ceremony at Mounts Ebal and Gerizim to emphasize the importance of the commitment decision. Why not have your group work out a similar ceremony, but using Luke 9:23-24? If they wish, material from Deuteronomy might be included.

Then actually have the ceremony your group designs as a concluding activity.

2. Or, emphasize the fact that the invitation to commitment remains open. Sometimes Christians feel that their sins and failures have disqualified them. But this is not true. Any believer can "return to the Lord your God and obey Him with all your heart" (Deut. 30:2).

STUDY GUIDE 22

Joshua 1–8

VICTORY PRINCIPLES

Overview
After the death of Moses, the people of Israel went on to conquer the Promised Land. This book tells the story, and demonstrates that God is well able to keep the promises He makes to His people.

▶ ***Joshua.*** Joshua, Israel's new leader, is the central personality in this book. He had always been the military leader in Israel (cf. Ex. 17:8-16). This has led some to believe that before the Exodus, Joshua was an Egyptian army officer. Josephus, a first-century Jewish historian, reports a tradition that Joshua once led an Egyptian army against Ethiopia.

Joshua played an important supportive role during Moses' leadership (cf. 24:13; 32:17; 33:11), and was one of only two adults who left Egypt to live long enough to enter Canaan, a privilege he won by his total faithfulness to the Lord (cf. Num. 14:6-9; 26:65; 32:11-12; Deut. 1:34-40).

▶ ***Canaanites.*** At the time of the Conquest, a variety of peoples were settled in smaller city-states in Canaan. The cities were well fortified, and the people warlike. But the design of the buildings, with established drainage systems, shows a high level of development. Also the metalwork and pottery of the peoples were advanced. And they carried on extensive trade with other nations. Yet for all their material advancement, the religion and morals of Canaan were degraded. Deuteronomy 18:9-13 lists some of the religious practices for which this people must now be dispossessed.

The diplomat paced the floor, thinking how to answer this latest dispatch from the East. How was he ever to sort out the conflicting reports! Which of the splinter parties was really loyal to his own nation? Was it the group in power now? Or were they just using the military and economic aid to feather their own nests? Of course they were corrupt, but would a different set of leaders prove any more effective? If he could only know which of the factions were under control of that other world power, then. . . .

He continued pacing.

If only he could see some light at the end of the tunnel.

The man we're watching is no Kremlin diplomat concerned with the Middle East. He is an Egyptian diplomat, pacing in an office in the city of Akhetaton, about the time of the Hebrew conquest of Palestine! And it is Palestine that is his concern. Far to the north of Egypt, the last decades have seen the rise of a powerful rival empire—the Hittites. Egypt and the Hittites came into conflict when the Hittites removed parts of Syria and Phoenicia from Egyptian control.

Syria and Palestine had been in Egypt's sphere of influence for some time. But now in many of the smaller city-states a nationalistic fervor was growing. Eager to cast off the imperialistic yoke of Egypt's influence, local princes already hoping to rebel and gain independence were encouraged by the Hittites. Conflict between rebels and loyalists broke out. Both sides sent letters to Egypt affirming their loyalty and accusing the other. Often both sides had lobbyists in the Egyptian court to look after their interests. Confused by the conflicting reports and the intrigue, the Egyptian state department seemed unable to distinguish between its friends and its foes.

Soon the influence and power of Egypt in Asia were sapped. Confused and uncertain, hesitant and indecisive, this once-great world power, though still one of the strongest nations of the ancient world, lost her grip over her former territories.

The Amarna Letters

This day in history, which sounds all too much like our own, is well known today because of the recovery of diplomatic correspondence between Egyptian government officials and various groups in Syria and Palestine. The ruins of Akhetaton, known now as Tell el-Amarna, have given up some 400 letters (written on clay tablets) since the first accidental discovery in 1887. In them, we get a revealing picture of an area which included the land that God's people, under the leadership of Joshua, were about to conquer.

Earlier we traced Bible history from Creation through the Exodus. In Genesis we saw God choose Abraham and give him covenant promises (Gen. 12; 15; 17). The Abrahamic Covenant was God's announcement of His purposes in our world. Abraham would have a host of descendants, some of whom would be formed into a special people (the Jews) through whom God would work out His plan. God promised Abraham He would set aside the land of Palestine for this people. Through this people God promised, looking forward to the Messiah (Christ), that "all the peoples of the earth" would be blessed.

The rest of Genesis tells the story of the line through which the promises would be fulfilled—Isaac, Abraham's son, and Jacob (later renamed Israel), Abraham's grandson. Genesis also tells how God providentially sent Joseph, 1 of Israel's 12 sons, down into Egypt to prepare that land for a coming famine, and to prepare a place for the family of Israel to stay and multiply.

As we trace the history of the Israelites beyond the Book of Genesis, we see that the chosen people were in Egypt for more than 400 years. After a time they were enslaved, and for decades experienced great hardship. Finally God sent a specially prepared leader, Moses, to bring Israel out of servitude and lead them to the land promised to Abraham.

Deliverance from Egypt was accomplished only by direct and miraculous divine intervention. God brought a series of plagues on Egypt in judgment. Finally Pharaoh, ruler of Egypt, did release Israel—only to change his mind and pursue them with an army. The army was destroyed at the Yam Suf (The Reed, or Red, Sea), which opened to permit the Israelites to cross, and then rushed together to drown the Egyptians. The now-freed slaves moved rejoicing out into the wilderness.

But centuries of servitude had weakened the fiber of the people. They consistently resisted and rejected God and Moses' leadership. As an aid to discipline, and to reveal God's moral character and expectations for His people, the Israelites were led to Mount Sinai. There the Law was given. The people were promised that while disobedience would bring discipline and disappointment, obedience would lead to blessing. Israel willingly accepted God's standards and promised to obey.

But Israel's promise was made too lightly. In fact, disobedience continued to distinguish the generation that came out of Egypt with Moses. Their rebellion reached a climax when the nation, poised on the border of the Promised Land, was commanded to go in. Moses sent 12 spies into the land to survey and to report. Ten of them returned, terrified by the strength of the fortified cities and by the stature of the inhabitants. Only 2, Joshua and Caleb, came back enthusiastic, confident that God would give them the land. Characteristically, the people of Israel listened to the 10 and doubted God. All the urging of Moses and Aaron and the insistence of Joshua and Caleb that they were well able to take the land went for nothing. The people would not obey.

Israel had made a basic choice. Because this people would not trust God or obey Him, that generation could not enter the Promised Land. God forced them back out into the wilderness. There the people of Israel wandered for 38 years, until the generation of adults who had refused to trust God died in the wilderness. All but Joshua and Caleb. These two men of faith survived, and over the years the old generation was replaced by a new one.

The new generation grew up with a greater trust in God. Tested in battle, they obeyed. Finally, as the Book of Deuteronomy describes, the new generation was once again camped outside the Promised Land, awaiting God's command to cross over the Jordan and to take their inheritance. In his last act as leader, Moses reviewed the love of God for His people and urged the new generation to keep His Law. This generation also stood, and made a personal commitment by accepting Law as their standard, and promising to obey the Lord. This time the promise was not made lightly. The discipline of the previous years had produced a committed band.

♥ ***Link to Life: Youth / Adult***
If your group is not familiar with the Old Testament story, summarize it, following the emphasis of the text (above). To understand Joshua, people need to know the sequence of events leading up to this point in history.

With the death of Moses and the appointment of Joshua to lead God's people on to victory, the adventure recorded in the Book of Joshua begins. And the Amarna letters? They tell us that God had quietly been at work, preparing the stage for Israel's Conquest.

During much of the 400 years that Israel was in Egypt, Palestine served as a land bridge between Egypt and a succession of world powers to the north. It had also been their battleground. The people of Israel, who multiplied from 70 people to more than 2 million in Egypt, could never have increased to such numbers if God had left them in the Promised Land. Then, just at the time when Israel was ready to enter that land, Egypt's power waned in Palestine. In the power vacuum which existed—into a land divided into petty kingdoms—God's people moved, ready to overcome peoples more numerous than themselves, but divided.

Diplomatic success and failure serves only to further the outworking of God's plan.

It's important to keep this point in mind. So often when we read the Bible we think of the people and events as distant, or somehow unreal. But the Egyptian diplomat in one of the luxuriously decorated brick buildings of Akhetaton who puzzled over the complex world situation is not so different from the State Department undersecretary in modern Washington. Their problems would be much the same. At night each would return to a suburban home, passing crowded and disorganized clusters of apartment houses. Cocktail parties and political maneuvering (if not between Republicans and Democrats, then between the Amon priesthood party and the party of Pharaoh), shaped the lifestyle then as now.

And even as emerging nations struggle today to establish their existence, so in Palestine the people of Israel were about to emerge as a nation, and to challenge a people long established there.

How real it all is! Just as real, just as living, as today's current events.

But what took place then has a unique timelessness. Events occurring in Washington today affect us and our future. But so do the events of Scripture. In the people and events described in God's Word, we discover timeless truths about ourselves and our relationships with God. The Bible's word of history becomes, by the activity of the Holy Spirit, God's voice guiding us today. As we listen, learn, and respond to One who speaks to us through the heritage of our sacred past, you and I can see our own years of darkness fade away, and welcome the days of glory that God intends to unfold for us.

Opening God's Word to Joshua is both to revisit a living history, and to open up our own lives to our loving God.

Commentary

Foundation for Conquest: Joshua 1–8

The Book of Joshua opens with the phrase, "After the death of Moses." There is a great transition here. It's the kind of transition that takes place when a young person leaves the family, and starts off on his or her own. Or when a marriage takes place, and the young couple leave their fathers and mothers to establish a new home.

For some 40 years—and for four entire books of the Old Testament—the man Moses had been the dominant figure in Israel. But now this people must strike out and face the challenge of the future without him.

It's helpful to look at these early chapters of Joshua and discover the resources that God provides for His people.

An equipped leader (Josh. 1). God does not want a leaderless people. But He needs leaders who are uniquely equipped.

Joshua's previous experience had prepared him for leadership. He had led the Israelite defense against an attack by the Amalekites (Ex. 17:8-16), indicating previous battlefield experience. It's likely he had served in the Egyptian army: foreigners were often enlisted in the military services. As 1 of the 12 spies, Joshua had learned firsthand the topography of Palestine. At that time his trust in God had led him to advise immediate attack when all the other spies but Caleb urged the people to disobey. Later, at God's direction, Joshua was invested with some of Moses' authority (Num. 27:20).

Usually the road to significant leadership is a long one, with many choices along the way. What you and I do with our less significant opportunities determines the part we'll play later!

But leadership demands more than character and experience. This first chapter of the book bearing Joshua's name makes it clear that the leader's relationship with God is crucial. Joshua had basic spiritual resources that are ours as well. How Joshua used the divine resources would make the difference between victory and defeat. What were his resources?

(1) *Joshua had a promise in God's stated purpose.* "I will give you every place where you set your foot, as I promised David" (Josh. 1:3). God's announced purpose was to give Israel the Promised Land.

(2) *Joshua had the promise of God's presence.* "As I was with Moses, so I will be with you; I will never leave you or forsake you" (v. 5). God had committed Himself to be with His servant and to take on Himself the burden of bringing success.

(3) *Joshua had the promise of God's faithfulness.* "You will lead these people to inherit the land I swore to their forefathers to give them" (v. 6). God had committed Himself to a cause, and He would not let His promise fail.

In view of these commitments made by God, there was only one thing required of Joshua: "Be strong and very courageous. Be careful to obey the Law My servant Moses gave you; do not turn from it to the right or to the left, that you may be successful wherever you go" (v. 7). Neither discouragement nor fear were to influence Joshua to hesitate or to disobey. If Joshua would live in close relationship to the Lord, being responsive and obedient to Him, victory was assured. The leader must be a person who follows. A person strong enough and courageous enough to follow God.

♥ ***Link to Life: Youth / Adult***
God's promises are intended to free us to follow the Lord. Ask your class to determine the promises in Joshua 1–9. Discuss: "How might having these promises have helped Joshua fulfill the commission of 1:7?" Then have teams look for promises of Jesus in John 14. When the promises have been found and discussed, go around the circle. Each person is to begin, "The promise of Jesus that will help me to obey God is ________." After specifying the promise, then each is to explain why he or she sees this having an impact on his or her life.

The emphasis in this first chapter on the vital role of obedience is repeated, not only in Joshua and in the Book of Judges which follows, but in every period of Old Testament history. Every event, every individual, reflects the basic principle: obedience brings victory, disobedience brings defeat.

Responsiveness to God, the willingness to live as He directs and to stay in close fellowship with Him, is not only a prerequisite for leadership, It is also prerequisite for any kind of blessing. Then and now.

♥ ***Link to Life: Children***
The stories of Joshua and the fall of Jericho are told to children of every age. How vital to make these stories and their lessons live for boys and girls.

One way to do it is with a tabletop adventure. Trace the events week-by-week on scenes constructed on construction-paper sheets laid end to end.

Make figures of chenille wire (pipe cleaners), and tape them on the paper. Use real objects where possible, and crayon in features like the Jordan River.

Here are a few of the scenes you might want to construct for these Joshua chapters: (1) Joshua kneels before the Angel of the Lord (chap. 1). (2) Rahab helps the spies escape (chap. 2). (3) The people construct a stone altar across the Jordan (chap. 4). (4) The people march around Jericho (chap. 6). (5) The walls fall down (chap. 6). (6) Achan hides his stolen booty (chap. 7). Israel wins at Ai (chap. 8). Be creative in constructing each scene: use a pile of rocks for the altar, dominoes or small blocks for the walls of Jericho, etc.

To help the children bring each lesson home, make small wire figures to attach to 3 x 5 or 4 x 6 cards. For instance, for Joshua 1 have a kneeling Joshua, and verse 7 printed on the card. Or give another reminder, like a piece of red yarn for chapter 2 or a small stone for chapters 3–4.

The theme of each story is of the

importance of obedience to God, and how obedience brings victory while disobedience brings defeat. What a practical message for boys and girls, who can show their love for Jesus by doing what is right.

Faith responds (Josh. 2). One of the most striking statements in the Bible was made by Rahab, a woman of Jericho who hid the Israelite spies.

Jericho was not a particularly large city. But it was strongly fortified. And most important, it controlled entry to the passes that led up into the interior of Canaan. Israel had to pass this way to reach the rest of the land.

While the people were shut inside the high walls of the city, they were still terrified. Rahab voiced their conviction when she said, "We have heard how the Lord dried up the water of the Red Sea for you when you came out of Egypt, and what you did to . . . the two kings of the Amorites east of the Jordan. When we heard of it, our hearts sank and everyone's courage failed because of you, for the Lord your God is God in heaven above and on the earth below" (Josh. 2:10-11). Rahab, a prostitute, heard and truly believed, for she acted on her conviction to save the spies. The rest, rather than turning to the Lord, locked themselves up, and trusted in stone walls.

First steps (Josh. 3–4). The Jordan River was in flood stage, blocking Israel from Palestine. These chapters tell how God began to demonstrate that He was with Joshua and with this generation. The flow of water stopped, and the people crossed on dry ground.

A stone altar was constructed from stones that had lain underwater, to serve as a reminder of this fresh wonder God performed. The miracle also served to authenticate Joshua as one who himself followed God's directions; one whom others could safely follow (3:7-8).

But there was also a great change about to take place. The text says that after their crossing, Israel ate some of the produce of the land. "The manna stopped the day after they ate this food from the land; there was no longer any manna for the Israelites, but that year they ate of the produce of Canaan" (5:12). This is both a fulfillment, and a challenge. God had brought them to a land where they would find plenty. Yet the manna that had given daily evidence of the Lord's care now ceased. From now on the people of Israel would have to walk by faith in the unseen, where before they had had visible evidence of God's presence.

We can look at what happened next at Jericho and Ai as powerful lessons to Israel and to us concerning the walk of faith.

Jericho—"point" (Josh. 5–6). When Joshua went to reconnoiter Jericho he was met by a Figure holding a drawn sword. This Figure announced that He Himself was "Commander of the army of the Lord" (5:14). Joshua bowed low, to await orders.

From a military standpoint, the orders this captain gave were ridiculous. Joshua was to march the people of Israel around the city of Jericho once a day for six days. On these circuits no one was to make a sound. On the seventh day, seven circuits were to be made. Then, at a signal, all the people were to shout. And, so the promise, when the people shouted, the walls of the city would fall down. Israel could then attack and was to utterly destroy the city, saving only those in Rahab's house. Nothing was to be salvaged. No booty was to be taken. All was to be destroyed.

Joshua may have felt foolish giving such orders. And Israel may have felt foolish too. Certainly, after a day or so of fearful observation, the people of Jericho would have become bolder and in relief have shouted out taunts and ridicule.

But Joshua was strong enough to do what he had been commanded. And the people too obeyed.

On the seventh day, when the people shouted with a great shout, the walls did come tumbling down.

It is this kind of belief, which expresses itself in obedience even when the nature of the command seems foolish or unclear, that is the kind of "trust" God calls all of us to have in Him.

Ai "counterpoint" (Josh. 7–8). At Jericho, one of the Hebrew warriors, a man named Achan, disobeyed God's command and took gold and silver. This hidden sin led to Israel's defeat at Ai, a minor city higher up the pass. Sin had broken fellowship with God, and the flow of divine power was interrupted.

Achan was sought out and he and his family were stoned. Perhaps the place Achan chose to bury his stolen treasure suggests a reason why the whole family had to die. He had buried the gold and silver and the garment he took "inside [his] tent." While he was responsible for his act, his family had been responsible to denounce that act of disobedience to God.

But why was Achan's sin deserving of the death penalty? Because like other sins that merited death under the Law, this one endangered the survival of Israel as a theocratic community. In Achan's case, the defeat might have so reduced the terror of the people of the land that they would gather against Israel (cf. Josh. 7:9). Perhaps more important, 36 men of Israel had died needlessly in the battle against Ai. The sin of Achan had caused the death of some of his companions.

After Achan was put to death, Ai was taken and completely destroyed.

A graphic lesson had been taught. Obedience to God was vital after all. Obedience brought victory; disobedience resulted in disastrous defeat.

With both these lessons deeply impressed, Israel stood as Joshua read the whole of the divine Law. The way of blessing and the way of curses was laid out before them all once again.

And so, with God's guiding truth again before them, the people of Israel went on to take the Promised Land.

TEACHING GUIDE

Prepare

Look back over your own experiences as a Christian. Can you identify personal Jericho's and Ai's?

Explore

1. Give a minilecture covering Bible history up to this critical point in time.
2. Or do a group character study of Joshua. Divide into teams, giving each team the verses noted in the *overview*. Discuss: "What do we learn from Joshua that we can apply to ourselves?"

Expand

Have one of your group members prepared to report—without comment—on the facts of the story of Jericho and Ai as told in Josh. 6–8. Let your group members ask any *factual* questions ("what happened?" but *not* "why?" or "how come?") until the situation is completely understood.

Then ask your group to pretend they are Israelites, one or two of whom may have known Achan, or have known one of the men who perished in the first attack on Ai, talking around a fire at night after the victory at Ai. The task: talk about what it all means, how you feel, and what you've learned.

Apply

Ask your group members to think back and identify any Jericho's or Ai's in their own lives. Encourage any who wish to share an experience he thought of, and what that experience has meant to him.

In closing, thank God that He gives us both victories and defeats, and teaches us to live close to Him.

STUDY GUIDE 23

Joshua 9–24

VICTORY WON

Overview

The story of the Book of Joshua is not so much the record of a Conquest, but the report of entry into rest.

The thrust of the book is summed up in 21:43-45: "And they took possession of [the land] and settled there. The Lord gave them rest on every side. . . . Not one of their enemies withstood them. . . . Not one of all the Lord's good promises to the house of Israel failed; every one was fulfilled."

- ***Militarily.*** The Conquest of Canaan is still studied in Israeli and other war colleges. It featured a quick attack in the center to divide the land, then forced marches and surprise attacks in Southern and then Northern campaigns. But the emphasis of the book on rest can be seen in this outline of Joshua.

Outline

I.	Preparation	1:1–5:12
II.	Central Campaign	5:13–9:27
III.	Northern, Southern Campaigns	10:1–12:24
IV.	The Land Divided	13:1–24:33

- ***Covenant Renewal.*** The covenant of Law defined the relationship between God as Israel's Ruler and the people as God's subjects. It spelled out how God expected His people to live and promised blessings for obedience. But each generation and individual had to ratify—to personally agree to—this national contract with God. Near his death, Joshua led the next generation in a service (Josh. 24), like the service led by Moses just before the Conquest (Deut. 27).

Commentary

Conquest: Joshua 9–12

After the Transjordan nations (those across the Jordan River to the east of Palestine) had been conquered, Joshua's campaign began with an attack on Jericho. This key city, just above the Israelite base of Gilgal, gave access both to the heart of Palestine and to Joshua's source of supply across the Jordan. It also controlled two trade routes up into the central highlands. In taking Ai and Bethel (8:17; 12:16), Joshua cut the land in two and was then able to campaign against a divided enemy. He dealt first with the Southern and then with the Northern kings.

The taking of Jericho first was thus of great strategic importance. And here divine intervention seemed essential. Leon Wood, in *A Survey of Israel's History* (Zondervan) describes Jericho's walls:

> [They] were of a type which made direct assault practically impossible. An approaching enemy first encountered a stone abutment, 11 feet high, back and up from which sloped a 35 degree plastered scarp reaching to the main wall some 35 vertical feet above. The steep smooth slope prohibited battering the wall by any effective device or building fires to break it. An army trying to storm the wall found difficulty in climbing the slope, and ladders to scale it would find no satisfactory footing. The normal tactic used by an army to take a city so protected was siege, but Israel did not have time for this, if she was to occupy all the land in any reasonable number of months.

Any impression we may have that Palestine was some rustic backwater and that Joshua's army was like some overwhelming horde of savages, is quickly dispelled by this description. The men of Palestine were acquainted with war; their offensive and defensive skills were highly sophisticated. But they had no defense against Israel's God.

Jericho's walls, which normally would have held off Israel for months or even years, fell down in a moment.

While God's power did provide victory in times of crisis, Joshua usually employed field tactics to defeat his enemies. Surprise attacks, forced marches, and flying columns which dashed ahead to cut off lines of retreat, were all tactics known by Hittite commanders of that day and used brilliantly by Joshua. As in Israel's Six-Day War with the Arab states, Israel, by aggressive tactics, defeated an enemy with forces much more powerful than its own.

The purpose of Joshua's campaign was not to destroy all the peoples living in Palestine, but rather to eliminate all effective opposition. The power of the Palestinian people to threaten the existence of Israel was to be crushed. Thus Joshua did not concentrate on the Conquest of land but on the defeat of enemy armies. Some of the cities against which the Israelites fought were taken and their populations destroyed. But other cities were not burned. Later those unrazed cities were reoccupied by survivors. However, the principal cities were "devoted" to God; they and their entire populations were completely destroyed.

Questions about the Conquest. Commentators have been universally impressed with Joshua's military strategy. The Israeli War College today features a study of his campaigns! But there are also questions the teacher of the Bible wants to explore.

(1) *The Gibeonites' deception (Josh. 9).* Peoples of one city in Palestine's central highlands resorted to trickery. Sure they were doomed otherwise, they sent representatives to Joshua with worn clothing, and dry, moldy food. Pretending they had come from a great distance, they begged for a treaty. The terms were attractive. "We are your servants" (v. 8), meant that this "distant" nation would be completely subject to Israel, in exchange for a promise that Israel would not war against them.

God had commanded His people to "make no treaty" with the peoples of Palestine. But He had said nothing about a treaty with people beyond its borders.

The Bible says that "the men of Israel sampled their provisions but did not inquire of the Lord" (v. 14).

They trusted the evidence of their eyes, and the word of strangers. They trusted their own ability and reason. And because they did, they failed to ask God for direction.

What a lesson for us. There are severe limits on our capacities. We should never make crucial, life-shaping decisions relying simply on our own wisdom. We, like Joshua, need to inquire first of the Lord.

After the treaty was made, Joshua learned that he and Israel had been tricked. The Gibeonites were actually near neighbors! But because the leaders had "sworn an oath to them by the Lord, the God of Israel," there was nothing they could do (v. 18). Too many decisions, once made, can never be taken back.

But even this situation was redeemed by God. When other inhabitants of the land heard of the treaty, they determined to attack the Gibeonite cities. In a surprise attack, Joshua shattered the besieging armies. God had turned Joshua's mistake in making the treaty into an opportunity for victory!

♥ ***Link to Life: Youth / Adult***

The experience of Joshua with the Gibeonites may well reflect our own. Outline the sequence of events in a minilecture: Joshua relied on self to make decision; Joshua learned too late the decision was wrong; God acted to redeem the situation.

Ask: "Have you seen this pattern in your own life?"

Give about three minutes for pairs to share experiences. Then discuss: "In your experience, did you have doubts about your decision? Why did you act without clear guidance—no time, didn't think to ask, or what? What do we learn about God from such experiences? What do we learn about ourselves, and about Christian decision-making?"

♥ ***Link to Life: Children***

Appropriate themes for telling this story to children are, "Don't forget to ask," or, "Ask when you aren't sure."

While boys and girls can ask God directly for guidance, the Lord has given children adults who better understand His Word and who have a developed Christian judgment to guide them. So why not have your boys and girls make up a number of stories about hard choices children like them have to make. Each should be a

"What-should-I-do?" kind of situation.

For instance: My friend wants me to give him answers when we take tests. He says he won't be my friend if I don't. What should I do?

In-class time might be used for this project. Then when the Sunday School department comes together, a panel of adults—a teacher, a parent, a pastor—can answer the question. Choose wise Christians, who can explain and draw on Bible knowledge in giving his or her answers.

(2) *The long day (10:12-14).* Israel made a surprise attack on an army gathered by five Southern kings. This enemy was routed and fled. During the panicked rout, the enemy soldiers were struck down by great hailstones falling from the sky, as well as by Joshua's men. Determined to crush their enemy before they could reach the safety of their walled cities, Joshua cried out, "Sun, stand still over Gibeon!" (v. 12) The biblical text reports, "The sun stood still, and the moon stopped" (v. 13).

Some have suggested that what happened here was a miracle involving refraction of light. The day was *apparently* lengthened. Others have argued that the request really was for the sun to "be silent"; that is, to stop shining so strongly that its heat would sap the strength of the pursuing Israelites. However, the language of the text, and particularly the statement that this day was unique and twice the normal length between noon and sunset, seems to indicate that the day was miraculously prolonged.

♥ ***Link to Life: Children***
God truly was a powerful Leader for His people Israel, who acted to help His people. God also helps boys and girls today, giving them strength to overcome in their own inner, spiritual battles.

Talk about the "right thing to do" in some of the situations the children described (see previous "link-to-life"). Ask the children whether doing the right thing seems hard or easy. Talk about why. Then tell the story of the miracles God did to help Israel. Let the children draw a bright yellow sun on a 3 x 5 card on which you've printed one of these verses, which give God's promise of the strength we need to win spiritual victories: 2 Samuel 22:33; Psalms 18:32; 29:11; 105:4.

Encourage the children to memorize their verses, and remember to ask God for His strength when it seems hard for them to do what is right.

(3) *Total destruction.* The ruthlessness with which Israel dealt with the Canaanites has raised a theological question, since the extermination was done at God's express command (cf. Deut. 7:1-5; 20:16-18; Josh. 11:20). How can this be reconciled with the New Testament picture of a God of love?

Materially and culturally the Canaanites had an advanced culture. Archeology has shown well-planned cities with homes of good design and construction. Drainage systems had been installed, trade was carried on with distant countries, skilled workmanship was shown in metals and pottery. But for all the cultural advancement, the Palestinian religious and moral life was in a great decline.

When Abraham lived in Palestine, there was no developed cult of Baal (a nature and fertility god). But over the centuries the worship of Baal and his female counterpart had come to dominate Canaan, and with this worship had come a host of associated immoral practices described in Leviticus 18. The sentence of destruction was passed to protect Israel from contamination by the surrounding peoples.

But it is also important to realize that the Canaanites were not destroyed out of hand. In Abraham's day there had been some knowledge of God (see Gen. 14:17-20). In fact, God refused to dispossess the Canaanites in Abraham's time because "the sin of the Amorites has not yet reached its full measure" (15:16).

We must look at the events of the Conquest in the light of divine judgment on sin. God did not command Joshua to destroy an innocent people. God chose to use Israel as the means by which He brought a well-deserved judgment on one of the most immoral cultures of the civilized world. And even within that context, those like Rahab who would turn to God could hope for deliverance.

And so, within a number of months, the army of the Lord completed the rout of the enemy and was ready to take its rest.

The Land Divided: Joshua 13–19
The majority of the Book of Joshua de-

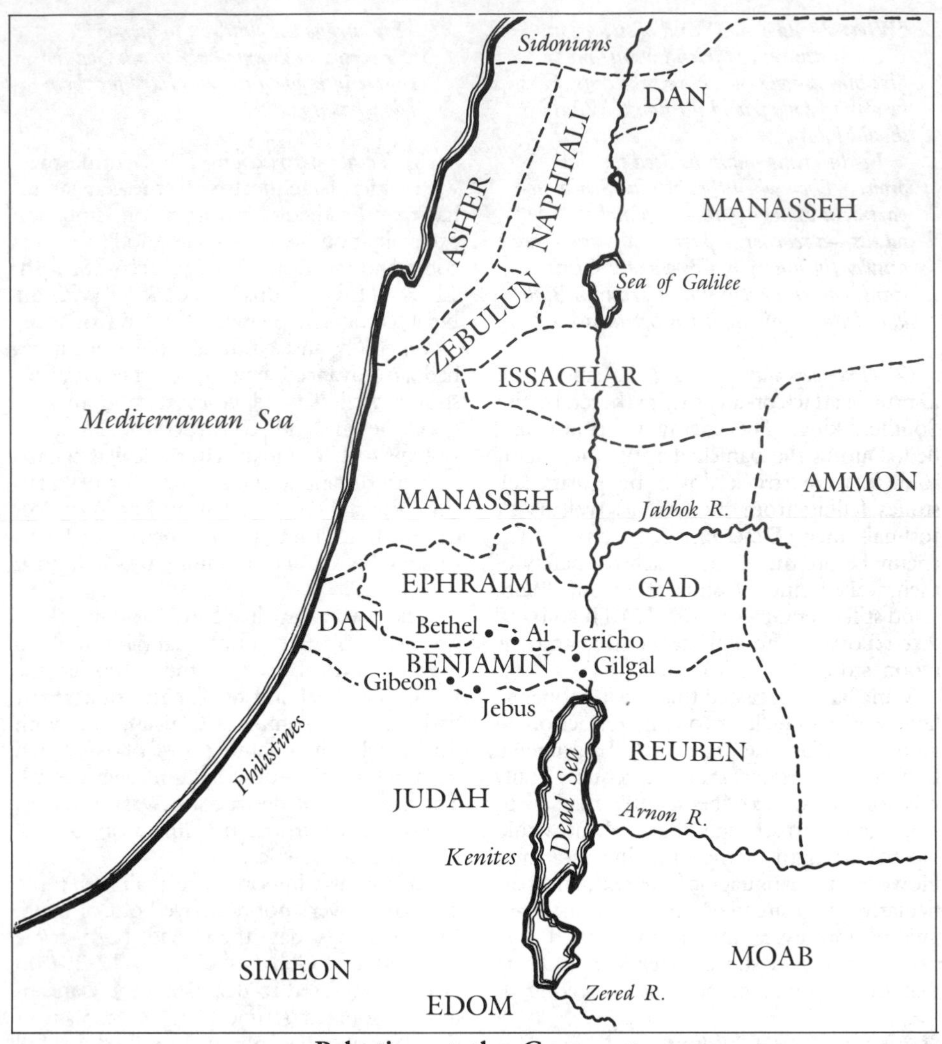

Palestine at the Conquest

scribes not the Conquest but the distribution of the inheritance to the 12 tribes of Israel. Large portions of territory were blocked out and the different tribes challenged to possess their land.

This often meant continuing to battle with Canaanites who still lived there. The power to resist Israel in a massive way had been shattered in Joshua's campaigns. Yet pockets of resistance were still found in each tribe's allotment. These mopping-up operations would keep God's people dependent on Him—and would make sure that they did not lose their skill in war.

With the victory won, the fighting men of those tribes which had settled across the Jordan but had come into the land with their brothers to help them fight, could return home. Throughout the occupied land of Palestine, the victorious Hebrews began to enjoy the rest which God had promised, and which through His faithfulness had now come true.

Rest's Lifestyle: Joshua 20–21

These chapters tell of the establishment of cities of refuge and of cities for the Levites within the allotments of the other tribes. These provisions remind us that the people of Israel were now to begin a lifestyle which was carefully planned and revealed by God long before the Conquest.

If you've studied the earlier books of the Old Testament, you're familiar with God's careful definition of His people's lifestyle. This definition included not only moral and religious injunctions; it also carefully structured every aspect of the new society.

The case law chapters (Ex. 20–24) spelled out a number of specific implications that the Ten Commandments had for life in the land. Commitment to love of God and to love of neighbor was to mark God's people as His own distinctive possession. As the people of Israel followed God's laws for holy living, then poverty, injustice, and all the social ills which warp human society could be dealt with compassionately.

In the lifestyle sketched by divine revelation there was no central government or administrative bodies. Obedience was to God. Elders had responsibilities in local communities. As Wood notes (*A Survey of Israel's History*), they "served as judges of persons who had killed someone (Deut. 19:12), conducted inquests (Deut. 21:2-8), heard family problems (21:18-26), settled matrimonial disputes (22:13-30; 25:7), and settled cases of controversy at the gate of the city (Ruth 4:2)."

Local courts shared cases with the elders, and when a case could not be settled, it was sent to the central sanctuary at Shiloh. There, before the tabernacle of the Lord, a court of priests and lay judges made a final and binding determination.

The tabernacle, which had been built to God's specifications and remained the symbol of God's presence with Israel, was now the great unifying center of Israel's life. Here the sacrifices commanded by God were made, and no sacrifices were to be made at any other location. Three times a year every healthy male citizen was to gather here for the feasts around which the worship and religious life of Israel centered.

The first of these feasts was the Passover (Ex. 12:1-13; Deut. 16:1-8), which began the religious year and commemorated God's deliverance of His people from Egypt. For seven days the people gathered (in April) to renew and reaffirm their commitment to the God of the Exodus.

At the close of the wheat harvest some 50 days later, a 1-day observation (called the Feast of Weeks, see Ex. 23:16; Lev. 23:15-22; Num. 28:26-31; Deut. 16:9-12) was held.

The third feast was a week-long commemoration in September-October of Israel's life in the wilderness. Families lived in tents or booths outside, and the occasion was called the Feast of Tabernacles (Ex. 23:16; Lev. 23:34-43; Deut. 16:13-15).

These three feasts were not, however, the only way in which the unity of the 12 tribes was maintained. There were other feasts they had in common, and all the tribes kept the Sabbath as a day of rest. Common customs and common laws, with a common language and history, bound Israel together as a larger family of God.

The common custom is well illustrated by the cities of refuge established by Joshua in obedience to God's earlier command through Moses. In Israel, a murderer was to be put to death. This sentence—already placed by God on one who killed another—was to be executed by a relative of the murdered man, "the avenger of blood" (Josh. 20:5).

But the Old Testament recognized an important distinction between premeditated murder and accidental death. The murderer was to be executed without fail. But one guilty of manslaughter was permitted to flee to a city of refuge. There he lived until the death of the high priest, after which he could return to his home without fear of retribution. There were six such cities scattered throughout the territories of the 12 tribes. These cities were the common possession of the whole people.

The common law is represented by the establishment of levitical cities through the land. When God established the tabernacle worship system, He set aside the family of Levi to serve Him. The descendants of Aaron served as priests; descendants of the other family members were singers, caretakers, and teachers. The role of teacher is particularly significant when we see the levitical cities placed in the allotments of the other tribes. Only the tribe of Levi did not receive its own territory. God was its portion. But they did live among the others, with men from the levitical cities taking their turn at serving in the central sanctuary. Taught themselves there, these men returned to serve as teachers of the Law throughout the land.

The tribes of Israel did retain their separate identities, and were directly responsible to God rather than to a central human authority. But the lifestyle God established for them constantly reaffirmed their unity as the special people of God, and provided for continuous instruction in His ways.

The structure of early Israel, so briefly described here, was a theocracy—a government in which God is the Head of state. The tragedy of Israel is that she did not continue in an obedient relationship with God. Soon Israel abandoned rest's lifestyle. The society broke down. Social injustice, poverty, unrest, conflict, fear, and pain all followed.

In God's church today, as in early Israel, our rest and peace depend on committing ourselves to trust in God—and to obedience.

The Empty Altar: Joshua 22

When the Reubenites, the Gadites, and the half-tribe of Manasseh which had chosen land across the Jordan were released from military service, they hurried home. But they stopped along the way to build an imposing altar beside the Jordan.

This startled the other Israelite tribes, who viewed it as apostasy! After all God had commanded that Israel worship in only one place, sacrifice at one altar, live by one Law, and recognize Him as the one and only God.

When an angry delegation confronted the Transjordan tribes and accused them of breaking faith with the God of Israel, their brothers explained.

The altar was not for sacrifice. It was built on the pattern God ordained as a witness to the unity of the tribes across the Jordan with their brothers in Canaan proper. The minority had feared that in time the river that divided them would be viewed as a separating barrier, and they would be denied a part in the worship of Yahweh.

These people named the altar: A WITNESS BETWEEN US THAT THE LORD IS GOD (22:34).

♥ ***Link to Life: Youth / Adult***

Give a minilecture covering the basic elements of the unity of Israel—the elements of common life which bonded this people together. Discuss: "Was the fear of the tribes across the Jordan that one day they might be viewed as 'others' rather than part of Israel, reasonable or not?"

After this discussion ask, "What is it that makes Christians one *today? What's basic to our faith?"*

Discuss also, "What things make us think of other Christians as different—and not like us? How have these things happened to separate us in view of all the things that make us one?

Joshua's Death: Joshua 23–24

Joshua had led Israel to victory and guided the people in establishing the theocratic society. In these concluding chapters, Joshua looked back, and he also looked ahead. In view of all that God had done for Israel, Joshua demanded total commitment. "Now fear the Lord, and serve Him with all faithfulness" (24:14).

Standing before this venerable saint who had led them to experience God's rest, the people reaffirmed their commitment to obey. And the biblical record echoes that commitment: "Israel served the Lord throughout the lifetime of Joshua and of the elders who outlived him and who had experienced everything the Lord had done for Israel" (v. 31).

Obedience to God had won them rest.

TEACHING GUIDE

Prepare

Read and meditate on Ephesians 4:3-6.

Explore

1. Begin with a minilecture on Joshua 9–10, outlining what happened with the Gibeonites. Use the "link-to-life" teaching idea on page 170 to help your group examine their own personal experiences.

2. Or give a minilecture on the elements of unity in Israel once they were in the land of promise.

Expand

1. Present the principle of guidance presented in Proverbs 3:5-6 and repeated in Psalm 37:4-5. Discuss how it related to the experience with the Gibeonites.

Then focus on Christian decision-making. Ask your group members to share experiences in which they have turned to God, and ways that He has communicated to them a sense of His will.
2. Or talk further about our relationships with other Christians who differ from your group. What are the specific things that bother your members about some they recognize as brothers and sisters? Why do these differences bother—how do they make group members feel?

What might serve as a modern WITNESS BETWEEN US THAT THE LORD IS GOD?

Apply
1. Tell each other about decisions which you sense a need for God's leading. Then pray together.
2. Or plan how you will affirm Christian unity in your relationship with other Christians.

STUDY GUIDE 24

Judges 1:1–3:6

WHEN JUDGES RULED

Overview
The book takes its name from the leaders who emerged to deliver and govern Israelite tribes during an era of moral decay.

The period probably extended from about 1390 B.C. to around 1050 B.C. when Saul was anointed king. In understanding this book it is important to note that a judge's influence was primarily regional, over a single tribe or several. The oppressors during this period lived on several different borders of Palestine, and their attack was directed on the tribes closest to them.

Judges can be outlined simply:

Outline

I. The Times Explained	1:1–3:6
II. Stories of Judges	3:7–16:31
III. Portraits of Decay	17:1–21:25

▶ ***Judge.*** The Hebrew word *sapat* is translated "judge" in this book. The word implies every function of government, not just the judicial. Thus the judges of this era were governors in the fullest sense. They were military leaders, with executive and legislative power as well as judicial power. Most important, the judges of Israel were divinely appointed to deliver God's people when the people turned from idols and returned to the Lord.

The stories of the heroic men and women of faith who served as judges in Israel during this period have delighted children, and contain many lessons on the spiritual life for adults.

■ A detailed verse-by-verse analysis is found in the *Bible Knowledge Commentary* on pages 376-384.

Commentary
The Book of Judges begins with an overview and ends with a summary. The first chapters of this book provide a brief analysis of why Israel's great promise was never realized. The middle section (Jud. 3:7–16:31) traces chronologically the history of the Judges and the conditions of their times. The final section summarizes and, through two case histories, vividly demonstrates the results of Israel's choice to abandon God's ways.

The key to understanding the decline recorded here is found in Judges 2:10: "Another generation [after Joshua] grew up, who knew neither the Lord nor what He had done for Israel." Israel's rest and blessing were dependent on obedience to God. But obedience in turn hinged on knowing the Lord—well.

The New Testament picks up this same theme. "Whoever has My commands and obeys them, he is the one who loves Me" (John 14:21). Obedience to God will result from relationship, and will depend on love. We do not coolly choose to obey in order to gain God's affection. It is only when we know that we are loved by God, and when we love Him in return, that love and trust awaken in us the capacity to obey.

The new generation, in drifting away from a personal relationship with God, inevitably lost the capacity to trust Him and to obey. Rest and blessing, contingent on living out the Law's lifestyle, were inevitably lost as well. These early chapters of Judges trace Israel's breakdown and record a revealing progression.

Incomplete obedience. Joshua had broken the ability of the Canaanites to organize resistance against Israel. Then the land had been divided among the tribes, and each tribe commanded to clear its own territory of enemies.

Archeological evidence combined with the biblical record indicates that Israel was successful in the hills of Palestine, but not in

Causes	Conditions	Consequences
1 – 3	3 – 16	17 – 21

Structure of Judges

the low-lying areas. The power of the remaining peoples was concentrated in the lowlands, and the Canaanites had adopted chariot warfare. Unable to cope with these chariots of iron, the tribes involved failed to drive the inhabitants out (Jud. 1:31, 34). Even more serious, when Israel was victorious they chose not to drive them out. "When Israel became strong," the author of Judges notes, "they pressed the Canaanites into forced labor, but never drove them out completely" (v. 28; see also vv. 30, 33, 35). The people of Israel valued slaves more than their covenant promise to the Lord!

God warned against this alarming tendency. Judges 2:1-4 tells of God's Angel speaking to all the people of Israel. He reminded them that the Lord had made a firm covenant with Israel and had kept His word in bringing them to the Promised Land. Then came the rebuke: "I said. . . . 'You shall not make a covenant with the people of this land, but you shall break down their altars.' Yet you have disobeyed Me. Why have you done this? Now therefore I tell you that I will not drive them out from before you; but they will be thorns in your sides, and their gods will be a snare unto you."

Apostasy. The wisdom of God in demanding that the Canaanites be driven out was demonstrated in what happened then. Influenced by the nature and fertility gods of the surrounding peoples, which appealed to the materialistic and sensual in their nature, the Israelites "followed . . . various gods . . . and bowed themselves unto them . . . they forsook [the Lord], and served Baal and the Ashtareths" (vv. 12-13).

Intermarriage. A third aspect of Israel's departure from God is seen in intermarriage (3:5-6). In this they not only denied their identity as a distinct and peculiar people of God, but also were further motivated to serve pagan gods. The distinctive lifestyle defined in the Law, which was intended to reveal the moral character of God and to set Israel apart from all other peoples, was abandoned in favor of the immoral lifestyle of the peoples of the land. Israel denied her heritage, her identity, and her God.

♥ ***Link to Life: Youth / Adult***
Write on the chalkboard, "Three Failures." Explain that while Joshua's generation followed the Lord, their children failed in three specific respects.

Ask teams of four or five to (1) locate and identify the three failures described in Judges 1:1–3:6, and (2) to describe several ways each failure might show up in a modern believer's life.

For instance, setting the Canaanites to taskwork was a materialistic *failure. Israelites valued slaves more than God. How does materialism show up in Christian experience today?*

(You might label the other two failures a spiritual *failure [incomplete love for God] and a* relational *failure [greater concern for what others will think or want than for God's will].)*

If you wish, list these on the board as hints for your group members, and then let them fill in the specifics from the Judges text.

Preview: Judges 3:7–16:31

Before you teach stories of the Judges, you'll want your group to be oriented to the characteristics of this dark period in Israel's history.

What do they teach us as a unit, apart from lessons apparent in each judge's story?

In these chapters the Book of Judges gives a chronological survey of events during the centuries of darkness which followed for Israel. God's Word had been abandoned and He Himself forsaken. The lesson that earlier generations had learned at Jericho and Ai forgotten, the people of Israel now had to be taught again and again and again. This time, instead of involving a single family (Achan's), the pattern of sin and subsequent judgment swept over the nation as a whole.

And there was a pattern. Seven repeated cycles of events are reported. The first scrip-

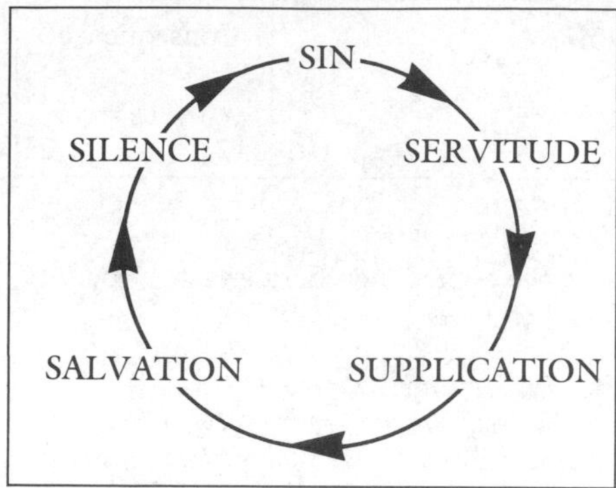

The Sinful Cycle

tural account reports that Israel fell into sin. As a result of sin, God brought judgment through the nearby nations, and God's people were forced into servitude. When the pressure became unbearable, Israel turned from her sin and cried out to God for deliverance. God heard Israel's prayers and a charismatic leader emerged to lead Israel—first to victory over the enemy, and then morally and spiritually as a judge. During this leader's life the people typically knew quiet and freedom from oppression. But all too soon, they slipped back into the sinful ways of the pagans around them. With that fall into sin, the cycle began all over again.

♥ ***Link to Life: Youth / Adult***
To understand this Bible book it is important to see that with each cycle, Israel appears to have become worse. And each subsequent judge had less spiritual impact, until Samson found himself unable to bring rest to the people, even though he was the most powerful of them all!

Use the workchart, "Analysis of Judges" in class. Work through the references, helping your group members find and note key words and phrases. Record them on the chart, and then discuss: "What is the portrait of Israel's experience during this period? What might the message of this book be for people today?"

The chronology. The length of time the Judges are said to have ruled adds up to 410 years. The actual period was probably about 335 years, since the time from Joshua's generation to the fourth year of Solomon (1 Kings 6:1) is itself about 410 years. The reason for the discrepancy between the actual and the apparent time span is that the ministry of the Judges overlapped to some extent (see Jud. 3:30–4:1 and 10:7-9). The various oppressors were not the world powers of the day, but the neighbors Israel had failed to drive out. One judge might have been occupied with a people to the east, while another was occupied with the peoples to the west. Thus we can't tell from internal chronology alone just how long the Judges served.

The shrunken territory occupied by Israel during this era, the seat of the various judges, and the location of the enemies mentioned in this book are shown on the map.

The judges. Twelve names are generally associated with the ministry of the Judges. For most of them the calling was both military and civil. A judge emerged (was "raised up" by God, 3:9, 15, etc.) in time of need, led Israel in throwing off an enemy yoke, and then usually continued as a supervisor of God's people. The judges, in most cases, were apparently successful in keeping their people from idolatry.

The Philistines. We meet these warlike people in Judges. They came to the south coast of Palestine, possibly from Crete, but certainly from the Aegean area. During the years 1200 to 1000 B.C. (part of the time of the Judges and during Saul's and David's reigns) they were the principal enemy of Israel. Their five key cities (Ashkelon, Gaza, Ashdod, Gath, and Ekron) controlled both land and sea trade routes, making the territory the Philistines occupied wealthy and highly desirable.

The Philistine society, in contrast to the tribal structure of Israel, was highly organized. These people knew the secret of making and maintaining iron weapons. This gave them a military advantage over Israel, which lacked both a source of iron ore and the technology to work it. Ultimately the Philistines were able to establish garrisons at strategic points within Israel, and by the end of the period of the Judges, had clearly embarked on a campaign to conquer the whole land.

Not until the time of David was this bitter enemy subdued. David reduced them to insignificance.

Thus these people, introduced here in Judges, play an increasingly significant role in the Bible books which follow.

	1	2	3	4	5	6	7
SIN	Did evil . . . Forgot Jehovah . . . Served Baalim					Again did evil . . . Many Gods	
SERVITUDE			Sold Israel to Jabin for 20 years				
SUPPLICATION		Cried to Jehovah					
SALVATION		Raised up Ehud					
SILENCE				Rest 40 years			No deliver-ance!
	3:7-11	3:12-30	4:1–5:31	6:1–8:32	8:33–9:57	10:6–12:7	13:2–16:31

Analysis of Judges

Judges for Today

Judges is the source of some of our most familiar Old Testament stories. The youngest of children have heard tales of Samson and Gideon—over and over again. In fact, the very familiarity of the stories from this book makes it likely that some will miss its message.

As in all of Scripture, God communicates His message to men in the selection and recounting of events as well as in explicit teaching. As we listen and respond to what God says, the message of the written Word becomes an adventure with the Living Word—Christ Himself! The written Word of God is the avenue through which God comes to us and invites us to enter into an ever-deepening relationship with Him.

Thus it's dangerous to treat familiar portions of the Bible simply as stories. All too soon "Bible stories" can take on a misty familiarity, associated with our childhood—and with Mother Goose fantasy. But the stories in our Bible are not fantasy; they are the rugged flesh and blood of reality. They are a living and powerful message to us from God, designed to captivate us as boys and girls—and to challenge us as adults.

When we do examine Judges with our hearts tuned to respond to God's Word, we find a powerful message indeed. Along with the demonstration of the basic theme (Ai, now magnified and repeated over and over again), we find in the experiences of men and women recounted here the promises and the warnings on which you and I must choose today to act—or to ignore.

This is the adventure of studying the Bible for adults: to study, to examine, and to hear God speak to us, as individuals today.

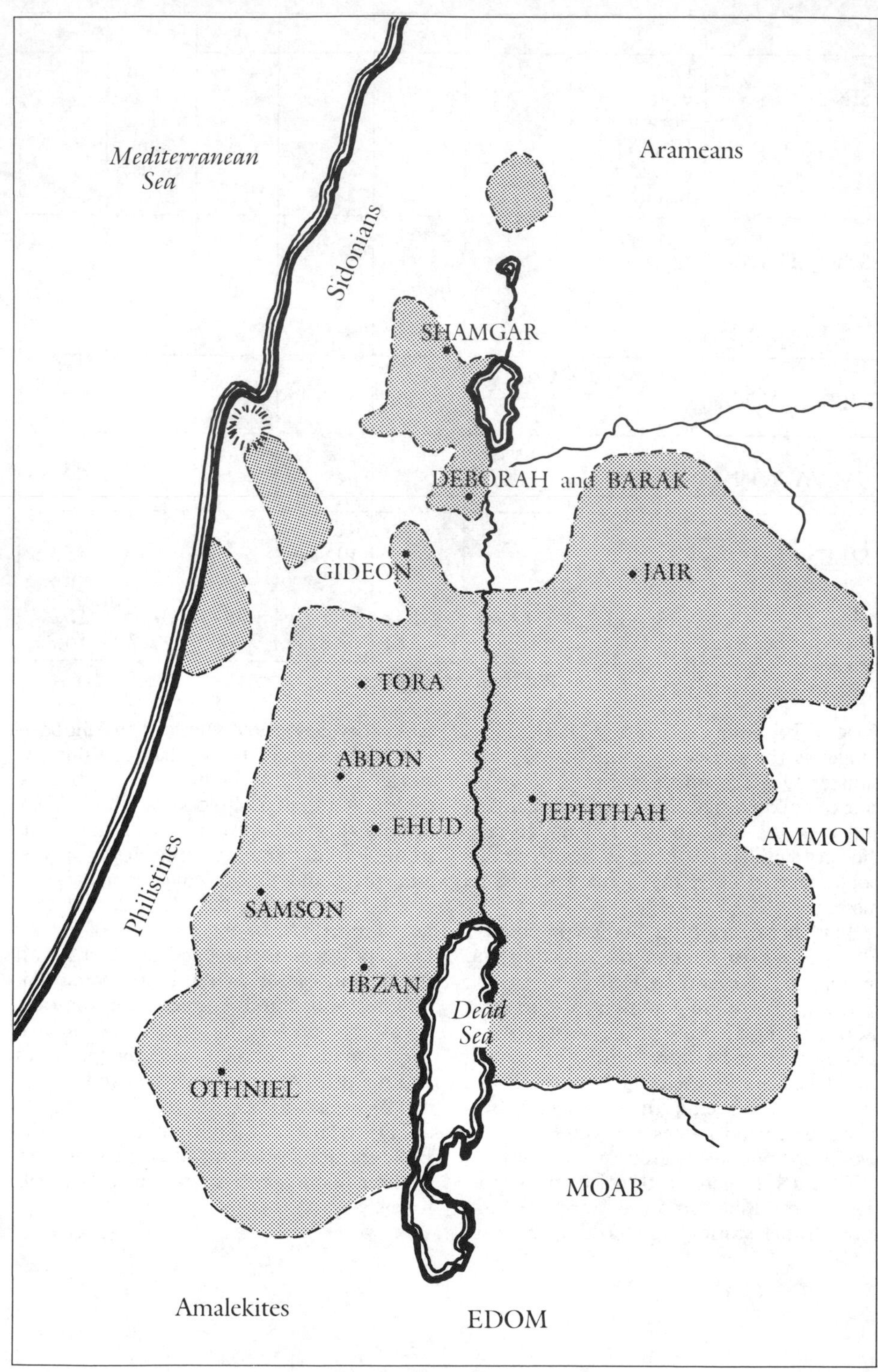

Israel in the Time of the Judges

NAME	OPPRESSORS	YEARS OF OPPRESSION and REST	REFERENCE
Othniel	Mesopotamians	48	3:7-11
Ehud	Moabites	98	3:12-30
Shamgar			3:31
Deborah/Barak	Canaanites	60	4–5
Gideon	Midianites	47	6–8
Tola		23	10:1-2
Jair		22	10:3-5
Jephthah	Ammonites	24	10:6–12:7
Ibzan		7	12:8-10
Elon		10	12:11-12
Abdon		8	12:13-15
Samson	Philistines	60†	13–16
TOTAL		407*	

† Some scholars would have Samson's 20 years running concurrently with the Philistines' 40 years.

*Abimelech, not a judge but a son of Gideon who set himself up as a king, ruled for three years (9:22) to bring the total number of years in the period to 410.

The Judges and Their Rules

TEACHING GUIDE

Prepare
Do the "Analysis of Judges" study suggested on page 178. What do you want your group to discover and to apply?

Explore
1. Give a minilecture orienting your group to the history of the Judges period and its main features. Use the charts to summarize key information.
2. Or put the "Sinful Cycle" chart on the chalkboard. Discuss: "Is this pattern typical of human experience? *Must* it be? What illustrates the 'normal Christian life' ?"

Expand
1. Have your group do an in-depth study of Judges 1–3. Use the suggestion given in the "link-to-life" idea outlined on page 177.
2. Or use the "Analysis" chart to get a picture of the period as a whole. Be sure to examine carefully with your group any obvious or hidden messages in the pattern we see here that can be applied to our lives today.

Apply
1. Suggest that each group member study the life of one of these judges, and be ready to report on lessons to be learned from him when you meet next.
2. Or give each person a card on which to write one lesson he or she will apply to his or her own life. Collect the cards and read aloud, to give your group a sense of what God has been saying to you.

STUDY GUIDE 25

Judges 3:7–16:31

HEROES AND HEROINES

Overview

The Book of Judges spans a period of several hundred years. During this time the people of Israel consistently turned away from God, seduced by the religions of the peoples they had been commanded to drive out of Canaan.

The "judges" of this era were charismatic leaders, who typically led one or several tribes to military victory over oppressing peoples. They then served as civil and religious leaders, and during their lives the people they judged typically remained faithful to the Lord.

The map on page 180 shows the reduced territory occupied by Israel during this period, the seat of each of the judges, and the lands of oppressing nations.

Study Guide 24 should be reviewed before teaching the life of any of the judges, who were the heroes and heroines of faith during a dark and tragic era in Israel's history.

▶ ***Biographical Study.*** There is great value in looking at the lives of Bible men and women. What do we look for? We observe their experiences: How do these mirror our own experiences? What errors did they make we can avoid? What positive choices can we imitate? We look at their character: What traits do we want to see developed in our own lives? How did that person grow and mature? We look at their relationship with God: What lessons can we learn? How did their faith find expression? What difficulties helped develop their trust in God? How was love for the Lord displayed? By their example, we learn and grow.

Commentary

The judges of ancient Israel have captured the imaginations of children in Israel and the Christian era. But there is much here for adults, as we lead biographical studies of these men and women of faith.

In studying this section of Judges we're guided by a principle of biblical interpretation we can call "selection and emphasis." All the events that God chose to have recorded in Scripture are there for a reason. But the story of some events is given more emphasis than others. This rightly draws our attention to those reports that the Bible emphasizes.

For instance, we can look at the number of verses given in this Bible book to the story of each judge.

Othniel	3:7-11	5 verses
Ehud	3:12-30	19 verses
Shamgar	3:31	1 verse
Deborah/Barak	4:1–5:31	55 verses
Gideon	6:1–8:35	100 verses
Tola	10:1-2	2 verses
Jair	10:3-5	3 verses
Jephthah	10:6–12:7	80 verses
Ibzan	12:8-10	3 verses
Elon	12:11-12	2 verses
Abdon	12:13-15	3 verses
Samson	13:1–16:31	96 verses

In terms of the impact of the judges on the men and women of their own times, each may have been equally significant. But in terms of the message for us in the life of these judges, it is clear that Deborah, Gideon, Jephthah, and Samson are more important to us. So in this unit we'll examine the message in each of their lives, and how to convey that message to children and to adults.

Deborah/Barak: Judges 4–5

Ancient civilizations were patriarchal in structure. In such societies, the role of men was emphasized. In many cultures women were viewed as nothing more than property, and were not permitted even to inherit the possessions of their husbands, much less given authority.

Israel too was patriarchal, but women were not oppressed there as in other lands. Women are even among the Old Testament prophets, who were called by God to be His spokeswomen.

Deborah was one of these special women, who even before the military victory over the Cannanites was "judging" Israel from Ramah.

The term "judging" is important if we are to understand this woman's importance. A judge was more than a person who settled disputes (which Deborah did: see 4:5). A judge in Israel exercised all the functions of a governor: he or she held executive and legislative authority, and often military authority as well. We can sense Deborah's authority as she "sends for" Barak, and he comes. It is only when Barak arrives that Deborah speaks in her role as prophetess, and tells him,"The Lord, the God of Israel, commands you."

The Lord's command. This area of Palestine had been oppressed for 20 years by a powerful Canaanite king. His power rested in military strength: the Canaanites had 900 chariots of iron.

These military chariots often had sharp blades attached to the hubs of their wheels: foot soldiers were devastated by the charge of these heavy vehicles, their whirring knives flashing.

God promised through Deborah to give Barak and just 10,000 Israelites a victory over the larger, better equipped Canaanite force.

Barak was willing to obey only if Deborah promised to go too. "If you go with me, I will go; but if you don't go with me, I won't go" (v. 8).

Clearly Deborah had won not only the respect of the leading men of her day, but also was held in awe by them. No one who observes Barak's response to Deborah could ever believe that women were, because of their sex alone, second class citizens in Israel. This woman was a leader; a leader on whom men like Barak had learned to depend.

Deborah's secret. While we have to believe that Deborah was an exceptional person in her own right, there was more to her leadership than her special talents. We can be sure she was wise and fair: the readiness of Israelites to trek to where Deborah held court so she could settle their disputes tells us that (v. 5). But what really made Deborah special, and won her the respect of the men of Israel, was her closeness to the Lord.

God spoke to this woman.

And God spoke through her.

She was one of those few spokesmen that God selected to communicate His will to His Old Testament people: Deborah was a prophetess (v. 4). It was Deborah's special relationship with God that was recognized by all the people, and that won her their respect.

And it was Deborah's closeness to God that led Barak to call for her to go with him.

Barak was willing to fight. But he wanted to be sure of God's presence. In this particular historical situation, it was Deborah who represented to Barak the very presence of God.

The victory. Deborah did go with Barak, and he led his forces to a stunning military victory. But even there Barak was directed and encouraged by Deborah (v. 14).

As if to underline the role of Deborah, a woman, and to protect her place, neither Barak nor his men killed the Canaanite leader, Sisera. He was killed by another woman, Jael, who drove a tent peg into his temple when he fell into an exhausted sleep! Women played the leading parts in this familiar story from the days when Judges ruled.

♥ ***Link to Life: Youth / Adult***

The story of Deborah raises the question of the role of women. Is the Bible really sexist, or are women valued and appreciated there?

Give a minilecture survey of the points made in the commentary. Then divide into teams to explore a biblical view of women.

For an Old Testament "ideal," have one team look at Proverbs 31. The group will discover that while the woman's life focused on the home, she had areas of freedom and responsibility (v. 13), made independent business decisions (vv. 13, 16, 18, 24), managed time and employees (v. 15), etc.

Have another team look at Romans 16. What did Paul say to and about women here? (Note how many of the 28 persons mentioned by name are women!)

Have a third team look at Acts 2:17;

1 Corinthians 12:7; and Galatians 3:26-28.

After discussing its passage, each team is to come up with five statements on "the general attitude of the Bible toward women."

[NOTE: This study should deal only with general attitudes—not with supposed limitations on the role of women in the church.]

Share team statements with the whole group.

Then divide into two groups, men and women. The men are to explore: How can we show appreciation for and recognition of the abilities and contributions of women? The women are to explore: How can we win the respect of and recognition of our abilities by men?

Gideon: Judges 6–8

In the days of Gideon, the Israelites in his area were oppressed by Midianites. The reason, explained by an unnamed prophet sent by the Lord to His people, was that they refused to listen to God but worshiped the pagan gods and goddesses of the land.

The familiar story of Gideon has lessons for us in almost every phase.

Gideon's call (Jud. 6:11-24). Young Gideon was openly skeptical when an Angel of the Lord appeared, called him "mighty warrior," and announced that the Lord was with him. Gideon wondered aloud first about God's presence. He was at that time hiding on his own land while he threshed grain from his own wheat, for fear a party of the enemy might come by and take it from him. Why was Israel in such a state if the God of miracles really was with them?

Gideon was also skeptical about his own prowess. Far from being a "mighty warrior," Gideon was a nothing: the least in the weakest clan in Manasseh.

Gideon was even skeptical about the promise of the Lord, "I will be with you," and about His promise to strike down the enemy (v. 16).

Gideon respectfully asked for a sign—that is, some miraculous evidence that what this stranger was saying was true. This should not be taken as a lack of faith. Deuteronomy 18 indicates that prophets in Israel—those who claimed to speak for God—could and should be tested. A prophet was supposed to make some statement which came true, giving supernatural indication he or she was God's spokesperson (Deut. 18:21-22).

Gideon prepared a young goat and flour as an offering, and when these were placed on a rock, the Angel caused fire to flare miraculously and consume the offering.

Gideon, now aware of the nature of his supernatural visitor, worshiped and honored the Lord.

Gideon's initial obedience (Jud. 6:25-40). Gideon was told to destroy the altar to pagan gods and goddesses erected by his own father for their town. He did it fearfully, at night, but he did obey. This initial act of obedience must have called for great courage. Each of us must begin our adventure with God in the same way. Great actions come only when we have been qualified by obeying in the smaller, local acts of obedience, which may seem frightening to us too.

When the townsmen wanted to kill Gideon for destroying their place of pagan worship, Gideon's father resisted. If Baal was truly a god, the father argued, let him fight his own battles. The only thing that happened was that Gideon won a new nickname: Jerub-Baal. "Let Baal fight him."

Baal did not, and when the enemy prepared to come in force as they had each harvesttime, to strip Israel of its winter food, God's Spirit came on Gideon and he summoned the four tribes in his area to send men to fight.

Gideon had begun to experience God's protection, and to sense His Spirit stir within him. And yet like us at times, Gideon needed reassurance.

Gideon begged the Lord to give that reassurance by putting out a fleece at night, asking that there be dew on it but none on the ground. When morning came, that was what had happened. But the next day, begging God not to be angry, Gideon asked that the sign be reversed. He wanted dew on the ground, but a dry fleece. Again God provided the reassurance.

Why wasn't this a presumptuous sin, a "putting God to the test" that the Bible forbids? (Deut. 6:16) The difference was that Gideon asked God in faith, humbly, seeking reassurance. The generation that had tested God earlier demanded that God prove Himself, and demanded it because they did not believe, not because they wanted reassurance.

God is very gracious in His dealings with His people. He was aware that Gideon felt a need for reassurance despite his faith. And God gave Gideon the reassurance that he asked for. When we need reassurance, God may very well deal with us in this same gracious way.

Gideon's victory (Jud. 7:1-25). Gideon had now been prepared by God for a stunning act of obedience. Thirty-two thousand men rallied in response to Gideon's call. God told Gideon this was too many, because the victory must be seen to be the Lord's. So Gideon told those who were fearful to leave. Twenty-two thousand left.

But on the march God told Gideon this was still too many. All but 300 were eliminated by the next test: anyone who took time to kneel at the riverside to drink was released. Only those so eager to meet the enemy that they dipped up water in their hands as they hurried through the waters could be kept!

Gideon did not now ask God for further reassurance. But the Lord provided it anyway! Gideon and a servant slipped near the enemy camp, and heard a man interpret another's dream about destruction of the Midianites!

The rest of the story is well known. Gideon gave his men trumpets and concealed torches. They surrounded the enemy camp, and when they suddenly shouted, the enemy were thrown into such confusion that they struck out at each other, running in panic.

Then the other Israelites hurried to join in pursuing the survivors.

Aftermath (Jud. 8:1-35). The power of the enemy was totally broken, and Gideon himself executed their leaders. Gideon dealt with jealousy and resentment in a wise and humble way (vv. 1-3). And, when Gideon was invited to establish a hereditary monarchy, he rejected the throne insisting that "the Lord will rule over you" (v. 23).

But Gideon's successes did corrupt him, in two ways. First, he made a golden ephod. In Israel an ephod was a priestly garment associated with worship. This act of Gideon suggests that he took for himself a priestly role which was to be limited to the family of Aaron. And he left his ephod in Ophrah, not at the tabernacle where alone God was to be worshiped. We read that, "all Israel prostituted themselves by worshiping it [the ephod] there, and it became a snare to Gideon and his family."

Second, while Gideon refused the title of king, he seems to have viewed himself as such a ruler. How do we know? Gideon named one of his sons Abimelech. The name means *abi* [my father] *melech* [is king].

Tragically, Gideon's attitude seems to have been transmitted to Abimelech.

This young man killed all the other sons of Gideon, and set himself up for a time as king. He and his coconspirators did not survive long. But one wonders how much of his ambition reflects the hidden attitude of his father.

Yet during Gideon's lifetime his area of Israel did worship the Lord. And on Gideon's death the people turned again to worshiping the Baals.

♥ ***Link to Life: Youth / Adult***

Set up the following list of "lessons for living" from Gideon's life. Ask group members to read the story of Gideon, and decide if the "lessons" are valid or not.

Then work through the passage together, discussing each part of Gideon's story and the "lessons" that might be drawn from it. In the discussion, any "lessons" that are not judged valid should be revised to reflect a principle that can be applied in our Christian lives. Possible "lessons" are:

(1) Skepticism is the enemy of spirituality.

(2) Humble and insignificant people can have a vital role in God's plan.

(3) Believers should never test God.

(4) Obedience in small ways can qualify us for larger ministries.

(5) God demands that our faith in Him be strong.

(6) Success holds special dangers for the believer.

(7) When God is on our side, numbers are meaningless.

♥ ***Link to Life: Children***

How do people obey God? Like Gideon, we need first to know what God wants us to do. Then we need to obey God, even when what God wants us to do is hard.

Gideon knew what God wanted by making sure (the fleece). We know what God wants by the full message of His written Word. Cut lambskin shapes from cardboard . Let the boys and girls add cotton "wool." On the back have each child write one thing he or she knows God wants him to do.

Gideon cut down the altar of Baal even though he was afraid of the people in his town. What things that we know God wants us to do are hard for us? What makes them hard for us? When Gideon did what God wanted, God protected him. Give your boys and girls a broken twig to carry, or to pin to their clothing. The broken twig will remind them that when Gideon did what God wanted and broke down Baal's altar, God took care of him.

Jephthah: Judges 10:6–12:7

Jephthah illustrates the fact that being a social outcast need not indicate the absence of a true faith in God. And that a person with an unhappy childhood need not grow up to be unsuccessful.

Jephthah, born out of wedlock, was rejected and driven away by his brothers even though they apparently grew up together. How difficult this family climate must have been for young Jephthah.

Outcast, Jephthah developed into the leader of a small military community. Later when his homeland was threatened by the Ammonites, the elders invited Jephthah to return and be their commander. No one had protected his rights when he had been driven out by his family. But now, in danger, his people wanted to use his skills.

It may have been surprising, when the delegation arrived, to hear this outcast speaking so familiarly of the Lord (11:9), as though they were closely acquainted. Apparently Jephthah had not rejected the God of the people and family who had rejected him!

Jephthah's letter to the Ammonite king was based on sacred history. He was well acquainted with the history of his people as well as God.

♥ ***Link to Life: Youth / Adult***

Set your group the task of looking at Jephthah's background as described in Judges 11:1-8. In view of his traumatic background and his disadvantages, what kind of person would you expect him to become?

After the group has developed its picture, discuss: "How was your own background like, or unlike, Jephthah's? What in your own personality do you trace to your early background and experience?"

Then study together verses 9-31. What kind of person did he actually turn out to be? What qualities seem surprising? How do you account for them?

Help your group members see that one's character and relationship with God do not depend on his circumstances alone, but on how he responds to them and to Him.

Most attention is usually focused on the question of whether Jephthah, who vowed to sacrifice to the Lord "whatever comes out of the door of my house to meet me when I return in triumph" (v. 31), actually did sacrifice the daughter who ran to meet him.

The answer is, no, he did not. How do we know he did not offer her as a human sacrifice? First, such sacrifice is forbidden in God's Law (Lev. 18:21; 20:2-5; Deut. 12:31; 18:10). Jephthah's letter to the Ammonites shows he was acquainted with sacred history, and would have known this basic worship principle. Second, no priest would have officiated at such a sacrifice, and Jephthah was not qualified by family line to serve as a priest. Third, there is an alternative established in Old Testament Law. A person or thing might be dedicated to the Lord for a lifetime of service (cf. Ex. 20:9; 1 Sam. 1:28; Luke 2:36-37). Fourth, the text indicates this in that the daughter asked for time to weep "because I will never marry" (Jud. 11:37). She was not looking forward to death, but to a celibate life dedicated to serving the Lord.

For all these reasons, we can be confident that Jephthah did not kill his daughter or offer her as a burnt offering in thanksgiving for Israel's victory over the Ammonites.

Samson: Judges 13:1–16:31

Samson, unlike Jephthah, began life with every advantage. His birth was announced by an angel, and he was given a godly upbringing by loving parents. In fact, from birth Samson was set apart to God. He was to live under the most special of all Old Testament vows, that of a Nazarite (see Num. 6).

Yet scanning the story of Samson reveals a tragic story. Though the Lord blessed young Samson (Jud. 13:24), this youth with every spiritual advantage was a spiritual failure.

First, Samson was dominated by sensual desire. That passion led Samson to desire a Philistine woman as a wife, which was strictly forbidden by God's Law. In addition, that passion led him to liaisons with prostitutes, like the one with the woman Delilah who betrayed him for money.

Second, Samson was motivated by pride and the passion for revenge. He was more moved by anger at personal affronts to strike out at the Philistines than he was moved by the suffering of the people he was supposed to lead (cf. 14:19-20; 15:7-8; 16:28).

Third, Samson led Israel for 20 years "in the days of the Philistines" (15:20). Samson, unlike other judges who gave their generations rest from their enemies, never threw off the enemy yoke. During his rule the Philistines still dominated Israel.

We can hardly imagine what Samson, with his great strength and godly heritage, might have been. If only he had lived out daily the formal commitment to God expressed in that Nazarite vow.

♥ ***Link to Life: Youth / Adult***
Why not have your group compare and contrast Jephthah and Samson? Ask them to look at three things: Advantages *(early life)*, Actions *(mature choices), and* Achievements *(results of their judgeship). Then develop a list of lessons to apply.*

TEACHING GUIDE

Prepare
Consider: Which of the judges examined in this unit are you most like?

Explore
1. You might make this a very special session by assigning, a week before your group meets, each of the judges to one of four teams. Give each team suggestions of how to study their character drawn from "link-to-life" ideas in this unit. Ask them to meet together as a team before your group meets. Then during your group time, have each team share what Christians can learn from the life of its judge.
2. Or, select one of the four judges to study together. Review each judge and the teaching suggestions in this unit. Then think about which of the four will relate most closely to the lives or experiences of your particular group.
3. Or, take four weeks for this study, and explore the life of one of these judges each time you meet. Such biographical studies can help Christians gain fresh insight and inspiration for their own personal walk with the Lord.

STUDY GUIDE 26

Judges 17–21

THE WAY OF DEATH

Overview
The last segment of Judges is not in chronological order. It, unlike the first, is a slice of life, summing up in two grim tales the personal impact on the men and women of this dark era of wandering from God.

Judges is divided into three distinct segments. The introduction (1:1–3:6) explains the causes for the centuries-long decline of the Hebrew people between about 1390 and 1050 B.C. The body of the book (3:7–16:31) tells stories of the judges whom God periodically sent to deliver His people from enemies and keep them faithful to Him. This final section might be titled portraits of decay (chaps. 17–21), or perhaps the way of death. As the stories here demonstrate, deserting God leads a people and individuals to a living death.

▶ ***Levites.*** This tribe in Israel had been set aside for the service of God. One family of the tribe of Levi, that of Aaron, was to serve as Israel's priesthood. The other families were helpers, worship leaders, and teachers of God's Law. But only the descendants of Aaron could offer sacrifices to God, and then only at the central place of worship where the tabernacle stood.

In this section of Judges we discover that even those who were to lead Israel in obedience to the Law had deserted it, for we meet a Levite who served as a family priest, served an idol forbidden by the Law, and deserted his benefactor when offered a richer position.

Commentary
"It's all right for you, if that's what you like," Danny told me. He was lying on his back in a hospital bed, his face pinched, still white from loss of blood.

We'd been talking about my conversion, and how a relationship with Jesus made a difference in my life. The day before our conversation, Danny had tried to commit suicide.

He'd taken a deer rifle and fired at his heart—and missed. Instead, he blew a hole through his side, a sofa, and a roof. Now the influence of the 13 downers he'd swallowed just before his attempt had worn off. But not the pain.

We talked and shared—about his life and mine—for several hours. We talked freely about God's desire to bring him the peace and fulfillment that only Christ can provide. It was then that Danny, with honest approval, gave me his blessing. "It's all right for you, if that's what you like."

Subjectivism.

Danny expressed the conviction of many today. All is relative; reality is subjective. The person who likes a religious lifestyle enjoys something that has meaning, "for him." The person with a drug culture lifestyle, like Danny, should be appreciated too. Both ways of life—and the many others open in our culture today—are perfectly fine for the person who chooses them. One is not objectively "better" than another; to insist that it is would be to intrude on another's freedom of choice.

To an extent, some court decisions in the United States reflect just this line of thought. Recently state legislatures have been puzzling over the question of whether homosexuals ought to be able to "marry" one another. The gay liberation movement aggressively demands the right to be different—and to have their particular difference accepted as an alternative, equally valid, morality. Some church bodies have even ordained homosexuals as ministers.

In one Western state, the madam of a well-known house of prostitution ran for the legislature—and was almost elected! Students in a Midwest seminary went to the board, to demand the same housing privileges for male and female students who live together as for those who are married! The "discrimination" outraged the students' moral sensitivities; an outrage foreshadowed by a young woman who told me some five years earlier that "immorality" had to do with exploitation of the poor—not with one's way of expressing himself or herself sexually. She was a seminarian too.

Not long ago a U.S. Congressman confessed to being an alcoholic (a fact long known by Washington politicians and newsmen). But he confessed only after successfully completing his reelection campaign; a campaign during which he lied again and again about the problem he later confessed. But, of course, there is also the Congressman who was reelected after being censured for an affair with an underage congressional page!

Danny had responded to my sharing about Jesus with honest appreciation and even with approval. He thought it was great—for me. But he himself was untouched. In his world, distinctions between right and wrong, true and false, illusion and reality, had long been blurred. With the moorings slipped, with each person taking whatever way seems right to him or her, Danny could not see that my testimony had anything at all to do with him.

A Biblical Absolute

Against subjectivism and relativism, the Bible presents a bold absolute. It affirms that there are universal moral principles on which the behavior of individuals and societies must be based. If this moral base is abandoned, the individual or the society will be destroyed.

Scripture's unyielding absolute is rooted in the presupposition that ours is a moral universe. God, who shaped and planned it all, is a moral Being. Creation's design expresses His moral character. This is true especially of the nature of man, which the Bible insists bears the stamp of the Eternal: the "image" of God planted in us at Creation. As a train is designed to run on tracks, the human personality is designed to function healthily only when stabilized by a steadfast morality. Individuals and societies which jump their moral tracks become increasingly bogged down—and ultimately are unable to function.

It would be wrong to think that morality is a stabilizing factor only for the believer. Righteousness is something that "works" for the believer and unbeliever alike. The Book of Proverbs puts it this way: "Righteousness exalts a nation; but sin is a disgrace to any people" (14:34). There are many such observations in Proverbs. "The unfaithful are destroyed by their duplicity" (11:3). "The wicked shall fall by his own wickedness" (v. 5, KJV). "The violence of the wicked will drag them away, for they refuse to do what is right" (21:7). In a moral universe, there are certain fixed moral laws which when violated bring destruction as a natural consequence. History is full of illustrations of this fact.

It is not that God *intervenes* to punish. It is simply that, given the nature of our universe, the abandonment of righteousness inevitably leads to dissolution of the personality or the society.

This, of course, is part of the tragedy of Danny. He had chosen a way that seemed right to him. Even his suicide attempt couldn't convince him that his way leads to death. Danny denied the Bible's revelation of reality and treated God's way as only one of many alternative and equally acceptable ways. This too is the tragedy of society after society and culture after culture. When a people choose a way that seems right to them, but a way which ignores the divine revelation of righteousness, that society is moving toward its downfall.

The Bible is not just for believers. The Bible reveals a reality with which every man must live. He can choose to accept reality and live in harmony with it. Or he can choose to reject reality and experience its crushing weight. In either case, each demonstrates that God's Word is true. And each society will bear witness.

The men of Joshua's day demonstrated the faithfulness of God's promise; their obedience brought victory and rest. In the days of the Judges, men turned away from righteousness to choose their own way. The fate of these men and the society which they developed now bear witness to the fact that rejection of the divinely ordained lifestyle brings despair, dissolution, and defeat.

Demonstration of the Theme: Judges 17–21

The middle chapters of the Book of Judges report external disasters that came on Israel.

Physical enemies, outside peoples, were sent by God to judge His people and bring them to repentance. These judgments were "extraordinary." That is, they were not direct natural consequences of Israel's sin but divine interventions. It does not always follow, when you or I sin, or when a nation abandons righteousness, that outside forces will overpower us.

What does always follow is inner deterioration. There is a loss of direction. There is growing conflict. These last chapters of Judges are added to show us what happened *within* Israel as a result of abandoning God's ways. It is, in fact, the inner deterioration that is the surest evidence. Abandoning God's standards sears the conscience and confuses the ability of the individual to distinguish between good and evil. No wonder Proverbs puts it the way it does. "There is a way that seems right to a man" (Prov. 14:12). But that "way" is one of illusion. Yet there is a hard reality; the end toward which man's "right way" leads is the reality of death!

Lost legacy (Jud. 17–18). The first of three stories steps outside of the earlier chronological sequence and into the intimate context of an Israelite family. Using the cameo, or slice-of-life approach, the author now moves on to demonstrate the impact of Israel's national apostasy on the lifestyle of individuals.

The first few verses of chapter 17 are enough to jolt us. If we're familiar with the lifestyle God defines for His people in the Mosaic Law, we're hardly prepared for what we see in this typical Ephraimite family. Verses 2 and 3 introduce Micah, a man who stole 1,100 pieces of silver from his mother and, moved by fear after overhearing his mother's curse on the thief, confessed. The curse was canceled by the mother's utterance of a blessing. Micah restored the silver, which was then dedicated to God to make idols for the household shrine!

Theft within the family? Superstition and fear? Worship of idols? Shrines in the house, and abandonment of the central sanctuary? Every one of these stands in stark contrast to the righteous way ordained by God for Israel. Every one of these is characteristic of the pagan culture Israel was to drive out and to supplant.

As we read on in the story, we see additional evidence that Israel had lost its moral bearings. Initial disobedience had led to an increasing loss of moral judgment. The ways of God were increasingly confused with and supplanted by the customs of the nearby pagans.

The story of Micah continues. Micah ordained one of his own sons to be a priest—again contrary to the Law. But when a wandering Levite (not one of Aaron's priestly line) passed by, Micah hired him to "be my father and priest" (17:10). Though Micah again violated instructions given in the Law, he was thrilled at the turn of events. "Now I know that the Lord will be good to me, since this Levite has become my priest" (v. 13).

Some time later a group of Danites (1 of the 12 tribes) was exploring for more land to occupy. They recognized the young Levite, asked his blessing, and shortly afterward located a city in a hidden valley that was occupied by a colony of Sidonians (inhabitants of the pagan city of Sidon, near Tyre). Reporting on the successful reconnaissance, the Danites recommended the young Levite to their tribe. Some 600 men stopped by on the way to the Sidonian colony and offered the young Levite a "promotion." The Bible tells us that "the priest was glad" (18:20) at this invitation. He stole the idol and other objects in Micah's shrine, and gladly left his employer behind.

Micah pursued, complaining bitterly about the theft of his gods and his priest. The Danites threatened him; the betrayed man slunk sadly back home. As for the Danites, they went on to the colony town, Laish, killed all the Sidonians, and the Levite's descendants served as their priests, ministering at a worship center featuring Micah's idol!

This story is told without comment or evaluation. None is required. Over and over again the pattern of life described stands in stark contrast to the pattern prescribed in the divine revelation. Godly ways were a legacy Israel seemed to have lost.

Moral decay (Jud. 19). The second story in this section of Judges does what no commentary could. We are shown vividly the moral and interpersonal implications of the loss of the divine legacy. In this story another Levite is featured.

We are told of the marriage of this other Levite to a secondary wife (a concubine), who angrily returned to her father's home after a spat. After four months, the Levite went to be reconciled to her—something welcomed by the father, as such a separation was both a reflection on his house and a threat to any bride price he may have received. After typical Eastern hospitality—a party of some five days—the Levite and his party left to return home.

As it was probably about three in the afternoon, they were unable to travel far. The Levite was unwilling to stop at Jebus (Jerusalem), for it was still occupied by pagans. Instead he went on to Gibeah, which was inhabited by Benjamites (1 of the 12 tribes).

But the man was offered no hospitality, except by a temporary resident from Ephraim. (This lack of hospitality violated basic Eastern custom.) That night the inhabitants of the city pounded on the door, announcing their intention to make the Levite a victim of homosexual assault! The Benjamites seemed on the verge of breaking in, so the Levite grabbed his concubine and thrust her outside to the men. The Scripture reports, "And they raped her and abused her throughout the night, and at dawn they let her go. At daybreak the woman went back to the house where her master was staying, fell down at the door, and lay there until daylight" (16:25-26).

In the morning when the Levite opened the door, he found the girl crumpled outside, her hands stretched out to grip the threshold—dead.

The ways that had seemed "right" to Israel led to the depths of depravity, to unbelievable moral decay, and to death. For far more than physical death is pictured in this dark incident.

**There is the death of love*. The Old Testament Law taught a person to love God and to love others as himself. Here was a Levite, who represented instruction in God's Law—selfishly thrusting his concubine out to a group of depraved perverts. The capacity to care for others dies when one deserts God's ways.

**There is the death of identity*. The Levite and the old man with whom he stayed both showed that they viewed women as something less than human. In the Creation, woman was taken from man's ribs as a vivid affirmation of her identity with man. Woman was created second, but is not secondary. She is of the same stuff as man; with man she bears the image of God and bears the privilege of dominion (Gen. 1–2).

With the loss of the divine viewpoint, which came with abandonment of Israel's legacy of Law, there came the loss of woman's identity. Distortion of the divine plan brought a measure of death to men and women alike, for in denying woman full humanity, man denies himself.

**There is a death of image*. Man was made in the image of God, with a personality to reflect the personality of the Creator. Even today, men choose to seek their identity in a supposed descent from the beasts—and choose to be ruled by their passions. Thus, the psalmists compare such men to brutes. Jude too sees them doing "by instinct, like unreasoning animals" the very things which destroy them (Jude 10). The depravity exhibited by the Benjamites clearly shows the degradation which comes when men lose sight of their divine image and deny their origins in Him.

The story of Micah and the Danites sets the stage for this tale of the Levite and his concubine. When men lose righteousness' way, depravity follows as night follows the waning of the day.

Conflict within (Jud. 20–21). These two chapters continue the story of the Levite and his concubine. Taking the body home, the Levite cut it into pieces and set the pieces throughout Israel. Shocked, the people gathered to hear the Levite's report (which carefully avoided mentioning his own cowardly part). Shocked as much by the way in which the Levite had dramatized the event as by the act, the tribes angrily agreed to punish Gibeah.

When the men of Benjamin would not surrender their relatives in Gibeah, a civil war resulted. Many thousands were killed, and the tribe of Benjamin was all but wiped out.

How different from the incident reported in Joshua 22, where all Israel was ready to war to keep some from beginning to sin! Here no discipline had been exercised to restrain sin from developing (the Law commands homosexuals be put to death). The war came when part of Israel proved unwilling to surrender murderers to justice.

Morality is never just an individual or personal thing. The strands which hold society together, which provide security for its members, are rooted in morality. When righteousness is abandoned and ways that "seem right" to men are allowed to substitute for the divine standards, the society itself has begun to rush down the road toward its own death.

On the Rock

Scripture does not argue or explain the universal truths which are God's firm expression of reality. Rather, the Bible tends to affirm—and to demonstrate. God's Word is true, not only because God is a trustworthy Person and it is He who has spoken, but also because the word which God speaks is in complete harmony with reality. That human experience conforms to the principles expressed in Scripture does not "prove" the Bible, but rather human experience serves to demonstrate Scripture's reliability and its relevance.

This is the function of this section of Judges as well, and the function of many Old Testament stories. They demonstrate and illustrate the reliability of the affirmations of God's Word. Through Moses and through Joshua, God had told Israel plainly that commitment to Him and to His ways would bring them blessing. "Righteousness exalts a nation" was true then, and it is true now.

But the same Word of God through Moses and Joshua had warned that disobedience carries within it the seeds of its own destruction. The time of the Judges graphically demonstrates this truth. The process of deterioration may take a longer or shorter time. The bitter and deadly fruit may require several generations to mature. But the Word of God is reliable. The death it foretells will come. Unshakable, and unbreakable, the Word expresses the realities by which human beings must live, whether they choose to live for God or not!

TEACHING GUIDE

Prepare

Read through Judges 17–21, and underline anything you see that is out of harmony with the life that God's Law prescribes.

Explore

As your group members arrive, have them read Psalm 12. Then discuss: "What kind of situation might have led the psalmist to express such feelings and views?"

Expand

Draw a continuum line on the chalkboard. Label the continuum line "righteous" at one end, "corrupt" at the other.

Divide into teams to read the events reported in Judges 17–21, breaking the chapters into sections (17–18; 19; 20–21).

When you come back together, decide where along this line your group members would place Israel during the time of the Judges.

Have each group justify its placement by references to the record in their portion of the Judges text.

Apply

1. One phrase which reappears in these chapters of Judges is, "In those days Israel had no king; everyone did as he saw fit" (21:25).

Today the courts in our country tend to define obscenity by what is known as the "standards of the community." In other words, what people in a community think is obscene is, what they think is not obscene, is not obscene.

What do you think of this rule? Is there a relationship between this phrase from Judges and the modern judicial principle? How can moral concepts rather than criminal acts be defined by law in a secular society like our own, where members of that society differ on what is right and wrong?

2. Or tell the story of Danny. How does the rejection of objective moral and religious standards affect individuals in our society?

STUDY GUIDE 27

Ruth

ISLANDS OF HOPE

Overview

The story of Ruth takes place in the time of the Judges (Ruth 1:1). The book tells a simple, beautiful story, that is even more compelling because of the spiritual darkness of the times.

The last chapters of Judges describe the tragic moral and spiritual state of the Jewish people during this era. They had lost track of the Law, perverted the worship of God, and slipped into moral depravity. The Book of Ruth reminds us that even in evil times a godly life is possible. There will always be believers who love and honor God even in sin-saturated societies.

Ruth herself is also important genealogically, for she was the great-grandmother of King David. Ruth is also an important reminder that, even though through the Old Testament era the Hebrews were God's chosen people, Gentiles like Ruth of Moab could find a personal relationship with the God of Israel.

▶ ***Kinsman-Redeemer.*** The story of Ruth also illustrates the meaning of the Hebrew word *ga'al,* which means to "play the part of a kinsman." In Old Testament Law, a near relative had the right to act on behalf of a person in trouble or in danger. When persons or possessions were in the grip of a hostile power, the kinsman might act to redeem (to win release and freedom). The marriage of Boaz to Ruth involved buying back Naomi's family land, and meant that their son would carry on Naomi's family line. Jesus, by taking on humanity, became our near Kinsman, with the right to redeem you and me.

Commentary

A teenager stands before the juvenile court judge. Who's to blame? The home? The society? The individual? Questions like these reflect one of the most significant disputes of our day: conflict between the notion that society shapes and determines the individual—and the notion that the individual bears full responsibility for his own acts. Pleas to juries, much of our social legislation, various schools of pyschology and sociology, and the supposed philosophies of political parties, all reflect the conflict between these two views.

How much of a person's choice is determined by social conditions and how much by the individual's free volition is a tangled question. There's no doubt that environment and society do have an impact on personality. This is one reason why Israel's lifestyle under Law placed so much emphasis on discipline. The people of Israel were to judge and cleanse themselves of sinful patterns which might emerge in the society. The people were jointly responsible to maintain a holy way of life. When righteousness did mark the lifestyle of the nation, the promised blessings included the eradication of social ills.

Israel, under Joshua, did maintain a just society. But there was no guarantee that individuals would continue to choose God's ways. The nation drifted away—away from trust in God and away from commitment to righteous paths. Israel increasingly became an *unjust* society, marked by all the sins and insensitivity we see portrayed in Judges 17–21. The society as a whole became ungodly.

What then about the individual? Did an unjust society, amplifying the tendency to evil that sin implants in every person, make it impossible for the individual to choose good? The last chapters of Judges might suggest this, for they give us insight into the deterioration of Israel as a whole, through descriptions of two people whose experiences reflect the condition of the nation.

But now we turn to a cameo portrait of

different individuals, and look into the private lives of Ruth and Boaz, two who lived in that same paganized culture. These individuals, private rather than public personages, reveal something of the freedom that each of us has to choose.

You and I live in what is, in many ways, an unjust and an unrighteous society. The standards of our day often reflect values and a morality which are tragically far from the divine ideal. But we, no less than Ruth and Boaz, also have the freedom to choose. Despite the pressures and temptations of our times, we too can live godly lives as we follow closely Jesus Christ, our Lord.

♥ ***Link to Life: Youth / Adult***
Put the following statement on a chalkboard: "Influences in our society today make it harder for a young person to live a godly life."

Ask your group to brainstorm, by listing quickly as many factors as they can think of that might lead a person to agree with this belief. (They will think of things like drugs, blatant sex on TV and in movies, pornography, violence, etc.)

Then ask: "What things in our society make it hard sometimes for the rest of us to live godly lives?" Record ideas on the chalkboard.

Finally, sketch the court scene with which this chapter opens. Ask: "In view of the influence of society, how responsible are individuals for their choices?" Let your class discuss this topic, but then move into the lesson to contrast Ruth and Samson, two who lived in the same dark days, but who made vastly different individual choices.

Two Who Chose

The Bible gives a surprising amount of space to the days of the Judges. Israel passed some 400 years in Egypt, but the Bible is silent about these centuries. Yet chapter after chapter portray, in depth, the life God's people lived during the 300 or so years of Israel's deterioration. It follows that God recorded these stories of men and women, as well as the tale of the nation, for an important purpose. Through the inspired record God communicates His message—to the generations of Israelites who lived later, and to us who live today.

Ruth (Ruth 1–4). When Elimelech took his wife, Naomi, and two sons to the land of Moab, one of Israel's traditional enemies, he was fleeing a famine. He was also leaving his heritage in Israel. During the following 10 years, Elimelech died and Naomi's two sons married Moabite wives. Within the decade the two boys also died, and Naomi, hearing that the famine time was past in Israel, determined to return home.

At first the two daughters-in-law intended to return to Israel with her. But Naomi urged them to stay in Moab. There seemed no hope of a marriage or a home for them if they returned with Naomi, who was by now a bitter widow. One of the two listened to Naomi's urging, and she returned to her people and their gods. But Ruth, the other, made one of the most touching and courageous statements of individual commitment recorded in Scripture. Abandoning her people and culture, Ruth chose to identify herself with Naomi, Naomi's then powerless people, and with Naomi's God (1:16-17).

The Book of Ruth tells of the return of the two women, and shows the results of Ruth's commitment.

First, however, we see Ruth's commitment expressed in her lifestyle. Even though Ruth was a foreigner, she was recognized as a good woman who had come to take refuge under the wings of the Lord God of Israel (2:8-13).

The story of Ruth continues with her meeting of Boaz, a relative of her dead husband. In Old Testament times, it was customary for a widow who did not return to her father's household to marry someone in her dead husband's family. The nearest kinsman had this privilege and obligation. The first child of such a second marriage was given the inheritance and name of the first husband, rather than inheriting from the actual father's holdings, particularly if the second husband had been previously married and had a family of his own.

With Ruth's reputation and her faith in God established, Boaz was drawn to this young widow. When, following Naomi's instructions, Ruth indicated her willingness to marry Boaz, he agreed to marry her and to take responsibility for Elimelech's inheritance.

It's easy to misunderstand some of the story here, unless we grasp something of the customs of those days. For instance, when Ruth went at night to the threshing floor where Boaz and his men were threshing wheat, and lay down at his feet, no immorality is suggested (3:6-9). This was a symbolic act expressing Ruth's willingness to place herself under the protection of Boaz.

Similarly the discussion at the gate, and the taking off of the sandal, reflect Old Testament customs. The city gates were where the older men gathered and where business could be transacted in front of many witnesses. Taking off the sandal and passing it had the same force in Israel in those days as signing a contract has in ours.

So Boaz quickly cleared away the legal requirements and married Ruth.

The last verses of the Book of Ruth contain a striking revelation: the child born to Ruth and Boaz (and "given" to Naomi as a grandson) was Obed, the grandfather of Israel's greatest and most godly king, David.

♥ ***Link to Life: Children***

Tell the story of Ruth. Then give your boys and girls crayons and paper to draw the part of the story they liked best.

Let the children show and explain their pictures. Then arrange the pictures in the sequence of their appearance in the story.

Talk about the choices Ruth made—the choice to go with Naomi, to follow God, and to be a good person when they came to Israel. Ask, "What if Ruth had not chosen to follow God, and had gone back to her gods?" (Illustrate by removing all the pictures of events that took place after this point.) "Ruth had to make the right choice for good things to happen to her."

Use this process to focus on the choice that fits your lesson aim: the choice to trust God, the choice of Naomi (a good person, a believer, etc.) as a friend, the choice to do the right thing, etc. By removing the pictures following the choice you help even young ones realize that good things follow good and right choices. But if we make the wrong choices, good things will not follow.

Samson (Jud. 13–16). Four Old Testament chapters are allotted to Ruth. Four are also devoted to Samson. Very possibly Samson was a contemporary of Ruth's son Obed, or of Ruth herself!

But what a contrast in the lives of these two who lived during the same era of Old Testament history.

Ruth had been born in a pagan home, and later, influenced by Naomi, had chosen to identify herself with Israel and Israel's God—even though at the time Israel was an oppressed people. Samson was born in Israel, and his birth was preannounced by an angel. His father and mother were godly believers. Their response to the angel clearly demonstrates that. When Manoah's wife told him an angel had spoken to her, Manoah prayed and asked that the angel be sent again to instruct them how to bring up the child. When the angel came, Manoah's first words were, "Now when your words are fulfilled, what is to be the rule for the boy's life and work?" (13:12)

The parents of Samson were taught that their boy was to be dedicated to God from birth, never to drink wine, or cut his hair, or eat any unclean thing. This pattern of life is defined in the Old Testament for those taking a special vow to God. Such persons were called Nazarites. From his birth, Samson knew an ideal environment. The Bible tells us that "he grew, and the Lord blessed him, and the Spirit of the Lord began to stir him" (vv. 24-25).

This promising start soon drifted into a disturbing pattern of life. Samson, for all his advantages, was a selfish and sensual man. He was not motivated by a concern for God's people; in fact, the Lord had to use his passion for a Philistine woman to move Samson to act against his people's enemies (see 14:1-4). Engaged to the girl he desired, Samson was tricked into the loss of a bet with guests at the wedding feast. Angry because the girl had betrayed the answer of the riddle over which he'd wagered, Samson paid—then disappeared in hot anger (v. 19). His bride was given to another man!

Furious, Samson took revenge by burning the Philistines' fields and by waging one-man guerilla warfare against Israel's oppressors. Instead of leading his people to throw off Philistine domination, Samson continued to act alone, being moved only by his thirst for revenge. Ultimately Samson's own people were forced to deliver him to their enemies, or face destruction! Samson went with them. But when the Israelites left, Samson broke off the bonds that held him and, grabbing a donkey's jawbone, used it as a weapon to kill a thousand enemies (15:10-15).

Samson was personally invulnerable. He possessed a supernatural physical strength so unnatural that the lords of the Philistines realized there must be some secret source—and perhaps some way to neutralize it. Samson's strength became his weakness: his dominance over others was based on physical prowess alone. But his weakness was the domination of his own personality by the desires of his flesh.

Samson became involved with a prostitute named Delilah, who was bribed by the Philistines to seek the source of Samson's power. Judges 16 tells how Samson foolishly betrayed his secret—his long hair, which had never been cut and which symbolized his Nazarite commitment. Once Samson's hair was cut, he was easily taken by the Philistines, blinded, and forced to grind grain at a mill in a Gaza prison.

Much later, the Philistines gathered to praise their god, Dagon, for giving them Samson, "the one who laid waste our land" (v. 24). Samson was brought in to be ridiculed. Leaning against the two middle pillars which bore the weight of the great temple, Samson, his hair now regrown, prayed for strength. With a mighty heave, Samson displaced the pillars, and the temple crumpled, killing Samson and about 3,000 of the enemy.

Samson had judged Israel for 20 years. Yet he is the only one of all the judges of whom it is not recorded that he brought rest to the land.

♥ ***Link to Life: Youth / Adult***

Divide into teams. Each team represents a group evaluating people for employment in an important leadership role.

Each team is to consider family background, moral character, ability to work with others on a team, and past accomplishments. Each team is to first discuss what weight to give each of these factors in their evaluation.

Using Ruth 1–4 and Judges 13–16 as source material, each team should work up a profile of the two candidates—Ruth and Samson. After deciding which person to hire, the teams should then go back and reevaluate their original weighing of factors. What is the most important thing to consider in evaluating another person?

The Family Factor: Deuteronomy 11:18-21

The portraits of Ruth and Samson in the days of the Judges focus our attention on another important issue. In each setting, we gain fascinating insight into families.

Ruth, brought up in a pagan home, turned from her upbringing to identify with Naomi, Naomi's people, and Naomi's God. Samson, child of a godly home, dedicated to the Lord, lived for himself. Even in his death, Samson's primary motive was selfish. "Strengthen me," Samson prayed, "and let me get revenge on the Philistines for my two eyes" (Jud. 16:28).

What can we conclude from the record? First, environment alone does not determine us for either good or evil. Neither being members of a sinful society nor a pagan family fixes our future. There is an element of freedom and of individual responsibility that must be accepted by each one of us. We cannot blame our parents for our choices. We cannot blame our friends. We cannot blame the moral state of the society in which we live.

A bad environment may make it more difficult to choose the right. But the individual still remains responsible for his acts. In the same way, a godly environment is no guarantee that one will choose wisely. We can take no comfort in our parents' faith. We need to make our own commitment lest we too wander from God.

Second, there seems to be an interplay in the era of the Judges between three factors rather than just two. It's not just the influence of society versus the individual's freedom to choose. There is a family factor as well. Judges and Ruth show us that even in a corrupt society there were godly men and women, and godly families. It also shows compellingly the fact that believers need to understand how to share their faith with the next generation!

Samson's parents, for all their personal piety, were not effective in sharing their faith with their son in any life-shaping way. Naomi, despite her unhappiness, communicated compellingly with her pagan daughter-in-law, Ruth.

How can parents, whose own relationship with God may be strong, communicate effectively with their sons and daughters? The Old Testament, reinforced by the New, suggests these principles:

Parental piety is a prerequisite (Deut. 11:18). God's command to adults is to "fix these words of Mine in your hearts and minds." This does not mean that a parent must be perfect, an "ideal" believer who never makes a mistake and never sins. Instead, it means that the parent's faith must mean more than Sunday expression; more than giving lip service to God and to His Word. Knowing a great deal about the Bible is not stressed here. What is important is that the parent be a person who himself or herself *responds to God's Word*. The parent needs to be building the messages of God into his or her own heart and soul. God's revelation is to shape the attitudes and values and behaviors of believers, as well as our beliefs.

Only a person who is growing in the Lord will be able to communicate his or her faith to others compellingly.

Intimate relationship provides a context (Deut. 11:19). The Scriptures focus on the privilege of communicating God and His ways to each new generation in the home. "Teach them to your children." Israel's lifestyle did include certain institutions, such as the cities of refuge and the levitical cities. But there were no educational institutions. There was no Sunday School for the nurture of a new generation, and no colleges for their instruction in the faith. The home, with its intimate and warm personal relationships, was the context in which God's Word was to be communicated.

The rest of Scripture shows us why the home is so important. Faith is best communicated when there is a love relationship between the teacher and learner. Where there is opportunity to observe the life, and participate in shared experiences, the values and the attitudes, the emotions that are associated with actions, all these are learned along with beliefs.

In the context of warm relationships there is a chance for the communicator to explain in words his or her inner feelings and thoughts.

In this whole process, faith's lifestyle is not just talked about: it is modeled, incarnated in the life of the older believer.

When the relationship is a continuing one, extending over the growing years, and not simply one of infrequent contact, faith's lifestyle can be gradually developed.

The critical relational factors shown throughout Scripture seem to be these: loving, being and staying close, sharing, communicating openly, and of course, living by one's commitment to God and His Word.

Somehow Samson's parents, for all their personal piety, were not successful in shaping a godly son. And Naomi, for all her disappointments in life, was able to influence Ruth to love her, and then to love her God.

Explicit teaching in daily life (Deut. 11:19). The Deuteronomy passage makes it clear that we are to teach God's Word. It also shows us when and how. We are to teach by talking about God "when you sit at home and when you walk along the road, when you lie down, and when you get up." The stress here is not laid on what we would call formal teaching—teaching with a teacher, a curriculum, a classroom, a particular time of day. The emphasis in the Bible is on informal teaching: on using God's Word to explain and interpret experiences we share in daily life.

The other morning a conflict flared up between my youngest son and my daughter. He said something thoughtless that hurt her feelings. After I spent 10 minutes of quieting and helping her, my son was angry with me. He felt she had taken his remark wrongly, and so it was her fault. I'd been altogether too comforting to suit him!

It took about half an hour to work things through with him, and help him see that his words had been thoughtless, and that he had really spoken in anger, selfishly. It took even more time to come to the place where forgiveness could be asked and given. Then we talked more about forgiveness, and that for the Christian it means that a confessed sin is truly gone. God's promise is "I will forgive their wickedness, and will remember their sins no more" (Heb. 8:12).

Later that day our youngest was going over to play with a friend with whom he'd had some conflict. Didn't it bother him to go over there again?

"No," he said. "When you've forgiven someone, you forget."

It is this kind of teaching of God's ways, using His Word to interpret and guide in daily experience, that is the key to effective Christian nurture. It was this kind of teaching which might have helped Israel to avoid the dark days of the Judges—if only the adults had first made their own choice to be faithful to God.

How good to know that when you and I trust God, and seek to obey Him, we *can* communicate our faith effectively to those who are near us, to those whom we love.

♥ ***Link to Life: Children***
In a minilecture cover the Deuteronomy principles of effective communication. Then list the three faith factors seen in this unit on the board: family, society, individual choice.

None of these determines *the others; each factor is important.*

Seated in a circle ask each member of your group to talk for two minutes on the role of one of these factors in his or her own life.

Observations on the Text
Ruth 1:1. Naomi's family lived in Bethlehem, which means "house of bread." Because of the apostasy of the age of Judges, God's blessing was withdrawn. There was no food in Israel even in the "house of bread."

Ruth 2:8-9. Boaz warned Ruth against gleaning grain in another's field, and explained, "I have told the men not to touch you." In Israel in the days of the Judges a woman was in real danger of rape!

Ruth 2:11. Boaz said to Ruth, "I've been told all about what you have done for your mother-in-law since the death of your husband." We can be sure that when we do good, our good reputations will spread.

Ruth 2:20. Ruth had not gone to Boaz's field by design. When Naomi heard his name, and that he had been kind to Ruth, she saw the hand of God, and praised the Lord. Naomi was an unhappy person. How good when we are unhappy to look for and to recognize the good hand of our God.

Ruth 4:15. When Ruth gave birth, the women of the community encouraged Naomi. "Your daughter-in-law, who loves you and who is better to you than seven sons, has given him birth." Nothing could replace Naomi's sons, of course. But what each of us needs is people who love us. Such love can make a person better to us than our relatives.

TEACHING GUIDE

Prepare
Read Ruth quickly, and write down five words that seem to you to best describe her.

Explore
1. How difficult is it today to make godly choices? Launch your group time with this question, following the discussion ideas developed in the "link-to-life" activity on page 194.
2. Or give a minilecture reviewing the conditions that existed during the era of the Judges, when the story of Ruth takes place.

Expand
1. Divide your group members into teams of four or five persons. They can work with a simple T-shaped chart, comparing and contrasting Samson and Ruth. Or let each team conduct an "executive search" and evaluate Samson and Ruth as candidates for employment. See the "link-to-life" idea on page 196.
2. Or raise the question: "Do godly parents always produce godly children?"

Let half the group look at Samson's origins and character, and half look at Ruth's.

Return to the whole group to discuss findings, and draw conclusions.
3. Give a minilecture on factors in family communication that can influence the faith and commitment of children.

Stress the fact that family, society, and individual choice are all important influences in personal spiritual development.

Apply
1. If your group members are parents of young children, share the story with which this unit concludes. Ask group members to share similar experiences that illustrate how they have used God's Word to guide their boys and girls in daily life situations.
2. Or ask group members to share about the impact of family, society, or personal choice on their own personality and Christian experience.

STUDY GUIDE 28

1 Samuel 1–8

ISRAEL'S LAST JUDGE

Overview
Samuel, Israel's last, greatest judge, was also a prophet (1 Sam. 3:20) and a priest (9:12-13). In his old age he served as God's adviser to Israel's first king, Saul. Samuel anointed Israel's greatest king, David.

Together the two Books of Samuel cover the history of Israel from the last quarter of the 12th century B.C. to the first quarter of the 10th. They explain Israel's transition from loosely associated tribes led by local judges to a unified nation led by kings.

The Book of 1 Samuel can be outlined as the story of two men, though the biblical focus soon shifts from the flawed Saul to his more godly successor.

Outline

I. Samuel	1–8
1. Early life	1–3
2. Defeat at Aphek	4–6
3. Mizpah	7
4. Demand for a king	8
II. Saul	9–31
1. Saul anointed	9–12
2. Saul rejected	13–15
3. Saul and David	16–20
4. David a fugitive	21–30
5. Saul's death	28, 31

First and 2 Samuel are rich sources of familiar stories. But even more important, they are a source of many lessons that can be directly applied to the lives of children, youth, and adults.

■ Excellent maps in the *Bible Knowledge Commentary* place the events reported in 1 and 2 Samuel.

Commentary
Samuel's Early Life: 1 Samuel 1–3
The right to be bitter (1 Sam. 1:1-20). Like many of us, Hannah was sure that she had the right to be bitter.

Life hadn't been fair to her. And every day, painful irritants reminded Hannah of her complaint.

Hannah was one of two wives of a man named Elkanah. The other wife, Peninnah, had children. But Hannah had none.

In ancient Israel, children were more than important: they were symbols of fulfillment. In Hannah's case her childlessness was a double burden. "Her rival kept provoking her in order to irritate her" (v. 6).

Year after year when Elkanah took his family to Shiloh to worship at the tabernacle there, Hannah met her family and friends—still childless. There her constant pain peaked, and she could hardly bear her fate. We can understand why Hannah felt bitter. She was denied something she wanted desperately.

Hannah's childlessness had at least two tragic effects. First, it colored her whole outlook on life. The Bible says that she was bitter. She wept often, and would not eat. She was "downhearted." And in her prayer to God, Hannah spoke of her condition as "misery." How tragic when we are so burdened that we're unable to experience the simple joys that enrich our lives.

Hannah's depression was so great that she could not even recognize evidences of the grace of God. Hannah had no child. But she had a husband who loved her and who was sympathetic. We can sense Elkanah's love in his words encouraging Hannah to eat: "Don't I mean more to you than 10 sons?" So often when we feel bitter and downcast we too are unable to sense, in the good gifts God has given us, evidences of His love and grace.

Hannah's perspective was so totally colored by her personal tragedy that she could not sense the beauty, the good, or grace with which God infuses every believer's life.

Finally, in her bitterness, Hannah took two vital steps. First, she took her bitterness to God. And second, in prayer she began to reorder priorities. Hannah made a commitment to dedicate the son she prayed for to the Lord. She no longer wanted a child just for herself. She began to look beyond her own needs, and to envision the good that meeting her need might do for others.

Hannah's prayer was a desperate one, so heartfelt that her lips moved, even though she was praying in her heart (v. 13). The high priest at the time, Eli, thought she was drunk and rebuked her. When she explained that she was praying out her anguish and grief, Eli blessed her and Hannah went away with a strange assurance. We read that she ate, and "her face was no longer downcast" (v. 18). That prayer of Hannah's was answered: she conceived and bore a child whom she named Samuel. A child who would grow up to become one of the most significant of all Bible characters.

♥ ***Link to Life: Youth / Adult***

Give your group members a study guide containing the following questions. Let teams of four or five work together to study 1 Samuel 1:1-20 and find answers.

- *How would you describe Hannah's emotional/mental state?*
- *What was the main cause of her condition?*
- *What other factors contributed to make her condition seem even worse?*
- *What evidences of God's love was Hannah given, but was unable to recognize?*
- *What characterized Hannah's prayer?*

When your group members have finished studying the passage, have the teams compare answers and insights. Be sure they note in Hannah's prayer both a free expression of her feelings, and a reordering of her priorities.

Work together to apply what you have discovered. See if you can develop "five ways to deal with discouragement or bitterness."

Praise for answered prayer (1 Sam. 1:21–2:10). When Samuel was weaned, which according to custom would have been about age three, he was taken to Shiloh and presented to Eli. Hannah told how she prayed for this child, and now he was given to the Lord for lifetime service.

It must have been painful for Hannah to leave Samuel. But Hannah's prayer, recorded in chapter 2, is a prayer of pure joy.

Perhaps even more significant, it is a prayer that shows a deep awareness of who God is. Hannah acknowledged God as holy (v. 2), as One who knows and weighs human deeds (v. 3). Hannah saw Him as the One who satisfies the needy (v. 5), who is Master of life and death, of poverty and wealth (v. 6). Her sense of the power and glory of God is summed up beautifully in these verses:

> For the foundations of the earth are the Lord's; upon them He has set the world. He will guard the feet of His saints, but the wicked will be silenced in darkness. It is not by strength that one prevails; those who oppose the Lord will be shattered.
>
> 1 Samuel 2:8-10

What a tremendous reorientation! The same Hannah who was so bitter and downcast that she could not even sense God's grace now saw the Lord clearly. In fact, she was able to praise God in a situation which some might expect would throw her back into despair—the loss of the very child she had prayed for!

What was so different? Hannah now was able to look beyond herself and her own needs. She could sense God's love now, and trust Him. And she could sense the future that God had for this first child she loved so deeply. Because Hannah truly had given her son to the Lord, she trusted God to care for him and to give him a fulfilling life.

♥ ***Link to Life: Youth / Adult***

Point out the pressure on Hannah as she gave up Samuel, and compare it to the pressure of childlessness. Yet Hannah reacted so differently to the two situations. Rather than being downcast, Hannah actually rejoiced (1 Sam. 2:1). Ask your group members to read individually Hannah's prayer (vv. 1-10). Ask each person to find one phrase which he or she believes may help to explain why Hannah was now able to rejoice rather than being bitter.

After everyone has shared, ask each person to identify one situation he or she faces that might cause bitterness or an-

guish. In pairs share the situation, and how the perspective expressed in Hannah's prayer might help him or her deal with it successfully.

♥ ***Link to Life: Children***
Tell boys and girls the story of Hannah's unhappiness and her prayer to God for Samuel. Tell how important having a boy or girl was to Hannah. Explain that Samuel was born as an answer to prayer. In dedicating Samuel to God, his mother and father were saying they wanted Samuel to grow up to love God and serve Him.

Then send home a "Tell me my story" sheet with your boys and girls. On one side duplicate "The story of Samuel's birth" as it is told in your Sunday School material. On the other side ask parents to write, "The story of [their child's] birth."

Moms and dads who have dedicated a son or daughter to the Lord can tell their boy or girl. Parents who have not yet taken this step may be encouraged to make a public dedication that will be particularly meaningful now to their older child.

The story of Hannah and Elkanah concludes with a single paragraph. Each year the two returned to the tabernacle to worship, bringing Samuel new clothes. But they did not come alone. God had opened Hannah's womb, and she bore three additional sons and two daughters.

What a wonderful reminder. It is impossible for us to out give God.

As for Samuel, the boy ministered before the Lord and was cared for by Eli the priest.

Eli's family failures (1 Samuel 2:12-36). While Eli himself was a dedicated and righteous man, his sons "had no regard for the Lord" (v. 12). This passage catalogs their sins as both ritual and moral. Ritually they violated regulations in the Law concerning the sacrifices that signified God's acceptance of sinners. In this they treated the Lord's offering with contempt, a very great sin in God's sight. Morally they were just as corrupt, quick to commit adultery, and ready to use violence as were the people that, as priests, they were called to serve.

While Eli rebuked his sons, they paid no attention. And Eli did no more than rebuke them. He did not even strip them of their priesthood, the least he might have done. As a result God sent a prophet to announce His judgment. The prophet outlined a series of tragic events that would take place "because you scorn My sacrifice and offering" and "honor your sons more than Me" (v. 29). No one in Eli's family line would grow old: his descendants would die in the prime of life. In the place of Eli and his line God would raise up "a faithful priest, who will do according to what is in My heart and mind" (v. 35).

Ultimately that faithful Priest is Jesus, who fulfills in Himself all that the Old Testament priesthood merely signified. In the immediate context Samuel, whose primary role was as a judge and prophet, did serve as a priest. And in the course of history the high priestly role was shifted from Eli's family line to another branch of Aaron's family (cf. 1 Kings 2:27, 35).

♥ ***Link to Life: Youth / Adult***
Do godly parents always produce godly children? It's clear that Eli failed with his sons. But ironically Samuel also had a similar failure! We read in 1 Samuel 8:1-3 that Samuel appointed his grown sons judges, but that they "turned aside after dishonest gain and accepted bribes and perverted justice." Samuel personally was a godly person, dedicated to God from his childhood. How do we explain his failure with his sons?

You might want to let your group members explore this theme by evaluating the following possible explanations.
(1) Busy parents don't give enough time to their children.
(2) Godliness in parents is not attractive to children.
(3) Godly parents expect too much of their children and turn them away.
(4) Godly parents are a good influence but influence cannot determine what a person will become.
(5) Children, like parents, have to make their own spiritual commitments.

After these explanations have been evaluated, give a minilecture. Point out first that we need to question the assumption that what a parent does can determine *a child's life. Each human being is in fact responsible for his or her own choices. Moms and dads should not blame themselves for their grown children's decisions. Second, we need to recognize that parents do influence. It seems significant that both Eli and Samuel showed favoritism to their sons in two ways. Each advanced his sons to positions of responsibility too quickly, and each failed to discipline or remove his sons when they went wrong. In essence each parent* protected his sons from the consequences of their wrong choices!

Follow up with a general discussion. "How are we likely to show favoritism to our children? How are we overprotective? What can we do to guard against these common parental faults?"

Samuel's call (1 Sam. 3:1-21). One of the most familiar of all children's stories is told in this chapter. Samuel heard a voice that he mistook as Eli's. Each time he ran to the old priest, he was told to go back to bed. Finally Eli realized that God was speaking to Samuel, and told Samuel that if the voice called again, he was to say, "Speak, Lord, for Your servant is listening."

Usually children are not told Samuel's message. For that message is a dark one. God told Samuel that the judgment of which He had warned Eli was coming soon. This was in fact a prediction of the future: a prediction which when announced by Samuel and fulfilled, marked him as a prophet, one who would speak God's message to His people. The passage observes that God continued to reveal Himself to Samuel, and that as Samuel grew up He "let none of his words fall to the ground" (v. 19). This phrase simply means that everything that Samuel foretold came true. As a result, Samuel was recognized as a prophet of God.

♥ ***Link to Life: Children***

Acting out Bible stories is fun for boys and girls. Pantomime this story. Let the boys and girls take turns running to Eli, returning to bed, and finally listening carefully to hear God's voice.

Afterward talk about what they have done and seen. How did each try to show he or she was listening? What shows another person we are listening to him? What shows God that we are listening to Him?

Samuel showed God he was listening (1) by going to a place where he could hear God speak. (2) By talking to God when he heard the Lord speak to him. (3) By doing what God said.

Help your boys and girls realize that they can live the Samuel Bible story that they have just acted out. They can go to God's Book, where we hear Him speak today. They can pray and talk to God when they read His Book. And, like Samuel, they can do what God tells them in the Bible.

You can also help each child make a "Listening" booklet. Fold a piece of construction paper horizontally. Print "Listening to God" on the outside. Let the boys and girls decorate the other three "pages" the fold creates, with scenes from the Samuel story. On the inside front have them draw a Bible. On the inside back draw praying hands. Encourage the children to read in the Bible this week and listen carefully to God. When they have found something God wants them to do, they can finish the booklet by drawing on the outside back cover what they have done to obey God.

You may want to suggest a Bible passage for the children to read. Choose one from a recent Sunday School lesson or a recent memory verse.

Defeat at Aphek: 1 Samuel 4–6

The Philistines were a sea people who settled along the Mediterranean coast around 1200 B.C. They established five major cities, from which they spread inland. These people maintained a military advantage from the time of Samson until the age of David. This was due to the fact that they alone in the area knew the secret of working iron. Their iron weapons were far superior to any weapons of the poverty-stricken Israelites.

Humanly speaking, war with the Philistines could only bring disaster. It's no wonder that, in the first battle mentioned in this section, Israel was defeated with about 4,000 men killed on the battlefield.

Israel's response was to bring the ark of the covenant into battle. This ark was to be kept in the tabernacle, the tent which served as Israel's worship center.

The ark contained several special items. It contained manna, the special food given to the people of Israel in their wilderness wanderings. Manna spoke of divine provision. The ark also contained the Ten Commandments, etched on stone tablets. They spoke of the covenant to which Israel was committed, and the holy way of life God set down for them. Even more important, the ark usually rested in the inner chamber of the tabernacle, the holy of holies. There, once a year, the high priest was to come to offer a blood sacrifice that made atonement for all the sins of Israel (cf. Lev. 16). Thus the ark spoke of the absolute holiness of God and of the need to hold God in awe and approach Him respectfully.

But in sending for the ark, the Israelites lost sight of its true meaning. They wanted the ark to serve as a magical talisman. Somehow God's presence was thought of as tied to the ark. If the ark were with them in battle, God must be with them as well. The ark, rather than symbolizing the holiness of God, was to manipulate God into sending a battlefield victory. For, if Israel lost, the ark would be lost! This was a blatant attempt to manipulate God!

Israel's act also revealed a pagan view of God. When the Philistines heard Israel shouting gladly when the ark was brought into their camp, these pagan peoples said "a god [had] come into the camp." How tragic that Israel had no more spiritual perception than the idolatrous Philistines. Neither saw beyond the symbol to realize that God is God of the whole earth, whose presence cannot be captured in any material object. And how revealing that Israel thought God could be manipulated by placing His ark in their vanguard.

In fact, the Israelites were again defeated. The two sons of Eli were killed. And the ark was taken captive.

The next events teach us that the God who cannot be manipulated *will* be honored as holy.

The ark was placed as a trophy in the house of the Philistine's deity, an idol they called Dagon. The idol fell, its extremities broken off. And the people of the Philistine city, Ashdod, were stricken with a painful disease. The ark was moved to another Philistine city, but again there was an outbreak of disease. Finally the Philistines hitched two cows that had recently calved to a new cart, put the ark on the cart, and turned the animals loose. Rather than going to their calves, the cows went straight to Israelite territory, lowing all the way.

The Philistines were healed. And the people of Israel rejoiced. But some of the Israel-

The Wanderings of the Ark of the Covenant

	HANNAH	ISRAEL	ME
The Tragedy	1 Sam. 1:1-2	1 Sam. 4:1-3	
Initial Response	1 Sam. 1:3-16	1 Sam. 4:10–6:20	
Outcome	1 Sam. 1:21–2:11	1 Sam. 6:21–7:14	
The Changes in Persons			

Comparison of Reactions to Tragedies

ite men peeked curiously into the ark. God struck them down, killing 70. The people of Israel still were not sensitive to the holiness of God. In fact, this three-chapter section of 1 Samuel records a painful lesson God taught to His people Israel, and through them teaches to us. Israel had failed to treat God with respect. Even Eli permitted his own sons to defile the priesthood. The people tried to manipulate God by bringing the ark to the battlefield "so that it may go with us and save us from the hand of our enemies" (4:3). This basically pagan view of the ark failed to sense that it was a symbol, pointing to God, but with no magical or divine power in itself.

Yet the ark was associated with God. It had been set apart to God, and as such was a holy thing. The Philistines discovered that Israel's God was supreme when He judged them and their god for treating the ark as a victory trophy. And when God's own people failed to show respect for the holy, they too were struck down.

Why? Because Israel desperately needed to recover a sense of the holiness and the power of God. Only when the people of God honored Him again could He bring His people blessing.

Mizpah: 1 Samuel 7

During the next 20 years Samuel led a spiritual revival. The Bible says that "all the people of Israel mourned and sought after the Lord" (v. 2). During this time the Israelites got rid of their idols, and confessed their sins to God.

When the revival was climaxed with a great assembly at Mizpah, the Philistines decided to attack. The terrified Israelites begged Samuel, "Do not stop crying out to the Lord our God for us" (v. 8). Now, with their sins purified, and with their trust in God Himself rather than in the ark that symbolized His presence, God acted. A terrible storm struck the Philistines. They fled in terror from this divine visitation, and the men of Israel pursued them, killing many. As a result of this decisive battle some of the land taken by the Philistines was recovered by Israel and the Philistines were unable to invade Israelite territory again during Samuel's lifetime.

♥ ***Link to Life: Youth / Adult***

Are tragedies necessary if we are to triumph? These chapters of 1 Samuel may suggest it. Give a minilecture, summarizing two of the tragedies recorded here. Point out that Hannah's personal tragedy led her to pray to God and to reorder her priorities. This in turn led to great blessings, as she recovered her vision of God and also was given a large family. Israel's defeat, and the death of the men who violated the sanctity of God's ark, were also tragedies. But the battle purged Eli's wicked sons from the priesthood, brought Israel a new awareness of the holiness of God, and led to a spiritual revival. That revival made it possible for God to give Israel military victory and peace!

After the minilecture, put the two left panels of the chart (p. 204) on a chalkboard. Let your group members check out each passage for details to complete them. Then ask each group member to think of tragedies in his or her own life. Looking back, can he or she find parallels not only with the tragedies, but with triumphs that grew out of them?

When your members have completed their charts, divide into groups of three or four to share stories.

Demand for a King: 1 Samuel 8

In Samuel's old age the people of Israel demanded a king. In part this was motivated by the fact that Samuel's sons were not like him. And Samuel took the request as a personal affront.

However, there were deeper motives. The people asked for a king so that "we will be like all the other nations, with a king to lead us and to go out before us and fight our battles" (v. 20). As God pointed out, this was an overt rejection not of Samuel but of the Lord Himself!

After all, it was God who had brought them out of Egypt. It was God who had given them victory at Mizpah. To ask for a human ruler showed an unwillingness to continue to rely on the Lord.

Samuel was displeased, and listed all the drawbacks to having a human ruler (vv. 11-18). But Israel insisted, and God told Samuel to listen to them, and to give Israel a king.

TEACHING GUIDE

Prepare

Meditate on how your personal tragedies may have helped deepen your awareness of God—and led to blessings.

Explore

1. Ask each member of your group to think of a personal tragedy or difficulty. When the incident is in mind, ask each to read 1 Samuel 1:1-20. Say, "Underline words or phrases that describe Hannah's reactions to her personal tragedy that *were like* reactions of your own."

When this is done, get in groups of five to share underlined items.

2. Or, if your group is made up of young parents, you may put on the chalkboard: "My children will turn out all right." Ask group members to assign a percent that they are sure this is true (e.g., 90 percent sure, etc.). Share responses, and discuss why the confidence level of different parents is high or low.

Expand

1. Use the "link-to-life" idea explained on pages 204-205. After a minilecture on the tragedies of Hannah and the nation, have your group complete the chart study.

2. Or use the "link-to-life" idea on page 201 to explore ways that we can influence our children toward godly choices.

Apply

1. Share the good things that God has brought into your lives through tragedies. Then close in a time of praise. Like Hannah, express your thankfulness to God for the love, strength, and wisdom that allows Him to use even pain to do good to His people.

2. Or spend time praying for your boys and girls, asking God to strengthen them as they grow to make the choices that will make them godly men and women.

STUDY GUIDE 29

1 Samuel 9–15

THE FLAWED KING

Overview

The story of Saul is a tragic one, yet one filled with important spiritual lessons. Young Saul was an attractive personality. But under the pressures of leadership he showed fatal flaws.

Saul's story is designed not to frighten us, as if we were like him. It is in Scripture to encourage us, for unlike Saul we will maintain a trust in God that enables us to triumph where he failed.

▶ ***King.*** The Hebrew word is *melek.* It is often translated "governor" or "chief" or "prince" as well as king. It indicates a person with civil authority. In biblical times this person had responsibility for all the functions of government—legislative, executive, and judicial. Israel's kings, however, were to be subject to God's Law personally, and to rule in harmony with that Law. Sacred history shows the powerful moral influence of both good and evil kings on the nations of Israel and Judah.

▶ ***Foolish.*** Samuel told Saul at one point that a decision he made to offer sacrifice to the Lord was "foolish." The word does not indicate a lack of intelligence, but a lack of moral and spiritual insight. The fool is impetuous, tends to rebellion, and insists on his or her own way. Only a growing relationship with the Lord and submission to Him can free us from the foolishness that is bound up in the heart of everyone—even children (Prov. 22:15). No wonder that "the fear of the Lord is the beginning of wisdom" (1:7).

Commentary

The Monarchy

Old Testament government. God's Old Testament people lived under two basic forms of national government. The first form was a theocracy. That is, God Himself served as Israel's King and Ruler. God gave His people a Law to live by (as legislator). God led His people in battle, often intervening miraculously to ensure victory when they trusted in Him (as chief executive). God made every individual and community responsible to hold each other accountable to perform the moral, social, and religious obligations set out in the Law (as judge). This understanding of the invisible God directly ruling His people was expressed by Samuel, who was shocked and outraged when the people demanded a human king. Samuel recalled the Israelites' reaction when they saw an enemy move against them: "You said to me, 'No, we want a king to rule over us'—even though the Lord your God was your King" (1 Sam. 12:12).

We might tend to excuse this demand for a visible leader to combat all too visible enemies, if it were not for history. For God, as King, had given His people human leaders. God had appointed Moses and Aaron, who brought this people's forefathers out of Egypt (vv. 6-7). Later, in the land, Israel had suffered oppression from human enemies. But oppression had come only when the people turned away from God. When Israel turned back to God, the Lord sent the leaders known as Judges: people like Gideon, Barak, Jephthah, and Samuel (vv. 9-11). Through leaders like these, God won military victories for His people. The Judges were charismatic leaders sent by God as an expression of the Lord's own kingship over Israel. They did not represent establishment of a different form of government.

But establishment of a monarchy *does* represent initiation of a different form of government. The human leaders to whom Israel would owe allegiance would, like the leaders of pagan nations around them, hold office not by virtue of God's call but by virtue of birth. Kings would pass the right to rule on to their children, with no consideration of ability or of moral character.

Israel's foolishness. When in Samuel's day the people of Israel called for a king, they performed a foolish act. That is, they showed a tragic lack of spiritual understanding.

First of all, Israel's call for a king was in fact a rejection of God's traditional role in her national life.

The desire of the people was for a king so that "we will be like all the other nations, with a king to lead us and go out before us and fight our battles" (1 Sam. 8:20). Yet God had called Israel *different* from all other nations. As Moses had said, "What other nation is so great as to have their gods near them the way the Lord our God is near us whenever we pray to Him?" (Deut. 4:7) It was Israel's direct relationship with the God of heaven that set her apart. In calling for a king, Israel in effect rejected God's direct rule, and denied her unique heritage.

Second, Israel's call for a king disregarded a basic aspect of covenant relationship with God. God had committed Himself to bless His people when they lived in harmony with His Law. God had said, "Walk in all the way that the Lord your God has commanded you, so that you may live and prosper and prolong your days in the land that you will possess" (5:33). This basic element of covenant relationship was unaffected by the introduction of a king.

Whatever the form of government, God's people would only know blessing when they obeyed!

When the monarchy was instituted, Samuel reminded Israel of this fact. "If you fear the Lord and serve and obey Him and do not rebel against His commands, and if both you and the king who reigns over you follow the Lord your God—good! But if you do not obey the Lord, and if you rebel against His commands, His hand will be against you" (1 Sam. 12:14-15). The form of government made no basic difference. Blessing could come only as a result of obedience of the whole people to the Lord.

Third, with a king as the visible head of the nation, many would begin to rely on him rather than on God. Reliance would shift from God to the standing army and the fortifications the king would build. Erosion of reliance on God alone became a real and present danger.

Fourth, institution of the monarchy introduced unnecessary danger. Power and influence were focused in a human leader; a single individual who in turn could influence the nation. An evil king with the power of life and death over his people could make wickedness appear to pay as he rewarded those who were loyal to him rather than to God. Just such a danger exists any time that people must live with divided loyalties.

Moses had foretold a day when the people would demand a king, and the Law established requirements designed to minimize the dangers. He said: "When you enter the land the Lord your God is giving you and have taken possession of it and settled in it, and you say, 'Let us set a king over us like all the nations around us,' be sure to appoint over you the king the Lord your God chooses. He must be from among your own brothers. Do not place a foreigner over you, one who is not a brother Israelite. The king, moreover, must not acquire great numbers of horses for himself or make the people return to Egypt to get more of them, for the Lord has told you, 'You are not to go back that way again.' He must not take many wives, or his heart will be led astray. He must not accumulate large amounts of silver and gold.

"When he takes the throne of his kingdom, he is to write for himself on a scroll a copy of this law, taken from that of the priests, who are Levites. It is to be with him, and he is to read it all the days of his life so that he may learn to revere the Lord his God and follow carefully all the words of this law and these decrees and not consider himself better than his brothers and turn from the law to the right or to the left. Then he and his descendants will reign a long time over his kingdom in Israel" (Deut. 17:14-20).

Israel's king was to subject himself to the King of kings. A king who would not be subject to God could and would bring disaster on the nation.

The coming king. The motives of the people of Israel in demanding a king were wrong. And they lacked the spiritual insight to see the implications of their request. Yet God granted it. Why?

At least two reasons can be suggested. The first reason is found in the fact that the three major institutions in Old Testament life each speak of Jesus. The priesthood was established to offer the sacrifices that affirmed and maintained relationship between God and sinful human beings. Jesus, as our High Priest, offered His own blood in history's ultimate sacrifice, making us forever acceptable to God. The prophet was established in Israel as God's spokesman, communicating His message to His people in time of need. Jesus is "the Prophet" spoken of in Deuteronomy 18, whose message both fulfills and supercedes that given by Moses. And the king was established in Israel as a ruler. Jesus is our present and coming King, who will surely establish His personal rule over this earth as well as the universe at large.

For us to understand the ministry of Jesus we need to sense the historic meaning of the priest, the prophet, and the king in Israel. Each of these offices was designed to help us grasp more of the role of Jesus in God's plan, and in our lives.

For this reason, then, that we might grasp the central role God intends for Jesus, it was necessary that Israel establish a monarchy and live under kings.

But there may be another, more subtle reason, that also points us to Jesus.

Throughout history human beings have assumed that if only a society might devise the *right form of government*, that society would become just and the people would enjoy the blessings of harmony and peace. Plato imagined his republic, and philosophers and dreamers since then have devised various plans for their utopias. But the Bible insists that our problems are not rooted in our forms of government, but in ourselves. Sin corrupts us all, and because of sin no form of human government can promise justice or peace.

Yet human beings continue to dream. And the Bible continues to testify that this dream is false! Israel sinned under Moses, the man of God. Israel sinned under the theocracy. Israel sinned under the monarchy. Israel sinned under Governor Nehemiah. Israel sinned as Rome's client state. And when Jesus returns, a world under Jesus' direct and righteous rule will again choose to follow Satan and rebel (Rev. 20:1-10).

In essence, history's many forms of government continually demonstrate that the problem with human society is not political, but personal. We do not need some new, inventive form of government to make us good. We need Jesus. We need the forgiveness of our sins, and an obedience to God that is expressed in a life of love for others.

God's willingness to let His people try different forms of government was at least in part intended to help them learn from their failures to turn away from man to find forgiveness in Him.

♥ ***Link to Life: Youth / Adult***

Ask your group members to evaluate the following forms of government: Dictatorship; Anarchy; Democracy; Communist; Monarchy. Which would you most like to live under? Which would you least like to live under? Why?

After each person has explained his or her choice, set up two conditions: (1) All members of the society are practicing Christians. (2) No members of the society are practicing Christians. Discuss: "Which form of government would be most effective under each of these conditions?"

After discussion explain the shift in governmental structures that took place when the monarchy was introduced in Israel. This form of government worked well when king and people were dedicated to the Lord. But when people or king were ungodly the nation met disaster. It is not the form of government that makes the difference in life, it is the relationship of the people of a nation to the Lord.

Lessons from the Life of Saul

Saul should have taught Israel the danger of relying on a human king. Every human being is flawed. Only God can be relied on fully.

Yet stories of Israel's first, flawed king continue to teach us important spiritual lessons.

Keys to success (1 Sam 9–11). Saul began his reign with notable success. What were the qualities that made his success possible? These chapters point up several.

**Humility.* Saul was initially free from a sense of self-importance. When told that God had chosen him as king, Saul protested. He pointed out that he was a member of the "smallest tribe of Israel, and is not my clan the least of all the clans of the tribe of Benjamin?" (9:21)

The same trait may have led Saul to hide himself among the baggage as Samuel later led the people through a process of divination—possibly using the Urim and Thummin by which God guided Israel. When he was brought out, the people were excited because he *looked* like a king, being a head taller than anyone in Israel. How good when we can remain humble, as Saul was, when others are impressed by some superficial trait.

**Restraint.* When Saul was proclaimed king a few "troublemakers" objected. In those times a monarch might have been expected to be angry, and act quickly to punish the affront. Saul however showed restraint and kept silent. It is a great personal strength when you and I can overlook criticism and even affronts.

**Godly concern.* The city of Jabesh Gilead, lying across the River Jordan, was besieged by the Ammonites. The purpose was to terrorize Israel, and humble this people who had just anointed a king. God's Spirit filled Saul with fury, and he commanded that all the men of Israel appear to fight the Ammonites. Saul responded in a godly way, for as king he was responsible to protect his people. How good when we too have a godly concern for others, and are willing to be responsible to help meet their needs.

**Wisdom.* Saul's army was large, but poorly armed. Only Saul and Jonathan had iron weapons when they faced the Philistines (13:22). The people of Israel were armed only with clubs, axes, and sickles!

So Saul had the people of Jabesh tell the Ammonites they would surrender the next day. That night he attacked the Ammonite camp from three sides. The surprise was complete, and the enemy force so completely shattered that "no two of them were left together" (11:11).

**Magnanimity.* After this victory the people remembered those who had slandered Saul earlier. They were eager to kill them to honor Saul, whom they credited with their stunning victory.

But Saul was magnanimous in victory. He refused to put them to death on the day that God had won such a victory for his people. What a lesson for us to learn. We need not rebuke others, for as we walk with God His evident blessings in events will rebuke them. We need not defend ourselves, for as we walk with God others sense God's blessing and they will speak up on our behalf.

**Praise.* Saul was not proud in his victory. Instead he led his people to give credit and praise to God. It was not Saul, the king said, but "the Lord [who] has rescued Israel" (v. 13). What an important lesson for you and me, for our victories too are won by the Lord, and are to issue in praise and celebration.

God's choice of Saul was a wise one. Saul was a man of many good qualities, and many of the traits we see in this 30-year-old are endearing.

♥ ***Link to Life: Youth / Adult***
Have your group take the role of a search committee for a pastor of a local church. One of the candidates is Saul. Work in teams of three or four to find in 1 Samuel 9–11 all the reasons why Saul should be recommended to the church by the committee.

Saul's flaws (1 Sam. 13–15). Saul was relatively young when he began to rule. (See the discussion of Saul's age on pages 443-445 of the *Bible Knowledge Commentary.*) Events early in his 40-year reign revealed flaws that had been hidden by the young king's many positive qualities. Several events demonstrate the nature of these flaws.

**Disobedience (13:1-15).* Saul established a small standing army, posting his men at Gibeah and Micmash to defend against Philistine attacks. These cities, which lie just a little to the east of Jerusalem, show how deeply the Philistines had penetrated into Israel's territory.

When Saul's son Jonathan attacked a Philistine outpost, this enemy assembled an overwhelming army that cut through Palestine to assemble near Gilgal, almost on the banks of the Jordan River! This invasion terrorized the Israelites, who forgot their recent victory. Saul called out his people to fight, but instead the men of Israel scattered, to hide in rocks and caves.

Earlier Samuel had predicted this situation, and had told Saul to wait at Gilgal seven days for Samuel to come and offer sacrifice. Saul had been told, "You must wait seven days until I come to you and tell you what you are to do" (10:8). So now Saul waited.

And he watched as members of his army slipped away! Saul did not know what he could do. But as the seventh day slowly passed, Saul felt he could not wait any longer.

Disobeying the word of God's spokesman Saul ordered a fire laid, and he himself, though not of priestly lineage, offered a burnt sacrifice to the Lord!

Saul had been effective in action. But he was unable to stand the pressure of waiting!

How like so many of us. As long as there is something to do, we're all right. But when there are pressures, when we don't know what to do and we have to wait, we too are tempted to act foolishly.

The smoke from Saul's sacrifice was no sooner drifting up into the skies than Samuel appeared. Shocked, the old prophet confronted the disobedient king. "You have not kept the command the Lord your God gave you," Samuel told him. "Now your kingdom will not endure" (vv. 13-14).

The biblical passage makes one striking addition. It reports that when Samuel left Gilgal, and Saul counted the men who were with him, they numbered about 600. Is this number significant?

Some years before Gideon had been called to deliver Israel from an enemy even more numerous. God gradually reduced his army, until only 300 remained. With the 300 God won total victory, and the enemy was routed.

I wonder. Did Saul, when the count was finally taken, remember Gideon? Did he wonder then, if he had only had the courage to wait, if God might not have given him a victory twice as great as Gideon's?

We will never know Saul's thoughts as he learned the number of the men who had remained with him. But we do know now the nature of Saul's flaw. Under pressure Saul would be unable to trust God. Under pressure Saul would be unable to wait. Under pressure, Saul would refuse to obey.

Saul's hypocrisy (1 Sam. 14). A sense of sin is intended to lead us to confession of our faults to God, and is to help us develop a compassionate sensitivity to others who may also fall.

A little later Jonathan again initiated an attack on a Philistine detachment that was deep in Israelite territory. Jonathan and his armor-bearer killed some 20 of the enemy in a half-acre area. The Philistines panicked, and the panic spread! As the Philistines ran, Saul and his men attacked!

As Saul sent out his men he commanded that no one taste food until evening. But as the running battle continued, Saul's men became weak from their exertion. Only Jonathan, who had not heard his father's command, snatched up a little honey as he pursued the enemy through a forest area.

That night, after the men had eaten, Saul wanted to continue his assault. But when he asked God for guidance, the Lord did not respond. Saul took this as a sign that someone had sinned. Again using the means God had provided for special guidance, Saul demanded to know who was at fault. The blame was fixed on Jonathan!

When Jonathan confessed that he had unknowingly violated his father's command, Saul was actually willing to put him to death.

Then the men of the army interceded. Should Jonathan die, who with God's help had routed the enemy? Never!

What an insight into the king. He was ready to kill a son he loved for violating his command. But the king had knowingly violated the command of God! Rather than making Saul sensitive to the weakness of others, he was harsh with those whose fault was less than his own!

Saul fought valiantly against Israel's enemies (1 Sam. 14:47-48). He won many victories. But Saul was never able to win the most important victory of all: a victory over his own inner weaknesses and flaws.

Flagrant disobedience (1 Sam. 15). God commanded Saul to battle the Amalekites, and to totally destroy this historic enemy. Saul was told to also destroy their possessions, including their flocks and other wealth.

Saul did lead his people to battle. But he spared Agag, the king, and the best of the sheep and the cattle.

Confronted by Samuel, Saul first tried denial: "The Lord bless you! I have carried out the Lord's instructions" (v. 13).

Next Saul offered an excuse, and attempted to shift the blame. "The soldiers . . . spared the best of the sheep and cattle to sacrifice to the Lord your God" (v. 15).

Disgusted now, Samuel told Saul, "Stop." Saul had disobeyed God, and that disobedience was evil in the eyes of the Lord. What God seeks in every person is not sacrifice, but a humble spirit, and a devotion to the Lord that is expressed in obedience.

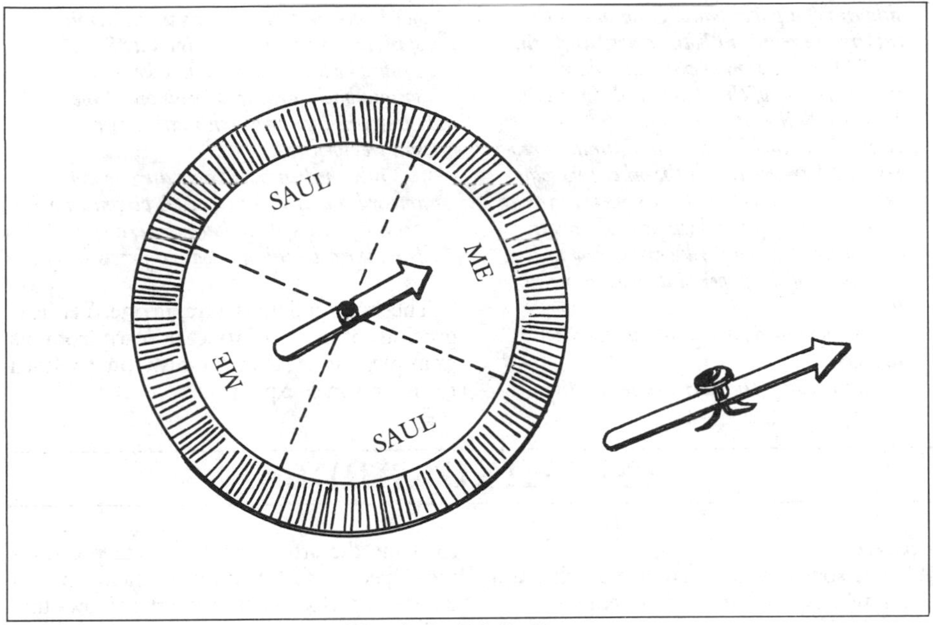

"Saul & Me" Game

Samuel's next words to Saul are addressed to every one of us as well:

> Does the Lord delight in burnt offerings and sacrifices as much as in obeying the voice of the Lord? To obey is better than sacrifice, and to heed is better than the fat of rams. For rebellion is like the sin of divination, and arrogance like the evil of idolatry. Because you have rejected the word of the Lord, He has rejected you as king.
>
> 1 Samuel 15:22-23

Only then did Saul confess his sin, and explain it honestly. "I was afraid of the people and so I gave in to them" (v. 24). But even this panicked confession seems to have been motivated by the fear that Samuel would leave and refuse to "honor me before the elders of my people and before Israel" (v. 30).

Even then Saul seemed more concerned about the opinion of his people than the opinion of God. He would confess his public sin privately. But he would not, as David later did, confess his public sin publicly.

And so we are shown the tragic flaws in Saul, a man who began so well but whose unwillingness to trust God robbed him of blessing, and ultimately filled him with fears not of an enemy but of his own people.

Still, there is one more word in the text of this chapter which, I believe, can comfort us. "Samuel went back with Saul, and Saul worshiped the Lord" (v. 31).

Saul was flawed. That flaw meant that he must be rejected as king over Israel. But the flaw did not mean that God rejected him personally. Saul, the sinner, could not be the leader he might have been. But Saul, the sinner, could find forgiveness and through forgiveness a personal relationship with the Lord.

♥ ***Link to Life: Youth / Adult***
Use the experiences of Saul to help your group members locate their own "pressure points." Divide into teams of three or four. Have half the teams study 1 Samuel 13, and half, 1 Samuel 15. Each is to determine the nature of the pressures that led Saul to disobey.

When your teams report, ask the group to imagine they are Saul, and to list all the arguments they can think of that Saul might have found to obey rather than disobey.

♥ ***Link to Life: Children***
Help your children make a "Saul and Me" game. Mark squares off along the out-

side rim of a paper plate. Color one of the squares, to represent both "start" and "finish." Divide the inner plate into four segments. In two of the segments draw a scene from Saul's life. Perhaps a fire to represent 1 Samuel 13, and an animal to represent 1 Samuel 15. In the other two segments have each child draw something that represents a way in which he or she obeys.

Loosely attach a cardboard arrow to the center of the paper plate with a metal brad.

Use coins or colored paper circles for markers.

After telling the stories of Saul's disobedience, introduce this game. A child spins the arrow. If it lands on a "Saul" square he must move his marker one square backward. If it lands on a "me" square he may move his marker two squares forward.

Only obedience will help anyone move toward the winner's circle. A person who disobeys is always going backward, away from the good things God has for us in life.

The story of Saul is a tragic one. Yet how gracious of the Lord to let us learn from his example, rather than to rush on to learn from personal experience.

TEACHING GUIDE

Prepare
What lessons has God taught you through times when you have disobeyed?

Explore
1. Work with a Choices chart. Draw a wavy line on a chalkboard or poster, labeled as in the sketch below. Ask your group members to name the arrows that indicate pressures most people feel that push them toward disobeying God. Then name the arrows that indicate encouragements to obey the Lord.

When this has been done, ask your group members to think of, but not name, the greatest pressure that they feel.

2. Or, have your group take the role of a search committee that is evaluating young Saul as a candidate for pastor. See the "link-to-life" activity on page 209.

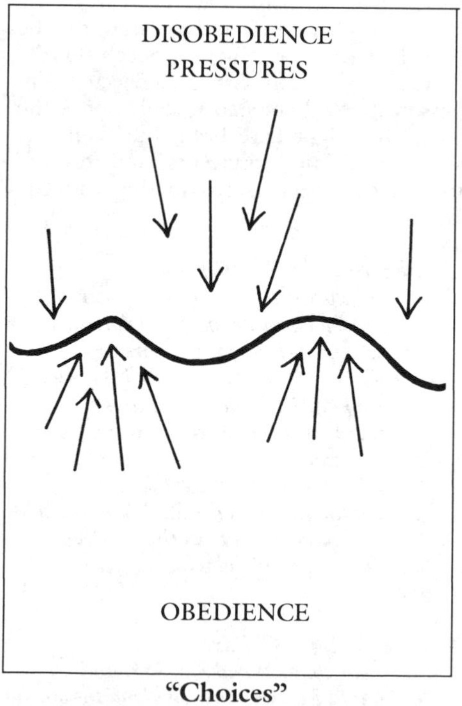

DISOBEDIENCE PRESSURES

OBEDIENCE

"Choices"

Expand
1. Pass out Choices charts drawn on 8 x 11 sheets of paper. Divide into study teams, assigning half the teams 1 Samuel 13 and the other half, 1 Samuel 15. Each team is to identify and label pressures on Saul that led him to disobey. Then each team is to develop counterpressures, which might have encouraged Saul to obey.

When the teams have completed their analyses, come together to share results.

2. Or, continue "gaming" selection of a pastor. Assume you now receive a report of how candidate Saul has functioned in his last leadership role. Explore 1 Samuel 13–15, and do a character analysis of Saul. Would Saul be a good candidate for pastoral leadership? Why, or why not? Saul did have many strengths. Under what conditions might Saul have been able to function well?

Apply
1. Give each person a copy of the Choices

chart. Ask each to identify one situation in which they feel pressure to disobey God. Have each identify and label the pressure arrows. Then have each identify and label encouragements that help them choose to obey.

2. Or, summarize. What should a group responsible to select spiritual leaders look for? How might they avoid calling seriously flawed individuals?

STUDY GUIDE 30

1 Samuel 16–31

THE MAKING OF A MAN

Overview

Israel's years of frustration came to an end with the death of Saul. God "sought out a man after His own heart and appointed him leader of his people" (1 Sam. 13:14).

David's appearance marks the dawn of Israel's ancient glory. During the life of David and his son Solomon, the covenant promise that obedience will bring showers of blessing was fulfilled.

These significant chapters of 1 Samuel relate the story of David's early years, and help us grasp the nature of the often painful process that God takes us through to prepare us for leadership. Many events of these years can be correlated with many of David's psalms, so that we can trace not only the outward circumstances but the inner emotional journey taken by this youth destined to be Israel's greatest king.

▶ ***Psalms.*** Hebrew poetry does not rely on rhyme or rhythm, but on the repetition and rearrangement of thoughts. This means that Hebrew poetry, unlike our own, is uniquely suitable for translation into any language! Another feature of the Psalms is their expressiveness: this poetry is a window on the soul. David and others freely share their emotions, and reveal their inmost thoughts. Whenever we study events in the life of David, it is important to look to the Psalms to understand what is happening inside as well as out.

■ A helpful map on page 452 of the *Bible Knowledge Commentary* traces David's flight from Saul.

Commentary

Greatness is something many people desire but few understand. Usually we recognize the great only after they have achieved. We call them "great" after their military victories have been won, their administrative skills have brought success, or their talents have gained awards. What we see is the finished product, not the process. So we tend to romanticize greatness.

The same thing happens in the Christian realm. The new believer, who dreams of the day he will do great things for God, or the individual who yearns for the day he will live a victorious life, have both romanticized spiritual greatness. They have missed the point that quality and character are forged in experience. Greatness comes only through a process that always contains an element of pain.

Too often we Christians yearn for the product—but try to avoid the process! In our rebelliousness we may miss the pathway that God intends us to take; the pathway that leads to maturity and to spiritual significance.

One of the advantages of a careful study of these passages of the Old Testament is that they counteract our romanticism. We may tend to hit only the highlights: to envision David merely as the shepherd boy who killed Goliath and went on to greatness. But the Scriptures draw us into a careful account of David and his greatness—and expose the suffering that marked his early life.

We have two rich sources to help us understand David's growth toward greatness. The first is the historical account of his life, found in 1 and 2 Samuel, in 1 Kings and in 1 Chronicles. The second source is the psalms that were written by David himself. These psalms portray David's rich emotional life, and reveal his attitudes and feelings at various stages of his life. We need to probe and explore both the historical and poetic sources, for David is the key to understanding the greatest period of Israel's national greatness. Even more, we need to probe and explore because David stands as a spiritual model for you and for me.

Like us, David was a man who often failed, who was subject to temptation and to sin. Like us, David knew despair and fear, doubt and loneliness. Like us, David had a personal relationship with the Lord—and found in that relationship the secret of living above and beyond his potential. As we explore David's life in this and following units, we'll study those qualities which can lift you and me to whatever greatness God calls us to in our own roles in life—in our work, in our homes, our churches, our circles of friends. In this study, we will come to better understand the process through which God is now at work to make us great.

The Early Years: 1 Samuel 16–17; Psalms 19; 23; 29

When we first meet David, we see him in the spotlight. David had come with food to Israel's encampment, where a citizen army was drawn up to fight the Philistines. But the whole army was immobilized by fear of a giant, Goliath, who was some nine feet tall and magnificently proportioned. Goliath had challenged Israel to send out a man for single combat. All Israel feared the giant's power.

Young David, probably still in his teens, was amazed. Certainly no pagan defying the army of the living God had a chance of victory! The Lord would deliver the man who accepted the challenge.

Saul heard about David's remarks. David was sent to the tent of this man who, as leader and the largest man in the nation, had been chosen to fight Israel's battles for them (1 Sam. 8:20). When David was brought before the king, he boldly affirmed that he would fight the giant and kill him. As a shepherd, David had battled lions and bears to preserve his sheep. Surely the Lord would deliver David from the hand of the Philistine giant, for David was going in the Lord's name, to battle now for His sheep!

We know the story well. David came without armor to meet the massive warrior. With a shepherd's sling, David hurled a stone which killed Goliath. Taking the giant's own massive sword, David then cut off his head. The demoralized Philistines fled, pursued by the triumphant Israelites.

♥ ***Link to Life: Children***

Boys and girls are familiar with the David and Goliath story. Here's a way to help them remember and rely on God's help in their own difficult situations. Let your index finger or thumb represent David. Let any young children who volunteer pretend to be Goliath. Ask: "Do you think giant Goliath can beat my tiny finger?" Then "wrestle," letting the child grip your finger or thumb, and press his or her hand down.

Explain. "My finger is much smaller than you are. But my finger is connected to my whole body. My finger is strong, because the body it is attached to is bigger than you. It was like that with David and Goliath. Goliath was bigger. But David was one of God's people, connected to God. God helped David win over Goliath.

"When you are afraid of something or someone who seems too big for you to win over, grab hold of your own finger (or thumb), and remember. You are connected to God too. God will help you win when you do what pleases Him."

The scene of David's triumph is not the beginning of his story. That beginning is rooted in the silent years David spent as a shepherd. It is rooted in the fear David must have felt of the wild beasts around him, and in the courage that was tested over and over again as David went out to meet his challenges. It is rooted in David's growing awareness and trust of God.

Insight into that beginning is also found in God's earlier word to Samuel. When Samuel was sent to anoint David as Israel's future king, Samuel had looked admiringly on David's tallest brother. God reminded His prophet: "The Lord does not look at the things man looks at. Man looks at the outward appearance, but the Lord looks at the heart" (1 Sam. 16:7).

David, though handsome, was not an impressive figure. But during the lonely years of shepherding, David had developed a heart for God. He learned to see God as *his* Shepherd (Ps. 23), sensing in his own care of his sheep aspects of God's care for His people. Living in the open, David also sensed God's greatness through His creation. Later David wrote:

> The heavens declare the glory of God;
> the skies proclaim the work of His hands.
>
> Psalm 19:1

This same theme is often echoed in David's psalms. For instance, in Psalm 29 David calls on men to ascribe glory to God for all that He reveals of Himself in nature.

> The voice of the Lord is over the waters; the God of glory thunders, the Lord thunders over the mighty waters. The voice of the Lord is powerful; the voice of the Lord is majestic.
>
> Psalm 29:3-4

The silent formative years, the weeks spent alone in the hills and valleys of Palestine tending sheep, deepened the youth's sense of God's greatness and power. David's heart responded to creation's revelation. His eyes saw the glory of the Lord.

Measured against this vision of the Lord, whose majestic voice spoke in the thunder, David saw Goliath in true perspective. The giant was merely a creature. The Lord is God.

♥ ***Link to Life: Youth / Adult***
Divide your group into three teams. Each is to study one psalm, and develop from that psalm a series of statements about the writer's concept of God. *That is, how does the psalm writer view God, or think about Him?*

When the teams have finished, ask each to describe the writer's concept of God for the others.

Then read aloud the familiar story of David and Goliath (1 Sam. 17:1-54). Ask: "How does David's concept of God, expressed in these psalms and developed during his early life as a shepherd boy, relate to this familiar Bible story?"

Then discuss: "What is our personal concept of God? How does our concept of God affect the way we respond to the giants (challenges) in our own lives?"

Early Advancement: 1 Samuel 18–22
David's stunning victory over Goliath brought its reward. David was taken into the household of Saul. There David had already established a reputation as the sweet singer of Israel, for his musical talents had soothed Saul, who was subject to demonic oppression (16:14-15, 23). Saul's question to Abner after David killed Goliath, "Whose son is that young man?" doesn't suggest that Saul did not know his young harpist. Saul's question concerned David's family line, as David's answer reveals: "I am the son of your servant Jesse of Bethlehem" (17:58).

But now David was given military command. Already jealous because of the people's praise of David for his victory over Goliath, Saul tried to kill David (18:10-11).

But as a commander, David had a continuing series of stunning successes (vv. 12-16). Finally Saul devised a plot to have David killed by the Philistines. Saul sent David into enemy territory, promising his daughter Michal would become David's wife if he succeeded. David carried out the "impossible" mission, and a disgruntled Saul fulfilled his part of the bargain.

First Samuel 19 and 20 tell of David's growing friendship with Jonathan, Saul's son. Jonathan knew God intended David to be king. The generous Jonathan gladly accepted God's will, and allied himself with David against his father. Finally the situation deteriorated so much that David was forced to flee for his life.

This was a time of intense strain for David. He knew great swings of emotion, as his situation alternated between times of public adulation, and periods when he lived as a fugitive. Psalm 59 tells us of David's feelings during this period, as he swings from fear to anger to hope. The psalm begins:

> Deliver me from my enemies, O my God; protect me from those who rise up against me. Deliver me from those evildoers and save me from bloodthirsty men.
>
> Psalm 59:1-2

Soon David's anger was aroused by the injustice of it all.

> Arise to help me; look on my plight. O Lord God Almighty, the God of Israel, rouse Yourself to punish all the nations; show no mercy to wicked traitors.
>
> Psalm 59:4-5

It seemed incomprehensible to David that God would let his enemies do such things to him. In fact, David was rather upset at the Lord for permitting it!

However, David found the strength to endure the growing pressure by reminding himself of who the Lord is, and by reaffirming his trust in God.

> I will sing of Your strength . . . for You are my fortress, my refuge in times of trouble. O my Strength, I will sing praise to You; You, O God, are my fortress, my loving God.
>
> Psalm 59:16-17

David had been anointed king by Samuel. But Saul ruled. David was not ready yet: he had to undergo further testing. Like his descendant, Jesus, David had to learn "obedience from what He suffered" (Heb. 5:8).

God uses stress in this way in all our lives. He does not rebuke our feelings of frustration or fear, or even anger. But God wants us to learn to bring our feelings and needs to Him, and to let the times of testing do their character-building work.

♥ ***Link to Life: Youth / Adult***
Duplicate Psalm 59, leaving off the superscription which identifies it as David's, "When Saul had sent men to watch David's house in order to kill him." Ask group members to read the psalm individually and (1) identify the sources of the writer's stress, (2) determine how the stress affects him, and (3) list what the writer seems to do in order to deal with his stress.

Share each person's insights with the group. Then discuss: "What seems to cause us most stress? How does it affect us? What positive benefits of stress are suggested in this psalm?"

Then give a minilecture, outlining the pressures on David during this period of time. Point out that David's stress caused him to turn to God. As David found refuge in God, he gained a deeper sense of God's love and was moved to praise (Ps. 59:16-17). The pressures in David's life forced him to probe to the depths of his relationship with the Lord, and this relationship with God was necessary equipment for his future role as Israel's greatest king.

Years of Persecution: 1 Samuel 23–31

The years following David's flight were agonizing ones. Saul, determined to kill David and establish a dynasty, pursued him. Cities which David helped to deliver from Israel's enemies were quick to betray their deliverer to Saul to gain the king's favor! The continual strain began to tell on the young leader; at times David knew deep despair and despondency.

The tremendous stress on David and his response to it are illustrated in the events recorded in 1 Samuel 26–27. Saul received a report of David's latest hiding place and rushed there with 3,000 men. The army camped near David; that night he and Abishai, a follower, eluded the sentries and stood over their sleeping enemy. Able to kill Saul with the king's own spear, David refused. God had chosen Saul. As God's anointed, Saul could not be murdered and the killer remain guiltless. God Himself had to depose Saul, in His own time. David disciplined himself to wait.

The next morning David stood on a nearby mountain crag and shouted down to Saul and his general, Abner. He showed them Saul's spear which he had taken away to demonstrate that he could have killed the sleeping king. Saul, admitting he was wrong, blessed David and stopped his pursuit. But this change of heart was only temporary, and David knew it would be!

Immediately after David's inner victory over what must have been a terrible temptation, David thought, "One of these days I will be destroyed by the hand of Saul" (1 Sam. 27:1). As is often the case with us, victory was followed by an emotional letdown. David was in despair.

In his despondency, David fled to the land of Israel's enemies, the Philistines. He was given a city by one Philistine lord, and from that city he and his men raided distant countries. David let the Philistines believe that his forays were against Israel. Soon David was viewed as a trusted servant of Achish, lord of the city of Gath.

Psalm 142 tells something of David's feelings during the time he hid from Saul and lived under the strain of constant persecution and pursuit. Reading this psalm today, we can sense the inner turmoil that David felt at this critical time. And we can see feelings reflected that we ourselves have known in times of stress.

> I cry aloud to the Lord; I lift up my voice to the Lord for mercy. I pour out my complaint before Him; before Him I tell my trouble. When my spirit grows faint within me, it is You who knows my way. In the path where I walk men have hid-

den a snare for me. Look to my right and see; no one is concerned for me. I have no refuge; no one cares for my life. I cry to You, O Lord; I say, "You are my refuge, my portion in the land of the living." Listen to my cry, for I am in desperate need; rescue me from those who pursue me, for they are too strong for me. Set me free from my prison, that I may praise Your name. Then the righteous will gather about me because of Your goodness to me.

Psalm 142

The years of suffering were forging David's character. God was applying pressures to the godly youth; pressures that would mature him into a man. David's experiences forced him to plumb the depths of his humanity—and to find that in every extremity God was his only refuge.

David often found himself in situations where the temptation to choose the easy way was great. At times David did choose wrongly. But in the great tests—like that moment when David stood over a sleeping Saul—David found the strength to choose what he believed to be God's will. It was this strength, this heart for God, which was at the core of David's developing character. It was this strength which made David great, as it can make you and me.

♥ ***Link to Life: Youth / Adult***
What role did others play in David's life during the difficult years? How do others affect us in our times of stress?

Have group members look at the following passages that describe the role of others in David's life during his years of persecution. Ask each group member to (1) describe the role played by the Bible person(s), and (2) name persons who play a similar role in his or her own experience.

The Bible characters and their roles are:

Jonathan	*(1 Sam. 23:15-18)*
David's men	*(1 Sam. 24:3-7)*
Abigail	*(1 Sam. 25:14-34)*
Abishai	*(1 Sam. 26:9-11)*

After individuals have completed this study, talk about their experience with modern counterparts. "What do others do that helps us in times of stress? What do others do that is not helpful? Can we see even unhelpful persons as God's gifts to us? How?"

♥ ***Link to Life: Youth / Adult***
Several psalms are correlated with this period in David's life. Ask for volunteers to read one of the following psalms, to correlate it with an event during this period, and to give a report during class. The psalms are Psalms 10, 13, 27, 34, and 142.

Storytime
These chapters which give us insight into the process by which David's mature character is shaped are filled with exciting stories which convey lessons of their own. Here are a few of these stories, and some of their lessons for us.

David and Jonathan (1 Sam. 20). Saul was determined that his son Jonathan be king, even though Samuel had secretly anointed David. Despite the close relationship between Jonathan and his father (cf. v. 2), Jonathan sided with David. He defended David when his father angrily demanded David's death (vv. 30-31). When Jonathan was convinced that Saul intended to murder David, Jonathan helped David escape.

This must have been a very painful dilemma. On the one hand, Jonathan loved and honored his father. His self-interest would have been served by David's death. But on the other hand, David was Jonathan's friend. And Jonathan's sense of right and wrong was violated by his father's acts. Jonathan worked through to a godly decision, and won the admiration of countless generations. David is often seen as this era's hero. But there is no more attractive or praiseworthy model of a godly man than Jonathan.

♥ ***Link to Life: Youth / Adult***
Together as a group list the various factors in the situation that must have made it hard for Jonathan to determine what to do. Then ask members to think of any situations in which they were in a similar dilemma, pressured by contradictory factors. Without being specific about their situations, ask members to list the kinds of things they had to consider.

Then discuss: "When in any such dilemma, how does a person go about making a decision? Are there any specific guidelines that can be developed from this chapter of 1 Samuel?"

David and Abigail (1 Sam. 25). When David was rebuffed by Nabal, whose flocks his men had protected, he was furious. In hot anger, he ordered his men to follow him to Nabal's house, intending to kill him and every male in his household.

But Nabal's men explained the situation to Abigail. She acted quickly, gathering food to take to David. When Abigail met David's force on the road, she begged his forgiveness, and urged him not to act hastily and "have on his conscience the staggering burden of needless bloodshed or of having avenged himself" (v. 31). David was wise and strong enough to relent, even though he had publicly announced his intention to punish Nabal.

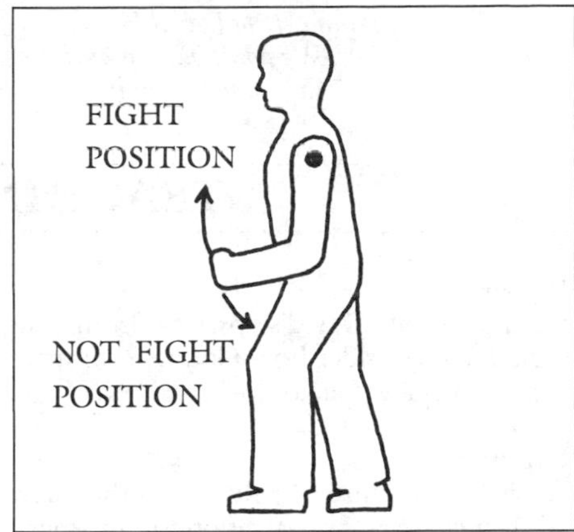

"Fight" Figure

♥ ***Link to Life: Children***

Children can understand David's anger. They get angry too. Often boys and girls want to strike out at siblings or friends as well as "enemies."

Here's an activity to use after telling this Bible story that will help children both learn how to be peacemakers, and learn to think before they fight.

From cardboard cut out several figures like that sketched above. Also cut out an arm with a clenched fist, to be attached to the figure with a brad so that it can swing up and down.

Divide your class into two groups. One group is to list things siblings or others do that make them angry. The other group is to list reasons why it's best not to fight.

Then give one of the "fight" group an assembled figure. He is a "David." He is to tell one of the reasons why boys and girls get angry, and raise the arm to fighting position. One of the members of the other group is to try to give reasons why it would be best not to fight. He or she is an "Abigail." Let the two talk about the problem. When the Abigail gives a reason the David thinks is a good one, he will swing the arm down.

This can be repeated with other things that make people angry, and with other reasons for not fighting.

David spares Saul's life (1 Sam. 26). When David had an opportunity to kill Saul, he held back. He reasoned, "Who can lay a hand on the Lord's anointed and be guiltless? As surely as the Lord lives . . . the Lord Himself will strike him; either his time will come and he will die, or he will go into battle and perish" (vv. 9-10).

David's trust in God was vividly demonstrated in his restraint. So too was his determination to do right, no matter how another provoked him.

The New Testament expresses this principle in a different way. We are to do good to those who persecute us so that we can be like the Lord, who does good to His enemies (see Matt. 5:43-48).

How important to learn to do good, even to those who try to do us harm.

♥ ***Link to Life: Children***

Make cardboard circles about the size of silver dollars. On one side write a possible result of acting lovingly to a person who is not kind or good to you. Among the results might be: we become friends, he or she is ashamed, he or she stops trying to hurt us, etc. On the other side write a possible result of taking revenge instead of being loving: we are punished, he gets madder, we fight a lot, he gets hurt, we get hurt, etc.

Let boys and girls invent situations where someone is unkind to them. Then play a coin flip game with each situation. The children can take turns flipping a cardboard coin. If it lands on the "loving" side, read the results, and let them tell some loving act they might do to gain that result. If it lands on the "not loving" side, read the results, and let them tell an unloving, revengeful act they might do to get those results.

Summarize by reminding them that

as God was taking care of David He is taking care of us. We don't have to hurt people who hurt us. We can be loving instead, as David was, and know that God will guard us.

TEACHING GUIDE

Prepare
Read one of David's psalms from this period and consider how God used difficulties to prepare David for greatness.

Explore
1. In a minilecture, briefly review the stages of David's days of preparation for greatness. Use the titles in the book (The Early Years, Early Advancement, Years of Persecution) to structure your talk. Emphasize the importance of process in preparation for spiritual significance. We cannot expect to become great unless we too go through a sometimes painful process of maturing.
2. Or, assign one or two psalms associated with each of the stages in David's life to different study pairs. Ask each pair to describe the psalmist's feelings at this point in time, his situation, and his relationship with God.

Give the minilecture suggested above. But as you finish describing each stage, ask relevant pairs to share what they have found in their psalm that adds insight.

Expand
1. Ask group members to give titles to their own life stages. Share personal stories in groups of four or five. Then discuss in the smaller groups: "How does my life parallel David's? How have my decisions been like his? Unlike his? What is God teaching me in the process He has planned for my life?"
2. Go back over these chapters and locate the critical decisions that David made. Which were wise? Which were unwise? Does a person have to make *all* right decisions to profit from pressure-packed times? (Note how God redeemed David's choice to settle in Philistine territory, and protected him from possible tragic results [1 Sam. 27:29].)

Apply
Find a verse in a psalm from David's years of preparation that expresses just how you feel about your own life just now.

Share the verse, and where you are just now in your spiritual journey.

Then close, praying for each other that God will use every experience to prepare you for spiritual significance, just as He used every experience to prepare David for greatness.

STUDY GUIDE 31

1 Chronicles 1–10

ROOTS

Overview

Historical roots are a vital element in our faith. We believe that God has acted in this world of space and time. The events that the Bible records are not myth or fantasy. They are in the fullest sense of the word, history.

One way in which the nature of Scripture as history is affirmed in our Bible is through genealogy. The Hebrew people kept careful records of their lineages. They traced that lineage not just to the tribes that sprang from Israel, but beyond that to Noah and even to Adam himself.

Most of the genealogies in the Old Testament are not complete. That is, they name *important people* in the family line, but do not name people in *every generation*. This generation-skipping characteristic of Hebrew genealogies was ignored by Bishop Usher, who by counting up the years of life ascribed to individuals in biblical genealogies, calculated that Creation took place in 4004 B.C.

What the genealogies *do* teach us, however, is that we must take the Bible seriously as history. The Bible is the story of real people. It is the record of God's actual interventions in time and space. It reports what has actually happened—reports that we are intended to take as fact, and to trust as an accurate record as well as to trust as God's revelation of truth to. man.

■ For a verse-by-verse discussion of the genealogies that explores names left out as well as names included, see *Bible Knowledge Commentary,* pages 592-603.

Commentary

The writer of 1 Chronicles is careful to provide detailed genealogical data. Much of the information in these chapters is drawn from other Old Testament passages. Why are these genealogies here?

The Books of Chronicles were written much later than the parallel Books of 1 and 2 Samuel and 1 and 2 Kings. They were in fact written during the Babylonian Captivity, after Judah had been destroyed and her people carried away captives. While the Books of Chronicles cover the same material as that covered in 1, 2 Samuel and 1, 2 Kings, Chronicles treats that material from a different viewpoint. While 1 and 2 Samuel set out to show the establishment of the Old Testament kingdom, 1 and 2 Chronicles set out to review the entire sacred history, from Adam to the day of the writer. With such a massive subject, selectivity is the key. So the chronicler moves quickly over the earlier historical ages, using the genealogies to summarize what God has done from Creation to the Kingdom Age. He then focuses on David's line and on temple worship. In Chronicles, Israel's evil kings are mentioned only when they come in contact with Judah. Even the writer's discussion of the Davidic line focuses on the good kings.

The Chronicles, then, are essentially a theological overview of kingdom history. They were written after the Exile, when Israel had fallen into such sin that the people were expelled from the Promised Land. The glory of David was remembered, but had long faded. Here the divine commentary recalls that glory, but not as a lost dream. Everything here is seen as evidence that God fulfills His commitment to His people, and will yet fulfill the promise of an everlasting kingdom.

The Genealogies: 1 Chronicles 1–10

The genealogies in 1 Chronicles 1–10 are included for several reasons. First, they are a simplified, almost shorthand way of reviewing the history of God's works, and of His special commitment to the family of Abraham, Isaac, and Jacob. Second, the genealogies provide evidence that the present generation has a valid claim to the divine

	1 Samuel	2 Samuel	1 Kings	2 Kings	1 Chronicles	2 Chronicles
Samuel	1:1–16:13; 25:1; 28:11-19					
Saul	9–11; 13–15; 17:32–19:24; 20:27-32; 22:6-19; 23:7–24:22; 26:1-21; 28; 31	1:1			8:1-39; 9:35–10:14	
David	16–27; 29–30	1–24	1:1-4, 15-35; 2:1-11		3:1-24; 11–29	
Solomon		12:24-25	1:28-48; 2:1–11:43		28:5-13, 20–29:1, 21-25	1–9
Kingdom Divided				12:1-33		10–11
Captivity for Israel				17:3-23		
Captivity for Judah				25:1-26		36:15-21

Overlap of Samuel, Kings, and Chronicles

promises. And third, they bring the reader through history up to the period on which the writer intends to focus: the era of the kingdom and the age of the temple.

We can outline these early introductory chapters by the key persons in the genealogies which they contain.

Outline

I. The Common Heritage: Adam to Abraham — 1:1-34
II. The Children of Esau — 1:34-54
III. The Children of Israel — 2:1–9:44
- A. Judah — 2:3–4:23
  1. To David — 2:3-17
  2. David's relatives — 2:18-41
  3. David's descendants — 3:1-24
  4. The rest of Judah — 4:1-23
- B. Simeon — 4:24-43
- C. Reuben — 5:1-10
- D. Gad — 5:11-17
- E. Levi — 6:1-30, 33-46, 50-52
- F. Issachar — 7:1-5
- G. Benjamin — 7:6-12
- H. Napthali — 7:13
- I. Manasseh — 7:14-19
- J. Ephraim — 7:20-29
- K. Asher — 7:30-40
- L. Benjamin (resumed) — 8:1–9:44
  1. Genealogies complete — 8:1–9:1
  2. Chief inhabitants — 9:2-9
  3. Priests, Levites — 9:10-34
  4. Saul's house (repeat) — 9:35-44
- M. The death of Saul — 10:1-14

The genealogies, then, with their emphasis on David's line, bring us to the theme that the writer will now emphasize: the kingdom, as the great divide in the history of God's unveiling of His purposes through Israel, the people of God.

The Review of History

What images and memories would the repetition of these genealogies, so boring to many of us moderns, have cast for the Hebrew reader? They would, essentially, have reviewed all of sacred history. Let's trace that history as it happened, and as it is reflected in the names of men long dead, but men who were vital in the unfolding of God's revelation of Himself and of His plan.

Creation. Genesis 1 and 2 provide the

context. We come to understand this universe we live in and our place in it. The Bible tells us that God created the material universe from nothing; all that exists must be understood in the personal framework that God Himself provides. The universe is not an impersonal "thing," but rather the planned expression of God's might and power and personality.

Genesis also explains man as being the focus and pinnacle of Creation—a creature made in the image of God and thereby vested both with significance and a derived glory. Man cannot be understood unless he is seen as irrevocably related to the eternal, though temporarily occupying space and time. Because man is made in God's image, each individual is of vital importance to God and special to Him.

So these earliest chapters of Scripture, represented by Adam in the genealogies, introduce us to ourselves and to our identity. They explain why each of us stands in need of a vital relationship with God. Without such a relationship to the God whose image we bear, each of us is incomplete. God made us for Himself, and we are restless and ill at ease apart from Him.

Sin. Adam in the genealogies also represents sin. The biblical account moves beyond the initial Creation and, in Genesis 3, shares the story of Adam's fall. This report accounts for the alienation and loneliness we each feel, as well as for the tugging power of sin to which we are each subject. In Adam, mankind chose to attempt life apart from God. Adam traded trust in his Creator for the empty privilege of choosing to do wrong. Ever since then, societies and individuals have shown the agonizing warping of sin-sick personalities.

When Adam sinned, something vital in each person died. Death, not life, became the experience of all men.

Sin's expression in Adam's family. The genealogies are silent concerning Cain and Abel, and the writer goes directly to Seth. But the silence is a painful one, for all remember the unnamed sons.

Chapters 4 and 5 of Genesis examine the impact of sin in Adam's own family. We see one son murder his brother and go on to establish a civilization in which harming others becomes a way of life.

Already in history events had begun to demonstrate the reality and the awfulness of sin. Satan had denied to Eve that sin led to death. Now man began to drink deeply of all that death really means—the dissolution of the personality, and the return of the body to dust.

God acted to cover Adam and Eve's sin. God had already introduced the idea of sacrifice. But since Adam had chosen sin, the ultimate meaning of this pathway would now become known. Adam had refused to trust; now God would demonstrate across the centuries and millenniums of human history how utterly true His words and warnings are.

Sin's outcome in judgment. As the race multiplied and spread across the earth, the expressions of sin we read of in Genesis 4 and 5 multiplied too. Then, when "every inclination of the thoughts of [man's] heart was only evil all the time" (Gen. 6:5), God acted to bring the judgment of the Flood on the human race (Gen. 6–9). Represented in the genealogies by Noah, this cataclysm communicated the fact that sin not only twists human experience, but also incurs guilt. And guilt forces a holy God to judge.

One family, Noah's, was borne over the waters and planted in a renewed world. Mankind was given a fresh start by a man who had enough faith in God to obey His instructions to build a boat.

History repeats itself. The next names in the genealogy, and Genesis 10 and 11, pick up the history of the race after the Flood. Again man disobeyed God. Rather than scattering to accept God-given dominion over creation (see 1:28), the postdiluvian people attempted to build a society without the Lord. So God scattered them Himself, confusing their language.

It was probably at the end of this period, around the time of Abraham, that Job lived. A godly man in an unnamed culture, Job illustrates early faith in God, and the loss of knowledge of God which came as the generations passed. God still cares for and deals with individuals, but sin has twisted the course of the race into unfruitful paths.

Abraham's call. Then comes a great name in the genealogical hall. With the introduction of Abram in Genesis 12, history took a new direction. God spoke to this pagan from Ur, and Abram responded. To Abram God gave a series of great promises, in a covenant explained in Genesis 12, 15, and 17. God announced the course of history ahead of time, as well as the purpose He would fulfill as history moves toward its intended culmination.

God announced that He would no longer work with man as a whole, but would work *for* all mankind through Abraham and his descendants. To these descendants God promised a specific land, Palestine. He also promised great blessings, and a special relationship with Him. God also promised that through this people would come One in whom the whole human race would be blessed.

From that time on, Abraham, his children, and his grandchildren began to view themselves as God's chosen people. God's purposes in history are to be worked out through them. These people are the key to understanding the past and the future; to understanding what has been, and what must surely be.

Captivity in Egypt. As the focus in the genealogies shifts to the sons of Jacob, whose name was changed to Israel, so the geographical location also shifts.

After three generations Abraham's descendants moved from Palestine, the land of covenant promise, to Egypt. There the people of Israel, named now for Abraham's grandson, waited for the next step in God's plan to unfold.

At first the Israelites were guests in Egypt. Then a series of political changes transformed their status, and they became slaves. As slaves, God's people suffered under harsh taskmasters. Because they multiplied so quickly, the Egyptians even initiated a policy of killing their male children when they were born.

Israel remembered the old stories of the God who spoke to their forefathers and who made great promises. But under the harsh reality of their immediate circumstances, the past they recalled and the future they dreamed of must have seemed tragically unreal.

Over generations of slavery, the people of Israel were humbled and crushed. They discovered through their suffering that there was no inherent strength in themselves that could win them freedom. Release could only come through the intervention of God.

Deliverance. God did intervene. Exodus tells us how God sent Moses to confront Pharaoh, Egypt's ruler. God's first demands that Pharaoh let His people go were refused. This brought a series of terrible judgments on the Egyptian people. Finally God struck down the oldest son in each Egyptian family. In terror, the Egyptians thrust Israel out of their country.

The redemption of Israel from Egypt by God's direct and personal intervention is a symbol of all redemption. What man cannot do to free himself from sin's slavery, God can do.

The redemption from Egypt also reaffirmed to Israel the faithfulness of God. God remembered His covenant with Abraham, and acted to keep His promises.

In order that Israel might always remember their need for God's intervention, the Passover feast was instituted. This annual time of remembering deliverance was designed to remind Israel that God is the source of their freedom.

In a series of continuing miracles, including the opening of the Red Sea for Israel and its closing to destroy a pursuing Egyptian army, God demonstrated His firm intention to free His people forever from the slavery under which they had suffered.

The Law. The name of Moses is forever linked with Law. Israel's redemption from Egypt freed God's people from external tyranny. But events soon demonstrated that this people was in bondage to an inner tyranny that was even more destructive. Sin sinks its roots deep into the personalities of even redeemed men and women. Once out of Egypt, God's people murmured and complained. They forgot His commitment to them, and they began to doubt and resist Moses at every turn.

God guided His people to Sinai. There God gave Israel a Law to set standards that revealed the Lord's own character, and showed them the way He expected His people to live. As told in Exodus 19—24, at Sinai God gave His people the Mosaic Law. This Law not only established moral standards, but also defined the distinctive lifestyle which God was to hold His people to, both for their benefit and as a testimony.

But, again, the Law provided an external standard. It did not change Israel within. The continuing story of the redeemed generation shows their inability to trust God, and the subsequent disobedience. Commanded to enter the Promised Land, Israel refused. The people were condemned to 38 years of wandering in the wilderness, until the generation that had known God's deliverance from Egypt died. Because of unbelief they were unable to enter into the promised rest.

The new generation. The men and women who had seen God's mighty acts in Egypt, but had refused to trust Him, died. Their children now stood poised on the edge of the Promised Land. In Deuteronomy, we hear Moses restate the Law and sketch again the lifestyle of trust to which God called His people. In Joshua we see the new generation respond to God and follow their new leader to victory.

The Promised Land was taken in a series of swift military moves, with God making His presence known on the side of His people at Jericho and in other actions.

With opposition of the people of the land rendered ineffective, the people of God settled into their promised rest.

Sin reappears again. Even though Israel moved into an ideal environment, in a social system designed by God to bless His people, the ancient specter of sin again appeared. The generations that followed drifted away from God and were marked by growing disobedience. Over the decades, the lifestyle of Israel deteriorated. God judged sin with the removal of His protection, and Israel's enemies gained ascendancy over the 12 tribes. Yet, when Israel turned to God, He sent deliverers or "judges" to free the people from their enemies and lead them back to His ways.

The more than 330 years that the Judges ruled were days of repeated ups and downs for Israel. But the trend of history was downward. The days of the Judges were dark days, days during which sin's dreadful dominion was demonstrated even under the divinely ordained system of government, the theocracy, which was potentially the best man has ever known.

The kingdom. Finally Israel demanded a new system of government. Israel's first king, Saul, demonstrated once again that the root of the sin problem is in man, not in society. But then God gave Israel a godly king, David. David led Israel to a foreshadowing of that glory which God told His people to expect.

It is here that the 1 Chronicles' genealogies end. "Saul died because he was unfaithful to the Lord; he did not keep the Word of the Lord and even consulted a medium for guidance, and did not inquire of the Lord. So the Lord put him to death and turned the kingdom over to David son of Jesse" (1 Chron. 10:13-14).

The Lesson

For the Israelite, a review of the genealogies was a review of sacred history itself. There were so many memories, captured there by familiar names.

The review of history was also a reminder to the Israelite of his heritage. As a descendant of Abraham, he was one of that special line chosen to be the focus of God's working in the world.

But for us, as we look back over Old Testament history as it is reflected in these names, there is another lesson as well. Our journey through Bible history reminds us that no changes in external conditions brought men to the condition of blessedness and dominion that God intends for man. Yet, human beings still struggle to find release and fulfillment without God, denying God's judgment that it is sin that has brought death, and that death still holds man and society in its unbreakable grip.

Looking ahead, in future studies we'll trace God's continuing revelation of His own solution to each individual's—and society's—need. We'll see in the continuing flow of history even more evidence that nothing apart from God's personal action in Christ can offer meaningful hope.

There is a personal message in this flow of history. The death we see expressed in history and in society grips you and me as well as others. You and I must turn from our own efforts and reject all the tempting solutions the world offers. We must seek God's intervention in our own lives. As the New Testament phrases God's message to the individual, "You were dead in your trespasses and sins, in which you formerly walked" (Eph. 2:1-2, NASB).

The passage, Ephesians 2, goes on to explain. "But God, being rich in mercy, because of His great love with which He loved us, even when we were dead in our transgressions, made us alive together with Christ" (vv. 4-5, NASB).

In the person of Jesus Christ, promised in the Old Testament and revealed in the New, God has acted to bring you and me the possibility of life, and to call us from the experience of sin's death to a new and abundant life in Jesus.

If we have heard the message of Bible history, our eyes have been turned away from ourselves and our own efforts to God. If we have heard the message of Bible history, we have recognized the reality of death, spiritual and physical. If we have heard the message of Bible history, we can begin to realize that our one and only hope is in God, our Creator and the Saviour of us all.

TEACHING GUIDE

Prepare
Which character in Bible history are you most like? Why?

Explore
1. Give a minilecture on the nature of Bible genealogies (as a generation-skipping record of important persons) and the reason why genealogies were so important to the Hebrew people.
2. Or ask your group members to write down the names of five *important* Bible characters who lived before King David.

Beside the names each person should jot down a note on why that person seems important to him or her.

Then share, writing down the names your group members have come up with. List these on the board, with a number noting how many of your group named each.

When you've completed your list, ask your group members to see how many of these names they can find in the genealogies of 1 Chronicles 1–10.

Expand
1. List on the chalkboard the different eras represented in the genealogies, as these are indicated in this chapter by *italicized* headings. As you work through these eras together, you might briefly sketch what happened in each. As you do, let your group members suggest spiritual lessons God taught during that time. In effect, this process will provide a simple but effective review of Bible history—just as the genealogies did for the people of the Old Testament.
2. Or, after your group members have searched for the names they listed, talk briefly about the writer's purpose and principles of selection. You can give a summary of the purposes of these genealogies as a review of history, and a reminder of the faithfulness of God, as well as reassurance to the living Jews that they truly are in the covenant line.

Apply
Ask each of your members to select one period or one name that seems to sum up his or her Christian experience. Then divide into groups of four or five. Each person is to tell which Bible person he or she chose, and to explain why.

STUDY GUIDE 32

2 Samuel 1–10; 1 Chronicles 11–19

DAVID'S TRIUMPHS

Overview
Now the Old Testament record focuses on David.

With the death of Saul, David's fortune changed. He was no longer a fugitive, and was quickly acknowledged as king by the southern tribe of Judah, his own tribe. In the north Ish-Bosheth, a surviving son of Saul, was propped up as king by the military leader, Abner.

Over the next years there were minor skirmishes between the two kingdoms. But David's strength showed itself, as did Ish-Bosheth's weakness. Then Ish-Bosheth was assassinated (and the assassins executed by an outraged David). It was seven and a half years after David had become king of Judah that he was recognized as king by all of Israel.

The story of David's triumphs is told in two Old Testament books, as shown in the outline below. From these books we grasp something of the significance of the accomplishments of this great leader, as well as great man of faith.

David's Triumphs

Period	2 Sam.	1 Chron.
1. King of Judah	1–4	
2. King of United Israel	5–10	11—19

▶ ***David.*** David's accomplishments as Israel's ruler are unmatched. He is a type of Jesus, who will rule as God's coming King. His personal qualities and faith provide examples for believers of every age.

Commentary
David's rule was strong and aggressive and his accomplishments were unparalleled. Other men of history have demonstrated military and administrative capacity, but David overshadows them all by the breadth and depth of his ability. To cap it all, David is one of the great men of faith.

To understand the significance of this remarkable man it is necessary to survey the accomplishments that are reported in these biblical passages, and to examine his role in Old Testament prophecy.

Events of David's Reign

David made king	2 Sam. 5:1-5 1 Chron. 11:1-3
David takes Jerusalem	2 Sam. 5:6-9 1 Chron. 11:4-9
David organizes the mighty men	1 Chron. 11:10–12:40
David defeats the Philistines	2 Sam. 5:17-25 1 Chron. 14:8-17
David brings the ark to Jerusalem	2 Sam. 6:1-12 1 Chron. 13:1-14; 15:1-15
David offers praise	2 Sam. 6:12-23 1 Chron. 15:6–16:36
David receives a covenant promise	2 Sam. 7:1-16 1 Chron. 17:1-15
David wins more victories	2 Sam. 8:1-14 1 Chron. 18:1-13
David organizes his government	2 Sam. 8:15-18 1 Chron. 18:14-17
David honors Mephibosheth	2 Sam. 9:1-13
David defeats the Ammonites	2 Sam. 10:1-19 1 Chron. 19:1-19

David's Accomplishments
Military achievements. Establishing the kingdom first of all required defeating Israel's enemies and setting up a perimeter of safety. As archeological digs have shown, up to David's time Israel was restricted to the hilly areas of Palestine; the rich plains were in the

hands of the ancient Canaanite peoples. Then, in a series of battles (2 Sam. 5; 8; and 10), David destroyed the power of the Philistines, Israel's principal enemy since the days of Samson. David's neutralization of the Philistines was complete; they never again posed any threat to God's people.

In a further series of battles, David brought Moab and Edom under his control. The kingdom of Israel proper then extended from north of the Sea of Galilee south to Beersheba and encompassed both sides of the Jordan River.

David's conquests set up a number of vassal states, which insulated Israel from distant potential enemies. These states also made available the natural resources of iron and coal which Israel needed to maintain military strength, and the conquered peoples provided the skills in metalworking which were not known in Israel. No longer would iron, the Philistines' ancient "secret weapon," be unavailable to the Hebrews!

Summarizing the position David had attained for Israel, Leon Wood *(A Survey of Israel's History,* Zondervan) notes of all the territory which acknowledged Israelite sovereignty, "This was the area which God had promised to Abraham for his posterity centuries before (Gen. 15:18). It did not rival the vast territories of Egypt, Assyria, or Babylonia in their empire days. But in David's time, Israel became one of the larger land areas then held, and David was no doubt the strongest ruler of the contemporary world."

Government organization. David quickly took steps to maintain all military and political gains. He instituted a creative military plan, under which 24,000 men were always under arms. The personnel roster rotated every month, according to 1 Chronicles 27:1-15, indicating that at least 288,000 trained men were ready for immediate service if needed. Yet David's structure enabled most of his army to devote most of their time to civilian pursuits. The core of David's military organization was 600 key commanders, his *gibborim* or "mighty men." Over these he had, in turn, a smaller general staff.

David's genius for organization showed itself in religious and civil areas as well. While we are not told of their duties, David apparently set a governor over each of the 12 tribal areas and also established a cabinet for the central government. Members' duties included supervision of his treasury, various agricultural departments, etc. (cf. 1 Chron. 27:25-31).

Centralization. Since the days of Joshua, the people of Israel had thought more in terms of tribal than national identity. This was the reason for David's ready acceptance by Judah, his own tribe, and the slower acceptance of the others. As king over the whole nation, David acted quickly to centralize the government. A key step was to choose a suitable site for the capital. David grasped both the religious and political significance of affirming Israel's identity as a single nation.

The city David selected was occupied at that time by Jebusites. It was so strongly fortified that its inhabitants boasted that the lame and the blind could defend it against David (2 Sam. 5:6). But David's army took the city by storm, overcoming those "lame and blind" defenders.

The city of Jerusalem was located on the border between Judah and the northern tribes. Selecting it was wise politically. David did not abandon his own tribe, nor did his choice suggest to the northern tribes a favoritism toward Judah.

Jerusalem then became David's capital. When David finally moved the ark of the covenant to that city, Jerusalem became the center of Israel's religious life as well.

Through David, God selected a city foretold in the Law. Jerusalem was "the place the Lord your God will choose from among all your tribes to put His name there for His dwelling" (Deut. 12:5). From that time on, Israel was to offer sacrifice only at Jerusalem and to appear there before the Lord at the time of the three special religious festivals.

The political and religious unification of the people around a central location, and establishment of a recognized central government, were two of David's greatest accomplishments. They involved a reorientation of the tribal lifestyle and thinking of the people.

Structuring worship. David's genius for organization also showed itself in his impact on Israel's religious life. Zadok and Abiathar served as chief priests and were members of David's cabinet. The priests and the Levites under them were organized into 24 shifts, each called to serve a brief time at

HAMATH
Lebo-Hamath
Byblos
SIDONIANS
ARAM ZOBAH
BETH REHOB
Damascus
Sidon
Zarephath
Dan
ARAMEANS
Tyre
MAACHAH
Kedesh
Megiddo
Ramoth Gilead
Bethshan
Shechem
ISRAEL
AMMON
Mahanaim
Rabbath Ammon
Joppa
Bethel
Jerusalem
Ashdod
Ashkelon
PHILISTINES
Hebron
MOAB
Gaza
JUDAH
Kir Hareseth
Beersheba
Kadesh Barnea
Tamar
Bozrah
EDOM
Teman
Kingdom Proper
Vassal States
Acknowledged Israelite sovereignty

David's Kingdom

the Jerusalem sanctuary (1 Chron. 24:1-19). Thus priests and Levites typically served two weeks a year. The rest of the time they lived at their homes.

David also was served by prophets, notably Gad and Nathan, who had a special ministry in instructing (and reproving!) the king.

David took a special interest in organizing the singers and musicians who served the tabernacle, and would later serve in Solomon's temple (25:1-31).

Many of the psalms which David wrote were used in public worship. His personal commitment was reflected in the fresh interest of Israel in the service of God during the years of David's reign.

David's reign was marked by many internal troubles. David was not always in a position to enforce his will on those with whom he shared power. At other times David's own actions brought disasters. But David's genius, committed to the service of God and enriched by God's Spirit, shaped Israel into a people who, for a brief time, knew glory.

Throughout David's long life, God's people stood on the pinnacle of long-promised power. In the transition that David effected, Israel moved:

1. from government by judges to an established monarchy.
2. from anarchy to a strong central government.
3. from a loose confederation of tribes to a unified nation.
4. from poverty and Bronze Age technology to an iron economy and to wealth.
5. from being a subject people to being conquerors.
6. from decentralized to centralized worship.

This transformation was God's work through David, and stands today as an example of what we can expect to see when Jesus comes again.

♥ ***Link to Life: Youth / Adult***

Outline in a minilecture the accomplishments of David as king. Be sure to list on the chalkboard the six accomplishments listed above.

Then brainstorm. If David does represent in Israel what Jesus will be for all humankind when He returns, what kind of changes can we expect to see on earth? What aspects of global life will Jesus change? If He makes changes on the pattern of David's ministry in Israel, what changes can we expect?

Let your group work together to portray the kingdom Jesus will establish then.

The Everlasting Kingdom

David has prophetic as well as historic significance. When the kingdom of Israel had been firmly established, David yearned to build a suitable temple for the Lord. But David was not permitted to build that house. Instead, God spoke to David (2 Sam. 7:12-16) and promised to build *David* a house! That promise of a Davidic dynasty is understood in the Old Testament to have the force of a covenant: an unbreakable promise or commitment made by God.

David was promised that after his death, a descendant of his would be established as ruler of a kingdom to be set up in God's name. God said, "I will establish the throne of his kingdom forever" (2 Sam. 7:13). David's line was promised the perpetual right to Israel's throne. Even though David's immediate descendant Solomon sinned in such terrible ways that he deserved to be set aside, the kings of Judah were always from the Davidic line. Because of David's faith, God did not treat his descendants as He had treated Saul's. Sin would be punished, but David's line would never be completely cut off.

God's promise to David is recognized in the Old Testament and the New Testament as an amplification of the ancient Abrahamic Covenant. The Davidic Covenant explains the means through which the earlier promises to Abraham will be fulfilled! As Psalm 89:3-4 expresses it:

> You said, "I have made a covenant with My chosen one, I have sworn to David My servant, 'I will establish your line forever and make your throne firm through all generations.' "

And again this great prophetic psalm affirms the certainty of God's promise.

> I will not violate My covenant or alter what My lips have uttered. Once for all, I have sworn by My holiness—and I will not lie to David—that his line will continue forever and his throne endure be-

> fore Me like the sun; it will be established forever like the moon, the faithful witness in the sky.
>
> Psalm 89:34-37

From this point on, for the Hebrew people and for the later prophets, David stood as the symbol and the ancestor of a coming King, destined to set up a lasting kingdom through which the whole world would be related to God (see especially Jer. 33:22, 25-26). God's formal promise was confirmed over and over again in such passages as Isaiah 9:6-7; Jeremiah 23:5-6; 30:8-9; 33:14-17, 20-21; Ezekiel 37:24-25; Daniel 7:13-14; Hosea 3:4-5; Amos 9:11; and Zechariah 14:9. We cannot understand the Old Testament or the hope with which godly Jews looked forward to the coming Messiah if we do not realize that they looked for a literal kingdom on earth, to be established and ruled over for an endless age by David's greater Son.

No wonder then that New Testament writers took such pains to demonstrate that Jesus of Nazareth is David's descendant, and thus genealogically qualified to mount his throne. We can also understand the confusion which arose when Jesus did not repeat David's military and political performance. Rather than throwing off the yoke of Rome as David had thrown off that of the Philistines, Jesus bowed His head and let Himself be led away and crucified. He who could have called on angel armies to release Him chose instead the shameful death of the cross.

Even after Jesus' resurrection, His disciples could not understand what had happened. They are recorded in Acts to have asked, "Lord, are You at this time going to restore the kingdom to Israel?" (1:6) Certainly God's rule of the universe and over the ages is recognized in both Old and New Testaments. But these men were concerned about that form of the overarching rule of God known not as the "kingdom" but as "the kingdom promised to Israel." As Jews they were curious about the destiny of their own nation.

Christ's answer contains no rebuke. The promises God has made will be fulfilled. So Jesus simply said, "It is not for you to know the times or dates" (v. 7). In Jesus, men of faith had correctly seen David's descendant who will one day establish an endless kingdom on earth. But they had not seen the centuries which lay between Jesus' first coming, with His suffering as man's Saviour, and His still-future second coming as Israel's—and the earth's—King.

It is important that you and I see Jesus as coming King. Right now He is our Saviour, and our Lord as well. But the day is coming when Jesus will be *Lord of all!* The careening course of modern history, rushing as it seems to toward disasters over which men have no control, points up our need to reaffirm the fact that history does have a goal. This very earth, the setting of man's first sin, will once again know the masterful touch of God's own hand. "I will proclaim the decree of the Lord," the psalmist says of that future day.

> He said to Me, "You are My Son, today I have become Your Father. Ask of Me, and I will make the nations Your inheritance, and the ends of the earth Your possession. You will rule them with an iron scepter; You will dash them to pieces like pottery."
>
> Psalm 2:7-9

The Old Testament picture of David, acting in his own might to establish Israel's glorious kingdom, is but a dim foreshadowing of David's Son, Jesus Christ, who will come again to act in even greater power and will establish a worldwide kingdom whose glory knows no end.

Notes on the Text

These chapters of the Old Testament are especially significant. They report a historical turning point. And they record a theological turning point. The kingdom David established is a foreview of a greater kingdom to be established by David's greater Son.

Yet even among these towering passages there are incidents that remind us of God's great compassion and love.

The ark is brought to Jerusalem (2 Sam. 6:1-15). When David tried to bring the ark of God to Jerusalem, it was carried on an ox cart rather than by Levites, as the Law instructed. The cart, jolting along the rough track, tipped and seemed about to fall. A man named Uzzah who was guiding the cart reached out to steady it—and was struck dead!

This event angered as well as puzzled David. It did not appear to fit with God's character, and a suddenly fearful David left the ark at the household of Obed-Edom.

But God blessed the household of Obed-Edom, and David's fears were relieved. David must also have studied the Scriptures or inquired of a prophet, for when David next tried to bring the ark to Jerusalem the Bible speaks of "those who were carrying the ark" (v. 13).

This time the ark arrived with a joyous David leading the company of dancing, shouting, praising worshipers.

What an important lesson David and all Israel were taught. You and I can revel in the love and compassion of our God. But we must always treat Him with respect! He who loves us is also the Holy One of Israel, and our love for Him should be tempered with a deep awe of who He is.

David and Mephibosheth (2 Sam. 9:1-13). When David was established as king, he set about investigating to see if any of Saul's family was still alive. It was common for ancient rulers to initiate such a search: most wanted to kill members of the previous ruling family who might one day challenge their reigns!

But David had a different purpose in mind. David wanted to find any family members still alive so he could show them "kindness for Jonathan's sake" (v. 1). The search turned up Mephibosheth, a son of Jonathan, who had been crippled in infancy. David not only made this lame grandson of Saul a member of his household, but also deeded to him Saul's extensive estate! Suddenly Mephibosheth's position was transformed from that of a helpless and poor cripple to a wealthy and powerful man who enjoyed access to the king and ate at his table.

What a picture of your state and mine! We, the children of one who made himself an enemy of God, crippling all his descendants, are suddenly taken from our helpless estate and brought into the very household of the Lord. We are made rich in Jesus, and through Him have direct access to the King of kings.

How great and how wonderful is this kindness, not only of David, but of the God whom he in this instance represents!

♥ ***Link to Life: Children***

Can we help boys and girls be like David and actively search for ways to be kind to others and show love? Here is a simple activity you can use to help develop the sensitivity of boys and girls.

On several paper plates draw faces to represent the following feelings: sadness (perhaps with tears flowing), loneliness (a straight mouth, eyes closed), worry (wrinkled brow, mouth turned down), and other emotions that might suggest a person needs help.

Show each face in turn. Ask the children to describe how the person represented feels. Talk about what kind of things might make someone feel that way. Talk too about how we might help a person who feels sad, lonely, or worried. Encourage the boys and girls to talk about their own experiences with these feelings.

After you've talked, let your class members role play. A child can choose one of the faces, and sit or walk in such a way that the emotion is also shown. For instance, a sad person might slump, or walk slowly. A lonely person might sit with shoulders humped and hands in pocket, etc.

Then let a volunteer talk to the person to find out what's wrong and see if he or she can help.

Remind your boys and girls that we can often see when another person needs our help by how he or she looks and acts. Encourage them to be like David, always looking for ways to help others and to search for ways to be helpers.

TEACHING GUIDE

Prepare

God used all of David's talents and abilities, so that even planning the government was a spiritual exercise. How is God using your abilities in your own work?

Explore

Give a minilecture, surveying the accomplishments of David. If you wish, duplicate the map of David's kingdom for your group members.

Expand

1. Look at the verses mentioned in the text that give insights into the kingdom of Jesus, David's greater Son:

Jer. 23:5-6	Jer. 33:22, 25-26
Jer. 30:8-9	Jer. 33:14-17, 20-21
Ezek. 37:24-25	Dan. 7:13-14
Hosea 3:4-5	Amos 9:11
Zech. 14:3-9	

Then brainstorm some of the implications of Jesus' return, using the approach outlined in the "link-to-life" on page 230.

2. Or, look with your group at the following psalms, which are prophetic portraits of the character and events associated with Jesus' coming as messianic King:

Psalm 45: a love song addressed to the King.
Psalm 46: a portrait of the Tribulation time during which all will be brought under the King's authority.
Psalm 47: a work picture of the joy earth will know under Christ's rule.
Psalm 48: praise to God who has finally fulfilled all His promises.

Apply

Read 2 Samuel 6:1-15 aloud. Let each group member imagine he or she was present as God struck down Uzzah, and saw David's reaction. How would he or she explain the event and David's response? How would he or she feel?

After sharing, challenge each person to remember that awareness of God's deep love for individuals must not be allowed to distract us from our awareness of who God is—and the awesome majesty of His plans not only for us but for Planet Earth.

STUDY GUIDE 33

2 Samuel 11–20

SAINT AND SINNER

Overview

David's greatness cannot hide the fact that he was very human. The two major stories told in these chapters of 2 Samuel reveal his weaknesses as well as the reality of his trust in and love for God.

▶ ***Sin.*** There are three major Hebrew word groups that communicate the concept of sin in the Old Testament. Each of them is illustrated in these chapters. In fact each of them is used in David's prayer of confession, Psalm 51.

The principle Hebrew word for sin, *hata',* means to miss the mark. It assumes the existence of a divine standard which, for some reason, a person does not live up to.

The other major terms also assume the existence of a divine standard and describe human actions in relation to it. *Pesa'* in the vocabulary of sin indicates a conscious revolt against the divine standard. And *'awon* is a deviation from or twisting of the standard.

In our NIV and NASB English versions, *hata'* is usually translated by "sin." *Pesa'* is rendered "rebellion" or "transgression." And *'awon* is "iniquity" or "guilt."

Strikingly, in Scripture the language of sin is also the language of redemption. The word *hatta't* means both "sin" and "sin offering." Thus it speaks both of human failure, and the wonderful provision by God of forgiveness through an offering that removes our guilt.

How beautifully both these realities are illustrated in David's life.

Commentary

Often it's crushing for us to discover that a person we admire has faults. An idealized parent disappoints. A friend we respect falls short. A political leader we support suffers his own particular Watergate. Discouraged and hurt, we feel a bitterness that is hard to overcome.

When we look in the biblical record at David, certainly one of history's exceptional men and one whose faith is mentioned in both Testaments, we discover that he too had feet of clay. The saint is revealed as a sinner. And we wonder, "Why does God hold up as examples men and women who have such obvious flaws?"

A look at David's life suggests a number of possible answers, some more satisfying than others. For one thing, through David we are reminded that God is a realist. His Book contains no "let's-pretend" whitewash of believers. Noting this, we may be helped to appreciate the fact that we can come to this God in spite of our own weaknesses. God won't overlook them. But He won't be crushed by our failures either. God knows that "we are dust" (Ps. 103:14).

For another thing, a revelation of saints' failures as well as successes helps us to identify with them. If a David or an Abraham were represented as spiritually perfect, you and I would hardly feel close or similar to him. The truths that God is teaching us through their lives might be seen but might not be thought of as relevant. After all, we might think, "That's all right for a spiritual giant like David! But what about poor, struggling me?" Then we discover that David struggled too. And sometimes he lost out to his weaknesses. David did know sin's pull, just as we do. His experiences *are* relevant to us!

The New Testament affirms, "No temptation has seized you except what is common to man" (1 Cor. 10:13). We are all bound up together in the shared ties of humanity. David knew the feelings and temptations that you know—and you know his! When the Bible accurately reports the failures and follies of God's saints, it demonstrates this common bond and encourages us to identify our own inner struggles with theirs.

Most importantly, when Old Testament saints are shown to be sinners, Scripture is expressing something basic about the Gospel. The good news of God's love for man is not, "Trust Me, and be freed of your humanity." The good news of God's love is that the Lord has committed Himself to deal with sin and to make us progressively more and more like Him. For progressive growth we always stand in need of God's grace and aid. God deals with sin by the means of forgiveness. The greatness of David is not in his perfection but in his willingness to face his sin and to return wholeheartedly to God.

How different from Saul! When Saul sinned, he begged Samuel to stay with him, that the people might not discover God's anger. When the Prophet Nathan confronted David concerning his sin with Bathsheba, David not only confessed immediately, but he even wrote a psalm used later in public worship, openly admitting his fault and sharing the inner anguish that accompanied loss of fellowship with God!

We cannot, and God did not, condone David's sins and failings. But we can praise God for moving David to share honestly with us. Through David we learn fresh lessons about the grace of God, and we are reminded that you and I are invited to come boldly to the Lord too that He may meet us—and our needs.

♥ ***Link to Life: Youth / Adult***

Read Genesis 3:7-10 aloud. Ask your group members to list three feelings of Adam and Eve in this situation. List their suggestions on a chalkboard.

Ask: "When you have feelings like these, what has usually been the cause?" After several have answered, explain the three words that the Hebrew language uses to describe sin (see overview). *Note that while sins and failures cause shame and make us, like Adam and Eve, want to avoid God, David's example teaches us that the way to deal with our failures is to hurry* to *God.*

David and Bathsheba: 2 Samuel 11–12

This familiar story recalls a time when David was in Jerusalem rather than with his campaigning armies. From the roof of his palace, David noticed a beautiful woman bathing, and he sent for her. When she became pregnant, he ordered her husband Uriah home from the front, so the adultery might not be discovered. But Uriah was a dedicated man: he would not enjoy the comforts of his home or wife while his companions were camped in the open before the walls of an enemy city.

Desperate now, David sent secret orders to his commander to place Uriah in an exposed position so the enemy might kill him. After Uriah's death, Bathsheba was taken into David's house as one of his wives. And the Bible tells us, "The thing David had done displeased the Lord" (2 Sam. 11:27).

Now came a confrontation between David and Nathan the prophet, who was sent to announce God's judgment on the king. David had violated the sanctity of the home; his own home now would produce evil.

This judgment needs to be seen as a natural consequence of David's act; his own disrespect for the divinely ordained family pattern would bear its own bitter fruit.

David's immediate reaction is revealing. Unlike others who struck out in anger against such prophets and condemned them, David immediately confessed his sin and admitted the rightness of God's judgment: "David said to Nathan, 'I have sinned against the Lord' " (2 Sam. 12:13).

David's confession brought him forgiveness. But it could not change the course of events his choices had set in motion. David would not die, but the child Bathsheba had conceived would die. One day David would go to be with the son whom the Lord had taken, but that son would never know David on earth (v. 23).

Scripture tells this story simply. All the facts are recorded. No cover-up is attempted. Meditating on the incident, David was led to make the fullest possible revelation of his inner thoughts and feelings. We find them in Psalm 51, a psalm later used in public worship! We see timeless themes in Psalm 51, and find guidance to help us realize how we ourselves are to approach God when we sin. As the analysis of this psalm shows, David's reaction is appropriate for us too when we fall short.

THE PENITENT'S PSALM

Have mercy on me, O God, according to Your unfailing love; according to Your great compassion blot out my transgressions. Wash away all my iniquity, and cleanse me from my sin.

For I know my transgressions, and my sin is always before me. Against You, You only, have I sinned, and done what is evil in Your sight, so that You are proved right when You speak and justified when You judge. Surely I have been a sinner from birth, sinful from the time my mother conceived me.

Surely You desire truth in the inner parts; You teach me wisdom in the inmost place. Cleanse me with hyssop, and I will be clean; wash me, and I will be whiter than snow. Let me hear joy and gladness; let the bones You have crushed rejoice. Hide Your face from my sins and blot out all my iniquity.

Create in me a pure heart, O God, and renew a steadfast spirit within me. Do not cast me from Your presence or take Your Holy Spirit from me. Restore to me the joy of Your salvation, and grant me a willing spirit, to sustain me.

Then I will teach transgressors Your ways, and sinners will turn back to You. Save me from bloodguilt, O God, the God who saves me, and my tongue will sing of Your righteousness.

O Lord, open my lips, and my mouth will declare Your praise. You do not delight in sacrifice, or I would bring it; You do not take pleasure in burnt offerings. The sacrifices of God are a broken spirit; a broken and contrite heart, O God, You will not despise.

Psalm 51:1-17

David had penetrated to the heart of the issue. His was no mere legal relationship with some "bookkeeper God" who cares only about balanced books. David did not rush to ask what he could do for God to make up for his sin! Instead David realized that God's concern is *personal* rather than *legal* in nature. A contrite heart means more to God than all anyone might possibly do for Him.

With David's heart attitude corrected, forgiveness could flow and the Spirit of God could work again to cleanse David. When he was cleansed, God would work through David to do good for Zion and for all his people.

♥ ***Link to Life: Youth / Adult***

Duplicate Psalm 51, leaving breaks between the verses that match the divisions on page 235 and this page. Ask group members to work in teams to title each section descriptively.

Then work as a whole group to sharpen these titles. By following this process and discussing how to best sum up the contents of each segment, your group members will develop a good understanding of the teaching of this important psalm.

Then read the story of David and Bathsheba aloud, trying to determine just which part of David's psalm is correlated with the ongoing experience described there.

If you wish, you might also give your group members a chance to mark mentally just where each is personally in relation to the psalm. Ready to admit guilt? Seeking forgiveness? Seeking restoration? In fellowship and ministering? Wherever a person is, the next step he or she needs to take is defined in the next segment of the psalm.

♥ ***Link to Life: Children***

Make a Forgiveness Wheel to help children learn to follow David's example. Use two paper plates. Cut a 1/4 section out of one, leaving enough of the center so it can be loosely attached to the other with a brad. Divide the bottom plate into quarters. On each draw a face, and write the following partial verses from Psalm 51.

Art	*Verse*
**angry face*	*"My sin is always before me" (v. 3)*
**praying face*	*"Blot out all my iniquity" (v. 9)*
**smiling face*	*"Restore to me the joy of Your salvation" (v. 12)*
**open mouth*	*"My tongue will sing of Your righteousness" (v. 14)*

Assemble the two plates so that when the top plate is rotated each of the above is shown in sequence. Go through this se-

quence several times, helping your boys and girls realize that when they feel guilty and ashamed they can confess sins to God and He will forgive them. Then they will feel good again, and praise the Lord.

Absalom's Revolt: 2 Samuel 13–19
David's children shared his weakness, but few demonstrated his redeeming characteristic of contriteness. David's lifestyle was one of responsiveness to God. In his infrequent departures, David remained open to correction.

Not so his sons. In these chapters we read of one son, Amnon, who seduced a half sister and then spurned her. The girl's brother, Absalom, plotted revenge and later killed Amnon. This son, Absalom, was then banished. Later, through the influence of David's general, Joab, the banishment was lifted. But David still refused to see Absalom.

David had two possible courses open here. He might have executed Absalom for murder, or he might have tried to restore him through confession and forgiveness. But David took neither course. Absalom's sin festered within the young man's personality.

In time Absalom began a careful campaign to woo the northern tribes of Israel and to alienate them from David. Amazingly, he succeeded! The tribes of Israel (those who had been the last to crown David king some decades before) swung their support to Absalom. Absalom, after having himself crowned, marched on Jerusalem. David was forced to flee for his life from the capital, with only his old companions remaining faithful—plus a band of mercenary soldiers whom David had employed for his personal guard just the day before! How deeply it must have cut him to see these mercenaries remain true to their commitment while his own people spurned him!

Second Samuel 13–19 traces the origin and the course of the rebellion, and reveals something of David's own doubt and discouragement. Without question, David examined himself and found many reasons why the Lord might be justified in removing him from the throne.

David fled toward Judah, aided by a few individuals. In the meantime, David's supporters in Zion gave bad advice to Absalom, which allowed David time to gather an army from his homeland. In the battle which followed, Absalom was killed—against David's orders.

The story ends with David crying out in agony and weeping over his lost son.

This experience was one of wrenching pain for David. And again David shared his innermost thoughts and feelings with us in the psalms. Psalm 3 emerges from the time of self-examination and self-doubt as David fled Jerusalem. It is short, yet its simple phrases take us deep into David's heart and show us how he handled one of those times which we all experience: a time when everything goes wrong and all seems hopeless.

Implications of the rebellion. David saw clearly that the fact of rebellion indicated that his people believed God was no longer with him. David was forced to examine that question, and recognized a certain justification for the accusation of Shimei that David was a "man of blood."

> O Lord, how many are my foes! How many rise up against me! Many are saying of me, "God will not deliver him."
>
> Psalm 3:1-2

Remembrance of God's past role in David's life. With his world tumbling down, David looked to God and characterized the relationship he had enjoyed with the Lord across the years. Each believer's past experience of God's blessing and lessons learned about the character of the Lord are a comfort when things go wrong.

Specifically David thought of God as his protector and strengthener ("the One who lifts up my head"). Even more significantly, David called God "my Glorious One." The earthly glory David attained—his status and wealth as Israel's king—were empty things to him. It was God and God alone in whom David gloried. David's final thought focused on God as One who answers prayer.

> But You are a shield around me, O Lord, my Glorious One, who lifts up my head. To the Lord I cry aloud, and He answers me from His holy hill.
>
> Psalm 3:3-4

Release from tension comes by turning it over to God. Then comes a striking revelation of David's commitment of himself to God. He lay down and went to sleep. Neither self-doubt nor anguish nor fear could hold him in its grip. Certainly David felt all these emotions. Yet, by focusing his attention on the Lord and who He is, David put his life in perspective and was freed to rest.

> I lie down and sleep; I wake again, because the Lord sustains me. I will not fear the tens of thousands drawn up against me on every side.
>
> Psalm 3:5-6

Such trust is not fatalism! One Stoic philosopher, a slave, is said to have been beaten and mistreated by his master. On one occasion when the master was twisting his leg, the Stoic warned, "If you keep on twisting my leg, you'll break it." The sadistic master maintained the pressure, and the leg snapped. The Stoic's only remark was, "See, I told you it would break."

David was hardly such a person. Nor should we be. To say that we trust in God and rest in Him never means that we do not care. And so we hear David give a last passionate cry, and trust the outcome to his God of deliverance.

> Arise, O Lord! Deliver me, O my God! For You have struck all my enemies on the jaw; You have broken the teeth of the wicked. From the Lord comes deliverance. May Your blessing be on Your people.
>
> Psalm 3:7-8

♥ ***Link to Life: Youth / Adult***

Describe the pressures on David during Absalom's revolt. Ask your group members to think of the time when their experience was most nearly like his.

Share about these experiences in groups of three to five.

Then introduce Psalm 3. Which verse or verses in this psalm most accurately reflects how each person felt during the experience just described?

Work through the psalm section by section, relating each verse to David's experience during the revolt. Discuss: "What can we learn from David about how to handle stress in our own lives?" (For instance, think about how God has delivered in the past. Remember that relationship with God is what is truly important [e.g., my Glorious One].)

The Godly Man

It's easy to emphasize one side of David's character at the expense of the other. Some tend to idealize David and explain away his faults. Yet David did have many weaknesses. We might well be horrified by the cruelty and selfishness David showed when he took Bathsheba and arranged for her husband's "accident." Can we ever reconcile this behavior with the brave and trusting shepherd boy, or the man who flung aside his dignity with his royal robes to dance for joy before the Lord? How can this David be the same young man whose days of shepherding taught him to view God as man's Shepherd, and who shared this beautiful insight with us in Psalm 23? Somehow we feel uncomfortable in the presence of a man who is both a sinner and a saint.

Yet, strikingly, David is portrayed as a man approved by God: one whose heart Scripture says was "fully devoted to the Lord" (1 Kings 15:3). David thus stands before us a unique example of how sin can distort the best of men, and how the best of men deal with sin in contrition and confession.

Even more, David stands before us as a testimony to God's love and His goodness. God's grace touched David. He forgave David's sins and enabled him for the task to which he was called.

How wonderful to realize that God yearns to deal with us this same way. For our sins, God has provided in Jesus Christ a full and free pardon, a forgiveness that blots out the past and opens up the future as well. Through the Holy Spirit who has come to dwell within, God has provided strength to enable us to meet life's challenges, fully equipping us for whatever life we are called to.

TEACHING GUIDE

Prepare
Consider: Why does God hold up as examples men and women who have such obvious flaws?

Explore
1. Explore the impact of sinning or falling short on your group members' experiences. Use the "link-to-life" suggestion found on page 235 to explore feelings and reactions.
2. Or, discuss the question posed in *Prepare*. How *can* such imperfect persons be held up to us in Scripture as examples? After your group has made a number of suggestions, you might give a minilecture on the material in the beginning of this chapter which deals with this subject.
3. Or, have your group read 2 Samuel 15:1-26. Have group members suggest how David must have felt at this time. When a number of feeling terms have been suggested, ask each individual to think of one time when he or she had similar feelings. Talk about these experiences in groups of three to five.

Expand
1. Pass out study sheets of Psalm 51, as explained in the "link-to-life" suggestion earlier. Follow the procedure developed there. Or, help your group members develop from Psalm 51 a step-by-step pattern for dealing with our personal sins.
2. Give a minilecture showing the relationship of Psalm 3 to elements of David's flight from Absalom. As each group member recalls personal stress experiences, ask him or her to pick one of the verses in Psalm 3 that he or she most closely identifies with. Share each member's choice, and ask each to explain why that particular verse was selected.

Apply
1. Work together from Psalm 51 to develop a step-by-step plan for dealing with personal sins and failures.
2. Or, work together from Psalm 3 to develop a step-by-step plan for dealing with stress.

STUDY GUIDE 34

2 Samuel 21–24; 1 Chronicles 21–29

INSIGHTS INTO DAVID'S REIGN

Overview

In these historical chapters the writers describe six incidents that are out of historical sequence.

The incidents give us further insights into David's reign and times. These incidents are:

Incident	*2 Sam.*	*1 Chron.*
Gibeonites avenged	21:1-14	
Philistine wars	21:15-22	
David's census	24:1-25	21:1-30
Temple plans		22–26; 28
David's giving		29:1-20
David's death	23:1-7	29:21-30

While lesser known, they too have very personal messages for you and me, and for those we teach.

▶ ***Mighty Men.*** These were military leaders of David's army. For a discussion of the organization of the military and civilian government, see Study Guide 32.

▶ ***Solomon.*** Solomon was 1 of 10 sons of David's eight major wives. The other sons were Amnon, Kileab, Absalom, Adonijah, Shephatiah, Ithream, Shammua, Shobab, and Nathan. Although 1 of 4 sons of David and Bathsheba, Solomon's exceptional qualities led many to encourage David to make him David's successor. The other named sons of David are Ibhar, Elishua, Eliphelet, Nogah, Nepheg, Japhia, Elishama, Eliada, and Eliphelet. These sons are named in 2 Samuel 3:2-5, in 1 Chronicles 3:1-9; and 14:3-7. In addition David had other sons by his concubines, or secondary wives.

Commentary

Each of the six incidents in these sections of our Old Testament adds insights into David and his rule. It is difficult to place them accurately in particular periods of David's life, except for those which clearly come near the end of David's reign.

Gibeonites Avenged: 2 Samuel 21:1-14

The Gibeonites had lived in the Promised Land long before the time of the Conquest. When Israel attacked Palestine, the Gibeonites resorted to a trick in a desperate effort to survive. They sent envoys, dressed in worn clothing and carrying aged supplies, to beg Joshua and the Israelite leaders for peace. In return for a nonaggression pact, the Gibeonites pledged to be subject to Israel.

Joshua and the others accepted this offer without taking time to consult with God. The Bible says, "Then Joshua made a treaty of peace with them to let them live, and the leaders of the assembly ratified it by oath" (Josh. 9:15). Three days later the Israelites learned that the Gibeonite cities were actually nearby, and were in fact part of Israel's inheritance. But then it was too late. "The Israelites did not attack them, because the leaders of the assembly had sworn an oath to them by the Lord, the God of Israel" (v. 18).

Despite the grumbling of the people, the leaders insisted that they abide by their oath, for it had been sworn in the name of the Lord. What Joshua did do was make the Gibeonites woodcutters and water carriers to serve the community of Israel and the altar of the Lord.

With this background we can understand the dynamics of the events recorded for us in 2 Samuel 21.

This passage tells us that there was a three-year famine in the land. When King David desperately sought for a reason from God, he learned the cause of the famine. "It is on account of Saul and his blood-stained house; it is because he put the Gibeonites to death" (v. 1).

This incident is not recorded in the Old Testament, and we do not know the reasons for Saul's act. We do know that Saul's own castle site was at Gibeah, about five miles north of Jerusalem, and that the Gibeonites lived nearby, about five and one-half miles northwest of Jerusalem. In his zeal to purge the land of foreigners, Saul had tried to annihilate them (v. 2).

This was a violation of the ancient treaty which had been sworn in God's name. The drought was now understood to be a divine punishment for a specific violation of God's Law.

So David asked the Gibeonites what he could do to make amends. The Gibeonites chose to have seven of Saul's sons or grandsons put to death.

The executions took place at harvesttime. When the absent rains returned, David knew that God would again answer prayer for his land.

David did however give the seven, and also the bones of Saul and Jonathan, burial in the tomb of Saul's father.

♥ ***Link to Life: Youth / Adult***
What are valid reasons for breaking your word to someone? Several passages in the Bible suggest that commitments are to be kept. Jesus condemned the Pharisees in part because they invented ways to keep their oaths from being binding (Matt. 23:16-22). Instructing His followers, Jesus said, "Do not swear at all," and went on to explain that each person's integrity should be such that his yes means yes and his no means no. More than that should be unnecessary for a man of integrity.

The death of Saul's descendants was harsh. And the text does not suggest that God approved. But Saul had intended genocide, despite the historic oath of protection sworn in God's name by an earlier Israelite leader. Brutality had engendered brutality in return, just as broken oaths destroy trust and gain a return of deceit.

Let your group members read this passage, and the background passages in Joshua, and try to explain what they read.

How tragic that what we sow we do reap. And how important to be trustworthy persons, whose yes can be counted on because of the depth of our integrity.

Philistines Defeated: 2 Samuel 21:15-22
In the Philistine wars David destroyed the power of these traditional and powerful enemies. Two things, however, are of note in the text.

In one battle David was in serious danger of being killed. After his rescue, his men insisted that he not go out to battle with them again. His life was too important to risk in battle. This reaction is understandable. But, on the other hand, if David had been leading his forces rather than standing on his rooftop the evening he saw Bathsheba, one of his great sins might have been avoided. Was remaining away from the battlefield the right thing to do? Or does it suggest a weakening of faith?

The other thing of note is the suggestion that Elhanan killed Goliath. Apparently the text has been corrupted here by dropping out the words "Lahmi the brother of [Goliath]" (see 1 Chron. 20:5).

David's Census: 2 Samuel 24:1-25; 1 Chronicles 21:1-30
This passage leads us to explore the Old Testament concept of causation—something that is difficult for Western minds to readily grasp.

The texts tell us the following story. God was, for some unstated reason, angry with Israel. He "incited David against them," and David ordered, "Go and count Israel and Judah" (2 Sam. 24:1). Though Joab resisted this order, David prevailed and the census was undertaken.

When this same story is told in 1 Chronicles, the text begins, "Satan rose up against Israel and incited David to take a census" (21:1). Here Joab's argument is stated even more strongly. This was a sinful act, which would surely bring "guilt on" David and the people he led.

When the census had been completed, God punished Israel in unnamed ways. But David realized that the fault was his. "I have sinned greatly by doing this," David confessed. "Now I beg You, take away the guilt of Your servant. I have done a very foolish [morally deficient] thing" (v. 8).

God gave David a choice of three punishments, each of which would fall on Israel. There would be three years of famine, three months of defeat, or three days of the "sword of the Lord"—a terrible plague in the land.

Heartbroken, David chose the least of the three evils: the plague.

The loss of life was terrible, and David had a vision of the destroying angel. He begged God to let the Lord's hand fall on him for he, David, was responsible. Instead, the angel commanded David to offer a sacrifice, and the plague was stopped.

In these two reports of this terrible event, responsibility for what happens seems to shift from person to person.

The people had done something to merit punishment. God incited David to a foolish act. Satan incited David to a foolish act. And David chose to act foolishly.

The question Westerns are likely to ask is, "Who is really to blame?" We want to fix responsibility in one place, and to excuse the other actors. But the Hebrews did not view moral causation in a Western way. *The Old Testament approach to morality takes it for granted that all are responsible.* That is, God was responsible for inciting David to take the census. He had His own purpose for this action, and that purpose was a righteous one. Satan was responsible for inciting David to take the census. And Satan had *his* own purposes for taking that action. And, *David* was responsible for taking the census. He too had his own purpose in mind!

In essence, each actor in this situation is viewed as both *free* and *responsible*. God incited David—but He was not responsible for David's choice. Satan incited David—but Satan was not responsible for David's choice. What God was responsible for was the act of inciting, and His reason for that act was a good, holy, and just reason. What Satan was responsible for was his act of inciting David. And Satan's reasons for his act flowed from his evil character: he was acting as the adversary and enemy of God's people. What David was responsible for was his decision to take the census. And David too had his own reasons, which commentators have suggested might have been pride, or a shifting of trust from God to military might.

We can diagram the above quite simply:

Person	*His responsibility*	*His reason*
God	He incited David	Righteous anger against Israel
Satan	He incited David	Hatred of God's people
David	He decided to take a military census	Pride or lack of trust in God

What is important to note here is that each party is responsible for his own acts. None "made" another do what he did. Each acted responsibly for his own good or bad reasons.

In the biblical view, *influences do not relieve a person of moral obligation.* Each individual is responsible for his own choices.

This is a difficult view for those who have been taught to excuse others so easily. Jimmy comes from a broken home. No wonder he steals. Mr. Bronson is an alcoholic. He was drunk when he hit that bicyclist. He'd never have done it if he'd been sober, so it's not his fault. Or, "My Suzie would never have given in if he hadn't pressured her so much."

In our society "mitigating circumstances" are assumed to at least partially excuse individuals, and the notion of full personal responsibility makes little sense. Yet in the Bible it is failure to hold people responsible for their actions which makes no sense. God has made human beings both free and responsible. It is true that temptations come, and that we are each subject to many influences. *But no influence determines our choices.* We are, and must ultimately, be held responsible for our actions.

David, despite the supernatural pressures on him, recognized and acknowledged his responsibility. And so must we, if we are to find, as David did, relief from guilt, and a way to halt the rippling effect of every sinful act.

♥ ***Link to Life: Youth / Adult***
Plan a courtroom role play. Let one member of your group prepare ahead of time to be "prosecuting attorney" and another to be "defense attorney." The crime is theft. The defendant comes from a broken home, and is a high school dropout.

There is no doubt that the defendant is guilty. The question is how responsible he or she is for the act, and what the sentence should be. The defense attorney argues for a light sentence on the basis of dimin-

ished responsibility. The prosecuting attorney argues for a heavier sentence.

After the summations, have the class discuss the arguments of each, and evaluate them.

Then look at the story of David's census in 2 Samuel and 1 Chronicles. How important is the biblical concept of full individual responsibility for one's actions, whatever the influences? How does such a view affect our own lives? How does it affect our relationships with God?

The story of the census concludes with David purchasing a threshing floor and animals to offer as a sacrifice. (The threshing floor was a flat, tabletop area of land where grain could be beaten and tossed. The wind blew out the chaff, letting the heavier kernels fall to the ground.)

Of particular note is one statement of David's to the owner, Araunah, who had offered to give the land and animals to the king. "No," David said. "I insist on paying the full price. I will not take for the Lord what is yours, or sacrifice a burnt offering that costs me nothing" (1 Chron. 21:24).

Temple Plans: 1 Chronicles 22–26; 28
David had yearned to build a temple for the Lord, but he had been rejected (cf. 22:7-8). Still, David was told that the desire was accepted. And David was told that his son, a man of peace to be called Solomon, would build the temple of the Lord.

But David was still concerned. Solomon was "young and inexperienced." So the worried father, like so many dads today when the time comes to turn over their businesses to their sons, gave Solomon advice. But also David went ahead and made preparations so Solomon wouldn't go wrong in building the temple when David was gone.

David gathered some 3,750 tons of gold and 37,500 tons of silver, along with uncounted amounts of wood, stone, and metals. David also assembled skilled workmen.

In addition David worked out with the leaders of the Levites their temple duties, and organized them into shifts. Still others were trained as musicians (1 Chron. 25).

In fact, David even gave Solomon detailed blueprints for the structure, and written instructions and drawings of each article of furniture.

"All this is in writing," David said, "because the hand of the Lord was upon me, and He gave me understanding in all the details of the plan" (28:19).

While the great Jerusalem temple was actually constructed during Solomon's reign, the vision and plans were David's.

David could not see his vision fulfilled. But that did not stop him from giving himself fully to that vision.

♥ ***Link to Life: Youth / Adult***
Often it is spiritual vision that sets apart those who accomplish great things for God from those who merely dream. Many a missionary has worked for decades in a difficult field without seeing a single convert. Yet his or her ministry has prepared the way for a great revival to come after his passing.

Ask your group members: "What can you think of that is so significant that you would spend your life working for it, even if it could not be achieved in your lifetime?"

David's Giving: 1 Chronicles 29:1-20
David's vision of the temple consumed his later years. At the end he could say, "With all my resources I have provided for the temple of my God" (v. 2). David added, "I now give my personal treasures of gold and silver for the temple of my God, over and above everything I have provided for this holy temple" (v. 3).

David's example stimulated all the leaders of Israel to give willingly, and "the people rejoiced at the willing response of their leaders, for they had given freely and wholeheartedly to the Lord" (v. 9).

This passage ends with prayer and with praise, and with this meditation: "But who am I, and who are my people, that we should be able to give as generously as this? Everything comes from You, and we have given You only what comes from Your hand" (v. 14).

The giving by David and by the people as well was truly, in this case, willing and "with honest intent" (v. 17). How beautiful David's request: "Keep this desire in the hearts of Your people forever, and keep their hearts loyal to You" (v. 18).

♥ ***Link to Life: Youth / Adult***
Have your group members study this passage and develop a plan to encourage giving

in your church. What seems to have motivated each giver mentioned in the text? What were the results of giving? What might you suggest to stimulate giving in your congregation?

When you have studied the passage, have the group work together to develop a list of recommendations on giving that might be presented to a church board or treasurer.

David's Death: 2 Samuel 23:1-7; 1 Chron. 29:21-30

Second Samuel reports the last words of David. Those words speak powerfully of David's awareness that he had been God's instrument. Even more, they speak of David's complete confidence that God had made an "everlasting covenant" with David's family, and that God would be loyal to that commitment. Because God truly is sovereign, David looked ahead with certainty, knowing that God had "arranged and secured . . . every part" (v. 5).

First Chronicles tells us that David then made final preparations for his departure. He saw to it that Solomon was acknowledged by all as the next king. Then, at the end of a 40-year reign, David died "at a good old age, having enjoyed long life, wealth, and honor" (1 Chron. 29:28).

And his son Solomon succeeded him as king.

♥ ***Link to Life: Youth / Adult***

Have your group members write their own epitaphs. Study David's last words in 2 Samuel and the last few verses of 1 Chronicles. Discuss: "What seemed important to David as he looked back? What were his feelings as he looked ahead to his coming death?"

Then give each member of your group a sheet of paper and ask each to write a two-paragraph "good-bye" to a loved one, or else to write an obituary column in which he or she looks back and looks ahead and summarizes his or her own life.

Read these to each other, and talk about what is really important to each. What kind of legacy would each like to leave others? What would make each feel, as David did, that his life had been meaningful and worthwhile?

TEACHING GUIDE

Prepare

Which of the incidents reported in these chapters has an important personal lesson for you? Write down the lesson God is teaching you through the selected incident.

Explore

1. Give a minilecture overview of the six incidents, including the following information on the practical themes of several. Then let your group members select one incident to focus on.

Gibeonites avenged. What does it mean to be a person of one's word? What can result from a loss of integrity?

David's census. How responsible are we for our choices? Can we ever shift responsibility to circumstance or to others who have influenced us, or are we fully responsible?

Temple plans. What is worth spending our lives working for, even though we may never see the results?

David's giving. What principles of giving should guide our own and our church's stewardship practices? How can we motivate our children to be givers rather than just receivers?

David's death. What would give us a sense of satisfaction were we to look back on our lives just before our deaths? What would give us a sense of confidence as we look ahead at that time?

2. Or, simply survey these themes, and then select one of them for your group to focus on, without giving them the option of choice.

Expand

Use the "link-to-life" activity suggested in the commentary with the passage you chose to emphasize to give you a start. Enrich and expand the process suggested to focus on your own teaching goals.

Apply

As you conclude, point out that the stories of the Old Testament are there to challenge each of us to examine our own lives and experiences. We can learn from David's successes and failures, and from other Bible characters, how to live more meaningful, more fulfilling, and more godly lives.

STUDY GUIDE 35

1 Kings 1–11; 2 Chronicles 1–9

SOLOMON THE KING

Overview

For 33 years David aggressively guided God's united people to greatness, forging a powerful empire. As David grew older, his sons disputed over the succession. But God had revealed to David that He had chosen Solomon to succeed him (see 1 Chron. 22:9-10).

David had shared this revelation with Bathsheba, Solomon's mother (1 Kings 1:13, 17). He had even announced it to the nation (1 Chron. 22:5; 29:1). Still, Solomon was not the oldest of David's living sons. There were older brothers who understandably disputed his right to the throne.

Finally, one of David's older surviving sons, Adonijah, took steps to gain the succession. Nathan the prophet and Bathsheba insisted that David act. David did. He made Solomon coregent. When Adonijah heard, his supporters deserted him and the young man rushed to the altar of sacrifice to claim sanctuary. His life was spared, and Solomon was secure on the throne.

Solomon's reign was a time of unparalleled wealth and greatness for Israel. No one dared attack the secure kingdom. It was also a golden literary age. We associate the Psalms with David. Solomon and his time are linked with the Proverbs. According to well-established tradition, Solomon also wrote Ecclesiastes and the Song of Songs.

These books give additional insight into Solomon, noted for his wisdom, but nevertheless a tragic figure who in his old age strayed from complete commitment to the Lord.

Commentary

The Era of Solomon

The years of Solomon's long reign seem to be years of growing glory for Israel. The traditional powers of the ancient world—the Egyptians and the Hittites—and the empires yet to appear—Assyria and Babylon—were not aggressive during either David's or Solomon's rule. David had expanded Israel's sphere of influence by war. Solomon was a diplomat, who held what his father had gained. During Solomon's reign, Israel's wealth and power were unmatched.

Strength for peace. One of Solomon's strategies for maintaining peace was to constantly strengthen Israel's military capacity. Like strategists in our day, Solomon wanted to deal with world problems through diplomacy, but he wanted to negotiate from a position of strength rather than weakness. He fortified key cities on the perimeter of Israel's territory and set up outer command posts to give early warning of possible enemy military buildups. In addition, Solomon developed a strong and mobile strike force, assembling some 1,400 chariots and 12,000 horsemen, and building stables for 4,000 horses. Solomon's chariot cities have been excavated and indicate the extent of the large standing army the king maintained.

This military readiness placed a heavy strain on the kingdom's financial resources. But throughout the years of Solomon's reign, Israel was at peace.

Diplomacy. David had won the respect of the great powers surrounding Israel. Solomon now moved to make alliances with them. His many marriages to foreign women were part of this diplomatic strategy; in that day such marriages were a normal way to seal an international alliance. Solomon's marriage to Pharaoh's daughter (1 Kings 3:1) shows the place Israel had won in the ancient world, as Egypt was a major world power.

Solomon also developed close ties with Hiram I, the Phoenician king of Tyre (ca. 978-944 B.C.). Again, marriage sealed the alliance. But trade between the two powers, with Tyre contributing her "cedars of Lebanon" and Israel providing wheat plus other foodstuffs, also bound them together. In addition, Solomon and Hiram jointly sponsored trade ventures that took ships representing Israel as far as India. This system of alliance and trade treaties was the key to Solomon's successful foreign relations program.

Economic conditions. Solomon was as aggressive economically as his father had been militarily. He invested in land and sea trade. He developed Israel's natural resources, setting up smelteries which excavation has shown brilliantly used prevailing winds to intensify the heat of the furnaces in which metals were refined. Solomon maintained a large court as well as a large army and built many public buildings. He also built the temple of the Lord, which his father had dreamed of and planned for. And that temple cost billions! While Solomon's sources of income were constantly being developed, his expenses still outgrew them. We are told that at one time he borrowed heavily from Hiram.

Solomon drew income from four major sources.

- *Taxation.* The country was divided into 12 districts (not along the old tribal lines), and the chief officer over each was primarily a tax collector. The bureaucratic demands grew so heavy that at Solomon's death the people cried out desperately for tax relief (12:3-4).
- *Trade.* Solomon's ships and caravans traveled to Africa, Arabia, and India, trading copper from his mines for many goods. He also became a middleman in selling military hardware, buying and selling chariots and horses for peoples to the north and south of Israel.
- *Labor conscriptions.* Solomon drafted laborers for his public works projects. At first the laborers were drawn from the foreign populations over which Israel ruled. Later, when more men were needed, he pressed Israelites into service as well. As such conscripts were expected to work for the government without pay, this was deeply resented.
- *Foreign tribute.* Income was also received from foreign countries. Some of this was annual tribute from subject states, while some was in the form of gifts from states desiring to remain on good terms with powerful Israel.

During Solomon's days Jerusalem became increasingly affluent. The wealth of the world flowed to Solomon's court and was reflected in the glory of the capital city. But bureaucracy grew as well. The nation's wealth was no longer based on the land and what it produced. Increasingly the government controlled the wealth of the land, and taxes drained wealth from the people and funneled expenditure through the central government. The glory was a superficial thing; prosperity was not for the people as much as it was at the expense of the people.

The temple. Solomon's most massive project was the building of the temple at Jerusalem. It was located on the site where Abraham had been commanded to sacrifice his son Isaac (Gen. 22:2). The gold used in its construction was worth over 2 ½ billion dollars—if gold were valued at only the old $35 per ounce. And 10 times as much silver as gold had been gathered by David before construction began.

The temple was similar to the tabernacle in structure, but was approximately twice as large. Built of stone, and paneled over with cedar, with the whole inlaid with gold, the temple was a strikingly beautiful building. It was fronted by two great pillars, each of which was topped with a flaming light at night to symbolize the mountaintop presence of Israel's God.

Solomon the Man

Scripture and archeology combine to provide an impressive portrait of Solomon's kingdom and his accomplishments. Three sources give us insight into Solomon the man during the early years of his brilliant reign.

Solomon's prayer (1 Kings 3:3-14). Early in Solomon's rule he was noted for his love for the Lord and his commitment to the Law. He "followed all of his father David's instructions" (v. 3, TLB). On one occasion after a great sacrifice had been made to the Lord, God spoke to Solomon in a dream and told him to make a request. Solomon's response was not only an affirmation of trust in God, but it was also an expression of sensitivity to the significance of his call as king. "Now, O Lord my God, You have made Your servant king in place of my father David. But I am only a little child and do not know how to carry out my duties. . . . Give Your servant a discerning heart to govern Your people and to distinguish between right and wrong. For who is

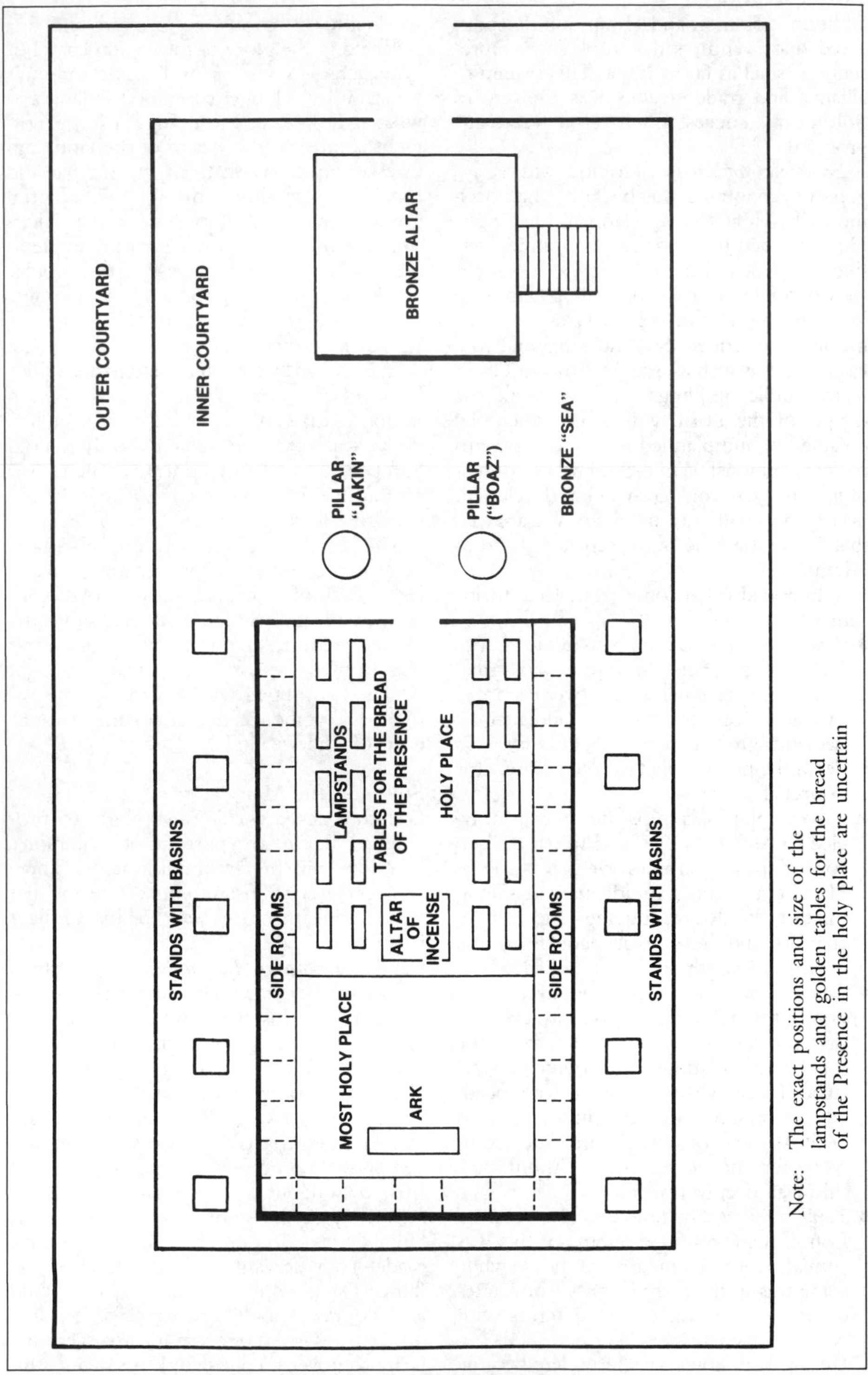

OUTER COURTYARD

INNER COURTYARD

BRONZE ALTAR

PILLAR "JAKIN"

PILLAR ("BOAZ")

BRONZE "SEA"

STANDS WITH BASINS

SIDE ROOMS

LAMPSTANDS

TABLES FOR THE BREAD OF THE PRESENCE

HOLY PLACE

ALTAR OF INCENSE

SIDE ROOMS

STANDS WITH BASINS

MOST HOLY PLACE

ARK

Note: The exact positions and size of the lampstands and golden tables for the bread of the Presence in the holy place are uncertain

Plan of Solomon's Temple

able to govern this great people of Yours?" (vv. 7-9)

This unselfish request was pleasing to God, and was granted. God said, "I will give you a wise and discerning heart, so that there will never have been anyone like you nor will there ever be" (v. 12). In addition, God promised glory and honor for which Solomon had not asked: "Both riches and honor—so that in your lifetime you will have no equal among kings" (v. 13).

The foundation for Solomon's later successes was laid here in his early meeting with God and in the love for God and for his people which led Solomon to seek wisdom to govern as God's regent.

♥ ***Link to Life: Children***

The story of Solomon's prayer for wisdom is followed immediately in 1 Kings by that of two women who both claimed an infant. When Solomon suggested the living infant be divided, the true mother wept and was willing to give up her son, while the other readily agreed. Solomon's prayer for wisdom had been answered, and that answer made him able to help the deserving.

To help boys and girls learn how to pray as Solomon did, bring 3 x 5 cards to class. Ask the boys and girls things they pray for, and list these on one side. For instance, a child might pray for a good grade on a test. This is the result they want. But if they were to follow Solomon's example, rather than praying for a good grade they might better pray, "Lord, help me study hard." If they do study hard, they will earn the good grade.

Look at the other prayers the boys and girls have reported. How can they get the results they want by praying for a godly quality or admirable trait?

How wonderful that good results do come when we pray to become better Christians and better people.

Solomon's temple dedication (1 Kings 8:1–9:9; 2 Chron. 5–7). Solomon called a great feast for all Israel when the temple was completed and ready for dedication. After a brief sermon to the people (2 Chron. 6:1-11), Solomon faced away from the multitude and knelt down to address God. Calling on God as a covenant-keeping Person, Solomon rehearsed some of the promises God had given His people, speaking both of God's commitment to discipline Israel when she sinned and to forgive and restore when Israel returned to the Lord. Calling on the Lord, Solomon asked that God's special presence might be focused in the now-completed temple.

"When Solomon finished praying, fire came down from heaven and consumed the burnt offering and the sacrifices, and the glory of the Lord filled the temple. The priests could not enter the temple of the Lord because the glory of the Lord filled it. When all the Israelites saw the fire coming down and the glory of the Lord above the temple, they knelt on the pavement with their faces to the ground and they worshiped and gave thanks to the Lord" (2 Chron. 7:1-3).

In this setting too we see Solomon in an excellent light, guiding his people in personal and national dedication to God. The Lord had made Solomon wise, and that wisdom was used to lead the nation closer to God.

♥ ***Link to Life: Youth / Adult***

At the dedication of the temple Solomon gave a brief sermon (1 Kings 8:15-21), made a long prayer (vv. 23-53), and concluded with a benediction (vv. 56-61).

Begin with direct individual Bible study. Ask each person to look for verses that might help to answer the following questions, and to place an appropriate symbol beside such verses.

What is Solomon's image of God? (Use a halo as a symbol.)

What is Solomon's view of people? (Use a stick figure as a symbol.)

What is important in man's relationship with God in prayer? (Use an R *as a symbol.)*

When each member of your group has read and marked the passage, divide into teams of five or six. Each team is to work out its own answer to the questions, based on what Solomon expressed in his prayer.

Hear team reports. Then discuss: "What do we learn here that can enrich our prayer lives?"

Literary achievements. A third source of insight into the first two decades of Solomon's rule is found in one of his great literary projects: the Book of Proverbs. Solomon wrote or collected over 3,000 of these practical sayings which sum up the Hebrew people's insights into life. Solomon's literary talents extended beyond this particular form: Ecclesiastes is a treatise in philosophy which sounds a note echoed by many moderns, and the Song of Songs is a love poem showing distinctive structure and depth. But it is the Proverbs themselves which give us our best insights into Solomon's character and his personal commitment during the first 20 or so years of his reign.

♥ ***Link to Life: Youth / Adult***
Have teams of four look at a chapter of Proverbs. Each team is to develop from evidence in its chapter a portrait of the character of the writer. Particularly, each is to list words suggested by their chapter that characterize the writer. (That is, the author is committed, generous, humble, etc.) Each is to be ready to demonstrate these conclusions from the text. Good chapters to use for this study are Proverbs 3, 10, 15, 16, and 22.

♥ ***Link to Life: Children***
The temple reminds us to worship the Lord in ways that are pleasing to Him. How else can we please the Lord? Let boys and girls look up proverbs from Solomon's time, and then draw a picture or make up and tell a story to illustrate one that they choose.

They may choose from the following: Proverbs 3:9, 27; 11:13; 14:31; 15:1; 16:32; 17:9; 19:17; 20:22. Be ready to explain any proverb younger children may not readily understand.

Solomon: An Evaluation: 1 Kings 11
It's appropriate that the Chronicles account of Solomon's life leaves out the events recorded in 1 Kings 11. Scripture affirms that God accepts us on the basis of faith, not works. Saving trust leads to the forgiveness of our sins. "Their sins and lawless acts I will remember no more" (Heb. 10:17) echoes Jeremiah 31:34. Now, in Chronicles, we see this principle in practice. History records that "as Solomon grew old his wives turned his heart after other gods, and his heart was not fully devoted to the Lord his God" (1 Kings 11:4). But the divine commentary on Solomon found in 1 Chronicles concludes with the account of his glory. The years of failure and decline are overlooked.

In this, the Chronicles are something like Hebrews 11, in which God catalogs the accomplishments of men and women of faith. Reading their history in the Old Testament we are often confronted by their weaknesses and failures—failures we dare not try to explain away. It's wrong to idealize biblical characters or to excuse their faults, or marshal our "scholarship" to show that the things they did were not so bad after all. But it is just as wrong to fail to recognize the fact that in forgiveness, God faces our sin, deals with it, and sends it to oblivion!

Solomon, like other Old Testament men of faith, trusted the God willing to send His Son to Calvary to deal decisively and eternally with human sin. In the blood of Christ, the unique answer to the fact of sin—yours and mine as well as Solomon's—has been given. God Himself paid sin's penalty in full. Now God exercises the freedom Christ has won for Him as well as for us. He accepts trust as the righteousness which we do not have. As for sin, God forgives.

Solomon, then, on the one hand stands before us an example of the forgiven man. On the other hand, he stands as an example of a man who chose a road on which he remained in constant *need* of forgiveness!

David is an example of the forgiven man as well. David sinned, was called to account, and was restored to fellowship. The wrong directions David took were turned again and again to the way of righteousness. Because David confessed and recognized his sin, his life with God was essentially one of continuing fellowship. Solomon, on the other hand, took a direction from which there is no record of a return. Because Solomon's relationship with God was founded on initial trust, as his early prayers clearly show, the forgiveness later won on Calvary was his. But because Solomon failed to confess, he wandered from the Lord and lived the last decades of his life out of fellowship.

What we learn from Solomon's life is that sin's impact on the individual and on others around him is utterly tragic. The basic relationship with God may not be broken by later acts of sin. Forgiveness may wash the empty years out of memory. But the contemporary loss in terms of human suffering is tragically great. The fantastic potential of a life completely given to God is lost. The person we could have been by denying our

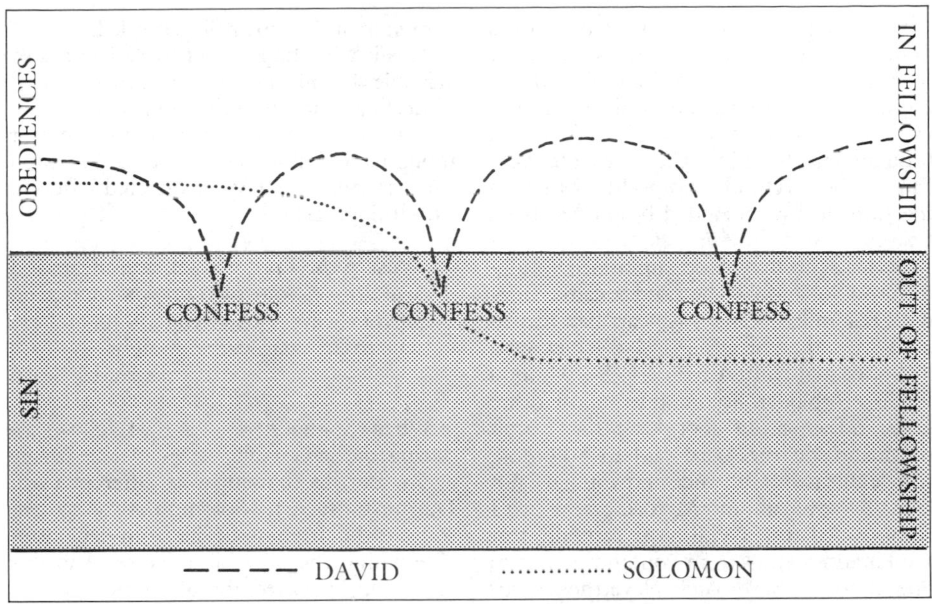

David's & Solomon's Life Paths

own passions in order to follow the Lord dissolves into a sigh.

♥ ***Link to Life: Youth / Adult***
Use the chart above to compare David and Solomon. In a minilecture point up the meaning of 1 Chronicles' failure to comment on Solomon's failure. But also point up the tragedy of what might have been, which always exists where believers stray from fellowship with the Lord.

Solomon's Strength

A simple New Testament warning helps us to understand Solomon—and ourselves. "If you think you are standing firm, be careful that you don't fall" (1 Cor. 10:12). We can never retreat from dependence on God. Those very strengths of character or personality that are ours are at the same time our points of vulnerability. Solomon's great strength was his wisdom. But Solomon's wisdom was also his weakness.

Solomon's diplomatic policies give clear examples. It certainly seemed wise to make alliances with surrounding nations and to seal those alliances in the normal way, with marriages. It also seemed wise to set up the mobile strike force of chariots, which was a keystone in Solomon's military defense. Yet both these "wise" courses of action are warned against in Deuteronomy. Telling Israel that they might set a king over them when they came into the land, Moses warned against choosing a foreigner. Then he added, he "must not acquire great numbers of horses for himself, or make the people return to Egypt to get more of them.... He must not take many wives or his heart will be led astray. He must not accumulate large amounts of silver and gold" (Deut. 17:16-17).

David had followed these injunctions. While he had several wives and concubines, there was nothing of the multiplication of Solomon (700 wives and 300 concubines). David also established a policy of incapacitating the chariot horses of the armies he had defeated, so they could never be used for war. David had carefully refrained from building up a chariot-based military.

Solomon reasoned that each of these new policies of his was prudent. He apparently failed to see the dangers inherent in each course—danger first that foreign wives might entice his heart from following God, and then that becoming a military superpower might lead him to trust his strength rather than rely on his God.

Solomon trusted his wisdom. Why not? His wisdom was renowned. God's warnings were apparently unrealistic. Human wisdom dictated a different course from the one commanded by God.

First Kings 11 tells us that God knows human strengths and weaknesses far better than any wise man. In Solomon's old age the women he loved did turn his heart away from the Lord toward their idols. Solomon brought into the Holy City itself the worship of the very gods and goddesses which the Lord had commanded be purged from Palestine!

Because of this, God announced judgment on Solomon. "The Lord became angry with Solomon because his heart had turned away from the Lord, the God of Israel, who had appeared to him twice (v. 9). Though He had forbidden Solomon to follow other gods, Solomon did not keep the Lord's command. So the Lord said to Solomon, "Since this is your attitude and you have not kept My covenant and My decrees, which I commanded you, I will most certainly tear the kingdom away from you and give it to one of your subordinates. Nevertheless, for the sake of David your father, I will not do it during your lifetime. I will tear it out of the hand of your son. Yet I will not tear the whole kingdom from him, but will give him one tribe for the sake of David My servant and for the sake of Jerusalem, which I have chosen" (vv. 11-13).

Solomon's failure to trust God rather than his own wisdom was destined to have a tragic impact on the people he led as well as on himself. No human trait, no matter how finely tuned, can function well apart from a relationship with God where that trait is fully submitted and committed. Solomon's wisdom, apart from God's special touch, led him in paths which "seem right to a man" but which led inexorably to death.

It is the same for us. However great our strengths, when we rely on them rather than on God, we're sure to fall.

We can track the impact of Solomon's defection in the events immediately following his death. The nation was split; and enemies made by Solomon's harsh policies, like Hadad the Edomite, attacked the Divided Kingdom from without. The wealth gathered by Solomon to Jerusalem created oppressed and oppressor classes within. The nation was wealthy, but many people lived in poverty.

It is never easy to discern from such facts what a person's defection from God does within him. Outward things can be measured, but the inner spirit can only be known if it is personally revealed.

This is why the Book of Ecclesiastes is so valuable. David, the emotional man, shared his feelings with us in the Psalms. Solomon, the intellectual man, now shared his inmost thoughts. In fellowship with God, Solomon had written, with a Spirit-directed wisdom, such things as:

> Trust in the Lord with all your heart and lean not on your own understanding; in all your ways acknowledge Him, and He will make your paths straight.
>
> Proverbs 3:5-6

When Solomon was out of fellowship during the later years of his life, he wrote again. But his thinking was different then. During those years Solomon chose to reason out the meaning of life from data available within the physical universe. And this reasoning, reported for us in Ecclesiastes, shows an out-of-fellowship Solomon despairingly conclude:

> Meaningless! Meaningless! . . .Utterly meaningless! Everything is meaningless.
>
> Ecclesiastes 1:2

As a man, Solomon started well, with a deep commitment to God. But Solomon's strength—his wisdom—also proved to be his weakness. He began to rely on his intelligence rather than on God's. As a result, his own spiritual life became deadened and his wives were able to turn him from the Lord. During his last years, this man who had expressed in Proverbs so many insights about life, attempted to find life's deepest meaning while ruling God out of his considerations!

Solomon had every opportunity to test the ways in which men today search for meaning. He probed the possibilities of the intellectual life. He abandoned himself to pleasure and luxury. He gathered great wealth, and built great buildings. He experienced an exciting and varied sexual life. He had power and status within and outside his kingdom. Yet all these things, when tasted, seemed flat and meaningless. None could give meaning or fulfillment to his life.

Even Solomon's final sayings in Ecclesiastes 12 do not represent a return to God. Instead they represent the best thinking of the natural man. Perhaps there *is* a God. If so, what more can man do than keep His commands? Possibly chapter 12 of Ecclesiastes represents a wistful look back on Solomon's own life and the days when he did fear God and keep His commandments; before the evil days came, the years drew on, and Solomon looked at all his glory and accomplishments and realized, "I find no pleasure in them" (v. 1).

And so Solomon died.

And left us a warning.

Beginning our life well is only half of it. Only a deep and close and continuing personal relationship with God can offer fulfillment. Only through continuing commitment can God's good purposes in our lives be achieved.

TEACHING GUIDE

Prepare

How has your life shown a growing commitment to God, rather than a Solomon-like decline?

Explore

Give a minilecture on the greatness of the Solomonic era and on the achievements of this great king. During the lecture do *not* mention his personal life or qualities.

Expand

1. Divide into two groups, which may be further subdivided into teams. One half should be assigned to study proverbs that reveal the heart of Solomon during the early years when he was in fellowship with the Lord (see "link-to-life," p. 250). The other half should be assigned passages in Ecclesiastes, and asked to also develop a character sketch of the writer. In Ecclesiastes they might read: 2:1-16; 6:1-12; 9:1-12.

When each team has developed its impressions of the writer, come together and compare. What words did each choose to describe Solomon? How are the differences to be explained?

2. Then read or review the material in 1 Kings 11 that describes Solomon's later years. Use the visual on page 251 to contrast David and Solomon, and underline the need for steadfast commitment.

Apply

Both Ecclesiastes and Proverbs are in effect expressions of a philosophy of life. Each reveals principles on which Solomon, at different stages of his life, felt people should live.

Ask your group members to write down five statements which sum up important principles on which each one tries to live: principles which express something of their own personal philosophy of life as Christians.

Then either have members share with your whole group, or divide into teams of five for sharing of the principles, and discussion of how the principles are applied in each person's life.

If you wish, you might collect what each person has written, and put them together as an affirmation of your group's Christian philosophy of life.

STUDY GUIDE 36

1 Kings 12–14; 2 Chronicles 10–12

THE KINGDOM DIVIDES

Overview
The division of David and Solomon's United Kingdom into two often hostile nations was truly one of history's turning points. In looking at the text which describes the division, we sense the spiritual apostasy which was part and parcel of the founding of the Northern realm, Israel.

In the entire history of the North, there is no godly king. In the history of the South, a kingdom known as Judah, there were only a few. Yet the kings in the Southern line were all descendants of David, for God's covenant-promise to Israel's greatest king was faithfully kept.

This era marks development of the prophetic ministry. Increasingly, prophets played a role in speaking out about the sins of the nation, and in calling God's people back to the Lord. Both North and South knew the ministry of these "men of God."

When teaching these turning-point chapters in the Old Testament, it is important to go beyond the immediate text to provide an overview of the future of each segment of the Divided Kingdom, and also to look ahead at the role to be played by the prophets.

▶ ***Charts.*** Charts like the one in this unit are important teaching tools. They permit you to present a large amount of information in a simplified, visual form. The charts in this text are intended not only for your instruction but also for your use in your teaching. So do feel free to duplicate them for your class or study group.

Commentary
With the division of the kingdom of Solomon, the Hebrew people were launched on a three and a half century decline, culminating in a final exile from the Promised Land. What happened during this extended period? And how did God's ancient people journey toward the edge of divine judgment?

Israel, the Northern Kingdom (931–722 B.C.).
The times of David and Solomon were days of glory for Israel. Blessed with power and prosperity, the united Jewish nation was a politically dominant force in the Middle East. But all was not well within Israel. In Solomon's later years, as the weight of his bureaucracy increased and his building projects multiplied, even his great income was not enough. Solomon increased the taxes on his people and drafted more and more men into labor levies. Discontent grew.

When Solomon died, Rehoboam, his son, went to Shechem to meet with the dissidents. These people came with the intention of making him king. Choosing a spokesman who had been Solomon's enemy (Jeroboam), the people promised to accept Rehoboam as king if he would lighten the tax burden. Foolishly, Rehoboam refused, promising rather to increase the burden. The 10 Northern tribes then openly rebelled, rejecting the Davidic dynasty's right to rule (2 Chron. 10). In place of Rehoboam, they recognized Jeroboam as king of Israel. When the Prophet Shemaiah turned back a loyalist army, a permanent division between the Southern and Northern tribes resulted. Two nations were now formed. They would afterward be known as Judah (the south) and Israel (the north).

As king of Israel, Jeroboam now faced a difficult political situation. The worship center for the Hebrew people was at Jerusalem, which was also the capital of the Southern Kingdom. Fearing that the people would return to the Davidic dynasty if they made the required annual pilgrimages to the temple, Jeroboam set up his own "iron curtain" between the two nations. And he went about setting up a rival religious system (1 Kings 12).

Jeroboam's false system counterfeited the pattern established by God in the Old Testament Law. He established worship centers at Dan and Bethel, but rather than erect temples, he put up idols—golden calves on whose backs the invisible God was imagined to ride. Jeroboam turned out the levitical priests who would not go along with his apostate plans, and ordained volunteers from among the people. And he set up his own priestly class and sacrificial system. Finally Jeroboam copied the great feasts of the Law in which all Hebrews were commanded to participate. He established his own festivals, set for different times than those ordained by God.

This false religious system had a dual impact on the Northern Kingdom, Israel. First, the godly slipped over into Judah and settled there, so they could worship the Lord as He had commanded. These immigrants were a significant number. At the time of the division Judah was able to mobilize only 180,000 men (2 Chron. 11:1). But just 18 years later, Judah's army entered the field with 400,000 fighting men (2 Chron. 13:2).

A second impact was on the character of the Northern Kingdom. The first king made a conscious and overtly rebellious decision to break with God and His Law. Each succeeding king continued in the pattern Jeroboam set! Israel, with only 19 kings during its brief existence, had nine different dynasties. Only eight kings died a natural death. Seven were assassinated, one was a suicide, one was killed in battle, one died of injuries suffered in a fall, and the last king, Hoshea, simply disappeared into captivity. The Bible says that they all "did that which was evil in the sight of the Lord."

With this kind of leadership, no wonder the people who remained in the apostate kingdom quickly fell into Baal worship and all sorts of injustice. God continued to send prophets to speak to Israel, but kings and people continued to resent the prophets' ministries and to reject their messages.

After a stormy history—during which Israel, however, did know material prosperity under strong rulers such as Jeroboam II and Omri (who established Israel's capital at Samaria)—Israel fell to the Assyrians in 722 B.C. The city of Samaria was totally destroyed and the people of Israel were deported. The Northern Kingdom disappeared from history; only the families who had settled in Judah kept the identity of the 10 tribes alive.

Judah, the Southern Kingdom (931–586 B.C.)

The dreary portrait of Israel's experience under the apostate kings is lightened when we look at Judah. Politically, the Southern Kingdom knew its ups and downs as conflicts with Egypt, Israel, and other surrounding states brought alternate victories and defeats. Spiritually, Judah was blessed with several godly kings. But she also knew the rule of apostate kings who followed Solomon's example and permitted pagan worship in the holy land. Queen Athaliah (841–835 B.C.) struggled to introduce the cult of Baal in Judah as her mother Jezebel had in Israel. Yet a succession of God-approved kings (Joash through Jotham) kept the extension of evil tendencies to a minimum.

Still, the great revivals under Kings Asa, Jehoshaphat, and Joash were unable to purify the land. Much local autonomy was retained, and the piety of the king did not guarantee the holiness of his people.

Hezekiah, one of the most godly kings, guided Judah during the critical time of Israel's destruction. He instituted drastic reforms to correct the idolatry of his father Ahaz, and thoroughly cleansed the land. He was certainly influenced by two great prophetic contemporaries, Isaiah and Micah.

Yet Hezekiah's own son, Manasseh, who ruled 55 years, was one of Judah's most evil men. He supported pagan worship, recognized the sacrifice of children to the Ammonite god Molech, and killed all who protested. Tradition tells us that Isaiah met his death at Manasseh's hands.

Despite a later revival under Josiah (640–609 B.C.), king during Habakkuk's day, the religious and moral deterioration was such that the revival made little impact on Judah. The graphic description by Jeremiah and Ezekiel (esp. Ezek. 8–11) of the way of life of God's people helps us see clearly why the announced judgment *had to* come.

And come it did. In a series of deportations, the surviving kingdom was wrenched from the land. The temple and the Holy

Two Kingdoms

ISRAEL

	Major Kings	Prophets
931	Jeroboam I	Ahijah[1] (Unnamed)[2]
909	Baasha	Jehu[3]
886	Omri	
874	Ahab	Elijah[4] (Unnamed)[5] Micaiah[6] Elisha[7] Obadiah
841	Jehu	
793	Jeroboam II	Jonah[8] Amos Hosea
722		Obed[9]

Assyrian Captivity

JUDAH

	Major Kings	Prophets
931	Rehoboam	Shemiah[10]
910	Asa	Azariah[11]
		Hanani[12]
872	Jehoshaphat	Jehu[13]
		Jahaziel[14] Eliezer[15] Elijah[16]
835	Joash	
		Zechariah[17] Joel
797	Amaziah	
791	Uzziah	
		Isaiah
750	Jotham	Micah
728	Hezekiah	
		Nahum
640	Josiah	Habakkuk
		Zephaniah Jeremiah
586		Ezekiel

Babylonian Captivity

1. 1 Kings 11:14
2. 1 Kings 13
3. 1 Kings 16
4. 1 Kings 17–2 Kings 2
5. 1 Kings 20
6. 1 Kings 22
7. 1 Kings 19–2 Kings 13
8. also 2 Kings 14
9. 2 Chron. 28
10. 2 Chron. 11–12
11. 2 Chron. 15
12. 2 Chron. 16
13. 2 Chron. 19
14. 2 Chron. 20
15. 2 Chron. 20
16. 2 Chron. 21
17. 2 Chron. 24

City were razed. Under the weight of this agonizing chastisement, God's people finally did come to repent in a foreign land. There they were purified of idolatry and, finally, a remnant returned from Babylon to the Promised Land to reestablish the Jewish homeland and to await the Messiah.

The Prophets

Reading the divine history, we quickly gain the impression that two groups of people are most significant during the time of the Divided Kingdom. One group is made up of rulers, whose deeds and misdeeds are chronicled. The other group is made up of prophets, whose voices were raised at critical times in each nation's experience. Who were these prophets, and what was their mission?

While the original sense of the word is unclear, its use in Scripture gives us a clear definition. A prophet is a spokesman for God. An incident in Exodus helps us to see this role. Moses had been called by God to deliver Israel, yet he feared that because he did not speak fluently he would not be able to move Pharaoh. God promised to give him Aaron his brother as "a mouth." "He will speak to the people for you, and it will be as if he were your mouth and as if you were God to him" (Ex. 4:16). This relationship is further described by God in 7:1: "See, I have made you like God to Pharaoh, and your brother Aaron will be your prophet."

As Moses was God's spokesman, Aaron was to be Moses'. In a similar relationship, prophets in the time of the two kingdoms served as "God's mouth."

The prophetic ministry was not one in which the spokesman's personality was blotted out in some ecstatic mystical experience. Each prophet retained his own individuality, his own personality, and peculiarities. Each spoke in his own historical and cultural context. Yet each was God's spokesman: each communicated God's own message.

Scripture gives us insights into how the prophets received their messages. At times they seem to have heard an external voice (cf. 1 Sam. 3:3-9). Often the voice was internal (Isa. 7:3-4; Hab. 2:2). Then again, the prophets were enabled to see spiritual realities invisible to others (Num. 22:31; 2 Kings 6:15-17). At other times the prophets saw visions (Ezek. 37; 40–48). The message was received in many ways, but the true spokesman recognized its source and confidently announced that what he had to say was "the word of the Lord."

Often, during the days of the two kingdoms, the ministry of the prophets was directed to the rulers. This was true in earlier days as well. Nathan the prphet rebuked David (2 Sam. 12), as did Gad (2 Sam. 24). It was Samuel, the prophet-judge, who ministered to Saul and anointed David king. Because the kings chose to move away from God, meetings between prophets and rulers often became confrontations. On the day that Jeroboam instituted his false religion, he was confronted by "a man of God... from Judah" (1 Kings 13:1). This prophet announced judgment on the altar Jeroboam was consecrating, foretelling the birth of Josiah, a king of Judah, who would one day burn the bones of the false priests on it. He gave a sign to prove that he was speaking by God's command: the altar would crack, and the ashes spill out. Angered, Jeroboam commanded that the young prophet be seized. But the hand he stretched out was gripped by paralysis: he could not lower it! And at that moment, the alter split.

Cowed, Jeroboam begged the prophet to ask God to release his paralysis, and the hand was restored. God's spokesman then made his announcements with unquestioned divine authority!

Such miracles or soon-fulfilled prophecies often authenticated the prophets. The influence they wielded is shown by the fact that Rehoboam turned back an army about to attack the rebels in Israel at the word of Shemaiah (2 Chron. 11). Even Jeroboam, when his son became ill, sent his wife to the Prophet Abijah to inquire of the Lord (1 Kings 14).

The ministry of the prophets was often resented by rebellious kings, and their messages were often rejected. But kings—godly and ungodly—and the common people as well, recognized these men as God's spokesmen and viewed them with awe and often fear.

How is it then that the prophets were unable to halt the slide of the two kingdoms into sin? Why was their ministry largely ineffective?

As today, the problem lay not with the Word but with the hearers. These spokesmen for God did deliver His message. But the people did not respond with faith. They recognized that the message and the messenger were from God, but this awareness did not lead them to commitment. Unwilling to submit to God's way, the people stubbornly held to their own paths. It is not, as Jesus reminds us, the one who hears the Word of God who is blessed. It is the person who *hears and does* who receives God's blessing (Matt. 7:24).

The men and women of the two kingdoms who took pride in their religious activities, their prophets, their temple, and holy places, were all too like men and women of today who confuse churchgoing with discipleship, and "Bible-believing" with obedience. In the prophetic call to God's people to respond to Him and wholeheartedly obey, we hear His invitation to us today—an invitation designed not to burden us, but to lead us safely away from the edge of personal judgment, toward which our willful choices would most certainly lead.

TEACHING GUIDE

Prepare
Jot down notes on what you see as the most important truths your group can learn from a review of the history of these two kingdoms.

Explore
Give a minilecture overview of the two kingdoms. Either duplicate the chart on page 256 on chalkboard or overhead, or make a copy of it for each of your students.

The minilecture is important background to the study of the biblical text.

Expand
1. Ask your group members to develop from 1 Kings 11:26–14:20 a personality profile of Jeroboam. How is he like or unlike modern politicians?
2. Or, examine and list from 1 Kings 12:26–13:6 the actions which Jeroboam took to establish his kingdom. What impact did each have on the future of his people? NOTE: Be sure your group members see each of the following elements of Jeroboam's false system:

A. Two calves of gold served as idols, even though the invisible God was supposed to be riding astride them. Jerusalem was replaced by Dan and Bethel as worship centers.
B. Priests not of the priestly line were appointed to serve at Bethel and Dan, as well as at "high places" (like roadside shrines).
C. A system of festivals that counterfeited those ordained by God were established.
D. Sacrifices were offered at the northern worship centers, which was again a direct violation of God's Law.

This whole pattern is summed up in 1 Kings 12:33, which contrasts the system Jeroboam devised in his own heart to replace that which had been devised and revealed by God.
3. Or, list at least 20 observations on prophecy by examining the ministry of the "man of God from Judah" (1 Kings 13).
4. Or, divide your group into three teams, each of which is to undertake one of the studies above. Give most of the hour for these studies, but save 8 to 10 minutes for final sharing.

Apply
If your group members have explored the text as suggested above, spend the last few minutes sharing. Do not ask what your study teams found. Instead, ask: "What did you personally learn that you can apply to your life from the passage you studied?"

STUDY GUIDE 37

1 Kings 15–22; 2 Chronicles 11–28

KINGS AND PROPHETS IN ISRAEL

Overview

The first 50 years of the Divided Kingdom saw sporadic conflict between the North and the South. King Asa of Judah even used the temple gold to bribe Ben-Hadad of Syria to break a treaty with Israel and to attack the North.

Within the Northern Kingdom, Baasha assassinated Nadab, and after killing Jeroboam's whole family, took the throne. While this fulfilled the words of a prophet against Jeroboam, Baasha also "did evil in the eyes of the Lord" and followed all the practices which Jeroboam had instituted. After a 24-year reign, Baasha was succeeded by his son Elah. Just two years later he was killed by Zimri, one of his generals, and Baasha's whole family was destroyed in its turn. The text says that Zimri "did not spare a single male" of Baasha's household, "whether relative or friend" (1 Kings 16:11). But Zimri himself ruled only seven days. Then the army proclaimed another commander, Omri, ruler. Zimri retreated to the palace and burned it to the ground around him.

After a brief civil war, Omri was established as king. Omri proved to be one of the strongest of Israel's rulers. But his son, Ahab, who was also a capable ruler, is infamous as one of Israel's most evil and selfish kings. Under Ahab the cult of Baal was reintroduced into Israel, and the royal family led a further moral and spiritual decline.

■ For a discussion of each of these rulers see the *Bible Knowledge Commentary*, pages 517-522.

Commentary

Israel was born in rebellion and nursed in apostasy. Yet there was worse to come.

A series of assassinations in 886 B.C. led to the crowning of Omri, a ranking army officer. Capable and aggressive, Omri quickly stabilized the nation. He built and fortified Samaria as capital and so impressed the Assyrians that a hundred years later Israel was known by them as the "land of Omri."

The Bible tells us little about Omri's reign (1 Kings 16:23-27), but archeology has added several important bits of information. An inscribed pillar, the Moabite Stone, found in 1898, reports that Omri conquered Moab and forced it to pay tribute to Israel. The marriage of his son Ahab to the Phoenician princess Jezebel indicates close relations with Phoenicia, a valuable trading ally for Israel. It is likely that much of the wealth of Samaria revealed by archeological expeditions has roots in the diplomacy and statecraft of Omri.

Yet in Scripture the focus clearly is not on the political and economic affairs of God's people. The focus instead is placed on the religious and moral dimensions of life. And here Omri's key significance seems to have been that he fathered Ahab who was, without question, the most evil ruler to that point.

Ahab's Reign

As a political and military leader, Ahab receives good marks. He was effective in defeating Israel's Syrian enemies. He joined in a coalition army which halted the invasion of a great Assyrian force under Shalmaneser III. And Ahab maintained the borders of his land. Assyrian records tell us that Ahab was able to contribute 2,000 chariots (the tanks of ancient warfare) to the coalition army, as well as some 10,000 foot soldiers.

Economically, Israel also prospered. The Phoenician alliance meant that sea trade routes were open to landlocked Israel, and the great "ivory house" Ahab built for himself (1 Kings 22:39) testifies to the land's prosperity.

Yet that same Phoenician alliance opened the door to introduction of Baal worship in

Israel. Ahab's marriage to Jezebel, a devotee of Baal, forced a direct confrontation. Jezebel was not satisfied with coexistence: she insisted that Baal worship replace any worship of Jehovah. She not only slaughtered the Hebrew prophets of Jehovah (18:4); she also imported hundreds of prophets of Baal to establish worship centers for this pagan deity.

Baal-Malquart, commonly called simply Baal in this part of Scripture, was the expression of Baal worshiped in Tyre, Jezebel's home city. The term *baal* simply means "owner" or "lord." In Canaan the baals were nature gods, regarded as owners of particular localities, and believed to control fertility. Thus good crops as well as the human birth rate demanded that a people remain on good terms with the local "owner" deity.

As Canaanite religion developed, it focused on the cycles of the year. And extreme cult activities were required to ensure the coming of the needed rains. A prominent feature of these rites was prostitution by both sexes (see Jud. 2:17; Jer. 7:9; and Amos 2:7). At times the rites even involved child sacrifice (Jer. 19:5). These orgiastic religious practices are well documented in hymns and poems from the period, which show a deadening moral depravity associated with the religious worship.

Jezebel and Ahab went about imposing this entire system on Israel, aggressively seeking to blot out the worship of Jehovah.

Standing against complete apostasy, and thwarting the attempt of those in power, was the best known of the Old Testament's speaking prophets, Elijah. With others, Elijah continually confronted the king and his pagan consort, and called Israel to commitment to God.

The Prophets: Deuteronomy 18:9-22
When, under Moses' leadership, God's people were about to enter the land of Palestine, God gave implicit instructions about supernatural guidance. The Canaanite peoples practiced witchcraft, consulted spiritualists, and used other means of divining the future. All such sources of information were forbidden to God's people, who had His Word to live by. In this key passage of Scripture, the people of Israel were promised that when God wanted to communicate with them, He would raise up a prophet (v. 15). These spokesmen for God would relay His Word to the people; the people were to listen and to obey.

This promise of prophetic guidance included several tests by which a true prophet of the Lord was to be recognized.

Recognizing prophets. Prophets whom God actually did send were marked off in several special ways.

1. The prophet was to be "from among your own brothers" (v. 15). No foreigner could speak to God's people in God's name; the Phoenician prophets of Baal were automatically ruled out.

2. The prophet would speak "in the name of the Lord' (vv. 20-22). Any prophet who claimed to have a supernatural message to communicate but delivered it as the message of another god was to be killed.

3. The prophet would predict events which invariably came true. Any self-proclaimed prophet whose message foretold a future event which did not happen could be safely ignored.

Bible history shows us that this test is very significant. Often when prophets spoke of events far distant in time, they would include information about things that would happen soon. When these near events came to pass as the prophet foretold, the hearers could trust the prophet's word. Thus the prophets of God were authenticated by the reliability of their messages.

In summary, then, the spokesmen whom God sent to His people would be Hebrews, they would announce their message as from the Lord, and their claim to be God's spokesmen would be authenticated by the fulfillment of their predictions.

One additional test is given in Deuteronomy 13—a test which warns against acceptance of the miraculous as sufficient proof of God's hand. The Bible says, "If a prophet . . . appears among you and announces to you a miraculous sign or wonder, and if the sign or wonder of which he has spoken takes place, and he says, 'Let us follow other gods . . .' you must not listen to the words of that prophet" (vv. 1-3).

The point made here is clear. A prophet's message must be in harmony with the written Word (see vv. 3-5). If the prophet truly spoke for God, his message would be in full harmony with previous revelation.

This is an important point for us to remember today, even as it was for Israel and for Judah. There *are* supernatural powers in conflict with God. A miraculous event or a fulfilled prediction is not in itself proof that God is behind the sign. The content of the message must always be measured against the teaching of the Word of God. Where the Word is in conflict with the messenger, the Word is to be given unquestioned precedence.

False prophets. In actual fact, Israel did know counterfeit prophets, even as today we know counterfeit religious leaders. Some were men who prophesied in the name of an idol (see 1 Kings 18; Jer. 2:8; 23:13). Other men pretended to be prophets to win the favor of rulers like Ahab, as in 1 Kings 22, when the false prophets were quick to give the king the message they knew he wanted to hear. Others very possibly spoke in God's name, but were sharing messages from a very different source.

In times when prophetic activity was high—as in the days of Ahab and Jezebel—it might have been easy for confusion to grow over who the true and false prophets were. Yet, marked off by the tests we have seen, and authenticated as well by the work of God within the hearer, God's spokesmen *were* recognized. The message they shared was known to come from God.

But all too often the message, like God Himself, was ignored.

♥ ***Link to Life: Youth / Adult***

Tell your group the following true story. "Beth's mother has gone to a spiritualist and palm reader. The woman informs her that her husband is overweight, and will die within the year. Distraught, Beth's mom calls her daughter and asks what she should do."

Ask your group to discuss in pairs what Beth should tell her mother.

After discussion read aloud Deuteronomy 18:9-13. God will not permit His people to seek guidance from any supernatural source other than Himself. God wants us to trust Him alone, and look to Him alone for direction. In Old Testament times that direction was provided through the prophets. Today we have the Scriptures and the Holy Spirit within us to show us God's way. We do not need, nor can we trust, any other source of information.

NOTE: Beth shared this passage with her mom, a Christian. Her mother did not visit the palm reader again. And Beth's dad is still living, some two years after this event.

Elijah

The biblical report of Ahab's reign is intertwined with a fascinating portrait of the prophets who constantly confronted him. In teaching these passages you'll want to look at each exciting story in the biblical text itself. Here, we want to review the highlights and give background that may make the Bible report clearer.

1 Kings 17:1-24. Nothing is said in Scripture about Elijah's background, except that he was a settler in Gilead. We meet Elijah when he suddenly appeared to announce to Ahab, "There will be neither dew nor rain in the next few years except at my word" (v. 1).

This particular judgment is significant. The Baal worship Ahab and Jezebel promoted was a fertility faith. The worship of Baal was thought to guarantee rains and crops. Now Elijah challenged Baal in the name of Jehovah at the very point where Baal's strength was supposed to lie!

It must have taken courage to go meet this wicked king who was a sworn enemy of the Lord and certainly capable of killing His prophets. But how much better to face our fears with trust in God than to run from them.

♥ ***Link to Life: Children***

Even children can find courage to face their fears when they trust God as Elijah did. After telling the Bible story, help boys and girls play a game of "What would Elijah do?" Have ready pictures of boys and girls and adults, cut from a catalog or magazine and backed with cardboard. Have also a picture of a Bible character who looks like Elijah cut from your Sunday School materials.

Before introducing the figures, ask the boys and girls to think of times when children might feel afraid. Situations may range from being in the dark to taking a test to waiting at a bus stop with bigger kids. It is important to work with situations that are real to your boys and girls, which they themselves suggest.

When a number of situations have been listed, remind your class of how Elijah faced the evil King Ahab even though he must have been afraid too. Then act out the different situations the children described, with the figure of Elijah taking the role of the fearful child. In each situation, ask the children, "What would Elijah do?" Try out different suggestions by having the figures act them out. Then replace the Elijah figure with the figure of a boy or girl, who puts into practice what the children have decided Elijah would do.

God's care of Elijah. Among children's favorite stories about Elijah are those that emphasize God's care of the prophet. During the terrible drought that struck Israel, the prophet was protected and provided for by the Lord. At first he was fed by ravens near a brook named Kerith. When the brook dried up, the Lord sent Elijah to Zarephath, outside of Israel in territory controlled by Sidon. There he met a widow about to eat her last meal with her son. Elijah asked her to feed him first, and promised that her jar of flour and jug of oil would never be used up.

Elijah lived with that widow and her son, eating that "last meal" every day, until the time came to return to Israel.

♥ ***Link to Life: Youth / Adult***
The story of Elijah illustrates both the meaning of the prayer Jesus taught His disciples, and of another teaching. The Lord's Prayer includes the words, "Give us today our daily *bread." And Jesus taught us not to be worried about tomorrow, but to trust a Heavenly Father to whom we are important. Surely, Jesus said, God would provide both food and clothing to meet our basic needs (Matt. 6:28-34).*

Ask your group members to imagine that each has only one day's food in the house, and is not sure where the next day's will come from. Each is to imagine his or her feelings and thoughts in this situation.

Then read the 1 Kings 17 story of God's care of Elijah. Work in teams to consider and list how Elijah's situation was similar *and how it was* different from *their own imaginary situation with one day of food.*

When lists have been completed, compare. You want them to be sure to note that both they and Elijah have the same relationship with God. Introduce both the Lord's Prayer and the Matthew 6 passage for further insights. How much of our life on earth really must *be lived by faith, for events truly are outside the realm of our control?*

1 Kings 18:1-46. The severe, three-year drought did not convince Israel of Baal's impotence. Ahab, rather than seeing himself as responsible, blamed the prophet who, although searched for, had not been found. Now Elijah was commanded to engineer a direct confrontation.

Ahab and Elijah met, and a test was agreed to. The people of Israel were invited to watch a supernatural contest between Elijah, the lone prophet of Jehovah, and some 450 prophets of Baal.

They met on Mount Carmel, where Elijah challenged Israel: "How long will you waver between two opinions? If the Lord is God, follow Him; but if Baal is god, follow him" (v. 21).

After a whole day of futile prayer, the pagan prophets were unable to bring fire to their altar. But God answered Elijah's simple prayer immediately, and in a blazing holocaust, the Lord burned not only the offering laid out on a water-soaked altar but also the very stones of the altar itself!

Convinced, the watching crowds killed the pagan prophets who had polluted God's people and His land.

Following this indication of Israel's return to God, Elijah announced return of the rains.

1 Kings 19:1-21. Elijah had experienced a great triumph. But while Ahab may have been momentarily cowed, Jezebel was not. When she heard what had happened, and how Elijah had killed all her prophets, the evil queen swore that she would have Elijah's life "by this time tomorrow." Suddenly, inexplicably, Elijah was stricken with terror. In an all-consuming panic he forgot his faith and simply ran.

Elijah's flight after victory shows us again the humanness of the prophets. Like us, their great triumphs were often followed by times of depression. Elijah's "up" at Carmel was followed by a desperate "down."

This passage is helpful in several ways. First, it helps us realize that the great people of the Bible truly were mortal, just as we are. We really can identify with them; they are not "spiritual giants" so unlike us that we cannot learn from their lives. Second, this chapter shows us how gently God dealt with the depressed Elijah. God did not rebuke, but offered support and comfort. We need not be ashamed of our own times of depression, but can turn to the Lord who truly does understand and care. And third, in the model of God's care for Elijah, you and I learn how we can be helpful to friends or family who may also be depressed.

♥ ***Link to Life: Youth / Adult***

Ask your group members to take the role of professional counselors. A person who is deeply depressed comes to them. Have members divide into teams of five to brainstorm for two minutes on: What can we do to help?

Let teams share their ideas. Then tell the story of Elijah, and of the depression he experienced after the great victory at Mount Carmel. Have the teams work together again to draw from 1 Kings 19 principles that suggest how God deals with depression, and how we might help people who are depressed.

The teams should note that:

God was not angry. Instead the Lord provided food to sustain *Elijah while he ran (vv. 6-9). Then God* spoke *to Elijah in a* "gentle whisper" *(v. 12). God* gave *Elijah* a simple task *to do, and also* reassured *Elijah that there were also others who remained faithful to the Lord (vv. 15-16, 18). Finally God* gave *Elijah* a companion, *Elisha, who would be with him and would one day take on his prophetic ministry.*

From these facts your group members should be able to develop ideas on how to help people who, like Elijah, experience depression.

Elijah's place in Scripture. C.E. DeVries, in the *Zondervan Pictorial Encyclopedia* (Zondervan), summarizes the many references to Elijah in later Scriptures.

> Malachi 4:5 foretold that Elijah would appear again before the Day of the Lord; this prediction has both New Testament and future fulfillment (cf. Rev. 11:6). The annunciatory angel declared to Zechariah that his son, John the Baptist, would go "before the Lord, in the spirit and power of Elijah" (Luke 1:17). Though John denied that he was Elijah (John 1:21), Jesus spoke of John as "Elijah who was to come" (Matt. 11:14; 17:10-13).
>
> Elijah appeared as a participant in the scene of the Transfiguration, when he and Moses discussed with the Lord the "departure" which Jesus was to accomplish at Jerusalem (Matt. 17:3; Mark 9:4; Luke 9:30-31).
>
> Paul, arguing for the principle of a remnant of Israel, referred to the 7,000 faithful worshipers in the time of Elijah (Rom. 11:2-4). The two witnesses of Revelation 11 are not mentioned by name, but the powers ascribed to them are those of Moses and Elijah (v. 6).

As we read the Old Testament stories about Elijah, it is helpful to realize that we are reading of a man whom the rest of Scripture marks out as particularly significant.

Authenticating miracles. A number of miraculous signs served to authenticate Elijah as God's spokesman. The seven signs recorded in these Old Testament passages are:

(1)	Elijah's word stops the rains.	1 Kings 17:1
(2)	Elijah's promise multiplies a widow's food.	1 Kings 17:14
(3)	Elijah's prayer restores the widow's son to life.	1 Kings 17:21
(4)	Elijah's prayer calls down fire on Mount Carmel.	1 Kings 18:38
(5)	Elijah's word restores rain to the land.	1 Kings 18:41
(6)	Elijah calls down fire on soldiers.	2 Kings 1:12
(7)	Elijah divides waters of the Jordan.	2 Kings 2:8

1 Kings 20:1-42. Elijah was not the only prophet who ministered in the days of Ahab. This chapter tells of an unnamed prophet who promised a terrified Ahab that God would deliver Israel from an overwhelming Aramean (Syrian) army under Ben-Hadad. God would act for Ahab, who refused to acknowledge Him, so that "you will know that I am the Lord" (v. 13). Ahab did follow the prophet's instructions, and Ben-Hadad was crushed.

The next year the Syrian king returned, convinced that while the Lord might be in control in the hills and mountains, He was not in control of the plains. So the Arameans would fight on the plains. The prophet told Ahab that the Lord would again provide a victory and demonstrate His power to Israel's enemy. Again, a great victory was won.

But with victory in his hand, Ahab reverted to type. Ahab released the captured Ben-Hadad, whom God had intended would die. The same prophet who had foretold the victories then told Ahab, "It is your life for his life, your people for his people" (v. 42). Rather than show any sign of repentance, Ahab was sullen and angry, and returned to his palace in Samaria.

1 Kings 21:1-29. Naboth owned a vineyard near the king's palace. Ahab wanted it for his own, and offered a fair exchange of land for the property. But Naboth would not sell.

The reason for Naboth's action should be understood. When the Promised Land was settled in the days of Joshua, each tribe and family was given land. This land was to be theirs perpetually. The land was not to be permanently transferred to any other owner (cf. Lev. 25).

Naboth's refusal to sell was a courageous act of obedience to God. Knowing the evil ways of the king and queen, Naboth must have determined to resist only after facing reasonable fears!

Ahab and Jezebel acted in character. Jezebel was given *carte blanche* by Ahab, and arranged to have Naboth falsely accused of cursing God and the king. When Naboth was executed, Ahab simply took possession of the field.

Again Elijah was sent to confront the king, and met him when Ahab went to inspect the vineyard that now was his. There Elijah pronounced a terrible doom on Ahab and Jezebel. Frightened now, the guilty Ahab at last humbled himself and "went around meekly." As a result, the disaster foretold was delayed—for three years.

1 Kings 22:1-53. The last chapter of this Old Testament book tells of the death of Ahab. In partnership with Jehoshaphat, king of Judah, Ahab attacked the Arameans. His own prophets were supernaturally informed that Ahab would win. But the source of their information was a "lying spirit" God permitted to deceive them. Micaiah, a prophet of Jehovah, announced the coalition's defeat and foretold the death of Ahab.

In the battle Ahab was killed, and just as Elijah had foretold, his blood was licked from his chariot by wild dogs.

The End of the Dynasty: 2 Kings 1:1–10:17

If we look ahead, what do we see as the outcome of the spiritual battle that took place between Elijah and those devotees of Baal, Ahab, and Jezebel?

Ahab's death did not put an end to Jezebel's efforts on behalf of Baal. The ruling family was still strong. But its days were limited.

After Elijah had been transported to heaven (2:11-13), his successor, Elisha, took up the battle. Leading the "sons of the prophets," whom many identify as men studying for spiritual leadership, and others believe were committed followers of a prophet, Elisha, throughout his life, played a significant role in the political, military, and spiritual life of the land. God continued to aid His people in their ceaseless warfare with Syria, and finally, in accordance with Elijah's earlier prophecy, the entire family of Ahab was exterminated by Jehu, who also totally wiped out the worship of Baal.

TEACHING GUIDE

Prepare

Read 1 Kings 17 through 22 rapidly, to get a sense of the interplay between the ruling family of Ahab and God's prophets.

Explore

1. Begin with a minilecture on the kings of Israel, focusing on the secular achievements of Omri and Ahab, and the Baal worship introduced from Phoenicia.
2. Or, have different members of your group read aloud 1 Kings 17–22. As they read, ask others to jot down their main impressions.

Expand
1. Review the marks of a true prophet (Deut. 13 and 18). Then have your group members examine Elijah's life to see how these marks were evident in his ministry. Discuss: "How do we evaluate spiritual leaders or Christian counselors today?"
2. Focus on lessons to be learned from a study of Elijah's life. You might want to look at the way he faced difficulties, the way he trusted God for daily needs, or the way God dealt with him in times of depression. Check the "link-to-life" suggestions in this unit for ideas.

Apply
Assign each of your students one group or individual seen in these Old Testament chapters to identify with. If he or she *were* that person or group, living in the time of Elijah, and a witness to the events reported in 1 Kings, what might he or she have learned that could be applied to modern lives?

Possible persons or groups for this identification activity:

Elijah	Ahab
The widow	Prophets of Baal
People of Israel	People of Judah
Ben-Hadad	Micaiah

STUDY GUIDE 38

2 Kings 1:1–8:15

DAYS OF ELISHA

Overview

Elisha was the apprentice and successor of Elijah. He too ministered in Israel, the Northern Kingdom. During Elisha's life, Ben-Hadad and then Hazael ruled Syria, building a powerful Aramean empire.

The Bible, however, focuses on Elisha and only secondarily on the political and military situation. Stories of Elisha and his miracles have been the source of thousands of sermons as well as stories for boys and girls.

▶ ***A Double Portion.*** When Elijah was taken into heaven alive, Elisha begged to "inherit a double portion of [Elijah's] spirit" (2 Kings 2:9). The request reflects Old Testament inheritance law: the oldest son and successor of his father was given a double portion. Elisha was asking to succeed Elijah as leading prophet in the land.

Interestingly, the Bible also reports twice as many miracles of Elisha as Elijah (14 compared to 7). They are: (1) separating the Jordan waters, 2:14; (2) healing spring waters, 2:21; (3) cursing jeering young men, 2:24; (4) filling ditches with water and winning a battle, 3:15-26; (5) multiplying a widow's oil, 4:1-7; (6) promising a pregnancy, 4:14-17; (7) raising a Shunammite's son from the dead, 4:32-37; (8) making poison harmless, 4:38-41; (9) multiplying loaves, 4:42-44; (10) healing Naaman the leper, 5:1-19; cursing Gehazi with leprosy, 5:19-27; (11) making an axhead float, 6:1-6; (12) blinding and trapping an Aramean army, 6:8-23; (13) showing his servant an angel army, 6:15-17; (14) and predicting an excess of food for besieged Samaria, 6:24–7:20.

Commentary

Elisha was farming when Elijah came to him. He was working a rich man's fields, plowing with the twelfth of 12 pair of oxen. Elijah threw his coat around Elisha, claiming him for his service, and walked on. Elisha was ready to follow, but begged permission to say good-bye to his parents.

Later Elisha killed the oxen he had been working with, and cooked them by burning his farm equipment. Literally "burning his bridges behind him," Elisha became Elijah's attendant and later, his successor.

During the years of Elisha, Israel was constantly threatened by a powerful Syria, led first by Ben-Hadad and later by Hazael. Ahab was dead, but members of his family still ruled, and like their father followed wicked ways. Elisha lived to command the anointing of Jehu as king of Israel. Jehu destroyed not only Ahab's family but also wiped out Baal worship in Israel.

The stories of Elisha give us insight into this critical period of Old Testament history, and help us to see God as One who remains involved in the lives of ordinary people even when the nation has strayed far from His ways.

Elijah's Appointment: 2 Kings 2

When Elijah was about to be taken by God, other prophets were aware of the coming event. Elisha refused to let Elijah go on his last journey alone.

On that journey Elijah asked his follower what he might do for him. Elisha quickly responded. "Let me inherit a double portion of your spirit" (v. 9). His later miracles showed he had been granted his wish.

What a contrast between Elisha, who served Elijah so faithfully, and Elisha's own companion, Gehazi. Later that servant of Elisha's would run after a man Elisha had helped, and beg for personal riches (2 Kings 5). Elisha's ambition was spiritual. He sought only strength and enablement to serve God.

♥ ***Link to Life: Children***
We can't expect boys and girls to have the spiritual maturity of an Elisha. But we can encourage them to pray as he prayed. One way is to suggest "matching prayers." Make up a list of things children might pray for that would reflect Elisha's spiritual concerns. For instance: pray to be a good friend, to be a good student, to be helpful, etc. In class have your boys and girls suggest things to add to your list.

Then give each a booklet made by folding a sheet of construction paper. Mark eight equal, paired segments on the inside back cover of the booklet. On the inside front cover write or have the children write your list of "Elisha" prayers.

Whenever your boys and girls pray for something they want, encourage them to match that prayer with a request for something on the Elisha list. Each can write down what he or she asked for first, and then, across from it, write the matching prayer from the list. Have stars ready to stick on each matching prayer when the children return their prayer record booklets.

The events reported in 2 Kings 2 clearly served to authenticate Elisha as Israel's premier prophet, and as God's spokesman.

Returning after Elijah had been taken up, Elisha struck the waters of the Jordan as his mentor had, and the waters divided. A watching company of the prophets understood the meaning of this act. "The spirit of Elijah is resting on Elisha" (v. 15).

Elisha then dealt with a spring whose poisonous waters killed any who drank from it and made the land unproductive. This healing of the waters authenticated him in the eyes of the people of the land (vv. 21-22).

Then, when some young men shouted out their ridicule, mockingly asking Elisha to "go on up" to heaven as he had reported Elijah went, Elisha called a curse down on them in the name of the Lord. Two bears came out of the woods and mauled 42! Elisha's power was established even in the eyes of his enemies.

Thus all who lived in Israel, prophets and common people and even enemies of the Lord, were forced to acknowledge that Elisha was the spokesman of God.

NOTE: Older versions suggest the "youths" who jeered Elisha were children. The Hebrew word indicates young men who were adults and fully responsible for their actions. Their jeering ridicule was not focused on Elisha's baldness, but on the notion that Israel's God was able to catch up the Prophet Elijah into heaven as Elisha had reported. What happened to this group was a warning to all the people of Israel to acknowledge and take to heart the fact that God is Lord in heaven and Lord on earth as well. The God of Elisha, the God of Israel, was not to be trifled with. Instead God was to be respected and obeyed.

If only the people of Israel had taken this graphic warning to heart, they might have been spared the tragedies and destruction which all too soon followed.

The Nature of Elisha's Miracles: 2 Kings 4

The series of miracles reported in this chapter are significant in several respects. First, they show the Old Testament prophet engaged not just in affairs of state but also in the lives of ordinary people. God is not just concerned with kings. God is concerned about the daily needs of everyone.

Second, these miracles seem to prefigure some of the miracles of Jesus. Elisha raised the Shunammite's son from the dead, and multiplied loaves to feed a hundred. These clearly foreshadow Christ's raising of the dead and feeding of thousands.

Third, each of these miracles was intended to enrich and save lives, just as every one of Jesus' miracles was performed to demonstrate the love of God rather than His justice or wrath.

Note each of the miracles, and some of its implications.

The widow's oil. A poverty-stricken widow appealed to Elisha for help. A creditor was about to make her two sons slaves to satisfy a debt. Elisha had the widow pour olive oil from her jar into all the empty jars her sons could borrow. The creditor was paid off, and the family lived on the excess proceeds from sale of the oil. The poor have always been, and will remain, a special concern of the Lord.

The Shunammite's son. A well-to-do woman, who lived in Shunem, welcomed Elisha whenever he passed by. She even had a room built for his exclusive use. Elisha wanted to show his appreciation. But the woman had no apparent needs. Then the prophet discovered one real need: the woman had no children, and her husband was old. Elisha promised her that she would have a child—and she did. Later, when the child grew sick and died, Elisha restored the boy to life.

How wonderful that God knows the deepest, hidden needs of our hearts, and is willing and able to satisfy those needs.

Poison stew. It was a time of famine, and a company of prophets gathered wild vegetables to make into a stew. One unknowingly gathered poison gourds. As the group began to eat the stew, the men cried out, "There is death in the pot!" Elisha mixed some flour with the stew, and told everyone to eat. The poison's power had been drawn.

Feeding a hundred. A few small loaves of bread were brought to Elisha. He told his servant to feed the company that was with him. Although there was not enough, Elisha announced God's promise: "They will eat and have some left over" (v. 43).

God *is* concerned and involved in our lives. As we look to Him, He meets our material needs. But He also looks deep within us, and meets the hidden needs of our hearts as well.

♥ ***Link to Life: Children***

We can count on God to help us in everyday life. And we can count on Him to answer prayer for us, as He did for Elisha.

How can we help boys and girls sense the Lord's constant provision and care, and give them a practical basis for expecting answer to prayer? We can apply a principle Paul expresses in Romans as he reminds us that God has given us Jesus. "How," Paul asks, "will He not also, along with Him, give us all things?"(8:32) Reminders of what God has done for us help us trust when we come to Him in prayer.

Work with the boys and girls to make a giant collage portraying "How God Shows His Care." Cut out pictures of the things God provides—food, clothing, housing, friends, toys, teachers, books, etc. Talk about how good God is to meet all our everyday needs. Assure the boys and girls they can count on God to answer prayer, because He shows us daily in the things He provides how much He loves us.

Naaman the Leper: 2 Kings 5

Few stories in the Old Testament show the complex interaction of people and personalities as this short report. The commander of the Aramean army, Naaman, suffered from leprosy. In his household there was a young girl, captured in a raid on Israel. The young girl told her mistress there was a prophet in Israel who could cure leprosy.

Like a modern cancer sufferer willing to try anything that offers hope of a cure, Naaman sought permission to go to Israel and seek a cure. A letter was sent by the king to Israel's king, simply saying that he was sending Naaman to Israel to be cured from leprosy.

The king of Israel was shaken. Only God could cure leprosy. The Syrian must be looking for an excuse to invade Israel!

Then a messenger came from Elisha, telling the king to send Naaman to him.

When Naaman came, Elisha didn't even bother to come to the door. He sent a message telling Naaman to wash seven times in the Jordan River.

Insulted, an angry Naaman headed toward home. "I thought that he would surely come out to me and stand and call on the name of the Lord his God, wave his hand over the spot, and cure me of my leprosy" (v. 11). The prophet hadn't acted as Naaman expected—so Naaman would go home.

On the way, his servants urged him to do what the prophet said. Still disgruntled, Naaman did obey—and when he came up the seventh time, "His flesh was restored and became clean like that of a young boy" (v. 14).

Naaman immediately returned to Elisha, and acknowledged God. "Now I know that there is no God in all the world except in Israel" (v. 15). Naaman urged the prophet to accept a gift, but he would not. But Naaman asked a gift for himself: as much of Israel's earth as two mules could carry. From now on Naaman would worship only Israel's God.

It was then that greed overcame Gehazi, Elisha's servant. He rushed after Naaman and begged about 75 pounds of silver and two sets of clothing in Elisha's name. He then hid the gifts, and returned to Elisha. Of course Elisha knew! Elisha announced, "Naaman's leprosy will cling to you and to your descendants forever" (v. 27).

What an interplay of personalities. And what a range of reactions to God.

The little slave girl kept her faith in a

foreign land, and spoke with confidence of the power of God's prophet.

Naaman, desperate enough to go to an enemy land, became angry because the prophet did not act as he expected. And then, when cured, totally committed to worship the Lord whom he realized had healed him.

Israel's king knew Elisha well, but he never thought of Elisha as the solution to the political problem posed by the Aramean king's letter.

Elisha wanted nothing but to be God's agent in whatever way the Lord chose to use him.

Gehazi, though familiar with the power of God that rested on his master, still supposed that he could safely lie in the prophet's name.

How like men and women of today. Some of us humble, pointing others to the Lord. Some of us doubtful, but still willing to taste and see His power. Some of us, familiar with evidence of God's presence, but never thinking of Him as the solution to our problems. Some of us, unconcerned about the material, finding fulfillment in spiritual ministries. Some of us, close to spiritual power, but never recognizing its extent or letting God cleanse us of greed.

♥ ***Link to Life: Youth / Adult***

Ask your class members to read 2 Kings 5 individually, and jot down observations about each person they meet there.

Then divide into teams, each of which is to focus on one of the following persons: the little Israelite girl, Naaman, the king of Israel, Elisha, or Gehazi.

From the story each team should try to define: What was this person's concept of God? How is this concept of God expressed in his or her actions? As a summary, each team member should write a paragraph or two about the person his or her team studied, trying to sum up that person's character.

Teams should then report their findings to the whole group.

Go around the circle and share: "What have I learned from one of these characters that I can apply to my own spiritual life?"

At War: 2 Kings 6–7

These two chapters of 2 Kings reveal Elisha's role in the ongoing conflict between Israel and the Aramean empire of Ben-Hadad.

First, Elisha regularly revealed the secret plans of the king of Aram (Syria) to the king of Israel. "Time and again Elisha warned the king" (6:10). When the king of Aram realized that his plans weren't being betrayed by one of his officers but by Elisha, he sent a strong force to capture the prophet. This force surrounded the town where Elisha was. When Elisha's servant saw the enemy army, he was terrified.

Then in one of the most wonderful events recorded in Scripture, Elisha prayed that his servant's eyes might be opened. Suddenly the servant "looked and saw the hills full of horses and chariots of fire all around Elisha" (v. 17). The prophet was guarded by an angelic army!

Angels. The Hebrew and the Greek words translated "angel" mean literally, "messenger." These messengers are directly created beings who do not reproduce or die (cf. Luke 20:34-37). While they are different from human beings, the Bible suggests that they are like us in many ways. Angels are known to be superior to humans, particularly in power and knowledge (cf. 2 Sam. 14:17, 20; Ps. 2:7; 2 Peter 2:11).

There are evil as well as good angels, though the evil angels are more commonly called demons in the Gospels. The Bible suggests that angels, like human beings, had freedom of choice. Some of them chose to follow Satan when he rebelled against God (cf. Matt. 25:41).

Hebrews suggests that the angels who remained faithful to God are His agents for good in human affairs. The Book of Hebrews calls them "ministering spirits" (1:14) who are commissioned to aid God's saints. The protective screen of angels that surrounded Elisha provide one example of the ministry of angels.

The Bible records a number of appearances by angels to human beings. At times they appeared in human form (cf. Gen. 18:2; Josh. 5:13; etc.). Daniel saw an angel as a brightly shining being, as did the women who went to Jesus' empty tomb (cf. Dan. 10:5-6; Luke 24:4).

Despite the many references to angels in the Bible, it is clear that Scripture does not focus on these beings. They are God's servants, but are not the central objects of His concern. Strikingly, God is concerned primarily with human beings. God the Son became a human being, not an angel. And His death was to redeem humankind. Though we are now a little less than the angels, in Christ we human beings will be catapulted far above them. As Scripture says, "Surely it is not angels [God] helps, but Abraham's descendants" (Heb. 2:16). In the end we will be lifted above the angels, to know the fullness of God's grace.

♥ ***Link to Life: Youth / Adult***
Lead your group in a concordance study of angels. A concordance is an important Bible study tool to which you can introduce any students who may not be familiar with it. A concordance lists, in alphabetical order, all significant Bible terms, showing where they appear in the Bible.

Use the above in a minilecture of background on angels. Then distribute concordances, or xerox copies of a concordance page on angels. Let your group members explore for some 15 minutes, and then come together to report what they learned about angels from a description of their appearances in the text.

NOTE: Be ready to deal with questions that may be raised about the "angel of the Lord." Many believe that this title indicates the Being who appeared was God Himself (cf. Gen. 31:11-13; 32:24-30; Ex. 3:6). Some believe that these were appearances of Jesus before His incarnation.

Blindness. The angels surrounding Elisha did not intervene—at least directly. The prophet prayed that the enemy would be stricken with a "blindness" that kept them from realizing where they were. Elisha then led them right into Israel's capital city, Samaria, where their eyes were opened and they realized they were captives.

At Elisha's instruction, the embarrassed captives were fed and then returned to their master. For a time the Arameans stopped raiding Israel's territory.

Famine. Later Ben-Hadad of Syria launched a full-scale attack on Israel. The capital city was under siege for such a long time that all food supplies were exhausted. Some who were starving had even eaten their own children (6:27-29).

In this situation the king of Israel began to blame Elisha, God's prophet! The king could not see that his own sins, and the sins of his family in introducing the worship of Baal into Israel, had brought on this disaster.

When the king came to confront Elisha, the prophet announced that the very next day food would be cheap in Samaria. One of the king's officers scoffed. Even if God sent food directly from heaven, what the prophet foretold could not happen!

But it did happen!

That night the Lord caused the Arameans "to hear the sound of chariots and horses and a great army." Supposing that the Egyptians and Hittites had come to rescue Samaria, the Arameans abandoned their camp and all its supplies and ran for their lives!

Meanwhile four lepers, crouching outside the city gate, decided they might as well surrender to the Arameans. If they stayed, they would die. If they surrendered, they might be spared. But when they arrived they found the enemy lines deserted. They wandered through the camp, eating and drinking, and picking up gold and silver and clothing to hide. Then they paused. It just was not right to enjoy so much food and wealth while their countrymen were starving. "This is a day of good news," they said, "and we are keeping it to ourselves" (2 Kings 7:9). When the report was carried to the king he feared the Arameans had laid a trap. But when some soldiers followed the trail of the enemy they learned that the Syrians truly had run. The starving people flooded out of the city and plundered the camp of the Arameans. Just as Elisha had foretold, food was suddenly plentiful and cheap.

And the officer who had laughed at the prophet's promise saw—but did not eat of that plenty. He was trampled to death by the people in their desperate rush to the food.

Hazael identified. When King Ben-Hadad became sick, he sent Hazael to ask Elisha if he would recover. Elisha wept when he looked piercingly at Hazael. Hazael was to tell Ben-Hadad that his illness was not fatal. But Elisha also told Hazael that he would one day be king of Aram (Syria). Elisha wept because he foresaw the devastation that Hazael and his armies would wreak in Israel.

Hazael delivered the good news to Ben-Hadad. But the next day Hazael suffocated the king, and took his throne.

Elisha ministered during trying days for Israel. Yet the prophet faithfully represented the Lord, offering help even to apostate Israel in the wars with the Arameans. At the same time, Elisha maintained a close and caring ministry to the common people of the land.

How amazing that, with countless incidents demonstrating God's love and His power, Elisha's ministry was largely rejected. Naaman, the Syrian general, needed only one touch of the Lord's power to acknowledge and worship God. But multiplied evidences failed to touch the heart of Israel's own king, or of most of the leading people.

An Israel that would not listen to God was surely doomed to destruction.

TEACHING GUIDE

Prepare

Read quickly, as if a novel, 2 Kings 1:1–8:15, and jot down your dominant impressions.

Explore

1. Ask your group members to list, without looking up, as many of Elisha's miracles as they can. What do the results suggest about their familiarity with this key Old Testament prophet?
2. Or, briefly sketch the political and international situation in Elisha's time as background for his miracles and ministry.
3. Or, tell your group members each has been suddenly told he or she must speak to a group about Elisha. Randomly assign each person one of the following passages. In 10 minutes each is to determine the point he or she will make in that talk, and the lesson he or she will try to drive home. The passages: 2 Kings 2:19-22, 23-25; 4:1-7; 5; 6:8-23, 6:24–7:20.

Expand

1. Develop the best known of the Elisha stories, that of the healing of Naaman. Use the "link-to-life" study process on page 269 to help your group members focus on application to their own lives.
2. Or, lead your group in a concordance study of the role of angels. See the process outlined in the "link-to-life," page 270.

Apply

Encourage each member of your group to tell one other person this week what he or she learned from the study of Elisha the prophet.

STUDY GUIDE 39

2 Kings 8:16–17:41

ISRAEL'S FALL

Overview

When Jehu became king in Israel in 841 B.C., the Northern Kingdom had some 119 years left. Jehu wiped out the family of Ahab and purged the land of Baal worship. But Jehu continued to support the counterfeit religion established at the time of the division of the unified kingdom some 90 years before.

Plagued by a series of weak and evil kings, Israel knew a brief glory only in the time of Jeroboam II, who began his rule in 793 B.C.

During the long decades, God did not desert His people Israel. He sent them suffering and defeat in an effort to turn them back to Him. And God sent Israel other prophets. In the days of Jeroboam II, three of the most powerful of the prophets—Jonah and Amos and Hosea—labored to turn Israel to the Lord.

Their efforts were in vain. The people of Israel hurtled on in their rush toward judgment. When destruction of the kingdom finally did come, and the Israelites were torn from the land by the Assyrians, the Scriptures make this sad comment:

> They forsook all the commands of the Lord their God and made for themselves two idols cast in the shape of calves, and an Asherah pole. They bowed down to all the starry hosts, and they worshiped Baal. They sacrificed their sons and daughters in the fire. They practiced divination and sorcery and sold themselves to do evil in the eyes of the Lord, provoking Him to anger.
>
> 2 Kings 17:16-17

The people of the North would not turn from evil, so evil came.

Commentary

The two major kings of Israel during the last half of its brief existence as a separate nation were Jehu and Jeroboam II.

Their stories provide the context for looking briefly at three prophets, whose ministries help us see the reason for the nation's fall.

Jehu: 2 Kings 9–10

Jehu was an army commander when a messenger came from Elisha to tell him that the Lord intended him to be king of Israel. The prophet who anointed Jehu gave him this commission: "You are to destroy the house of Ahab your master, and I will avenge the blood of My servants the prophets and the blood of all the Lord's servants shed by Jezebel. The whole house of Ahab will perish. I will cut off from Ahab every last male in Israel—slave or free. . . . As for Jezebel, dogs will devour her on the plot of ground at Jezreel, and no one will bury her" (9:7-10).

When Jehu told his fellow officers what the prophet had said, his fellow officers immediately proclaimed him king.

Jehu acted decisively to establish his claim. When King Joram came out to meet Jehu, the soldier killed him with a single arrow. His body was thrown in the field of Naboth, whom Ahab and Jezebel had murdered.

Moving quickly, Jehu rushed to deal with Jezebel, the queen mother. She taunted him from a high window, calling him Zimri (another regicide, who had ruled only seven days before dying in flames). But Jehu was no Zimri. He ordered the wicked Jezebel thrown from the window, and Jehu went in to dinner. When he finally ordered her body disposed of, he found that she had been eaten by wild dogs, as the Lord had foretold.

The only way that Jehu could establish his own rule was to destroy the whole family of Ahab. But Jehu was not about to open himself to later criticism. He sent a message to the families that were raising the king's sons. They could choose a leader and fight for the old royal family. Or they could kill their wards and demonstrate loyalty to Jehu.

Frightened, the leading men of the kingdom murdered the royal sons. Now the responsibility for wiping out his predecessor's line was shared.

At first Jehu's revolt was probably seen simply as a coup by an ambitious military man. So when Jehu announced his commitment to Baal, and called all Baal worshipers and priests to come to Baal's temple for a great celebration, all appeared. Jehu then had every one of them killed, and had the temple of Baal burned to the ground.

God rewarded Jehu for carrying out His intended judgment, and promised that this man's dynasty would last four generations. But Jehu did not turn to God. And he continued worship of the golden calves established 90 years earlier at Bethel and Dan.

Jehu did not follow up his early decisive acts with similar leadership. His destruction of Baal worship, which had been imported from Phoenicia, must have strained relations with that nearby state. Both the Assyrians and the Arameans remained powerful during his era, and Jehu's 28-year reign was a time of political decline for Israel.

Jeroboam II was fourth in Jehu's line. The Old Testament says very little about him, passing quickly over his time in 2 Kings 14:23-29, and giving him brief mention in 1 Chronicles 5:17. Yet we know from archeology that Jeroboam II was a vital, aggressive ruler.

The *Word Bible Handbook* (Larry Richards, Word) describes his age in these words:

> The later reign of Jeroboam II was a time of exploding prosperity for Israel. The earlier destruction of the military power of Syria had enabled Jeroboam to expand his kingdom, even taking over the old capital of Aram, Damascus. Now Israel controlled the important trade routes which crisscrossed Palestine, linking the ancient world. Their multiplied revenues made Israel rich. But the wealth was distributed unequally. The old aristocracy of nobles and the new merchant class kept the wealth for themselves. They demanded luxury goods and residences, and the pattern of life in Israel began to change. More and more people left the country and drifted toward the cities and towns. For the first time towns in the Northern Kingdom became overpopulated.
>
> The concentration of wealth stimulated economic corruption. Heavier and heavier taxes were laid on workers. The wealthy became land-hungry, forcing out the small farmers and building great estates. Many of the poor were forced to sell themselves and their families as bondservants, becoming no better than serfs on lands that had once been their own. Even the small merchants were corrupted, and it became common for them to use unjust weights to measure out purchases. The process of corruption was accelerated by the failure of the justice system. Rather than acting to protect the poor, judges took bribes from the rich and so joined the oppressors! The old middle class began to disappear, and the society was increasingly divided into the oppressed poor and the very rich.
>
> In this situation the rich showed no sense of responsibility to the poor. Instead of showing compassion and concern, they seemed bent on depriving the poor of all rights and property. The heartlessness of the rich is well expressed in one angry charge hurled by Amos—these people are willing "to sell . . . the needy for a pair of sandals" (2:6). Luxury footwear meant more to the wealthy of Jeroboam II's day than did the suffering of fellow human beings.

Religiously, economically, and socially, Israel had become an unjust society. Again the summary in 2 Kings 17 written after Israel's deportation is succinct. "The Lord warned Israel and Judah through all His prophets and seers: 'Turn from your evil ways. Observe My commands and decrees, in accordance with the entire Law that I commanded your fathers to obey and that I delivered to you through My servants the prophets.' But they would not listen" (vv. 13-14).

Three Prophets

Three of the prophets that are dealt with in detail in future units in this book spoke out during the time of Jeroboam II. Each of their messages constituted both a warning and a promise to the people of Israel. And each prophecy contains warnings and promises for us, who in many respects live in a time of prosperity much like that of Jeroboam's.

Jonah. Jonah is not only known from his book. He is also mentioned in this section of 2 Kings that traces the decline and fall of Israel in the North.

Jonah was somewhat unusual. He was a popular prophet. The reason is seen in the text. "He [Jeroboam II] was the one who restored the boundaries of Israel from Lebo Hamath to the Sea of Arabah, in accordance with the word of the Lord, the God of Israel, *spoken through His servant Jonah son of Amittai, the prophet from Gath Hepher*" (2 Kings 14:25, italics added).

Jonah was popular because he foretold good things for Israel. And Jonah was also a patriot.

It was particularly difficult then when Jonah was sent to Nineveh to warn that city of coming judgment. Jonah was unwilling to go. Jonah 4:2 explains that Jonah was afraid that the people of Nineveh might heed him and repent, and that the Lord would withhold judgment. Jonah didn't want that! Nineveh was capital of mighty Assyria, which had raided Israel before and which would later be the agent of Israel's destruction. So rather than going overland to Nineveh, Jonah found a ship going in the opposite direction!

We all know the story of Jonah's repentance in the belly of the great fish. And we remember that he finally did go to Nineveh and deliver his message. We also remember the results: the people of Nineveh repented, and God withheld His judgment. The last we see of Jonah is the angry and discouraged prophet slumped on a hill overlooking the city, deaf to God's explanation of His concern for the children and even the dumb animals who would have perished with the responsible adults.

But if we are to understand the impact of Jonah's ministry in Israel, we need to see his adventure as God's object lesson. Soon Amos and Hosea would appear. They would detail the sins of Israel, and call the people to return to the Lord. *The mission of Jonah to Nineveh provided proof that if only a people would repent, they could be saved.* But despite the example of Nineveh, the people of Israel simply would not respond to the prophets of the Lord.

It was their failure to repent that made judgment inevitable!

Amos. Amos was one of the poor that the wealthy in Israel despised. Amos was a citizen of neighboring Judah, where he worked caring for sheep and a stand of sycamore trees. We know that Amos was poor, for sycamores were to the poor what figs were to the rich.

Though neither a prophet nor the son of a prophet, Amos responded to God's call and trudged in his rags across the border into Israel.

There he must have visited the cities that had grown up around the worship centers at Bethel and Dan. He must have walked past the great houses, seen the luxury goods in stores outside of which the poor crouched. Walking through the market he must have noticed merchants mix chaff with the grain they sold, or slyly exchange honest weights for lighter ones when they measured out the purchases of the poor.

Angered by the heartlessness and the materialism, Amos boldly identified the sins for which God was about to judge the Northern society. In his rebuke we can hear God's evaluation of man's greed, and a powerful expression of the divine values that had been expressed for centuries in the Law.

> For three sins of Israel, even for four, I will not turn back My wrath. They sell the righteous for silver, and the needy for a pair of sandals. They trample on the heads of the poor as upon the dust of the ground and deny justice to the oppressed. Father and son use the same girl and so profane My holy name. They lie down beside every altar on garments taken in pledge. In the house of their god they drink wine taken as fines.
>
> Amos 2:6-8

> You hate the one who reproves in court and despise him who tells the truth. You trample on the poor and force him to give you grain. . . . You oppress the righteous and take bribes and you deprive the poor of justice in the courts. Therefore the prudent man keeps quiet in such times, for the times are evil.
>
> Amos 5:11-13

Based on this indictment, Amos announced the sure approach of divine judgment.

Yet, the example of God's gracious dealing with Nineveh, not even His own people, should have offered hope! And Amos made this hope plain in a clear, well defined promise.

> Seek good, not evil, that you may live. Then the Lord God Almighty will be with you, just as you say He is. Hate evil, love good; maintain justice in the courts. Perhaps the Lord God Almighty will have mercy on the remnant of Joseph.
>
> Amos 5:14-15

Hosea. We know little about the prophet. What we do know is heartrending. Hosea was called to suffer the pain of commitment to a faithless wife—a prostitute. His experience graphically reveals the meaning of Israel's religious apostasy. Just as Hosea's wife would not remain faithful to her marriage covenant, so God's people had abandoned Him.

The imagery of sexual unfaithfulness is appropriate in this case. The religions which the Israelites followed were nature faiths. They sought to influence fertility in lands and animals as well as humans by sexually stimulating the gods, whose passions were thought to overflow as fertility on earth. So the pagans of Palestine engaged in all sorts of sensual excess in an effort to arouse their gods.

So idolatry and sexual promiscuity were closely linked in Hosea's day. And God, through the anguished prophet, communicated something of His own anguish at His rejection by an Israel that ran after pagan, sensual faiths.

Hosea announced proof upon proof of Israel's abandonment of God and His Law.

> There is no faithfulness, no love, no acknowledgment of God in the land. There is only cursing, lying, and murder, stealing and adultery; they break all bounds, and bloodshed follows bloodshed.
>
> Hosea 4:1-2

Despite all this, God continued to pour out His love on Israel. In a beautiful passage Hosea describes God's loving care.

> When Israel was a child, I loved him, and out of Egypt I called My son. But the more I called Israel, the further they went from Me. They sacrificed to the Baals and they burned incense to images. It was I who taught Ephraim to walk, taking them by the arms; but they did not realize it was I who healed them. I led them with the cords of human kindness, with ties of love; I lifted the yoke from their neck and bent down to feed them.
>
> Hosea 11:1-4

Even so, God was anguished at the thought of giving Israel up and handing His people over to her enemies (11:8-11). Though Israel's sin demanded punishment, ultimately this people would return to Him and beg forgiveness.

Then, "I will heal their waywardness and love them freely, for My anger has turned away from them" (14:4).

But Israel was as unmoved by the pleas and the pain of Hosea as the nation had been by the angry denunciations of Amos. And Israel remained blind to the promise implicit in God's gracious treatment of Nineveh.

The prophets spoke.

But Israel would not hear.

Concern for Justice

All the Old Testament prophets, those sent to Judah as well as Israel, had a deep concern for justice. It is one of the repeated themes of the Old Testament.

Too often evangelical Christians have made a distinction between what is seen as God's concern for souls and His concern for social issues. The distinction rests on several assumptions.

First is the belief that the basic issue each individual must resolve is one of relationship with God. Will a person come to faith, and receive the forgiveness that salvation provides? Until that issue is resolved, all else seems irrelevant. Eternity is what counts.

A second belief is that attention given to social conditions steals attention from the eternal. Some have become so focused on society that concern for man's relationship with God has been lost.

A third belief is that the only real solution for social injustice is transformation of individuals through personal relationship with Jesus Christ. If injustice and oppression are an expression in society of the sin that mars humanity, then the way to make a difference is to challenge men to deal with their sin in a personal, life-transforming way. Thus, for many Christians, aggressive evangelism *is* an expression of concern for justice, and if successful, this will change society.

While there is a measure of validity in each of these arguments, they do not justify a withdrawal from the social justice arena! There are other factors we must consider.

1. A believers' concern for justice is not associated with utopian political or social theory. The Christian does not seek to "do justice" because he expects to bring in the kingdom of God. Long after Israel had demonstrated that the people had lost all concern for others and had adopted materialistic values, Micah cried out to individuals:

> He has showed you, O man, what is good. And what does the Lord require of you? To act justly and to love mercy and walk humbly with your God.
>
> Micah 6:8

When, in England, William Wilberforce initiated his long campaign to outlaw slavery in the British empire, he did not act as a social reformer. He was moved by Christian compassion: he acted because he *cared* about those helpless chattels that the majority in his day viewed as scarcely human. In working for justice, in showing loving-kindness, in committing his health and fortune to the betterment of his oppressed fellowman, this man uniquely pleased and honored God.

It is not some utopian dream but a practical concern for people that drives us to seek justice.

2. It is tragically wrong to view the Christian's concern for justice as something to be valued or devalued on the basis of its contribution to evangelism. The church has often done this. We have said, "Send doctors—that we might break the power of the witch doctor and win the lost."

These statements implicitly assign to justice a value based on the *end* it is supposed to achieve. Thus "doing justice" is viewed as a means to an end, and when it does not seem to promote that end (evangelism), it is roughly thrust aside.

But is concern for the oppressed and the hungry a tool? How do we differ from the Pharisees if our commitment to do right by all men is conditional on whether we believe our actions will help us gain other ends? No, we "do justice" because it is right.

3. It's an amazing thing that concern for people's social and material needs is conceived as somehow intrinsically different from concern for their souls. But the Bible does not describe man as composed of an immaterial "soul" captured in a physical body. Instead it speaks of the breath of life breathed into the body God prepared so that "man became a living soul" (Gen. 2:7, KJV). Human beings experience life as a unity: we do not separate our selves from our bodies, or from our souls.

It follows that when we come in contact with others, we are to reach out to them in love and love them fully. We are to care about their *every* need. There may be little we can do to change basic conditions in our society. But we are not to hold back in loving because one sort of need is "social" and another "spiritual." If minority children in our neighborhood need tutoring, we do not ignore that need because such a thing in our church would not be "religious." If an inner-city store gouges the poor who cannot shop elsewhere, we don't keep silent because the injustice is only bodily and not related to the soul. If pornography is openly sold in a shop near a school, we don't just ignore it.

Simply put, the Christian has a commitment to justice, simply because doing justice is right.

4. Probably the most compelling reason that Christians today need to be committed to doing right by others is this: that's the kind of person God is. God Himself is just. He is committed to doing right by all. God, as the Old Testament clearly reveals, does care deeply when injustice and indifference to others are accepted elements in an individual's or society's lifestyle.

As the New Testament adds, "Religion that God our Father accepts as pure and faultless is this: to look after orphans and widows in their distress and to keep oneself from being polluted by the world" (James 1:27).

Our study of the Old Testament prophets brings us face-to-face with a dimension of faith that our generation has tended to overlook. The prophets' constant emphasis and

God's constant call to Israel teaches us that we need to have a concern for the whole person. A concern that God feels deeply, as He calls us today as then to "hate evil, love good, and maintain justice in the courts" (Amos 5:15).

TEACHING GUIDE

Prepare

Consider: How is a godly commitment to doing justice demonstrated in my life?

Explore

1. In a minilecture summarize briefly the history of Israel during its last 100 years. Include a review of how Jehu came to power, and describe the economic and political resurgence under Jeroboam II.
2. Or, ask three of your group members to prepare to take the roles of Jonah, Amos, and Hosea. Each should quote from his book to give a feel for the message. Then each can give a brief review of the issues which so concern him and the Lord.
3. Or, write on the board, "Christians should be involved in justice issues." Ask the group members whether they agree or disagree. After discussion, ask each person to list what he or she thinks "justice issues" are. Then compare the lists.

Expand

1. Select passages from Amos and Hosea. Duplicate them, or have your group members read them from their own Bibles. Work in threes from these passages to answer the following questions: What would it have been like to live in Israel in this period? What characterized Israel religiously? What characterized Israel socially?
2. Divide the group into teams to look through Amos and Hosea to locate the "justice" issues your group identified earlier. As they search, each team should add to the list, and note those things which the prophets emphasized. After reporting, discuss: "How do we today show a disregard for, or a concern for, justice?"
3. Discuss the pro and con arguments for involvement in social justice issues raised in the last section of this unit. Do not try to bring everyone to agreement. But when viewpoints have been expressed, remind your group that injustices that the people would not correct were a basic cause of the fall of that kingdom, and of the judgment of God.

Apply

What do your members know that is happening in your community today that involves injustice? What should Christians do about it?

STUDY GUIDE 40

2 Kings 19–24; 2 Chronicles 29–32

JUDAH, THE SURVIVING KINGDOM

Overview

Judah existed as a separate kingdom from 931–586 B.C. Like Israel, Judah experienced national ups and downs. Spiritually Judah was blessed with several godly kings. But Judah was also ruled at times by apostates. Queen Athaliah (841–835 B.C.) attempted to bring Baal worship into Judah as Jezebel, her mother, had brought it into Israel. While Baal worship was never established in Judah, and the land knew great revivals under Kings Asa, Jehoshaphat, and Joash, the people were never completely committed to the Lord.

Hezekiah, one of the most godly of Judah's kings, guided this nation during the critical period when Israel was invaded and destroyed. Hezekiah instituted drastic reforms to correct the idolatry of his father Ahaz. Under the influence of two great prophets, Isaiah and Micah, he thoroughly cleansed the land.

Yet Hezekiah's own son, Manasseh, who ruled for 55 years, was one of Judah's most evil rulers.

Despite a later revival under Josiah (640–609 B.C.), religious and moral deterioration continued. Jeremiah and Ezekiel graphically describe the way of life of Judah's people—a way of life that helps us see clearly why God's judgment had to fall on Judah too.

As we look at highlights of Judah's history, the kings who struggled to lead Judah back to God, and the prophets God sent to warn His own, we learn more of the love of God—and more of that godly way of life that can bring blessing even today to you and to me.

Commentary

When Solomon's kingdom was torn in 931 B.C., the Southern Kingdom, Judah, comprised considerably less territory and had a much smaller population than the Northern Kingdom. In the initial years of conflict between the two kingdoms, however, many from Israel drifted across the border. These were people committed to the worship of Jehovah, and they remained faithful to the Jerusalem temple and to the Law which ordained worship there. They rejected Bethel and Dan as worship centers, and refused to have the counterfeit priests ordained by Jeroboam I make their sacrifices.

Then, as the decades passed, the once-united nation accepted its divided state. And, tragically, any initial claim of Judah to a special godliness was gradually lost.

Of Judah's 19 kings, Scripture marks out 8 as "good." Characteristically, some of these kings stimulated revivals. Yet the fact that the Southern Kingdom even needed revival, plus the Bible's description of the sins that were put away, tells us that the citizens of Judah were all too quick to fall into the same apostasy that plagued Israel.

Revival

Asa (2 Chron. 14–16). Asa removed idols from the land, and purged the male prostitutes who were associated with their worship. Asa also deposed his grandmother (the queen mother) because she had made an idol of Asherah. Encouraged by the Prophet Azariah, Asa led the people of Judah to renew their covenant promises to God.

Yet Asa did not remain fully committed to God. In his later years Asa imprisoned the Prophet Hanani for rebuking him, and Asa failed to turn to God for aid when he was ill (2 Chron. 16).

Jehoshaphat (2 Chron. 17; 19–20). This son of Asa also followed the Lord. Like his father he attempted to root out the worship of Baal and removed many "high places." These high places (*bamoth*) were elevations set aside for pagan worship. Each contained an altar featuring idols. Sometimes the Hebrews would set aside a high place for the

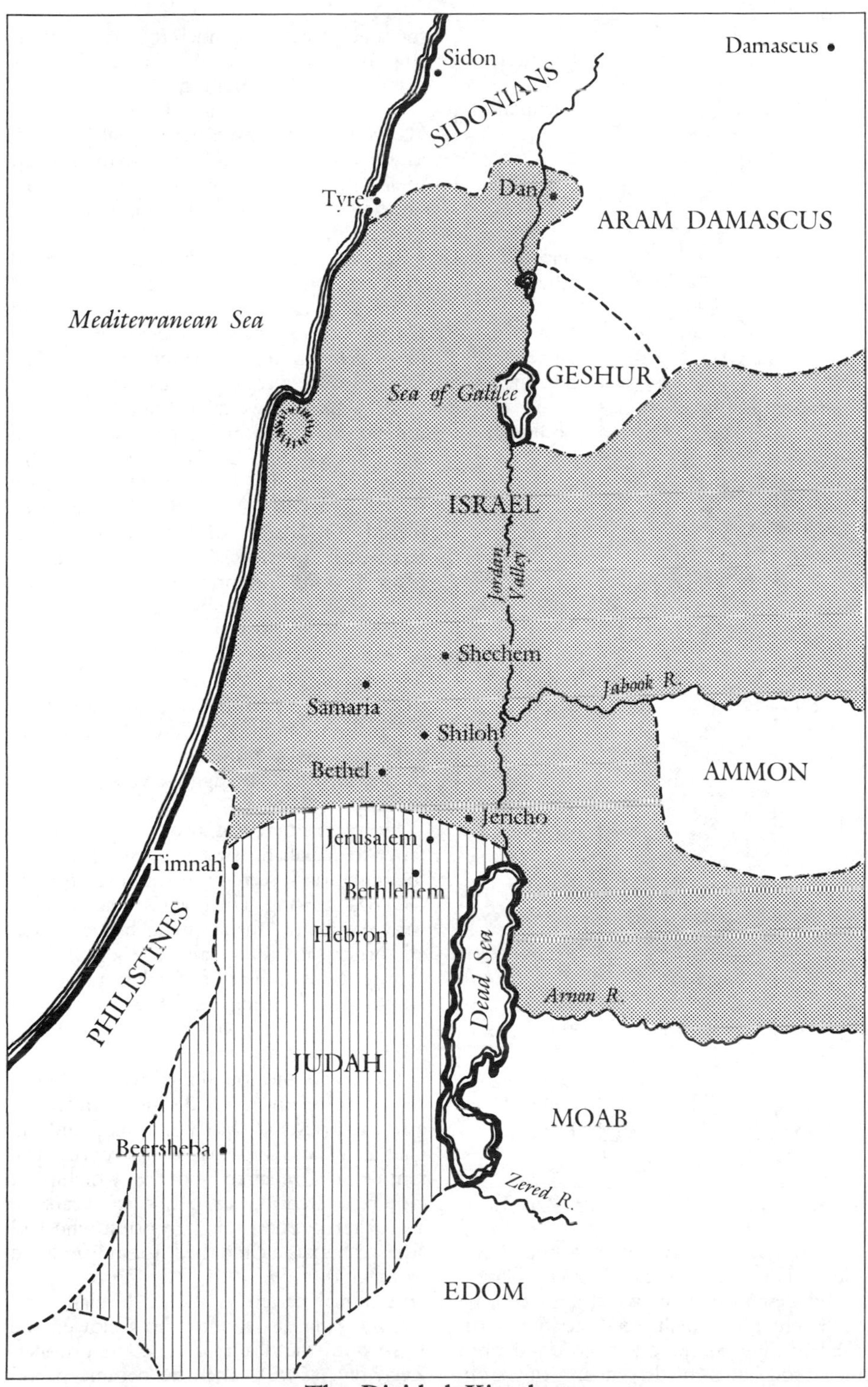
Damascus
Sidon
SIDONIANS
Tyre
Dan
ARAM DAMASCUS
Mediterranean Sea
GESHUR
Sea of Galilee
ISRAEL
Jordan Valley
Shechem
Jabook R.
Samaria
Shiloh
Bethel
AMMON
Jericho
Jerusalem
Timnah
Bethlehem
PHILISTINES
Hebron
Dead Sea
Arnon R.
JUDAH
MOAB
Beersheba
Zered R.
EDOM

The Divided Kingdom

	JUDAH Major Kings	Prophets
931	Rehoboam	Shemiah
910	Asa	Azariah
		Hanani
872	Jehoshaphat	Jehu
		Jahaziel
		Eliezer
		Elijah
835	Joash	
		Zechariah
		Joel
797	Amaziah	
791	Uzziah	
		Isaiah
750	Jotham	Micah
728	Hezekiah	
		Nahum
640	Josiah	
		Habakkuk
		Zephaniah
		Jeremiah
586		Ezekiel
	Babylonian Captivity	

Judah's Major Kings and Prophets

worship of the Lord and would ordain local priests. This practice was in direct violation of Old Testament Law, which insisted on a single center for worship and sacrifice (Jerusalem, during the kingdom era) and on a priesthood staffed by descendants of Aaron, Moses' brother. The pagan associations of the high places were much too strong; worship there soon took on characteristics of occultism and immorality.

So Jehoshaphat's attack on the high places was undertaken out of zeal for God, as was his insistence that the Levites resume their ministry of traveling to teach the "Book of the Law" throughout Judah (2 Chron. 17:9).

Jehoshaphat's faith was demonstrated powerfully when the Moabites and Ammonites invaded Judah. He turned to God in prayer, and fully trusted His promise of deliverance. On the morning of battle Jehoshaphat encouraged his army, "Have faith in the Lord your God and you will be upheld; have faith in His prophets and you will be successful" (20:20). He then led his army out, praising God for what the Lord was about to do. That trust in God was well placed. As Judah's little army marched out to meet the overwhelming enemy force, the Moabites and Ammonites began fighting each other! The enemy were dead when Judah's forces arrived.

Joash (2 Chron. 23–24). The kings after Jehoshaphat were evil, and set an example that the people of Judah gladly followed. Athaliah, a daughter of Jezebel (the pagan wife of Israel's King Ahab) came to the throne in Judah and aggressively promoted the cult of Baal.

However, there was a core of godly resistance to Athaliah. After six years, Jehoiada, the high priest, secretly crowned seven-year-old Joash as king. The boy had been hidden six years from Athaliah, who had executed all other possible claimants of Judah's throne. Now military and religious leaders combined to bring about a coup, and Athaliah was quickly executed (22:10–23:15).

Joash and the four kings who followed him were relatively good kings. Under Joash, the priests of Baal were killed and pagan altars and idols were destroyed. The temple was repaired and the worship of God reinstated. But in Joash's later years, he also faltered. After the high priest who had advised him as a child died, Joash wandered from God.

A similar pattern is seen in Uzziah, who became king at 16 and who followed the Lord until the death of his court prophet, Zechariah (26:5). Then he became proud and God struck him with leprosy.

♥ ***Link to Life: Children***
Children can identify with the boy king who wanted his people to love God. And this Bible story can be immediately applied in a simple, relevant way.

After telling the Bible story, let one of your boys or girls be "King Joash." One of Joash's most important orders was to make God's house beautiful again. Let your pretend king give this same command: "Make God's house beautiful."

The boys and girls can then pick up and store materials, dust, wash fingerprints from the doorjamb, etc.

Hezekiah (2 Chron. 29–32). Hezekiah reigned during the critical years of Assyrian world domination. The vast armies of this northern power invaded the Middle East again and again, dominating the nations there and in fact wiping out Israel as a nation in 722 B.C.

Judah too was threatened. But from the very beginning of Hezekiah's reign, "in the first month of the first year," this king had shown great zeal for the Lord. The temple, which had been defiled and all but abandoned, was reconsecrated, and the 25-year-old king determined to renew his generation's covenant with the Lord. For the first time in decades, Passover was celebrated in Jerusalem, and the people were so moved that the festival was extended seven extra days! As a result of that worship experience, the people returned to destroy the pagan altars and high places throughout their land.

When Assyrian forces threatened Jerusalem, Hezekiah showed his faith by turning immediately to God. Again God acted to aid His people, bringing death to the enemy soldiers.

How tragic that on the death of this godly king all the good he had done was quickly overthrown by his own son, Manasseh, who was undoubtedly one of the most wicked of Judah's rulers, though in his later years Manasseh did return to the Lord.

Josiah (2 Chron. 34–35). The last godly king of Judah, Josiah, also led a revival. He became king at 8, and at 16 began to seriously seek God. At 20, Josiah began to purge Judah of idolatry (yet again!). He also ordered another restoration of the temple, during which a copy of God's lost Law was found.

Josiah was shaken by what he read, for he realized how far God's people had departed from the Lord. The king acted immediately, calling all his people together and leading them in another service of covenant renewal, promising to follow the Lord and keep His commands. The Passover was instituted yet again, and Josiah kept on seeking to lead Judah to worship God until his death in battle against the Egyptians.

♥ ***Link to Life: Children***
Josiah is another child king your boys and girls will enjoy pretending to be. The highlight of his rule was discovery of a copy of the then-lost Law of God in the temple when it was being repaired.

This time your boy or girl "King Josiah" can give a different command: "Remember what God's Book says, and do it."

Have small scrolls prepared by gluing the ends of an 8" long paper strip to two dowel sticks. Then roll the paper up on the sticks. In response to "King Josiah's" command, your boys and girls can write a selected Bible verse on their scrolls to take home.

Print on the chalkboard memory verses taught during this quarter. Let each boy and girl choose one to print on his or her scroll.

Using memory verses for this activity provides a helpful review. And do be sure to talk with each child about how he or she can put the verse chosen into practice in his or her life the coming week.

Josiah's revival, like that led by other kings, brought the people nearer to God. But only for a time. Again, after his death, the people drifted quickly away, turning down that tragic path that could lead to only one thing—the edge of judgment.

♥ ***Link to Life: Youth / Adult***
What characterizes revivals? Here are some of the elements seen in the revivals led by Judah's kings. Write this list on a chalkboard. Have group members in teams of three or four develop modern parallels. That is, describe one or more corresponding elements that we might observe in a revival that took place in our own day.

Elements to list on the board are:
Tear down pagan altars

Destroy "high places"
Renew covenant with God
Send Levites to teach the Law
Turn to God when in danger
Praise God even before the battle is won
Repair the temple
Worship joyfully

When teams have developed parallels and have shared them with the group, discuss: "How many of these characteristics of revival do we experience now? Are we in revival, or do we need a revival today?"

Regret

It's difficult to look at Judah's history without experiencing a deep sense of regret. We do rejoice at the stories of revival and renewal. But we are saddened by the tragic state that called for revival: a state of spiritual decline and deadness that was all too often the normal state of affairs in Judah.

Under its later kings Judah, the surviving kingdom, knew both trial and triumph. As in the Northern Kingdom, increasing prosperity led to the neglect of faith. Ahaz, Judah's king during the years preceding the destruction of Samaria, committed himself to evil. He promoted Baal worship and even engaged in infant sacrifice (2 Chron. 28:3). He also established a pagan altar in the Jerusalem temple itself, making this the official place of sacrifice. He finally closed the temple, to force his people into the kind of pagan worship that he desired.

Micah, a contemporary prophet, cried out against Judah in those days just before the downfall of Israel.

> You have observed the statutes of Omri and all the practices of Ahab's house, and you have followed their traditions. Therefore, I will give you over to ruin and your people to derision; you will bear the scorn of the nations.
>
> Micah 6:16

How little difference could be seen between the sins of the Northern Kingdom and the lifestyle of "godly" Judah! And prophet after prophet sent, along with the pious kings, to lead Judah back to God were rejected or ignored.

Isaiah. Isaiah, who lived during the reigns of Uzziah, Jotham, Ahaz, and Hezekiah, called Judah a

> sinful nation, a people loaded with guilt, a brood of evildoers, children given to corruption. They have forsaken the Lord; they have spurned the Holy One of Israel and turned their backs on Him.
>
> Isaiah 1:4

In one of the Old Testament's most poignant images, Isaiah shares the song of the vineyard, God's plaintive cry over a nation gone astray.

> I will sing for the one I love a song about his vineyard: My loved one had a vineyard on a fertile hillside. He dug it up and cleared it of stones and planted it with the choicest vines. He built a watchtower in it and cut out a winepress as well. Then he looked for a crop of good grapes, but it yielded only bad fruit. Now you dwellers in Jerusalem and men of Judah, judge between me and my vineyard. What more could have been done for my vineyard than I have done for it? When I looked for good grapes, why did it yield only bad?. . . The vineyard of the Lord Almighty is the house of Israel, and the men of Judah are the garden of His delight. And He looked for justice, but saw bloodshed; for righteousness, but heard cries of distress.
>
> Isaiah 5:1-4, 7

Habakkuk. Habakkuk wrote in yet another time of revival, during the time of Josiah. Yet the first chapter of his short book indicates how troubled this prophet was with social and moral conditions in Judah. He was so troubled that he cried out to God, unable to grasp how God could permit the violence and injustice he saw everywhere. Despite a godly king whose whole heart was dedicated to the Lord, Habakkuk still cried out:

> How long, O Lord, must I call for help, but You do not listen? Or cry out to You, "Violence!" but You do not save? Why do You make me look at injustice? Why do You tolerate wrong? Destruction and violence are before me; there is strife, and conflict abounds. Therefore the law is paralyzed, and justice never

> prevails. The wicked hem in the righteous, so that justice is perverted.
>
> Habakkuk 1:2-4

The revival may have touched the hearts of the king and of Habakkuk, but the majority in Judah were unaffected; sin still marked the society.

And what about the days just before judgment fell? Listen to Jeremiah, as he looked back on the captivity of the Northern Kingdom, seeing it as a special lesson to Judah—a unique call to the South to repent. The words of Jeremiah clearly show that all the revivals of the Southern Kingdom, even the greatest under Hezekiah and Josiah, had not touched the hearts of God's chosen.

> "Have you seen what faithless Israel has done? She has gone up on every high hill and under every spreading tree and has committed adultery there. I thought that after she had done all this she would return to Me but she did not, and her unfaithful sister Judah saw it. I gave faithless Israel her certificate of divorce and sent her away because of all her adulteries. Yet I saw that her unfaithful sister Judah had no fear; she also went out and committed adultery. Because Israel's immorality mattered so little to her, she defiled the land and committed adultery with stone and wood [e.g., was involved in idolatry]. In spite of all this, her unfaithful sister Judah did not return to Me with all her heart, but only in pretense," declares the Lord.
>
> Jeremiah 3:6-10

In Judah, the outward form of religion was correct. But the form was deceptive. In their hearts, the people of Judah had drifted far from God.

♥ ***Link to Life: Youth / Adult***
How do we measure religious commitment? Ask your group which of the following is the best *indicator of true spirituality:*

A. News Item: *56 percent of Americans consider themselves "born again"*

B. Statistic: *More Americans attend church regularly in the '80s than did in the '70s*

C. News Item: *Catholic bishops urge unilateral ban of the bomb*

D. Advertisement: *Revival extended extra week! Come experience moving of God's Spirit!*

After discussion, ask what is inadequate about each of these items as an indicator of spirituality.

Then against the background of Judah's periodic revivals, look at the words of the prophets quoted in this unit. Ask your group, from these quotes, to develop their own list of measures of spirituality.

♥ ***Link to Life: Youth / Adult***
Help your group apply the measures of spirituality they developed.

Ask them to write a series of headlines for news items as they might appear if (a) they reported how members of your local congregation were experiencing true revival, if (b) they reported how your whole community were living close to God, and if (c) our country was to experience life-changing revival.

After sharing and discussing headlines, discuss ways that your group members, as individuals and together, can help make some of those headlines come true.

Review

When we look back over the history of Judah, we do more than read of men long dead and empires whose remains are now little more than dust. When we look back we discover spiritual forces that are at work in people today. We see reflected in the actions of men and women then the very choices that we face. And in what happened to them, we sense both promise and warning. We can choose today to follow God, and know blessing. Or we can choose to turn away, and know the pain of judgment and defeat.

The revivals reported here point the way to blessing. Like Judah's godly kings we can commit ourselves afresh to our relationship with God. We can learn to depend on prayer. And we can praise, even before our battles have been won, because we are confident in God's love.

The regrets the prophets express warn us as well. Each testifies to a fact noted in 2 Chronicles 20:33: "The people still had not set their hearts on the God of their fathers." God today as then is never satisfied with a superficial faith. He yearns now as then for full heart-commitment to Him. In our lives today we may be superficially good, and even respected by friends at church. But only a full, complete love for God that issues in a holy life can be acceptable to the Lord.

TEACHING GUIDE

Prepare
Read in 2 Chronicles about one of the revivals discussed in this unit. Imagine you were there, living in Jerusalem and close to the king. How would you have felt? What might your role have been? How would the revival have affected your life?

Explore
1. Draw the time-line chart on the chalkboard. Use it to review the spiritual history of Judah. As you talk of the godly kings, draw the wavy line which indicates Judah's periods of revival and decline. Discuss: "If we each drew a time line of our own lives, showing our personal spiritual experiences, would it be similar to or different from this chart of Judah's spiritual experience? How?"
2. Ask your group members for their impressions of revival and its characteristics. What do they think of when they hear of a "revival"? See "link-to-life" idea on page 283.

Expand
1. Engage in direct Bible study of the revivals reported in 2 Chronicles. Assign teams of several group members *one* of the passages that report revival. Each team is to list characteristics of the revival as it is reported in the biblical text. The passages to assign are 2 Chronicles 14–15; 17; 20–21; 23–24; 29–32; 34–35.
2. Or list the characteristics of revivals found in the earlier "link-to-life" activity. Have your group brainstorm as to what contemporary parallels would mark a revival today.
3. Or present the headlines suggested in "link-to-life." Use them to help your group explore the question of what are valid indicators of revival and a close spiritual relationship with the Lord.

Apply
1. Summarize the words of the prophets God sent to Judah in a minilecture. Remind your group that God is not concerned with a superficial faith that exists as a veneer of religion. God seeks a heart-commitment to Him, and that heart-commitment will be expressed in the total life—the commitment to righteousness and holiness in all things—of the true believer.
2. Or have your members work in pairs to write headlines that might appear if revival were a reality in your church, community, and/or nation.

When the headlines have been shared, discuss: "What might we do to help headlines like these come true?" See "link-to-life," page 283.

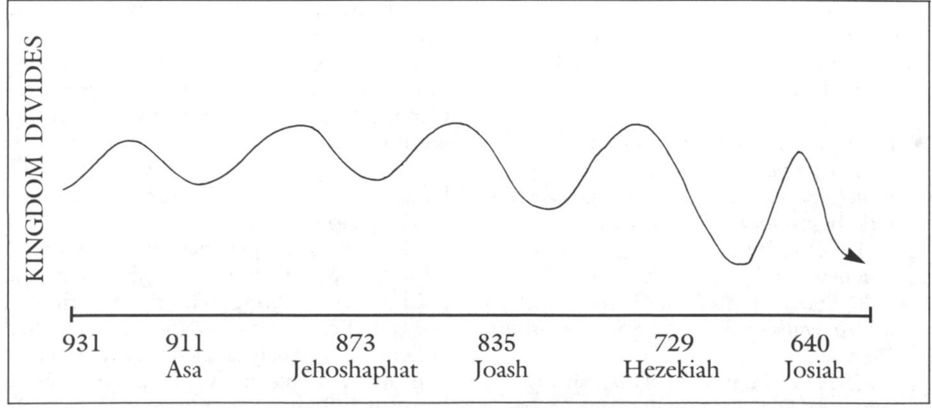

Judah's Spiritual History

STUDY GUIDE 41

2 Kings 25; 2 Chronicles 33–36

JUDAH'S FALL

Overview

The reign of Manasseh was the beginning of the end for Judah. Even though at the end of his 55-year rule he "told Judah to serve the Lord, the God of Israel" (2 Chron. 33:16), he himself had led the people too deeply into idolatry.

A revival under Manasseh's grandson, Josiah, failed to redirect the nation to God.

Two prophets, Jeremiah and Ezekiel, ministered to Judah during her last days. By hearing their words against the background of historic events we can sense the spiritual condition of Judah which made the Babylonian Exile a divine necessity.

▶ ***Babylonians.*** The city of Babylon lies some 50 miles south of modern Baghdad. The impressive capital of one of the ancient world's greatest empires has been studied intensively by archeologists.

▶ ***Nebuchadnezzar.*** He was the son of the founder of the Neo-Babylonian empire. He personally led the armies of Babylon in a series of wars against Egypt that crushed that ancient power and established Babylonian mastery of the Middle East. When the last kings of Judah rebelled, Nebuchadnezzar destroyed the city of Jerusalem and Solomon's magnificent temple. His established policy was to resettle troublesome people, and so Nebuchadnezzar ordered the Exile of the people of Judah. Daniel tells us much about this great pagan ruler who finally acknowledged God.

Commentary

During the reign of Manasseh (2 Chron. 33:1-20) the Southern Kingdom, though threatened, survived the Assyrian invasion that had swept Israel away. And there had been a religious revival at that time under Hezekiah. But Manasseh, Hezekiah's son, plunged Judah into the same kind of idolatry that the Northern Kingdom had known under Ahab and Jezebel. The temple was polluted with pagan altars, and the occult was promoted by the king. Child sacrifice to Molech was even practiced in the Hinnom Valley near Jerusalem!

Tradition tells us that Isaiah spoke out against the king—and was executed, as were many other pious leaders who dared to protest (2 Kings 21:16).

Manasseh's 55-year reign did not bring prosperity to Judah. In 678 B.C. he and 21 other kings made a compulsory visit to swear allegiance to Assyria. Later Manasseh apparently involved Judah in a rebellion with Moab and Edom against Assyrian control, and the king was taken prisoner to Assyria. There, the Bible tells us, Manasseh "humbled himself greatly before the God of his fathers" and was returned to Judah by the Assyrians. "Then," the text adds, "Manasseh knew that the Lord is God" (2 Chron. 33:12-13). After his release the repentant king attempted to institute his own reforms. He cleansed the temple, threw down centers of idolatry in Jerusalem, and "told Judah to serve the Lord, the God of Israel" (v. 16).

But the people of Judah did not respond. This nation too had passed beyond the edge of judgment; only death and destruction lay ahead.

♥ ***Link to Life: Youth / Adult***

Sometimes people put off salvation, pointing to the thief on the cross as evidence that "it's never too late" to be saved.

Read 2 Chronicles 33:1-13 to your group. Then put a simple T-shaped chart on the chalkboard. On one side write "Manasseh" and on the other "the thief on the cross."

Ask your group members to compare and contrast these two repentant sinners.

After they have done so, ask: "What does this tell us about God? What does this tell us about salvation?"

Then introduce the problem of those who want to wait to accept Christ, arguing from such late conversions that they don't have to become Christians "yet." How might they be answered?

When your group members have shared ideas, read verses 12-17, emphasizing verses 16-17. Manasseh may have known a personal conversion. But he could not do anything about the impact of his evil days on others! He was saved. But it was too late for Manasseh to undo the harm his wickedness had done to his nation.

Discuss and apply: "More than our own salvation depends on turning to Jesus now."

The Last Days

Date	Event
686	Manasseh becomes sole king
648	Josiah born
642	Amon succeeds Manasseh as king
640	Josiah becomes king
633	Josiah at 16 seeks after God
628	Josiah at 20 begins reforms
627	Jeremiah at 20 called as a prophet
621	Mosaic Law found in temple
612	Nineveh destroyed as Nahum prophesied
609	Josiah slain in battle at Megiddo; Jehoiakim becomes king
605	Babylon defeats Egypt at Carchemish; Nebuchadnezzar becomes king of Babylon; First deportation to Babylon includes Daniel
604	Nebuchadnezzar receives tribute in Palestine
601	Nebuchadnezzar defeated near Egypt
598	Jehoiakim set aside Jehoiachin rules December 9 to March 16, 587; is then deported April 22 to Babylon
597	Zedekiah becomes king in Judah; Ezekiel taken to Babylon
588	Babylon lays siege to Jerusalem on January 15
587	Jeremiah imprisoned (Jer. 32:1-2).
586	Zedekiah flees July 18; Destruction of Jerusalem begins August 14
581	Gedaliah killed and Jews migrate to Egypt against God's command October 7

Jeremiah

One of the two prophets who gives us insight into the last days of Judah is Jeremiah. The prophet was born about 648 B.C. and grew up as a contemporary of godly King Josiah. He lived only about two miles from Jerusalem, and was a member of a priestly family. He would have been intimately acquainted with the political situation in Judah.

At age 20, in 627 B.C., God told Jeremiah that he was to be His prophet. Jeremiah objected that he was too young, but God answered:

> Do not say, "I am only a child." You must go to everyone I send you to and say whatever I command you. Do not be afraid of them, for I am with you and will rescue you.
>
> Jeremiah 1:7-8

But while given this promise, Jeremiah was also warned. His ministry would be one of judgment and punishment! He would be hated and unpopular. But out of the anguish God would bring a new hope.

> See, today I appoint you over nations and kingdoms to uproot and tear down, to destroy and overthrow, to build and to plant.
>
> Jeremiah 1:10

This call set the tone for Jeremiah's long life. Obeying this call, Jeremiah urged his countrymen to surrender to Babylon, whom God showed him was the instrument of divine chastisement. But this demand was viewed as treason! Jeremiah was imprisoned, his life was threatened, and his words were constantly rejected by God's people.

What, through the eyes of Jeremiah, can we learn about the last days and the final sins of Judah that led to the Babylonian Captivity?

Jeremiah's Messages under Jehoiakim

In the fourth year of Jehoiakim's reign Nebuchadnezzar defeated the Egyptians at Carchemish, firmly establishing the Babylonians as the dominant world power. Hostages were taken by the victorious Nebuchadnezzar, whom Jeremiah identified as the servant God had chosen to judge Judah and the other nations of Palestine. Jeremiah predicted a lengthy Captivity, to last for 70 years, and at God's command made a written record of his sermons and prophetic messages.

This scroll fell into the hands of King Jehoiakim, who ordered it burned and who commanded the arrest of the prophet and his secretary, Baruch. Even under arrest Jeremiah continued to utter the dire warning, adding a prediction of the death of Jehoiakim and of the certainty of Babylonian victory (Jer. 36:27-32).

Messages from this dark period are filled with despair. God's heart was moved for His people, but they simply *would not* respond!

Jeremiah 11:1–13:14. God's convenant and oath given to Israel when the people came up from Egypt are reviewed, and the falseness of this generation to its oath is exposed. God would surely "uproot and destroy it" (12:17).

Jeremiah 14:1–15:21. The despair in this message grows out of the realization that it was now too late for God's people to turn to Him. God told Jeremiah not even to pray for his countrymen, and said, "Even if Moses and Samuel were to stand before Me, My heart would not go out to this people. Send them away from My presence! Let them go!" (15:1)

Four kinds of doom had been determined, and destiny had been sealed.

> Those destined for death, to death; those for the sword, to the sword; those for starvation, to starvation; those for captivity, to captivity.
>
> Jeremiah 15:2

Jeremiah 23:1-40. The religious leaders whom God sent to care for His flock had instead scattered them. Their lying prophecies and promises would bring them everlasting reproach.

Jeremiah 26:1-24. Jeremiah related an incident from early in Jehoiakim's reign, when He had offered pardon if only the people would return to God and "listen to Me, and follow My Law, which I have set before you . . . listen to the words of My servants the prophets, whom I have sent to you again and again" (vv. 4-5).

The leaders then actually encouraged the people to shout for Jeremiah's death, for the "crime" of speaking against their city in God's name! The one man who dared to speak up in support of Jeremiah, Uriah, was himself hunted down and later killed by Jehoiakim. Yet Jeremiah was delivered, as God had promised at the time of his call.

The Final Decades: 597 B.C.—581 B.C. The second group of captives was taken to Babylon in 597 B.C. At that time, 25-year-old Ezekiel, a member of an important priestly family, was taken to Babylon along with those distinguished men whom Nebuchadnezzar wanted to remove from political influence in their homeland. Some five years later, in 592 B.C., Ezekiel was called as a prophet (Ezek. 1:2).

Ezekiel had a unique two-part ministry. He prophesied warnings of Jerusalem's destruction between 592 and 586 B.C. His last message of this era, reported in Ezekiel 32, was delivered in April of 585 B.C., just after the city and its temple fell.

Then, some 13 years later, the prophet took up a new ministry—a ministry of hope and comfort.

But as we explore the fall of Judah, it is the first part of Ezekiel's ministry on which we need to focus. And particularly on a vision concerning God's temple, reported in chapters 8–11.

Ezekiel was sitting with the elders of the Jews in Babylon when he was suddenly caught up by an angelic visitor and taken in a vision to Jerusalem. There he was shown what was happening in the very temple in which the exiles put their trust, confident that God would never permit the destruction of the building which had been His place of presence on earth.

The vision demonstrated how foolhardy such a hope was, for Ezekiel saw God *removing* His presence from the temple! The shell of gold and marble that remained afforded no protection for God's sinning people!

Ezekiel 8:4-18. Ezekiel was taken to the temple where he perceived the "glory of the Lord" (the sign of His presence) in the holy of holies. But Ezekiel was told to look away from God and to observe what the men of Judah were doing in the temple itself.

He was taken through a secret passage into a hidden chamber, where the elders of Israel worshiped idols and "crawling things and detestable animals" (most likely the gods of Egypt that Jehovah had shown so powerless at the time of the Exodus). In the hidden chamber, the priests and elders offered incense, imagining that "the Lord does not see us; the Lord has forsaken the land."

Then Ezekiel was guided to the gate of the temple, where he found women involved in the worship rites of the mother/son cult of Tammuz.

Then, in the inner court he found 25 men facing *away* from the temple (see 2 Chron. 6:20), praying toward the sun, the chief god Ra of the Egyptian pantheon.

The pollution of the temple by the Hebrews showed how far all had fallen. "Therefore," God said, "I will deal with them in anger. I will not look on them with pity or spare them" (Ezek. 8:18).

Ezekiel 9:1-11. Then a striking thing happened. Six angelic figures with weapons in hand approached, and "the glory of the God of Israel went up from above the cherubim, where it had been, and moved to the threshold of the temple" (v. 3). God's presence was preparing to leave!

The executioners were given instructions—first, to mark off those individuals who were ashamed and who mourned over Judah's faithlessness, and then to strike out among the rest and "kill, without showing pity or compassion," those who had defiled the Lord's sanctuary.

Ezekiel 10:1-22. Cherubim, a guard of honor, now approached the temple, and the glory of the Lord moved out to the threshold of the temple. As the honor guard stood ready, the glory of the Lord left the temple threshold and paused above it.

Ezekiel 11:1-21. Ezekiel was now lifted and brought to the place from which the glory looked back toward the temple. From this perspective, he saw the faces of the 25 who had earlier been worshiping the sun. Among them he recognized the key religious and political leaders of God's people! Commanded to prophesy against them, Ezekiel spoke . . . and at his words one leader fell dead.

The prophet in turn cried out, "Ah, Sovereign Lord! Will You completely destroy the remnant of Israel?"

God's answer was both comforting and foreboding. Not all His people would be destroyed. Those in Captivity would be kept secure and would be regathered one day to the Promised Land. But for those "whose hearts are devoted to their vile images and detestable idols," there would be a complete end.

Ezekiel 11:22-25. With this announcement the cherubim lifted up their wings and the glory of the Lord left not only the temple but the city itself, hesitating briefly over the mountains east of Jerusalem.

God had left His sinning people to the fate that, in their hardness of heart, they themselves had chosen.

♥ ***Link to Life: Youth / Adult***

"America is a Christian nation. God will never let godless enemies defeat us."

Put this proposition, held by many, to your group. Do they agree, or disagree? Why? Allow time for a thorough discussion. Then sketch the situation in Judah around 590 B.C. The Jews argued that God's temple in Jerusalem was their protection. God would never let the city fall as long as the building that bore His name was there.

Have your group members study Ezekiel 8–11 to answer these questions: "What was happening to the 'glory of God'? What were the people of Judah doing in the temple? What does Ezekiel 9:4 teach us?"

On the basis of this study, return to the question of the Jews' conviction that the temple would protect them. What was wrong with this idea? Then apply it to the present day: What principles can we apply here to evaluate the idea that God will protect "Christian" America?

Back in Judah, it was stunningly clear by 597 B.C. that all Jeremiah had prophesied for the past 30 years was true. The most distinguished families in Judah had been taken to Babylon in the first of three deportations. Zedekiah, Judah's last king, was destined to rule only 11 more years.

During these last 11 years, Jeremiah continued his warnings. He advised submission to Babylon, since God had chosen this pagan power to discipline His people. But despite the evidence of fulfilled prophecies, the Jews and their leaders refused to listen. Zedekiah rebelled against Babylon, and in 586 B.C. the city of Jerusalem fell. Zedekiah's children were executed while he watched, and then he was blinded. The last thing he saw on earth was their deaths.

Temple treasures were transported to Babylon; then both the city and the temple were razed. All but the poorest people of the land were taken into Captivity, and Gedaliah was appointed as governor over the remnant. Jeremiah too remained there to guide the people with a word from God.

In yet another uprising in 581 B.C., Gedaliah was killed along with the small Babylonian occupation force. The remaining Jews were terrified of the revenge they were sure must come. They fled toward Egypt, and Jeremiah was forced to come with them. On the way, they begged Jeremiah to seek guidance from God, and promised to do whatever he told them.

The word picture of this event is a fitting climax to decades of rebellion.

The people, "from the least to the greatest" [important and insignificant] respectfully approached the 67-year-old prophet. "Please hear our petition," they said, "and pray to the Lord your God for this entire remnant. For as you now see, though we were once many, now only a few are left. Pray that the Lord your God will tell us where we should go and what we should do" (Jer. 42:1-3).

Jeremiah agreed to pray, and the people promised, "May the Lord be a true and faithful witness against us if we do not act in accordance with everything the Lord your God sends you to tell us. Whether it is favorable or unfavorable, we will obey the Lord our God, to whom we are sending you, so that it will go well with us, for we will obey the Lord our God" (vv. 5-6).

But the message with which Jeremiah returned was not what the remnant expected! They were told not to fear the king of Babylon: God would keep them from punishment and would restore their lands. They were definitely *not* to flee to Egypt, for if they did, sword and famine would overtake them and they would die with no survivors.

What was the reaction to this promise of protection? As soon as Jeremiah finished telling the people these words of the Lord, the leaders "and all the arrogant men" shouted at Jeremiah, "You are lying! The Lord our God has not sent you to say, 'You must not go to Egypt to settle there.' But Baruch son of Neriah is inciting you against us to hand us over to the Babylonians, so they may kill us or carry us into exile to Babylon" (43:2-3).

Rejecting God's Word, the few Jews who remained plunged on into Egypt, dragging the reluctant Prophet Jeremiah with them!

In Egypt, Jeremiah continued to minister, reminding the people of the sins of their fathers that had brought them judgment, and warning against the punishment that must fall on them in Egypt. Their response demonstrates the justice of God, who acts in judgment only when His people have gone too far. For this people, there was no hope of response or change: they were committed to sin.

> Then all the men who knew that their wives were burning incense to other gods, along with all the women who were present—a large assembly—and all the people living in Lower and Upper Egypt, said to Jeremiah, "We will not listen to the message you have spoken to us in the name of the Lord! We will certainly do everything we said we would. We will burn incense to the Queen of Heaven and will pour out drink offerings to her just as we and our fathers, our kings and our officials did in the towns of Judah and in the streets of Jerusalem. At that time we had plenty of food and were well off, and suffered no harm. But ever since we stopped burning incense to the Queen of Heaven and pouring out drink offerings to her, we have had nothing and have been perishing by sword and famine."
>
> Jeremiah 44:15-18

A saddened and angry Jeremiah then made a final statement.

> Did not the Lord remember and think about the incense burned in the towns of Judah and the streets of Jerusalem by you and your fathers, your kings and your officials and the people of the land? When the Lord could no longer endure your wicked actions and the detestable things you did, your land became an object of cursing and a desolate waste without inhabitants, as it is today.
>
> Jeremiah 44:21-22

The final calamity then fell. Pharaoh Hophra, the Egyptian king who had welcomed Judah, was given over to his enemies. The sword and famine destroyed the Jewish colony that had committed itself to perform their vows, not to God who loved them, but to the pagan idols that had been their downfall.

And Jeremiah?

Tradition tells us that the old prophet found his way to Babylon, and there completed his book, including his eyewitness story of the last days of Judah, recorded for the exiles—and for us.

TEACHING GUIDE

Prepare

Meditate on Ezekiel 9:4: "Go throughout the city of Jerusalem and put a mark on the foreheads of those who grieve and lament over all the detestable things that are done in it." What do these words of God to destroying angels have to say to American Christians today?

Explore

1. Put the time chart (beginning of study guide) on the chalkboard. In a minilecture cover the events of the last days of Judah, and show the relationship of the two major prophets, Jeremiah and Ezekiel, who ministered during that tragic era.
2. Or begin with a study of Manasseh, comparing this evil man who repented late in life to the thief on the cross. Help your group members see that while it is never too late for an individual to turn to Christ, the harm that person does to others while he or she delays cannot be remedied. How important to accept the Lord when we first hear the message of salvation, and then spend our lives to affect others positively for Him.

Expand

1. What factors led to Judah's downfall? Divide your group into three teams. Each can examine a different section of Scripture to develop impressions of the spiritual state of the people when judgment came.

Assign the following passages to the teams, for quick reading and to record impressions:

- Team 1: Jeremiah 12, 23, and 26
- Team 2: Ezekiel 8–11
- Team 3: Jeremiah 42–44

2. Or focus on the Ezekiel passage, and the false hope of the people of Judah in the temple. What God is always concerned with is the spiritual and moral state of His people—not material things or even civilizations as such. Explore with your group the relationship of the Jews' confidence in their temple with the confidence of some modern Christians in "Christian America." Be sure to note that while wicked civilizations fall, God continues to watch over the individual who trusts in and obeys Him.

Apply

1. Have your group members imagine themselves as believing citizens of Judah just before its fall. How would they have felt? What would they have feared? What would have given them hope?

Then go around the circle and ask each person to complete this statement: "Today the hope that I have as I look ahead. . . ."

2. Or, conclude the session by going around the circle, asking each member to complete the following: "I think that the most important message Judah's fall contains for us today is. . . ."

STUDY GUIDE 42

Selected Scriptures

THE BABYLONIAN CAPTIVITY

Overview

The Babylonian Captivity was a turning point for the people of Judah. The last decades of Judah's existence saw the culmination of the idolatrous tendencies so obvious in God's people since their entry into the land nearly 900 years earlier. Generation after generation had refused to heed the warnings of the prophets, and continued to rebel against God and His Law. The defeat by Babylon and Exile to the capital of that great empire was, however, not the end, but a new beginning!

As we examine the experience in Babylon we note: (1) A new emphasis on Scripture, reflected in the synagogue and in the scribal movement, and (2) an end to idolatry. After the Jews returned to their land they never again worshiped false gods. In later years many would die rather than bow down to conquerors' gods.

The Captivity then is a turning point—but only in some ways. The remnant of the exiles who chose to return to their land under Cyrus the Persian soon drifted from full commitment. All too often they ignored prophets sent to them, as their fathers had. And, with the exception of words against idolatry, we see the same themes in the postexilic prophets as those in the warnings of God's preexilic spokesmen. The hearts of God's people never did turn fully to the Lord. Only the coming Messiah would resolve the deepest problem of Israel and humankind—winning the invisible war between sin and commitment that has raged from Adam and Eve's first portentious step out of the will of God.

Commentary

On the fall of Jerusalem in 586 B.C. a third deportation of Judah's citizens took place. The captives who trudged toward Babylon represented all but a scattering of Jews. Soon even that remnant would flee to Egypt after murdering their governor and a small Babylonian garrison.

Nebuchadnezzar had developed a policy of resettlement for troublesome ethnic groups in his empire. If a people rebelled, he simply took them from their homeland. This decisive act was intended to neutralize their patriotism, and in time to blot out their identity as a separate group. In an age when the gods of a people were thought to own their particular territory, deportation also had the impact of undermining their religious faith. Typically exiles began to worship the gods and goddesses of any new land they were settled in. In the ancient world it was only politic to be on good terms with the deities who "owned" the area in which one lived!

Only Israel's God, who had revealed Himself as God not of a territory but of the entire earth, could survive in the hearts of a displaced people.

In fact, the deportation ordered by the Babylonian king Nebuchadnezzar had an effect opposite of that which he intended. In Babylon the faith of the Jewish people was strengthened! And new institutions grew up which would keep that faith vigorous and alive through the centuries that lay ahead.

We can best picture the Babylonian Captivity and its meaning in the sacred history if we look at four themes: the causes of the Captivity, the setting of the Captivity, great personalities of the Captivity, and finally, outcomes of the Captivity.

Causes of the Captivity

Sometime during the reign of Josiah and after his attempt at revival (628–609 B.C.), the Prophet Habakkuk complained to God about the moral situation in Judah.

There had been a return to religion stimulated by the efforts of the godly king. But the revival had not touched the hearts of God's people, so the prophet cried out:

> How long, O Lord, must I call for help, but You do not listen? Or cry out to You, "Violence!" but You do not save? Why do You make me look at injustice? Why do You tolerate wrong? Destruction and violence are before me; there is strife and conflict abounds. Therefore the Law is paralyzed, and justice never prevails. The wicked hem in the righteous, so that justice is perverted.
>
> Habakkuk 1:2-4

In the few decades that followed the Josian era this situation deteriorated, and Judah turned completely to idolatry. Jeremiah sobbed over the way the people of Judah and their children remembered how to worship idols—but not how to worship God.

> Judah's sin is engraved with an iron tool, inscribed with a flint point, on the tablets of their hearts and on the horns of their altars. Even their children remember their altars and Asherah poles beside the spreading trees and on the high hills.
>
> Jeremiah 17:1-2

Near the end Ezekiel was given a vision, and saw the priests and the elders of Judah in the temple itself—worshiping pagan gods!

> I went in and looked, and I saw portrayed all over the walls all kinds of crawling things and detestable animals and all the idols of the house of Israel. In front of them stood 70 elders of the house of Israel.
>
> Ezekiel 8:10-11

Each of these quotes, and the words of other prophets who ministered in the dark days just before the Captivity, shows the depth of the spiritual deterioration that caused the Captivity. As God explained to Habakkuk, a prophet puzzled and troubled that God would permit such wickedness in a people called by His name, "I am raising up the Babylonians, that ruthless and impetuous people, who sweep across the whole earth to seize dwelling places not their own" (Hab. 1:6).

Habakkuk understood.

> O Lord, You have appointed them to execute judgment; O Rock, You have ordained them to punish. Your eyes are too pure to look on evil; You cannot tolerate wrong.
>
> Habakkuk 1:12-13

This then was the cause of the Babylonian Captivity. A God too pure to look on while evil reigns, a God who cannot tolerate wrong, finally acted to punish and judge His sinning people.

♥ ***Link to Life: Youth / Adult***

Is our suffering punishment for sin?

Many fear that any sickness or financial reversal is a sign that God is punishing them. God does punish. But the Old Testament prophets help put such experiences in perspective.

Have half your group look at Habakkuk's complaint (1:2-4), at God's answer (vv. 5-11), and at Habakkuk's interpretation (vv. 12-13).

Have the other half of your group look at a parallel in Isaiah, where that prophet identified Assyria (which destroyed the Northern Kingdom, Israel) as the "rod of My anger." In that passage note the purpose for which Assyria is dispatched (Isa. 10:5-12), and the result (vv. 20-23).

After each team has read and talked about its passage, put the following on the board. Each team is to agree *or* disagree *with each statement, and to demonstrate its conclusion from the text:*

(1) The slightest sin is likely to bring divine punishment.

(2) Suffering may lead people to rely more on God.

(3) When a Christian has troubles, he or she can be sure God is acting to punish.

(4) Serious, continuing sin for which one does not repent is most likely to bring punishment.

(5) God is unfair in the ways He chooses to punish His people.

The Setting of the Captivity

It would be a mistake to imagine that the Babylonian Captivity was a time of continual hardship for the Jewish people. In fact, it was a time of relative peace and prosperity!

The captives were taken to the capital city of Babylon itself. They were settled there in several districts. The best known of these

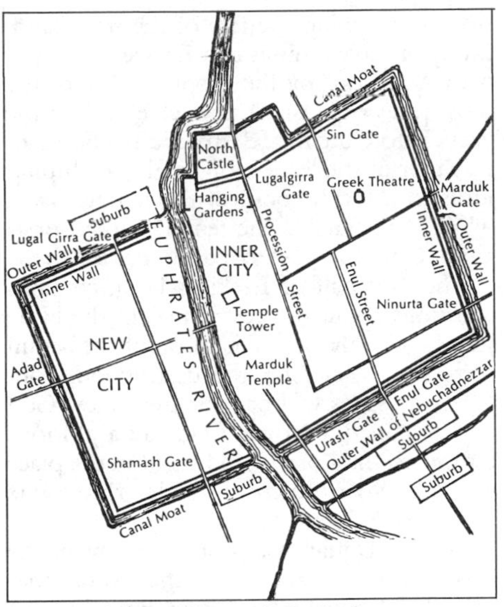

The City of Babylon
Taken from the Zondervan *Pictorial Encyclopedia of the Bible,* Merrill C. Tenney, editor. © 1975, 1976, the Zondervan Corporation. Used by permission.

was called Tel Aviv, by the river (actually the canal) Chebar. The typical exile very likely owned his own home, and had enough property to grow garden crops (cf. Jer. 29:4, 7; Ezek. 8:1; 12:1-7). The land they lived on was fertile, and under irrigation. In the early days many may even have sent money back to Jerusalem!

Archeologists have found that the Babylonians recognized three classes of citizens. The first was *Awelin,* free men of the upper classes. *Mushkenu* were free men also, but of lower classes. The third class, *Wardu,* were slaves. The Jewish captives who settled in Babylon were probably *Mushkenu;* free, but not influential.

We do know that many of the Jews were prosperous. They worked on the king's building projects, and some at least entered business as merchants. The Babylonians kept careful records, and recovered records show Jewish names on copies of various business transactions. At least one trading house was owned and operated by Jews.

The favorable treatment of the Jews is reflected in the records of Babylon that tell us King Jehoiachin was released from prison there, and given court apartments. Babylonian records of the food and oil ordered for the king, his sons, and servants have been recovered!

Another indication of the favored treatment given the Jews is that, by the time a return to Jerusalem was permitted by Cyrus the Persian, many Jews decided to stay in Babylon. They were unwilling to trade their material success for the risky business of settling in the now-empty and desolate land God had given their forefather, Abraham!

Finally, we know from Jeremiah and from Ezekiel's writings that the Jews were allowed much self-government. The community had its own elders, and in them priests and prophets continued to play an influential role.

But despite the material benefits of life in Babylon, those who loved God still experienced those decades as punishment. God's people were far away from the land of promise, uprooted from their past, and far from the place where the promised Messiah was to appear.

The Book of Lamentations captures something of the anguish of spirit that can exist within even when every possible material need has been met. The writer pictured Jerusalem in tears, saying:

> See, O Lord, how distressed I am! I am in torment within, and in my heart I am disturbed, for I have been most rebellious. Outside the sword bereaves; inside, there is only death.
>
> Lamentations 1:20

And the captive responds to Jerusalem's cry with a cry of his own.

> I am the man who has seen affliction by the rod of His wrath. He has driven me away and made me walk in darkness rather than light; indeed, He has turned His hand against me again and again, all day long. He has made my skin and my flesh grow old and has broken my bones. He has besieged me and surrounded me with bitterness and hardship. He has made me dwell in darkness like those long dead.
>
> Lamentations 3:1-6

It may seem strange, but despite his comforts the godly Jew walking in the magnificent city of Babylon felt isolated and alone.

Babylon truly was a beautiful city. Nebuchadnezzar ruled there for some 43 years. And he was more than a conqueror. He was a builder. His buildings included temples, streets, walls, and entire districts of the great city. The Greeks identified the hanging gardens of Babylon as one of the ancient world's seven wonders. These gardens were built in terraces on a man-made mountain looming high over the flat Babylonian plains.

Nebuchadnezzar was proud of his building projects. An inscription describes one of them:

> Huge cedars from Lebanon, their forests with my clean hands I cut down. With radiant gold I overlaid them, with jewels I adorned them. . . . The side chapels of the shrine of Nebo, the cedar beams of their roots I adorned with lustrous silver. Giant bulls I made of bronze work and clothed them with white marble. I adorned them with jewels and placed them upon the threshold of the gate of the shrine.

The materialists among the Jews might have been captivated by the glory of Nebuchadnezzar's city, the hub of that world's greatest empire. But the hearts of the godly were empty, yearning instead for the land that was the focus of the past and future working of their God.

Great Personalities of the Captivity

There are a number of people linked with this era of sacred history. It helps to put the period in perspective to see the role of each.

Jeremiah. Jeremiah was born about the time of Josiah, the last godly king of Judah. His ministry extended for nearly 50 years. He lived to witness the destruction of Jerusalem and the temple, and to see the final apostasy of the remnant that remained as they fled to Egypt. Jeremiah's harsh warnings against the sins of Judah, and narratives about his conflict with various Jewish leaders, give us clear insights into the spiritual and moral conditions that made the Exile a divine necessity.

Ezekiel. The Babylonians ordered three deportations of Jews from Judea. The first, in 605 B.C., involved leading members of the aristocracy, and promising young people who could be trained for government posts in the Babylonian bureaucracy.

Ezekiel was a member of a priestly family, and in Babylon was given a number of visions concerning the fate of the homeland. Many of the warnings that Ezekiel conveyed were acted out by the prophet. One of the most powerful visions of Ezekiel during the years before the final destruction in 586 B.C. was that of the leaders of Judah worshiping idols in a secret room of the temple itself, while men outside the temple turned *away* from God to pray to pagan deities.

The first half of Ezekiel's book contains warnings about the destruction of the Holy Land and holy city. The second half, begun some 13 years after the destruction, contains messages of hope for the exiles. God had ordained a return. One day a glorious temple to the Lord would stand in the place of the Solomonic temple that was destroyed.

Daniel. Daniel was just a teen when he was taken to Babylon in the group that included Ezekiel. But Daniel and three of his friends were placed in the king's school—an academy designed to prepare promising young people from throughout the empire for administrative posts. There Daniel came in contact with King Nebuchadnezzar himself, and had a dramatic impact on that ruler's life and relationship with God (see Dan. 2 and 4).

Daniel continued in administrative roles for some six decades! He may have been influential in guiding Cyrus to change the Babylonian policy of exiling ethnic groups from their lands, and thus opening the door for the Jewish people to return to their homeland.

The famous story of Daniel in the lions' den happened when the prophet was an old man, over 80 years old, around 536 B.C.

Ezra and Nehemiah. In the first year of Cyrus, who overthrew the Babylonian Empire and set his own Medo-Persian Empire in its place, a decree was issued permitting captive peoples to return to their homelands. A group of Jews returned that very year (538 B.C.), commissioned by that ruler to rebuild the Jerusalem temple. Ezra led a second group that returned some 80 years later, in 458 B.C.

Nehemiah came with a third, very small group in 444 B.C. to serve as governor. His drive and commitment led to a rebuilding of the walls of Jerusalem and to a temporary revival.

Esther. Esther is also set in the era of the Persian Empire. The events take place between the third and twelfth years of Xerxes (483–471 B.C.). The Book of Esther tells how an enemy determined to wipe out the Jewish people, but were thwarted by Esther, who had providentially become Xerxes' queen. This action took place some 70 years after the first group of Jews had returned to their homeland.

As we collate the stories of men and women associated with this period, we make several significant discoveries.

First, the Captivity was not a single event, but rather took place through a series of deportations of Jews to Babylon. Groups were taken in 605 B.C., in 597 B.C., and 586 B.C. The first deportation took upper-class persons. The second seems to have focused on artisans and leaders. And the third, of about 70,000 persons, included all but the "poor" who later fled to Egypt.

Second, the "return" was not a single event or mass movement. Two large groups of people moved from Babylon to the Holy Land, the first in 538 B.C. and the second some 80 years later in 458 B.C. During this period and beyond it there were more Jews outside of the Holy Land than in it!

Third, the focus of history had shifted from the land of Palestine itself to the Gentile world powers who controlled it. Daniel and Esther point up the fact that the events which shaped the experience of the Jews in tiny Judea were themselves shaped in the centers of world power, not in Palestine. The land is religiously significant, not politically.

Only a few, and those the most faithful and religiously motivated, returned to Palestine to establish a Jewish presence in the land God had promised to Abraham so long ago.

The Outcomes of the Captivity

God used the Captivity to filter from His people those whose hearts had turned from Him.

This filtering process had two aspects. First, Ezekiel had warned that the sinful person would die in the coming invasion of Judea. But the person who turned from evil and to the Lord would live through the terror of that time (see Ezek. 18). So on the one hand, death itself removed many who were unresponsive to God, leaving a remnant more willing to hear His words.

Second, the blessings of the Captivity also served to separate the godly from those less attuned to spiritual things. There was no repetition in Babylon of the slavery an earlier generation had known in Egypt. In fact, the material prosperity many experienced in Babylon was one way that God distinguished between the spiritual and unspiritual. Writing of the first return Ezra said that "then the family heads of Judah and Benjamin, and the priests and Levites—*everyone whose heart God had moved*—prepared to go and build the house of the Lord in Jerusalem" (Ezra 1:5, italics added). The spiritually motivated returned. The materially motivated stayed in Babylon where life was now comfortable and safe.

So both suffering and blessing were means by which God separated out those individuals who were fully committed to Him.

♥ ***Link to Life: Youth / Adult***

How does God purify a people? Ask your group members to imagine that each of you has no *problems. Each has all the money he or she will ever need. Each is assured of good health. Each has a happy home life and a satisfying job.*

From this description ask each member to predict the spiritual state *of the group as a whole 10 years from this date.*

After each person has had a chance to make his predictions, discuss: "What do most of you seem to expect would result from unmixed blessings? Why do you expect this result? What personal experiences may support your conclusions?"

Then look at what happened to the Jewish people in Babylon. Give a minilecture covering conditions, report on the returns. While some 50,000 people did come back in the first return, there were far more Jews who stayed in Babylon than there were who returned! Material prosperity often saps spiritual commitment!

The Captivity also had an impact on Jewish institutions. There were three major results of the Captivity on the life of the people as a whole.

A new center for religious life developed in Babylon. This center was the synagogue, a word which simply means "gathering." Without a temple as a focus for worship, smaller groups began to meet for worship and for study of the written Word.

There is little documentary evidence, but it is likely that the passion for study of Scripture which existed in later Judaism was stimulated in this period (see Ezra 7:10). In the synagogue the study of the Word began to take priority over the worship rituals and ceremonials which had been the focus of Israel's spirituality while the temple stood. When the temple was rebuilt, the passion for study continued to exist side by side with ritual.

Second, a scribal class developed. The Book of Ezra tells how this man "devoted himself to the study and observance of the Law of the Lord, and to teaching its decrees and laws in Israel" (v. 10). Ezra's later authority in Judah derived not from his membership in a priestly family line but from his ability to understand and to interpret Scripture.

Interpretation was needed. By this time the Jewish people spoke Aramaic, while the Old Testament is written in Hebrew. Thus the student of the Old Testament was both a translator and an interpreter.

Gradually the role of these men who studied Scripture was magnified. Their writings and interpretations were collected and studied, and their explanations of the Law began to carry the weight of the Scriptures themselves. By the time of Jesus, the Pharisees believed that the oral tradition they used to interpret Scripture went back to Moses himself! This was the tradition of men which Jesus condemned as all too often making the Law empty of its true meaning (cf. Matt. 15:3-6).

Still, the scribal movement in its origins was healthy. The people of God began to study and listen to the Law and to the prophets that their forefathers had so long ignored and rejected.

Third, the Babylonian Captivity put an end to idolatry. No longer would the worship of idols be attractive to the Jewish people. Later attempts to force idolatry on the Israelites would in fact lead to fierce, angry rebellions against foreign powers.

And so the Captivity had its desired impact. Wickedness was punished, and idolatry expunged from the hearts of Israel. A new generation, purified first by bloodshed and then by prosperity, returned to establish a Jewish presence in the Promised Land.

And the people returned with two new and powerful institutions which would shape the future. There was the synagogue, where the people could gather to worship God and to study His Word. And there were the scribes, many motivated by the most pure desire to know and to love God, and to teach God's people His ways.

The fact that the scribal movement deteriorated into the excesses of the Pharisaism of Jesus' time should not blind us to the fact that a desire to know and teach the Word of God is good. Nor should it blind us to the fact that again a good start, made by a new and dedicated generation, was about to drift into failure and sin.

How great a testimony Old Testament history bears to the need of humankind for the Saviour! The best of men, the best of starts, without the full forgiveness and new heart that Jesus brings, and apart from the power He gives us through His Spirit, is sure to end in failure again and again.

TEACHING GUIDE

Prepare

Review the history of this period. Put the time-line chart on page 297 on a chalkboard or overhead before your group meets.

Explore

It is best to cover material of this type in a lecture, and then let learning activities that involve your group members focus on application.

Use the chart to orient your group members to the events of the period, covering the four aspects of the Captivity discussed in this chapter: causes, setting, great personalities, and outcomes.

Expand/Apply

Select an application activity which best suits the needs of your particular group. Possible approaches include:

1. Is all trouble punishment? As your group members examine the experience of Israel and the words of the prophet, they will see that the Captivity came only after continu-

Captivity and Return

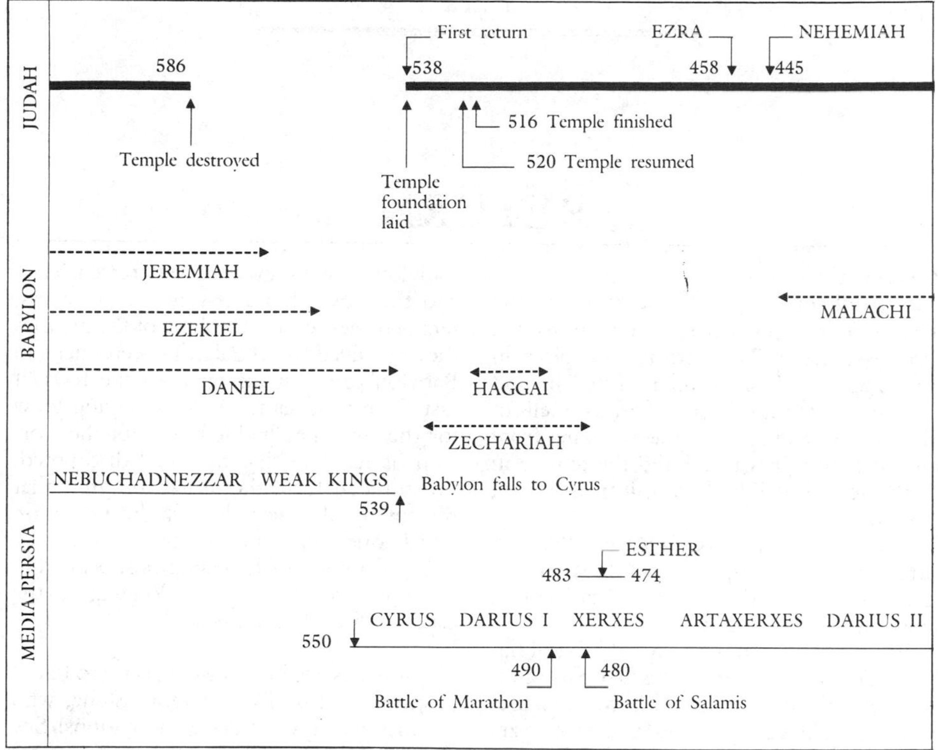

ing apostasy by God's people. Use the approach suggested in "link-to-life" on page 292, to help your group members think through this practical issue. Note too that God's punishments resulted in good for His loved but sinning people.

2. What is the impact of prosperity on spirituality? The question is raised by the fact that the majority of Jews chose to stay in Babylon rather than return to their homeland. Explore the question with your group, using the "link-to-life" process on page 295.

3. Or ask your group members to suggest lessons the history of this period might have for Christians today, and discuss their ideas.

STUDY GUIDE 43

Ezra

RETURN!

Overview

The Book of Ezra tells the story of the return of the Jews from Babylon to the Promised Land. This return took place in two stages. A first group returned in 538 B.C., the first year of Cyrus. Ezra 1–6 tells of that return, and spans some 23 years, from the edict of Cyrus to rebuild the temple in Jerusalem until its completion (from 538–515 B.C.).

A second return took place some 80 years after the first group arrived. This smaller group was led by Ezra, author of the biblical book that bears his name.

Ezra is associated with several biblical figures. The story he tells in the first part of his book is intimately linked with the ministries of the Prophets Haggai and Zechariah. Ezra himself was a contemporary of Nehemiah.

The chart in this lesson, reproduced from the Scripture Press *Bible Knowledge Commentary,* puts the events and personalities of this period in perspective.

The Book of Ezra develops several themes. It affirmed the belief of the people of Judah who returned: that one day God would establish the nation again and set up a promised glorious kingdom. And it emphasized the importance of rebuilding the temple, so that God might be worshiped according to the Law. Ezra also expressed the importance of commitment, and called for reform of a people who wished to claim God's covenant promises.

- The *Bible Knowledge Commentary* contains an excellent discussion of the Book of Ezra on pages 651-671.

Commentary

God's chosen people had sinned. And the Lord had brought the Babylonians to crush the nation and tear her people away from the Promised Land. In a series of deportations the Hebrews had been taken to far-off Babylon. There they were well treated. They had their own homes, went into business, retained their customs. Many of the luxuries they had lived for in Palestine were theirs in Babylon too. But for many of the Jews, it just wasn't the same. A deep longing grew for the land they had left, and for the worship of Jehovah that they had discounted. For some at least, the realization grew that the intangibles were in fact the values on which one's life must be based.

In the poetry of Lamentations, penned in Babylon, we can hear the longing of the captives for their homeland.

> How deserted lies the city, once so full of people! How like a widow is she, who once was great among the nations! She who was queen among the provinces has now become a slave. . . . Joy is gone from our hearts; our dancing has turned to mourning. The crown has fallen from our head. Woe to us, for we have sinned! Because of this our hearts are faint, because of these things our eyes grow dim for Mount Zion, which lies desolate, with jackals prowling over it. You, O Lord, reign forever; Your throne endures from generation to generation. Why do You always forget us? Why do You forsake us so long? Restore us to Yourself, O Lord, that we may return; renew our days as of old unless You have utterly rejected us and are angry with us beyond measure.
>
> Lamentations 1:1; 5:15-22

Despite increasingly improved conditions in Babylon, the Jewish people could not wipe away the image of their humiliation. The songs of Lamentations are a constant reminder that, for the people of Judah as for all of us:

> The worldly things men set their hearts

upon turns ashes or it flourishes, and soon, like snow upon the desert's dusty face is gone.

The Rubaiyat of Omar Khayyám

In the darkness of the Captivity, misery turned the people of God in a new direction. Men poured over the writings of the prophets and of Moses, seeking to understand what had happened. Out of this return to the Word of God grew the synagogue, the local gathering place for the Jews. And out of the return to the Word grew hope!

Hope Stirs

There was a sound basis for the rebirth of hope. The Prophets Jeremiah and Ezekiel, just before the Exile, not only warned of judgment but also spoke of the faithfulness of God to His covenant promises. God would return the people to the Promised Land (Jer. 31). His covenant with Abraham would be kept; the temple would be rebuilt (Ezek. 40–44).

Jeremiah's writings had indicated that the Captivity would last for only some 70 years (Jer. 25:11-21; 29:10). Over a century and a half before that, God had even given through Isaiah the very name of the ruler who would initiate the return: Cyrus.

> [It is I] who says of Cyrus, "He is My shepherd and will accomplish all that I please; he will say of Jerusalem, 'Let it be rebuilt,' and of the temple, 'Let its foundation be laid.' "
>
> Isaiah 44:28

And God had spoken again through Isaiah about this pagan ruler, calling him His own anointed!

> "I will raise up Cyrus in My righteousness: I will make all his ways straight. He will rebuild My city and set My exiles free, but not for a price or reward," says the Lord Almighty.
>
> Isaiah 45:13

We can imagine, then, the excitement in the Hebrew community in Babylon as word of a Persian conqueror named Cyrus drifted into the capital! By 550 B.C. Cyrus had formed a large domain known in history as Medo-Persia. Bent on world conquest, Cyrus defeated Babylon's ally, Croesus, and in 539 B.C. took Babylon itself—without a fight! There, in October of 539, Cyrus was welcomed by the people of Babylon as a liberator, and accomplished an amazingly easy transfer of power. Truly God had made "all his ways smooth"!

Then, in the first year of his rule, Cyrus announced a startling reversal of Babylonian resettlement policy. We have portions of his decree recorded in the Bible.

> This is what Cyrus king of Persia says: "The Lord, the God of heaven, has given me all the kingdoms of the earth and He has appointed me to build a temple for Him at Jerusalem in Judah. Anyone of His people among you—may his God be with him, and let him go up to Jerusalem in Judah and build the temple of the Lord, the God of Israel, the God who is in Jerusalem. And the people of any place where survivors may now be living are to provide him with silver and gold, with goods and livestock, and with freewill offerings for the temple of God in Jerusalem."
>
> Ezra 1:2-4

The darkness was lifting. The Jewish people were about to go home.

The First Return: Ezra 1–3

Not everyone was eager to return to Judah. While many of the Jews had reexamined their values and made a fresh commitment to God, a great number of those who prospered in Babylon were again enmeshed in materialism.

Ezra's report makes it clear that those who did return were spiritually motivated: those "whose heart God had moved—prepared to go up and build the house of the Lord" (1:5). They did receive enthusiastic support from the rest of the Jewish community. They were given gold, silver, and beasts of burden. In addition, all the treasures of the first temple, that had been carried off to Babylon, were now returned by Cyrus (vv. 6-11). So the 42,360 Israelites—plus their 7,337 servants—did not return as paupers. They were well equipped to rebuild the temple and to reestablish Jerusalem.

Ezra, who told us about the pilgrimage of 538 B.C., was not among that company. He had not yet been born. But, some 80 years later, Ezra would follow this first group's path from Babylon to the Holy Land.

The leader of the first group was a man called Zerubbabel (his Hebrew name), or Sheshbazzar (his Chaldean name: see 5:16). He and the high priest, Jeshua, guided the people back to their homeland and, once there, quickly began work on the temple. First, though, they erected an altar and reinstated the sacrifices that God had prescribed through Moses. And they kept the Feast of Tabernacles.

In May they began to lay the foundation of the new temple. As soon as the foundation was finished, they called the people together to celebrate. The Bible tells us that "with praise and thanksgiving they sang to the Lord: 'He is good; His love to Israel endures forever' " (3:11). Those shouts of joy were mingled with tears, as the older men who could remember the glory of Solomon's temple compared its magnificence with the modest dimensions of the new. But the shouts of joy and tears could not really be distinguished: the celebration was so great that only triumph rang through.

What mattered was not the size.

What mattered was that once again a temple to God was being built!

The temple. Why was the temple so important to the Jews? And what was the significance of this rebuilding?

In the ancient world, deities were associated with particular locations, viewed either as the home or a favorite haunt of the god. Thus temples were constructed as residences for the god or goddess manifested there, and it was assumed that the deities found these residences acceptable. No wonder the pagan Cyrus referred to Jehovah as "the God who is in Jerusalem" (1:3).

This did *not* underlie the meaning of the temple in Israel. As Solomon had asked in his prayer of dedication of the first temple, "Will God really dwell on earth? The heavens, even the highest heaven, cannot contain You. How much less this temple I have built!" (1 Kings 8:27)

Still God did promise Israel that in a special sense He would focus His presence with the Jews through the temple. Even as early as Moses' day, God indicated that one day the Lord would choose a place "as a dwelling for His name," and that that place was to be the only location for offering sacrifices (Deut. 12:11). The central place of worship would be a unique unifying element for Israel.

Three times a year the Jews were to gather to worship there, reaffirming their common faith and common heritage as God's covenant people.

By limiting the sacrifices of Israel to this one location, the Jews were also protected from the pattern of pagan worship common in the Near East. That pattern saw local gods and goddesses worshiped in each community—on high hills, in sacred groves, and secluded caves. The single place of worship set aside to meet Jehovah was thus a unique affirmation of the oneness of God and of the commitment that Israel was to maintain to Him and to Him alone. In the words of Moses, chanted in every synagogue even today:

> Hear, O Israel: The Lord our God, the Lord is One. Love the Lord your God with all your heart and with all your soul and with all your strength.
>
> Deuteronomy 6:4

In the public worship of Israel as in the heart of the believer, there was to be room for only One.

But the significance of the temple is not fully seen even in this great distinctive. There was a portrait of God imbedded in the temple design. As in the tabernacle that preceded it, the pattern given by God spoke of access into God's presence through the blood of sacrifice. The design also spoke of worship, divine guidance, and supernatural supply. In the pattern of the building and its courts, the believing Jew could see reflected realities about his relationship with God.

These important roles of the temple in the faith of the Old Testament would be enough to explain the drive to rebuild that motivated the thousands who enthusiastically left Babylon and headed home. But as we read more deeply in Ezra, and hear the contemporary message of the Prophet Haggai, we learn that there was a deeper reason yet that the returnees felt that they *must* rebuild the temple of their God.

Good Intentions: Ezra 4–6; Haggai 1:1–2:9

The foundation of the temple was laid in 537 B.C. in the flush of the Jews' first enthusiasm. But almost immediately opposition stirred.

The material in Ezra 4 is out of sequence historically. But it was placed there to support and demonstrate Ezra's theme. Opposition grew . . . and the people of God succumbed!

When Nebuchadnezzar had taken the people of Judah from Palestine, he had brought other settlers in. These new peoples carried over much of their old religions, but as a matter of course they had also adopted the God of the new land. They did not know Him personally. They were not His covenant people. But as they lived in His land, it was considered only proper to worship Him.

So when the Jews returned to rebuild the temple of God, these foreigners wanted a part. "Let us help you build," they said, "because, like you, we seek your God and have been sacrificing to Him since the time of Esar-haddon king of Assyria, who brought us here" (v. 2).

This request was flatly denied. "You have no part with us," Zerubbabel and Jeshua and the other leaders replied (v. 3). And they were right! These were not people of Abraham's line. They were not children of the covenant. Thus, unless they were willing to first become Jews, they could have no part of a ministry that God had committed to His own and only to His own.

The reply angered the Samaritans (a name for these strangers that was carried on into the New Testament period). They immediately began to oppose the Jews, and even sent paid lobbyists to government centers to block further work on the temple (v. 5). They were so successful in this that for some 16 years the temple remained no more than a foundation!

During these years, the people built homes for themselves. They planted fields and laid out vineyards. Apparently they even spent much of the funds committed to them for construction of the temple! But they did not prosper, despite all their hard work. They had permitted opposition to divert them from their commitment to God and their initial enthusiasm for the Lord had drained from their hearts.

♥ ***Link to Life: Youth / Adult***
Taking a stand for the truth is seldom popular! Let the experience of the returning Jews stimulate a discussion of unpopular stands that Christians may (and perhaps should!) make today.

Sketch the situation in Judah, identifying and explaining these elements (seen in Ezra 4:1-5):

(1) request *(let us help build);*
(2) rejection *(you have no part in our God);*
(3) resistance *(we will try to stop you).*

Be sure you explain why the stand taken by the Jews was right: the temple was a place of worship only for God's covenant people. Also note the forms resistance took: discouraging, frightening, slandering, and organizing political pressure.

Then divide into teams to develop at least five *issues on which Christians might reject a request of a modern group, and as a result risk rejection and/or persecution. For instance, join our "gay rights" march, give to X project, etc.*

With issues identified discuss: "What happens when we are pressured for a stand against something we believe as Christians is right? How are we pressured? How do we react? What could or should we do?" Note particularly that the people of Judah gave in *to the pressure! Haggai 1:3-11 describes the result of surrender.*

On September 1, 520 B.C., the Prophet Haggai recalled Judah to the task of building the temple. Discouraged by opposition to their spiritual mission, the people had redirected their efforts to making a living. In the process they had forsaken God as their central concern. And so Haggai shouted out that September day these jolting words:

> This is what the Lord Almighty says: "These people say, 'The time has not yet come for the Lord's house to be built.' . . . Is it a time for you yourselves to be living in your paneled houses, while this house remains a ruin?" Now this is what the Lord Almighty says: "Give careful thought to your ways. You have planted much, but have harvested little. You eat, but never have enough. You drink, but never have your fill. You put on clothes, but are not warm. You earn wages, only to put them in a purse with holes. . . . Why?" declares the Lord

> Almighty. "Because of My house, which remains a ruin, while each of you is busy with his own house."
>
> Haggai 1:2, 4-6, 9

The first flush of commitment to God had been dissipated by difficulties, and in their efforts to meet material needs the people had forgotten the spiritual.

In a series of jolting exhortations, Haggai, joined by Zechariah, stirred the people of Israel to action. Once again Zerubbabel and Jeshua led the people to build. The opposition of the Samaritans was overcome (Ezra 5–6), and in four years the restored temple stood on the site of the temple which had been burned in 586 B.C.

It was 516 B.C.

The 70 years foretold by Jeremiah had passed. With the temple rebuilt, Israel was once again officially in the Promised Land.

♥ ***Link to Life: Youth / Adult***
Old Testament history often illustrates New Testament principles. Read the preceding quote from Haggai to your group. Ask: "If Haggai were preaching this sermon in our church today, he would not be speaking about rebuilding the temple. But what do you think he would *be exhorting us to do?"*

Discuss the ideas that group members suggest. Then note that Haggai's exhortation implied a promise, which the prophet stated clearly when the rebuilding was done: "From this day on I will bless you" (Hag. 2:19).

What New Testament principle is seen in these historic events? One Jesus stated clearly. "Seek ye first the kingdom of God, and His righteousness; and all these things shall be added unto you" (Matt. 6:33, KJV).

But what was it that motivated the people to return to building the second temple? It was not just the promise of material blessing. If materialism had motivated these people, they would have stayed with the comforts that had been theirs in Babylon. In his sermon Haggai went on to share God's promise for the future. "I will shake the heavens and the earth. I will overturn royal thrones and shatter the power of the foreign kingdoms" (Hag. 2:21-22). When the "shaking of the nations" took place, Messiah, the promised deliverer, would appear! And according to Ezekiel, He would stand in the temple, for it would become "the place of My throne and the place for the soles of My feet. This is where I will live among the Israelites forever" (Ezek. 43:7).

What motivated the people to rebuild the temple was the hope that one day soon the promised Messiah would walk on Zion's hill. And to hasten His coming, the temple in which He was destined to stand must be there!

The Second Return: Ezra 7–10

In the seventh year of Artaxerxes Longimanus, 458 B.C., just 58 years after the completion of the temple, Ezra led a group of some 1,500 men and their families back to Palestine.

In Ezra's day, Palestine was part of a larger governmental unit, the satrapy of Abarhahara (see map), and was ruled by a Persian subgovernor. Times had been difficult in Judah. To reconstruct the agricultural base for their economy, the people had scattered from Jerusalem and had built smaller communities throughout the land. Even the Levites, dedicated to temple service, had built homes and cleared land. The walls of Jerusalem had not been rebuilt, and the people had begun to intermarry with the pagans of the land. This last act was a serious breach of Old Testament Law, which insisted that God's people maintain a separate identity. This was a very practical law: history demonstrates over and over again that when the Israelites intermarried with pagans, the sure outcome was the introduction of idolatry.

Ezra was no political reformer. He was, however, a teacher, "for Ezra had devoted himself to the study and observance of the Law of the Lord, and to teaching its decrees and laws in Israel" (7:10). There was no doubt in Ezra's mind that a fresh start for God's people could be found only in a return to God's Word.

The last chapters of Ezra focus on three highlights.

Artaxerxes' decree (Ezra 7:11-28). When Ezra returned he came with a number of significant concessions from the king.

Funds were granted so that sacrifices could be offered in Jerusalem for Artaxerxes and his sons. Those in temple service were declared free from taxes. Ezra was given the

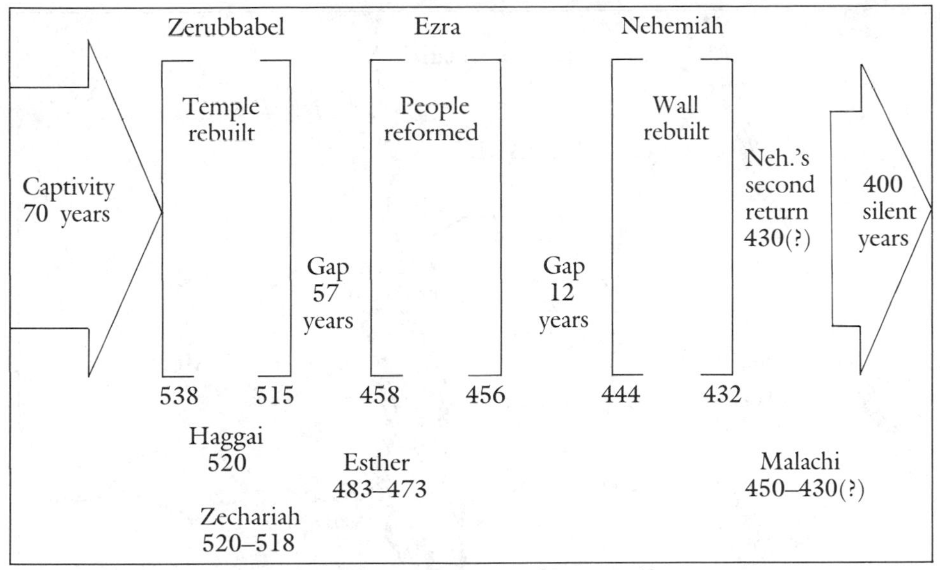

The Three Returns from Exile

right to appoint magistrates and other government officials, and the Old Testament Law was affirmed as the civil as well as the religious code of the land!

Praising God "who has put such a thing as this in the king's heart" (v. 27, NASB), Ezra and his company, after a time of fasting, set out for the homeland.

♥ ***Link to Life: Children***

You can help boys and girls appreciate Ezra's prayer, reported in 8:21-23. The road to Judah was a dangerous one. But Ezra was ashamed to ask the king for a guard of soldiers. After all, Ezra had told the king that God took care of people who looked to Him, and that God would be angry with people who did not honor Him. So Ezra chose to trust God, and led all the travelers in a time of prayer.

After telling this story, introduce a game: "Whom do you trust?" Have 10 3 x 5 cards marked and ready. Two will say "God" on the top. Four will say "friends" and four "adults." On the back of two of the friends *cards print "helps" and on two print "not home, can't help." On two of the* adults *cards print "helps" and on two, print "too busy to help." On the back of the "God" cards print "helps us always."*

Let your boys and girls imagine a situation in which they might ask God or others for help. As a child suggests a situation, he is allowed to draw a card (*without looking) from the pile. He or she looks at the back to see whether or not the person helped—and then tells* how *the person helped.*

For instance: "I need help to get ready for a test." If he draws a friend or adult "helps" card, he might say, "My friend read questions and I tried to answer them." If a God card, "God helped me remember to turn off the TV and study."

If a "helps" card is drawn, say, "Sometimes others do help us." If a "not help" card is drawn, say, "Sometimes others let us down." If a God card is drawn, say, "God always helps us when we ask Him."

"Whom do you trust? It's good to ask others for help. But the One we can always count on to help us is God."

Ezra's prayer (Ezra 9:6-16). When Ezra arrived in Judah he found that the people of Israel had not kept themselves separate from the peoples of the land, but had begun to intermarry with them. Not only was intermarriage commonplace, but the spiritual and political leaders in Judah were the worst offenders!

Deeply shaken, Ezra tore his clothing and his hair—a sign in that time of intense grief and/or anger—and slumped down before the temple. At evening he rose, then fell on his knees and prayed.

Ezra's prayer was a prayer of confession. And as he wept aloud, a large crowd gath-

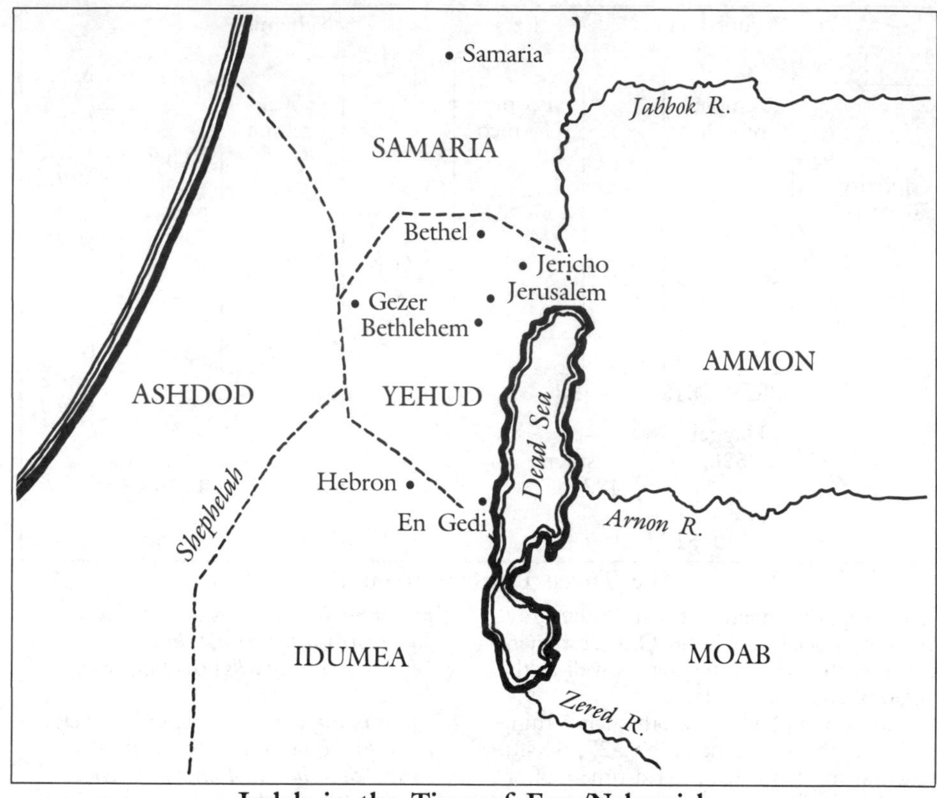

Judah in the Time of Ezra/Nehemiah

ered. They too began to weep bitterly! The Spirit of God was using the anguish of Ezra to touch the hearts of His people. Revival was about to break out!

♥ ***Link to Life: Youth / Adult***
Have your group members analyze Ezra's prayer, not only as a model of confession of sin, but also as a key to modern revival.

Divide into teams of three to five. Each paragraph of the prayer (Ezra 9:6-15) should be titled to reflect its content. For instance:

- *6-7 Ezra identifies with his sinning nation.*
- *8-9 Ezra affirms God's grace and goodness.*
- *10-12 Ezra pinpoints the commands the people have broken.*
- *13-15 Ezra recalls past punishments and expresses fear of God's righteous anger.*

Discuss together the pattern seen in this prayer which prepared the people of Judah for spiritual revival. Then give 10 minutes for each person to write out *a prayer in this same pattern, identifying areas in which church or country need to follow Ezra's example, and in confessing sin, open hearts for a spiritual revival.*

The people's response (Ezra 10:1-15). The people were deeply affected by Ezra's empassioned prayer. They volunteered to repent, and to make a solemn covenant (a contract or promise) to send away their pagan wives and their children, and so purify their nation.

At a great assembly of all the people, Ezra confronted the nation with its unfaithfulness, and the whole assembly responded, "You are right!" Investigating teams were set up, and all the men who had married foreign wives divorced them and sent them away.

The nation was, once again, fully committed to God's Law.

For a time.

TEACHING GUIDE

Prepare
The temple served as the measure of spiritual commitment in the life of those who returned to Judah from Babylon. What in your life serves as the measure of your own spiritual commitment?

Explore
In a minilecture supplemented with the chart, The Three Returns from Babylon, review the return from Babylon. Be sure to touch on the earlier prophecies that assured the Jews that God would bring them back to their land, and read the Isaiah prophecies actually naming Cyrus.

You will also want to briefly comment on the significance of the temple as the measure of spiritual commitment for those who first returned—and the messianic implications of rebuilding. To rebuild the temple was an affirmation of faith in God's promise of a future for their people and their land.

Expand
1. One study focus might be on the response to the opposition described in Ezra 4–6. How quickly the spiritual fervor disappeared when opposition developed!

Use the "link-to-life" idea to identify issues on which Christians should take unpopular stands today—and to discuss how we should meet opposition such stands might arouse.

2. Or focus on Ezra's prayer of confession and the return to God's Law which it stimulated.

Use the "link-to-life" idea to help your group members understand that a deep sensitivity to and concern about sin is vital if God's people are to turn to Him wholeheartedly. Help your members identify, as they write their own prayers of confession, issues in the church and the country about which believers today should be concerned.

Apply
Ask your members to skim Ezra 8:15-34 or 9:1-5 to identify some trait in Ezra that they would like to see developed in their own lives. Then go around the circle and have each person tell what he sees in Ezra that he or she would like to see in his or her personality, and tell why.

STUDY GUIDE 44
Nehemiah

REBUILDING

Overview
The Book of Nehemiah continues the story of the Jewish exiles who returned to their homeland after the Babylonian Captivity. As told in the Book of Ezra, a group of about 50,000 returned to Judah in the first year of Cyrus, conquerer of Babylon (538 B.C.). The temple at Jerusalem was rebuilt by this group. Ezra himself led about 1,500 more back some 80 years later (458 B.C.). Ezra's spiritual leadership led to a vital reform: those who had married foreign women divorced them and recommitted themselves to their covenant relationship with God.

The events recorded by Nehemiah took place some 12 years later (446 B.C.). Nehemiah came as a governor appointed to lead his people, with the express purpose of rebuilding the walls of the Holy City.

Outline

I.	The Walls Rebuilt	1–6
II.	The Covenant Renewed	7–12
III.	The Sins Purged	13

▶ ***Covenant.*** The covenant referred to in this unit is the Mosaic Law. The Law was viewed as a formal contract that defined the relationship between God and His people.

▶ ***Walls.*** Cities in the ancient world were walled for protection. The walls were also symbols: Unwalled cities merited contempt. Walled cities were seen as significant. Nehemiah could not stand the thought that the city of God should not have walls, and committed himself to rebuild them.

Commentary
Hollis was a good man: a sincere Christian, well liked by everyone who knew him. Yet whenever there was an altar call in the church he attended—an invitation to those who felt a need to rededicate themselves to the Lord—Hollis was always the first to respond.

It was hard to understand why. One of his sons was a friend of mine when we were teens. In the time I spent in their home I saw no evidence of faults or failings. My parents were sure that Hollis was the last man in that congregation who needed rededication. Yet in his own heart Hollis must have felt a need for new beginnings and must have seen each altar call as an opportunity for a fresh start.

As an adult, I've yearned many times for a fresh start myself. Not that my spiritual commitment or relationship has changed dramatically. But somehow, many little things get warped and twisted. Habits develop, ways of thinking and feeling and responding intrude that do not fit with what I want to be. I'd like to wipe them all out and start again, with a sense of freshness and restoration. I'd like to make a new beginning.

I suspect that the desire for a fresh start is something each of us experiences. Too often little failures, or large ones, are the source of such a sense of need.

Somehow we feel that if we had *really* committed ourselves to God that last time, we'd not need a fresh start now. Our lives would be consistent experiences of victory; steady journeys upward. It's painful to discover that even after sincere dedication we can fall. Somehow our hearts tend to drift, until we're jolted into awareness that we need yet another new beginning.

It was a jolt for men like Ezra and Nehemiah to discover that Israel too needed fresh beginnings. The people of God had returned to the Promised Land with great expectations; they enthusiastically journeyed hundreds of miles to rebuild the temple . . . and stopped with bare foundations. Stirred up by Haggai and Zechariah, they made a fresh beginning and completed the temple, to be ready for the Messiah. But the years passed. The Messiah did not come. And the old patterns of life, the old materialism, the old values, crept in.

There was no excuse.

It was wrong.

But it did happen to them—just as it happens to you and me. When a people or an individual does drift from God, it's time for recommitment. Time for the fresh start that God is always willing to give us when we return to Him.

♥ ***Link to Life: Youth / Adult***

Briefly tell the story of Hollis and his response to calls in his church for recommitment. Ask your group members to jot down one or two words that tell how they think Hollis felt. Then brainstorm: "What kinds of things make people feel the need for a fresh start?"

When many items are listed, discuss: "How do you suppose God feels about our need for fresh starts? Our requests for fresh starts?"

Nehemiah: An Overview

It was only 12 years after Ezra's return that Nehemiah came to Judah. Nehemiah was a high official at the Persian court who, out of concern for Jerusalem, asked for and was given permission to serve as governor of that minor district. He served in Jerusalem 12 years, returned to Persia, and then came to Judah a second time to govern there.

Unlike Ezra the priest, Nehemiah exercised political power. Yet his colorful and decisive leadership dealt with more than restoring respectability to Jerusalem by rebuilding its walls. Nehemiah also committed himself to purifying the lifestyle of God's people and bringing them into conformity with God's Law. It is striking to realize that even with Ezra in Judah, teaching the Word of God to the people, the Jews had drifted from full commitment. By Nehemiah's time intermarriage was again a problem, and doing business on the Sabbath Day was an established way of life. It was time for another fresh start for God's people.

Nehemiah's day. I suppose for most who read the Bible, the ancient Jewish state might seem to be a broad and extended kingdom.

Actually, in her days of greatness Israel never ranked in size with the empires and kingdoms of the Near East. In Nehemiah's day this always-small land had shrunk even more; the district of Yehud (Judah) included only some 800 square miles! It extended north and south about 25 miles, and east and west about 32. The tiny size of Judah and the plight of the exiles, who were surrounded on every side by hostile peoples, makes it easier for us to understand why Jewish morale so often ebbed, and why opposition from neighbors was usually all that was necessary to cause them to abandon a project.

Nehemiah's decision to live on this insignificant parcel of land rather than to continue in his important position in the capital of the great Persian Empire seems especially dramatic, and is a measure of this man's commitment to God.

Nehemiah's boldness. The people of Judah were discouraged about themselves and their future. Not Nehemiah! On his return to Judah he surveyed the tasks to be accomplished and laid his plans quietly (Neh. 2:11-16). Nehemiah then boldly called the people of Israel to rebuild the walls of Jerusalem "and we will no longer be in disgrace" (v. 17). The response of the people was immediate—but so was the reaction of the Jewish opponents. They were greatly displeased that "someone had come to promote the welfare of the Israelites" (v. 10).

"Bold" seems to be the best word to use to describe Nehemiah's character. A catalog of the challenges he had to face, and his response to them, makes it clear that in spite of Judah's weakness Nehemiah was unimpressed by problems.

Nehemiah's commitment. Nehemiah brought great energy and courage to the building of the walls. The success of this project led to a dramatic change in the attitude of the people of Judah. Their self-respect had been recovered by their victory over their enemies; their awareness of God's presence had been stirred. Gathering together to celebrate and praise God, Nehemiah put forward Ezra the scribe "to bring out the Book of the Law of Moses, which the Lord had commanded for Israel" (8:1). All the people gathered to hear as Ezra read and interpreted the words. (NOTE: The interpretation was necessary because by this time the language of the people was Aramaic, not the classical Hebrew of the Old Testament documents. Ezra and the other teachers had to read in the original, translate, and explain.)

This reading of the Law by Ezra took some seven days, and culminated on the eighth day with a worship service. The Jews recovered their sense of identity as God's people. And they went on to express fresh commitment by a written covenant (Neh. 10), which the leaders of the people signed. This covenant reflected the specific areas in which the people had drifted from God—and expressed their intention to observe the commands of the Lord that they had previously ignored.

In a great outpouring of praise, temple service was restored, and the ministers of the temple moved back to Jerusalem from their farms.

Nehemiah had not only led the people of Judah to rebuild the walls of their city; he had led them to renewed commitment to God and to His revealed will.

Then comes Nehemiah 13.

Nehemiah had returned to Persia to report to the king. It is uncertain how long he was away, but when Nehemiah returned he was stunned by what he found. The fresh-start promises had been broken once again!

- The people bought and sold on the Sabbath.
- A guest room for one of Judah's pagan enemies had been prepared in the temple of God itself.
- Once again Jews had married foreign wives. "As for their children, half spoke in the language of Ashdod, and none of them was able to speak the language of Judah, but the language of his own people" (v. 24, NASB).

Nehemiah's shock did not keep him from acting as boldly as ever. "I rebuked them," Nehemiah reported, "and called curses down on them. I beat some of the men and pulled out their hair. I made them take an oath in God's name and said: 'You are not to give your daughters in marriage to their sons, nor are you to take their daughters in marriage for your sons or for yourselves'" (v. 25). And as for the grandson of the high priest, who was one of those who had married a foreign woman, "I drove him away from me" (v. 28).

Even the Levites who served the temple had returned to their land—because the people no longer paid their temple tithes.

And here the Book of Nehemiah ends. "So I purified the priests and the Levites of everything foreign, and assigned them duties. . . . Remember me with favor, O my God" (vv. 30-31).

Observations on the Text

The Book of Nehemiah is a rich source of personal insights. It helps us discover how to make that fresh start we so often feel we need. And it shows us how to continue, unshaken, on a godly path despite opposition. Here are some of the highlights of this book to emphasize in studying and teaching it.

Practical prayers. Nehemiah was a man of action. But his prayer life was not neglected. Instead, Nehemiah seems to have blended practicality and spirituality in an impressive way.

**Prayer of confession (1:4-11).* An effective prayer life is rooted in right relationship with the Lord. Our insight into Nehemiah's prayer life is launched in chapter 1, with his prayer of confession. Like Ezra before him (Ezra 9:6-15), Nehemiah identified with his people and accepted responsibility for their failures. He confessed their—and his own—disobedience and weaknesses. And Nehemiah prayed for strength to make a fresh start in obedience.

♥ ***Link to Life: Youth / Adult***

A prayer of confession is the way for us to make fresh starts in our own spiritual lives. This is why Hollis continued to respond to altar calls in his church. He was sensitive to his failures, and looked to God for cleansing and renewal.

A similar prayer is found in Ezra 9:6-15.

To help your group members see how to make such a "fresh-start" prayer themselves, have them work in teams to compare the Ezra 9 and Nehemiah 1 prayers. If you wish, list the following elements to look for: express sense of failure, affirm God's grace, pinpoint broken commands, remember results of failure, seek present aid.

Discuss the insights of the work teams. Then give each group member a 3 x 5 card. Ask each to write down a step-by-step process telling "How to Make a Fresh-Start

Prayer," which can be kept handy in their Bibles. (If you wish, work out the step-by-step process and put it on a chalkboard for each to copy.)

**Prayers of action (2:4; 4:9; 6:9).* Nehemiah lived and worked under great pressure. Yet he remained conscious of God's presence with him. Awareness of God's presence is seen in three brief prayers. We know they were brief, because they were uttered in Nehemiah's heart as he carried on his mission.

Nehemiah stood in the presence of Artaxerxes, the absolute monarch of Persia whose displeasure meant death. While asking this ruler to release him from his duties so he could rebuild his ancestral city, Nehemiah "prayed to the God of heaven, and . . . answered the king" (2:4-5). Back in Judah Nehemiah learned of a plot by surrounding peoples to come and fight those rebuilding the walls. "But we prayed to our God and posted a guard day and night to meet this threat" (4:9).

Later those nearby sent lying reports back to the capital of Persia, and used them to try to frighten Nehemiah. But Nehemiah simply prayed, "Now strengthen my hands," and kept on (6:9).

This is practical prayer. It is prayer by a person who relies on God—but who keeps on giving his or her best efforts to the task at hand.

How much we need to learn from Nehemiah's prayer life. We need to let confession launch us on a fresh start, and then rely fully on God while we keep on with our daily work.

♥ ***Link to Life: Children***

Boys and girls can learn early to pray as Nehemiah did, asking for help with hard things, then keeping on with their work. After teaching the Nehemiah story, give each child a 4 x 6-inch piece of cardboard. Let them trace a circle in its center, using a quarter or half-dollar for the pattern. Let each child then pick one color to represent prayer, and another color to represent work. Each can color one side of their piece of cardboard with the prayer color, and the other with the work color. Then cut out each circle.

Suggest that the boys and girls carry the circle with them in pocket or purse. Whenever they have a hard thing to do, they can touch the circle and be reminded to ask God for help—and keep working on the hard thing. Suggest the larger cardboard rectangle be placed at home in a place where they often do hard things. It can remind them that the way through their troubles is found in prayer and hard work. The circles and cardboard rectangles will help your boys and girls remember God's presence, and help them look to Him for help while they do their part.

Meeting opposition. Nehemiah's determination to rebuild the walls of Jerusalem is seen in the way he dealt with opposition. And this opposition came from many different avenues. The chart lists the problems Nehemiah had to overcome—and what he did in each situation. What is impressive is first that opposition came from every possible source—and that in each case Nehemiah refused to be distracted from his goals. Nehemiah knew where he was going—and he permitted nothing to stand in his way.

This is important to us too. We need to know our spiritual and personal goals. And then as problems arise, we need to deal with them in such a way that we keep on making progress toward our goals.

♥ ***Link to Life: Youth / Adult***

How does a person set and reach goals? Research has shown an interesting phenomenon. People who write *down goals and make lists of things to do generally achieve their goals.*

Have your group members study Nehemiah 2:11–6:19. From what they read they are to develop and write down Nehemiah's list of goals and "things to do."

You can then review the list of problems and responses (chart), and point out how having a clear goal, and planning what needs to be done to reach it, helped Nehemiah be a spiritually significant person.

You may want to give each member a sheet of paper on which to write down one goal, and these "to-do" lists: this year, this month, this week, tomorrow. Then share goals and plans in pairs.

♥ ***Link to Life: Children***

Looking ahead to set goals and plan is important for adults. It is important for

Problem	Response
• ridicule by enemies	• asked God to vindicate them; ignored the ridicule
• plot to attack the builders	• set half the people to work, half to guard with arms in hand
	• encouraged Israel to remember the Lord
• poorer Jews borrowed from wealthy; they could not repay creditors while working on walls	• got wealthy to remit interest, return the lands taken as security
	• set example by supporting himself rather than demanding the governor's allowance
• invited to a "counsel" (trap) by the enemies	• refused to be distracted; kept building the walls
• Shemaiah the prophet hired by enemies to frighten Nehemiah into hiding in the temple	• refused to hide from possible assassins; set example of courage
• threatened with a letter to Artaxerxes saying Nehemiah planned rebellion	• replied that the enemy had a good imagination; kept on with the work

Nehemiah's Problems and Responses

children to look back—to have a sense of what they have accomplished. Nehemiah seems to have done this often: it confirmed his sense of accomplishment and his commitment to the Lord (cf. 5:19; 6:14). To encourage your boys and girls to commitment, give each a one-month "calendar," ruled with squares to represent each day. Let each child pick one task he or she needs to do faithfully (perhaps study, help with dishes, make his or her bed, help with younger child, etc.). Have each child write his selected task on the top or bottom of the calendar. Then give each 30 gummed stars. Tell the children that at the end of each day, if they have done their job, they can give themselves a star for that day.

How good it is to look back and like Nehemiah to know we have been faithful in doing something that pleases the Lord.

Covenanting with God (Neh. 9:1–10:39). Nehemiah had a spiritual impact on the people he governed. Rebuilding the walls of Jerusalem had given the people a new sense of their identity as God's people. Success despite opposition had helped them realize that their God truly was among them, as small as their people and land had become. And then Nehemiah had the whole people assemble to hear the Word of God read and explained by Ezra (8:1-18). The new sense of God's presence, combined with the realization of what God required, led to national repentance and recommitment.

The national prayer (Neh. 9) of repentance follows a familiar pattern. What is new is that the people determined to make a "binding agreement" with God, even putting it in writing and affixing their seals to the document. The contents of this document are repeated in 10:28-39.

The commitments listed there reflect both the sins that had been committed, and the intentions of the people of the land to correct them.

How important that we too clearly define our intentions as we make fresh starts in our spiritual lives. Good but unspecified intentions are not likely to result in reform. When we clearly define what a fresh spiritual commitment may mean in terms of how it will affect our lives, we are far more likely to follow through.

Facing discouragement (Neh. 13). Nehemiah had made a commitment to Artaxerxes to return to the Persian capital at a set time. He did so, and stayed for an unspecified time. Then Nehemiah returned.

He was shocked and discouraged when he came back. The people of Judah had not followed through on their written commitments. The house of God was neglected; the Levites were forced back to the land because the tithes that would have supported them as they served at the temple had not been paid. The people again violated the Sabbath by working and trading. And again the men of Judah had married foreign wives.

How discouraging it must have been. And yet Nehemiah's personal commitment never flagged. He again confronted the sins of his people, and again demanded that they live up to their earlier commitments.

It is discouraging for us when others may not maintain a high level of spiritual commitment. But it is no excuse. Nehemiah shows us that whatever others may do, the individual who is fully committed to the Lord can live a holy life—and can affect the lives of others for good.

TEACHING GUIDE

Prepare
Read through the Book of Nehemiah as you might read a story or newspaper article. Afterward, jot down your dominant impressions of this godly man. What traits do you want to see in group members?

Explore
1. Give a minilecture overview of the period. You may want to make a sketch of the map in Study Guide 43 to put Judah's condition in perspective. Explain why building the walls was so important to Nehemiah.
2. Or tell the Hollis story and help your group members identify the feelings that lead believers to sense a need for a fresh start. See the "link-to-life" suggestion on page 307.

Expand
1. Develop "fresh start" and "staying power" prayer patterns. Nehemiah's "fresh start" prayer was a prayer of compassion. Use the process outlined in "link-to-life," page 308, to teach the process.

Nehemiah's "staying power" prayers were practical, quick prayers that showed reliance on God while he kept on with his task. Point out that if we continue to be aware of God's presence and rely on Him in our hard times, we'll have the courage to keep on with our work and to reach our goals, as Nehemiah did.
2. Or help your group members explore the importance of setting goals and working systematically to accomplish them. Nehemiah 2–6 can help your group members learn how to establish this vital practice. See "link-to-life, page 309.

Apply
Look with your group at Nehemiah 10, where the people wrote down spiritual commitments: promises of what they would do to serve God better. Give five minutes for each person to write out personal commitments. Close in prayer that each might have the strength of Nehemiah to carry them out.

STUDY GUIDE 45
Esther

GOD'S PROVIDENTIAL CARE

Overview

Events in this book are set in the era of the Persian Empire, sometime between 483 and 471 B.C. Xerxes the Great ruled: the same Xerxes who invaded Greece, but was thrown back.

Chronologically Esther comes between the return of a first group of Jews to Judah from Babylon (538 B.C.) and the return of a second group led back by Ezra (458 B.C.).

Events are set not in Babylon but at Susa, which lay closer to the Persian Gulf. Archeologists have not recovered documents that mention either Esther or her uncle, Mordecai. But the detailed descriptions of Persian court practices and customs in Esther have been shown to be completely accurate.

The Book of Esther is unusual in that nowhere is God mentioned. Yet again and again the story told there shows our sovereign God working quietly, behind the scenes, shaping events so that His good purpose for His people is achieved.

Another important contribution of Esther is to document what happened to the Jews who did not return to Judah. Esther 3:8 shows that they had scattered throughout the empire "among the peoples in all the provinces" of the empire, and that there they kept "themselves separate."

■ See the verse-by-verse commentary on Esther in the *Bible Knowledge Commentary,* pages 699-713.

▶ ***Providence.*** The word is not in the Bible. But the doctrine that God is in full control of all events is taught—and is illustrated fully in Esther.

Commentary

The Book of Esther should be read at a single sitting, and read as a story. It *is* a story, filled with drama and excitement, with plots and subplots. And most exciting of all, this story is true!

And, like the rest of Scripture, the Book of Esther has a living word for us today as well.

We can sense the impact of this great book by looking at three aspects: the story, the heroine, and the message.

The Story

Xerxes (Zurk-seez) was holding one of the drinking parties for which history tells us he was famous. When his wife ignored a command to visit the party, Xerxes set her aside. There would be no "women's lib" in Persia!

Immediately a search was begun for a new queen, while the king gave his attention to the four-year process of gathering an army to invade Greece. It was not until after his defeat in the west that Xerxes finally chose a new queen. When he did, he chose Esther, the adopted daughter of a minor court official named Mordecai.

The book then tells of the anger of a high court official named Haman when he thought he had been slighted by Mordecai. Haman determined to have his revenge. He would not only have Mordecai executed: he would have his entire race exterminated! When Haman asked Xerxes for permission, it was granted casually!

But Mordecai had earlier warned the king of a plot on his life, and somehow his reward was overlooked. One night Xerxes could not sleep, and had the record of his rule read. Mordecai's act was reported there, but no reward was mentioned.

Meanwhile, Mordecai had urged Esther to speak to the king for her race. She was afraid, but risked the anger of Xerxes, who was known for his instability and rages. She asked Xerxes and Haman to her apartments for dinner the next day. At that dinner, she requested the king's and Haman's presence at a second dinner the following day.

The morning of the second dinner, Haman came to the palace and was asked advice on how to honor someone the king wished to reward. Haman, thinking he was the one to be honored, outlined what should be done—and then was commanded by Xerxes to personally lead Mordecai, clad in the king's own robes and riding a royal horse, through the capital, shouting loudly that this was one the king wished to honor.

Then at dinner Esther accused Haman of wickedly plotting against *her* race, and revealed that she was a Jew. When one of the king's servants volunteered that Haman had actually had a gallows erected on which to hang Mordecai, whom the king had ordered him to honor, Xerxes had Haman and his sons hanged there instead.

According to custom, once a royal decree had been published, it could not be revoked. So Xerxes gave Mordecai his seal and told him to write any decree in Xerxes' name that would correct the situation. The new decree simply gave the Jews the right to organize, and to protect themselves by killing those who planned to kill them. No victims could be plundered, so the motives of the defenders could not be greed.

When the appointed day came the Jews did defend themselves and many of their enemies were killed. Mordecai became a powerful figure in the empire, and used his position to promote the welfare of his people.

The great deliverance reported in Esther is celebrated today by the Jewish people on March 13 and 14, and is known as the Feast of Purim.

♥ ***Link to Life: Youth / Adult***

To get the impact of the Book of Esther it should be treated as it is—an exciting but true story. If you have an especially good reader in your group, have him or her simply read the story aloud from the Bible. This may take about half your group time. But reading will give all a unique feel for and sensitivity to this book.

If you wish, you might divide up into listening teams. Team one: Listen for turning points. What were key events on which future happenings depended? Team two: Listen for Esther's character. What kind of person was she? What were her strengths and weaknesses? Team three: Listen for Mordecai's character. What kind of person was he? What were his strengths and weaknesses?

After the reading, have listening team members discuss together what they heard. Then have each listening team share with the rest of the group.

Esther

Esther was an orphan girl brought up in the home of her uncle, Mordecai.

As a young woman Esther was presented to the palace as a candidate to replace the deposed queen of Xerxes. She was pleasant as well as beautiful, and became a favorite of the eunuch in charge of the king's harem. He advised Esther, and by following his advice she pleased the king more than the others. As a result Xerxes made Esther queen, and proclaimed an empire-wide holiday.

Esther seems to have been a responsive and compliant personality, eager to please people in authority. Esther 2:19-20 tells us that she even continued to respect Mordecai and follow his instructions, just as when he was bringing her up.

The picture we have is of an attractive but somewhat uncertain young woman. She is eager to please others, but perhaps not one who was used to taking personal initiative or responsibility.

It must have been particularly difficult for Esther when suddenly the fate of her people appeared to depend on her taking responsibility, and acting with strength and initiative.

Chapter 4 of the book describes Esther's time of stress. When the king's decree to destroy the Jews was published, Mordecai, like other Jews throughout the kingdom, wept and tore his clothing, to show the intensity of his grief and to humble himself before the Lord.

When Esther heard of Mordecai's behavior, she sent a trusted servant to find out what was wrong. Mordecai explained the situation and gave the servant a copy of the edict, with instructions to show it to Queen Esther "and explain it to her" (v. 8). Mordecai also urged Esther to go to the king and beg for mercy for her people.

Esther listened to the explanation. But she was unwilling to go to the king! She reminded Mordecai what everyone in the kingdom knew: "that for any man or woman who approaches the king in the inner court without being summoned the king has but one law: that he be put to death. The only exception to this is for the king to extend the gold scepter to him and spare his life. But 30 days have passed since I was called to go to the king" (v. 11).

Mordecai answered bluntly and perhaps a little harshly. "Do not think that because you are in the king's house you alone of all the Jews will escape. For if you remain silent at this time, relief and deliverance for the Jews will arise from another place, but you and your father's family will perish. And who knows but that you have come to royal position for such a time as this?" (vv. 12-14)

Mordecai's response seems to confirm the picture of Esther as a rather unsure and timid person, whose advancement rested not so much on her character as on her beauty and her eagerness to please. Now her uncle warned her harshly. If she did not act, the Jews would survive somehow. But she would not. And Mordecai added the thought that perhaps God had been at work in the circumstances of her advancement: she may have come to her royal position for just such a time as this.

Esther finally decideed. She asked Mordecai to have all the Jews fast for three days. She and her staff would fast too. Then she would risk going to the king, "even though it is against the law." And, she added, "If I perish, I perish" (v. 16).

There are several things to encourage us in this story. First, even a person not noted for courage can rise to the occasion when it is necessary. Esther was able to act against her normal character. The possibility to live beyond our normal potential exists for all of us.

Second, when a person faces his or her fear, that fear can be dealt with. The text suggests that Esther was still—and understandably—afraid. Yet she faced her fears and determined to act anyway. Esther would do what she had to do, realizing that she could not control the outcome.

Finally, Esther determined to act in faith. While "prayer" is not mentioned in the text, fasting was associated in Israel with appeals to God for deliverance from danger and other religious observances (cf. Jud. 20:26; 2 Chron. 20:3; Ezra 8:21; Neh. 9:1). Esther realized that what happened to her depended entirely on the will of God.

Esther then approached the king. He raised the gold scepter, sparing her life, and called her to him. Though the king urged her to make a request, Esther hesitated. Instead of telling him the situation and appealing for her people, Esther invited Xerxes and Haman to her apartments for supper. There, at a second banquet, she accused Haman and begged for her own life and the lives of her people. The king flew into one of the rages for which history says he was famous. When a servant volunteered the information that Haman had built a gallows for Mordecai, "who spoke up to help the king" (7:9), Xerxes had Haman hanged on it.

Mordecai had been right. Esther had come to her royal position "for such a time as this."

While the traits that led to her rise were traits that made it more difficult for her to act with initiative, she found the inner strength to do what was right when act she must.

How good to realize that, like Esther, we are not trapped even by our weaknesses. God uses us as we are, placing us where we can serve Him and others. If a time comes that we must step out of character to do His work, the Lord will give us the grace to live beyond our capabilities.

♥ ***Link to Life: Children***

The story of Esther can help boys and girls to choose God's way by trusting Him when afraid, just as Esther did. After telling the story, draw a diagram of the palace, perhaps like that on page 315. Point out that Esther was afraid to go to the inner court where the king was. Put a gummed star on the "inner court" in the diagram. Point out that Esther knew it was right to try to save her people. So she trusted God and did what was right, even though she was afraid.

Then ask your boys and girls to draw a diagram of some place where they may be afraid. This can be a place at home, or in school, or in their neighborhoods.

Have each child explain his drawing and tell where and why he or she is sometimes afraid. When a child has explained, put a star(s) on the place(s) identified, as you did on the palace diagram. Say: "I know you'll be brave and do what's right when you're afraid, Julie, just as Esther did."

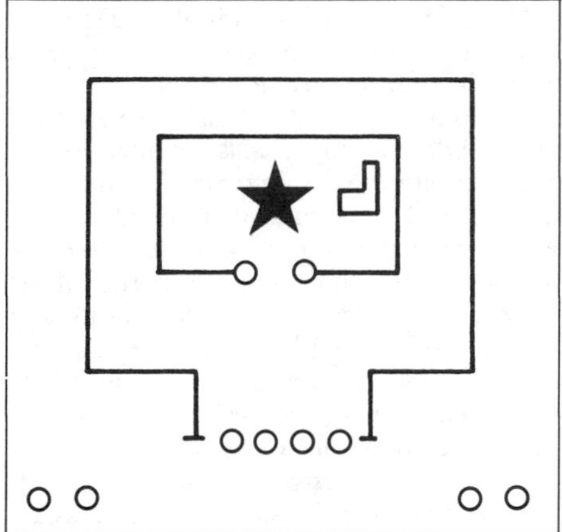

Palace

You may want to give each child one or more gummed stars to put in the home or school location where they are afraid, as a reminder in that situation to be like Esther and do what is right when afraid.

The Lesson of Esther

The greatest contribution of the Book of Esther is to our appreciation for God's providential care.

Bible miracles demonstrate God's ability to intervene directly in space and time. God is not limited in His power but is fully capable of controlling what happens in our "real" world. The wonders of the Exodus, with its miraculous plagues on Egypt, its passage through the Red Sea, and the daily manna God supplied, were obvious interventions by God on behalf of His people.

But the obvious miracle is not the norm in Scripture. Instead history, like our own daily life, tends to flow in a "natural" way. There is a process, a sequence of events in which causes lead to effects, and both cause and effect can be traced and understood.

To some people the flow is simply one of chance. You "happen" to meet a person waiting in a line, and that "happens" to lead to a job where you "happen" to meet a person who becomes your spouse. How lucky, people say.

To the ancient Greeks the flow of cause and effect seemed more grim. The Greeks tended to fix on tragedy, and so believed in a mindless "fate" that ruined the hopes of people no matter what they did. It was still all chance. Not good luck, but bad luck. And there was nothing a person could really do to affect those things that shaped and influenced his life.

And then, in Esther, we see another view. The God of miracles, who has at times intervened in obvious supernatural acts to benefit His people, is also at work in the flow of "natural" events as well! God superintends the "chance" experiences that prove to be the turning point in the lives of individuals and in the history of nations.

This is the Christian doctrine of providence: the conviction that the God of the Bible is in full control of the details of every life.

As we look at Esther we can see a number of turning points: events on which the story and its resolution hinge. We can, in effect, see God setting the stage for happenings that led to the deliverance of His people, the Jews.

What are some of the turning points, the indicators of a God of providence at work, in this Bible book?

- Mordecai, a minor court official, adopted his beautiful niece when her parents died. He was in position to have her presented as a candidate for queen.
- Vashti, the queen, refused to appear at Xerxes' command, causing her to be deposed.
- Hegai, the eunuch in charge of Xerxes' harem, took a liking to Esther and helped her win the king's approval.
- Mordecai uncovered a plot against Xerxes, and through Esther saved the king's life. But the king "overlooked" a reward for Mordecai.
- When Haman consulted diviners to pick the ideal time to carry out his plot to destroy the Jews, the lot fell on a time 12 months later. This delay gave Mordecai and Esther time to counter the plot (see 3:7).
- Mordecai urged Esther to act, calling on her to realize that she might have come "to royal position for such a time as this" (4:14).
- The night before Xerxes and Haman were to come to Esther's banquet, the king was unable to sleep. He ordered the chronicles of his reign to be read to him, and "happened" to come across the record of Mordecai's discovery of

the plot against Xerxes' life. The king asked how Mordecai was rewarded, and when he learned no reward was given, Xerxes determined to honor him.

- When Esther accused Haman at her banquet, one of the king's attendants told of a gallows Haman had built for Mordecai. The furious king ordered Haman to be hanged on it.

In all these things, and especially in the timing of the events so that one circumstance led "naturally" to another, each turning point channeled history to the reported end. The Jewish people were saved.

But, we might ask, what about the events that led to the danger initially? What about Mordecai's refusal to honor Haman, which first aroused his anger and placed the Jewish people in danger?

We can draw two possible conclusions here. Perhaps Mordecai's pride should be blamed, for his actions placed his whole people in danger. Many events in our world flow directly from human sinfulness, and while God rules in all things, He need not be held responsible for willful human actions.

But another conclusion is also suggested. Even if Mordecai acted in foolish pride when he refused to honor Haman, God seems to have used Mordecai's weakness for good. For the Bible tells us that in the months between issuing the decree to kill the Jews and the time that Mordecai and Esther were able to reverse it, that "in every province to which the edict and order of the king came, there was great mourning among the Jews, with fasting, weeping, and wailing. Many lay on sackcloth and ashes" (4:3). The danger led Jews everywhere to turn to God wholeheartedly!

This is a perspective that each of us needs to gain. Even the disasters that strike us are intended for our good. God is in control, and He is able to sanctify even our tragedies.

And so Esther teaches us many lessons about God's providential care. The events from which our lives and the history of nations are woven are not subject merely to change. They rest in the hands of a God who cares for us; a God who sometimes permits pain, but who is well able to transform pain into joy as we rely fully on Him.

TEACHING GUIDE

Prepare

What events in your life show God's providential care?

Explore

Read the Book of Esther aloud to your group, as you might read a story. See "link-to-life," page 313, on how to set up listening teams that will focus on different aspects of the story.

Expand

1. Do a character study of Esther, drawing particularly from Esther 4:1–5:8. What was Esther like? What were her weaknesses? What were her strengths? What does Mordecai seem to have thought of her? Would it be easy or hard for Esther to take initiative and to take a personal risk on behalf of her people?

What is one encouraging thing you see in Esther's story that can be applied to your own life?

2. List on the chalkboard the turning points identified in this unit. Or have your group members suggest the turning points after hearing the Book of Esther read.

Explain the doctrine of providence, and show how this story with its many "chance" happenings illustrates providence.

Then have each group member think of a time in his or her life when a similar set of events proved turning points in his or her life. Write down the "chance" events that set a new direction.

In groups of three to five, share what each person has jotted down, and discuss: "How do these events illustrate God's providential care? What has God done in your life or through you that hinged on the events you wrote down?"

Apply

Discuss: "Does the person who knows God see Him more clearly in miracle or in providence? Why might some find it hard to sense God's hand in seemingly 'chance' events?"

Close in prayer that your group members will learn to recognize God in all the events of their lives.

STUDY GUIDE 46

Job

THE SUFFERER

Overview

The Book of Job is very old. The dialogue section is written in the most difficult and archaic Hebrew in the Old Testament. There is no mention here of the Law, no reference to Abraham or to the covenants. The book should probably be dated to the time of the patriarchs, sometime between 2100 and 1700 B.C.

The Book of Job, written before the time of Moses, gives us insight into what people knew about God before mankind had been given a written revelation. Job suggested that human beings knew God as personal and transcendent, Master of the world He created. As Creator of men, God permits us freedom of choice and thus holds human beings morally responsible. As a moral being Himself, God punishes evil and rewards those who do right. But God is loving. He can be approached through sacrifice. And God forgives sinners who repent and turn to Him. Yet even though through tradition and vision Job and his friends knew much about the Lord, ultimately He remained hidden.

In the Book of Job the mystery of God's working with human beings is explored through the suffering of the hero, a good man, who like his friends simply cannot understand why God permits him to suffer if he is truly innocent.

Outline

I.	Prologue: Satan's Test	1:1–2:10
II.	Dialogue with Friends	2:11–31:40
III.	Elihu's Contribution	32:1–37:24
IV.	The Lord Speaks	38:1–41:34
V.	Epilogue: Job Restored	42:1-16

Commentary

Prologue: Job 1:1–2:10

When we meet Job we're immediately impressed. He was a surprisingly pious man, and a very wealthy one. As was common in those days, Job served as a family priest. We note that his material wealth had not led him to pride, but seemed to have deepened his sense of humility and his awareness of sin. In fact, Job regularly offered sacrifices to God to cover possible hidden sins of his family. Job knew nothing against his sons, but he did know the deceit of the human heart.

Our own impression of Job has surprising corroboration. While we're visiting the man, God Himself is pointing Job out to Satan!

Job 1:6-12 depicts a striking scene. Satan presented himself to God and made his report (vv. 6-7). At this time God directed Satan's attention to Job. "There is no one on earth like him," the Lord commented. "He is blameless and upright, a man who fears God and shuns evil."

Satan responded. Job's piety had certainly been profitable! "Have You not put a hedge around him?" Then Satan proposed a test. If God would only *take away* the blessings Job had been given, Satan said, "he will surely curse You to Your face" (v. 11). And so the ground rules for a test were laid. God would permit Satan to attack the protected believer, and Satan would try to force from Job's tortured lips a rejection of the Lord.

What happened then is too familiar. In a single day all that Job had was torn from him. His oxen and donkeys were rustled by Sabeans and his herders were killed. His sheep were destroyed by fire falling from heaven. His camels were lost to a raiding band of Chaldeans. And a tornado struck the house where his 10 children were feasting, and all the young people were killed. And the Bible tells us, "Job got up and tore his robe and shaved his head [signs of mourning in the East]. Then he fell to the ground in worship" (v. 20). Total tragedy had not torn a denial of God from Job's lips, nor did his anguish lead him to charge God with wrong.

But Satan was not done. When on another day God pointed out that Job "maintains his integrity" (2:3), Satan cynically asked for the ultimate test. "A man will give all he has for his life" (v. 4). So God permitted Satan to touch Job's person. For any extremity short of death, Job was in the tempter's power.

The extremity of the physical suffering Job underwent is hard for us to imagine now. But we have a witness. Job's wife was finally moved to beg Job to "curse God and die" (v. 9), and so find death's release. But to Job the Lord is still God. Satan met his defeat, for "in all this, Job did not sin in what he said" (v. 10).

This is the last time we see Satan in the Book of Job! The initial test is over. But Job's suffering does not end! In fact, Job's suffering seems to intensify. We have to conclude that there is more involved here than a personal battle between God and Satan with Job as a helpless pawn.

In fact, the Book of Job can be best understood if we see it as a cosmic court scene where Job had his sincerity and integrity questioned by Satan, the "prosecuting attorney," and found his own friends acting as witnesses against him. God acted as Judge, and finally vindicated Job. The tension, however, revolves around a single question: Why do the righteous suffer? And this question moves naturally into a consideration of the nature of God.

So the Book of Job does not simply invite us to observe Job's suffering. It calls us to enter, with him, into a pain-filled struggle to understand our own suffering as well.

♥ ***Link to Life: Children***

God permits the troubles that we have. But usually He protects us from troubles. Use the imagery in Job to help boys and girls sense God's care.

Build a "living hedge." Have boys and girls hold hands and form a circle. Let one child stand in the center of the circle. Then have a sign on a string labeled "troubles." Put it around your neck, and pretend to try to reach through the "living hedge" to the child in the middle.

Point out that God builds a hedge around people who trust Him. The only way we can be touched by troubles is if God opens up the hedge and lets them through. (Act this out too with your living hedge.)

Let different children take the protected place in the center. Talk about thanking God for His protection from troubles. Talk too about how Job thanked God even when the Lord opened up the hedge and let troubles in. Job believed that God loved him even in his troubles. We can keep on trusting God even when He permits us to have troubles.

♥ ***Link to Life: Youth / Adult***

Before your group members come in, write on the chalkboard: "Satan has only limited power to harm us." Also have written "Job 1:1–2:10."

As members enter ask each to read the Job passage and underline phrases that suggest the statement written on the board is true.

The Three Friends: Job 2:11–31:40

Outwardly unmoved by his troubles, Job inwardly was in turmoil. As the days of agony continued, his inner doubts and fears must have been far more excruciating for Job than the physical pain. He was a man who had built his life on piety and honesty. Now the God he had served had turned against him. Certainly the timing and the method of the losses Job suffered made it clear: this was the hand of the Lord.

The question that tormented Job was "Why?" When three friends came from their homes to comfort and console Job, they hardly recognized him. In tears they sat with him for seven days and nights, so moved by his suffering that they could not bring themselves to speak. Then, plagued by the tormenting questions within, Job began a dialogue that continues through the next 28 chapters of the book that bears his name.

Because the Book of Job is written in difficult poetry and with unfamiliar imagery, the best way to teach it may be by summarizing the arguments of the participants, and by putting their thoughts in modern language. As we do, we can understand their difficulties as they struggle with the problem of suffering and evil in human experience. For these were people like you and me, who feel the heat of suffering's flame and are desperate to at least understand what they cannot avoid.

♥ ***Link to Life: Youth / Adult***
To teach this major section of the book, you have permission to make copies of the dialogue that follows. Give members of your group the roles of Job, Eliphaz, Zophar, and Bildad. Then read this as a play, while your group members watch and listen.
To help them listen carefully you might ask some to jot down notes on the ideas about God held by these men. Others might jot notes on how they explain suffering, or why the idea that the innocent can suffer is so hard for any of them to accept. Some should listen to Job's feelings, to sense just why he was in such inner anguish.

Job (3:1-26)

"I'm sorry I was ever born. Why didn't I die at birth? I'd have been better off. At least there's no misery then.

"I knew things were going to no good. I was afraid of something like this all along.

"I'd be better off dead than suffering all this trouble."

Eliphaz (4:1–5:27)

"I've got to answer that. Remember how you counseled other people? Remember how you held out hope to those who would walk in integrity?

"After all, the innocent don't perish. God punishes the sinner. If I were you, I'd turn to God.

"God is clearly chastising you, and when you turn to Him, He'll restore you."

Job (6:1–7:21)

"If you only knew how much God is making me suffer! I wish He'd crush me and get it over with!

"As for you, Eliphaz, you're a lot of help. Show me what I've done wrong! I tell you the truth: I just can't be suffering chastisement. I've been good.

"Oh, how I'm suffering! I just can't keep quiet any longer. I tell you, I'm terrified! I'd rather die in a minute.

"Why does God let this happen? If I'd sinned He could have pardoned it. What's happening to me?"

Bildad (8:1-22)

"That's a terrible way to talk! Is God ever unjust? Never!

"If you were pure and prayed to God, He'd surely pardon you.

"Just think back. Our fathers taught us that the man who forgets God is the one who fails. But God doesn't punish the upright. So you're bound to come out all right if [*aside*] you're upright."

Job (9:1–10:22)

"I know what you're saying is true. But how can anyone really have any standing with God? He's so far above us. What can I say to Him? How can I reach Him?

"I wish I could. I wish I could plead my innocence in some court. But who's going to judge between me and God? I say I'm righteous, but God still afflicts me.

"And no one can judge, can make Him stop whipping me.

"I wish I could die.

"God, cut it out!

"I didn't do anything. Show me where I sinned. You know I'm not wicked.

"If I were, I'd deserve punishment. But I don't. Why did You ever let me grow up to be mistreated like this, and then just to die?"

Zophar (11:1-20)

"How can you expect to be justified talking like that?

"Why, you're full of boasting.

" 'I'm just,' you say. 'I'm pure,' you blab.

"Ha! If God would talk, He'd tell you! God knows. He sees secret sin.

"But there's still hope. Get your heart right with God, and He'll still accept you. But watch out. There's no escape for the wicked. Their only hope is death."

Job (12:1–14:22)

"You guys are so smart. You sure know it all.

"Well, I know just as much as you.

"I know God has all wisdom and power.

"I know He sets people up, and knocks them down. Sure God is working in our lives.

"Oh, I wish I could talk to God about it. You stick up for God, and say I must be wrong. Well, you're wrong! You're unfair, on His side.

"I know I'm right. I'd say it to God's face as well as to yours. I'm right. I haven't done wrong.

"O God, it's not fair! Men are so frail. So weak. Stop it! Don't do this to me. You're wearing away all my hope!"

Eliphaz (15:1-35)

"Job, you've been rambling on like a fool. Why, that kind of talk itself condemns you.

"You don't know everything. God is wiser than you.

"Remember what we know about God.

"It is the wicked man who suffers.

"It is the proud man God brings low—the man who boasts against God.

"It's the godless who suffer in the end."

Job (16:1–17:16)

"Oh, you're a miserable bunch of comforters.

"Whether I talk like this or keep quiet, I still suffer.

"The fact is, God's against me. He's delivered me to the ungodly. He's putting unbearable pressure on me.

"Scoff if you will. But let heaven and earth be my witness. It's not happening because of my guilt.

"People spit on me. They mock me. You mock me with your arguments.

"My only hope is to die. Let my moldering body find rest as dust."

Bildad (18:1-21)

"Why keep on trying to justify yourself? We all know it's the wicked man who suffers terrors and falls into calamity.

"And, oh, the wicked will suffer!

"Their families will die—no one will carry on the family name.

"The wicked will dash in terror toward death. Surely this is the horrible fate of the man who doesn't know God."

Job (19:1-29)

"Stop it! Stop it! I'm not wicked. Oh, for justice—simple justice.

"But there's no hope. God's crushed me. Even you, even my relatives, have turned against me.

"Everyone says, 'God is punishing Job.' Have pity, friends. Have pity. Why do you persecute me like God does?

"I wish my side were published. Someone would vindicate me. But you—you're afraid to take my side!"

Zophar (20:1-29)

"That's enough!

"Don't you know that ever since men have been on earth that the wicked only get away with sin for a time?

"They might seem to prosper, but in the end the wicked man's life is one of gall and bitterness. His possessions will be gone, his children dead. He won't keep on prospering. God will unleash all the fierceness of His wrath on him.

"That's what always happens to the wicked man.

"Get that, Job? To the wicked man!"

Job (21:1-34)

"Listen. Listen, and then mock. But now listen and be surprised.

"You talk about the end of the wicked. Well, look around. We each know wicked men who do prosper. They get old. They see their grandchildren. Their houses are safe, nothing bad seems to happen to them.

"God doesn't use His rod on them. Why, they mock God! They say, 'Why serve God? We're doing all right without Him. Where's the profit in prayer?'

"How often do folks like this really get what they deserve?

"Oh, you say, they get it in the end.

"But *when?* Why, God's children seem to suffer more than the ungodly!

"*Who* repays the wicked? Your answers are all lies!"

Eliphaz (22:1-30)

"Well, what good is it to God that you're so righteous? Do you suppose He's clapping and jumping up and down over your goodness?

"Why does He reprove you, then?

"Let's face it. This has happened because you're a big, wicked, terrible sinner.

"God knows. He sees things we didn't, things you've done at night, skulking about.

"But now you've shown your true colors. Who said, 'What's the profit in prayer?' Why, that's your own heart talking. You hypocrite!

"Listen, Job, seek God now. Listen to Him. If you return to God and put away your sins, He'll restore all the good things you had.

"Pray. God will hear you.

"God saves the humble man, the innocent. Turn from your sin. You can still be delivered."

Job (23:1–24:25)

"I wish I could talk to God. He'd have to

listen. I'm right. I am innocent. God would have to agree.

"But He's hidden—He's hiding.

"I've done right.

"I've done His will.

"I've kept His commandments.

"Why does He do this to me? I'm terrified!

"God knows what's happening, but He doesn't act. People are murdered. People steal. People commit adultery. And the poor suffer.

"And the wicked prosper! God upholds them. Be honest. It's true.

"Prove me a liar."

Bildad (25:1-6)

"God is always right. We men, how can we be just with God? How could we, worms that we are, explain His actions?"

Job (26:1–27:12)

"How you've helped poor, weak me. Thanks!

"I know God's power—His majesty. How far beyond our conception His might is.

"But as God lives, He's treating me unjustly.

"I won't lie, even for God.

"I won't confess sin.

"I have been righteous. I'll hold to that fact as long as I live.

"I'll never admit it's my fault."

Zophar (27:13–28:28)

"I say it again. God does indeed judge the wicked.

"Wealth is hidden in a mine, deep underground, out of sight. But it's there. God's ways aren't to be compared with wealth—sapphires, gold, rubies—for value. But God's wisdom may be as hard to seek out.

"But remember, Job, He is God! As for us, it is enough to know that 'the fear of the Lord is wisdom, to leave evil is understanding.' "

Job (29:1–31:40)

"I've never done any wrong. If I have, convict me. I'll take my punishment.

"But I haven't.

"I am clean.

"That's all I have to say."

Job's morality. Throughout the dialogue Job insisted that he was righteous. Several of Job's speeches indicated the principles of right and wrong by which this man lived. When Job served as a judge, seated with other elders at the city gates, he "rescued the poor who cried for help, and the fatherless who had none to assist him" (29:12). Job searched out any who were defrauding or taking advantage of the poor. He "broke the fangs of the wicked, and snatched the victims from their teeth" (v. 17). Job took an active role in crusading for what we today call social justice. In our modern world he would have been an aggressive enemy of city slum landlords and economic oppression.

Job's sexual life was also pure. His public and private morality matched. He did not lust after the virgins or envy his neighbor his wife (31:1, 9). Job rejected falsehood and dealt honestly with all. No thumb on the scales for Job; what he sold he always weighed out fairly, giving full measure. If any of his employees had a complaint, Job listened and never rejected the cause. (If only management and labor had this attitude today!)

If any poor had need, if any strangers were hungry, if any were perishing for lack of clothing, Job met their need. Though rich, Job avoided the great hazard of the materialist. He put his confidence in God, not in his wealth. Job even avoided prideful joy in his riches. Never was Job false to God by lifting possession or idols above the Lord.

No wonder the Scriptures tell us God pointed Job out to Satan as a unique servant, and affirmed, "There is no one on earth like him; he is blameless and upright, a man who fears God and shuns evil" (2:3). Job was truly an admirable man.

Yet it was a man like this which divine judgment seemed to strike. In Job's case, it was not an evil man who suffered at God's hand, but a good man. In the face of this mystery, Job and his friends were forced to examine the foundations of their faith, and to question their very concept of God.

And this is what the Book of Job asks us to do: to risk confronting mystery. To be willing to admit that perhaps the idea we have of God may not be God at all!

♥ ***Link to Life: Youth / Adult***

Today many people like Job's friends try

to explain suffering as punishment for sin. And they urge the sufferer to confess and get right with God. Ask your group members if they have ever known such "comforters." What is wrong with the hasty conclusion that when anything bad happens God is punishing? What other explanations for trouble might there be? How should they respond to a well-meaning but mistaken comforter?

Elihu's Contribution: Job 32–37
Job's three friends had held fast to their brittle concept of God, sure that God *must* act to punish sin and reward good—now. Because they admitted no freedom of action for God, they concluded that Job had sinned and his troubles were a divine judgment.

The tragedy was that Job agreed with this assessment! He could find no explanation other than sin for suffering. Yet Job knew that he had not sinned. Impaled on the agonizing dilemma, Job was forced to go further and further and to question God's justice. Finally he faced the fact that in this world the evil do *not* always suffer. And that at times believers may have more difficulties than unbelievers!

This line of reasoning was fearfully rejected by the three. Job *had to* be forced to admit he had sinned, or they must change the picture of God they had hung in their hearts to worship.

But then a young observer broke in. Elihu had been silent as the older men talked. But Elihu had been frustrated by their circular argument. Finally, about to burst, Elihu broke in.

The three friends had reasoned syllogistically: Suffering is punishment for sin; Job was suffering; therefore Job was being punished for some sin. Job rejected the conclusion, but could not reject either premise! Now, what Elihu did was to show that the premises need not be accepted! *God may use suffering to instruct as well as to punish* (33:19-30).

Elihu couldn't say just *why* God had permitted Job's suffering. But Elihu had shown that suffering is not *necessarily* punishment for sin.

Elihu went on to point out that no one will be able to really understand God. He simply is too great to fit into our categories. We can, however, be sure that He is great in power and justice, and that His character is marked by a "great righteousness He does not oppress" (37:23).

God Speaks: Job 38–41
Elihu had prepared the way. Then God spoke. But in speaking God neither reassured His servant, nor explained the reason for Job's suffering. Instead God revealed His omnipotence (38:1–40:2), and then compared His power with human frailty (40:10–41:34). No one can demand to meet God on equal terms. God and man simply are not equal. God is the Lord. And human beings mere creatures of the dust.

Job suddenly understood. He accepted his position as a creature before the Creator, and asked no more for a confrontation.

> I spoke of things I did not understand, things too wonderful for me to know. . . . My ears had heard of You but now my eyes have seen You. Therefore I despise myself and repent in dust and ashes.
>
> Job 42:3-6

The confrontation was over. Job had bowed his knee. Job had recognized God as God. Beyond this, the questioning sufferer had received no answer.

Epilogue: Job 42
The conclusion of the story (42:7-16) seems to many to be an anticlimax. Job's wealth is restored double. He has seven more sons and three more daughters. And Job is told to pray for his three friends because, God said to them, "You have not spoken of Me what is right, as My servant Job has" (v. 7).

Thus the Book of Job leaves us with more questions than when we began. But perhaps it suggests answers.

How did Job speak what was right, and his friends incur God's anger in the dialogue? Perhaps because only Job was willing to test his concept of God against his own experience and observation. True faith is no retreat from reality, but a willingness to face mystery. Job's three friends were unwilling to admit the possibility that their understanding of God might be imperfect. Is it possible that their trust was not in God but in an image they had constructed in His likeness?

Why did Job suffer? No answer is given in the text. But there are clues. For instance, at the beginning Job cries out that what he feared has come upon him (3:25). Can it be that Job's relationship with God was flawed by a fear that blocked full trust and love? Certainly Job's meeting with God replaced hearing with sight. Job lost all trust in his own righteousness as the basis for a standing with God (42:6), and simply bowed down before the Lord.

Deep release and freedom are available for us too when we let God's perfect love cast out our fear and no longer think of what we do as having merit in God's eyes. Like Job we need to trust in the Lord and to abandon reliance on any righteousness of ours.

What do we learn about our suffering? One message is clear. We wrong God if we fall into the way of thinking of Job's three friends. We wrong God if each trial of ours is excused by condemning ourselves for supposed sins. Instead, we need to approach God with trust in His love and His righteousness. His purposes will be just and what He does in our lives will be for our good.

The New Testament adds special insight here. In 1 Peter God assures those who suffer for doing right that, when such suffering does come, it is a special purposive act of the Lord. Christ also suffered though He was innocent, and through that suffering accomplished the wonderful purpose of bringing us to God (see 1 Peter 3:13-18).

We may not know exactly why Job suffered, or why we sometimes suffer. But we can know that the suffering of God's own is purposive, intended for good. Like Job, and like Jesus, when suffering comes we must simply trust.

TEACHING GUIDE

Prepare

Read through the dialogue section in this unit again, to sense Job's feelings. How many in your group may be suffering because they can't understand why God is letting them suffer?

Explore

1. Ask, "Have you ever wondered why God was permitting you to suffer?" Ask two or three who have to tell about the experience. Ask particularly how they felt; why the uncertainty made the suffering even more painful.

Then ask what others who wanted to help said or did. What was most helpful? What was least helpful?

2. Or put an outline of Job on the board, and tell briefly what happened in the first and second sections.

3. Or have your group members read Job 1:1–2:10, and write down questions these chapters raise about God, questions they raise about Satan, and questions they raise about suffering.

Compare the questions your group has come up with. Be sure someone has noted the most important question: Why did the suffering continue after Job passed the test and Satan met his defeat?

Expand

1. Explain the dialogue section of the book, and pass out copies to those who will take the parts of Job, Elihu, Eliphaz, Zophar, and Bildad.

Read the dialogue as a play.

After the reading, discuss what the group has noted in listening. Be particularly sensitive to Job's feelings and why his experience is marked by such inner torment as well as physical pain.

2. After the play and discussion, summarize Elihu's contribution, and Job's reaction to God's sudden self-revelation, as well as the return of Job's wealth.

Apply

1. As a group make a list of insights from Job that might help if and when suffering comes to members of your group. The list might be in a "to do" and "not to do" form.

2. Or, based on Job, determine how you might serve as godly comforters to people experiencing tragedy. Again, developing a "to do" and a "not to do" list may prove a good way to go about it.

If time permits, try role play. Let volunteers try to comfort "sufferers" from your class as these recall past or present experiences of suffering.

STUDY GUIDE 47

Psalms 1–73

PATTERNS OF PRAYER

Overview

The Psalms have a wonderful capacity to capture the reality of our human experience. Dr. Samuel Schultz notes in *The Old Testament Speaks* (Harper and Row) that "they express the common experience of the human race. Composed by numerous authors, the various psalms express the emotions, personal feelings, attitudes, gratitude, and interests of the average individual. Universally, people have identified their lot in life with that of the psalmists."

In every experience of our own, no matter how deep the pain or how great the frustration or how exhilarating the joy, we can find psalms which echo our inmost being; psalms which God uses to bring comfort or to confirm release.

The Psalms were written over an extended period of time, most probably coming between 1000 and 400 B.C. They were written by different authors, and at several times new groups of psalms were added to the collection. Seventy-three of the psalms were written by David. Forty-nine are anonymous.

The psalms were used in public worship in Israel, as well as for private devotions. They show us how intimate and free our relationship with God can be, as we share every thought and feeling with Him.

▶ ***Selah.*** This word appears 71 times in the psalms. The word means "to lift up" and most believe it is a musical sign, perhaps of a pause.

■ The *Bible Knowledge Commentary* discusses interpretation of the psalms and comments on each of the 150 on pages 779-899.

Commentary

The era of David brought not only political but also literary revival. Many of the psalms recorded in Scripture come from David's own pen, and many others were written during his reign.

The 150 psalms are organized into five books, which represent four later collections added to the first worship book. Book I (Pss. 1–41) is Davidic, compiled prior to his death. Book II (Pss. 42–72) was most likely added in the era of Solomon. Books III and IV (Pss. 73–89; 90–106) were probably collected during the Exile, and Book V (Pss. 107–150) in the time of Ezra. This last book is the most liturgical.

The various books of Psalms, then, are not organized by content but by the time they were added to the official worship collection. It is likely that many if not most of the psalms were used before the official compilations were made.

The structure of the books is just one of several things we need to understand before we look into this wonderful Bible book.

Hebrew poetry. Unlike English poetry, which emphasizes rhyme and meter, Hebrew poetry relies on other characteristics for its impact. These are parallelism, rhythm, and figures of speech.

Parallelism. English verse manipulates sound, and emphasizes rhyme and meter. Hebrew poetry repeats and rearranges thoughts rather than sounds. There are several types of parallel arrangement of thoughts, with three being basic.

**Synonymous parallelism* indicates verses in which the same thought is repeated in different words.

> But God in heaven merely laughs!
> He is amused by all their puny plans.
> Psalm 2:4 (TLB)

**Antithetical parallelism* indicates verses in which a thought is emphasized by a following contrasting thought.

> The lions may grow weak and hungry, but those who seek the Lord lack no good thing.
>
> Psalm 34:10

**Synthetic parallelism* indicates a pattern of adding thoughts to explain or develop an original expression.

> He is like a tree planted by streams of water, which yields its fruit in its season and whose leaf does not wither.
>
> Psalm 1:3

When reading the Psalms or any other Hebrew poetry, it is important to be aware of parallelism. Our understanding of the text, and our interpretation of it, hinges on sensing this thought pattern.

Rhythm. In the original text there are accent marks, which indicate stress to be placed on words and phrases. But this rhythm is not metrical, and it cannot be distinguished in English translations.

Figures of speech. Hebrew poetry, like the Hebrew language itself, uses vivid images, similes, and metaphors to communicate thoughts and feelings. These, like parallelism, are easily translated into other languages, even though at times idiomatic uses may be obscure.

In reading Hebrew poetry then, and especially in reading the Psalms, we need to be sensitive to these literary distinctives. We need to be aware of the role of repetition and imagery in the Psalms, and discover their meaning in these characteristics.

♥ ***Link to Life: Youth / Adult***

If you want to help your group learn how to understand the role of parallelism in the Psalms, explain the three basic types of parallelism using the illustrations given. Then pass out copies of Psalm 1. Have group members work in pairs to identify the type of parallelism found in each verse. (These are: verse 1, synthetic; verse 2, synonymous; verse 3, synthetic; verse 4, synthetic; verse 5, synthetic; verse 6, antithetical.)

Then, if you wish, ask each person to pick a favorite psalm and analyze its structure. Come together and share: "Does knowing how Hebrew poetry works give any added insights to the familiar psalm's meaning? Does it change any ideas previously held?" Have group members illustrate from their psalms as they share.

Themes of the Psalms. While the books of Psalms are not organized by topics but by the era they were added to the official collection, the Psalms do show a number of repeated themes. So we can classify some psalms by their content.

What types of psalms have been identified? Here are the major types.

**Praise psalms.* These focus on the person of God and praise Him by describing His nature or His qualities. This type of psalm is illustrated by Psalms 33, 103, and 139, and by such expressions as:

> Praise the Lord, O my soul; all my inmost being, praise His holy name. Praise the Lord, O my soul, and forget not all His benefits. He forgives all my sins and heals all my diseases; He redeems my life from the pit and crowns me with love and compassion.
>
> Psalm 103:1-4

**Historical psalms.* These review God's dealings with His people. Illustrations are Psalms 68, 78, 105, and 106, and such expressions as:

> In spite of all this, they kept on sinning; in spite of His wonders, they did not believe. So He ended their days in futility and their years in terror.
>
> Psalm 78:32-33

**Relational psalms.* These psalms explore the personal relationship which exists between God and the believer. They are illustrated by Psalms 8, 16, 20, 23, and 55, and such expressions as:

> Keep me safe, O God, for in You I take refuge. I said to the Lord, "You are *my* Lord; apart from You I have no good thing."
>
> Psalm 16:1-2 (italics added)

**Imprecatory psalms.* These are psalms in which the worshiper calls on God to overthrow the wicked. Among them are Psalms 35, 69, 109, and 137. They contain such expressions as:

> May those who seek my life be disgraced

and put to shame; may those who plot my ruin be turned back in dismay. May they be like chaff before the wind, with the angel of the Lord driving them away.

Psalm 35:4-5

**Penitential psalms.* In these the psalmist expresses sorrow over his failures and confesses his sins to God. Examples are Psalms 6, 32, 51, 102, 130, and 143. They contain expressions like:

O Lord, do not rebuke me in Your anger or discipline me in Your wrath. Be merciful to me, Lord, for I am faint; O Lord, heal me, for my bones are in agony. My soul is in anguish. How long, O Lord, how long?

Psalm 6:1-3

**Messianic psalms.* These psalms refer in some way to Christ, who is to come from David's family line. Many such psalms are indicated by references in the New Testament. Psalms which the New Testament indicates refer to Christ are Psalms 2, 8, 16, 22, 40, 45, 69, 72, 89, 102, 109–110, and 132. Others also may have messianic elements or make prophetic references.

**Liturgical psalms.* These are psalms which were used in Israel's worship at specific times of the year or on special occasions. While most of the psalms were used in public worship, these are linked with such events as coming up to Jerusalem for one of the annual festivals. Liturgical psalms may be illustrated by Psalms 30 (used in the dedication of the temple), 92 (a psalm for the Sabbath), and Psalms 120–134.

♥ ***Link to Life: Youth / Adult***

You may want to have your group sample the various types of psalms which are found in this great prayer and praise book.

As group members arrive, pass out assignment slips. Have as many of each slip as needed for everyone to have a slip. Ask your group members to look in the psalms listed for two illustrations of the thought expressed on their slip. On the slips have written:

- *What about God really moves me? Psalms 33, 103, 139*
- *What about the past teaches me about my today? Psalms 68, 78, 105*
- *What's it like to be really close to God? Psalms 16, 23, 55*
- *How do I feel when others mistreat or persecute me? Psalms 35, 69, 137*
- *What do I say when I know I've failed and fallen short? Psalms 32, 51, 130*

When your group members have chosen passages, read the questions aloud, and have those assigned that question read their verses. Then talk briefly about that type of psalm.

♥ ***Link to Life: Children***

Boys and girls will be familiar with and love Psalm 23, about their own personal relationship with God. The imagery of sheep and shepherds has spoken for nearly 3,000 years to people of all ages.

To help the children sense how loving and gracious God the Good Shepherd is, play a "sheep and shepherds" game. It's best to play this game as a department rather than as a single class.

Let three or four of the children be shepherds. They are told to love their sheep, and help take them to food and water and keep them safe.

Let the rest of the children be sheep—BUT—tell several of the children privately that they are "curious sheep." They are good sheep, and like their shepherds. But now and then they become curious and want to go look at things. Tell several others privately that they are "independent" sheep. They have minds of their own, and want to do what they want to do, when they want to do it.

Now tell the shepherds that they are to take their flock of sheep out of the room (their pen) to find cool water (a drinking fountain?), and rich grass where they can eat and drink. Afterward they are to lead the sheep back to their pen where they can get a good rest.

As the situation develops, the "shepherds" will soon become frustrated with the curious and independent sheep!

Back in the room, talk about what happened. How did the good sheep feel? How did the curious? The independent? How did the shepherds feel?

Point out that God is the Good Shepherd. We are wise when we follow Him. But even when we go astray God keeps on loving us, and cares for us always.

Then read and talk about the wonderful images of the twenty-third Psalm. Your boys and girls will have a deeper grasp of what it means for the Lord to be their Shepherd. And they will have a fresh desire to follow Him to the safe, beautiful places He will lead them.

Personal Messages from the Psalms

The Book of Psalms has long been recognized as a guidebook for prayer. As we read the psalms, there are a number of very personal messages about prayer that come through with clarity and beauty.

It's all right to be human. The Bible tells us that in Creation God viewed man, the culmination of His creative work, and affirmed that work as "very good" (Gen. 1:31). Man, the Bible says, was made in God's image, and we are taught to value our humanity. As people we do bear a certain likeness to the Lord.

Sometimes, aware that sin has entered the race and warped mankind out of the intended pattern, Christians have come to view their humanity with shame and guilt rather than pride. A person who tends to locate the identity of mankind in our character as sinners, rather than in our nature as those who bear God's image, is likely to repress human feelings and emotions. Struggling for "control," such people may be uncomfortable with strong emotions and may attempt to hold them down or to deny them.

The Bible really does teach us to affirm our value and worth as human beings. Psalm 8 speaks in wonder that God should have created man "a little lower than the heavenly beings" and "crowned him with glory and honor." Hebrews 2:10 echoes the thought that we are never to let slip the awareness that God's intention in Christ is to bring "many sons to glory." Christ calls Himself our brother; He was "made like His brethren in all things" (2:17, NASB). Far from being ashamed of his humanity, the Christian is free to rejoice in who he is, knowing that in Creation and in redemption God has affirmed our worth.

Such teaching passages might help us grasp this affirmation about man intellectually. But we are gripped by it when we read the Psalms! For here we see our own inner experiences openly shared without shame or hesitation, and we discover that God values man's inner life enough to record this dynamic record of it in His own Word.

When we read the Psalms and see in them our own emotions and struggles, we find a great release. It *is* all right to be human. It *is* all right to be ourselves. We need not fear what is within us or repress the feeling side of life.

There's a way out. One reason why emotions frighten us is that many people do not know how to express or release them. In our culture, the recognition and expression of feelings is not encouraged—especially of negative feelings. Feelings are feared. To feel anger well up within and to sense that we're on the verge of losing control is a frightening thing.

For Christians there is the added pressure of the notion that it's wrong to feel anger or sense tension. "If only I were a good Christian," we're liable to tell ourselves. "If only I were really trusting the Lord." So we feel guilt over the emotions that well up, and then, all too often, we try to deny this very important aspect of personhood.

Reading the Psalms carefully, however, we note that they often trace a process in which the writer begins with strong and almost uncontrollable feelings. We see how he struggles with them, and we see how he brings his feelings to God or relates them to what he knows of the Lord and His ways. In reading Psalms, you and I can learn how to handle our emotions creatively, and how to relate feelings to faith.

Psalm 73 is a good example of this "working through" process. It begins with the writer confessing that he has become envious of the wicked—certainly not an unusual experience when we face difficulties and then see everything going well for the person who cares nothing about God!

The psalmist shares:

> I envied the arrogant when I saw the prosperity of the wicked. They have no struggles; their bodies are healthy and strong. They are free from the burdens common to man; they are not plagued by human ills. Therefore pride is their necklace; they clothe themselves with violence. . . . They say, "How can God know? Does the Most High have knowledge?" This is what the wicked are like—always carefree, they increase in wealth.

> Surely in vain have I kept my heart pure; in vain have I washed my hands in innocence. All day long I have been plagued; I have been punished every morning.
>
> Psalm 73:3-6, 11-14

How hard it seemed! What good was it to be good? Frustration, envy, self-pity—all had gripped Asaph, the Levite who wrote this psalm, and who now faced rather than repressed his inner state.

The passage goes on to explain how the writer handled these feelings. First of all, he tried to think the problem through, but "it was oppressive to me" (v. 16). He went to God with his problem, to pray at His sanctuary. There God gave him an answer. Asaph's thoughts were directed to the end toward which the sinner's life leads.

> Surely You place them on slippery places; You cast them down to ruin. How suddenly they are destroyed, completely swept away by terrors! As a dream when one awakes, so when You arise, O Lord, You will despise them as fantasies.
>
> Psalm 73:18-20

The easy life of the scoffers had led them to forget God, and their success had not permitted them to sense their need of Him. The very wealth and ease which Asaph had envied were "slippery" places that Asaph's trials helped him to avoid!

This new perspective changed Asaph's feelings. His past feelings were "senseless and ignorant; I was a brute beast before You" (v. 22). His emotional reactions in this case had not corresponded with reality. Yet, when God showed Asaph reality, his emotions changed.

> Yet I am always with You; You hold me by my right hand. You guide me with Your counsel, and afterward You will take me into glory. Whom have I in heaven but You? And being with You, I desire nothing on earth. My flesh and my heart may fail, but God is the strength of my heart and my portion forever.
>
> Psalm 73:23-26

Real life always holds such struggles for us. There is nothing wrong with them. The emotions we feel then are not bad; they are part of being a human being. The glory of the believer's privilege is that, because he knows God, his emotions can be brought into fullest harmony with reality. You and I can face all of our feelings—and find freedom to be ourselves with the Lord. What a privilege to be ourselves with God, and to experience His gentle transformation!

We can be honest with God. This is a third great message of Psalms. Just as we need not repress our feelings, we need not try to hide our feelings from God. He loves us and accepts us as we are—yet always so creatively that we are free to grow toward all that we want to become.

How freeing to realize that God's love is unconditional. He is concerned about every aspect of our lives, inviting us to share all that we are with Him, that in return He might share Himself with us and bring us to health and wholeness.

Psalms, then, speaks directly to our inner lives. The patterns of relationship we find there guide you and me in our prayer lives.

Like the poetry of other peoples, Hebrew poetry is not designed so much to communicate information as to share the inner life and feelings of its writers.

This characteristic of the Psalms is very important to us, and is a dynamic aspect of divine revelation. Through the Psalms we are able to see the men and women of Scripture as real people, gripped by the feelings that move us. We are also able to sense a relationship with God that is deeply personal and real. Every dimension of the human personality is touched when faith establishes that personal relationship. God meets us as whole persons—He touches our feelings, our emotions, our joys and sorrows, our despair and depression. Faith in God is not just an intellectual kind of thing; it is a relationship which engages everything that we are. Thus, in the Psalms we have a picture of the relationship to which God is calling us today—a relationship in which we have freedom to be ourselves, and to share ourselves freely with the Lord and with other believers.

♥ ***Link to Life: Youth / Adult***
Have your group members jot down one or two emotions they have experienced strongly in the past week. The emotion may be positive (joy, thankfulness, etc.) or

negative (anger, envy, loneliness, etc.). Then give the group time to scan the Psalms, looking for short passages in which the writer shares and expresses those feelings.

Then go around the circle. Ask each to describe the feelings he or she identified, and tell a bit about the circumstances that caused them. Then read the verses selected from the Psalms.

After all have had a chance to share, discuss: "What does finding our feelings in the Psalms mean to us personally? What does finding them there tell us about God's attitude toward us and our humanness? What does finding them there say about the validity of human emotions?"

TEACHING GUIDE

Prepare

Read and reread your favorite psalm. Meditate on what it has meant in your life.

Explore

1. Plan a minilecture overview of the Psalms, including the themes of the Psalms, the nature of Hebrew poetry, and the personal message of the Psalms directed to our prayer life. If you wish, include in your lecture a discussion of Psalm 73.
2. Or, use learning activities that will help your group sense how to study the Psalms. Use the analysis activity suggested in "link-to-life," page 326. This will help them in their future reading of this vital Old Testament book.
3. Or, sample the content of the Psalms. Use the "link-to-life" idea on page 327 to examine the different themes that can be found in the psalter; themes that can be found in each of our lives as well.

Expand

Have your group members study Psalm 73. Ask each to look at the psalm individually, and jot down in his or her own words some *five* sentences that explain what is happening.

When completed, share insights with the group.

Then point out that this psalm records an experience which moved the writer to prayer. In fact, the psalm traces the inner experience of a person who brought his feelings to God—and found that God changed those feelings!

Then work as a group to make a list of "what we learn from Psalm 73 about prayer."

Apply

Ask each person to pray silently, expressing his or her feelings now to the Lord.

STUDY GUIDE 48

Psalms 74–150

PATTERNS OF PRAISE

Overview

The Hebrews knew the Book of Psalms as the Hallel, the Book of Praises.

In Study Guide 47 we looked at the Psalms as a guide to prayer. We saw the warm and open sharing by the psalmists, finding examples of the intimacy you and I are to have in our relationships with the Lord.

But the focus of the Psalms is not really on human experience. The focus of the Psalms is on God. As Christians today approach this great book we meet the Lord in a special way, and we are taught how to worship and praise Him.

▶ ***Praise.*** There are a number of Hebrew and Greek words in the Bible rendered "praise." In each Testament praise is our response to God's revelation of Himself, an acknowledgment of His character and His acts. But it is more. Praise is our expression of delight in God Himself; our expression of the love we feel as we consider, "How Great Thou Art."

▶ ***Hebrew Poetry.*** Hebrew poetry rests not on rhyme and rhythm but on parallelism (repetition and sequencing of thoughts) and on imagery. While English poetry cannot be easily translated into another language, Hebrew poetry has been rendered into every language, with none of its power or passion lost. Study Guide 47 explains how Hebrew poetry works, and shows you how to teach youth and adults to understand it.

■ For a discussion of each psalm in this wonderful Book of Psalms see the *Bible Knowledge Commentary,* pages 779-899.

Commentary

While the Psalms tell us much about ourselves, they are also of great benefit in their revelation of God as they guide us into worship.

Classification of Psalms. There are many ways in which commentators have attempted to classify the Psalms. One approach, discussed in the last unit, is by content. We analyze the themes that seem to recur. For instance, there are a number of *messianic psalms* which speak of Christ. There are *imprecatory psalms* which call for judgment against enemies. There are psalms of praise and penitence and worship. Such classification systems do help us categorize individual psalms. But the systems do not help us organize the book as a whole.

Actually, we probably should not expect to find a careful or logical structure to the Bible's collection of psalms. Life is complex, filled with surges of joy and contrasting times of stagnant depression; of moments enriched by worship of God and times strained by difficulty and despair. The Book of Psalms shares the complexity of life itself, reflecting in organization as well as content the complexity of our human condition.

Yet one way of classifying the Psalms is of special interest. It is a classification by use. For instance, many psalms have titles, such as *mizmore* or *shir.* These words refer to ways that the psalm was integrated into the life and worship of Israel. The 57 psalms entitled *mizmore* were sung to the accompaniment of stringed instruments and were used as public worship songs. There are 30 *shir,* a word meaning secular or sacred song. Other psalms, such as *ma'aloth* (songs of ascent) were sung by pilgrims on the way to Jerusalem for the three compulsory annual feasts (Pss. 120–134).

Simply noting the title may not be of great value in understanding individual psalms. Yet, together the titles give us an engaging picture of the use of these psalms by Israel and a suggestion for their use in our own day. The titles recall a picture sketched by one of the sons of Korah (a levitical group dedicated to temple musicianship).

> These things I remember, as I pour out my soul: how I used to go with the multitude, leading the procession to the house of God, with shouts of joy and thanksgiving, among the festive throng.
>
> Psalm 42:4

Perhaps this is the image we ought to keep in mind as we approach the Book of Psalms. Keeping festival. Coming with praise and rejoicing to our God.

Keeping festival. This is one of the lost arts of believers, who are called to celebrate relationships with God. Such celebration comes not because of our feelings alone, but it comes when we realize just who God is and all that He means for us.

One contemporary definition of worship, suggested by Chapel of the Air speaker David Mains, helps us focus on a secret of keeping festival. Worship, says Pastor Mains, is essentially "ascribing worth to God for who He by nature is." At heart, worship is focusing our attention on God. It is praising the Lord for one of those qualities or characteristics which set Him apart in His perfection and His glory.

There are many psalms which give us insight into how to worship. For example, each of Psalms 93 through 99 selects one quality of God to emphasize and for which to praise Him. In Psalm 95, the writer is taken up with the greatness of God, and calls all men to worship and respond to Him:

> Come, let us sing for joy to the Lord; let us shout aloud to the Rock of our salvation! Let us come before Him with thanksgiving and extol Him with music and song. For the Lord is the great God, the great King above all gods. In His hand are the depths of the earth, and the mountain peaks belong to Him. The sea is His, for He made it, and His hands formed the dry land. Come, let us bow down in worship, let us kneel before the Lord our Maker; for He is our God and we are the people of His pasture, the flock under His care.
>
> Psalm 95:1-7

Lifted up, our own eyes are given a fresh vision of who God is, and our spirits are borne along with the psalmist as we give God our own heart's praise as well.

This sequence of short psalms helps us see what potential there is for worship in contemplation of God and His qualities.

Psalm 93 praises God as reigning King:

> The Lord reigns; He is robed in majesty; the Lord is robed in majesty and is armed with strength. The world is firmly established; it cannot be moved. Your throne was established long ago; You are from all eternity.
>
> Psalm 93:1-2

Psalm 94 praises God as the One who acts in justice and vengeance:

> O Lord, the God who avenges, O God who avenges, shine forth. Rise up, O Judge of the earth; pay back to the proud what they deserve. How long will the wicked, O Lord, how long will the wicked be jubilant?
>
> Psalm 94:1-3

In Psalm 96 the focus is on God as Saviour:

> Sing to the Lord a new song; sing to the Lord all the earth. Sing to the Lord, praise His name; proclaim His salvation day after day. Declare His glory among the nations, declare His marvelous deeds among all peoples.
>
> Psalm 96:1-3

And so the psalms continue, on and on. For our God *is* splendid. We never reach the end of probing His nature, or of discovering in Him that which calls forth our praise.

It is in the psalms' clear focus on the person of God that the deepest meaning of this book of Scripture is to be found.

♥ ***Link to Life: Youth / Adult***
One exciting value of the Book of Psalms is its capacity to enrich our image of God. Why not launch class with a brainstorming session? Ask your group to see how many qualities or characteristics of God they can suggest in four minutes. Write their ideas (loving, gracious, forgiving, powerful, etc.) on the board.

Then have each group member scan Psalms for four minutes, and jot down words used there to talk of or describe God.

Make another group listing on the chalkboard, beside the first list. Which is longer? Compare items: which items are on both lists? What images from the Psalms were not suggested by your class members in the brainstorming?

Point out that one great value of the Book of Psalms is that as we read we learn more about who our God is. If we read the Psalms regularly, our appreciation for who God is will grow.

Patterns for Praise

When we look at the different Hebrew words translated "praise" and their use in the Psalms, we gain further insight into how you and I can worship and praise the Lord. Here are the primary Hebrew words, and their meanings, as discussed in *The Expository Dictionary of Bible Words* (Richards, Zondervan).

Each of the Hebrew words, while with its own emphasis, shares common elements. These are:

(1) Praise is addressed to God or His "name." God Himself, His attributes, or His acts are the content of our thoughts, words, and songs.
(2) Praise is linked with the believing community's joy in the person of God. Most praise in the Old Testament is corporate, though an individual certainly could praise God in private. Most praise comes from those who are filled with a sense of joy in who God is and in how deeply He is committed to His people.
(3) Praise exalts the Lord. It is in praise that the believer implicitly acknowledges creaturely dependence on God and explicitly acknowledges God's greatness and goodness.

Among the Hebrew words that share in this common core of meaning are these.

Hallel. In various forms this word means "to acclaim," "to boast of," "to glory in." The word expresses a deep satisfaction to be found in exalting the acts and the qualities of the Person being praised.

This verb is used primarily in the plural. This suggests that the joy of recognizing God's greatness is to be shared by God's people. Those who love God come together to rejoice in the Lord, and to exalt Him together.

We sense this particularly in Psalm 65, which expresses how good it is to exalt God and to sense His greatness.

> Praise awaits You, O God, in Zion; to You our vows will be fulfilled. O You who hear prayer, to You all men will come. . . . You answer us with awesome deeds of righteousness, O God our Saviour, the hope of all the ends of the earth and of the farthest seas, who formed the mountains by Your power, having armed Yourself with strength, who stilled the roaring of the seas, the roaring of their waves, and the turmoil of the nations. Those living far away fear Your wonders; where morning dawns and evening fades You call forth songs of joy.
>
> Psalm 65:1-2, 5-8

Yadah is translated "to praise," "to give thanks," and "to confess." This word and related terms emphasize our acknowledging of God's works and of His character, often in contexts which emphasize human failure and need.

Psalm 107 illustrates this emphasis in its opening verses.

> Give thanks to the Lord, for He is good; His love endures forever. Let the redeemed of the Lord say this—those He redeemed from the hand of the foe, those He gathered from the lands, from east and west, from north and south. Some wandered in desert wastelands, finding no way to a city where they could settle. They were hungry and thirsty, and their lives ebbed away. Then they cried out to the Lord in their trouble, and He delivered them from their distress. He led them by a straight way to a city where they could settle. Let them give thanks to the Lord for His unfailing love and His wonderful deeds for men, for He satisfies the thirsty, and fills the hungry with good things.
>
> Psalm 107:1-9

Typically, *yadah* is praise as an acknowledgment of God's goodness. The sense of exultation implicit in it is seen in Psalm 118.

> Shouts of joy and victory resound in the tents of the righteous: "The Lord's right hand has done mighty things! The Lord's right hand is lifted high; the Lord's right hand has done mighty things!" I will not die but live, and will proclaim what the Lord has done. The Lord has chastened me severely, but He has not given me over to death. Open for me the gates of righteousness; I will enter and give thanks to the Lord. This is the gate of the Lord through which the righteous may enter. I will give You thanks, for You answered me; You have become my salvation.
>
> Psalm 118:15-21

Zamar means "to sing praise," "to make music." This word suggests the use of musical instruments in praising God, and is found only in Bible poetry. Once again, songs of praise focus on who God is and on what He has done. So David called on Israel in Psalm 9:11 to:

> Sing praises to the Lord, enthroned in Zion; proclaim among the nations, what He has done.

Sabah, in certain forms, means "to praise or commend." This too is directed to the Lord. The word suggests adoration, the deepest kind of loving praise. Both who God is in His essential nature and God's wonderful works for us.

> Great is the Lord and most worthy of praise; His greatness no one can fathom. One generation will commend Your works to another; they will tell of Your mighty acts. They will speak of the glorious splendor of Your majesty, and I will meditate on Your wonderful works. They will tell of the power of Your awesome works, and I will proclaim Your great deeds. They will celebrate Your abundant goodness and joyfully sing of Your righteousness.
>
> Psalm 145:3-7

And so in these words, illustrated in praise songs, we sense the nature of praise as praise is revealed in the Old Testament and particularly in the Psalms. Praise is God's people, gathered to adore and to give glory to God, for all that He is and for all that He has done. Praise is God's people, gathered to remember His works, and to focus attention on Him. Praise is the overflowing joy of a people whose vision is filled with the beauty and the glory of their God.

♥ ***Link to Life: Youth / Adult***
In a minilecture explain and illustrate from the Psalms the nature of praise. Emphasize the common elements, but also the unique emphases of the Hebrew praise terms.

Then pass out pens and paper. Ask each person to write about six lines expressing his or her praise to God. Each can select one of the Hebrew terms, and shape his praise poem/song to reflect its emphasis. To help, put the following summary of the terms on the board:

Praise is
- *(1) addressed to God*
- *(2) an expression of shared joy*
- *(3) exalting the Lord and His works.*

Hallel *emphasizes joy as we exalt God together.*
Yadah *acclaims God's goodness.*
Zamar *expresses praise in song.*
Sabah *expresses adoration.*

How Great Thou Art
In this discussion I've noted that praise is directed *to* God. And praise is focused *on* God. It involves the believer concentrating on just who the Lord is, and how the Lord has acted to bring blessing to humankind.

One psalm which draws these elements together in a clear and beautiful way is Psalm 103, reproduced here from the *New International Version.* As you read it, note how clearly it expresses who God is in His essential nature, and how His many qualities affect the psalmist's life and relationship with the Lord. This psalm is included here, for you to duplicate to use in your group as described below.

Psalm 103

Praise the Lord, O my soul;
all my inmost being, praise His holy name.

Praise the Lord, O my soul,
and forget not all His benefits.
He forgives all my sins
and heals all my diseases;
He redeems my life from the pit
and crowns me with love and compassion.
He satisfies my desires with good things
so that my youth is renewed like the eagle's.
The Lord works righteousness
and justice for all the oppressed.
He made known His ways to Moses,
His deeds to the people of Israel:
The Lord is compassionate and gracious,
slow to anger, abounding in love.
He will not always accuse,
nor will He harbor His anger forever;
He does not treat us as our sins deserve
or repay us according to our iniquities.
For as high as the heavens are above the earth, so great is His love for those who fear Him; as far as the east is from the west, so far has He removed our transgressions from us.
As a father has compassion on his children,
so the Lord has compassion on those who fear Him; for He knows how we are formed, He remembers that we are dust.
As for man, his days are like grass,
he flourishes like a flower of the field;
the wind blows over it and it is gone,
and its place remembers it no more.
But from everlasting to everlasting
the Lord's love is with those who fear Him, and His righteousness with their children's children—with those who keep His covenant and remember to obey His precepts.
The Lord has established His throne in heaven, and His kingdom rules over all.
Praise the Lord, you His angels,
you mighty ones who do His bidding, who obey His word.
Praise the Lord, all His heavenly hosts,
you His servants who do His will.
Praise the Lord, all His works
everywhere in His dominion.
Praise the Lord, O my soul.

Like other psalms of David, Psalm 103 emphasizes God in relationship with human beings. That is, God is not seen simply as a distant power. He is not an awesome "other." He is not a watchmaker God, who set the universe in motion and then withdrew, having lost interest in the processes of life which He began. God is a Person who is revealed most clearly in His loving approach to humankind. God is known best as He is seen drawing near to you and me, eager to forgive, filled with parental compassion, continuing always to love those who have turned to rely on Him.

♥ ***Link to Life: Youth / Adult***

Have your group study Psalm 101. The goal of this study will be to discover just how the psalmist sees God, and how he responds to the One who has such love for us.

Duplicate Psalm 103 as it appears here. Give a copy to each group member. Ask each to underline words or phrases *which tell what God is like.*

Let pairs compare to be sure that each expression has been identified.

Then read aloud the call to praise in verses 20-22. Ask each person to select from the psalm the one quality of God that he appreciates most; the one which moves him most to praise.

Go around the group, having each person tell the quality of God expressed in Psalm 103 which he or she selected, and tell briefly why this quality of God is important to him or her.

When all have shared, go around again, letting each person praise God in sentence prayers for the quality he or she selected.

How enriching the Psalms are! How clear the image of God that they portray. It is almost impossible to read these great praise poems without feeling our own emotions surge and our own hearts tuned to praise our God.

Truly God is great and wonderful. As we come to appreciate Him, and to express our appreciation in praise, our lives are greatly enriched.

TEACHING GUIDE

Prepare
Read and meditate on Psalm 103. Sense with the psalmist the loving-kindness of God, and let your heart respond to Him with David in adoration and praise.

Explore
1. Launch the session by listing together qualities of God. Then have group members scan the Psalms to see how the psalmists viewed the Lord. Use the process suggested in "link-to-life," pages 332-333.
2. Set up teams of two or three members. Each is to look at one psalm (from 93–99), and determine its theme. When teams report, explain that the focus of worship psalms is on the person of God and His qualities.

Expand
1. Give a minilecture on the nature of praise, illustrating from the Psalms. Follow the guidelines suggested in "link-to-life," page 334. Having your group members write their own verses to capture the emphasis of various Hebrew praise terms will enrich their appreciation for the Lord and how to worship Him.
2. Work together to plan a worship service for your church. Find out the theme and passage for an upcoming sermon. What quality or trait of God is closely related to the sermon theme? Then find music, addressed to God, that picks up this trait. Also select an appropriate psalm, or construct a responsive reading from several psalms. Your group may also wish to write a prayer, or plan other service elements which would help your congregation praise God together.

Apply
1. Together do the study of Psalm 103 outlined earlier. This activity will help your group members personalize their praise as each shares his or her personal appreciation for one of our God's wonderful qualities.
2. Or pick any quality of God or any aspect of His nature. Have each group member write just two or three lines in praise of that aspect or quality. Then go around the circle, reading the verses written in sequence in concluding worship of the Lord.

You may want to put your group's verses together and create their own psalm, which can be typed and duplicated so each member can have a copy.

STUDY GUIDE 49

Proverbs 1–9

WISDOM'S CHILD

Overview
The Book of Proverbs is a collection of sayings, intended to serve as a guide for daily life. The sayings cover many different topics, exploring attitudes and relationships, and evaluating such things as wealth, poverty, and power.

The Proverbs reflect a kind of literature that was common in ancient times. Many of the sayings in this book were written or collected by Solomon, some 950 years before Christ. Proverbs 25:1 suggests that the collection as we have it was completed in the days of King Hezekiah, about 700 B.C.

While the sayings in the book are not organized by topic, Proverbs has been outlined as follows.

Outline

I.	Praise of Wisdom	1–9
II.	Solomon's Proverbs	10–22:16
III.	Collected Sayings	22:17–24:22
IV.	More Sayings	24:23-34
V.	More Proverbs of Solomon	25–29
VI.	Sayings of Agur	30
VII.	Sayings of Lemuel	31

▶ ***Proverb.*** The Hebrew word is *masal.* It includes brief sayings as found in this book, and also the extended parables and vivid illustrations found so often in the Old Testament.

■ The *Bible Knowledge Commentary* contains an extended discussion of Proverbs, which includes both an introduction to this kind of literature and a verse-by-verse explanation of individual proverbs. This helpful and thorough study guide to the Book of Proverbs is found on pages 901-974.

Commentary
All Scripture is given to us by God's inspiration (2 Tim. 3:16). But not all Scripture has the same purpose, and different literary forms are to be interpreted differently. For instance, a passage like Ephesians 1 gives specific and direct teaching about relationships between the Persons of the Godhead and the part of each in redemption.

A psalm like Psalm 3 looks into David's experience and shows us how trust in God enabled him to rest in a time of great stress. A passage like Joshua 5–6 gives a narrative account of historical events, reporting to us how God worked in a specific space-time situation in the past. Each of these literary forms is different; each has a different purpose and value and use. To affirm that each is inspired by God tells us that the Holy Spirit superintended the writing and the recording so that what is communicated to us is both reliable and relevant. We have in words the message God intended us to have, and that message will have meaning for our lives.

But we need to remember that different literary forms are designed to communicate different messages, especially when we come to the Book of Proverbs. For these proverbs, as all proverbs, have characteristics of their own which we need to understand as we interpret and apply them.

Characteristics. What are some of the distinctive characteristics of the Proverbs? Commentators list these:

1. The pithy sayings recorded here *express* general truths, but do not attempt to *explain* them. The *how* and *why* simply are not in view. Likewise, the Proverbs do not argue. They give no closely reasoned defense of their position. Instead, they simply assume that the reader will see the point and agree.

2. Proverbs has a universalistic rather than particularistic application. Nowhere does the term *Israel* appear. Unlike the Law, which was spoken to Israel, these sayings

are viewed as relevant to all people of all times. The general principles expressed here are universally valid.

3. The outlook of the Book of Proverbs is comprehensive. These sayings probe all experiences and relationships.

4. It is important to realize that the Proverbs are *generalizations*. That is, they express the normal course of events. Like other general principles, they do have exceptions. Frequently this same trait will be seen in New Testament sayings. For instance, 1 Peter 3:13-14 deals with the normal course of events when a person does what is good. "Who is going to harm you if you are eager to do good?" Peter asked. But then the apostle went on immediately to examine the exception. He spoke of the unusual circumstance in which a person does the right thing and still suffers for it. In his argument Peter called on us to keep on trusting God, and to remember that God has a purpose in everything that happens. After all, Jesus too did only what was right, and yet He suffered unjustly. But out of the injustice—out of the suffering of the Cross—God wrought salvation, bringing from death new life and new good for Christ and all mankind.

So general statements do have exceptions, and the Proverbs should not be taken as divine promises or guarantees. Proverbs does not deal with the special events of life, but rather with the normal course of events. Proverbs tells us then how things usually work out in human experience.

5. It is rather striking that the Book of Proverbs, dealing with such a broad range of subjects, does not include any "unscientific" statements. For instance, Proverbs 6:6-8 accurately describes the social structure of the ant, something that shows acute insight and careful observation.

6. Unlike other proverbs in the Orient, biblical proverbs reveal a distinctively high morality. Proverbs gathered by archeologists from other sources indicate that the sayings of the people who lived near Israel tended to focus on sex—and to treat it grossly.

The first four of these often-noted characteristics of Proverbs helps us to understand and interpret the Book of Proverbs itself. Studied in this context, the book becomes a very practical and helpful guide to thinking about the life issues which many of us face. The last two characteristics help us very much in understanding Solomon, the chief writer. He remained, for all his marriages, a moral man who, during most of his reign at any rate, was not obsessed with sex. Solomon was also a careful scientific observer, a man whose research, even while ruling a nation, surpassed that of Aristotle. Scripture tells us that Solomon "was the author of 3,000 proverbs and wrote 1,005 songs. He was a great naturalist, with interest in animals, birds, snakes, fish, and trees—from the great cedars of Lebanon down to the tiny hyssop which grows in cracks in the wall. And kings from many lands sent their ambassadors to him for his advice" (1 Kings 4:32-34, TLB).

Content. The Book of Proverbs has been broken down into from 4 to 10 sections by different commentators, revealing that, like Psalms, this collection is not clearly organized by content or progression of thought. However, two major divisions are very plain. The first nine chapters are a discussion of wisdom, with wisdom often personified.

Chapters 10–31 include several collections of proverbs which involve application of this wisdom to many life situations. As one commentator has suggested, this section contains the "philosophy of the practical life." *The Zondervan Pictorial Encyclopedia of the Bible* gives a number of groupings of the Proverbs by topics.

The content of Proverbs can be grouped according to topics discussed; for example: social evils (22:28; 23:10; 30:14); social obligations (18:24; 22:24-25; 23:1-2; 25:6-7, 17; 27:6-10); poverty (17:5; 18:23; 19:4, 7, 17); concern for the poor (14:31; 17:5; 18:23; 19:7, 17; 21:13; 22:2; 30:14); laziness (12:27; 20:13; 26:14-15); wealth as secondary (11:4; 15:16; 16:8, 16; 19:1; 22:1) but important (10:22; 13:11; 19:4).

Domestic life is a frequent topic (18:22; 21:9, 19; 27:15-16; 31:30); relationships between parents and children are discussed (10:1; 17:21, 25; 19:13, 26; 20:7; 23:24-25); the importance of friendship is stressed (18:24; 22:24-25; 25:17).

No less than four types of fools can be discerned in Proverbs: (1) the simple fool who is still teachable (1:4, 22; 7:7-8; 21:11); (2) the hardened fool (1:7; 10:23; 12:23; 17:10; 20:3; 27:22) who is obstinate; (3) the arrogant fool, the scoffer who rejects all attempts at enlightenment (3:34; 21:24; 22:10; 29:8); (4) the brutish fool (17:21; 26:3; 30:22; cf. Ps. 14:1).

Royal conduct is a topic (16:12-14; 19:6; 21:1; 25:5; 28:15; 29:14). Cheerfulness is enjoined (15:13-15; 17:22; 18:14). The use of the tongue is discussed (10:20; 15:1; 16:28; 21:23; 26:4). Other personal habits are mentioned (11:22; 13:7; 22:3; 25:14; 26:12; 30:33). Finally, some aspects of the concept of life are discussed—its fountain (9:11; 13:14; 14:27); its path (6:23; 10:17; 15:24); and life itself (11:30; 12:28; 13:4, 12).

This wide-ranging book, then, is a source of many insights which God chose to share with us through His sacred Word.

For individual and group study, Proverbs remains one of our least explored but richest heritages in the Old Testament.

♥ ***Link to Life: Youth / Adult***
It's important to launch a study of Proverbs with a minilecture on its characteristics. Believers should not take its sayings as promises or commitments by God, but need to understand that in this book the Lord is dealing with the normal course of events. Exceptions to such statements as "a generous man will prosper" and "all hard work brings a profit" do exist.

So list the characteristics of the Proverbs on the board, and explain how to read and apply this distinctive literary form.

Wisdom: Proverbs 1–9

The first part of Proverbs examines the nature of wisdom, and applies wisdom to specific issues. But what according to the Bible *is* wisdom? And how will the wise person live?

The nature of wisdom. The Hebrew word group that expresses the idea of wisdom has as its root the verb *hakam.* Words in this group occur in the Old Testament over 300 times!

Hakam deals with an individual's approach to life itself. It is practical in nature, and yet is spiritual. For, biblically speaking, "wisdom" provides the insight to master life's challenges through a responsive personal relationship with God. In essence wisdom has to do with choosing what is right and good as we live our daily lives.

A wise person is one who is sensitive to the Lord and who subjects himself to God. A wise person will apply guidelines revealed by God and make his daily decisions based on these truths. In its deepest meaning "wisdom" unites God's words and everyday experience, and it is only in the way a person lives his life that wisdom can be demonstrated.

Proverbs 2 sums up this perspective.

> For the Lord gives wisdom, and from His mouth come knowledge and understanding. . . . Then you will understand what is right and just and fair—every good path. For wisdom will enter your heart, and knowledge will be pleasant to your soul. . . . Wisdom will save you from the ways of wicked men, from men whose words are perverse.
>
> Proverbs 2:6, 9-10, 12

In Scripture then there is a clear distinction drawn between intelligence and wisdom. One may have great intellectual capabilities. But unless a person accepts the words of God and applies them to make his or her choices in life, that person can hardly be called "wise." There is, in fact, many an intelligent person who makes wrong moral choices and thus, in biblical terms, is a fool!

The Book of Proverbs is intended to be a word to the wise. It is a book with a moral foundation, designed to help us make godly choices. Thus the book's opening explains that the Proverbs are:

> For attaining wisdom and discipline; for understanding words of insight; for acquiring a disciplined and prudent life, doing what is right and just and fair.
>
> Proverbs 1:2-3

In Scripture morality always has spiritual roots. Thus Proverbs says that:

> The fear of the Lord is the beginning of knowledge, but fools despise wisdom and discipline.
>
> Proverbs 1:7

"Fear" in this context is not terror but respect. The person who has a deep respect for God, who acknowledges Him as Creator and Lord, is the one who will listen attentively to God's Words and will apply them daily. For this reason wisdom begins with faith in God. But for a person of faith to be wise, he must act with full trust in God and live according to that Word.

♥ ***Link to Life: Youth / Adult***
Divide into two teams. Give each team its own assignment without letting either know that of the other. One team is to describe *"the most intelligent person in the world" by listing his traits. The other team is to describe "the wisest person in the world" by describing his traits.*
When the descriptions have been completed, come together and share, listing the traits side by side on a T-shaped chart.
Then discuss: "What are significant similarities? What are differences? How do we explain the differences?"
Use the discussion to launch a minilecture on "wisdom" as it is conceived of in Scripture, and illustrated in Proverbs.

The message of wisdom. The first nine chapters of Proverbs are devoted to a description of wisdom, which is often personified as a woman. The text discusses the benefits of wisdom, warns against folly, and describes the wise way.

In teaching this book you can let your group members sample especially significant and familiar verses, in order to get a feel for this vital spiritual trait.

Proverbs 1: Warnings. This first chapter exhorts the reader, as a son might be exhorted by his father, against rejecting wisdom. The thrust of the passage is that those who do, and thus turn to moral evil, set foot on a pathway that leads to destruction. As a result:

> Since they hated knowledge and did not choose to fear the Lord, since they would not accept my advice and spurned my rebuke, they will eat the fruit of their ways and be filled with the fruit of their schemes.
>
> Proverbs 1:29-31

Benefits of wisdom (Prov. 2–3). On the other hand, the person who gains wisdom wins many benefits. Among those mentioned are deliverance from the ways of wicked men (2:12), deliverance from the adulteress (v. 16), a long life (v. 21), a good name and prosperity (3:2), health (v. 8), wealth (vv. 9-10), safety (v. 22), grace (v. 34), and honor (v. 35).

These chapters make it very clear that wisdom is moral in nature, for they specify some of the choices that wisdom will lead a person to make. The wise person will receive wisdom from the Lord and as a result will choose:

- against the ways of the wicked (2:12);
- against involvement in adultery (v. 16);
- for goodness and righteousness (v. 20);
- for love and faithfulness (3:3);
- for disciplined giving to God (v. 9);
- for giving to the needy (vv. 27-28);
- against plotting to harm anyone (v. 29);
- against false accusations (v. 30);
- against envy (v. 31).

While situations may arise in which it seems expedient to make a different kind of choice, the wise person will:

> Trust in the Lord with all your heart and lean not on your own understanding; in all your ways acknowledge Him and He will make your paths straight.
>
> Proverbs 3:5-6

Wisdom's priority (Prov. 4). The reader is exhorted to value wisdom above everything. One who loves wisdom (that is, the whispered word from God which directs us into right paths), will always be watched over. "Wisdom is supreme"; the writer insisted, "therefore get wisdom" (v. 7).

In this world there are many values competing with the biblical. Many may look attractive and seem desirable. But one should only listen to wisdom, and act in accord with wisdom. Thus the writer says:

> Above all else, guard your heart, for it is the wellspring of life. Put away perversity from your mouth; keep corrupt talk far from your lips. Let your eyes look straight ahead, fix your gaze directly before you. Make level paths for your feet and take only ways that are firm. Do not swerve to the right or the left; keep your foot from evil.
>
> Proverbs 4:23-27

Warning against adultery (Prov. 5). Much attention is given to adultery in these early chapters. The sexual dimension of life seems to be one which is a test for moral discipline (v. 11). This does not suggest a negative view toward sex. On the contrary, the writer speaks poetically of married love, and encourages the reader to "rejoice in the wife of your youth" (v. 18).

> A loving doe, a graceful deer—may her breasts satisfy you always, may you ever be captivated by her love.
>
> Proverbs 5:19

But, because a man's ways are examined by the Lord, evil deeds always ensnare a person so that:

> He will die for lack of discipline, led astray by his own great folly.
>
> Proverbs 5:23

Warnings against folly (Prov. 6:1-16). There are several things that the writer views as foolish. One who consistently makes such choices is sure to be sorry. Among the foolish things men do is to guarantee loans made to another (vv. 1-5), and to sleep when one should be at work (vv. 6-11). Some things are foolish in a moral sense, because they are evil and hated by the Lord. On this list of moral folly are:

> Haughty eyes [pride], a lying tongue, hands that shed innocent blood, a heart that devises wicked schemes, feet that are quick to rush into evil, a false witness who pours out lies, and a man who stirs up dissension among brothers.
>
> Proverbs 6:17-19

More against adultery (Prov. 6:20–7:27). In this extended passage the writer again warns against adultery. The commandments of God will guide the wise, "keeping you from the immoral woman" (v. 24). It is no more safe to touch her than to play with fire (v. 27).

Perhaps the most significant statement here is:

> For the prostitute reduces you to a loaf of bread.
>
> Proverbs 6:26

Human beings are made in the image of God, and are to be valued and protected. Prostitution is an offense against both the seller and the buyer, reducing the human being to a commodity. People are not things to be used. Each individual man and woman is special, made in God's image, and is to be loved and protected.

The believer can hardly become involved in any *user* relationship, in which the value of another person is reduced by treating that other as a thing.

Wisdom's appeal (Prov. 8). In this segment personifying wisdom as a woman, she appeals to the reader to make her their choice.

> I love those who love me, and those who seek me find me. With me are riches and honor, enduring wealth and prosperity. My fruit is better than fine gold; what I yield surpasses choice silver. I walk in the way of righteousness, along the paths of justice, bestowing wealth on those who love me and making their treasuries full.
>
> Proverbs 8:17-21

Wisdom contrasted with folly (Prov. 9). Wisdom bases her character on fear of the Lord and knowledge of the Holy One. While her ways involve rebuke and discipline, the way of wisdom is rewarding.

On the other hand Folly is undisciplined, and without knowledge. While her appeal may seem attractive on the surface, and many turn in at her door,

> Little do they know that the dead are there, that her guests are in the depths of the grave.
>
> Proverbs 9:18

In wisdom and folly the Book of Proverbs sketches the most basic decisions a human being can make. We must each make a commitment to God and His ways, and live faithfully by that commitment, or wander down other paths.

Only commitment to God can lead to blessing. Any other path is folly indeed, for such paths lead to disappointment and to death.

TEACHING GUIDE

Prepare
Select one proverb from this section and put it into practice for one week. Be prepared to share the proverb and how you applied it when your group meets.

Explore
1. Give a minilecture on the Proverbs as a literary form, to show how this affects our understanding of this important Old Testament book.
2. Divide your group members into equal teams to see which can list the most "sayings" that capture the practical wisdom of our culture. For instance, "Well begun is half done," "A stitch in time saves nine," etc.

Then discuss whether these sayings are always true, usually true, sometimes true, or seldom true. Talk about what they are intended to communicate, and how they differ from, say, a scientific textbook.

Then give your minilecture on characteristics of the Proverbs, showing how to interpret and understand them.

Expand
1. Discuss the nature of "wisdom." Use the activity explained in "link-to-life," page 340. As your group members contrast wisdom and intelligence, they will be sensitive to the contribution of Proverbs to their own lives and relationships with God.
2. List on the chalkboard the topics of chapters 2–9 of Proverbs. List them in question form, and let your group members form teams to study the chapter of each person's choice. Each team is to find out how the chapter answers the question, and each member is to select one proverb he or she thinks can be applied this week in his or her life.

The questions:

Chapter 2:	How is wisdom "moral"?
Chapter 3:	How is the person with wisdom better off than others without it?
Chapter 4:	How great a priority should wisdom have?
Chapters 5–7:	How is adultery unwise?
Chapter 8:	How is wisdom appealing to us?

When the teams have finished, come together to share what each has learned. Supplement team reports with insights from the commentary section of this unit.

Apply
Talk about the proverb you chose and applied to your life this past week. Then let everyone share the proverbs they selected, and mention briefly how they expect to relate to them this coming week.

STUDY GUIDE 50

Proverbs 10–31

WISDOM'S WAY

Overview

The Book of Proverbs is what is known as "wisdom literature." In Scripture, wisdom is a moral and practical quality: wisdom guides the individual of sound character to make decisions which are both right and beneficial.

The Book of Proverbs begins with a section written in praise of wisdom (chaps. 1–9). The rest of the chapters contain brief, often unrelated sayings that sum up wisdom's way in a number of issues of human life.

Here we find the writers speaking out on marriage, work, poverty, raising children, and a number of other topics that are relevant to everyone's life.

Because of the structure of Proverbs, one of the best ways to study or teach this book is by choosing a topic and then locating each proverb dealing with it. When the observations of the writers are considered together we can gain considerable insight into issues that concern us all.

Proverbs are not intended to be understood as promises or divine guarantees. They are general principles: descriptions of how things normally work out in this life not only for the believer but for all human beings. While each of us may experience exceptions to the general principles stated in this Old Testament book, we can still rely on the Proverbs for guidance in living our daily lives.

■ For a verse-by-verse commentary on individual Proverbs in chapters 10–31 see *Bible Knowledge Commentary*, pages 925-974.

Commentary

The Book of Proverbs typically makes a number of observations on its topics. While each individual proverb provides insight, the best way to see what wisdom suggests in such areas as child-rearing or interpersonal relationships or dealing with money is to draw together all the proverbs that touch on a topic.

This characteristic of Proverbs suggests several teaching approaches which you can apply in working with your group. Each section in this unit will illustrate a different way to help your group members explore and profit from the wisdom shared with us in this special book of the Old Testament.

But first, what are some of the things that are dealt with in Proverbs? The *Bible Knowledge Commentary,* also published by Victor Books, contains this comprehensive list. General topics include:

fear of the Lord	gluttony, food
wives	husbands
mothers	fathers
kings, rulers	children
friendship	slaves
orphans and the needy	prostitutes
business dealings	hypocrisy
stealing	rebuke

In addition the book identifies and comments on many positive, wise, or beneficial traits. Among them are:

wisdom	life
knowledge	work
diligence	orderliness
success	self-control
faithfulness	obedience
honesty	integrity
justice	fairness
truth	honor
encouragement	purity
love	peace
kindness	mercy
joy	generosity
good company	hope
wealth	friendliness

soberness	virtue
trust	pleasure
quietness	contentment
teachableness	

Other traits are viewed as negative, wicked, or foolish (morally warped and harmful). Among these traits are:

folly	wickedness
death	ignorance
laziness	disorderliness
failure	anger
unfaithfulness	rebellion
cheating	deceit
injustice	unfairness
lying	deception
dishonor	criticism
impurity	slander
strife	jealousy
hatred	cruelty
greed	sadness
anxiety	bad company
animosity	enmity
poverty	shame
drunkenness	unfriendliness
worry	misery
talkativeness	envy
unteachableness	pride

While this list is not inspired, and thus others may organize the topics differently, it does suggest one good way of studying Proverbs. It's possible to look at this book of wisdom and go about listing those things which make a positive contribution to living the good life—and those things which have a negative impact on our experiences.

♥ ***Link to Life: Youth / Adult***
Divide into pairs, giving each pair one or two chapters of Proverbs to explore (use chapters 10–29). Ask each pair to read its chapter(s) to identify what is good, *and what is* bad. *This may be morally good/bad or experientially good/bad (that is, desirable, undesirable).*

When the pairs have finished, work together to construct a group list of topics in Proverbs.

But don't stop with the list. Have each pair select one of the topics listed, and spend about 30 minutes locating several verses that deal with that topic. Thus while poverty *may be a bad thing, what does Proverbs say about it? Where does poverty come from? How are others to treat the poor? What is the poor person to do?*

Poverty in Proverbs

Jesus commented at one time, "The poor you will always have with you" (Mark 14:7). Today as in other ages what to do with and for the poor is a matter of debate. Does our welfare system really help the poor? Does it encourage rather than fight poverty? Are the poor to blame for their condition, or is society? What is the believer's obligation to the needy, and how is that obligation to be met? Questions like these are difficult to answer, because the issues involved are complex. Yet Proverbs—like the rest of the Bible—has much to say about the poor and oppressed in society.

Following is a list of proverbs from chapters 10–29 which deal with this issue. Look at them, and then note how they can be used to develop a perspective which can help guide us today in our approach to the question of poverty in our society.

First, Proverbs makes it clear that some poverty is a matter of bad choices. There are constant warnings against laziness, sleep, and a love of pleasure. Diligence leads to wealth, and hard work brings a profit. A person's financial condition is something for which he or she is largely responsible.

But poverty isn't always a man's fault. At times poverty may be the result of others' choices. "A poor man's field may produce abundant food, but injustice sweeps it away" (13:23). Even hard work is no guarantee one will not become poor. At times the poor are exploited by others, and rulers (laws, social structures) can be oppressive. So poverty is a complex phenomenon. It is linked with an individual's personal choices, but all are also vulnerable to society and to the criminal behavior of others.

Proverbs seems especially concerned with the relational impact of poverty. It creates individuals and a class of people who are outcasts, ascribed little or no value by others. This depersonalizing impact of poverty is seen in the way the poor are shunned by their neighbors, plead uselessly for mercy, and are avoided even by their friends. The Bible universally teaches that each human is precious to God, of great personal worth and value. How tragic that we tend to measure our own value and the value of others by what they possess.

"Lazy hands make a man poor, but diligent hands bring wealth" (10:4).

"The wealth of the rich is their fortified city, but poverty is the ruin of the poor" (10:15).

"One man gives freely, yet gains even more; another withholds unduly, but comes to poverty" (11:24).

"One man pretends to be rich, yet has nothing; another pretends to be poor, yet has great wealth" (13:7).

"A man's riches may ransom his life, but a poor man hears no threat" (13:8).

"He who ignores discipline comes to poverty and shame" (13:18).

"A poor man's field may produce abundant food, but injustice sweeps it away" (13:23).

"The poor are shunned even by their neighbors" (14:20).

"All hard work brings a profit, but mere talk leads only to poverty" (14:23).

"He who oppresses the poor shows contempt for their Maker, but whoever is kind to the needy honors God" (14:31).

"He who mocks the poor shows contempt for their Maker" (17:5).

"A poor man pleads for mercy, but a rich man answers harshly" (18:23).

"Better a poor man whose walk is blameless than a fool whose lips are perverse" (19:1).

"Wealth brings many friends, but a poor man's friend deserts him" (19:4).

"A poor man is shunned by all his relatives—how much more do his friends avoid him! Though he pursues them with pleading, they are nowhere to be found" (19:7).

"He who is kind to the poor lends to the Lord, and He will reward him for what he has done" (19:17).

"Better to be poor than a liar" (19:22).

"Do not love sleep or you will grow poor; stay awake and you will have food to spare" (20:13).

"If a man shuts his ears to the cry of the poor, he too will cry out and not be answered" (21:13).

"He who loves pleasure will become poor; whoever loves wine and oil will never be rich" (21:17).

"The rich rule over the poor, and the borrower is servant to the lender" (22:7).

"A generous man will himself be blessed, for he shares his food with the poor" (22:9).

"He who oppresses the poor to increase his wealth and he who gives gifts to the rich—both come to poverty" (22:16).

"Do not exploit the poor because they are poor and do not crush the needy in court, for the Lord will take up their case and will plunder those who plunder them" (22:22-23).

"For drunkards and gluttons become poor, and drowsiness clothes them in rags" (23:21).

"A little sleep, a little slumber, a little folding of the hands to rest—and poverty will come on you like a bandit and scarcity like an armed man" (24:33-34).

"A ruler who oppresses the poor is like a driving rain that leaves no crops" (28:3).

"Better a poor man whose walk is blameless than a rich man whose ways are perverse" (28:6).

"He who increases his wealth by exorbitant interest amasses it for another, who will be kind to the poor" (28:8).

"A rich man may be wise in his own eyes, but a poor man who has discernment sees through him" (28:11).

"He who works his land will have abundant food, but the one who chases fantasies will have his fill of poverty" (28:19).

"A stingy man is eager to get rich and is unaware that poverty awaits him" (28:22).

"He who gives to the poor will lack nothing, but he who closes his eyes to them receives many curses" (28:27).

"The righteous care about justice for the poor, but the wicked have no such concern" (29:7).

"The poor man and the oppressor have this in common: the Lord gives sight to the eyes of both" (29:13).

"If a king judges the poor with fairness, his throne will always be secure" (29:14).

Still, there are compensations for the poor. For instance, it is better to be poor and honest, than to be a rich exploiter of others. The poor like the rich have eyes with which to see—and at least the poor man's children aren't likely to be kidnapped! (v. 8) But there is more. The Lord has a special concern for the poor, and will take up their case against the oppressor. God intervenes to frustrate the desires of the person who misuses the poor.

What then is our attitude to be toward the poor? For one thing, "The righteous care about justice for the poor" (29:7). The righteous are willing to be involved in issues that touch on the lives of the needy. In addition, the good man is willing to use his own resources to supply the poor with food, or to lend to the needy. This is done as an act of piety, knowing that "he who is kind to the poor lends to the Lord, and He will reward him for what he has done" (19:17).

Each believer as an individual and as a citizen has a responsibility to God to love other human beings. Proverbs makes it clear this includes the poor.

♥ ***Link to Life: Youth / Adult***
Guide an in-depth study of this or another topic dealt with in Proverbs. Select or let your group members select topic(s) of interest. Use a concordance to find relevant proverbs. Then, from the selected proverbs, develop summary statements like the preceding discussion of poverty.

Topics that your group members might choose to study, and key words to look up in the concordance, are:

- child-rearing: *child, children, mother, father;*
- husband/wife relationships: *wife, woman;*
- talking: *talk, words, tongue, lips;*
- money: *rich, wealth, prosperity;*
- work: *work, works, labor.*

Teams can work together on these or other topics. When relevant proverbs have been located and discussed, each team should write out *a few paragraphs summarizing the viewpoint expressed in Proverbs, and suggesting how it relates to Christians today.*

The Noble Wife: Proverbs 31:10-31
One famous passage in Proverbs is the epilogue in chapter 31 which describes the "wife of noble character." It is a particularly fascinating refutation of the notion that it is "biblical" for the wife to stay home and take care of the house while the husband works.

In Old Testament times as in earlier days in our own country, families lived an agricultural life. The husband's work focused outside, in the fields. The wife's work focused around the household. But both husband and wife contributed through their areas of responsibility to the well-being of the family. In carrying out those responsibilities the woman often acted in just the same roles as the man, but in her area of responsibility.

Proverbs 31 takes us back to that time, and in the description of the noble wife shows how fully the woman's potential as a person was used in biblical times.

This section of Proverbs is reproduced here, so you can duplicate it for distribution and group study.

> A wife of noble character who can find? She is worth far more than rubies. Her husband has full confidence in her and lacks nothing of value. She brings him good, not harm all the days of her life. She selects wool and flax and works with eager hands. She is like the merchant ships, bringing her food from afar. She gets up while it is still dark; she provides food for her family and portions for her servant girls. She considers a field and buys it; out of her earnings she plants a vineyard. She sets about her work vigorously; her arms are strong for her tasks. She sees that her trading is profitable, and her lamp does not go out at night. In her hand she holds the distaff and grasps the spindle with her fingers. She opens her arms to the poor and extends her hands to the needy. When it snows, she has no fear for her household; for all of them are clothed in scarlet. She makes coverings for her bed; she is clothed in fine linen and purple. Her husband is respected at the city gate, where he takes his seat among the elders of the land. She makes linen garments and sells them, and supplies the merchants with sashes. She is clothed with strength and dignity; she can laugh at the days to come. She speaks with wisdom, and faithful instruction is on her tongue. She watches over the affairs of her household and does not

eat the bread of idleness. Her children arise and call her blessed; her husband also, and he praises her: "Many women do noble things, but you surpass them all." Charm is deceptive, and beauty is fleeting; but a woman who fears the Lord is to be praised. Give her the reward she has earned, and let her works bring her praise at the city gate.

Proverbs 31:10-31

What's so impressive in this description? Several things. First, the wife had several areas of responsibility, and in them she exercised a great deal of personal freedom. She was buyer of materials relating to the home and family, carefully examining them in making her selection (v. 13). She also had purchasing discretion: her activities earned money, and she was able to spend it as she chose. Thus she "considers a field and buys it; out of her earnings she plants a vineyard" (v. 16). The wife sold the excess her household produced to local merchants (v. 24), and was a good enough businesswoman to "see that her trading is profitable" (v. 18). She has total responsibility for her earnings, including the right to give generously to the poor and the needy (v. 20). Like her husband, she feels a sense of concern and responsibility for those who are less fortunate.

While the wife is engaged in these activities, she does not do all the work alone. In fact, she is an employer, supervising both her family and "her servant girls" (v. 15). In essence the noble wife is management, with all the responsibilities of management. She must hire and fire. She must supervise and plan. She must organize so that the raw materials and supplies needed for the work to be done are present. And she must also market the goods her staff produces!

These are heavy responsibilities, and like other management positions can't be accomplished in an eight-hour day. So she gets up early (v. 15) and often must work late (v. 18).

There are, however, many rewards. Her children appreciate her, and her husband praises her. When her husband takes his place among the men of the city, he is respected for his wife's accomplishments! (v. 23) While he does not derive his identity from her, neither does she derive her identity from him. That is, she is not known as "banker Jones' wife." Her own accomplishments have merit and she has the respect of all for whom she is as a person (v. 31).

And along with that respect she wins a reputation for wisdom, so that others come to learn from her, asking her advice and thanking her for her instruction (v. 26).

The picture of the wife's role here in Proverbs is striking. The woman, like the man, is expected to use all her abilities. The woman, like the man, has great personal freedom and great personal responsibility. The woman, like the man, is worker, manager, buyer, and seller. She is as much "in business" as her husband, and she both has and uses all the mental and intellectual capacities that make for success.

We cannot study this passage in Proverbs and support the notion some have that the wife is to stay at home and clean house, prepare dinner, and ask her husband's permission to make any kind of purchase! And we cannot support the idea that working is a violation of the woman's God-given role.

In a fascinating way this passage in Proverbs invites us into an aspect of Old Testament life and culture which no other passage reveals. We need to study this passage carefully as we consider the question of women and their role in the modern world.

♥ ***Link to Life: Youth / Adult***

List several statements about the role of women, and ask group members whether they agree or disagree with each. You may also ask: "What other statements might we list that sum up viewpoints on women and their role?"

Starter statements might include:

- *Woman's place is in the home.*
- *Women are emotional, men intellectual.*
- *Women don't make good managers.*
- *Women need careers as much as men do.*
- *Women should find their satisfaction in taking care of their husbands and children.*

After your group members have discussed these statements and have suggested others, challenge them to study Proverbs 31:10-31 to find specific support for their opinions.

Don't be concerned if members disagree heatedly. This is a controversial issue. But one on which the perspective provided here in Proverbs should be considered.

The Book of Proverbs is unique in the canon of Scripture. Its collection of sayings are general, practical, and moral guidelines that anyone can apply to enrich his or her life. While its sayings do not constitute promises or guarantees from God, those sayings do give insights in how you and I can live happy and holy lives.

TEACHING GUIDE

Prepare
Pick one topic that interests you personally, and see what the Book of Proverbs has to say. Do a concordance study, or quickly scan chapters 10–29.

Explore
1. Ask your group members to make up their own proverbs on a selected topic (poverty, child-rearing, etc.). Then go around the circle telling each other your "proverbs." Encourage both humorous and serious contributions.
2. Or if this is your first study of Proverbs, give a minilecture on how to interpret this book, drawing on material in the previous unit.

Expand
1. Launch an in-depth study of a theme in Proverbs. Use one of these "link-to-life" suggestions:
(a) explore the content of Proverbs by dividing into teams to discover what this book considers to be wise/good and foolish/bad. See the "link-to-life" idea on page 344.
(b) Or, focus on one theme developed in Proverbs, by leading your group in a concordance study. The discussion of poverty in this unit and the "link-to-life" approach outlined on page 346 show how to conduct this kind of study.
2. Or lead your group in a study of the woman's role in biblical times, as outlined in the "link-to-life" suggestion on pages 347-348.

Apply
Have each group member write a single paragraph summing up what applying the wisdom drawn from your Proverbs study would mean for him or her. If you have time, let your group members read their paragraphs aloud.

STUDY GUIDE 51

Ecclesiastes

THE SEARCH FOR MEANING

Overview

Tradition tells us that this book was written by Solomon near the end of his reign. Linguistic study has revealed word choices and literary characteristics which fit Solomon's era, and support the traditional view that the writer, who claims to be king in Jerusalem and the wisest of men, was Solomon himself. In addition, the fact that in Solomon's old age he turned aside to worship the gods of his foreign wives adds support to this view.

Ecclesiastes is unlike any other Old Testament book, and has no parallel in other literature of the biblical world. Ecclesiastes is philosophical discourse. But more. Ecclesiastes makes no claim to bring man a word from God. Instead the writer specifically states that he includes only what he can determine by reason, and limits himself to data that is available "under the sun." The doctrine of inspiration guarantees that this book conveys the message God intended we receive but, as we will see, does *not* guarantee that all Solomon's statements are true!

▶ ***Vanity.*** This traditional KJV rendering of a key word in this book is correctly translated by the NIV as "meaningless." Solomon's search for meaning in life apart from God and divine revelation was futile. Like modern existential philosophers, Solomon concluded that life is meaningless. How good to know that God's revelation of Himself and His purposes give a meaning to your life and mine which can be found in no other source.

Commentary

David's son, Solomon, was crowned king of a united Israel just before his father's death. The young Solomon was given a unique gift from God: wisdom. He was certainly an intelligent man, and while his father extended Israel's kingdom by conquest, Solomon maintained the gains without war, through diplomacy.

But Solomon's strength was also his weakness. Solomon tended to trust in his wisdom rather than in the guidelines given in God's Word. Deuteronomy looked ahead to the future monarchy and said that "the king moreover, must not acquire great numbers of horses for himself or make the people return to Egypt to get more of them. . . . He must not take many wives, or his heart will be led astray. He must not accumulate large amounts of silver and gold" (Deut. 17:16-17).

David had followed these injunctions. He did take several wives, but nothing like Solomon's multiplication (700 wives and 300 concubines). David had established a policy of cutting the tendons of enemy war horses so they could not be used in battle, and refused to build a chariot-based military establishment. But Solomon reasoned that these were prudent policies. He failed to see the danger in each—that foreign wives might entice him from wholly following God, and that by becoming a military superpower he might trust his might rather than God.

Solomon trusted in his wisdom. Why not? His wisdom was renowned. God's warnings seemed unrealistic: wisdom dictated a different course from the one commanded by God.

First Kings 11 shows us how much wiser God was than this wisest of men. In Solomon's old age the women he loved did turn his heart from the Lord and toward their gods. Solomon brought into the Holy City itself the worship of the very gods and goddesses which the Lord commanded be purged from the land!

Because of this God pronounced judgment on Solomon. "The Lord became angry with Solomon, because his heart had turned away from the Lord, the God of Israel, who had appeared to him twice. Although He had forbidden Solomon to follow other gods, Solomon did not keep the Lord's command. So the Lord said to Solomon, 'Since this is your attitude and you have not kept My covenant and My decrees, which I commanded you, I will most certainly tear the kingdom away from you and give it to one of your subordinates. Nevertheless, for the sake of David your father, I will not do it during your lifetime. I will tear it out of the hand of your son. Yet I will not tear the whole kingdom from him, but will give him one tribe for the sake of David My servant and for the sake of Jerusalem, which I have chosen' " (1 Kings 11:9-13).

Thus Solomon's failure to trust God rather than his own wisdom had a tragic impact on his nation.

But Solomon's defection also had a tragic effect on him. Cut off from God by his own choice, left with only his wisdom to guide him, Solomon set out to find life's meaning apart from the Lord. This is why the Book of Ecclesiastes is so valuable. David, the emotional man, shared his feelings with us in the Psalms. Now Solomon, the intellectual man, shares his reasonings and inmost thoughts.

While Solomon lived in fellowship with God he wrote proverbs that reflect a Spirit-directed wisdom, such as:

> Trust in the Lord with all your heart and lean not on your own understanding; in all your ways acknowledge Him, and He will make your paths straight.
>
> Proverbs 3:5-6

When Solomon was out of fellowship during the later years of his rule, he wrote again. But this time his thinking was different. During these later years Solomon chose to attempt to reason out the meaning of life from data available within the physical universe. It is this reasoning, this exploration of the world in which man lives by unaided human reason, that we have recorded for us in Ecclesiastes.

Ecclesiastes Overview

Different kinds of biblical literature must be understood within the framework of their purpose and form. Poetic expression, for instance, should not be taken in the same way as a carefully reasoned teaching paragraph in a New Testament epistle. In order to understand any passage of Scripture, it is important to define its purpose and frame of reference. We need to remember this when we approach the Book of Ecclesiastes.

Ecclesiastes is different from any other book of the Bible. While it is included in the category of "wisdom literature" (with Job and Proverbs), it remains unique. Wisdom literature is universal in its scope; it does not dwell on the covenant, the election of Israel, redemption, prophecy, sacred history, or the temple. Its focus is on man the creature, his life on earth, and the inscrutability of God and His ways. Ecclesiastes goes beyond the other wisdom literature to emphasize the fact that human life and human goals, as ends in themselves and apart from God, are futile and meaningless.

Key phrases. There are three key phrases which help us understand the Book of Ecclesiastes.

(1) Twenty-nine times the writer used the phrase "under the sun" to define the limits he chose for his search. Only data which the senses can test and probe would be considered. Nothing from beyond this space-time universe would be considered. Nowhere in Ecclesiastes is Moses or Scripture or any form of revelation mentioned. Verse 13 of chapter 1 illustrates the limits that Solomon set for himself: "I devoted myself to study and to explore by wisdom all that is done under heaven."

(2) The second key phrase appears seven times and reflects the same limitation. Solomon said that, "I thought in my heart" or "thought to myself" in reaching his conclusions. His methodology was empirical, but all the data he gathered was evaluated by the standard of his own intelligence. In this book Solomon recognized no higher wisdom than his own; he never looked beyond the conclusions unaided intelligence can draw.

(3) The third key word appears 34 times! It is "meaningless," a term translated in other versions as "vanity" or "emptiness." Solomon's determined effort to make sense of human life led him to the same tragic conclusion of many modern philosophers. Life is absurd. There is no meaning or purpose in human experience. There may be fleeting joys. But ultimately, above the doorway through which men are born into

this world and the doorway through which they exit is written the same phrase: "Meaningless, meaningless, everything is meaningless."

This is not the overall witness of Scripture! God looks beyond the brief years human beings live on earth, and reveals our true destiny. Human beings were created in His image, touched by the eternal. Each of us has a future that extends beyond the limits of time itself. We will exist forever—with God, or separated from Him. In light of this heritage, and this destiny, each human life has tremendous meaning and each individual immeasurable worth and value. When we know God and hear His Word we affirm with Him that life is filled with meaning.

But Solomon here was looking for meaning *within* time—in fact, within the span of a man's lifetime on this earth. Using the intelligence Solomon had been given by God, he extended his great powers to the limit. But no matter how hard Solomon searched, he could find no satisfying purpose for life—within the limits he had set. Within these limits, life *does* become absurd and meaningless, and no one has any prospect of personal fulfillment.

Interpreting Ecclesiastes. When we know the context in which this book of Scripture was written, we are immediately warned not to draw doctrinal conclusions from Ecclesiastes. We can safely draw such conclusions from a Pauline epistle, for instance, or from the Book of Exodus. But what is recorded in Ecclesiastes is Solomon's reasoning. It is not necessarily the divine viewpoint!

How then do we interpret this book of the Bible?

(1) *We recognize it as a report of human reasoning.* We remember that this book communicates what Solomon thought, not what God reveals. As such, it may well contain many truths. But the conclusions Solomon reached will not necessarily express God's own thoughts or His will.

(2) *We remember that in this book inspiration means simply that Solomon's reasoning was accurately recorded.* Inspiration does not guarantee that everything recorded here is truth.

(3) *We rely on the whole revelation of God for interpreting problem passages.* Where a conclusion or insight in this book seems questionable, it is important to compare it with the rest of Scripture, which does reveal God's thoughts through men rather than describe as Ecclesiastes does the best reasoning of human beings.

When we approach Ecclesiastes in this way, the book gives us a penetrating insight into the emptiness of Solomon's last years. And a deep awareness of how tragic life is for all those who search for its meaning apart from our God.

♥ ***Link to Life: Youth / Adult***

To help your group members come to grips with the unique nature of this book, list the following on the chalkboard. Ask the group, "Which of these things is in the Bible?"

- *Don't be overrighteous.*
- *A live dog is better off than a dead lion.*
- *The dead know nothing.*
- *You will not surely die.*

After group members have expressed opinions, ask: "Are these statements true?"

Then look at each separately. The last *statement ("You will not surely die") is in Genesis 3:4. It directly contradicts Genesis 2:17—and it was said by Satan! Inspiration of the Bible guarantees that this is what Satan actually said, but it does not guarantee that what Satan said is true!*

The other three are in Ecclesiastes: in order, in 7:16; 9:4 and 9:5. Like the Genesis 3 statement, these expressions also are not necessarily *true!*

Go on then and explain the uniqueness of this book which records the reasoning of Solomon, not revelation from God!

Observations on the Text

The Book of Ecclesiastes can be outlined quite simply. It contains a prologue which states the writer's theme, two major sections, and then an epilogue.

Outline

I.	Prologue	1:1-11
II.	Theme Proven	1:12–6:12
III.	Deductions	7:1–12:8
IV.	Epilogue	12:9-14

Prologue (Ecc.1:1-11). Solomon clearly stated his theme:

> "Meaningless! Meaningless!" says the Teacher. "Utterly meaningless! Everything is meaningless."
>
> Ecclesiastes 1:2

The cycle of nature repeats endlessly as generations come and go. There is nothing new, nothing unique, and those who die are soon totally forgotten by the generations that succeed them. The endless repetition of sunrise and sunset suggested to Solomon that human life itself has no meaning.

Theme proven (Ecc. 1:12–6:12). In this first major section of the book Solomon marshaled evidence that supported his conclusion. All the evidence was drawn from Solomon's own experience and his observations. All the evidence was limited to what human beings can test by their senses within the limits of the physical universe. We can trace his argument, and see all the avenues that Solomon followed in his vain attempt to find a meaning for his life apart from God.

**The avenue of knowledge (1:12-18).* Solomon at first devoted himself to intellectual pursuits, and to learn all he could about everything "done under heaven" (v. 12). After years of study he concluded that learning is "chasing after the wind" (v. 14), because the more he learned about the nature of things, the more sorrow and grief he experienced.

**The avenue of pleasure (2:1-11).* Solomon created gardens and parks, amassed wealth, collected a harem of beautiful women. He said:

> I denied myself nothing my eyes desired;
> I refused my heart no pleasure.
>
> Ecclesiastes 2:10

And while Solomon was involved in his construction or projects he was distracted for a time. Yet when he looked back, and evaluated the many things he had achieved, he realized that it was all meaningless.

**The avenue of achievement (2:12-16).* In all Solomon's activities he proved himself superior to others. He had achieved, and surpassed all others. But while he felt that wisdom was better than folly, he couldn't help noting a terrible reality.

> The fate of the fool will overtake me also.
>
> Ecclesiastes 2:15

Solomon realized that he would die, and in time be forgotten just as the fool would die and be forgotten. How meaningless then to feel that contrasts between people can give life meaning.

**The avenue of work (2:17-26).* Solomon looked back at the energy and enthusiasm with which he had approached his work as king, and everything seemed to have the taste of ashes. He said, "I hated life, because the work that is done under the sun was grievous to me" (v. 17). Solomon's problem was that everything he had accomplished and worked for he must soon leave to someone else—"and who knows whether he will be a wise man or a fool?" (v. 19)

Solomon was not suggesting a life of idleness and abandonment. In fact, he said a "man can do nothing better than to eat and drink and find satisfaction in his work" (v. 24). But in an ultimate sense this too is meaningless.

**The avenue of natural cycles (3:1-15).* Solomon looked at the natural cycles of nature, life, and society. He found that time and time again what had been was repeated in the experience of the individual, the culture, and in nature. Yet these cycles in nature and human experience could offer no help in Solomon's search for meaning.

Why? Because, Solomon said, God "has also set eternity in the hearts of men" (v. 11). There is no way that the cycles of time, repeated as they are, can satisfy, because eternal meanings cannot be found in time's cycles.

**Injustice demonstrates meaninglessness (3:16-22).* Solomon discovered wickedness in man's treatment of man. He tried to explain it, arguing that someday God would bring good and evil people to judgment. But limiting himself to what he observed, he could not accept this thought. "Man's fate is like that of the animals" (v. 19). Both simply die, and their deaths seem to be the same in nature. "Who knows," Solomon said, "if the spirit of man rises upward and if the spirit of the animal goes down into the earth?" (v. 21)

**Human suffering gives evidence of meaninglessness (4:1-16).* When Solomon saw all the oppression to which people were subject, and noted their tears, he decided that "the dead, who had already died, are happier than the living, who are still alive" (v. 2). In the context of human suffering, those with friends are better off than those who are alone. But ultimately all are vulnerable.

**God is hidden (5:1-7)*. Solomon realized from the evidence of Creation that God must exist. He also was convinced that it was dangerous not to honor God: one should stand in awe of the Lord.

But God is distant and hidden. "God is in heaven, and you are on earth" (v. 2). So respect for the hidden God cannot be translated into a personal relationship which might give life meaning.

**Riches cannot provide meaning (5:8–6:2)*. No one really has control over his own possessions, for there are always authorities with power to take it from us. And there are many other reasons why riches are meaningless. First, the one loving money never really gets enough. Second, "as goods increase, so do those who consume them" (5:11). Third, the one with riches will worry about protecting them.

But ultimately, human beings who enter the world naked leave the world the same way, and as they bring nothing with them so they take nothing away.

What weighed so heavily on the heart of Solomon (then one of the world's richest men!) was that "God gives a man wealth, possessions, and honor, so that he lacks nothing his heart desires, but God does not enable him to enjoy them" (6:2).

Money does not bring happiness, and when death comes all one possesses passes to another.

**Life itself is meaningless (6:3-12)*. Grimly Solomon drew this section of his discourse to an end. The stillborn child was better than the person who lived, had a hundred children, and died in his old age. Life itself was a restless state. Ultimately no one could say what was "good" for a man in this life, and no one could tell what would happen on earth after a person was gone.

♥ ***Link to Life: Youth / Adult***

Ask your group to list things which people think of as giving life meaning. Among the things they suggest will probably be money, power, status, pleasure, etc.

Ask: "Have you ever tried to find meaning for your life in one of these things? What happened?"

After sharing, divide into teams to discuss why *these things are not able to provide life with meaning.*

After team members have listed their ideas, let them compare with Solomon's findings in parallel passages of Ecclesiastes.

Deductions to be derived (Ecc. 7:1–12:8). Solomon had proven to his own satisfaction that no real meaning could be found to human life. Still, he believed that some things are better than others. In the latter part of this book, then, Solomon gave suggestions to his readers.

He was still convinced that life was meaningless. But he did want to suggest rules for living the best life possible.

**Preferred ways (7:1-12)*. Given the meaninglessness of life Solomon was still aware that some experiences were better than others. For instance—and perhaps surprisingly—Solomon said sorrow was better than laughter. And the house of mourning better than the house of pleasure. Essentially, Solomon saw sorrow and mourning as more realistic, and thus less likely to lead to disappointment.

He also said that patience was better than pride, and noted that both wisdom and money could shelter human beings from troubles.

**Fatalism is to be adopted (7:13-14)*. Since no one has control over his future, good and bad must be accepted, with the good enjoyed while present.

**Extremes are to be avoided (7:15-22)*. A person should not be "overrighteous" or "overwise"—or "overwicked." Solomon was aware that there is "not a righteous man on earth who does what is right and never sins" (v. 20). He supposed that the middle road of avoiding all extremes was the best road to take. To be overwicked would lead to an early death. To be overrighteous to the torments of guilt.

**Wisdom is preferable (7:23–8:1)*. While wisdom cannot penetrate or learn "the scheme of things" it was clear to Solomon that wisdom, here as moral insight, was to be preferred. One who engaged in folly (an act that was morally perverted or twisted) would discover only that wickedness was stupid and folly was madness.

**Submission to authorities is better (8:2-10)*. One who does not obey will be harmed by temporal authorities. In this world where misery weighs heavily on every man there is no reason to ask for more by disobeying the king.

**Reverence for God is better (8:11-13)*. People are naturally twisted toward evil. No matter that Solomon had seen wicked men survive; "I know that it will go better with God-fearing men, who are reverent before God" (v. 12).

**Good things are better (8:14-15)*. The good things of life which persons enjoy cannot give life meaning. But it is better to enjoy them while we live than not to experience their pleasures.

**Enjoy life while it's possible (9:1-12)*. In view of the common destiny of the wicked and the good, for death awaits all, Solomon could only say, "Enjoy life with your wife, whom you love, all the days of this meaningless life that God has given you under the sun—all your meaningless days" (v. 9). Work hard, for there will be nothing for you to do in the grave, and death may catch you soon and unaware.

**Wisdom's ways are better (9:13–10:20)*. But wisdom will never protect a person. Fools are advanced by rulers, and a wise man's contributions will often be forgotten.

**It's better to prepare for the future (11:1-6)*. While no one can tell what the future will hold and no one can control the future, it's better to prepare for it rather than to be idle and wait until disaster strikes.

**Enjoy your youth (11:7–12:8)*. Ahead of every person is only darkness, lying with blind eyes under the earth unable to see the sun. But there is no use dwelling on this future. The phrase, "Remember your Creator" (12:1), is not a call to religious commitment but a suggestion that youth realize they are simply created beings, placed within creation and given capacity to enjoy what has been made. Thus Solomon said, "Be happy, young man, while you are young, and let your heart give you joy in the days of your youth" (11:9). Do it while you can, because the days of trouble will come and the years approach in which you will say, "I find no pleasure in them" (12:1). With age comes the awareness that Solomon's discovery is true for all:

> "Meaningless! Meaningless!" says the Teacher. "Everything is meaningless."
>
> Ecclesiastes 1:2

Epilogue (Ecc. 12:9-14). Solomon's conclusion has a different tone. He suggested, "Fear God and keep His commandments, for this is the whole duty of man" (v. 13). Ultimately it is God who will "bring every deed into judgment, including every hidden thing, whether it is good or evil."

TEACHING GUIDE

Prepare
Have you ever felt the kind of despair that Solomon's book communicates? Was there a special occasion, or a particular cause?

Explore
1. Use the "link-to-life" idea on page 351 to introduce the book. See if your group members recognize several sayings as from the Bible, and realize that they are not necessarily true. Then go on to show how the Book of Ecclesiastes is not intended to be taken as a divine revelation of truth.
2. Or give a minilecture on the book, and on Solomon's spiritual decline. Then ask your group members to locate statements in the book with which they *disagree*.

Expand
1. Examine the reasons Solomon gave as basis for his belief that life is meaningless. Use the teaching idea in "link-to-life," page 353. See how many of the reasons Solomon gives your group members can suggest from their own personal experience.
2. What "guidelines to the good life" could you give to a person who is not a believer? Make a list from Ecclesiastes 7:1–12:8.

When your group has developed a list, discuss: "How much would this really help another person?"

Talk together about the need for each person to find meaning in personal relationship with the God we know through Jesus Christ.

Apply
Brainstorm situations in which a Christian might use the Book of Ecclesiastes. Under what conditions might it be helpful in dealing with non-Christians? With other believers? In our own lives?

STUDY GUIDE 52

Song of Songs

CELEBRATION OF LOVE

Overview

This unusual Bible book makes no theological statement. It unveils no fresh revelations. It makes no mention of the divine Law, or the Lawgiver. And it seems to have little or nothing to say about our personal relationship with the Lord.

The first verse of the book identifies Solomon as its author. While some have challenged this, there is no doubt that this book held a place in the Hebrew canon of Scripture long before the Christian era, and most likely dates from the Solomonic era of 970-930 B.C.

The greatest debate over the book focuses on how it should be interpreted. Is this simply a great lyric love poem? Or is it intended to tell us something about God? If it does not speak of God, then why would it be included in the Scriptures?

Perhaps because of the uncertain nature of the book's message and perhaps because of its intimate portrayal of human love, the Song of Songs is seldom taught in our classes or churches.

The NIV translation adopts the view that Song is a love poem. It identifies the probable speakers, and the chorus of friends who speak as background for the dialogue between lover and beloved. Using this version makes it easy to follow the flow of the poem, and to grasp its structure.

- The *Bible Knowledge Commentary* contains a thorough discussion of the book and gives a helpful verse-by-verse commentary. It is helpful in explaining the many images Solomon uses.

Commentary

The *Word Bible Handbook* (Richards, Word Inc.) contains a succinct description of the various historical approaches taken to interpret this difficult Old Testament book. That description is repeated here by permission of the publisher.

Among the approaches suggested for interpreting the Song, three have gained strong support historically.

(1) Allegorical. Many Jewish rabbis saw the Song as an allegory of God's relationship with Israel. Early Christian interpreters took the same approach, but applied it to the relationship between the church and Christ. With this approach a phrase like "black but comely" in 1:5 [KJV] was taken to mean black with sin, but made beautiful by conversion. A phrase like "between my breasts" in 1:13 was seen as a reference to the Old and the New Testaments.

The primary problem with such interpretation, that there is no objective way to check interpretive flights of fancy for literal meanings, are deemed to be irrelevant. Some versions of the Bible in English reflect the allegorical approach to this book in chapter headings, as: 1–3, The mutual love of Christ and the church; 4, The graces of the church; 5, Christ's love to us; 6–7, The church professes her faith and desire; 8, The church's love to Christ.

(2) Typical. In the twelfth century A.D. a tradition began which held Song to be what it seems, a love poem, but with typical meaning, meant to help us understand the relationship of Christ and the church. This view is held by many today. But there is no indication in Song of Songs or other passages of Scripture to suggest a type is intended.

(3) Literal. Those who see Song of Songs as a celebration of love as God intended it to be experienced by a man and woman, have held different views about the book's structure. To some it seems just a collection of love poems. To others it tells a unified story. The great

scholar Franz Delitzsch suggested it is a drama, telling the story of King Solomon falling in love with a girl from one of Israel's northern villages. He meets her while traveling incognito, returns to the capital, and later returns in splendor to carry her back to Jerusalem.

This dramatic view is reflected in the NIV, which marks out the alternating speeches of the beloved (the bride) and lover (Solomon), and infrequent refrains spoken or sung by a chorus of her friends. The structure fits the Hebrew text, and the determination of who is speaking is made by the gender (male, female) of the Hebrew pronouns.

Because of its poetic and dramatic nature, it is not possible to outline Song of Songs effectively. However the following generally accepted structure helps fit together the story told in the book.

1–2:7	The bride longs for her bridegroom. They meet and praise each other.
2:8–3:11	As their love grows, the bride praises the groom, using figures in nature.
4:1–5:1	The lover comes and praises the bride.
5:2–6:3	The lover has gone away and the bride expresses her longing for him.
6:4–8:14	The lover returns, the marriage is consummated (7:1–8:4), and the happiness of the couple celebrated.

The third view was held in the early church, and is still held by many today. For many reasons, this seems to be the best for us to accept as well.

Biblical View of Sex

If we accept the third view, that Song of Songs is in fact a poem written in celebration of married love, we are invited to look more closely at the biblical view of sex.

It is striking to note first of all that the Bible does not trivialize sex. In other cultures in the area and era of the Bible, little sexual restraint was shown. Graphic language and many specific terms for sex organs and activities fill the religious and secular poetry of nearby pagan lands.

In contrast, the Bible speaks circumspectly about sex. No specific terms are found in the Bible for sex organs. Euphemisms such as "to know" and "to lie down" are used to describe intercourse. While this biblical restraint is notable, it does not suggest a puritan attitude toward sexuality. Instead the sexual nature of human beings is affirmed in the Bible, and the care with which sexual matters are spoken of affirms the mystery of and special nature of the sexual relationship. By restraint the Scriptures guard the mystery and sanctity of intimate experience; an experience that is sacramental in nature and not to be treated as mere animal function, as in ancient paganism and modern-day "adult" publications.

Scripture, of course, forbids sex out of marriage, both adultery and premarital. It also forbids prostitution. A number of passages in the Law, but particularly Leviticus 18, define sexual limits.

Yet when it comes to marriage, the biblical message is one of freedom rather than restriction. No passage in Old or New Testaments regulates sexual practices within marriage. Instead the Bible affirms the joys and values of human sexuality. To question the rightness of sex in marriage, Paul teaches, is to follow "things taught by demons" (1 Tim. 4:1). It's clear from the Creation story that God is pro sex, for He is the One who created them "male and female" (Gen. 1:27).

At times Christians have adopted an ascetic, negative view of sex. Even in Bible times some felt that marriages should be "spiritual," and that normal sexual relations between Christian husband and wife should be abandoned. Paul dealt with this question in 1 Corinthians when he wrote:

> The husband should fulfill his marital duty to his wife, and likewise the wife to the husband. The wife's body does not belong to her alone but also to her husband. In the same way, the husband's body does not belong to him alone but also to his wife. Do not deprive each other except by mutual consent and for a time, so that you may devote yourselves to prayer.
>
> 1 Corinthians 7:3-5

In the account of the original Creation, God created Eve from Adam's rib, shaping her, like Adam, in God's own image to be a suitable companion for Adam. The two, man and woman, are capable of experiencing a unique oneness, that meets the deepest inner needs of each, and that oneness is both sealed and symbolized by sexual intercourse. For that reason, Paul was unwilling to have husbands and wives deny each other the celebration of oneness that is married sex.

It's clear from Paul's New Testament writings that he believed there are reasons for men and women to remain unmarried. He himself had chosen this course. But Paul was not antisex. For those whom God leads to unite with another, sex is sacramental, designed by God not only for pleasure but also to express the intimacy of the bond that exists between husband and wife.

In the context of the biblical affirmation of sex, the Song of Songs takes on a special role. As a love poem it is designed to help us sense the joy, and join in the celebration of that which is essentially good. Delicately, and sensitively, we are invited in the Song of Songs to sense the nature of a pure sensuality: a sensuality that releases the believer to fully enjoy the gift of sex within the context of marital commitment.

TEACHING GUIDE

Prepare
Read through the Song of Songs, sensing its power as a love story and love poem.

Explore
1. Read Song aloud as a dramatic poem, using the NIV text. A woman should read the role of the beloved, a man the role of lover. The group can read the "friends" verses in unison as a chorus.

Such a reading will give your group a unique feel for this poem in celebration of married love.

2. Or give a minilecture on the ways in which Song of Songs has been interpreted historically.

To demonstrate the problem with an allegorical interpretation, divide into teams of three persons. Each team is to look at Song 5:1-7, and develop detailed suggestions about what the thoughts and action in their sections really mean.

After 5 to 10 minutes, have teams share their ideas with the group.

Then discuss the similarities and differences between the teams' ideas. What do they suggest about allegorical interpretations?

Expand
1. Ask your group members to write brief paragraphs summing up a "biblical view of married sex."

Then, without reading the paragraphs, take a poll. How many of your group members think that the Bible has a generally positive view of sex in marriage? How many think that the Bible takes a generally negative view?

Ask for group members to volunteer the passages or teachings on which their view is based.

2. Or ask your group members to develop a series of statements on Christian sexuality. Divide into teams to look at the following passages, giving each team a different passage to read and discuss: Genesis 1:26-31; 2:20-25; 1 Corinthians 7:1-38; and 1 Timothy 4:1-5.

Apply
1. If you did not do the group reading of Song to launch this session, do it as a concluding activity, so that your members can sense the celebration which is an appropriate response to God's gift of sexuality and marriage.

2. Or ask your members to read through this book silently, marking passages or phrases that seem to them to express the tone of celebration.

STUDY GUIDE 53

Selected Old Testament Scriptures

UNDERSTANDING THE PROPHETS

Overview

The prophet served a major role in Old Testament times. Prophets were God's spokesmen, sent to give supernatural guidance to individuals and to the nation.

God through Moses had warned His people not to seek guidance from occult sources (cf. Deut. 18). In that passage God promised to send prophets to unveil His will. These prophets were to be authenticated by foretelling future events. What the true prophet foretold would surely happen.

The primary message of the Old Testament prophets was to the men and women of their own time. And the authenticating signs could be observed by their contemporaries. But many of the Old Testament prophets looked far beyond their own times and their writings convey a sweeping vision of the then-distant future. Many of these prophecies concern Jesus in His first coming. Others concern events hundreds of years future to the prophets, but events now far in our past. But perhaps most of the far-view prophecies concern the time of the end.

As we read the written works of the prophets in our Old Testaments, we are struck by common end-time themes that recur again and again in both the Major and Minor Prophets. While we do not have enough data to speak with certainty about the details of what still lies ahead, we surely have enough to see the future's broad outlines.

In this introductory unit we survey the future through themes that are repeated again and again by the Old Testament prophets.

Commentary

The roots of prophecy are found in the covenants of the Old Testament. The word covenant (*b'rit*) means a contract, oath, or promise. When God first spoke to Abram in Ur He made a personal commitment, expressed in a covenant which explained what God intended to do. In that first great covenant promise, God said He would:

- *make Abraham a great nation* (fulfilled in the Jewish and Arab races who trace their origins to Isaac and Ishmael).
- *bless Abraham* (fulfilled in God's daily care and in counting Abraham's faith as righteousness).
- *make Abraham's name great* (fulfilled in the respect paid him by Jews, Christians, and Muslims).
- *bless those who treat Abraham's people well and curse those who do not* (fulfilled in history and illustrated in the fate of Nazi Germany).
- *bless all the families of the world through Abraham* (fulfilled in Jesus, the Saviour, who is a Jew), and finally
- *give Abraham and his descendants the land of Palestine* (still unfulfilled in its defined extent!).

The land "from the river of Egypt to the great river, the Euphrates" (Gen. 15:18) has in historic times been partially occupied by the Hebrew people, but in its defined extent has never yet been theirs.

As the centuries passed, the original covenant stated in Genesis 12 and restated in chapters 15 and 17 was further defined by additional covenant promises. The Davidic Covenant promised that a descendant of David's would rule: "Your throne will be established forever" (2 Sam. 7:16). Permanent, endless rule of Israel's Promised Land was guaranteed to One from David's family.

Again centuries passed, and both Northern tribes (Israel) and Southern tribes (Judah) were torn from Palestine by foreign conquerors. Did this mean the ancient covenant promises were set aside? Had the sins of the Jews led God to withdraw His promised blessings?

To answer this question, the Prophet Jeremiah was told to announce a New Covenant. God had not changed His mind!

> "Restrain your voice from weeping and your eyes from tears . . ." declares the Lord. "They will return from the land of the enemy. So there is hope for your future," declares the Lord. "Your children will return to their own land."
>
> Jeremiah 31:16-17

In this New Covenant promise, God announced His intention to change the hearts of His people in a great national conversion.

> "I will put My Law in their minds and write it on their hearts. I will be their God, and they will be My people. No longer will a man teach his neighbor, or a man his brother, saying, 'Know the Lord,' because they will all know Me, from the least of them to the greatest," declares the Lord. "For I will forgive their wickedness and will remember their sins no more."
>
> Jeremiah 31:33-34

While God's commitment to keep His promises remains firm, the Lord also added a special set of promises and warnings for each generation of Israelites. The Law covenant did not speak of the time of the end, but spoke to people who would live in the centuries before the end came.

In the Law God gave each generation this commitment: Those who obeyed Him and kept His commandments would be blessed in their present, even as all humanity will be blessed at history's end. And those generations and persons who failed to obey would suffer divine judgment.

Imbedded in the promises and the warnings found in Deuteronomy 28, are portraits of national poverty, defeat, and exile! In a striking way this chapter pictures exactly what has happened to the Jewish people—*often!*

It happened when Assyria defeated Israel.

It happened when Babylon defeated Judah.

It happened when Rome finally crushed the Jews in A.D. 70.

And yet, with its warning of defeat and exile Deuteronomy contains a promise of restoration to the land.

> When all these blessings and curses I have set before you come upon you and you take them to heart wherever the Lord your God disperses you among the nations, and when you and your children return to the Lord your God and obey Him with all your heart and with all your soul according to everything I command you today, then the Lord your God will restore your fortunes and have compassion on you and gather you again from all the nations where He scattered you. Even if you have been banished to the most distant land under the heavens, from there the Lord your God will gather you and bring you back. He will bring you to the land that belonged to your fathers, and you will take possession of it. He will make you more prosperous and numerous than your fathers. The Lord your God will circumcise your hearts and the hearts of your descendants, so that you may love Him with all your heart and with all your soul, and live.
>
> Deuteronomy 30:1-6

One of the great questions debated by Christians with differing prophetic views is whether or not this Deuteronomy 30 promise was fulfilled in the return from Babylon some 500 years before Christ.

The answer is "yes"—and "no"!

Certainly the return from Babylon was a fulfillment of God's Deuteronomy promise. But it was not a *complete* fulfillment. How do we know? We know because after the return took place, the postexilic prophets repeat the same themes we find in Deuteronomy and in the prophets who spoke before the Babylonian Captivity. For instance, Zechariah said:

> This is what the Lord Almighty says, "Once again men and women of ripe old age will sit in the streets of Jerusalem, each with cane in hand because of his age. The city streets will be filled with boys and girls playing there." This is what the Lord Almighty says, "It may seem marvelous to the remnant of this people at that time, but will it seem marvelous to Me?" declares the Lord Almighty. This is what the Lord Almighty says, "I will save My people from the countries of the east and the west. I will

> bring them back to live in Jerusalem; they will be My people, and I will be faithful and righteous to them as their God."
>
> Zechariah 8:4-8

How significant Isaiah's statement, made long before the first Exile, seems.

> In that day the Lord will *reach out His hand a second time* to reclaim the remnant that is left of His people.
>
> Isaiah 11:11, italics mine

What then do we conclude? First, that the prophet's picture of still-future events is rooted in the covenant promises God has given His Old Testament people. Second, that themes repeated by prophets before and after the Babylonian Captivity, while partially fulfilled in the return from that exile, have a more complete fulfillment ahead.

And third, when we see themes, rooted in the covenants, repeated in the prophets of all Old Testament eras, we can assume that these repeated themes foreshadow events that are still future to our own times.

♥ ***Link to Life: Youth / Adult***

Help your group see the pattern of scattering and return defined in Deuteronomy 28–30. A minilecture should accomplish this.

Then ask: "Does this passage describe something in history, or something yet future?" After discussion, divide into study teams to look at the following passages which deal with the scattering and return of the people of Israel.

Have your teams note carefully. Is the final return natural or supernatural? Where are the people who return found? How is this event like or unlike the return described in Ezra and Nehemiah?

The passages: Isaiah 11:11-12; 14:1-3; 27:12-13; 43:1-8; 49:16; 66:20-22; Jeremiah 16:14-16; 23:3-8; 30:10-11; 31:8, 31-37; Ezekiel 11:17-21; 20:33-38; 34:11-16; 39:25-29; Hosea 1:10-11; Joel 3:17-21; Amos 9:11-15; Micah 4:4-7; Zephaniah 3:14-20; Zechariah 8:4-8.

After reports, locate each prophet on a timeline. What are the implications of seeing the same theme repeated before and after the Babylonian Exile and return?

The Old Testament covenants provide that Testament's basic orientation to the future. What the prophets describe is essentially how God's promises to Abraham will be kept. The prophets do not change those purposes, but expand and develop themes found in the original covenants.

What then are recurring themes that tell us more about this regathering the Bible speaks of as a prelude to giving Israel her Promised Land?

A Great Tribulation

Few themes linked with history's end have drawn so much attention. Few are so emphasized in the Old Testament. When the prophets speak of the "Day of the Lord" (a phrase which like "that day" indicates the time of the end and God's active involvement in it), they often sound much like Amos:

> Woe to you who long for the Day of the Lord! Why do you long for the Day of the Lord? That day will be darkness, not light. It will be as though a man fled from a lion only to meet a bear, as though he entered his house and rested his hand on the wall only to have a snake bite him. Will not the Day of the Lord be darkness, not light—pitch-dark, without a ray of brightness?
>
> Amos 5:18-20

While the "Day of the Lord" as a theological term encompasses all that happens in the extended period during which God fulfills His promises and brings history to its conclusion, the emphasis in most Old Testament passages is on the dark time of tribulation and judgment initiating that day.

The Day of the Lord is pictured as a terrible time for humanity; an era of purposeful judgment. Earth is wasted and emptied, its inhabitants devastated. There is gloom and darkness, trouble and woe, for God's wrath is fully expressed against sinning humankind (cf. Deut. 4:30-31; Isa. 2:19; 24:1, 3, 6, 19-21; 26:20-21; Jer. 30:7; Dan. 9:27; 12:1; Joel 1:15; 2:1-2; Amos 5:18-20; Zeph. 1:14-15, 18).

According to the Old Testament, pagan nations and God's people are both to experience the divine judgment, for this Tribulation is worldwide. As Jeremiah said:

> "Look! Disaster is spreading from nation to nation; a mighty storm is rising from the ends of the earth." At that time those slain by the Lord will be everywhere from one end of the earth to the other. They will not be mourned or gathered up or buried.
>
> Jeremiah 25:32-33

Yet, with all the stunning terror of the Tribulation time, it is clear that it is intended to lead to deliverance.

> How awful that day will be! None will be like it. It will be a time of trouble for Jacob, but he will be saved out of it.
>
> Jeremiah 30:7

> I will take note of you as you pass under My staff, and I will bring you into the bond of the covenant. I will purge you from those who revolt and rebel against Me.
>
> Ezekiel 20:37-38

> "In the whole land," declares the Lord, "two-thirds will be struck down and perish; yet one-third will be left in it. This third I will bring into the fire; I will refine them like silver and test them like gold. They will call on My name and I will answer them; I will say, 'They are My people,' and they will say, 'The Lord is our God.' "
>
> Zechariah 13:8-9

The time of trouble leads to this consummation. It is intended for cleansing (see also Rev. 7:9; 14:4) and intended as preparation for national conversion of Israel (cf. Ezek. 20:37-38; Zech. 13:1, 8-9).

So worldwide Tribulation does lie ahead. But even this most terrible of times is intended by God for good, and will move history toward His intended end.

The dark threads of prophetic warning about events associated with the time of the end can best be appreciated simply by reading. So prepare a "responsive reading" from the following passages:

Day of the Lord: Isaiah 2:12; 13:6; Ezekiel 13:5; 30:3; Joel 1:15; 2:1, 11, 31; Amos 5:18-20; Obadiah 15; Zephaniah 1:7, 14; Zechariah 14:1; Malachi 4:5.

Tribulation: Deuteronomy 4:30-31; Isaiah 2:19; 24:1, 3, 6, 19-21; 26:20-21; Jeremiah 30:7; Daniel 9:27; 12:1; Joel 1:15; 2:1-2; Amos 5:18-20; Zephaniah 1:14-15, 18.

The Cast of Characters

When the prophets spoke of history's end there are certain characters or powers which have leading roles.

Political powers. The Old Testament suggests that several power blocks will exist as the end time approaches. These include:

**The West.* This power block is seen in Daniel 2:41-42; 7:7; and 8:9-26. It seems to be a coalition of 10 states, some weak and some strong, who come under the influence of a political leader who will counterfeit the Messiah. These states occupy territory roughly that of the Roman Empire of Jesus' day.

**The North.* This represents a second great confederacy. It is described in Isaiah 30:31-33; Ezekiel 38:1–39:25; Daniel 11:40; Joel 2:1-17; and other passages. Nations called in the Old Testament Gog, Magog, Rosh, Meshech and Tubal have been identified as territory currently including Russia, Iran, certain Arab states, East Germany, and some Asian peoples.

**The East.* This power is mentioned in Revelation 16:12, and indicates a coalition of Asian powers.

**The South.* This is the final area, mentioned in Daniel 11:40. This is Egyptian or North African territory, and is the first power block to be confronted by the West and destroyed by it.

Teachers of prophecy make much of the fact, that for the first time in some 19 centuries of the Christian era, the political shape of our world fits the distribution of powers described in the Old Testament.

The personalities. The dominant personality associated with the end time is a person known as the Antichrist. He is described in great detail, and will be the leader of the Western power block. His character and his activities are presented in Ezekiel 28:1-10 and Daniel 7:7-8, 20-26; 8:23-25; 9:26-27; 11:36-45 as well as in the New Testament passages such as 2 Thessalonians 2:3-10 and Revelation 13:1-10.

While the Antichrist will at first appear to be a friend of Israel, he will quickly turn against her and set himself up as god (Dan. 9:27; 11:36-37). Israel itself will become a battleground.

Patterns. While exact details and sequences are difficult to follow, an extended passage in Ezekiel has been understood by many to give a general sequence of the events that lead to the intense persecution and culminating judgments of history's end. In brief, the passage (Ezek. 38–39) suggests the following senario.

**Ezekiel 38:1-6:* The invaders are identified as Russia and her confederates, coming from the "far north" (v. 6) with many peoples.

**Ezekiel 38:7-9:* Israel's people, having returned from "many nations," will finally be dwelling securely (possibly because of the treaty with the West).

**Ezekiel 38:10-14:* In spite of a Western protest the invaders will sweep down on defenseless Israel to plunder her.

**Ezekiel 38:15-16:* The invading army will be successful, covering the land like a cloud. Like other earlier invaders, these too are called to a ministry of judgment, purging Israel.

**Ezekiel 38:17-23:* In a great cataclysm, God will act to destroy the invading army. The destruction will be so startling and its supernatural origins will be recognized by all: "And so I will show My greatness and My holiness, and I will make Myself known in the sight of many nations. Then they will know that I am the Lord" (v. 23).

**Ezekiel 39:9-11:* The remaining war materials will become a resource for Jewish rebuilding. The battle will be followed by cleansing and forgiveness of Israel.

According to this interpretation, the destruction of Russia leaves a power vacuum and the West, led by Antichrist, is free to occupy Palestine and the adjacent oil fields of the OPEC nations.

If we sum up the events linked with these major characters in Old Testament prophecy, we come up with the following general outline of the time of the end.

(1) Israel makes a treaty with the Antichrist and occupies her land in false security.
(2) Russia invades Palestine.
(3) Russia and her allies are destroyed.
(4) The Antichrist breaks his treaty with Israel and the West occupies the land.
(5) A world government is formed under the Antichrist.
(6) All nations gather to battle around Jerusalem.
(7) Jesus returns to destroy the Gentile world powers and to rule.

The Glorious Kingdom

The last event on the list above is perhaps the most significant theme of the prophets. They speak powerfully of a coming kingdom, governed by a ruler who is to come from David's line.

The coming king. The titles of this coming king make it very clear that the One of whom the prophets speak is Jesus, God Himself come in human form.

Here are some of those titles:

Jehovah (Isa. 2:2-4)
Mighty God (Isa. 9:6)
The Judge (Isa. 11:3-4)
Lord Almighty (Isa. 24:23)
The King (Isa. 33:17)
Our Lawgiver (Isa. 33:22)
Your God (Isa. 52:7)
The Redeemer (Isa. 59:20)
The Lord our Righteousness (Jer. 23:6)
Ancient of Days (Dan. 7:13)
The Most High (Dan. 7:22)
Prince of princes (Dan. 8:25)
The Anointed One (Dan. 9:25-26)
The Lord (Micah 4:7)

In the earliest days, the promised throne was said to be the Lord's own (1 Chron. 28:5; 2 Chron. 9:8; 13:8). The King is "God with us" (Isa. 7:14), to be born of a virgin in Bethlehem (Isa. 7:14; Micah 5:2). This Ruler's authority will extend to the entire earth (Ps. 2:8; Isa. 11:9; 42:4; Jer. 23:5; Zech. 14:9), even though it will be centered in Jerusalem (Isa. 2:1-3; 62:1-7; Zech. 8:20-23). Ruling over a converted Israel (Isa. 11:11-12; 14:1-2; Jer. 23:6-8; 32:37-38; 33:7-9; Ezek. 37:21-25; Micah 4:6-8), the King will bring peace to Gentiles as well as to Israel (Pss. 72:11, 17; 86:9; Isa. 55:5; Dan. 7:13-14; Micah 4:2; Zech. 8:22).

This prophetic theme makes it increasingly clear that the King must be God Himself, a truth made especially plain in Isaiah 9:6-7.

> For to us a Child is born, to us a Son is given, and the government will be on His shoulders. And He will be called Wonderful Counselor, Mighty God, Everlasting Father, Prince of Peace. Of the increase of His government and peace

> there will be no end. He will reign on David's throne and over his kingdom, establishing and upholding it with justice and righteousness from that time on and forever.
>
> Isaiah 9:6-7

His wonderful rule. What will the restoration, of which the Old Testament speaks, be like, and how does it describe the earthly kingdom of the Messiah? The most famous description is found in Isaiah 11:1-9.

> A shoot will come up from the stump of Jesse [the father of David], from his roots a Branch will bear fruit. The Spirit of the Lord will rest on Him—the Spirit of wisdom and of understanding, the Spirit of counsel and of power, the Spirit of knowledge and of the fear of the Lord—and He will delight in the fear of the Lord. He will not judge by what He sees with His eyes, or decide by what He hears with His ears; but with righteousness He will judge the needy, with justice He will give decisions for the poor of the earth. He will strike the earth with the rod of His mouth, with the breath of His lips He will slay the wicked. Righteousness will be His belt, and faithfulness the sash around His waist. The wolf will live with the lamb, the leopard will lie down with the goat, the calf and the lion and the yearling together; and a little child will lead them. The cow will feed with the bear, their young will lie down together, and the lion will eat straw like the ox. The infant will play near the hole of the cobra, and the young child put his hand into the viper's nest. They will neither harm nor destroy on all My holy mountain, for the earth will be full of the knowledge of the Lord as the waters cover the sea.
>
> Isaiah 11:1-9

In this lengthy passage we see images repeated again and again. The supernaturally endowed ruler brings peace. The poor and the oppressed are cared for at last, while the wicked are judged. In many ways, the Messiah's rule has a wonderful impact on human experience.

- In place of *war* there will be *peace* (Isa. 9:4-7; 32:17-18; Ezek. 34:25, 28; Micah 4:2-3).
- In place of *sin* there will be *holiness* (Isa. 29:18-23; 35:8-9; Zeph. 3:11; Zech. 14:20-21).
- In place of *misery* there will be *comfort* (Isa. 29:22-23; 61:3-7; 66:13; Jer. 31:23-25; Zech. 9:11-12).
- In place of *injustice* there will be *justice* (Isa. 42:1-4; 65:21-23; Jer. 31:23, 29-30).
- In place of *sickness* there will be *healing* (Isa. 29:17-19; 35:3-6; 61:1-2; Jer. 31:8; Micah 4:6-7).
- In place of *ignorance* will be *knowledge* of the Lord (Isa. 11:1-2, 9; 41:19-20; 54:13; Hab. 2:14).
- Instead of *early death* there will be *preservation* (Isa. 41:8-14; 62:8-9; Jer. 23:6; 32:27; Ezek. 34:27; Joel 3:16-17; Zech. 8:14-15; 9:17; 14:10-11).
- Instead of *poverty* there will be *prosperity* (Isa. 4:1; 65:21-22; Ezek. 34:26; Joel 2:21-27; Amos 9:13-14; Zech. 8:11-22; 9:16-17).

All these and other blessings are promised by the Old Testament prophets—when the King finally reigns.

♥ ***Link to Life: Youth / Adult***

Give group members large sheets of paper and crayons. Ask each person to select three *passages or verses from the following list. After reading the selected passages, each is to* draw a picture of the Old Testament's promised kingdom. *Each will incorporate images drawn from the passages he or she selected.*

When the pictures have been completed, go around the circle and ask each person to share what he or she has drawn and what the features represent.

This simple approach should help your group develop a comprehensive view of the Old Testament kingdom in prophecy.

Passages from which to select:

Isaiah 2:1-4	*Daniel 2:31-45*
4:2-6	*7:1-28*
9:6-7	*9:1-3, 20-27*
11:1-13	*12:1-4*
24:1-13	*Hosea 3:4-5*
32:1-5, 14-20	*Joel 2:18–3:2*
33:17-24	*3:9-21*
35:1-10	*Amos 9:9-15*
52:7-10	*Obadiah 9-15*
60:1–61:6	*Micah 4:1-5*
66:15-23	*Zephaniah 3:8-20*

Jeremiah 22:1-8	*Haggai 2:1-13*
31:1-27	*Zechariah 2:1-13*
33:14-26	*6:11-13*
Ezekiel 20:33-42	*8:1-8*
34:20-21	*9:9-10*
36:22-36	*12:1-10*
37:1-28	*14:1-21*
39:21-29	*Malachi 3:1-5*
	4:1-6

There are then a number of themes common to the Old Testament prophets, which look forward to a time which is still future to us today.

We read in the prophets of a terrible time of judgment, marked by trials and tribulation for the entire earth. We read of wars that ravage the earth, and power blocks of nations that seem to match the great powers of our own time. We read of the Antichrist, and of God's appointed and coming King. And we read of a glorious kingdom which that King will establish on earth.

Surely, while many elements of these Old Testament prophecies have at least partial fulfillment in history, at no time have they combined to constitute fulfillment of God's covenant promises.

Whatever we may think of these promises from the vantage point of the cross, it is clear that God's Old Testament people, like the prophets, looked forward to a real fulfillment in history of the events that they described.

It is also clear, as we read the Old Testament prophets today, that when we meet these repeated themes again and again, we need to know that they are part of a cohesive and consistent view of a future that God's prophets believe the Lord intends for the race He chose to be His own.

TEACHING GUIDE

Prepare

In view of the international situation today, how important is it to you to believe that God is in control of the future, and that each day moves us closer to His intended end?

Explore

This unit gives an orienting interview to prophetic themes that anyone who studies the Old Testament prophets will meet again and again. It should be taught as an overview, in preparation for looking more deeply into the individual prophets and their particular messages.

So begin this session with a responsive reading, developed from passages which describe the Great Tribulation (see "link-to-life," p. 360).

Expand

1. Give a minilecture overview of the major elements in Old Testament predictive prophecy as outlined in this unit.
2. Pass out crayons and paper, and have your group members draw impressions of the coming kingdom as it is described in three passages they select from the list on page 363. Comparing and explaining pictures should give a powerful impression of the good things God has ahead for humankind.

Apply

Raise the question of whether there are indications in the New Testament that this Old Testament picture of the future is to be accepted by the church. After discussion, close with another responsive reading, which you develop from the following New Testament passages: Matthew 24; Romans 11:1-2, 16-27; 2 Thessalonians 2:1-8.

Then close in prayer, thanking God that, whatever lies ahead, His good purposes for mankind—and for each of us—will surely be realized.

STUDY GUIDE 54

Isaiah 1–6

THE HOLY ONE

Overview
Isaiah is one of the most significant of Old Testament books. Isaiah spoke out to Judah during the critical years of Assyrian expansion, when the Northern Kingdom, Israel, was destroyed.

Isaiah is especially significant for (1) his revelation of God through powerful, vital names (such as Holy One, God the Judge, etc.); for (2) his clear vision of Jesus the Messiah; for (3) his Servant theme; and (4) for his powerful visions of history's end.

The book is divided into two major segments, written at different periods of Isaiah's life.

Outline

I.	Visions of Judgment	1–35
	1. Israel's Holy One	1–6
	2. Book of Immanuel	7–12
	3. Oracles of judgment	13–24
	4. God's sure purposes	25–35
II.	Historical Interlude	36–39
III.	Visions of Splendor	40–66
	1. Beyond the Exile	40–48
	2. Servant of the Lord	49–55
	3. Redemption's need	56–59
	4. Restoration	60–66

Isaiah's great contribution to modern Christians is his majestic portrait of God and of our Lord. As we meet God in this great prophetic book we are moved to awe—and to worship.

■ Were there two Isaiahs? How many prophecies about Jesus does this book contain? For answers to these and many other fascinating questions see the verse-by-verse exposition in the *Bible Knowledge Commentary*, pages 1029-1121.

Commentary

So man will be brought low and mankind humbled, the eyes of the arrogant humbled. But the Lord Almighty will be exalted by His justice, and the holy God will show Himself holy by His righteousness.

Isaiah 5:15-16

To the Jews, Isaiah was the greatest of the prophets. The commentator Karl Delitzsch called Isaiah the "universal prophet."

Probably no other Old Testament document has been more deeply studied than the Book of Isaiah. Certainly none has had more books and articles written about it. The New Testament alludes to it over 250 times and quotes Isaiah specifically at least 50 times!

There are several reasons for this fascination with Isaiah. As literature, Isaiah has been called the "climax of Hebrew literary art." In content, it deals in a sweeping way with the great themes of the Old Testament. Judgment and hope, sin and redemption, find clear expression here. Christians have been fascinated by the picture of Jesus the Messiah drawn by this man who wrote so many centuries before Christ's birth. The picture of the suffering Messiah in Isaiah 53 has been critical in our understanding of Jesus' Calvary death.

Isaiah has also been a source of controversy. The book is divided into two distinct halves, set apart by a historical interlude. The first half of Isaiah announces judgment; the second half seems to assume the judgment has passed and that hope has come. Were these two sections of Isaiah written by the same person? Or was a "Second Isaiah" added later on? Conservatives have argued persuasively that the whole book was written by Isaiah the son of Amoz, whose ministry extended over some 60 years from 739 to about 681 B.C.

This was a critical period of Old Testament history. Israel, the Northern Kingdom, was overwhelmed by Assyria. Judah was threatened as well. What was God's message to a nation and people threatened by a Gentile world power? How were His people (and how are we) to live in the face of the powers of the world around them?

But the primary reason for reading Isaiah is to see the Lord. Certainly we've seen God in other Old Testament books. We've seen His power in the Exodus, His righteousness in the Law, His justice in the Book of Judges. But somehow it's as though we saw God *through* the events recorded. He is there, but as a shadow; glimpsed, but not fully revealed, in His actions in history. In Isaiah the veil of history is pulled aside and we see God directly, revealed in all His glory.

It's as if we set out at night to explore a new land, holding up our flickering candles to light the darkness. We see, but not clearly. And then torchlight more brilliant than the sun fills the sky, and what had been only outline becomes solid and real. In the light of that torch, we see clearly for the first time. Isaiah's distinctive ministry is to lift high the torch, to show us, in brilliant clarity, the God men grope after.

For all of us who desire to know God in a deeper and fuller way, the Book of Isaiah holds great promise. As you study it with your group, you will together be filled with wonder at the greatness and majesty of our God. You will be moved to praise and to hope, as God lifts high the torch of revelation to show us . . . Himself!

♥ ***Link to Life: Youth / Adult***

Launch your study of Isaiah in a simple way which will help your group members sense the value of this great book in developing a more adequate vision of God. As people come in assign the following brief readings. When the session is ready to begin, do the first reading yourself and have others follow in sequence.

Introduce each reading with a statement: "Our God is a [Holy God, etc.]" and read the appropriate verses. The readings and introductions are:

- *Holy One, Isaiah 5:15-16*
- *Sovereign Lord, Isaiah 8:13-15*
- *God the Judge, Isaiah 11:3-5*
- *God, our Salvation, Isaiah 26:1-4*
- *Everlasting God, Isaiah 44:6-8*
- *The Living God, Isaiah 41:10, 13*
- *Lord of Glory, Isaiah 60:1-3*

After the readings, open in praise to God for who He is.

Then introduce Isaiah, pointing out that we meet God in a special way in this book, and will come to appreciate Him deeply as we study.

"I Saw the Lord": Isaiah 6

The year was 739 B.C. It was the twelfth year of Jotham's coregency, three years after the death of Israel's great king, Jeroboam II. According to tradition this may have been the actual year in which, on the banks of the Tiber River across the Mediterranean, Rome was founded!

In Judah it was the year King Uzziah died.

For Isaiah, it was the year he saw the Lord.

These events were turning points for both Judah and Isaiah. For Judah Uzziah's death marked the beginning of the end of peace and prosperity. Assyria had begun to expand westward. Israel joined with Syria to stave off an attack and then tried to force Judah into a coalition with them against Assyria. Judah refused to go along, so Israel and Syria attempted to replace Judah's king with a man of their own choosing. Finally, King Ahaz of Judah called on Assyria for support against his two local enemies, only to find himself threatened by this voracious helper. Ultimately, Israel became a puppet state and then suffered complete destruction (722 B.C.), and Judah was left exposed on her northern and western flanks.

Within the land there was a deepening spiritual decline. Uzziah had begun as a godly king, and "as long as he sought the Lord, God gave him success" (2 Chron. 26:5). Growing military success, however, made Uzziah proud. He turned away from God, was struck with leprosy, and retired to a separate house for his final years. Jotham, his son, ruled for him. Jotham "did what was right in the eyes of the Lord" (27:2) and during his 16-year reign enjoyed continued political and military success. But he had little influence on the practices of Judah's people. The Bible tells us that they "continued their corrupt practices" (v. 2). The sins against which Isaiah would cry out were deeply entrenched in the lifestyle of

Judah as well as of Israel!

Uzziah's death was symbolic. He who had begun so well and had found prosperity in obedience had been struck by the dread disease of leprosy. An appearance of health and strength remained for a time, but the disease was at work within the body of the king; its marks became more and more visible as the ravages of that dread sickness took their toll. Finally, destroyed within and without, Uzziah died; his pride and his disobedience brought judgment on him.

Isaiah pointed out that Judah was also diseased, just like her king, because she too had deserted the Lord.

> Ah, sinful nation, a people loaded with guilt, a brood of evildoers, children given to corruption. They have forsaken the Lord; they have spurned the Holy One of Israel and turned their backs on Him.
> Isaiah 1:4

Isaiah graphically describes the advanced stages of leprosy:

> Your whole head is injured, your whole heart afflicted. From the sole of your foot to the top of your head there is no soundness—only wounds and welts and open sores, not cleansed or bandaged or soothed with oil.
> Isaiah 1:5-6

Judah's sickness, like that of Uzziah, had to end in death. The year Uzziah died was a pivotal time for Judah. She had a last opportunity to choose between life and death. And Judah's choice, like Uzziah's, had been made.

Yet this was the year Isaiah saw the Lord!

We read about his vision in chapter 6 and recognize that the prophet has been called to a lifelong work. From this time on, Isaiah would lift high the torch to reveal God to his people, and to us. He would proclaim the God who stands behind all history, the God who wants us to know and love Him. In the year Uzziah died, Isaiah saw the Lord, and his whole life and perspective were transformed. As ours too can be.

Isaiah's description (Isa. 6:1-4). Perhaps Isaiah had come to the temple to pray or to offer sacrifices. We're not told. All we know is that suddenly the veils were stripped away and Isaiah "saw the Lord seated on a throne, high and exalted" (v. 1). He was surrounded by angelic beings. The foundation shook, smoke filled the temple, and God's brilliance blazed as the beings cried out:

> Holy, holy, holy is the Lord Almighty; the whole earth is full of His glory.
> Isaiah 6:3

Isaiah was filled with dread. He was confronted with the reality which God's people had ignored: the God of Israel is holy.

Isaiah's response (Isa. 6:5-9). When Isaiah saw God's holiness, he also saw his own condition. With all his pride and his self-righteousness stripped away, Isaiah cried, "Woe to me! . . . I am ruined! For I am a man of unclean lips, and I live among a people of unclean lips" (v. 5). Against the stark holiness of God, Isaiah suddenly saw his whole lifestyle as a perhaps unwitting but nevertheless real expression of an inner wickedness.

But then God acted. One of the angelic beings touched Isaiah's lips with a live coal from the altar, announcing, "Your guilt is taken away and your sin atoned for" (v. 7). The altar fires, which would one day flare up with Jesus' blood, now brought Isaiah covering of sin and release from guilt. Pronounced holy by the Holy One, Isaiah could now stand before the Lord.

♥ ***Link to Life: Youth / Adult***

Divide into teams of three. Each person is to tell the others something of what led up to his or her conversion experience.

After sharing, have your group members, still in teams, read Isaiah 6:1-7. What points of comparison *do members find between their own conversion experiences and this experience of Isaiah? What* differences?

Returning to the whole group, explore: "How might this powerful conversion experience have affected Isaiah? How did it make him feel about himself? About God? How might this experience affect his values and future commitments?"

Isaiah's vision of God, and his experience of cleansing, prepared him for a lifetime of ministry. When Isaiah heard God ask, "Whom shall I send? And who will go for Us?" he responded immediately. "Here I am. Send me!" (v. 8)

♥ ***Link to Life: Children***
In Isaiah's vision of God the prophet saw Him as bright and awesome. We have no way to capture or represent this vision. Yet we do need to move beyond words to help boys and girls sense the awesome greatness of the Lord, and to worship Him as Holy One and Saviour.

One way to do this is with a 100-plus watt light bulb. Let boys and girls feel the heat (warmth), and see that the bulb is too bright to look into directly. God is holy, too bright to look at. But God loves us and, like the light bulb, sheds the light of His salvation so we can come to know Him, and can see the way that we should go.

Encourage the children to think of God's holiness and love when they notice a light bulb, and thank God for being bright and holy, and warm.

Isaiah's commission (Isa. 6:10-13). Isaiah was now charged with a staggering task. He was to speak God's Word to a people who had made an irrevocable choice and warn them of the certainty of judgment. He was to point out their blindness and their unwillingness to listen. Isaiah had to face the fact that God's people would remain deaf and blind to the Lord's message for another hundred years.

> Until the cities lie ruined and without inhabitant, until the houses are left deserted and the fields ruined and ravaged, until the Lord has sent everyone far away, and the land is utterly forsaken.
> Isaiah 6:11-12

Only then would God's people finally hear. Only then would they read the words of Isaiah the prophet and see the Holy One who reveals sin and brings forgiveness.

What a burden for Isaiah to bear. He knew the men and women he walked beside were doomed; he realized the supernatural power with which his words were endowed and that all his prayer concern would not break through to reach the hardened hearts of his generation. But what a blessing to know that another day would come! Someday, when Isaiah himself had been laid to rest and all the people who spurned God had returned to dust, other generations would pour over Isaiah's words and find God's Spirit quickening them to life with the Holy One of Israel.

And so it happened. Isaiah prophesied judgment, and it came. But generations of believers before Christ poured over Isaiah's words and found a vital hope. And generations after Christ have returned to this book to renew their vision of the Lord.

One exciting archeological find, the Dead Sea Scrolls, gives us insight into how accurately the prophet's words have been preserved. The Qumram community hid their sacred library some 180 years before Christ. The library was discovered in 1947. Apparently Isaiah, along with Deuteronomy and Psalms, were especially loved by these Old Testament believers. Among the finds was a copy of Isaiah, the first copy of any Old Testament book from the pre-Christian era. Before this time our earliest text of the Hebrew Bible dated from around A.D. 1100. The striking fact is that the text of the scroll authenticates the Hebrew text of our Bible; except for minor differences in vocalization, spelling, and the presence or absence of an article ("the," "that"), this ancient text is the same as the text of some 1,300 years later! God has preserved across the centuries an accurate text of His Word so that you and I can read our Old Testament with the confidence that what we see on its pages is a translation of the very words the authors penned.

Three Sermons: Isaiah 1–5

These first chapters of Isaiah contain three sermons that, together, give us a picture of Isaiah's early ministry. They also underline the holiness theme that culminates in Isaiah 6. Each sermon gives us insight into the spiritual condition of God's people, a condition of great concern to the Holy God.

An indictment (Isa. 1). This first sermon is both an indictment and an appeal in which God described the sins that characterized the lifestyle of His people. In choosing the way of sin, Judah had "spurned the Holy One of Israel" (v. 4). Living in sin is an act of rebellion, a deliberate choice to turn against God.

God's complaint against Israel focused on her lack of concern with justice. Isaiah cried out to this people:

> Your hands are full of blood; wash and make yourselves clean. Take your evil deeds out of My sight! Stop doing wrong, learn to do right! Seek justice, encourage the oppressed. Defend the cause of the fatherless, plead the case of the widow.
>
> Isaiah 1:15-17

Judah still maintained the appearance of religion. She continued to worship; offered sacrifices; held Sabbaths, solemn convocations, required festivals, and appointed feasts. But her heart was far from God; her life was, in fact, dedicated to ungodliness. God said Judah must be purged so that once again Jerusalem may be known as the City of Righteousness.

> Zion will be redeemed with justice, her penitent ones with righteousness. But rebels and sinners will both be broken together, and those who forsake the Lord will perish.
>
> Isaiah 1:27-28

♥ ***Link to Life: Youth / Adult***
We know that God is holy. But what is it that people do which is an affront to holiness? Lead your group members to study Isaiah 1, to first identify what is unholy, *and then together to describe a "holy life" for God's people.*

A description of judgment (Isa. 2–4). Isaiah saw beyond time to the end of history when the glory God intends for His purified and holy people will be theirs (2:2-5; 4:2-6). The promise is rich in beauty. God will judge between nations; swords will be beaten into plowshares and spears into pruning hooks. No more will men train for war. The Lord will wash, cleanse, and shelter. Jerusalem will become "a refuge and hiding place from the storm and rain" (v. 6).

But before that time judgment will come!

> The Lord Almighty has a day in store for all the proud and lofty. . . . The arrogance of man will be brought low and the pride of men humbled. . . . Men will flee to caves in the rocks and to holes in the ground from dread of the Lord and the splendor of His majesty, when He rises to shake the earth.
>
> Isaiah 2:12, 17, 19

The prosperity Judah had come to trust would be stripped away. Those who had crushed their brothers and ground down the faces of the poor would experience the full meaning of being crushed and ground down.

♥ ***Link to Life: Youth / Adult***
Work as a group to define from Isaiah 2:1-5 and 4:2-6: "What is God straining to accomplish among us?" *When your members have arrived at consensus, work in teams. Study the rest of chapters 2–4, to determine: "What in our lifestyle blocks God's goal of cleansing and peace?" And, "What actions can we expect to take against such behavior?"*

Judgment vindicated (Isa. 5). A farmer planted grapevines, intent on harvesting a crop of choice fruit. But despite all the farmer's care, the yield was only sour and bitter grapes.

Applying this figure, Isaiah confronted the people of Judah. They were themselves God's tender plantings, but the fruit they had produced was bitter.

> He looked for justice, but saw bloodshed; for righteousness, but heard cries of distress
>
> Isaiah 5:7

So God will act. He will vindicate His holiness. He will not permit the people called by His name to tarnish His glory, or to splatter His character with their filth.

> The Lord Almighty will be exalted by His justice, and the Holy God will show Himself holy by His righteousness.
>
> Isaiah 5:16

Those who have rejected the word of the Lord will feel His anger burn and will see His hand raised to strike.

It is then that we find the report of Isaiah's personal experience with God, recorded in Isaiah 6. Isaiah too saw the Holy One of Israel. But, unlike Judah, Isaiah dropped to his knees and confessed his sinfulness. Unlike Judah, Isaiah felt the burning touch of forgiveness, which did not bring pain but healing, and a renewed relationship with God.

What a portrait for us. God comes to us

as the Holy One. We can fall to our knees before God, acknowledge our sins, and discover that holiness heals. Or we can turn our backs on the vision as Judah did, and know that in spurning the Holy God we invite a dreadful, certain fate. For God *will* be exalted. The Holy God *will* show Himself holy. In forgiveness or in judgment, God's holiness is revealed.

How then will His holiness be revealed in you and me?

TEACHING GUIDE

Prepare

Skim through the first six chapters of Isaiah, jotting down words and phrases that help you sense the holiness of God.

Explore

1. As your group members arrive assign readings that introduce them to some of the names of God found in Isaiah, that help make this great Old Testament book so significant. See the "link-to-life" idea on page 366.
2. Give a brief overview of the book, using the outline and other information at the beginning of this unit. You may want to supplement this overview with material from the *Bible Knowledge Commentary.*

Expand

1. Have group members share their conversion stories in preparation for looking at Isaiah's conversion story in chapter 6. Follow the plan provided in "link-to-life," page 367.
2. Follow up by examining either Isaiah 1 or Isaiah 2–4. The experience of King Uzziah serves as a mirror for the nation. Israel's sin was likened to the king's leprosy; the judgment that would fall on Israel if they did not repent is like the judgment that fell on Uzziah when he turned away from following the Lord. Either of these two studies will help your group members sense the necessity of responding to God as Isaiah did. For those who accept forgiveness, God's holiness is healing. For those who will not turn to the Lord, holiness destroys.

Apply

Several verses imbedded in the dark portrait of Judah's sin offer us hope. For instance, "Tell the righteous it will be well with them, for they will enjoy the fruit of their deeds" (Isa. 3:10).

Read this and these other verses in closing: 1:18-19; 2:5; 5:16.

Close with sentence prayers, suggesting each person express thanks for one of the truths reflected in the verses just read. Also, suggest that this week each person choose one of these verses to memorize.

STUDY GUIDE 55

Isaiah 7–12

IMMANUEL

Overview

During the 60-year ministry of Isaiah he served God under both godly and ungodly rulers. One of the wicked rulers was Ahaz, who even sacrificed to the pagan gods of surrounding nations.

Yet it was during the rule of Ahaz that one of the most powerful of Isaiah's great promise-prophecies was uttered. It was to this king who had turned away from the Lord, and who in this represents all humankind, that Isaiah was sent with a clear promise that one day God Himself would take on human form. One day a virgin would have a Child, and He would be the Son of God.

Against the background of Judah's sin, and despite the dark warnings of judgment Isaiah was commissioned to bear, the promise of Immanuel shone through the ages as a bright, eternal hope.

▶ ***Sign.*** Isaiah told Ahaz to ask God for a "sign." Old Testament prophets often authenticated their messages by making a prediction or performing a miracle which proved God spoke through them.

▶ ***Virgin.*** The Hebrew word speaks of a young unmarried woman. But the Greek of the New Testament and the rabbi's translation in the LXX uses a word which definitely means "virgin."

▶ ***Immanuel.*** This word is unusual. We might render it, to give it its true emphasis, "WITH US is God!" Thus the construction of this name captures the wonder of the Incarnation itself, that the God of glory would actually become a Man.

Commentary

In Isaiah 7–12 we not only meet the Immanuel, the One God promised would come to bring everlasting righteousness, we are also reminded that our God is Sovereign. He will accomplish all He purposes, for none can stay His hand.

Thus Isaiah says:

> The Lord Almighty is the One you are to regard as holy. He is the One you are to fear, He is the One you are to dread, and He will be a sanctuary; but for both houses of Israel He will be a stone that causes men to stumble and a rock that makes them fall. And for the people of Jerusalem He will be a trap and a snare. Many of them will stumble; they will fall and be broken, they will be snared and be captured.
>
> Isaiah 8:13-15

Isaiah told us very little of himself. He would only say that he and his children were signs to Israel from the Lord (v. 18). The prophet, after the brief but revealing picture of his call, submerged himself in his message and told us nothing about his own feelings. When we meet him next, holding his infant son Shear-Jashub in his arms, he was confronting King Ahaz outside Jerusalem. Even the name of his son is a message: it means "a remnant will return" (7:3).

Ahaz

Jotham, son of Uzziah, ruled for some 16 years and then was succeeded by his son, Ahaz. While Jotham had followed the Lord's ways, Ahaz "did not do what was right in the eyes of the Lord" (2 Chron. 28:1). He adopted the apostate ways and faith of the Northern Kingdom, Israel, even erecting images of Baal and sacrificing his own sons in the fire.

Politically, the times of Ahaz were marked by constant crisis. Tiglath-Pileser, ruler of Assyria, was expanding his power westward. Egypt, which had counterbalanced the power of northern empires for centuries, was now weak. Syria and the

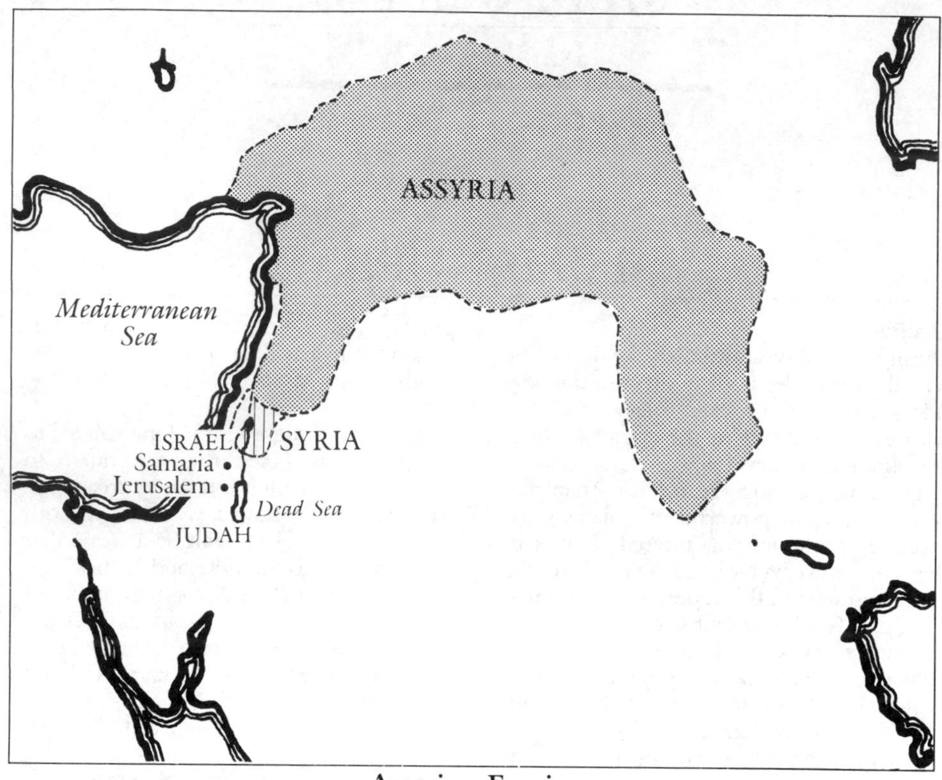

Assyrian Empire

Northern Kingdom, Israel, were struggling to form a defensive alliance against Assyrian encroachment. Ahaz was pressured to join the coalition. He refused.

Determined to replace Ahaz with a puppet king who would cooperate with them, Rezin of Syria (whose capital was Damascus) and Pekah of Israel (whose capital was Samaria, Isa. 7:8-9) decided to attack Judah. They forced Ahaz's hand, and he sent envoys to Assyria, begging for help against his nearby enemies. This was all the excuse Assyria needed. Soon the Middle East was plunged into a complex and fratricidal war.

The first action was a battle between Judah and the combined powers of Israel and Syria. In a crushing defeat, some 120,000 of Judah's soldiers were killed. Another 200,000 women and children were taken captive but, through intervention of a prophet sent by God (see 2 Chron. 28:8-15), these were released and were returned to Judah.

When Assyria responded to Ahaz's plea for help, she swept down to crush both Damascus and Samaria, and then turned on Judah, her ally! Tiglath-Pileser came against Ahaz and "gave him trouble instead of help" (v. 20). Ahaz was forced to strip the land of its wealth to buy off Assyria (v. 21) and Judah became in effect a satellite nation that reflected the policy of its powerful neighbor.

Bitterly angry at God, Ahaz closed the Jerusalem temple, stripped it of its remaining treasures, and cut up even the golden vessels dedicated to God's worship. He "offered sacrifices to the gods of Damascus, who had defeated him; for he thought, 'Since the gods of the kings of Aram have helped them, I will sacrifice to them so they will help me' " (v. 23).

The Promise: Isaiah 7

Before the days of battle came, God sent Isaiah with his infant son Shear-Jashub to meet Ahaz "at the end of the aqueduct of the Upper Pool, on the road to the Washerman's Field" (v. 3). He was to review the political situation and warn Ahaz of the danger from Judah's neighbors. God was still the Sovereign Lord, while Judah's enemies were mere men. God promised, "It will not take place, it will not happen," but then went on to warn Ahaz. "If you do not stand firm in your faith, you will not stand at all" (vv. 7, 9). The plot to replace Ahaz came to nothing. Judah was defeated, but Ahaz remained king.

The sign (Isa. 7:10-14). God then instructed Ahaz to ask for a sign.

God had indicated ways that a prophet's message could be tested. The Hebrew prophet was to speak in the name of the Lord (not in the name of a false god), and his word was to *invariably come true*. If the word did not come true, or if the foretold event did not happen, that person was not a true prophet (see Deut. 18:17-22).

But what of a prophet who foretells a distant event that may take place long after he and his listeners have died? It was common in such cases for the prophet to speak also of contemporary things, so that the message could be authenticated as God's own.

Isaiah's demand that Ahaz ask for a sign, then, was not unusual. But Ahaz replied, "I will not ask; I will not put the Lord to the test" (Isa. 7:12). At first this reply might seem almost pious. But it was hardly that! Not only was Ahaz insincere in his mocking quotation of Deuteronomy 6:16, he was also disobeying a direct command of God through His prophet. We can't hear the sneer that undoubtedly filled this apostate king's voice, but we can recognize Isaiah's sharp rebuke. "Is it not enough to try the patience of men? Will you try the patience of my God also?" (Isa. 7:13) In anger, Isaiah went on to announce a sign, but a sign that would come long after Judah was broken under the enemy. "The Lord Himself will give you a sign: The virgin will be with Child and will give birth to a Son, and will call Him Immanuel" (v. 14). The name *Immanuel* means "God with us."

God is determined to act in human history. Petty kings' dreams of conquest, or their fears for preservation, are meaningless. One day the true King, God Himself, would take on human form. When God became Man *with* us, then the fears of Ahaz and all the glory of the kingdoms of this world would dissolve in the revelation of God's true glory. The King would enter history as a Man, born of a virgin. When He, the ultimate sign, appeared, all nations would recognize the majesty and wisdom of the Sovereign God.

The judgment (Isa. 7:15-25). When would the Immanuel come? Isaiah set no date. In fact, Isaiah immediately shifted to give a "near view" prophecy which would authenticate his exalted vision of the coming Deliverer.

Holding out his son, Shear-Jashub, Isaiah continued. Before the child he held in his arms was weaned (v. 15), the two nations that Ahaz feared most would be laid waste and Judah herself would undergo oppression by Assyria, on whom Ahaz had pinned his hope.

By refusing to remain still and trust God, Ahaz would initiate a chain of events that would bring Assyria into the area, and lead to devastating judgments on Palestine. Poverty would replace plenty. Briars and thorns would grow in the once-cultivated fields. Assyria would carry off Israel into captivity while Judah would be beaten down. But even this terror would not cure Judah or bring her back to God. Finally, when Babylon had conquered Assyria, then Judah would know Captivity.

♥ ***Link to Life: Youth / Adult***

Study Isaiah 7:3-17 with your group. This passage contains a clear Old Testament prophecy about Jesus' birth. Lead your group step by step through verses 3-9, explaining the political situation.

The "65 years" in verse 8 has been taken to indicate Rezin's age (65 years old), for the destruction foretold came quickly.

Then concentrate on verses 10-17. Point out that the Lord specifically told Isaiah to take Shear-Jashub with him. This is explained by Isaiah's reference to his infant child in verse 15.

The Two Kingdoms

In reading Isaiah it's important to remember that the Hebrew people were divided into two nations, a Northern Kingdom (Israel) and a Southern (Judah), which was Isaiah's home. Though God spoke through Isaiah *about* the Northern Kingdom and, indeed, about all the surrounding powers, Isaiah's ministry remained directed to Judah. Israel had had a succession of evil kings; not one godly man broke the pattern. Judah had seen revival under kings such as Asa and Jehoshaphat.

The fate of Israel stood as a vivid object lesson to Judah. If Judah were to choose the evil ways of her sister Israel, her fate must surely be the same. Judah was warned when Sargon tore the Israelites from the Promised Land in 722 B.C. God had demonstrated His principles of judgment in an unmistakable way. Now God's warnings to Judah would come to pass just as His pronouncements against the Northern Kingdom had. History would bear terrible testimony to the trustworthiness of God's Word.

How carefully then Judah should heed every message. How quickly Judah should repent. But, in spite of all the evidence, Judah *would not*. She saw, but she did not perceive. She heard, but she would not listen. Like her king, Judah would choose to spurn God's offer of a sign.

The Immediate Future: Isaiah 8
Isaiah and his wife had another son, named Maher-Shalal-Hash-Baz. The name means "quick to the plunder, swift to the spoil," and points to the impending judgment on Israel. Within months Syria and Israel were crushed, their capitals plundered, and their people deported. The armies of Assyria flowed over the borders of Judah to flood that nation, rising swiftly from feet to knees to waist and shoulders, right up to the very head itself, Jerusalem. The waters would recede, but Judah was left a disaster (vv. 6-10).

The people of God needed to forget their fear of men, of Rezin and Pekah who terrorized Ahaz but who soon were to die, and to fear God who judges iniquity. Isaiah cried out:

> The Lord Almighty is the One you are to regard as holy, He is the One you are to fear, He is the One you are to dread.
> Isaiah 8:13

He would be a sanctuary to any who would turn to Him, but if Judah refused to return, the God they spurned would bring about their brokenness. Yet instead of turning to God, the people turned to mediums and spiritualists, to consult the dead on behalf of the living (vv. 11-22).

The Fixed Purpose: Isaiah 9:1–10:34
In spite of the coming disaster, God's intention to bless His people and bring them holiness had not been changed. One day the Promised Child would be born. One day the Promised Son would be given. He, whose names are Wonderful Counselor, Mighty God, Everlasting Father, and Prince of Peace, will reign on the Davidic throne over a cleansed world.

> Of the increase of His government and peace there will be no end. He will reign on David's throne and over His kingdom, establishing and upholding it with justice and righteousness from that time on and forever. The zeal of the Lord Almighty will accomplish this.
> Isaiah 9:7

On the throne where Ahaz, that unworthy descendant of David now sat, another King will reign. He will establish the righteousness and the justice that every act of Ahaz denied. And of His kingdom there will be no end.

Yet before the final kingdom comes, much history will intervene. The course of history, as well as its appointed end, is fixed by the Sovereign Lord. Israel and its capital Samaria would be destroyed by her enemies.

> Yet for all this, His anger is not turned away, His hand is still upraised.
> Isaiah 9:12

The elders and the prominent men who led Israel into sin, and the prophets who lied for them, would be killed.

> Yet for all this, His anger is not turned away, His hand is still upraised.
> Isaiah 9:17

Those who had defrauded the poor and made unjust laws for their own profit would lose all their wealth and cringe among the captives, or fall among the slain.

> Yet for all this, His anger is not turned away, His hand is still upraised.
> Isaiah 10:4

Then, when His judgment had been executed to the full, God would judge the persecutors! God had given Assyria power to be the disciplining rod against the Lord's willful people. But Assyria would fail to recognize God, so she had to suffer punishment "for the willful pride of [her] heart and the haughty look in [her] eyes" (v. 12). God would be recognized, finally, as the Holy One of Israel.

And now, in the quietness following judgment's raging storm, the remnant would look up and at last see God. How great a day, when they "truly rely on the Lord, the Holy One of Israel" (v. 20).

In the end, the powers of this world will be lopped off like branches, and the burden will be lifted from the shoulders of God's people. In the end history will turn to destiny, and the plans and promises of our Sovereign Lord will be perfectly fulfilled.

The Righteous Land: Isaiah 11–12

> He will not judge by what He sees with His eyes, or decide by what He hears with His ears; but with righteousness He will judge the needy, with justice He will give decisions for the poor of the earth. He will strike the earth with the rod of His mouth; with the breath of His lips He will slay the wicked. Righteousness will be His belt and faithfulness the sash around His waist.
>
> Isaiah 11:3-5

We may find it hard to be comfortable with God revealed as Righteous Judge. We have experienced the inequities in our judicial system, and we've been bombarded with rationalizations that seek to establish one set of laws for the influential and another for the have-nots. Our sense of justice has become warped.

In a recent article on white-collar crime several businessmen and lawyers who had been sentenced to prison for fraud involving hundreds of thousands of dollars were quoted. They argued bitterly that, for them, the shame of exposure was enough. Certainly they did not deserve imprisonment like "common criminals"!

Too often the newspapers report a rape case brought to trial in which the victim becomes the defendant on the witness stand, subject to insinuations that she invited the crime against her.

Of course, we must have due process of law, and sometimes even the guilty will be set free on a technicality. After all, in an imperfect society we can't always be certain about guilt. Human eyes and ears are not always reliable witnesses. Perhaps more importantly, human emotions make us anything but impartial. Because it is so hard to be objective and never to waver from an absolute standard of righteousness, we find it difficult to accept the judicial system of the Sovereign Lord, who is *absolutely* just!

Justice. We can't read the Old Testament without becoming convinced that God cares about all people and that He expresses His concern by a deep commitment to justice. Justice is hardly an abstract code. The Law of God has always been associated not with arbitrary rules but with life and with how people can best express love for each other.

God's concern for all people is clear in this sampling of levitical law:

> When you reap the harvest of your land, do not reap to the very edges of your field or gather the gleanings of your harvest. Do not go over your vineyard a second time or pick up the grapes that have fallen. Leave them for the poor and the alien. I am the Lord your God.
>
> Do not steal. Do not lie. Do not deceive one another. . . .
>
> Do not defraud your neighbor or rob him. Do not hold back the wages of a hired man overnight. Do not curse the deaf or put a stumbling block in front of the blind, but fear your God. I am the Lord.
>
> Do not pervert justice; do not show partiality to the poor or favoritism to the great, but judge your neighbor fairly. . . .
>
> Do not seek revenge or bear a grudge against one of your people, but love your neighbor as yourself. I am the Lord.
>
> Leviticus 19:9-18

Against the background of the good and just life God planned for His people, Isaiah exposed the corrupt lifestyle of Israel and Judah.

> The vineyard of the Lord Almighty is the house of Israel, and the men of Judah are the garden of His delight. And He looked for justice, but saw bloodshed; for righteousness, but heard cries of distress.
>
> Isaiah 5:7

God has determined to bring terrible judgments on His people. But His acts throughout history have never been vindictive. Nor have they been primarily deterrent. Rather, they have been acts of *judgment.* God's goal is to establish justice.

Messiah. Violence had become a way of life in Israel and Judah. As we remember Ahaz sacrificing his own sons to pagan gods, we can more easily accept the picture of God trampling out the grapes of wrath in His holy anger against such bestial sins. So lest we forget what is really involved in the events Isaiah portrays, we are shown Messiah.

Messiah's person (Isa. 11:1-3). The house of David was a lofty tree felled by judgments of the Lord. From the stump (note: Jesse was David's father) springs a branch (an Old Testament symbol of the promised Messiah). God's own Spirit will fill Him with wisdom, understanding counsel, power, and knowledge. He will be in complete harmony with the holy character of God.

Messiah's task (Isa. 11:3-5). The task of this one sent from God is to judge. Edward Young comments:

> The principle function of a ruler is to judge, and to reign with authority. How will this King, One who so delights in the fear of Yahweh, carry out His function of judging? To ask that question is to answer it, for His judging will be completely unlike that of previous rulers on David's throne. His judgment will not be based upon the ordinary sources of information open to men, namely, what men see and what they hear. Such means, the eyes and the ears, can bring at best an outward impression. For absolute justice, there must be absolute knowledge (*The Book of Isaiah,* 3 vols. [Grand Rapids: Eerdmans]).

When God acts in judgment He sees perfectly into the heart of every man and into the heart of every issue. Remembering it is God who is the Judge, we must forever turn our thoughts away from temptation to judge Him!

Isaiah reassures us concerning the Messiah-Judge: "Righteousness will be His belt and faithfulness the sash about His waist" (v. 5). Archeology tells us what this description means. In biblical times wrestlers wore belts. The object of the match was for each opponent to seek to wrest the other's belt away. Later, the figure of a belted man came to indicate any person ready to face a contest or to engage in a struggle.

Isaiah pictured the poor and needy of the land moaning on the mat, as human arrogance and pride bruised the neck with a cruel boot. Man is no match for sin and injustice. But wait! Stepping into the arena comes a man belted for battle. His belt is woven of dual strands of righteousness and faithfulness. No man or demon will ever snatch that belt from Him!

Restoration (Isa. 11:6-9). Now follows one of the most famous and moving of all passages of Scripture. After the judgment, when Messiah has won His victory, righteousness and peace will be restored.

> The wolf will live with the lamb, the leopard will lie down with the goat, the calf and the lion and the yearling together; and a little child will lead them. . . . The lion will eat straw like the ox. The infant will play near the hole of the cobra. . . . They will neither harm nor destroy on all My holy mountain, for the earth will be full of the knowledge of the Lord as the waters cover the sea.
>
> Isaiah 11:6-9

The Gentiles (Isa. 11:10-16). In the days following Messiah's judgment victories, the hostility between Judah and Israel will be healed, and all God's people will rally to Him. From every nation to which judgment has scattered them, the chosen of God will return to experience the blessings of messianic rule.

Songs of praise (Isa. 12:1-6). The chapter concludes with two brief psalms. When God's judgment work is done and sin has tasted final defeat, how God's people will rejoice and sing His praise!

TEACHING GUIDE

Prepare
As you read through these chapters of Isaiah, mark phrases or passages that deepen your awareness of who God is.

Explore
1. Give a minilecture covering the political situation as it affects this section of Isaiah. Use the map in this guide to illustrate.
2. Work step-by-step through the Isaiah 7 prophecy of Jesus' virgin birth. The Hebrew term "virgin" (*alma*) is used six times in the Old Testament and never of a married woman. It is translated in the Septuagint (the pre-Christian Greek translation of the Old Testament) and in the New Testament by *parthenos,* which does mean "virgin."

Expand
Either divide into teams for independent study and reports, or select one of the following to look into as a group.

1. *Isaiah 8.* Earlier chapters (1; 5) tell how we are to respond to each other. How are we to respond to *God?*
2. *Isaiah 9:8–10:19.* What does "God's anger" really mean? What does this passage suggest about it?
3. *Isaiah 9:1-7; 10:20-34.* God's promise of destiny has great meaning for all mankind. How are we to live while waiting for the end?
4. *Isaiah 11–12.* What is "justice"? What is the purpose of a criminal justice system in society?

Apply
Have members read aloud the following brief passages, and suggest that each person choose one of them to memorize this coming week. The passages:

Isa. 8:12-13 Isa. 9:6-7
Isa. 10:20 Isa. 11:1-3
Isa. 12:1-3

STUDY GUIDE 56

Isaiah 13–39

JUDGMENT AND SALVATION

Overview

The first part of the Book of Isaiah is filled with visions of judgment. Yet there are flashes of light: brilliant visions of a bright glory that splashes through the overcast. Isaiah 11 and 12, which picture the Messiah, are such bright visions. And yet, in this first half of Isaiah, the dark clouds quickly close in again, and all is dark and gray. Thus the first part of this great prophetic book which we are studying is rightly called a book of judgment.

▶ ***Fulfilled Prophecy.*** Several of Isaiah's prophecies have been fulfilled in clear and striking ways. Of course, the promise of the Virgin Birth (Isa. 7:14) was fulfilled in Jesus. But Isaiah's warnings about what would happen to Babylon and Tyre, great cities in the prophet's time, have also been literally fulfilled. As you meet such prophecies in Isaiah, check the *Bible Knowledge Commentary* for details of their fulfillment. Use this information to enrich your group's study of this exciting Bible book.

Commentary

Immediately after the bright hope that shone through Isaiah 11 and 12, darkness closed in. Oracles of judgment are like lowering clouds that make the landscape seem dark and grim. It is hard to remember the sunlight when we read words like these:

> The rising sun will be darkened and the moon will not give its light. I will punish the world for its evil, the wicked for their sins. I will put an end to the arrogance of the haughty and will humble the pride of the ruthless.
>
> Isaiah 13:10-11

> The shouts of joy over your ripened fruit and over your harvests have been stilled. Joy and gladness are taken away from the orchards; no one sings or shouts in the vineyards; no one treads out wine at the presses, for I have put an end to the shouting.
>
> Isaiah 16:9-10

> See, the Lord is going to lay waste the earth and devastate it; He will ruin its face and scatter its inhabitants—it will be the same for priest as for people. . . . The earth will be completely laid waste and totally plundered. The Lord has spoken this word.
>
> Isaiah 24:1-3

The Oracles: Isaiah 14–24

We have now come to a series of divine declarations, or oracles, concerning surrounding nations. The great world powers of Isaiah's day (and coming powers like that of Babylon) who have set themselves against God will be themselves set aside as God's judgment brings them low. Only the righteous kingdom of the Messiah will remain.

God raised up these nations to be instruments of judgment against His people (5:26-30; 7:18-20). Now Isaiah identified these powers and exposed their sin. They had arrogantly gone beyond God's boundaries in punishing Israel. Even Babylon, which would fulfill the course begun by Assyria, would be unable to stand. All worldly powers directed against God and His purposes will be cut off.

THE ORACLES

Isa. 13:1–14:23	Against Babylon
Isa. 14:24-27	Against Assyria
Isa. 14:28-32	Against Philistia
Isa. 15–16	Against Moab
Isa. 17	Against Damascus
Isa. 18	Against Cush
Isa. 19	Against Egypt

Isa. 20	Against Egypt & Cush
Isa. 21:1-10	Against Babylon
Isa. 21:11-12	Against Edom
Isa. 21:13-17	Against Arabia
Isa. 22	Against Jerusalem
Isa. 23	About Tyre
Isa. 24	Portrait of judgments

Those who deny the possibility of prophetic foreknowledge argue that the name *Babylon* was substituted for *Assyria* by some later scribe. Those who believe the prophet was inspired by God realize that Babylon would consummate the scattering of God's people initiated by Assyria.

Two elements of this prophecy (13:1–14:23) have drawn much attention. Many have seen in the destruction of the boastful king (14:12-21) a portrait of Satan's fall from heaven (Luke 10:18). Of one thing we can be sure. *Every* arrogant power, whether in Satan, in kings, or in you and me, that exalts itself against God . . . falls under sure judgment.

Another element deserving comment is the picture of a deserted Babylon:

> She will never be inhabited or lived in through all generations; no Arab will pitch his tent there, no shepherd will rest his flocks there. But desert creatures will lie there, jackals will fill her houses. . . . Hyenas will howl in her strongholds, jackals in her luxurious palaces.
>
> Isaiah 13:20-22

Today there is only an empty wilderness where Babylon once stood. The Lord is a great Judge, and His judgment is sure.

About Egypt (Isa. 19). God's judgment is not only sure, it is purposive. After judgment, God brings restoration and healing.

> In that day there will be an altar to the Lord in the heart of Egypt. . . . The Lord will make Himself known to the Egyptians, and in that day they will acknowledge the Lord. . . . They will turn to the Lord, and He will respond to their pleas and heal them.
>
> Isaiah 19:19, 21-22

However stern the judgment of God seems, however terrible the vision of God as Judge, beyond the darkened clouds the sun of blessing still shines.

♥ ***Link to Life: Youth / Adult***
Isaiah 24 summarizes the judgment theme. Use it as a responsive reading to launch the group study. If you wish, use a minilecture to summarize highlights in chapters 14–24. While it is possible to focus on an interesting theme within these chapters (such as Satan's fall, 14:12-15; or on fulfilled prophecies about Babylon or Tyre), in a survey of the Book of Isaiah itself, the responsive reading will effectively sum up this section's theme.

God, Our Salvation: Isaiah 25–35

I remember as a teenager walking home one night after a high school game. Clouds hid the moon, and a damp breeze cut through my thin jacket. Just as I reached the flowerbed bordering our yard, I felt a jolt of terror.

Out of the total black of the peony bushes a mysterious shape rose, with a deep threatening rumble. I jerked back, poised to run, and then I recognized him! It was my own dog, Ezra! Half asleep, he'd failed to recognize me and had risen stiff-legged and growling. In the dark I failed to recognize him as well. What a relief for each of us to recognize the other as his own!

In a way, that incident gives us a clue to this section of the Book of Isaiah. God has risen as a dark specter, a strange and terrifying shadow. Every way Isaiah described God—the Holy One, the Sovereign Lord, the great Judge—promised sure judgment. But Israel did not recognize nor claim relationship with the God Isaiah knew.

Now Isaiah reminded his people. God will not always remain a stranger.

> We have a strong city; God makes salvation its walls and ramparts. Open the gates that the righteous nation may enter, the nation that keeps faith. You will keep in perfect peace him whose mind is steadfast, because he trusts in You. Trust in the Lord forever, for the Lord, the Lord, is the Rock Eternal.
>
> Isaiah 26:1-4

A God to be trusted (Isa. 25–27). The first words of Isaiah 25 introduce, for the first time, a tone of *personal relationship.* God's people respond to Him, saying:

> Surely this is our God; we trusted in

> Him, and He saved us. This is the Lord, we trusted in Him; let us rejoice and be glad in His salvation.
>
> Isaiah 25:9

The people delight in their new relationship.

> Yes, Lord, walking in the way of Your laws, we wait for You; Your name and renown are the desire of our hearts. . . . Lord, You establish peace for us; all that we have accomplished You have done for us. O Lord, our God, other lords besides You have ruled over us, but Your name alone do we honor.
>
> Isaiah 26:8, 12-13

In these chapters we see Judah view God for the first time as the source of her salvation. Prophetically, this follows the time of judgment; personally, the recognition can come at any time to anyone who chooses to trust God. The benefits of seeing God, the Holy One, as the source of salvation are described in these brief chapters.

**Praise replaces fear (25:1-5)*. Realizing at last that God is "my God," the believer is moved to:

> Exalt You and praise Your name, for in perfect faithfulness You have done marvelous things, things planned long ago.
>
> Isaiah 25:1

The faithfulness of the Saviour God is itself a shelter from the storm, and a shade from the heat of the coming judgments.

**Joy replaces tears (25:6-12)*. The portrait is of a banquet of rich food and aged wine set by God Himself for all peoples. The Sovereign Lord will wipe away all tears, and those who trusted Him will cry out, "Let us rejoice and be glad in His salvation" (v. 9).

**Peace replaces oppression (26:1-6)*. The society salvation builds will be righteous, made up of individuals who trust God. Those whose minds are steadfastly fixed on God will have perfect peace, "for the Lord, the Lord, is the Rock eternal" (v. 4).

**Righteousness replaces wickedness (26:7-11)*. The redeemed person yearns for God and desires to walk in His ways. This longing for God, rather than the Law, or fear of punishment, produces righteousness. The renewed person will want God to be the center of his thoughts and his hope.

**Humility replaces pride (26:12-18)*. God's people have been haughty and arrogant, but coming to know God will make them see that "Lord, You establish peace for us; all that we have accomplished You have done for us" (v. 12).

One especially poignant passage describes how redeemed Israel will recognize that she failed to accomplish God's purpose. Rather than being a witness to surrounding lands, Israel chose to follow pagan ways:

> We were with child, we writhed in pain, but we gave birth to wind. We have not brought salvation to the earth; we have not given birth to people of the world.
>
> Isaiah 26:18

God will redeem His people. And He Himself will undertake the ministry of world redemption through His Son.

**Life replaces death (26:19-21)*. Because of God, the dead will wake to joy. Isaiah encourages those who know God as their Saviour to:

> Go, my people, enter your rooms and shut the doors behind you; hide yourselves for a little while until His wrath has passed by.
>
> Isaiah 26:20

God is the Saviour, but He is also the great Judge. Salvation will come, but in a little while, when His wrath has passed by.

♥ ***Link to Life: Youth / Adult***

The future of Israel as a saved nation, described in Isaiah 25–26, seems to recapitulate the experience of individual believers. Divide your group into teams of five people. Either ask them to outline the chapters, or provide the outline used here: praise replaces fear, joy replaces tears, peace replaces oppression, etc.

Each team is to first identify what salvation will mean to redeemed Israel. Then have each person talk about his or her personal experience as a Christian. What has salvation meant to him or her, and how has the Christian experience paralleled the future of which Isaiah speaks?

**The day of wrath (27:1-13)*. This section concludes with another sketch of judgment, but without the hints of terror seen in earlier passages. Through judgment there will come blessing. "In that day a great trumpet will sound. Those who were perishing in Assyria and those who were exiled in Egypt will come and worship the Lord on the holy mountain in Jerusalem" (v. 13). The revelation of our Saviour God brings deliverance.

Woes (Isa. 28–31). The predominant theme of the first half of Isaiah is one of darkness. Israel had forsaken the way of the Lord and had become, not a light to the nations around her, but *like* the pagan peoples. Her ways were ways of arrogance and oppression, war and injustice, of terror of enemies within and without.

But not only was the earth dark. Black clouds of judgment swept across the face of the heavens. A warrior girded for battle, so massive that he seemed to block out the very sky, appeared. The Holy God, the Sovereign Lord, the great Judge, was about to do battle with arrogance and oppression.

Isaiah cried out a warning, but his people were so committed to wickedness that they did not even glance up! Hearing, they failed to hear. Seeing, they failed to perceive. They responded neither to Isaiah's portraits of judgment nor to his brief, flashing portraits of the glory that will be theirs when the restoring fire has purged the land.

Isaiah then announced that the Holy One is God our Saviour; the Judge is the Deliverer. The nation still did not turn to God, but there was some individual response. Some looked away from themselves long enough to see God and find in Him personal deliverance and peace. The individual will have to endure while God judges the nation. But the individual who trusts in God will have security even when:

> The Lord is coming out of His dwelling to punish the people of the earth for their sins. The earth will disclose the blood shed upon her; she will conceal her slain no longer.
>
> Isaiah 26:21

Isaiah had to return to the theme of woe because, while individuals might respond to his revelation of a Saviour God, the nation as a whole did not. They were unwilling to listen to the Lord's instruction and demanded the prophet be silent. The people shouted out to Isaiah, "Stop confronting us with the Holy One of Israel!" (30:11) Because the nation rejected God, all the terrors of His judgment will surely come upon them. The woes are pronounced on those who reject salvation's offer.

**Woe to Ephraim (Isa. 28).* The message to the Northern Kingdom, Ephraim, was to rest in God (v. 12). Unresponsive to the personal dimension of God's message, they had twisted the Word of God into empty legalism. Stripped of His living presence, the Word of the Lord became:

> Do and do, do and do, rule on rule, rule on rule; a little here, a little there—so that they will go and fall backward, be injured and snared and captured.
>
> Isaiah 28:13

We too can distort Scripture. God's message is not a system of rules to imprison us, but calls us to a personal relationship which grows into a loving and holy lifestyle.

**Woe to David's city (Isa. 29).* God's people were blinded because they had devoted themselves to a life of ritual observance (v. 1). God complained:

> These people come near to Me with their mouth and honor Me with their lips, but their hearts are far from Me. Their worship of Me is made up only of rules taught by men.
>
> Isaiah 29:13

How often the revealed faith gets slowly buried as we interpret and repeat our interpretations. Soon we lose the reality of God in the confusing structures of our traditions. Then, beneath all the outward piety, our hearts turn from God. We devise plans in the darkness and think, "Who sees us? Who will know?" (v. 15)

How strange that religion itself can so easily rob us of our sense of God's presence.

**Woe to the obstinate nation (Isa. 30).* Looking with love on His straying people, God invited them to return. "In repentance and rest is your salvation, in quietness and trust is your strength" (v. 15). But:

> They say to the seers, "See no more visions!" and to the prophets, "Give us no more visions of what is right! Tell us pleasant things, prophesy illusions. Leave this way, get off this path, and

> stop confronting us with the Holy One of Israel!"
>
> Isaiah 30:10-11

They had stubbornly closed their eyes to Isaiah's vision of God. Yet the Lord longed to be gracious (v. 18). He will answer when they finally do cry out to Him (v. 19). But as long as a people reject the Lord, they will know only woe.

**Woe to those who rely on Egypt (Isa. 31).* When people have turned from God, in what will they trust? The people of Isaiah's day trusted the military might of their ally, Egypt, and fastened on emptiness.

> The Egyptians are men and not God; their horses are flesh and not spirit. When the Lord stretches out His hand, he who helps will stumble, he who is helped will fall; both will perish together.
>
> Isaiah 31:3

When we lose sight of God, our perception of reality gets distorted. The fact is that the unseen things are far more real than the seen. The material things on which we fix our hope when we wander from God are bound to disappoint—and to bring woe.

Salvation's certainty (Isa. 32–35). Isaiah affirmed that God is Salvation:

> See, a King will reign in righteousness and rulers will rule with justice. Each man will be like a shelter from the wind and a refuge from the storm, like streams of water in the desert and the shadow of a great rock in a thirsty land.
>
> Isaiah 32:1-2

Isaiah told the fruit God's righteousness will produce and reviewed the work of the destroyer. He described the judgments that would finally overthrow the oppressor nations. Then Isaiah pictured the joy of the whole world breaking into bloom, warmed by the glory and splendor of our God. And the fruit will be righteousness.

In the early chapters of his book Isaiah focused on the corruption and unrighteousness that marked the people's lifestyle. Now he portrayed the righteousness that will mark the lifestyle of the redeemed. When the Spirit of God is poured out on humankind:

> Justice will dwell in the desert and righteousness live in the fertile field. The fruit of righteousness will be peace; the effect of righteousness will be quietness and confidence forever.
>
> Isaiah 32:16-17

Those who draw on God's rich store of salvation can live in the presence of the consuming fire. Who can reside with the Holy One?

> He who walks righteously and speaks what is right, who rejects gain from extortion and keeps his hand from accepting bribes, who stops his ears against plots of murder and shuts his eyes against contemplating evil—this is the man who will dwell on the heights.
>
> Isaiah 33:15-16

♥ ***Link to Life: Youth / Adult***

In chapters 28 to 31 Isaiah identified hindrances to trust in God. These range from a legalistic approach to Scripture (chap. 28) to ritualism (chap. 29) to stubborn rejection of God's Word (chap. 30) to reliance on material rather than spiritual resources (chap. 31).

Briefly outline the topics for your group. Then let individuals choose one of these themes to look at more intensively. Form one team for each chapter and topic. The teams are to answer the following questions, and then report to the whole group. What is the main teaching of the chapter? What can we do to avoid the danger of which Isaiah warns? How does a person with this problem think or act? What is the most important single verse? How does what Isaiah said apply to believers today?

A Historic Interlude: Isaiah 36–39

In these chapters of historical narrative Isaiah told of an Assyrian invasion of Judah that swept up to the very walls of Jerusalem. But Judah had a godly king, Hezekiah, who appealed immediately to God. God responded to Hezekiah's prayer. He struck the Assyrian army before it could reach Jerusalem. The city was saved, and during the life of Hezekiah, Judah knew peace.

Why is this historical interlude, described fully in 2 Chronicles 32, included here? As an object lesson!

Isaiah had desperately urged God's people to open their eyes to Israel's Holy One, and turn to Him with their whole hearts. The Northern Kingdom of Israel totally refused—and was destroyed. But godly King Hezekiah of Judah chose to trust God the Holy One. Despite the fact that God is Judge and men sinful, Hezekiah was sure that the Lord was committed to do His people good. So Hezekiah looked to God—and the deliverance God brought to Jerusalem is evidence to all people of all time that our God, while the awesome Judge of sinners, is Saviour of all who appeal in faith to Him.

TEACHING GUIDE

Prepare

Read Isaiah 36–39 devotionally. What do you find there for which you want to praise the Lord?

Explore

Begin your session with a responsive reading of Isaiah 24, to capture the sense of judgment which pervades the first 10 chapters of this section.

Expand

1. Work in teams to discover in Isaiah 25 and 26 parallels between the salvation God promised to Israel and the salvation that we experience as believers today. See the "link-to-life" suggestion on page 380.
2. After hearing reports on parallels to Old Testament and present personal salvation, let members select hindrances to trust to study in new teams. Identify the hindrances, found in Isaiah 28–31. Then follow the procedure given in "link-to-life," page 382.

Apply

1. Tell briefly the story that Isaiah included in chapters 36–39. Highlight how these historic events underlined and emphasized the message of the prophet.
2. Or close by reading selected verses from these chapters that are suitable for memorization. Appropriate verses include:

Isa. 25:1	Isa. 29:13	Isa. 33:5-6
Isa. 25:9	Isa. 30:15	Isa. 33:15-16
Isa. 26:3-4	Isa. 32:1-2	Isa. 35:3-4

STUDY GUIDE 57

Isaiah 40–48

THE EVERLASTING GOD

Overview

Some argue that the second half of Isaiah was written by a person other than Isaiah the son of Amoz. There is a dramatic change in theme and emphasis. But the real reason for postulating two Isaiahs lays in the refusal of liberal scholars to accept the supernatural. Isaiah spoke of Babylon before that city was capital of a world power. He even named Cyrus, the Persian who overcame Babylon. Only God could have known ahead of time.

Why do conservatives maintain the unity of this great book? • The Jews treated this book as a unity and believed Isaiah wrote it. • New Testament writers who quote Isaiah treat passages from the first and second halves the same. • Jesus, given the "scroll of the Prophet Isaiah" read from 61:1-2 (Luke 4:17-19). • Similar passages occur in both parts of the book (cf. 1:15 with 59:3; 30:26 with 60:19). • The book maintains a strong theological unity, and uses terms and names of God in both sections unique to Isaiah. • Prophetic utterances often foretell distant events. The predictive elements in Isaiah are in full harmony with the Bible's general supernaturalism. • The two-Isaiah theory was not introduced until the 18th century. It was offered by antisupernaturalists to explain away the predictive accuracy of the book. That view has no basis in history, nor is compelling evidence found in Scripture.

How good to know that in the Word of God we have revealed truth. The God who speaks through Isaiah was well able to tell the future then, and still speaks to us today.

Commentary

> This is what the Lord says—Israel's King and Redeemer, the Lord Almighty: I am the first and I am the last; apart from Me there is no God. Who then is like Me? Let him proclaim it. Let him declare and lay out before Me what has happened since I established My ancient people, and what is yet to come—yes, let him foretell what will come. Do not tremble, do not be afraid. Did I not proclaim this and foretell it long ago? You are My witnesses. Is there any God besides Me? No, there is no other Rock; I know not one.
>
> Isaiah 44:6-8

With Isaiah 40 we move into the second half of Isaiah, and immediately burst into a fresh and joyful world. A tone of optimism and celebration pervades these last chapters of the prophet's work. We hear that tone in the very first words of Isaiah 40:

> Comfort, comfort My people, says your God. Speak tenderly to Jerusalem, and proclaim to her that her hard service has been completed, that her sin has been paid for, that she has received from the Lord's hand double for all her sins.
>
> Isaiah 40:1-2

In this half of Isaiah the prophet seems to *look back on* judgment past. The prospect of terror is gone. Now comes the promised joy. Isaiah looks beyond even the Babylonian Captivity of Judah, still a hundred years in his future. There Isaiah sees Babylon's power shattered by Cyrus of Persia (Isa. 45–46). He looks even beyond this to the restoration of all things. In prophetic vision Isaiah sees history's end, when God will say to His redeemed people:

> Forget the former things; do not dwell on the past. See, I am doing a new thing! Now it springs up; do you not perceive it? I am making a way in the desert and streams in the wasteland. . . . To give drink to My people, My chosen, the people I formed for Myself that they may

proclaim My praise.

Isaiah 43:18-21

In the new world, former things will not be remembered or come to mind. God will make all things new.

♥ ***Link to Life: Youth / Adult***
What kind of God speaks to us in Isaiah 40–48? As your group members come in give each one of these nine chapters to skim. Ask each to select a few verses that express God's nature and character as He reveals it here.
Then when class opens, have each person read in turn the verse he or she has selected as an introduction to this powerful Old Testament section.

Pivotal Themes
Isaiah's looking back at terrible judgment from the perspective of the joyful experience of God's promised blessings brings two pivotal themes of Scripture into fresh focus.

Theme 1: Scripture as revelation. In Isaiah one dramatic means that God used to reveal Himself is through His names. But there came a point in time when God also revealed Himself in man's language. God communicated Himself to us through words spoken by prophets and recorded in written form in the Scriptures. Through the written Word, we too are invited to know and trust God.

We can watch an individual's actions. We can learn his titles. But we can never know his motives or his feelings, what is in his heart, unless he explains himself to us in words.

The Apostle Paul made this point in 1 Corinthians. "For who among men knows the thoughts of a man except the man's spirit within him? In the same way no one knows the thoughts of God except the Spirit of God." Paul went on to point out that in the Bible we have knowledge not in "words taught us by human wisdom but in words taught by the Spirit" (1 Cor. 2:11, 13). Scripture is far more than the record of man's groping after God. It is more than human theories of the meaning of history. The Bible, as prophet after prophet has proclaimed, is the recorded Word of God. It is His revelation, through which we come to know Him as He shares His inmost thoughts with us.

Isaiah 40–48 presents one aspect of God's inmost thoughts: His intentions. We are given a unique insight into God's person as we read these words about His plans for man's better tomorrow:

> I the Lord will answer them; I, the God of Israel, will not forsake them. I will make the rivers flow on barren heights, and springs within the valleys. I will turn the desert into pools of water, and the parched ground into springs. I will put in the desert the cedar and the acacia, the myrtle and the olive.
>
> Isaiah 41:17-19

God intends to restore the shattered land and the shattered people, so He may bring a celebrating people back to Himself.

We do not study the Bible just to gain information. We come to Scripture to meet God. *If we truly want to know God, you and I must look into the Word of God and listen to Him share what is in His heart. We must look beyond the darkness of our todays to catch a vision of the bright sunshine of God's promised tomorrow.*

How can we be sure it's really Him we see in Scripture, and not some dream or strange vision drawn from an overactive imagination? This was a problem for Israel as well as for modern man to which God gave a distinct answer. He challenged Judah concerning the idols on which she had fixed her hope:

> Bring in your idols to tell us what is going to happen. . . . Declare to us the things to come, tell us what the future holds, so we may know that you are gods.
>
> Isaiah 41:22-23

Then God established His unique claim:

> I foretold the former things long ago, My mouth announced them and I made them known. . . . I told you these things long ago; before they happened I announced them to you so that you could not say, "My idols did them. . . ." From now on I will tell you of new things, of hidden things unknown to you.
>
> Isaiah 48:3, 5-6

God announced through the prophets

what would happen in Israel's history; invariably His words came true. God has verified His trustworthiness through fulfilled prophecy. Just how accurate prophecy has proven to be is something we'll see in the next unit as we consider the Servant of the Lord. For now, we simply want to note that the Old and New Testaments alike speak with sure conviction that the words recorded are God's. They accurately reveal Him. Prophecy not only vindicates God's claim of self-revelation; it moves the expression of God's good intentions for mankind beyond *possibility* to *certainty!* In Scripture's statement of God's plans, we meet *Him*, and we read history before it happens!

♥ ***Link to Life: Youth / Adult***
Prophecy is presented here as something which makes our God unique, and which gives us great confidence in the Word of God.
Here is a list of Old Testament prophecies. Your group members will enjoy a "prophecy search." Give teams slips of paper on which the following Old Testament prophecy references are written. The team which locates the most fulfillments in the Gospels in six minutes *wins.*
Prophecy references to use: Isaiah 7:14; 9:1-2; 9:6-11; 11:1; 53:1; 53:9; 53:12; Micah 5:2; Zechariah 9:9; 11:12-13; Psalms 22:1; 22:18; 31:5; 34:20; 69:21.

Theme 2: God as ever-living. How can we be sure that what is portrayed by Isaiah will come to pass? He has an answer for us in God's revelation of Himself as everlasting. He Himself will be present in the future to keep the wondrous promises He gives.

But Israel and Judah had turned aside from the living God to follow *idols!* Isaiah in these chapters contrasted the power of God with the ineffectiveness of idols:

> To whom, then, will you compare God? What image will you compare Him to? As for an idol, a craftsman casts it, and a goldsmith overlays it with gold and fashions silver chains for it. A man too poor to present such an offering selects wood that will not rot. He looks for a skilled craftsman, to set up an idol that will not topple.
>
> Isaiah 40:18-20

But God is no idol that must be nailed down so it won't topple (41:7). God sits enthroned above the earth. He looks down and sees mankind as we see grasshoppers, insignificant below Him (40:22).

How foolish the idol maker. He cuts down a tree, uses some of it to build a fire and cook his food, and then he makes an idol from the rest.

> He . . . fashions a god and worships it; he makes an idol and bows down to it. Half of the wood he burns in the fire. . . . From the rest he makes a god, his idol. . . . He prays to it and says, "Save me; you are my god."
>
> Isaiah 44:15-17

To bow down to a block of wood! And to choose such gods when the Living God, the Maker of heaven and earth, presents Himself to us to be known and worshiped, to be our Healer and Redeemer. The Lord says:

> Before Me no god was formed, nor will there be one after Me. I, even I, am the Lord, and apart from Me there is no savior. I have revealed and saved and proclaimed.
>
> Isaiah 43:10-12

I have revealed. I have saved. I have proclaimed.

It is the Living God who has revealed Himself to us in His Word. On Him Isaiah based all his hope and his confidence. A vision of the Everlasting God dominated Isaiah's thoughts. The Everlasting God, the First and the Last, the Living One whom we meet in Isaiah 40–48, is the One on whom all our hopes must rest.

Purposes of the Living God: Isaiah 40–48
In these opening chapters we are shown God's intentions and reassured that what He intends will come to pass.

> I am God, and there is no other; I am God, and there is none like Me. I make known the end from the beginning, from ancient times, what is still to come. I say: My purpose will stand, and I will do all that I please.
>
> Isaiah 46:9-10

What, then, does God please to do?

Comfort (Isa. 40). In this chapter God is seen coming with power. But He does not come to judge. Instead:

> He tends His flock like a shepherd: He gathers the lambs in His arms and carries them close to His heart; He gently leads those that have young.
>
> Isaiah 40:11

He who will never grow weary or tired is now seen giving strength to weary people, renewing their strength. God's intentions for us are good; He cares for His sheep.

Help (Isa. 41). The idols in which Israel and Judah trusted are vain things. But God Himself will lead His people to a time of rejoicing:

> I will strengthen you and help you; I will uphold you with My righteous right hand. . . . For I am the Lord, your God, who takes hold of your right hand and says to you, "Do not fear; I will help you."
>
> Isaiah 41:10, 13

Fully restore (Isa. 42–43). In these chapters God contrasts the past and the future. When all the former things have been put behind, there will be a new song of praise for God's people to sing. Then the Lord Himself, apart from whom there is no savior, will be their Redeemer, bringing them forgiveness and joy.

> Yes, and from ancient days I am He. No one can deliver out of My hand. When I act, who can reverse it?
>
> Isaiah 43:13

To be forever (Isa. 44). God committed Himself to restore Jerusalem and to stand forever as Israel's King. In this chapter is the most devastating critique of idolatry in all of Scripture. Because our God is not an empty man-made idol, we can even now:

> Sing for joy, O heavens, for the Lord has done this; shout aloud, O earth beneath. Burst out into song, you mountains, you forests and all your trees, for the Lord has redeemed Jacob, He displays His glory in Israel.
>
> Isaiah 44:23

To destroy Babylon (Isa. 45–48). Looking beyond the current Assyrian danger the prophet foresaw the end of another nation, Babylon. It would be another hundred years before Babylon would carry Judah away captive even as Sargon had carried away Israel.

For unaided men, this kind of prophecy seems impossible. In fact, scholars who dismiss the possibility of propositional revelation have argued that someone other than Isaiah must have written the latter half of his book. But God reminds us in these very chapters:

> I foretold the former things long ago, My mouth announced them and I made them known; then suddenly I acted, and they came to pass.
>
> Isaiah 48:3

The Bible presents God as the Living God, the Everlasting One, who not only announces the future but who acts to bring about foretold events. If we accept the possibility of a Living God, as opposed to a mere expression of man's imagination or need, then there is nothing terribly unlikely about the prophet looking *back* on a day that is still future to his own time. After all, it is God who speaks through him. The Living God who is always present with His people is in a unique position to *know*.

The Living God speaks to us now and, in His promise of restoration, reveals Himself to us as a God of endless love.

TEACHING GUIDE

Prepare

Read through Isaiah 40–44 quickly. Then jot down several words or phrases that seem to you to express the vision of God given in them.

Explore

1. Have class members select one or two verses from each chapter which unveil something special about God's nature or character. Read them consecutively as a

worshipful opening to this week's session. See "link-to-life," page 385.

2. These chapters contain striking prophecies—and make powerful statements about prophecy.

To check out the authenticating power of the prophetic word, play the six-minute "prophecy search" game explained in "link-to-life" on page 386.

Then read and discuss Isaiah 41:22-23; 46:9-10; 48:3, 5-6. What do these passages tell us about the significance of prophecy in revealing the nature of God?

Expand

Read and study Isaiah 44 together. This classic chapter discusses the folly of idolatry. Your group will want to answer the following questions: (a) What are some modern idols? (b) What is the contrast between modern idols and the Living God? (c) What is the most important thing that God seems to want to get across in this chapter?

Apply

Reproduce on sheets of paper the following verses. Ask each person to select a "most significant verse to me." Go around the circle so each can share why he or she chose the verse he did. Verses are:

- Isa. 40:11
- Isa. 40:28-31
- Isa. 41:13
- Isa. 43:1-2
- Isa. 46:10-11

STUDY GUIDE 58

Isaiah 49–54

GOD'S SERVANT

Overview
Isaiah powerfully portrayed the awesome greatness of Israel's Sovereign Lord. In power the Holy One of Isaiah will come to:

- enforce obedience
- blot out injustice
- exercise kingly power
- judge the earth
- fulfill the covenant promises
- be welcomed by Israel
- win the allegiance of mankind.

Now, suddenly, Isaiah introduced a different theme. The King will be a Servant! As Servant, He will:

- be obedient
- suffer injustice
- will not raise His voice
- will become a covenant
- will be rejected by Israel
- will be mocked and spit on.

And, at the climax of these revelations, is the explicit picture in Isaiah 53 of the Servant's substitutionary death!

The contrast between Isaiah's image of the Sovereign Lord, acting in power, and his image of the Servant, suffering for others, was puzzling to Old Testament saints. But now, in Jesus, we at last understand the unity of God's plan. Jesus suffered, but will return in glory. And, in Isaiah's vision of a Suffering Servant, we see our Lord more clearly—and we better understand our calling to be servants too.

▶ ***Servant.*** In Old Testament thought it was not demeaning to be a servant. One Hebrew term, *sarit,* suggests that the "servant" serves an important person to whom he is close, and that what the servant does is truly significant.

Commentary

> And now the Lord says—He who formed me in the womb to be His servant to bring Jacob back to Him and gather Israel to Himself, for I am honored in the eyes of the Lord and my God has been my strength—He says: "It is too small a thing for you to be My servant to restore the tribes of Jacob and bring back those of Israel I have kept. I will also make you a light for the Gentiles, that you may bring My salvation to the ends of the earth." This is what the Lord says—the Redeemer and Holy One of Israel—to Him who was despised and abhorred by the nation, to the servant of rulers: "Kings will see You and rise up, princes will see and bow down, because of the Lord, who is faithful."
>
> Isaiah 49:5-7

A Servant?
At first the title "Servant" seems out of place among all the splenderous titles which Isaiah gave God: The Holy One. The Redeemer. The Sovereign Lord. The Everlasting God. All these names seem so much more appropriate to that Person who is unveiled in this great prophetic book. Yet "Servant" may most fully display the glory and wonder of our God.

The title is one that Jesus chose for Himself and held out His lifestyle as a model for His disciples to adopt. When the Twelve, hungry for splendor, argued over who would be greatest, Jesus called them together and said:

> You know that the rulers of the Gentiles lord it over them, and their high officials exercise authority over them. Not so with you. Instead, whoever wants to become great among you must be your servant, and whoever wants to be first must be your slave—just as the Son of man did not come to be served, but to serve, and to give His life as a ransom for many.
>
> Matthew 20:25-28

Jesus saw Himself and His mission in the perspective of servanthood. Indeed, He is The Servant of the Lord spoken of by the Prophet Isaiah and by New Testament writers. Paul wrote in Philippians that Jesus:

> Being in very nature God, did not consider equality with God something to be grasped, but made Himself nothing, taking the very nature of a servant, being made in human likeness. And being found in appearance as a man, He humbled Himself and became obedient to death—even death on a cross!
>
> Philippians 2:6-8

Such passages, with Isaiah's portrait, give us several distinctive impressions of the Servant.

- His desire was to serve God.
- His stance before men was one of humility.
- His mission was to bring others deliverance.
- His servanthood involved great personal suffering.
- His strength came from God, who upheld Him in and through His mission.

How greatly these qualities contrast with the lifestyle of Israel, against which Isaiah cried. Her attitude was arrogant and proud. Her goal was to gather wealth and comforts for herself. She chose whatever pathway seemed to promise the easiest life. She failed to rely on God, but relied instead on her own strength or on alliances with pagan nations. Only the servant relies on and knows God.

The servant. There has been much debate over just who Isaiah's servant really is. In some cases the prophet seems to refer to Israel. In other cases the reference is clearly to the Messiah. Some have insisted that *every* servant passage is essentially messianic and thus speaks of Christ.

Looking through the whole Scripture, it is clear that the idea of "the Servant of the Lord" is *not* reserved for the coming Messiah alone. Various prophets speak of themselves as the Lord's servants (2 Sam. 7:19; 1 Kings 18:36). David and even Nebuchadnezzar (Jer. 25:9) are identified as servants of the Lord. The nation Israel is also specifically identified as God's servant (Isa. 49:3). But when Israel failed to fulfill her servant role, Isaiah turned to reveal a messianic Servant who would come and accomplish salvation (v. 6).

The New Testament uses the term "servant" to refer to the people of God in general (Acts 4:29; Rev. 2:20). It also is used in reference to the community of Israel (Luke 1:54). But most often in the New Testament the title "servant" refers to Jesus (Matt. 12:18; Acts 3:13; 4:27, 30).

In the New Testament each believer-servant ministers to the whole community of faith, taking as his example the Lord's own servant life (cf. Mark 10:43; 1 Cor. 4:5 with Mark 10:35-45; Matt. 23:8-12; John 13:1-17).

THE Servant. Just as it's clear that Isaiah used "servant" to designate more than one group of individuals, it is also clear that among the servants of the Lord there is One who has a preeminent place. This Servant, unlike others, never fails to do the will of the Lord. This Servant draws on God's strength and accomplishes His purpose. This Servant is clearly the promised Messiah, the One through whom all of God's purposes for Creation will be fulfilled. Isaiah 52:13–53:12 is a clear Old Testament prophecy of Christ's death and even explains its meaning. This passage is referred to explicitly in the New Testament some 10 times (Matt. 8:17; Luke 22:37; John 12:38; Acts 8:32-33; Rom. 10:16; 1 Peter 2:22, 24-25).

What is particularly striking in Isaiah is the fact that the God revealed in all His glorious splendor is also the God of the Incarnation. He comes to be Servant as well as King.

This paradox is captured in Philippians 2. The passage describes Jesus' willing descent from glory to take on the form of the Servant, and as a servant to be obedient even to death. But His death is a return to glory. Because He served:

> Therefore God exalted Him to the highest place and gave Him the name that is above every name, that at the name of Jesus every knee should bow, in heaven and on earth and under the earth, and every tongue confess that Jesus Christ is Lord, to the glory of God the Father.
>
> Philippians 2:9-11

The Lord is the Servant. The Servant is Lord.

Lessons from servanthood. Jesus taught that we who believe in Him need to follow His steps, and serve one another as He served us (see 1 Peter 2:21; John 13:3-17; Matt. 20:26-28). Christ called us to be servants who are faithful in our appointed tasks (see Matt. 24:45–25:30). Paul exhorts us to develop the servant's attitude (Phil. 2:1-4).

The same lessons are found in the Old Testament. God called Israel to be His servant, the agent through whom He could make Himself known to mankind. Israel arrogantly turned away from the path of obedience to the Heavenly Lord. Rather than reveal God to the nations, Israel became like the nations, and her value to God and to man was lost.

But God did not discard His servant Israel; instead He acted to redeem her. God Himself entered the world as Immanuel, the Servant. In salvation's ultimate act of obedience, He died for Israel and called all humankind back to God. In the Servant of the Lord we find our deepest revelation of the character and love of God, for in the Servant we meet the one who sacrifices Himself for the good of mankind.

What does all this mean for us? We too are called to be servants, walking in Jesus' steps. As we commit ourselves to the Heavenly Lord, He will strengthen and direct us, and through us do good to all men. God's servants find fulfillment and meaning in life. But beware! The servant ministry requires a servant's heart. We must rely fully on God, and prize Jesus' attitude of humility if we are to know exaltation by the One who rewards all who choose to obey Him.

♥ ***Link to Life: Youth / Adult***
Matthew 20:25-28 offers us a powerful explanation by Jesus of servanthood. In the passage the way of the servant is contrasted with the way of "Gentile rulers" who exercise power and authority.

Place a T-shaped chart on a large chalkboard. Title the left side "servant," the right "ruler." Divide your group into teams of four. Each is to find contrasts *and* comparisons *that this passage may suggest between the servant and secular rulers. Contrasts need not be specifically in the text, but may be suggested by the images themselves. After about eight minutes, come together to list comparisons/contrasts on the chart.*

Then discuss: "What does it mean to be a servant of God today? What are specific ways that we can be servants in our homes? Our churches?"

Servant Portraits in Isaiah

Isaiah contains a number of brief references to a servant (41:8-9; 42:19; 43:10; 44:1-2, 21, 26; 45:4; 48:20). In addition there are four major passages (42:1-9; 49:1-6; 50:4-10; 52:13–53:12). It is helpful in understanding these middle chapters of Isaiah to look at them through the Servant's eyes. What are the characteristics of a servant?

Israel, the servant chosen by God (41:8-9), failed to realize that one who receives God's grace becomes an agent of grace. Missing this meaning of the covenant, Israel, with haughty disdain, stubbornly chose a lifestyle of selfishness and wickedness. Now Isaiah introduced a Servant who was totally unlike Israel, a Servant who would pick up the shambles of the unfinished task and would redeem not only Israel but all mankind.

Isaiah 42:1-9

"Here is My Servant." These words commence a unique unveiling. The One who accomplished God's purposes would be no bold conqueror. Instead the One who established justice on earth would be a Servant who:

> Will not shout or cry out, or raise His voice in the streets. A bruised reed He will not break, and a smoldering wick He will not snuff out.
>
> Isaiah 42:2-3

The initial imagery is understandable. The Servant would not be strident or attract attention to Himself as He went about His mission. Humility, not forcefulness, would identify Him.

But what of the second? What of the bruised reed and the smoldering flax?

The Hebrew language does not describe with abstract concepts, but with vivid word pictures. The images of the bruised reed and smoldering wick would have been understood by Isaiah's readers. The bruised reed conjured up the picture of a shepherd, who selected a reed from which to make a shepherd's pipe (flute). The shepherd cut the reed, then gently tapped the back with a smooth stone. Rotating the reed, he continued tapping. He had to be gentle, because if he bruised the reed with the stone it would be worthless as an instrument. He would have to toss it away and begin all over again.

The same was true of smoking flax. In Isaiah's day the lamp was a small bowl of oil in which a bit of flax was dropped as a wick. After a time, the flax became encrusted with carbon. The wick began to sputter and to smoke. Such a wick was useless, to be plucked from the bowl and tossed out.

To the Servant of the Lord, the worthless of the world have great value! He will not casually snap the bruised human twig or discard the useless human flax. Instead, He commits Himself to bring them justice, and to bring them hope.

Isaiah moved on. The Creator of the heavens and earth had committed Himself to walk beside the Servant and would make the Servant Himself be a covenant:

> To open eyes that are blind, to free captives from prison and to release from the dungeon those who sit in darkness.
>
> Isaiah 42:7

Isaiah 49:1–50:3

The first seven verses of this section reintroduce the servant theme. Israel herself had been called by God to be "My servant, Israel, in whom I will display My splendor" (49:3). But Israel was forced to confess that she had failed, and fallen far short of that purpose (v. 4). Then came a new revelation: One who was formed in the womb to be God's Servant will gather Israel again to the Lord (v. 5) and, beyond that, will become:

> A light for the Gentiles, that you may bring My salvation to the ends of the earth.
>
> Isaiah 49:6

In spite of the Servant's initial rejection by the world, God has not rejected Him. God will act through Christ in total faithfulness to His expressed purpose of doing good for all men (v. 7).

Restoration (Isa. 49:8-26). The Servant had been introduced. Now Isaiah described the healing and restoration God will accomplish through Him. The captives will return; they will shout for joy; the Gentiles will honor the chosen people. In the punishment of oppressors:

> All mankind will know that I, the Lord, am your Saviour, your Redeemer, the Mighty One of Jacob.
>
> Isaiah 49:26

While Israel was in Captivity she despaired God's favor. But had God ever divorced Himself from Israel? (50:1) Is God too weak to rescue? (v. 2) No. Through the ministry of the Servant restoration will come, and lost hope will turn to joy.

Isaiah 50:4–52:12

This passage begins with a further unveiling of the Servant (50:4-10). He was committed to *obedience*. While Israel stubbornly refused to respond to the Lord, the Servant would be completely responsive to God's will.

Isaiah 50:4. Because the Servant listens intently and obediently "morning by morning," He has wisdom to "know the word that sustains the weary." Obedience qualifies and marks the Servant as He pursues His ministry.

Isaiah 50:5. The open ear (to hear) comes with obedience. The Servant could hear God's voice because "I have not been rebellious; I have not drawn back."

Isaiah 50:6-7. The choice to obey God brought the Servant into conflict with men. But even the most degrading of insults failed to shame or deter Him. "I set My face like flint." Total commitment rests on total confidence in God. "I will not be put to shame."

Isaiah 50:8-9. Rather than react vengefully, the Servant waits for God's vindication. Because the Sovereign Lord helps the Servant, no case against Him can stand. Every human opponent will "wear out like a garment," while God remains forever the same.

Isaiah 50:10. The Servant's obedience provided the example for Israel. All who fear the Lord will obey the word of the Servant and trust in the name of the Lord. Those who rely on God, as the Servant relied, will have deliverance.

Isaiah 51:1-16. Salvation is everlasting. How comforting the Servant's message to those "who pursue righteousness and who seek the Lord." When God's people listen to the Servant, justice, righteousness, and peace will light the world. How good to know that "the cowering prisoners will soon be set free" (v. 14).

Isaiah 51:17-21. Wrath is past. In the first half of Isaiah, the prophet saw the grim prospect of God's coming day of retribution. But he calls those who have experienced wrath to awake! (v. 17) God takes from their hand the cup of judgment that makes them drunken. Now He calls out to them through the Servant:

> Awake, awake, O Zion, clothe yourself with strength. Put on your garments of splendor, O Jerusalem, the Holy City. . . . Shake off your dust; rise up, sit enthroned, O Jerusalem.
>
> Isaiah 52:1-2

The good news is, God reigns! His return to Zion will cause the people to break out into songs of joy.

The way of obedience to God is not a path to bondage but to *freedom.* The ministry of the Servant breaks the chains from the necks of God's people.

Today too many are enslaved. They are enslaved to anxiety, to passion, to greed, to fear of others, to self-doubt. The Servant offers them freedom. But to find the true freedom that God provides we who have trusted Jesus must walk the path He walked, and become willing servants of our God.

♥ ***Link to Life: Youth / Adult***

Here's a way to help your group members discover for themselves the exciting truths revealed in Isaiah's "servant" passages. Use this study before giving any lecture input on the Servant of the Lord in Isaiah.

Divide into teams of four or five people. Ask each team to read these "servant" references in Isaiah and answer the following questions:

Isaiah 43:8-9
Isaiah 43:10
Isaiah 44:1-2, 21, 26
Isaiah 45:4
Isaiah 48:20
Isaiah 49:1-6
Isaiah 50:4-19

- *Who is the servant referred to in this passage?*
- *What do we learn about servanthood?*
- *What do we learn about THE Servant?*

After reports, discuss: "What would it mean for me to live a servant life today?"

Isaiah 52:13–53:12

This passage, which focuses on the suffering of God's Servant, unmistakably describes and explains the meaning of the death of Jesus Christ. It is one of the most vivid and important of all Old Testament prophetic passages, and might well be the focus of a separate group session.

What are the most powerful teachings of this final, and central, servant passage in Isaiah?

Isaiah 52:13-15. The wisdom of the Servant led Him to make choices that seem foolish to men. He chose a path, obedience, that led to intense and terrible suffering. When finally men do understand, an awed and stunned humanity will at last begin to sense the depth of the love and holiness of our God.

Isaiah 53:1-3. Those looking for the glorious King of Old Testament prophecy will despise the Servant, who had "no beauty or majesty to attract us to Him." To those hungry for outward glory, what attraction could there be to One who was despised, rejected, sorrowful, and familiar with suffering?

Looking ahead Isaiah realized that the people of Messiah's own time would hide their faces from Him in shame, considering Him of no value or worth.

Isaiah 53:4-6. Isaiah went deeper into the great misunderstanding. As the Servant's obedience led Him into deeper and deeper suffering, and finally death, His contemporaries were convinced that He had been "stricken [and thus rejected] by God." In fact, the suffering He underwent was for the sins of God's people. He took our place, bearing our weaknesses and sorrows. He was pierced for our transgressions, crushed for our iniquities, punished for our rebellion, and took on His shoulders the iniquity of us all.

The Servant's great act of self-sacrifice brought peace, healed, and lifted the sin-guilt from us.

Isaiah 53:7-9. Isaiah pointed out that the Servant's suffering was voluntary. No word of complaint passed His lips. In verses 8 and 9 Isaiah described what would actually happen to Jesus some 700 years after! He was taken from arrest (*otzer,* "oppression") to an unjust trial. He died a painful death, and yet was given honorable burial among the rich. Because He had done no violence, nor was any deceit in Him, the Servant was spared the final disgrace intended by His enemies.

Isaiah 53:10-12. We should not ignore the responsibility of the wicked men who plotted the Servant's death. But we must also realize that God Himself chose this course for His Servant. And that the Servant freely elected to become a guilt offering, and thus be both priest and sacrifice.

This passage tells us the startling results for the Servant. Though He died, as the sacrifice must always die, the Servant will

see His offspring prolong His days
be the Agent who carries out God's will for men
see the light of life
gain great satisfaction
take His place among the great
gain the treasures associated with victory.

How could a dead man continue past the time of His self-sacrifice and gain all these rewards? The resurrection of Jesus gives God's historical, definitive answer. God raised His Servant to life again; death could not hold Him captive.

But there are exciting results for men as well. We are beneficiaries of the Servant's sacrificial act. We become His offspring, and because of Jesus take our place as children of God. We experience justification, and find in the Servant of the Lord the freedom from the sins He bore in our place.

♥ ***Link to Life: Children***

Jesus died so that we might become God's children. Even young children can grasp enough of God's saving love to respond to the offer of salvation. But how can we explain faith's response to the Lord? Here's one way.

Have a coin or some other thing of value for each child in your class. Put the coins on a low table beside name cards. Explain that the coins are gifts. Anyone who wants to receive the gift can get up, find his name card, and take the gift reserved there for him or her. If some children do not go get their gift, tell them again they may pick it up. But do not *pick it up for them.*

Then explain: "Jesus died so we could each have our sins forgiven and become God's children. This too is a gift." Have the boys and girls close their eyes, and imagine that this gift is right in front of them too. Let them imagine reaching out to take God's gift.

Then thank God for the gift that we have received from Him.

TEACHING GUIDE

Prepare

Read and meditate on Isaiah 53.

Explore

1. Give a minilecture contrasting Isaiah's exalted images of the Sovereign Lord with his images of the Servant (see *overview*).
2. Or launch with team studies of brief "Servant" passages (see "link-to-life," page 393).

Expand

1. What are the implications of the choice of a servant lifestyle? Use a T-shaped chart to record group members' insights gained from Jesus' words in Matthew 20:25-28.
2. Or read through Isaiah 53 together, letting your group members make observations on what they see in the text.

Divide into three study groups. Each group will look at different New Testament passages which refer to this key Old Testament chapter. Each group should then summarize what the New Testament says about it or its teaching.

Team 1: Matthew 8:17; Luke 22:37; Romans 10:16; 1 Peter 2:22.

Team 2: John 12:38; Acts 8:32-33; Romans 15:21; Hebrews 9:28; 1 Peter 2:24-25.

Team 3: Hebrews 10.

Apply

Ask each person to select one phrase from Isaiah 53 which expresses something important Jesus has done for him or her. Give two additional minutes for each to meditate on the selected phrase.

Then close with sentence prayers. Ask each to use this form: "Jesus, thank You for serving me in Your death and (fill in the selected phrase). In response, help me to serve others by . . . (complete as desired)."

STUDY GUIDE 59

Isaiah 55–66

LORD OF GLORY

Overview

The last chapters of Isaiah's great work are rich in promise. They begin with an invitation to experience redemption (Isa. 55–59), and conclude with a picture of the glory that will come with history's end (Isa. 60–66).

Isaiah had already touched on many aspects of God's eternal purpose. At the time of fulfillment:

- The Sovereign Lord will come with power (40:10).
- The Holy One of Israel will bring judgment on earth (41:14-15).
- The God of Israel will make the barren land rich (41:17-18).
- The warrior Lord will triumph over all His enemies (42:13).
- The Saviour will bring all Israel back from captivity to the Promised Land (43:5-6).
- Israel's King will blot out their transgressions (v. 25).
- The Redeemer will pour out God's Spirit on Israel's descendants (44:3-4).
- The Servant will not only restore Israel, but Gentiles as well will know God's salvation (49:6).
- The Lord will comfort Israel and bring her joy (v. 13).
- The Sovereign Lord will cause the Gentiles to acknowledge the favored position of Israel as God's chosen (v. 22).
- The Righteous Lord will establish justice, and a holy people will light the way for all nations (51:4-5).

Now, further enriching and expanding our vision of the future, Isaiah went into more detail about what will happen on earth when the Sovereign Lord comes to embrace His own and make all things right.

Commentary

Timeless Principles: Isaiah 54–59

Before defining what lies ahead, Isaiah unveiled some of the timeless principles that are expressed in God's dealings with men.

Invitation (Isa. 55). The nation to whom Isaiah preached failed to respond to the prophet's message. The kingdom kept firmly on its road toward divine judgment. But Isaiah also *gave an open invitation to individuals!* He called out to everyone who recognized his or her need:

> Come, all you who are thirsty, come to the waters; and you who have no money, come, buy and eat!
>
> Isaiah 55:1

The person who hears the invitation is to respond in faith, and come into a covenant relationship with God. In that relationship, the benefits of the promise (which will one day be given to all) will become the present possession of the individual now.

> Give ear and come to Me; hear Me, that your soul may live. I will make an everlasting covenant with you, My faithful love promised to David.
>
> Isaiah 55:3

This invitation is open to all, including the wicked man, who is to forsake his way and his evil thoughts. To every individual who comes, God promises mercy and pardon (v. 7).

It is at this point that God declares, "My thoughts are not your thoughts, neither are your ways My ways" (v. 8). God does not deal with us on our terms, but on His. Jesus picked up this same theme in His instruction to His disciples to love their enemies.

> [God] causes His sun to rise on the evil and the good, and sends rain on the righteous and the unrighteous. If you love those who love you, what reward will you get? Are not even the tax collec-

tors doing that? And if you greet only your brothers, what are you doing more than others? Do not even pagans do that? Be perfect, therefore, as your Heavenly Father is perfect.

Matthew 5:45-48

God initiates relationship with those who are His enemies, and He does so with love. As His people, we too are to take the initiative and to love aggressively. In order to have this kind of loving involvement with others, we must look to God for our example, because loving enemies is foreign to humankind.

God's invitation to the wicked promises that when they respond to Him, life-change will follow. They will have joy, peace, and fruitfulness (Isa. 55:12-13).

♥ ***Link to Life: Youth / Adult***
Write Isaiah 55:8 on the chalkboard. As your group members come in, ask them to make guesses about how *God's thoughts are not like ours, or His ways like our ways.*

Then read verse 7, which is linked to 8 by the "for." It is God's willingness to have mercy on and pardon the wicked that sets Him apart.

If you wish, explore the implications of Matthew 5:45-48 for us today. How can we be more like God by adopting His attitude toward people who have made themselves our enemies?

The excluded are welcomed (Isa. 56). In chapter 55 individuals within the chosen nation respond to God and find the blessings to which most citizens are blind. Now the prophet made it clear that more than the chosen people are invited to experience salvation:

> Let no foreigner who has joined himself to the Lord say, "The Lord will surely exclude me from His people." And let not any eunuch complain, "I am only a dry tree."
>
> Isaiah 56:3

According to the Mosaic Law both foreigners and eunuchs were excluded from worship. There was the promise that someday, at the time of the end, all nations could taste God's salvation. That blessing was to await the work of Messiah.

But God wants to let the excluded know that they are welcome *now*.

> "Their burnt offerings and sacrifices will be accepted on My altar; for My house will be called a house of prayer for all nations." The Sovereign Lord declares—He who gathers the exiles of Israel: "I will gather still others to them besides those already gathered."
>
> Isaiah 56:7-8

History shows this principle in operation. Rahab in the days of Joshua, Ruth in the later day of the Judges; these were pagans who responded to God and found a place in His love. Even that wicked city, Nineveh, which repented under the prophetic preaching of Jonah, finds a place in the Bible record.

The New Testament explains that those once "excluded from citizenship in Israel and foreigners to the covenants of the promise, without hope and without God in the world" have now been "brought near through the blood of Christ" (Eph. 2:12-13). The unexpected dimension of God's promise is His intention to "create in Himself one new man out of the two, thus making peace" (v. 15). Not only are the excluded welcomed, they are welcomed on the same terms and to the same inheritance as the chosen!

We have a tendency to deal with the excluded as if they were really different from us; so different that to be acceptable they must first become like us. God accepts each person as he is, whether foreigner or eunuch, and brings him and us together into the New Covenant that Christ *is*. When we evaluate others on the basis of how they are different from us, rather than seeking to affirm our potential oneness in and through Christ, we miss the wonder of our covenant-keeping and covenant-making God.

Restoration is possible (Isa. 57). Why do righteous people sometimes pass from the scene when they are most needed in society? Isaiah's insight into this question is:

> The righteous are taken away to be spared from evil. Those who walk uprightly enter into peace; they find rest as they lie in death.
>
> Isaiah 57:1-2

In contrast, the majority of Israel could not be considered righteous. In fact, God declared Israel to be the offspring of adulterers, prostitutes, and sorceresses! (v. 3) She had turned from God, who had entered into a marriage covenant with her, and had actively, even lustfully, sought out foreign gods (vv. 4-9). Since God did not act in judgment immediately, Israel assumed she was safe. But God warned that He would expose her "righteousness and works" and that neither would save His wayward people (v. 12).

God says, however, that restoration is possible. "The man who makes Me his refuge," He explains, "will inherit the land and possess My holy mountain" (v. 13). God will restore and build up His people when their lifestyle and attitude are acceptable.

> I live . . . with him who is contrite and lowly in spirit, to revive the spirit of the lowly, and to revive the heart of the contrite.
>
> Isaiah 57:15

God promises peace, healing, guidance, comfort, and an attitude of praise to those who depend on Him (vv. 18-19). While there is no peace for the wicked (vv. 20-21), a right relationship with God will bring inner, and even international, peace.

Reality not ritual (Isa. 58). Ritual and ceremony had a significant place in Israel's worship of the Lord. But faith is not summed up in ritual. Too often a Christian's lifestyle can become simply following a pattern of "religious" duties.

In Isaiah's day the people fasted and carefully followed the prescribed rituals, even as they complained that God did not seem to hear their prayers. God's answer?

> Yet on the day of your fasting, you do as you please and exploit all your workers. Your fasting ends in quarreling and strife, and in striking each other with wicked fists. You cannot fast as you do today and expect your voice to be heard on high.
>
> Isaiah 58:3-4

What kind of "fasting" does God call us to? Isaiah went on, relaying this timeless message from God.

> Is not this the kind of fasting I have chosen: to loose the chains of injustice and untie the cords of the yoke, to set the oppressed free and break every yoke? Is it not to share your food with the hungry and to provide the poor wanderer with shelter?
>
> Isaiah 58:6-7

The one who finds restoration and peace in covenant relationship with God will express that commitment by sharing God's love with people. His worship may contain ritual elements, fastings, and festivals. These are not wrong. But at the heart of the believer's lifestyle must be a loving representation of God to the world.

God Himself must redeem (Isa. 59). How bad is bad, and what is God going to do about evil? Isaiah summarized the iniquities which had separated Israel from God. The only way to get the full impact of the strength and beauty of his words is to read the passage, sensing the power of verses 1-15.

Note how far Israel strayed from God's intention for her:

> The way of peace they do not know; there is no justice in their paths. They have turned them into crooked roads; no one who walks in them will know peace.
>
> Isaiah 59:8

God Himself must intervene and redeem. His own arm must work salvation. When the Redeemer comes to Zion and the covenant is established, then not only will sins be forgiven but the words of God and His Spirit will become one with God's people.

Where there is sin, oppression, injustice, or thoughtless arrogance that dismisses and discards other human beings, then God must act. For those who remain hardened there will be retribution (59:18), but God's deepest desire is to redeem. And so we are called to enter into a covenant of peace and personal relationship with God. He then will change the hardness of our hearts, and plant within us His living Word.

♥ ***Link to Life: Youth / Adult***
Seeking parallels between Old Testament and New Testament passages can be one of the most rewarding approaches to Bible study. List on the chalkboard these

chapters and titles. Let your group members choose one to study with a friend. As they read, each pair is to come up with at least five *verses or passages from the New Testament (or Old) which suggest the same truths.*

When each pair has had about 10 minutes, reassemble. Work through each chapter, having group members read relevant verses and telling the New Testament parallel.

Portrait of History's End: Isaiah 60–66

> Arise, shine, for your light has come, and the glory of the Lord rises upon you. See, darkness covers the earth and thick darkness is over the peoples, but the Lord rises upon you and His glory appears over you. Nations will come to your light, and kings to the brightness of your dawn.
>
> Isaiah 60:1-3

Isaiah's prophecy lifted high the torch, which is the Lord Himself!

Now, in the last chapters of Isaiah, we catch a glimpse of the day toward which history is moving. When we reach that goal, we will see and share His glory, as all life's mysteries find final resolution in joy.

The sleepers awake (Isa. 60). The feeling we get reading Isaiah 60 is that God's people have been dozing and dreaming as they drifted along the stream of time. Then, cutting through their dreams comes a vibrant call:

> Arise, shine, for your light has come, and the glory of the Lord rises upon you.
>
> Isaiah 60:1

Israel's newly opened eyes see a stunning sight. From all around the sons and daughters that were lost are gathering. The riches of the nations are brought to Israel. They see God's glorious temple not on time's horizon, but here!

> You will look and be radiant, your heart will throb and swell with joy.
>
> Isaiah 60:5

The once-forsaken and hated shake off depression as they become the pride of mankind. Most wonderful of all, in those days of splendor God promises:

> The sun will no more be your light by day, nor will the brightness of the moon shine on you, for the Lord will be your everlasting light, and your God will be your glory. Your sun will never set again, and your moon will wane no more; the Lord will be your everlasting light, and your days of sorrow will end.
>
> Isaiah 60:19-20

Ruins restored (Isa. 61–62). The good news of time's end focuses on restoration. The man of God is anointed:

> To bind up the brokenhearted, to proclaim freedom for the captives and release for the prisoners.
>
> Isaiah 61:1

All who mourn are comforted with the word that the ancient ruins will be restored and devastated lands made fruitful.

Isaiah made it clear that this picture of restoration is not primarily physical but spiritual: Its first concern is to clothe men "with garments of salvation, and arrayed . . . in a robe of righteousness" (v. 10). When the Lord makes "righteousness and praise spring up before all nations" (v. 11), then the days of endless blessing will come. When the Saviour steps into full view:

> They will be called the holy people, the redeemed of the Lord; and you will be called sought after, the city no longer deserted.
>
> Isaiah 62:12

The land and the people will be filled with praise.

Yearnings satisfied (Isa. 63–64). These chapters begin with God's great saving acts at the end of time. His purifying judgments precede the days of blessing (63:1-6).

When God has completed His final act of judgment, His restored people will praise Him (vv. 7-10).

> I will tell of the kindnesses of the Lord, the deeds for which He is to be praised, according to all the Lord has done for us.
>
> Isaiah 63:7

Then comes a recapitulation of their feelings before they had experienced God's salvation (63:11–64:12). They remember the times of sin, of repentance, of desire for God once again to "rend the heavens and come down" (64:1). In the prophet's eyes, God had already acted. All those longings had now been filled. The emptiness was only a dim memory. For the glory of the Lord *had* come down, and His splendor shone all around.

God's response reviewed (Isa. 65). Now God responded to the cry of His people. Throughout history God had revealed Himself, though His people had stubbornly rejected the message. To those who rejected, judgment came:

> But as for you who forsake the Lord and forget My holy mountain, who spread a table for fortune and fill bowls of mixed wine for destiny, I will destine you for the sword, and you will all bend down for the slaughter; for I called but you did not answer, I spoke but you did not listen.
>
> Isaiah 65:11-12

To those who respond to God's message, He will give bountifully:

> Behold, I will create new heavens and a new earth. The former things will not be remembered, nor will they come to mind. But be glad and rejoice forever in what I will create, for I will create Jerusalem to be a delight and its people a joy.
>
> Isaiah 65:17-18

The glory of God, and His presence, makes all things new.

Judgment and hope (Isa. 66). The Book of Isaiah ends with a repetition of the twin themes that mark not only his messages but the writings of all the Old Testament prophets.

God sets before men a clear vision of two pathways. One leads to judgment, the other to hope. Each man chooses the path he will follow. Of those who turn from Him the Lord says:

> They have chosen their own ways, and their souls delight in their abominations; so I also will choose harsh treatment for them and will bring upon them what they dread.
>
> Isaiah 66:3-4

Yet the birthpangs of judgment can bring forth joy. The Lord says a day will come when all people who have responded to Him will live in fellowship with each other and with their God:

> I will extend peace to her like a river. . . . As a mother comforts her child, so will I comfort you; and you will be comforted over Jerusalem.
>
> Isaiah 66:12-13

Those two ways, to judgment and to hope, remain open today. And what lies at the end of each is known.

> "As the new heavens and the new earth that I will make will endure before Me," declares the Lord, "so will your name and descendants endure. From one New Moon to another and from one Sabbath to another, all mankind will come and bow down before Me," says the Lord. "And they will go out and look upon the dead bodies of those who rebelled against Me; their worm will not die, nor will their fire be quenched, and they will be loathsome to all mankind."
>
> Isaiah 66:22-24

The place to which each pathway leads is sure. The choice remains ours.

TEACHING GUIDE

Prepare

After reading the chapters, return and meditate on Isaiah 65:17-25.

Explore

1. As students come in ask them to guess *how* God's thoughts and ways are different from ours (Isa. 55:8). Use the approach outlined in "link-to-life," page 397.

2. Graphically illustrate the impact of Jesus' return on society. Have group members read Isaiah 59. Then give each one a full sheet of the day's newspaper. Ask each to *carefully cut from the paper* any items that

would *not* be found in a newspaper after Jesus' kingdom has been instituted.

Then tape the newspaper pages around the room. The gaps will graphically illustrate how different this world will be when Jesus reigns!

Then brainstorm. Can you list headlines for stories that might replace the ones you have cut out?

Expand

1. Find parallels between principles expressed in Isaiah 55–59 and familiar New Testament truths. See the "link-to-life" suggestion on pages 398-399.
2. Together work through Isaiah 64–65. Discuss each section and give each a title that will serve both to summarize and outline the passage.

Apply

To conclude this week's study, organize the following possible memory verses into a responsive reading.

Isaiah 60:19-20	Isaiah 66:12-13
Isaiah 65:17-18	Isaiah 66:22-23

STUDY GUIDE 60

Jeremiah 1–26

MAN WITH A MISSION

Overview

The dominant theme of Jeremiah is that of national sinfulness and looming judgment. Jeremiah's 40-year ministry spanned the final days of Judah's existence as an independent nation. He constantly warned his nation to submit to Babylon, a nation which God had appointed to discipline His people. As a result he was hated as a traitor to his people, and his life was often threatened.

Yet Jeremiah lived to see his words come true. This man, often called the weeping prophet because of the personal anguish he knew in his ministry, witnessed the utter destruction of Jerusalem and of the temple that he, like other godly Jews, loved.

The Book of Jeremiah is often outlined with the following five divisions.

Outline

I.	Jeremiah's Mission	1–10
II.	The Broken Covenant	11–20
III.	Judgment Nears	21–29
IV.	New Covenant Promises	30–39
V.	Jerusalem Fallen	40–51
	Historical Appendix	52

Jeremiah is difficult to outline because the book is an anthology of sermons, delivered during the rule of various kings of Judah. To teach the book it is probably best to take the approach adopted here: to look at the sermons delivered under each king rather than go chapter by chapter.

■ For a verse-by-verse commentary see the *Bible Knowledge Commentary*, pages 1123-1206.

Commentary

The reign of Manasseh (686–642 B.C.) was the beginning of the end for Judah.

The Southern Kingdom, though threatened, survived the Assyrian invasion and had a religious as well as political resurgence under Hezekiah. But Manasseh, Hezekiah's son, plunged Judah into the same kind of idolatry that the Northern Kingdom had known under Ahab and Jezebel. The temple was polluted with pagan altars, the occult was promoted by the king, and child sacrifice to Moloch was practiced in the Hinnom Valley near Jerusalem.

Tradition tells us that Isaiah spoke out against this king and was executed, as were other pious leaders who dared to protest (2 Kings 21:16).

Manasseh's reign did not bring prosperity to Judah. In 678 B.C., he and 21 other kings made a compulsory trip to swear allegiance to Assyria. Later Manasseh apparently involved Judah in a rebellion of Moab and Edom against Assyrian control, and was taken to that great empire as a prisoner. There, the Bible tells us, Manasseh "humbled himself greatly before the God of his fathers," and was returned to Judah by the Assyrians. "Then," adds the text, "Manasseh knew that the Lord is God" (2 Chron. 33:10-13). Following his release Manasseh attempted to institute his own revival. He cleansed the temple, threw down the centers of idolatry in Jerusalem, and "ordered Judah to serve the Lord God of Israel" (v. 16).

But the people did not respond. Judah too had passed beyond the edge of judgment, and destruction was now sure.

Jeremiah

Jeremiah was born about 648 B.C. and grew up as a contemporary of Manasseh's grandson, Josiah. Living only about two miles from Jerusalem, and coming from a priestly family, Jeremiah would have been intimately acquainted with the political situation in Judah.

At age 20, in 627 B.C., God told Jeremiah that he was to be His prophet. Jeremiah objected that he was too young, but God answered:

> Do not say, "I am only a child." You must go to everyone I send you to and say whatever I command you. Do not be afraid of them, for I am with you and will rescue you.
>
> Jeremiah 1:7-8

Thus commanded, Jeremiah was told that his ministry was to be one of judgment and punishment, but also would bring a unique recovery of hope:

> See, today I appoint you over nations and kingdoms to uproot and tear down, to destroy and overthrow, to build and to plant.
>
> Jeremiah 1:10

This call set the tone for Jeremiah's long life. Obeying his call, he urged his countrymen to surrender to Babylon, whom God showed him to be the instrument of His chastisement. Such a demand could be viewed only as treason. So Jeremiah was imprisoned, his life threatened, and his ministry constantly rejected by God's people.

Jeremiah lived and ministered under a succession of kings: first, godly King Josiah, and then a series of ungodly rulers: Jehoiakim, Jehoahaz, Johoiachin, Zedekiah, and Gedaliah. His book can best be understood and the progress of his times viewed if the various messages and sermons are organized according to the king in whose reign each was spoken.

In this unit and the next, we will look, through the eyes of Jeremiah, at the last days of the surviving kingdom. We will trace in his words the final sins which brought on the Babylonian Captivity.

♥ ***Link to Life: Children***
Bring a glass milk bottle or metal box to class to make a "time capsule." Explain how sometimes people try to save special things so others who live thousands of years from now will be able to see how we lived and what was important to us. Let your boys and girls talk about what they would like to send to people 2,500 years from now.

Then think about what could happen to keep your "time capsule" from reaching the future. It could be lost, destroyed, people then might not be able to read or understand what we send, etc.

Then explain: "Jeremiah's prophecy was written over *2,500 years ago! The king then tried to destroy what Jeremiah wrote (cf. Jer. 36:1-32). But what Jeremiah said is God's Word. God protected His Word. What Jeremiah said came true, and we have his words in our own language today!"*

The Bible, the Word of God, is itself a miracle, preserved through the ages and kept safe to teach you and me how to love and serve God.

Jeremiah's Ministry under Josiah 626–609 B.C.

Josiah was 8 years old when he became king. At 16 he began to seek God, and by 20 Josiah initiated a vigorous religious revival. The idols introduced by Manasseh were purged, and Josiah ventured out into the countryside to cleanse the whole land.

This four-year project completed, Josiah set about repairing the temple in Jerusalem and, as had happened in an earlier day, the lost books of Moses were again recovered. When the books were read, Josiah was horrified to discover the curses God had placed on the very lifestyle that Judah adopted (Deut. 28:15-68). Josiah set about immediately to find out what God intended. The Prophetess Huldah was consulted, and she told the king that all the judgments would surely come on Judah, but because of his own relationship with God the days of his reign would be peaceful.

Josiah was relieved by Huldah's words, and even more committed to the Lord. He gathered all the people to hear the words of God's Book read aloud. The king himself renewed the covenant with God, promising to respond and keep God's words with all his heart. And 2 Chronicles 34:32 tells us that Josiah caused (made!) all present in Jerusalem to take the same promises.

Thus, under Josiah, the ancient feasts and worship were reinstituted. Thus too Habakkuk, the troubled Levite whose thoughts are recorded in the book that bears his name, came to Jerusalem and took a leading role in the revival of public worship.

But Habakkuk was a worried, deeply concerned man. In spite of the outward signs of revival under Josiah, Habakkuk sensed the deep-seated evil which still revealed itself on

Jeremiah's Times

686—Manasseh becomes sole king

648—Josiah born

642—Amon succeeds Manasseh as king

640—Josiah becomes king

633—Josiah at 16 seeks after God

628—Josiah at 20 begins reforms

627—Jeremiah at 20 called as prophet

621—Mosaic Law found in the temple

612—Nineveh destroyed as Nahum prophesied

609—Josiah slain in battle at Megiddo;
Jehoiakim becomes king

605—Babylon defeats Egypt at Carchemish;
Daniel, others taken hostage to Babylon;
Nebuchadnezzar becomes king of Babylon

604—Nebuchadnezzar receives tribute in Palestine

601—Nebuchadnezzar defeated near Egypt

598—Jehoiakim set aside; Jehoiachin rules from December 9 to March 16, 597 and is deported April 22 to Babylon

597—Zedekiah becomes king in Judah

588—Babylon lays seige to Jerusalem on January 15

587—Jeremiah imprisoned (Jer. 32:1-2)

586—Zedekiah flees July 18; destruction of city begins August 14; Gedaliah killed and Jews migrate to Egypt against God's command October 7

the hills of Judah and in the injustices which marred his society.

Reading Jeremiah's messages, we can see more clearly why Habakkuk was troubled. Very likely he heard Jeremiah speak, witnessed the sins the weeping prophet pointed out, and came to see Judah from the divine perspective.

What, then, would Habakkuk have heard as Jeremiah ministered during Judah's last revival under godly King Josiah?

Jeremiah's Messages During Josiah's Reign

2:1–3:5	On Judah's sinful heart
3:6–6:30	Jerusalem to be destroyed
7:1–10:25	Ruin and exile coming
18:1–20:18	Message on the potter

Jeremiah 2:1–3:5. Jeremiah denounced Judah's sin in defiling the land with Baals and other false gods. "My people have committed two sins," Jeremiah cried as God's spokesman. "They have forsaken Me, the spring of living water, and have dug their own cisterns, broken cisterns, that cannot hold water" (2:13).

Jeremiah 3:6–6:30. This impassioned appeal by Jeremiah to return to God supported Josiah's attempt at revival. Promising a "pleasant land," Jeremiah, in God's name, begged his people to return and "only acknowledge your guilt" (3:13). Unless there would be such a return, Jeremiah could envision only one future:

> I looked at the mountains, and they were quaking; all the hills were swaying. I looked, and there were no people; every bird in the sky had flown away. I looked, and the fruitful land was a desert; all its towns lay in ruins before the Lord, before His fierce anger.
>
> Jeremiah 4:24-26

Jeremiah 7:1–10:25. As the outward signs of return to God began to be seen in the restored temple, Jeremiah stood in its gates and warned against trust in ritual.

"Reform your ways and your actions," the spokesman cried, "and I will let you live in this place. Do not trust in deceptive words and say, 'This is the temple of the Lord, the temple of the Lord, the temple of the Lord!' If you really change your ways and your actions and deal with each other justly, if you do not oppress the alien, the fatherless or the widow and do not shed innocent blood in this place, and if you do not follow other gods to your own harm, then I will let you live in this place" (7:3-7). Again, the choice Judah had to make was fully explained and the consequences examined. If there was no response to "the Lord, who exercises kindness, justice and righteousness on earth" (9:24), then surely Judah would be dragged away into Captivity.

Jeremiah 18:1–20:18. This last message associated with the days of Josiah reflected the prophet's growing awareness that Judah *had* made her choice. Whatever God warned or commanded, only one response could be expected. "But they will reply, 'It's no use. We will continue with our own plans; each of us will follow the stubbornness of his evil heart' " (18:12).

Watching a potter shape a clay pot on his wheel, Jeremiah saw the vessel spoiled—and the clay remade into another vessel. Unresponsive Israel had not obeyed: now it must become a formless lump which later *will* respond to the potter's hand. Taking a pottery bowl, Jeremiah was sent to confront the leaders and inhabitants of Jerusalem. He broke the jar before them and informed them that God had determined to break the city in just the same way, for it too was beyond repair.

When the chief priest heard of Jeremiah's words, he had the prophet beaten and put in stocks as a humiliating punishment. Eventually released, Jeremiah defiantly announced destruction of both the city and priest.

Yet the last verses of chapter 20 help us realize how much the prophet himself suffered in his rejection. Very probably these words also reflect his deep despair, for the godly King Josiah had recently been killed in battle. When Josiah fell, Jeremiah's hope was also destroyed. The full realization that he must live through the last days of the surviving kingdom, prophesying warnings to a people who would not listen, must have come home with stunning force.

No wonder the mourning prophet's feelings burst out in agonized expression:

> Cursed be the day I was born! May the day my mother bore me not be blessed! Cursed be the man who brought my father the news, who made him very glad, saying, "A child is born to you—a son!" May that man be like the towns the Lord overthrew without pity. May he hear wailing in the morning, a battle cry at noon. For he did not kill me in the womb, with my mother as my grave, her womb enlarged forever. Why did I ever come out of the womb to see trouble and sorrow and to end my days in shame?
>
> Jeremiah 20:14-18

♥ ***Link to Life: Youth / Adult***
Open class with a minilecture overview of Jeremiah's life and times. Focus on the revival that took place under Josiah.

Emphasize the dedication shown by Josiah, without mentioning the general unresponsiveness of Judah.

Then have different teams read and discuss the four messages of Jeremiah given during Josiah's reign. Each is to seek to determine from the prophet's words the depth and nature of this "revival."

After reports are given, discuss: "What are valid indicators in our day of true national dedication to the Lord?"

Jeremiah's Ministry under Jehoiakim 609–598 B.C.

In the fourth year of Jehoiakim's reign, Nebuchadnezzar defeated the Egyptians in the battle of Carchemish. This firmly established the Babylonians as the dominant world power. Hostages were taken by the victorious Nebuchadnezzar, whom Jeremiah identified as the servant God had chosen to judge Judah and the other nations of Palestine. He predicted a great Captivity, which would last 70 years. At God's command, Jeremiah made a written record of his sermons and his messages.

King Jehoiakim ordered the scroll burnt and commanded the arrest of the prophet and his secretary, Baruch. Even under arrest, Jeremiah continued to utter the dire prophecies which God commanded, adding a prediction of the death of Jehoiakim and the certainty of Babylonian victory (Jer. 36:27-32).

Jeremiah's Messages During Jehoiakim's Reign

11:1–13:14	The broken covenant
14–15	Prayers are fruitless
16–17	Jeremiah's celibacy
22	The king rejected
23	False prophets charged
25	Nebuchadnezzar, God's servant
26	Jeremiah threatened with death
35	Example of the Recabites
45	Promise to Baruch
46–48	Against foreign nations

Under Jehoiakim's evil rule the last hope for Judah ebbed away. The messages delivered during these years are full of darkest despair. God's heart is moved for His people, yet they *will not* respond.

Jeremiah 11:1–13:14. God's covenant and oath given to Israel when His people came up from Egypt to freedom were renewed, and the falseness of this generation to its oath was exposed. God would surely uproot that nation, "uproot and destroy it" (12:17).

Jeremiah 14:1–15:21. Much of the tone of despair in these messages is rooted in the growing realization that it was now too late for God's people to turn to Him. God warned Jeremiah not even to pray for his countrymen, and said, "Even if Moses and Samuel were to stand before Me, My heart would not go out to this people. Send them away from My presence! Let them go!" (15:1)

Four kinds of doom had been determined, and destiny had been sealed. They will go—

> Those destined for death, to death; those for the sword, to the sword; those for starvation, to starvation; those for captivity, to captivity.
>
> Jeremiah 15:2

Jeremiah 16:1–17:27. In view of the approaching judgment, Jeremiah was warned against taking a wife or having sons "in this place." In the Lord's goodness, His faithful servant would be spared the agony of seeing his own flesh and blood suffer in the coming invasion.

Jeremiah 22:1-30. Jeremiah visited the king to entreat him to practice justice, and when the king replied that he would not listen, Jeremiah pronounced judgment. No child of Jehoiakim would ever sit on the Davidic throne or rule in Jerusalem.

Jeremiah 23:1-40. The religious leaders whom God sent to care for His flock had instead scattered them. Their lying prophecies and promises would bring them everlasting reproach.

Jeremiah 25:1-38. Nebuchadnezzar was now identified as the invader about whom Jeremiah had been warning for some 23 years. Not only Judah, but also the surrounding nations, would suffer at his hand, for God had determined to use the Babylonians to punish the sins of Palestine.

Jeremiah 26:1-24. Jeremiah related an incident from early in Jehoiakim's reign, when he had offered pardon if only the people would return to God and "listen to Me, and follow My law, which I have set before you, and . . . listen to the words of My servants the prophets, whom I have sent to you again and again" (26:4-5).

The leaders then encouraged all the people to shout for Jeremiah's death for the "crime" of speaking against their city in God's name! The one man who dared to speak up in support of Jeremiah, Uriah, was himself hunted down and later killed by Jehoiakim. Yet Jeremiah was delivered, as God had promised at the time of his call.

Jeremiah 35:1-19. As an object lesson, Jeremiah gathered a family called the Recabites, who had been commanded generations earlier by their dead clan leader not to drink wine. They had faithfully obeyed.

Jeremiah pointed out the tragic difference: the Recabites had faithfully obeyed a man, while Judah faithlessly disobeyed God Himself! For their faithfulness the Recabites were promised God's constant favor. And Judah was promised judgment.

The nation had made its choice. Jeremiah would live to see the foretold results of his countrymen's sins. He would continue to raise his voice to guide them and show them the way of least pain. It was possible that the severity of Judah's judgment would bring men to their senses and lead them to return to God.

Only the Words of Jeremiah Will Be Spoken Aloud the Rest of This Session

To sense the burden and message of this great prophet, we will speak only Jeremiah's own words for the rest of this session.

Open to Jeremiah 1. Each of us will be free to read those sections we have underlined as significant in our reading. I will begin by reading from Jeremiah 1. Then, as you wish, read aloud from your own underlined portions.

We will work through the following chapters in sequence, reading brief sections in or out of order.

Jeremiah 1
Jeremiah 2:1–3:5
Jeremiah 7–10
Jeremiah 11:1–13:14
Jeremiah 16–17
Jeremiah 23
Jeremiah 26

When our reading is complete, we'll take a few minutes for silent prayer. Then share any portion of Scripture that you have memorized which seems appropriate to you as a prayer to be offered to God.

TEACHING GUIDE

Prepare

Read several of the sermons that Jeremiah gave during each reign in preparation for this group session.

Explore

1. Give a minilecture of the era of Jeremiah. You may want to reproduce both the chart of Jeremiah's times, as well as the charts of Jeremiah's sermons during the rule of Josiah and Jehoiakim.
2. Try a truly unique session, which will let your group members sense the dark message of Jeremiah in a powerful way. After giving a brief introduction to Jeremiah's times, divide the following chapters among your members: Jeremiah 1; 2:1–3:5; 7–10; 11:1–13:14; 16–17; 23; 26; 35. Each is to read his or her chapters and *underline* significant verses.

Then distribute the Only Words handout (above), and together do as it directs.

Expand

1. Or have teams read Jeremiah 14–15, 16–17, 23, and 26. Each team should reconstruct the spiritual condition of Judah from its chapter(s).
2. Or focus on Jeremiah as a person. How must it have been for a godly person like Jeremiah to minister in such a sick and sinful society?

Let Jeremiah 20:14-18 sensitize your group further to the prophet's despair. Then read selections from chapters 16–17 and chapter 1.

What does Jeremiah's faithful ministry despite personal suffering teach us about how to deal with our own times of depression or despair?

Apply
Review the story of the Recabites (chap. 35). God honors faithfulness. As the Recabites were faithful to the command of their clan leader, we are to be faithful to the Word of our living God.

STUDY GUIDE 61

Jeremiah 27–29; 34–52

EDGE OF JUDGMENT

Overview

Jeremiah's book contains many sermons and prophetic messages given during the last three decades of Judah's existence. These messages are recorded out of chronological order. The chapters studied in this unit are from the final decades before the Babylonians totally destroyed Jerusalem.

In 605 B.C. Nebuchadnezzar's Babylonian army defeated the Assyrians at Carchemish. Judah, like other Palestinian states, was forced to send hostages to Babylon.

In 601 B.C., Nebuchadnezzar attempted to invade Egypt, but was defeated. Jehoiakim of Judah now allied his nation with Egypt. But in 598 B.C. Nebuchadnezzar returned, determined to discipline the fickle Palestinian states. Jerusalem surrendered in 597 B.C., and another larger group of 10,000 captives was deported to Babylon, along with the wealth of the city.

When a new Pharaoh began to rule in Egypt, Zedekiah, king for Judah's last 11 years, rebelled against Nebuchadnezzar again. Now the army of Babylon placed Jerusalem under siege. In 586 B.C. the city was finally destroyed and the beautiful temple of Solomon burned.

The passages in Jeremiah we explore in this unit are messages and reports from the final years of Judah, under King Zedekiah.

These last chapters of Jeremiah also tell of the flight of the last few Jews from Judah to Egypt. This flight was in direct disobedience to the Lord, who warned the people to remain in Judah. To the very end, the people of Judah remained unwilling to listen to God.

Commentary

By 597 B.C. it was stunningly clear that all Jeremiah had prophesied for the past 30 years was true. The most distinguished families in Judah were taken to Babylon in the first of three deportations. Zedekiah, Judah's last king, was destined to rule only 11 more years.

During these 11 years, Jeremiah continued to warn God's people. He advised submission to Babylon, since God had chosen this pagan power to discipline His people. But in spite of the evidence of fulfilled prophecy, the Jews and their leaders refused to listen. Zedekiah rebelled, and in 586 the city fell. Zedekiah's children were executed while he watched, and then he was blinded so that the last thing he saw was their deaths. Temple treasures were transported to Babylon; both city and temple were razed. All but the poorest of the land were taken into Captivity, and Gedaliah was appointed as governor over the remnant.

Jeremiah's Messages During Zedekiah's Reign: Jeremiah 21–29; 34; 37–39

Zedekiah had been warned. Jeremiah continued to faithfully announce God's message. But Zedekiah and the people of his time were as unready to listen as were the people of Jehoiakim's time.

A brief survey of the prophet's messages shows how clearly God's Word had come to the men and women of the stubborn city of Jerusalem.

Messages In Zedekiah's Time

Chapter 21	Advice for the king
Chapter 24	Zedekiah abandoned
Chapter 27	Judah must submit
Chapter 28	God's iron yoke
Chapter 29	Letter to the exiles
Chapter 34	Judah's broken covenant
Chapters 37–39	Jerusalem's fall
Chapter 49	The nations warned

Events of Gedaliah's Rule

Chapters 40–42	The flight to Egypt
Chapters 43–44	In Egypt

	Later
Chapters 50–51	The judgment of Babylon

Jeremiah 21. As the Babylonian invasion force approached, Zedekiah asked Jeremiah to see if the Lord might "perform wonders for us as in times past so he will withdraw from us" (v. 2). Jeremiah told the king that God would actually "fight against you with an outstretched hand" (v. 5).

Jeremiah warned the people of Jerusalem to desert the city, and surrender to the besieging Babylonians! His warning, "Whoever stays in this city will die by the sword, famine or plague" (v. 9) was crystal clear. But to the people of his time it seemed "unpatriotic."

Jeremiah 24. The message of surrender was not a new one. Earlier Jeremiah had had a vision of two baskets of figs. One basket had good figs, the other "so bad they could not be eaten" (v. 2). Jeremiah interpreted the vision to the people of Judah. The good figs were the people taken into Captivity by the Babylonians; the bad figs, those who remained in Judah. Those who remained in Jerusalem would experience sword and famine and plague "until they are destroyed from the land I gave to them and their fathers" (v. 10).

Jeremiah 27–28. Early in the reign of Zedekiah, Jeremiah made a yoke of straps and crossbars, and put it on his neck. This symbolized submission to Babylon. Jeremiah was told to send word to all the surrounding kings as well as to announce his message to Zedekiah. God had determined all must serve Babylon. Any who refused would be destroyed. And Jeremiah clearly warned against any "prophet" who might speak otherwise.

Almost immediately a prophet named Hananiah contradicted Jeremiah. Speaking in the presence of the leaders and the people, Hananiah, claiming to speak in God's name, announced

> "I will break the yoke of the king of Babylon. Within two years I will bring back to this place all the articles of the Lord's house that Nebuchadnezzar king of Babylon removed from here and took to Babylon. I will also bring back to this place Jehoiachin son of Jehoiakim king of Judah, and all the other exiles from Judah who went to Babylon," declares the Lord, "for I will break the yoke of the king of Babylon."
>
> Jeremiah 28:2-4

Jeremiah's response is instruction. He affirmed his own desire that what Hananiah had said would come true. For Jeremiah *was* a patriot: he took no pleasure in the doom of his fellow-countrymen. But Jeremiah reminded all there that according to Scripture, the prophet of God "will be recognized as one truly sent by the Lord only if his prediction comes true" (v. 9; cf. Deut. 18:14-22).

Jeremiah left, but soon the Word of the Lord came to him, and he returned to confront Hananiah.

> Listen, Hananiah! The Lord has not sent you, yet you have persuaded this nation to trust in lies. Therefore, this is what the Lord says, "I am about to remove you from the face of the earth. This very year you are going to die, because you have preached rebellion against the Lord."
>
> Jeremiah 28:15-16

The very next verse tells us that just two months later, Hananiah was dead!

Yet even with this clear vindication of his role as God's messenger, Jeremiah's word continued to be ignored by God's unresponsive and sinful people.

♥ ***Link to Life: Youth / Adult***

The confrontation between Jeremiah and Hananiah is dramatic. It is so dramatic that it offers a special opportunity to vitalize your group session.

Before the group meets work with others to dramatize the events described in Jeremiah 28. Either script the scene beforehand, or ad-lib, but only after each participant has studied the events thoroughly.

Stop the drama after the first confrontation in which the two contrasting messages are presented by Jeremiah and Hananiah. Ask the rest of the group which prophet they would believe, and why?

Then play out the scene where Jeremiah announced Hananiah's coming death.

Discuss: "Even when Hananiah died within months, Judah did not believe Jeremiah or repent. Why do you think this was? How can this incident be applied to our own day and lives?"

Jeremiah 34. In an attempt to win God's favor Zedekiah made a promise, and forced others in Jerusalem to promise to free their Hebrew slaves. Enslaving a fellow Jew violated Old Testament Law, which permitted binding a countryman to a maximum of seven years of service (Lev. 25:39-55).

Almost immediately the people of Judah went back on this commitment, and "took back the slaves they had freed and enslaved them again" (Jer. 34:11).

Jeremiah was commissioned to announce the "freedom" that God had determined for this wicked people, who would not repent even though disaster was obviously near. The freedom they had was " 'freedom' to fall by the sword, plague and famine" (v. 17).

Jeremiah 37–39. These chapters describe the end of the city, and Jeremiah's treatment by his frantic countrymen. His insistence that the Jews surrender led to the accusation that Jeremiah intended to desert to the Babylonians.

Jeremiah was arrested and beaten, and put in a dungeon. Many of the officials insisted Jeremiah be put to death. The king made a weak effort to save him, but finally gave in. Jeremiah was lowered into an empty cistern, where he sank deep into the mud. Later another official moved the king to release Jeremiah. In a final interview with the prophet, Zedekiah was told his last hope. If he would surrender to the King of Babylon, the city would not be destroyed, and the king and his family would live.

But Zedekiah still would not act. Pleading fear of the Jews who had gone over to the Babylonians, he decided to fight on. The king would survive, but his city and his family, as well as his officials, would die.

Zedekiah swore Jeremiah to secrecy. But the words of Jeremiah soon came true. Though the king fled by night, he was quickly captured by the Babylonians. After seeing his sons killed, the king was blinded and taken in chains to Babylon.

Jeremiah was released by the Babylonians, and on Nebuchadnezzar's orders was well treated.

God's promise to rescue Jeremiah from danger had been kept. The prophet survived. But his city was destroyed.

Under Gedaliah: Jeremiah 40–44

After the city had been destroyed and most of the Jews transported to Babylon, Nebuchadnezzar appointed Gedaliah as governor over the small remnant. He also left a small Babylonian occupation force in Judah. Jeremiah chose to remain behind, still committed to his mission of guiding his people with God's Word.

But the Jews again rebelled! In yet another uprising Gedaliah was killed along with the Babylonian garrison. Terrified at the revenge this act must surely bring, the remaining Jews fled toward Egypt. Jeremiah was forced to go along. Though they asked Jeremiah to seek God's guidance for them, they again rejected God's Word.

The portrait Jeremiah sketches of that incident is a fitting climax to the decades of Judah's denial of God. Looking back on it, we see the people "from the least to the greatest" respectfully approach the 67-year-old prophet. "Please hear our petition," they said, "and pray to the Lord your God for this entire remnant. For as you now see, though we were once many, now only a few are left. Pray that the Lord your God will tell us where we should go and what we should do" (42:1-3).

Jeremiah agreed to pray, and the people promised, "May the Lord be a true and faithful witness against us, if we do not act in accordance with everything the Lord your God sends you to tell us. Whether it is favorable or unfavorable, we will obey the Lord our God, to whom we are sending you, so that it will go well with us, for we will obey the Lord our God." (vv. 5-6).

But the message Jeremiah returned was not what the remnant expected. They were told not to fear the king of Babylon: God would keep them from punishment and restore them to their lands. They were definitely *not* to flee to Egypt, for if they did, sword and famine would overtake them and they would die there with no survivors.

As soon as Jeremiah finished telling the people these words of the Lord, the leaders "and all the arrogant men" shouted at Jeremiah. "You are lying! The Lord our God has not sent you to say, 'You must not go to Egypt to settle there.' But Baruch son of Neriah is inciting you against us to hand us over to the Babylonians, so they may kill us or carry us into exile to Babylon" (43:2-3).

Rejecting God's Word, and the lessons of their history, these people plunged on into Egypt, dragging the prophet with them.

In Egypt, Jeremiah continued to minister, reminding the people of the sins of their fathers that had brought the judgment and warning against the punishment that must come to them in Egypt. Their response demonstrated the justice of God, who acts only when there is no hope of response or change in His people. Judah had gone too far in its commitment to sin.

> Then all the men who knew that their wives were burning incense to other gods, along with all the women who were present—a large assembly—and all the people living in Lower and Upper Egypt, said to Jeremiah, "We will not listen to the message you have spoken to us in the name of the Lord! We will certainly do everything we said we would: We will burn incense to the queen of heaven and will pour out drink offerings to her just as we and our fathers, our kings and our officials did in the towns of Judah and in the streets of Jerusalem. At that time we had plenty of food and were well off, and suffered no harm. But ever since we stopped burning incense to the queen of heaven and pouring out drink offerings to her, we have had nothing and have been perishing by sword and famine."
>
> Jeremiah 44:15-18

A saddened and angry Jeremiah then made a final statement.

> Did not the Lord remember and think about the incense burned in the towns of Judah and the streets of Jerusalem by you and your fathers, your kings and your officials and the people of the land? When the Lord could no longer endure your wicked actions and the detestable things you did, your land became an object of cursing and a desolate waste without inhabitants, as it is today.
>
> Jeremiah 44:21-22

And now again calamity befell the remnant. Pharaoh Hophra, the Egyptian king who had welcomed Judah, was given over to his enemies. Sword and famine destroyed the Jewish colony that had committed themselves to perform their vows not to the God who loved them but to the pagan idols that had been their downfall!

And Jeremiah?

Tradition tells us that he found his way to Babylon and there completed his book, including his eyewitness account of the last days of Judah, recorded for the exiles—and for us.

Hope

The messages recorded in the Book of Jeremiah during these decades show God's continuing concern for His people. He hates and will punish rebelliousness. But Jeremiah has offered these powerful reminders that God remains faithful to His ancient covenant promises.

Seventy years (Jer. 25). Jeremiah had warned Judah for some 23 years, speaking again and again of the judgment that would surely come. Speaking again of the "desolate wasteland" which the whole country would become, Jeremiah made an important announcement. The judgment to come did not signify a final rejection of the Jewish people. The devastation of Judah and the Exile itself would last only 70 years.

"When the 70 years are fulfilled, I will punish the king of Babylon and his nation" (v. 12).

Hope and a future (Jer. 29). Jeremiah also wrote a letter to the exiles in Babylon, telling them to seek the peace and prosperity of their captors. "Pray to the Lord for it, because if it prospers, you too will prosper" (v. 27).

Now the prophet added a specific commitment to the earlier announcement of 70 years. " 'When 70 years are completed for Babylon, I will come to you and fulfill My gracious promise to bring you back to this place. For I know the plans that I have for you', declares the Lord, 'plans to prosper you and not to harm you, plans to give you hope and a future' " (vv. 10-11).

A New Covenant (Jer. 30–33). Moses gave Israel the Law Covenant, which promised blessing to Israel if only the people would trust and obey the Lord. The history of Israel and Judah had demonstrated over and over again in the nearly 1,000 years between Moses and Jeremiah that the Jews *could not* obey God.

Despite punishments and discipline, despite times of blessing in revivals, despite

God's miraculous interventions showing His people His power and His goodness, the Jews had again and again turned their backs on God and His covenant.

Now Jeremiah looked ahead and saw a New Covenant, not like the Mosaic in that one day God will write His law not in stone but in the hearts of His people. Then, moved by an inner transformation, the people will truly serve God. Their sins will be forgiven, and they will honor God with their lives.

Taken together, the identification of a limit on the Exile, the promise of both judgment on Babylon and restoration to the land for the Jews, with the vision of a New Covenant, must have been encouraging to the godly Jew who was swept up with his fellow-citizens and torn from the Promised Land.

We may fail God.

God may punish us.

But God does not desert that people who are called by His name, and whom He owns as His own.

TEACHING GUIDE

Prepare

Read Jeremiah 29 and 43 carefully, listening to sense not only the agony of Jeremiah's day but also the implications of what he wrote for us today.

Explore

1. Begin with a dramatization of Jeremiah's confrontation with Hananiah, described in the "link-to life" on pages 410-411.
2. Choose brief, selected readings from other chapters in this section. The readings should sum up warnings given by Jeremiah to Judah during the time of Zedekiah. Introduce the readings briefly, but let Jeremiah's words speak for themselves.

Expand

1. Give a minilecture on the fall of Jerusalem. Summarize what happened to Zedekiah, and to the remnant who rebelled against Gedaliah. Emphasize their response to Jeremiah's final directions from God.

Then ask your group to assume they are Jews in Babylon who hear this report. How will they feel? What might they think of their people? What conclusions might they draw about God's attitude toward them now?

2. Have teams look at the promise of the 70-year span determined by God for the Captivity (Jer. 25; 29).

Discuss: "What does this tell us about God?" Also share: "What are times when Christians need to be reminded that God has 'a hope and a future' in His plans for us as well?"

Apply

Conclude, thanking God that He is a Person who remains faithful to us even when we are not faithful to Him. We may experience discipline as Judah did. But God will never desert His own.

STUDY GUIDE 62

Jeremiah 30–33

THE NEW COVENANT

Overview

Most of Jeremiah's life was spent ministering in a country whose doom was sealed—and obvious. His words were dark with warning. And Jeremiah lived to see the terrible things he foretold come true. The city founded by David, and the temple built by his son Solomon, were destroyed, and most of Judah's citizens died in the siege or in Egypt where the remnant fled.

The Jews who remained were transported to Babylon. There, torn from the Promised Land, and suddenly aware of the depth of their sins against God, they lived in material comfort but spiritual pain. Had God, the God of Abraham, really abandoned His people? Had God rejected them because of their unfaithfulness?

Many Christians, when troubles come and sins are remembered, may ask the same question. Are my troubles evidence that God no longer accepts me? That I am abandoned by the Lord?

The answer of Jeremiah to the people of Judah comforts us too. God had Jeremiah announce His plan to make a New Covenant with the people of Israel. A New Covenant which would lift Israel—and you and me—to a new and vital relationship with our God.

▶ ***Covenant.*** In Old Testament times a *b'rith* (covenant) was a formal and binding instrument. Between nations it was a treaty; between business partners it was a contract. Between a ruler and citizens it was a constitution. But when God made His covenants with Israel the *b'rith* was a promise: a commitment made by the Lord.

Commentary

With the destruction of the temple and the final flight of the few Jews who remained in Palestine, all hope for Israel seemed dead.

But each of the two great prophets who spoke to this people had a message of hope! That generation was experiencing punishment for sin. But another generation would come. And, in time, God's people would be returned to the Promised Land. There they would know the fullness of the blessing God yearned to pour out on the exiles.

The people torn from Judah had placed their trust in idols. Now they were called to return to God, and trust Him and His ancient covenants.

The Covenants

The identity of Israel has always been rooted in history. And the key to understanding that history is to grasp the meaning of what the Old Testament calls the "covenants."

The Abrahamic Covenant. God called Abraham out of Ur of the Chaldees, and led him to Palestine. There an original promise given to Abraham at the time of his call (Gen. 12) was reaffirmed and expanded (Gen. 15; 17). When we look at these early Genesis promises to Abraham and his descendants, we note several basic elements.

- Abraham was to be progenitor of a great nation.
- Abraham was to be blessed and his name made great.
- Abraham was to be the source of blessing for the world.
- Abraham's treatment by others was to be the criteria for their own blessing or cursing.
- Abraham's descendants are to possess the land of Palestine.
- Abraham's descendants are to have a special relationship with God "throughout their generations."

These promise elements, found in Genesis 12, 15, and 17 are the core of Hebrew identity. They are the solid rock on which the entire Old Testament is founded. All the Old Testament writers and prophets shared the common conviction that God is at work in history, carrying out His plan, and that His plan is unveiled in the covenant promises given to Abraham and his descendants.

The Davidic Covenant. The promise given to Abraham revealed the basic outline of God's plan and purpose for Israel. As the centuries rolled on, God, at various times, revealed additional insights into His plan.

In the time of King David a special aspect of that eternal plan was unveiled. David, as king over a resurgent and united Israel, had occupied most of the land promised Israel in the Abrahamic Covenant. When David expressed his desire to build God a house (temple), God responded by promising instead to build David a house (family line). God promised that there would always be a descendant of David qualified to sit on Israel's throne until finally one of his line would be confirmed as King forever (2 Sam. 7). A Deliverer for Israel and for mankind would be born of David's line. One day this Deliverer would assume the throne of His forefather and reign not only as King over Israel but also over the entire world. In His day there would be peace—a peace that would never be broken.

After David's time the prophets added fresh insights about this coming king. Micah and others told God's people that the king would actually be their God: that from Bethlehem, the city of David, "One will come for Me, One who will be Ruler over Israel, whose origins are of old, from ancient times." This One would come to "shepherd His flock in the strength of the Lord, in the majesty of the name of the Lord His God." It is this One who "will be our peace" (Micah 5:1-5).

And so the purpose of God, a purpose that will one day be realized, had been explained to God's people. Through their Messiah, God's anointed Successor to David, would come deliverance for Israel and for all mankind. All history, the prophets believed, was marching to that intended end.

But now, joltingly, the people of God had been torn from the Promised Land! The kingdoms of Israel and Judah were no more! How could God then fulfill His promises? David's family no longer lived in Bethlehem. There was no throne for a royal descendant to mount. The very existence of the nation that God had promised Abraham had ceased, and the conqueror, rather than to suffer divine judgment, seemed only to prosper!

The believing Jew, who had anchored his faith in God, and who found his identity in the ancient covenants, was stunned by the Exile. Had God cast off His people? Had the very covenants themselves been set aside because of the abominations committed by God's people?

The Mosaic Covenant. Part of the answer to these soul-searching questions of the exiles is found in an understanding of the nature of another covenant: the Covenant of Law.

Both the Abrahamic and Davidic Covenants were in fact promises, or sworn oaths. God simply stated there what He intended to do and bound Himself to it by using the cultural contract form, the *b'rith.* Neither of these covenant promises hinged on any human action. Whatever God's people might do, God had announced His purposes and revealed His plan. He would accomplish all He intended to do.

The Mosaic Covenant is a promise too. But it is significantly different from the Abrahamic and Davidic Covenants. The Law Covenant spells out how God's people are to live in fellowship with Him. It shows Israel how to love the Lord and to love their neighbor. In this covenant God also bound Himself with promises. He promised to bless His people *if they obeyed Him.* And He promised to punish His people if they disobeyed. Here, for the first time, God's intentions were made contingent on human behavior. The obedient generation would be blessed and the disobedient would suffer the discipline its actions deserved.

There are two other important differences between the Law Covenant and the Abrahamic/Davidic Covenants. Those two Covenants focus on history's end. That is, they will be fulfilled *in the future.* The Law and its associated promises dealt with the present experience of each generation of Israelites. If a generation lived by God's Law, it would experience *now* the blessings intended for Israel at history's end. If a generation rebelled against God and rejected His Law it would experience *now* divine discipline.

The last way in which the Law Covenant

Relationship between Law and Other Covenants

Other Covenants	Law Covenant
1. Express divine commitment as a promise/oath.	1. Express divine commitment as a promise/oath.
2. Expressed purpose not related to human actions.	2. Express purpose *is* linked with actions of His people in obeying or disobeying His commandments.
3. Focus is on the future and what God intends to do at history's end.	3. Focus is on the present and how God will treat living generations.
4. The covenants state an unchanging purpose and intention of God and will not be changed.	4. The Law is temporary, to be replaced by a better, New Covenant.

differs from the others is that it alone served a *temporary* function. Law, as we will see, was intended to guide God's people only until the promised Messiah came. Then a new and vital way of relating to God would be introduced. We can summarize the comparisons and contrasts between the Law and the other Covenants on a simple chart.

When we grasp the relationship between the Abrahamic/Davidic Covenants and the Law Covenant, we too can grasp the wonderful truth that Jeremiah and his contemporary Ezekiel both emphasized for the exiles.

The Exile was a punishment. It was discipline, brought on by decades of disobedience. But, however long the sufferings of the exiles might last, *the Exile in no way changed the purposes or abrogated the promises of God.* The people had been torn from the land? Then God would bring their children back!

Through disobedience living generations had forfeited their own blessing. Yet in some future generation God would bring to pass all that He had promised from the beginning. Rather than cast doubt on the future of Israel, the Exile should have reassured! In fact, the Exile demonstrated conclusively that *God does keep His Word!*

How? Look back at these words from the Book of Deuteronomy, penned nearly a thousand years before the Babylonian invasion. How these words of Moses must have echoed through the minds of the people of the Exile:

> The Lord will drive you and the king you set over you to a nation unknown to you or your fathers. There you will worship other gods, gods of wood and stone. You will become a thing of horror, and an object of scorn and ridicule to all the nations where the Lord will drive you. . . . Because you did not serve the Lord your God joyfully and gladly in the time of prosperity, therefore in hunger and thirst, in nakedness and dire poverty, you will serve the enemies the Lord sends against you. He will put an iron yoke on your neck until He has destroyed you.
>
> The Lord will bring a nation against you from far away, from the ends of the earth, like an eagle swooping down, a nation whose language you will not understand, a fierce-looking nation without respect for the old, or pity for the

young. . . .

Then the Lord will scatter you among all nations, from one end of the earth to the other. There you will worship other gods—gods of wood and stone, which neither you nor your fathers have known. Among those nations you will find no repose, no resting place for the sole of your foot. There the Lord will give you an anxious mind, eyes weary with longing, and a despairing heart. You will live in constant suspense, filled with dread both night and day, never sure of your life. In the morning you will say, "If only it were evening!" and in the evening, "If only it were morning!"—because of the terror that will fill your hearts.

Deuteronomy 28:36-37; 47-50; 64-67

Yet words from this same book bring comfort:

When all these blessings and curses I have set before you come upon you and you take them to heart wherever the Lord your God disperses you among the nations, and when you and your children return to the Lord your God and obey Him with all your heart and with all your soul according to everything I command you today, then the Lord your God will restore your fortunes and have compassion on you and gather you again from all the nations where He scattered you. Even if you have been banished to the most distant land under the heavens, from there the Lord your God will gather you, and bring you back.

Deuteronomy 30:1-4

The unchanging purposes of God will be fulfilled and His covenants will be kept. A generation might die in exile. But Israel will be preserved and will be brought back to the land God has promised.

♥ ***Link to Life: Youth / Adult***
Brainstorm with your group the doubts and fears people have when tragedy or sickness comes.

Explain the uncertainties of the exiles, whose promises from God were linked to the land God had promised Abraham and his family.

Then let teams look at the Deuteronomy passages quoted in this lesson. How might they have answered a Jew in Babylon who felt doubts and fears like those you brainstormed?

After hearing team ideas, explain the nature of God's covenants, using the chart "Relationship between Law and other Covenants."

The New Covenant: Jeremiah 30–33

God chose Jeremiah, the prophet of doom, to bring Israel yet another expansion of the Abrahamic Covenant. At a time when the Hebrew people were torn from their land, as foretold a thousand years earlier by Moses, God through Jeremiah added a fresh revelation of how He intended to keep His ancient promises.

The timing was significant. There could be no doubt now. God had *not* cast off Israel forever. The content is significant too. Earlier God had explained that He would keep His promises to Abraham through sending a Messiah, a man of David's family, anointed as King. Now God explained that His plan involved replacing the Mosaic system with a New Covenant that would plant righteousness within the personality of every believer.

Jeremiah 30:1-11. God promised that His people Israel would be brought "back . . . to the land I gave their forefathers to possess" (v. 3). In that final regathering, "David their king, whom I will raise up for them" (v. 9), will lead them to serve the Lord. In the Exile God intended to chasten them justly, but said He would "not completely destroy" them (v. 11).

Jeremiah 30:12-24. The wound of God's people was incurable and their iniquity was great. As a result, the Captivity was an absolute necessity. But again, the promise was restated. Israel would return and "you will be My people, and I will be your God" (v. 22).

Still, God's wrath must be experienced until the purification of His people had been completed. "In the days to come you will understand this" (v. 24).

Jeremiah 31:1-14. The blessings of the time of regathering are described, and the promise made that the full extent of the Promised Land will be theirs (see also v. 23; 32:44; 33:6-7, 12-14).

Jeremiah 31:28-34. But the heart of the New Covenant is not seen in the reaffirmation of the ancient promises. It is seen in the unveiling of an unexpected dimension of God's plan. God will replace the old Mosaic Covenant, under which the Law was written in stone tablets and men were commanded to "do," with a New Covenant under which God's righteousness will be written on the hearts of believers, and human beings will be enabled to "be"!

That covenant stipulation, found here and quoted in Hebrews 8:8-12, reads:

> "The time is coming," declares the Lord, "when I will make a New Covenant with the house of Israel and with the house of Judah. It will not be like the covenant I made with their forefathers when I took them by the hand to lead them out of Egypt, because they did not remain faithful to My covenant, and I turned away from them," declares the Lord. "This is the covenant I will make with the house of Israel after that time," declares the Lord. "I will put My laws in their minds and write them on their hearts. I will be their God and they will be My people. No longer will a man teach his neighbor, or a man his brother, saying 'Know the Lord,' because they will all know Me, from the least of them to the greatest. I will forgive their wickedness, and will remember their sins no more."
>
> Hebrews 8:8-12

With this great promise, yet another aspect of the Abrahamic Covenant unfolds. The time is coming when Israel will be born again, and a new heart given to God's people. Only then, when the least of them to the greatest shall truly know the Lord, will God's intention to bless humankind be fulfilled.

Jeremiah 32:1-44. With the city of Jerusalem under siege, Jeremiah purchased a field, and buried the deed in an earthen pot so that it would "last a long time" (v. 14).

This action demonstrated to the people of Jerusalem that even though the city would fall and the people be carried into Captivity, "houses, fields and vineyards will again be bought in this land" (v. 15).

Jeremiah's prayer (vv. 16-25) is a highlight of this chapter, as is God's response: "I will surely gather them from all the lands where I banish them in My furious anger and great wrath; I will bring them back to this place and let them live in safety. They will be My people, and I will be their God. I will give them singleness of heart and action, so that they will always fear Me for their own good, and the good of their children after them. I will make an everlasting covenant with them: I will never stop doing good to them, and I will inspire them to fear Me so that they will never turn away from Me" (vv. 37-40).

Jeremiah 33:1-13. Again came the promise of restoration. "I will bring Judah and Israel back . . . as they were before. I will cleanse them from all the sin they have committed against Me, and will forgive all their sins of rebellion" (vv. 7-8).

Jeremiah 33:14-22. The Davidic Covenant was reaffirmed, and David was promised never to "fail to have a man to sit on the throne" (v. 17). This promise was *not* that a descendant of David would always rule in Jerusalem. It was simply that there will always be a valid claimant—until finally, in fulfillment of all the covenant promises, Messiah reigns.

Jeremiah 33:23-26. With the reaffirmation of the Davidic Covenant comes also reaffirmation of God's intention to accomplish His purposes through the physical seed of Abraham—the peoples of Israel and Judah. Keeping the promises made to the descendants of Abraham, Isaac, and Jacob is just as certain as the fact that night follows day. "I will restore their fortunes and have compassion" (v. 26).

And so through Jeremiah, the man who announced the Exile, came the great promise of regathering, and the promise too of a New Covenant. One day God will act, and then the laws once engraved in stone will be rewritten on the very hearts of men born again into living relationship with God.

The New Covenant Today

Jeremiah's announcement did not in fact *make* a New Covenant with Israel. It simply promised that, in time, a New Covenant *would be* made. Until that time, the old, Mosaic Covenant remained in force. It is much like engagement and marriage: engagement is a promise that a couple *will* marry, but it is not a marriage itself. Until the marriage has taken place, each of the two remains single.

For hundreds of years the Jewish people

looked forward to the time when the New Covenant would be made. When finally it was made, Israel tragically failed to recognize it, for the nation refused to acknowledge Jesus as the long-promised Messiah.

The night before Jesus' death, He explained its meaning to His closest followers. At the Last Supper Christ said, "This is My blood of the New Covenant, which is poured out for many for the forgiveness of sins" (Matt. 26:28).

There were several types of *b'riths* in Old Testament times. The most binding was a "covenant of blood": one confirmed by the death of a sacrifice, and by those making the commitment passing between the severed halves of the sacrificed animals (cf. Gen. 15:6-21). The blood of Jesus not only won our salvation. That blood confirmed in an unmistakable way God's oath, promising forgiveness to all who would believe in Jesus.

But it is important to realize that Jesus' death *made* the New Covenant. That is, the death of Jesus was the confirming oath, the promise of what God will do in the future. The death of Jesus did not *fulfill* the promise, for the New Covenant with the house of Israel promises a national renewal and conversion.

Like the Abrahamic and Davidic Covenants, the total fulfillment of the New Covenant awaits history's end!

How then do we explain the fact that today the forgiveness you and I experience through faith in Jesus is ours through the New Covenant? How do we explain the fact that God is, even now, at work writing His Law on *our* hearts as the Holy Spirit works an inner transformation? (2 Cor. 3:18)

The answer is found in a principle implicit in the Law. The blessings promised in the Abrahamic Covenant were to be Israel's at history's end. But any generation might experience those same blessings through obedience.

Today, the full blessing of mankind under the New Covenant also awaits history's end for its ultimate fulfillment. But until that time, you and I can experience the promised blessings through faith. God, so good and loving, gives us today what He intends to pour out on all mankind when Jesus comes again.

TEACHING GUIDE

Prepare
Read and meditate on Hebrews 8:1–10:22, which indicates that we today *do* experience the benefits of the New Covenant.

Explore
1. Think together about how people react to tragedy or suffering. How might the people of Judah have reacted to the extreme suffering associated with the Exile?

Use the approach of the "link-to-life" on page 417.

2. Or, ask group members to picture themselves in Babylon, with their nation and temple destroyed. Then play a tape, on which are recorded verses selected from Jeremiah 31–33. Discuss: "What does this message mean to you? Why is it something you especially need to hear just now?"

Expand
1. Give a minilecture explaining the biblical covenants. Use the chart in this lesson to summarize.
2. Put on the chalkboard the basic elements of the Abrahamic Covenant. Then divide into teams to read and study Jeremiah 30–33. Each team is to *link what Jeremiah says* with the original covenant promises. How are original promises expanded? How are God's intentions further explained?

Apply
Make copies of Hebrews 8:8-12 to distribute to your group. Ask members to underline benefits of the New Covenant we experience as Christians.

Close thanking God for both forgiveness, and for the new heart and life He gives us.

STUDY GUIDE 63
Lamentations

MOURNING IN A STRANGE LAND

Overview
Times of discipline are never enjoyed—by children or by God's people. The Book of Lamentations, written during the years Judah spent in exile in Babylon, shares the inmost feelings of the Jews who had been torn from their land and separated from the now-destroyed temple because of their rebelliousness and many sins.

This Old Testament book is composed of five somber poems.

They were probably written within a few years of Jerusalem's destruction. Tradition says that Jeremiah himself found his way to Babylon from Egypt, and wrote these anonymous words.

These poems were read aloud by the Jews in mid-July, on a date set to commemorate the fall of their Holy City, Jerusalem.

Outline

I.	Jerusalem in Mourning	1:1-22
II.	Jerusalem in Ruin	2:1-22
III.	Call for Renewal	3:1-66
IV.	Restitution to Come	4:1-22
V.	A Cry for Relief	5:1-22

Each chapter of Lamentations has 22 verses or a multiple of 22 because each verse or group of three verses begins with a different letter of the 22-consonant Hebrew alphabet.

■ The *Bible Knowledge Commentary* has excellent charts that illustrate the distinctive structure of Lamentations. The chart on page 1209 also lists parallels between the experience of Judah and the disciplines foretold by God in Deuteronomy 28.

Commentary
When Jeremiah finally made his way to Babylon, he found the Hebrew people in far better condition than most of us might imagine. There were no concentration camps. There was no slave labor, as there had been in Egypt. Instead, the exiles were settled in southern Mesopotamia near the river (canal) Chebar, southeast of Babylon. They enjoyed royal protection and a great amount of self-government. They married, kept in touch with Jerusalem (Jer. 29:1), met to worship and discuss, and kept the Sabbath. A.C. Schultz describes their lives in the *Zondervan Pictorial Bible Encyclopedia* (Vol. 2, p. 427).

> Some of the captives were used to supply labor for Nebuchadnezzar's building projects, at least in the beginning of the Exile. Some of them enjoyed special prerogatives. They could own their homes and land, and enjoyed the produce of their gardens (Jer. 29:5, 7; Ezek. 8:1; 12:1-7). This would enable them to provide for some of their physical needs. Some of the captives apparently made an adequate living in other ways (Zech. 6:9-11), and even entered business in the "land of merchants," as Babylon was known (Ezek. 17:4, 12). The Hebrew banking house of Murashu appears in the inscriptions. The lists of captives receiving royal support includes along with the Hebrew names the skilled trades in which some of them worked. Jeremiah 29:5-7 indicates that they were so successful financially that they were able to send money to Jerusalem, and when the exiles were given permission by Cyrus to return home, they refused because according to Josephus, "they were not willing to leave their possessions" (Antiquities XI.i.3). This materialism on the part of some of the exiles led to conformity to the customs of the Babylonians and cultural assimilation. The tendency to assimilate included the adoption of the Aramaic language and the acceptance of

idolatry and participation in pagan ceremonies, even to sacrificing their sons on pagan altars (Ezek. 14:3-5; 20:31).

Yet the experience was for many of the exiles an increasingly bitter one. After the destruction of Jerusalem and its temple, when all hope of return seemed gone, the people of Israel began to realize how much they had lost. The birthright they had so lightly traded away for pagan Baals and Asherahs suddenly seemed precious. Israel realized at last that if they were not God's people, they had no identity. If they no longer retained the promises, life had no meaning.

This sense of loss is communicated in the brief Book of Lamentations, which tradition tells us was written by Jeremiah himself.

> How deserted lies the city, once so full of people! How like a widow is she, who once was great among the nations! She who was a queen among the provinces has now become a slave. Bitterly she weeps at night, tears are upon her cheeks. There is none to comfort her among all her lovers. All her friends have betrayed her; they have become her enemies. After affliction and harsh labor, Judah has gone into exile. She dwells among the nations; she finds no resting place. All who pursue her have overtaken her in the midst of her distress. . . . Her foes have become her masters; her enemies are at ease. The Lord has brought her grief because of her many sins. Her children have gone into exile, captive before the foe. All the splendor has departed from the daughter of Zion.
>
> Lamentations 1:1-3, 5-6

Looking at the change, the captives finally appreciate the lifestyle that God had planned for them under His own care. Lamenting now, the people sorrowed for what they had once scorned.

> The Law is no more, and her prophets no longer find visions from the Lord. The elders of the daughter of Zion sit on the ground in silence; they have sprinkled dust on their heads and put on sackcloth. The young women of Jerusalem have bowed their heads to the ground. My eyes fail from weeping, I am in torment within, my heart is poured out on the ground because my people are destroyed.
>
> Lamentations 2:9-11

Suddenly the material things that had tempted Judah seemed meaningless to many. In setting their hearts on wealth, they had seemed for a time to gain the whole world. But they had lost themselves.

Impact of the Exile

The tears shed by Judah in Babylon proved fruitful. The repentance of the people brought many benefits to God's people, and in significant ways shaped the nation up to, and even beyond, the time of Christ.

A remnant. As Josephus pointed out, the materialists among the Jews found in Babylon a place to prosper financially. Those wealthy men and women settled down to enjoy their wealth, untroubled by questions about the ultimate meaning of their lives. When the time came for God's promise of a return to be fulfilled, only those who were moved by a great religious commitment were ready to go. These returned, eager to lay the foundation of a new temple, and to rebuild Jerusalem. They believed that only when God's people were again in the Promised Land could Messiah come.

Thus the decades in Babylon, like the destruction of the wicked in Jersualem some 70 years earlier, served to cleanse and purify the nation.

That the purification process was accomplished is demonstrated by the fact that, in spite of tremendous pressures later, the Jewish people successfully resisted every effort to make them give up their Law and accept Hellenic (Greek) culture.

The tendency to chase after the gods of the people around them was thoroughly purged by the Exile.

The written Law. Prior to the Captivity, the Levites had been responsible for teaching the Law to the people. This function was shared with the priests, who were the Law's official interpreters.

But the religious life of the people had centered around the festivals and the temple and its sacrifices. With the temple now destroyed, and no place where sacrifices could be offered, the emphasis of the exiles shifted to the study and interpretation of the Law and the Prophets. God's Word, which the people had refused to hear, was now studied intently and devoutly.

An example of this revival of biblical studies is seen in Ezra, who "devoted himself to the study and observance of the Law of the Lord, and to teaching its decrees and His laws in Israel" (Ezra 7:10). Later scribes would amass volumes of traditions supposedly containing an "oral law" given to Moses on Sinai. That tradition would, by the time of Jesus, rob much of the written Law of its power and meaning. But during the Captivity and the years immediately following, the hearts of many in Israel were set to study, to do, and to teach God's Book. Clearly, all that had happened to the people of Israel and Judah had happened in accordance with what had been written. Clearly too, if one wished to live in harmony with God and to experience blessing rather than judgment, the Word of God must be taken to heart.

This fervor for the Law, even though later twisted and misguided, was one of the positive outcomes of the Exile.

The synagogue system. While there is no definite evidence of the existence of the synagogue as an institution prior to the Hellenistic Age, it seems most likely that its origins go back to the time of the Babylonian Captivity.

With the temple gone, groups of faithful people met in homes in their Exile, and when Israel returned to its homeland, this new institution seems to have been retained. Many modern excavations indicate that before the Christian era the synagogue was the center of town life. Here the sacred Books were read and often interpreted by a rabbi. Here the townsmen gathered to work out legal-political problems, guided by the books of revelation. In fact, on the return from Babylon by Persian royal decree, the Law of Moses was made civilly binding on the Jews living west of the Euphrates.

By Jesus' day, each town was also responsible for seeing that the children learned to read the sacred Word, so that on becoming an adult, each male might take on responsibility for himself and community welfare.

The synagogue system has continued to our own day. This institution, springing from the Exile, maintains a continuing impact on Judaism.

In each of these ways, the Captivity proved of lasting benefit to God's people. It purged Israel of her tendency to idolatry. It refocused Israel's attention on the Word of God. It shaped institutions which in the future would hold the Jewish people together when a much greater and longer exile should come. God's punishments, like His blessings, are designed to bring good to His beloved people.

Demonstration of Principle

It is helpful to look at Judah's experience in Babylon as a demonstration of a basic principle of God's dealing with His Old Testament people.

The Deuteronomy warnings (chaps. 28–29) made it clear that responsiveness to God's Law was the condition for blessing of a given generation. The promises contained in the covenants would one day surely be fulfilled. But in the meantime, blessing for each generation was mediated through obedience to the Law. That same passage made it clear that a physical relationship to Abraham was not enough in itself to guarantee blessing. Each link in the line of descent must exercise an obedience-producing faith in God. And whatever might happen to a given generation, it would in no way change God's commitment to the purposes announced in His Word.

In Jeremiah's time, the Jews were led into captivity. *But God's promised purposes were unaffected.* Much later, just after the time of Christ, a Roman invader would destroy Jerusalem and another temple. As a result, the Jewish people would again be scattered through the nations. There, "among those nations you will find no repose, no resting place for the sole of your foot. There the Lord will give you an anxious mind, eyes weary with longing, and a despairing heart" (Deut. 28:65). The words of Deuteronomy have echoed through our centuries, describing in mournful tone the experience of the Jewish people in the last 1,900 years. In Spain, in Poland, in Russia, in Nazi Germany—in whatever land—God's people have found no rest. Only in our day, with the return to Palestine and the establishment in 1948 of a Jewish state, have we heard the bones rattle and watched the flesh and sinews and skin take shape.

The announcements of Jeremiah and his contemporary Ezekiel, repeating the promises of God on which Israel's identity was founded in a time of Exile, give renewed assurance. God will surely do for His people in our day *all* that His Word reveals is our destiny.

It seems clear that the messages of the prophets who first warned Judah, and then shared great promises, help us as we study the Old Testament. *God is faithful.* Surely God will hold fast to the purposes He has announced. In some way, though the details are known only to Him, all that He has promised in the Old and New Testaments will undoubtedly come to pass.

TEACHING GUIDE

Prepare
Think of a time when you were aware of being disciplined by God. How did you feel during this time?

Explore
1. As your group members arrive, have on the chalkboard: "How does it feel to be disciplined by God?"

Ask each person to jot down one or two feeling words in answer to that question. Then ask each to find phrases in Lamentations which reflect those feelings.

When all have scanned the book and found several illustrations, come together to share the emotions and the verse selected from Lamentations.
2. Or, read Psalm 32:3-4, and ask group members to guess *why* the writer had those feelings. Then read verse 5, and point out that while being disciplined by God a believer experiences many difficult emotions. Ask: "How would you describe feelings you have had when you felt God's discipline?"

When feelings have been expressed, read selected verses from Lamentations so members can sense the depth of the Jews' feelings of guilt and suffering.

Expand
1. In a minilecture cover the situation of Judah in Babylon, and outline the good things which resulted from this time of discipline. Discuss: "How does the history of the Exile help us gain perspective on our own times of suffering or discipline?"
2. Review Deuteronomy 28 and its description of what would happen to the Jews if the nation sinned. How might God's faithfulness to His Word of warning bring comfort to people undergoing discipline?

Apply
Share any good things that have resulted in your own life from times when God has disciplined you.

STUDY GUIDE 64

Ezekiel 1–24

PRINCIPLES OF JUDGMENT

Overview

The prophecies recorded in this book were first uttered by Ezekiel between July 593 B.C. (Ezek. 1:1-2), and April 571 B.C. (Ezek. 29:17).

These were tragic years for the Jewish people (called "Israel" in this Old Testament book). Twenty-three years before Nebuchadnezzar became ruler of Babylon, Jeremiah had warned Judah that the Babylonians would crush their country and had counseled surrender. God's people rejected Ezekiel's message, even after 605 B.C., when the Babylonians destroyed Assyrian power and slowly crushed the Jewish state by a series of invasions.

Ezekiel had been taken captive with others during the first Babylonian invasion. While Jeremiah continued in Palestine to prophesy Judah's doom, Ezekiel preached this same message to those already in Exile.

The first part of Ezekiel's book is made up of messages delivered before the final destruction of his homeland. The later part of the book is made up of messages given after Jerusalem and the temple had been razed.

Outline

I.	Prophecy against Judah	1–24
II.	Prophecy against Nations	25–32
III.	Prophecy of Restoration	33–39
IV.	Prophecy of the Temple	40–48

■ For a discussion of the many technical questions raised by the Book of Ezekiel, see the *Bible Knowledge Commentary*, pages 1225-1317.

Commentary

At the time of the first deportation of Jews from the Promised Land, 25-year-old Ezekiel was taken to Babylon. Ezekiel was a member of an important priestly family, taken as captives with other distinguished persons whom Nebuchadnezzar wished to remove from political influence in their homeland.

It was five years after this transportation, in 593 B.C. (see Ezek. 1:2), that Ezekiel received his call to be a prophet.

Ezekiel had a unique two-part ministry. Between 592 and 586 his messages contained warnings about Jerusalem's destruction. His last message of this era, reported in chapter 32, was delivered in April 585 B.C., just after the city and its temple were destroyed.

For the next 13 years Ezekiel was silent. Then, in April 571 B.C., the prophet took up a new ministry. Now his message was one of hope, promise, and comfort for the exiles.

In this unit we focus on the first part of Ezekiel's ministry—a ministry in which he struggled in Babylon with the same unbelief that met his contemporary Jeremiah in Judah. Both men fought to lead God's people to accept Captivity as part of God's plan for His people.

The Book of Ezekiel has four natural divisions, reflected in the outline in the *overview* of this unit. Within the first section, the focus of our present study, there are several major sermons.

Messages before 586 B.C.

(Chaps.)	(Event)
4–5	Pictures of siege
6–7	The land desolate
8–11	God's glory withdraws
12	Exile symbolized
13	False prophets charged
15–16	Jerusalem allegories
17–19	Leadership allegories
23	The two sisters
24	Death of Ezekiel's wife

Ezekiel is interesting to teach as well as

relevant and valuable for believers today.

His eccentric method of symbolically acting out his teachings offers us an unusual opportunity for some creative teaching methods.

But most important, his message on the glory of God, and on human responsibility, are vitally relevant to every believer.

Symbolic Acts: Ezekiel 4–5

The most striking features of Ezekiel are the symbolic acts that accompanied the prophet's messages.

Ezekiel did not simply speak of a coming siege of Jerusalem: he obtained a large brick, sketched a city on it, and like a child in a sandbox, raised earth siege works against it. Lying on his side, Ezekiel gazed at the besieged city, with each day representing a year in God's program of discipline.

To represent the fate of the people still in Palestine, Ezekiel carefully shaved off his hair and beard. With greatest care he weighed and divided the hairs of his head. One-third of his hair he placed in the center of his sandbox city and burned. This represented those who would die when the Babylonians finally overran Jerusalem. Ezekiel spread another third on the ground around the city, and attacked it with a sword. Finally Ezekiel took the last third of his hair and tossed it high, to be scattered by the wind. This represented those who would be taken to surrounding nations and scattered across the face of the earth.

The exiles must have gathered in wonder to watch these strange actions of Ezekiel. They would then listen as God's spokesman explained their meaning. The message was clear. There would be no "next year in Jerusalem" for those taken to Babylon.

♥ ***Link to Life: Youth / Adult***

Replay Ezekiel's symbolic representation of Jerusalem's siege, reported in chapters 4–5. Use a brick to represent the city, and Legos or other children's building toys to construct siege works.

As group members come in, be on the floor, gazing silently at the siege scene.

Say nothing, but when all have come, play a tape recorded composite of the message of Ezekiel, using Ezekiel 5:8-12.

Have your group members quickly read through Ezekiel 4–5, to list each act and what it symbolized.

Then debrief. How did group members feel when they came in? Why might Ezekiel's approach have been necessary? (cf. 2:3) Are there issues today that may need to be dramatized to gain the attention of Christians or non-Christians?

The Glory of God Withdraws: Ezekiel 8–11

The Book of Ezekiel is impressive in its revelation of God as transcendent—that is, as highly exalted above all material creation. In the very first chapter of his book, Ezekiel told of a vision which he had from God: a vision which we can hardly understand but which conveys powerfully a sense of God's awesome majesty. In a series of phrases and images Ezekiel helps us realize that the God he saw is not only powerful beyond all power as we know it, but is totally different from anything that we know in our acquaintance with the things of space and time.

God came to Ezekiel in "an immense cloud with flashing lightning and surrounded by brilliant light." The figures glimpsed at its center looked like "glowing metal" and their burnished, winged forms and faces were like nothing ever seen or dreamed of. Sparkling, rimmed wheels spinning within wheels rose and fell with these creatures. But the focus of the vision towered above these beings. Against the background of an "expanse, sparkling like ice and awesome," was the central figure of the Almighty. His figure, shaped like a man, was ablaze, and from Him emanated a brilliant light.

Completely awed by "the likeness of the glory of the Lord" Ezekiel fell facedown.

The word "glory" is a significant one in the Old Testament. The Hebrew word, *kabod*, comes from a root that means "heavy" or "weighty." It suggests what is impressive or worthy about a person or thing. The term is often associated in ancient cultures with kings, who possessed both high position and great wealth.

In the Old Testament the phrase "the glory" or "the glory of God" is closely linked with God's revelation of Himself. As here in Ezekiel, the imagery of a blazing splendor, or flaming holiness to mark His presence, is often used (cf. Ex. 16:10; 2 Chron. 7:1-2).

Yet neither raw power nor burning holiness can express the glory of our God. When Moses begged to see God's glory, he was told, "I will cause all My goodness to pass in front of you" (Ex. 33:19). "Glory" is also associated with the acts by which God redeemed Israel from slavery in Egypt (Num. 14:22), and even with Creation (Ps. 19:1).

The *Expository Dictionary of Bible Words* (Richards, Zondervan), says that:

> "Glory" implies more than a disclosure by God of who He is. It implies an invasion of the material universe, an expression of God's active presence among His people. Thus, the Old Testament consistently links the term "glory" with the presence of God among Israel in tabernacle and temple (e.g., Ex. 29:43; Ezek. 43:4-5; Hag. 2:3). God's objective glory is revealed by His coming to be present with us, His people, and to show us Himself by His actions in the world.

It is this powerful concept, of the awesome, transcendent God present and active with His people, that is captured by the term "glory." And thus when Ezekiel saw in a vision the glory of God actually departing from the Jerusalem temple, the prophet knew that Judah's doom was truly sealed!

When Ezekiel had this vision he was seated with the elders of the Jews in Babylon. Suddenly caught up by an angelic visitor, he was taken in his vision to Jerusalem. There he saw what was happening at that moment in the temple in which the exiles had placed their trust, confident that God would never permit the place where His presence rested to be destroyed.

The vision demonstrated how foolhardy their hope was, as Ezekiel observed God removing His presence from the edifice constructed by Solomon. The remaining shell of marble and gold could afford no protection to God's sinning people.

Ezekiel 8:4-18. Ezekiel was taken to the temple, where he perceived the glory of the Lord, the visible sign of His presence, in the holy of holies (the inner sanctuary of the temple). But in the vision Ezekiel was told to look away from God, and to observe what the men of Judah were doing in the temple.

He was taken through a secret passage into a hidden chamber. There the very elders of his people worshiped idols and "crawling things and detestable animals." These most likely represented the gods of Egypt, with whom the Israelites were seeking a political alliance against the Babylonians. Yet it was the gods of Egypt that the Lord had shown so powerless at the time of the Exodus! There, in the hidden chamber, priests and elders offered incense, imagining that "the Lord does not see us: the Lord has forsaken the land."

Then Ezekiel was guided to the gate of the temple, where he found women involved in the worship rites of the mother/son cult of Tammuz.

Then, in an inner court, Ezekiel found 25 men facing *away* from the temple (see 2 Chron. 6:20), praying toward the sun, the chief god Ra of the Egyptian pantheon.

The pollution of the temple by the Hebrews showed how far they had fallen: "Therefore," God said, "I will deal with them in anger. I will not look on them with pity or spare them" (Ezek. 8:18).

Ezekiel 9:1-11. Then a striking thing happened. Six angelic figures with weapons in hand approached, and "the glory of the God of Israel went up from above the cherubim, where it had been, and moved to the threshold of the temple" (v. 3). God's presence was about to leave!

The executioners were given instructions—first to mark off those individuals who were ashamed and mourned over Judah's faithlessness, then to strike out among the rest and to kill, without showing pity or compassion, those who defiled the Lord's sanctuary.

Ezekiel 10:1-22. Cherubim, a guard of honor, now approached the temple, and the glory of the Lord moved out to the threshold. As the honor guard stood ready, the glory of the Lord left the temple threshold and paused above it.

Ezekiel 11:1-21. Ezekiel was then lifted and brought to the place from which the glory looked back toward the temple. From this perspective, Ezekiel saw the faces of the 25 who had earlier been worshiping the sun. Among them Ezekiel recognized the key religious and political leaders of God's people! Commanded to prophesy against them, Ezekiel spoke . . . and at his words one leader fell dead.

The prophet cried out in anguish. "Ah, Sovereign Lord! Will You completely destroy the remnant of Israel?" (v. 13)

God's answer was both comforting and foreboding. Not all His people would be destroyed. Those in captivity would be kept secure and regathered one day to the Promised Land. But for those "whose hearts are devoted to their vile images and detestable idols," there would be a complete end.

Ezekiel 11:22-25. With this announcement the cherubim lifted their wings and the glory of the Lord left not only the temple but the city itself, hesitating briefly over the mountains east of Jerusalem.

God had left His sinning people to the fate that, in their hardness of heart, they themselves had chosen.

♥ ***Link to Life: Youth / Adult***
Review with your group the dedication of the temple by Solomon, at which time "the glory of the Lord filled the temple. The priests could not enter the temple of the Lord because the glory of the Lord filled it. When all the Israelites saw the fire coming down and the glory of the Lord above the temple, they knelt on the pavement with their faces to the ground, and they worshiped and gave thanks to the Lord" (2 Chron. 7:1-3).

Read also the warning given by God at that dedication (2 Chron. 7:19-22).

Then with your group work through Ezekiel 8–11, noting how the actions of the Israelites made it certain that the threat of God to uproot Israel and reject the temple would be carried out.

Then discuss: "What lesson was there for Ezekiel's contemporaries in his vision? What lessons were there for future generations of Israelites? What lessons or principles can we draw from this passage for believers today?"

Personal Responsibility: Ezekiel 18

There are many indications in Ezekiel and in Jeremiah that God's judgment is selective. While all must suffer when a nation is defeated and its people taken captive to a strange land, God continues to deal with individuals.

We see this theme in Ezekiel 9, in which individuals who were ashamed of Judah's unfaithfulness were marked off by the destroying angels before they went about their work to "kill, without showing pity or compassion," the rest. The survivors in the national holocaust were carefully selected by the Lord!

Against this background the attitude of many in Judah, who lightly shrugged off the warnings of God's prophets, is difficult to understand. And yet the nation continued to quote a proverb that said, "The fathers eat sour grapes, and the children's teeth are set on edge." We might phrase it, "Mom ate a lemon, and her children puckered."

But however the proverb is phrased, it *dismisses the notion of personal responsibility.* It suggests a fatalism which dulls the moral sensibilities. If tragedy was about to come to Judah, her people seemed to say, there was nothing they could do: it would come because of the sins and failings of their parents.

This moral and spiritual fatalism was both an insult to God and a snare to His people. The notion that God might bring disaster on the innocent was an affront to His justice. And the notion that nothing could be done became an excuse for further excesses. Why repent, if judgment would come anyway? Why not simply take whatever pleasure or profit they could from the present moment, if there was nothing they could do to alter the future?

This attitude, so deeply ingrained in the people of the prophet's day, helped to make the Israelites so unresponsive to God's words of warning and exhortation.

But in Ezekiel 18 the Lord makes something abundantly clear. What the individual does *will* make a difference! An individual's choices may not have an impact on the fate of his or her nation, but those choices will surely have an impact on his or her own fate!

Soul. A phrase that is often repeated in this chapter confuses many about just what God is saying. That phrase is "the soul who sins is the one who will die" (vv. 4, 20).

Assuming that "soul" here means that permanent, immortal element of the human personality which survives death, some have taken Ezekiel's words to be about eternal destiny. The sinning soul, they have understood, will suffer eternal punishment.

But the Hebrew *nephesh* does not indicate "soul" in that sense. Instead it is often used in Hebrew as an intensive personal pronoun, meaning the person himself. Here, as in other places in the Old Testament, the meaning is simply "the person." Thus Ezekiel's warning was simply this: "The person who sins is the one who will die."

But what "death" was Ezekiel speaking of? Ezekiel spoke of physical death: the person who sinned would be killed in the coming holocaust when the Babylonians overran the nation and shattered Jerusalem!

Who would live? Ezekiel then went into a thorough explanation of who would live and who would die. The person who was "righteous" in terms of obedience to the Law's commands would live.

> "He does not eat at the mountain shrines or look to the idols of the house of Israel. He does not defile his neighbor's wife or lie with a woman during her period. He does not oppress anyone, but returns what he took in pledge for a loan. He does not commit robbery but gives his food to the hungry and provides clothing for the naked. He does not lend at usury or take excessive interest. He withholds his hand from doing wrong and judges fairly between man and man. He follows My decrees and faithfully keeps My laws. That man is righteous; he will surely live," declares the Sovereign Lord.
>
> Ezekiel 18:5-9

This statement of the divine standard of behavior contains nothing new. Every clause is found written in the divine Law; every expectation has been repeated by the prophets.

In the same way, the sinful behavior of the person who would die had been declared wicked from the beginning (see Ezek. 10–13). Ezekiel asked, "Will such a man live? He will not! Because he has done all these detestable things, he will surely be put to death and his blood will be on his own head" (18:13). Even if such a person had a righteous parent, he would die, for each individual was responsible for, and would be dealt with according to, his own actions.

Repentance and change. The prophet then went on to take several mixed cases. Suppose a person who has been wicked repents and begins to keep God's commands? God says, "If a wicked man turns away from all the sins he has committed and . . . does what is just and right, he will surely live" (v. 21).

This statement answers one of the major confusions of our own time. People tend to think of circumstances as something that *determine* human choices. We think that if a person had a troubled childhood, his later actions are both explained and excused. "His parents were drunks. No wonder he beats his wife now and then." Or, "Her folks never made it past third grade. No wonder she talks in classes and won't pay attention."

Now, it is clear that childhood experiences and the other circumstances of our lives *influence* us. But they do not *determine* our futures. Each of us is free enough to make responsible choices. And each of us will be judged by the choices we do make.

Thus we each know of individuals who are like the ones Ezekiel described. We know the godly son of the wicked father, who somehow turned away from the way of life he had always known to find God and godliness. And we each know of the sinning children of godly parents.

And now Ezekiel said that the individual who had chosen righteousness would not share the guilt of the father—nor benefit from the godliness of the father unless he too chose good (vv. 19-20).

With this message of responsibility Ezekiel has a powerful word of hope. Even the person who *has been wicked* and made wrong choices can repent and change! A wicked person can "turn away" from all his sins, turn to good, and live (v. 21).

But the possibility of change cuts both ways. A person who had done what is good may stray from righteousness. If a righteous man "turns from his righteousness and commits sin and does the same detestable things the wicked man does, will he live?" (v. 24)

We can summarize the message that Ezekiel had for individuals in Judah on a simple chart.

Live	Die
good man	wicked man
good man with wicked parent	wicked man with good parent
wicked man who repents and does good	good man who changes and does evil

♥ ***Link to Life: Youth / Adult***
Use the chart to present and summarize the content of Ezekiel 18. Be sure to explain the meaning of "soul" in this context, and the life or death issue with which the prophet dealt. Also use verses 5-9 to explain that "good" in this context means a person who makes moral and interpersonal choices according to what God says is right in His Word.

Then put the following on a chalkboard. Ask your group members to agree *or* disagree *that each sums up adequately a lesson or principle taught in this chapter. If group members* disagree, *work together on restatements that* will *express a principle we can apply in our own lives today. The statements:*

- *God actively watches over those who do what is right.*
- *Our moral choices may sometimes influence our future.*
- *We can't be held responsible when childhood influences cause our later sins and failures.*
- *Once you've started down a wrong path, there's nothing anyone can do to change you.*
- *Good people become immune to temptations that drag others into sin.*
- *When a person does wrong he should blame the devil.*
- *A person's will gets so weakened by sin he or she just can't change.*

Warnings, and Hope: Ezekiel 1–24
The first section of Ezekiel, composed of messages and visions concerning Judah's doom, were dark warnings indeed. Yet even in them we sense an exciting hope.

First, we catch a glimpse of the glory of God. One so powerful and transcendent cannot be thwarted by any occurrences here on Planet Earth. Whatever our situations may be, we can rest in the assurance that God is all-powerful, and that God remains in control.

Second, we learn that even in a time of national disaster God continued to care about, and to watch over, individuals. God preserved the good in Israel despite the terrible disaster that befell the country. What is more, the words God sent His prophet to utter conveyed good news to each individual. To the godly Jew Ezekiel's words were a promise. God would watch over him or her whatever came. And to the wicked, Ezekiel's words were both a warning and an invitation. The pressures they must have felt now under the threat of re-invasion by the Babylonians were nothing compared to the death and destruction that lay ahead. In view of that certain future, God's willingness to accept the person who would repent shone bright. It is never too late to change.

It is never too late—until the judgment comes.

TEACHING GUIDE

Prepare
Read Ezekiel 18 thoughtfully. To whom do you think such a message might be directed?

Explore
1. Give a minilecture of Ezekiel's times.
2. Or, actually act out as Ezekiel did the siege of Jerusalem as your group members enter. See "link-to-life," page 425.

Expand
1. Divide your group into teams of five or six people. Each team is to determine one Bible truth that is vital for people of today to understand. After choosing, each team should plan one way a prophet like Ezekiel might dramatize or symbolize that message today.

For a variation on this, pick a topic like abortion or pornography. Have your teams suggest at least one message to our society on the selected topic that Scripture conveys. Then plan how they might symbolize that message, as Ezekiel so powerfully presented his message to his contemporaries.
2. Or, focus on Ezekiel's message on personal responsibility. Use the "link-to-life" idea on page 429 to explore the teaching of Ezekiel 18.

Apply
Share: "Which of the principles derived from Ezekiel 18 is most meaningful to me? Why?"

STUDY GUIDE 65

Ezekiel 25–48

PROPHECIES OF HOPE

Overview
The ministry of Ezekiel had two separate thrusts. The prophet, one of the exiles in Babylon during the decade before Jerusalem was razed, warned the Jewish community there of the coming destruction. There was no hope that God would relent: the Jews would be torn from their homeland and the temple as well as their cities would be destroyed.

The destruction of Jerusalem silenced the prophet. For 13 years he remained silent. And then Ezekiel took up yet another prophetic mission. Now Ezekiel's words contained a message of hope. God would surely bring His people back to the Promised Land, and once again they would be planted in the place where God intended to bless the descendants of Abraham.

In this unit, we look briefly at some of Ezekiel's messages about the nations surrounding Israel. And then we look closely at the prophetic words of hope—words about a future for Israel which lies ahead of our day as well as Ezekiel's!

The chapters in this unit cover material represented by II-IV of the following outline.

Outline

I.	Prophecy against Judah	1–24
II.	Prophecy against Foreign Nations	25–32
III.	Prophecy of Restoration	33–39
IV.	Prophecy of the Temple	40–48

■ Why will there be sacrifices in a temple erected after Jesus returns to earth? His one sacrifice of Himself was sufficient. See the discussion in the *Bible Knowledge Commentary*, page 1305.

Commentary
The different themes of Ezekiel's ministry are carefully organized in his book. The earlier prophecies against Judah, explored in the last unit, are found in the first 24 chapters of his work. Ezekiel's prophecies against foreign nations, about Israel's restoration to the land, and about a temple to exist at the time of Israel's Messiah, are also grouped together.

Prophecies Against the Nations: Ezekiel 25–32
The ancient covenant promise that God gave to Abraham echoes throughout the Old Testament. The Jews discovered their identity in their relationship with God as His chosen people. They saw their destiny in God's promise to Abraham of the land that had been called Canaan, and across the centuries has been known as Palestine, Judah, and Israel. Now Ezekiel showed that he, as well as other prophets, explained God's dealings with pagan nations through another aspect of that ancient promise.

One of the several promises that God made to Abraham was, "I will bless those who bless you, and whoever curses you I will curse" (Gen. 12:3). This promise was now recalled as Ezekiel announced doom for the nations around Judah who delighted or participated in her fall.

Edom's doom would come "because Edom took revenge on the house of Judah and became very guilty by doing so" (Ezek. 25:12).

Philistia would suffer "because the Philistines acted in vengeance and took revenge with malice in their hearts, and with ancient hostility sought to destroy Judah" (v. 15).

Tyre would fall "because Tyre has said of Jerusalem, 'Aha! The gate to the nations is broken . . . now that she lies in ruins I will prosper' " (26:2).

Egypt would be crushed because, "You have been a staff of reed [e.g., a useless ally] for the house of Israel. When they grasped you with their hands, you splintered and you tore open their shoulders; when they leaned on you, you broke and their backs were wrenched" (29:6-7).

Thus the prophet reminded the Jews that the ancient covenant promises were still valid, despite their own wickedness. God kept His Word. Those who through history have sought the welfare of Jerusalem have prospered, and those who have been the enemy of the Jewish people have declined.

Against Tyre. One of the most fascinating of Old Testament prophecies concerns the future of Tyre.

This Phoenician city-state was rich in Old Testament times. Built largely on an island lying in the Mediterranean Sea just off the Lebanese coast, Tyre seemed to be impregnable. The ships of Tyre ruled the seas, and their trade brought her vast wealth. Yet Ezekiel warned that even the island state was not safe.

Nebuchadnezzar attacked the mainland settlements of Tyre, and as Ezekiel foretold, "set up siege works against you" (26:8). While the island city surrendered in 573–572 B.C., it was not destroyed. The rest of Ezekiel's prophecy did, however, come true! Here is what Ezekiel foretold—and how it actually happened.

> They will break down your walls and demolish your fine houses and throw your stones, timber, and rubble into the sea. I will put an end to your noisy songs, and the music of your harps will be heard no more. I will make you a bare rock, and you will become a place to spread fishnets. You will never be rebuilt, for I the Lord have spoken, declares the Sovereign Lord.
>
> Ezekiel 26:12-14

Much later, in 332 B.C., Alexander the Great led his small Macedonian army against the great Persian Empire. When Alexander marched along the coast to attack Tyre, that people refused to surrender. They simply retreated again to their island, sure their fleets would protect them against any possible attack.

But Alexander did not attack by sea. Instead he threw the stones, timber, and rubble of the shoreside communities into the sea—and built a causeway out to the island on which Tyre lay! Attacking over the land bridge that he had built, Alexander and his forces completely destroyed the city. As the prophet of God had said, the land was cleared down to bare rock.

Today one can visit that war-torn coast and see the causeway containing the ruins of ancient Tyre. A person can stand on the bare rock of the shore, and watch fishermen spread their nets. For the city of Tyre has never been rebuilt, as God through Ezekiel foretold.

The "king of Tyre." Ezekiel 28 contains a message to the "ruler of Tyre," and also a "lament concerning the king of Tyre."

There is no doubt that the ruler is a human being. But many feel that the "king" referred to in these passages is not human at all. Instead they believe the "king," identified in the text as a "guardian cherub," is none other than Satan himself.

If this interpretation is correct the passage looks back to an age before the creation of human beings, when Satan held an important position in the angelic order, stationed where Eden lay. Again, if this interpretation is correct it also describes the very origin of evil itself! What does the passage suggest?

Satan's original state (Ezek. 28:12-15). The "king of Tyre" is described as the model of perfection, full of wisdom and perfect in beauty (v. 12). In that state the "king" was "in Eden, the garden of God," and was adorned with "every precious stone."

The phrase placing this "king" on "the holy mount of God" suggests a high position, as mountains in the Old Testament are associated with power and authority.

Satan's fall (Ezek. 28:15-17). The next verses examine the origin of evil in the universe. God did not create evil, in the sense of wrongdoing. Even Satan was "blameless in your ways from the day you were created till wickedness was found in you."

Pride in his own beauty and splendor led to Satan's downfall, corrupting the perspective of this being and leading him to violence and sin.

As a result the "king" was expelled from his high position and thrown to the earth.

Satan's future (Ezek. 28:18-19). Satan will be destroyed by the flames of his own consuming evil, and his "horrible end" will be witnessed by all creation.

♥ ***Link to Life: Youth / Adult***

While this section of Ezekiel is inter-

esting and significant in satanology, (a study of Satan), it has little to do with the thrust of this powerful prophetic book. So you will probably not want to deal with it unless you are teaching a special session on Satan. In that case, you will probably want to use this passage, with Genesis 3, Job 1, Isaiah 14, and possibly Matthew 4, and Revelation 20:7-10, to develop a more fully orbed picture of this truly evil being.

To teach on Satan, place a series of questions on the chalkboard. Then distribute the various chapters to teams from your group. Each team is to see what answers its passage suggests to the questions, if any. The questions:

- *Who is Satan?*
- *Where did Satan come from?*
- *What is Satan's relationship to evil?*
- *What is Satan's attitude toward God?*
- *What is Satan's attitude toward human beings?*
- *What do we know about how Satan operates?*
- *What is Satan's final destiny?*
- *What is God's attitude toward Satan?*
- *How should Christians think and feel about Satan?*
- *How vulnerable are believers to this wicked being?*

Prophecies of Restoration: Ezekiel 33–39

It was 13 years after the destruction of Jerusalem and its temple that Ezekiel took up his new ministry as a prophet of hope. The Captivity that God had ordained for the Israelites was not permanent. A remnant would surely return to the land. In God's own time and in His own way, God would keep the promises He had made to Abraham and to David.

Many conservative scholars are convinced that the pictures here of a return to the land refer not simply to the exiles in Babylon but express a basic pattern in God's dealing with Israel. According to this understanding, the pattern of scattering and regathering we see in the Old Testament operates even today! Thus the scattering of the Jewish people in A.D. 70, after the destruction by the Romans of Jerusalem and the temple, is a reflection of what happened some 500 years later. That scattering lasted not just for 70 years, but has extended to nearly 2,000! And, many believe, the establishment of the state of Israel in 1948 was the first phase in a regathering yet ahead, but described graphically in Ezekiel 37.

But there are several regathering themes in these important Old Testament chapters.

The watchman (Ezek. 33). Ezekiel compared the ministry of the believer sensitive to God's truth to that of a city watchman set on a high wall to guard against enemy attack. It was the watchman's duty to blow the trumpet and warn of danger so the city inhabitants could prepare for the attack.

Those who heard the warning might not respond. But that was their responsibility. It was the responsibility of the watcher to give warning.

This principle is often applied to Christian witness in our preaching. You and I cannot be responsible for how a person responds to the Gospel. But we are responsible to share the Good News. Like the Lord Himself, we can say, "I take no pleasure in the death of the wicked, but rather that they turn from their ways and live. Turn! Turn from your evil ways! Why will you die?" (v. 11)

Shepherds and sheep (Ezek. 34). In this prophetic message Ezekiel condemned those spiritual leaders of his people who were supposed to shepherd them, but rather than caring for the flock of God, "clothe yourselves with the wool and slaughter the choice animals," ruling brutally for their own profit rather than for the good of the sheep.

This message has a dual emphasis. First God said of the shepherds, "I am against [them] and will hold them accountable for My flock" (v. 10). The predatory shepherds will be removed, and the sheep rescued from their care.

Then the Lord said, "I Myself will search for My sheep and look after them" (v. 11). This personal commitment is to be fulfilled by Jesus, who spoke of Himself as the Good Shepherd in John 10, in words that reflect Ezekiel's emphasis.

> I Myself will tend My sheep and have them lie down, declares the Sovereign Lord. I will search for the lost and bring back the strays. I will bind up the injured and strengthen the weak.
>
> Ezekiel 34:15-16

But associated with the Lord's coming to shepherd His people is the promise of a regathering to the land! The Shepherd God will bring the sheep back from the nations "and I will bring them into their own land. I will pasture them on the mountains of Israel" (v. 13). There the "house of Israel," who are "My people," will be blessed endlessly (v. 30).

The mountains of Israel (Ezek. 36). In this unique prophetic message God speaks to the mountains of the Promised Land. The mountaintops, polluted by Israel's pagan worship and shamed by the trampling feet of enemy armies, have suffered divine judgment along with God's people.

But in the future Israel will be cleansed and spiritually transformed. In that day the desolate land will be resettled, to become cultivated and fruitful, no more a waste.

Here too is a striking prophecy of spiritual rebirth, one which parallels Jeremiah's great prophecy of a New Covenant.

> I will take you out of the nations; I will gather you from all the countries and bring you back into your own land. I will sprinkle clean water on you, and you will be clean; I will cleanse you from all your impurities and from all your idols. I will give you a new heart and put a new spirit in you; I will remove from you your heart of stone and give you a heart of flesh. And I will put My Spirit in you and move you to follow My decrees and be careful to keep My laws. You will live in the land I gave your forefathers; you will be My people, and I will be your God.
>
> Ezekiel 36:24-28

An image of the regathering (Ezek. 37). So far each passage we've looked at in this section associates the spiritual renewal and revitalization of Israel with both God's direct action, and a return of the people to the Promised Land. Now a spectacular prophecy outlines steps associated with that regathering.

Ezekiel is taken by the Spirit to a valley. Scattered over it are millions of bones, dried and lifeless on the ground. At God's command, Ezekiel cried out for the bones to hear the Word of the Lord. In response there was a great rattling, and the bones came together. Sinews grew, and flesh and skin covered them. Then, last of all, the winds breathed life into the restored beings, and they "stood up on their feet, a vast army" (v. 10).

God explained the vision to Ezekiel. "These bones are the whole house of Israel. They say, 'Our bones are dried up, and our hope is gone; we are cut off' " (v. 11). Ezekiel was to inform the nation that God will open the graves (e.g., the lands to which Israel has been scattered) and will bring them back to the land of Israel. The restored people will at first be lifeless. But God will act again. "I will put My Spirit in you and you will live, and I will settle you in your own land" (v. 14).

Is this a description of modern Israel, a secular state whose citizens generally do not believe in the God of the Old Testament? Will the spiritually dead people one day be converted by a wonderful act of God's Spirit and, restored to their ancient relationship with the Lord, experience fulfillment of the Old Testament prophecies? This is what many Christians believe. And it may well be exactly what Ezekiel teaches us in this significant section of his book.

Certainly the rest of Ezekiel's picture of restored Israel has not yet had a historic fulfillment. For when that day comes, "My servant David [that is, the Messiah, who will come from David's family line] will be king over them" not just for one generation but "forever" (vv. 24, 26).

Gog and Magog (Ezek. 38–39). These two chapters describe an invasion of Israel mounted from the North. The ancient place names in these chapters have been identified. Many are currently located in the Soviet Union. Others are those loosely aligned today with Russia: Iran, Libya, and Turkey as well as the Sudan and northern Ethiopia. This coalition of states will invade as "a great horde, a mighty army" (38:15). While the attack will succeed initially, God will personally intervene and destroy the invading army (vv. 18-23). The war material left behind by the invaders will supply Israel for years, and it will take seven months to dispose of the bodies of the crushed enemy. And, God said to Ezekiel, "From that day forward the house of Israel will know that I am the Lord their God" (v. 22). For then "I will pour out My Spirit on the house of Israel, declares the Sovereign Lord" (v. 29).

Interpreting prophecy. Each of the images

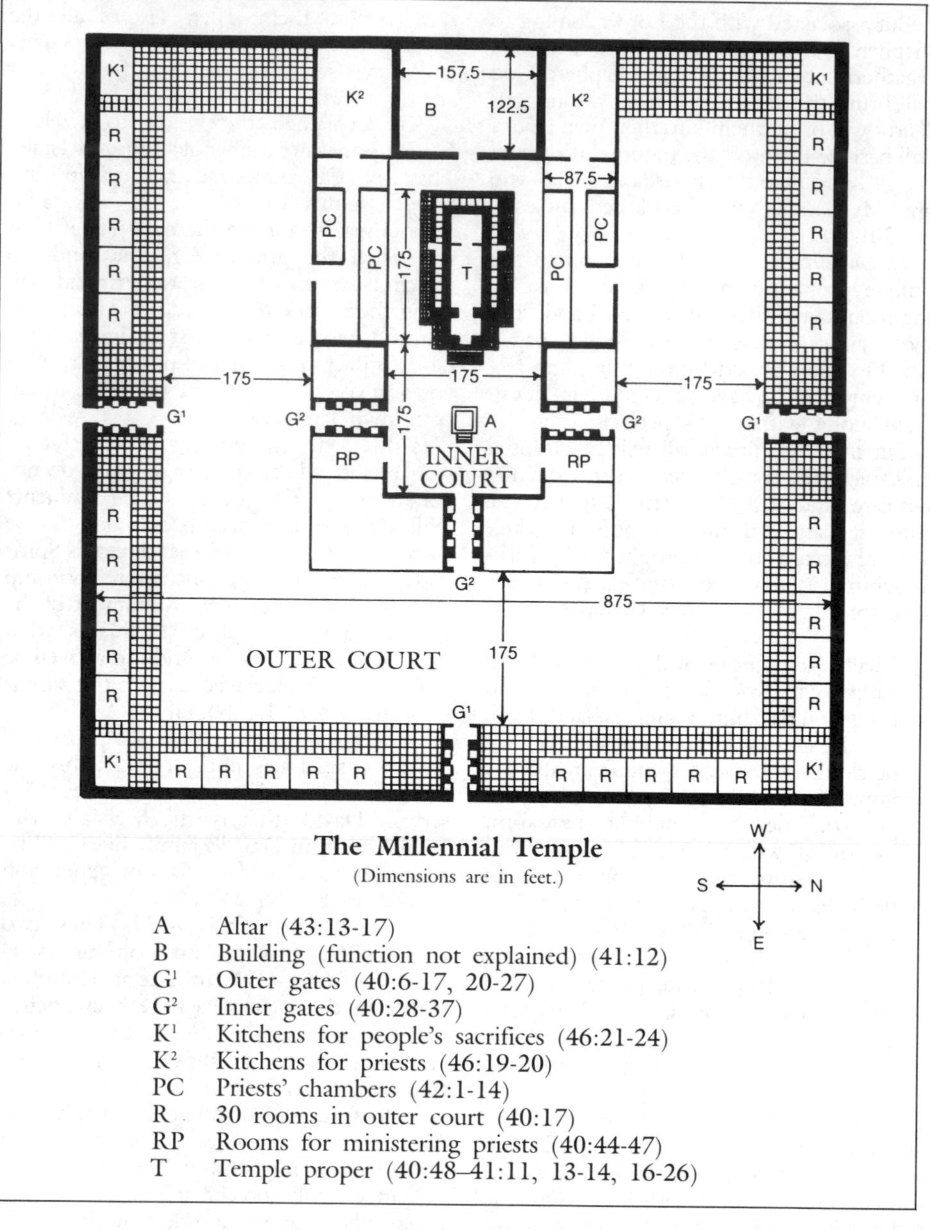

The Millennial Temple

(Dimensions are in feet.)

A	Altar (43:13-17)
B	Building (function not explained) (41:12)
G¹	Outer gates (40:6-17, 20-27)
G²	Inner gates (40:28-37)
K¹	Kitchens for people's sacrifices (46:21-24)
K²	Kitchens for priests (46:19-20)
PC	Priests' chambers (42:1-14)
R	30 rooms in outer court (40:17)
RP	Rooms for ministering priests (40:44-47)
T	Temple proper (40:48–41:11, 13-14, 16-26)

in this section is prophetic in that each deals with events still future to the writer. So how are we today to take these vivid images? Are they images intended to convey spiritual truth about living close to God, or are they intended to outline what will literally take place on earth? While this issue is debated by sincere Christians, it is fascinating to note these facts:

(1) Other Old Testament prophecies, like that concerning Tyre, and like the many concerning Jesus' first coming, have been fulfilled in a literal way. The pattern established by already-fulfilled prophecy suggests a literal fulfillment.

(2) Again and again these prophecies speak of Israel, and the physical seed of Abraham, Isaac, and Jacob are clearly intended. It is true that Christians today are members of the spiritual family of Abraham

(Rom. 4:16-17). But this does not make Christians "Israel."

(3) Again and again these prophecies also speak of the Promised Land in the most literal possible way. The spiritual renewal they foretell is *invariably* linked by Ezekiel with a return of the people to inhabit the Promised Land.

(4) Ezekiel linked the events he foresaw with the establishment of a Davidic ruler on Israel's throne. We know that that ruler is Jesus, the promised Messiah, God the Shepherd. We also know that He has not yet in any literal way established kingly authority in Israel—but that Jesus will return. While many different themes are associated with Jesus' return, it is surely possible that the fulfillment of Davidic Covenant promises are included.

♥ ***Link to Life: Youth / Adult***

Let your group members explore these prophecies and debate their meaning. Divide the chapters between study teams. Each team is to find evidence for *and* against *this position: "The prophecies of a regathering for Israel were fulfilled when the people returned to Judah from Babylon."*

Do not try to get complete agreement on this question. But do assemble evidence.

Then discuss: "If most of what Ezekiel was speaking of is still in the future, what might this mean for Christians? Based on current events, how far in the future do you think fulfillment lies?"

The Future Temple: Ezekiel 40–48

The rest of the Book of Ezekiel is composed of a detailed description of a temple to be built in Jerusalem in the day of restoration. The description intermingles the natural and supernatural, picturing a world that is distinctly not like our own—a world in which "the Lord is there" (48:35).

The temple described, and the passages dealing with its various features, are shown on the chart on page 434.

Much of the controversy surrounds the description here of a sacrificial system—a system which is unnecessary because Christ's one sacrifice in making the New Covenant has perfected all who believe in Him (Heb. 10). Why then, at a time when "the Lord is present," should animal sacrifices be necessary?

The best way to look at the sacrifices and ceremonies of Ezekiel 42–46 seems to be to take them as memorials; constant and joyous reminders of the redemption which Christ has secured. In this context the prophecy of Ezekiel is parallel to the vision in Isaiah 60. There will be a glorious kingdom, to be realized only through God's personal presence among the redeemed when the "tabernacle of God is with men" (Rev. 21:3, KJV).

How rich life will be when Jesus returns, and the full meaning of Ezekiel's promise is experienced by all: "I will no longer hide My face from them, for I will pour out My Spirit on the house of Israel" (Ezek. 39:29).

TEACHING GUIDE

Prepare

What does Ezekiel 34 suggest to you about your teaching ministry?

Explore

1. The thrust of this section is prophetic. Yet there are two "lesson" chapters that can be directly applied to Christians today. Divide into teams to come up with three "lessons for living" from the assigned chapter(s).

- Chapter 33: What do we learn about witnessing?
- Chapter 34: What do we learn about spiritual leadership?

2. Or, you may wish to jump from Ezekiel 28 into a study of Satan. If either of these two approaches seems better suited to the needs of your group, feel free to take the one you like best.

Expand

1. If you wish to explore the main prophetic thrust of these chapters, begin with a minilecture on the prophecy against Tyre. Read the prophecy in the text, and then tell how it was literally fulfilled in 332 B.C. by Alexander's Greek army.

2. Raise the question of how to understand the prophecies in Ezekiel 33–38. Have your

group members form teams to look at specific chapters, looking for answers to questions posed in the "link-to-life" on page 435. Remember you are not trying to win an argument or have your group members make points. Instead you want to help them consider carefully all the evidence in these chapters and draw a reasonable conclusion.

If you wish, however, you might conclude the discussion with a summary of the principles for interpreting prophecy.

Apply

If Ezekiel *were* speaking of modern Israel, Russia, Libya and other Middle Eastern states, how should we respond? What difference would believing the end is near make in our values? Choices? Priorities?

STUDY GUIDE 66

Daniel 1–6

DANIEL'S LIFE

Overview

The Book of Daniel contains the personal history and visions of the future of Daniel, a Jew deported to Babylon as a teenager in 605 B.C. There Daniel was trained, with young people from other conquered nations, to become administrators in the empire of Nebuchadnezzar.

The book is divided into two natural parts:

Outline

I. Daniel's Life and Work	1–6
II. Daniel's Prophetic Visions	7–12

The Book of Daniel is written in two languages: 1:1–2:4a, and 8:1–12:13 are in Hebrew. The rest of the book, 2:4b–7:28, is written in Aramaic. Archeology has shown that other writings of the same time share this trait.

The name "Daniel" means "God is my judge." The first six chapters of this important Old Testament book show how the conviction represented by Daniel's name guided his actions from youth through old age. Committed to pleasing God alone, this man was unshakable in his determination to do what he knew was right.

The book, written in the first person, gives an insider's view of the administration of three great empires Daniel served. While some have challenged Daniel's authenticity because of the accuracy of its fulfilled prophecy, this unit reviews some of the evidence which shows it truly was written by Daniel in his own time.

■ For verse-by-verse comments, see the *Bible Knowledge Commentary*, pages 1323 to 1375.

Commentary

The Bible is a book of history. Archeological discovery after discovery has shown just how accurate it is. We can trust Scripture's historical accounts.

But the Bible is more. Among its amazing claims is the clear expression of confidence that its writers and prophets were inspired by God to predict the future. Sometimes these predictions are narrow and specific, touching the life of an individual or the near future of a city or nation. But often prediction involves vast and sweeping panoramas, encompassing the destiny of not only the nations of our world but of the universe itself. In the next unit we'll look at the shape of history ahead as the Bible describes it in one of the most fascinating of Bible prophetic books.

But how confident can we be that the Bible's picture of history ahead is accurate? Probably the best way is to look closely at the life and writings of one man: Daniel.

Daniel

As a young teenager, Daniel and several friends were taken to Babylon in the first group of captives (605 B.C.). There Daniel was trained with young men from other districts of the far-flung empire for the Babylonian civil service. Through a series of events recorded in his book, Daniel was advanced to the highest positions in the administration of three empires, and his lifetime spans the entire period of Judah's Captivity.

Five incidents illustrate Daniel's relationship with these world rulers: his decision not to defile himself with pagan foods (chap. 1: ca. 602 B.C.); his interpretation of Nebuchadnezzar's first dream (chap. 2: ca. 595 B.C.); his interpretation of Nebuchadnezzar's second dream (chap. 4: ca. 567 B.C.); his reading of the writing on Belshazzar's wall, when Daniel was at least 80 (chap 5: ca. 539 B.C.); and his being cast into the lions' den (chap. 6: ca. 537 or 536 B.C.).

In addition Daniel experienced, at least four times, special revelations of the future. Those recorded in chapters 7–9 were probably given during Belshazzar's reign, while those in chapters 10–12 were in the first and third years of Cyrus' rule.

Of particular note is the fact that the Book of Daniel is written half in Hebrew and half in Aramaic, the language of the Gentile world of Daniel's day. The Aramaic portion, chapters 2:4b–7:28, seems to concentrate on Gentile issues.

Daniel the man. Daniel is portrayed as a distinctly committed and humble man. Though he rose to the highest governmental rank, and was familiar with several world rulers, Daniel maintained his daily walk with God. His character is mentioned several times by Ezekiel, a contemporary of his, who compared Daniel's righteousness to Noah's and Job's (cf. Ezek. 14:14, 20). Daniel was set up by Ezekiel as the standard against which to measure wisdom (28:3). When jealous enemies tried to set Daniel aside from his administrative posts, they could find no areas of weakness except that he was faithful to God. Their attempt to turn Daniel's commitment to their own advantage—and how that attempt backfired!—is recorded in the famous story of Daniel and the lions' den.

Daniel's times. Probably the Book of Daniel has been given more critical scrutiny than any of the prophetic books of the Old Testament. Some scholars have believed that it was not written by Daniel at all, but by an unknown author about 165 B.C. The main reason for this belief is the amazing detail with which Daniel outlines history from the days of the Roman Empire to at least the time of Antiochus in the 160s. Those who cannot accept the idea of supernatural revelation of the future have been forced to seek some other explanation for Daniel's accuracy!

Yet the book itself claims to be Daniel's work, and Jesus authenticates his prophecies (see Matt. 24:15; Mark 13:14). Fragments of Daniel's book have been found in the Qumran documents—a cache of Old Testament books dating from the early first and second centuries A.D.—and it is highly unlikely that "fiction" would have been included among that community's treasure-house of Scripture.

Actually, as Leon Wood points out, many recent archeological discoveries strongly support the Daniel authorship and the Exile dating. Wood summarizes:

> The author shows remarkable knowledge of Babylonian and early Persian history, such as would be true of a contemporary like Daniel. In the fourth chapter Nebuchadnezzar is presented correctly as the creator of the Neo-Babylonian Empire. In the fifth chapter Belshazzar is set forth as co-ruler of Babylon, a fact only recently demonstrated by archeological research. In the sixth chapter, Darius is presented as ruler of Babylon, even though Cyrus was the supreme ruler of Persia. Cyrus is now known to have appointed one Bubaru in this capacity, with whom Darius may well be identified. In the second chapter (cf. vv. 12-13, 46), Nebuchadnezzar is shown to have been able to change Babylonian laws which he had previously made (such a change is now known to have been possible in Babylonia); whereas in the sixth chapter (cf. vv. 8-9, 12, 15) Darius is presented as not having been able to do this (such a change is now known to have been impossible in Persia).
> (*A Commentary on Daniel,* Zondervan)

The supernatural. The only serious question left concerning the authenticity of Daniel has to do with the likelihood of the supernatural. The book describes several notable miracles. God delivered Shadrach, Meshach, and Abednego (three Jewish fellow-captives) from a fiery furnace. Through Daniel, God not only interpreted Nebuchadnezzar's dream; he even described the dream when Nebuchadnezzar refused to reveal it to his "wise men" advisers. The mouths of a den of hungry lions were closed by angelic intervention to preserve Daniel's life; then opened to crush the bones of Daniel's enemies. Nebuchadnezzar was struck with seven years' madness, and when he recovered his throne was returned.

How likely are these amazing events? How much confidence can we place in these miracles?

This is, of course, the same argument raised against prophecy. No living human being can possibly know the outline of the future, and surely not in the detail given in the Book of Daniel. If we reject the idea that

God exists or that He acts in the world of men, then of course we have to seek some other explanation for miracles. We have to suppose that people who describe historical events live *after* the events have happened and not before.

But once we admit the possibility of the supernatural; once we accept the fact that God may actually *not* be standing impotently on the outside of space and time—then everything changes! *If God exists, and if He is the kind of God the Bible describes, then there is nothing impossible about miracles and nothing unlikely about prophecy.*

In fact, the Bible records four great but relatively short outbursts of miracles. The first was the time of miracles associated with the deliverance of Israel from Egyptian bondage (the Exodus Age). The second was the days of Elijah and Elisha, shortly after Israel's unified kingdom had been shattered into two. The third was focused in the time of Daniel. And the fourth was the day of Jesus and the early church. Through most of recorded time God has not chosen to intervene in obvious ways. He has chosen instead the quiet providential manner of guiding events illustrated so powerfully in the Book of Esther.

Why then the periods of miracles? Some have suggested that miracles may be associated with times of deep-set resistance to God, or times of questioning God's power. In Daniel's time the miracles certainly had both these functions, of witness and reassurance. To the Babylonians, a god was evaluated by the size of the nation which worshiped him and the power of that nation's army. How could the God of insignificant Judah, whose people had been led away in humiliation, be anything but insignificant too?

And then, as Daniel recorded the series of miraculous interventions, we see a gradual change in the attitude of the Babylonian rulers. Finally even Nebuchadnezzar himself is seen praising and honoring the Most High:

> His dominion is an eternal dominion; His kingdom endures from generation to generation. All the peoples of the earth are regarded as nothing. He does as He pleases with the powers of heaven and the peoples of the earth. No one can hold back His hand or say to Him: "What have You done?"
>
> Daniel 4:34-35

We can see how such rulers' public decrees acknowledging God must have comforted their captives. Had their God lost power, or lost His love for them?

No, even in Captivity they were not abandoned! Even here God acted and in His miracles gave continuing testimony to His involvement in their lives.

You or I may choose to hold a view of God that denies Him the power to intervene in space and time, or that at least doubts His will to do so. But it is clear that the writers of the Bible held no such limited view. The God of the Bible chose to stand behind the scenes of history for the most part. But when He chooses, He can and will intervene. And even behind the scenes, He is the Author and Director of the play. So history moves, purposefully, toward the great climax He has planned.

Impact on His Own Time

Like all Old Testament prophets, Daniel had a great impact on his own era. Unlike most, Daniel's impact was primarily on the very highest ranks of *pagan* rulers!

Earlier, the experience of Jonah had shown that God cares for pagan peoples as well as for His chosen community of Israel (see especially Jonah 4). In Daniel we see God acting in grace in the lives of pagan individuals, to bring them to a knowledge of Himself. The apparent conversion of Nebuchadnezzar is among the most striking of all Old Testament events, particularly when contrasted to Pharaoh's response some thousand years earlier.

At the same time, Daniel must have had several very vital influences on the captive Israelites. His early example of commitment to God (Dan. 1) was an encouraging testimony to the fact that the believer could remain true to his faith in a pagan culture—and still find acceptance and even advancement. Rather than withdrawing from his world, Daniel influenced the course of events!

Often questions are raised today about the validity of Christians in politics. Shouldn't the true believer withdraw from the system, particularly when to get ahead seems associated with compromise and questionable "yokes" with unbelievers?

While this is not a simple question, the experience of Daniel demonstrated that when God calls a believer to a role within the power structure of society, that individual can both remain true to God *and* influence the course of history.

It is possible, as some have suggested, that the influence of Daniel even extended to drafting Cyrus' decree permitting the first groups of Jews to return to Jerusalem to rebuild the temple. If so, it must have been one of the final—and most satisfying—acts of Daniel's long and useful life.

Daniel's righteousness, described by Ezekiel as being legendary in his own day, stood to the exiles as a beacon, pointing them toward the way to live for God no matter where they might be.

One final influence on his own people must have come from the prophetic sections of the book Daniel authored (chaps. 7–12). Daniel was old when these sections were introduced. The Jews had been in Babylon for a generation or more. After the passage of decades, the majority would have settled down to seek the best possible adjustment to their fate. Many would have been born and grown to maturity there, knowing nothing of their homeland or their God except what was passed on by their parents. For a great many of that generation, Hebrew was a foreign tongue; a scholar had to explain in Aramaic what the original text said.

But God's people were not meant to settle down in a foreign land. Destiny awaited them, and the whole world, in Palestine!

Someday Messiah would come. Someday the kingdoms of this world would be shaken. Someday all worldly glory would be shattered. There would come one "like a Son of man" (7:13). To Him, the Ancient of Days would make a great presentation. Looking ahead in a great vision of the night, Daniel saw destiny.

> He was given authority, glory, and sovereign power; all peoples, nations and men of every language worshiped Him. His dominion is an everlasting dominion that will not pass away, and His kingdom is one that will never be destroyed.
>
> Daniel 7:14

Observations on the Text

A youth's commitment (Dan. 1). Old Testament dietary law specified certain foods no Jew was to eat. When Daniel was taken to Babylon he and three companions determined to keep God's Law and refused "to defile" themselves with the royal food and drink.

His native wisdom and tact are shown in this incident. He requested permission from the chief official (no "demands" or sullenness here!), and proposed a test when he understood the fears of that official that a limited diet might harm Daniel's health.

We too can learn much from this teenager. We too want to be committed to doing what is right. But we also need to show sensitivity to others. In most cases commitment can be expressed in cooperation, and need not provoke confrontation.

♥ ***Link to Life: Children***

God's people today are also special. We are supposed to do what is right and to stay away from things that are forbidden. Boys and girls, like young Daniel, can dare to do what is right.

What do the boys and girls you teach think of as right (but hard) things to do, and wrong things to keep away from? Have your class members pretend that Daniel is coming to visit them. Let them make a list to show Daniel things children today do because they are right, and another list of things they stay away from.

When the children's lists of right and wrong things to do has been completed, ask each to pick out one thing *they will dare to do or not do, like Daniel. Give each child willing to "dare" an I DARE pin to wear during the week to remind him to show Daniel's courage and faithfulness.*

To make I DARE pins, cut half-dollar sized circles from heavy cardboard. On one side glue heavy aluminum foil. Attach a small safety pin to the other side with scotch tape. Use nail polish to print "I DARE" on the foil side.

Courage rewarded (Dan. 3). The events reported in this chapter probably happened when Daniel was away from the capital. But his three Jewish companions, also officials in the government, were in Babylon when Nebuchadnezzar set up a giant golden idol and commanded all to worship it. All who would not were to be thrown in a blazing furnace. The three Jews—Shadrach, Meshach and Abednego—refused to bow.

Courageously they expressed both faith and commitment: "The God we serve is able to save us from it, and He will rescue us from your hand, O king. But even if He does not, we want you to know, O king, that we will not serve your gods or worship the image of gold you have set up" (vv. 17-18).

God *did* deliver His three worshipers. A fourth figure appeared in the center of the flaming furnace, to be with the three. And even though the heat of the fire was so great it killed those who cast them into the furnace, the three returned without even the scent of burning on their clothing.

Nebuchadnezzar was impressed not only with the rescue, but with the fact that the three "were willing to give up their lives rather than serve or worship any god except their own God" (v. 28).

♥ ***Link to Life: Children***

It often takes courage to choose to do things we know will please the Lord. Taking that courageous stand is one way that we witness for the Lord.

But what gives us the courage? We Christians need to know that God is with us, and that God can help. As you emphasize the faith of the three young Jewish believers, here's a simple way to help your boys and girls remember that God is with them when they face a hard choice.

At home practice holding up three fingers, bending the little finger and holding it down with your thumb. Then try to pick up a pencil, hold a fork, or do some other task. It is almost impossible to do.

In class, show the three fingers to your boys and girls, naming one Shadrach, one Meshach, and one Abednego. Explain that they were not afraid, because they believed God was with them (hold up the little finger too).

Have your children hold down their little fingers with their thumbs, and try to pick up pencils or do other tasks. Explain that the three knew they couldn't to anything alone, just as our three fingers don't work well without the fourth!

Then have them release their little fingers, and try the same tasks. God was the fourth Person in the fire with His three servants. With God there the three were able to live even in the fire. Because God is with us too, we can have courage in our difficult situations.

Encourage the children, when they feel anxious or afraid, to grip their right hand and look at all four fingers. They can remember that God is with them too and because He is there, they can be courageous instead of afraid.

Nebuchadnezzar's pride (Dan. 4). God revealed Himself to Nebuchadnezzar in several ways. He learned of God through Daniel's interpretation of an early dream (Dan. 2). He saw God's power to save at the incident of the fiery furnace (chap. 3). And in another dream God warned the great king of judgment due to his great pride (chap. 4).

This dream, interpreted by Daniel, also came true. The king, swelling with pride at his accomplishments, was suddenly stricken with madness. When his mind was restored, and his kingdom with it, Nebuchadnezzar at last praised and honored and glorified God as the Most High. It is likely that Nebuchadnezzar's confession recorded here represents a true conversion.

There are many exciting lessons to be drawn from God's dealing with the Babylonian conqueror. We see evidence that God did care about pagan individuals. We see evidence that believers in public positions can have influence—on individuals and on national policy. How rich the personal recollections of Daniel are in lessons for us.

♥ ***Link to Life: Youth / Adult***

Divide into teams to look at the incidents reported in Daniel 2, 3, and 4. Each team is to look at the same material from a different viewpoint, and to answer its "key question." Questions are:

- *Group 1: What demonstrates God's care for Nebuchadnezzar as a person?*
- *Group 2: What qualities in believers influenced Nebuchadnezzar?*
- *Group 3: What changed Nebuchadnezzar's attitude toward the God of little, defeated Judah?*

When each group has answered its question, ask each to take 8 minutes and develop a list of lessons we can learn and apply to our own lives from these chapters.

Delivered from lions (Dan. 6). The story of

Daniel in the lions' den is familiar to all of us. What may not be well known is that at the time Daniel was over 80 years old, and chief administrator of the Persian Empire.

Daniel's enemies tried to trap the aged saint through his faithfulness to God. But God was also faithful to him. The lions were unable to touch Daniel. But those who had falsely accused Daniel were quickly killed when the angry ruler had them cast into the same den.

♥ ***Link to Life: Children***
Have your boys and girls draw pictures of the famous Daniel and the lions' den story, picking the scene they prefer. Print on each picture, "When I am afraid, I will trust in You."

Then have the children draw a picture of a time when they *were afraid, or may still be afraid.*

Let each child tell about his completed picture. Remind them, "How good to know that God is with us when we are afraid, just as He was with Daniel." Let each child print the same verse on his contemporary picture.

Send both pictures home, to be put on bedroom walls as a reminder that God is faithful now as He was in Daniel's day.

TEACHING GUIDE

Prepare
What is one trait of Daniel's you would like to see mature in your own life?

Explore
1. Give a brief overview of the life and times of Daniel. You may want to supplement your minilecture with introductory material from a commentary like the excellent *Bible Knowledge Commentary* (Victor).

Touch particularly on lines of evidence which demonstrate that the book truly is Daniel's composition.

2. Or, ask your group members to assume they are high officials in an all-conquering empire. What impression would they form of the god of a tiny, defeated nation whose captive citizens were an insignificant minority in their population?

List impressions, and reasons for them, on the chalkboard.

Expand
1. Assign one chapter of Daniel 1 through 6 to pairs of group members. Each pair is to identify choices of believers in God which suggest they did *not* share the Babylonian view of the Lord, and to identify acts of God which began to change the Babylonians' impression of the Lord. In what specific ways would that impression have changed: that is, what insights into who God is and what He is like would each incident provide an observer?

Share team discoveries, and then work together to answer this question: "What does the Book of Daniel teach us about God?"

2. Or, examine God's interaction with Nebuchadnezzar. What do chapters 2–4 tell us about God's concern for the lost in Old Testament times, and about how believers might exercise influence even in difficult circumstances? See the "link-to-life" idea on page 441.

Apply
Go around the circle. Ask each person to pick a trait of Daniel which he or she admires, and tell why that trait is important for Christians today.

STUDY GUIDE 67

Daniel 7–12

DANIEL'S PROPHECIES

Overview

Much of Scripture is predictive. This means that we cannot ignore a study of prophecy. In addition, the accuracy of biblical predictions sets God aside from all that men have ever called "god." As Isaiah says, what pagan deity can:

> Declare to us the things to come, tell us what the future holds, so we may know that you are gods.
>
> Isaiah 41:23

Yet God can say through His prophet both that "the former things have taken place" and that "new things I declare; before they spring into being I announce them to you" (42:9).

The Book of Daniel contains some of the most spectacular prophecies, *because many of them have been fulfilled*—but hundreds of years after Daniel recorded them! Other prophecies of Daniel are yet to be fulfilled! And Jesus Himself told His followers to watch for an event "spoken of through the Prophet Daniel" (Matt. 24:15).

Some of the prophetic themes you meet in this book concern world empires from Babylon to the time of Christ, the coming of Messiah, and the days of the Antichrist.

■ For a careful, verse-by-verse exploration of Daniel's prophecies see the *Bible Knowledge Commentary*, pages 1323-1375.

Commentary

It is clear from Isaiah's words to the people of his day that one function of prophecy is to encourage God's people to trust Him. Predictions which *always are fulfilled* are clear indications that there is something beyond nature. And fulfilled prophecies also indicate that the supernatural either knows the future—or controls events in this world.

But prophecy in Scripture is more than evidence of the existence of God. Prophecy says something about God's involvement in the lives of His people.

Deuteronomy 18:9-22. This passage contains one of the most significant instructions given by Moses just before Israel passed over the Jordan River into the Promised Land. God's people had just been delivered from Egyptian slavery; they were about to enter a settled land with a culture marked by a profusion of gods and goddesses. These were mainly nature gods, associated with the cycle of the seasons and the fertility of the land and people. Some of the practices associated with this faith, called by God "detestable practices," are seen in the divine prohibition against practice of the occult.

> Do not learn to imitate the detestable ways of the nations there. Let no one be found among you who sacrifices his son or daughter in the fire, who practices divination or sorcery, interprets omens, or engages in witchcraft, or casts spells, or who is a medium or spiritist or who consults the dead. Anyone who does these things is detestable to the Lord.
>
> Deuteronomy 18:9-12

There was then, and still is, a deep human attraction to the occult. Each of us at times senses the frustrations of the limits of our nature; each of us wants some insight, some guidance, some kind of supernatural assurance that our choices are good ones, or that at least everything will come out all right. Tarot cards and Ouija boards may be different means than were used by the ancients, but the purpose is the same. Astrology has hardly changed at all. Through these means people reach out to grasp at something beyond the natural, at something supernatural to bring them aid.

In this Deuteronomy passage God strictly

forbids an appeal to the occult by His people. Yes, there *is* a supernatural world, and through the occult it may be contacted. But the contact is with evil, not with good!

What is more, the believer is *not* cut off from contact with the supernatural. In fact, contact is invited—with God. God seeks a *personal relationship* with man. This is not a relationship initiated by us through questionable intermediaries, but a direct relationship initiated by God. The breakthrough into the supernatural is made by Him from His side of the barrier, not by us from our side. So Deuteronomy promises just the kind of guidance and help we would long for. Moses went on:

> The Lord your God will raise up for you a prophet like me from among your own brothers. You must listen to him. . . . I [the Lord] will put My words in his mouth, and he will tell them everything I command him.
>
> Deuteronomy 18:15, 18

The prophetic movement in Israel was not primarily to authenticate the supernatural. Rather it developed in fulfillment of God's promise to speak to His people whenever they needed fresh guidance. God committed Himself to speak to the Old Testament believers through the prophets.

The prophets' ministry. Tracing through the Old Testament, we can see several characteristics of the prophets' ministry. First, it was primarily religious. The prophets did not normally speak about when to plant crops or when to harvest. They occasionally guided military activities. But their main focus was on the ongoing relationship of the people with their Lord. Again and again we hear the prophets rebuke sin, and promise restoration if the people will return to God.

Second, we note that the prophet's words always spring from the context of their own times, and are addressed to their contemporaries.

Third, as we will see, Old Testament prophecy is definitely predictive. It is teleological: it looks forward to an end, a culmination. What is said to a contemporary generation is said *in view of a destiny* which the prophet sees as fast approaching.

Old Testament prophecy was not an everyday kind of thing. In those days as in ours, the believer was to walk by faith in obedience to the written Word. Yet whenever history seemed to take a turn away from God, or when special help and guidance was necessary, God's promised messenger did appear.

The messenger. The Bible speaks of false and true prophets, and tells us how to distinguish them. A true prophet was (1) from your countrymen (Deut. 18:18), a Hebrew; (2) spoke in Yahweh's name rather than in the name of a pagan god or goddess; and (3) his commission was validated by fulfilled prediction.

> You may say to yourselves, "How can we know when a message has not been spoken by the Lord?" If what a prophet proclaims in the name of the Lord does not take place or come true, that is a message the Lord has not spoken.
>
> Deuteronomy 18:21

Here is a decisive test. What the prophet predicts must *always* come true! If his predictions do not come to pass, then his words can be discounted, and he need not be heeded.

This helps us account for an interesting phenomenon. Even those prophets who deal with the most far-flung future, focusing nearly all their attention on the end of time, also utter short-term prophecies. It is these prophecies, whose accuracy can be authenticated by the prophets' contemporaries, which establish him as God's spokesman.

No wonder the Book of Daniel records not only the miraculous interpretation of Nebuchadnezzar's first dream, but also the prophecy of Nebuchadnezzar's madness. Within a year, what Daniel foretold did come to pass; within seven more the king was restored to his throne, and then he recognized God as Lord. With Daniel's credentials established by prophecies that could be tested within the prophet's own time, Daniel's portraits of the far future would be studied with wonder—and with belief.

It is even more striking for us, looking back over the centuries, to see the accuracy with which Daniel outlined centuries of world history between his own day and the coming of Jesus. Surely God can boldly proclaim:

> See, the former things have taken place,

> and new things I declare; before they spring into being I announce them to you.
>
> Isaiah 42:9

Daniel—History Ahead: Daniel 7–8
These two chapters contain prophecies which came to Daniel as visions, and were interpreted by him. Each has to do with the same events; the doubling of the prophecy being a sign of its certainty.

It is clear that the focus is on governments; on four world empires. The first is that of Nebuchadnezzar; the second is Cyrus' Media-Persian Empire; and the third is the Greek (Hellenistic) Empire won by Alexander the Great and, on his death, divided among four of his generals. The fourth empire is not identified, but in the sequence of history it is clear that this must be Rome.

It is also clear that the visions of Daniel 7 and 8 correspond with the vision of the great statue recorded in Daniel 2.

Each of these three prophetic teachings focuses on the Gentile world powers that were to rule as history moved toward its culmination. In each teaching, the fourth empire is to be replaced by a kingdom set up by the Lord of heaven.

In Daniel 2, we have the picture of a stone cut without tools from a mountain, which dashes the previous governments into pieces and grows to fill the whole earth.

In Daniel 7, we have the picture of the Ancient of Days seated in judgment, destroying the final enemy. Then, "with the clouds of heaven," a "Son of man" comes to receive dominion and glory and the kingdom. He rules forever.

In Daniel 8, we again see the final enemy destroyed by the Prince of princes . . . but only after the very sanctuary of God has suffered revolting sacrilege (v. 13).

This later prophecy is not explained to Daniel, for his angelic interpreter reports that "the vision concerns the time of the end" (v. 17).

It is in fact these prophecies, with their accurate portrayal of the history of the fifth through second centuries B.C., that have led many to question Daniel's authorship of the book. How could such details as the death of Alexander and the division of his kingdom be told *before* the fact? To anyone unwilling to admit the supernatural, there must be some alternate explanation. Espe-

	Babylon (605–538 B.C.)	Medo-Persia (538–331 B.C.)	Greece (331–146 B.C.)	Rome (146 B.C.–A.D. 476)
Daniel 2:31-45 Dream image (603 B.C.)	Head of gold (2:32, 37-38)	Breast, arms of silver (2:32, 39)	Belly, thighs of brass (2:32, 39)	Legs of iron Feet of iron and clay (2:33, 40-41)
Daniel 7 First vision: Four beasts (553 B.C.)	Lion (7:4)	Bear (7:5)	Leopard (7:6)	Strong Beast (7:7, 11, 19, 23)
Daniel 8 Second vision: Ram and goat (551 B.C.)		Ram (8:3-4, 20)	Goat with one horn 8:5-8, 21) Four horns (8:8, 22) Little horn (8:9-14)	

Fulfilled Prophecies in Daniel 2, 7–8

cially in view of the *detailed* accuracy of the prophecy, commented on here in this extended quote from Leon Wood's *Commentary on Daniel* (Zondervan, p. 211f).

> 8:8 Thus "the he-goat became very great; but when he was strong the great horn was broken, and in place of it came up four winds of heaven."
>
> *Became very great.* This is the same phrase as used regarding the ram in verse 4, except for the addition of "very." It could be translated "did very great things," but the thought would still be that the goat became very great, so as to be able to do them. The addition of the adverb, "very," is apparently meant to indicate that the he-goat became greater than the ram.
>
> *Great horn was broken.* Daniel does not state what happened in the vision to cause the great horn to be broken, but this detail is not needed to see the intended symbolism. Alexander dies when he had just subjected all Medo-Persia to himself. On returning to Babylon from the east, he was taken with a severe fever, and in June 323 B.C., died at the age of 32. He had left his country over 11 years before, and apparently never returned. He was taken in death, a young military genius, cut off at the height of achievement and power.
>
> *Four prominent horns.* Where the great horn had been, Daniel now saw four take its place. The word for "prominent" is the same as that used in verse 5, but it is used here without the preceding construct word "horn." Its use appears to be adverbial, giving the literal translation, "there came up prominently four in its place." This development is symbolic of the dividing of Alexander's vast holdings between four of his generals: Cassander receiving Macedonia and Greece; Lysimachus, Thrace and much of Asia Minor; Seleucus, Syria and vast regions to the east; and Ptolemy, Egypt. For a while a fifth, Antigonus, held territory in Asia Minor, but in 301 B.C. he was overthrown. It should be noted that the imagery employed in the vision does not imply, correctly, that Alexander himself divided the empire. He did not: the fourfold division came rather as a result of extensive fighting among the generals during 22 years.
>
> *The four winds.* Reference is to the four directions. Cassander to the west, Lysimachus to the north, Seleucus to the east, and Ptolemy to the south.

The Coming Prince: Daniel 9:24-27

Just how accurate is Bible prophecy? How sure can we be we've correctly understood a particular passage? The Book of Daniel gives unique evidence for Bible prophecy's amazing accuracy in one specific prediction that *does* (unlike most other predictions) specify the time factor. In fact, the timing is so clear that this prophecy gives us a great insight into God's overall plan as well as an explanation of why the promised destiny, the Messiah's kingdom, has not yet arrived!

In the years before the turn of the century Sir Robert Anderson, a lay theologian and Bible teacher in Great Britain, could not agree with Germany's "higher critics," who attacked the accuracy and dating of many Old Testament documents. Anderson determined to study the subject, working from the language of Scripture itself and from archeological discoveries. Thus, for instance, he used the 360-day sacred Jewish calendar rather than the Julian calendar in computing time.

Working carefully, Anderson was able to pinpoint the exact date from which, according to Daniel 9, a specific period of time was to be counted.

> Seventy "sevens" are decreed for your people and your holy city to finish transgression, to put an end to sin, to atone for wickedness, to bring in everlasting righteousness, to seal up vision and prophecy and to anoint the Most Holy. Know and understand this: From the issuing of the decree to restore and rebuild Jerusalem until the Anointed One, the ruler, comes, there will be seven "sevens," and sixty-two "sevens." It will be rebuilt with streets and a trench, but in times of trouble. After the sixty-two "sevens," the Anointed One will be cut off and will have nothing. The people of the ruler who will come will destroy the city and the sanctuary. The end will come like a flood: War will continue until the end, and desolations have been decreed. He will confirm a covenant with many for one "seven," but in the

Purpose: Destiny

- to finish transgression
- to make an end of sin
- to make atonement for iniquity
- to bring in everlasting righteousness
- to seal up vision and prophecy (i.e., to fulfill it)
- to anoint the most holy place

Chronology

69 SEVENS OF YEARS (360 days each = 173,880 days)		70TH WEEK
445 B.C. Decree to rebuild Jerusalem (Neh. 1–2; Dan. 9:25)	A.D. 32 Messiah cut off (Dan. 9:26)	A.D. ? Period of prophetic culmination

Support for the Time Gap

1. It is characteristic of Old Testament prophecy in general (e.g., Isa. 61; Luke 4).
2. The language of Daniel 9:26—"After the sixty-two 'sevens,' the Anointed One will be cut off."
3. History: "The people of the ruler who will come" (not the enemy prince himself) "will destroy the city and the sanctuary" (Dan. 9:26). This happened in A.D. 70 when a Roman army under Titus destroyed Jerusalem.
4. The New Testament (Matt. 24) expects that the events of the seventieth week are yet future.

The Seventy Weeks

> middle of that "seven" he will put an end to sacrifice and offering. And one who causes desolation will place abominations on a wing of the temple until the end that is decreed is poured out on him.
>
> Daniel 9:24-27

Sir Robert took each statement of Scripture and sorted out the dates involved. The salient aspects of this interpretation are included on the chart with these the critical elements.

Weeks. The word is *shabua,* and literally means "sevens." The Jews used this term for weeks and also for a "sabbath of years" or seven years (see Gen. 29:27; 2 Chron. 36:21). Using the Hebrew religious year, Anderson determined that a period of 490 years was divided into two separate time periods: 69 weeks (or 173,880 days) and 1 week (or 2,520 days). When did the countdown begin? And when did this first period of 69 weeks end?

Dating. Three decrees made the Jews' return to Palestine possible. The first, issued by Cyrus in 538 B.C., had to do with the rebuilding of the house of God (2 Chron. 36:22-23; Ezra 1:1). The second, issued by Darius in 521 B.C., also related to the temple (Ezra 6:3-8). The only decree that was concerned with rebuilding Jerusalem itself was issued in the twentieth year of Artaxerxes, 445 B.C. (Neh. 2:1). What is more, we know the month! Anderson proceeds to assign a day:

> The Persian edict which restored the autonomy of Judah was issued in the Jewish month of Nisan. It may in fact have been dated the 1st of Nisan, but no other

> day being named, the prophetic period must be reckoned, according to a practice common with the Jews, from the Jewish New Year's Day. The seventy weeks are therefore to be computed from the 1st of Nisan, 445 B.C. (*The Coming Prince,* Kregel).

Computing carefully, Sir Robert concluded that the 69 weeks of years would have ended on April 6 of A.D. 32—"that fateful day on which the Lord Jesus rode into Jerusalem in fulfillment of the prophecy of Zechariah 9:9; when, for the first and only occasion in all His earthly sojourn, He was acknowledged as 'Messiah the Prince, the King, the Son of David' " (p. 122).

History's end? We all know the events that followed on the heels of the Triumphal Entry. The proclaimed Messiah, Jesus, was in a few short days scorned by the very crowds who had cheered Him; He was "cut off" by execution. Out of the Crucifixion came the Resurrection, and with the Resurrection came a new and previously undisclosed turn to history.

God's plan was proving to be more complex than had been imagined. The promised Deliverer now chose *to put off* the seventieth week, the culmination of history, so yet unborn generations would have the opportunity to benefit from His work on the cross. Forgiveness for the sinner, not only establishment of a righteous kingdom, was shown in a fresh and startling way to be God's concern.

And what of the seventieth week? What of the events detailed so carefully in Daniel 10 and 11, and referred to in Daniel 8 as history's climax? If we take Bible prophecy seriously—and these amazing fulfillments tell us we must—then we must also take seriously the Old Testament's portrait of the time of the end.

That time, the last seven years of history, is still ahead. We wait for it. And it rushes toward us. We cannot avoid a destiny in which the entire universe will take part. We must come to grips with destiny, and with its implications for us.

The Seventieth Week: Daniel 11–12

Much of Daniel's revelation of the future focuses on the seventieth week: the time of the end, when history is about to experience the divinely planned culmination. Yet again, sufficient details are given concerning past history to support the complete accuracy of Daniel's prediction and to give us confidence that the unfulfilled portion will be fulfilled with the same careful attention to detail.

Daniel 11:2-4. This describes again Alexander's rise and the future division of his conquest between the four generals.

Daniel 11:5-20. Here Daniel predicted struggles between the Ptolemys (Egypt: the South) and the Selucids (the North), up until the time of Antiochus Epiphanes (ca. 175-164 B.C.). A study of the history of the intervening period shows just how literally and in what careful detail each aspect of this prophecy was fulfilled.

Daniel 11:21-35. In this section the outrages of Antiochus, who launched a crusade against the Jewish faith, are predicted. As is common in Bible prophecy, the description of this disaster shifts from the prototype Antiochus to a description of the final enemy of God's people, the Antichrist.

Daniel 11:36-45. In this passage a new personality, who is like Antiochus in his drive to persecute God's people, is introduced. With supernatural aid this individual wins great military victories and exalts himself above every god. These prophecies fit the portrait given elsewhere of the Antichrist, a satanic counterfeit of the promised Ruler of righteousness. In spite of his great victories, "he will come to his end" (v. 45).

Daniel 12:1-4. Daniel's interpreter now went on to speak of that period when the enemy will be unveiled, calling it a "time of distress such as has not happened from the beginning of nations until then" (v. 1). In spite of the Great Tribulation by which those days are marked, deliverance comes to God's people. The period culminates in a bodily resurrection to "everlasting life" (v. 2). This is the first scriptural usage of this term—a common one in the New Testament. It is not, however, the first reference to a bodily resurrection (cf. Job 14:11-14; 19:25-27; Pss. 16:10; 49:15; Isa. 25:8; 26:19; Hosea 13:14). The resurrection of the ungodly is also spoken of here as a restoration "to shame and everlasting contempt" (Dan. 12:2).

Daniel 12:5-13. The final section of the Book of Daniel seems to give a general chronology of this time of the end. Of particular note is the time period of 1,290 days specified in verse 11, just 30 days beyond half of the last seven-year period of foretold history. Why the extra 30 days? The reason is uncertain, though some have suggested that they refer to the time of judgment for the nations mentioned by Jesus in Matthew 25:31-46 as following the Great Tribulation period.

Whatever the reason, if we take the pattern of fulfilled prophecy as our guide, we can expect these to be literal days; and that when history overtakes prophecy, every detail will be seen and understood.

TEACHING GUIDE

Prepare

What does the fact that God knows and controls the future mean to you? What do you want this wonderful truth to mean to your group as you study Daniel this week?

Explore

1. Put a three-column chart on the chalkboard, labeling the first column "1 year," the second "5 years," and the third "100 years."

Then ask several members of your group to "prophesy" local, national, or international events to happen this year, within 5 years, and in the next 100 years.

Record their "prophecies" and then discuss: "How great is the likelihood of any or all of these actually happening?"

2. Point out that biblical prophecy is completely accurate. Illustrate this with minilectures on *both* Daniel's prophecies about world empires, and his prophecy concerning the date of the appearance of the Messiah. Duplicate the charts in this chapter to hand out or to show on the overhead to illustrate your lectures.

Expand

Some of Daniel's prophecy seems to focus on the "seventieth week"—the last seven years with which Daniel's prophecy of the Messiah deals. That seven years is still future. But what is to happen during it?

Like other biblical prophecy all the details are not clear. But your group members can discover much by looking in teams at these passages—and trying to answer the following questions.

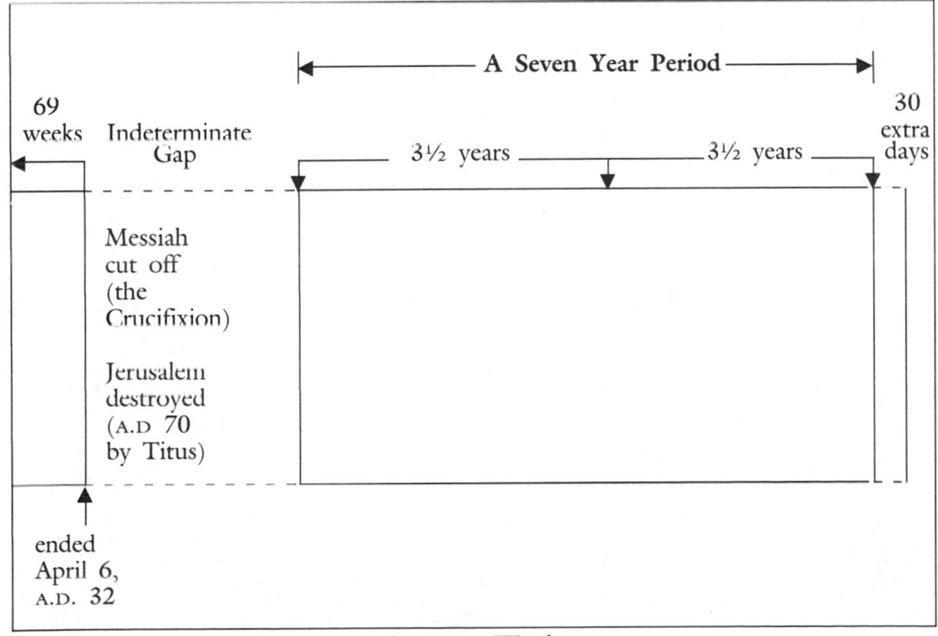

Seventy Weeks

Daniel 2:33-45 Daniel 9:27
Daniel 7:7-28 Daniel 11:36-45
Daniel 8:23-25 Daniel 12:1-13

• What time frame is in view, and how is it divided? • Who are the chief characters in the final drama, and what are their parts? • What events will take place in the final "week of years," and what can we tell of their sequence? • What will *follow* the "last week"?

Again, remember that details, like order and sequence or timing of prophesied events, are often unclear. So we should not be dogmatic in our interpretation of prophecy. What we can do is to discover major events, and then wait until history unveils the details.

You may want to use the "End Time" chart to help your group summarize.

Apply

Share: "How does it make you feel to realize that current events are under God's control, and moving toward a future which He has planned?"

STUDY GUIDE 68

Hosea

SPIRITUAL ADULTERY

Overview

Hosea lived and ministered in Israel in the days of the Divided Kingdom. He preached during the later years of Jeroboam II, a time of great material prosperity (about 753–723 B.C.).

Hosea's mission was both special and painful. He was called to experience the anguish caused by an unfaithful wife: a wife whose sexual adultery mirrored the spiritual adultery of the nation Israel, which had been unfaithful to the Lord by worshiping idols and rejecting the holiness in His Law. The names of his children were chosen by God as reminders of Israel's unfaithfulness.

The outline of the Book of Hosea reflects the prophet's calling.

Outline

I. Unfaithful Wife	1–3
II. Unfaithful People	4–14
A. Sins denounced	4–8
B. Doom announced	9–10
C. Love affirmed	11
D. Discipline	12–13
E. Blessing	14

▶ ***Grace.*** The Book of Hosea illustrates powerfully the Old Testament concept of grace. The Hebrew word *hesed*, often translated "mercy" in the KJV and "loving-kindness" or "steadfast love" in recent translations, indicates God's total commitment to be faithful to those He has chosen. The people of Israel, like Hosea's wife, were unfaithful in their relationship with the Lord. But God would remain faithful, first disciplining Israel, but then restoring them to an intimate relationship with Himself.

■ For a verse-by-verse study of Hosea, see the *Bible Knowledge Commentary*, pages 1377-1407.

Commentary

Unfaithful Wife: Hosea 1–3

There are many experiences that cause us pain. But one of the most painful of all must be the unfaithfulness of a marriage partner.

For Hosea, who married "an adulterous wife," that pain was not just something occasioned by a single fall. Hosea's wife Gomer practiced unfaithfulness as a lifestyle. Ultimately she left the prophet and their three children, to live with a series of other men. Yet Hosea continued to care for her.

♥ ***Link to Life: Youth / Adult***

Begin with a "counseling case history." Ask your group members what advice they would give to Mr. H. Mr. H.'s wife has left him and their three children (two of them teens). She's moved to another town, and has been living with a series of different men. Even though Mr. H. has tried repeatedly to get her to return, and even helped her out financially when she has had money problems, she just laughs at him. Still, Mr. H. can't seem to accept what has happened, and dreams of getting his wife back.

"What advice would you give Mr. H.? How would you justify your advice biblically?"

Let your group discuss this thoroughly. Some may believe he should get a divorce (he does have grounds). Others may call for continuing forgiveness. Don't express a personal opinion, but let your members explore options.

While Hosea could have validly divorced his wife under the Law, this was something he simply could not do. Despite the anguish he felt, Hosea continued to love Gomer.

This was admittedly unusual. Hosea had been called by God to demonstrate both the

Lord's personal pain and His utter faithfulness. Hosea did demonstrate God's character and His commitment by his continuing faithfulness to his prostitute wife.

Surely God must have given Hosea the grace to live through this agonizing experience!

We don't know how many years Hosea lived this way—rejected, feeling agonizing pain, but continuing to love.

Hosea 1–3 tells us that the prophet was called by God to "take to yourself an adulterous wife" because "the land is guilty of the vilest adultery in departing from the Lord" (1:2). It is likely that this revelation was given Hosea *before* his marriage, and that Gomer may have been an active prostitute before she became a bride. If so, Hosea, like Isaiah and Jeremiah and Ezekiel, was warned in advance of the personal cost of obedience to the Lord.

Chapter 2 is a poem, expressing both Hosea's and God's feelings as they experienced a beloved's unfaithfulness. The choice of adultery to represent spiritual unfaithfulness is purposive. When God brought Israel into the Promised Land, He told His people they were to supplant a corrupt civilization. The religion of the land was essentially a fertility faith that linked the land's fruitfulness to the supposed sexual activity of gods and goddesses. When the male lord or owner god (Baal) and his consort (Astarte, or Asherah) engaged in sex, the land was stimulated to produce crops. The fertility of animals and people too was assumed to be linked to the sexual activity of these nature gods.

As an expression of this belief, the worship of the pagan gods and goddesses at local shrines and high places was typically marked by drunkenness and orgy. Male and female prostitutes joined in erotic acts intended to sexually stimulate the gods, and make the land fertile.

By the time of Hosea, many of the practices of Canaanite worship were actually integrated with the worship of the Lord. Local shrines were erected, and religious celebration often involved debauchery. So idolatry and sexual looseness were actually linked in Hosea's day. The imagery of Israel as the adulterous wife of the Lord was appropriate, for adultery was often an integral part of the pagan worship experience.

There is another close link between adultery and idolatry.

Adultery is unfaithfulness in what is intended to be a lifelong commitment. Marriage is intended to bond a man and woman together for their lifetimes. One who turns from his or her partner to others has violated that commitment.

God too calls His people to a lifelong commitment. Believers are to be totally faithful to God, and not to waver in their allegiance to Him. In Old Testament times unfaithfulness to God often was seen in idolatry. But it was also expressed in injustice—in a violation of the divine Law motivated by a greed for wealth or material possessions.

Whatever it may be that leads a person to turn from a commitment to a life-partner or to God, that unfaithfulness will cause great pain. Just as it caused Hosea pain. Just as it has caused unnumbered husbands and wives pain. Just as the unfaithfulness of God's people to Him has caused Him intense pain as well.

Yet Hosea 3 tells us that finally, after years of unfaithfulness, God told the prophet, "Go, show your love to your wife again, though she is loved by another and is an adulteress. Love her as the Lord loves the Israelites, though they turn to other gods" (3:1).

Following God's instructions the prophet found Gomer. She apparently had been forced finally to sell herself as a bondservant. Hosea paid the price to buy back her contract, and then took her home "to live with me" (v. 3). In this Hosea acted as God Himself would act. There would be a terrible time of separation as Israel was torn from her land. But God would remain faithful, and finally would bring His people back to their land. "Afterward," the prophet is told, "the Israelites will return and seek the Lord their God and David their king. They will come trembling to the Lord and to His blessings in the last days" (v. 5).

♥ ***Link to Life: Youth / Adult***

After your group has debated how to advise Mr. H., tell the story of Hosea and Gomer. Explain the link in Old Testament times between adultery and idolatry. Explain too that Hosea's call to remain faithful to her was a call to represent God to unfaithful Israel.

Then discuss: "Is Hosea's faithfulness

to an unfaithful wife a model for Christians? What is the place of forgiveness in cases of unfaithfulnes in Christian marriage? Under what conditions should Hosea's experience not *be considered normative?"*

NOTE: If no one else makes this observation, note that God expressly called Hosea to his wife and his life. Each Christian is to respond to Jesus' guidance in his or her own life. Saints like Hosea can lead us to think of our personal situations in fresh ways, and to consider various options. But we must each ultimately be led by Jesus to the choices He wants us to make in our own lives, except where a clear yes or no in Scripture makes His will plain.

God's Unfaithful People: Hosea 4–14

The first ruler of the Northern Kingdom, Jeroboam I, had set up a false worship system that counterfeited the sacrifices, the priesthood, the worship center, and the annual worship festivals established in God's Law. Each ruler of Israel continued this evil, and some actively promoted idolatry. The kings also promoted a materialistic life. Thus Hosea was right when he charged Israel's rulers, saying, "All their leaders are rebellious" (9:15).

In the days of Hosea Israel was a prosperous nation. Her aggressive ruler, Jeroboam II, multiplied his country's territory and defeated her enemies. Control of trade routes brought unexpected wealth. Yet the political life of Israel was marked by murders, intrigues, and many other evils. The wealthy oppressed the poor, and those in authority accepted their bribes. In every significant way, Israel was a land whose people had proven completely unfaithful to the Lord.

Now the prophet moved from his own experience with Gomer to show the parallels that existed in the Lord's relationship with Israel.

Sins denounced (Hosea 4–8). Among the violations of God's laws that called out for judgment were cursing, lying, murder, stealing, and adultery (4:1-2). The people even practiced ritual prostitution in conjunction with their adultery (vv. 4-14). The arrogance of this people was so great that they could never find God (5:1-7). Surely a terrible time of wrath would come (vv. 8-12).

Hosea contrasted Israel's words and her verbal repentance with her actions. It was what she did rather than what she said that demonstrated the nature of her heart attitude. And what marked Israel's lifestyle? Deceit and thievery (7:1-2), and royal drunkenness and intrigue (vv. 3-8). To such a people "repent" was an empty word, and whatever this people said they simply had not returned to God (vv. 9-16).

As a result, judgment would come like a tornado and tear up God's people (8:1-14).

♥ ***Link to Life: Youth / Adult***

What constitutes spiritual adultery or unfaithfulness to the Lord? Have teams examine Hosea 4–5 and 6–7. Each is to list *the sins that Hosea described.*

Then each group is to try to define "spiritual unfaithfulness" for contemporary Christians. We do not worship idols. How then does a person exhibit unfaithfulness in his or her relationship with the Lord?

After each team has defined spiritual unfaithfulness, come together to share and compare findings.

Doom announced (Hosea 9–10). Hosea warned that judgment must come "because of all their wickedness" (9:15). The people of Israel (called Ephraim in this book because Jeroboam II was from the tribe of Ephraim) had rejected God. Now they would be rejected by Him and "they will be wanderers among the nations" (v. 17).

Love affirmed (Hosea 11). In one of Scripture's most beautiful chapters God expressed His continuing love for His people. They had hurt Him deeply. But God could not help loving them.

> When Israel was a child, I loved him, and out of Egypt I called My son. But the more I called Israel, the further they went from Me. They sacrificed to the Baals and they burned incense to images. It was I who taught Ephraim to walk, taking them by the arms; but they did not realize it was I who healed them. I led them with cords of human kindness, with ties of love; I lifted the yoke from their neck and bent down to feed them. . . . How can I give you up, Ephraim? How can I hand you over, Israel? How can I treat you like Admah? How can I make you like Zeboiim? My heart is changed within Me; all My compassion

> is aroused. I will not carry out My fierce anger, nor devastate Ephraim again. For I am God, and not man—the Holy One among you.
>
> Hosea 11:1-4, 8-9

Discipline (Hosea 12–13). The judgment which Israel was about to experience was terrible. But it would not lead to final destruction.

But discipline there *must* be. God must "punish Jacob according to his ways and repay him according to his deeds" (12:2).

Again Hosea recounted some of the sins of the people which called for judgment.

> The merchant uses dishonest scales; he loves to defraud. Ephraim boasts, "I am very rich; I have become wealthy. With all my wealth they will not find in me any iniquity or sin [that is, wealth can be used to bribe the judges so they acquit me]."
>
> Hosea 12:7-8

Only a return to God, demonstrated by a commitment to maintain love and justice, could win a reprieve.

Yet, despite evidence of God's love, Israel would not respond. The God who once "cared for you in the desert" (13:5) would turn on them like a fierce beast (vv. 7-8).

> The people of Samaria [Israel's capital] must bear their guilt, because they have rebelled against their God.
>
> Hosea 13:16

Final blessings (Hosea 14). Even though the sins of Israel had been their downfall, they could return to the Lord.

> Say to Him: "Forgive all our sins and receive us graciously, that we may offer the fruit of our lips."
>
> Hosea 14:2

That day of return will surely come. And when it does, God makes His wayward people a promise.

> I will heal their waywardness and love them freely, for My anger has turned away from them.
>
> Hosea 14:4

TEACHING GUIDE

Prepare
Consider how great God's faithfulness is in the light of our unfaithfulness to Him.

Explore
1. Open class with a discussion of the case of "Mr. H.," whose wife has deserted him and their three children. See the "link-to-life" idea at the beginning of this guide.
2. Tell the story of Hosea, and his years-long suffering before a reconciliation with Gomer.

Go back then and reevaluate the earlier discussion. Especially explore whether or not Hosea's commitment (like God's) to an unfaithful partner is to be considered normative for believers today whose spouses might prove unfaithful.

Expand
1. Work in teams to define spiritual unfaithfulness. What do we learn from Hosea 4–8 that helps us understand how moderns might be unfaithful to God? How moderns might be more faithful to God? See "link-to-life," page 453.
2. Or, raise the question: "How does God feel about us when we have failed Him?" Ask your group members to find one verse in Hosea 11 which expresses God's feelings when we are unfaithful, and one verse there which expresses His attitude toward us.

Compare verses, asking each person to explain why he or she made a particular choice.

How good to know that God has a deep and tender love for us, and that when we turn to Him He forgives us freely.

Apply
Place the last verse of Hosea on the chalkboard:

> Who is wise? He will realize these things. Who is discerning? He will understand them. The ways of the Lord are right;

the righteous walk in them, but the rebellious stumble in them.

Hosea 14:9

Go around the circle and ask each person to make one observation on what this verse says to him or her after your study of Hosea.

	Adultery	**Prostitution** (Fornication)
OT	*nā'ap̱*	*zānâh*
NT	*moicheia*	*porneia*
differences	usually refers to men relations with a married person not spouse not a professional prostitute death penalty appropriate	usually refers to women relations outside of marriage often a professional prostitute death penalty not appropriate
similarities	both are forbidden by God both are used figuratively to represent spiritual and moral unfaithfulness both merit and will receive divine punishment	

STUDY GUIDE 69

Joel

FINAL JUDGMENT

Overview

No date is given by Joel, son of Pethuel, for his ministry. He mentions a still-standing Jerusalem. The enemies he speaks of are those of Judah before the Babylonian Captivity. But we cannot fix the exact time of his writing.

The structure of Joel is simple. The prophet is moved by a plague of locusts, sent as divine discipline. He envisions a great act of judgment at history's end which will purify his people and lead to national conversion.

Many powerful phrases and wonderful promises dot this brief Old Testament prophetic book.

"Rend your heart, and not your garments" (Joel 2:13).

"I will repay you for the years the locusts have eaten" (v. 25).

"I will pour out My Spirit on all people" (v. 28).

Against the background of a series of superficial revivals in Judah, Joel uttered a call for deep commitment to God—and described the blessings that total commitment would bring.

▶ ***Locusts.*** Nine Hebrew words are translated "locusts" in English versions, suggesting the importance of these terrifying insects. They multiplied at an incredible rate, swarming together in clouds that blotted out the sun. Every living plant was stripped to the ground where they passed. One swarm that crossed the Red Sea in 1899 was estimated to cover 2,000 square miles! What an appropriate symbol of devastation! No wonder locusts who visited Judah suggested final judgment to Joel.

Commentary

When Solomon's kingdom was torn in 931 B.C., the Southern Kingdom, Judah, comprised considerably less territory and had a much smaller population than the Northern. In the initial years of conflict between the two kingdoms, however, many from Israel drifted across the border. Committed to the worship of Yahweh, they remained faithful to the Jerusalem temple and to the festivals that God had instituted through Moses. They rejected Bethel and Dan and the counterfeit priesthood ordained for the North by King Jeroboam I.

But as the decades passed, the once-united nation accepted its divided state. And any initial claim of Judah to a special godliness was lost.

Of Judah's 19 kings, Scripture marks out 8 as "good." Generally these kings stimulated revivals. Yet the fact that the Southern Kingdom even needed revival, plus the Bible's description of the sins that were put away, tells us that Judah tended to fall into the same apostasy that plagued Israel.

King Asa, who ruled from 911–870 B.C. (2 Chron. 14–15), removed idols from the land as well as the male prostitutes associated with their worship. He also deposed his grandmother as queen mother because she had made an idol to Asherah. Encouraged by the Prophet Azariah, Asa led the people of Judah to renew their covenant promises to God.

Yet Asa himself did not remain committed to God. In his later years, he imprisoned the Prophet Hanani for rebuking him, and he failed to turn to God for aid when he was ill (2 Chron. 16).

Jehoshaphat, Asa's son, also followed the Lord. Like Asa, he attempted to root out the worship of Baal and removed many "high places." These high places (*bamoth*) were elevations set aside for pagan worship. Each contained an altar featuring idols. Sometimes the Hebrews would set aside a high place for the worship of the Lord and would ordain local priests. This practice was

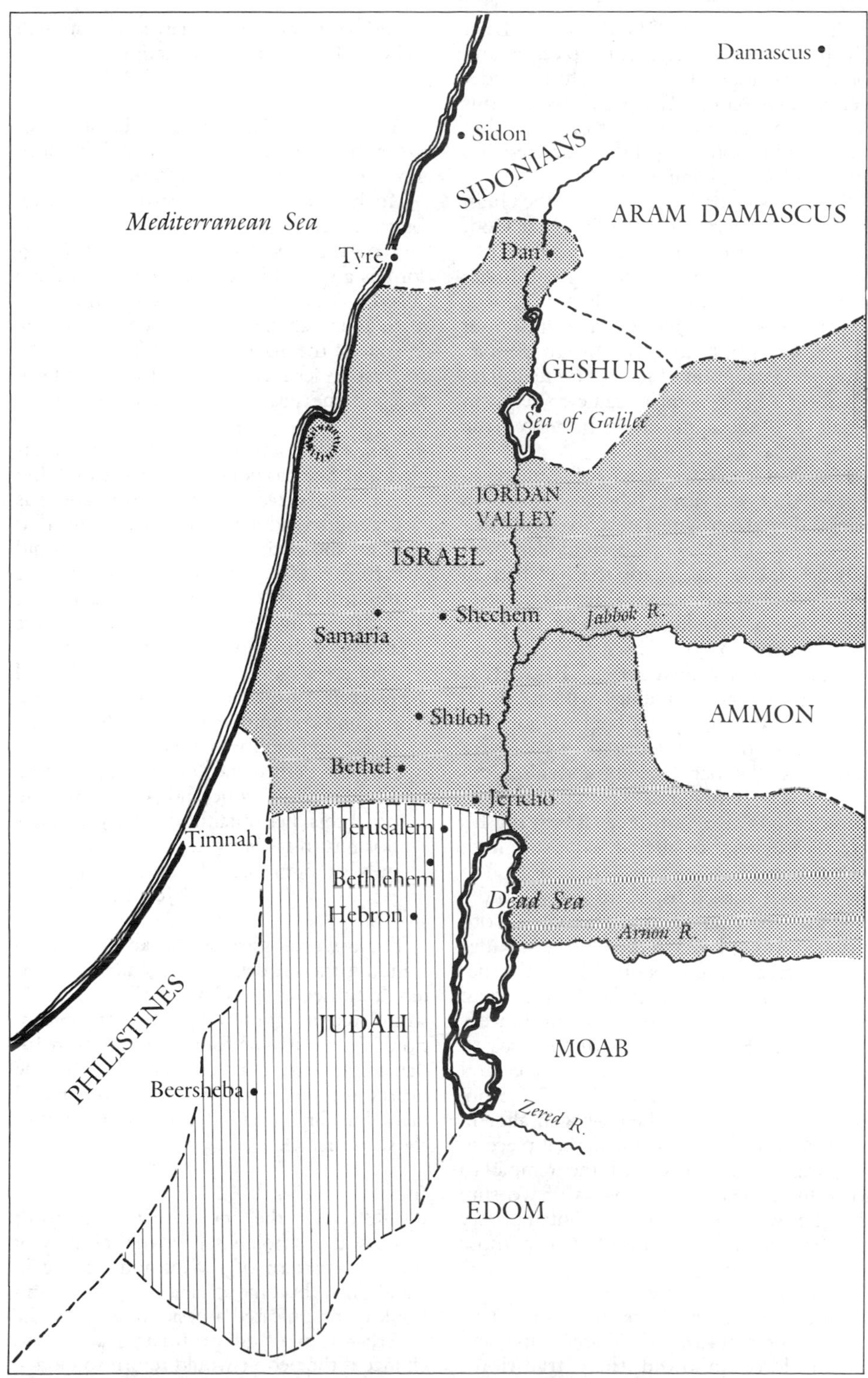
Damascus
Sidon
SIDONIANS
Mediterranean Sea
ARAM DAMASCUS
Tyre
Dan
GESHUR
Sea of Galilee
JORDAN
VALLEY
ISRAEL
Samaria
Shechem
Jabbok R.
Shiloh
AMMON
Bethel
Jericho
Timnah
Jerusalem
Bethlehem
Hebron
Dead Sea
Arnon R.
PHILISTINES
JUDAH
MOAB
Beersheba
Zered R.
EDOM

The Divided Kingdom

in direct violation of Old Testament Law, which called for a single worship center and for a priesthood drawn entirely from descendants of Aaron. The pagan associations of worship were much too strong: worship there would soon take on the characteristics of occultism and immorality.

So Jehoshaphat's attack on the high places was undertaken out of zeal for God, as was his insistence that the Levites resume their ministry of traveling throughout Judah to teach the "Book of the Law" (17:9).

The next kings of Judah were evil, and set an example gladly followed by the people. Athaliah, a daughter of Jezebel (wife of Israel's King Ahab), actually came to reign in Judah, and she aggressively promoted the cult of Baal.

However, there was a core of godly resistance. After six years, Jehoiada, the high priest, secretly crowned seven-year-old Joash as king. The boy had been hidden from Athaliah for six years, for she had had all other possible claimants to the throne executed. But now military and religious leaders combined to bring about the coup, and Athaliah was executed (cf. 22:10–23:15).

Joash and the four kings who followed him were relatively good kings. Under Joash (835–796 B.C.) the priests of Baal were killed and the pagan altars and idols destroyed. The temple was repaired, and worship of God was reinstituted. But in Joash's later years, he also faltered. After the high priest who had crowned and advised him died, Joash turned aside from the Lord.

Under the later kings, Judah knew both trial and triumph. As in the Northern Kingdom, increasing prosperity led to the neglect of faith. Ahaz, Judah's king from 732–715 B.C., the years preceding the destruction of Samaria, committed himself to evil. He promoted the worship of Baal and even engaged in infant sacrifice (2 Chron. 28:3). He also established a pagan altar in the Jerusalem temple as the official place of sacrifice. Finally he closed the temple to force his people into the ways of worship that he wanted. Micah, a contemporary prophet, cried out against Judah in those days:

> You have observed the statutes of Omri and all the practices of Ahab's house, and you have followed their traditions. Therefore I will give you over to ruin and your people to derision; you will bear the scorn of the nations.
>
> Micah 6:16

How little difference could be seen between the sins of the Northern Kingdom and the lifestyle of "godly" Judah!

Much later, as the destruction Micah foretold actually struck, Jeremiah looked back on the captivity of the Northen Kingdom as a special lesson to Judah—a unique call to revival. The words God communicated to Jeremiah clearly indicated that all the revivals of the Southern Kingdom, even the greatest under Hezekiah and Josiah, had not touched the hearts of God's chosen.

> "Have you seen what faithless Israel has done? She has gone up on every high hill and under ever spreading tree and has committed adultery there. I thought that after she had done all this she would return to Me but she did not, and her unfaithful sister Judah saw it. I gave faithless Israel her certificate of divorce and sent her away because of all her adulteries. Yet I saw that her unfaithful sister Judah had no fear; she also went out and committed adultery. Because Israel's immorality mattered so little to her, she defiled the land and committed adultery with stone and wood. In spite of all this, her unfaithful sister Judah did not return to Me with all her heart, but only in pretense," declares the Lord.
>
> Jeremiah 3:6-10

These words give us the key to understanding the burden of Joel. Judah had often "returned to God" in a series of revivals stimulated by godly kings. But "in deception." The outward form of religion in Judah might have been correct then. But the hearts of the men and women of Judah had drifted as far from God as had the hearts of those of Israel.

Joel

By 830 B.C., the approximate date most conservative scholars set for the ministry of Joel, the pattern of revival and decline in Judah had become clear. Just as Jonah's book communicated a basic message to the North—a message promising a second chance if the people would return to God—so the Book of Joel contained a basic message to Judah. Through the decades of ups and downs, of revival and apostasy, the words of Joel would echo in the ears of a "religious" people as a call for *wholehearted* return. Superficial reform, or ritual revival, could never bring the blessing that would follow true revival. Listen to Joel's words, as his message is made perfectly clear.

> "Even now," declares the Lord, "return to Me with all your heart, with fasting and weeping and mourning." Rend your heart and not your garments. Return to the Lord your God, for He is gracious and compassionate, slow to anger and abounding in love, and He relents from sending calamity. Who knows? He may turn and have pity and leave behind a blessing—grain offerings and a drink offering for the Lord your God. Blow the trumpet in Zion, declare a holy fast, call a sacred assembly. Gather the people, consecrate the assembly; bring together the elders, gather the children, those nursing at the breast. Let the bridegroom leave his room and the bride her chamber. Let the priests, who minister before the Lord, weep between the temple porch and the altar. Let them say, "Spare Your people, O Lord. Do not make Your inheritance an object of scorn, a byword among the nations. Why should they say among the peoples, 'Where is their God?' " Then the Lord will be jealous for His land and take pity on His people.
>
> Joel 2:12-18

Joel's message breaks naturally into two sections. The first, 1:2–2:17, is words of the prophet himself rather than a divine revelation.

Apparently a series of calamities, especially a great swarm of locusts, had struck Judah. Joel looked on this insect horde as a forerunner of even more terrible punishments. Unless God's people came to *genuine* repentance. Both the locusts and the human enemy they might foreshadow were recognized by Joel as being led by Yahweh Himself. Only destruction could follow should God's people waver between holiness and evil; between the Lord and the sensual pagan gods of Canaan.

The second section of Joel (2:18–3:21) contains Yahweh's response. God promised that after His people returned to Him "with all your heart" they would know the fullness of blessing promised under the ancient Abrahamic Covenant. The land would overflow with produce (2:19, 21-26; 3:18). Judah's enemies would be overcome (2:20; 3:1-17, 19-20). God Himself would be among His people in a unique way (2:27), and they would be regathered from the lands in which they have been scattered (3:5-7). Great spiritual blessing would be poured out on all mankind as a consequence of the return of God's people to Him (2:28-32).

The message of Joel can be summarized in three simple statements.

(1) *Calamities are God's warning of judgment to come.*

(2) *Heed these warnings, and return to God with all your heart.*

(3) *When you return to God, God's fullest blessings will be poured out on you and on all people.*

Judah, which had become a land of superficial religion, had in Joel's prophecy a basic message that would be reflected in the ministry of each prophet God would later send. But the revivals that did follow would never penetrate to the heart, or call forth the full commitment of God's people. Like her sister kingdom to the North, Judah would appear at public worship and pretend, but then would slip away to the high places and be unfaithful to her God.

Predictive Elements

There are elements in Joel's prophecy which modern scholars believe firmly refer to events that lie in our own future. And the great promise of the pouring out of God's Spirit, partially fulfilled and surely illustrated on the Day of Pentecost (see Acts 2:14-36), is something that has already come to pass. But we need to be careful. Very often Old Testament books are studied solely to isolate their indications on the future, and to discover details which can be slipped into our eschatological charts.

There *is* a still-future dimension to many Old Testament writings. In some prophetic books, large sections are specifically devoted to pictures of the future.

But when we read an Old Testament prophet such as Joel, we must realize that first of all, *each prophet presented a message to the people of his own time.* Joel and the rest were God's spokesmen to a living people. Each message was shaped to his own historical setting and conditions. Whatever picture Joel may give of the future, we need to concentrate on the book's purpose *in that historical setting* if we are to understand its basic message for us today.

With Joel, that message is clear. To a land that knew many superficial revivals, God's prophet communicated a vital truth. *Superficial religion and a divided heart can never satisfy God.* Any revival that substitutes emotionalism, with repeated altar calls and repeated failures, is no pattern for our relationship with God. To know God and to be His people calls for full commitment.

Christ's invitation in the Gospel is not just to return, but to return with all our heart. Complete commitment remains God's unchanging avenue to blessing.

TEACHING GUIDE

Prepare
Select from Joel one verse which seems to you to best sum up the message *most needed* by your group members.

Explore
Begin with a minilecture, sketching the historical context of Joel's message. You'll want to review the pattern of revivalism seen in Judah—and the evidence that these returns did not represent a true *national* return to the Lord.

Explain that Joel called for a *wholehearted* return to God rather than a superficial revival.

Expand
1. Put the following outline of Joel on the chalkboard:

I. The Locust Plague	1:1–2:27
II. The Day of the Lord	2:28–3:21

Explain how the actual plague of locusts, a contemporary judgment on Judah, stimulated the prophet to a vision of final judgment and to his warning of Judah.

List the three themes of that message given in this unit. Ask group members to select *one* of the three to explore. Those who select the same theme can work together to discover just what Joel said about this subject and to prepare a report for your other group members.

The themes are:

(a) *Calamities are God's warning of judgments to come.*

(b) *Heed the warnings, and return with all your heart.*

(c) *When you return, God's fullest blessing will be poured out on you and all people.*

2. Or, understanding the basic thrust of Joel's ministry, work in teams to select *key verses* on the following themes:

- God judges sin.
- God demands full commitment.
- God blesses those who commit themselves to Him.

Each team is to select key verses and plan a *five-minute message* around them, which might be given to a modern Christian community.

After the planning stage, have each team select one spokesman, who will then share that five-minute message with your group.

Apply
Have each group member select one verse from Joel which seems most important to him or her personally. As you close, share verses and a brief word about why the verse is or has been important to you.

STUDY GUIDE 70

Amos

LET JUSTICE ROLL

Overview
Amos was a herdsman in Judah when called by God to preach against the social and economic sins of the Northern Kingdom, Israel. He spoke in the reign of Jeroboam II, near 760 B.C.

Amos, a poor man who cared for sycamore trees (whose fruit was a food of the poor), traveled to the worship centers of Israel, where the rich idled, to proclaim God's condemnation of their distorted values.

The Book of Amos is a rich source for Christians today. In the words of this ancient prophet we catch a very special glimpse of God as One who cares intensely for the poor. We also sense His deep commitment to personal and social justice. The emphasis of the New Testament on personal relationship with God and individual salvation does nothing to lessen God's deep concern for justice and holiness in society.

Outline

I.	Judgment Coming	1:1–2:16
II.	Indictment Entered	3:1–6:14
III.	Visions of Warning	7:1–9:10
IV.	Kingdom Visions	9:11–15

▶ ***Justice.*** This vital Old Testament term is also translated "righteousness" in our English versions. Its basic meaning is that of harmony with a standard by which right and wrong can be measured. In the Old Testament this standard is God's revealed Law.

■ For a verse-by-verse commentary on the important Book of Amos, see the *Bible Knowledge Commentary*, pages 1425-1452.

Commentary
The fitful warfare with Syria, which had flared up time and time again since the days of Elijah and Elisha, was over. The 100-year feud was settled and the military threat ended when Damascus came under the sovereignty of Jeroboam II. Israel's territory almost reached the borders of the United Kingdom of David's day.

An economic explosion accompanied the military success, as spectacular as the stunning revival of West Germany and Japan after World War II. Israel now controlled ancient trade routes, and expansion gave rise to a new social class of wealthy merchants. Wealth created a demand for the many luxuries available from all over the known world.

Pressured by the influx of wealth, jolting social changes took place. The population began to shift from farms to cities and towns. Class distinctions crystallized, with the rich bent on piling up profits at the expense of their poorer brothers. Exorbitant prices were charged; poor farmers were dispossessed so that the rich might build up great estates. A heartless unconcern for the sufferings of the oppressed marked the well-to-do.

Homer Harley, writing in his *Commentary on the Minor Prophets* (Baker), portrays the social conditions sketched by Amos:

> The luxury of the wealthy class in Israel is clearly indicated by the prophet as he speaks of their "couches" and "silken cushions" (3:12), of their "winter house" and "summer house," and the "houses of ivory" (ivory inlay and ornamentation), and of "the houses of hewn-stone" (3:15; 5:11). The voluptuous women were spoken of as "kine [cows] of Bashan," who insisted that their husbands provide ample wine and other luxuries for their feasts, even if the poor had to be crushed in order to provide them (4:1-3). Their feasts were characterized by

> revelry, songs, music, choice meats, and the best of wines to satiate their lusts, and by cushions and silken tapestries upon which to recline (6:1-7). These luxuries were enjoyed by the wealthy, whose eyes were closed to the afflictions and needs of the poor (6:6).

The moral condition of the nation was clearly revealed by the prophet's shock at the cruel treatment of the poor by the rich, at the covetousness, injustice, and immorality of the people in power, and at the general contempt for things holy (2:6-8). Trampling on the poor, taking exactions of wheat (5:11), afflicting the just, taking a bribe, and turning aside from the needy (v. 23) stirred the indignation of the prophet, and gives us insight into the morals of the day. These people were ready to "swallow up the needy" and "to do away with the poor of the land"—that is, to let them die (8:4).

In political circles there was tumult and oppression, violence and robbery (3:9-10). People hated any judge who would reprove them or speak uprightly (5:10).

Then suddenly, against this background of prosperity and oppression, a man who knew poverty appeared from Judah. For a few short months, he denounced the sins of Israel and promised judgment.

Amos was a native of Tekoa, a town about 12 miles south of Jerusalem. A farmer and herder, he had spent his life caring for sheep and harvesting the sycamore fig, the "food of the poor." He was used to hard work and accustomed to a frugal life. He stood in sharp contrast to the "beautiful people" of Israel.

Shocked by the moral, social, and religious situation in the Northern Kingdom, Amos stood at Bethel (the center of worship established over a century before by Jeroboam I) and denounced the lifestyle of Israel. In a series of scathing sermons, he confronted the wealthy and ruling classes, exposed their sins, and pronounced in flaming anger the punishment that God was to impose.

Amos' anger was but a pale reflection of God's own wrath. Yet the prosperous of Israel were unmoved. To these proud and selfish men, unconcerned about the misery of those they oppressed, Amos must have seemed some wild fanatic. He was out of touch with modern times—perhaps simply jealous that he was himself poor and not one of the favored few!

Later, Jesus would comment to His disciples, "How hard it is for the rich to enter the kingdom of God!" (Luke 18:24) Prosperity promotes values in deep conflict with what God Himself says is important. How hard it is to have wealth and status, and retain perspective!

♥ ***Link to Life: Youth / Adult***

To launch your group meeting give out 8 x 11 sheets of paper and pens or crayons. Ask each person to draw a cartoon depicting an "injustice."

When cartoons are completed, let each person show and briefly describe his or her sketch. Then discuss: "What is injustice? Do we see injustice in our society? Where?"

Explain that in the Book of Amos we see reflected an unjust society, and in the prophet's message learn much about God and a holy lifestyle.

The Book of Amos

Our Old Testament Book of Amos is a carefully organized compilation of the message which Amos, God's spokesman to the rich society, delivered in the Northern Kingdom. An outline helps us see its development, and guides us in reading it today.

Outline

I. Judgment Announced
   A. On surrounding nations — 1:3–2:3
   B. On Israel and Judah — 2:4-16
II. Sermons of Indictment
   A. First sermon — 3:1-15
   B. Second sermon — 4:1-13
   C. Third sermon — 5:1–6:14
III. Declarations of Judgment
   A. Judgment averted: locusts — 7:1-3
   B. Judgment delayed: fire — 7:4-6
   C. Judgment determined — 7:7-9
   D. Amaziah's opposition — 7:10-17
   E. Judgment imminent — 8:1-14
   F. Judgment executed — 9:1-10
IV. Restoration Promised — 9:11-15

As you and your group follow this outline, the pattern of Amos' preaching becomes sharp and clear.

Outlining. Outlining is one of the basic methods of Bible study, and is particularly helpful here. The goal in outlining is to trace a writer's thoughts, and also to highlight what is important.

For instance, in the first chapter of Amos each of Amos' pronouncements against the nations follows a particular pattern:

(1) Declaration of judgment
(2) Cause of judgment
(3) Description of judgment.

In speaking against Damascus and Gaza, and then Judah and Israel, this pattern is consistently followed.

What seems to be the underlying cause of the judgment pronounced on God's own people?

In Judah, the cause is simple: "Because they have rejected the Law of the Lord and have not kept His decrees" (2:4).

For Israel, the cause is expressed in much greater detail. There the focus of God's concern is placed squarely on similar violations expressed as social injustice, as the breakdown of morality, and as repudiation of God and His Word. How graphic the words of Amos are:

> For three sins of Israel, even for four, I will not turn back My wrath. They sell the righteous for silver, and the needy for a pair of sandals. They trample on the heads of the poor as upon the dust of the ground and deny justice to the oppressed. Father and son use the same girl and so profane My holy name. They lie down beside every altar on garments taken in pledge. In the house of their god they drink the wine taken as fines.
>
> Amos 2:6-8

What specifically do these charges reveal?

"They sell the righteous." The rights of the poor, carefully protected in the Old Testament Law, were regularly violated. This institutionalized injustice had turned away the "humble" from following God's way of love and obedience. It is hard for the oppressed to love the oppressor!

"A father and his son." This may be a reference to use of the same temple prostitute. If so, it was a flagrant violation both of God's command to worship only Him, and a revelation of the gross immorality involved in pagan worship.

"Garments taken in pledge." Here Amos returns to his central theme of injustice. The Law demanded that if a poor man's cloak were taken as a pledge against a loan or debt, it was to be returned to him before night, since the cloak was also his blanket (Deut. 24:12-13). But in Israel, such cloaks were piled around the altars as resting places for wealthy worshipers!

"The wine taken as fines." Wine that had been extorted as taxes or fines from the poor was used in the very centers (wrongly) set aside to worship God! Thus, even God was made to seem a party to oppression.

This explanation of the cause of judgment on Israel sets the stage for our reading of the book, and it immediately draws attention to the causes of God's wrath.

♥ ***Link to Life: Youth / Adult***

We learn much about a person's character by discovering what makes him or her angry. It is the same with God. We can gain great insight into the character of our Lord by seeing what moves Him to wrath.

Ask teams of three or four group members to look at the following verses. What qualities of our God do these verses reveal? (Amos 3:7; 4:2, 6-11, 13; 5:4, 6, 8, 21-22; 6:8; 7:2-3, 5; 9:2-4, 7)

When each team has worked through and discussed the verses, come together and share insights. What common portrait of God might you develop together?

Amos Today

The Book of Amos, expressing as it does God's outrage against a society that had become insensitive to justice—a society that materialistically exalted profit over people—has been identified as one of the most significant of prophetic books for us today. Certainly we too experience unequalled prosperity. Surely, there are great class distinctions in our society. And surely too there is oppression—oppression that has not been touched by institutionalizing a financial dole to the poor.

Perhaps most important, Amos helps us review our own values. He asks the question: Do our lifestyles reflect the heart of God? Or do we share the selfish heart of the indifferent of Amos' day?

Oppression. Reading through Amos, we realize that God's anger constantly flashes out against those who oppress others. The poor of the land seem very precious to Him. The indifferent attitude of men and women concerned with only profit and their own pleasures deeply offends God.

The Old Testament Law made careful and explicit provision for meeting the needs of *all* God's people. When a man sold himself or one of his family into servitude, it was not *slavery*. He would later be released and restored to his ancestral land (Lev. 25). Widows and others without means of support were provided for. Each farmer was to allow gleaning, the gathering of part of his harvest by the poor. All grain that fell to the ground was to be left for the poor. Fruit of the vine and tree was not to be completely harvested by the owner. There was no welfare roll in Israel; the poor maintained their self-respect and worked for what they received. The man who had plenty made the excess available to the less fortunate. No wonder the Old Testament promised that, should Israel obey God's Law "there should be no poor among you" (Deut. 15:4-5).

God's Law was a charter for a truly just society.

Those laws, and God Himself, were now being denied by God's people. Love for neighbor and respect for the poor had long been forgotten. In their place had come deep social cleavage; brutal oppression was undertaken for material gain.

Justice. Significant also is the insight Amos gives us into the nature of justice and righteousness. Too often we think of these qualities as related to rules of behavior—to what a person does or does not do.

Amos, reflecting the Old Testament Law, focuses our attention on God's concern for people. The purpose behind the laws governing society takes on fresh meanings. The laws were given that each person, rich and poor alike, might be treated with fairness and compassion. In essence, Amos helps us see that the concept of God being just is in fact an affirmation that God is committed to do right by all people. What is more, God's own deep commitment to justice leads Him to require that in human society we also maintain a commitment to do right by all.

Ritual. The thrust of Amos' message is the announcement of God's judgment on Israel for injustice.

Israel had never abandoned the worship centers erected by Jeroboam I in violation of God's Law. She still bowed down before golden calves. What is more, Baal worship had again crept into the land. Altars were built on high ridges of land in honor of the ancient nature gods, and around them the old immoralities were practiced still—in the name of religion.

The ritual, even when performed in God's supposed honor, horrified the Lord.

> For I know how many are your offenses and how great your sins. You oppress the righteous and take bribes and you deprive the poor of justice in the courts.
>
> Amos 5:12

God's demand focused not on restoring the appropriate forms of worship, but on returning again to His values. A people who worship God acceptably must share God's commitment to do right by all.

> Seek good, not evil, that you may live. Then the Lord God Almighty will be with you, just as you say He is. Hate evil, love good; maintain justice in the courts. Perhaps the Lord God Almighty will have mercy on the remnant of Joseph.
>
> Amos 5:14-15

It is the heart of man with which God is concerned. In turning away from God, Israel lost touch with the divine values. Rejecting righteousness and justice, God's people abandoned themselves to wealth and pleasure and to oppression of the poor.

And to punishment.

Israel had passed beyond the edge of judgment.

TEACHING GUIDE

Prepare

Read through Amos at one sitting. How much of God's indictment of Israel might be included in an indictment of our society today?

Explore

1. Have your group members draw cartoons representing "injustice." See "link-to-life," page 462.
2. Give a minilecture on Amos and his con-

cern for justice. Then work in teams of three or four to see what God was concerned about—and to discover what His concerns tell us about God's own character. See "link-to-life," page 463.

Expand

Outlining is a basic and very helpful approach to Bible study. What a person does is to try to summarize the major thought of a paragraph or even a sentence, and state that thought in such as way that with other summary sentences it can actually trace the thought of a passage.

Begin by explaining outlining and putting the outline of Amos found on page 461 on the chalkboard.

Then have your group members work in pairs to outline *in detail* one of these three passages: Amos 3:1-15; 4:1-13; or 5:1–6:14.

When completed, let each pair discuss what they discovered about Amos' message through this study approach.

Apply

Go back to the cartoon activity. How might group members change their cartoon renderings of "injustice" after studying Amos?

Conclude by agreeing on a clear and powerful statement on justice that will reflect the commitment of group members to God's values. Begin, "We care about justice, and so we will. . . ."

STUDY GUIDE 71

Obadiah and Nahum

WARNING TO ENEMIES

Overview

The Books of Obadiah and Nahum are seldom taught today. Each is a prophetic warning against an enemy of ancient Israel. The great contribution of each to believers today is to underscore the fact that God does make moral judgments—and He acts on them!

These books also remind us of the faithfulness of God to His covenant promises to Abraham. The God who promised to bless those who blessed the Hebrew people and to curse those who cursed them is powerfully illustrated in these two short Old Testament books.

The three-chapter Book of Nahum has yet another value. It demonstrates powerfully that God is in full control of history. In a series of detailed prophecies against Nineveh, the capital of Assyria, Nahum foretold accurately just how the great city would one day fall. How good that prophecy constantly shows the total trustworthiness of the Word of God.

The date that Obadiah was written is uncertain, and has usually been placed either around 840 B.C. or 585 B.C. Nahum probably ministered between 885 B.C. and 667 B.C.

■ The *Bible Knowledge Commentary* contains a discussion of the date each of these early prophetic books was written, as well as a verse-by-verse commentary on the text of each.

▶ ***Jealous.*** Nahum spoke of God as "jealous." A weakness in human beings, when "jealousy" is ascribed to God it indicates His zeal for and commitment to His people.

Commentary

We live in a world where many things seem tragically unfair. Libya sponsors terrorist attacks that maim innocents. The Iranian regime arms children and sends them against Iraq to be massacred. Communist and right-wing regimes alike suppress freedom, and brutalize their citizens. Countries like Afghanistan are crushed by invaders while the United Nations hesitates to even complain.

In a world like ours, it is easy to wonder whether God is concerned with international injustice. It might have been easy for such questions to arise in Bible times too. The people of Israel and Judah suffered under hostile enemies. And this people possessed wonderful promises of divine protection! It would be particularly troubling for those who saw themselves as "God's people" to know persecution. Where, they must have wondered, was the God of Abraham and Isaac and Jacob? Where was the God of Moses and the Exodus? Where was the God of the all-conquering king, David?

The background of promise. When God first appeared to Abram in the land of Ur, he made that patriarch a series of wonderful promises. Genesis 12, 15, and 17 define these promises, and put them in the cultural framework of a "covenant." "Covenant" (*bri't* in Heb.) is an inclusive but important term. In Old Testament times it was the general word for "agreement," with its particular meaning and character defined by the context of its use. In business a *bri't* would be a contract. In international law it would be a treaty. In personal relationships it would be a firm commitment. In the context of God's relationship with human beings, it is best understood as a promise, or oath. In making a covenant with human beings God is expressly stating what He will surely do, and how He will surely act.

Among the features of this covenant or promise that God made to Abraham was to bless those who blessed his descendants (e.g., who treated them well) and to curse (punish) those who cursed his descendants (e.g., who mistreated them).

Later the Law added further insights. If God's people would obey Him, they would be prosperous and would also defeat their enemies. But if God's people turned from the Lord and disobeyed Him, they would know both poverty and defeat (see Deut. 28).

Again and again the pattern outlined by the Mosaic Law was replicated in the history of God's people. When they wandered God used enemy nations, along with famine and plague, to discipline them. *But this principle in the Law of Moses in no way supplanted the promise stated to Abraham!*

Indeed, the nations God used to discipline His people went beyond what God had in mind, for the pagan enemy sought not to punish but to destroy! As God said through Isaiah:

> Woe to the Assyrian, the rod of My anger, in whose hand is the club of My wrath! I send him against a godless nation, I dispatch him against a people who anger Me, to seize loot and snatch plunder, and to trample them down like mud in the streets. But this is not what he intends, this is not what he has in mind; his purpose is to destroy, to put an end to many nations.
>
> Isaiah 10:5-7

Thus God will punish the proud oppressor of His people, and will fulfill the promise He made in ages past to Abraham. The Assyrian and other enemies sought to curse God's own people. Now they would suffer His anger, for God's promises are sure.

Two Enemies

The Books of Obadiah and Nahum announce the doom of two separate nations who were enemies of Israel. In each case the basis of judgment was the same: the enemy had mistreated God's own, and the Lord was committed to punishing them.

Edom. Edom was a nation lying just south of the Dead Sea. It was settled by descendants of Esau, Jacob's brother. Like Easu, his descendants had shown themselves hostile to the Jews. When the Hebrews left Egypt under Moses, the Edomites denied Israel passage through their lands (cf. Num. 20:14-20). Moses avoided battle with the army of these distant kinsmen, and took a lengthy route around their nation.

Later, in the time of King David, the Edomites warred against Israel. They were defeated and became a subject people. But the next several hundred years showed constant warfare between these people and Israel, until in the fifth century B.C. the Edomite kingdom was destroyed.

Later the descendants of Edom, then known as Idumeans, were forcibly converted to Judaism. Herod the Great, the brutal founder of the Herodian line which ruled in Jesus' time, was an Idumean.

But this lay far in the future as Obadiah penned his brief, one-chapter book—the shortest book in our Old Testament. At that time, very probably around 844 B.C. when Jerusalem was attacked by a coalition army of Arabs and Philistines, the Edomites had delighted in the disaster.

Their own capital was Sela, or Petra. This city was literally carved into rock, and could be entered only by a narrow canyon easy to defend. Their own supposedly impregnable situation led both to pride and to contempt for Israel. Obadiah depicted their attitude:

> The pride of your heart has deceived you, you who live in the clefts of the rocks and make your home on the heights, you who say to yourself, "Who can bring me down to the ground?"
>
> Obadiah 3

God announced woe against them, and destruction "because of the violence against your brother Jacob" (v. 10).

The particular offense is clearly specified. They will be judged because of what happened:

> On the day you stood aloof while strangers carried off his wealth and foreigners entered his gates and cast lots for Jerusalem, you were like one of them. You should not look down on your brother in the day of his misfortune, nor rejoice over the people of Judah in the day of their destruction, nor boast so much in the day of their trouble. You should not march through the gates of My people in the day of their disaster, nor look down on them in their calamity in the day of their disaster, nor seize their wealth in the day of disaster. You should not wait at the crossroads to cut down their fugi-

> tives, nor hand over their survivors in the day of their trouble.
>
> Obadiah 11-14

God, then, will be true to His promises. The Edomites, who cursed His people Israel, would be punished.

But the prophet then went on to expand his message to include all nations and people who despise the Lord and His inheritance! He spoke of a Day of the Lord "near for all nations" (v. 15). One day the ancient promises will be fully kept, and when the house of Jacob possesses its inheritance "deliverers will go up on Mount Zion to govern the mountains of Esau. And the kingdom will be the Lord's" (v. 21).

Nineveh. Nineveh was the capital of the Assyrian Empire, which dominated Palestine and much of the ancient world from around 930 to 612 B.C., counter-balanced in the south by Egypt.

It was this people who, in 722 B.C., swept down on the Northern Kingdom of Israel. The Assyrians battered down the walls of Samaria, Israel's capital, and took the people away, resettling them away from the Promised Land.

The Bible has much to say about this terrible, warlike pagan nation. Isaiah particularly contains many passages that foretell Assyria's doom (cf. Isa. 10:5-19; 17:12-14; 18:4-6; 30:27-33; 37:21-35).

The little three-chapter Book of Nahum contains detailed prophecies about the doom of Israel's ancient enemy.

The book begins with a statement about God's character, which is to be revealed in the judgment on Nineveh.

> The Lord is a jealous and avenging God; the Lord takes vengeance and is filled with wrath. The Lord takes vengeance on His foes and maintains His wrath against His enemies. The Lord is slow to anger and great in power; the Lord will not leave the guilty unpunished.
>
> Nahum 1:2-3

The doom came because Nineveh, in destroying Israel, had plotted against the Lord (v. 9). Therefore:

> The Lord is good, a refuge in times of trouble. He cares for those who trust in Him, but with an overwhelming flood He will make an end of Nineveh; He will pursue His foes into darkness.
>
> Nahum 1:7-8

What is perhaps most striking about this book is the detail with which the destruction of Nineveh is foretold. Written between 667 and 655 B.C., about 50 years before the city fell, the book gives details of the three-month siege and fate of the once-powerful city. These details are summarized in an excellent chart in the *Bible Knowledge Commentary* (Victor), which is reprinted on the next page.

The powerful images of terrible judgment about to fall on Nineveh remind us that God stands against all oppressors, not just the enemy of His people Israel.

What then do we gain from a study of these two almost-forgotten books of the Hebrew prophets? While there may be little that is directly relevant to our day, there surely are lessons.

We learn that God is faithful to His promises. God's Old Testament people may have wondered why deliverance seemed to take so long. And they may have felt at times that God had truly abandoned them to enemies intended only to discipline them. Yet these two prophetic books are evidence that God did not abandon even His sinning people. The judgment may have been delayed, but it did come. And judgment was just, based on ancient principles clearly laid down. So even though we may not see a particular promise fulfilled quickly, we can be sure that God will keep every commitment He has made to us.

We also sense something of the justice of God, whose wrath is aroused by that human pride and injustice which causes one people to disregard the rights of another, and declare war on them. There may well be such a thing as a just war. But any war in which righteous objectives are set aside merits the judgment of our God.

Fulfillments of Nahum's Prophecies

Nahum's Prophecies	Historical Fulfillments
1. The Assyrian fortresses surrounding the city would be easily captured (3:12).	1. According to the Babylonian Chronicle the fortified towns in Nineveh's environs began to fall in 614 B.C. including Tabris, present-day Sharif-Khan, a few miles northwest of Nineveh.
2. The besieged Ninevites would prepare bricks and mortar for emergency defense walls (3:14).	2. A.T. Olmstead reported: "To the south of the gate, the moat is still filled with fragments of stone and of mud bricks from the walls, heaped up when they were breached" (*History of Assyria.* Chicago: University of Chicago Press, 1951, p. 637).
3. The city gates would be destroyed (3:13).	3. Olmstead noted: "The main attack was directed from the northwest and the brunt fell upon the Hatamti gate at this corner. . . . Within the gate are traces of the counterwall raised by the inhabitants in their last extremity" (*History of Assyria,* p. 637).
4. In the final hours of the attack the Ninevites would be drunk (1:10; 3:11).	4. Diodorus Siculus (ca. 20 B.C.) wrote, "The Assyrian king . . . distributed to his soldiers meats and liberal supplies of wine and provisions. . . . While the whole army was thus carousing, the friends of Arbakes learned from some deserters of the slackness and drunkenness which prevailed in the enemy's camp and made an unexpected attack by night" (*Bibliotheca Historica* 2. 26. 4).
5. Nineveh would be destroyed by a flood (1:8; 2:6, 8).	5. Diodorus wrote that in the third year of the siege heavy rains caused a nearby river to flood part of the city and break part of the walls (*Bibliotheca Historica* 2. 26. 9; 2. 27. 13). Xenophon referred to terrifying thunder (presumably with a storm) associated with the city's capture (*Anabasis,* 3. 4. 12). Also the Khosr River, entering the city from the northwest at the Ninlil Gate and running through the city in a southwesterly direction, may have flooded because of heavy rains, or the enemy may have destroyed its sluice gate.
6. Nineveh would be destroyed by fire (1:10; 2:13; 3:15).	6. Archeological excavations at Nineveh have revealed charred wood, charcoal, and ashes. "There was no question about the clear traces of the burning of the temple (as also in the palace of Sennacherib), for a layer of ash about two inches thick lay clearly defined in places on the southeast side about the level of the Sargon pavement" (R. Campbell Thompson and R.W. Hutchinson, *A Century of Exploration at Nineveh.* London: Luzac, 1929, pp. 45, 77).
7. The city's capture would be attended by a great massacre of people (3:3).	7. "In two battles fought on the plain before the city the rebels defeated the Assyrians. . . . So great was the multitude of the slain that the flowing stream, mingled with their blood, changed its color for a considerable distance" (Diodorus, *Bibliotheca Historica* 2. 26. 6-7).
8. Plundering and pillaging would accompany the overthrow of the city (2:9-10).	8. According to the Babylonian Chronicle, "Great quantities of spoil from the city, beyond counting, they carried off. The city [they turned] into a mound and ruin heap" (Luckenbill, *Ancient Records of Assyria and Babylonia,* 2:420).
9. When Nineveh would be captured its people would try to escape (2:8).	9. "Sardanapalus [another name for King Sin-shar-ishkun] sent away his three sons and two daughters with much treasure into Paphlagonia, to the governor of Kattos, the most loyal of his subjects" (Diodorus, *Bibliotheca Historica,* 2. 26. 8).
10. The Ninevite officers would weaken and flee (3:17).	10. The Babylonian Chronicle states that "[The army] of Assyria deserted [lit., ran away before] the king" (Luckenbill, *Ancient Records of Assyria and Babylonia,* 2:420).
11. Nineveh's images and idols would be destroyed (1:14).	11. R. Campbell Thompson and R.W. Hutchinson reported that the statue of the goddess Ishtar lay headless in the debris of Nineveh's ruins ("The British Museum Excavations on the Temple of Ishtar at Nineveh, 1930–1," *Annals of Archaeology and Anthropology.* 19, pp. 55-6).
12. Nineveh's destruction would be final (1:9, 14).	12. Many cities of the ancient Near East were rebuilt after being destroyed (e.g., Samaria, Jerusalem, Babylon) but not Nineveh.

TEACHING GUIDE

Prepare
Review the important concept of covenant by referring to other discussions in this book (see *Index*).

Explore
1. Place the following statement on the chalkboard, and when your group members have come in ask them for their reactions. "The existence of aggressor nations is a strong argument against the belief that God is in control of history."
2. Or in a brief lecture compare the theme of these two prophets. Include in your overview a discussion of the Abrahamic Covenant on which each bases his assurance that God will act, and his explanation for the fate of Israel's enemy.

Expand
1. Duplicate and pass out the chart of prophecies concerning Nineveh. Look together at the detailed description and fulfillment of Nahum's prophecy.

Discuss: "What can we learn about God's control of history from the prophet's description of Nineveh's fall before the event?"
2. Or raise the question of the validity of the Abrahamic Covenant in modern international politics. Should the U.S. support Israel because God is committed to bless those who bless His Old Testament people? Or can the present state of Israel be compared with biblical Israel?

Apply
1. Divide into teams to read through Obadiah and Nahum 1. Each team is to find at least three verses or phrases which might contain a message to us today as well as to the people of the prophet's day.

Then share the messages each team has found. Discuss: "Are the messages for today related to the main theme of each book? Are there modern parallels between the issues that concerned the people of each prophet's day and issues that concern contemporary Christians?"
2. Share: "Was there any message in either of these books that was especially for you?"

STUDY GUIDE 72

Jonah

GOSPEL OF THE SECOND CHANCE

Overview

The Book of Jonah dates from the 8th century, probably around 760 B.C. Unlike the other minor prophets, this book is written as a story of the prophet's personal struggle with God over a mission on which he had been sent.

Each chapter in this small but important Bible book is rich in application to the Christian life. The book can be outlined to reflect its nature as a historical narrative telling Jonah's story.

Outline

I.	Jonah's Disobedience	Chap. 1
II.	Jonah's Submission	Chap. 2
III.	Jonah's Mission	Chap. 3
IV.	Jonah's Motives—and God's	Chap. 4

Among the many wonderful contributions of this short book are: God in grace gives His people a second chance. God's warnings contain an implicit promise of blessing if we repent. God's motives are shaped by a deep love for all people.

▶ ***Repentance.*** The concept of repentance is important in both Old and New Testaments. We can sum up the basic meaning: repentance means "a change of heart and life." While repentance is popularly linked with sorrow and prayer, the basic meaning is one of a change of life direction. A person who repents turns from his old ways to wholeheartedly commit himself to doing the will of God. Is repentance linked with salvation? Yes. But the life-change expressed by "repentance" is a result of saving faith in God, not a condition of our salvation.

Commentary

Some 40 years before the Assyrians destroyed the Northern Kingdom, the Prophet Jonah was sent from Israel to save the enemy capital.

Jonah lived and ministered during the golden age of the Northern Kingdom. Under Jeroboam II, a weakened Israel saw a dramatic resurgence of power, and Jonah had a significant role in this recovery. Second Kings 14 tells us that while Jeroboam "did not turn away from any of the sins of Jeroboam son of Nebat [the first Jeroboam]," nevertheless, "he . . . restored the boundaries of Israel from Lebo Hamath to the Sea of the Arabah, *in accordance with the word of the Lord, the God of Israel, spoken by His servant Jonah* son of Amittai, the prophet from Gath-Hepher" (2 Kings 24–25, italics mine).

Jonah apparently had a patriotic and popular ministry. He must have enjoyed the favor of both Jeroboam II and his fellow citizens.

No wonder the divine command to go to Nineveh, the capital of the empire that for decades had terrorized the people of Israel, came as a jolting shock. The Bible indicates that Jonah reacted immediately to the divine commission. "Jonah ran away from the Lord and headed for Tarshish" (Jonah 1:3).

The prophet had acted as God's spokesman when the message was good for his people. But he was unwilling to carry a message to an enemy who might do his country harm!

The Story

We are all familiar with Jonah's experience. Going to the seaport of Joppa, he took a ship for Tarshish, in Spain. This was as far from Nineveh as the prophet could travel!

♥ ***Link to Life: Children***

We can all understand Jonah's feelings. Boys and girls too have times when they simply do not feel like obeying. As you teach the familiar story, help your class identify with Jonah's feelings before you emphasize the need to obey God or parents, even when we do not feel like obeying.

How? Tell the first part of the story, and explain why Jonah did not want to go to his country's enemies. Then let your boys and girls act it out, using figures made of Popsicle sticks. "Jonah" will hear what God has to say, will mutter and complain, and then go to the seashore and pay the captain for a ticket to Tarshish.

Talk about how Jonah must have felt. Then let the children use the stick figures to act out times when they don't feel like obeying either. What do they say then? How do their voices sound? What do they do?

Then go on with the story, pointing out that Jonah did obey when he was disciplined. How much better to obey even when we don't want to, than to have to go through a hard time, as Jonah did.

But God stayed with His runaway. A storm struck, which terrified even the ship's experienced crew. Recalling that Jonah had told them he was fleeing from God (1:10), the mariners took Jonah's advice and reluctantly threw him over the side. The storm calmed immediately, and Jonah sank beneath the waves.

Slipping down, Jonah's body entangled by the fronds of giant, 50-foot-long seaweeds, the prophet was sure that death was God's judgment on his disobedience. Then, suddenly, Jonah found himself swallowed by a giant fish. He lost consciousness—later waking to realize he still lived and that the fish had been prepared by God to save his life. Later, Jonah penned a psalm about this experience:

> When my life was ebbing away, I remembered You, Lord, and my prayer rose to You, to Your holy temple.
>
> Jonah 2:7

The giant fish bore the repentant prophet back the way he had come, and vomited him up on dry land. And the Bible tells us, "Then the word of the Lord came to Jonah a second time: 'Go to the great city of Nineveh and proclaim to it the message I give you' " (3:1-2).

Obediently now, Jonah trudged toward the enemy capital to fulfill God's command.

The Nineveh of Jonah's day was a great city; counting its suburbs, it took three days to walk through it. That first day, Jonah began to shout out the message God gave him. "Forty more days and Nineveh will be destroyed" (v. 4).

The pagan people of Nineveh did not laugh at this strange little Jewish fanatic. Instead they "believed God. They declared a fast, and all of them, from the greatest to the least, put on sackcloth" (v. 5). The message of coming judgment had immediate effect, and brought a wholehearted repentance.

Scholars who have studied Assyrian history have suggested possible reasons for this response. Under Adad-Nirari III (ca. 810–783 B.C.) the Assyrians had begun a trend toward monotheism. And just before the probable time of Jonah's arrival, a great plague had marked the reign of Assurdan II (ca. 771–754 B.C.). Whatever the contributing factors, the Assyrians did respond to God's messenger. King, nobles, and slaves fasted, mourned, and prayed, humbling themselves before God.

And when God saw that they turned away from their wicked way, God "had compassion and did not bring upon them the destruction He had threatened" (v. 10).

♥ ***Link to Life: Children***

Both Jonah and Nineveh reveal an important Bible principle. A person or nation who returns to God will be welcomed by Him. God is good, and will forgive us when we do wrong.

After telling the story of Jonah and of Nineveh, talk about how glad God feels when people come to Him to be forgiven. Let the boys and girls think of feeling words that express His attitude—loving, happy, not angry, etc. Then distribute paper and crayons. Ask each child to draw a picture of how he or she thinks God looks when a person comes to ask for forgiveness.

When the pictures are completed, let each tell about his or her picture. Then suggest the pictures be put up on the child's bedroom wall at home. Whenever he or she does something wrong, the picture can remind him or her that God will gladly forgive.

After delivering his message of impending doom, Jonah slipped out of the city.

Finding hilly ground to the east, he settled down to wait and to see what God would do. Nothing happened. And Jonah reacted with anger and bitterness. His complaint opened up the motive for his earlier flight to Tarshish. "O Lord, is this not what I said when I was still at home? That is why I was so quick to flee to Tarshish. I knew that You are a gracious and compassionate God, slow to anger and abounding in love, a God who relents from sending calamity" (4:2).

Jonah, who had prophesied before on behalf of "my own country" now asked God to take his life rather than let him live to remember that he might have been used to deliver his country's enemy!

So Jonah settled down, despite the intense heat, to wait out the 40 days, still hoping to see Nineveh destroyed. God then caused a plant to grow which was large and succulent enough to shelter the prophet. And Jonah was "very happy" (v. 6). But the next day God caused a worm to attack the plant, and it withered away. That day was agonizing, with a scorching wind and a sun that beat unmercifully down on Jonah's head. Exhausted by the sun and heat, the suffering Jonah begged God to let him die, insisting that he had every right to be angry about the plant as well as about his mission to the city.

The book concludes with God's words of instruction to Jonah—words the prophet faithfully recorded though they constitute a sharp rebuke. Jonah cared about the plant, a thing of transitory existence at best. But God responded, "Nineveh has more than a hundred and twenty thousand people who cannot tell their right hand from their left, and many cattle as well. Should I not be concerned about that great city?" (v. 11)

God's compassion extends to all. People are truly important to Him.

♥ ***Link to Life: Youth / Adult***
The Book of Jonah shows several ways that our choices can take us in relationship to God. Put on the chalkboard the arrow chart showing Jonah's direction in each of the chapters of this short book. Then:
(a) ask each group member to determine privately (not to be revealed to the group) which arrow represents where he or she is now. Then (b) as a class, look together at each chapter and list several characteristics of Jonah when moving in the directions shown on the chart.

Messages of Jonah for Today
The Book of Jonah is far more complex than it seems at first glance. The basically simple story communicates messages to us on several different levels.

The relationship between God and unbelieving nations. On one level, Jonah portrayed God's way of dealing with Gentile nations while working with Israel through His covenant and Law. It is clear from the Book of Jonah that God has *not* simply "set aside" the nations as unimportant, or their peoples as without value. Note:

(1) God clearly cared about the Gentiles during this era in which the Jews were his chosen people. God's heart was moved with compassion for Nineveh and its inhabitants.

(2) God also maintained a moral relationship with those who were not His own. The Ninevites were responsible for their actions, and God took the responsibility to judge them when they sinned. It is also clear

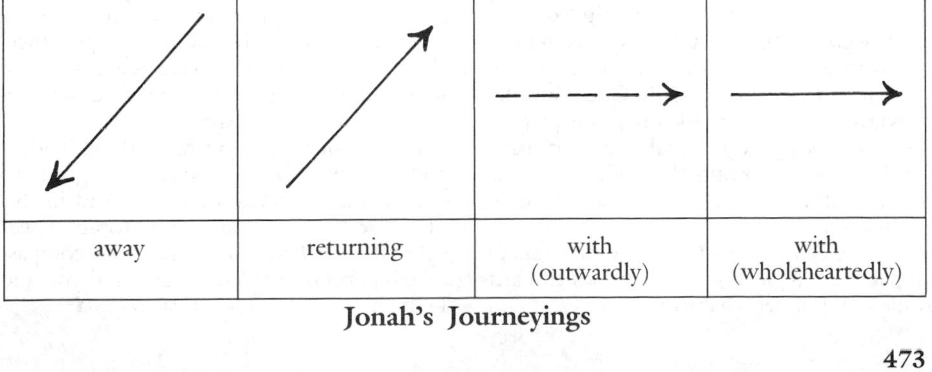

chapter 1	2	3	4
↙	↗	- - - - →	———→
away	returning	with (outwardly)	with (wholeheartedly)

Jonah's Journeyings

from the response of the Ninevites that they were aware of what constituted wickedness. While God did not hold them responsible for Israel's Law, they were being judged on the basis of the light they did possess (see Rom. 2:12-16).

(3) It is also clear that God gave the people of Nineveh sufficient information about Himself and His intentions for them to respond to Him. We must never think that even pagan peoples have *no* light.

(4) Finally, we see striking evidence that God was—and is—responsive to the unbeliever as well as the believer. He heard the prayer of these men even though they were without a basis for personal relationship with Him. God's goodness extends far beyond our understanding.

We must be careful not to push these observations too far. Yet it is important to realize that while God was dealing with the Hebrew people throughout the course of Old Testament history, and while they *are* His chosen people, God still maintained a supervisory relationship with all. And God still did care for all.

The relationship between God and Jonah as an individual. Two striking relationships are illustrated. The first has to do with God's commitment to His own. Jonah ran away from God, willfully and consciously disobeying the divine command. God's response was to *stay with* His runaway. God disciplined Jonah, but only to bring the straying prophet back into renewed fellowship with Him. And after Jonah had returned to the Lord, God gave Jonah a second chance.

The idea of a second chance is something we often lose sight of. We tend to feel that sin and disobedience disqualify us from further service. Jonah shows us how full and free God's forgiveness really is. He forgives and *restores*. In fellowship with God again, we can be both useful and fulfilled.

A second important message communicated to us in the relationship between God and Jonah has to do with God's attitude toward the believer. Jonah was a prophet with a message, but Jonah was not just a tool. After the prophet's work was done, God continued to deal with Jonah as an individual.

And God's concern was focused not on Jonah's behavior, but on his values and attitudes—his inner character.

The Book of Jonah shows Jonah as a man without compassion for his enemies. He did care about "us." But he wished only evil on "them." While Jonah obeyed God when given his second chance, his heart was not in tune with the Lord. Yet it is our heart that God cares about; He seeks not mere obedience, but that we *become like Him.*

Jesus taught in the Sermon on the Mount, "Love your enemies" (Matt. 5:44). And Jesus pointed out that in loving our enemies, we reflect the nature of the Heavenly Father, who gives His rain to just and unjust alike.

That was no new revelation!

The Book of Jonah reverberates with the same message: God has compassion on all people, even those who make themselves His enemies and the enemies of His people. The believer *is* to be like God, in His love for and valuing of all persons.

The relationship between God and Israel. The nation Israel had known the ministry of many significant prophets, all warning them to return to God. And, like Jonah, Israel had resolutely run the other way!

Following Jonah, or perhaps contemporary with him, Amos shouted out his pronouncements of judgment on the wickedness of God's people. In the experience of Jonah, Israel was given two significant object lessons to reveal to them God's willingness to forgive.

First, Jonah himself demonstrated the willingness of God to restore fellowship, and to work with the repentant individual. If Israel would follow Jonah's course and return to God, the nation could expect its compassionate God to bless and restore her as well. Second, was the example of the Ninevites. Their response and the delay of judgment demonstrated the kind of response that is always appropriate to a message of judgment. There must be a turning from the wicked way, and a wholehearted humbling before the Lord in repentance. With such repentance comes relief from the sentence of judgment. The foretold evil does not come to pass.

In the Book of Jonah, both individual and national object lessons were given to the men and women of Israel. And in this object lesson a promise of restoration was extended to them. God's heart of compassion had been revealed. Israel—and you and I—*never need fear to return to God.*

The more we explore this book, the more we see. Once again, God has communicated many vital principles and messages to you and to me and to the people we teach.

♥ ***Link to Life: Youth / Adult***
Sometimes when working through a book, using a chart on which to record observations is a most helpful Bible study method. You can duplicate and distribute the chart on page 473.
First have each individual read through the book, and jot down notes where indicated. Then work together to
(a) title paragraphs and chapters,
(b) choose a term that summarizes the characteristics of God and Jonah unveiled in each chapter, and (c) agree on the "main message" of each chapter.

A Special Note
One of the important contributions of Jonah has to do with the interpretation of prophecies concerning judgment. God did *not* do to Nineveh what He announced through His spokesman. Does this mean that Jonah was a false prophet, because what he announced did not come to pass? Does it mean that God changed His mind about the destruction of the city?

It seems clear from the Book of Jonah that prophecies concerning judgment *as they relate to a given generation* are intrinsically conditional; they depend on the response or lack of response to the message.

Perhaps it is best to think of prophecies of judgment in terms of "intercept points." As shown in the figure, judgment comes when a person or nation passes through the warning zone and reaches a point at which judgment *must be imposed.* If those approaching judgment turn back, they do not experience the judgment they surely would have known had they continued in their sinful ways. God did not "change His mind" at all. The people changed direction!

Prophecy, like all revelation, strips away the illusions that cloud men's minds and demonstrates reality. We live in a moral universe, governed by a moral Being. The moral principles on which this universe operates are very similar to the physical laws which govern matter—the principles that give our universe stability. Drop a rock, and according to the physical law of gravity, it will fall—not rise. If we sin or seek by fraud to gain security, anxiety will come. If we choose to ignore such warnings, as individuals and nations have, we inevitably come to the edge of divine judgment.

Prophetic warnings announce what will happen when that edge is passed. Sometimes the announcement comes too late; impending judgment is upon us. Sometimes the Word comes before we reach the brink, and warns us away. If we respond, then we avoid the fall. God has not changed His mind; we have changed our ways.

Jonah, a short and simple book, continues to be rich in meaning for you and me, just as it was significant for the people of the prophet's time.

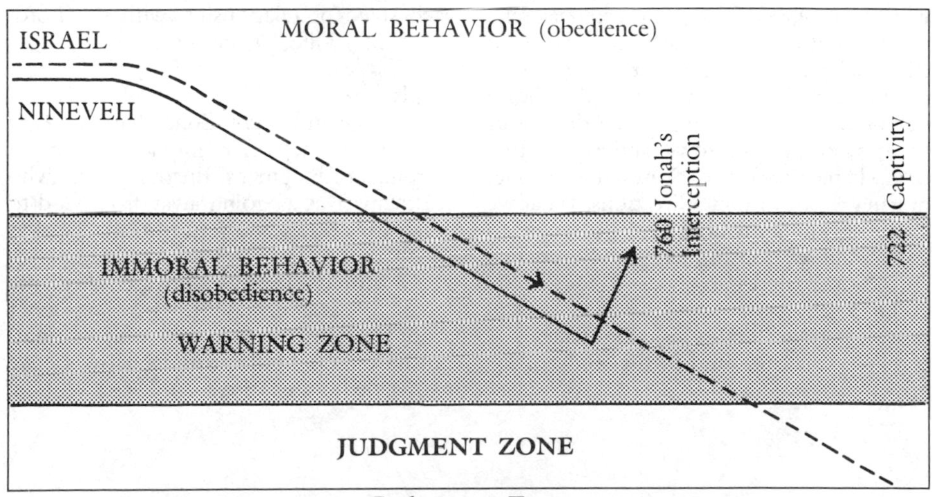

Judgment Zone

Chapter titles ➧							Nineveh's Repentance				
Notes ➧											
Paragraph titles ➧										Jonah's complaint	
	1:1-3	4-10	11-16	17	2:-19	10	3:1-4	5-9	10	4:1-5	6-11
God, characterized by His actions ➧					Deliverer						
Jonah, characterized by his actions ➧	Disobedient										
Main messages ➧											

The Book of Jonah

TEACHING GUIDE

Prepare
Look at the arrow chart on page 473. Where are *you* right now in your own relationship with the Lord?

Explore
1. Put on the chalkboard the four arrows shown on the chart on page 473. Explain what each represents in our personal relationship with God, and ask each person to choose the arrow that *best represents* his or her present state. (Promise that the choice will *not* be revealed later.) Then draw four squares *around* the arrows, and explain that each chapter of Jonah shows the prophet moving in one of these directions. What we learn from Jonah is how to evaluate and to correct our relationship with the Lord when correction is necessary.
2. Or briefly summarize the three sets of relationships dealt with in Jonah (pages 473 to 474), as background to the study of the book.

Expand
1. Work together on the chart study suggested in "link-to-life," page 475. When your group has a complete knowledge of the content you can move to explore meaning.
2. Return to the Jonah's Journeys chart, and together list characteristics of Jonah at each stage of relationship with the Lord. See "link-to-life," page 475.

Apply
1. Use the Judgment Zone chart (p. 475) to explain the offer implicit in divine warnings of judgment. Encourage any who see themselves as going away from God to accept this offer, and return to the Lord as Jonah did.
2. Or discuss Jonah's outward obedience (chap. 3) and its conflict with his inner attitude. "Can we today do what is right, but have an ungodly attitude? How are we to deal with this situation?"

STUDY GUIDE 73

Micah

GOD'S OFFER OF PARDON

Overview

The Prophet Micah ministered to the Southern Kingdom, Judah. He lived in the time of Isaiah, during the reigns of Jotham, Ahaz, and Hezekiah (742–687 B.C.). His careful dating of his ministry lets us know this historical background of his words. Micah was respected in his own time, and King Hezekiah responded to his preaching (see Jer. 26:17-19).

Though he lived in a time of religious revival, Micah's visions reveal that a time of dark judgment lies ahead for God's people before the dawn of a heavenly kingdom can come.

The major thrust of Micah's message was against social sins that existed in both Israel (Samaria, Israel's capital) and Judah. He spoke against the greedy nobles who defrauded the poor of their land, and who were quick to evict widows. This social oppression was reflected in Micah's passionate call for a return to doing justice.

There are many parallels in the messages of Isaiah and Micah, and the message of each can be seen in the other. For instance, compare:

Micah	*Isaiah*	*Micah*	*Isaiah*
1:9-16	10:28-32	4:7	9:7
2:1-2	5:8	4:10	39:6
2:6, 11	30:10	5:2-4	7:14
2:12	10:20-23	5:6	14:25
3:5-7	29:9-12	6:6-8	58:6-7
4:1	2:2	7:7	8:17
4:4	1:19	7:12	11:11

■ For a verse-by-verse discussion of this important Old Testament book, see the *Bible Knowledge Commentary*, pages 1475-1492.

Commentary

It has always been a great temptation for the true believer to rely on his orthodoxy.

We see it in our own time. In a New Mexico church a young ministerial intern found his marriage hurting. His wife left and returned to her parents' home. The pastor called the young man in, and rather than offering support and help to repair the broken relationship, demanded his resignation. Unsatisfied by the letter of resignation that was submitted, the pastor rewrote the letter and sent his version out to the congregation over the young man's signature. He then insisted the intern simply disappear. There would be no farewells or good-bye gatherings.

When the people began to probe and to ask why they had not had a chance to express appreciation for the young man's ministry, the pastor held an exorcism in the church, banning the devil who was manifesting himself in the "critical spirit" of the people!

Though this pastor's actions showed a total and calloused disregard for the deep need and the pain of the young couple, he could always justify his action. After all, wasn't he biblically "right"?

The Pharisees operated on this same principle. Jesus was criticized—not for His miracles of compassion and healing, not for His capacity to touch unresponsive people and bring them into relationship with God—but because He did not wash His hands the way the Pharisees thought was "right," or because His disciples disregarded a tradition of men (not a word from God) and plucked ears of grain to eat as they walked through a field on the Sabbath. To the Pharisees, being "right" was an excuse to justify any and all comment, however unloving it might be.

We need to remember this tendency of the religious to justify themselves when we look at the Book of Micah. For Micah gave a prophetic warning—not to wayward Israel but to orthodox Judah!

Background

Micah was a contemporary of Isaiah. He and Isaiah both prophesied to Judah, the Southern Kingdom, at the time when Israel was carried into captivity by the Assyrian king, Sargon II. Most date Micah's ministry around 730 to 700 B.C.

These were tense days for Judah. Even though led by godly King Hezekiah, who worked wholeheartedly to bring revival, the Assyrian menace constantly loomed over little Judah.

As was characteristic, Hezekiah's rule brought a form of revival, but it was superficial. It did not touch the hearts of the people. Yet the combined ministry of these three godly men—Micah, Isaiah, and Hezekiah—was used by God to pull His people away from the edge of judgment. The Assyrians did indeed invade Judah. Following Sargon's death, Sennacherib captured some 46 Judean cities (including most of those named by Micah in chapter 1), and according to Assyrian records shut up Hezekiah in Jerusalem "like a bird in a cage."

But the city itself was delivered. Despite the continuing threat, God protected the remnant of His people. The incipient sin we see portrayed in the Books of Isaiah and of Micah had not yet matured. God would hold off judgment; His people would have yet another chance.

Being "right." It is clear that even under the preaching of Micah and Isaiah the mass of Judah's population still did not grasp the reality of their situation. Hezekiah had initiated great religious reforms. Most people assumed that this ritual reformation was what had protected them from their enemies.

This was one illusion the people of the Northern Kingdom never had.

The Northern Kingdom was founded with a false religious system, with counterfeit worship centers at Bethel and Dan, where counterfeit priests offered counterfeit sacrifices before counterfeit altars on counterfeit holy days. The whole ritual of the nation's official faith was *wrong.* Yet even this unorthodox approach to Yahweh's worship was not the dominant faith in the days Assyria invaded. It was the worship of Baal and Asherah, with pagan excesses committed on every height of ground, which gave abundant evidence of Israel's religious apostasy.

The social evils, the materialism, and the oppression which marked the society of the Northern Kingdom merely demonstrated the departure from God to which Israel's religion blatantly testified.

With the reforms instituted by Hezekiah, Judah's religious observances could not be faulted. Her official faith—or state religion, if you will—was beautifully orthodox. The house of God had been cleansed, the priests sanctified for ministry. Jerusalem altars erected to heathen deities were destroyed and the commanded feasts and sacrifices observed. The ways of praise instituted by David were restored; psalms were again sung. Throughout the tribal lands of Judah and Ephraim and Manasseh, the pillars and altars to Baal were crushed and burned. The orthodox faith of the Old Testament was scrupulously observed, and Judah took great comfort in the notion that her faith was "right."

The heart. Micah does not seem to have been impressed. Looking beneath the externals of ritual and form, Micah evaluated the heart of God's people and found it as perverse and ungodly as the heart of the men of the North:

> Hear this, you leaders of the house of Jacob, you rulers of the house of Israel, who despise justice and distort all that is right; who build Zion with bloodshed, and Jerusalem with wickedness. Her leaders judge for a bribe, her priests teach for a price, and her prophets tell fortunes for money. Yet they lean upon the Lord and say, "Is not the Lord among us? No disaster will come upon us." Therefore because of you, Zion will be plowed like a field, Jerusalem will become a heap of rubble, the temple hill a mound overgrown with thickets.
>
> Micah 3:9-12

Judah was placing its confidence in the outward orthodoxy of its ritual—just as many of us today place our confidence in the orthodoxy of our doctrine. But God demands more.

Micah, in words that seem to echo Amos' message to the people of the North, urged a return to God that would be demonstrated in a change of heart—a change of heart that would necessarily issue in a lifestyle of love and justice, of compassion and caring for their fellowmen as they walked close to God.

> With what shall I come before the Lord and bow down before the exalted God? Shall I come before Him with burnt offerings, with calves a year old? Will the Lord be pleased with thousands of rams, with ten thousand rivers of oil? Shall I offer my firstborn for my transgression, the fruit of my body for the sin of my soul? He has showed you, O man, what is good. And what does the Lord require of you? To act justly and to love mercy and to walk humbly with your God.
>
> Micah 6:6-8

Orthodoxy is never enough. Being right with God will be expressed in godly and compassionate living.

In a very real way, Micah is a book that speaks directly to us in our day. We are "right" in our doctrine. We are "right" in much of our practice. But our orthodoxy is an empty shell, a basis for even greater judgment, unless God's truth has warmed our hearts and moved us into relationships with individuals and with our society in which we do justice, love kindness, and walk humbly with our God.

♥ ***Link to Life: Youth / Adult***
Have the following statements on the chalkboard as group members enter. Ask your members to choose the one statement *which best sums the confidence a Christian can have in his or her personal relationship with God.*

- *We worship the right way.*
- *We believe what is true.*
- *We love kindness and justice.*

Discuss the choices and the reasons given for them. But do not *express a personal position. Simply contrast Israel and Judah at this time in history, and move into the study. You may want to return to these statements later in the session.*

Micah's Message
Seen in the context of its time, Micah's message takes on special significance. We can see the structure of the book and message by tracing the following outline.

Outline

I. Immediate National Judgment Coming
  A. Judgment announced 1:2-5
  B. Judgment described 1:6-8
  C. Judgment explained
    1. As amputation of a diseased limb 1:9-16
    2. As correcting of injustice 2:1-13
II. Principles and National Purpose
  A. Sin will bring judgment 3:1-12
  B. Ultimate blessing sure 4:1-8
  C. Scattering to come first 4:9–5:1
  D. Messiah to carry out God's plan 5:2-15
III. Pardon for Individuals Proclaimed
  A. A plea to see God's side 6:1-5
  B. How to return to God 6:6-8
  C. The need for punishment 6:9–7:6
  D. The believer's experience
    1. In time of judgment 7:7-10
    2. In terms of eternity 7:11-20

We can trace the thoughts of this significant Old Testament book.

Micah, identified in 1:1 as a prophet who ministered in the reigns of Jotham, Ahaz and Hezekiah, launched immediately into his message concerning Samaria and Jerusalem.

Judgment (Micah 1:2-5). Judgment was announced, as God was seen stepping out from His holy temple. To God both Samaria, the capital of the Northern Kingdom, and Jerusalem, capital and site of the temple in the South, were rebellious high places!

Explanation (Micah 1:9–2:13). The explanation of the judgment was given under two figures. The first was a graphic analogy (1:9-16). Samaria's idolatry and rebellion were likened to a wound which would not heal. Instead, the wound filled with pus, and infection and inflammation spread. Finally, there was no recourse but to amputate the wounded limb and all the surrounding body that had been infected. According to Micah's description, the infection had spread to reach "the very gate of My people, even to Jerusalem" (v. 9). When the Assyrians came, the cities between the Northern Kingdom and Jerusalem would be taken too, "for the transgressions of Israel were found in you" (v. 13).

The second picture seems to imply a set

of balances (2:1-13). There is a point and counterpoint structure to the passage:

sin described	*balancing judgment*
2:1-2	2:3-5
2:6-11	2:12-13

First, as in Amos, God focused attention on Judah's injustice, describing men who lie awake scheming to defraud their neighbors. Therefore, God said (v. 3), calamity would come on the family of Judah, and the fields the oppressors plotted to gain would be distributed to "apostates"—to a pagan people whom the victorious Assyrians would resettle in Israel.

Second, Micah spoke of the reaction of the people to his prophetic ministry. They said, "Do not prophesy" (v. 6), and then they spoke out with their own versions of God's message. And this from people who "strip off the rich robe from those who pass by" (v. 8) and who evict widows! They were ready to listen to a drunkard, but would not hear the Word of the Lord. The result? God must balance their sin with judgment.

> I will surely gather all of you, O Jacob; I will surely bring together the remnant of Israel.
>
> Micah 2:12

Then, gathered together in the midst of their pastures, God Himself would lead a robber band to break in and drag them out and away.

God *is* just. His holiness demands that the sin of His people be balanced by judgment.

With the immediate fate described and justified, Micah turned to a restatement of the principles found earlier in God's Word. While God has committed Himself as the holy God to punish sin, He has also committed Himself to the ultimate good and blessing of His people.

Review of sins (Micah 3:1-12). Graphically, Micah reviewed the sins that marred the lifestyle of God's people. He pictured their injustice as a brutal cannibalism (vv. 2-3) in which the very life of the poor was torn from them. He sketched the prophets as gross gluttons, always willing to cry, "Peace," and promise good news if their mouths were filled, but who were enemies of him "who puts nothing in their mouths" (v. 5, NASB). Gluttony, not God, was the source of their messages. Their leaders took bribes, the city was filled with violence, and yet because of the presence of the temple where their empty rituals were repeated, they "lean upon the Lord" (v. 11). The temple, polluted by their sins, would one day lie in ruin—and their empty hopes with it. God's holiness remains unchanged. Sin *will* be judged.

God's promise (Micah 4:1-8). When the judgment came, it should not be interpreted as total repudiation. Looking ahead to the end of history, Micah conveyed God's promise that the whole world will come to Jerusalem to learn of God and His ways, and that in those days God Himself will rule. Implements of war will be reshaped to harvest the bounty of the earth, and all men will live in peace and plenty.

Whatever comes, God will preserve a remnant of His people so that the time of promised blessing may be assured.

Babylon (Micah 4:9–5:1). But the present was to be a time of agony when Judah would be displaced. The Exile of Judah would not be at the hands of Assyria, but of Babylon (v. 10). From Babylon, God's people would be regathered.

Scattering and regathering, scattering and regathering—this is the pattern of judgment which Israel and Judah will experience until God finally brings all His promises to pass.

The Messiah (Micah 5:2-15). At this point Micah introduced the Messiah—the promised One on whose coming all the plans and purposes of God hinge. He would be born as a man in Bethlehem (v. 2), even though His "goings have been . . . from everlasting" (KJV). When Messiah comes, He will shepherd His people, deliver the scattered remnant, destroy Israel's enemies, and change the heart of God's people to root out all that has been associated with their sin.

Most of the Old Testament deals with the national experience of God's people. Judgments are announced on the Hebrew nation: promises tell of a national regathering. The corporate responsiveness or unresponsiveness of the nation as a whole is clearly the basis of God's dealing with His people.

Often the question is raised: What about the individual? Didn't God care about individuals in Old Testament days? Was the godly person swallowed up in judgment that was determined because of national sin?

Micah helped us to answer such questions, and to see that throughout history God has retained concern for the individual. In every age, God's overall working in history and society harmonizes with His love for each person.

What, then, does God say to the individual who lives in an unjust society and whose experience is shaped by environment?

God's perspective (Micah 6:1-5). The message to individuals began with a plea to realize that God *did* have a valid case against Israel. God had brought His people out of Egypt, ransomed them, gave leaders to guide them, protected and guarded them that they might "know the righteous acts of the Lord" (v. 5), i.e., that they might obey and experience all the good things which God would then be free to shower on them. But Israel had turned away, bored with God and His ways.

The righteous person will see the situation from God's perspective, even when the judgment brings him personal affliction.

God's requirements (Micah 6:6-8). What can the individual who recognizes the righteousness of God's cause do? "He has showed you, O man, what is good. And what does the Lord require of you? To act justly and to love mercy and to walk humbly with your God" (v. 8).

Necessity of judgment (Micah 6:9–7:6). Reviewing again the sins of the society in which the just live, God pointed out that He *must* act to judge it. "Can I justify wicked scales and a bag of deceptive weights?" (6:11, NASB) No, punishment must come. And when it does, the just in that society must undergo the same experience as the unjust.

Believer's response (Micah 7:7-20). How then is the believer to respond in times of judgment? Micah gave two answers.

First (vv. 7-13), suffering in such a time is to be expected. It is just. The individual *does* bear responsibility for his society (v. 9). Yet during such a time of discipline the true believer will not lose hope in God: "Though I fall I will rise; though I dwell in darkness, the Lord is a light for me" (v. 8).

Second (vv. 14-20), the believer takes comfort in his confidence in God's commitment to bring him good in the end. We think in terms of eternity; the godly Jew characteristically thought of a national restoration. In either case, God *will* do what He intends and bring us everlasting good. The sufferings of this time are not fit to be compared with the glory to come. So Micah concluded:

> Who is a God like You, who pardons sin and forgives the transgression of the remnant of His inheritance? You do not stay angry forever but delight to show mercy. You will again have compassion on us; You will tread our sins underfoot and hurl all our iniquities into the depths of the sea. You will be true to Jacob, and show mercy to Abraham, as You pledged on oath to our fathers in days long ago.
>
> Micah 7:18-20

TEACHING GUIDE

Prepare

Meditate on Micah 6:8. What does it suggest that God yearns to see in the lives and character of your group members?

Explore

1. Tell the true story of the intern and pastor related at the beginning of this unit. Discuss: "Was the pastor right or wrong? Did he or did he not have a biblical view of marriage? Is it possible to be 'right' and 'wrong' at the same time?"
2. Or, as your group members enter, place on the chalkboard the three ideas contained in "link-to-life," page 479. Talk about them, and then contrast for your group the orthodoxy of Judah and the heresy of Israel.

Expand

1. Duplicate for your members the outline of Micah in the commentary. Divide into teams to explore the three major sections of the book, and to report back on key thoughts or verses there.
2. Or have group members paraphrase Micah 3:9-11, as if it were being written to a contemporary Christian congregation. What would Micah have to say to people of our day?

You may want to select added short pas-

sages for this kind of modernizing paraphrase, which helps us sense the power of the prophet's words and their relevance to us today.
3. Or work through the book together, following the outline. You may want to make this a minilecture, or simply make sure that your group members discover the main points made by the prophet in each section.
4. Or compare the parallel verses in Isaiah and Micah (see list at beginning of study guide), and develop your own portrait of this orthodox but ungodly people.

Apply
Return to the questions raised at the beginning of the group session. How might elements in each sentence be combined to present a view with which Micah would agree?

STUDY GUIDE 74
Habakkuk

CHALLENGES TO FAITH

Overview
The Book of Habakkuk explores the question of why—and whether—God permits evil to exist unpunished. It is best to place this prophet, unknown except through his book, in the days of Josiah (639–597 B.C.). Habakkuk was troubled by the sins he saw in Judah despite the religious revival. God showed the prophet that He was about to bring the Babylonians down on His people as a punishment.

But Habakkuk raised another question: How can the holy God use a wicked people as a tool?

This small book has great value for us today. We too see the wicked apparently flourish, and may have questions about God's justice. If we do, we find God's striking answer in Habakkuk!

We also find something else: the secret of survival when national or personal troubles come.

Outline

I.	The Prophet's Cry	chap. 1
II.	Principles of Judgment	chap. 2
III.	Personal Faith	chap. 3

▶ ***Hebrew.*** The Hebrew language is a picture language. It enriches its presentation of concepts by the use of graphic descriptions which, while easily translated, may not be as clear to modern readers as to those of the author's own times. The Book of Habakkuk is particularly graphic in some of its portrayals. To express the meaning most sharply, the text quoted in this unit is my own translation. It is not intended to replace but to supplement study in other versions.

Commentary
Habakkuk's Cry: Chapter 1
It seems that the twenty-first year of the reign of godly King Josiah would have been a time of joy for any worshiper of the Lord. Especially for a man like Habakkuk, a Levite, devoted to God's service. Yet Habakkuk, who may have been a temple worship leader, was deeply troubled when the events recorded in his book took place.

It was a time of revival. But it was also an age of sin.

Josiah's revival. The king had come to the throne of Judah at age 8. At 16 he began to seek the Lord, and at 20 purged idolatry from Jerusalem. In the process of repairing the temple, Hilkiah the priest had discovered a copy of the Book of the Law—that Book which God had given Israel through Moses, and which had been lost during the rule of a series of evil kings. When Shaphan, the scribe, read the book, he hurried to Josiah (2 Kings 22:10).

The Book had a tremendous impact on the king. It contained not only the history of the nation's call by God, but also gave explicit instructions on how to live. And at the end of the lost Book, in the section we call Deuteronomy, was a list of curses that God would call down on Israel if His people forsook Him and His Law.

The king was terror stricken. No one living could remember a day when Judah had known and obeyed the commands found in this Book! Immediately Josiah humbled himself before God and prayed for mercy. He determined to publish the divine Law throughout his realm. As king, Josiah made a solemn promise to Yahweh to keep His commands and His statutes with all his heart.

Publish God's Word Josiah did. He required everyone to hear the Book read, and that very year he reinstituted the Feast of the Passover. Josiah led all Judah to keep it, with great rejoicing (23:21-22).

An age of sin. Habakkuk and the people of Judah were now exposed to the Word of

God. On the one hand this was exciting for a man like our prophet. Each word told Habakkuk more of his God, and the more he heard, the more exalted God, the Holy One, became in Habakkuk's eyes. But as Habakkuk began to see the perfect holiness of God, he became more and more concerned about the imperfections and sins of God's people. True, idolatry was gone, and men now worshiped Yahweh. Josiah was working tirelessly to promote knowledge of the Lord in his kingdom. But it was also clear that the religious reformation was superficial. The hearts of the men and women who came to worship at the Jerusalem temple were much the same as when they had bowed before pagan altars!

Simply knowing the Law did not produce holiness. God's people were not obeying the commands of their God.

To Habakkuk this situation was intolerable. Here was Judah, a people called by the name of God, blessed with the Law of God, daily bringing shame on His holy name by flagrant disregard of what was right. They twisted and perverted the Law, and even did violence against those who tried to walk by it.

This is Habakkuk's burden when we turn to the first chapter of his book. He opens his heart and mind to us, and expresses a complaint that must have been constantly on his lips.

> How long, O Lord, must I call for help, but You do not listen? Or cry out to You, "Violence!" but You do not save? Why do You make me look at injustice? Why do You tolerate wrong? Destruction and violence are before me; there is strife, and conflict abounds. Therefore the law is paralyzed, and justice never prevails. The wicked hem in the righteous, so that justice is perverted.
>
> Habakkuk 1:2-4

The condition of violence and perverted justice is difficult for us to understand today. Why, if the king was righteous, was the Law benumbed and justice ever absent? The answer is found in the way law was administered in the Judah of Habakkuk's day.

While the king's power may have been supreme in Jerusalem, where he reigned through his personal officers, outside the capital the administration of justice was a local affair. There was no code of statutory law administered by trained officials and enforced by public police. Cases were brought by individuals before local elders, who sat at each city's gates. The plaintiff and defendant each brought witnesses to give evidence, and each pled his own case.

There were many ways that such justice could be perverted. False witnesses were easy to hire in Judah. Or a friendly lie might be told for a neighbor in return for the promise of similar help later. And the men who made the decisions were not above a bribe; many went out of their way to seek them. By sheer weight of numbers, those who tried to keep the Law and do justice might be overwhelmed and defrauded by the wicked around them. Justice was administered, but it was a perverted and crooked sort of justice.

Still, Habakkuk's thoughts lay not so much with the people as with God. He was not moved as much by anger as by concern for the glory of God. How could the holy God let His people go on like this and dishonor Him? Must not God move to remedy the situation? Must He not move the hearts of the people as He had moved Josiah's, and bring Judah to love and obey Him? Must not God be glorified in the sight of all the heathen?

♥ ***Link to Life: Youth / Adult***
Write several brief scenarios on 3 x 5 cards. Pass them out to teams of three or four as group members enter. Have on the chalk board this question:

What will people think of God?

Scenarios may go something like these two:
Investigative reporters discover that an elder in X church owns a local pornographic bookstore. The pastor and other leaders of the church defend him. "He's always given generously to our building program," the pastor is quoted as saying.

A young man is beaten and robbed by three drug users. An acquaintance tells his friends, "He had it coming. He stopped going to church a couple months ago. I guess God was punishing him."

After your teams have discussed each

scenario, draw them together again. Do not hear reports, but share Habakkuk's situation, with the wicked surrounding the righteous and perverting God's Law despite the religious revival.

How would they feel if they were Habakkuk? What questions does the holiness of God raise for us in our own day?

In 626 B.C., which may have been a few brief years before the problem began to torment Habakkuk, Nabopolassar, a Chaldean prince, led a rebellion and defeated the Assyrians outside the city of Babylon. He took the city, and established the Neo-Babylonian Empire. The Assyrians repeatedly tried to dislodge him, but fighting fiercely on the defensive, Nabopolassar maintained his hold on the city. Even if Habakkuk had been informed of this situation in far-off Babylon, he could hardly have foreseen the developments that less than two decades would bring.

By 620, Nabopolassar would form an alliance with the Medes, a fierce people on Assyria's northeastern border. This coalition would make great inroads in Assyrian territory. Soon Assyria would be fighting for existence. Within five years of Habakkuk's experience, Egypt, Assyria's ancient enemy, would see such danger from the Medo-Babylonian axis that she would even send an army to Assyria's support!

Just 2 years after that, in 614 B.C., the Medes took the ancient capital of Asshur. By 612 the allies assaulted Nineveh, the impregnable citadel of Assyria, and destroyed it within three months. This was the death of Assyria. It was now merely a matter of time before the terror that the name of Assyria had raised in the hearts of generations of Hebrews would be transferred to the name of Babylon. Within another 15 years, Nebuchadnezzar, Nabopolassar's greater son, would begin a series of deportations that by 586 B.C. would leave the temple in Jerusalem a smoking, crumbling ruin.

All this Habakkuk could not know. But Habakkuk's God *did* know, and as Habakkuk wrestled with his problem, God spoke to this man so concerned with the Lord's glory.

God would not permit His people to keep on sinning. God was even then preparing an instrument He would use to chastise them.

> Look at the nations and watch—and be utterly amazed. For I am going to do something in your days that you would not believe, even if you were told. I am raising up the Babylonians, that ruthless and impetuous people, who sweep across the whole earth to seize dwelling places not their own. They are feared and dreaded people; they are a law to themselves and promote their own honor. Their horses are swifter than leopards, fiercer than wolves at dusk. Their cavalry gallops headlong; their horsemen come from afar. They fly like a vulture swooping to devour; they all come bent on violence. Their hordes advance like a desert wind and gather prisoners like sand. They deride kings and scoff at rulers. They laugh at the fortified cities; they build earthen ramps and capture them. Then they sweep past like the wind and go on—guilty men, whose own strength is their god.
>
> Habakkuk 1:5-11

All this Yahweh told Habakkuk was coming, straining and hastening toward Judah. And all this, God said, was His work! He was raising up the Chaldeans (the Babylonians), and He was riding at the head of this dreadful scourge.

To Habakkuk, who understood the holiness of God and who saw beneath the facade of Judah's apparent reform to its inner depravity, there were no doubts about justice. And there was no retreat to a fuzzy concept of love that robbed God of His holiness and left Him the emasculated image honored by the wishful thinkers of all ages. Habakkuk knew God's love for His people. And Habakkuk recognized the cancer of sin that now infected the body of Yahweh's beloved.

Sin had led to Habakkuk's original complaint. The surgery the divine Physician decreed warranted no recriminations. No, Habakkuk looked into the face of his God and saw the Lord's unchanging purpose. He saw love—expressed as chastisement.

> O Lord, are You not from everlasting? My God, my Holy One, we will not die. O Lord, You have appointed them to execute judgment; O Rock, You have ordained them to punish.
>
> Habakkuk 1:12

But though Habakkuk accepted the rightness of the decreed punishment, he was now faced with an even greater puzzle. That puzzle is expressed in his next words.

> Your eyes are too pure to look on evil; You cannot tolerate wrong. Why then do You tolerate the treacherous? Why are You silent while the wicked swallow up those more righteous than themselves? You have made men like fish in the sea, like sea creatures that have no ruler. The wicked foe pulls all of them up with hooks, he catches them in his net, he gathers them up in his dragnet; and so he rejoices and is glad. Therefore he sacrifices to his net and burns incense to his dragnet, for by his net he lives in luxury and enjoys the choicest food. Is he to keep on emptying his net, destroying nations without mercy?
>
> Habakkuk 1:13-17

Surely the God who had spoken earlier to His troubled servant would speak again. So Habakkuk chose a place to watch and wait.

> I will stand at my watch and station myself on the ramparts; I will look to see what He will say to me, and what answer I am to give to this complaint.
>
> Habakkuk 2:1

God's Answer: Habakkuk 2

The message of a coming invasion was not new. Isaiah had foretold that it must happen one day (Isa. 39). The startling thing about the revelation to Habakkuk was that the day of judgment was on his people.

When God next spoke to Habakkuk, the message of immediacy was repeated.

> Then the Lord replied: "Write down the revelation and make it plain on tablets so that a herald may run with it. For the revelation awaits an appointed time; it speaks of the end and will not prove false. Though it linger, wait for it; it will certainly come and will not delay."
>
> Habakkuk 2:2-3

Then, after commanding Habakkuk to publish God's sentence, the Lord turned to Habakkuk's own problem. He revealed to Habakkuk why even the success of the wicked can never tarnish the glory of God.

Dissatisfaction (Hab. 2:4-5). The wicked man suffers from a fatal flaw that drives him on, seeking a satisfaction he can never find. In essence God told His prophet that the Babylonians' successes would only feed the flames of their desires. As passion is inflamed, the emptiness within is enlarged, and the wicked man is driven to push further into sin in a vain attempt to find satisfaction.

Thus the Chaldeans embarked on a course that, for all their victories, led only to frustration and self-enslavement. In Habakkuk's words:

> See, he is puffed up; his desires are not upright—but the righteous will live by his faith—indeed, wine betrays him; he is arrogant and never at rest. Because he is as greedy as the grave and like death is never satisfied, he gathers to himself all the nations and takes captive all the peoples.
>
> Habakkuk 2:4-5

Repayment (Hab. 2:6-8). The course the wicked choose offers no inner satisfaction no matter how "successful" such people seem. And there is another principle at work that demonstrates God is actually actively judging sinners *now.* The wicked person arouses hostility, and one day those he harms will turn on him:

> Will not all of them taunt him with ridicule and scorn, saying, "Woe to him who piles up stolen goods and makes himself wealthy by extortion! How long must this go on?" Will not your debtors suddenly arise? Will they not wake up and make you tremble? Then you will become their victim. Because you have plundered many nations, the peoples who are left will plunder you. For you have shed man's blood; you have destroyed lands and cities and everyone in them.
>
> Habakkuk 2:6-8

No security (Hab. 2:9-11). The drive which led the wicked to seek wealth or power at the expense of other people was a drive for security. Yet wealth and power could never really protect anyone. All that this lifestyle was sure to gain was dashed hopes and guilt.

> Woe to him who builds his realm by unjust gain to set his nest on high, to escape the clutches of ruin! You have plotted the ruin of many peoples, shaming your own house and forfeiting your life. The stones of the wall will cry out, and the beams of the woodwork will echo it.
>
> Habakkak 2:9-11

Material things decay (Hab. 2:12-14). What will happen to those who pile up material things, and build cities in this world to promote their own glory? All they build will fall into ruin. What a judgment—that the builders build for nothing! The earth is destined to be filled with the knowledge of the Lord, not with monuments to murderers!

> Woe to him who builds a city with bloodshed and establishes a town by crime! Has not the Lord Almighty determined that the people's labor is only fuel for the fire, that the nations exhaust themselves for nothing? For the earth will be filled with the knowledge of the glory of the Lord, as the waters cover the sea.
>
> Habakkuk 2:12-14

Repayment in kind (Hab. 2:15-17). All man's plots for self-promotion at the expense of others led directly to appropriate consequences:

> Woe to him who gives drink to his neighbors, pouring it from the wineskin till they are drunk, so that he can gaze on their naked bodies. You will be filled with shame instead of glory. Now it is your turn! Drink and be exposed! The cup from the Lord's right hand is coming around to you, and disgrace will cover your glory. The violence you have done to Lebanon will overwhelm you, and your destruction of animals will terrify you. For you have shed man's blood; you have destroyed lands and cities and everyone in them.
>
> Habakkuk 2:15-17

How striking. Habakkuk had feared for the glory of God, concerned at the success of the sinner. He had worried that puny men would exalt themselves, and boast of victories over God. *Yet every sinful act brings its own judgment, natural consequences of wickedness that mark the personalities of the sinner, and shape the circumstances of his later life.* No need to fear for God! The idols of the men of every age are empty things of no value for anything.

> Of what value is an idol, since a man has carved it? Or an image that teaches lies? For he who makes it trusts in his own creation; he makes idols that cannot speak. Woe to him who says to wood, "Come to life!" Or to lifeless stone, "Wake up!" Can it give guidance? It is covered with gold and silver; there is no breath in it. But the Lord is in His holy temple; let all the earth be silent before Him.
>
> Habakkuk 2:18-20

The idols of men, whether of wood and stone or of wealth and success, hold out no hope. God is in His holy temple. *God* is Judge. And God is judging sinners even now!

♥ ***Link to Life: Youth / Adult***

Make copies of each brief chapter 2 segment, titling it as in the text (e.g., dissatisfaction, repayments, etc.). Give an overview of the thrust of this chapter; explain that in it God told the prophet why the wicked did not "get away with" sin even though they might appear happy and successful.

Break into teams, each of which is to look at one *of these segments. Each is to answer the following questions: "What happens within or to the wicked person? What modern illustrations of this principle, in individuals or nations, can you think of?"*

Personal Faith: Habakkuk 3

The answer God gave Habakkuk in chapter 2 satisfied the prophet. He began to realize that the wicked of every age make choices which guarantee their downfall—and misery. Whatever heights the wicked reach the evil person can never be satisfied. And the course he takes in its pursuit will trip him up: the enemies he inevitably makes will treat him as he has treated them.

Satisfied, Habakkuk now was ready to welcome the coming invasion.

> Lord, I have heard of Your fame; I stand in awe of Your deeds, O Lord. Renew them in our day, in our time make them known; in wrath remember mercy.
> Habakkuk 3:2

But then God gave Habakkuk a stunning experience. He transported the prophet back in time, and let him witness from the divine viewpoint a series of other judgments wrought by the Holy God.

The first image was of God proceeding from Sinai, following the course His people took after receiving the Law.

> God came from Teman, the Holy One from Mount Paran. His glory covered the heavens and His praise filled the earth. His splendor was like the sunrise. Rays flashed from His hand, where His power was hidden. Plague was before Him; pestilence followed His steps. He stood, and shook the earth; He looked, and made the nations tremble. The ancient mountains crumbled and the age-old hills collapsed. His ways are eternal.
> Habakkuk 3:3-6

Then the vista changed, and Habakkuk saw God reach the tents of Israel that were spread near Midian. He saw the Israelites embracing the women and idols of that land. And Habakkuk saw the terrible plague God sent sweeping through the camp; he saw the writhing and the agony of those who felt the fury of God.

> I saw the tents of Cushan in distress, the dwellings of Midian in anguish. Were You angry with the rivers, O Lord? Was Your wrath against the streams? Did You rage against the sea when You rode with Your horses and Your victorious chariots? You uncovered your bow, You called for many arrows.
> Habakkuk 3:7-9

Then Habakkuk was shown a panoramic view of God's cataclysmic judgments, from the time of the Flood throughout sacred history.

> In wrath You strode through the earth and in anger You threshed the nations. You came out to deliver Your people, to save Your anointed one. You crushed the leader of the land of wickedness, You stripped him from head to foot. With his own spear You pierced his head when his warriors stormed out to scatter us, gloating as though about to devour the wretched who were in hiding. You trampled the sea with Your horses, churning the great waters.
> Habakkuk 3:12-15

The vision over, Habakkuk, who had prayed so lightly for judgment to come, now understood what that judgment would mean. At last he knew the terror of the angry, holy God.

> I heard and my heart pounded, my lips quivered at the sound; decay crept into my bones, and my legs trembled. Yet I will wait patiently for the day of calamity to come on the nation invading us. Though the fig tree does not bud and there are no grapes on the vines, though the olive crop fails and the fields produce no food, though there are no sheep in the pen and no cattle in the stalls.
> Habakkuk 3:16-17

And this judgment was coming on him.

Habakkuk had looked at the coming judgment from God's viewpoint alone. His concern had been for God's glory, and not for men—not even for himself.

But Habakkuk was a man, and must face the Chaldean terror.

We need to picture Habakkuk, standing on some mountain trail, as he came to this realization. Trembling and overcome, his eyes caught a glimpse of movement above him. There, on a higher crag, the prophet caught a glimpse of a mountain goat, surefooted despite the danger on the heights.

And then Habakkuk realized the nature of faith's calling. He too was to walk on the heights, to live only a step from disaster, as his nation fell in ruins around him.

> Yet I will rejoice in the Lord, I will be joyful in God my Saviour. The Sovereign Lord is my strength; He makes my feet like the feet of a deer, He enables me to go on the heights.
> Habakkuk 3:18-19

Habakkuk had reached the pinnacle of faith.

TEACHING GUIDE

Prepare
What do you think is meant by the phrase, "The righteous man will live by his faith"? (Hab. 2:4)

Explore
1. On the chalkboard write: "Why do the wicked have it so good?" Discuss: "Do the wicked have it good? Why, or why not?"
2. Or use the "link-to-life" idea on pages 484-485 to help your group members understand Habakkuk's initial concern.

Expand
1. Use the "link-to-life" idea on page 487 to help your group explore principles of God's present judgment in the lives of the "successful" wicked.
2. Or give a minilecture showing the consequences of sinful choices in our here and now. We do not need to wait for eternity for justice to be done, whatever the appearances may be.

Apply
Share Habakkuk's vision of the human meaning of God's judgment, seen in chapter 3.

Focus on the conviction that the prophet came to: that no matter how terrible what happens, God will guard his footsteps.

Draw on a chalkboard a jagged mountain height, where it is dangerous to walk. Ask each person to determine what his own personal mountain crag involves, then to close his eyes and thank God that the Lord will guide his feet.

STUDY GUIDE 75

Zephaniah

JUDGMENT COMING

Overview

Zephaniah has been called the "prophet of universal judgment." He looked far ahead, and described a day when God will judge, and history will demonstrate His sovereignty.

Outline

I. Judgment on Judah	1:1–2:3
II. Judgment on the Nations	2:4-15
III. Jerusalem's Future	3:1-20
A. Near judgment	3:1-7
B. Eternal kingdom	3:8-20

Zephaniah was a descendant of Judah's King Hezekiah. He preached in the time of Josiah, another godly king. Zephaniah's portrait of the idolatry in Judah suggests that he spoke in Josiah's early years, as that child-king was growing up and before his revival of 621 B.C.

Zephaniah's structure reflects common elements in the books of all the minor prophets. Thus the book gives us a springboard from which to look at aspects of the future seen by all the Hebrew prophets.

▶ ***Judge.*** The Hebrew words translated "judge" and "judgment" are derived from *din* and *sapat*. These synonyms imply all functions of government; executive and legislative as well as judicial. Thus the prophets affirmation that "God is Judge" suggests that He is the ultimate Ruler of the universe as well as its moral arbiter. Because God is in total control of this universe He can and will come to punish sin and, ultimately, to establish righteousness.

Commentary

In studying Old Testament prophetic books it is important to pay attention to their structure.

It is true that each prophet had a message for his contemporaries. In general when we study the major or minor prophets, it's best to explore them from this viewpoint. By looking at the message of a prophet for the people of his own day, we discover what might be called the universal message of that prophet: the message that God has through His Word for believers of all times.

Still, as we read the prophets, we cannot help but notice that there is a striking similarity in the way these works are organized. Simply put, they generally (1) start with words of warning to the living generation, (2) move on to announce a coming judgment, (3) add an invitation to the living to repent and be restored, and (4) conclude with a portrait of the distant future.

This final section may focus on the tragedies of what is commonly called "the Day of the Lord" or "that Day." Often this time when God intervenes and acts directly to judge sin is spoken of as a day of darkness and terror. Yet there is also glory ahead. And often the prophets move beyond the time of judgment to show a brighter aspect of the Day of the Lord. For all agree that that day will close with the establishment of peace and of righteousness. In almost every case, the last words of a prophet's writings are words of hope.

The Book of Zephaniah illustrates that structure, and helps us grasp the outline of most of the minor prophets. It reminds us that if we want a picture of the end of time, we can turn to the ending of almost any of the minor prophets (the majors are Jeremiah, Ezekiel, Isaiah, and Daniel) and find there descriptions of what the prophets believed lay ahead.

Zephaniah

The Book of Zephaniah clearly demonstrates the common structure, and picks up most of the prophetic themes. Note the pattern mentioned earlier.

Words of warning to the contemporary generation (Zeph. 1:2-13). Zephaniah launched into a stern and powerful warning:

> "I will sweep away everything from the face of the earth," declares the Lord. "I will sweep away both men and animals; I will sweep away the birds of the air and the fish of the sea. The wicked will have only heaps of rubble when I cut off man from the face of the earth," declares the Lord.
>
> Zephaniah 1:2-3

In the next verse Zephaniah explained the reasons why his generation must be judged. God's people were sunk deep in idolatry. And they had filled the temple of their gods "with violence and deceit" (v. 9).

Announcement of coming judgment (Zeph. 1:14–2:15). Zephaniah moved on to portray the "great Day of the Lord" which is "near and coming quickly" (1:14).

His initial description is of its bitterness:

> That day will be a day of wrath, a day of distress and anguish, a day of trouble and ruin, a day of darkness and gloom, a day of clouds and blackness, a day of trumpet and battle cry against the fortified cities and against the corner towers.
>
> Zephaniah 1:15-16

And Zephaniah made it clear that while Judah, a "shameful nation," will experience all the distress ordained because "they have sinned against the Lord," the day of judgment will also see the punishment of pagan nations. Much of chapter 2 details God's description of the judgment coming on Philistia (vv. 4-7), Moab and Ammon (vv. 8-11), Cush (v. 12), and Assyria (vv. 13-15).

An invitation to repent and be restored (Zeph. 2:2-3). Imbedded in the announcement of judgment is a typical invitation. Before the terrible day came and the wrath of God swept everything away, individuals are told to:

> Seek the Lord, all you humble of the land, you who do what He commands. Seek righteousness, seek humility; perhaps you will be sheltered on the day of the Lord's anger.
>
> Zephaniah 2:3

A picture of the far future (Zeph. 3:1-20). Zephaniah turned now to a picture of the more distant future. He continued describing the Day of the Lord, now as it will affect Jerusalem specifically.

He described a great warlike assembly of nations and their destruction under the fierce anger of the Lord. In the process God will "remove from this city those who rejoice in their pride" (v. 11).

> But I will leave within you the meek and humble, who trust in the name of the Lord. The remnant of Israel will do no wrong; they will speak no lies, nor will deceit be found in their mouths. They will eat and lie down and no one will make them afraid.
>
> Zephaniah 3:12-13

With these words Zephaniah moved beyond the dark clouds of divine judgment to portray the bright day judgment will bring. He saw Jerusalem glad and rejoicing, and he said, "The Lord, the King of Israel, is with you" (v. 15). In that day God will save, and:

> The Lord your God is with you, He is mighty to save. He will take great delight in you, He will quiet you with His love, He will rejoice over you with singing.
>
> Zephaniah 3:17

The book concludes with another promise which is repeated again and again in the prophets:

> "At that time I will gather you; at that time I will bring you home. I will give you honor and praise among all the peoples of the earth when I restore your fortunes before your very eyes," says the Lord.
>
> Zephaniah 3:20

♥ ***Link to Life: Youth / Adult***
List on the chalkboard the four structural elements the author says are characteristic of the books of the minor prophets. Have group members work in pairs to (1) identify the verses in Zephaniah that go with each structural element, and (2) sum up what this prophet says about each.

Discuss: "What are major impressions you have about the future as sketched by Zephaniah?"

End Time Themes
The structure of this book, like those of the other minor prophets, ends with a vision of the distant future. And strikingly each of the prophets, major and minor, repeats again and again the same themes.

The prophets all speak of a regathering of Israel: with Zephaniah they promise that God will "gather those who have been scattered" to "bring you home" (3:19, 20).

The prophets all describe a time of terrible distress and tribulation: with Zephaniah they describe a time when "the whole world will be consumed by the fire of My jealous anger" (v. 8).

The prophets all describe a glorious kingdom to be established after the judgment: with Zephaniah they see a time when "the Lord, the King of Israel, is with you" and Israel will be exalted, for God "will give you honor and praise among all the people of the earth" (vv. 15, 20).

These elements are repeated so often that, while details of time and sequence are undefined, a clear portrait of the time of the end as seen by the prophets can be drawn. Thus it's helpful, not just for an understanding of Zephaniah but to sensitize Christians to the message of the prophets, to look at each of these themes separately.

A final regathering. While hardly a popular view in modern Arab countries, it is the conviction of the prophets that history's end will find the Jews in possession of the Promised Land.

This conviction is rooted first of all in the ancient Abrahamic Covenant, under which God guaranteed Abraham's descendants possession of Palestine "from the river of Egypt to the great river, the Euphrates" (Gen. 15:18). In historic times this territory has been *partially* occupied by the Hebrews. But even under Kings David and Solomon Israel has never possessed the full extent of the Promised Land.

Yet this promise is repeated in the Old Testament, at various periods of history. One of the most significant repetitions is in Jeremiah 31. In that prophet's time the people of Judah were all torn from their land, and taken away captive to Babylon. Yet Jeremiah conveyed this message from God:

> "Restrain your voice from weeping and your eyes from tears, for your work will be rewarded," declares the Lord. "They will return from the land of the enemy. So there is hope for your future," declares the Lord. "Your children will return to their own land."
>
> Jeremiah 31:16-17

The Book of Deuteronomy explains that when God's people turn from Him to idols and immorality they will be expelled from their land (Deut. 28:36-37, 64-68). Yet that same powerful passage contains the promise of regathering, which is echoed by all the prophets (Deut. 30:1-10).

The fact that the theme of regathering is found in prophets before and after the Babylonian Exile, along with the fact that for nearly 2,000 years the Jewish people have been scattered among the nations, indicates that the Day of the Lord with which the regathering is associated still lies ahead.

Isaiah looked beyond the Babylonian Captivity and the return of the Jews in the fifth century B.C. to say:

> In that day the Lord will reach out His hand a *second time* to reclaim the remnant that is left of His people from Assyria, from Lower Egypt, from Upper Egypt, from Cush, from Elam, from Babylonia, from Hamath and from the islands of the sea. He will raise a banner for the nations and gather the exiles of Israel; He will assemble the scattered people of Judah from the four quarters of the earth.
>
> Isaiah 11:11-12 (italics mine)

What do the other prophets say about the regathering which they see associated with history's end? Here are passages in which this theme is found: Deuteronomy 28–30; Isaiah 14:1-3; 27:12-13; 43:1-8; 49:16; 66:20-22; Jeremiah 16:14-16; 23:3-8; 30:10-11; 31:8, 31-37; Ezekiel 11:17-21; 20:33-38; 34:11-16; 39:25-29; Hosea 1:10-11; Joel 3:17-21; Amos 9:11-15; Micah 4:4-7; Zephaniah 3:14-20; Zechariah 8:4-8.

A Great Tribulation. Of all the themes associated with the prophetic view of destiny, that of a final Tribulation is given the most attention. As Amos warned those who speak lightly of the Lord's coming,

> Woe to you who long for the Day of the Lord! Why do you long for the Day of the Lord? That day will be darkness, not

> light. It will be as though a man fled from a lion only to meet a bear, as though he entered his house and rested his hand on the wall only to have a snake bite him. Will not the Day of the Lord be darkness, not light—pitch-dark, without a ray of brightness?
>
> Amos 5:18-20

The terrors of this time are graphically described by some of the prophets. For instance:

> A Day of the Lord is coming when your plunder will be divided among you. I will gather all the nations to Jerusalem to fight against it; the city will be captured, the houses ransacked, and the women raped. Half of the city will go into Exile but the rest of the people will not be taken from the city. Then the Lord will go out and fight against those nations, as He fights in the day of battle. On that day His feet will stand on the Mount of Olives, east of Jerusalem, and the Mount of Olives will be split in two from east to west, forming a great valley. . . . You will flee by my mountain valley. . . . Then the Lord my God will come, and all the holy ones with Him.
>
> Zechariah 14:1-5

Yet despite the terror of that day it is clear that the prophets see it as a time of purification. It is a day of wrath and judgment, but it will lead to deliverance.

Here are sample descriptions from some of the prophets.

> Behold, evil is going forth from nation to nation, and a great storm is being stirred up from the remotest parts of the earth. And those slain by the Lord on that day shall be from one end of the earth to the other. They shall not be lamented, gathered, or buried.
>
> Jeremiah 25:32-33, NASB

> Alas! for that day is great, there is none like it; and it is the time of Jacob's distress, but he will be saved from it.
>
> Jeremiah 30:7, NASB

> And I shall make you pass under the rod, and I shall bring you into the bond of the covenant; and I shall purge from you the rebels.
>
> Ezekiel 20:37-38, NASB

> "In the whole land," declares the Lord, "two thirds will be struck down and perish; yet one third will be left in it. This third I will bring into the fire; I will refine them like silver and test them like gold. They will call on My name and I will answer them; I will say, 'They are My people,' and they will say, 'The Lord is our God.' "
>
> Zechariah 13:8-9

What else do the prophets say about the time of distress, and the faithful remnant who will be purified and preserved through it? For images of the Great Tribulation, see Deuteronomy 4:30-31; Isaiah 2:19; 24:1, 3, 6, 19-21; 26:20-21; Jeremiah 30:7; Daniel 9:27; 12:1; Joel 1:15; 2:1-2; Amos 5:18-20; Zephaniah 1:14-15, 18. For the promise of a remnant to be preserved see Isaiah 1:9; 4:3-4; 6:12-13; 10:21; 26:20; 51:1-11; Jeremiah 15:11; 33:25-26; 44:28; Ezekiel 14:22; 20:34-38; 37:21-22; Hosea 3:5; Amos 9:11-15; Zechariah 13:8-9; Malachi 3:16-17.

A king and kingdom. The prophets do not end history on a dark note. Instead they are caught up with visions of glory. Each sees a Ruler, whose titles reflect His divine nature, who will bring blessings to the people of the earth.

Typical of these prophecies is this powerful vision of Isaiah of the characteristics of Messiah.

> For to us a Child is born, to us a Son is given, and the government will be on His shoulders. And He will be called Wonderful Counselor, Mighty God, Everlasting Father, Prince of Peace. Of the increase of His government and peace there will be no end. He will reign on David's throne and over his kingdom, establishing and upholding it with justice and righteousness from that time on and forever. The zeal of the Lord Almighty will accomplish this.
>
> Isaiah 9:6-7

Some of the most beautiful pictures of that time, a coming Messianic Age, are found in Isaiah. Here, from chapter 11, is one of the best known.

> A shoot will come up from the stump of Jesse; from his roots a Branch will bear fruit. The Spirit of the Lord will rest on Him—the Spirit of wisdom and of understanding, the Spirit of counsel and of power, the Spirit of knowledge and of the fear of the Lord. . . . He will not judge by what He sees with His eyes, or decide by what He hears with His ears; but with righteousness He will judge the needy, with justice He will give decisions for the poor of the earth. He will strike the earth with the rod of His mouth; with the breath of His lips He will slay the wicked. Righteousness will be His belt and faithfulness the sash around His waist. The wolf will live with the lamb, the leopard will lie down with the goat, the calf and the lion and the yearling together; and a little child will lead them. The cow will feed with the bear, their young will lie down together, and the lion will eat straw like the ox. The infant will play near the hole of the cobra, and the young child put his hand into the viper's nest. They will neither harm nor destroy on all My holy mountain, for the earth will be full of the knowledge of the Lord as the waters cover the sea.
>
> Isaiah 11:1-9

Lord of hosts (Isa. 24:23, NASB)
The Lord (Micah 4:7)
Your God (Isa. 52:7)
The Most High (Dan. 7:22-24)
The Lord our Righteousness (Jer. 23:6)
Mighty God (Isa. 9:6)
Ancient of Days (Dan. 7:13)
The King (Isa. 33:17)
Messiah the Prince (Dan. 9:25-26, KJV)
The Judge (Isa. 11:3-4)
The Redeemer (Isa. 59:20)
The Lawgiver (Isa. 33:22)
Prince of princes (Dan. 8:25)

Titles of the Coming King

What do the prophets say about this time of a glorious kingdom established on earth by God Himself? Vivid images of that time are found in Isaiah 2:1-4; 4:2-6; 9:6-7; 11:1-13; 24:1-23; 32:1-5, 14-20; 33:17-24; 35:1-10; 52:7-10; 60:1–61:6; 66:15-23; Jeremiah 31:1-27; 33:14-26; Daniel 2:31-45; 7:1-28; 9:1-3, 20-27; 12:1-4; Malachi 3:1-5; 4:1-6; Ezekiel 20:33-42; 34:20-31; 36:22-36; 37:1-28; 39:21-29; Hosea 3:4-5; Joel 2:28–3:2, 9-21; Amos 9:9-15; Obadiah 15-21; Micah 4:1-5; Zephaniah 3:8-20; Haggai 2:1-9; Zechariah 2:1-13; 6:11-13; 8:1-8, 20-23; 9:9-10; 12:1-10; 14:1-21.

When Will These Things Be?

Christians are divided on their interpretation of the visions of the prophets. Some Bible students are convinced that the promises are true, but are to be understood as a symbolic expression of the work of Christ in the hearts of the believers of this age. Others take the words of the prophets at face value, and look for a literal fulfillment in history.

There is no doubt that the prophets thought in literal terms, and did not foresee the Christian era. So, when studying the Old Testament, if we want to look through the prophets' eyes we need to take their words in their plain and literal sense.

If we do this, we can construct a picture of what they foresaw for the future. We cannot tell just *when* the things they spoke of will take place. But we can see what they foresaw, and be assured that the future rests firmly in the hands of our great God.

TEACHING GUIDE

Prepare

Read through Zephaniah, to underline phrases that reflect the themes noted in this unit.

Explore and Expand

At times a Bible book is more important for understanding basic biblical teaching than for direct application to believers' lives.

Zephaniah, while relevant as a reminder that God is Judge and will punish sin, is a book that helps us grasp both the structure of Old Testament prophetic books, and themes that we meet again and again in the prophets. To guide your group to understand both structure and themes, lead an unusual "self-study" group this week.

1. Give an overview of the structure of Old Testament prophets and have group members find this structure in Zephaniah (see "link-to-life," page 491).

2. Have duplicated the verses the author gives on each of the three major Old Testament prophetic themes. Briefly explain each theme, and let your group members select *one* theme to explore with others. Form teams to examine each theme by looking up the verses.

Apply

Use the last 10 or 15 minutes for groups to report on what they have learned, and to share dominant impressions.

STUDY GUIDE 76
Haggai

PUTTING GOD FIRST

Overview
Haggai was a prophet who spoke to the tiny Jewish community which had settled again in the Promised Land after the Babylonian Captivity. Little is known of the prophet. Jewish tradition suggests he was a priest.

Three things set this prophet's work apart. First, each message is carefully dated. We can place his preaching of each sermon recorded in this book to the day! Second, the people acted on his exhortation! While many Old Testament prophets saw no real response to their ministries, this prophet saw the Jews heed his words. Third, rebuilding the temple is linked with the "shaking of the nations"—the coming of Messiah to establish the kingdom promised by the Lord.

This book, whose theme is putting God first, has a special message for those we teach as well as its message to the men and women of Haggai's day.

Outline

August 29, 520 B.C.	1:1-15
October 17, 520 B.C.	2:1-9
December 18, 520 B.C.	2:10-19
December 18, 520 B.C.	2:20-23

Ezra and Nehemiah contain narrative descriptions of the return. The Prophet Zechariah was a contemporary of Haggai. They mention many of the same people, such as Zerubbabel (who was governor of the Jewish community) and Joshua (who was high priest).

■ For a verse-by-verse commentary see the *Bible Knowledge Commentary*, pages 1537-1544.

Commentary
Some 50,000 people returned to Judah from Babylon. They settled in a tiny portion of the Jews' ancient heritage, centered on Jerusalem. There they found their once-fertile lands ruined. What had once been forested was stripped of its trees and grasses. What had been fertile crop land was now wilderness. In addition, the little remnant, struggling to clear its land, was met with a series of natural disasters. There were droughts and storms. Crops planted in hope were harvested in despair, as not even the seed was recovered.

It was this situation that the Prophet Haggai described when he preached his first sermon on August 29, 520 B.C., to a people who had gathered in Jerusalem for a religious festival.

> Now this is what the Lord Almighty says: "Give careful thought to your ways. You have planted much, but have harvested little. You eat, but never have enough. You drink, but never have your fill. You put on clothes, but are not warm. You earn wages, only to put them in a purse with holes in it. . . .
>
> "You expected much, but see, it turned out to be little. What you brought home, I blew away. Why?" declares the Lord Almighty. "Because of My house, which remains a ruin, while each of you is busy with his own house."
>
> Haggai 1:5-6, 9

The First Message: Haggai 1:1-15
The people had returned to Judah in 538 B.C., some 16 years before Haggai first spoke out. They had come with the specific intention of rebuilding the ruined temple of their God. The people had quickly laid the foundation of the temple, but then enthusiasm had flagged. Their efforts shifted to preparing houses to live in, and to clearing fields so crops might grow. For over a decade work on the temple had been abandoned, and even the funds they had brought

with them for the building program were spent on a futile effort to make the little community self-sufficient.

In essence, the people of Judah had forgotten that it is the call of the believer to put God first. Blessing follows full commitment—blessing cannot be found apart from it.

Haggai's first message, then, was a call to recommitment. It was an explanation of dashed hopes, for through Haggai the Lord now explained what had been happening.

> "You expected much, but see, it turned out to be little. What you brought home, I blew away. Why?" declares the Lord Almighty. "Because of My house, which remains a ruin, while each of you is busy with his own house. Therefore, because of you the heavens have withheld their dew and the earth its crops."
>
> Haggai 1:9-10

♥ ***Link to Life: Youth / Adult***

Tape record this "appeal" from a radio or TV preacher. Play it, and ask your group members to evaluate:

"You have to put God first! You have to show God you love Him! You have to be willing to sacrifice if you're going to be blessed! That's why I'm begging you to put that $100 in the mail today. Or even that $1,000. You say you're too poor? You don't have that kind of money? Well, maybe the reason you're poor is because you haven't put God first! Maybe He's holding back financial blessing just to teach you that God and His ministries have got to come first! Oh, yes, that's the pattern, brother and sister. Give to God first, even when it's a sacrifice. And then, yes then, *God will bless you."*

Discuss: "What's your reaction to this kind of appeal? What is right about it? What may seem wrong? Would you send that $100 or $1,000? Why, or why not?"

Then *give the background and read together Haggai's first sermon (1:2-11). Discuss: "How is this sermon different from the one we've just heard on tape?" (Note it had to do with an earlier commitment that had been abandoned, and was uttered by a prophet who spoke expressly at God's command in a specific situation.)*

How did the people of Judah respond to Haggai's August sermon? His book tells us that "the whole remnant of the people obeyed the voice of the Lord their God and the message of the Prophet Haggai, because the Lord their God had sent him. And the people feared the Lord" (v. 12). God worked in the hearts of His people (vv. 13-14), and within the month work on the temple was resumed!

♥ ***Link to Life: Youth / Adult***

Put on a chalkboard a sketch of the "foundations of the temple" (drawn simply as a rectangle). Point out that the foundations of Judah's commitment had been laid, and that God withheld blessing because the people had not carried through on their commitment. They had been distracted by the "cares of life" and had not put God first.

Ask each person to look quietly at the rectangle, and meditate for 90 seconds. Have the foundations of any special commitment to God been laid in their own lives—foundations on which they have not built while going about other business?

Make no other comment, but move on with the rest of this study.

The Second Message: Haggai 2:1-9

The people had worked for nearly two months when Haggai received another message from God. This was a message of encouragement: encouragement that took several forms.

First, the postexilic temple did not compare in size or beauty with the temple of Solomon which Nebuchadnezzar had destroyed. It must have been discouraging for the people to compare what they were able to do with what David and Solomon had accomplished with the resources of a wealthy and powerful kingdom. Yet God announced through Haggai that "the glory of this present house will be greater than the glory of the former house" (v. 9).

How true these words proved to be! It was not expansion and beautification of the temple hundreds of years later under Herod that the Lord had in mind, however. It was the fact that in the person of Jesus, God Himself would come to this temple of the exiles, to preach His good news of salvation and peace. The glory of the second temple is that the very Son of God stood on its porches, and beautified it with His presence.

But there was another, pressing need for encouragement. The Jewish remnant was poor. How could they build and decorate a temple that would be worthy of the Lord? Speaking to this issue, the Lord said through Haggai, "The silver is Mine and the gold is Mine" (v. 8).

The Book of Ezra tells us how God solved this problem. The peoples of the land objected to the Jews' rebuilding program, and tried to stop it (Ezra 5:1-17). But a search of empire records showed that Cyrus had actually commanded that the temple be rebuilt! As a result, orders came from the present king, Darius, that the house of God was not only to be built, but that *the full cost was to be paid by the royal treasury, through taxes collected in the Trans-Euphrates province* (6:1-12). In essence, the enemies of the Jewish people bore the expense of rebuilding their temple!

How ironic. And how clear a demonstration that we need never hold back from full commitment to our God. Truly the silver and the gold *are* His.

God provides what we need to complete any task to which He calls us.

♥ ***Link to Life: Youth / Adult***

Ask your group to brainstorm. What are some of the fears that hold people back from following through on commitments to the Lord? List their ideas on the chalkboard. Then give a minilecture, explaining the Ezra background that helps us see the significance of Haggai's word from God, "The silver is Mine and the gold is Mine."

Then return to the list on the chalkboard. How do the words of Haggai and the experience of the people help us deal with each fear listed on the board?

There is a third thread of encouragement in Haggai's message. He speaks of the future, saying, "In a little while I will once more shake the heavens and earth, the sea and the dry land" (Hag. 2:6). This imagery of shaking the heavens and earth is associated with history's end and divine judgment. Isaiah cried:

> Men will flee to caves in the rocks and to holes in the ground from dread of the Lord and the splendor of His majesty, when He rises to shake the earth.
>
> Isaiah 2:19

The writer of Hebrews picks up this imagery in chapter 12.

> At that time [on Sinai] His voice shook the earth, but now He has promised, "Once more I will shake not only the earth but also the heavens." The words "once more" indicate the removing of what can be shaken—that is, created things—so that what cannot be shaken may remain.
>
> Hebrews 12:26-27

It is important to put God first now, for ultimately only what we do for Him will not be shaken and destroyed when Jesus returns. And it was important for the people of Haggai's day to look ahead, to realize that only what they did for the Lord would remain.

Yet perhaps the most important encouragement was given in these words: " 'Be strong, all you people of the land . . . and work. For I am with you,' says the Lord Almighty" (Hag. 2:4).

The Third Message: Haggai 2:10-19

In the age before the Exile, the Jewish people had been confident that Jerusalem at least was safe. After all, wasn't God's temple there? Surely God must protect the place He had chosen for His name to dwell.

This thinking had been wrong! The Babylonians had come, sacked the city, and destroyed the temple.

Now, as the new temple was being constructed, Haggai was sent with a special message to that generation.

The message came in a distinctive way. The prophet was sent to ask the priests about a point of Law: "If a person carries consecrated meat in the fold of his garment, and that fold touches some bread or stew, some wine, oil or other food, does it become consecrated?" (v. 11) The answer was no.

He asked another question: "If a person defiled by contact with a dead body touches one of these things, does it become defiled?" (v. 13) The answer was yes.

What is Haggai's point? Simply this. The presence of God's holy temple could not make the people holy. In fact, according to the Law, even the touch of a sinful and defiled people should make the temple itself *un*holy! The people of Judah must not put their hope in their own supposed holiness, or in the supposed holiness of the house of God.

What basis then is there for hope? Haggai's response is, essentially, God's grace.

God is good to us, not because we deserve it, and not because His presence makes us holy, but simply because He has chosen to bless us. "Whatever they do and whatever they offer there [in the rebuilt temple] is defiled," God said (v. 15). And yet, God was determined to pour out His blessings on this people who had at last put Him first!

> "Now give careful thought to this from this day on—consider how things were before one stone was laid on another in the Lord's temple.
>
> When anyone came to a heap of twenty measures, there were only ten. When anyone went to a wine vat to draw fifty measures, there were only twenty. I struck all the work of your hands with blight, mildew and hail, yet you did not turn to Me," declares the Lord. "From this day on, from this twenty-fourth day of the ninth month, give careful thought to the day when the foundation of the Lord's temple was laid. Give careful thought: Is there yet any seed left in the barn? Until now, the vine and the fig tree, the pomegranate and the olive tree have not borne fruit.
>
> "From this day on I will bless you."
>
> Haggai 2:15-19

According to Old Testament law a person who was ceremonially (ritually) "defiled" or "unclean" was not permitted to approach or worship God. Explain Haggai's point—the temple would not make Judah a holy community. But their obedience in building it, their demonstration of readiness to put God first, freed God to give them gracious, unmerited blessings. What is more, God committed Himself to do just this!

How like our own experience. Even when we are fully committed to the Lord, and express that commitment in obedience, the blessings we experience are not merited, but evidence of the overwhelming grace of our God.

The Last Message: Haggai 2:20-23

The last message of Haggai, given on the same day as the promise of divine blessing, looked far ahead.

Zerubbabel, though of the royal line, was not Judah's king. The little district of Judah was merely a minor region, one of the Persian Empire's 120 great provinces! Yet the word is directed to Zerubbabel as a representative of the kingly line.

Though insignificant now and for centuries to come God will one day act:

> Tell Zerubbabel governor of Judah that I will shake the heavens and the earth. I will overturn royal thrones and shatter the power of the foreign kingdoms. . . . On that day . . . I will take you, My servant Zerubbabel son of Shealtiel . . . and I will make you like My signet ring, for I have chosen you.
>
> Haggai 2:21-23

The rebuilding of the temple, like the restoration of the Jews to their land, is but a reminder of the greater promises that God has given His ancient people. The day will come when this earth is shaken, and when the kingdom is possessed by Jesus, David's greater Son.

TEACHING GUIDE

Prepare

Are unfulfilled commitments keeping you from an experience of the gracious blessing of God?

Explore

1. Play a tape representing a radio preacher's appeal for funds for evaluation by your group members (see "link-to-life," page 497).
2. Or give a minilecture outlining the situation before Haggai began to speak. Ask each group member to write out what he or she might expect God to say to this particu-

lar generation. Then compare with the prophet's first message (Hag. 1).

Expand

1. Examine fears that people have concerning full commitment to the Lord. Then look at how God provided financially for poverty-stricken Judah so that the temple could be built. See "link-to-life," page 498.
2. Or give a minilecture, explaining each sermon. Then divide into teams, each of which is to examine one sermon and list applications for people of today.

Apply

Draw a sketch of a foundation on the chalkboard. Ask your group members to meditate on any commitments they may have made to God, but like Judah, have set aside because of daily life concerns.

Then close in prayer, thanking God for His willingness not only to supply what we need to finish building, but also His gracious willingness to bless us as we are obedient to Him.

STUDY GUIDE 77

Zechariah

WORDS OF HOPE

Overview
Zechariah is called "the prophet of hope." He looks at the future for the Jewish people during the coming centuries of pagan empire, and to the age of Messiah.

Outline

Part I

I.	Introduction: A Call to Return	1:1-6
II.	Eight Visions and Oracles	1:7–6:15
	1. False security	1:7-17
	2. Retribution	1:18-21
	3. Protection	2:1-13
	4. High priest ordained	3:1-10
	5. Resources	4:1-14
	6. Punishment of evil	5:1-4
	7. Purification	5:5-11
	8. Priest/King united	6:1-15
III.	Messages on Fasting	7:1–8:19
	1. The question	7:1-3
	2. First sermon	7:4-14
	3. Relevant sayings	8:1-8
	4. Second sermon	8:9-17
	5. Answer	8:18-19
IV.	Conclusion: Longing for God	8:20-23

Part II

V.	God's Intervention	9:1–11:17
	1. Triumph	9:1-8
	2. The King arrives	9:9-10
	3. Prosperity	9:11–10:1
	4. Rebuke of leaders	10:2-3
	5. Restoration	10:3–11:3
	6. Good Shepherd's Fate	11:4-17
VI.	Final Intervention of God	12:1–14:21
	1. Jerusalem rejoices	12:1-9
	2. The One pierced	12:10–13:1
	3. Leaders rejected	13:2-6
	4. Shepherd killed	13:7-9
	5. Cataclysm	14:1-15
	6. Lord, King of all	14:16-21

Commentary
While Daniel in Babylon was being given the "coming Prince" prophecy of Daniel 9, God spoke to the little community in Palestine by the Prophet Zechariah. With his contemporary Haggai, Zechariah was used by God to stimulate the completion of the temple. Even more, he brought words of hope to the Jews. Daniel warned of hundreds of years under a succession of Gentile world-rulers. Zechariah stressed the continuing concern of the Lord for His people and the final vindication of the Jewish hope. Messiah would come, and all the families of the earth would appear at Jerusalem to worship Him (Zech. 14:16).

As we study what might be called the Old Testament's springtime teachings, we find several values in Zechariah's 14 chapters.

Major Themes Repeated
When I taught Old Testament survey in the graduate school of Wheaton College, I used to give a pop quiz when we came to Zechariah. I asked my students to tell where they thought each of the following passages might be found:

> Though I scatter them among the peoples, yet in distant lands they will remember Me. They and their children will survive, and they will return. And I will pour out on the house of David and the inhabitants of Jerusalem a spirit of grace and supplication. They will look on Me, the One they have pierced, and they will mourn for Him as one mourns for an only child, and grieve bitterly for Him as one grieves for a firstborn son. I will gather all the nations to Jerusalem to fight against it; the city will be captured, the houses ransacked, and the women raped. Half of the city will go into exile, but the rest of the people will not be taken from the city.

This was, of course, a "trick" quiz. Each of these passages sounds very much like a theme from one of the prophets who lived and spoke in Israel or Judah before the Babylonian Captivity. These former prophets warned of a "scattering among the nations" and told of a regathering to follow. They spoke of a change of heart associated with Messiah's coming. And they warned that enemy nations would assemble to battle and eventually would overwhelm Jerusalem. We might think that these prophecies were at least in part fulfilled in the Babylonian Captivity. Nebuchadnezzar's armies besieged and finally destroyed Jerusalem, and the people were scattered through pagan lands. God acted to bring back a remnant from the nations where they were scattered; the temple and city were rebuilt.

But what is so striking about these prophecies is that *each one comes from Zechariah* (10:9; 12:10; 14:2). Each was spoken *after* the exiles had, in large part, already returned!

Zechariah, looking ahead, saw essentially the same future for Judah that the earlier prophets had seen. The interlude in Babylon had not completely fulfilled the warnings of an end-time scattering and regathering, or of a great end-time war against God's people and His city.

This is an illustration of what has been called the "law of double reference." Zechariah's generation could rightly see themselves in the portrait of judgment and restoration; yet the ultimate fulfillment of the prophetic word still looked beyond their own experience.

How do we explain the repetition of these themes and the up-and-down experience of Judah? We see the earth as a stage on which God has set a drama to work out good and evil, the reconciliation of justice and love. The play has been written and the script placed in the actors' hands. We can see in the Scripture the amazing resolution planned by the Author. But God does not wait for the final production to demonstrate His genius. History contains a number of dress rehearsals. The playwright's plan and the principles of reality that underlie the last act are woven into Judah's experience again and again so you and I can look back into history and see them illustrated. We can also look forward and understand what is to come.

And we can invite the actors to the after-celebration He has always had in mind for them!

The fact that the warnings, promises, and principles found in the pre-exilic prophets are also found in the postexilic prophets should not surprise us. *No experience up until the arrival of destiny itself can exhaust the meaning of these prophets' words. The ultimate focus of all prophecy is the time of the end.*

♥ ***Link to Life: Youth / Adult***
Write the three verses quoted from Zechariah (10:9; 12:10; 14:2) on the board. Ask class members to guess
(1) what the prophet is talking about, and
(2) what prophet(s) wrote them.
Listen to suggestions, and ask why a particular time or prophet was chosen.
Then point out that each comes from Zechariah, using the chart on page 503 to highlight the implications.

Forms of Prophecy

Zechariah also illustrated the variety of forms in which Old Testament prophecies were given. Here we find vision and symbolic action, principles expressed in institutions like the temple, poetic expressions, prose statements, reports of experiences, and oracles delivered with the certainty of "thus says the Lord."

Visions. The first part of the Book of Zechariah (chaps. 1–6) reports eight visions given to the prophet. These are in most cases either interpreted or applied by an angelic messenger. The vision of the flying scroll (5:1-4) was typical. Here Zechariah reported seeing a flying book, or scroll, about 30 feet by 15 feet in size! The angel explained: "This is the curse that is going out over the whole land . . . every thief will be banished, and . . . everyone who swears falsely will be banished." The Lord Almighty declares, "I will send it out, and it will enter the house of the thief and the house of him who swears falsely by My name. It will remain in his house and destroy it, both its timbers and its stones" (vv. 3-4).

Clearly God was acting in a distinct (and new?) way to administer justice severely and fairly. To what period of time does this vision apply? That is something we can't tell from the vision—but may be able to determine by looking at the broader context of

PRINCIPLE	PRE-EXILE		POST-EXILE	
	Isaiah	11:11-12	Isaiah	66:20-22
		14:1-3	Ezekiel	39:25-29
Deuteronomy 28:1-2	Jeremiah	16:14-16	Zephaniah	3:14-20
13-15		23:3-8	Zechariah	8:4-8
36-37	Ezekiel	11:17-21		
45-46	Joel	3:17-21		
	Amos	9:11-15		
	Micah	4:4-7		

Scattering & Return

the seven visions with which it is associated. Again, remember that the time factor in prophecy is normally open and relatively uncertain.

Symbolic acts. The prophets often take as a starting point an institution, persons, or events from their own day as a launching pad for prophecy. Thus Joel, for instance, spoke of a great plague of locusts from his own time but used the devastation of the insects to portray the greater devastation that invading hordes would work on the Promised Land at history's end.

In Zechariah 6:11 we hear the prophet told to make a crown of gold and silver and set it on the head of Joshua, the high priest. While there is direct reference to a role for Joshua in presiding over the restoration of the contemporary temple, there is clearly a typical meaning as well, in which Joshua stands for another Person yet to come. This is made clear immediately by the title "the Branch," which was recognized by the Jews as a messianic reference, for it was used in this way by Isaiah (cf. Isa. 4:2) and Jeremiah (cf. Jer. 23:5; 33:15).

What then was God saying about the Messiah through this incident and the words of coronation?

1. Messiah the Branch will build a future temple.
2. Messiah the Branch will rule as King.
3. Messiah the Branch will also have the office of Priest, uniquely combining these two roles.
4. Messiah the Branch will bring together Jew and Gentile in common worship of the Lord.
5. Messiah the Branch will fulfill prophecy and validate the revealed Word.
6. Messiah the Branch will bring in full obedience to the voice of the Lord.

One of the striking aspects of this prophecy is the apparent impossibility of its fulfillment! The coming King was to be of the tribe of Judah. But priests were to come only from Aaron's family line. Thus it would be impossible for one man to be both priest and king; the two offices were kept forever separated. But when Jesus died, a new priesthood was established "after the order of Melchizedek" (see Heb. 5). Thus the impossible *did* happen . . . and this "impossible prophecy" demonstrated anew the trustworthiness of the Word of God.

A prophetic message (Zech. 7–8). In an extended section that seems to include four distinct themes or mini-messages, Zechariah answered a question raised by the men of Bethel. They had wondered if they needed to keep on fasting on the anniversary of the destruction of Jerusalem now that the city had been restored.

They were rebuked and asked, "When you fasted and mourned in the fifth and seventh months for the past 70 years, was it really for Me that you fasted?" (7:5) Were their fasts caused by sorrow for their sufferings, or did they indicate repentance and concern for their treatment of God?

The prophet reminded the people of Judah of God's requirements for holiness, and then of His promise of restoration. This message is meant to bring hope in their discouragement, and to fix their thoughts on the rejoicing that will be theirs when Messiah comes.

Again we see the emphasis on destiny. Present discouragement must be evaluated in view of the certainty of ultimate blessing when God's promises to His people are finally fulfilled.

The oracles (Zech. 14). The last part of Zechariah is clearly focused on the culmination of God's plan. This is seen with great clarity in chapter 14, which describes the return of Messiah in great glory to consummate the divine program.

Many unusual details are introduced here, details sometimes repeated in other prophetic portraits.

1. There is to be a final siege of Jerusalem (vv. 1-2).
2. There is to be an appearance of the Lord on the earth, resulting in great topographical changes (vv. 3-8).
3. There will be a divine kingship established (vv. 9-11).
4. There will be punishment of Israel's enemies (vv. 12-15).
5. There will be a great conversion of the Gentile world to the Saviour (vv. 16-19).
6. There will then be an experience of true holiness reflected in the purity of the worship offered the Lord (vv. 20-21).

It is clear from this quick review that not only are the prophetic forms many, but that each seems to lean forward. Each has in view, even when dealing with contemporary problems, the ultimate solution to human needs when the Messiah comes to rule over the kingdoms of this world.

There is certainly no doubt or hesitation in the prophet's portrayal. There's a great day coming. A day of deliverance and restoration. Our present experience must be evaluated in view of what God is doing in our world, and in view of the destiny toward which history is swiftly carrying the universe itself.

♥ ***Link to Life: Youth / Adult***
Have your group members sample the prophetic styles found in this book. Divide into teams, each of which is to look at one of four prophetic types:

- *A vision* — *5:1-4*
- *A symbolic act* — *6:9-15*
- *A prophetic message* — *7:1–8:17*
- *An oracle* — *chapter 14*

Each team should study its passage, and then determine: (1) Is it easy or hard to understand? (2) What does this passage teach? (3) As this was written after the Babylonian Captivity and return, when has or will it take place?

TEACHING GUIDE

Prepare
Work through the book using the outline in *overview.* If you have questions on this difficult book's visions, consult a verse-by-verse commentary, like the *Bible Knowledge Commentary,* pages 1545-1572.

Explore
1. Let your group members guess the source and time of the three quoted prophecies at the beginning of this chapter. See "link-to-life," page 502.
2. Or distribute the outline of Zechariah (see *overview*) and summarize its contents. Supplement your remarks with information from a commentary.

Expand
1. Divide into teams to look at four types of prophecy ("link-to-life," page 504).
2. Or look at the detailed outline of the future suggested by Zechariah 14. Which elements have had at least partial fulfillment in history? Which elements have not yet happened?

Apply
How important was prophecy to God's Old Testament people? How important is it to us today? Share.

STUDY GUIDE 78

Malachi

LOVE GROWN COLD

Overview

This last of the Old Testament prophets ministered in Judah between 460 and 430 B.C. His words sketch a tragic picture of the little company that had returned from Babylon to settle there over 115 years before.

The temple had been completed, and the people worshiped there, following the prescribed rituals and offering the required sacrifices. Haggai and Zechariah were gone, and the religious enthusiasm these prophets stimulated had now drained away.

Nehemiah's ministry as governor, during which he held the Jews in Judah to the Old Testament Law that they were so prone to break, was over. The complaints that Malachi recorded indicate the same sins still plagued God's people.

And Malachi's blunt report of God's words (the Lord speaks in 42 of the 55 verses in this book) exposes the attitude of those whose love for God has grown cold. How important for us, when God seems distant or unreal, to remember the message of Malachi.

Outline

I.	The Chosen People	1:1-5
II.	Neglect God	1:6–2:9
III.	Break Commitments	2:10-16
IV.	Doubt God's Presence	2:17–3:5
V.	Deny God's Significance	3:6–4:3
VI.	Closing Exhortation	4:4-6

■ For a verse-by-verse commentary see the *Bible Knowledge Commentary*, pages 1573-1588. In particular, see the discussion of the promise that Elijah will come *before* the Day of the Lord.

Commentary

Malachi, the last book of the Old Testament is a discouraging document. The days of Ezra and Nehemiah were past, and no imprint seemed to be left on the people of Judah. Again we find them sliding down toward sin and spiritual lethargy, trapped in the old patterns, but now completely indifferent to Malachi's call for another fresh start.

Haggai ended his ministry in 520 B.C. with words of hope: the kingdoms of this earth were about to be shaken, and God's servants would be worn by Him as a signet ring, " 'for I have chosen you,' declares the Lord Almighty" (Hag. 2:23). Malachi ended nearly a century later, on a note of warning and near despair. God must send another Elijah to His people before the great and terrible day of the Lord; the people must be reconciled not only to Him but to one another, "or else I will come and strike the land with a curse" (Mal. 4:6). Reading this book, the last testimony to the men and women of the return, a peculiar realization grows. God's people have lost their vision of God, and of their own future.

This is important for us to grasp, because the principle applies to us as well as to Israel. We too are forced to live with imperfection—our own imperfection as well as that of those around us! It is so easy to become discouraged when we try and try again, and still seem to fail.

I remember the frustration my children felt when they were younger. Paul wanted to push our old man-powered lawnmower when he was 5. And he couldn't. When he was 12, he wanted desperately to beat me at basketball. And he couldn't do it (then). Tim sometimes felt deep frustration because he couldn't draw as well as his older brother who is an artist. He tried, but his hands just couldn't form the lines as he saw them in his mind's eye. From the first stumbling steps of the toddler, and his tears when he falls, on through the teenage athlete's crushing defeat, life teaches us that we haven't arrived yet.

And still, with each child, I've known that destiny lay ahead. "Soon you'll grow tall. Soon. . . ."

It never seemed soon.

And yet each child knew it was true.

I think there's an important analogy here for us in our spiritual experience. We are not yet what we shall be. And what we shall be always lies just beyond our grasp . . . our destiny is always ahead. Yet we can stretch out now, straining toward it. What's more, we're not doomed to remain as we are until destiny comes. We can grow toward it: *God calls us to grow toward it*. Like the toddler who stumbles, we are called to get up, to put our hand in our Father's, and to try again. In spite of our stumbling steps, each one we do take does bring us closer to what will be.

When we lose sight of our destiny, and when we fail to grasp the reality of growth, our motivation to live for God begins to die. This is what happened to the people of Judah in Malachi's day. They had looked inward, lost sight of the destiny ahead, and abandoned hope for personal growth and change.

♥ ***Link to Life: Youth / Adult***

Prepare your group for a study of Malachi by "dreaming." Ask each member to jot down where he or she wants to be in 10 years. Explain that "where you want to be" should include all one's goals—personal, financial, and especially spiritual—the kind of person you want to be.

After each has jotted down his or her dream, share these in groups of four or five.

Then explain that what we find in Malachi is a definition of what can keep an individual or a people from realizing its dreams of growth and change.

Malachi

Little is known about the prophet himself. But his writings give us a sharp portrait of conditions in Judah. The hard years seem to have passed. The city and its walls had been raised, the temple rebuilt. Prosperity as well as relative independence from the peoples around had returned. God's people had settled down to live the "good life" in the land of Palestine.

But with blessing had come a peculiar reaction. The sense of need for God had receded; yearning for the coming destiny had disappeared. God Himself was ignored, even despised. All the meaning of life seemed summed up in the experience of the good things of this world's "now."

Malachi's book is organized around a series of seven sarcastic questions posed by the people of God in response to his words to them. These questions show a definite rejection of the divine viewpoint; they show how far Judah's loss of a sense of destiny had caused them to drift spiritually.

In looking at these questions, it is easy to see some of our own attitudes reflected. In God's response we can hear His call, inviting us to turn our steps again toward *our* destiny.

Love lost (Mal. 1:1-5). The Book of Malachi begins with an affirmation: " 'I have loved you,' says the Lord" (v. 2). What a starting point in our relationship with God! It is not that we loved God. He loved us and, acting in love, He delivered His people.

Yet the people of Malachi's day replied with a plaintive whine: "How have You loved us?" It is as though a child, used to plenty, complains because he's been denied some new toy. With all the evidence of history and with all their present prosperity, Judah could still claim to be uncertain of God's love!

God's answer is to point to the fact that He *chose* their ancestor Jacob over his twin Esau (who was the ancestor of the people who even then surrounded Judah). God's love was demonstrated primarily in that He chose to establish a relationship with His people; love draws us to Himself.

The phrase, "Esau I have hated" (v. 3), bothers many. It seems best to understand this expression not as a statement of feeling or attitude but as a *legal* term. In that day a father used this terminology in legally designating one son to inherit his possessions while decisively rejecting the claim of another. By custom such a rejected son really was loved. And he was given resources to make his own way. But the legally "loved" son inherited.

God has shown His love for us in that He has chosen us to inherit all that He has and is, for we are His people, and He is our God.

Honor denied (Mal. 1:6-9). God's complaint against Judah is that, though He has called this people into a relationship with

Himself, the people have refused to honor Him. This goes beyond disrespect; they have despised God's name (v. 6). As the prophet pointed out, a son honors his father—and God had been a Father to Judah. A servant shows respect to his master; and God was rightly called "Lord" and "Master" by His people. Why then was God treated in Judah as unimportant?

The people of Judah react to this charge with another caustic reply. You can almost hear the tone of outraged innocence. "How have we despised Your name?"

In answer God simply pointed to the mildewed bread on His temple's altar; to the ill and injured animals offered as sacrifices. Why, these people were offering to God what they would never dare to present to a human governor!

Worship defiled (Mal. 1:10-14). Worship essentially is an expression of our awareness of who God is; it is honoring and praising Him for Himself. Any true worship must honor and exalt the Lord.

Now we are shown the priests and the Levites of Malachi's day, who were to be closest to God and to serve Him (and in return be provided for from the sacrifices and offerings brought to the temple), complaining about their lot. They were unsatisfied with the offerings that God had chosen for Himself; they wanted the cuts of meat that others ate. They were bored with worship (v. 13). And the people constantly sought to swindle God out of what they had vowed to Him.

Obedience ignored (Mal. 2:1-12). In this passage God reminded Judah that in the Sinai Covenant He promised the obedient that He would bless them. The Law outlined His plan for holy living, but this people had not taken God's ways to heart (v. 2). If they had only chosen to live by the Law, they would have known life and peace and righteousness (v. 5). But the very priests charged with teaching God's way denied it—first with their actions (v. 8) and then in their distorted teaching of God's truth (v. 9).

This corruption could not be overlooked. In spite of their relationship with the Lord as His people, they were faithless and cruel to one another, and faithless to the God they claimed as their common Father, for they persisted in marrying pagan wives who worshiped foreign gods.

Prayer unanswered (Mal. 2:13-16). When God warned Judah that He would not answer prayers, the people responded with a complaint: "Why?" They had prayed fervently, flooding the altar of God with tears. Why then didn't God pay attention to their offerings?

Here another sin of the people, and another evidence of their hardheartedness is brought into focus. This society had adopted divorce as a lifestyle. This is not divorce stimulated by a partner's sin or unwillingness to maintain the marriage covenant. It is divorce motivated by lust—by an older man's desire for a new and younger wife! This kind of faithlessness is something that God cannot stand.

Evil affirmed (Mal. 2:17–3:4). Malachi's charge that Judah had "wearied the Lord with your words" is met with another sarcastic inquiry. "How have we wearied Him?" (2:17) Malachi's answer went to the roots of another symptom of spiritual sickness. "By saying, 'All who do evil are good in the eyes of the Lord' " (v. 17).

How quickly humanistic values replace God's revelation of true goodness and purity. In modern doubletalk, pornographic movies are called "mature," and campaigns are launched to present homosexuality as an alternative and perfectly acceptable lifestyle. In Malachi's day too society slipped into the practice of calling evil good.

This last charge led Malachi to a promise and a warning. He spoke of the coming of God, but warned, "Who can endure the day of His coming? Who can stand when He appears?" (3:2) Destiny, in the person of God's messenger, was approaching, and He would purify the land by judgment. *Then* the offerings of the remnant would be pleasing to God.

When we refuse to purify ourselves, God must act for us. It is not pleasant to be placed over what Malachi calls the "refiner's fire" (v. 2). The fire that removes impurities burns while it cleanses.

Return rejected (Mal. 3:6-12). Approaching the end of the dialogue, God now confronted Judah with a call to restoration. " 'Return to Me, and I will return to you,' says the Lord Almighty." But the hardened people responded, "How are we to return?" (v. 7) The meaning of the question is clear: "What do You mean, *return*? Why, we've never strayed!"

So again God brought into focus evidence of Judah's desertion of His path. They had been robbing God of the tithes and offerings commanded in the Law. They could return by once again putting God first, and—if they did—God would open the very windows of heaven and pour out blessings. Not because they "paid" for them, but because, when God's people are close to Him, He enjoys doing them good.

The Lord denied (Mal. 3:13-15). One final word remained. God called Judah to account for saying harsh things about Him personally. And again came the whining reply, "What have we said against You?" The answer is simple. "You have said, 'It is futile to serve God. What did we gain by carrying out His requirements and going about like mourners before the Lord Almighty?' " (vv. 13-14)

This people had *chosen* to set God aside as irrelevant; they had determined to pay Him no more attention. They might go through the motions. After all, appearance at the temple was one of those things well-bred people did! But in their hearts there was no longer a place for God.

Malachi ended with two special notes. First, he reported that while the society refused to turn to God, there were individuals who "listened and heard." And Malachi told us that their names were recorded in God's record book (3:16-18). " 'They will be Mine,' says the Lord Almighty, 'in the day when I make up My treasured possession.' "

And Malachi shared a promise. "Surely the day is coming" (4:1). It will come, burning like a furnace, and then all the arrogant will be like chaff. Destiny does lie ahead for the good and the evil alike. Destiny is ahead for those who look for it, and those who look away. We may not welcome destiny, but we can not escape it.

♥ ***Link to Life: Youth / Adult***

To reach personal spiritual goals—and other healthy goals that can be achieved only through God's blessing—we need to avoid the attitudes and actions that we see revealed in Malachi.

Lead your group in a chart study of this book, looking together at each section of the book as discussed in the commentary.

As you look at each section, first identify the issue *that Malachi dealt with. Then look at the patterns of thought and behavior that revealed the attitude of the people of his day toward this issue.*

Finally, in the third column of the chart, jot down modern parallels. What contemporary attitudes and acts would show that we have become lukewarm, as did the Jews of Malachi's day?

Malachi Study Chart

Issue	Judah's pattern	Modern patterns

Destiny

The Christian's destiny is ultimately found in resurrection. On that wonderful day, you and I will be transformed, to bear the image of our Saviour. We shall be like Him, John told us, for we shall see Him as He is (1 John 3:2). And as we wait, we have His promise. God's Holy Spirit, given to us, is even now working an inner transformation, shaping us to be more and more like Jesus (2 Cor. 3:18). Our destiny (resurrection) lies ahead, but as we live close to Jesus, we experience something of that destiny even now.

The Old Testament vision of destiny was not sharp and clear as far as the individual was concerned. But the people of Judah, as the Hebrews of every era, did possess wonderful promises. God would act in their future—and they too could live in expectation, loving God, responding to His Word, experiencing present blessings.

How wonderful that you and I, like God's people of every age, can set aside the attitudes that destroy our dreams of what we will become. And whatever the characteristics of our day, we can be like "those who feared the Lord," and "talk with each other" (about Him), knowing that the Lord listens and hears, and that we who honor Him now will know the fulfillment of our dreams as destiny draws near to you and me.

TEACHING GUIDE

Prepare
Jot down where you personally want to be in 10 years.

Explore
1. Have each of your group members jot down, and then share, where each wants to be in 10 years. See the "link-to-life" explanation on page 506.
2. Or have several group members read Malachi as a dramatic reading. Two or three can speak the mock questions of the Judeans, another can read the words of God which Malachi quotes, and another can read those which are the prophet's. This method is especially effective with a short book like Malachi where there are a number of distinct voices. This will also motivate a careful pre-group meeting study of the book by those who prepare the dramatic reading.

Expand
Do the chart study suggested in "link-to-life," page 508. Working as a group, define the issue involved; look at how the underlying attitude of the people was expressed in their acts, and suggest ways this attitude might be expressed in our day.

This chart study will provide a mastery of the material in Malachi, and serve as a solid foundation for application.

Apply
Look at the chart, and transform the negatives into positives. That is, suggest how a person can grow in commitment to the Lord. For instance, the people of Malachi's day ignored God's love as expressed in His choice of their nation. We can remember God's love, expressed in Jesus, who has loved and saved us. Or note that the people of Malachi's day withheld their best from God. We can give Him our best.

STUDY GUIDE 79

Between the Testaments

THE SILENT YEARS

Overview

The quiet drama of Jesus' birth in Bethlehem was the culmination of centuries of special preparation. The world into which Jesus was born had been uniquely designed. His birth was "when the time had fully come," as Paul wrote in Galatians 4:4.

We can trace that preparation in the history of those centuries that immediately preceded Jesus' birth. When we do, we appreciate even more fully how significant the incarnation of Jesus was—the whole world was quietly molded by God to make everything ready for the birth of His Son, and for the spread of His Gospel.

Everything we read in that history focuses our attention on the birth, life, death, and resurrection of God's Son. Everything after leads us to look back on the living of this one life as the most significant event the world has ever known.

It's no wonder that so much of our New Testament is composed of the Gospels—four tellings of the story of that one life. Each Gospel looks at Jesus from a slightly different perspective, telling His story in a way that a different segment of the population of Jesus' world could best appreciate, and come to believe in the Saviour.

In this study guide we'll see how history itself converged to shape a world ready for Jesus' birth. And we'll catch a glimpse of the differences that make each of the familiar Gospels special and unique.

Commentary

One World: 350–4 B.C.

The world of Christ's day was unified in a way it had never been before. A common language provided a medium by which the Gospel could be quickly spread. A single political power maintained its massive authority, and wiped out old national boundaries, freeing men to travel safely throughout the known world. These unique conditions were vital in the later spread of the new faith.

Alexander. Alexander the Great had been responsible for the spreading of the overarching culture and language of this worldwide civilization. Alexander, a Macedonian, had set out over three centuries before Christ to conquer the world. His goal was to spread Greek culture, which he firmly believed was superior to all others. By 333 B.C. he had conquered the whole of Syria and Palestine; by 331 he had added Egypt. The whole vast Persian Empire was his. But in 323, after touching India itself, Alexander died. His holdings were divided between four generals, and the unity that Alexander envisioned was shattered.

In the East, Egypt and Palestine were held by Ptolemy and his descendants. Syria was ruled by the Seleucids. There was constant struggle between the two powers; finally in 198 B.C., Jerusalem and the Jews came under the sway of the Seleucids.

Rome. Following Alexander's day, the city on the Tiber River in Italy continued to expand its influence. Each new conquest led to further conquests as the Romans sought more distant borders to insulate their empire's heartland. Gradually the borders pushed outward to include what is now Spain, France, parts of Germany, part of Britain, and the Black Sea coast of Asia Minor. Ultimately the Roman Empire extended from Spain to Armenia and from Britain to the Sahara.

By Jesus' day the whole Western world was knit together by Rome's Empire—a single unit over which Rome maintained control. But the language and culture were Greek (Hellenic). Alexander's dream had been realized—through the agency of another race!

But Rome herself had not been stable. In the last ineffective days of the Republic (a form of government under which the Ro-

The Roman Empire in the Time of Christ

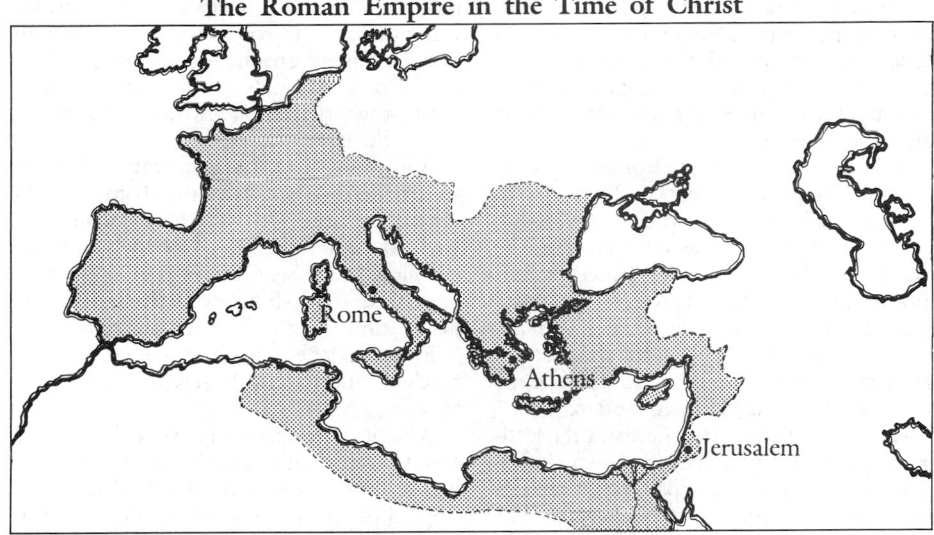

mans were supposedly led by a senate of many legislators) the central authority had broken down. In times of emergency, generals like Pompey and Julius Caesar, who won the loyalty of the armies they led, assumed the real power. After the assassination of Julius Caesar in 44 B.C., the Empire drifted into a decade of civil wars. The decisive battle was fought at Actium in 31 B.C. The victor, Octavian (Augustus) became Rome's "first citizen" and virtual dictator.

Augustus, with his other gifts, was a brilliant administrator. He succeeded in bringing to the Roman Empire a period of unmatched stability and prosperity. Thus the world into which Jesus was born had known some 25 years of Roman peace (the *Pax Romana*)—a peace imposed by the power of Roman arms, and maintained by the administrative and political genius of the emperor.

The Days of the Hammer Palestine: 198-4 B.C.

The ancient world was seldom a quiet one. Wars and rivalries troubled even the least significant backwaters. For decades wars had scarred Palestine and helped shape in Israel a special hunger for the promised messianic King.

In the early division of Alexander's empire, as we have seen, Palestine fell to the Ptolemies. This house seemed genuinely concerned about Alexander's dream. They developed the city of Alexandria, Egypt as a center of culture and learning. The largest library in the world was established there, and Jewish rabbis labored there to translate the Old Testament into the Greek language. The version they produced is known as the Septuagint.

But in 198 B.C. control of Palestine shifted to the Seleucids (Syria), who adopted an aggressive policy of Hellenization, imposing Greek culture, language, and religion. After a series of wars much like those through which Herod would later come to power, rule of the Seleucid Empire passed to Antiochus IV Epiphanes. He determined to unify the diverse peoples under his control through Hellenization. His program included religious unification, but unification around the worship of himself as *theos epiphanes,* "the manifest god."

Antiochus set up his own high priest in Jerusalem, selling the office to the highest bidder, who plundered the temple riches to pay off his bribe. In the meantime, Antiochus defeated the Ptolemies, and even occupied Egypt. There Antiochus, at the head of his victorious army, was confronted by a representative of Rome who commanded Antiochus to vacate Egypt's rich land. Antiochus had spent 12 years as a hostage in Rome, and knew Rome's power well. Cowed, he turned back. But Antiochus was now furious, and he determined to concentrate on making Palestine a buffer state between Syria and Egypt. Immediately he began a crash program to Hellenize the Jews.

Antiochus desecrated the Jerusalem temple, offering on the altar a pig in sacrifice to Zeus. And he forbad the practice of the Jewish religion. With this single command he sought to destroy the ancient Hebrew faith and lifestyle.

In Jerusalem, many Hellenized Jews accepted Antiochus' commands. But not so in the villages. In the small village of Modein, a priest, Mattathias, was ordered to make sacrifice to Antiochus. He refused. When another Jew volunteered to make the sacrifice, Mattathias killed the traitor and the Syrian legate, and fled into the Judean mountains with his five sons. This began the Maccabean rebellion in 166 B.C.

Mattathias died in 166 B.C., and the leadership passed to his third son, Judas. Judas, nicknamed Maccabeus ("hammerer"), led a growing revolt against the Seleucids. The dramatic exploits of the Maccabees, as they were popularly known, can be read in the apocryphal books of 1 and 2 Maccabees, which are included in Roman Catholic versions of the Bible. At one point Judas defeated an army sent by Antiochus. Soon the entire country was under Maccabean control!

But there were still inner struggles between bitterly divided Jews. After the death of Antiochus (163) and a defeat of the Jews by Lysias (the general placed over Palestine), Syria guaranteed the Jews religious freedom in 162 B.C. But Judas now insisted on political freedom as well, and the battle continued to 160. Judas appealed to Rome for protection, and his request was granted. But before Rome could step in, a swift Syrian attack led to a Jewish defeat and to Judas' death.

Other sons of Mattathias took up the struggle, and a long line of Maccabean (also called Hasmonean) leaders resulted. Though internal rivalries plagued the land, Judea finally realized a degree of autonomy as the Seleucids gradually lost their power and authority.

But in 63 B.C., when two Hasmonean rulers contended for control of Judea, and both appealed to Pompey (a Roman general) for support, Palestine was firmly annexed as part of the Roman world, just as Syria had been in 65 B.C. Soon Egypt too would know Rome's sway (30 B.C.).

The Maccabees' vision of a free and independent Palestine had been buried by the inexorable march of history. But the dream was not lost. Its roots were sunk deep in Old Testament prophecy and promise. One day God's Messiah would appear. And then—then the empire would be *theirs!*

So the land waited.

Augustus, good administrator that he was, ordered a census of the Roman world for tax purposes. In Palestine, Joseph went back to his hometown of Bethlehem to be enrolled. Mary, who was of the same family line, went with him, even though it was nearly time for the birth of her first child.

Entering the city, the young woman reached out to clutch Joseph's arm. "It's time."

And it was time. The time had "fully come" according to God's plan and according to His working in events (Gal. 4:4).

All history had converged on this moment. Augustus in Rome would never dream that God had guided him to power to bring world peace. Alexander never imagined that God was using him to establish a common language as a medium through which a new revelation of God's grace could be communicated to all men. Even Antiochus in his maddest dreams could never know that, in the rise and fall of the Maccabeans, whose revolt he caused, Israel would be led to realize anew that only in the prophet's promised King could she have hope.

Perspectives

Today few of us know much of the world of Jesus' day. For us the focus has shifted from Rome to Bethlehem. The records that detail the histories of the nations and leaders of the then-known world have either been lost or forgotten by the common man. But millions pour over another record; a record that documents the course of one solitary life.

We ourselves fail to realize how much of our New Testament is given to four portraits of our Lord. In one Bible on my desk just now, 102 pages of text cover the four Gospels, while 134 pages record the rest of the New Testament! Why this emphasis, and why four portraits?

Reading the Gospels, it's clear that each writer selected and organized his material for a distinct purpose. Matthew, Mark, and Luke all cover similar material in their three portraits of Jesus. For this reason, they are

Jesus' Life on Earth

Emphases	Birth	Victor	Moral Teacher	Miracle-worker	Contro-versialist	Leader	Prophet	Suffering Saviour
MATTHEW	1–3	4	5–7	8–9	10–17	17–20	13, 21–25	26–28
MARK				1–5	6–8	9–12	13	14–16
LUKE	1–3	4	6	5; 7–8	19–20	9–18	21	22–24

JOHN—emphases on **Controversialist, Leader,** and **Saviour** throughout

	Kingdom Emphasis	Turning Point	Cross Emphasis
MATTHEW	4–15	16	17–28
MARK	1–7	8	9–16
LUKE	4–9	9:22-27	9:28–24
JOHN	—	—	1–21

called the "synoptic" (meaning to give an account from the same point of view) Gospels.

Mark. Mark is generally agreed to have been the first Gospel written, probably penned in Rome for Gentile believers. Jewish coloring is absent, and where Palestinian customs are included, Mark explains them for a non-Jewish audience. The book is brief—a mere 661 verses, and seems to be a fast-moving, eyewitness account of Jesus' life, with great emphasis on the Passion Week and on Christ's culminating act of redemption.

Both Matthew and Luke probably took Mark as a guide, in that they seemed to generally follow his chronology and sequence of events, though each made changes in emphasis.

Luke. Luke is the most comprehensive Gospel, covering more of Christ's life than any other. Luke seemed particularly sensitive to Jesus' humanity, stressing His relationships with men in need, and including individuals left out in other accounts. Luke mentioned 13 women not found elsewhere in the Gospels. He also included several case histories of men whose ways of life made them social outcasts, yet who were transformed by Jesus' touch.

Luke's stated aim (Luke 1:1-4) was to provide a clear, accurate historical account. He combined detail with a beautiful and sensitive portrait of the personality of Jesus, and of Jesus' love for all men.

Matthew. The first of the Gospels in our New Testament was probably written after Mark, and has a distinct and clear purpose. It was written to demonstrate to the Jew familiar with the Old Testament that Jesus is indeed the Messiah. Because of this emphasis, Matthew is the bridge between Old and New Testaments.

In addition, Matthew gives great prominence to Jesus' teaching, with five blocks of teaching included which are absent from Mark.

John. John's Gospel is distinctly different, and focuses on presenting Jesus as the Son of God. Where Matthew and Luke launch the story of Jesus with His birth, John traces the origin of our Lord back into eternity itself (John 1).

In keeping with his purpose, John selected incidents and events that were different from those reported by the other three evangelists. John reported different speeches, usually ones set in Judea. These are often long, theological, and argumentative. Against the background of Judean unbelief, Jesus presented Himself as the Bread of heaven, the Giver of life, the true Light, and the ultimate Truth.

From the very earliest days of the church, Matthew, Mark, Luke, and John have been accepted as apostolic accounts of Jesus' life and ministry. They have always been viewed as one collection. Through these ancient eyewitness accounts, we are uniquely introduced to Jesus.

In these Gospels we meet our Lord. In these accounts of His words and actions, we realize that, as on this Man all history seems to converge, so on Him we too must converge our faith and our lives.

We recognize Jesus here as Israel's promised King.

We acknowledge Him as our Redeemer.

And we puzzle over His words and ways, struggling to understand them that they might mark out our pathway to a life lived in union with our God.

TEACHING GUIDE

Prepare

For more background look up the following in a Bible dictionary or encyclopedia: Alexander the Great, Augustus Caesar, Antiochus (IV) Epiphanes, the Maccabees, Hellenistic culture, and Pax Romana.

Explore

1. Ask group members to share: As they think back over their lives, can they see anything which might be viewed as God's preparation, helping each become the person he or she is, or become ready for the work he or she is doing?
2. Before your group meets, ask individuals to look up and report on the topics identified in the *prepare* section. Encourage each to focus on the role his or her topic played in preparing the first-century world for the birth of Jesus and the spread of the Gospel.

Expand

1. Explain the emphasis that the New Testament places on the life of Christ by giving so much of its space to the four Gospels. Then use the chart on page 513 to survey the themes found in each of the four, and show the general emphasis of each.
2. Duplicate and distribute to each group member a copy of the detailed analysis of the Gospel's contents found on pages 515-517. These can be used for any study of any Gospel to quickly locate parallel passages.

Apply

1. Return to the discussion with which you launched your group. Does God's work in shaping the history of the world for His purpose carry any message for us today? What might be suggested by the length of time taken? By the integration of many different factors?
2. Is God at work in our own day in world events? What events do you believe show His shaping hand?

	Matthew	Mark	Luke	John
I. Birth and Childhood (4/5 B.C.)				
Genealogy of Jesus	1:1-17		3:23-38	
Birth of John the Baptist			1:5-25, 57-80	
Jesus' Birth Foretold (Mary)			1:26-38	
Jesus' Birth Foretold (Joseph)	1:18-25			
The Birth of Jesus	2:1		2:1-7	
Angels Announce the Birth			2:8-20	
Jesus Presented at the Temple			2:21-39	
The Wise Men Come	2:1-12			
The Family Flees to Egypt	2:13-23			
Childhood, and Visit to Temple			2:40-50	
Growth to Manhood			2:51-52	
II. Preparation for Public Ministry (A.D. 29)				
John the Baptist's Preaching	3:1-12	1:1-8	3:1-20	
Jesus Is Baptized	3:13-17	1:9-11	3:21-22	
Jesus Tempted in the Wilderness	4:1-11	1:12-13	4:1-13	
III. Beginning of Jesus' Ministry				
John Points Out Jesus				1:19-34
The First Disciples Attracted				1:35-51
The First Miracle: Water to Wine				2:1-12
Jesus Cleanses the Temple				2:13-25
Jesus Explains "Born Again"				3:1-21
John Testifies about Jesus				3:22-36
John Imprisoned			3:19-20	
Jesus Travels in Samaria				4:1-42
IV. Great Galilean Ministry				
Jesus Arrives	4:12-17	1:14	4:14	4:43-45
Heals Nobleman's Son				4:46-54
Calls First Disciples	4:18-22	1:16-20		
Jesus Heals the Sick	8:14-17	1:21-34	4:31-41	
Jesus Travels and Preaches		1:35-39	4:42-44	
Jesus Performs Many Miracles	8:1-4; 9:1-35	1:30–3:12	5:1–6:19	
Jesus Confronts Pharisees	12:1-21			
The Twelve Appointed		3:13-19	6:12-16	
The Sermon on the Mount	5–7		6:20-49	
Jesus Heals a Soldier's Servant	8:5-13		7:1-10	
Jesus Raises a Widow's Son			7:11-17	
John the Baptist Doubts	11:2-19		7:18-35	
Jesus Anointed by a Prostitute			7:36-50	
Jesus Makes Another Tour			8:1-3	
Jesus' Family Protests	12:46-50	3:31-35	8:19-21	
Jesus Speaks in Parables	13:1-53	4:1-34	8:4-18	
Jesus Performs a Series of Miracles	8:14-17; 9:18-34	4:35–5:43	8:22-56	
Jesus Rejected at Nazareth	13:54-58	6:1-6		
Disciples Sent Out to Preach	9:36–11:1	6:7-13	9:1-6	
John the Baptist Executed	14:1-12	6:14-29	9:7-9	
The Twelve Return		6:30-32	9:10	
Jesus Feeds 5,000	14:13-21	6:33-44	9:11-17	6:1-14
Jesus Walks on the Sea	14:22-33	6:45-53		6:15-21
Jesus Teaches on "Uncleanness"	15:1-20	7:1-23		

Detailed Harmony of Gospels

	Matthew	Mark	Luke	John
Jesus Near Tyre and Sidon	15:21-28	7:24-30		
Jesus Heals Near Decapolis	15:29-31	7:31-37		
Jesus Feeds 4,000	15:32-39	8:1-10		
Jesus Warns against Pharisees	16:1-12	8:14-21		
Jesus Heals a Blind Man		8:22-26		
Jesus Affirmed as the Christ and Son of God	16:13-26	8:27-37	9:18-27	6:68-69
Jesus Transformed	17:1-13	8:38–9:13	9:28-36	
Jesus Heals Epileptic Boy	17:14-21	9:14-29	9:37-43	
Jesus Predicts His Death and His Resurrection	17:22-23	9:30-32	9:43-45	
Jesus' Last Galilean Ministry	17:24–18:34	9:33-50	9:46-50	7:1-9
V. Judean and Perean Ministry				
Journey to Jerusalem	19:1-2	10:1	9:51-62	7:10
At the Feast of Tabernacles				7:11-52
The Woman Taken in Adultery				7:53–8:11
Jesus Claims Deity				8:12-59
Jesus Heals a Man Born Blind				9:1-41
Jesus Claims to Be the Good Shepherd				10:1-21
72 Followers Sent to Preach			10:1-24	
Story of the Good Samaritan			10:25-37	
Jesus in Mary and Martha's Home			10:38-42	
Jesus Teaches a Prayer			11:1-4	
Jesus Accused of Satanic Empowerment by Pharisees			11:14-54	
Jesus Warns against Pharisee Attitudes and Values			12:1-59	
Jesus at Feast of Dedication				10:22-39
Jesus Warns His Listeners			13:1-35	
Jesus Dines with a Pharisee			14:1-24	
Jesus Tells Cost of Discipleship			14:25-35	
Jesus Teaches on God's Compassion			15:1-32	
Jesus Teaches His Disciples			16:1–17:10	
Jesus Raises Lazarus				11:1-44
Enemies Plot to Kill Jesus				11:45-54
VI. Jesus Travels Toward Jerusalem				
Jesus Teaches About His Return			17:20-37	
Jesus Teaches About Prayer and Faith			18:1-17	
Jesus Teaches on Divorce	19:1-12	10:2-12		
The Rich Young Ruler	19:16–20:16	10:17-31	18:18-30	
Jesus Predicts His Death	20:17-19	10:32-34	18:31-34	
Jesus Teaches on Leadership	20:20-28	10:35-45		
Events Near Jerusalem	20:29-34	10:46-52	18:35–19:28	
Jesus Arrives at Bethany				11:55–12:11
VII. Jesus' Last Week, Passover A.D. 33				
Sunday				
The Triumphal Entry	21:1-9	11:1-10	19:29-40	12:12-19
Jesus Views the City	21:10-11	11:11	19:41-44	
Monday				
Jesus Curses a Fig Tree	21:18-19	11:12-14		
Jesus Cleanses the Temple	21:12-13	11:15-19	19:45-48	
Healings in the Temple	21:14-17			

	Matthew	Mark	Luke	John
Tuesday				
The Fig Tree Is Withered	21:19-22	11:20-25		
Jesus Challenged by the Elders	21:23–22:46	11:27–12:37	20:1-44	
Pharisees Condemned by Jesus	23	12:38-40	20:45-47	
The Widow Gives Her Mite		12:41-44	21:1-4	
Greeks Try to See Jesus				21:20-36
Jews Reject Jesus' Claims				12:37-50
Jesus Teaches on History's End	24–25	13:1-37	21:5-38	
Jesus Predicts Crucifixion	26:1-5	14:1-2		
Jesus Anointed by Mary	26:6-13	14:3-9		12:2-8
Judas Agrees to Betray Jesus	26:14-16	14:10-11	22:3-6	
Wednesday				
Thursday				
The Passover Meal Held	26:17-29	14:12-25	22:7-22	13:1-38
The Last Supper Teaching				14–16
Jesus' High Priestly Prayer				17
Prayer at Gethsemane	26:36-46	14:32-42	22:39-46	18:1
Jesus Arrested	26:47-56	14:43-52	22:47-53	18:2-12
On Trial before Annas				18:12-14, 19-23
On Trial before Caiaphas	26:57-68	14:53-65	22:54	18:24
Peter Denies the Lord	26:69-75	14:66-72	22:54-62	18:15-18, 25-27
On Trial before the Sanhedrin	27:1	15:1	22:66-71	
Suicide of Judas	27:3-10			
Friday				
On Trial before Pilate	27:11-14	15:2-5	23:1-5	18:28-38
Taken to Herod			23:6-12	
Returned to Pilate	27:15-26	15:6-15	23:13-25	18:39–19:16
Mocked by Soldiers	27:27-30	15:16-19	22:63-65	
Led to Calvary	27:31-34	15:20-23	23:26-32	19:16-17
Jesus' Crucifixion	27:35-56	15:24-41	23:33-49	19:18-37
Jesus' Body Buried	27:57-60	15:42-46	23:50-54	19:38-42
Saturday				
Women Visit the Tomb	27:61	15:47	23:55-57	
A Guard Set over the Tomb	27:62-66			
Sunday				
The Women Return	28:1-8	16:1-8	24:1-12	20:1-10
VIII. Resurrection Appearances of Jesus Christ				
To Mary Magdalene		16:9-11		20:11-18
To the Other Women	28:9-10			
Report by the Guards	28:11-15			
Two Unnamed Disciples		16:12-13	24:13-32	
Peter			24:33-35	
The 10 Apostles		16:14	24:36-43	20:19-25
The 11 Apostles				20:26-31
By the Sea of Galilee				21:1-14
Questioning of Peter				21:15-25
The Disciples, in Galilee	28:16-20	16:15-18		
The 11 at Olivet			24:44-49	
At the Ascension	28:18-20	16:19-20	24:50-53	

STUDY GUIDE 80

Introduction

MATTHEW'S GOSPEL

Overview

Matthew's Gospel was viewed as the most important by the early church, and is the Gospel most frequently quoted by writers of the first three centuries. Its date is much argued, but all agree it was produced in the first century, a few or several decades after Jesus' death.

The Gospel of Matthew is directed primarily to the Jewish people. At least 130 direct references or allusions to the Old Testament have been identified. The book shows that Jesus truly is the messianic King of Old Testament prophecy. It is designed to help the believing Jew understand what has happened to the kingdom the prophets link with Him.

There are several unique features of Matthew. Of 1,068 verses in this Gospel, 644 contain words of Jesus. Thus more than three fifths of the Gospel is a report of Christ's sayings. Among them are 35 parables. Matthew also emphasizes both Jesus' ethical teachings, and His eschatological teaching (teaching about the future). Matthew's Gospel records 20 of Jesus' miracles, 3 of which are found only in this Gospel (Matt. 9:27-31, 32-33; 17:24-27).

Perhaps the most striking feature of this Gospel, however, is the fact that while it affirms Jesus as Israel's promised King, it also presents Him as a Servant. In Jesus, and in Jesus only, glory and humility, power and gentleness, are perfectly combined.

■ For a discussion of the use of sources, and of outstanding characteristics of this Gospel, see the *Bible Knowledge Commentary*, pages 13-17.

Commentary

When we look at any of the Gospels in our New Testament, we're sure to read of persons, parties, and institutions which were as familiar then as the Kennedys, the Republicans and Democrats, and the postal service are to us today. When we meet these in the Gospels they sound familiar, but most of us may not be sure just what the terms meant in first-century days. So, before we look at a few specific characteristics of Matthew's Gospel, let's look at terms we'll meet in any Gospel that help us to understand the New Testament world.

Parties and Sects

The Gospels tell us about priests and rulers, about Pharisees and Sadducees and Herodians. They mention Galileans and Samaritans. Who were these groups, and what did they stand for in Jesus' world?

Priests. The priesthood was an Old Testament institution, established in the time of Moses. Priests were required to be descendants of Aaron, Moses' brother. These priests were the only ones authorized to offer sacrifices, and were to instruct the people in the meaning of the divine Law. While the priesthood was originally a religious office, by the time of Jesus some priests also exerted political influence. The high priest was the president of the Sanhedrin (the Jewish governing body), giving him both religious and political power. The "chief priests" (mentioned 64 times in the New Testament) were temple officers with seats on the Sanhedrin, who also had significant political influence. They should be distinguished from the ordinary priests, like Zechariah (Luke 1:5) who simply carried out their religious function.

The high priest and chief priests, and the aristocratic families from which they came, generally opposed Jesus and later the Apostles.

Rulers. This word, used a number of times in the Gospels, usually indicates members of the Sanhedrin or others with political influence.

Pharisees. While this party arose in the

time of Maccabees, its members liked to trace the origin of their teachings to the time of Moses. The name means "separated." It may have been used first in mockery of their resolve to separate themselves from the political parties in their nation. It also surely reflected their determination to separate themselves from sinful practices and to zealously follow God's Law.

The Pharisees were the conservatives of Jesus' day. They held to the authority of the written Law, but also to the authority of the oral traditions that interpreted Mosaic Law and taught how it should be applied. While the Pharisees were truly the orthodox of Judaism in Jesus' day, theirs was a sterile faith. Again and again Jesus had to confront them, showing that their piety was legalistic and hypocritical. In their eagerness to exalt the written Law they missed the love for and mercy toward others the Law was intended to establish.

Tragically, these first-century conservatives would not respond to Jesus. He did not fit their preconceived notions of how the Messiah should behave, and His interpretations of Scripture, which cut through human tradition to original meaning, were not in harmony with their rigid beliefs.

Sadducees. This was the liberal party of Jesus' time. It may have had close links with the priesthood, and was solidly represented in the Sanhedrin.

The Sadducees acknowledged only the Books of Moses as Scripture, denied the existence of angels, and believed in neither resurrection nor the immortality of the soul. They owed their place to their ability to fit in with the pagan power structure, and were not against secularizing their nation and Judaism.

They were in accord with the Pharisees only in their dislike of Jesus, and plotted with them to have Christ killed.

Scribes. The scribes were the scholars of both the Pharisean and Sadducean parties. They were simply authorities on the Law, who were highly respected by the people for their devotion to the study and interpretation of the Old Testament. However, Jesus came in conflict with them as He attacked, not the Law, but accepted scribal interpretations of it.

Herodians. This party was political rather than religious in character. It was linked with the ruling family of Herod, and supported Roman rule. The Herodians were against any political change which might threaten them and their collaboration. They opposed Jesus not so much on religious grounds but because they feared Him as a revolutionary. They saw His claim to be the Messiah as a political threat.

Galileans. This was a political party, as well as a geographical designation. The "Galileans" were what we would call today "freedom fighters," who opposed the Romans and the Hellenization of their land.

Jesus came from Galilee, as did His closest followers. But only Simon the Zealot had been previously associated with the revolutionary "Galilean party."

Samaritans. These inhabitants of the district of Samaria (see map) were descendants of peoples imported after the Assyrians defeated the Northern Kingdom of Israel in 722 B.C. Most of the Jewish people then had been removed, and mixed races had been settled there from many parts of the Assyrian Empire. These people adopted the God of the new land, Yahweh, but continued to worship their old gods as well. Much later, when a small group returned from Babylonian Captivity to resettle Judea, the Samaritans wanted to participate in rebuilding the Jerusalem temple. Their offer was rejected. By the time of Jesus, a deep hostility existed between the Jews and Samaritans. Often people traveling between Judea and Galilee would take a much longer route rather than travel through Samaria.

Palestine. The Palestine of Jesus' time was divided into several districts.

The whole area included in the several districts is only some 140 miles long. In the north it reaches only 23 miles inland from the sea; in the south, about 80. Palestine in Jesus' day was essentially only a tiny mote in the vastness of the Roman Empire.

Galilee. This district was some 60 by 33 miles in area. It held the Sea of Galilee, and many of the places associated with the ministry of Jesus, such as Nazareth, Capernaum, Cana, and Bethsaida.

Samaria. This district lay between Galilee and Judea, and at its greatest extent was 56 miles long and 47 miles wide. Its cities are seldom mentioned in the Gospels, as Jesus' ministry during His lifetime was primarily to the Jewish people, who did not live here.

Judea. Though only 57 miles wide and about 45 miles in length, Judea was the

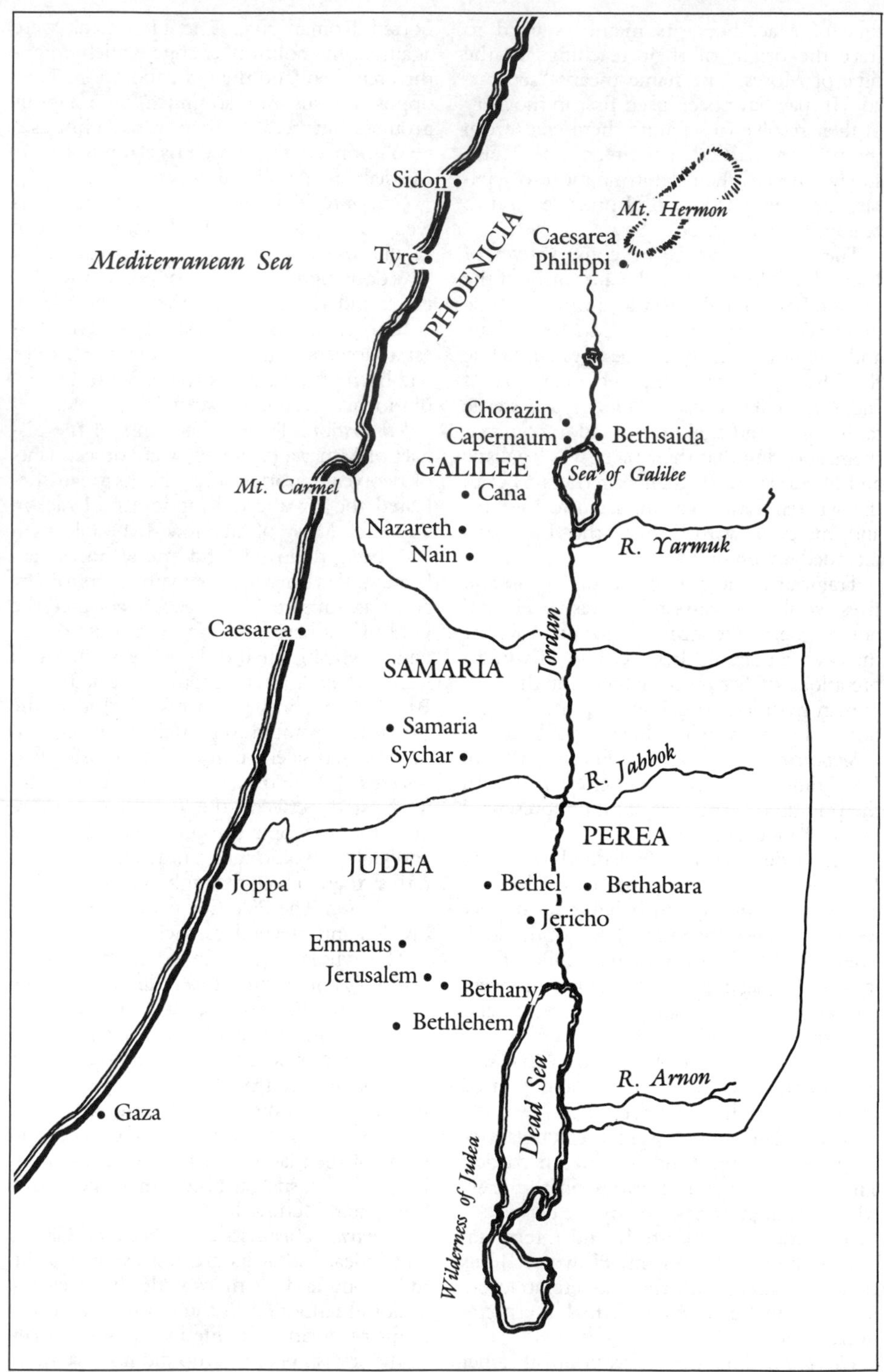

Palestine in the Time of Jesus

The Herodian Family

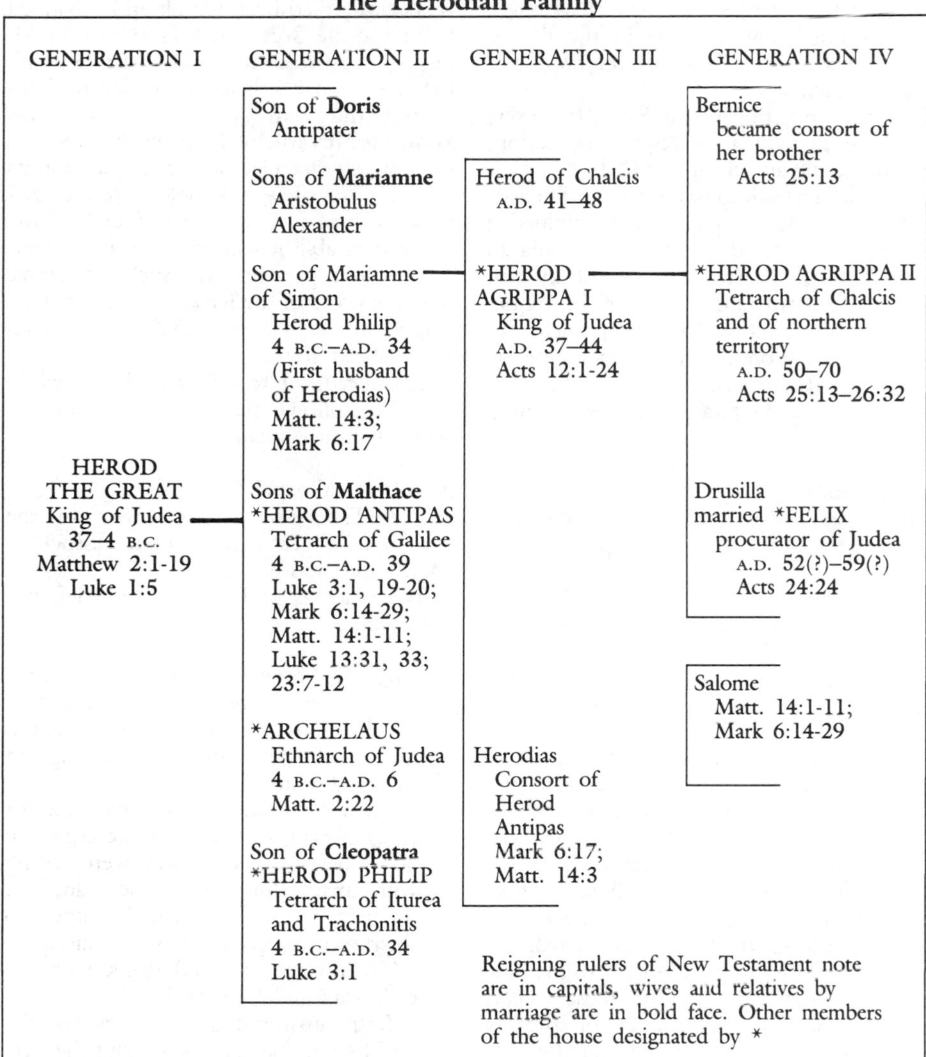

center of Jewish life. It held Jerusalem, with its beautiful temple. Other Judean localities prominent in the Gospels include Bethlehem, Bethany, and Emmaus.

While the geography of Palestine is varied, with mountains and hills, valleys and fertile plains, it is hard for us to grasp just how small this land truly is. Yet it was here, in a land whose entire population was smaller in New Testament times than the Jewish community in a modern city like New York or Chicago, that the most significant of history's events took place. As in so many things, size here gives no true indication of significance.

Political Situation

The political situation in Palestine was complex, with various overlapping authorities. The Romans held overarching power, represented in Judea by the procurator, Pontius Pilate. Members of the family of Herod the Great, who ruled at the time of Jesus' birth, held various positions of authority over different parts of Palestine. Herod Antipas was Tetrarch of Galilee. Herod Philip, a son of Herod the Great and Cleopatra, was Tetrarch of Iturea. Herod Agrippa I was king of Judea from A.D. 37–48. The chart traces the Herodian family's role in the life of Palestine during the Gospel and New Testament church era.

In addition, the Jewish Sanhedrin exercised authority over the Jewish population, administering and enforcing Old Testament Law (with its traditions/additions). The Romans taxed the people, and maintained a military force in the Fortress Antonia in Jerusalem. But day-to-day administration of law lay primarily in the hands of the Sanhedrin, who could order any punishment short of execution. Execution had to be ordered by Rome, which is why the Jews brought Jesus to Pilate after condemning Him in their own courts.

Institutions

The Gospels also introduce us to several institutions familiar to the people of Jesus' day.

The Sanhedrin. This governing body of the Jews was both religious and political in character. The Law of the Old Testament was civil as well as religious. The Sanhedrin, headed by the high priest and composed of the "chief priests," scholars of Scripture, and lay members, governed the Jewish population in Palestine, and also had authority over Jews anywhere in the Roman Empire.

The synagogue. When the temple was destroyed in 586 B.C. by Nebuchadnezzar, the Jews were taken captive to Babylon. There they began to meet in small groups on the Sabbath to study the Scriptures and worship God. When the people returned to the land and the temple was rebuilt, these weekly meetings of local communities for study of God's Word continued. Wherever the Jewish people found themselves in the Roman Empire, and many were scattered throughout it, they met together around the Word of God each Sabbath.

Jesus Himself attended synagogue. Luke tells us of one incident in which He was asked to read, and went on to explain a passage from the Old Testament (Luke 4:16-30). Paul and other early missionaries typically went to the synagogue first when they visited any city in the Roman Empire. There they too were often invited to speak, and could share the Gospel with God's ancient people.

The temple. In Jesus' day, the temple that had been rebuilt by the exiles some 500 years earlier had been rebuilt and expanded by Herod the Great. Herod's 40-year building program was intended in part to pacify the Jews. But it was also intended to demonstrate the greatness of this ruler who was known for his cruelty. Many of the events of the Gospels take place at the temple or in its environs. The Jewish people were required to appear at Jerusalem for several of the festivals established in the Old Testament. Jesus often preached on such occasions. And members of the Jerusalem church worshiped in the temple daily, and preached there about Jesus.

This beautiful temple was destroyed in A.D. 70, following another revolt by the Jews against Roman power.

Matthew's Gospel

Author. The writer of this Gospel was the person called Levi in his own Gospel, in Mark, and in Luke.

The story as told in Luke is brief, but powerful.

> After this, Jesus went out and saw a tax collector by the name of Levi sitting at his tax booth. "Follow Me," Jesus said to him, and Levi got up, left everything and followed Him.
>
> Then Levi held a great banquet for Jesus at his house, and a large crowd of tax collectors and others were eating with them. But the Pharisees and the teachers of the Law who belonged to their sect complained to His disciples, "Why do you eat and drink with tax collectors and 'sinners'?"
>
> Jesus answered them, "It is not the healthy who need a doctor, but the sick. I have not come to call the righteous, but sinners to repentance."
>
> Luke 5:27-32

The placement of this incident is significant. Jesus had just healed a paralytic, and announced that He has power to forgive sins (vv. 17-26). Now He called Levi, who was publicly identified as a tax collector and who associated with "sinners." This identification was accurate. Tax gatherers had to bid for their positions, and made their profit by extorting extra from their fellow-countrymen. As collaborators with Rome and as dishonest oppressors, tax gatherers were despised by the general populace.

Now Jesus not only invited one of these men to become His disciple, but even went to a party of "sinners" held in His honor!

Jesus' explanation that He came to call sinners to repentance is magnificently borne out by subsequent events. This "sinner," Levi, became the Matthew whose Gospel launches our New Testament. Jesus, who forgives sins through the power of His forgiveness is able to transform sinners into righteous women and men.

♥ ***Link to Life: Youth / Adult***

Another parallel incident shows that forgiveness is transforming, and not simply overlooking faults.

Have your group first look at Luke 5:17-26. The Pharisees objected to Jesus announcing sins were forgiven on theological grounds: only God can forgive sins. Some objected on practical grounds: forgiveness is too easy. They even said, "Then a person could just go out and sin all he wants, and ask for forgiveness. It can't be that easy."

Explain why tax collectors were considered "sinners" in New Testament times. Have teams look at the calling of Levi, explaining that he later became known as Matthew. How might Luke 5:27-32 be an answer to this "practical" objection?

If your group members do not note that the transformation of Levi into Matthew demonstrates that forgiveness has transforming power, have them read also 19:2-10, the story of Zaccheus. This chief tax collector, when converted, paid back those he had cheated four times the amount, and gave half of his possessions to the poor. The forgiveness that Jesus offers us, and that the Gospels testify to, truly does possess transforming power.

Content

Matthew's Gospel is marked off from the others by several emphases. Each Gospel, of course, tells the story of Jesus. But each Gospel writer lays a particular stress on issues that most concern his intended readers.

Matthew's Gospel, intended for Jewish readers, has these distinctive features.

Multiple Old Testament quotes and allusions. There are some 53 direct Old Testament quotes in Matthew's Gospel. In addition 76 allusions, or general references, have been identified. Several of the direct quotes are linked with Jesus' birth, while many others are associated with His death. Among the latter, intended to show that the death of the Messiah is in harmony with Old Testament revelation, are: Matthew 26:31 (Zech. 13:7); Matthew 27:9-10 (Zech. 11:13; Jer. 32:6-9); Matthew 27:35 (Ps. 22:18); Matthew 27:39 (Ps. 22:7); Matthew 27:43 (Ps. 22:8; 71:11); Matthew 27:40 (Ps. 22:1-2).

In addition there are a number of allusions in these same chapters, notably: Matthew 27:6 (Deut. 23:18); Matthew 27:31 (Isa. 53:7); Matthew 27:60 (Isa. 53:9).

Extended moral teachings. More than any other Gospel writer, Matthew reported the moral teaching of Jesus as Christ challenged His listeners to examine their values, and to set fresh priorities in their relationships with God and their fellowmen. This is particularly set forth in the Sermon on the Mount, found in Matthew 5–7.

Expectations for the future. Jesus also spoke much about the future. He insisted that life's meaning cannot be summed up in our experience in this world. The wise person will lay up treasures in heaven, not on earth. Jesus warned also about hell, speaking more often about it than about heaven! But in addition Jesus did look ahead to events yet to take place on earth. In the extended prophetic discussion found in Matthew 24–26 Jesus shared a vision of the future of this earth held in common by the Old Testament prophets.

In these and all the other themes that are prominent in Matthew, this disciple is concerned with telling the story of Jesus in such a way that His identity with the Messiah of the Old Testament is unmistakable.

Matthew, and only Matthew of the four Gospels, focuses on demonstrating that this Man who lived and died as a servant truly was the Old Testament's promised King.

TEACHING GUIDE

Prepare
Make up handouts for your group summarizing background information on the Gospel period. Include the map and chart of the Herods. Check in the *Bible Knowledge Commentary* (New Testament) for additional material for a lecture overview.

Explore
1. Start with a quiz. List on the board the following topics. Have each person jot down *one thing he or she knows* about that topic. List: Judea, Priests, Pharisees, Galileans, Samaritans, Sanhedrin.

Let group members share what they jotted down. Then pass out any note or information sheet you may have prepared, and give your group background information they need to understand New Testament meanings.

2. Continue your overview by handing out both a map of Palestine in New Testament times, and the chart showing the various generations of the Herodian family, and references to that family in the Gospels. These can be used throughout your study of Matthew, or any other Gospel.

Expand
Let your group members break into teams to preview some of the distinctive features of Matthew's Gospel.

One team can look up the Old Testament quotes in Matthew 26 and 27. Another team can scan the moral teaching of Jesus in Matthew 5–7. A third team can look at Jesus' teachings on the future of our world in Matthew 24.

Give each team time to read and make notes on its passage. Then return and discuss: "What were your major impressions?" And, "How do you see this emphasis related to Matthew's primary concern, that the Jewish people see Jesus as the Messiah of the Old Testament?"

Don't be concerned if the answers to this last question are not sharply in focus. In your study of Matthew the answers will become increasingly clear to all group members.

Apply
Use the "link-to-life" idea on page 523 to sense the power of the forgiveness Jesus brings us in the lives of Matthew and Zaccheus. How good to realize as we study this wonderful Gospel that we are not simply reading history, but instead meet the living Saviour, who intends to transform us as well.

STUDY GUIDE 81

Matthew 1–2

THE BIRTH OF JESUS

Overview

Matthew was concerned that his readers acknowledge Jesus as the promised Messiah of Israel. Several features of the first two chapters demonstrate his theme. The genealogy we find in Matthew 1 traces Jesus' human ancestry back to Abraham, through David, whose offspring was promised an eternal throne. Matthew referred to acknowledged messianic passages to show that the details of Jesus' birth were in full harmony with the Old Testament. Matthew also emphasized the fear of King Herod, who knew that the promised Deliverer of the Jews was destined to be King. The people of Jesus' time expected the coming Deliverer to be a mighty Ruler—and Herod feared the Infant might grow up to threaten his own throne. How little Herod understood of Jesus' kingdom—and of Jesus' purpose on earth. And how clearly we come to understand it as we trace Matthew's revelation of Jesus as truly a King, but a King who came to suffer and to serve.

▶ ***Magi.*** These Persians were members of a scholarly class that had existed from the time of Daniel. They accurately interpreted the appearance of the star that marked Jesus' birth, and came to honor Him.

▶ ***Genealogies.*** Hebrew genealogies often skip generations. The record in Matthew 1 includes representative persons who serve to demonstrate Jesus' claim to the Davidic throne.

Commentary

Genealogy of a Man: Matthew 1:1-17

Genealogy is the first emphasis in the Gospel of Matthew. When we think of Jesus, we must realize that we are dealing with a Man. The Person who came from heaven (John 1:1-2) was also fully human, and it is His heritage as a human being that Matthew wants us to first understand.

Sometimes we hesitate here. Somehow being human doesn't seem all that special. We picture humankind as sinful, and recall the vast distortions that sin has swept into our individual and societal experience. We even find ourselves ashamed of our humanity at times. How far this attitude is from Scripture!

At Creation, God made two striking affirmations. One, "Let Us make man in Our image, after Our likeness" (Gen. 1:26, KJV), tells us that our identity is not rooted in this world but in eternity. We bear the image-likeness of God: human nature can only be understood by reference to God, not to some supposed animal predecessor. Only man, of all creation, shares something of the likeness of God as a true Person.

The second affirmation, "Let them have dominion" (Gen. 1:26, KJV), affirms that human beings were created to rule! We were born to be kings.

Even the entry of sin, while it has warped our capacity to rule wisely over creation, and even to rule our own passions, has not changed this destiny. The Psalmist David caught a glimpse of our destiny and expressed his wonder in Psalm 8:

> When I consider Your heavens, the work of Your fingers, the moon and the stars, which You have set in place, what is man that You are mindful of him, the son of man that You care for him? You made him a little lower than the heavenly beings and crowned him with glory and honor. You made him ruler over the works of Your hands; You put everything under his feet.
>
> Psalm 8:3-6

God created human beings—for dominion.

Probably the strongest emphasis on this

truth in the New Testament is found in Hebrews 2. There the writer quotes Psalm 8, and notes "in putting everything under him [man], God left nothing that is not subject to him. Yet at present we do not see everything subject to him. But we see Jesus, who was made a little lower than the angels, now crowned with glory and honor because He suffered death" (Heb. 2:8-9).

We may not be able to see the glory of that destiny to which God calls us. But we see Jesus glorified—and we realize that the pathway we too must take to dominion is marked by servanthood and suffering.

In Jesus we see our destiny realized. Jesus, the Man of Galilee, fulfilled the destiny of humanity by becoming King, and in doing so was "bringing many sons to glory" (v. 10). Jesus in His death and resurrection was bringing you and me to the place where we could experience our destiny—where we can know the dominion God has always intended human beings to know. Jesus is King of kings. And we are the kings over whom, and with whom, He reigns. Just what the nature of that reign is, of His and of ours, is something we learn about in the Gospel of Matthew.

Old Testament expectations. God's Old Testament people had dimly realized that dominion was their destiny. But they tended to think of dominion in a national sense, as that prophesied time when the nation Israel, under the promised Jewish Messiah, would be exalted over all the nations on earth. Their sense of destiny was accurate. God did make such promises. But their sense of destiny was limited. God intended far more through the ministry of the Messiah than Israel expected.

So it was very important that Matthew, who wrote primarily to the Jews, establish the right of Jesus to the throne promised the Messiah. (This word, Messiah, refers to the Hebrew practice of anointing kings and others to office with oil. Messiah means "anointed one.")

Two genealogical elements were critical if Matthew was to demonstrate Jesus' right to reign. The first was a relationship with Abraham (Matt. 1:1). It was from Abraham that Israel's awareness of her destiny sprang. God called this man from Ur of the Chaldees, and sent him to Palestine. There God gave Abraham great and special promises. These included the promise of possession of the land of Palestine forever, a great people to live in it, a special relationship with God for Abraham's descendants, and ultimately a descendant (seed) through whom all the peoples of the earth would be blessed (see Gen. 12; 15; and 17).

These promises were given in the form of a covenant (a contract, or oath). They would be fulfilled through one Man, who must come from Abraham's line. The genealogy in Matthew proves that Jesus comes from the covenant line.

The second significant genealogical element is the relationship to David. Later in Israel's history God promised to David that the Messiah would come through his family line. The ultimate King would be born from the family of David, Israel's greatest king. In tracing the genealogy of Jesus from Abraham and from David, Matthew was demonstrating Jesus' right to rule. Jesus' genealogy not only established Him as a true Man, but also was the foundation of His claim to the throne of Israel as the promised Seed of David.

In this genealogical record, the focus of Matthew's Gospel becomes even more clear. We are invited to look into this great book, to see Jesus as King. Through Matthew's portrait of our Lord, you and I will learn what dominion involves—and how to realize in Jesus the destiny God holds out to humankind.

♥ ***Link to Life: Youth / Adult***

Set your group the challenge of explaining the difference between the genealogical list in Matthew and the one in Luke. Print the names side by side.

Your group may note that the line differs from David on, though both go back to David. Why? Jeremiah records a decisive rejection of Jehoiachin (Matt. 1:11): "No man of his seed shall prosper, sitting upon the throne of David and ruling anymore in Judah" (Jer. 22:30).

What scholars believe is that Matthew gave us the genealogy of Joseph "the husband of Mary, of whom was born Jesus, who is called Christ" (Matt. 1:16). Luke gave us the genealogy of Mary. As Jesus was without human father, His claim to the throne of David was established through His mother, who came from a different branch of the Davidic line which had not been rejected by God!

The King? Matthew 1:18-25
One problem that Matthew faced in structuring his Gospel for the Hebrew reader was to show that Jesus really was the expected Messiah. Jesus did not seem to be the King the Jews pictured. He did not set out to crush the Roman Empire. He did not act to set up the expected earthly kingdom. He did not behave as the Jews thought their King should behave.

Theologically, then, Matthew had to answer several critical questions which the Jewish skeptic would naturally ask. Such questions as: "Is Jesus really the Messiah? Then why didn't He fulfill the prophecies about the kingdom? What has happened to the promised earthly kingdom of Israel? And, if the kingdom is not for now, what then is God's present purpose?" Each of these questions is answered in Matthew. And Matthew, very much aware of his readers' concerns, immediately tackled the first of these four critical questions.

One of Matthew's approaches to reaching Hebrew readers was to use extensive quotes from the Old Testament. In his 53 direct quotes and many allusions, Matthew draws from no less than 25 of the 39 Old Testament books! Clearly, Matthew was determined to bridge the gap between the Old and the New.

It's very significant to look at the contexts of the quotations used by Matthew in these first two chapters. When we return to them, we see that Matthew insisted his readers view Jesus as the expected King.

Matthew 2:6 quotes from Micah's prophecy that the coming Ruler will be born in Bethlehem (Micah 5:2). In context that Old Testament prophecy speaks of the Messiah, whose origins lie hidden in eternity. He is to rule in Israel in the name of Yahweh, and to be great to the ends of the earth. It is through this Person that Israel is to find peace.

Matthew 2:2 alludes to Jeremiah 23:5. The promised Messiah of the Jews was to be God and man. He is called in this context "The Lord Our Righteousness" (v. 6), and was to be born of David's line. The prophet said that He will reign over a regathered people, who had been scattered over the world. This person is to reign as King, and in His days Judah and Israel will dwell safely.

Matthew 2:23 looks back to Hosea 11:1, and its prophecy that the Messiah will be called a Nazarene. The context emphasized Messiah's descent from David's line. It said that He will judge and rule with divine wisdom. His rule will bring destruction to the wicked. Gentiles as well as Jews will rally to Him, and in His day the earth will be filled with a knowledge of the Lord. Even the realm of nature is to know unheard of peace.

There are no less than 16 references to the Old Testament in these first two chapters of Matthew. It is clear that Matthew drew from prophecies which affirmed that the Jesus he described was indeed the Messiah Israel had been expecting. Jesus, the Man who lived so quietly, who raised no army, who taught and healed, and who was dragged unprotestingly to an agonizing death, truly is the expected King of glory.

Later the Jewish rabbis would try to explain the jolting contrast between the suffering Saviour and the expected King by postulating two Messiahs: one, Messiah ben David who was yet to come, and who would rule; and two, Messiah ben Joseph, who had perhaps fulfilled the Old Testament prophecies associated with messianic suffering. Yet who would have imagined before Jesus was born and lived His unique life that the pathway to glory led through suffering and self-emptying? Who would have dreamed that the concept of royalty and dominion contains an ingredient of brokenness? Certainly the Jews of Jesus' day, looking for the coming glory, did not see the majesty of suffering. And all too often, you and I miss this dimension as well!

Matthew did not miss it. Matthew made it plain that the Jesus about whom he spoke to us *is* the King of glory. And with this fact firmly established, Matthew went on to describe a King who served; a King whose majesty is enhanced by suffering. A King who shows us how to experience the dominion for which God has destined us—through a servanthood like His own.

♥ ***Link to Life: Youth / Adult***
Have your group members imagine themselves a rabbinical committee in Jesus' lifetime. Examine some of the passages to which Matthew referred in marshaling evidence that Jesus is the promised Messiah.

Look at the specific verses and their context as well. What points would you list in favor of accepting Jesus as the Messiah? What points would you list against so acknowledging Him?

Discuss: "Why would it have been hard for people of Jesus' time to immediately recognize Him as the Messiah? What would the evidence of Jesus' life and ministry have added to help you make this decision? Looking back, can you reconcile the apparent conflict in evidence? How?"

Again, point out that in your studies of Matthew, the Gospel writer's answers become more and more clear. But in referring to the Old Testament, Matthew wanted to be sure everyone understood that Jesus of Nazareth has come in fulfillment of the ancient prophecies.

♥ ***Link to Life: Children***

Junior-age boys and girls can sense both the unexpectedness of Jesus coming to be our Saviour, and the fact that God's inspired words come true in every detail.

Tell your class that a very special visitor is coming. Describe him or her as very important, very powerful, very rich. Tell the children you are going to draw a picture of this person too. Have them draw a picture of what they think this powerful, rich, and important person will look like.

As they draw their pictures you draw a picture too—of a small, quiet, woman (perhaps the Queen of England). Did their pictures look like yours? Talk about how easy it is when we know some things about a person, but not everything about him or her, to imagine he or she will be different than we expect.

The people of Jesus' day did not expect their promised King to be like Jesus. He used His power to heal rather than make war. He helped people, instead of making them obey Him. But everything the Bible says about Jesus is true, and will come true.

Work with your curriculum to help the Juniors find Bible verses that told about Jesus long before He was born.

Two Models: Matthew 2

It's striking. Matthew no sooner introduced us to Jesus, Son of Abraham, Son of David, Israel's destined King, than he introduced us to another ruler. "After Jesus was born in Bethlehem in Judea, during the time of Herod the King" (2:1). No two men could ever stand in starker contrast.

Herod. Herod the Great was the founder of a dynasty that played a key role in Gospel history. We meet four generations of Herods in the New Testament. It is the founder, who ruled from 47–4 B.C., who was then aged and nearing the end of his life, whom we meet in Matthew 2.

Herod's father had attached himself to Julius Caesar's party, been made a Roman citizen, and appointed procurator (ruler) of Judea. Herod and his brothers were given government roles, but a decade of battling followed before Herod was proclaimed king of Judea by Rome, and was able to enforce his rule. As king, Herod was both brutal and decisive, punishing or executing his enemies, and rewarding his friends. Rivals were murdered. When the decisive battle for the Roman Empire was fought between Anthony and Octavian (later to become "Augustus"), Herod gained the victor's friendship and was given control of additional lands.

While Herod's power was growing, his control over himself and his family was slipping. Herod had married 10 wives and had a number of sons. While these sons schemed to gain the throne, his wives hatched plots and counterplots. Herod became more and more suspicious and paranoid, even torturing his sons' friends to discover any plots against his own life. Herod's own character as a plotter who never hesitated to resort to murder was being reproduced in his family, and this led to the aging tyrant's own sense of terror and fear. Herod finally had the two sons of his favorite wife, Mariamne, executed by strangulation in the very city where he had married their mother 30 years earlier. Antipater, Herod's oldest son and designated heir, tried to poison his father and was put in chains.

When nearly 70 years old, Herod was stricken with an incurable disease.

It was at this time, shortly before his death, that Herod heard of wise men who were seeking to worship the newborn King of the Jews. Herod summoned the wise men and made them promise to report the whereabouts of the child so he could "go and worship Him" (Matt. 2:8). The dying man still struggled to grasp the power that had brought him and his family only suspicion, hatred, and death!

God warned the wise men to return home another way. And God warned Joseph to flee with the Christ Child to Egypt. Herod, realizing that the wise men had returned to the East without reporting to him, had all the male children of Bethlehem two years old and under killed!

It was then only a few days before Herod's own death. Five days before he expired, Herod had his son Antipater executed. Then he called all the leading Jews of his territory to his palace. When they came, he imprisoned them, giving orders that they were all to be killed the moment he died. He wanted to ensure that there would be national mourning at his death, rather than rejoicing!

Herod's dream of power and glory had turned into a nightmare. The desperate king struggled to the last to maintain control over his kingdom, long after he had lost control over himself. And so he died.

Jesus. As the hateful old man was living his last days in the splendor of a marble palace, a Child was born in a stable. There, surrounded by the warmth of the animals which shared His birthplace, Jesus entered our world and became a part of a family so poor that Mary had to offer two doves rather than the prescribed lamb as the sacrifice for her purification.

The Child would grow up in a small town far from the seat of power. He would become a carpenter, to live and labor in obscurity for 30 years. Finally, as a young Man, the Carpenter from Nazareth would stand on a riverbank to be recognized by John the Baptist as the Lamb of God, destined to take away the sin of the world. For three years Jesus would walk the roads of Palestine, teaching and healing. He would raise no army. He would seek no earthly glory. He would ultimately humble Himself and accept death at the hands of selfish men who saw Him as a threat to their place and their power.

And yet, through it all He would be a King.

A Servant King.

A King in whom you and I find, not only our redemption, but a pathway to the unique dominion over ourselves and our circumstances to which God has destined humankind.

♥ ***Link to Life: Children***

While Herod refused to worship Jesus, many welcomed Him and came to offer the Babe their love, their worship, and their gifts.

Let your class members imagine that they were following the wise men, looking for the newborn Saviour. Give each a Christmas card. On the outside back ask each to draw a picture of a gift he or she would have wanted to give to Jesus. On the inside, have each write to Jesus how he or she feels about Him.

How good it is this Christmas season to offer Jesus our love and our worship. And to express our thanks with tangible gifts.

The Choice

In contrasting Herod and Jesus, Matthew implicitly presented his Jewish readers and us with a distinctive choice. We can see *dominion* in terms of outward power and splendor, as Herod did, or we can look beyond the external to distinguish the inner core of greatness.

There was nothing wrong with the picture the Jews had of the messianic kingdom. Later Matthew reported Jesus' own affirmation that an outward expression of the kingdom was still to come. Even after the Resurrection, the disciples could not shake their longing for the days of the coming glory. "Are You at this time going to restore the kingdom to Israel?" they asked. Gently Jesus responded, "It is not for you to know the times or dates" (Acts 1:6-7). That kingdom will come, in God's own time.

But until then Jesus remains King. And dominion is ours—if we choose it in Him. If we can only shake the Herod dream, and see in Jesus' humility the key to greatness and true glory, you and I can find a distinctive freedom that the world around us, stumbling over the external, can never understand. It is a journey toward just this kind of inner freedom and power that we take as we trace the Messiah's steps with Matthew, the writer of this Gospel.

Jesus *is* King of kings.

In Him, we grasp our title deed to rule.

TEACHING GUIDE

Prepare
What do *you* expect from your relationship with Jesus? How often do you suppose Christians are as surprised about what faith brings into their lives as the Jewish people were surprised that their Messiah chose a path of suffering and servanthood?

Explore
1. Launch with a review of the genealogy in Matthew 1. Compare it with the genealogy in Luke, and explain their differences. Tell how the Jewish people used genealogies to establish family line and rights to position. If Jesus were the Messiah, He *must* come from David's line—and does!
2. Divide your group into teams, to serve as members of a rabbinical court of Jesus' day. Their task is to examine the prophecies which Matthew referred to as evidence that Jesus is the Messiah. They should follow the procedure outlined in "link-to-life" on pages 527-528.

For part of this activity you will draw on your group members' general knowledge of the life of Jesus. If your group is made up of new Christians, or those unfamiliar with the Bible, you may need to draw additional evidence that Jesus is the Messiah from His miracles, teaching, death, and resurrection, to present to them.

While we can understand the reasons why so many in Jesus' time failed to recognize the Messiah in the quiet Carpenter, there is no excuse for their failure to respond to this Person who was so clearly attested by miracle and word as sent by God.

Expand
1. Discuss: "Jesus' first coming did literally fulfill prophecy. But the people of His day did not realize it until later, because they had developed false expectations. How likely are we to be similarly mistaken about features of His second coming? Can we be sure that when Jesus returns He will do exactly what modern writers on prophecy say He will do? Why, or why not?"
2. Jesus is contrasted with Herod in Matthew 2. Each seems to have a very different view of what is involved in "dominion"—e.g., in power, authority, rule.

Have your group work together to brainstorm differences between Herod's and Jesus' views of dominion. For instance, Herod saw it as power over others. He saw it as something to be maintained by fear and murder. He saw it as outward glory. What does the life of Jesus suggest about Christ's view?

After developing as many contrasts as possible and listing them, see if your group can come up with a common definition of "dominion."

Apply
Ask each group member to identify one area in his or her life in which he is satisfied that his attitude is more like Jesus' than like Herod's. Pray quietly, as each asks the Lord to help him or her experience dominion over his or her own passions rather than over others.

STUDY GUIDE 82

Matthew 3–4

JESUS' PREPARATION

Overview
Matthew's Gospel skips over Jesus' childhood and adolescence. From the birth story it moves directly to introduce Jesus' ministry. But Matthew gives two chapters to the theme of preparation.

The first preparation theme focuses on the preparation of the Jewish people for Jesus. Matthew 3 reports the preaching of John the Baptist, who announced the approach of the Messiah, and who baptized with water those who wished to publicly repent.

Matthew 4 tells of the personal preparation of Jesus. Our Lord overcame three temptations, demonstrating His sinlessness and His complete commitment to God. With His humanity and His obedience both established, Jesus is seen to be qualified to teach others how to live in intimate union with God.

▶ ***Repentance.*** Both John and Jesus called on people to "repent, for the kingdom of heaven is near" (Matt. 3:2; 4:17). "Repent" (in Greek, *metanoia*) means to change one's mind and attitude. It is a decision which changes the total direction of one's life.

▶ ***Baptism.*** The word is an intensive form of the Greek *bapto*, and means "to immerse." In the New Testament it is a technical theological term with different meanings (see Matt. 3:11). This unit looks at "John's baptism." For a discussion of the others see my *Expository Dictionary of Bible Words* (Zondervan).

Commentary
In A.D. 28 one of the Old Testament prophets returned. It had been nearly 400 years, and God had been silent. Malachi, the last of those Old Testament greats, closed his book with a promise—and a warning. "Behold I will send you Elijah the prophet before the coming of the great and dreadful Day of the Lord. And He shall turn the heart of the fathers to the children, and the heart of the children to their fathers, lest I come and smite the earth with a curse" (Mal. 4:5-6, KJV).

Thus, the Jews had been guided to turn their eyes ahead, and look for the day of Messiah's coming. They were promised a forerunner, someone to warn them and turn their hearts back to God's ways. Implicit in Malachi's words was a choice. Unless the hearts of God's people were turned, the Messiah's coming would not bring Israel the expected blessing, but would bring a curse.

Later Jesus would tell crowds that John, then executed by Herod (a son of Herod the great), was the greatest of all the prophets and was, in fact, a messenger sent to prepare Messiah's way. And Jesus added these words: "If you are willing to accept it, he is the Elijah who was to come" (Matt. 11:14). Israel did not accept John's Elijah-ministry. Their hearts would not turn. The golden opportunity slipped by. The Messiah's body came to fit a wooden cross rather than an ivory throne, and Israel was destined to know another 2,000 years of scattering, of ghettos, of pogroms, of unrealized hopes. History would now pivot to focus on the second coming of Messiah. The fulfillment of Malachi's words would await another Elijah.

John: Matthew 3:1-12
John's background. Luke 1 tells us about John's birth. He was born into a priestly family. His father, Zechariah, was one of the many politically unimportant men who served the temple two weeks a year, and lived the rest of the time at his own farm in the countryside. Probably John was trained for the priestly ministry as well. The privi-

lege was passed on from father to son, reserved by Old Testament Law for the descendants of Aaron.

Perhaps John, like Habakkuk, was shaken by the ritualism and emptiness of the religion of his day. We do know that from birth John was filled with the Holy Spirit. Then, as an adult, John left home to live in the wilderness. He ate wild honey and protein-rich locusts, and wore a scratchy shirt made of camel's hair. When the time was right, John began to preach beside the Jordan River.

John's ministry. John's stern and bold preaching echoed the messages of earlier prophets. They too had condemned sin and called God's people back to the way of holiness outlined in Old Testament Law. But there were differences.

The content of John's message was not really new. Luke 3:10-14 gives specific content: to each group or individual who came for guidance, John's prescription was a return to the righteousness and the love expressed in God's Law.

But several things about John's preaching *were* new. There was its sense of urgency. "Hurry," John urged the crowds who came out to hear him, or simply to gaze at the spectacle. "Repent, for the kingdom of heaven is near" (Matt. 3:2). John focused the attention of his listeners not on some distant future, but on the immediate situation.

Another new focus in John's ministry was on the personal responsibility of the individual for his own actions. There had always been a thread of teaching on personal responsibility in the prophets' messages. But now John warned against any hope anchored in relationship to Abraham. "Do not think you can say to yourselves, 'We have Abraham as our father' " (v. 9), he cried, and then urged each individual to repent and to show by his changed life his inner, personal commitment to God.

The third new element was baptism, as a sign and symbol of repentance. Baptism had been known in Judaism before. But John transformed baptism, giving it fresh moral and eschatological significance. One who was baptized by John confessed his sins, identified himself with the renewal of the kingdom under the coming Messiah, and committed himself to live a holy life.

There was a final unique aspect to John's preaching. John recognized himself as the forerunner, sent to prepare the Messiah's way. Seven times the New Testament records John's announcement that the One to follow him will be greater than he (Matt. 3:11; Mark 1:7; Luke 3:16; John 1:27, 29-30; Acts 13:25). The warning—and the invitation—were both given.

And the crowds came. They listened. Many were baptized. Many, particularly those of the religious elite who were quick to put themselves in the forefront of any popular movement, could see no harm in the rite. But they were withered by John's angry denunciation of them as a "brood of vipers" (Matt. 3:7).

Soon everyone in the tiny land of Palestine had heard of God's firebrand in the desert. They gossiped excitedly about whether he might be the Messiah, and they waited to see what would come next!

♥ ***Link to Life: Youth / Adult***

Tape record a dramatic reading of John's preaching and his interaction with the crowds as found in Luke 3:7-18. Open your group session by playing it, and explaining the "new" elements in John's preaching.

If you wish, work together to develop a different tape, expressing what John might say if he were to preach to our generation.

Jesus' Baptism: Matthew 3:13-17

"Then Jesus came from Galilee to the Jordan to be baptized by John" (v. 13).

Here a fascinating confrontation took place. John objected! It would more appropriate for Jesus to baptize John; John was sure that Jesus did not need his repentance-oriented rite.

It is tempting here to think that John recognized Jesus as the Messiah. But the Bible tells us that the day *after* the baptism John pointed out Jesus as the Messiah to two of his followers, and said, "I would not have known Him, except that the One who sent me to baptize with water told me, 'The Man on whom you see the Spirit come down and remain is He who will baptize with the Holy Spirit" (John 1:33). All the four Gospels agree that John saw the Holy Spirit in dove form descend on Jesus when our Lord came up from the water after baptism. Clearly then, John did not object to Jesus' baptism on the grounds of His messiahship.

The mystery may be resolved when we realize that John and Jesus were probably related. Their mothers were very close (cf. Luke 1:36-45). Probably the two young men, both now about 30, had spent much time together, meeting each year as their families came to the three annual feasts in Jerusalem at which all males over 12 were to appear. And they must have exchanged visits during the rest of the year, as relatives and friends do everywhere. No, John's objection to baptizing Jesus may have been based on a simple fact: John knew that Jesus had no need to repent! John knew that Jesus' life was in fullest harmony with the laws and the ways of God—in fuller harmony even than his own!

Jesus overcame John's objection. It is only right, Christ pointed out, to identify oneself with right things (Matt. 3:15). Entering the water with John, Jesus was baptized, thus identifying Himself fully with John's message as well as with the men and women who flocked to receive that baptism because they *did* need it so badly.

The baptism of Jesus launched His public ministry. But it did even more than that. It demonstrated how fully Christ as a Man identified Himself with humanity. One of the central doctrines of the Christian faith is that of *Incarnation*. Isaiah had foretold it: "A virgin shall conceive, and bear a Son and shall call His name Immanuel" (Isa. 7:14, KJV). The name, giving it the emphasis of its Hebrew form, means "*With us* is God!" God, in the person of the Child of promise, would fully identify Himself as a human being. In every way this promised individual would be God, yet would be God *with us*.

Both Matthew and Luke report the birth of Jesus and explain how Mary, before her marriage to Joseph was consummated, miraculously conceived through the direct intervention of God. The Child was in a totally unique sense the Son of God—God Himself, come to enter the race of man in the only way in which He could become truly human. Jesus is fully identified with us in our humanity. He is God, and He is Man.

Hebrews 2 points out that it was fitting for Jesus to be like us in every way, including His subjection to human weaknesses and His susceptibility to suffering. "Since the children have flesh and blood," the writer explained, "He [Jesus] too shared in their humanity" (Heb. 2:14). Dying, Jesus could then deliver us from our lifelong slavery. God's concern for humanity drove Jesus to "be made like His brothers in every way" (v. 17) and, becoming a faithful High Priest, He offered Himself as the expiation for our sins. The writer to the Hebrews concluded, "Because He Himself suffered when He was tempted, He was able to help those who are being tempted" (v. 18).

The full humanity of Jesus is a basic teaching of our Bible. It was necessary for Jesus to be truly human for Him to become our sacrifice. It was necessary for Jesus to be truly human for Him not only to free us from lifelong bondage, but also to aid us in our own temptations and sufferings.

No wonder John, meeting his relative Jesus on the Jordan riverbank, protested against baptizing Him. John recognized Jesus as a good and righteous Man. Jesus Christ, as a Person, was so completely identified with humanity, that even one most impressed with His spiritual qualities never dreamed He was the Son of God!

There is a lesson here for each of us. What do we look for when we are seeking evidence of God's work in our lives, or in another's? Some startling, miraculous sign? Something that sets the person apart from all other men? Or are we looking for a work of God within: a work of God that produces the love, joy, peace, patience, kindness, goodness, faithfulness, gentleness, and self-control which God values so highly (cf. Gal. 5:22-23). Are we looking for a person who is different, or for a person who demonstrates the very best of what humanity can be? How strikingly our Lord's experience with John points it out. The spiritual person is, in fact, the most humane, and human of us all!

Then, once the voice of God had spoken from heaven, "This is My Son, whom I love; with Him I am well pleased" (Matt. 3:17), John realized the obvious.

Of course Jesus is the Messiah! Of course this most perfect Man had to be the promised Redeemer. The virgin had brought forth a Son, a Son who was the "with us" God. God had identified Himself in every way with humanity. God had come at last, to free us and lift us up to share His throne.

♥ ***Link to Life: Youth / Adult***
There have been several theories advanced to explain Jesus' baptism. List each, and ask your group to read Matthew 3:13-17 and determine which best seems to fit the facts. After they have discussed, you can introduce the perspective shared in the commentary above, if the group has not seen it. The theories:

(a) Jesus was seeking forgiveness.

(b) Jesus was dedicating Himself to His mission.

(c) Jesus was entering the priestly office.

(d) Jesus at this point became God's Son, when the Spirit anointed Him.

(e) Jesus was identifying Himself with John's message and his movement.

♥ ***Link to Life: Children***
Ask your boys and girls: "How do your parents show they are pleased with you?" (Make a list of the ways they suggest.) Then ask: "What do you do that pleases your mom and dad most?" (Again make a list.) Then read or tell the story of Jesus' baptism, and the Holy Spirit descending in the form of a dove, while God said aloud how pleased He was with Jesus. Explain that God sent His Son to be our Saviour, and Jesus was willing to obey His Father.

Young children can trace and color a dove form cut from cardboard. Print "I love Jesus too" to help them remember God's approval of His Son for His readiness to become our Saviour.

The Temptation: Matthew 4:1-11

If the baptism of Jesus impresses us with the complete identification of the Saviour with us in our humanity, His temptation stretches our minds to grasp the depths to which Jesus stooped.

In theology, Jesus' self-humbling is called the *kenosis*: the emptying. Paul develops it briefly in Philippians 2, speaking there of Jesus "who, being in very nature God, did not consider equality with God something to be grasped, but made Himself nothing, taking the very nature of a servant, being made in human likeness. And being found in appearance as a man, He humbled Himself and became obedient to death—even death on a cross!" (vv. 6-8) Simply stated, the Bible affirms that when Jesus entered our world He set aside the power and the privileges of Deity. He consciously limited Himself to live here as a man. Even the miracles Jesus would later perform would be attributed by Him to the power of the Spirit (see Mark 3:22-30). The emptying process Paul described is one of progressive humiliation. Jesus . . .

- emptied Himself
- was born in man's likeness
- was obedient even when it meant death
- accepted even the shameful death of an outcast criminal!

Tempted as a man. When we read about the temptation of Jesus in Matthew 4, we have to read the story against the background of the *kenosis*. When a physically weakened Jesus, after 40 days of fasting in the desert, was tempted by Satan, He did not seek strength from His divine nature to resist! The very first words of Jesus in response to Satan's initial temptation sets the tone.

"If You are the Son of God," Satan challenged, "tell these stones to become bread." Jesus answered with a quote from Deuteronomy: "Man does not live on bread alone, but on every word that comes from the mouth of God" (Matt. 4:2-4). Note the first word.

"*Man* does not live by bread alone!"

Addressed as the Son of God, Jesus affirmed His intention to live on our earth as a human being. Subject, as you and I are, to the hungers and drives and needs which throb within us and seek to pull us into sin, Jesus met every one of Satan's temptations. Rejecting the privilege that was His by virtue of His deity, Jesus cast His lot fully with you and with me.

It is because of this great act of self-emptying that you and I can find hope. Jesus overcame temptation—as a human being! Because Jesus met temptation in His human nature, you and I can find victory too, by meeting our temptations as He met His!

The three temptations. There are three temptations recorded in Matthew, as there are in Luke. But the order differs between the two Gospels. Each writer reported the experience of Jesus with a view to highlighting the culminating test from his own perspective.

Luke, whose focus is on Jesus as a warm and real human being, saw the temptation to throw Himself down from the temple pinnacle (and so prove the Father was with Him) as the culminating test. We all have times when we feel deserted by God; when things have gone wrong and we doubt His continued concern for us. As the Old Testament passages quoted by Jesus stress, the issue in this temptation was that of putting God to the test, to see "is the Lord among us or not?" (Ex. 17:7)

But Matthew saw this temptation as less significant for Jesus than the vision Satan spread before Christ of all the kingdoms of the world. "All this I will give You," the tempter enticed, "if You will bow down and worship me." The Man born to be King was shown the kingdoms that would be His, and was reminded that they could become His *now*. All the suffering would be avoided—all the anguish, all the rejection, all the pain of a death in which the weight of the world's sins would bear down on the sinless One.

And again Jesus chose. "It is written: 'Worship the Lord your God, and serve Him only' " (Matt. 4:10). Complete commitment to the will of God was Jesus' pathway to the throne. There could be no shortcuts. There could be no other way.

Before Jesus could rule, He had to learn by experience the fullest meaning of submission to the Father's will. The crown lay beyond the Cross.

♥ ***Link to Life: Youth / Adult***

A helpful study can be made of the temptations. Put on the chalkboard a three-column chart. Label the first column "source." In each temptation, what seems to have been the particular human vulnerability which Satan attacked? (For instance, the challenge to make bread was a temptation because Jesus was hungry: it was directed against His physical nature and needs.) Label the second column, "victory principle." Jesus in each case returned to the Old Testament to select a biblical principle to act on. (For instance, "Man shall not live on bread alone" teaches that we are not to let the physical dominate, for as spiritual beings we are attuned to God, and can choose to live by His Word.) Label the third column "additional temptations." Brainstorm with your group to list the kinds of things that tempt human beings that flow from each of the three sources you identify.

For a more detailed discussion of each temptation, see study guide on Luke 4.

♥ ***Link to Life: Children***

Draw a face on poster board. Cut out holes where the eyes would be. On a strip of paper make two black round dots to represent the pupils of one's eyes.

In class show the face, and manipulate the eyes so the person seems to be looking furtively to each side.

Tell your children that this boy (or girl) is about to do something he knows is wrong, and is looking to see if anyone is watching. Ask them to guess what he is about to do.

Make a list of their guesses. These will suggest some of the things that may be temptations to your boys and girls.

Talk about why children and grown-ups too sometimes want to do things they know are wrong.

Tell the story of Jesus and how He remembered God's Word, and chose to do what is right.

Return to your face, and make the eyes look up. *When we are tempted to do something wrong, we can remember that God will help us, and make the right choice as Jesus did.*

As a project, let each child copy your face, and draw the eyes looking up as a reminder to look to God's Word for help to obey Him when he or she is tempted.

Lessons for Living

Matthew 4 concludes with a brief sketch of Jesus as He launched His public ministry. Jesus took up John's theme and preached that the kingdom was near at hand (Matt. 4:17). He chose disciples (vv. 18-22). He went about Galilee teaching in the synagogues and healing (vv. 23-24). Soon the crowds that had followed John swirled around our Lord.

But Matthew gives us only the briefest sketch of these events. He does not seem concerned here with the public ministry. All the hurry, all the excitement, all the converging of the crowd eager to see miracles and hear the Man who spoke of God with such authority, seem unimportant compared to two initial portraits of the King. First there is the picture of Jesus submitting to John's baptism, identifying Himself fully with humanity. And then comes the picture of an emptied Jesus—suffering, tested, opening Himself to the full force of temptation in His vulnerability as a human being.

What is the meaning of this emphasis for us? We see at least four lessons immediately brought home.

(1) Jesus truly was determined to be a servant. The Incarnation did not mean that Jesus stopped being God, but that He had freely set aside His rights as Deity. The outward exercise of power and glory was not essential to Jesus' majesty. In choosing to empty and to humble Himself, Jesus displayed God's pathway to dominion.

How different from our way. When Cathy and Earl met and fell in love, she determined to become the center of his world. Gradually, she shut out his old friends. After they were engaged she became even more adept in manipulating him to keep him for herself. Cathy took Herod's route in search of power. Manipulating, selfish, she always was trying to control.

Cathy wanted to fill the throne of Earl's life. She wanted to be queen—but a commanding and not a servant queen.

How different with Jesus. Whatever dominion may involve, and whatever it means for us to reign, our destiny is not to be found in selfishness, but in self-emptying.

(2) Jesus' full identification with us in our humanity offers hope. If Jesus had overcome the tempter in His nature *as God*, we could hardly expect to overcome. We are not divine. But Jesus met Satan's tests *as a human*. So we can dare to trust that our dominion destiny includes power to overcome!

Ted, a young man, feels helpless. He sees himself as trapped, overwhelmed by a life that is out of control. Yet seeing Jesus become vulnerable—and victorious!—can change Ted's outlook. "Because He Himself suffered when He was tempted, He is able to help those who are being tempted" (Heb. 2:18). In Jesus the human, you and I realize that we may be vulnerable, but we do have hope.

(3) Jesus' response to the tempter spotlights resources that you and I can draw on to overcome. In each case, Jesus went back to the Word of God and found a principle by which He chose to live.

This is important. It is not simply "the Word" that is our resource. It is the commitment to live by the Word. It is resting the full weight of our confidence on what God says, and choosing in each situation to do that which is in harmony with His revealed will.

This same resource which Jesus used to overcome is our resource too. But we must use Scripture Jesus' way.

(4) Jesus is portrayed in Matthew 3 and 4 as a Person in full control—of Himself! In fact, we might even view this as the central message of these chapters. Jesus demonstrated His right to reign over us by proving that He had authority over the worst of man's enemies—Himself.

Certainly Israel had known in Herod a king who had absolute power over others, but was powerless to control his own hatred and fears. Since then, in our Napoleons and our Hitlers and Stalins, we've seen again and again that enslaving others brings the ruler no freedom within.

Yet it is exactly here that our dominion rule as kings under the King of kings must begin. We must gain power over ourselves: power to humble ourselves, power to submit to God, power to give up our rights, power to obey. Jesus demonstrated just this kind of authority. In His humanity, Jesus was exalted above the greatest men our world has ever known. Jesus alone fully controlled the world within.

No wonder Matthew wants us to grasp this truth. Jesus has overcome! He is worthy to be proclaimed King.

TEACHING GUIDE

Prepare
Which of the temptations that Jesus overcame is most like temptations that trouble you? How can you apply the scriptural principle Jesus drew on to overcome your temptations?

Explore
1. As your group comes in, have on the chalkboard: What does "incarnation" mean? What does Jesus' incarnation mean *to you*? Let your members briefly discuss.
2. Give a minilecture explaining the Incar-

nation. Use Philippians 2 to show that Jesus chose to live here as a true man, and to limit expression of His divine nature.

Expand

1. Examine the baptism of Jesus by listing the theories outlined in "link-to-life," page 534. Use the method outlined there.
2. Study the temptations of Jesus, supplementing the "link-to-life" idea on page 535 with material from Luke.

Apply

Review the four lessons for living suggested in this guide. Let each person share which lesson is most important to him or her, and why.

STUDY GUIDE 83

Matthew 5

THE BEATITUDES

Overview

Matthew 5–7 contains Jesus' famous "Sermon on the Mount." In the context of Matthew's argument that Christ is the expected Messiah-King, this sermon takes on special importance. In giving His moral teaching, Jesus announced as mankind's destined Ruler the lifestyle to be adopted by all who submit to Him.

In this particular study of Matthew 5 we focus on the Beatitudes—a series of "blessed are" or "happy are" statements. The issues explored by Jesus deal with the basic values which human beings adopt and live by. Jesus' point is that the values of this world do not lead to blessing. Instead blessing comes through living by values which the world despises, but which God holds dear.

▶ ***Blessed.*** Both Old and New Testaments speak of the "blessed." In the Old Testament, and especially the Psalms, the "blessed are" statements describe qualities in a person which bring him or her God's blessing. Here in Matthew the Greek word is *makarios*, which means "happy." Is there a difference? Yes. The Old Testament describes blessings that *will come* to the godly person, and emphasizes material goods. Jesus focused on the *present state* of persons who adopt values and attitudes which permit them to know, now, the inner touch of God in their present lives.

Commentary

Matthew tells us that, after Jesus' baptism, "Jesus began to preach, 'Repent, for the kingdom of heaven is near' " (4:17). Book after book has been written exploring Jesus' "kingdom" emphasis, puzzling over the exact thrust of all His words.

God as King over all. All agree that the Bible pictures God as King over all His creation. In this sense God is sovereign, marking out the course of cultures and the process of the ages. In a universal sense, everything and all times are to be viewed as God's kingdom: a realm over which He exercises control.

It is also true that the Old Testament brings another focus to God's kingly rule. God in a special way rules over Israel: He is Israel's true King (Deut. 33:5; 1 Sam. 12:12), and Israel is His kingdom (1 Chron. 17:14; 28:5). In a distinctive sense, God involved Himself in the control and direction of Israel's destiny.

When we read in the New Testament that Christ is "Head over everything for the church, which is His body" (Eph. 1:22-23), we have a parallel to the Old Testament emphasis. The rule of God extends over all—but finds special focus in His concern for His own.

God's future reign. A reading of the Old Testament makes it plain that there is more involved in talk of a kingdom than God's overarching rule. God promised through the prophets that a day would come when He will set up an everlasting kingdom on earth, and personally rule from Zion (Isa. 24:23; Micah 4:6; Zech. 14:9-17). Daniel and Isaiah added their descriptions: the King will be God, and yet of David's line. When the Messiah comes, the rule of God will find visible and overwhelming expression as God openly exercises His once-hidden power.

It was this kingdom the Jews expected and yearned for. And it was this kingdom which is described in the prophecies which Matthew relates to Jesus.

So we can hardly doubt what Jesus' listeners pictured in their minds when Jesus announced the good news that the kingdom was at hand. His listeners were sure He meant the eschatological expression of the rule of God. They thought "kingdom of heaven" must mean God's revelation of His power and goodness through Messiah's righteous, endless rule.

Near? It is here that many hesitate. Jesus said that the kingdom of heaven was "near." Yet, 2,000 years have fled since that announcement, and the visible earthly kingdom Jesus' hearers expected has not come. So some have stepped back, and denied the Old Testament vision. They have tried to make the "kingdom of heaven" simply another affirmation that God is in charge, after all.

But why then did Jesus say that the kingdom was finally "near"? Why the urgency? Why, if God has *always* exercised that kind of rule? Clearly some other aspect of the kingdom than God's universal rule must be drawing near.

Particularly significant is the Greek word translated "near." It can mean "at hand," or "has arrived." Was Jesus' announcement of the kingdom an affirmation that in His own coming, God's kingly action was already breaking in uniquely on time and space?

Usually we think of "kingdom" as a place. The "kingdom of Liechtenstein" is geographically defined: a tiny bit of land. Certainly the Old Testament picture of God's ultimate kingdom does involve a place: Palestine is the center from which the Messiah will rule, and the whole earth will be His kingdom's limitless extent. However, in rabbinic literature, kingdom emphasis is not on a *place* but on *action!* "The kingdom of heaven" speaks of that divine action which breaks into our universe and marks out events as God's accomplishment.

No wonder Jesus taught His disciples to pray and say:

> Your kingdom come, Your will be done on earth as it is in heaven.
>
> Matthew 6:10

Jesus' disciples, then and now, are to look to God to act on earth just as He acts in heaven itself, to bring His will to pass.

It is most likely, then, that Jesus' announcement of the kingdom had a dual emphasis. On the one hand, Jesus was announcing the nearness of the promised eschatological kingdom in which God will act visibly and dramatically to enforce His will. That kingdom was near in the person of the promised King!

On the other hand, Jesus also was announcing that the kingdom had arrived! In the personal presence of Jesus on earth, God had acted to take a hand in human affairs. In Jesus, God was already bringing to humankind His final gift of deliverance, and dominion.

The Sermon on the Mount: Matthew 5:1-11

The impact of the kingdom message does not strike us with the same force that it would have struck the believer of Jesus' day. We have the entire New Testament revelation; we're aware that Jesus acts today in our lives through the Holy Spirit.

But to the men and women who heard Jesus teach, this kingdom concept was new and powerful. They were used to looking ahead to a future when God would act. Jesus' kingdom message made them realize that God was already exercising kingly authority. We can expect God to act *now* to work out His will in you and me!

This kingdom emphasis on an active God underlies what we call the Sermon on the Mount. Only those who throw the full weight of their confidence on God as a King who acts in and for them *now* can ever locate the courage to live the startling lifestyle Jesus laid out for His disciples (Matt. 5:1).

Interpreting the sermon. There have been various approaches to interpreting the Sermon on the Mount. Some are clearly designed to suggest we need not take its teachings seriously.

(1) One view sees the sermon as a salvation message for the world. By "being good" an individual can live in harmony with God and earn His approval.

Only a person who is blind to his own sin and who ignores Jesus' command to repent can see the sermon as portraying a way to find God.

(2) Another view insists that Matthew 5 contains "kingdom truth." The ways of living portrayed there are the ways men will live when Jesus returns to reign. But they are not practical for us until then.

Too often this approach, which has a certain validity, is used to excuse behavior and attitudes that fall far short of the standard Jesus expressed here.

(3) A third view suggests that the sermon is addressed primarily to the church. This too has some validity. But it overlooks the fact that at this stage in Jesus' ministry,

Israel, and not the church, was central.

(4) A fourth view synthesizes and provides a better balance. First, the sermon is to be seen as a detailed exposition for Jesus' hearers of what repentance (which literally means a "change of direction" or "about face") involves. Second, it does picture life in the eschatological kingdom. When God is in full charge, at the end of time, everyone *will* live by these guidelines. Third, we have in the Sermon on the Mount the most detailed exposition of God's ethical standards given in the Word. Because these standards reflect God's character and reveal His will, they are relevant to us today as well as in the future kingdom.

(5) To these traditional interpretations we need to add a fifth. *The Sermon on the Mount describes the way in which men are freed to live when they commit themselves to the kingship of Jesus!* When men of any age realize that *in Jesus* the kingdom is "near" to them, they are free to abandon themselves totally to God's will, confident that, as they obey, He will act to shape events.

The Kingdom Now

When Wayne Adams began to dream of making available high-quality art with a subtle yet powerful Christian message, the vision seemed impossible. Wayne had no background or contacts in the art world. And he had no money to finance such a venture.

But Wayne began to pray. Within weeks, believers with all the needed skills were located. Wayne also prayed for funds and left his well-paying job to concentrate on the dream. He sold his car to get enough for a start. When his house was burglarized, insurance payments met other needs. By December 2,000 prints of the first painting, *Born Again*, were completed.

For a number of years Christian bookstores carried Witness Art paintings, and many Christian homes featured these lovely testimonies to some of the great realities of our faith.

Looked at from a "sensible" point of view, everything Wayne did to launch his venture was foolishness. He left his job. He entered a field in which he was less than a novice. He sold his car when the money ran out, and used insurance funds to pay the bills of his project rather than refurnish his home. Everything that Wayne did *was* foolish—unless God's kingdom has broken into our world, and unless God Himself acts in our lives to accomplish His will. Given the reality of God's rule, a person like Wayne, who sets the Lord on the throne of his life, is not foolish but wise.

The Bible makes it clear just how wise Wayne was. According to Colossians, God in Christ "has rescued us from the dominion of darkness and brought us into the kingdom of the Son He loves" (1:13). The Christian has been torn from Satan's grasp and planted firmly in a relationship with God in which Christ is King—a relationship in which Christ acts in our lives.

The Sermon on the Mount is for men who have chosen to be Jesus' disciples and have freely submitted themselves to the King (Matt. 5:1). In it Jesus explains to His disciples of every age what living as a citizen of heaven's kingdom involves. As it meant for Wayne, living in the kingdom means for us, abandoning the ways of the world to adopt a diametrically different set of values and commitments.

New values (Matt. 5:1-12). When first heard by disciples, the familiar words of the Beatitudes must have sounded jolting and strange. Familiarity has made them palatable today; their stark challenge to our deepest notions about life is easily passed over. But that first time the challenge must have been almost overwhelming.

What Jesus did in these few verses was to set up a new system of values by which His people are to live. Implicit is a rejection of the values which lie at the core of human civilizations and which shape most individual personalities.

It is difficult to live in our world, to look at men and women who live by the values in the column on the right (chart, p. 541), and be unaffected. We admire this world's "beautiful people." Their sophistication, looks, pleasures, and importance draw us. We appreciate the values which their lives express. That whole package of values is appealing to us because we tend to associate those values with fulfillment. To be and behave like the people who have status in our society becomes our dream.

Jesus shatters such dreams and rejects such goals in the Beatitudes. He sets up a whole new package of values, proclaiming that in *these* you and I will find fulfillment. Not in pleasure, but in longing. Not in

The Beatitudes: Matthew 5:3-10

Jesus' Values		Countervalues
BLESSED ARE THOSE WHO . . .		**BLESSED ARE THOSE WHO ARE . . .**
(v. 3)	are poor in spirit	self-confident competent self-reliant
(v. 4)	mourn	pleasure-seeking hedonistic "the beautiful people"
(v. 5)	are meek	proud powerful important
(v. 6)	hunger for righteousness	satisfied "well adjusted" practical
(v. 7)	are merciful	self-righteous "able to take care of themselves"
(v. 8)	are pure in heart	"adult" sophisticated broad-minded
(v. 9)	are peacemakers	competitive aggressive
(v. 10)	are persecuted because of righteousness	adaptable popular "don't rock the boat"

satisfaction, but in hunger. Not in popularity, but in commitment to an unpopular cause. Not in competition and "winning," but in helping others win their way to peace.

The first Beatitude illustrates. "Blessed are the poor in spirit," Jesus said. Blessed are those who do not approach life with confidence in themselves or reliance on their gifts and talents, sure that they are competent to meet life's challenges. Blessed instead are those who approach life *without* such self-based confidence, "for theirs is the kingdom of heaven." Not, theirs "will be" the kingdom of heaven. But, theirs *is* the kingdom of heaven. In approaching life humbly, and with full reliance on the King, we open up our lives to His direction. We open up our present and future to Jesus' kingly action.

Commitment to kingdom values brings us to the place where we ask the King to reign in our lives. When Wayne Adams surrendered his competencies to God, depending on the Lord to shape events, Wayne responded to the leading of the King and committed himself to the values of the kingdom. In becoming one of the poor in spirit, Wayne discovered the reality of Jesus' promise: "Theirs *is* the kingdom of heaven."

♥ ***Link to Life: Youth / Adult***
Give each group member a copy of the Beatitudes chart. Work in pairs to add other "countervalues" which stand in contrast to the values Jesus teaches in the Beatitudes.

Then work together to fill in a master chart with your group members' insights.

New behaviors (Matt. 5:13-16). Our values are always expressed in our actions. What is truly important is the way values find expression in our daily lives.

This is what Jesus alludes to in two brief word pictures. Those who hold kingdom values will witness to those around them the reality of the kingdom. "You are the salt of the earth," Jesus said. In Palestine, flakes of salt form on the rock shores of the Dead Sea at night. In the morning the sun rises. Under its heat the salt loses is saltiness. It blends with the shore and loses its distinctiveness.

"You are the light of world," Jesus went on. Lamps are designed to be put on a lampstand in full view, not to be hidden.

Both these word pictures help us realize that the values which we hold as citizens of Jesus' kingdom are to find expression in our behavior, so that our difference from men of the world will be made plain. Those who come to know us will gradually realize that we are different because of our relationship with our Father "in heaven" (v. 16). The kingdom of heaven is to break into our world, today, through you and me!

Case histories (Matt. 5:17-42). Jesus' kingdom teaching focused first on values and then on the behaviors through which values are expressed. Our Lord went on to give a number of illustrations. This "case history" approach is in full harmony with Old Testament practice. After the Ten Commandments are recorded in Exodus 20, for example, the next few chapters are devoted to illustrating them with examples.

In this sermon Jesus began (Matt. 5:17-20) by explaining that His teaching is not contrary to Old Testament Law. It is intended to "fulfill it." That is, Jesus would explain the Law's true meaning. The kingdom lifestyle that Jesus promoted fulfilled the Law's requirements by producing a righteousness that "surpasses that of the Pharisees and teachers of the Law" (v. 20).

Each of the following case histories demonstrates how the Law is to be "fulfilled" (that is, truly and accurately explained). In each case Jesus shifted the focus of attention from the behavior that the Law dealt with to intents and motives. Here the King works in the hearts of men, changing the values and the behaviors from which behavior springs. In Jesus' kingdom any outward conformity without an inward commitment is unthinkable!

What about murder? Jesus located the root of murder in anger and hatred (vv. 21-26). Rather than nurse anger, which may lead to murder, the kingdom citizen is to value peacemaking. He is to take the initiative to be reconciled to his brother. Later John would write, "Anyone who hates his brother is a murderer" (1 John 3:15).

Adultery? In its true meaning Law does not just speak against the act, for God is concerned with lust itself (Matt. 5:27-30). Jesus sarcastically suggested to men quick to excuse themselves by claims that "I saw her, and couldn't help myself," that they try to rid themselves of their problem by plucking out the offending eye! Impossible? Surely. And so again the issue is focused on the place where the problem lies: "in the heart."

Divorce? Moses permitted it, but Jesus called for lifetime commitment (vv. 31-32).

Promises? Make your word binding by signing a contract—and feel free to break a promise sealed with a handshake? (vv. 33-37) No, be the kind of person whose yes always means yes, and whose no means no.

What about revenge and repaying those who harm you? (vv. 38-48) The Law says you can insist on your rights and on repayment. But in the kingdom, God's blessing rests on the merciful. In relationships with people, the kingdom citizen is called on to be like the Father in heaven and to love even enemies. Does this deny justice? Not at all! It recognizes the fact that in the kingdom, *God* is the One who acts. Paul later put it in these words: "Do not take revenge, my friends, but leave room for God's wrath, for it is written: 'It is Mine to avenge; I will repay,' says the Lord" (Rom. 12:19).

Abandoning the values and the instincts which lie at the root of man's society, the kingdom citizen is to build his life on those peculiar values Jesus taught, values that seem all too shabby to most people. Poverty of spirit? Mourning, meekness, hunger for righteousness? Mercy, purity, peacemaking, willingness to be persecuted on God's account? Yes. On these values Jesus invites His hearers to build new lives.

♥ ***Link to Life: Youth / Adult***
Divide the "case history" illustrations in

Matthew 5 among teams of three or four. Each is to examine its case, and to determine how any of the values seen in the Beatitudes are expressed in the action Jesus calls on us to take.

When teams have had time to study and think, come together as a group and discuss each case.

Ask: "If we truly adopt Jesus' values as expressed in the Beatitudes, what other kinds of changes can we expect to see in our lives?"

♥ ***Link to Life: Children***

Ask your boys and girls to think of a time when someone hurt them. Then ask: "What was that person like?" List their descriptions on the chalkboard.

Ask: "Is is all right to hurt them back?" Let the children express their opinions, which will probably support repayment in kind.

Then tell them what Jesus said about how to treat enemies. Explain that a person who hurts others is like the individuals they have just described (point to the chalkboard list). Do they want to become that kind of person?

Jesus wants us to be like our Father in heaven. How is He different from the person who hurts others? Make another list beside the first.

It may seem all right to pay back a person who hurts us. But then we will be acting like him, and not like God. The Lord wants God to be our example, not a bad person.

Why not give each child a hand mirror, on which you have glued a bright yellow "halo." Encourage them when they feel like paying someone back to hold the mirror so the halo is over their head, and remember they don't have to be like the bad person. Because they love Jesus, they can be like God.

The Risk

There are two things that are immediately striking about this part of Jesus' Sermon on the Mount. First of all, a person who takes the call seriously and attempts to live as a kingdom citizen takes a great risk. Each of the countervalues of the world seems to have great survival value!

If you aren't competitive and aggressive, how can you get ahead? If you can't take the practical course, and make the expedient choice, you're asking for trouble!

Jesus' sermon calls men to abandon this whole approach to life and to walk out of step with society. We are called to abandon "wisdom" for responsiveness to God's will —whatever the apparent cost. And this involves risk.

The second thing we see in the sermon is the impossibility of the standards Jesus maintains. In shifting attention from behavior to values and motives, Jesus sets righteousness even farther from us than it was before! You and I may have been relatively successful in controlling our behavior. But what about our desires? Our thought lives? Our emotions and feelings toward others? If righteousness in the kingdom means purity in the inner man, each of us is helpless!

But this is just the point of Jesus' announcement. The kingdom is "at hand"! In Jesus Christ, God has begun to take that action which culminates in our total freedom. In the ultimate expression of the kingdom, Jesus will reign over a renewed earth. But even before Jesus returns, believers of every age have been "brought" by God to the "kingdom of the Son He loves" (Col. 1:13). You and I are in a relationship with God in which He acts for us. When we grasp this, when we open up our lives to Jesus' royal control, He will break into the pattern of our daily lives and into the very heart of our character. Owning Jesus as King, we turn our fears over to Him and seek to rebuild our lives on that which He finds valuable.

Jesus is King. We can take the risk.

TEACHING GUIDE

Prepare

What does it mean to you that Jesus is "at hand" in your life today?

Explore

There are many significant and probably unfamiliar concepts introduced in this study guide. So you will probably want to launch your group meeting with a minilecture.

Cover first of all the concept "kingdom." Remember that in biblical thought "kingdom" is essentially a realm in which a ruler exercises control. As you and I relate to Jesus as our King, He is increasingly free to exercise control within us, and in our circumstances.

Then cover the various views of the Sermon on the Mount. The fifth view expressed seems to capture its purpose. This sermon describes how human beings are freed to live in any age when they commit themselves fully to Jesus. When we realize that *in Jesus* the kingdom is near *us*, we can abandon ourselves totally to Jesus, sure that as we obey He will shape circumstances and events.

Expand

1. Duplicate for each group member the chart of the values expressed in the Beatitudes. Have teams look at each value and countervalue. Each team is to see if it can suggest other countervalues, that the world adopts but that Jesus' exposition of blessing calls us to reject.

Discuss the values present on the duplicated list, and values that your group members added.

2. Return again to teams to look at the examples Jesus gave to illustrate His values in operation.

Introduce the assignment by noting that true values always find expression in behavior (the point of Matt. 5:13-16). Show too that in these cases Jesus "fulfills" (that is, gives a true and full explanation) of what the Law of God actually *means*, even though it speaks in terms only of behavior. Note that each case focuses on *intent and motive* and not just acts.

Ask each team to select one of the following cases, and to determine which of the values expressed in the Beatitudes it illustrates. The cases: Matthew 5:21-24, 27-30, 31-32, 33-37, 38-42, 43-48.

When done, have each team share what it has seen.

Apply

Jesus' call in the Beatitudes is to reject the values this world lives by to choose another, contrasting set of values. Discuss: "What kinds of risks can you see in totally adopting Jesus' values as your rule of life? What would make you willing to take such risks?"

STUDY GUIDE 84

Matthew 6–7

KINGDOM LIFESTYLE

Overview

These chapters continue Jesus' extended teaching called the Sermon on the Mount. In chapter 5 Jesus gave the moral basis for life in His kingdom: Jesus' people are transformed from within, and their godly values are expressed in a holy life that fulfills not just the letter of the Law, but its spirit and intent. In chapters 6–7 Jesus described the lifestyle of those who live in His kingdom.

The major emphases in these chapters indicate that the person who lives, in any age, as a citizen of heaven's kingdom will:

- seek to please God, who sees in secret, rather than men who judge by what is on public view.
- trust God completely to meet material needs, and so concentrate on God's kingdom and righteousness.
- express trust in God in prayer, and by looking to Him to meet every need.
- act on and obey the words of Jesus, which are the only sure foundation for the kingdom lifestyle.

Christians who develop the lifestyle Jesus explains in these two exciting New Testament chapters will experience the presence and the power of our God.

▶ ***Kingdom.*** A "kingdom" is a realm in which the will and power of a king are expressed. We live in the kingdom Jesus rules when we do His will. Then He will act in our lives and circumstances.

Jesus' listeners were hungry for the kingdom. His message was a jolting one, yet many followed and listened eagerly. They sensed that this Man, who taught with authority, had to know the way to the experience for which they yearned.

That hunger, that longing, is something you and I can understand. We've yearned for a fuller experience of God. We too have been looking for the kingdom where Jesus reigns and acts. All too often we've missed it. All too often we've concluded, wrongly, that the kingdom is wholly future, only to be known when Jesus comes again.

Part of the reason why we tend to look at the kingdom as future only is that we've missed the kingdom when we've looked back into history. Our view of history is distorted, a caricature that has little resemblance to reality. Often the caricature is drawn something like this: "Everything was great as long as the apostles lived. Then it got bad, with the church hardening into a dead and restricting institution paganized by Rome. Then Luther and Calvin brought the Protestant Reformation, and it was alive again for a while. But soon that drifted into deadness as well. Today we're just holding on (sometimes with a feeble grip), waiting till Jesus comes."

This portrait of church history is faulty. It comes in part from the tendency of historians to focus on the institutions, the popes, the cathedrals, and the books written by establishment men to sum up the wisdom of their age. But neither Thomas Aquinas' *Summa* nor John Calvin's *Institutes* expresses the kingdom! The kingdom is expressed in the living witness to Jesus which the Holy Spirit has burned into the lives of those whose hearts turn to the Lord.

For instance, in the twelfth century, the Waldensians, the Poor Men of Lyons, appeared. They gave the Bible to the people in the common language, stressed repentance and conversion, and also emphasized living a Christian life guided by all Scripture—and especially by the Sermon on the Mount.

Long before Luther, John Huss led a great revival in Prague; a revival later forced underground by the persecution which led to Huss' death. For 300 years an underground church existed in Bohemia, with the Gospel passed quietly from father to son, from grandparent to grandchild. Finally these people found refuge in Germany on the estate of Count Nicholas Ludwig von Zinzendorf. Now called Moravians, this group provided impetus for a great missionary movement leading to revivals in Germany, Holland, the Scandinavian countries, France, Switzerland, and America, as well as England. It was Moravian missionaries who met John Wesley while on a ship going to America and introduced him to the possibility of personal faith in Jesus Christ. So, many years before Luther, small prayer and Bible-study groups dotted Germany; when God called Luther to the Reformation leadership, followers had already been prepared.

Today the United States sends out thousands of missionaries across the world. But as late as 1800, there was no missionary movement to reach abroad. Then in 1806, students at Williams College in Massachusetts began to discuss their part in sharing the Gospel with the non-Christian world. A sudden rainstorm sent them dashing into a haystack. Praying there together, God called the first American missionaries. Adoniram Judson, Luther Rice, and Samuel Mills were to lead a host of young men and women, who crossed the oceans to take the Gospel to the world.

These illustrations, which can be multiplied to touch every century and every nation where the Gospel has taken root, bear a striking similarity. A movement of God began in a quiet, hidden way. As far as what has become known as "church history" is concerned, the movements often lie outside the worldly events historians choose to record. Yet the haystack, not the cathedral, is most likely to be characteristic of the kingdom!

True, these movements have often forced their way into the history books. A city set on a hill cannot be hid; a light placed on a candlestick cannot be ignored. But all too often, whether the movement has been Catholic or Protestant, the historical record is one of persecution and antagonism and fear. As in Jesus' day, institutions tend to teach the traditions of men rather than those of God. And such institutions feel threatened by the kingdom.

The kingdom comes into conflict with the world, even as Jesus ultimately was forced into open conflict with the religious men of His day, who demanded, with insistent shouts, "Crucify Him!"

Commentary

Recognizing the Kingdom: Matthew 6:1–7:23

It would be wrong to conclude from what I've just shared that the kingdom of heaven is always in contrast with the established or institutional church. The Wesleyan revival led to the formation of the Methodist Church. The touch of the kingdom was not removed as soon as this church became institutionalized. Today there are Methodist churches which are living expressions of the kingdom—and Methodist churches which know no touch of kingdom life.

The point made by church history is that institutions can never be *identified* with the kingdom. The kingdom can sweep into man's edifices—and sweep out again. To perceive the kingdom, we must look beyond outward appearances to the fleshed-out life of Christ in His body.

This is hard for seekers to grasp. You and I, who are looking for the kingdom of Jesus and are eager for Him to reign in our lives, often become confused. We look to the wrong things for light to guide us. *It is exactly this tendency to miss the inner reality of the kingdom in the outward trappings of religion which Jesus dealt with in the next section of the Sermon on the Mount.*

Jesus gave four warnings—warnings against plausible pathways which will inexorably lead us farther and farther away from the kingdom's presence in our daily lives.

Visible piety (Matt. 6:1-18). "Be careful," Jesus says, "not to do your 'acts of righteousness' before men, to be seen by them" (v. 1).

It's a very natural thing to want to be appreciated as men and women of God, and to be looked up to with respect. It's healthy to want to be a leader. But there are many religious games that people of every age play, which draw them away from the reality of the kingdom.

In Jesus' day, one game was to have a trumpeter announce when someone was going to give alms (charity) to the poor. The poor would come—and so would a host of admiring observers. Everyone would watch as the giver earned a reputation for piety and generosity.

Another common game was played with prayer. When a man wanted to pray, he would go to a busy street corner or a well-filled synagogue and stand, to pray aloud.

Often he would pray prolonged and wordy prayers, giving evidence to all that he was pious. Even when men took a vow to go without food, they would be sure to look pained, and would rub dirt into their faces so all could see how much they were suffering for God!

These games were not played for God. They were played for other men, to be seen by them, and to win a reputation with men for piety.

Tragically, many in Jesus' day thought that such people were truly pious! They felt that the way to find the kingdom was by imitating such public acts. Thus an earnest seeker could be drawn into a hypocritical, "play-acting" lifestyle.

In contrast, three times in this passage Jesus instructs, "But when *you* give to the needy, do not let your left hand know what your right hand is doing, so that your giving may be *in secret*. Then your Father, who sees what is done *in secret* will reward you" (vv. 3-4, italics added). And about prayer, "Go into your room . . . and pray to your Father, who is unseen. Then your Father, who sees what is done *in secret* will reward you" (v. 6, italics added). Fasting too is to be seen only by "your Father, who is unseen; and your Father, who sees what is done *in secret*, will reward you" (v. 18, italics added).

It is tremendously important for us to grasp the impact of this repeated emphasis. Kingdom reality cannot be measured by the external things which, done to be seen by men, are singled out in each age as evidence of spirituality.

In one of the churches I attended as a young Christian there were a number of external measurements: attendance at the meetings of the church, praying in King James English at prayer meetings, teaching in the Sunday School, carrying tracts to hand out at the subway station, refraining from smoking and drinking and movies—and from close association with anyone who did indulge in the forbidden three. Most men and women in our little church conformed to these externals. Yet, I know now that beneath the surface of public piety many suffered the emptiness and pain of alienation, and were unfulfilled. I know also that when I struggled to find reality through conforming, I too wandered away from the reality.

What then is the authentic road? If we are to look away from the ways our culture measures public piety, to what do we look? Jesus' answer is that we are to look to an "in secret" relationship with God as our Father. We are to cultivate awareness that He is present, though unseen, and we are to act to please this One who sees us *in secret*.

How significant is the four-times repeated "in secret"? The world around us does not see the Father. Even our brothers and sisters may see no visible sign of God's presence. In this age, before Jesus comes in power, the kingdom and the Father exist "in secret." But the God who sees us in secret does reward us. The God who sees us *is*, and He does act in the world of here and now.

If we seek the kingdom, we dare not let the traditions of the men of our age draw us away from the God who *is*. It is our secret life with Him which is the key to our experience of the kingdom.

♥ ***Link to Life: Youth / Adult***

Write on the chalkboard, "Games Christians Play." Have your group members read Matthew 6:1-6, 16-18 and identify "games" played by the religious of Jesus' time. Divide into teams of five. Each team is to locate the three "games" described here by Jesus. They are to define the rules *of each game, and how a person might count a* score.

When this has been done, ask each team to describe at least three similar games modern Christians play. Again they are to define the rules of the game (tell how *it is played), and tell what constitutes a score.*

Come together as a whole group to share. Then discuss: "Why do people play these games? How do they keep us from experiencing the kingdom of Jesus? What are the rules to play by if we are serious about living for Jesus rather than for the approval of others?"

♥ ***Link to Life: Children***

Two themes are developed in this section which can be helpful to children and are treated in children's curriculum.

GIVING. Give each child five coins. Have cut-out pictures from magazines of: food, housing, clothes, several toys, a hungry child. Place covered cans or boxes, with a slit in the top, in front of each picture.

Let your class look at and talk about the pictures and what each represents. Tell your boys and girls each is to decide how to use his or her coins. As each comes to "spend" his or her money, you and the others in class turn your backs.

After each has used his coins, talk about how we use money. Some goes to buy things we need to live. People also buy fun things. But we need to think too about people who are hungry or need to learn about Jesus. Explain that no one looked as another used his coins, because God is the only One we should think about watching us as we decide how to use our money.

PRAYER. What do we talk to God about? Make a Lord's-Prayer booklet. Younger ones can color pictures you have drawn and duplicated; older children can illustrate their own. We talk to God about:

- *Himself—Matthew 6:9-10 (God in heaven, earth)*
- *Our needs—Matthew 6:11 (loaf of bread, plate of food)*
- *Forgiveness—Matthew 6:12 (two people hugging, hands clasped)*
- *Protection—Matthew 6:13 (large figure protecting smaller)*

Children can write or print phrases from the Lord's Prayer on their booklets.

Material success (Matt. 6:19-33). Jesus' second warning focused on possessions. In His day, even the disciples believed that wealth was a sign of God's blessing. Thus, the rich man was viewed as being close to God, while the poor man was somehow thought of as being under His judgment. Jesus put material possessions in a totally different frame of reference in this passage of the sermon.

"Do not store up for yourselves treasures on earth" (v. 19). Instead, treasures are to be laid up in heaven. Once again we are confronted by the fact that the kingdom in our day is in secret. It cannot be measured by material achievement or any of our other standards of "success."

Jesus went beyond warning against such a measurement of His kingdom. He said, "Do not" lay up such treasures. Jesus explained why by pointing out that a concentration on material success would lead to the darkened eye and the divided heart. The eye is the organ of perception through which our whole personality is guided (vv. 22-23). If we focus our vision on what the world calls success, our perception will be distorted and the light of God's revelation of reality will be blocked out. Our whole personality will be darkened.

What's more, our will is affected as well. God and "success" will compete in our personalities, and our values will be shaped by a commitment to one or to the other. "You cannot serve both God and Money" (v. 24).

Then Jesus went beyond, to lay bare the basic issue. Jesus said we are not even to be anxious about necessities! We reject the laying up of earthly treasures, and we reject concern about what we will have to eat and drink! (v. 31) Living in the kingdom means abandoning our very lives to the Father's care so that we can concentrate on seeking "first His kingdom and His righteousness" (v. 33).

How can we find the courage to abandon our lives to God's care? Jesus' illustration answers us. God feeds the birds and clothes the flowers—and you and I are of infinitely more value to our Father! His power orders every detail of the world in which we live; knowing His power and knowing His love for us, His children, we abandon ourselves to His loving care. We know that He will meet our needs.

♥ ***Link to Life: Youth / Adult***

Put on the chalkboard a simple illustration linking Jesus' words about the healthy eye and His words about anxiety (see p. 549).

The pagan sees only things he needs, and is anxious because he can rely only on himself to get them. The person living in Jesus' kingdom senses, in God's care of birds and flowers, the unseen Father. Secure in the Father's love, the kingdom citizen trusts, and focuses his efforts on pleasing God.

Authority (Matt. 7:1-14). "Do not judge" are the warning words which mark off the third section of Jesus' guidelines for kingdom seekers. It is directed at those who see in the kingdom the right to exalt themselves above their fellow citizens, who are named "brothers" here.

The first warning dealt with seeking approval of men rather than God.

The second warning dealt with having

What Does our Eye See and What Does It Mean?

concern for the goods in this world, rather than abandoning such concerns to seek the kingdom and righteousness.

The third warning deals with relationships within the kingdom.

This warning is a vital one; in human society we always go about setting up a "pecking order." We try to settle the question of who has control or influence over another. The whole "chain of command" approach of the military and the business world reflects the concern human beings feel for authority. The right to judge another is a right which the human heart naturally yearns for.

This is true in the church as in any group. Church history is in a real sense a report of the struggle for control over others in the name of religion. This is not true only in the papal distortions of the Middle Ages. It is true in the local Protestant church of today, where a pastor or a board member may struggle to impose his will on his brothers and sisters. Or where a gossip may claim the right to exalt himself or herself over the person whose reputation is smeared. Pushing others down seems such an easy way to raise ourselves up.

But if we are to find the kingdom, we have to abandon all claims to a right to judge. "Do not judge," Jesus said, and for all time He destroyed the pretentions of anyone who would seek to exalt himself over others in the kingdom (vv. 1-6).

Instead Jesus taught another attitude: that of humility and servanthood. "Ask," Jesus said, commanding us to take the position not of a judge but of a supplicant. We are to approach life in the kingdom with a deep sense of our need for God's good gifts—and with full confidence that our loving Father will supply us with all we need (vv. 7-11). What is more, in bowing down to God we also bow down to our brothers. We commit ourselves not to judge them but to serve them: "In everything, do to others what you would have them do to you" (v. 12).

This truly is a narrow gate. But it leads us to life—the life of the kingdom, now (vv. 13-14).

♥ ***Link to Life: Youth / Adult***

Set your group members to work in pairs to write descriptions of "a really fine Christian," "a good Christian," "a lukewarm Christian" and "a backslidden Christian."

Compare these descriptions. Then read Matthew 7:1-5 and discuss: "What does it mean to 'judge'? What 'measure' did we use in trying to decide who is a 'good' and who a 'better' Christian? Would we like these measures applied to us? Why, or why not?"

After the discussion, point out that Jesus told us not to try to measure others, or establish a Christian "pecking order." Romans says the only debt we owe others is to love them (Rom. 13:8). In Jesus' kingdom we are to think and do good, not to fall into the trap of judging others.

False leaders (Matt. 7:15-23). Jesus concluded His warnings by focusing on men who will claim Jesus as Lord, but who will seek to use and to savage His flock. How will the false prophet be known? Not by what he says so much as by what he is and does. "By their fruits you will recognize them" is how Jesus put it (v. 20). In context, the bitter fruits are obvious.

Men will come, claiming Jesus as Lord and offering to lead the way into His kingdom. But their lives will be marked by a public rather than a private kind of piety. Their lives will show a concern for, rather than disinterest in, material things. And their lives will be marked by the claim of the right to judge their brothers and sisters.

When these marks are seen, we have Jesus' declaration that, no matter what mighty words they accomplish in His name, "I never knew you" (vv. 22-23). Such men cannot lead us into an experience of the kingdom.

The Kingdom Found: Matthew 7:24-29
Jesus' message concluded with a simple yet powerful illustration, which focuses our attention on the one road to experience the kingdom of Jesus now.

> Therefore, everyone who hears these words of Mine and puts them into practice is like a wise man who built his house on the rock. The rain came down, the streams rose, and the winds blew and beat against that house; yet it did not fall, because it had its foundation on the rock. But everyone who hears these words of Mine and does not put them into practice is like a foolish man who built his house on sand. The rain came down, the streams rose, and the winds blew and beat against that house, and it fell with a great crash.
>
> Matthew 7:24-27

We stand at a fork in a road that leads only two ways—Jesus' way, or another. We too have heard the words of the King. We see the pathway He set out as leading to the kingdom.

In Matthew 5, we heard Jesus focus the issue on our inner lives, and we explored the values by which we are called to live. In Matthew 6 and 7, we see how to distinguish between true and false pathways to the kingdom. What have we learned?

We have learned that to live in Jesus' kingdom, we must abandon concern for the approval of men, and learn to care only for the approval of God. We have learned that we can find release from anxiety over necessities, and so be free to concentrate our attention on righteousness. And we have learned that we are to be humble before God and our brothers: we are not to judge, but to take our place with them as supplicants before God.

Will we find the kingdom if we follow this pathway?

Of course we will. For we will be walking in the footsteps of the King!

TEACHING GUIDE

Prepare
Which lesson in this sermon is most important to you personally? Which do you think your group members need most?

Explore
1. Have group members list facts from church history. Record on chalkboard. Then ask: "How are the things you have listed related to Jesus' kingdom?"

2. Or explain the "hidden" nature of the kingdom as the author reviews church history at the beginning of this study guide. Point out that in Matthew 6 and 7 Jesus showed us how to recognize—and find—the way to personal experience of His kingdom.

Expand
1. Have teams work together to define

"games Christians play." Follow the approach outlined in "link-to-life," page 547. Help your group members realize that our "in-secret" relationship with God, and constant awareness of His presence, helps us make the choices that keep us on the kingdom pathway.
2. Use the illustration included in "link-to-life," page 548, to help your group members quickly grasp the main point of the passage. Then work as a group to list *paired contrasts* between the person who is anxious and concerned about necessities and the person who is more concerned about God's kingdom and righteousness. Lead your group to think in terms of values, choices, actions, attitudes, etc.
3. Or focus on the problem of judging. Use the "link-to-life" process outlined on page 549.

OPTION: You may choose to divide into three teams or sets of teams to do each of the three studies suggested. If so, save time for a report from each team or set of teams as a review of the whole passage.

Apply
Sum up the teaching of this section, and then read, without comment, Matthew 7:24-27. Close by asking each to pray silently.

STUDY GUIDE 85

Matthew 8–11

THE AUTHORITY OF THE KING

Overview

This extended section of Matthew builds on the Gospel writer's earlier presentation. Matthew showed that Jesus is the One the Old Testament prophets told would come: He fit the prophecies. Matthew showed that Jesus demonstrated in His baptism and temptation dominion over the inner sin which entangles other men: He can lead us to victory. Matthew reported Jesus' Sermon on the Mount: Jesus explained how to live as a citizen of the heavenly kingdom.

Now Matthew moved on to establish clearly the authority of the King. The miracles that Matthew now reported do more than authenticate Him as God's Messenger. They demonstrate the extent of His authority: over sickness, nature, demons, sin, and even over death itself.

Surely this One is to be followed completely, by those who own Him as King. What a privilege to be disciples of our wonderful Lord!

▶ ***Authority.*** The Greek word expressing the idea of "authority" is *exousia*. It is also translated in English as "power."

The basic meaning of *exousia* is that of "freedom of action." A person with authority has greater freedom to act than a person under authority. The greater the authority, the greater the freedom of action. Jesus in the New Testament is shown to be a Person with *complete* authority. No one or no thing can place restrictions on Jesus' freedom to act—for good—in your life and mine.

Commentary

The live TV audience broke into laughter each time one of the cast asked the "pastor" a question. Why? Well, each time his answer was the same: a decisive "perhaps"!

It is funny. On TV. But not in real life. Kay found that out as she went the rounds of her Christian friends, asking their advice and counsel. Some said one thing. Some said another. No one seemed to be too sure. The uncertain and conflicting ideas confused rather than helped.

No wonder the crowds who listened to Jesus' Sermon on the Mount were stunned. No, not so much by what Jesus said. That hadn't really sunk in yet. The words of the sermon would be remembered and talked about, until finally the new way of life Jesus sketched gradually became more clear. What the crowds who heard Jesus were astonished at was His tone of *authority*. They were "amazed at His teaching, because He taught as One who has authority, not as their teachers of Law" (Matt. 7:28-29). Christ claimed the King's right to govern His people; He spoke with authority. Now all would ask, did He really *have* the authority He claimed?

Authentication: Matthew 8:1–9:34

The next events seem to merge in a fast-paced narrative. The acts of the King are traced as, over and over, they demonstrate the validity of Jesus' claim to authority.

Willing and able (Matt. 8:1-13). Immediately after Jesus' descent from the mount on which He spoke His sermon, a leper met Him. He said, "Lord, if You are willing, You can make me clean" (v. 2). This man sensed Jesus' power, but was uncertain whether Christ would use that power for his sake. Jesus reached out and touched the leper, healing him. The King *is* willing to exercise His authority to help humankind.

Entering the city of Capernaum, a Roman officer met Jesus to ask for the healing of a servant. Christ offered to go with the Roman, who objected. "I do not deserve to have You come under my roof" (v. 8). Instead the Roman asked Jesus merely to speak the word. Jesus spoke; the servant was healed. Jesus is able.

♥ ***Link to Life: Children***
Draw pictures of people who are far away who still help us. For instance, a person who makes electricity, a person who cooks the bread we buy at the grocery, the farmer who milks cows, etc. We can't see these people, but they do help us in many ways. Put the pictures the children draw together to form a booklet. On the last page have a picture of Jesus or of the centurion's sick servant. Leave the booklet in class for early comers, to remind them that though we do not see Jesus, He is real and He does help us in many ways.

Power over all (Matt. 8:14–9:31). The next event shows Jesus' authority over *all* the powers to which you and I are subject.

Sickness	Jesus heals	8:14-17
Nature	Jesus stills a storm	8:23-27
Demons	Jesus casts them out	8:28-32
Sin	Jesus forgives	9:1-8
Death	Jesus makes alive	9:18-26

There is nothing to limit the authority of Jesus, who has demonstrated His power over everything under which you and I are crushed! This Man *is* able to speak "as One having authority" (7:29, KJV)—because He does!

♥ ***Link to Life: Children***
The Bible contains images to help us sense how fully God's forgiveness blots out our sin. Among them is the image of sins "sealed up in a bag" (Job 14:17).

After telling the story of Jesus forgiving sins (Matt. 9:1-8), help each child write down one bad thing he has done on a slip of paper. Then put all the slips of paper in a bag, and cover up the bag so it cannot be seen.

Jesus takes away our sin so completely that it is hidden from everyone, even from God. When sin is forgiven it is really gone, and gone forever.

There are three very special riches for us in this extended passage.

(1) *Under authority.* The Roman soldier speaking to Jesus said, "I myself am a man under authority, with soldiers under me. I tell this one, 'Go,' and he goes" (Matt. 8:9). He said this to explain the confidence he had in Jesus which enabled him to ask Jesus to heal from a distance, by the mere speaking of a word. His point was this: As a soldier, his authority over others was *derived.* It was his relationship in the chain of command which gave this military man his power. When he spoke, all the power of Rome's mighty empire, under whose authority he stood, spoke through him.

And what about Jesus? How was Jesus able to speak and have nature, demons, and even death jump to obey? Because here on earth Jesus also operated under authority; the authority of God. When Jesus spoke all the limitless power of God Himself spoke through Him.

It's like this today. We can trust Jesus. The full power of Almighty God is His.

(2) *New wineskins.* A fascinating dialogue here is inserted in Matthew 9:14-17. John the Baptist's disciples had noted that Jesus was unlike their master. They came to ask why. Jesus explained, and added, "Neither do men pour new wine into old wineskins. If they do, the skins will burst, the wine will run out and the wineskins will be ruined. No, they pour new wine into new wineskins" (Matt. 9:17).

You and I cannot stuff Jesus or our experience with Him into our old ways of thinking and living. Life with Jesus is a new and exciting thing. He Himself wants to fill us, to expand our personalities, and to reshape us to fit who He is. When Jesus, the Man with all power, comes into our lives, we are privileged to open ourselves up to newness.

(3) *Dead and blind.* Through these two chapters the acts of Jesus follow a progression. Each portrait shows Christ as having power over a greater enemy than the last: sickness, nature, demons, sin, and then death itself.

Why then does an instance of healing the *blind* follow the raising of the ruler's daughter? For our sakes! You and I can find the faith to believe that Jesus will make us fully alive when He returns. But how often we look at the dead dimensions of our present lives with despair. The blind men were living—but with dead eyes. When they begged for healing, Jesus asked, "Do you believe that I am able to do this?" (Matt. 9:28) They did believe. Jesus touched their eyes. And where the moment before there had been death, now there was sight.

Jesus comes into our lives with hope *for*

today. If your personality has died to the capacity to live, or has shriveled in bitterness, or if you have lost the capacity for compassion, Jesus asks, "Do you believe that I am able?" We can answer, "Yes!" Jesus does have the power to revive the deadened areas of our lives.

♥ ***Link to Life: Youth / Adult***
In a minilecture note the progression of the miracles reported in Matthew 8:1–9:32. Then ask your group members to read this passage individually. Each is to find two insights which can be applied by Christians to enrich life today.
After about 15 minutes have the group members come together, to minister to each other through their insights.

To really understand the significance of the extended passage we've been considering, we need to note one of its peculiarities. Throughout this sequence of events Jesus referred to Himself as "the Son of man." He did not use the term in the Sermon on the Mount. The first occurrences are here.

The term "Son of man" is found in both the Old Testament and the New. In the New it is used 94 times, and, with 5 exceptions, always by Christ of Himself. Clearly Jesus affirms something important about Himself in His selection and use of this term.

On the one hand, of course, the phrase "Son of man" emphasizes Jesus' full humanity. But even greater significance is found in the fact that, as in Matthew 9:6, "Son of man" signifies Jesus' redemptive work and mission. In the term "Son of man" Jesus presents Himself as the Victor, for He accomplished all that man was intended to do, and becomes all that man was intended to be.

The demons recognized and spoke to Jesus as the "Son of God" (8:29). They were right; they knew Him for who He is. The whole Bible makes it very clear that the One who became Man at Bethlehem truly is the Creator God. John insisted that Jesus is God, coexisting with the Father from the beginning (John 1). Jesus does not hesitate to claim equality with God (John 17). Paul's writings affirm Jesus as God, along with the Father and the Holy Spirit. The Old Testament prophecy identifies Jesus as the "Father of eternity" (a phrase meaning the source or originator of eternity itself!) and speaks of the Child to be born as "a Son . . . given" (Isa. 9:6, KJV). The name Immanuel, as we have seen, means, "With us is God." Jesus had every right to speak of Himself as the Son of God, for that is who He is.

Yet Jesus chose another title for Himself: "Son of man." A Man, with God's prerogative of forgiving sin. A Man, with power to heal and to give life. A Man, yet Victor over death.

In Jesus the very power of God entered the mainstream of humanity, and in Jesus' authority as the Son of man you and I find an anchor for our hope. Many years ago Johann Burger (1598–1662) caught a vision of the authority of the Son of man, and expressed it in the hymn, "Jesus Lives, and So Shall I."

Jesus lives and reigns supreme;
　And His kingdom still remaining.
I shall also be with Him,
　Ever living, ever reigning.
God has promised: be it must;
　Jesus is my hope and trust.

The Man with all power lives today. His kingdom does remain. With Him, we also shall reign. Then—and now.

Shared Authority: Matthew 9:35–10:40

Jesus' authority had been established by His miracles. Then He did an amazing thing. "He called His twelve disciples to Him *and gave them authority*" (10:1, italics added).

Immediately after establishing His own authority, you and I are shown that Jesus intended to share that authority with His followers.

It was human need that moved Jesus to this unexpected decision. Matthew 9:35-38 pictures Jesus continuing His itinerant mission, teaching and healing. Everywhere there were crowds; everywhere Jesus saw men and women who were "harassed and helpless, like sheep without a shepherd" (v. 36). Moved, He turned to His disciples. "Ask the Lord of the harvest, therefore, to send out workers into His harvest field" (v. 38). Jesus determined to multiply His ministry by sending His disciples to every place where He Himself wanted to go.

It must have seemed exciting to His disciples. To be men, themselves harassed and helpless a short time before, and suddenly to have power! "Heal the sick," Jesus told them. "Raise the dead, cleanse those who have leprosy, drive out demons" (10:8). With it all, they were to share the good news that the long-awaited kingdom was at hand. But the thrill and pride must have been dampened as Jesus went on to explain the lifestyle of men who were given the gift of power.

The disciples were not to go in pomp or in luxury. They were to live among their fellowmen as Jesus did—humbly, as servants. And while Jesus' disciples were given authority over sickness, death, and demonic power (v. 8), they were not to coerce men. Some people would receive them; some would hate them. The disciples' role was to use authority to serve.

Lifestyle then. This chapter gives us deep insight into discipleship and helps us see ourselves as kingdom citizens who have power—but who humble ourselves to serve. Note these features of Jesus' instructions:

- Disciples were to be dependent on God, not on their own wealth or possessions, for necessities (vv. 8-11).
- Disciples were to give all men the freedom to accept or reject them and their Lord (vv. 12-15).
- Disciples were to expect and to endure persecution from those who rejected and hated their Lord (vv. 16-25).
- Disciples were to remember their great value to God the Father, and do His will without fear of men (vv. 26-33).
- Disciples were to expect conflict, even in their own homes. In everything, Jesus is to be put first, and pain is to be borne just as Jesus bore the pain of His cross (vv. 34-39).
- Disciples could know they brought great gifts to men, who would be rewarded for their responses to the Father and His children (vv. 40-42).

How very different from the life we expect of a man with power! Instead of wealth, there was self-chosen poverty and dependence. Instead of exercising power over others, disciples extended to all men freedom to choose. Instead of honor and praise, the disciple was often persecuted and maligned. Jesus chose to empty Himself to win us victory as the Son of man. So too disciples are called to wear the humble garb of servants as the badge of their God-given authority.

♥ ***Link to Life: Youth / Adult***

"Discipleship" in Jesus' time was the basic way Jewish leaders were trained. They lived with their master, and learned by observing—then imitating—him. After their years of training were complete the disciple could be recognized as a teacher.

While "disciple" is used in several ways in the Gospels and in Acts, its basic meaning is that of learning to be like one's teacher (cf. Luke 6:40).

Divide your group into teams of four or five. Each team is to study Matthew 10 and write at least six statements which describe how a disciple will live. Then each team is to suggest one incident from Jesus' life which illustrates each statement.

Finally, each team is to suggest two ways *that we might practice discipleship in our own times.*

Shattered Expectations: Matthew 11

Like chapter 10, Matthew 11 is completely discourse. While Matthew 10 is addressed to the disciples, chapter 11 is addressed to the crowds—crowds who, struggle as they will, cannot see in Jesus their coming King.

The dialogue was initiated by disciples who had come from John the Baptist. The great prophet and forerunner of Jesus was in prison. Soon he would be executed by Herod, his head a prize won by the sensuous dance of a girl with whose mother Herod was living in sin. John had recognized Jesus at His baptism when our Lord was clearly marked out for him by God. But now even John was wondering.

Why? Because John too expected the King and kingdom to burst on Israel with outward power. Not even John had expected the coming of a servant King!

Jesus' answer was to direct John's disciples' attention to the acts of mercy He was performing. "Go back and report to John what you hear and see: The blind receive sight, the lame walk, those who have leprosy are cured, the deaf hear, the dead are raised, and the Good News is preached to the poor" (Matt. 11:4-5). John would grasp the meaning. John, like Jesus, was steeped in the lore of the Old Testament. His thoughts would turn to Isaiah 35 and he would remember that prophet's words about the glory and the majesty of God (v. 2).

> Behold, your God will come with vengeance; the recompense of God will come, but He will save you. Then the eyes of the blind will be opened, and the ears of the deaf will be unstopped. Then the lame will leap like a deer, and the tongue of the dumb will shout for joy.
>
> Isaiah 35:4-6, NASB

John envisioned the glory primarily as recompense; as the day of God's judgment. But the glory of God was also to be seen in the tender care of Messiah for men and women in need. John did not understand then that the servant ministry of Christ had to come first. But the report reassured him. Jesus *was* doing what the Scriptures foretold that Messiah would do.

The crowds were not so easily satisfied. Jesus spoke then of John, and said that if they would accept it, "He is the Elijah who was to come" (Matt. 11:14). Clearly Jesus claimed to be the Messiah whom John announced (vv. 7-15).

But the people of Israel were unable to make up their minds. They were repelled by John's austerity and demand of repentance—he took his religion a little too seriously. Yet they were tempted to dismiss Jesus because, in contrast with John, Jesus lived a normal life and was a friend of tax collectors and "sinners" (v. 19). Like people today, they wanted to have a God who fits *their* expectations. Yet, like changeable children, they could not make up their minds what He should be like. Each time a new candidate appeared, they changed the rules! (vv. 16-19)

Then Jesus uttered His first recorded words of warning and judgment. He spoke of the cities where His miracles had been done, and announced a coming woe. Even pagan Tyre and Sidon, even licentious Sodom, would have repented and believed if a messenger from God had come with such powerful authenticating works as His. But Israel had hesitated—and hesitated still. Israel simply refused to commit herself to her King (vv. 20-24).

The chapter closes with a prayer, and with an invitation. Israel's rejection of the King was also part of the Father's "gracious will." The nation might refuse its King, but all who labor and are heavy laden are called to come to the Saviour.

"Come to Me," Jesus invited, "and I will give you rest. Take My yoke upon you and learn from Me, for I am gentle and humble in heart, and you will find rest for your souls. For My yoke is easy and My burden is light" (vv. 28-30).

The word picture is a beautiful one. The yoke of Jesus' day was a fitted collar-like frame, shaped to rest on the neck and shoulders of two animals. Teamed together, the task was far easier for two oxen than for one. And if one were a young ox, how much easier to have an older, stronger companion to share the burden. To men who called for God's King to reign over them, Jesus offered to be God's Servant, yoked in harness with them.

Today, taking up the yoke that links us to Jesus, we too find rest. We walk beside Jesus. We learn from Him. And because our older, stronger, all-powerful Companion takes His fullest share of all our burdens, when we are linked to Jesus our burdens truly are made light.

TEACHING GUIDE

Prepare
Study Matthew 10. What do you learn about being a better disciple of our Lord?

Explore
1. Give a minilecture overview of these chapters, stressing the two major themes of Jesus' authority and of Jesus' explanation of discipleship.

2. List on the chalkboard the sequence of Jesus' miracles, and the areas over which they demonstrate His authority.

Over sickness	Matthew 8:14-17
Over nature	Matthew 8:23-27
Over demons	Matthew 8:28-31
Over sin	Matthew 9:1-8
Over death	Matthew 9:18-26

Discuss: "What were His observers intended to learn from these miracles? Which would be most impressive? Is there any significance in the sequence?"

Don't draw conclusions, but let this discussion launch closer study of the text.

Expand

1. Divide into teams to look in Matthew 8:1–9:32 for insights to apply to our lives today. See "link-to-life," page 554.

2. Or focus on discipleship and what the disciple's life is like. Use the method explained in "link-to-life," page 555. Be sure to emphasize the fact that the life of discipleship to which Jesus calls us is essentially *His own* kind of life! He asked nothing of us that He was unwilling to do Himself.

Apply

Challenge those who hesitate over discipleship to remember two things. First, Jesus has authority of all that could harm us. And second, we will be yoked to Him (Matt. 11:25-30).

STUDY GUIDE 86

Matthew 12:1–15:20

HARDENING OPPOSITION

Overview

Matthew now comes to his initial explanation of what happened to the promised messianic kingdom.

Matthew's Gospel flows logically from his theme: that Jesus is the Messiah of the Old Testament.

Chapters 1 and 2 reported the birth of Jesus, and demonstrated its harmony with Old Testament messianic prophecy.

Chapters 3 and 4 affirmed Jesus' full identity with humanity—and His victory over every human weakness. Surely this Person can lead us to victory too.

Chapters 5–7, the Sermon on the Mount, contained Jesus' explanation of the lifestyle appropriate for those who choose to live in His kingdom.

Chapters 8–11 proved Jesus' authority over all that binds human beings. And it also shows that in Jesus, authority is expressed through servanthood—in both Master and disciples.

Now, in chapters 12–15, we learn of the response of the nation to Jesus and His message. That response is one of growing opposition, spearheaded by the Pharisees. The Jewish leaders rejected the Lord—and in a series of parables Jesus introduced a modification of the kingdom. If the nation will not welcome the King, individuals who do welcome Him into their lives will live in an unexpected, a mystery form, of Jesus' kingdom.

How wonderful that Jesus is still willing to welcome individuals. How wonderful that His hidden kingdom still exists today!

Commentary

The other night I listened to a late night talk show on which two well-known radio personalities were talking about visits each had made to the South American land of the Aucas. These were the jungle peoples who in the late '50s speared five missionaries—some of whose wives and children later went to live among them and won them to Christ. One of the radio personalities told how impressed he had been with the translated testimony of a converted chief, who had earlier taken 35 human heads, and by the fact that the actual killers of the five missionaries had not only become Christians but were now themselves missionaries to other jungle tribes.

Both men were tremendously impressed by their trips and these jungle peoples. Their interest and curiosity had been challenged—but not their commitment. Faced with the necessity of making a personal choice, neither had responded. And one was clearly hostile.

It must have been something like this in Jesus' day. When Christ first came on the scene, teaching and healing, many were drawn to Him. He was a curiosity, Someone to be impressed with and to talk about. Even the leaders of the people viewed Jesus as God's messenger (John 3:2). But as Jesus' message became more clear, and as He confronted each hearer with the challenge to *choose*, attitudes began to change. Jesus' Sermon on the Mount spoke of the kingdom in unexpected ways. Jesus' own behavior did not fit the popular notion of the coming King. His authenticating miracles could not be denied. But as Jesus continued teaching, He exposed more and more clearly the sinfulness of current attitudes and ways. The leaders particularly became hostile. Jesus was no longer a curiosity. He had become a threat, demanding that they choose between His revelation of God and His ways, and their own dearly held beliefs.

Jesus' authority had clearly been demonstrated in His miracles; He exercised authority over *all* the powers that hold men in bondage. It was clear that no Pharisee or Sadducee had similar authority. Yet their resistance grew. They *would not* believe.

In the men of Jesus' day we see a contemporary issue drawn as well. Rejection of Christ is seldom a choice which hinges on lack of knowledge. Rather, as the issues become more and more clear, our response to truth hinges on our will. We must *choose*. For the non-Christian it becomes a choice to abandon hope in oneself and trust Jesus alone to bring him or her into a family relationship with God. For the Christian there is also a choice. A choice to follow the servant King and to adopt the lifestyle of the kingdom, or to hold onto the attitudes and values and beliefs and behaviors of the world. In tracing growing opposition in these chapters of Matthew, we see some of the issues facing all men—you and me as well. And we are confronted by our own necessity to choose.

♥ ***Link to Life: Youth / Adult***
Share with your group the story of the two radio personalities who interviewed Auca converts—were most impressed by their conversions—and refused to believe. Discuss: "What things are most likely to keep people who understand the Gospel from believing in Jesus?" After sharing, summarize, and then record your group's ideas.

Attack: Matthew 12

The men who seem to have spearheaded the growing opposition to Jesus were the Pharisees. Along with the Sadducees, traditionally their rivals, this band of rigid and committed men were quick to see the great gap between Israel's present lifestyle and Jesus' kingdom truth.

The Pharisees. The name comes from a root meaning "separated." The movement apparently began some two centuries before Christ, and focused on resistance to hellenization of the Jews. The Pharisees were earnestly concerned with the Law and with keeping its minutest detail. But the Pharisees tended to emphasize the "oral law" of the Torah (Pentateuch). This oral law was composed of a vast number of interpretations and explanations of the Old Testament, which over the years continued to grow and grow. Tragically, the oral law increasingly focused on trifling details. For instance, the command not to work on the Sabbath was expanded and illustrated with hundreds of explanations and exceptions. According to the Pharisees' oral law, a person was allowed to spit on rocky ground on the Sabbath. But he could not spit on soft or dusty earth; the spittle might move the dirt and that would constitute plowing, for it might make a furrow! Thus the oral law often robbed the written Law of its real message—a message of godly concern for others. Jesus once rebuked the Pharisees for their practice of "giving" all of their possessions to the temple (to be taken over after their deaths), and then telling poor parents or other relatives that they owned nothing with which to help *them*. God's command to "honor your father and mother" was thus pushed aside in favor of this merely human tradition.

We can see in the New Testament many evidences of the Pharisees' scrupulous concern for the minor details of legalism (Matt. 9:14; 23:16-19, 23; Mark 7:1-13; Luke 11:42). What we often miss is that the movement itself did have healthy roots.

The Pharisees had separated themselves from the rest of Israel because of a deep concern for righteousness. They yearned for the arrival of the kingdom in which God and His ways would be honored in holiness. Until that time, in search of personal holiness, the Pharisees joined communes of others with the same longing. These Pharisees were neither educated nor upper-class men. Instead, they were characteristically middle class, without formal education in the interpretation of the Law. In their closed communities they lived under the direction of a scribe (an expert in the Law), and they sought to separate themselves in order to find righteousness by keeping the whole Law. This high level of commitment won them the admiration of the common people, and gave this group, which in Jesus' day numbered about 6,000, great influence.

Later Paul would write something about the Jews which was characteristic of the Pharisees: "For I can testify about them that they are zealous for God, but their zeal is not based on knowledge. Since they did not know the righteousness that comes from God and sought to establish their own, they did not submit to God's righteousness" (Rom. 10:2-3). In their attempt to find righteousness through legalism, they missed the Old Testament's message of righteousness through faith (cf. Gen. 15:6). The Pharisees became so committed to their own notions of what God's will must be that when the Son of God appeared to reveal the Law's true meaning, they refused to listen. For the Pharisees to respond to Jesus would have meant admitting that the principles on which they had built their lives, and which gave them their distinctive identity, had been wrong. They simply could not and would not abandon themselves, even though it was God who called.

We can sympathize with the Pharisees. Some of us too have had an honest concern for the things of God without real understanding.

But then Jesus confronts us, and calls us to abandon all that we once held dear and true that we might rebuild our lives on Him, and learn His kingdom lifestyle. Too often we too hold back. Dare we surrender all we thought we had and were in order to become something new, just because the King commands and promises?

The Pharisees would not, and could not, make this surrender. They insisted on holding on to their own ideas rather than submitting to the King. Their rebellion against the lordship of Jesus led, not only to their own destruction, but it contributed to the suffering of the nation that they influenced.

Attack (Matt. 12:1-24). We see the Pharisees' mindset in three incidents reported in this chapter. Walking through the grainfields, the disciples plucked and ate wheat kernels. The Pharisees shouted to Jesus, "Hey! They're breaking the Law!"

The "Law" they referred to was the oral law's interpretation of that act as "harvesting." And the disciples were "harvesting" on the Sabbath! But the Old Testament itself never interprets Sabbath Law to demand going hungry.

A little later Jesus entered a synagogue of the Pharisees (v. 9). There He was confronted by a man with a withered hand. This confrontation was apparently arranged by the Pharisees so that they "might accuse" Him (v. 10). So they challenged Jesus. "Is it lawful to heal on the Sabbath?" Jesus responded by pointing out the value of a man to God, and added, "It is lawful to do good on the Sabbath" (v. 12). Jesus then healed the man—and the Pharisees went out and began to plot how to kill Him!

♥ ***Link to Life: Children***
What makes Sunday special? The Pharisees tried to keep the Sabbath by restricting what a person could do on that day. Help children avoid this sterile approach to worship. Emphasize the things we do *to make Sunday special. Include of course going to Sunday School and church. Let the children add other things as well. Do they have family traditions—visiting relatives, taking family trips, etc.—that bond the Christian family closer together?*

Later Jesus was seen healing, and the crowds wondered aloud if He was the Messiah. Then the Pharisees, hardened in their rejection of Jesus, began a slander campaign against Him. "It is only by Beelzebub, the prince of demons, that this fellow drives out demons" (v. 24).

Jesus' response (Matt. 12:25-50). Much of this chapter is devoted to Jesus' response to the attack of the Pharisees. Responding to the first attack (on the disciples plucking grain to eat as they walked), Jesus pointed out that even God's laws (to say nothing of the oral traditions intended to explain them) are not intended to be rigid, unyielding rules. God is concerned with "mercy and not sacrifice": His Laws are intended to provide a framework for the expression of love. The disciples were guiltless in this situation, for they acted only to meet real need. Their freedom from guilt was pronounced by He who is "Lord of the Sabbath" (v. 8).

The second incident also is revealing. The Pharisees were willing to *use* a man with a withered hand to trap Jesus. They were totally unconcerned about his personal tragedy and his feelings. Jesus' response, affirming God's valuation of individuals, showed up their hardheartedness for what it was. No wonder these men plotted to kill Jesus. In their pursuit of self-righteousness, the Pharisees had lost the deep concern for others that characterizes God. Their religious zeal had, in fact, led them to become *ungodly* (un-Godlike) persons!

With their ungodliness clearly revealed, in contrast to our Lord's own compassion and love, the Pharisees had no choice. They had to either face their sinfulness and abandon the legalistic search for righteousness that had produced it, or to strike out against the One who pierced their pretentions and revealed their lack of love. They chose to strike out.

Several important issues were raised by

Jesus in the extended response He made to the Pharisees and their followers.

**The unforgivable sin.* The Pharisees rejected the evidence of Jesus' miracles and even claimed that Satan's power was behind them. This blasphemy was unique in history; never before had God's Son, standing among men as a Man, by the power of the God's Holy Spirit, performed such obvious authenticating signs. Speaking against the source of Jesus' power was, first of all, a recognition of its supernatural origin, and second, a hardened rejection of Jesus Himself. Completely hardened now, this desperate attack demonstrated the fact that the Pharisees had made their choice. They no longer hesitated. They were committed *against* the Son of God. Their choice, made in the face of all the unique evidence which Jesus Himself had presented to them, was irrevocable: they had chosen to step beyond the possibility of repentance.

**Idle words.* Matthew 12:36 reports Jesus' warning against "careless words." This is *not*, as some have taken it to be, a reference to chitchat in contrast with "edifying" talk about God. Actually, Jesus is pointing to what is recorded in these very chapters.

The Pharisees, in reacting to the disciples' plucking of the grain and in challenging Jesus concerning the withered hand, had carelessly exposed their hearts! The Pharisees were so careful to appear pious. But in criticizing the disciples and in using the man with the withered hand, they had spoken unthinkingly words which revealed their hearts. No wonder verses 34-35 preface the warning about careless words with this statement:

> Out of the overflow of the heart the mouth speaks. The good man brings good things out of the good stored up in him, and the evil man brings evil things out of the evil stored up in him.
>
> Matthew 12:34-35

What is in a man's heart will be inadvertently expressed in his words, for "out of the overflow of the heart the mouth speaks" (v. 34).

We can hide our bitterness and lack of compassion. We can disguise hostility under a cloak of religiosity. We can even be rigorously "separated" from all sorts of cultural "sins." But when our reactions and our words reveal a Pharisee-like contempt for men and women whom God loves, our ungodliness is revealed.

The section of dialogue closes with Jesus' refusal to give Israel any more miraculous signs as proof of His identity, and with a renewed warning that judgment must surely come. Nineveh, a pagan land, responded to Jonah's preaching. The pagan Queen of Sheba responded to Solomon's instruction. But Israel had refused to respond to Jesus, though He is greater by far than either Jonah or Solomon.

By turning away from the King, Israel opened herself up to emptiness and a terrifying fate. No longer could physical descent from Abraham be considered a mark of standing with God. Each individual had to see that his relationship was personal, and would hinge on doing the will of the Father in heaven (vv. 46-50).

♥ ***Link to Life: Youth / Adult***
Give your group members a minilecture on the Pharisees. Then introduce the "careless word" principle of Matthew 12:36. Ask your group to look at the three incidents in this chapter (disciples gather grain, withered hand, Jesus associated with Beelzebub), to see what they can discern of the Pharisees' hearts from these incidents.

The Parables: Matthew 13:1-52

The same day that Jesus spoke out, warning His hearers of the tragedy which rejection of the King and kingdom was to bring on them, He sat in a boat to teach the gathering crowds. He "told them many things in parables" (v. 3).

There are a multitude of parables in the Bible. The word itself means to "set alongside," and it is a normal pattern of Scripture to illustrate by setting concrete and familiar illustrations alongside abstract concepts (cf. 2 Sam. 12:1-7; Jud. 9:8-15; and Isa. 5:1-7 for Old Testament examples). Sometimes parables are allegories, such as the story of the Good Samaritan through which Jesus answered the man who wondered aloud, "Who is my neighbor?"

But there is something very different about the parables recorded in Matthew 13. Rather than illuminating what Jesus said, they seem almost to obscure it!

Why then did Jesus speak in parables?

Parables of the Kingdom

The Parable	Expected Form	Unexpected Characteristic
1. Sower 13:3-9, 18-23	Messiah turns *Israel* and all *nations* to Himself	*Individuals* respond differently to the Word's invitation.
2. Wheat/tares 13:24-30, 37-43	The kingdom's righteous citizens *rule over* the world with the King.	The kingdom's citizens are *among* the men of the world, growing together till God's harvesttime.
3. Mustard seed 13:31-32	Kingdom *begins* in *majestic glory.*	Kingdom *begins in insignificance;* its greatness comes as a surprise.
4. Leaven 13:33	Only righteousness enters the kingdom; other "raw material" is excluded.	The kingdom is implanted in a different "raw material" and grows to fill the whole personality with righteousness.
5. Hidden treasure 13:44	Kingdom is *public* and for all.	Kingdom is *hidden* and for individual "purchase."
6. Priceless pearl 13:45-46	Kingdom *brings all valued things* to men.	Kingdom demands *abandonment* of all other values (cf. 6:33).
7. Dragnet 13:47-50	Kingdom begins with initial separation of righteous and unrighteous.	Kingdom ends with final separation of the unrighteous from the righteous.

There are several hints in the text. Asked this question by the disciples, Jesus said, "Though seeing, they do not see; though hearing they do not hear or understand" (v. 13). The crowds, in rejecting Jesus' clear presentation of Himself as their King, had closed their eyes to truth. Now Jesus would speak less clear words to them, lest they be even more responsible.

It is also possible that Jesus adopted parables here to keep His listeners concentrating on the choice they had to make for or against Him. We need to remember that the Israelites had a clear notion of what the kingdom would be like. They would not be shaken from this single conception to accept new truth, which might modify their expectations. Jesus later explained to His disciples that the parables were spoken to *them* (v. 16). What they dealt with was a dimension of the kingdom which was not the subject of earlier Old Testament revelation. The parables, Jesus said, fulfill this prophecy:

> I will open My mouth in parables; I will utter things hidden since the Creation of the world.
>
> Matthew 13:35

These parables deal with dimensions of the kingdom which Israel did not suspect existed. They deal, in fact, with those dimensions of the kingdom which you and I experience today and will experience until, at the return of Jesus, the Old Testament's prophesied kingdom rule *is* established.

No wonder the disciples, themselves steeped in the Old Testament's lore, were also puzzled and had to ask Jesus, "Explain to us the Parable of the Weeds in the Field" (v. 36). Only later could they look back and see in Jesus' words the portrait of a time between the Lord's resurrection and the establishment of the earthly kingdom in its expected form. These, then, are parables of *contrast*. By contrast they illuminate key differences between the prophesied kingdom reign and the present servant form of the kingdom over which Jesus now rules.

Jesus concluded His seven parables with a question: "Have you understood all these things?" (v. 51) Afraid to say no, the Twelve nodded yes. Both the old and the new are elements in the kingdom which Christ came to bring. Only later would they begin to understand the deep implications for the church of the unexpected form of the kingdom which Jesus expressed in His parables.

♥ ***Link to Life: Youth / Adult***
Duplicate the parables chart to give your group members. Then assign teams two or three parables each. Each team should read its parables in the text, check with the chart, and then list at least three applications of the principle Jesus expressed in a parable to the church today or to Christian life and experience.

Resistance: Matthew 13:53–15:20
The failure to respond to Jesus was becoming open resistance to Him and to His teachings. When Jesus returned to His hometown, He was resented rather than honored (13:57).

John's death at the hands of Herod (14:1-12) added its dampening effect. The early mood of expectancy Jesus' ministry had stimulated was evaporating. The Pharisees had taken sides against Him. Jesus had not acted as the expected King should. The hated Herod had even executed Jesus' cousin John—and Jesus had done nothing. Instead of mounting a vengeful attack on Herod and Rome, Jesus "withdrew . . . to a solitary place" (v. 13).

The crowds followed Jesus. Waiting. Though Jesus would no longer perform miracles as authenticating signs to demonstrate the validity of His claim, He continued to be moved by compassion. Thus Jesus continued to heal—because He cared. And, when the crowds around Him were hungry and there was no source of food nearby, Jesus distributed five loaves and two fish—and fed the thousands who had come.

Late that night Jesus met His disciples on the sea (Matt. 14:22-32). They'd taken a boat; He walked across the waters to them. The rejecting Pharisees and doubting crowd would receive no more such proofs of the King's authority. But the believing disciples would continue to receive miraculous reassurance. So it is even today. The evidence men seek—and then reject when given—is withheld. But the believer who walks with Jesus sees constant evidence that God is ever near.

♥ ***Link to Life: Children***
The story of feeding thousands and of Peter's walk on the water are known by most children. Let older boys and girls work together to write a one-act play. Have them read the story carefully. Have them write down a list of characters (they can include imaginary persons as well as those in the text). Then have them write what each person might say and do. Also have them include a scene in which people who witnessed the event talk about it afterward, expressing what they have learned and thought about Jesus.

This section of the story of Jesus closes with the Pharisees returning to Jesus once again. Hating Him as they did, the Pharisees still seemed driven to come and, through confrontation, to find some justification for their stand.

Again the Pharisees attacked at a point developed in the oral law. "Why do Your disciples break the tradition of the elders? They don't wash their hands [ceremonially] before they eat!" (15:2)

Again Jesus bluntly confronted them, seeking to reveal to them the emptiness and hypocrisy of what they had substituted for the heart of God's revealed Law.

"Why do you break the command of God for the sake of your tradition?" (v. 3) Jesus asked. Their whole approach to life "invalidated the Word of God" (v. 6, NASB) for the sake of their tradition; they were setting aside the intent of God for the sake of a legalistic self-righteousness! Lashing out at these religious men, Jesus cried:

> You hypocrites! Isaiah was right when he prophesied about you: These people honor Me with their lips, but their hearts are far from Me. They worship Me in vain; their teachings are but rules taught by men.
>
> Matthew 15:7-9

Again Jesus focused attention on the heart (vv. 10-20). It is not what a man eats or how he washes that defiles. It is the heart of man that defiles, and it is this with which the King and the kingdom deal. Only Jesus can heal the diseased heart, and His work must be done within.

Coming to the kingdom we must abandon all that we have relied on to perfect ourselves. We must abandon all we are into the hands of the King. We may, like Israel, long for the outward pomp and glory of

God's future power. Yet, we must surrender all this for now. If we recognize Jesus as our King, He must be given our individual personality over which to reign.

TEACHING GUIDE

Prepare
Read what Jesus says about the heart (Matt. 13:33-37 and 15:10-20). What is there here that can guide your prayers for your group members?

Explore
1. Tell the Auca story and ask: "What is most likely to keep people who understand the Gospel from trusting Jesus?" See "link-to-life," page 559.
2. Give a minilecture on the Pharisees. Have your group members study Jesus' confrontations with them, and discover how the "careless word" principle Jesus stated applied to the Pharisees' unwitting revelation of their hearts. See "link-to life," page 561.

Expand
1. Distribute copies of the parables chart. Let your group members use it in teams to study two or three of Jesus' parables, and to develop applications to today's church and to Christian life.
2. Or examine carefully what Jesus said in His discussion of the heart, and what this means to us today. Then summarize in a single sentence the major lesson we can draw.

Apply
Discuss: "How can we help each other avoid the perils of Phariseeism in living out our faith in Christ?"

STUDY GUIDE 87

Matthew 15:21–17:27

THE TURNING POINT

Overview
These chapters contain the theological turning point in Matthew's story of Jesus and His ministry. The King was rejected by His whole people, not just by the leaders. It was not that they opposed Jesus: they simply refused to commit themselves to Him.

But the rejection was real. From here on Jesus spoke not so much of His kingdom as of His cross. And Jesus began to lay out more clearly the way of life to be adapted by those whom faith bonds to Him.

These chapters also pose several puzzling questions: Why did Jesus speak of a foreign woman as a "dog"? What is the cross Jesus' disciples are called on to bear? What are, or were, the keys to His kingdom? How did Peter line up with Satan against Christ? What is the firm foundation against which even the gates of hell cannot prevail?

These, and other questions, are answered as we explore this critical segment of Matthew's story of the life of Christ.

▶ ***Faith.*** In these chapters "faith" comes into clear focus. While the term is used in different ways in both Old and New Testaments, faith is essentially a personal, trusting response to God, who speaks words of promise. Faith is our inner response to the Good News that God loves us, and in Jesus has made a way for us to live forever with Him. What a promise! Our God is so trustworthy we need not hesitate to trust ourselves to Him.

Commentary
One afternoon on a flight to Denver I sat next to an orthodox rabinnical student. As we talked, it became clear that I was seated next to a worthy successor of the Pharisees. Like them, he believed that the oral law was given at Sinai; that the complete Jewish faith and lifestyle were communicated then and never have been modified since. He challenged me about the very incident we looked at in the last study guide: If Jesus were a Rabbi, how could He have justified eating grain on the Sabbath? I explained Jesus' answer: that the oral law is human tradition. As Lord of the Sabbath, Jesus rejected incorporations which actually drained the Law of its intended meaning.

He smiled. Clearly his confidence that he had the entire truth was as unshaken as had been the assurance of the Pharisees of Jesus' day. The way of the Law was the way of life.

Assurance that one knows the whole truth about God's plans and intentions, and that there can be no possible variation which we have not grasped, is always dangerous. If you and I adopt this attitude, we shut ourselves off from new insights from the Word of God and are in danger of ignoring God's Spirit as He seeks to teach us. When we close our minds and hearts and insist that we have all truth, any suggestion of new truth frightens and shakes us.

We can understand, then, that what we are about to see in Matthew 15–17 had great potential to disturb both Jesus' countrymen and His disciples. Jesus went on to further explain the unexpected form of the kingdom which His death and resurrection would install, and which He had already introduced (Matt. 13).

Let's trace through what we've seen in Matthew to date, and note how a shift in Jesus' kingdom-teaching has taken place.

As opposition grew, that particular expression of the kingdom for which the Jews looked receded. Increasingly, Jesus began to speak about an expression of God's kingdom on earth which was unexpected: which had been "hidden from the Creation of the world" (v. 35).

The point of national decision seems to have been reached with an event recorded in 16:13-21. Great crowds had continued to come to hear Jesus and to rejoice in His healings (15:31). In Caesarea Philippi, Jesus asked His disciples, "Who do people say the Son of man is?" (16:13) The disciples reported a variety of ideas. Some thought Jesus was John the Baptist come back; others suggested Elijah or Jeremiah or another of the ancient prophets. This was high praise! Clearly Jesus was regarded as one who was under the blessing and authority of God. But still Israel did not recognize Jesus as the promised Messiah and Son of God. They would not bow down to Him as their King!

Jesus then turned to His disciples and asked, "Who do you say I am?" (v. 15) It is on this foundation—recognition of Jesus Christ as both Messiah and Son of the living God—that any expression of the kingdom must be based. On this foundation, Jesus said, "I will build My church" (v. 18). Then Jesus charged the disciples to tell no one that He was the Christ and, the Bible says, "From that time on Jesus began to explain to His disciples that He must go to Jerusalem and suffer many things . . . and . . . be killed, and on the third day be raised" (v. 21).

From that time the message of the "kingdom at hand" was subordinated to the message of the Cross.

From this point also the Book of Matthew shows a definite shift in emphasis. Jesus increasingly stressed principles on which the present (between Resurrection and return) form of the kingdom would operate.

Focus on Faith—Matthew 15:21–16:12
The section begins with a significant incident. Jesus was met by a Canaanite woman who pleaded with Him to heal her daughter. Jesus refused, saying "I was sent only to the lost sheep of Israel" (15:24). This is a tremendously important saying. What is more, it is not an isolated statement. When Jesus gave authority to the Twelve to preach and heal, He told them, "Do not go among the Gentiles or enter any town of the Samaritans. Go rather to the lost sheep of Israel" (10:5-6).

This, of course, fit the expectations of the Jews. They knew that they were God's chosen people. As the seed of Abraham, they were possessors of God's covenant promises. When the Messiah came, He would reestablish the Davidic kingdom and rule from Jerusalem, regathering all Israel to share His glory with them. Of course, with the kingdom established, the knowledge of God would fill the earth. Then even the Gentile nations would look to the Messiah (Isa. 11). But the Messiah was *Israel's* King. Just as Israel belongs to God in a special way, (Hosea 11:1-5; Micah 6:3-5), so the Messiah belongs to Israel (Jer. 31; Micah 4:1-5). Until rejected by the people of Israel, Jesus conscientiously made Himself available to them. John put it this way: "He came to that which was His own, but His own did not receive Him" (John 1:11).

Strikingly, the Canaanite woman recognized Jesus for who He is. She addressed Him, "Lord, Son of David," thus giving Him His full messianic title. Rebuked by Jesus, she asked for the crumbs which, overflowing from Israel's future table, would bless the world. Jesus answered, "Woman, you have great faith! Your request is granted" (Matt. 15:28).

The kingdom benefits which Israel as a nation rejected when she refused to recognize her King would be made available to all men—on the basis of faith.

Matthew 15:29–16:12 continues to portray Jesus as offering Himself to Israel. He healed, He fed crowds, He continued to warn against the Pharisees who had been unable to interpret the many signs of the King's presence.

And then Jesus asked the fateful question: "Who do men say that the Son of man is?" And the disciples' report confirmed what had already been made clear. The nation had rejected Jesus. Peter's confession of faith, "You are the Christ, the Son of the living God" (16:16), was a confession which Israel could not and would not make.

Refocused: Matthew 16:13-28
These few verses, coming as they do at the turning point in Matthew's portrait of the life of Christ, have been an object of controversy through much of church history. What is the foundation on which the church will be built? What are the "keys of the kingdom" (v. 19) that Jesus handed to Peter? What are the denial of self and the taking up of one's cross which Jesus said would enable a person to find himself?

The foundation (Matt. 16:17-18). After Peter's affirmation, Jesus called Peter blessed. God had revealed Christ's identity to him. And Jesus went on to say, "On this rock I will build My church" (v. 18).

The ancient church fathers gave various interpretations of this statement. Some said that the rock on which the church was founded was Peter. Others insisted that the name Peter (*petros*, which means "little stone") could hardly be identified as a foundation rock. Other fathers have argued that the church is founded on Peter's *confession*: it is the faith in Christ which Peter professed which is the church's foundation. Still others have seen this as a reference to Christ Himself. Jesus the Christ, the Son of God, is the foundation.

The Epistles seem to support this third conclusion. "No one can lay any foundation other than the one already laid, which is Jesus Christ" (1 Cor. 3:11). Christ Himself, the Messiah and Son of God, is the Foundation of the church and the kingdom.

The keys (Matt. 16:19). What then about the gift of the "keys of the kingdom" and the promise that "whatever you bind on earth will be bound in heaven, and whatever you loose on earth will be loosed in heaven"? What are the keys, and what are the loosing and binding?

Here again there have been disagreements. To some these verses are clear evidence that the church, as made visible in the Roman pontiff, is the "Vicar of Christ on earth." It is held that the power of making binding decisions has been delegated to Peter and his successors. But this notion came late in church history, after the bishop of Rome gained dominance over the other bishoprics.

Other scholars have noted that Peter was chosen by God to open the door of the Gospel to each of the two major groups of mankind recognized in his day. At Pentecost, Peter preached the first Gospel sermon to the Jews. Later still, God chose him to speak to Cornelius, the first Gentile to become a part of the body of Christ (Acts 10–11). Yet, this does not explain binding and loosing.

One thing is clear in the New Testament: Jesus is Head over all things for the church which is His body (Eph. 1:22-23). Jesus was not surrendering His position to any individual or group of men. If we realize our direct link with Jesus as our Head, this will suggest the best solution to the puzzle. How do we on earth speak with such authority? Only because we on earth are, through Jesus' presence within us, an extension of Christ Himself! Our Head, who directs us, acts through His body on earth to loose and bind authoritatively. How fully, then, you and I need to be committed to Christ's lordship, and how fully we need to obey Him. As believers respond to Jesus' direction, the kingdom continues to express its presence on earth.

Jesus' response to the disciples' confession was pointed and striking. He confirmed their awareness that He is the Messiah and Son of God, and announced His intention of building on this reality a "church," literally a "called-out assembly." Moreover, this church is to be the lived-out expression of heaven on earth. In our relationship with Jesus we are to express the kingdom in our generation's "here and now." The destiny of the believer is to *express* the kingdom. We bind and loose; we affirm forgiveness of sin and its retention. We speak God's Word, not on our authority, but on the authority Christ shares with us as He shared it with these disciples He once sent out two by two (cf. Matt. 10).

The portrait given here is an overwhelming one. To *be* the kingdom! To reflect Jesus in our world! To express Him, His grace and His judgments! This is who we are called to be—and become.

This is who we are.

To become (Matt. 16:24-28). Knowing that as kingdom citizens we are to reflect the King may make us feel guilty or unworthy. It is not meant to. Instead, it is meant to help us sense our calling, and respond joyfully to follow our Lord. There *is* a gap between our present experience and our calling. Recognizing the gap, Jesus told His disciples, "If anyone would come after Me" (v. 24). If we want to follow Jesus, we are invited to, and are shown the results.

What results? "Whoever loses his life for Me will find it" (v. 25). This puzzling statement is made more clear when we realize that the word translated "life" here, and "soul" in some translations, reflects a common Hebrew usage. The words (*nephesh*, in Hebrew and *psuche*, in Greek) can mean "soul" or "life." But in Hebrew and in the Greek translation of the Old Testament, the words are often used as a reflexive pronoun. Thus, Jesus warned not of losing one's life, but of losing *oneself*!

"Whoever loses himself for Me," Jesus was saying, "will find himself." And "what good will it be for a man if he gains the whole world and yet forfeits his . . . [self]?" (v. 26) What "self" was Jesus speaking of? Jesus was speaking of who you and I can become if we choose to follow Him!

You and I *can* choose to turn away from all that kingdom citizenship offers. If we do, we will never become what Jesus yearns to make us. Or we can follow Jesus and lose the self we are—the self that feels guilt and shame for so many failures. In following Jesus, you and I can become closer to what we yearn to be.

What does it take? How do we follow Jesus? "He must deny himself and take up his cross and follow Me" (v. 24).

Each of these phrases is significant:

**Self-denial*. It would be a mistake to see self-denial as refusing pleasures or joys. The Bible says that God "gives us richly all things to enjoy" (1 Tim. 6:17, KJV). And one of the Pharisees' criticisms of Jesus was that He went to parties! No, self-denial is far more significant than this. It involves a denial of the values, the attitudes, and the emotions of which Jesus spoke in the Beatitudes. For example, bitterness is rooted in the old self and is to be denied. As Christ speaks to us when we are bitter, insisting that we let forgiveness wash away our anger, all that's old in us fights against that choice. Pride, competitiveness, and self-pity all struggle within to direct our reactions. To deny these natural pressures within ourselves involves denying the self we are, in order to follow Jesus. To deny these natural pressures and to choose to forgive helps shape the self that only Jesus can help us become.

**Daily cross*. It is significant that Jesus did not ask us to take up *His* cross. Instead Jesus teaches us to be willing to take up *our* crosses. Why the symbol of the cross? No, not because it indicates suffering. The Cross speaks of Jesus' willing choice of that which was God's will for Him. What our crosses symbolize is our willingness to make daily choices of God's will for us—whatever that will may prove to be.

**Follow Me*. This is the heart of Jesus' invitation to us. Follow. But not at a distance. Not as someone searching for tracks, to trace a figure long disappeared over the horizon. No, Jesus' "Follow Me" means "*Keep close* to Me." Only when we are close to Jesus can we find the strength for self-denial; only when we are close to Jesus can we sense His daily guidance in our lives.

Denying the old self, choosing daily the Father's will, and keeping close to Jesus, we will—as the first disciples did—find our true selves.

Coming Glory: Matthew 17

Jesus' talk of His coming death was deeply disturbing to the disciples (16:22-23). Disturbing too was the choice Jesus then set before His followers. "If *anyone* would come after Me" (v. 24). There was no overpowering "coming" here, to sweep all Israel to a promised glory. Instead, each individual had to face his own private Gethsemane. "Shall I follow the King?" The pathway on which the King walked, a way of self-denial and daily cross, was tremendously less appealing than the expected Old Testament kingdom.

Yet, Matthew 16 closed with Jesus making another puzzling statement. "Some who are standing here will not taste death before they see the Son of man coming in His kingdom" (v. 28). The next verse says, "After six days Jesus took with Him Peter, James, and John . . . and led them up a high mountain by themselves" (17:1). Some of the disciples, but not all, were about to see the glory all will share when Jesus comes into His promised kingdom.

There on the mountain Jesus was "transfigured before them. His face shone like the sun, and His clothes became as white as the light" (v. 2). There too appeared Moses (who had died) and Elijah (who had been taken up into heaven without passing through death) to talk with Him. The present pathway for Jesus led to the Cross. *But the Cross was the doorway to Glory.*

♥ ***Link to Life: Children***

How can we illustrate the Transfiguration for boys and girls? Draw a figure of Jesus on regular typing paper. Back the paper with black construction paper, but cut out of the black a silhouette that matches the drawn figure. Tape the black silhouette back.

In class hold up the sheet of paper, white side out, to show the figure of Jesus. Explain that when Jesus lived here He lived like any other human being. But on the Mount of Transfiguration Jesus showed His splendor as God. Hold the sheet of paper up against a light, take out the silhouette, and let the light shine through. On the Mount, Jesus' true nature as God shone through His human form, and the disciples knew again how wonderful Jesus is.

On the way down the mountain, Jesus warned the three disciples not to share this experience with anyone until He had been raised from the dead. Impressed by the vision and eager for that time of glory to arrive, they seemed disturbed by the fact that Elijah, the forerunner, hadn't accompanied them. They asked, "Why then do the teachers of the Law say that [before the messianic kingdom is established] Elijah must come first?" (v. 10) Jesus answered that Elijah will come first (v. 11). But He also said that if Israel had responded to Jesus, John the Baptist's ministry would have been considered to fulfill the Elijah prophecy.

As the disciples were coming down from the mountain, a crowd led by a man with an epileptic son met Jesus and the three disciples (vv. 14-20). The other disciples had tried to cure the son but had failed. Now the father appealed to Jesus. Jesus responded. A faithless and perverse generation had rejected Jesus as King—and yet constantly sought His help!

Later the disciples asked Jesus why they had been powerless to help. Jesus answered, "Because you have so little faith" (v. 20). The people of Israel, because of faithlessness, were unable to enter the kingdom. And the disciples, who had entered the kingdom through recognition of the King, were unable to experience kingdom power for the same fault: lack of faith.

To enter the kingdom, and to live victoriously in it, faith is required.

The final incident in this sequence (vv. 24-27) sums up in a unique way the message Jesus had begun to communicate to His unresponsive people. The Old Testament established a half-shekel tax to be paid to the temple by each adult male. Met by tax collectors, Peter was asked if Jesus paid the tax, Peter blurted out, "Yes,"

At home, Jesus asked Peter, "From whom do the kings of the earth collect duty and taxes—from their own sons or from others?" (v. 25) Peter gave the obvious answer: "From others." "Then," Jesus said, "the sons are exempt."

What was Jesus' point? The Jews had assumed that because they were the physical descendants of Abraham, they had a special relationship with God and a unique claim on Him. But the very fact that God taxed the Jews to maintain the temple demonstrated clearly that they were *not* sons! The physical basis on which the Israelites thought they could claim relationship with God was inadequate, and it had always been so! Men who so confidently claimed Abraham as their father (John 8:33) had failed to realize that Abraham's relationship with God was rooted in faith, not in the Law. They rejected that very quality of the man, whose descendants they claimed to be, which had made Abraham God's man.

Without faith, that generation lost for Israel and for mankind the very kingdom whose living expression you and I are called today to be.

By faith.

TEACHING GUIDE

Prepare

Review all the "puzzles" in this passage, and be sure you understand their solutions.

Explore

1. Give your group members a minilecture on the significance of these "turning-point" chapters in Matthew's report of Jesus' life.
2. List on the chalkboard the "puzzles" to be found in this section of Scripture. Include:

- Why wouldn't Jesus help a Canaanite?
- What is the foundation on which the church is built?
- What are the keys to the kingdom, and who holds them?
- What is denying yourself?
- What is "your cross"?
- What made Jesus angry when a father asked help for his son?

Let each person in your group select two of these puzzles to explore. Each person will serve on two teams. Give the first teams, formed around each person's *first* puzzle choice, about 20 minutes to look in the passage and to discuss. Then form new teams around each person's *second* puzzle choice.

Then come together as a group to share insights. Supplement your group members' discoveries from the commentary in the text, and from other commentaries such as the Victor *Bible Knowledge Commentary*, pages 55-61.

Apply

Finally, use the last few minutes to express: "What have I learned from this study that I can apply to my own life?"

STUDY GUIDE 88

Matthew 18–20

THE WAY TO GREATNESS

Overview

Each Gospel writer takes the events that he reports and arranges them to develop themes he seeks to emphasize. This characteristic is especially clear in Matthew 18–20, which explores the theme of greatness in Jesus' kingdom.

The sequence begins when the disciples ask Jesus about greatness. It proceeds, through stories Jesus tells about greatness, to incidents that show the emptiness of notions about greatness held by the religious of Jesus' day, to a final demonstration by Jesus Himself of the stunning truth that greatness is found in servanthood.

What an important passage to teach members of your group. We find greatness in a servanthood like Jesus' own.

▶ ***Servant and Slave.*** Both Old and New Testament terms are often translated by either "servant" or "slave." Yet there are special emphases in each. In Hebrew the root *'abad* can indicate voluntary work or forced service. Its derivative, *'ebed* means either servant or slave. But *sarat* indicates significant service, important because one serves an important person in a close personal relationship, doing that which is truly important. In the New Testament *douleuo* indicates submission of the will, as in slavery. We Christians are slaves of Jesus, for we submit to Him. But *diakoneo* means serving by giving personal help to another. Christian servanthood means willingly submitting to the will of God, and freely offering help to others.

Commentary

Sometimes we apologize for dreaming great dreams. As a young Christian, I had dreams of becoming another Apostle Paul, just as dedicated to Christ and the Gospel. My dreams were foolish and immature. But I'm sure they were not wrong.

Neither were the disciples wrong when they came to Jesus to ask about greatness. "Who is the greatest in the kingdom of heaven?" (Matt. 18:1) they inquired. Their simple question launched a series of teachings and events which show us in a unique way just how different spiritual greatness is from all that we expect.

It's all right for you and me to want to be great. But we must first grasp what greatness *is*. The vision we often have, looking up to the famous preacher holding large crowds spellbound, or the sensitive counselor whom all respect, or the brilliant teacher all flock to hear, can actually blind us to the fact that a journey toward greatness is a journey *down*, not up!

First Steps: Matthew 18

The disciples' request to know who was greatest in the kingdom stimulated a totally unexpected reply. "He called a little child and had him stand among them. And He said: 'I tell you the truth, unless you change and become like little children, you will never enter the kingdom of heaven' " (vv. 2-3).

Faith (Matt. 18:1-5). The child is the living embodiment of several truths which the disciples of Jesus had missed. The first truth involves faith, a theme developed in Matthew 15–17. Seeking greatness, the disciples must humble themselves, as one of the little ones who "believe in Me."

The people of Israel did not respond when Jesus called them to Him. They stood off at a distance, reserving judgment. When Jesus called the child to Him, the child responded immediately. Without pride, humble and trusting, the child accepted Jesus' invitation at once.

Greatness comes only when we humble ourselves to trustingly respond to our King's every call.

Concern for "little ones" (Matt. 18:6-35). Jesus then lashed out at those who cause little ones to sin (vv. 6-9). This world is the kind of place in which temptations to sin are bound to come, but "little ones" are to be protected. So Jesus warned, "See that you do not look down on one of these little ones" (v. 10). Who are the "little ones"? All of us who, like children, have responded to Jesus' invitation and put our trust in Him. But, like children, we are to remain little ones in our attitudes toward God—to remain responsive to Jesus' every word.

The three following illustrations show us how to live with each other to preserve the quality of childlike responsiveness to Jesus in ourselves and others.

**Matthew 18:10-14.* Like sheep, little ones who go astray are to be searched for and restored to the fold. The Palestine shepherd gave each sheep in his flock a name and knew each sheep individually. Rather than driving his flock, the shepherd led. The sheep, knowing his voice, followed him (cf. John 10:3). When a young lamb wandered away, the shepherd left the flock in the sheepfold and braved any weather to find the lost one. Climbing over rocks, searching each crevasse, the shepherd gave himself freely to find the lost one. Finding it, the shepherd gave no thought of punishment, but knew joy that the lost one was restored.

Faith does not make you or me great. But responding to Jesus' call to care about His little ones who stray does. Caring enough to greet them with joy rather than recrimination, with love rather than condemnation.

**Matthew 18:15-22.* Here Jesus changed the simile. Little ones are sheep—but little ones are also brothers.

"If your brother sins against you, go and show him his fault" (v. 15), Jesus began. Temptations to sin must surely come, as Jesus had already pointed out (v. 7). Even with men of faith, sin will intrude, with all its hurts and pains, to break the fellowship of the family. Such failings are not to destroy family unity. A brotherly desire for reconciliation can keep God's little ones from turning away from Him.

This troubled Peter, who asked, "How many times shall I forgive my brother when he sins against me? Up to seven times?" (v. 21) Christ's answer: "Seventy times seven" [i.e., "always"].

Faith does not lift us above the possibility of sin. But forgiveness can cancel sin's impact on family relationships.

**Matthew 18:23-35.* Once again the simile shifted. Here we the little ones are seen as servants. Christ, our King, has forgiven us a great debt. In His patience and love, He has treated us gently and lovingly. As servants of such a King, we are now called on to have patience with our fellow believers (v. 29). Failure to have such patience and to extend forgiveness will cut us off from our experience of God's forgiveness. This is not because God is unwilling to forgive. It is because forgiveness is like a coin: it has two sides. We cannot have "heads" (receive forgiveness) without having "tails" (extend forgiveness) too.

Faith does not elevate our status: we are servants, subject to the will of God. And we are to treat our fellow servants as God treats us.

♥ ***Link to Life: Children***

We have so much. We can give to others. No, we're not rich in money, or rich in possessions. But we are rich in the forgiveness God has showered on us.

Cut out from newspapers or magazines many pictures of cars, of food, of clothes, etc. In class give one child all the cars, another all the food, another all the clothes, etc.

Then ask each to give you one *of the things he or she has been given so many of.*

"*We may not* really *have a lot of cars, or clothes, or food. But each of us has been given a lot of one thing by God.*"

Explain how God has forgiven each of us for every sin. We have been given so much forgiveness that when someone does something wrong that harms us, we can give him some of the forgiveness we have received.

Greatness? The disciples must have been stunned by this discourse. They had asked about greatness, but Jesus spoke only about God's little ones! They had been thinking about great deeds and high position, but Jesus had spoken of sheep and brothers and servants. What did all this have to do with greatness?

Much, for them and for us. To be great in Christ's present kingdom, you and I must first of all take our places as God's little ones—and learn to see our fellow believers in the same way. In our desire to excel, we must never forget that we are sheep, prone to go astray, always in need of our Shepherd's tender care. We must never forget that all other Christians are brothers, and seek to live with them in fullest harmony. We must never forget that we are simply servants living with (not *over*) fellow servants. And we must treat all others with that same patience and forgiveness which Jesus shows us.

One of the most poignant passages in Scripture pictures the Apostle Paul ministering to God's little ones. Paul reminds the Thessalonians:

> We were gentle among you, like a mother caring for her little children. We loved you so much we were delighted to share with you not only the Gospel of God but our lives as well, because you had become so dear to us. . . . You know that we dealt with each of you as a father deals with his own children, encouraging, comforting, and urging you to live lives worthy of God, who calls you into His kingdom and glory.
>
> 1 Thessalonians 2:7-12

Do you want to be great? Then take your place among God's little ones, and love them into God's kingdom.

♥ ***Link to Life: Youth / Adult***
Give a short overview of the focus of Jesus on "little ones." Then break into three teams. Each team is to look at one of the images (sheep, family, servants), and to (1) describe the kind of person *who most needs this teaching, and (2) describe specifically how it will help that person. Each team should mention several situations in which the typical behavior of the person will be changed if the "living with little ones" principle is applied.*

Another Way? Matthew 19:1–20:16
Jesus' ideas about greatness are revolutionary. Soon they were contrasted against the ideas of the religious of His day; ideas still popular in our day. And still wrong.

The way of the Law (Matt. 19:3-15). The Pharisees are still the classic example of those zealous for God who expect to find spiritual greatness by rigid adherence to both biblical and human standards of righteousness. These proponents of strict legalism appeared to test Jesus, apparently bringing up a subject which Jesus had spoken on before. "Is it lawful for a man to divorce his wife for any and every reason? (v. 3) Jesus' answer goes back to the Creation account. He pointed out that God intended marriage to unite two persons as one; thus divorce is not His intention.

Immediately the Pharisees struck back. "Why then did Moses command that a man give his wife a certificate of divorce?" (v. 7) The Law permitted divorce. Jesus' answer had to be wrong.

Christ's response reveals the root of legalism's error. "Moses permitted you to divorce your wives because your hearts were hard" (v. 8). Yes, God permits divorce to a sinful humanity which so often falls short of His ideal. But the Law is not a way of some higher or superior righteousness! The permission to divorce shows how willing God is to accommodate His ideal in consideration of human weakness and sin!

The Pharisees' legalism led them to ask the wrong question. They did not ask, "How can we restore the broken relationships which bring such agony into marriage?" No, they asked instead, "When is it all right to permit hurting people to separate?" They did not care about broken hearts, crushed by rejection. The Pharisees took refuge instead in legalism, missing the meaning of the Law by setting up rules as to when it should and should not apply.

The disciples also missed Jesus' point. Jesus had been teaching about greatness, and had shown that true greatness is to restore the straying lamb, to exercise patience, and to continue ever ready to forgive. Others too are God's little ones, and may need years of tender love to help them grow. Failing to relate Christ's teaching on greatness to this legal issue, the disciples blurted out, "In that case, it's better not to marry!" Even they were unwilling to commit themselves totally to another person.

Jesus then spoke to the disciples. The choice not to marry is for some, but "only those to whom it has been given" (v. 11). Within marriage, all who can live by the way of greatness should choose it (v. 12).

Again Jesus drew children around Him. "Let the little children come to Me, and do not hinder them," He said to His disciples (v. 14). The incident is significant. A Jewish person became "a child of the Law"—that is, responsible to relate to God through the Mosaic Law—at 12. These "little children" were too young to be under Law, yet they could come to Jesus. What God wants is not legalists, but people in intimate personal relationship with Jesus, who will respond willingly to His voice.

The way of "goodness" (Matt. 19:16-30). Immediately after this a young man came up to Jesus and asked, "What good thing must I do to get eternal life?" (v. 16) This young man was a good person, one whose goodness was expressed in his honest observation of the Law. But Jesus challenged him on one point. "Sell your possessions and give to the poor, and . . . come, follow Me" (v. 21).

The young man turned away.

No. This was not a universal command to sell all, given to all the rich. Instead it was a challenge to this individual who measured his goodness by his dealings with other men. Yet, this humanistic benevolence avoids the first commandment: "You shall have no other gods before Me" (Ex. 20:3, NASB). How do we know? Jesus' words were a command from the young man's God. Hearing them, the young man rebelled and put wealth first.

All human goodness fails at this same point. It is good enough to do good to others, but it is not enough. God must be the center and focus of our lives.

As the young man went sadly away, Jesus remarked that wealth makes it difficult to enter the kingdom. The disciples, who, like others in their culture, viewed wealth as evidence of God's favor, asked in astonishment, "Who then can be saved?" The answer? "With man this is impossible, but with God all things are possible" (Matt. 19:25-26).

At this point, Peter blurted out yet another foolish question. The disciples had left all to follow Jesus. What would they gain? Jesus accommodated His answer to their need. They were still concerned about the kind of greatness that involves status and power. Jesus reassured them. "At the renewal of all things, when the Son of man sits on His glorious throne, you who have followed Me will also sit on twelve thrones, judging the twelve tribes of Israel" (v. 28). But, Jesus added, *This is not for now!* For now, "Many who are first will be last and many who are last will be first" (v. 30).

The way of hard work (Matt. 20:1-16). A final parable was added to explain the "last-first" comment. Jesus pictured a landowner who went out early in the morning and hired men to work in his harvest. Later he went out and found more standing idle. He sent them out into his fields as well. Several times during the day this pattern was repeated.

At evening, those who had worked the full day were dismayed to find that others who had worked only two hours received as much pay as they! When they complained, the landowner explained that they were paid what they had agreed on that morning. As for the rest, their reward was a matter not of what they had earned, but what was given by the owner out of generosity. The last had been first.

Like each of the workers in Jesus' parable, we have been invited to serve in His kingdom. What is important is our response to the King when He calls us to our individual tasks. Greatness is not measured by how long or hard we may work trying to gain a reward.

Greg found this out at a Faith/at/Work retreat. For eight years he had directed an evangelistic mission which flooded 70 countries with college students. He labored 16 and 18 hours a day, and his feeling of worth and value was directly related to the length of his day. At the retreat, Greg was confronted by a small group who revealed that they saw him as a man with a "Messiah complex." He was someone who thought he was called to save the world all by himself. Greg broke into tears. For the first time he realized that all his Christian life he had been trying to earn God's favor, caught up in an endless struggle for acceptance. During that week, Greg discovered that he *is* one of God's little ones.

Currently a pastor in Colorado, Greg is now free to respond when God calls, and is finding a rich reward in the conversion and growth of many whom the Lord touches through him.

In the kingdom of Christ's present reign we *are* called to greatness. But we will not find it along the roads that many of the religious have traveled. Christ has another way, marked out for all of us who humbly accept our places as His trusting little ones.

♥ ***Link to Life: Youth / Adult***
How would a person traveling one of the three wrong roads to greatness explain his or

her expectations? Give your group members a "starter" statement that might be made by each individual. Have them add as many more similar statements of explanation as they can. Here are some starter statements:

- *I expect to surpass others by figuring out just what every rule in the Bible means and doesn't mean.*
- *I expect to win God's favor by the way I treat other people.*
- *I expect God to be pleased with me because I give more time to His work than others do.*

The Servant Leader: Matthew 20:17-28 Again Jesus took the Twelve aside and spoke to them of His death. "We are going up to Jerusalem, and the Son of man will be betrayed to the chief priests and the teachers of the Law. They will condemn Him to death and will turn Him over to the Gentiles to be mocked and flogged and crucified. On the third day He will be raised to life!" (vv. 18-19) In the context of teaching on greatness, Jesus focused the attention of His disciples on His own choice to give His life.

We see why. Immediately afterward, the mother of James and John, two of the Twelve, came to Jesus to ask for the right- and left-hand seats in the coming kingdom for her sons. These two seats represent power and honor. Momma was politicking for her boys.

It's clear from the context that James and John had asked her to intercede, and were standing close by to hear the Lord's answer. "You don't know what you are asking," was Jesus' weary reply. "Can you," He said, turning to the two listening disciples, "drink the cup I am going to drink?" (v. 22) Authority and power in the kingdom are not what the disciples imagined. The leader will influence others, but he will perform his ministry in the same way that Jesus chose to perform His. Still not understanding, James and John eagerly insisted that they were able to drink Jesus' cup. "You will do that," Jesus replied. But the power and position they yearned for was something Jesus would not promise.

When the other 10 disciples heard, they were indignant at James and John. So Jesus called all 12 around Him, and gave what is probably the most significant instruction recorded in the New Testament about spiritual leadership.

> You know that the rulers of the Gentiles lord it over them, and their high officials exercise authority over them. Not so with you. Instead, whoever wants to become great among you must be your servant, and whoever wants to be first must be your slave—just as the Son of man did not come to be served, but to serve, and to give His life a ransom for many.
>
> Matthew 20:25-28

In this short passage, Jesus once and for all put to rest the pretentions of the spiritual leaders of every age to that kind of "power" which demands the right to command others.

The secular ruler. Jesus set up two models or examples of leaders. The one model was provided by the secular ruler of Jesus' day, the emperor or king or governor who "exercises authority over" others. There are many characteristics of this style of leadership, some made explicit in the text, and others implicit in the example chosen.

For instance, there is a distinctive relationship between the leader and the led: the secular ruler "exercises authority *over*." When I was in the Navy, my commanding officer, Lieutenant Kahle, was about five feet two inches tall, a full foot shorter than I. It was the most peculiar sensation, standing in front of Lieutenant Kahle and still feeling that I was looking up! There is a relational distance between the leader and the led in the secular world.

Another significant characteristic is implied in both the phrases "lord it over them" and "exercise authority." The secular ruler has the ability to enforce his will. He has sanctions to make sure that his orders are obeyed. This was certainly true in my Navy days. If I had not responded to orders, my liberty (time off) could have been canceled. I could have been brought up before the captain's mast (an informal court). I could have been court-martialed. Punishments ranging from restriction to the base, to the forfeiture of my pay, to imprisonment, assured my conformity. Secular leaders have this kind of power.

A third significant characteristic implicit in both the above has to do with *how* leadership is exercised. From his position above, using his power to enforce, the secular ruler *leads by command*. He simply tells others what to do, and they do it.

The servant leader. Jesus chose a servant as the countermodel for His followers. Nothing could be farther from our idea of greatness or leadership. We tend to see, as did the disciples, the pomp of power. The TV cameras focus on the great seal of the United States, a hushed quiet falls, the band in the background plays "Hail to the Chief," and the announcer's voice is heard: "Ladies and gentlemen, the President of the United States." We feel that is greatness. That is what being a leader is all about.

But then Jesus directs our attention to a quiet person standing off camera; a person in overalls with the working tools of his trade. And Jesus says *that* is greatness! That is what being a leader is all about.

This graphic contrast must have jolted the disciples just as it jolts us. Yet Jesus clearly wants us to see each of these people as leaders. Each of them is to be seen as having authority and the power to move other men. What, then, are the significant contrasts between the two?

While the secular ruler is above those he leads, Jesus said, "Not so with you" (v. 26). Instead of relational distance, there is relational closeness. The Christian leader must seek to be one with those he or she is called to serve.

Instead of "exercising authority" as a ruler who demands and enforces conformity, the Christian leader is to abandon coercion. Jesus said firmly and plainly, "*Not so with you.*" Force, manipulation, demand—all are ruled out in the way by which the servant leader exercises Christian authority. Outward force can produce conformity, but it can never produce that inner commitment which moves people to choose to follow Jesus.

How, then, does the servant lead? By serving! The secular ruler speaks the commands, but the spiritual leader demonstrates by his example the kingdom way of life into which he is called to lead others. No wonder Peter picked up this same theme and wrote as an elder to fellow elders, "Be shepherds of God's flock that is under your care . . . not lording it over those entrusted to you, but being examples to the flock" (1 Peter 5:2-3). By serving, the Christian leader demonstrates the greatness of the love of God, and gently motivates others to follow him. "Whoever wants to be first must be your slave—just as the Son of man did not come to be served, but to serve, and to give His life as a ransom for many" (Matt. 20:27-28).

♥ ***Link to Life: Youth / Adult***

Put a T-shaped chart on the board. On the right write "secular ruler" and on the left, "servant leader." Give your group eight minutes to work in pairs to develop comparisons and contrasts explicit or implied in Matt. 20:25-28 between the two kinds of leadership. Then list their insights on the chalkboard. After you have a clear description of servanthood, discuss: "How do we exhibit this kind of spiritual leadership in our daily lives and relationships?"

♥ ***Link to Life: Children***

In the passage Jesus tells us to follow His example. Even boys and girls have an impression of what Jesus is like and how they can be like Him. Draw on what your class already knows about the Lord. Ask each to use crayons and draw a picture of Jesus doing something kind. Have your boys and girls tell about their pictures, and describe what Jesus is doing. Encourage them to talk about why Jesus is doing what He is.

Then ask each to draw another picture, showing him or her doing something like *what Jesus did. Again, have the children talk about their pictures.*

Encourage them to remember what Jesus is like, and to let Him keep on being their example of how to live with others.

A Last Example: Matthew 20:29-34

The disciples had asked about greatness in Jesus' present kingdom. Jesus had answered them—fully. Greatness involves humbling ourselves and taking our place as one of God's little ones. Greatness involves accepting others as little ones too: seeking to restore when they go astray, having patience, and always being willing to let forgiveness wash away the hurts that sin must bring. Greatness also involves rejecting the attractive but destructive ways in which religious people often seek greatness. Legalism, good deeds, hard work—none of these can produce greatness in Christ's kingdom.

Finally, Jesus has given us His own clear prescription for greatness. Learn how to lead others *as a servant*. Be one of those men or women who choose to drink Jesus' cup and give up their lives for the sake of others.

Then Matthew recorded a deeply moving incident that helps us sense what Jesus' kind of greatness is. As Christ and the disciples were leaving Jericho, a great crowd followed. Two blind men, sitting by the road, heard that Jesus was passing by. They cried out to Him. The crowd callously told them to shut up. But the two only called louder.

And Jesus stopped.

Jesus was on His way to Jerusalem, toward His trial and crucifixion. He was burdened by great crowds who did not care, and by disciples who did not understand. But Jesus set aside His own burdens and need to respond to this call for help. "Jesus had compassion on them and touched their eyes. Immediately they received their sight and followed Him" (v. 34).

Jesus stopped—for the individual in the crowd.

Jesus cared—for the outcasts whom the crowd considered worthless.

This is greatness. To touch in compassion, and to give ourselves for others as their servant, for Jesus' sake.

TEACHING GUIDE

Prepare

Who is the "greatest" Christian you know personally, using the criteria Jesus establishes in this chapter?

Explore

1. Give your group an overview of the theme of greatness as it is developed in this passage. Explain the links between each incident and teaching, so they will sense how it all fits together in a unified whole.
2. Have group members work in teams to describe the kind of person who most needs the teaching implicit in each incident in Matthew 18. See the "link-to-life" activity on page 573.

Expand

1. Put the T-shaped chart suggested on page 576 on the chalkboard. Let your group members work together to compare and contrast the servant and the secular ruler. After this is done, discuss: "How does servanthood find expression in our daily lives today? Why does Jesus stress 'Not so with you?' What would be wrong with mixing servant and secular methods in leading others? In what ways does our church follow the servant model? In what areas does our church need to move away from a secular approach to spiritual leadership?"
2. Or work on listing statements that might be made by those who have adopted one of the false roads to spiritual greatness that Jesus looks at in Matthew 19 and 20. See "link-to-life," pages 574-575.

Apply

Read aloud Matthew 20:29-34. But first, ask each person to visualize the scene and to imagine how Jesus must have felt as He turned toward Jerusalem and His ultimate rejection and crucifixion. Ask each to pray quietly that God will help him or her follow the example of Jesus, who truly "gave His life," not just on Calvary, but daily, to meet the needs of others.

STUDY GUIDE 89

Matthew 21–23

CONFRONTATION

Overview
Jesus was welcomed by the Jerusalem crowds; hailed as the Messiah on what Christians call "Palm Sunday." Jesus' enemies were aroused by this event, and renewed their attacks. Jesus silenced them—and in turn boldly condemned their wickedness and hypocrisy.

In these chapters we find many of Jesus' most familiar parables. And we find the clearest exposition in the Bible of legalistic pathways which falsely promise spiritual growth. Religious people are all too prone to walk these promising paths, which actually lead to spiritual emptiness and to judgment.

▶ ***Praise.*** The joyful response of the people to Jesus that first Palm Sunday is a beautiful illustration of praise. Several Hebrew words and concepts enrich our grasp of this richest of words in the vocabulary of worship. *Halal* means "to acclaim," "to glory in," and expresses deep satisfaction in exalting God's wonderful acts and qualities. *Yadah* suggests acknowledging God's works and character, often with thanksgiving. *Zamar* means to "sing praise" or "make music," while *sabah* expresses praise or commendation. What delight we can have in responding to God and His works with growing love and praise.

▶ ***Woe.*** In both Testaments this is an exclamation of grief or denunciation. How tragic. For those who love and praise Jesus there is joy. But for the rest, as Jesus' words in Matthew 23 reveal, there is only woe.

Commentary
We have a tendency today to see gentleness as weakness.

This tendency probably explains, at least partially, why people of all times tend to draw back from Jesus' picture of leadership as servanthood. "But," they object, "we want leaders who are *strong*. We want leaders with authority!"

The fact of the matter is that only in Christ's kind of servanthood do we find true spiritual strength. Gentleness is *not* weakness. Compassion is becoming to the King.

So it is not Mr. Milquetoast that Jesus sets before us as our example, but Himself. In these next chapters of Matthew, which portray Jesus in direct conflict with His enemies, we see our Lord speak out boldly in His full authority as King. In dealing with little ones the Leader is gentle. In facing foes, He is bold.

The Triumphal Entry: Matthew 21:1-17
It was the Passover week, a few brief days before the Crucifixion. Coming to Jerusalem, Jesus sent two of His disciples to bring a donkey and colt to Him for a long-prophesied entry into Jerusalem. Isaiah and Zechariah had both spoken of it:

> Your King comes to you, gentle and riding on a donkey, on a colt, the foal of a donkey.
>
> Matthew 21:5

Without pomp, humble and on a humble beast of burden, the King would come.

On this day the crowds that soon would turn against Jesus swelled with enthusiasm for Him. "Hosanna to the Son of David!" they shouted. "Blessed is He who comes in the name of the Lord!" (v. 9)

Christ moved purposefully to the temple. There He went into the court, which was to be reserved for prayer, and found merchants.

The Old Testament ruled that only unblemished animals might be offered in sacrifice. The priests set up a very lucrative trade in "approved" lambs and pigeons. Animals brought from the country for sacrifice might easily be disapproved by priestly inspectors, and worshipers forced to buy from the temple merchants. What had been set aside for prayer had become a "den of robbers" (v. 13).

As Jesus stood in the cleansed temple yard, the blind and the lame came to Him and He healed them. With even greater enthusiasm, the crowds proclaimed "Hosanna to the Son of David!" The chief priests and the scribes saw all these wonderful things which Jesus did and "they were indignant" (v. 15). Hardened as ever, the leaders were totally unwilling to acknowledge Jesus as their King.

♥ ***Link to Life: Youth / Adult***
There are a number of Old Testament references associated in some way with Matthew 21:1-17. Have group members look up these verses, and see what insights they give into the significance of the events reported by Matthew.

The Old Testament passages are: Exodus 30:13; Leviticus 1:14; 2 Kings 9:13; Psalms 8:2; 118:26; Isaiah 56:7; Jeremiah 7:11; Zechariah 9:9.

♥ ***Link to Life: Children***
How are we to praise God? The New Testament speaks of shouts of joy, of cheering, excitement, and pleasure about the "wonderful things" that Jesus did. And this shouting was led by children (Matt. 21:15).

Ask your boys and girls to tell about the "most wonderful thing" Jesus did. Use construction paper to make pennants. Let each child draw a picture of His "most wonderful" event on the pennants.

Then together wave the pennants, and "cheer" for Jesus!

The Emptiness of Legalism: Matthew 21:18–22:14

When evening fell, Jesus and His companions went across the valley to Bethany for the night. The next morning an incident occurred which gives us the key to understand the events which follow.

On the way back to Jerusalem, Jesus saw a fig tree and went over to it, as if to pluck some fruit for breakfast. Though the foliage was luxuriant, there was no fruit. Jesus uttered a curse, and "immediately the tree withered" (21:19). Impressed, the disciples asked, "How did the fig tree wither so quickly?" (v. 20) Jesus' explanation was simple: "Faith."

The fig tree of Israel which *appeared* luxuriant had produced no fruit. It was to wither away, its fruitlessness to be exposed. Faith was to provide a better way.

Immediately on entering the city, Jesus began a series of confrontations and teachings which reveal why the legalism of the Jewish leaders, like the hypocritical fig tree, produced only appearances rather than fruit.

Empty of authority (Matt. 21:23-27). In Deuteronomy, the Jewish people were told to take disputes to their rulers for them to settle. The elders of the people challenged Jesus and asked by what authority He was acting. Christ asked them a question: "John's baptism—where did it come from? Was it from heaven or from men?" The elders were thrown into confusion. If they said "from heaven," Jesus would condemn them for not listening. But if they said "from men," the crowds who held John was a prophet might even attack them! Unwilling and unable to take a stand, or exercise the authority they claimed to have, these men replied, "We don't know" (v. 27).

Untouched by changed lives (Matt. 21:28-32). Jesus then told a parable, which He explained. The leaders were like a son who professes obedience but in practice will not do what the father has asked. Even when the leaders saw sinners respond and change their ways (the disobedient son in the parable later repented and chose to do his father's will), still the leaders did not respond.

They were untouched by the evidence of transformed lives, because they did not, in fact, care about people or about their relationship with God.

The desire for personal power (Matt. 21:33-46). What then *did* the leaders care about? Jesus launched into another parable, about an owner who leased his vineyard to tenants. They were to care for it and then give the owner his share of the profits. When messengers were sent to the tenants, they beat and stoned and killed them. Finally the owner sent his own son. The tenants' reaction? "Come, let's kill him *and take his inheritance!*" (v. 38)

Again the parable was devastatingly clear. The Old Testament speaks often of Israel as

God's vineyard (cf. Isa. 5:1-7). The servants God sent were the prophets, which earlier generations had rejected and often killed. Now, in Jesus, the Son had come. And the reaction of the rulers had been to plot to kill Him!

The Jewish leaders might speak of their pure and holy reverence for God and His Law. But, in fact, their motive was one of lust for personal power. That passion would not permit them to take their place with God's other little ones.

And so Jesus pronounced judgment. "I tell you that the kingdom of God will be taken away from you and given to a people who will produce its fruit" (Matt. 21:43).

Pretentions withered (Matt. 22:1-14). Before this scornful exposé, all the pretentions of the Pharisees withered, just as had the leaves of the fig tree. Looking ahead to the day when Jesus will come into His kingdom, Jesus used the common picture of a marriage feast (cf. Rev. 19:7). Those who were invited have refused to come. They will be replaced by others, both bad and good, who do respond to the King's call. As was the custom, those coming are to be provided with a wedding garment by the Father. Anyone seeking to "crash" this feast will be recognized immediately; his own clothes will not be acceptable. And he will be cast "into the darkness" (Matt. 22:13).

♥ ***Link to Life: Youth / Adult***
In a minilecture cover the parables in Matthew 21, and show just how they expose the religious leaders of Jesus' time.

Each of these has a single major point; explain that point clearly.

But the Parable of the Wedding Feast with which this sequence culminates makes more than one point! Have teams of three or four read Matthew 22:1-14, and jot down all *the points Jesus seems to be making.*

Counterattack: Matthew 22:15-46

The religious leaders were desperate now. And they were afraid of the reaction of the people against them if they took direct action against Jesus (21:46). So they determined to try to entangle Jesus in a way that might weaken His popularity.

The Pharisees (Matt. 22:15-22). The strength of the Pharisees was their complete commitment to the Law, and their rejection of all that was Gentile and foreign. The Greek culture which influenced the Sadducee party was totally rejected by the Pharisees, who had a reputation with the people for standing firm for Jewish ways. So a delegation of Pharisees approached Jesus, hoping to trap Him.

"Tell us then," they asked. "Is it right to pay taxes to Caesar or not?" (v. 17)

The Pharisees must have been very pleased at their cleverness. If Jesus directed them *not* to pay taxes, the Roman overseers could be informed and might take action. If Jesus said they *should* pay taxes, the Pharisees were sure He would lose popularity with the people. The insult of paying taxes to Rome through tax collectors, who normally took two or three times what was due, uniquely roused the hostility of the Jews.

Jesus asked His enemies for a coin. When the Pharisees gave a coin to Jesus, He asked them whose inscription and picture it bore. "Caesar's," the Pharisees said. "Give to Caesar what is Caesar's," Jesus responded, "and to God what is God's" (v. 21). Stunned, the Pharisees left Him and went away.

The Sadducees (Matt. 22:23-33). Sadducees have been mentioned earlier in Matthew. But we have not yet focused on them.

For about a hundred years, the Sadducees and the Pharisees were competing parties in Palestine. The word Sadducee seems to come from a root meaning "judge." They were, however, an aristocracy, which controlled the high priesthood and thus gained political power.

Like many an aristocracy, they were exclusive and proud. Theologically they were liberals who rejected the oral law exalted by the Pharisees, and who also rejected such doctrines as that of resurrection and angels. They were the kind of people who were tempted to adjust their views to the "modern" notions of the educated men of their world.

Though in conflict with the Pharisees, the Sadducees had to accommodate themselves to them because of the Pharisees' influence over the masses. But when Jesus appeared, these traditional enemies quickly arrived at a truce. Their mutual hatred and fear of Jesus brought them together.

Now the Sadducees raised one of those hypocritical questions with which they had long taunted those who believed in resurrection. They spoke of a woman who had been successively married to seven brothers. "At the resurrection, whose wife will she be?" (v. 28) the Sadducees asked. Jesus' response was a rebuke, pointing out that these proud men were strangers both to the Scriptures and to God's power. In the resurrection, people will not marry. And as far as resurrection is concerned, the Scriptures reveal God as One who *is* (not *was*!) the God of Abraham, Isaac, and Jacob. God is God not of the dead, but the living.

The lawyer (Matt. 22:34-45). Once again the Pharisee party attempted to trap Jesus. This time a lawyer (one who was an expert in oral and written Law) asked Jesus to name the first and greatest commandment. Answering, Jesus then asked the Pharisees a question in return.

"What do you think about the Christ [Messiah]? Whose Son is He?" (v. 42) The Pharisees answered correctly: "David's." Then Jesus asked, "How is it then that David, speaking by the Spirit, calls Him 'Lord'?" (v. 43)

The point is, of course, that no human father calls his son Lord, for in the culture of the Middle East the son always owed deference and respect to his father. David's descendant is more than human. He is, in fact, as the Old Testament foretells, the Son of God. Only if David's "son" is his God does David's acknowledgment of Him as Lord make sense.

The Pharisees were unable to utter a single word. They simply went away, and no one dared to challenge Jesus to a debate again.

The Scribes and Pharisees Denounced: Matthew 23

Then, in one of the most scathing indictments imaginable, Jesus cataloged the faults of the Pharisees—faults of which all of us must be wary; particularly those who stand in places of spiritual leadership.

What was wrong with Phariseeism?

- They preached, but did not practice (v. 3).
- They acted only to be seen and admired by others, not to please God (v. 5).
- They were proud, seeking to be prominent and exalted over others (vv. 6-9). Because they rejected servanthood and humility, they were themselves rejected by God (vv. 10-12).
- They were hypocrites who neither responded to God nor let others respond (vv. 13-15).
- They were blind guides who played with man-made rules and missed the great realities of faith (vv. 16-22).
- They were hypocrites who made a great to-do over strict tithing of the leaves of tiny herbs like mint and dill, but who neglected great matters like justice and mercy (vv. 23-24).
- They were hypocrites who focused on outward appearances, when within they were filled with greed and pride (vv. 25-27).
- They were just like their fathers (e.g., predecessors) who, when they had authority, killed the prophets and wise men God sent to Israel. In this generation's rejection of Jesus, the blood guilt of the ages was coming to rest on them (vv. 28-36).

Yet, against the background of this indictment, we see one last touching portrait of Jesus. As He condemned these hypocrites, His heart broke for them and for the crowds who would soon scream for His death.

In anguish, Jesus cried out:

> O Jerusalem, Jerusalem, you who kill the prophets and stone those sent to you, how often have I longed to gather your children together, as a hen gathers her chicks under her wings, but you were not willing. Look, your house is left to you desolate. For I tell you, you will not see Me again until you say, "Blessed is He who comes in the name of the Lord."
>
> Matthew 23:37-39

♥ ***Link to Life: Youth / Adult***

What is a "hypocrite"? The Greek word denotes someone acting out a part in a play. In Greek drama the actors held masks over their faces. Each mask was painted to represent the character the actor played. In real life, a "hypocrite" is a person who masks his real self, while he plays a part for his audience.

Have your group members read Matthew 23 individually. Each is to describe the actions and motives of a religious hypocrite. *Discuss: "How can we recognize hypocrisy in ourselves? In others?"*

TEACHING GUIDE

Prepare
If you had observed Jesus during the days reported in Matthew 21–23, what words or incident would have most impressed you? Why?

Explore
1. As your group members enter, have on the chalkboard: "When do you think Christians have the right or obligation to be bold in confronting others?" Discuss briefly before moving to explore Jesus' confrontation of the religious leaders of His day.
2. Read together the Triumphal Entry passage (Matt. 21:1-14). Then look up Old Testament prophecies which focus on this event, to see what added insights your group might gain into the significance of this event. The passages are listed in "link-to-life," page 579.

Expand
1. Summarize the incidents reported in Matthew 21:18-46, and explain the single point each makes. Then have teams study the Parable of the Wedding Banquet (22:1-14), which makes several points. Each team should try to find many different points which Jesus makes here. See "link-to-life," page 580.
2. Or explain the background of the word "hypocrite," and work with your group to discover the characteristics of religious hypocrisy as demonstrated in the Pharisees and other leaders of Jesus' time.
3. Or from Matthew 23 develop a set of 10 positive commands for Christian leaders. (Note that the points Jesus makes *against* the Pharisees can be reversed to become positive guidelines.)

Apply
Share: "Which of the positive commands the group developed from Matthew 23 seem most important to you personally? Why?"

STUDY GUIDE 90

Matthew 24–25

THE FUTURE OF THE KINGDOM

Overview

Much of the Old Testament speaks about what will happen in the future. And much of that prophecy focuses on a promised kingdom, over which God rules. Jesus also spoke about that coming kingdom, and His words are reported in the Gospels.

Christians do differ on how to interpret the Bible's prophetic portions. But in Matthew 24 and 25 we have several clues. First, Jesus was asked—and answered—several specific questions about what is to come. Second, Jesus referred to events foretold by the Old Testament prophets to explain His answers. In view of this and other features of the passage, it seems best to take Jesus' words in their plain sense. The message will not always be clear, but what Jesus said is not to be taken as symbolic of this Church Age. Here Jesus was answering the one question that Matthew's Jewish readers felt must be addressed.

What *has* happened to the kingdom of which the Old Testament speaks?

▶ ***Daniel.*** Jesus referred in this passage to the prophecies about the future found in Daniel. Daniel's prophecy is unusual because it predicts the very day that Messiah will triumphantly enter Jerusalem and also predicts an unexpected "cutting off" of Messiah—and a gap between His appearance and establishment of the kingdom.

Commentary

Many people have enjoyed playing games with the Bible, raising all sorts of objections and pointing out all sorts of supposed errors. The foolish raise silly objections that can be easily answered: Where did Cain get his wife? Doesn't the Bible say the earth is flat? How can you believe the Bible since it talks about the sun going around the earth?

This kind of superficial objection is easily explained, particularly as the queries are obviously raised by people who know nothing about the Bible. Any serious student of Scripture can raise far more basic and difficult issues. Without a doubt, one of the most difficult is this: What happened to the prophesied Old Testament kingdom? If God did not keep His word about establishing that kingdom, how can we trust anything in the Word?

The question troubled the disciples. Jesus had told them He was approaching a Cross, not a crown. They could not grasp what was happening. They were sure God's Word is trustworthy, but not at all sure how He would keep His promises if He, the King, were to die.

This concern of the Twelve surfaced as Jesus led them away from the temple after announcing judgment on the Pharisees. Glancing at the towering temple building, Jesus remarked that each stone of the temple would be thrown down, and "not one stone here will be left on another" (Matt. 24:2). This destruction was accomplished four decades later in A.D. 70 by a Roman army under Titus, a general who would later become emperor.

That evening the disciples came to ask Jesus about the future, about that time when Christ would come again and the age would close. In answering them, Jesus gives us our answers as well.

The Future

The Bible speaks a great deal in both Old and New Testaments about the future. Some "prophecy" in both Testaments involves forthtelling: communicating a message from God. But most prophecy involves foretelling which involves telling what will happen *before the historical events occur*.

Foretelling may involve either near events or events that are far distant to the prophet's day. Thus, Jeremiah spoke both of the death of a false prophet, Hananiah (Jer. 28), to take place within one year, and of a New Covenant to be made with the house of Israel which was actually ratified hundreds of years later by Christ at Calvary (Jer. 31).

Prophecy's promise. What is important to note, however, is that in prophecy the *time elements and sequences* are seldom clear. This was Peter's point in 1 Peter 1:10-11, when he noted that the prophets themselves puzzled over "the time and circumstances" the Spirit who inspired their words intended. The prophets had insights into the foretold events, but they could not fit them together.

This is a very important thing to remember when we study prophecy. We do not really know the time when prophesied events will happen, or even the exact sequences. Thus, it is always dangerous to attempt to erect tight prophetic systems in which we confidently sequence the future according to clues provided in the Word. Prophecy is not designed to give us a "future-history book" which can be written before the events. While we do know the broad outlines of the future from Scripture, we can never be too sure about the systems we construct from them.

As a matter of fact, an approach to prophetic studies which majors on constructing systems misses something basic about Bible prophecy. Bible prophecy is meant to have an impact on the present. Prophecy is designed to have a penetrating impact on our lives and values now. Thus, when Peter spoke of the fact that our present universe will one day be dissolved in fervent heat, he did so to challenge values: "Seeing then that all these things shall be dissolved, what manner of persons ought ye to be?" (2 Peter 3:11, KJV) When Paul spoke so beautifully of the Rapture in Thessalonians, it is not so that you and I might argue over whether it comes in the middle or at the beginning of the Tribulation. It is so that we might "encourage each other" (1 Thes. 4:18) with the realization that when Jesus comes, all believers will be together in Him. The dead we mourn will be our eternal companions. When John spoke of Jesus' return it was not to locate it in relation to Daniel's seventieth week, but to help us realize that "when He shall appear, we shall be like Him; for we shall see Him as He is" (1 John 3:2-3, KJV).

Thus, when we come to a study of the future in any part of the Bible we want to be careful to resist the temptation to speculate on details, and instead seek to discern the major emphasis of the passage. We need to keep the *purpose* of the prophetic passage in clear view.

Relationship between Old Testament and New Testament prophecy. When looking at New Testament prophecy, and particularly at prophetic segments of the Gospels, it is important to be very clear about the relationship between events foretold in the two Testaments.

First, we need to remember that there is full harmony between the Old Testament and the New Testament in prophecy, as in all things. The New Testament does not replace the Old. Thus, we have Christ's own affirmation in Matthew's Gospel that the kingdom, expected on the basis of the Old Testament, *will* come. "I tell you the truth, at the renewal of all things, when the Son of man sits on His throne, you who have followed Me will also sit on twelve thrones, judging the twelve tribes of Israel" (Matt. 19:28). Matthew 24:15 confirms that the future foretold by Daniel and associated with setting up the "everlasting kingdom" will come to pass. There is no doubt that Jesus expected, and promised, a time "when the Son of man comes in His glory, and all the angels with Him, He will sit on His throne in heavenly glory" (25:31)

The glorious kingdom of the Old Testament, expected by Israel and by the disciples themselves, *will surely come*.

Second, since the New Testament does not supercede or replace the Old, we can accept the broad outline of the future developed in the Old Testament as the basic framework within which to understand the teachings of the New. God has not gone back on His Word. Instead, He has demonstrated a greater complexity and variety to His eternal plans and purposes than were earlier revealed.

God's prophetic plan for the "time of the end" as given in the Old Testament involves:

- nations of the earth divided into power blocks.
- the Western power block headed by the Antichrist.
- increasing tension over the Middle East, leading to a treaty in which the Western powers guarantee the integrity of the Jewish state.

- increasing worldwide troubles and disasters, gradually intensifying.
- tremendous tribulation for Israel, involving persecution by the Western powers and finally invasion and desolation by the Northern.
- personal coming and intervention of Christ, the Messiah, who will defeat Israel's enemies and set up a righteous kingdom worldwide.

It is helpful as we read Christ's portrait of the future in Matthew to remember this outline, and to notice that Jesus is clearly speaking within that Old Testament framework.

Third, we want to note that the New Testament provides not a revision of God's plan but rather an addition to it. This, of course, was the point of Jesus' quote of Psalm 78:2 in Matthew 13:35: "I will utter things hidden since the Creation of the world." This is also what Paul was referring to in Colossians where he spoke of himself as a minister charged with making fully known "the mystery that has been kept hidden for ages and generations, but is now disclosed to the saints" (Col. 1:26).

In short, then, the answer to the question of, "What has happened to the kingdom?" is, "Nothing!" It is still coming.

The Old Testament speaks of both a suffering and a reigning Messiah, but makes no clear time distinctions. The whole intervening age between the Messiah's resurrection and return is not a subject of Old Testament prophecy, but a new dimension of God's eternal plan introduced by Jesus during His lifetime as the "unexpected form of the kingdom." It is the Age of the Church.

With this background, we can go back to look at Matthew 24 and 25. We realize immediately that the questions which stimulated this discourse were asked from an Old Testament frame of reference. Matthew 24 and 25 are, in fact, Jesus' affirmation that the glorious kingdom which Israel expected will surely come. If we understand the content of Old Testament prophecy, we have no doubts about the meaning and impact of Jesus' words here.

Jesus' Words of Prophecy: Matthew 24:1–25:30

These chapters contain Jesus' answers to three questions posed by His disciples. "Tell us," they asked, "[1] when will this happen, and [2] what will be the sign of Your coming and [3] of the end of the age?" (24:3) The questions were answered, but in reverse order.

Signs of the end of the age (Matt. 24:4-26). The picture given in this section of Matthew 24 is of a time of increasing tension, disaster, and disturbance. Wars and rumors of wars, earthquakes, increasing wickedness, and persecution of Jesus' followers are all involved.

None of these is in itself striking: there have always been wars, and earthquakes often dot the news with tragedy. But there are aspects of this picture which make it the description of a unique time which is the subject of much Old Testament prophecy.

- The common disasters were identified by Jesus as "the beginning of birth pains" (v. 8).
- Events Jesus spoke of are identified in the Old Testament Book of Daniel as taking place in the seven-year period just before the Messiah will establish His earthly kingdom (v. 15).
- The Tribulation which is said to come then will be a "great distress, unequaled from the beginning of the world until now and never to be equaled again" (v. 21).

In the Old Testament this time of worldwide trouble is given various names: "the time of Jacob's trouble," "that day," "the Day of the Lord," and "the Tribulation." Against this Old Testament background, the disciples would quickly identify the time of which Jesus spoke.

What will be the sign of Your coming? (Matt. 24:27-31) Jesus' answer to this question was far less specific. There is, in fact, no single "sign" identified. Yet, several striking characteristics of Jesus' return are given.

First, Jesus' coming will be visible, seen as clearly as spectacular lightning from horizon to horizon (v. 27). That visible appearance will follow immediately after the Tribulation, and will be accompanied by great and dramatic physical disturbances in the heavens. There will be an unidentified "sign" in the heavens, with deep mourning as the Son is seen to return in power and great glory (v. 30). Jesus' coming will initiate an angelic regathering of His elect (for this Old Testa-

Matthew's Teaching on the Kingdom

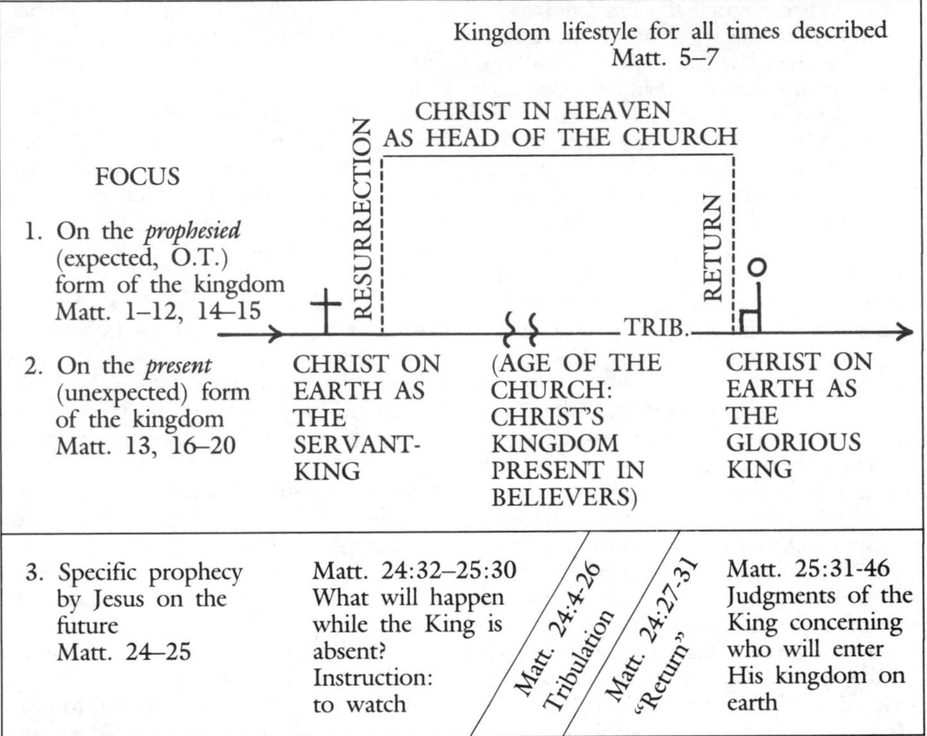

ment context, see Isa. 27:13; Zech. 9:14).

When will this be? (Matt. 24:32–25:30). Jesus answered this third question exhaustively. But only after saying, "No one knows about that day or hour, not even the angels in heaven, nor the Son, but only the Father" (24:36).

Nevertheless, it is this question Jesus chose to explore in greatest depth. It is the answer to this question which has the most significance for the disciples and for us.

This generation will certainly not pass away (Matt. 24:32-35). The Tribulation events previously described are like buds on a tree before the leaves come. The bud is evidence that the time of flowering is near. But one thing Jesus promised: "This generation will certainly not pass away" (v. 34) till all He has spoken of comes to pass.

What "generation" is Jesus speaking of? The term used here does not indicate people alive at that day, but Israel as a race. (Some interpret it to mean the living generation actually undergoing the Tribulation time.) By either interpretation this was Jesus' promise of preservation. The time of trouble will not be the end of the Jewish people or of mankind.

What then did Jesus say about the time of His coming, and the time *until* His coming?

Watch for His coming (Matt. 24:36-44). As in Noah's day, before the Flood swept everything away, the people living in the day just before Jesus returns will be involved in their own affairs, blind to the significance of happenings around them.

Because the day when the Son will come is unexpected, we are to "watch." "So," Jesus said, "you must be ready, because the Son of man will come at an hour when you do not expect Him."

Responsible servants (Matt. 24:45-51). What is to be done by servants who are looking for the Lord's return? They are to remember they have been given responsibility in their Master's household.

The danger Jesus warned against is a real one. He said, "But suppose that servant is wicked and says to himself, 'My master is staying away a long time.' . . . The master . . . will come . . . when he does not expect him" (vv. 48-50). Faithfulness involves taking proper care of God's household, knowing that the Lord will appear at an unexpected time.

The ten maidens (Matt. 25:1-13). This is the well-known story of the 10 maidens who took lamps and went to meet the bridegroom who was coming for his bride. Unprepared for a long wait, 5 ran out of oil when the bridegroom was delayed.

Again, Jesus warned, "Watch, because you do not know the day or the hour" (v. 13).

The talents (Matt. 25:14-30). The Parable of the Talents again emphasizes the same elements. A lord leaves on a journey, making his servants responsible for his possessions. While he is away, the servants are to use the gifts they have been given for the benefit of their master. One day the master will return, and then there will be an accounting.

Each of these stories drives home an important point: What God has promised will come to pass. But our time is not to be spent dreaming of that future day. It is to be spent in the service of our absent Lord who has entrusted His possessions to us. Christ the King has entrusted to us this unexpected and unprophesied form of His kingdom.

Being ready for His coming means being involved as servants in the ongoing ministries committed to us by our Lord.

The Gathering of the Nations: Matthew 25:31-46

Then Jesus turned again to His second coming. "When the Son of man comes in His glory, and all the angels with Him, He will sit on His throne in heavenly glory" (v. 31). Christ went on to discuss the ministry of judgment He will undertake at that day. Again in the Old Testament, roots of the picture He sketched are clear. Christ looked ahead to describe a prophesied time when all the nations on the earth will be gathered before Him.

The peoples of the world will be separated into two groups, one destined to enter the kingdom over which the Messiah will rule. The term "nations" here does not refer to national groups but to the Gentile world in contrast to "brothers of Mine." These Jewish brothers, who will have suffered in the Tribulation, will have been naked, hungry, thirsty, imprisoned, and sick. And some will have reached out to them, while others ignore them.

This passage does not picture the time of final judgment. Instead, as the text indicates, judgment is announced for a generation of men living at Jesus' coming. The prize is not eternal life, but entrance into the kingdom that God has prepared for Gentiles as well as for believing Israel (v. 34).

The Old Testament picture of the future is *not* wrong, for the promised kingdom will come when the King returns. And we can leave the details of that time to God.

There is for us a different focus in life. You and I expect His return, and so we wholeheartedly serve Him. We minister as servants in a household which He has left with us, until He comes to take up His throne.

TEACHING GUIDE

Prepare

Remember that in the text, 37 verses contain Jesus' prophetic utterances—while 55 verses are given to His exhortations on how to live until the time of return comes.

Explore

1. Give a minilecture orienting your group members to aspects of Bible prophecy explained in this study guide. You may also check the *index* for the source of additional material on interpreting Bible prophecy.
2. Or use the chart in this study guide to summarize the picture of the future expressed both in Old Testament prophecy and by Jesus here in Matthew 24.

Expand

It is clear that most of this section of Matthew concerns a time when the King is absent. Jesus obviously focuses our attention, in a series of stories, on what is to happen during this period of time (Matt. 24:32–25:30).

What is most important to Jesus is not that we know the prophetic timetable, but that we understand how we are to live while we are waiting for Jesus to come back.

List common elements in each of Jesus' stories on a chalkboard:

- the key figure is absent.
- the time of his return is uncertain.
- servants are responsible for the absentee's possessions.
- there is an emphasis on watching.
- servants are to be evaluated for what they do while the key figure is gone.

Divide your group into teams, giving each one story to examine. Each should look at each of these aspects, and see what specific lesson Jesus seems to be communicating to us today.

When each team has drawn all the lessons it can from its passage, come together and share findings.

Apply

Discuss: "What specifically can I do to please Jesus while we await His return?"

STUDY GUIDE 91

Matthew 26–27

JESUS' TRIAL AND DEATH

Overview

Each of the Gospel writers speaks in detail of the last few days of Jesus' life. The Cross, with the Resurrection which followed, is clearly the focus of the Gospel story.

Each of the Gospel writers adds details not included by the others. By studying the four accounts, we can know what happened almost hour by hour.

For instance, we know that Jesus had not just one trial, but six! He was taken from court to court, examined (at times in actual violation of Jewish Law), and shunted off to another jurisdiction. Finally He was condemned by Pilate, the Roman governor, who alone had authority to pronounce the death sentence.

Jesus' religious trials

Before Annas	John 18:12-14
Before Caiaphas	Matthew 26:57-68
Before the Sanhedrin	Matthew 27:1-2

Jesus' civil trials

Before Pilate	Luke 27:66–23:7
Before Herod	Luke 23:8-12
Before Pilate	Luke 23:13-25

While the Gospels tell the story of Jesus' death, we need to look to the Old Testament and to the Epistles to explain its meaning. How good to lead our group to sense once again the wonder of what Jesus did on Calvary for you and me. How great the price of our salvation.

Commentary

If Jesus' prophetic picture of the kingdom's future has its roots in the Old Testament, what is about to happen has even deeper roots. All of revelation focuses on the events of the next few days: Millennia and centuries of time strain forward to it, while additional millennia and centuries find meaning by looking back to it.

Matthew puts it in perspective as he gives us Jesus' words: "As you know, the Passover is two days away" (Matt. 26:2).

Passover

The Passover marked the Jewish new year: it was the time of beginnings for Israel. The annual festival recalled a historic event which marked a true spiritual beginning for God's Old Testament people.

Exodus 11 and 12 record the story. Great plagues had ruined the land of Egypt in Moses' day, but they had failed to move Egypt's ruler to let Israel, then a slave race, go. God then determined a final judgment. But He instructed each Hebrew family to select a lamb, to be kept in the home for four days. On the fourth day the lamb was to be killed, and its blood sprinkled on the doorposts and lintel of each Jewish home. The lamb itself was to be roasted and eaten.

The night this happened, God's death angel swept through the land of Egypt. Each home unprotected by the blood of the lamb suffered the loss of its firstborn son. But the homes marked out by the blood of the Passover lamb were safe.

Impelled by the horror of the multiple deaths, Pharaoh released the Jews. Israel had been redeemed by death from slavery, to fulfill its destiny as the people of God.

And God commanded the Jews, each year after this event, to commemorate it by reenactment. Fresh lambs were slain, fresh blood sprinkled, and each generation was taught again the lesson that freedom could come only through the shedding of the blood of the lamb.

This Passover. This Passover, Jesus was about to fulfill the deepest meaning of the Old Testament celebration rite. Passover not only looked back to the Exodus; it looked forward to the Cross. "The Passover is two days away," Jesus said, "and the Son of man will be handed over to be crucified" (Matt. 26:2).

John the Baptist had foreseen it that day back at the River Jordan. "Look," he said, "the Lamb of God, who takes away the sin of the world!" (John 1:29) For three to four years after this Jesus had been among the Jewish people, teaching, healing, caring. But then, when Passover came, like the lambs that represented Him, Jesus had to die. He had to die that through His death those who sprinkle His blood by faith on the doorposts of their hearts might know the ultimate freedom. Through the blood of Christ we are freed from sin and from sin's power—freed even from the fear of death.

The culminating act of service and self-giving had been clearly taught in the Old Testament, even apart from the Passover symbolism. We see it, for instance, in Isaiah 53. The death of Christ and its meaning are so clearly portrayed in this passage that we can hardly believe we are reading words penned over 600 years before Jesus' birth!

> He grew up before Him like a tender shoot, and like a root out of dry ground. He had no beauty or majesty to attract us to Him, nothing in His appearance that we should desire Him. He was despised and rejected by men, a Man of sorrows, and familiar with suffering. Like one from whom men hide their faces He was despised, and we esteemed Him not. Surely He took up our infirmities and carried our sorrows, yet we considered Him stricken by God, smitten by Him, and afflicted. But He was pierced for our transgressions, He was crushed for our iniquities; the punishment that brought us peace was upon Him, and by His wounds we are healed. We all, like sheep, have gone astray, each of us has turned to his own way; and the Lord has laid on Him the iniquity of us all. He was oppressed and afflicted, yet He did not open His mouth; He was led like a lamb to the slaughter, and as a sheep before her shearers is silent so He did not open His mouth. By oppression and judgment He was taken away. And who can speak of His descendants? For He was cut off from the land of the living; for the transgression of My people He was stricken. He was assigned a grave with the wicked, and with the rich in His death, though He had done no violence, nor was any deceit in His mouth. Yet it was the Lord's will to crush Him and cause Him to suffer, and though the Lord makes His life a guilt offering, He will see His offspring and prolong His days, and the will of the Lord will prosper in His hand. After the suffering of His soul, He will see the light of life and be satisfied; by His knowledge My righteous Servant will justify many, and He will bear their iniquities. Therefore I will give Him a portion among the great, and He will divide the spoils with the strong, because He poured out His life unto death, and was numbered with the transgressors. For He bore the sin of many, and made intercession for the transgressors.
>
> Isaiah 53:2-12

The Last Days: Matthew 26–27

The culminating events occurred with tragic swiftness. Matthew describes them.

Jesus was anointed with expensive ointment, an act symbolic of preparation for burial (26:6). Judas slipped away to make an arrangement with the chief priests to betray Jesus to them when the crowds were not present. He settled on a price: 30 pieces of silver (vv. 14-16).

When morning came, Jesus sent His disciples to arrange a hall where they would eat the Passover meal together (vv. 17-19). That night, after the meal and before the discourse recorded in John 13–16, Judas left again to finalize plans for Jesus' betrayal (Matt. 26:20-29).

On the way out of Jerusalem, Jesus told the disciples that they would all flee and leave Him to face His fate alone. Peter led a chorus of objectors: no, all would die with Him before they would desert Him! (vv. 30-35)

Arriving at a garden called Gethsemane, Jesus asked His disciples to wait as He went aside to pray. This deeply moving prayer, in which Jesus expressed the agony He felt approaching the Cross, is recorded for us by Matthew (vv. 36-39). But the disciples were too tired to be moved. They drifted off to sleep.

Christ, feeling the utter loneliness of the condemned, urged them to stay awake to watch with Him. But again they dozed off as Christ returned to prayer (vv. 40-46).

Then the light of flickering torches was seen, and sounds of an armed mob was heard. Led by Judas, the mob hung back until he advanced to identify Jesus with a kiss (vv. 45-50). Immediately the crowd surged forward, and servants of the priests roughly pinned Jesus' arms behind Him!

Bravely, Peter drew a sword and struck out! "Put it away," Jesus told him. If Christ had intended to resist, angel armies could have been summoned. "But how then would the Scriptures be fulfilled that say it must happen in this way?" (v. 54) When Jesus turned to face the mob, the disciples scattered (vv. 51-56).

Then began the long night of trials. Jesus was taken first to the high priest's home, where the council was gathered to try Him at night (an illegal act under Jewish Law). Witnesses were brought forward to accuse Him, but even their lies could not raise an issue meriting death. Finally the high priest asked Jesus directly: "Tell us if You are the Christ, the Son of God" (v. 63). Christ answered: "Yes, it is as you say. But I say to all of you: In the future you will see the Son of man sitting at the right hand of the Mighty One and coming on the clouds of heaven" (v. 64). The high priest rightly recognized this as an affirmation by Jesus of Deity, at which he cried out, "Blasphemy!" And blasphemy is a crime for which the Old Testament prescribes death (vv. 57-65).

The court then passed its judgment. "He is worthy of death" (v. 66). Immediately they began to treat Jesus as a convicted felon, slapping Him and spitting on Him and mocking Him (vv. 66-68).

Meanwhile, Peter was sitting outside the high priest's house. Peter had run. But he still had enough courage to trail the crowd that guarded Jesus. Yet, when Peter was accused by a serving maid and then other bystanders of being a follower of Jesus, Peter denied it with a curse! Then a cock crowed, and Peter remembered that when Jesus told the disciples they would scatter, Christ had also told Peter that he would deny the Lord three times before morning. Sobbing uncontrollably, Peter stumbled away into the dawn (vv. 69-75).

Back inside, the rulers of the Jews had a problem. The Romans ruled Palestine. While the Jews had a large measure of self-government, they did not have the authority to execute. So the leaders packed Jesus off to Pilate, the Roman governor.

Meanwhile, Judas had discovered that Christ was actually condemned to death! Hurrying back to the temple priests, Judas returned the 30 pieces of silver, and wailed, "I have sinned, for I have betrayed innocent blood" (27:4). Unmoved, these men whose office made them mediators between sinners and God, coldly replied, "What is that to us? That's your responsibility" (v. 4). Throwing down the money, Judas rushed out—and hanged himself. And the priests, ever careful to keep the letter of the Law whose spirit and intent they daily distorted, argued over the blood money which it was not "lawful" to put back into the temple treasury! At last they decided to use the money to buy a burial ground for indigents (vv. 3-10).

Jesus then stood before the Roman governor. There He admitted that He was indeed King of the Jews. Beyond this, Jesus refused to defend Himself (vv. 11-14).

Pilate was clearly unhappy with the situation. Even while sitting on his judgment seat, a messenger from Pilate's wife arrived, told Pilate of a dream she had had, and warned Pilate to have nothing to do with "that innocent man" (v. 19). Squirming, Pilate offered the crowd, which had by then gathered, a choice. He would release Jesus or Barabbas, a murderer who was also sentenced to death. And the crowd, urged on by the leaders, shouted out that Barabbas should be freed. As for Jesus, "Crucify Him!" (v. 22)

Pilate tried to reason with the mob. But their only response was to chant, repeating over and over again with bestial rhythm, "Crucify Him!"

Overwhelmed by the passion of the mob, Pilate feared a riot. Historic research suggests that Pilate held his post due to the influence of a man who had recently been executed in Rome. Terrified that the Jews would now accuse him of supporting some other "king" than Caesar, Pilate permitted Jesus' execution. And the Jews accepted the implications of Pilate's symbolic hand-washing: "His blood be on us and on our children" (v. 25).

Then Pilate released Barabbas, and turned Jesus over to the soldiers to be beaten and mocked in preparation for His execution (v. 26-31).

On the way out of the city to the killing

grounds, Jesus stumbled and fell under the weight of His cross. A visitor to the city, Simon, was pulled from the crowd by the soldiers and made to carry it for Him.

At the place of execution, called Golgotha, a sign was nailed to the cross, reading THIS IS JESUS, THE KING OF THE JEWS (v. 37). When all was ready, Jesus refused a drugged drink designed to lessen the pain. Prostrate on the wooden post, spikes were driven through His living flesh. Then, with a tearing jolt, the pole was lifted—hung poised—and dropped into the hole prepared to receive it.

Jesus, King of the Jews, hung outlined against the sky, flanked by two dying criminals.

Jesus, who walked the lanes of Palestine to heal the sick and feed the hungry, to free men and women tormented in the grip of demons, was hanging in suspended agony as passersby paused to watch—and ridicule (vv. 32-44).

Suddenly, about noon, grim darkness blotted out the sun. A hush fell. Near three in the afternoon the figure on the cross convulsed, and cried out: "My God, My God, why have You forsaken Me?" (v. 46) "What's happening?" the watchers whispered to each other. One ran to Him, to again offer Him the drug. Others held back. "Leave Him alone. Let's see if Elijah comes to save Him." Ghoulishly curious, strangely uninvolved, they watched as the drama unfolded.

Then came another cry from the cross—a cry like a triumphant shout. The figure jerked—then slumped in relaxation against the brutal metal restraints. Finished with His work, Jesus had dismissed His spirit (vv. 45-50).

♥ ***Link to Life: Youth / Adult***
Help your group experience the events at Calvary in a totally new way. Give each an 8½ x 11 sheet of paper, containing a sketch of Calvary hill with the three crosses. Have pairs read Matthew 27:32-56. Each pair is (1) to identify the individuals and groups who witnessed the Crucifixion, and (2) to locate them on the hill, according to their relative distance from Jesus.

When this is done, ask each person to meditate for a moment on which of the witnesses he or she feels was most like him or her. Then, ask each to speak as that person, *telling what he or she saw and how he or she felt.*

Move around the room, letting each person tell of the Crucifixion from the viewpoint of the person he or she chose.

The very moment Jesus died, the temple curtain, which cut off access to the holy of holies, was torn in two from top to bottom. An earthquake struck, rocks were ripped apart, old tombs opened, and dead men and women stood. Stunned and awestruck, the Roman officer in charge of the execution detail, blurted out, "Surely He was the Son of God!" (v. 54)

At evening Pilate received a rich man who asked for the privilege of burying Jesus' body. Gently, the servant King's form was laid to rest in a tomb hewn from rock. A great stone was rolled to block the door—and Jesus' sorrowing followers departed (vv. 57-61).

Unmoved by these events just as they had been unmoved by Christ's miracles, the leaders of the Jews hurried to Pilate. They told him of Jesus' talk of rising from the dead, and urged the Roman governor to place a military guard over the tomb to keep the disciples from stealing the body. Soldiers were assigned from troops detailed to the high priest's guard. The boulder was sealed, the guard set.

And the chief priests and Pharisees retired. Triumphant? Afraid? We do not know. But surely Jesus Himself was dead. There was nothing to do but wait.

And so, these men desperately believed, His story had at last come to a fitting end.

Why?

All Christians from the earliest days of the church have looked to Jesus' cross and resurrection as the central facts of the Christian faith, through which the incarnate God reconciled us to Himself. Peter, in his first sermon, said that this Jesus was "handed over to you by God's set purpose and foreknowledge"—and loosed from death because it was impossible for death to keep its hold on Him" (Acts 2:23-24). Only much later would this question be asked: "Why was Jesus' death essential in God's 'definite plan'?"

Atonement theories. One of the first theories advanced saw Jesus' death as a ransom price paid to the devil, in whose kingdom mankind lived enchained. But Christ died not to pay, but to "destroy him who holds the power of death—that is, the devil" (Heb. 2:14). Christ's death was no price paid to Satan but a battleground on which Satan met decisive defeat.

Anselm of Canterbury (A.D. eleventh/twelfth century) probed more deeply to explore why God's love is expressed through atonement. The *Zondervan Pictorial Encyclopedia of the Bible* (Tenney) summarizes Anselm's answer expressed in *Cur Deus Homo* (Why did God become man?):

> His answer was that though prompted by His love to redeem us, God must do so in a manner consistent with His justice. The necessity of the Atonement, then, is an inference from the character of God. Sin is a revolt against God and He must inevitably react against it with wrath. Sin creates an awful liability and the inexorable demands of the divine justice must be met. The truth that God is love does not stand alone in the Bible. The God of the Bible keeps wrath for His enemies (Nahum 1:2); He is "of purer eyes than to behold evil" (Hab. 1:13, KJV). The God of Jesus is to be feared as One "who can destroy both soul and body in hell" (Matt. 10:28). "The wrath of God," Paul wrote, "is being revealed from heaven against all the godlessness and wickedness of men" (Rom. 1:18).
>
> Therefore the death of Christ is the way in which God shows that He is righteous in forgiving sins and justifying him who has faith in Jesus (Rom. 3:24-26). God justly demands satisfaction for one's sins, and since by Christ's death satisfaction is given, the sinner is forgiven and punishment remitted.

Anselm's theory, of vicarious or substitutionary Atonement, has dominated orthodox tradition. Christ's death is seen as *for* us, and *in our place*.

A third theory, which has characterized liberal Protestantism, is the "moral influence" theory. This also has its roots in the eleventh and twelfth centuries. According to this theory, Jesus' death demonstrates God's forgiving love, and stirs up a responding love in men, which leads them to repent of their sins.

Scripture's testimony. Scripture itself speaks with a clear and unmistakable voice about the death of Christ and its meaning. It is so clear that "Atonement theories" hardly seem needed: the Word is explicit.

> In fact, the Law requires that nearly everything be cleansed with blood, and without the shedding of blood there is no forgiveness.
>
> Hebrews 9:22

> This Priest [Christ] . . . offered for all time one sacrifice for sins. . . . Because by one sacrifice He has made perfect forever those who are being made holy.
>
> Hebrews 10:12, 14

> [Jesus said,] "This is My blood of the covenant, which is poured out for many for the forgiveness of sins."
>
> Matthew 26:28

> God demonstrates His own love for us in this: While we were still sinners, Christ died for us. Since we have now been justified by His blood, how much more shall we be saved from God's wrath through Him!
>
> Romans 5:8-9

> God presented [Jesus] as a sacrifice of atonement, through faith in His blood. He did this to demonstrate His justice, because in His forbearance He had left the sins committed before unpunished—He did it to demonstrate His justice at the present time, so as to be just and the One who justifies the man who has faith in Jesus.
>
> Romans 3:25-26

> For God was pleased to have all His fullness dwell in [Jesus], and through Him to reconcile to Himself all things, whether things on earth or things in heaven, by making peace through His blood, shed on the cross. . . . But now He has reconciled you by Christ's physical body through death to present you holy in His sight, without blemish and free from accusation.
>
> Colossians 1:19-22

> But now in Christ Jesus you who once

> were far away have been brought near through the blood of Christ. For He Himself is our peace.
> Ephesians 2:13-14

> He Himself bore our sins in His body on the tree, so that we might die to sins and live for righteousness.
> 1 Peter 2:24

> To Him who loves us and has freed us from our sins by His blood.
> Revelation 1:5

> He died for all, that those who live should no longer live for themselves but for Him who died for them and was raised again. God . . . reconciled us to Himself through Christ . . . not counting men's sins against them.
> 2 Corinthians 5:15, 18-19

> God made Him who had no sin to be sin for us, so that in Him we might become the righteousness of God.
> 2 Corinthians 5:21

Bearing the full weight of our sin, and in our place, Jesus shed His blood. To set us free.

♥ ***Link to Life: Children***
Boys and girls can understand that Jesus has paid for our sins. Modern signs visualize what used to be spelled out. For instance, "no turns" is indicated by an arrow, set in a circle with a bar across it (see sketch). After telling about Jesus' death to take the punishment for our sins and save us from eternal death, have your boys and girls make up their own signs telling what Jesus has done for us.

First, on half a potato carve a cross so that it sticks out from the surface (see illustration). Have your boys and girls draw pictures in circles about the size of the potato to suggest punishment or death.

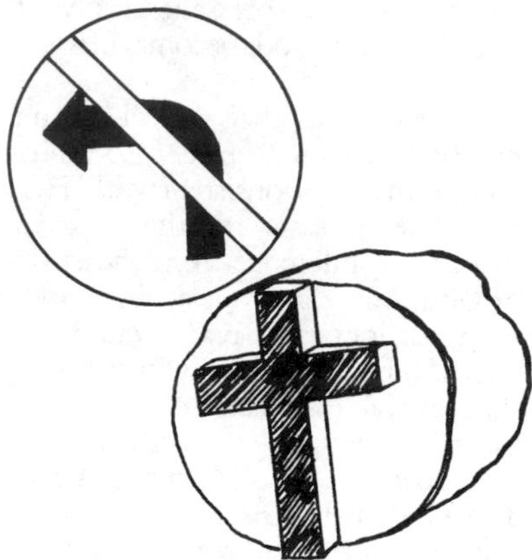

Then let each press the potato on a stamp pad, and stamp over the picture he has drawn. It is the cross that cancels our punishment and cancels the power of death. Because of Jesus, we are on the road to heaven and the good news is, "No punishment!" "No death!"

TEACHING GUIDE

Prepare
Read Matthew 26 and 27 as though hearing the story for the first time. How does the story make you feel?

Explore
Have pairs read the report of the events at Calvary. Use the identification activity explained in the "link-to-life," page 592 to help your group members enter into the Calvary events in a new way.

Expand
1. Sketch the three theories of the Atonement mentioned in this chapter. Then have your group members read through Isaiah 53 carefully. From this passage, what would you say in answer to Anselm's question, *Cur Deus Homo?*
2. Or have your group members use a concordance to look up verses like the ones quoted at the end of this study guide that tell of the meaning of Jesus' death. Use "blood" as the key word. From these verses, how would your group sum up the meaning of Jesus' death on the cross?

Apply
Pray together, expressing your praise and thanks to Jesus for His sacrifice, and for the forgiveness that death assures you and all who believe.

STUDY GUIDE 92

Matthew 28

ALIVE, FOREVERMORE

Overview

The resurrection of Jesus is one of the best attested events of history. What happened that Resurrection morning, and who saw our risen Lord?

Three women at tomb	Luke 23:55–24:9
Peter, John see empty tomb	John 20:3-10
The women see Jesus	Matt. 28:9-10
Peter sees Jesus same day	Luke 24:34
Two on Emmaus road	Luke 24:13-31
The Apostles, Thomas absent	Luke 24:36-45
The Apostles, Thomas present	John 20:24-29
Seven at Lake Tiberius	John 21:1-23
Five hundred in Galilee	1 Cor. 15:6
James in Jerusalem	1 Cor. 15:7
Many at Ascension	Acts 1:3-12
Paul near Damascus	Acts 9:3-6
Stephen at stoning	Acts 7:55
Paul in the temple	Acts 22:17-19
John on Patmos	Rev. 1:10-19

There were so many witnesses that even though Jesus' enemies started a rumor that Christ's body had been stolen, they could not stop the news of the Resurrection from sweeping the nation, and then the world.

Today we have nearly 2,000 years of church history to demonstrate the validity of our faith. The resurrected Jesus has proved His presence to His people in every age. But do the members of your group grasp just what the reality of Jesus' resurrection means to them, and to other Christians? That is the focus of this study of Matthew 28: the meaning of Resurrection, now.

Commentary

Enemies and friends of Jesus waited. On the third day after His execution, two Marys went to see the tomb. They were shocked to come to a deserted garden.

The guard the Jewish elders had posted was gone. The stone that had sealed the entrance of the tomb was rolled away. Sitting on it was an angel, whose appearance had jolted the guard to insensibility, and who now spoke to the women. "Do not be afraid, for I know that you are looking for Jesus, who was crucified. He is not here; He has risen, just as He said" (Matt. 28:5-6).

The Resurrection

The Resurrection was an unexpected event. Though the Lord had foretold His resurrection, the disciples were unprepared. They even found it hard to believe when the reports began to come in. During the 40 days that Jesus met with the disciples after the Resurrection, many proofs were given. Paul reports:

> For what I received I passed on to you as of first importance: that Christ died for our sins according to the Scriptures, that He was buried, that He was raised on the third day according to the Scriptures, and that He appeared to Peter, and then to the Twelve. After that, He appeared to more than 500 of the brothers at the same time, most of whom are still living, though some have fallen asleep. Then He appeared to James, then to all the Apostles, and last of all He appeared to me also, as to one abnormally born.
>
> 1 Corinthians 15:3-8

The resurrection of Christ is one of the most thoroughly attested facts of history, not only through the written documents of the Scriptures, but also by the transformation of the disciples. From a group of men cowering in a locked room for fear of the Jews (John 20:19), these men were transformed into bold and joyful witnesses of the resurrection of their Lord. The historical

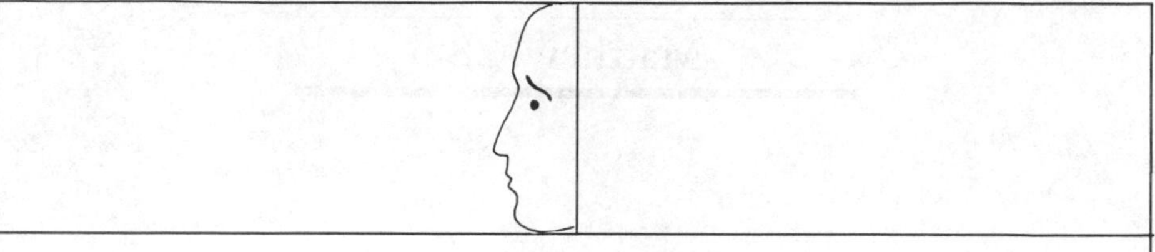

Resurrection means . . .

"If the Spirit of Him who raised Jesus from the dead is living in you, He who raised Christ from the dead will also give life [now!] to your mortal bodies through His Spirit, who lives in you" (Rom. 8:11).

So . . .

"Forgetting what is behind and straining toward what is ahead, I press on toward the goal to win the prize for which God has called me heavenward in Christ Jesus" (Phil. 3:13-14).

fact reported in Scripture, accepted by faith by believers, is a cornerstone of our faith.

Resurrection's place in the New Testament. The New Testament gives the resurrection of Jesus a central place. Each of the Gospels climaxes with a description of this great act of God. The earliest preaching of the Gospel takes the Resurrection as its keynote (cf. Acts 2–5; 7; 10). Paul in 1 Corinthians 15, argued that Christianity stands or falls with the Resurrection, the decisive turning point in mankind's history. Dying, Jesus won us forgiveness. Rising, He presents us with all the benefits of a renewed life (cf. Rom. 4:25; 5:9-10; 8:1-2; 1 Cor. 1:30).

♥ ***Link to Life: Youth / Adult***

Prepare a study sheet like the one illustrated above. When you pass it out, ask your group members to look back over their lives, and think of faults, failures, and sins that have defeated them. Then have them draw features on the backward-looking face at the top of the page, to show how they make them feel, and write one *emotion or feeling that such recollections cause them.*

Share the pictures drawn, and the feeling words each person has written.

Then look together at the verses on the page. Jesus' being raised to new life promises new power to us for our present (mortal) lives. So we can literally forget our past sins and failures, and set out to experience the new life Jesus gives us.

Ask each person to draw features on the lower *face, showing how it feels to have the promise of power for godly living. Have each jot down one area in his or her life in which newness is important.*

Resurrection's nature. Christ's resurrection was the resurrection of a real body of flesh. Jesus' followers recognized His face and voice (Matt. 28:9; Luke 24:31; John 20:16, 19-20; 21:12). His body was touched by them (Matt. 28:9; Luke 24:39; John 20:17, 27). He ate with them (Luke 24:30, 42-43; John 21:12-13). He Himself pointed out that "a ghost does not have flesh and bones, as you see I have" (Luke 24:39).

Yet His resurrection body showed a unique freedom from the limitations placed on us today. He appeared among them in a locked room (John 20:19), and vanished at will (Luke 24:31). He ascended into heaven before the disciples and many witnesses (Acts 1). Though made of flesh and bone, Jesus' resurrection body is called by Paul "spiritual"—not immaterial, but controlled by or responsive to the Spirit (1 Cor. 15:44). In 1 Corinthians 15, Paul described Christ's body as imperishable, glorious, powerful, incorruptible, immortal, and victorious. And we are promised that our resurrection state will be like His.

♥ ***Link to Life: Children***
Ask your boys and girls how they would tell if something they saw was a ghost. After they have listed characteristics, explain that at first some of the people who saw Jesus alive again after He was killed thought He was a ghost. Ask how the children would tell someone they saw was not *a ghost.*
Then go through the evidences in the Gospel: Jesus ate, prepared a meal for the disciples, could be touched by them, etc.

Matthew's Emphasis: Matthew 28:16-20
Each of the four Gospel writers gives extensive space to the Resurrection, and each has its own particular emphasis. Matthew's emphasis is in fullest harmony with the theme and thrust of his book. Jesus, the glorious King who lived as a servant, did establish a kingdom. Christ's last recorded words in Matthew echo the command of the King to the servants He leaves in charge of His possessions:

> All authority in heaven and on earth has been given to Me. Therefore go and make disciples of all nations, baptizing them in the name of the Father and of the Son and of the Holy Spirit, and teaching them to obey everything I have commanded you. And surely I will be with you always, to the very end of the age.
>
> Matthew 28:18-20

All authority. It's important to realize first of all that Jesus' kingdom does exist today. The fact that the Old Testament visible form of the kingdom has not yet been established in no way means that Jesus' power or authority over this earth are limited. The fact is that Jesus reigns now.

His kingdom exists alongside and within human cultures and societies, focused in the men and women in whom Jesus' Spirit dwells. His quiet, unobtrusive rule is nevertheless totally real. Nothing can happen in heaven or on earth except by His will.

Just as Jesus chose during His days on earth to give men freedom to respond to or to reject Him, the pattern of our world today shows a similar freedom. When Christ returns, His righteous ways will be *imposed.* Today, He permits men to choose. How tragic that most men choose the ways of sin. Even so, Jesus continues on the throne. And Jesus does intervene today on our behalf as we choose to live by His will.

♥ ***Link to Life: Children***
To "witness" is simply to give personal testimony. It is as we give testimony to Jesus that others, hearing of Him, make their own personal choice. So "making disciples" is not a process of forcing the Gospel on others. It is a process of sharing Good News in attractive, positive ways.
Help your boys and girls give a simple, positive witness to their friends and family, and so do their part even now to "make disciples." How? Cut crown-shaped badges from cardboard. On the base print "I choose." Then help your boys and girls cover the rest of the crown with bright, aluminum or metal foil. Tape a safety pin to the back of the crown so it can be worn on shirt or blouse.
Explain that the badge indicates "I choose King Jesus." If someone asks about the badge, a child can explain that Jesus died and came alive again, and He is both Saviour and Lord. The badge says that the child has chosen Jesus, and reminds others that they can choose to be Jesus' followers too.

Make disciples. Jesus' command to us as servants, left in charge of our Lord's possessions while He is away, is very specific. When Jesus returns and sits on His glorious throne, Christ will impose righteousness on the whole world. Until then, the kingdom continues as a hidden thing, revealed only to the eyes of faith, and experienced only by those who follow in the footsteps of the King.

Christ's words to the disciples in Matthew 16 and 28 give us direction for our lives. "If anyone would come after Me," He told the Twelve, "he must deny himself and take up his cross and follow Me" (16:24).

In following Jesus we find not an earthly kingdom but ourselves. We become new men and new women, whose lives are being transformed, and whose personalities are being reshaped to reflect the love, the compassion, and the character of the King.

Making disciples who will be like the Master (Luke 6:40) is the calling which you and I have from our Lord and King.

All nations. The kingdom of God in its present form cuts across all languages and boundaries and societies. Men of every culture are called, not to become like those of some other nation, but to become like Jesus and to reflect Him in their own lands. Baptism, which speaks of identification, is to be into the Father, Son, and Holy Spirit—not into the "Western world" or into America's idea of the church.

Thus, Christ's kingdom is universal, and the Sermon on the Mount is a unique expression of a reality that cuts across all cultures. Unlike the coming kingdom, which will shatter the kingdoms and the cultures of this world, the kingdom today *infuses.* God's kingdom today touches men, shaping within them Christ's unique concern and love for others. Individuals from every land and age respond, and, in becoming followers of the King, demonstrate the transforming power of Christ in fresh and ever-living ways.

Teaching them to observe all that I have commanded you. The disciple expresses allegiance to his King through obedience. Christ's instructions to His disciples about their own lifestyles are to be communicated to each new generation of believers. The Sermon on the Mount, the way of greatness, the challenge to watch and to serve while the Master is away, are all basic to the Gospel today.

In Matthew, we have been shown a way of life, amplified in the rest of the New Testament but unmistakably clear in the Gospel. In Matthew's portrait of Jesus, we have a model of the men and women you and I are to be.

Jesus lived and died as a *servant* King. In the words of this final command, "Obey everything I have commanded you," we hear echoes of Jesus' earlier words.

> It is enough for the student to be like his teacher, and the servant like his master.
> Matthew 10:25

> Whoever wants to become great among you must be your servant, and whoever wants to be first must be your slave—just as the Son of man did not come to be served, but to serve, and to give His life as a ransom for many.
> Matthew 20:26-28

I am with you always. It's important as we face the meaning of Christ's kingdom and His kingship over us, to realize that we are not left alone to do the impossible. Christ has all authority, and Christ promises to be with us. What is impossible for us is fully possible for Him. We are free to follow, for we do not follow alone.

It is this reality that Paul writes of in Romans 8:11: "If the Spirit of Him who raised Jesus from the dead is living in you, He who raised Christ from the dead will also give life to your mortal bodies through His Spirit, who lives in you." Christ was raised from the dead by the power of God. That same resurrection power is available to overcome the deadness in our lives. Because Christ promises to be with us always, we know that His power is always ours.

The King lives.
And reigns.
In us, as in all the world.

The Breaking: Luke 24:13-35

There is a Resurrection story in Luke which helps us grasp the uniqueness of Matthew's picture of Jesus—and of the kingdom of which you and I are a part.

On that Resurrection Day, two disciples were returning to their Emmaus home, about seven miles from Jerusalem. They were talking about the events of the Passion Week, and the strange reports of the morning.

As they walked they were joined by a third Person. He questioned them about what had been happening. As they strode along together, the two told the Stranger about Jesus, who they had hoped was to redeem Israel. How amazed they were now at the report that Jesus had been seen alive again!

Then the Stranger interrupted: "How foolish you are, and how slow of heart to believe all that the prophets have spoken! Did not the Christ have to suffer these things and then enter His glory?" (Luke 24:25-26) Then He traced the Old Testament prophecies that foretold the events of that week and of His coming.

When they arrived at the village, the two urged their Companion to stay for a meal and the night. Seated, He took the bread and blessed it—and broke it. And their eyes were opened. They recognized Jesus!

There's something about the breaking of the loaf of bread. The rich odor of its goodness fills the room. The odor awakens hunger—a hunger that demands satisfaction. All this is known in the breaking of the bread.

This is also how Jesus is known. King He is. But at Passover, Jesus identified Himself as "bread." "This is My body, which is broken for you" (1 Cor. 11:24, KJV).

Had Jesus come in glory first, we would have known His power. But God's great love is not known in Jesus' glory, but in His brokenness. Not in the throne, but in the Cross. Not in might, but in servanthood.

As the rich warm odors given off in the breaking of the bread invite men to the feast, it is in the servanthood of Jesus we are shown God's love, that we sense His invitation to draw near.

So it is in our lives.

There will be time enough for glory when Jesus comes. Today the hidden kingdom is revealed in us, as we, following our King, humble ourselves to serve.

Humble and broken, as was our Lord in the service of His fellowmen, we best fulfill His last command.

TEACHING GUIDE

Prepare
Read 1 Corinthians 15. How important does Paul say that a literal resurrection is to our faith?

Explore
1. Hold a discussion on the question: "How do we really *know* that the resurrection of Jesus took place?"
2. Give a list of the witnesses included in this study guide's *overview* to each of your group members. Divide the references among the group, so each can look up and read at least one.

Some have suggested that these witnesses would have had no motive to lie. If Jesus were *really* dead, they would have been in despair, and at best all they could expect was persecution and a death like their Lord's. Only conviction that the Resurrection was real could have transformed Jesus' followers from despair to joy, and given them the courage to witness in Jerusalem, and then throughout the world.

Expand
What does the Resurrection mean for us *now*? Use the study sheet and process outlined in "link-to-life," page 596 to help your group members sense the transforming power the Resurrection unleashes for believers to appropriate.

Apply
Go around the circle, asking each person to finish this open-ended statement: "Because Jesus lives, I. . . ."

STUDY GUIDE 93

Introduction

MARK'S GOSPEL

Overview
Papias, about A.D. 140, expressed the view of the early church about this, the shortest of all our Gospels. He wrote: "Mark, being the interpreter of Peter, whatsoever he recorded he wrote with great accuracy, but not however in the order in which it was spoken or done by our Lord."

Like the other Gospel writers, Mark organized his material to achieve a specific purpose. In Mark's case, this purpose was to introduce Jesus through a simple, vivid narrative, to converts from the Roman world. Writing in the blunt, ordinary language of the common people, Mark focused attention on Jesus' acts (rather than His teachings). About half of the book is devoted to the last eight days of Jesus' life.

In this introductory session, you'll guide your group members to look at some of the things that make this short Gospel so special: the fascinating story of its young author, the confrontation of Jesus with demons, the response of observers to Jesus' miracles, and the special insights which the Book of Mark provides into the emotions of Jesus.

- An excellent discussion of the date of Mark (probably before A.D. 70), the authorship, the sources Mark may have used, evidence that the Book of Mark was probably written in Rome for Gentile Roman Christians, and Mark's theological themes, is found in the Victor *Bible Knowledge Commentary*, pages 95-101.

Commentary
Writings from every center of early Christianity support the belief that this short Gospel was written by John Mark, a young man mentioned no less than 10 times in the New Testament.

Nearly all the material in Mark is found also in Matthew and Luke. Mark seldom quoted the Old Testament. He explained Jewish customs and terms for Gentile readers (cf. Mark 7:2; 12:42), used Latin terms not found in other Gospels (cf. Mark 6:27; 12:15, 42), and used Roman rather than Jewish systems for calculating time (cf. Mark 6:48; 13:35).

Like so many in our own day, the ordinary people in the Roman world were not interested in abstracts. What gripped them was the evidence of accomplishment, not lengthy discourse. Thus Mark adopted a vigorous style, giving in his fast-paced narrative vivid images of Jesus in action. What impresses us as we read Mark today is the vitality and energy of Jesus, the sense of urgency that marked His activity (often heightened by Mark's repeated use of "and immediately"), and the power that Jesus exudes not only in His miracles but in His confrontations with opponents.

The men and women of the early church must have been impressed, as we are today, with Mark's vision of Jesus as a real human being, totally involved in carrying out His mission, always in command as He moved purposefully to His culminating ministry on the cross.

John Mark
John Mark is mentioned 10 times in the New Testament. The references are: Acts 12:12, 25; 13:5, 13; 15:37, 39; Colossians 4:10; 2 Timothy 4:11; Philemon 24; 1 Peter 5:13. From them we can reconstruct the story of his life, and particularly the fascinating incident which led to the splitting up of the Apostle Paul and his earliest companion and Christian friend, Barnabas.

As a young person from a wealthy Jerusalem home, John Mark must have listened often to the preaching of Peter and the other disciples, who met often in his home. He became a believer, and was serious enough about his faith to travel from Jerusalem to Antioch to be with the Apostle Paul and his partner, Barnabas. When these two set out on their first missionary journey, Mark traveled with them.

But missionary life seems to have been too difficult for young Mark. We are told that when the team reached Perga, in Pamphylia, Mark returned to Jerusalem. Although we are not given any details, Mark's departure was clearly viewed by Paul as desertion. Mark was one of those whose commitment faltered, and Paul was hardened against him.

We known that Mark's departure was harshly judged by Paul because later, when a second missionary trip was being planned, Paul utterly refused to permit Mark to come along. But Barnabas, ever living up to the meaning of his name as a "son of consolation" (or "encouragement"), wanted to give young John Mark another chance. The dispute between Paul and Barnabas grew so heated that the two parted, and Paul took Silas on the second journey, while Barnabas took Mark and went to Cyprus.

How heated this dispute must have been is understood when we grasp the nature of the relationship between Paul and Barnabas. When Paul had first been converted, only Barnabas had been willing to associate with this man who had been such a bitter enemy of Christianity. Years later it was Barnabas, a leader in the church at Antioch, who had taken a long journey to find Paul and bring him to Antioch to serve with the leadership team there. It was these two who had started out together on the first of several missionary journeys. Paul, who had gained so much personally from the sensitivity and compassion of Barnabas, was bound to Barnabas by a deep love and trust, developed over years of shared ministry.

Yet when it came to taking John Mark on another missionary journey, Paul adamantly refused. And Barnabas, convinced John should be given another chance, would not give in either. John Mark, who had deserted the two earlier, became the occasion for a bitter dispute that separated two Christian brothers who had loved one another deeply and well.

But the story of John Mark does not end here. Some years later Mark was with Peter in Rome (called "Babylon" in 1 Peter 5:13). And after a few more years, Mark was with Paul in Rome! During Paul's final imprisonment in Rome, he wrote to Timothy, "Get Mark and bring him with you, because he is helpful to me in my ministry" (2 Tim. 4:11). Apparently the division between Paul and Mark had been healed. Barnabas was right. What Mark needed was a second chance. Through a loving, supportive relationship with the mature Barnabas, young Mark became a Christian leader that even Paul learned he could rely on!

What a lesson for you and me. Are we discouraged at times because of our own lack of progress in the faith? Or because of the weakness of the commitment of those we minister to? Let's learn the lesson of Mark, who was given a second chance, and who became a "helpful" Christian: a person whom God used to write the second Gospel, a book which bears his name.

♥ ***Link to Life: Youth / Adult***

Divide into teams of five. Give each team a list of the 10 references to Mark in the New Testament. Each is to develop the story of Mark's life from these references. The stories should include a sketch of Mark's character, his effect on others, turning points in his life, etc. When the teams have finished, share their findings.

Then discuss: "Have you ever felt rejected by Christians because of a personal failure? Have you ever rejected others because of real faults or failings? Who is our best example in such situations: Paul, or Barnabas? Why? What is the most important lesson to be gained from a study of Mark's life that you can apply to your own life?"

Jesus' Miracles

Mark's Gospel is significantly shorter than the others. Yet while Matthew and Luke each mention 20 of Jesus' miracles, Mark—half their size—speaks of 18 specific miracles and refers 10 additional times to miracles that are not described in any detail. A list of the miracles in Mark shows:

1. Demon-possessed man healed	1:23-28
2. Peter's mother-in-law healed	1:29-31
3. Leper healed	1:40-45
4. Paralytic healed	2:3-12
5. Withered hand healed	3:1-5
6. Storm stilled	4:35-41
7. Demon-possessed man healed	5:1-20

8.	Jairus' daughter raised	5:22-43
9.	Bleeding woman healed	5:25-34
10.	5,000 fed	6:35-44
11.	Jesus walks on sea	6:45-52
12.	Woman's daughter healed	7:24-30
13.	Deaf and dumb man healed	7:31-37
14.	4,000 fed	8:1-9
15.	Blind man healed	8:22-26
16.	Epileptic boy healed	9:14-29
17.	Blind men healed	10:46-52
18.	Fig tree cursed	11:12-14

The 10 general references to other miracles performed by Jesus are: 1:32-34, 39; 3:9-12, 22; 6:2, 5, 7, 13, 14, 53-56. The words used to describe all these miracles are "wonder," "power," "sign," and "miraculous deed."

♥ ***Link to Life: Youth / Adult***
Give your group members a copy of the list of miracles. From this list, what can be learned about Christ's miracles? (Your members might note that most are healing. Miracle stories are concentrated in the first half of the book, etc.) Discuss: "What do our findings tell about the role of miracles in Mark?"

The nature of miracles. A number of Greek words are associated with miracles in the Gospels. *Dunamis,* often translated as "miracle," is from a root that means "power." This word focuses attention on an event as an explosive demonstration of God's own power. *Semeion* is "sign." This word indicates that the miraculous event links the doer of the act with the divine. The New Testament also uses *ergon,* "work," where miracles are clearly meant.

These words each reflect Old Testament terms. There *mopet,* found only 36 times, means a "wonder" or "miracle." It is used primarily of God's personal intervention through miracles in Egypt to free His people, Israel. *'Ot* means "miraculous sign." Each of the plagues on Egypt is called an *'ot.*

In both Testaments, miracles are unmistakable acts of God—interventions whose nature or whose timing demonstrate God's action in our world of space and time. In each Testament, there was no question in the minds of observers that what they saw was in fact a supernatural act.

In the Old Testament the word indicating this is *pala'.* It is a word describing the impact of miracles on the observers; the sense of awe and amazement at the unmistakable evidence that God has demonstrated His reality in this universe.

No wonder the Old Testament encourages believers to remember what God has done as a source of comfort and confidence. We "remember the wonders He has done, His miracles," and we declare "His marvelous deeds among all peoples" (1 Chron. 16:12, 24).

What is particularly striking in the Gospel accounts of Jesus' miracles is that His fellow countrymen, steeped in Old Testament lore, responded with the same stunned amazement of past generations.

The words Mark uses to describe this reaction emphasizes the stunning impact of Jesus' miracles. *Thaumazo* is usually translated "amazed" and suggests utter astonishment. Yet amazement doesn't automatically produce faith!

Existemi mixes astonishment with anxiety. The miracles of Jesus were so out of the ordinary that they created fear as well as wonder.

Thambeo indicates actual fright. Three times Mark tells us that Jesus' miracles frightened observers (1:27; 10:24, 32).

In fact, the works of Jesus were astonishing and frightening to those who did not believe in Him. As those who believed listened and watched this Man of Galilee, and realized just who He is, His wonders seemed only fitting. He *was* their God; as He had acted in ages past, so He acted now.

There were many differences between the miracles of Jesus and those who claimed to be able to do "magic" in the ancient world. The works of Jesus were performed simply. He used no spells or incantations. He spoke, and His word was enough. His works were performed in public, observed by friend and foe alike. Nicodemus spoke of the ruling Jewish council when he said, "*We* know that You are a Teacher who has come from God. For no one could perform the miraculous signs You are doing if God were not with him" (John 3:2, italics added).

But perhaps most importantly, magic in the ancient world was seen as a mode of controlling or harming others. It was used *against,* rather than *for,* them. But all of Jesus' miracles were exercised on behalf of others, to free them from sickness, pain, and spiritual bondage.

In performing His miracles, Jesus not only demonstrated His power, but also showed the overwhelming love of God for humankind.

What a wonder those miracles were. They documented the reality of God's power to act in man's world, they authenticated Jesus as God's Son, and they revealed in unmistakable ways the love and compassion of God for individual human beings. In the Old Testament God had acted to free the nation Israel. In Jesus He acted to release individuals from the physical and spiritual impact of man's ancient enemy—sin.

♥ ***Link to Life: Youth / Adult***
Divide the miracles that Mark reports, assigning an equal number to teams of three or four group members. Each team is to analyze its miracles. Particularly each should look for: nature of the miracle, purpose of the miracle, method of performing the miracle, response of onlookers to the miracle, miracle's relationship to spiritual needs as well as physical needs, other observations.

When the teams have completed their analysis, record results on a large chalkboard chart that includes each category.

Discuss: "What is the most important lesson people of Jesus' day might have drawn from His miracles? What is the most important lesson for us today?"

Jesus and Demons

Some of Jesus' most notable miracles involved casting out demons, and releasing the demon-possessed from their malignant influence.

What do we know about the demons of which the New Testament speaks?

Most ancient cultures believed in demons who had an evil influence on humans. It is striking in view of the prevalence of this belief that demons are only mentioned twice in the Old Testament (Deut. 32:17; Ps. 106:36-37). Yet the Gospels are full of reports of demons and demonic activity.

Some have suggested that this is because Satan marshaled his forces against Jesus during His life on earth. It does not seem unreasonable that the level of demonic activity then *was* unusual. Perhaps the charge of the Jewish leaders that Jesus was in league with the prince of demons was stimulated by the unusual amount of demonic activity associated with Christ's earthly ministry (cf. John 7:20; 8:48-52).

What we do know is that demons *were* active while Jesus walked the earth. We also know that they demonstrated their hostility toward humankind by harming rather than helping individuals they influenced. Many sicknesses and madness are linked with demon oppression (cf. Mark 1:32; 5:16-18).

We know little about these beings who are called demons or "evil spirits" in the New Testament. The only supernatural beings whose origin and future Scripture speaks of are Satan and the angels who followed him in his rebellion. Regarding these beings, Jesus said, there was "eternal fire prepared for the devil and his angels" (Matt. 25:41). It seems most likely that the demons of the Gospels were actually fallen angels, followers of Satan, and like him, the determined enemy of God and His people.

Several things are significant in the many confrontations that took place between Jesus and demons. First, they invariably knew Him to be the Son of God. Second, they immediately submitted to Him. There was no question that demons could not withstand Jesus: even these evil beings were subject to His authority. Third, Jesus always acted to release human beings who suffered from their evil influence. There is no record that Jesus ever abandoned any person who was demon-possessed or demon-oppressed.

Today many have questions about demons and demon-possession. It is clear from Scripture that demons are real. They can bring misery and cause sickness. But Jesus remains Lord, with authority and power far beyond that of wicked spirits. We can remain confident as we live close to Jesus that He will guard us. As the Apostle John wrote, "The One who is in you is greater than the one who is in the world" (1 John 4:4). It is hard to imagine even Satan himself settling into any relationship with a person indwelt by the Spirit of our Lord.

♥ ***Link to Life: Youth / Adult***
Brainstorm with your group. What questions do people have about demons? Make a list including all the questions your group members can come up with.

Then together examine the following passages in Mark: 1:23-28; 3:20-30; 5:9-20; 7:26-30; 9:17. Based on what your group members can see in these passages, how would they answer the questions they have just listed?

Jesus and His Emotions

Mark is unusual in that in describing Jesus' acts he often spoke of Christ's emotions. Mark wrote about Jesus as a Person who knew grief, who experienced both anger and compassion. He mentioned Christ's hunger and His exhaustion. We find these mentioned in passages like Mark 3:5; 4:38; 6:6, 31; 7:34; 8:12; 10:14, 21; and 11:12.

Perhaps most striking is the fact that several times Mark refers to Jesus' anger, using at least four Greek words. In Mark 3:5 the word is *orge,* a strong term indicating wrathful indignation. In 9:25, the word translated "rebuked" (*epitimao*) means to angrily reproach. In 10:14 the word rendered "indignant" is *embrimaomai,* which indicates irritation and annoyance.

Jesus was not unmoved by human suffering. But neither was He unmoved by sin in any of its expressions.

These passages raise the question of the anger of God, something spoken of in the Old Testament as well as the New. Both Testaments use similar words to describe God.

But the anger of God is never like a human temper tantrum, nor is it capricious. It is God's righteous response to specific human failures and sins. The *Expository Dictionary of Bible Words* (Richards, Zondervan) says that:

> The Old Testament sees God's anger in a positive rather than negative light. God's anger expresses itself in rebuke and discipline (Pss. 6:1; 38:1; 78:31-38). It is God's righteous reaction to those who persecute His people unjustly (Ex. 15:7; Ps. 7:6). His anger is provoked by wicked deeds (Ps. 106:29). The psalmist says, "Surely Your wrath against men brings You praise, and the survivors of Your wrath are restrained" (Ps. 76:10). God's anger is thus viewed as completely justified, and also as ultimately of benefit to people.
>
> But the Bible does not present anger as an essential characteristic of God. In fact, God's wrath is set aside when God forgives (Ps. 85:2-3), and even His acts of anger show restraint (Ps. 78:38). Compared to His favor, which lasts a lifetime, God's anger is momentary (Ps. 30:5). God intends only good to humanity, and when it is necessary to act in anger, the intention to do good is never lost.

We can gain special insight into the anger of God by noting in Mark's Gospel just what it is that stimulates the Lord's anger, and the control over this emotion which He exhibits.

♥ ***Link to Life: Youth / Adult***

Ask your group members if they agree or disagree: "We cannot see the 'angry God' of the Old Testament in the loving Jesus."

Then explain the three terms that express Jesus' anger. Look together at each incident. "What stimulated Jesus' anger? How is this related to Jesus' love? How is the anger of Jesus like or unlike the anger we most often feel?"

Mark's Jesus

There are many attractive things about Jesus as Mark portrays Him. Jesus is a Man of action, yet a Man with deep feelings and emotions. Jesus takes sides: He readily uses His power to help the helpless, and withstand the individuals and forces who would enslave human beings. Jesus in Mark's Gospel remains a servant, dedicated to actively doing His Father's will in the service of humankind.

Yet half of this brief Gospel is given to describe the final eight days of Jesus' life. It is the final act of service that Jesus offered us that is the most significant to John Mark.

Perhaps John Mark's portrait of the strong Jesus is so powerful because Mark himself knew he was weak. Mark, who had failed himself, and had found in Jesus the strength to overcome, reveals to us the Jesus who can act dynamically in our lives.

TEACHING GUIDE

Prepare
Review the material in Study Guide 79. If this is your first group study of one of the Gospels, draw from the general information provided there to sketch the setting for Jesus' life.

Explore
1. Give a minilecture on Mark's distinctives, some of which you will sample in this group meeting.
2. Or briefly introduce John Mark. Then use the inductive study explained in the "link-to-life" on page 601 to learn more about Mark, and to learn from his life.

Expand
1. Introduce your group to New Testament miracles in a minilecture. Then either survey the miracles of Jesus reported by Mark in a superficial way ("link-to-life," p. 602), or analyze and chart data that helps you discover more of what miracles reveal about the Lord ("link-to-life," p. 603, column 1).
2. Or let your group members express their questions about demons, and discover what you can about them by looking at incidents reported in Mark, guided by the questions in "link-to-life," page 603, column 2.

Apply
Share around the circle: "What would you most like to learn about Jesus from your study of this Gospel?"

STUDY GUIDE 94
Mark 1–5

THE AUTHENTIC SAVIOUR

Overview
Mark's Gospel is the shortest of the four. In powerful prose, Mark tells story after story about Jesus.

Many of the stories bear the mark of eyewitness testimony. The early church believed that Mark, a close companion of Peter, reported what Peter had witnessed, and represents Peter's testimony to the life of his Lord.

Distinctives of Mark are explored in the introduction to this Gospel.

The Gospel can be simply outlined. After a brief introduction (1:2-13), Mark links together stories around simple, clear themes.

Outliine

I.	Introduction	1:2-13
II.	Jesus Authenticated	1:4–5:43
III.	Jesus in Conflict	6:1–8:26
IV.	Jesus' Instructions	8:27–10:52
V.	Journey toward Calvary	11–13
VI.	Death and Resurrection	14–16

▶ ***Healing.*** Mark records a stream of healings in the opening chapters of his Gospel. Christians have often wondered, is there healing for us today? The Bible clearly indicates that God *can* heal. But in New Testament times God did not always heal even His most faithful servants (see 2 Cor. 12:7-10). When one of Paul's dearest friends was ill, the apostle did not "heal" him, but rather prayed and waited for God's answer (cf. Phil. 2:26-28). What Jesus' healings assure us of is that, whatever our need, God cares!

Commentary
The Gospels of Matthew and Luke each carefully describe the miraculous birth of Jesus, and events associated with it. In Mark, Jesus bursts on the scene unexpectedly, as He must have appeared in His own land. We meet Jesus only as an adult, launching into His ministry in a flurry of vital activity. But Mark makes sure that we do understand who Jesus is.

Authenticated by God: Mark 1:1-13
Mark immediately stated that his Gospel was "about Jesus Christ, the Son of God." Quickly Mark went about marshaling his evidence.

There was a man named John who appeared, baptizing in a desert area in Judea. His message, foretold in the Old Testament, concerned a Person who was to appear. And, "at that time" Jesus came from Nazareth in Galilee and was baptized.

Mark reported that as Jesus was coming up out of the waters after being baptized, John saw heaven "torn open" and the Spirit of God descending on Jesus. And John heard a voice from heaven, saying, "You are My Son, whom I love; with You I am well pleased."

Jesus was first authenticated by God Himself. And John the Baptist was the witness to that authentication. With this beginning, Mark initiates chapters intended to authenticate Jesus as God's Son.

Authenticated by Power: Mark 1:14-39
Witnesses (Mark 1:14-20). Mark first tells us that Jesus selected 12 disciples. This was important to his story, for the disciples would serve as witnesses to the acts which authenticated Jesus as Son of God.

The role of the disciples as witnesses was emphasized. After the resurrection of Jesus the eleven apostles gathered to select a replacement for Judas Iscariot. According to Peter, "it is necessary for us to choose one of the men *who have been with us the whole time* the Lord Jesus went in and out among us, *beginning from John's baptism* to the time when Jesus was taken up from us. For one of these must become a witness with us of His resurrection" (Acts 1:21-22, italics added). The disciples, who accompanied Jesus at all times, would be able to give an eyewitness account of His whole life and ministry, firmly establishing the historical roots of the faith.

There was no room in early Christianity for myth and rumors. The story of Jesus was no hearsay account, based on what someone said that another person heard from a friend. What Jesus said and did was heard by thousands, but in particular there was a group of disciples who saw it *all*—and who in God's time not only traveled the world telling what they had seen and heard, but also saw to it that the story was written down accurately and carefully.

It is no wonder then that Mark notes the calling of the disciples at this point in his story. He wants us to know that witnesses who can authenticate everything he has to tell were actually there.

When we hear of scholars who search for the "historical Jesus," trying to separate strands of the Gospel report into what "really happened" and what was supposedly added later, we need to remember that Mark takes special care to assure us that the Jesus of the Gospels *is* the historical Jesus. What Mark and the other Gospel writers reported is what actually happened, and their accounts are supported by the eyewitness testimony of people who were there.

What was it that the witnesses saw as Jesus launched His ministry that authenticated Him as Son of God?

An evil spirit driven out (Mark 1:21-28). It was Jesus' teaching that first amazed the crowds. Mark, typically, does not tell us *what* Jesus was teaching: simply that He did teach. And those who heard were amazed, because Jesus "taught them as One who had authority, not as the teachers of the Law" (v. 22).

In Jesus' time anyone who wished to be recognized as a rabbi (teacher) went through a recognized process of training. He became a disciple of a rabbi, and from him learned the mass of oral traditions and interpretations which had grown up around the Law. It was common for a rabbi to refer to tradition; to discuss the notion of rabbi this and rabbi that. It was what the long dead had said that the living referred to when teaching. And then Jesus appeared. And when Jesus taught, He did not hedge His words by references to others. He spoke plainly, powerfully, as One who possessed authority on His own.

The word "amazed" here does not suggest belief. In fact, it suggests skepticism. But, Mark says, "just then" a man possessed with an evil spirit cried out. The spirit identified Jesus as "the Holy One of God!" And Jesus commanded the spirit to come out of him. Shrieking, the spirit obeyed.

News of this act spread. Jesus gave His "new teaching . . . with authority!" And He "even [gave] orders to evil spirits and they obeyed Him."

Even the evil spirits who hated Jesus testified to the fact that He is the Son of God. Jesus' disciples, and the people of Capernaum were witnesses.

Jesus heals (Mark 1:29-34). The first healing Mark reported was of Peter's mother-in-law. But that evening, the ministry of healing was extended to the "whole town," which gathered at the door. This time Jesus' power over the sicknesses that bind humanity authenticated Him as the Son of God. And again the witnesses were, first the disciples, and then the "whole town."

Prayer (Mark 1:35-39). What was the source of Jesus' power? The town did not know. But the disciples did. Mark tells us that "very early in the morning, while it was still dark, Jesus got up . . . and went off to a solitary place, where He prayed." Christ's intimate personal relationship with the Father was the source of His power. This intimacy, witnessed by the disciples, also authenticated Christ as the Son of God.

From there, Mark concludes, Jesus traveled with His disciples to nearby villages, until He had traveled throughout Galilee. Everywhere He went Jesus preached, and His acts of power publicly authenticated Him as the Son of God.

♥ ***Link to Life: Children***

Mark's vivid stories are a favorite source of Sunday School lessons for boys and girls. In this passage we not only sense Jesus' power, but also His need for prayer. It was Jesus' closeness to God the Father that gave Him the strength to act as He did.

Boys and girls too need to be close to God to find strength to do what is good and right. Prayer can bring them close to God, as it kept Jesus close to His Father.

How can you demonstrate to children the importance of prayer? Point a flashlight at a sheet of paper held up across the room. The light will show, but dimly. Gradually bring the paper closer to the light, and note how the light seems stronger and stronger.

Prayer brings us closer and closer to God, the Source of our strength. The closer we are, the stronger His light will shine in our lives.

Authenticated by Compassion: Mark 1:40–3:12

The first set of stories Mark told focused on the emotion of amazement aroused by Jesus' acts of power. Now, in another series, Mark focused on the emotions which moved Jesus, and on the impact of His interventions on the lives of individuals. In this series we realize that Jesus truly was God in the flesh, for He showed God's own concern for individuals who live in bondage.

The healing touch (Mark 1:40-45). Mark had spoken of the crowds. Now he spoke of individuals. The first person Mark mentioned was a leper who came to Jesus, begging Him on his knees.

Leprosy was especially terrible to a Jew. More than what we call leprosy (Hanson's disease) was designated by this name in Bible times. The word was used of any chronic or infectious skin disease. Leprosy was serious in Israel not only because it caused physical pain, but because it made a Jew ceremonially "unclean" (see Lev. 14). Such a Jew could not participate in worship and was to be isolated from others in the Hebrew community.

The leper who approached Jesus had very probably not known the touch of another's hand for years, as all around him were repelled by his disease.

No wonder he was hesitant as he came to Christ and said, "If You are willing, You can make me clean" (Mark 1:40). The leper did not question Jesus' power. But he did question Jesus' willingness to act for him, an outcast.

Mark tells us that Jesus was "filled with compassion." The Greek word used here makes it clear that he was deeply moved. Jesus reached out His hand and actually touched the man! He said, "I am willing," and with a word cured the incurable disease.

With that touch Jesus answered for all time the doubts of those who wonder if God really cares. Jesus not only met the physical need. He understood the loneliness and psychological pain this man must have experienced, and with His touch dealt directly with that inner pain.

A paralytic healed and forgiven (Mark 2:1-12). The next story also focused on an individual. The man was a paralytic, brought to Jesus by friends. Confident that Jesus did care and could heal, the friends actually dug through the roof of a home where Jesus was teaching in order to bring the man to Him.

Jesus, in response to this faith, announced not only healing but also the forgiveness of the man's sins! This was too much for some of the "teachers of the Law" who were now listed by Mark as among the observers. These teachers were "thinking to themselves" that Jesus words about forgiveness of sins were blasphemy, because "who can forgive sins but God alone?"

They were right, of course. Only God can forgive sin. But Jesus is God the Son!

Jesus answered their unspoken objection in a graphic way. Which is easier: to tell a paralyzed man that he is forgiven, or to heal him? The answer is clear. It is far *easier* to speak of forgiveness. Who could possibly look into a man's heart to see if he was forgiven? It's easy to say, "You're forgiven," because who could really tell? How different to say, "Take up your bed and walk." Everyone can see, then, if the speaker has authority!

Not waiting for an answer, Jesus told the paralyzed man to get up, and walk home. "In full view of them all," the paralyzed man got up and walked away! Jesus' authority as God the Son to forgive sin was authenticated by a healing that took place not just in front of Christ's followers, but in front of His enemies as well!

Levi called (Mark 2:13-17). But is it true that there is no public evidence of Christ's inner work in a human life? Mark focuses our attention on yet another individual. The man was Levi, a tax collector. Tax collectors in New Testament times collaborated with the Romans and often profited by what they extorted from their fellow-countrymen. They were linked by all with other "sinners" from various outcast classes, like prostitutes.

Jesus not only called Levi to become one of His disciples, but even went to his home. There, at a party in His honor, Jesus mixed comfortably with the "sinners" of society.

The Pharisees, witnessing this, were scandalized. In response Jesus simply said, "It is not the healthy who need a doctor, but the sick. I have not come to call the righteous, but sinners" (v. 17).

What is significant about this story is, of course, the fact that the man called "Levi" here is elsewhere called Matthew! He was not only 1 of the 12 disciples, but wrote the Gospel identified by his name!

Jesus' power as Son of God was authenticated not only by healing sickness and disease, but by healing the sin which infects every human being. Jesus came to call sinners. And when His touch is felt on a human life, the sinner responds by becoming a new and righteous man.

Lord of Sabbath (Mark 2:18–3:6). In each of the stories in Mark 2, Pharisees or teachers of the Law have a prominent part. Why?

The people of Israel were truly zealous for God. But their zeal had been misdirected. They thought that God would be pleased if they rigorously kept the details of His Law. In their focus on the details, they missed the real meaning and purpose of God's ancient commands. Our saying, "They couldn't see the forest for the trees," was doubly true of the Pharisees and religious leaders of Jesus' time.

This theme is introduced as Jesus is asked His view on fasting. The disciples of the Pharisees and John the Baptist fasted. What about Jesus' disciples? Did they fast too? Jesus dismissed the question, pointing out that His new wine (His "new teaching") could not be poured into old wineskins. The patterns of thought and religion which characterized Israel were out of harmony with the message Jesus had to share.

Two incidents demonstrate Jesus' focus. Christ's disciples plucked some heads of grain as they followed Him through a grainfield. This was allowed in the Old Testament Law: a hungry person could eat from another's field as he passed by, but could not carry anything away. But this was the Sabbath. And to the Pharisees, who classified the act as "work," the act seemed a violation of the Sabbath Day.

Jesus dismissed their complaint. He did not point out that this interpretation was not found in Scripture but in mere human tradition. Instead, Jesus went back to the Old Testament and noted that even David, when hungry, ate of the shewbread located in God's tabernacle. Though this bread was supposed to be eaten by the priests alone, David was not charged with a sin because he had acted out of real need.

So, Jesus explained, "The Sabbath was made for man, not man for the Sabbath." In other words, God was not angered when real need drove a human being to violate a ceremonial aspect of Old Testament Law. People are more important to God than ritual observances. And this, Jesus said, He now established as One who is "Lord of the Sabbath."

At another time Jesus found a man with a shriveled hand when He entered a synagogue. The Pharisees had apparently planted him there, intending, if Christ should heal him, to accuse Jesus as a Sabbath-breaker. Jesus confronted them. He asked, "Which is lawful on the Sabbath: to do good or to do evil, to save life or to kill?" The Pharisees had no answer—but they were unmoved.

Deeply angered by the stubborn heartlessness of these men, Jesus restored the cripple.

And the Pharisees "went out and began to plot with the Herodians how they might kill Jesus" (3:6).

Mark concluded with another of his typical summary paragraphs. Jesus traveled, taught, healed, and expelled evil spirits who continued to cry out, "You are the Son of God."

What is the significance of this sequence in Mark's story of Jesus? Mark wanted his readers to realize that Jesus is authenticated as the Son of God by His demonstration of God's deep compassion for human beings. He heals our diseases. He forgives our sins. And He shows us that what God desires is not a legalistic relationship with human beings but a relationship marked by loving concern. The love which infused the Law at its giving had been lost sight of as God's people thought of it as rules to follow in order to please God rather than as guidelines showing them how to love Him and one another.

And the Pharisees? They were witnesses of the authenticating marks of Jesus' compassion. And by their reaction they demonstrated to all that their approach to religion was devoid of the love that marks the character of God.

♥ ***Link to Life: Children***

Stories in this section also are children's favorites. Here's a review activity focusing on the compassion they show, and the example they give of how we can please God. On a paper plate divided into quarters, print: Touch (1:40-45); Forgive (2:1-12); Be friends (2:13-17); Help (3:1-12). Cut a picture from your curriculum to illustrate each Bible story, and paste it in the appropriate quarter. Attach a cardboard arrow with a brad, so it can be spun to point to any quarter.

You are now ready to play the "We Care!" game with your boys and girls.

Remind the boys and girls of the Bible stories. Let them take turns spinning. Each is to make up a story about a person who needs to be touched, forgiven, have friends, or be helped, and tell how a child might care for that person.

Authenticated by Personal Authority: Mark 3:13–5:43

Mark began this new section with a list of those Jesus appointed as His official apostles (sent ones). He then launched into a series of stories which demonstrate that the Son of God's personal authority is absolutely unlimited. There is only one possible explanation for His acts and His words.

False explanations (Mark 3:20, 25). The excitement had grown in Galilee, until Jesus was constantly surrounded by crowds. Shouting, shoving people pressed so close that Christ and His disciples could not even find an opportunity to sit down and eat! These people did not try to explain Jesus: they simply mobbed this new celebrity.

When His family heard, they rushed to Him. "He is out of His mind," was their theory. What had happened to this quiet, hard-working carpenter Son and Brother, to make Him run around the country drawing crowds! It seemed so unlike Him!

The "teachers of the Law" who came down from Jerusalem to check out this phenomenon had another theory. "He's demon-possessed!" They tried to explain Jesus' supernatural powers by saying that they were from Satan rather than God.

Jesus exposed the ridiculous theory by pointing out that His powers had been used *against* Satan's minions. What ruler would start warfare between his own subjects? Only if a strong homeowner had been rendered powerless could another carry away his possessions. Jesus' works were done in the power of the Holy Spirit, not of Satan.

Only one conclusion fit the facts. Jesus is the Son of God: His personal authority as God's Son is the only explanation for all He said and did.

Authoritative teaching (Mark 4:1-34). Now Mark gave a sample of Jesus' teaching.

The word Jesus spoke was like seed scattered by a farmer. When the word took root in "good soil" it produced much fruit. Those who hear Jesus are likened to various soils. Some are like stony ground, on which the seed initially sprouts but cannot grow because there is no place for it to take root. Any trouble or persecution brings rejection of the Word. Others allow concern for the affairs of this life to choke out the spiritual. But on those who are "good soil" (responsive to the Word) it produces a rich crop.

This longer parable is followed by a series of enigmatic statements. Lamps are to be put on stands, not covered with a bowl. The kingdom of God grows gradually, like a planted seed. Taking in the crop awaits harvesttime. The tiniest of seeds can grow into a large garden plant.

Jesus' parables were not explained to the crowds, but "when He was alone with His disciples, He explained everything" (v. 34). The truths hidden in the parables of Jesus were understood by the disciples, and those that relate to the church are woven into the teaching of the Epistles.

Personal authority demonstrated (Mark 4:35–5:43). Now, in his report of a series of miracles, Mark showed us in their ascending significance the full extent of Christ's personal power.

Asleep at sea, Jesus was aroused by His terrified disciples when a "furious squall" struck their fishing boat. He rebuked the storm . . . and suddenly the waters were completely calm! Jesus has power over nature.

♥ ***Link to Life: Children***

Have your boys and girls draw a picture of the favorite part of this Bible story, and talk about why they like that part. (Most will choose a dramatic storm scene.)

Then ask how the disciples must have felt before Jesus awoke. How did they feel after He stilled the storm?

Ask each to draw another picture: of a

time when they are glad that Jesus is with them as He was with the disciples in the boat. Have each tell about his picture, and thank God together that Jesus is present when they are afraid.

In the next story in this sequence Mark told how Jesus cast many demons out of a man, sending them into a herd of pigs. Jesus has power over evil spiritual beings and forces.

Then Jesus was urged to go to help a dying daughter. On the way He was touched by a woman who had suffered from chronic bleeding for 12 years. She was healed simply by touching Jesus' clothes, and confessed the faith that brought her to Jesus. Even the physical illnesses which bind us and are one of the most obvious results of the Fall submit to Jesus.

When Jesus arrived at the home of Jairus, the man who had begged Him to come to his daughter's aid, she had died. Entering the house with the parents and the disciples, Jesus took her by the hand—and restored her to life! Jesus had power not only over sickness, but over death itself.

Jesus does have personal authority. All that Jesus said and did authenticated Him as the Son of God.

Those who first read Mark's Gospel, as we who read it today, must have been convinced. Jesus is just who Mark claimed Him to be in his first words. What we have read truly is about "Jesus Christ, the Son of God" (Mark 1:1).

TEACHING GUIDE

Prepare

Read Mark 1–5 through quickly. What are your major impressions of Jesus?

Explore

1. When your group members come in have Mark 1:1 written on the chalkboard. Ask each to quickly read through Mark 1–5, and select the "most compelling evidence that Jesus *is* the Son of God."

2. Explain that Mark, like the other Gospel writers, reported what really did happen, but may sequence events to support a particular emphasis. Chronological sequence isn't the only valid way to organize material.

Then outline the organizing principle of authentication as it functions in these chapters. Jesus was:

- authenticated by God (Mark 1:1-13);
- authenticated by power (Mark 1:14-29);
- authenticated by compassion (Mark 1:40–3:12);
- authenticated by personal authority (Mark 3:13–5:43).

Together work through the first of these sections, pointing out the nature of the authentication and the importance of witnesses.

Expand

1. Break into teams to examine the other three "authenticating" segments. Each team is to look at the nature of the authenticating words, guided by the section titles. Each is also to note the witnesses. Finally each team should try to explain just how the incidents reported are linked to each other.

Do *not* follow up these studies by having each team report its findings to the others.

2. Have each group member select *one* incident from these chapters as his or her favorite. Each is then to read and reread his or her incident, and *write down* two or three "lessons for living" that can be learned through it.

Apply

Form teams of four. Each person should share the "lesson for living" that he or she drew from a Mark incident that is most important to him or her personally, and explain why this lesson has personal value.

STUDY GUIDE 95

Mark 6:1–8:30

JESUS' CONFLICTS

Overview

The first few chapters of Mark show us that Jesus is the authentic Son of God. Still, the people to whom Jesus came and showed His powerful proofs did not acknowledge Him! Why?

In two cycles of stories, Mark reveals the reason for Israel's rejection, and demonstrates the response that all must make to Jesus, the Son of God. In these chapters Mark invites us to look at two kinds of hearts. There is the hardened heart of Jesus' followers, who could not seem to grasp the meaning of what they saw. And there are the distant hearts of Jesus' enemies, who refused to even look. Yet Mark also shows us faith, a principle which can open our eyes and our hearts to spiritual reality.

Here, as in the rest of his Gospel, Mark's style is not to preach. Mark simply tells what happened, carefully linking story with story to lead us to discover in Jesus alone a power that can cleanse and renew us.

▶ ***Heart.*** The theological meaning of "heart" is established in the Old Testament. The "heart" is the conscious self, the inner core of the individual. Jeremiah portrayed the heart as "deceitful above all things and beyond cure" (Jer. 17:9). Every dimension of the human personality has been infected by sin. But only the willfully hardened or distant heart is beyond the power of Christ to change.

Commentary

There has never been any real question about Jesus' authority. The question has always been how human beings will respond to Him. Many throughout history have heard the evidence and hesitated. Others have heard and actively opposed the Gospel. But always one key alone has released the power of the Saviour to operate in the life of the individual.

The Issue Drawn: Mark 6:1-44

Unbelief (Mark 6:1-6). After Jesus' reputation had been well established, He returned to His hometown of Nazareth. When Jesus taught in the synagogue, His words created the familiar "amazement," an amazement linked with doubt rather than faith. As Jesus' fellow-townsmen listened they began to resent Him. How was Jesus better than they? Wasn't He just the village carpenter? Didn't His mother and brothers live next door? Why should Jesus be given such wisdom, and the power to do miracles?

Mark says they "took offense at Him." The word is a strong one. It indicates anger, shock, and even revulsion.

Among these friends and neighbors Jesus did no miracles, except for a few healings. And Mark comments, "He [Jesus] was amazed at their lack of faith."

In this short story Mark established the theme of this section of his Gospel. Mark would examine the response of people to Jesus the Son of God. And he would go about explaining their amazing lack of faith.

The Twelve instructed (Mark 6:7-13). Jesus continued traveling, teaching from village to village. Then He determined to send out the Twelve, giving them authority over evil spirits. Jesus gave them significant instructions. They were to carry nothing for the journey, but depend on those to whom they came. But "if any place will not welcome you or listen to you, shake the dust off your feet when you leave as a testimony against them" (v. 11). The disciples were to preach the Word. Each person was free to welcome or reject the message. But the disciples were to "leave" those who would not respond, and were to "shake the dust off your feet . . . as a testimony against them."

The disciples went out, teaching, healing, and driving out devils. With such abundant evidence of the authority and compassion of Jesus, who would refuse to believe?

Belief is not faith (Mark 6:14-29). Mark interrupted his narrative to tell a story which established a vital principle. Belief, as the realization that certain things are true, must never be confused with "faith."

As more and more stories about Jesus reached King Herod, speculation about Him grew. Some said that Jesus was Elijah; others, another of the ancient prophets. But Herod was convinced that Jesus was John the Baptist, raised from the dead.

Herod had imprisoned John who condemned the king for an illicit relationship he established with his brother's wife. The woman, Herodias, hated John and wanted to kill him. But Mark tells us that Herod "feared John and protected him, knowing him to be a righteous and holy man" (v. 20).

But when Herodias' daughter danced at Herod's birthday party, and he offered her any reward, she asked for the head of John the Baptist.

Herod looked around. All his guests had heard his promise. Their opinion seemed terribly important to him then. Though he didn't want to do it—and though he knew it was wrong—Herod ordered John's execution.

In Greece, hundreds of years before Christ, the philosopher Plato speculated that if only a person knew "the good," he would do it. Herod's act showed how wrong Plato was. It is not enough to know what is good. It is not enough to believe the right things. A person must commit himself to what he knows is right. A person must trust God enough to believe that He exists, and that it is God's opinion that counts; that His will must guide ours.

Herod believed that John was a prophet. He even liked to listen to John's teachings, just as the people of Israel believed that Jesus was a Prophet and crowded around to hear Him speak and to witness His miracles.

But when the time for decision arrived, *mere belief must be transformed into faith.* There must be commitment! A person must not look around, and try to please those who are watching. A person must face the fact that only God's opinion counts, and in the firm conviction that God is and that He is a rewarder of those who seek Him, that person must commit himself to what is right.

See the Son of God (Mark 6:30-44). Now Mark told another story, one that linked the authenticating marks of Jesus' divine sonship which we noted in the first five chapters.

Crowds followed Jesus out into a wilderness place. Out of compassion He taught them until late in the day. Then, realizing the people must be hungry, Jesus fed some 5,000 men, plus uncounted women and children, from five small loaves and two fish. Jesus' miracle combined the power and the compassion of God, and reminded Mark's readers that this One truly is the Son of God. Surely we cannot only believe in Jesus; in total faith we can commit ourselves fully to Him as God's only begotten Son.

♥ ***Link to Life: Youth / Adult***

Introduce Plato's notion that one who truly knows "the good" will choose it. Do your group members think this is true, or false? Why?

After discussion, ask them to read Mark's report of the beheading of John the Baptist (Mark 6:14-29). From the story discuss: "What did Herod know as 'the good'? What evidence is there that he had this knowledge? How did Herod choose against what he himself believed? What in the text suggests Herod's motives for his choice?"

Sketch the progression in 6:1-44 to show how this story is linked to Mark's theme.

A Matter of the Heart: Mark 6:45–7:37

Hardened hearts (Mark 6:45-56). Jesus sent His disciples ahead by boat so He might have time alone to pray. When the wind came up later that night, Jesus went to join His followers, walking on the water. When the disciples saw His figure amid the waves, they cried out in fear, thinking He was a ghost.

Jesus moved toward them, speaking reassuringly. When He reached them, He climbed over the side into the boat, and the winds died down.

Then Mark gave stunning information: "They were completely amazed, for they had not understood about the loaves; their hearts were hardened" (6:51). Even Jesus' disciples, who had witnessed every miracle and heard every teaching, did not fully realize who Jesus is!

We shouldn't be surprised that the

crowds who heard Him and witnessed a few of His miracles hesitated to commit themselves to Jesus. We shouldn't be surprised that the religious leaders were skeptical. Even those closest to Jesus did not fully grasp who this Person they had committed themselves to truly is!

With this story Mark focuses our attention on the heart. As we noted in the overview of this passage, the heart in Hebrew thought is the sum total of the personality, the essence of the individual. It is the testimony of Scripture that the heart of man was tragically warped by the Fall. Sin has darkened human understanding, twisted human motives, crippled human will, distorted human emotions. The grip of sin on each of us is deadly, trapping us in a dark realm of illusion where we can hardly glimpse the truth. Even the disciples of Jesus, who had been so close to Him, were crippled by darkened and hardened hearts.

It is not enough for Jesus to show Himself to be the Son of God. Somehow Jesus must deal with deadened, hardened human hearts.

Distant hearts (Mark 7:1-23). There was no accusation of malice or willful ignorance implied in Jesus' diagnosis of the disciples' hardened hearts. But when the Pharisees and some of the teachers of the Law came to observe Jesus, Christ diagnosed them as victims of an even more terrible spiritual disease.

These men, who took pride in keeping the Law's most minute detail, noted that Jesus' disciples ate with "unclean" hands. Mark explained for his Gentile readers. They were eating with *ceremonially* unwashed hands.

This ceremonial washing was not part of the Mosaic Law. It was instead an interpretation, an application. But the Pharisees held that such oral traditions had the same force as Scripture itself, and so religiously followed the rite. Hands were dipped in water, then raised so that the water ran down the arms and off the elbows. And this was repeated a prescribed number of times. It was unthinkable for the Pharisee to eat until he had completed the required ablutions.

The Pharisees immediately challenged Jesus. As a Rabbi (a Teacher) with His own disciples (students, followers), Jesus was responsible for their behavior. So in asking why His disciples did not wash, the Pharisees were really attacking Jesus. How could Jesus permit them to abandon the traditions of the elders and violate the oral law to which the Pharisees were committed?

Jesus bluntly called them hypocrites and quoted a passage of Isaiah which He said spoke of them:

> These people honor Me with their lips, but their hearts are far from Me. They worship Me in vain; their teachings are but rules taught by men.
>
> Mark 7:6-7

The Pharisees had substituted man-made rules for relationships with God. And their rules actually "set aside" the commands of God!

Jesus illustrated. God commanded everyone to honor father and mother. But one interpretation of a regulation about dedicating possessions to God allowed the individual to technically "give" his possessions to God, while using them throughout his lifetime!

However, since what he possessed was technically dedicated to the Lord, he was released from any obligation to help needy parents financially. But this interpretation, this "tradition of the elders" clearly violated both the letter and intent of one of God's Ten Commandments!

How could "religious" people invent such subterfuges? Only if their hearts were far from God; only if they were using religion for their own purposes rather than acting out of real dedication to the Lord.

Jesus went on to explain. In essence, "clean" and "unclean" aren't concerned with externals at all! It isn't what affects the body that makes a person "unclean." No, "what comes out of a man is what makes him 'unclean.' For from within, out of men's hearts, come evil thoughts, sexual immorality, theft, murder, adultery, greed, malice, deceit, lewdness, envy, slander, arrogance, and folly. All these evils come from inside and make a man 'unclean.' "

The Pharisees, with their exaltation of externals and ignorance of the inner meaning of the Law, demonstrated by the very traditions they held so dear that their own hearts were far from God. The tradition of corban (dedication of property to God) revealed that their hearts were full of greed, deceit, and evil thoughts.

And when Jesus held up the mirror of truth to these men whose hearts were so far from God, they hated Him!

Faith, the key (Mark 7:24-37). The disciples' hearts had been willing, but hardened. The Pharisees' hearts had been unclean, tragically far from God. What can be done to heal such sin-infected hearts?

The answer most Jews of Jesus' time would have given was simply to appeal to the covenant. God had made promises to Abraham, and the Jews of Jesus' day were Abraham's descendants. Thus the Jews believed that, because of their physical descent from Abraham, God owed them! They were His people, weren't they? As long as they kept the Law (as best they could) everything would be all right.

And then Mark told of a meeting with a pagan woman, a Greek, born in the Phoenician (coastal) part of Syria. This woman had no basis for any claim on Jesus. She was not a descendant of Abraham. And yet she came to Christ to beg Him to drive a demon from her daughter.

At first Jesus refused. It wasn't right to take what belonged to the family and toss it to their dogs. The Jews *did* have a special claim on God through the covenant promises He had made!

But the woman answered, "Even the dogs under the table eat the children's crumbs." What the children would not eat, but let fall to the ground, could be eaten by others.

Jesus dismissed her, "You may go; the demon has left your daughter."

And the woman went home to find her daughter healed.

What had happened? The disciples, the crowds, and the Pharisees had seen Jesus' miracles and heard His teaching, and still held back. They would not eat this spiritual food spread so generously on their tables. But this woman had believed! Driven by her need, she came to Jesus and acknowledged Him as "Lord." She knew He could heal and expected Him to be gracious even though she had no claim on His grace.

This, and this alone, is the key.

We must recognize Jesus as Lord. We must come to Him, recognizing that we have no claim on His grace, but expecting Him to be gracious. When we do, Jesus Himself will heal our diseased hearts, and bring us new life.

Mark concludes this section with yet another story. Jesus was brought a man who was deaf and could hardly talk. His physical senses were as blocked as the spiritual senses of Israel! Jesus took the man aside and said to his senses, "Be opened." And they were! His senses were functioning at last; he was in touch with the world and able to speak.

How wonderful that this same Jesus changes our hearts, and opens our spiritual senses. Those who come to Him with faith, acknowledging Him to be Lord, will be spiritually healed and made truly well.

♥ ***Link to Life: Youth / Adult***
Summarize the meaning of "heart" and briefly discuss the disciples' "hardened" hearts. Then have your group examine Jesus' confrontation with the Pharisees (7:1-23). Divide into teams, each of which is to answer the following questions: "What characterizes the 'heart far from' God? How did Jesus recognize people with such hearts? How does one's approach to religion indicate his or her heart is far from God?"

The Focus of Faith: Mark 8:1-30

Mark again let events speak for themselves, and marshaled his evidence in logical sequence.

He began by showing us the striking reaction of the people in Jesus' hometown. Christ's teaching and the report of His miracles had stimulated active resentment rather than praise and faith! Why? The story of Herod's relationship with John the Baptist illustrated. Herod knew that John was a "righteous and holy man" (6:20). But Herod had acted against this knowledge and ordered John executed. His belief that John had been sent by God had produced no inner commitment to do the will of God. Belief in Herod had not been transformed into faith.

As for Jesus, He continued to perform compassionate miracles. Those who came and who saw what He did had to believe. But would they respond with faith?

In another cycle of stories Mark noted that even Jesus' disciples struggled with hardened hearts that could not fully grasp the impact of what they saw. The natural hardness of sin-infected hearts made faith's full commitment difficult even for those who loved and followed Jesus. We should not be surprised that it was so difficult for those who witnessed what Jesus did to make life's most significant decision and fully commit themselves to Him.

But for some, more than simple hardness of heart was the problem. For the religious leaders the problem lay in the fact that their hearts were "far from" God! Their religion was an external thing; their traditions were masks for their unwillingness to obey God's commands. And their hearts, as revealed in their traditions and acts, were filled with greed, deceit, arrogance, and a host of other evils.

How different they were from the pagan woman who came to Jesus so humbly and begged His aid. She did not trust in her relationship with Abraham; she had none. She did not mention the Law. She simply came to Jesus, acknowledged Him as Lord, and hoped in His grace.

Now, in a final sequence of stories, Mark brought the issue into clear focus, and taught that we must respond to Jesus with faith.

Another miracle (Mark 8:1-13). Mark reported another familiar miracle. Jesus was followed for three days by crowds who now had nothing to eat. Moved by compassion, He shared His concern with the disciples. They were upset since they were in a remote place. Even if they had the money, where would they get enough bread to feed so many?

Again Jesus multiplied a few loaves and a few small fish, and fed thousands—with basketfuls left over. This miracle again expressed both the power and compassion which marked Jesus clearly as the Son of God.

And Mark tells us that "the Pharisees came. . . . To test Him, they asked Him for a sign from heaven" (v. 11). The word "sign" means "miracle." And Jesus' whole ministry had been marked by miracle after miracle, as these men well knew! Mark said that Jesus sighed deeply. These men had all the evidence they needed, yet they would not believe.

The yeast of the Pharisees (Mark 8:14-21). In a boat with His disciples Jesus warned the Twelve against the "yeast of the Pharisees and that of Herod." The disciples, who had forgotten to bring lunch, misunderstood. Exasperated, Jesus reminded them of His miracles multiplying the bread and fish. "Are your hearts hardened? Do you have eyes but fail to see, and ears but fail to hear? . . . Do you still not understand?"

What was Jesus speaking of? The "yeast" of the Pharisees and of Herod are those heart attitudes which distort and permeate the personality. The externalism of the Pharisees, and the concern for the opinion of others that both they and Herod showed, are enemies of faith. For true faith calls on us to make a full commitment to our God, and to make the choices which please Him.

Beginning to see (Mark 8:22-26). Mark told a significant story. A blind man was brought to Jesus. Jesus spat on the man's eyes and touched him. "Do you see anything?" Jesus asked.

The blind man looked around. "I see people; they look like trees walking around."

Once more Jesus put His hands on the man's eyes. His sight was restored, and then he "saw everything clearly."

How like Jesus' relationship with His disciples! These followers of Jesus did see. It was simply that because of hardened hearts, they did not yet see clearly. But the Pharisees, like Herod, whose hearts were far from God, could not see at all!

Who is Jesus? (Mark 8:27-30) Then came the final incident, which both ended this section of Mark's Gospel and began the next.

Jesus asked His disciples, "Who do people say I am?" The Twelve reported the views of the crowds. Everyone agreed that Jesus was one of the prophets; they disagreed on which one Christ most closely resembled. Then Jesus asked, "But what about you? Who do you say I am?"

Peter answered for them.

"You are the Christ."

And with this response, Peter focused on the central issue of our faith.

Who is Jesus?

When we, with Peter, have faith that Jesus is the Christ, the Son of God, we have established a personal relationship with God. Like the blind man and like the disciples themselves, we may not see clearly at first. But as we continue to trust Jesus and respond to Him, our hearts will melt, and our vision clear. We will know the truth and do it, for Jesus and Jesus alone can transform the human heart.

TEACHING GUIDE

Prepare
Make notes on the relationship of each incident Mark reports to the others in this section of his Gospel.

Explore
1. Have group members discuss: "Why do so many people not believe the Gospel?" Jot down the theories suggested on a chalkboard.
2. Give a minilecture on the heart. If you wish to include more information than is provided in this study guide, see: Matthew 6:21; 12:34; 15:18-19; Romans 1:21-32; 10:8-13; 2 Corinthians 1:22; Galatians 4:6.

Expand
1. Divide into teams to study Herod's execution of John the Baptist. Use the process outlined in "link-to-life," page 613. Be sure that your group members note the basic difference between belief and faith. Belief acknowledges certain things to be true. Faith involves a commitment to what is believed in, so that a person acts on it out of a desire to please God.
2. Or divide into teams to study the Pharisees, and the "heart far from God" which they illustrate. The "link-to-life" on page 615 structures this study.
3. Return to the question with which you launched the session. What now seem to be the most likely reasons why many who hear the Gospel do not respond?

Apply
Mark 5:24-30 and 8:27-30 focus our attention not on faith in general, but on faith in a Person. It is coming to Jesus and acknowledging Him to be Lord that is the key to our transformation.

The hardened heart will melt and spiritual sight be restored as we commit ourselves to Jesus as the Christ, the Son of God, and follow Him.

Close in brief sentence prayers, in which each group member can express to Jesus faith, trust, or renewed commitment.

STUDY GUIDE 96

Mark 8:31–10:52

TEACHING HIS DISCIPLES

Overview
The key to this section of Mark is the repeated note that Jesus "began to teach" and "was teaching" His disciples. Also, five of the six times in Mark that Jesus' disciples call him "Teacher" are found in Mark 9 and 10.

What was happening *before* the events reported in these chapters? Wasn't Jesus teaching then?

Jesus did teach as He traveled from village to village, healing and casting out demons. But it was the crowds that He was teaching. Often that teaching was in parables. Mark does not report this teaching in detail. But what he does tell us suggests that Jesus' teaching was both about Himself and about life in His kingdom.

In this section there is a significant shift. The ones Jesus taught were the disciples. While He began to teach them about His coming death and resurrection, the focus of His teaching is not how to live in Israel's expected kingdom, but on how to live as His disciples now.

The great value for us in these chapters of Mark is to be found in the fact that, as believers, we too are called to be Christ's disciples. How good to learn more of how to live for Him.

▶ ***Disciple.*** The Greek word means "pupil" or "learner." In its most intense sense discipleship suggests a total commitment to stay close to and to obey the person chosen as one's teacher.

Commentary
In each of the synoptic Gospels (Matthew, Mark, and Luke) one question Jesus asked His disciples marks a turning point. That question is, "Who do people say I am?" (Mark 8:27: see also Matt. 16:13; Luke 9:18)

The disciples reported what the people were saying, people who had seen Jesus' miracles, listened to His teaching, been restored by His healing power, and eaten of the bread and fishes He had multiplied. Everywhere people were convinced that Jesus was among the greatest of the prophets, and might even be one of the ancients restored to life!

And then the synoptic Gospel writers each tell us that Jesus asked His disciples, "But who do *you* say that I am?"

Peter answered for them all.

"You are the Christ."

What is so significant about this incident is that three Gospels tell us that from this point there was a shift in Jesus' ministry. Only then did Jesus begin to teach His disciples about His coming death. In fact, from this point on Jesus focused His ministry more and more on instructing the Twelve.

Why? Because these men acknowledged Jesus for who He is: the Christ, the Son of God. The compliments of the crowds who linked Jesus with the greatest of Old Testament saints fell far short, for they failed to acknowledge Him for who He is. Those compliments in fact constituted a *rejection* of Jesus, a damning with faint praise.

There is no way that people who will not *believe* in Jesus can really profit from His instruction. Without the personal relationship with God which is established by faith, what a person *does* is completely irrelevant. It is only as we believe *and* obey that Jesus can fill our lives with newness. It is only faith *and* obedience that can transform.

And so Jesus now turned to instruct the little core of men who did believe, as you and I believe, how to live as disciples and so to please our God.

Life Through Death: Mark 8:31–9:13
Jesus' coming death (Mark 8:31-33). Matthew, Mark, and Luke agree. As soon as

Peter expressed the disciples' conviction that Jesus truly is the Christ, Jesus began to "teach them that the Son of man must suffer many things and be rejected by the elders, chief priests, and teachers of the Law, and that He must be killed and after three days rise again."

This blunt, clear teaching upset the disciples. They didn't want Jesus to die. Peter even took Jesus aside and began to "rebuke" Him!

Christ spoke sharply. "Out of My sight, Satan," Jesus said. And He added, "You do not have in mind the things of God, but the things of men."

This last phrase is especially important. What seems right and reasonable to human beings is often totally out of harmony with God's ways. We must learn to trust the wisdom of God, even when it seems to go against all that seems wise or best to us.

Choosing "death" (Mark 8:34-38). Jesus immediately applied what He had said to discipleship. God had determined Jesus' own death on the cross. Through that death will come new life for Jesus (He will "after three days rise again") and also new life for those who believe in Jesus. But God had also determined that the way for disciples to *experience* that new life was through a self-denial like Jesus' own!

He told the Twelve that if they were to "come after Me," they must also deny self, take up their cross, and follow Jesus.

The disciple's cross is the choice of God's will for the individual, even as Jesus' cross was God's will for Him. Self-denial is a rejection of human wisdom and desires that may conflict with God's will. And "following" Jesus is staying close to Him, living in intimate daily relationship, by adopting His own commitment to please God.

What hinges on this kind of discipleship? Jesus said that the person who rejected discipleship and held on to his (old) life will lose it, while the person who loses his (old) life will save it.

While this may seem complicated, the point is simple and vital. A person who rejects discipleship will never know what he or she might have become if his or her life had been turned over to Jesus. Only if we commit ourselves fully to Him, and make the disciples' daily choice of obedience, can we discover the new life relationship which Jesus makes possible for us!

♥ ***Link to Life: Youth / Adult***

Give each person in your group a sheet of paper and have colored crayons available. Tell each that he or she is going to create a picture of the ideal person; the truly beautiful person; the person he or she would like to become.

The pictures need not be portraits: they can be shapes, form, a scene, etc. However, each color and shape should represent something in a person which the artist admires and desires to see developed more fully in himself or herself.

When the drawings are complete, have each show and explain his or her picture. If your group is larger than 10, divide into smaller groups for this sharing.

Then raise the question: "How can we actually become this 'ideal' person we want to be?" Introduce Mark 8:31-38.

Glory follows (Mark 9:1-13). Again the sequence of events is important. Jesus had just told the disciples of His coming death and resurrection, and pointed out that the disciples too could be transformed if they would only give up their old lives for Him. Then Jesus told them, "I tell you the truth, some who are standing here will not taste death before they see the kingdom of God coming with power" (v. 1).

While many have puzzled over the meaning of this saying, in each Gospel it is followed by a report of Jesus' visit six days later to the Mount of Transfiguration. There, with Peter and James and John watching (note just "*some* who are standing here"), Jesus "was transfigured before them. His clothes became dazzling white, whiter than anyone in the world could bleach them" (vv. 2-3).

The glory that lay ahead for Jesus, a glory to be visible to all when "the kingdom of God come[s] with power," was shown to the three disciples.

The Bible tells us that Elijah and Moses appeared and talked with Jesus, while a voice from heaven said, "This is My Son, whom I love. Listen to Him."

The disciples were given a glimpse of the splendor to come after the Cross. Death truly was the pathway to glory.

The incident was intended not only to reassure the disciples. It is intended to reassure you and me as well. The daily cross of the disciple is hard to bear. Often we will be called on to make choices that seem to us to involve great cost. What we need to remember is that beyond each cross God calls on us to bear, and beyond the little death that obedience may seem to involve, lies the splendor of transformation. Just as Jesus' cross was the pathway to glory, so obedience is the pathway to transformation for you and for me.

The disciples did not yet understand the meaning of what they had seen. They had not even grasped the fact that Jesus would be crucified, and they discussed what "rising from the dead" might mean. But rather than asking Jesus, they moved to safer ground, and raised a theological question: "Why do the teachers of the Law say that Elijah must come first?"

Theological questions and discussion surely are not wrong. But what is most important is in simple faith to take heed to the words that were heard on that mountain. "This is My Son, whom I love. Listen to Him."

If we simply listen to Jesus, and do what He says, our lives will be transformed.

Pathways to Power: Mark 9:14-50

Jesus then went on to instruct His disciples in the kind of life they would be expected to live. Mark reported just a few of Jesus' teachings, giving us brief and pithy accounts of His sayings. Yet each is distinctively helpful as we try to live our own Christian lives in the twentieth-century world.

Prayer (Mark 9:14-32). When Jesus and the three came down from the Mount of Transfiguration, they found milling, shouting crowds. The disciples and some teachers of the Law were arguing loudly, while people in the crowd shouted out their comments. But when they saw Jesus all ran to greet Him.

Quickly the story came out. The disciples had been asked to cast an evil spirit from a child, but were unable to. When the child was brought to Jesus, the spirit saw Him and "immediately threw the boy into a convulsion."

The father begged, "If You can do anything, take pity on us and help us."

Jesus fastened immediately on the first phrase.

" 'If You can'?"

Hadn't Jesus been teaching and healing literally for years in Galilee? Could there be any doubt?

The answer was, of course there was doubt! People had witnessed what Jesus did but would not commit themselves fully to Him. The man's response to Jesus' statement that "everything is possible for him who believes" was certainly true of the majority in Israel. "I do believe; help me overcome my unbelief."

There was faith, but it was mixed with an unbelief that needed to be overcome.

Jesus rebuked the evil spirit, which shrieked, violently convulsed the child, and left him. Jesus took the near-dead child by the hand and lifted him to his feet.

Perhaps the first lesson for us in this story is that God does not demand perfect faith in people. We *do* believe. But we still need help for our unbelief. Jesus accepts even imperfect faith and generously works His miracles in our lives. As we continue to grow in our relationships with Him, He does indeed "help our unbelief," gradually replacing it with a more perfect trust in Him.

But there is another lesson as well. The disciples who had been unable to help were troubled by their powerlessness. Afterward they asked Jesus privately, "Why couldn't we drive it out?"

Jesus answered, "This kind can come out only by prayer."

For the challenges of our lives as Jesus' disciples we must rely, not on our own strength, but completely on God's. And we express that dependence most perfectly in prayer.

Servanthood (Mark 9:33-37). On the road to Capernaum Jesus' disciples had been arguing about which would be greatest. Christ called the Twelve together and said, "If anyone wants to be first, he must be the very last, and the servant of all."

Greatness is not to be found in self-exaltation, but in self-humbling. Spiritual significance is not won by concern for oneself, but by concern for others. It is only as we give that we receive God's praise.

When Jesus told the disciples to welcome the little children in His name, He illustrated the nature of servanthood. In the Roman world, the "little child" was placed under the authority of slaves. They might be loved, but were of little account until they reached their maturity. But to Jesus, the least important in society were valuable indeed.

In our servanthood, we value the least of men, not just those whom the world considers important.

Nonjudgmentalism (Mark 9:38-41). When the disciples saw a person they did not know driving out demons in Jesus' name, they told him to stop! After all, weren't *they* Jesus' disciples? What right did anyone else have to use His name?

Christ rebuked them, pointing out that no one who does good in Jesus' name one moment can speak against Jesus the next. Even a person who does the simplest good in Jesus' name will be rewarded.

How often through church history Christ's people have forgotten these words to disciples. We are not to condemn others who act in Jesus' name just because they are not part of our group, or our church. Those who act in the name of Jesus are with us, even if they are not of us.

Harmony (Mark 9:42-50). Jesus warned that disciples must do nothing to cause "one of these little ones who believe in Me to sin." In a series of strong statements, Jesus emphasized how terrible sin is. The imagery of cutting off the hand that causes sin, etc., is not meant literally but instead emphasizes the necessity of a decisive rejection of sin.

Disciples are to be "salt," a preservative. If the disciple does not live in harmony with Jesus and with others, but sins or causes others to sin, the disciple will be worthless as salt, and unable to fulfill his or her function.

Sin, in ourselves or in others, is serious. It shatters the harmony that is to exist between us and God, and within the Christian community.

How, then, does Jesus instruct His followers to live as disciples? They, and we, are to live a life of prayer and of servanthood. We are to live with our fellow believers in a nonjudgmental way, a way that promotes harmony by personally rejecting temptations to sin, and being careful not to cause brothers and sisters to sin either.

♥ ***Link to Life: Youth / Adult***
Put this outline on the chalkboard: Prayer: 9:14-32; Servanthood: 9:33-37; Nonjudgmentalism: 9:38-41; Harmony: 9:42-50. Let each group member select one of these four subjects to research in a team. Each team is to identify at least one principle for living as a disciple. Then each team is to list as many situations as possible in which acting on this principle is important to Christians today.

There are a number of enigmatic statements in this section, and your group members may have questions. Read the passage carefully and if you have questions that are not answered in this survey, consult the excellent Bible Knowledge Commentary *(Victor) which discusses each verse (see pp. 144-148).*

Threats to Discipleship: Mark 10:1-52

Jesus had shown His followers several keys to living as disciples. Now in a series of incidents that Mark linked together, Christ warned against pathways that have attracted the religious of all the ages. Jesus' disciples, today as then, must be careful not to fall into these spiritual traps.

Legalism (Mark 10:1-16). Again Jesus was met and questioned by some Pharisees. As always, they raised a legal question to "test" Jesus. There is one Greek word that suggests a "test" which is administered from a desire to prove the genuineness of the article tested. That word is *not* used here. The Pharisees did not wish to approve Jesus; they wished to discredit Him.

Each of the Gospel writers reports words of Jesus on marriage. He must have spoken of it often. So when the Pharisees raised the question again to "test" Christ, we can assume that they already knew His position.

Their question: "Is it lawful for a man to divorce his wife?"

This was intended as a trap. If Jesus said no, He would seem to speak against the Law of Moses. If He said yes, He would apparently contradict His own often-expressed commitment to a permanent relationship.

Jesus answered by referring to the Law in which they claimed to trust. "What did Moses command you?"

And they spoke of the "certificate of divorce" that the Mosaic Law permitted.

Jesus' response showed a totally different perspective on the Law than was held by the Pharisees. The Pharisees held that the Law was "the" standard of perfection. They believed God had given that perfect standard to mark out the way of salvation. And they also believed that they, by their zealous effort to keep the Law, would win His approval.

Jesus had a different perspective. He explained, "It was because your hearts were hard that Moses wrote you this law." Look back to Creation, Jesus taught, and you will see God's intention. Marriage is to be a lifelong commitment.

The reference to hard hearts is a reference to sin. It was only because sin warped and distorted this most intimate of relationships that Moses permitted divorce. God was willing to *lower* His standards, to provide imperfect human beings with a way to escape a destructive marriage. Divorce law, then, *proved that Law itself was not the ideal standard the Pharisees thought it to be!* In fact, Law involved a *lowering* of God's standards, permitting men who fell far short of His true ideal to continue in fellowship with Him.

What Law does is to show how far short we fall of the divine ideal, and reveal our need for salvation (cf. Rom. 3:19-20). The Pharisees' assumption that one could be saved by works of the Law, or even win God's approval by legalistic dedication, was completely wrong!

Later the disciples asked about the incident. His answer again focused on the heart, and suggested that the law on divorce was being used simply to change an older mate for a younger one. Anyone who divorces and remarries commits adultery. It is not conformity to the letter of the law, but intent, that God judges.

How careful we must be not to let our living relationships with Jesus be translated into frozen rules that ignore the motives of our hearts and are insensitive to the true desires for our God. And how very careful we must be not to legalistically "test" our brothers as the Pharisees constantly tried to test Jesus, not to approve but to discredit Him.

This sequence ends with another story. People were bringing little children to Jesus. The disciples objected, and tried to send the parents away. But Jesus indignantly commanded them to "let the little children come to Me, and do not hinder them, for the kingdom of God belongs to such as these." He went on to add that "anyone who will not receive the kingdom of God like a little child will never enter it."

What did Jesus mean? In Judaism a "little child" was not considered to be under the Law. Not until one's thirteenth birthday was a person old enough to begin to relate to God through the Law. To receive the kingdom like a "little child" meant to reject Law as a way of entering God's kingdom, and to rely instead as children did on the love and grace of the God who had made great promises to His people.

Humanism (Mark 10:17-34). The "rich young man" who came to Jesus addressed Him as "good Teacher" and asked what he must "do" to inherit eternal life. These provide the key to understanding the next danger to the disciple: humanism.

Jesus immediately challenged the young man's assumptions. Why did he call Jesus "good" and add a merely human title? Didn't he realize that only God is truly "good"?

This is, of course, the key error of humanism. It seeks goodness in human motives and actions, without realizing that only God is good.

To help the young man discover his error for himself, Jesus asked about the commands listed on the second tablet of the Law.

When Moses brought God's Ten Commands down from Mount Sinai, they were written on two stone tablets. The first tablet contained commands that related to loving God. The second tablet contained commands related to loving other human beings. Now Jesus quoted only from the second tablet as He spoke of the commands not to murder, commit adultery, steal, give false testimony, or defraud, and to honor mother and father. This, the young man said, he had done since he was a boy.

This young man was not lying. He *had* been a truly good person. "Jesus looked at him and loved him."

But then Jesus spoke of a great lack. And He told the young man to sell everything, give it to the poor, and then follow Jesus.

The young man's face fell, and he went away sad "because he had great wealth."

What happened here? This young man who represented the best humanism has to offer—a truly "good" (by human standards) person—had related correctly to his fellowmen. But the very first commandment says, "You shall have no other gods before Me" (cf. Ex. 20:3). Jesus' instructions to sell all was a vivid demonstration that this lovely young man, so sensitive in his dealings with others, actually did have another god before

God: his money. When the Son of God commanded him to sell his possessions, he made his choice—money.

How hard it was for this rich young man to give God His proper place. Humanistic good—an honest consideration of other people—is not really costly. But putting God first may demand our everything!

The disciples again misunderstood. When Jesus remarked on how hard it is for the rich to enter His kingdom, the disciples were stunned. Surely wealth was a sign of God's approval! If the wealthy found it difficult, who then could be saved?

Jesus answered, "With man this is impossible." No matter how kind and considerate the humanist may be, mere human goodness can never win entrance to God's kingdom. But, "All things are possible with God" (Mark 10:27). In Jesus Himself God has made a way for His lost ones to return.

Still the disciples misunderstood. Fascinated with riches, Peter wondered aloud. "We have left everything to follow You!" Jesus nodded and made Peter, and you and me a promise. In abandoning everything we will without fail receive "a hundred times as much in this present age." In Christ we become the possessors of all things. But many who seem "first" in this life will be last in God's kingdom, and those whom men account "last" will be first.

♥ ***Link to Life: Children***

It's not wrong to possess things. What is wrong is to value earthly treasures more highly than we should. Today boys and girls are constantly tempted by sophisticated marketing to want things that have no real value.

Watch a couple of children's TV shows and look at the back of cereal boxes to discover what advertisers are trying to make children want now. Obtain pictures of half dozen or so of the most currently wanted items.

Paste one picture on one side of a 4 x 6 card. On the other paste or draw a picture to represent: friends, school, church, missions (a needy person), etc.

Then play "Choose One." First show each side *of one card. Have the children talk about why they like the thing on each side (for instance, GOBOTS, and friends). Then ask the children if they could have only one of these two, which would they choose?*

After the choice is made, talk about why each child chose as he did. Why didn't they choose GOBOTS? (Get broken, lost, can't talk to or care about us, etc.)

How important that we learn to choose the things that are truly important to us, the good gifts God has given us rather than the things advertisers try to make us think we need.

Authoritarianism (Mark 10:35-45). The third danger to discipleship is the desire for the wrong kind of authority within the believing community. James and John were eager for positions of power in Jesus' coming kingdom. Jesus warned them that one who sought position in His kingdom must be ready to drink from Christ's cup and to be baptized with His baptism. In this He spoke of complete dedication to God's will, and the suffering that this might entail.

Jesus warned them, however, to abandon the notion of "authority" as it was understood in the secular world. There the rulers "lord it over" others and "exercise authority over them." It is not to be this way in Jesus' kingdom. The person who is great is the one who gives himself to serve others, even as Jesus came to serve and to give His life (vv. 43-44).

There is to be no hierarchy in the church! The greatest is the lowest: the one who dedicates himself not to be served by those to whom he gives orders, but to give service that they might become all that God wants them to be.

The blind see (Mark 10:46-52). Again Mark closed a section with report of a miracle. But what a special miracle. A blind man was given his sight, and was told, "Your faith has healed you."

It is the same with us. Jesus gives us the spiritual sight to see the emptiness in legalism, the futility of mere humanism, and the error of hierarchialism. What is it that truly can heal the disciple and lead him along the pathway of power? Jesus answers us in His words to the blind who now can see. "Go, your faith has healed you." And as with Bartimaeus, "immediately he received his sight and followed Jesus along the road."

TEACHING GUIDE

Prepare
In which area is your own discipleship most actively expressed: Prayer? Servanthood? Nonjudgmentalism? Harmony?

Explore
1. Ask each person to write down a single statement explaining what a *disciple* is and does.

Share ideas and discuss your group members' ideas.
2. What do your group members yearn to become? Help them explore how discipleship promises personal transformation, and sense what they can become through full commitment to Jesus Christ. Use the "link-to-life" activity explained on page 619.

Expand
1. What are the pathways that Jesus marked out to spiritual success for disciples? "Link-to-life" on page 621 suggests a way to study Mark 9 and learn about the role of prayer, servanthood, nonjudgmentalism, and interpersonal peace.
2. Or look at the three detours that lead disciples astray as they seek to follow Jesus.

Before your group meets, assign three different members one of the different detours found here: legalism, humanism, and authoritarianism. Work through the passage each is assigned with him or her. Then in class ask each for a five-minute summary of his or her theme.

After reports are heard, have these three people serve as a panel, to answer any questions on the passage he or she reported on.

Apply
In closing ask your group members to meditate quietly for about two minutes on the statement: Discipleship is a choice.

STUDY GUIDE 97

Mark 11–13

THE LAST WEEK

Overview

As the last week of Jesus' life on earth begins, Mark brings three distinct themes into focus.

In Mark 11 we gain insight into the mission of the Messiah. On Palm Sunday Jesus was hailed as the Promised One. He cleansed the temple, signifying His ministry of purifying religion. He cursed the fruitless fig tree, which symbolized a ritualistic Israel, and explained the power of personal faith.

In Mark 12 we see the futility of Israel's approach to faith explained in great detail. Jesus showed us by contrast how living by faith can please God.

In Mark 13 we have the only prophetic section in this Gospel. Jesus spoke of the end of the age. No one knows just when the events He spoke of will happen. So we are to be on guard, always attending to our assigned task as we expect Christ's imminent return.

There are many familiar stories in these chapters of Mark's Gospel. And there is much to learn from each, as well as from the way Mark linked them to demonstrate his larger themes.

▶ ***Pharisees, Sadducees.*** You can find background information on these two religious groups of Jesus' time in the introduction to the Gospels, Study Guide 79.

■ See the *Bible Knowledge Commentary* pages 155-173, for a verse-by-verse commentary on each incident.

Commentary

The scene now shifts to Judea. It was the last week of Christ's life, and Jesus now appeared in Jerusalem. This is the traditional center of Old Testament faith. But it is also the center of the corruption of that faith. In a series of incidents and confrontations Jesus demonstrated how the pure religion of the Old Testament had been corrupted, and in those confrontations helps us better understand the relationship that you and I today are to maintain with our God.

The Messiah's Mission: Mark 11:1-26

Triumphal Entry (Mark 11:1-11). Jesus told His disciples where to obtain a colt on which He would enter Jerusalem. Mark did not refer to it, but this fulfilled Zechariah's prophecy that He who is King of Israel will enter in just this way (Zech. 9:9). Jesus now presented Himself in Jerusalem as the promised Messiah.

As Jesus moved slowly toward the city gate, the crowds waved branches and shouted praises. They recognized Him as Messiah: "He who comes in the name of the Lord" (Mark 11:9).

When Jesus entered Jerusalem He went directly to the temple. He did not go to the Fortress Antonia or to Herod's palace. Secular power was not the concern of the Messiah of Israel at this time.

Jesus' choice of the temple established immediately that His first concern was religious. The focus of Jesus' concern was the faith of Israel as a people of God, not the fate of Israel as a nation.

Jesus "looked around at everything." After making this evaluation Jesus left. But He would return the next day.

Cleansing the temple (Mark 11:12-26). On the way back to Jerusalem the next day Jesus saw a luxuriant-looking fig tree. But the tree had only leaves and not fruit. Jesus cursed the tree: "May no one ever eat fruit from you again." He then passed on into the city.

Entering the temple area (its outer courts), Jesus "began driving out those who were buying and selling there." After He had overturned tables and chased out the merchants, Jesus taught, quoting the Old Testament:

My house will be called a house of prayer for all nations.

Mark 11:17

The religious leaders of Judah had made God's house a "den of robbers."

The two incidents are intimately linked. The fig tree represented Israel. Often in the Old Testament the image of a vine or tree is used to represent God's people. In these images God spoke of the fruit which He expected His planting to produce. In Isaiah 5:7 we read that the fruit He desired from the house of Israel, the "garden of His delight," was justice and righteousness.

But like the fig tree, Israel had produced no fruit! Therefore like the fig tree the nation would be cursed, and no one would "ever eat fruit from you again."

But why the link of this incident with the temple which Jesus looked over, and where He returned to drive out merchants? Because in the Judaism of Jesus' day, as in much of Old Testament history, the temple and its ritual were assumed by the Jews to provide special standing with God. The people could do anything they wanted in the temple—even robbing the poor in its very courts by forcing them to buy "approved" animals for sacrifice at inflated prices. They trusted in ritual, unaware that God was unimpressed with great edifices and cared only for hearts tuned to love Him and one another.

The next morning the fig tree had withered away. Its deadness was now exposed, even as Jesus was about to expose the deadness of Israel's religion.

Jesus told the disciples the truth. The true power of religion is not found in buildings or ritual, but in a personal relationship with God which is expressed in faith. The person who trusts God completely can move mountains! We are to pray, believing. We can be sure as we focus our trust in God that we will receive what we ask.

But there is a horizontal aspect to faith as well as a vertical. We are to forgive anyone we have something against when we stand praying. The true religion Jesus the Messiah promotes calls for both love for God and love for our fellowmen.

♥ ***Link to Life: Youth / Adult***

Give an overview of the linkage of the incidents in these chapters. Then have your group members turn to Jeremiah 7:1-11, to which Jesus alluded when He said that the Jews had made God's house a "den of robbers."

The people of Jeremiah's day trusted in the temple (e.g., as long as His temple is there, God must *protect us). The temple of Jeremiah's time was destroyed by the Babylonians, along with Jerusalem. Only a moral and spiritual reformation—not a ritual faith that ignored morality—could have saved them.*

From this passage ask your group members to define what is wrong with a merely ritual religion. What seem to be the assumptions of the worshipers about what pleases God? What seems to be the lifestyle of the people? From what the Lord criticizes, what can we assume He seeks from His worshipers?

Israel's Futile Faith: Mark 11:27–12:44

Mark had established in his first two stories about Jesus' acts in Judea a theme he then developed. How can it be that Israel's faith, rooted in God's Old Testament revelation, had become futile and empty? What was it that had distorted in practice the beauty of the faith God Himself revealed?

Empty of authority (Mark 11:27-33). The "chief priests, the teachers of the Law, and the elders" composed the ruling council of Israel. This group had the power to judge both religious and civil matters in the Jewish community. They even claimed, and exercised, the right to expel people from the synagogue (cf. John 9:22; 12:42).

Since these leaders of the community had never commissioned or recognized Jesus, they liked to think that He spoke without any real religious authority. This, despite the fact that the people were amazed just because Jesus *did* speak as a Man with authority, unlike their official leaders (cf. Mark 1:22).

Now, after Jesus had driven the money changers from the temple, a delegation of leaders challenged Jesus. By what authority was He acting? And who gave Him authority to do what He did?

Jesus asked them one question that exposed how empty of "authority" these so-called spiritual leaders really were. Jesus asked them whether John's baptism was from heaven or from men.

Now, a person who has spiritual authority must derive it ultimately from God. So one who exercises authority must refer to God and God's will in making his decisions. But when these religious leaders discussed Jesus' question, they immediately referred not to God but to the people. "If we say, 'From men.'. . ." The text notes, "They feared the people, for everyone held that John really was a prophet."

Ultimately, they who claimed to be the final court of spiritual appeal, answered Jesus, "We don't know."

No religion which appeals to mere human opinion in making its determinations can have real authority or power. The faith of Israel in Jesus' day was futile because it had exchanged the authority of God and His Word for mere human opinion!

No religion which looks to public opinion to determine its stand can ever be vital and real.

Misuse of authority (Mark 12:1-12). Jesus then told a parable about a person who prepared the land and planted a vineyard. He rented it out to some tenant farmers, and left on a trip. But when he sent servants to collect his share, the servants were beaten and some were even killed. Finally the man sent his only son, saying, "They will respect my son."

Instead the tenants chose to kill the heir, so "the inheritance will be ours."

The leaders realized that Jesus had spoken the parable against them, and were even more determined to arrest Him. They had not used their authority as God's agents to serve Him at all! They had misused their authority, seeking only their own benefit. Their fathers had been willing to kill God's servants, the prophets, and now this generation was eager to kill His only Son!

Hypocrisy (Mark 12:13-17). The fact that the religion of Israel was now marked by hypocrisy is demonstrated in the next incident.

The Pharisees and Herodians came to try to trap Jesus. The Herodians were a political party that believed in accommodation with the Romans. To them Jesus seemed a dangerous revolutionary. Both these groups, usually opposed to each other, feared Jesus and hated Him passionately.

When they came to Jesus their hypocrisy was made plain in multiple ways. They addressed Jesus as a "man of integrity" who teaches "the way of God in accordance with the truth." They did not believe what they were saying; they said it only to "set Jesus up" for their trap.

They asked Jesus whether or not the Jews should pay taxes to Caesar. The trap was simple. If Jesus told them to pay taxes, He would lose favor with the people who hated Rome. If Jesus told them *not* to pay taxes, He could be accused to the Romans, and would be executed!

Yet this trap was itself a hypocritical one. It was shown to be even more hypocritical when Jesus had to ask *them* for a coin! Here these men were trying to trap Jesus and accuse Him of collaboration with the enemy, and they were the ones who were profiting financially from the Roman occupation, for they were the ones who possessed Roman money!

Jesus avoided their trap by pointing to the portrait and inscription on the coin. These were Caesar's? Then let Caesar have what belonged to him, and give God what belongs to God.

What is it that belongs to the Caesars of this world? Only material things: things that have no lasting value and cannot really reflect the issues of life. And what belongs to God? Our heart, our soul, our love, our obedience, our whole being.

Let Caesar have his *things*, but give God your heart.

The religion of Jesus' day was empty and meaningless because it was all hypocrisy and show. The men who led His people were not moved by a passion for God.

Without understanding of Scripture (Mark 12:18-27). Now the Sadducees—the "liberals" of Jesus' day, who denied the resurrection and life after death, along with angels and miracles—tried to trap Jesus. They raised a hypothetical case. Here's a widow who has been married, in turn, to each of seven brothers. "At the resurrection," they asked (subtly ridiculing this doctrine in which they did not believe), "whose wife will she be?"

Jesus' answer affirmed the authority of Scripture. Their error arose from the fact that "you do not know the Scriptures or the power of God." Jesus explained that there is no marriage in heaven: the saints there, like the angels, will not wed. But as for resurrection, Jesus pinned His teaching on the tense of a verb. God said to Moses, "I *am* the God of Abraham, the God of Isaac, and the God of Jacob." God did not say, "I *was*" their God! Obviously then Abraham, Isaac, and Jacob must be living when God spoke those words, even though they had died physically centuries before.

What a tremendous confidence we can have in Scripture! Even the tenses of words are rooted in reality, and one can trust each phrase to express divine truth.

The Sadducees, like the liberals of every age, were quick to discount the authority of the Word of God. And just because of this fault, they and their religion were "badly mistaken."

Without focus (Mark 12:28-37). There was another fault in the ritual religion practiced by the Jews in Jesus' day. They cluttered up their faith with hundreds of rules derived from traditional interpretations of biblical Laws. But somehow all these laws seemed just as important as all the others. Don't spit on sand on the Sabbath (because you might inadvertently "plow a furrow") was treated with the same importance as "love your neighbor."

When one of the teachers of the Law saw that Jesus was answering well, he raised what to Him was an honest question. "Of all the commandments, which is the most important?"

Jesus answered, " 'Love the Lord your God with all your heart and with all your soul and with all your mind and with all your strength.' The second is this: 'Love your neighbor as yourself.' There is no commandment greater than these."

With this answer Jesus provided the focus for faith which Israel had lost. All of the laws which were so important to the Jews, all the ceremonies and rituals, must be placed in perspective by the realization that man's central duty is to love God and to love neighbors.

The man affirmed what Jesus had said. "To love [God] with all your heart . . . and to love your neighbor as yourself is more important than all burnt offerings and sacrifices" (v. 33).

Jesus said to him, "You are not far from the kingdom of God."

Only when the focus of our faith is squarely on loving God and our neighbor do we even approach the kingdom of our God. Israel's faith was futile because in the preoccupation of the religious with ritual and ceremony and tradition, the true heart of God's revelation of Himself in Law had been totally missed.

The total inability of the religious leaders to understand the Scriptures or its focus is now illustrated by Jesus. The teachers of the Law say that Christ is the Son (descendant) of David. This is clearly true. But how do they explain David speaking of his descendant as "my Lord?"

The crowd was delighted, not because they knew the answer, but because Jesus had shown up the hypocrisy and spiritual fraud of those proud men who claimed to be so much better than common men.

Greed (Mark 10:38-44). The final condemnation drew attention to the true motives of the religious leaders of Israel. These men who loved to be treated with respect because of their superior piety actually "devour widows' houses and for a show make lengthy prayers." They were outwardly religious, but within were moved only by greed.

Jesus and His disciples sat down to watch worshipers contribute money to the temple treasury. Some who were wealthy "threw in" large amounts. The sound of the heavy coins told everyone how much they were giving, and they threw in their offerings with force to make sure all could hear. They were outwardly religious.

But then a widow timidly "put in" two tiny coins, almost worthless. Jesus pointed her out, and said, "This poor widow has put more into the treasury than all the others. They all gave out of their wealth; but she, out of her poverty, put in everything—all she had to live on."

What a difference. The size of the gift the rich could give might impress men. But what they gave was really nothing to them: it cost them not one moment of discomfort. It was no sacrifice at all. But the gift of the widow impressed God. She gave all.

A religion practiced by greedy men who get their wealth by oppressing the poor is a meaningless faith, no matter how much they may "give" to God. What God wants is our love, for out of love we will be willing to give Him not a "tip," but our all.

♥ ***Link to Life: Youth / Adult***
Give a minilecture showing the relationship of each incident in this section to Jesus' theme of the reasons why Jewish religion had become fruitless.

Then tell your group they have been appointed to a "renewal committee" at their church. They are to study this chapter of Mark's Gospel to develop a renewal and revitalization program. From the problems identified by Mark, the committee is to specify modern parallels—and then develop "action ideas" a congregation might take to help its members develop a more vital, fruitful relationship with God.

If your group is large, you might form "subcommittees" (teams) to examine individual incidents.

The End of the Age: Mark 13

This chapter contains Mark's longest report of any connected discourse by Jesus. It closely parallels the report in Matthew 24 and 25 (see Study Guide 90).

Jesus warned of terrible tragedies which will be part of human experience while He is away. Finally there will come events foretold in the Book of Daniel and by other Old Testament prophets (Mark 13:14-32). As the end nears there will be "days of distress unequaled from the beginning when God created the world, until now" (v. 19).

That day will close with "the Son of man coming in clouds with great power and glory" (v. 26).

Jesus concluded His predictions about the future with the statement, "This generation will certainly not pass away until all these things have happened" (v. 30). Since that generation is long dead, what could Jesus have meant?

The term translated "generation" here can mean those currently living. But it also can mean a family or national *line*. Jesus had begun His discourse by predicting the destruction of the temple in which the Jews took such pride. Within the lifespan of the generation then living, the temple Herod had spent 40 years beautifying and expanding was destroyed completely. It was destroyed by the Romans in A.D. 70 in response to yet another Jewish rebellion. The generation that had heard Jesus teach and witnessed His miracles—and had rejected the Son of God—lived to see their city razed and their temple destroyed.

What happened to the Jewish people then? For thousands of years they were scattered throughout the world, with no homeland to call their own. And yet they survived. And they maintained their separate identity. That "generation," as represented in the Jewish people (the family and national line) "will certainly not pass away" until *all* the things Jesus spoke of actually take place.

But what about those who believe in Jesus during the interim? Jesus gives His followers this warning: "Be on guard! Be alert!" No one knows when the Lord will come, so each of us must be alert and about his assigned task.

And what, then, must we be alert for? Why, we must be alert that the very things which crept into the religion of Israel and sapped it of its vitality do not slip into the practice of our faith!

How good it is to know that, until Jesus does return, you and I can worship Him, with others, in Spirit and in truth.

TEACHING GUIDE

Prepare

What distortion of biblical faith in Israel seems most likely to be a danger for your group members as well?

Explore

1. Play a tape recorded reading of Isaiah 5:1-7 as Old Testament background. Then tell the story of Jesus cursing the fig tree. Against the Old Testament background, what do your group members suppose the fig tree represents? What was Jesus communicating in His curse of the fruitless tree?

2. What is the background of the "den of robbers" accusation leveled by Jesus against those who bought and sold in the temple? Look with your group members into Jeremiah 7, guided by the approach outlined in "link-to-life," page 626.

Expand

1. Give most of your group time to a study of the specific attitudes and viewpoints revealed as Jesus confronted the religious leaders of His time. Let your group serve as a "renewal committee" to identify elements

in "religion" which are destructive to a biblical faith. Based on what your group members discover, what practical suggestions might they give a local congregation to guard against the errors that crept into Judaism? See "link-to-life," pages 628-629 for ideas on how to go about this study.
2. Cover Mark 13 in a *brief* minilecture, keeping your focus on Jesus' command to His present disciples to watch, and be ready for His return.

Apply
Name one thing that you are doing now to guard against any of the attitudes that sapped the spiritual strength of Judaism.

STUDY GUIDE 98

Mark 14–16

JESUS' DEATH AND RESURRECTION

Overview
Each of the Gospel writers gives us much detail about the last evening Jesus spent with His disciples, and about the trials which led up to His execution. Yet few Christians are aware of the exact sequence of events, or of their locations. In this study, the events reported by Mark and the other Gospel writers are located for you and your group members on a large map which you can duplicate for them to have.

In this *Teacher's Commentary* each Gospel's report of Jesus' death and resurrection is given a slightly different treatment, designed to reflect the emphasis of the Gospel.

In the study of Matthew, we explore the meaning of Christ's death as a sacrifice for sins. In that study we answer the theologian's question, "Why did God become man?"

In this study of Mark's Gospel we emphasize the sequence of the events on the day Christ died.

In the study of Luke's Gospel we focus on evidence that, throughout the experience, Jesus remained in control. He *gave* His life; it was not taken.

In the study of John's Gospel we examine Christ's instructions to His disciples at the Last Supper, and the striking confrontation Jesus had with Pilate, the Roman governor.

Through each of these studies we come to appreciate more the suffering of Christ, and sense more of the love He showed to you and me at Calvary.

Commentary
The events associated with Jesus' trials and death took place in and around Jerusalem. While there is debate concerning some of the specific locations, such as the location of Joseph's tomb, we have a great deal of information on the specific places Jesus traveled to on that fateful night.

Jerusalem in the time of Jesus was a typical walled city. The "lower city," built along a steep hillside, was filled with crowded tenement-type structures. The upper city contained the larger city homes of the wealthy, like Caiaphas, the high priest and the beautiful palace of Herod.

It was the temple, however, which dominated the city, and was the focus of the faith of all Jews in every land. Immediately next to the temple was the Fortress Antonia, where a Roman army contingent was stationed and Pontius Pilate held court. Directly across from the temple, separated from it by the deep Kidron Valley, and up on the side of the Mount of Olives lay the Garden of Gethsemane, an olive orchard where Jesus often stopped to rest and pray. On the other side of the city, just outside the city walls, was the public execution grounds, Golgotha—the place of the skull. Many believe that a tomb nearby, hewn into the living rock and matching perfectly the description given in the Gospels, is the very tomb which Joseph of Arimathea surrendered to the Saviour.

This, then, was the setting for those familiar yet terrible events that we know so well as Jesus, near the end of His life on earth, approached the Cross.

Tuesday and Wednesday: Mark 14:1-11
Jesus passed the two days between His confrontation with the Jewish leaders and His final day on earth with friends in Bethany. There He was anointed by a woman who poured expensive perfume on His head. This was a "beautiful thing" done in preparation "for My burial." The woman may not have understood, but she did love the Lord and expressed that love by giving.

Judas, on the other hand, "went to the chief priests to betray Jesus to them" for the promise of money.

What a contrast. The woman gave generously because she loved Jesus: Judas be-

Jerusalem at the Time of Jesus

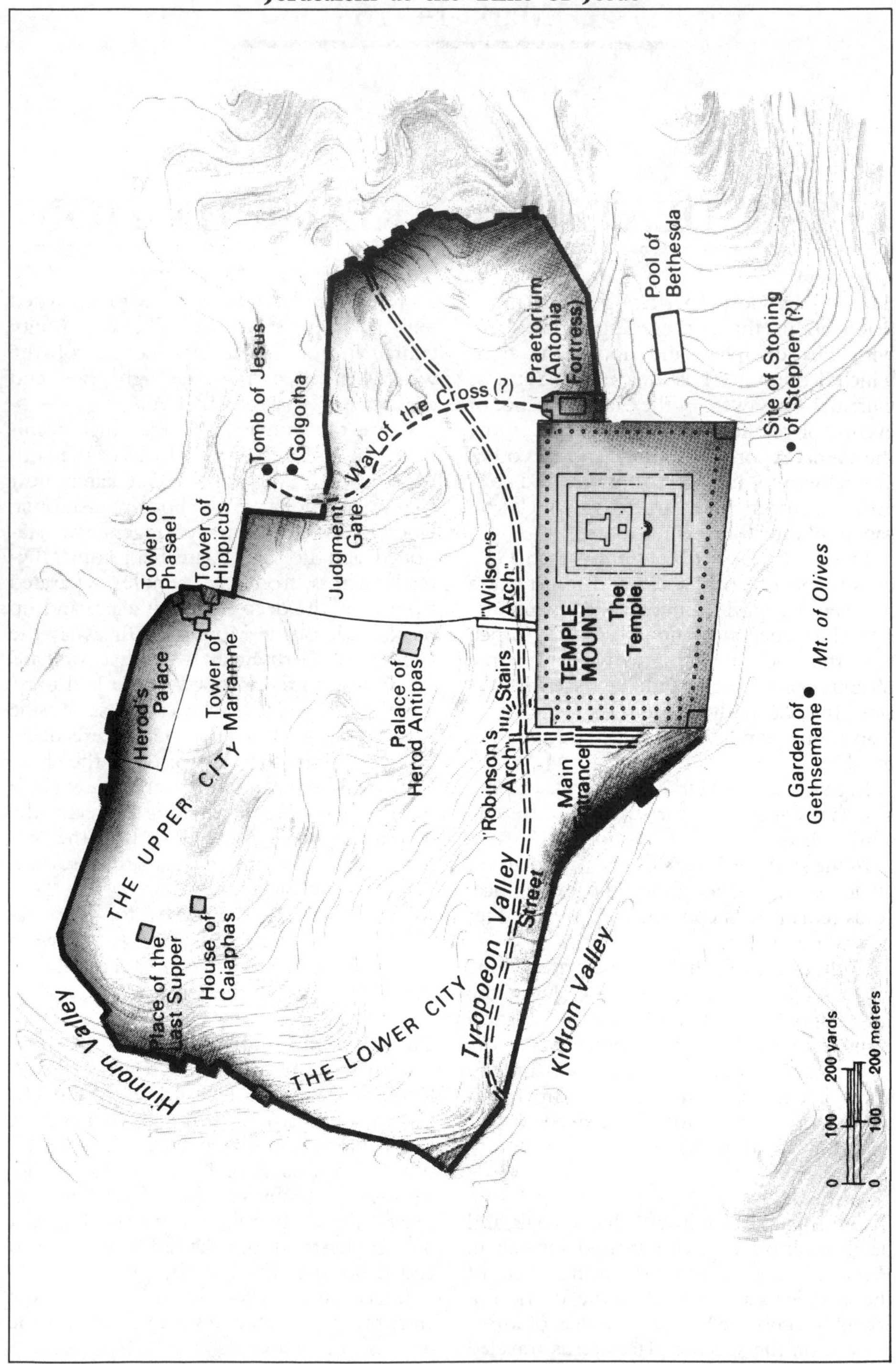

Taken from Zondervan *Pictorial Bible Dictionary*. Edited by Merrill C. Tenney. © 1963, 1964, 1965, Zondervan Publishing House. Used by permission.

trayed Jesus because he loved money.

♥ ***Link to Life: Children***
It is important for all of us to link giving with love for Jesus. We can help boys and girls make this connection by letting them help decorate our offering plate, or create special offering envelopes. For the first, have each child write on a paper plate, "I love Jesus" and decorate the plate with hearts, or whatever scene they may wish. For the second, have each child scotch tape two 4 x 6 cards together. Tape three sides, but leave one side untaped so money can be slipped into it. Again let each child in your class write, "I love Jesus" on the envelope and decorate it appropriately. Then each week use a different child's decorated plate or offering envelope to take up the collection, letting the child who made it take up the offering. Pray with the children, thanking Jesus that because you love Him you want to give to Him all.

Thursday: Mark 14:12–15:1

The Passover meal (Mark 14:12-26). That Thursday Jesus and His followers met in a room in a house in Jerusalem's upper city. John's Gospel tells us in great detail what Jesus taught His disciples there. Mark simply tells us that Jesus, seated at the table, told the Twelve that one of them was about to betray Him. Judas then slipped away to go to the chief priests.

Mark tells us that then Jesus broke bread and told the disciples, "This is My body." And He took the cup, saying, "This is My blood of the covenant, which is poured out for many." After they sang a hymn, they left the house where they had eaten and went to the Mount of Olives.

It was night, and the little party probably went down steps that still lead down the steep hillside near the house of Caiaphas into the valley. Traveling back along the Hinnom Valley into the Kidron, they moved up a path that climbed the Mount of Olives to the Garden of Gethsemane.

Peter's denial predicted (Mark 14:27-31). On the way Jesus remarked that soon all the disciples would desert Him. Peter was incensed. "Even if I have to die with You, I will never disown You." But Jesus told Peter that that very night he would disown Christ three times—three times before the rooster crowed.

	Matthew	Mark	Luke	John
Thursday				
The Passover Meal Held	26:17-29	14:12-25	22:7-22	13:1-38
The Last Supper Teaching				14–16
Jesus' High Priestly Prayer				17
Prayer at Gethsemane	26:36-46	14:32-42	22:39-46	18:1
Jesus Arrested	26:47-56	14:43-52	22:47-53	18:2-12
On Trial before Annas				18:12-14, 19-23
On Trial before Caiaphas	26:57-68	14:53-65	22:54-65	18:24
Peter Denies the Lord	26:69-75	14:66-72	22:54-62	18:15-18, 25-27
On Trial before the Sanhedrin	27:1	15:1	22:66-71	
Friday				
On Trial before Pilate	27:11-14	15:2-5	23:1-5	18:28-38
Taken to Herod			23:6-12	
Returned to Pilate	27:15-26	15:6-15	23:13-25	18:39–19:16
Mocked by Soldiers	27:27-30	15:16-19	22:63-65	
Led to Calvary	27:31-34	15:20-23	23:26-32	19:16-17
Jesus' Crucifixion	27:35-56	15:24-41	23:33-49	19:18-37
Jesus' Body Buried	27:57-60	15:42-46	23:50-54	19:38-42
Saturday				
Women Visit the Tomb	27:61	15:47	23:55-57	
A Guard Set over the Tomb	27:62-66			
Sunday				
The Women Return	28:1-8	16:1-8	24:1-12	20:1-10

Events of Trial, Crucifixion, and Resurrection in Gospels

Gethsemane (Mark 14:32-42). It was now late at night. The tired disciples could hardly stay awake. But Jesus was in anguish, so tormented by His knowledge of what was about to come that He was "overwhelmed with sorrow." Jesus needed their companionship, but the disciples' eyes were so heavy they kept nodding off.

Finally Jesus wakened them. At the base of the hill, torches could be seen, and the sounds of a mob stumbling up the hill could be heard.

Jesus arrested (Mark 14:43-52). Judas was leading the armed crowd that had been sent by the religious leaders to seize Jesus. He identified Christ with a kiss, and the men roughly grabbed hold of the Lord.

Other Gospels tell us that it was Peter who then bravely drew a sword and struck out. His blade grazed the head of a servant of the high priest, cutting off his ear. Again, another Gospel tells us that Jesus picked up the severed ear and replaced it. As Jesus rebuked the mob, His terrified disciples all slipped away and fled.

Most believe that the "young man, wearing nothing but a linen garment" who was following Jesus was John Mark himself, the author of this Gospel. When the mob seized Jesus, Mark was so terrified he fled "leaving his garment behind him."

On trial before Annas. Jesus was taken back through the Kidron Valley and up the Hinnom to the steps that led up the hill toward Caiaphas' house. John tells us that He was taken first to Annas, who is also called the high priest. In fact, Annas was high priest emeritus, and was the father-in-law of the current high priest, Caiaphas. He exerted such influence that Luke, in Acts 4, spoke of Annas as high priest.

After a preliminary examination in which Jesus was struck in the face (John 18:22), Christ was sent on to Caiaphas.

On trial before Caiaphas (Mark 14:55-65). The home of the high priest was large, with a handsome courtyard. There the leadership gathered to determine how they might get rid of Jesus. The leaders interviewed those who volunteered to give false testimony against Jesus, but their testimony was not consistent.

Finally the high priest asked Jesus bluntly, "Are You the Christ, the Son of the Blessed One?" Jesus answered, "I am." To the leaders this was blasphemy: Jesus had claimed to be God Himself! And the penalty for blasphemy was death.

Jesus had not yet been officially condemned. The "trial" had been more of a hearing, but a hearing before those who would soon serve as judges. By the time the Sanhedrin met in official session the verdict would be settled.

In the meantime, some began to spit at Jesus, and to strike Him with their fists. In the Jerusalem house that tradition says was that of Caiaphas there is a dark, dungeon-like basement. It may be that the guards who Mark tells us then beat Christ took Him down into that shadowy room.

Peter denies Jesus (Mark 14:66-72). Peter alone of all the disciples had followed the mob that took Jesus all the way back into Jerusalem. There some recognized Peter as one of Jesus' followers. And when Peter spoke, his accent betrayed him as a Galilean. The frightened Peter swore again and again that he did not even know "this Man you're talking about."

It was then the cock crowed . . . and Peter remembered that Jesus had known about his denial. Crushed, Peter "broke down and wept."

On trial before the Sanhedrin (Mark 15:1). Mark 15:1 sums up what Luke 22:66-71 describes. Early in the morning, just before dawn, Jesus was brought back before the Sanhedrin, now officially constituted. Jesus was asked again if He were the Christ, the Son of God. Again Jesus affirmed that He is.

Now the verdict was officially passed. Jesus was guilty of blasphemy for claiming to be God.

There was only one problem, not recognized by the Sanhedrin. Jesus *is* God. The court had met, and had condemned—itself.

Friday: Mark 15:2-46

Jesus before Pilate (Mark 15:2-15). The Jews, like other peoples in the Roman Empire, were granted a great degree of self-government. Of course, local laws were subordinate to Roman law. But only a Roman citizen had access to Roman courts. So most of the civil as well as religious disputes in Judea and Galilee were settled by the Jewish court.

But the Sanhedrin lacked one very important power. It had no authority to execute.

It was for this reason that Jesus was now

sent, under guard, to the Fortress Antonia to appear before Pilate. It was very early. But it's possible that even that early in the morning Jesus was taken outside the city, through the narrow valleys, to approach the fortress without being observed. The Jewish leaders would not have wanted to rouse the city that had hailed Christ as the Messiah just a few days earlier.

Luke tells us that after an initial appearance before Pilate, Jesus was taken to Herod Antipas. Herod was technically ruler of Galilee. Sending Jesus to Herod was a courtesy, and Luke tells us that Herod appreciated it. In fact, the gesture healed a rift that had developed between the two.

But Herod, after Jesus disappointed him by performing no miracle, returned Christ to Pilate. After all, only Pilate had the power of life and death.

Each of the Gospels tells us how hard Pilate tried to avoid condemning Jesus. But Pilate, technically the ruler of this subject people, was unwilling to offend them.

To satisfy the crowd Pilate went against his own conscience, and ordered Jesus' crucifixion!

Mocked by soldiers (Mark 15:16-23). Jesus was then turned over to the military to be prepared for crucifixion. This involved beating, designed to weaken the victim. In this case the soldiers took great delight in mocking Jesus. These Roman soldiers were auxiliaries, probably Franks and Gauls marched across the empire from France to serve in hot, dusty Palestine. They neither understood nor liked the Jews. To ridicule and torment one who called Himself King of the Jews must have stimulated their smoldering hostility and cruelty.

The Crucifixion (Mark 15:24-32). Jesus was taken by a direct route from the Fortress Antonia to the execution ground outside the city. This was located on a major road, where all would profit by seeing what happened to criminals under Roman rule.

Crucifixion was a method of execution that Roman law ordained for the worst of criminals. No Roman citizen could be executed in this way.

The crucified did not die from the wounds in their hands or ankles. The blood in the suspended victims, especially one who had suffered much loss of blood from whippings, was forced into the lower body. The pulse rate increased; after agony which might have lasted for days, the victim died from lack of blood circulating to the brain and heart.

As Jesus suffered crucifixion's excruciating pain, the soldiers on the execution detail gambled for His clothing, while onlookers either mocked or sorrowed. Even the thieves who were crucified too "heaped insults on Him."

Jesus' death (Mark 15:33-41). Jesus hung on the cross from about 9 A.M. to noon. Then, at noon, a terrible darkness blotted out the sun. After three more hours, at about 3 P.M., Jesus cried out, "My God, My God, why have You forsaken Me?"

This cry reflects the real anguish of the cross.

It was not the physical pain that tormented Jesus. It was the fact that, when our sin was laid on Jesus, He was made sin for us (2 Cor. 5:21). At that moment, for the first and only time, the Father turned away from the Son, and Jesus experienced the full meaning of the alienation from God that sin must always cause.

A moment later, the work of redemption done, Jesus "breathed His last." The Saviour was dead.

"The curtain of the temple was torn in two from top to bottom." This curtain cut off the holy of holies, the temple's most inner room, which could only be entered once a year by the high priest, bearing sacrificial blood. This curtain was visible evidence in Old Testament religion that there was no direct access to God for the worshiper. The tearing of the curtain showed that now, through the death of Jesus, the way to God was open to all.

Jesus is buried (Mark 15:42-46). The Jewish Sabbath began at sundown Friday. The death of Jesus moved His followers to act quickly. Joseph of Arimathea, a council member but a believer, hurried to beg Pilate for Jesus' body. Pilate checked to be sure Jesus was actually dead; death usually took much longer. When the death was confirmed by the commander of the execution party, Pilate gave the body to Joseph.

Joseph had to hurry. Rushing back to Golgotha, he wrapped Christ's body in some linen cloth and placed it in his own nearby tomb. The burial must be completed before Sabbath.

It was.

And suddenly the stunning reality must

have struck all of those who loved Jesus. He was gone. He was really gone. As the cut stone circle was rolled up to cover the tomb door all their hopes died as well.

Sunday Morning: Mark 16:1-8
Jesus had been put in the garden tomb without normal preparation of the body. So Sunday, when the Sabbath with its restrictions on what one might do had passed, three women brought spices intending to rewrap and anoint Jesus' body.

They were uncertain. A military guard had been set on the tomb, and a seal on the stone. Who would roll the stone away so they could slip into the rock-hewn tomb?

But when they reached the garden the stone had been rolled away! Inside the tomb there was a "young man" (an angel) waiting for them. "Don't be alarmed," he announced. Jesus is no longer there. "He has risen."

The women, trembling and bewildered, set off to deliver a message to Peter and the disciples. Jesus is alive. "He is going ahead of you into Galilee. There you will see Him, just as He told you."

Jesus had died, yes.

But Jesus lives!

The Cross was not the end, but a new beginning—for us all.

TEACHING GUIDE

Prepare
Read through these Mark chapters, tracing events on the map. If you wish, check parallel passages that supplement Mark's report.

Explore
Duplicate and give out to your group members both the map of Jerusalem and also the list of events associated with the trial and death of Jesus.

Quickly set the scene, explaining the map and reviewing each of the events in sequence.

Expand
1. Ask each group member to select *one* incident listed on the sequence chart. Each person is to study his incident carefully, to re-create the scene in his or her mind. Identify those who were present. Try to sense their feelings, outlook, attitudes. What were Jesus' feelings in this situation? What did He do and say? Why did He speak or act as He did? What does this particular incident say to us today? How should it affect us today?

After some 15 or 20 minutes, meet together as a group and go through the events in sequence, with each person speaking on his or her segment.

2. Some in your group may be curious about Mark 16:9-20. Is this disputed section of Mark's Gospel really part of the original text? Is it, as many believe, a later addition?

The *Bible Knowledge Commentary* contains an excellent summary, and concludes that it is best to consider these verses part of canonical Scripture.

However, our goal in this study—to place the events of Thursday through Sunday in perspective and to locate them on the map of Jerusalem—is achieved without going into these verses.

Apply
Share: "Which of the incidents in these chapters moves you most? How are you affected by it?"

STUDY GUIDE 99

Introduction

LUKE'S GOSPEL

Overview

The Gospel of Luke is the longest book in the New Testament. It was written by Luke the physician, a companion of Paul on several missionary journeys (cf. Acts 16:10-17; 20:5–21:18; 27:1–28:16). Luke is the only author of a New or Old Testament book who was probably a Gentile rather than a Jew.

The early church fathers noted the emphases common to both Paul and Luke. Each emphasized the universality of salvation. Even Luke's parables focused on the response of individuals to God's grace, while Matthew's parables concerned the kingdom. Luke, like Paul, spoke often of faith, of repentance, of mercy, and of forgiveness. Thus Irenaeus held that Luke, Paul's companion, "put down in a book the Gospel preached by him," and Origen called Luke "the Gospel commended by Paul." If Mark was the "interpreter" of Peter, Tertullian wrote, Luke was the "illuminator" of the Apostle Paul.

For instance, "grace" is found some 146 times in the New Testament. Of these, all but 21 are in the writings of Paul and Luke. And 190 of the 243 occurrences of "faith" are found in the writings of these two.

It's not surprising, then, that this Gospel, like Paul's ministry, is a Gospel directed to the Gentiles, and particularly for the better educated Hellenists. In some of the most beautiful literary Greek found in any ancient writing, Luke tells the story of Jesus, a true human being who is the Son of God.

Commentary

Tradition tells us that Luke was a physician, who practiced in Antioch. The first Gentile church was established there, and Luke may have been a member during the time Barnabas and Saul (as he was called then) were part of the leadership team. It is clear from the use of "we" in Acts (after 16:10) that Luke often traveled with the missionaries and was a witness of what he wrote.

Perhaps the most fascinating feature of Luke is the beauty of its language. Paul wrote elegant Greek, and displayed a rich vocabulary. About 250 Greek words that Luke used are found *only* in this Gospel in the whole New Testament. And there are another 61 words used only in the Book of Acts, also written by Luke.

In addition, much of the material in Luke's Gospel is found only here, with no parallel in Matthew, Mark, or John. To see its extent, it's helpful to use a highlighter and mark the following passages, identified by W. Graham Scroggie:

Luke 1:1–3:2
Luke 3:10-15, 23-28
Luke 4:1a, 13b, 14a, 15-30
Luke 5:1-11, 17, 29-39
Luke 6:11a, 12b, 17a, 24-26, 33-34, 37b, 38a
Luke 7:3-5, 7a, 10-17, 20-21, 29-30, 36-50
Luke 8:1-3, 12b
Luke 9:9b, 18a, 28b, 29a, 31-33, 43, 44a, 51-56, 61-62
Luke 10:1, 8b, 17-20, 25-26, 28-42
Luke 11:5-8, 12, 27-28, 37-38, 40-41, 44-46a, 53-54
Luke 12:1-2, 13-21, 29b, 32-33a, 35-38, 41, 47-50, 52, 54, 57
Luke 13:1-17, 22-23, 25-27, 31-33
Luke 14:1-25, 28-33
Luke 15:3, 6-32
Luke 16:1-12, 14-15, 19-31
Luke 17:3-5, 7-19, 20-22, 28-30, 32, 37a
Luke 18:1-14, 31b, 34, 43b
Luke 19:1-28, 37, 39-44
Luke 20:16b, 20b, 26a, 35a, 36b, 38b, 39
Luke 21:12a, 18-19, 21b, 22-23b, 24-25b, 26a, 28, 34-38

Luke 22:3a, 15-16, 19b-20, 27-32, 35-38, 40, 43-45a, 48b, 49, 51, 53b, 61a, 65-68
Luke 23:2, 4-15, 22b, 23, 27-31, 34a, 39-43, 45a, 46, 48, 51a, 53b, 56
Luke 24:4a, 7, 8a, 11-53

We sense the special contribution that Luke makes to our knowledge of Jesus and His teaching when we realize that in these passages above are 15 parables found only in Luke. Only here do we read about the Good Samaritan (10:30-37), the Rich Fool (12:13-21), the Lost Coin (15:8-10), the Prodigal Son (vv. 11-32), the Rich Man and Lazarus (16:19-31), and many others.

What else is special in Luke's Gospel? Over half the verses in this Gospel contain words of Jesus. Forgiveness and individual response to the Saviour are emphasized in this Gospel written for Gentiles. Luke's concern was not the future of Israel, but personal salvation.

In a most significant sense Luke is the Gospel of the Good News for each individual human being born into our world.

While we will explore many of the special emphases of Luke in the following studies of his Gospel, there is one important theme that deserves special study. That theme is the theme of prayer, for Luke, more than any other Gospel, emphasizes this dimension of the Christian life.

Scroggie, in his *Guide to the Gospels* (Revell), notes that prayer-lessons are taught in this Gospel by exhortation and by illustration. This introductory session provides a good opportunity to explore prayer, and at the same time to sense the uniquely personal aspect of Luke's beautiful telling of the Gospel story.

♥ ***Link to Life: Youth / Adult***

Pass out a list of the verses that are unique to Luke. Assign each group member one chapter, and have him or her mark and then read the verses in that chapter which are unique to Luke.

Then share, chapter by chapter, what each person has found.

When all have shared, discuss: "How much does Luke contribute to our understanding of Jesus? What seems to be Luke's special emphasis or thrust?"

Supplement your group members' insights with minilectures as needed. Your goal is to help your group sense the warmth of Luke's writings, and his emphasis on the individual, on grace, forgiveness, and love.

Prayer

The Bible has much to say about prayer. To understand its essence we need to return to the Old Testament and New Testament languages, and see how biblical terms are used to describe this special relationship between man and God.

Hebrew words for prayer. There are a number of different words for prayer in Hebrew. *Palal,* translated "pray," emphasizes the dependence and humility of the person praying, and is an appeal for God to act on the need being presented. *'Atar* emphasizes the intensity with which a person prays. *Sa'al* means to "ask" or "to inquire" and is often used by those seeking God's guidance. Again, dependence on God is viewed as very important. *Paga'* suggests intercessory prayer; asking God to help another. *Hanan* is a cry to God for mercy, asking Him to act in grace and meet a need.

Each of these terms in the Old Testament shows us that prayer is an expression of personal relationship. God is recognized as Creator and Redeemer, One who is able to act in this world and One who will act on behalf of His people. The Old Testament saint who came to God in prayer approached Him humbly, sure that he was completely dependent on God, just as a little child is dependent on his or her parents.

Prayer in the Old Testament is not really a matter of ritual religion. God can be approached at anytime, anyplace. Prayer is an expression of a living, vital relationship between God and His worshiper. Its answer depends not so much on how the worshiper prays, but on the grace and kindness of a God who cares.

Greek words for prayer. As in Hebrew, several different Greek words are associated with prayer. *Proseuchomai* is the general term for prayer. In the New Testament it takes on the warmth of conversation, losing the formal "calling on a deity" characteristic of classical Greek culture.

Aiteo means "to ask for or request." The New Testament often emphasizes the fact that God hears and responds to the requests of His people.

Deomai means "to ask" or "to beseech."

This word places stress on the need which motivates prayer. The person speaking to God is hurting, and cries out for help to Jesus or the Father. The word is also used of intercessory prayer for others.

While there are other words used commonly of prayer, these are the central ones.

But again it is how the words are used in the New Testament that gives us our insight into prayer. Here, as in the Old Testament, it is clear that prayer is an expression of relationship. We who have a personal relationship through faith with Jesus Christ have immediate access to God the Father, and can "approach the throne of grace so that we may receive mercy and find grace to help us in our time of need" (Heb. 4:16). In addition, Jesus promised that as we remain close to Him, we can "ask whatever you wish, and it will be given you" (John 15:7).

It is wrong, then, to assume that prayer is like an obstacle course which believers must successfully negotiate if we are to receive answers from God. What have been called "conditions" for answered prayer are not conditions at all. What are they? They are promises, showing us that as we live in intimate relationship with the Lord we can have confidence that God will hear and answer our prayers. Thus if we are not living in disobedience (Deut. 1:43-45), unconcern (Isa. 58:7-9), or treating others unjustly (1:15-17), we can rest assured that prayer is no meaningless exercise for us. In the same way the New Testament reassures us. We who seek, knock, and ask are heard (Matt. 7:7-8). When we agree on a matter with others, we can be sure God will act (18:19). When we pray "in Jesus' name," identifying with His character and purposes, we can be sure the prayer is in God's will and will be answered.

How wonderful these assurances are. As we live close to our God, in a warm and dependent relationship, we can share every need and desire with Him and know that God who cares, will answer us.

♥ ***Link to Life: Youth / Adult***

Have each of your group members write down anonymously one question he or she has about prayer.

Collect the questions, and have one of your group write them on the chalkboard.

At this point you may want to give a minilecture on prayer terms. If so, ask your group to listen for concepts that suggest answers to one or more of the questions on the board. When you're done, let them tell you any insights gained which relate to questions on the board.

Exhortations to Pray

Prayer was important to Jesus. Luke tells of nine times when Jesus prayed (Luke 3:21; 5:16; 6:12; 9:18; 9:29; 10:21; 11:1; 22:39-46; 23:34, 46). Seven of these incidents are reported only by Luke.

It's not surprising, since Jesus found prayer so important for Himself, that He often exhorted His followers to pray. Let's see what we can learn about prayer from the exhortations that Luke records.

Prayer for enemies (Luke 6:27-36). Jesus called on His followers to act as sons of the Most High should, modeling their relationships with others on the way God treats human beings. In a familiar passage Jesus encouraged us to actively love our enemies, doing good for those who hate us and praying for those who mistreat us. The call to do good demonstrates the importance of action; the call to prayer demonstrates the importance of heart attitude.

Prayer and ministry (Luke 10:1-3). Jesus urged His disciples to be aware of the need and readiness of people for the Gospel. A plentiful harvest awaited, but there was such a need for workers. Here two things are linked: the call to pray, and the command to go. How striking that those who pray that God will send forth workers become the very workers to whom Jesus says, "Go."

But perhaps it is not such a surprise. It is the person who spends time with God in prayer who is closest to Him, and best able to hear His voice and recognize His call.

Prayer and needs (Luke 11:9-13). Jesus promises, "Ask and it will be given to you; seek and you will find; knock and the door will be opened to you."

The exhortation suggests deep need and uncertainty. And Jesus' comment is intended to assure us that God is eager to listen to our requests and to respond. What human father, Jesus asked, who, if his child needed food, would hand him a snake? How foolish to assume that a human father, who is by nature sinful and bent toward evil, will act more lovingly toward his children than God, the perfect Father, will act toward us.

Again we see the significance in prayer of personal relationship. It is out of confidence that God does love us that we come to Him. And we can come confidently. We can depend on God, who loves us, to give what we need, and to open the door to the future He has in mind for you and me.

Prayer and God's character (Luke 18:1-7). Jesus encouraged prayer by making a comparison (11:9-13). A human father, as imperfect as he may be, gives good gifts to his children. God is a Father too, but a perfectly good Father. How confident then we can be that He will give us what we need when we appeal to Him.

Jesus told a story that reveals something of God's character by contrast (18:1-7). The story of the "unjust judge" underlines the fact that God, unlike him, is a just Judge.

The parable introduces a judge who cares nothing for God or others. It also introduces a widow who had been defrauded, and begged the judge to grant her justice.

The indifferent judge simply ignored the woman's pleas. But the woman would not give up! She kept knocking on the judge's door, and waiting to plead with him on the streets. The judge couldn't go anywhere without the woman showing up and bothering him.

Finally he gave up. He would grant her justice, not because he cared about her, but simply because he didn't want to be bothered anymore!

Jesus asked us to think for a moment about God. How unlike the unjust judge He is! He acts for us because He *does* care, both about us as individuals and about what is right. Remembering these facts should encourage us to keep on praying, and never give up. Let's not be discouraged when God says, "Wait," and our prayers seem unanswered. God will see that His chosen ones get justice. How good to have this assurance as we "cry out to Him day and night."

♥ ***Link to Life: Youth / Adult***
Analyze this story as a group, by raising and answering the following questions:

- *What does the widow stand for?*
- *Why does she appeal to the judge?*
- *Why does she keep after him?*
- *How is the judge like and unlike God?*
- *What did Jesus want us to learn from the story?*
- *How does Jesus want the story to affect our behavior?*
- *What* kind *of prayer is particularly in view here?*

Prayer Illustrations

In addition to the exhortations, Jesus also told stories which illustrate truths about prayer. Two familiar ones are particularly helpful.

The need for persistence (Luke 11:5-8). Several of Jesus' exhortations to prayer encourage persistence. In this story Jesus used a familiar device: He described a person who was so obviously *unlike* God that a quality of the Lord's which encourages us in prayer seems obvious.

In this story that individual was a "friend." It is important to note that there was no family or intimate relationship implied in "friend." The person might simply be a neighbor, an acquaintance.

At any rate, when the friend was approached at midnight with a need, the friend wasn't very friendly. "Don't bother me," is the shouted response. "The door is already locked, and my children are with me in bed." It's clear that the friendship isn't worth the slight inconvenience involved in opening the door and giving the neighbor needed bread.

But Jesus observed, if you *keep on knocking,* your friend *will* get up and help. He'll not do it for friendship. He'll do it because you are persistent in banging on his door, and he can't get back to sleep.

How unlike God.

God does not sleep. He never locks the door against us. He is always eager and ready to help.

How terrible that we should even inadvertently think of God as like a selfish, heartless person who for any reason would be unwilling to help.

Our attitude in prayer (Luke 18:9-14). In a familiar parable, Jesus told of two men who came to the temple to pray. One was a Pharisee who stood up and prayed "about himself." His prayer was nothing more than a rehearsal of all the things that he did and did not do. He prayed proudly, sure that God must admire such a righteous individual.

The other person was a tax collector. In that day the tax collector was a social outcast. Most were dishonest, and all were counted among Israel's "sinners."

This man could hardly bring himself to approach the temple, and then did not look up. Instead he beat his breast, aware of his need, and cried, "God, have mercy on me, a sinner."

Jesus told His listeners that the tax collector went home justified—not the Pharisee.

The attitude shown here is basic not only for salvation but also in prayer. A person who seeks to be counted innocent by God can hardly come boasting of his actions. We are all sinners. The self-righteous individual will hardly be willing to submit to God's righteousness, which is given on the basis of faith rather than works. For a person to be accepted and acquitted by God, there must be acknowledgment of need and an appeal solely to God's grace as a basis for hope.

It is the same in all prayer. God answers our prayers, not because we deserve His help, but because He is gracious and loving. The root of answers to prayers is sunk deep in the loving and merciful nature of our God; it never grows out of our merely human goodness.

How wonderful then, to know that we can come to God humbly, relying only on His grace. How wonderful that our God *is* gracious, and that He will answer our prayers simply because He cares.

TEACHING GUIDE

Prepare
Mark in your own Bible the parts of Luke which are unique to his Gospel, and read them through quickly. What a wonderful Gospel this is that you are about to teach!

Explore
Give a brief minilecture on special features of Luke's Gospel. You may want to supplement material in this study guide with information in the excellent *Bible Knowledge Commentary* (see pages 199-201).

Expand
1. During this session in which you introduce your study of Luke to your group, your goal should be to both familiarize group members with the distinctives of this Gospel, and to encourage enthusiasm for coming studies.

Probably the best way to do this is to follow the "link-to-life" suggestion on page 638. Distribute lists of material found only in Luke's Gospel. Assign one chapter to each group member. Each is to mark verses and passages found only in Luke, and then to read them carefully.

Let each member share the unique material found in his or her chapter. Then discuss, "What seems special about this Gospel? What seems special about its tone? Its emphases?"

2. If you have time after the introductory survey of Luke, follow the plan suggested on page 639 to launch a study of prayer as it is taught in Luke.

Select from the several "link-to-life" activities suggested in this section, studies which seem to you to best answer questions about prayer your group members generate.

Apply
Discuss: "In view of the emphases of Luke's Gospel, in what way do you expect to profit from our study of it?"

STUDY GUIDE 100

Luke 1:1–3:22

REBIRTH OF HOPE

Overview
Luke's Gospel provides many details about events associated with the birth of Jesus. In these first chapters we find:

- the birth of John the Baptist foretold;
- the birth of Jesus foretold;
- Mary's Magnificat (a hymn of praise);
- the birth of John the Baptist;
- the birth of Jesus;
- the witness of the shepherds;
- Jesus presented as an Infant at the temple;
- Jesus as a Boy visiting the temple;
- the ministry of John the Baptist.

In providing all these details Luke showed us how important it is to establish for his Gentile readers that Christ was no ordinary man. The Gospel itself hinges on the fact that Jesus is the virgin-born Son of God.

▶ ***Elijah.*** The Old Testament closes with the promise that God will "send you the Prophet Elijah" before "the Lord comes" (Mal. 4:5). Luke reported that an angel told Zechariah, John's father, that the son to be born to him will "go on before the Lord, in the spirit and power of Elijah" (Luke 1:17). John's call and ministry authenticated Jesus as the Christ.

▶ ***Virgin Birth.*** Isaiah 7:14 established that the Messiah would be virgin born. Mary conceived by the Holy Spirit, so that the Child Jesus was "the Holy One" who must be identified as "the Son of God" (Luke 1:35).

Commentary
Had there been newspapers in the Roman Empire almost 2,000 years ago, some of the headlines that month might have been:

KING ARTAXUS NEAR DEATH
GRAIN SHIPS DOCK, ROME RIOTS END
NINE PIRATE SHIPS SUNK BY SIXTH FLEET
ATHENS STUDENTS CLASH WITH POLICE
OLYMPIC WRESTLER STILL IN COMA
REPORT ANGELS SIGHTED IN JUDEA

Such headlines look very much like the headlines in our newspapers today. For the world of the New Testament was a world very much like ours.

There were wars.

There was sickness.

There was poverty and injustice.

There were people who struggled to keep on living, living by habit long after they had lost any sense of purpose, meaning, or goal.

It was a world like ours, populated with people like ours. *But God had made preparations.* God was about to burst into this world of men. Jesus was about to be born, and after His birth our world, despite all its poverty and injustice, wars and terrorists, has never been the same.

The world that was. God has never desired the kind of world men have made. The Bible tells us that God worked carefully with men. Yet when "He looked for justice, [He] saw bloodshed; for righteousness, [He] heard cries of distress" (Isa. 5:7). Even the people of Israel, who had been given God's laws and had been sent prophets to guide them, twisted life out of shape. The people of Israel were brothers, but in the passion of selfishness they too cheated one another, lied, and tried to use each other. Yet, the more life fell under the control of sin, the emptier life seemed, and the more frustrated people became (cf. Isa. 59).

So God judged the sin of His people. History records a series of defeats and years of foreign captivity. And then, though living in their own land, God's people were crushed under the weight of the Roman

Empire. That empire extended over the whole of the Western world. Rome had brought world peace—but with peace came heavy taxes, armies of mercenaries stationed in every land, Roman culture and values, the gladiatorial games, slavery—and misery.

There were still wars.

There was still poverty and injustice.

People still struggled to live, and kept on living by habit long after they had lost all sense of purpose or meaning in life. Not all the power of Rome, nor the progress of our modern technology, have been able to satisfy the basic need all people share to find life's meaning. Neither Rome nor computers have been able to break the bondage of sin that constantly expresses itself in individual life and society.

But something unique was about to happen in an insignificant province in Rome's wide-spread empire. The birth of a Baby would do what no authority or invention of man could. One day that Babe, full grown, would say, "I have come that they may have life, and have it to the full" (John 10:10).

In the birth of Jesus, God acted decisively to bring new life to individuals and transformation to human cultures. In the person of Jesus, God has extended humanity an invitation to new life.

To every person who lives by habit, without direction or meaning or real hope—to you and me—Jesus' birth offers a fresh newness, a life turned around and transformed by the power of God.

This is what the Gospel of Luke is all about: a transformed life. In Luke Jesus is presented as the transformer, with a message of new life for all the world, and with a special message of newness for believers. As we study this exciting book, we and your group members will discover more and more of what it means to *really live*. You will learn and teach the *how* of that full life Jesus promises, and show how that promise can be fulfilled in our daily experiences.

And this is something we all need to learn. Desperately.

♥ ***Link to Life: Youth / Adult***

The "headlines" at the beginning of this study guide reflect actual events that took place about the time Jesus was born. Share them. Then distribute the day's newspaper and ask group members to find similar modern headlines. Read these; then discuss: "What difference has the birth of Jesus made to society? Why did Jesus say, 'I have come that they may have life, and have it to the full'?"

Then have each person write down three things that he or she associates with a "full life." Promise that during this study of Luke's Gospel you will find help to experience the fullness of life that Jesus came to give to you and me.

Responses to God's Involvement: Luke 1

The Old Testament foretold the coming of a day when God would step into this world of darkness to bring light and hope. A Child would be born, a Son given (Isa. 9:6), and that One would bear the name Immanuel, "With us is God!"

But the announcement that the time was at hand was met with varied reactions.

Zechariah (Luke 1:5-25). Zechariah was a priest who lived in a little hillside town in Judea, except for the two weeks a year when his shift was on duty at the Jerusalem temple. It was during one of these weeks of duty that he was chosen by lot to enter the temple to burn the evening incense. Entering, Zechariah was jolted to see an angel of the Lord standing beside the incense altar! Quieting Zechariah's fears, the angel told him that his prayers had been answered, and his childless wife would have a son to be named John.

Zechariah's response to this announcement was one of hesitation and doubt. "How can I be sure of this? I am an old man and my wife is well along in years." *Zechariah's doubt was based on his understanding of nature!* He had failed to take God into account!

How often we hesitate to believe for the same reason. Answer *my* prayer? "Well, the way things normally work out. . . ." How wonderful that our God is not restricted to the usual, or bound by the merely natural. Our God is a God of the unusual, and the sooner we see God as He is, the more quickly our lives will be transformed.

Certainly Zechariah should have seen the unusual in the angel's appearance. Not only was John's birth announcement supernatural, everything said about the baby marked him off from others.

**John's person*. John was to be one of God's great men, filled with the Holy Spirit and set apart from birth.

**John's ministry*. John was to turn many of his countrymen to God. The angel's reference to the "spirit of Elijah" made it perfectly clear to anyone familiar with the Scriptures that this babe was to be the forerunner of the Messiah. John's birth announcement was at the same time an announcement that God was at last ready to act—God was about to intervene in the world of men!

**John's significance*. There was such a need for John's ministry! To prepare Israel for the Messiah he would be used by God to "turn the hearts of . . . the disobedient to the wisdom of the righteous" (Luke 1:17). How greatly such a ministry was needed is illustrated in John's later preaching (cf. Luke 3:1-20). There were many "disobedient" in John's day, as in ours. Many were uncaring, defrauding others. Many used violence or brutality to extort, and lied for one another in court (cf. vv. 12-14). John was to face this world of sin, and to prepare the hearts of men for the forgiveness and the transformation that Jesus, who came after him, would bring.

Knowing all this from the angel's announcement, Zechariah still hesitated. He still doubted. And because of his hesitation, the Angel Gabriel (1:19-20) announced that he would be unable to speak until the day of John's birth.

After the months of silence, the day came. John was born. Zechariah's tongue was loosed, and he praised God.

Mary (Luke 1:26-56). The Angel Gabriel had another announcement to make. Some months after he had spoken with Zechariah, Gabriel was sent to Nazareth, and there appeared to a young engaged woman named Mary.

Like Zechariah, Mary was startled and upset at the angel's appearance and his greeting. But, reassuring Mary of God's love, the angel told her she would have a Son. This Child would be the "Son of the Most High." He would be of the Davidic line, and would be King over Israel, fulfilling the Old Testament covenant promises. In this one Person, Deity and humanity would be perfectly blended. In this one Person, all the promises of God and all the purposes of God for humankind would be fulfilled.

Like Zechariah, Mary too blurted out a question. "How will this be, since I am a virgin?" (v. 34) The angel's response echoed another Old Testament prophecy: "A virgin shall bear a child, and you will call his name Immanuel" (Isa. 7:14). There was to be no human father. The power of the Holy Spirit was to supernaturally invest an ovum with the germ of life, and the Child to be born would be God the Son (Luke 1:35).

To this explanation Mary had only one response. "I belong to the Lord, body and soul, let it happen as you say" (v. 38, PH).

What a beautiful faith! Zechariah, godly and mature (vv. 5-6), had doubted the possibility of birth because of his age. This young girl, certainly still in her teens, never hesitated or doubted a *supernatural* birth, though she was single!

There is a blessing for those of us who learn to believe in spite of doubt. There is blessing for those of us who respond as Mary did with perfect, childlike trust.

♥ ***Link to Life: Youth / Adult***
Have your group members read Luke 1 silently to decide which person, Zechariah or Mary, each feels he or she is more like. *Then go around the circle, asking each to tell which person he or she chose, and what characteristic made him or her feel like the one chosen.*

You can continue this study by putting a T-shaped chart on the board, and listing comparisons and contrasts between Zechariah and Mary. Then summarize: "What do we learn from each person's experience about our own walk with God?"

Mary's faith-response is even more striking when we realize that, according to Old Testament Law, her pregnancy while still single might well be dealt with by stoning! And certainly her fiancé, who would know the child was not his, would hardly go through with the marriage. Yet all these things Mary was willing to trust God to work out!

Instead of worry, joy filled Mary's heart. And her praise song, known as the Magnificat (vv. 46-55), was filled with praise for God and with a vivid awareness of His greatness and love. What was Mary's vision of God?

[He] has done great things (v. 49).
Holy is His name (v. 49).
His mercy extends to those who fear Him (v. 50).

He has performed mighty deeds (v. 51).
[He] has lifted up the humble (v. 52).
He has filled the hungry (v. 53).

Mary knew God as a God of power and a God of concern, the One who cares enough for the humble and the hungry to reach down and to meet human need.

Perhaps this helps to explain Mary's response to the Lord. She had a clear vision of who God is. She knew Him as a God who cares . . . who cares enough to act. May we each know God so well!

♥ ***Link to Life: Youth / Adult***
Ask each group member to jot down three images that he or she has of what God is like. Then read Mary's Magnificat, and jot down her *images of what God is like. Compare: How are the two visions of God alike? How do they differ?*

The Birth of Hope: Luke 2
Mary's faith was not misplaced. God sent His angel to Joseph too (Matt. 1:19-21), and that good man determined to complete the marriage contract. The two wed, but the marriage was not consummated until the birth of Jesus.

The birth (Luke 2:1-7). As the time of Jesus' birth approached, Caesar Augustus had declared an empire-wide census. So all the people of Palestine went to the towns of their births to be registered. This brought Joseph and Mary, both of whom were of Davidic lineage, to Bethlehem. Though in the late stages of her pregnancy, Mary probably rode a donkey along the dusty roads and waited in weariness as Joseph tried to find accommodations when they reached their destination.

The inns were filled, but Joseph found a sheltered stable, possibly a cave behind an inn. There, in the most common of circumstances, to the simple sounds of animals shifting their weight and munching their straw and contentedly swishing their tails, Jesus was born.

It was a strange unobtrusive birth. No doctors crowded around, no gilt couch held the laboring mother, no fine linens covered the Infant. In simplicity the Baby was born, the quiet was broken by His cries, and His exhausted mother, her labors ceased, wrapped Him in a cloth and lay back to sleep, resting Him beside her where He could sense her warmth and be comforted by it.

We sometimes yearn for great and startling evidences of God's presence. "Oh," we think, "if only I could see miracles now, as in Bible days. If only something *great* would happen to me!" How we long for the sensational.

And how much we have to learn.

For the greatest miracle of all, God's greatest work, was done in quietness and in the simplicity of daily life common to millions of men. A look at the stable, and we may well wonder: Do the great things God wants to do in us and for us bear the same stamp? The stamp and seal of commonness . . . of God's mighty, yet unobtrusive, work in the lives of women and of men?

♥ ***Link to Life: Children***
What made Jesus' birth special? Help your boys and girls make a "surprise" card to show their moms and dads. Cut a sheet of construction paper as indicated in sketch. In the center (x) put a seal or picture of the Baby Jesus. Then fold down each flap, one at a time, placing on each a symbol or picture that tells us something special about Jesus' birth. Your boys and girls can suggest special things: born in a manger, announced by angels, etc. You can also tell them other very special things. The Bible said He would be born in Bethlehem hundreds of years before the event (cf.

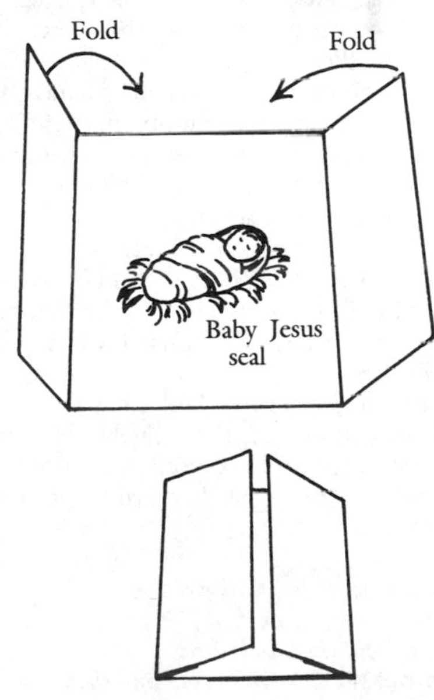

Micah 5:2). The Bible also told ahead of time that God would be Jesus' Father (Isa. 7:14), and He would be the Son of God.

The pictures and symbols (such as the Bible for prophecy) colored on each flap are clues to the "surprise" inside. Let your boys and girls unfold the flaps one at a time, show and tell about what is pictured on each, letting parents "guess" what the surprise is.

Each flap reminds us that Jesus truly is special. No other child ever born into our world could possibly be pictured in the center of this surprise card.

Shepherds and angels (Luke 2:8-20). While the manger was silent, the hills outside Bethlehem resounded with shouts of joy. Far away, where it would not be observed by the crowds, a heavenly celebration was taking place. Choirs of angels shook the air with joyful shout and song, and as though unable to contain the good news, an angel appeared in a brilliant ball of light to shepherds in those fields, crying, "Good news. . . . Today in the town of David a Saviour has been born to you. . . . Christ the Lord" (vv. 10-11).

But why to shepherds?

Perhaps because shepherds would understand. The Saviour, now lying in the quiet manger, was to be the Lamb of God. And as the Lamb, He was destined to die for the sins of the world, to die for these very shepherds as their Saviour. So perhaps shepherds, who cared for the young lambs, who sat through cold dark nights in the fields to guard and protect their flocks, might understand the shepherd's heart of God the Father—might glimpse what it meant for Him to give His one Lamb for all.

So as the hills throbbed and echoed with the remembered songs of joy, the shepherds left their sheep and hurried off to view God's Lamb.

They found Him. And they told Mary and Joseph about the angelic visitation. Leaving, they told everyone who would listen what the angels had said about this Child.

♥ ***Link to Life: Children***

The shepherds praised God by telling others about the Good News the angels had told them. We can praise God and show love for Him the same way.

Suggest to your boys and girls they show their "surprise" cards to a friend who does not go to church. Use it to explain how special Jesus is, and that He was born to be our Saviour.

Then let them select a friend or relative to send the card to. Younger children can get help from parents to write a note explaining the card, and why Jesus is the only Person it could possibly be about.

Dedicated at the temple (Luke 2:21-38). Once more, before the years of silence during which Jesus would grow to adulthood in Nazareth, God gave the parents a special sign.

On the eighth day of Jesus' life on earth, the time for circumcision, Jesus was brought to the temple to be presented to the Lord. Every firstborn son was to be so presented, dedicated to God and to His service. And then the son was to be redeemed (purchased back) with a blood sacrifice. The Law commanded a young bull or a lamb for parents who could afford such an offering. But the poor were allowed to bring two young birds. Joseph and Mary offered only the sacrifice of the poor.

But as they moved toward the altar they were met by Simeon, a man who had eagerly looked forward to the coming of the Saviour, and who had been shown by the Holy Spirit that this Child was the One! Simeon took the Baby Jesus in his arms and praised God.

His praise was echoed by Anna, an 84-year-old woman who had served the Lord in the temple with prayer and praise, and who now told everyone in Jerusalem about Jesus, assuring them that the Saviour had been born.

Jesus' childhood (Luke 2:39-52). Only Luke mentioned Jesus' childhood. He simply said that the child grew and became strong; He was filled with wisdom, and the grace of God.

At age 12 Jesus went up to the temple, where He amazed the teachers of the Law by His understanding. But the most striking note is that afterward, Jesus "went down to Nazareth with [His parents] and was obedient to them" (v. 51). Though the Son of God, and far beyond His parents in understanding even as a Child, Jesus fulfilled the commandment that ordained, "Honor your father and your mother." And so Jesus grew physically and in wisdom, being appreciated by God and by others.

All this Mary stored up in her heart. She must have watched her Son as He grew. She watched as He learned the carpenter's trade from Joseph, His earthly father. She watched as He moved in anonymity around the obscure town where the family was settled. She watched, and wondered. And waited.

♥ ***Link to Life: Children***
Let your boys and girls think of times when children think they know better than their parents, and tell what they might say. (For instance, "It's bedtime"—"But I'm not sleepy!" "Do your homework first"—"I want to watch this TV show first." "Eat your vegetables"—"I want dessert." Etc.)

Let them discuss: "How often are parents right? How often are children right? What should boys and girls do when they are sure they are right and parents wrong?"

Then tell the story of Jesus, who as the Son of God was wiser than His parents, but obeyed them because He wanted to please God and keep God's Word. How important for us to follow Jesus' example, and honor our moms and dads.

The Baptist's Ministry: Luke 3:1-22
Then the days of obscurity came to an end.

It began with John, who broke out of the desert like an old-time prophet, boldly announcing God's Word an challenging his hearers to a complete change of heart.

John's words were straightforward, and pierced to the heart of his hearers. He called them a brood of snakes. He warned them not to keep on trusting in their ancestry; their own hearts must be right with God. When they cried out, asking what they should do, John told them plainly, and in telling them John revealed the ways that they hated and hurt one another.

John's message was simple. *There must be a change in your hearts.* God is about to act; judgment is coming. And you must have a new life!

There must be forgiveness first, for there has always been sin. There must be baptism next, as a public sign of a choice to turn from sin (v. 3). And then there must be a whole new lifestyle—a new life that is lived in harmony with God and with holiness, a new life that breaks completely with sin.

And John had one other message.

The Saviour-Messiah was coming. The One who would make all this possible was approaching. He would be here soon (v. 16).

And then Jesus did come. He stood in the waters and, by baptism, identified Himself with the people and with the stand for righteousness that this act symbolized. As He came up, God's voice was heard from heaven: "You are My Son, whom I love; with You I am well pleased."

And, being about 30 years old, Jesus began the work that was to bring the possibility of a truly new life to you and to me.

♥ ***Link to Life: Youth / Adult***
Return to the headlines from modern newspapers you may have looked at earlier. Now compare them with the needs and problems reflected in John's preaching (Luke 3:1-20).

Jesus seeks to deal with them not by new legislation, but by bringing inner transformation and change.

TEACHING GUIDE

Prepare
Pray now that during this series of studies in Luke your group members will experience more of the new life Jesus came to bring.

Explore
1. Share the New Testament "headlines" given at the beginning of this study guide. Let group members find similar headlines in today's papers. Discuss: "What difference has Jesus' coming really made?" Raise the question about "full life," for individuals suggested in "link-to-life," page 643.
2. Or look at the reactions of Zechariah and Mary to angelic announcements. Have your group members identify as "more like" one or the other of the two. Go on to explore what we can learn from the experience of each. See "link-to-life," page 644.

Expand

1. The concept that we have of who God is will be one key to our responsiveness to Him. Ask your group members to jot down three images that come to mind when someone speaks about "God." Then together study Mary's Magnificat to find her images of the Lord. Discuss: "How are the images each jotted down like or unlike Mary's? What about Mary's view of God helped her to be so responsive to Him?"

2. Or examine the content of John the Baptist's preaching (Luke 3:1-20). Compare it with articles in one of today's newspapers. Then examine what John presents as the *solution* (e.g., an inner change of heart, repentance, linked to the coming Messiah who will baptize with the Holy Spirit).

There may be little we can do about injustice in the world at large. But we can act now to let Jesus change our hearts and lives, and so purify our own corner of His world.

Apply

The Book of Luke is about new life. Ask each to share what "new life" means to him or her. Each can share either what he or she *has* experienced, or what he or she expects to experience through relationship with Jesus.

STUDY GUIDE 101

Luke 3:23–4:44

OVERCOMING TEMPTATIONS

Overview

Matthew and Luke each paid careful attention to Jesus' temptation by Satan. The Temptation is important to the theme of each Gospel. The King must rule: the perfect Man must possess self-control. Because Jesus has overcome, we can have complete trust in the Son of God. And, because He met temptation in His human nature, He has given us an example which reveals the secret of overcoming to you and me.

This is our focus in this important study: the secret of victory over our temptations.

▶ ***Temptation.*** The same Greek and Hebrew words are translated as "test," "trial," and "temptation." In the New Testament "temptation" in every instance is *peirazo* or *peirasmos*.

The Expository Dictionary of Bible Words (Richards, Zondervan) says "a temptation is a difficult situation, a pressure that brings a reaction through which the character or commitment of a believer is demonstrated" (p. 593).

James made it clear that temptations are not in themselves evil (James 1:13-15). God permits such situations to prove and improve our faith. The evil is not in the situations God permits but in responding sinfully to them. Temptations are not designed to trap, but to approve us. God even provides a way with every temptation to overcome it (1 Cor. 10:13).

Commentary

I remember how trapped I felt in high school. It started well. I was running up a flight of stairs and bumped into our football coach. When he got up he said, "I can't wait till you come out for football!" I went out for football. But I was clumsy. I fought it out for a tackle position with my friend, Kayle Craig, and lost. He was a good guy, and I was glad for him. But it was embarrassing when he'd get his 5′2″ frame under by 6′1″ frame, and I'd flop like a beached whale.

So I went out for baseball, and discovered that whenever I did happen to hit a pitch, it popped softly 20 feet to the right of second base. Soon, in our practice game, seven guys on the other squad would be standing there by second, waiting for the putout. Fortunately, I got plantar warts on my right heel and was able to withdraw gracefully.

I had similar successes in my social life. For one thing, I have very peculiar hair. It grows out a dozen different directions, and earned me the nickname, Bushman.

I still had my personality, of course. But that didn't help much. I was so shy that I couldn't look a girl from my class in the eye. If I were downtown and saw one coming, I'd cross the street, or look down, or find something interesting in a store window, just so I wouldn't have to greet her.

Things didn't change much in college. I did learn to play Ping-Pong. And once I took a girl on a long walk on a winter night in Yellow Springs, Ohio. We went out to the city dump, where we threw snowballs at the jumble of cans, to hear the rats jump and scurry.

After two years in college I joined the Navy. A lot of things happened there. After two more years I became a Christian, and joined a little church. I felt better. Before, I'd gone to movies on 42nd Street in Manhattan—two or three triple features a day—and was very lonely. Now I had Christian friends, decided to study for the ministry, became president of our youth group, and just before discharge from the Navy, met a girl on Saturday night, proposed the next Wednesday, and a few months later married.

It was a new beginning all right. But, living in our little house trailer in Saline,

Michigan I discovered it wasn't all that different after all. My boyhood home had been quiet; we didn't get excited. My new wife felt things intensely, and expressed her feelings. When she did, I ran and hid, unable to help her. I felt afraid.

Perhaps all of us feel that way at times. Boxed in. Trapped. Inadequate. Struggling for freedom from our faults and weaknesses; for the freedom to live successfully with loved ones and associates.

When we do have those feelings, it is exciting to realize that Jesus promises us His eternal life, *now*. In fact, even before Jesus began to speak to the people of His day about the new life He offered, Christ gave them a demonstration of the power and the freedom that He Himself had and that He came to offer to us all.

Christ's Ancestry: Luke 3:23-38

Ancestry was very important to the Jewish people. They traced their lineage back to Abraham. Their whole identity as a people rested on the fact that God had given Abraham promises (Gen. 12; 15; 17) which they, as his descendants, had inherited.

While Jesus' sudden appearance in Judah was not supported at the time by genealogical evidence, both Luke and Matthew felt it was important to show that, on the human side of His nature, our Lord was both in the Abrahamic line of promise and in the Davidic royal line. He was qualified to take the throne that God promised to the Messiah.

We need to note just two things about the genealogy before moving on. First, as is common to biblical genealogies, this one skips. It does not necessarily record each generation; a "son of" someone, in Hebrew usage, might be a grandson or great-grandson. Only the notable in the family need to be mentioned. Thus we cannot estimate times or dates by using Bible genealogies.

The second thing is that this genealogy differs in significant ways from the genealogy in Matthew. Why? Most Bible scholars believe that Luke gives the genealogy of Mary (who was also of the royal Davidic line), while Matthew traces the family of Joseph. Thus by both His mother and His earthly father, Jesus had a right to the throne of Israel.

Jesus' Temptations: Luke 4:1-13

It was important as Jesus launched His public ministry to establish His claim to be the Transformer. Jesus was One who would bring new life to people. But before Jesus offered others new life, *He proved in a personal demonstration that a new life was possible!*

Jesus showed His own freedom from the inadequacies and the sin which trap you and me. In proving that freedom is possible, Jesus gives each of us hope.

The first temptation (Luke 4:1-4). Jesus was led by God after His baptism into the desertlike country where no one lived (vv. 1-2). He was there for 40 days, without food.

Jesus had to prove that new life was a reality in Him.

Those were hard days for the 30-year-old Nazarene. He ate nothing, and the Bible says that afterward He was hungry (v. 2). Physically, Jesus was drained of the natural resources inherent in our bodies.

It was then that the devil came to Him with the first temptation. There are several things to note about it.

"If You are the Son of God. . . ." Satan initiated his attack, not by asking a question, but by making a statement.

There are a number of uses of *if* in every language, but the Greek language usually makes it clear the kind of *if* that is meant. One *if* means doubt: "Well, if you think so, but I can't see it myself."

Another *if* means *since*. Suppose an employer comes home every evening from work and complains about a particular secretary. She's inefficient. She comes to work late. She misfiles things. Finally his wife gets so upset she blurts out, "Well, *if* you're the boss, why don't you fire her?"

This *if* says *since*. Because you are the boss, act like the boss!

This is the kind of *if* that Satan uses here. "Since You are the Son of God, act like God and command these stones be made bread!"

"Man does not live on bread alone." Jesus' response is a thrilling one. He quoted this Scripture, and in selecting the particular verse Jesus identified Himself fully with us. *"Man"* does not live on bread alone. In choosing this verse Jesus told us plainly. *Jesus did not meet the testings of Satan in His deity; Jesus met each test in His human nature as a true man.*

In this we find hope. If Jesus had responded to temptation in His divine nature, there would have been no help here for you and me. Jesus' victory would have proved nothing but that God is greater than Satan. But Jesus was born into our world to live as a human being, and to be hungry and tired, misunderstood and hurt, as we all have been. So Jesus met every temptation *as a man*, and in His victory He showed us the possibility that we will win victory too.

What Jesus did as a man, using the resources available to every believer, *we* can do. The principles on which Jesus' victory was based are principles by which you and I can live too.

"It is written." The next thing to note is that, to find victory, Jesus went to Scripture. And He used God's Word in a particular way.

As a young Christian, I was told that the Bible would give me victory over sin. Yet I was often gripped by a particular temptation. I'd quote a verse that I thought was appropriate—but as soon as I stopped quoting, I found I surrendered to the temptation!

Why? I was using the Bible as something like a Hindu prayer wheel, saying words over and over by rote as though there were something magical in the words themselves.

Jesus' use of Scripture was very different. He went back to the Old Testament, saying in effect, "Here is a principle to live by . . . and I will live by it." *Jesus chose to act on what God's Word revealed to be God's will.*

So it always must be with the Bible. God's Word is given us to be *lived.* We are to be hearers, but not only hearers. We are to do what it says (James 1:22). It was in doing God's Word that Jesus found His victory, and it is in doing God's Word that we shall find ours.

What then was the principle on which Jesus acted? This particular temptation of Satan was focused on Jesus' physical nature. Christ, after fasting for 40 days, was hungry. In response to the temptation, Jesus recalled, "Man does not live on bread alone." Christ had been led into the wilderness by the Spirit. He had been led to fast. Now He would not let His physical needs or urges dominate: Jesus would choose instead to continue to do the will of God.

The physical is one avenue of temptation for all of us. Some are ruled by gluttony. Others are firmly in the grip of sexual appetites. One young man and his wife felt led by God to go to a Texas seminary. They arrived, and settled into a small seminary apartment in August, as the temperature hovered over 100 degrees. Within four days they decided God hadn't called them to *this* school, after all. It was simply too hot.

Yes, you and I do have physical needs. And it is all right to satisfy them. But we are more than our bodies. We are more than our sensations. Life for us is far more than the satisfaction of bodily urges and needs. For all of us who feel trapped in a pleasure-seeking society, dominated by our desires, Jesus' victory offers us new hope. The physical *need not dominate in our lives, either!*

With God's help, we can choose to live by the Word of God.

The second temptation (Luke 4:5-8). Then Satan approached Jesus from a different direction. He showed Christ all the kingdoms of the world in a moment of time, and offered them and their glory to the Messiah-King, if He would only bow down to Satan.

Some have felt that this temptation involves worldliness—and have defined worldliness as a desire to possess things, and as the pride of possession. Yet there is more involved in this test than that.

First, we have to realize that authority over all the kingdoms of this world is Jesus' destiny. He is King of kings (1 Tim. 6:15) and to Him one day every knee shall bow and every tongue confess that Jesus Christ is Lord to the glory of God the Father (Phil. 2:10-11).

Certainly what God has planned for Jesus cannot be, in itself, a bad thing—or worldly.

We have to believe also, that it would be a good thing for us if Jesus were to rule. Would there be wars and killings today if Jesus were in charge? Would there be sickness or cancer? Would there be crime, or discrimination, or injustice? Of course not! For the Bible says that "of the increase of His government and peace there will be no end. He will reign on David's throne and over His kingdom, establishing and upholding it with justice and righteousness . . . forever" (Isa. 9:7). The history of the world would have been very different if Jesus had surrendered to Satan's temptation—there would have been peace. There would have been good things.

But this was just the strength of the temptation! It was compelling, because what it seemed to offer seemed so very good!

It's not strange when we think about it. The most powerful temptations are those that involve good things. Not many of us would be tempted if someone said, "Hey, let's go out and commit murder." Or, "Let's have a drunken orgy." Or, "Let's go worship Satan." Oh, no. It is the *good* things that tempt most of us, not the obviously evil.

When Marv was invited to move to Illinois from California, he was troubled by one thing. He had no winter clothes for his three young children, and no money to buy any. Could he move and expose his children to the cold?

Marv's temptation involved a good thing. Shouldn't he have considered the welfare of his children? Oh, yes, it is good desires that make our testings most painful.

How did Jesus respond to His temptation? He again returned to Scripture, and drew from it a principle on which He was willing to stake His life. "Worship the Lord your God and serve Him only" (Luke 4:8). Jesus would not worship Satan. And *Jesus would not serve the good! God's will alone was to determine!*

Choosing God's will was costly. Yet, God intended and still intends to give Jesus the kingdoms of this world. But the pathway to the crown led Jesus by way of the Cross. Suffering preceded glory. Knowing this, Jesus turned His back on the "good," and chose to live by God's will.

You and I know, of course, that the Cross brought a greater good. Jesus might have brought peace to earth as King, but as dying Saviour Jesus brought us peace with God, and eternal life. All the suffering was worth it! God had our greater good in mind as He directed Jesus toward the scourgings and the thorny crown; toward the brutal pain of nails driven into yielding flesh.

It is always this way. God's will brings us the greater good. Marv chose to bring his toddlers to Illinois, even though they had no money, because he felt God wanted the family there. And the warm clothes came—as a gift.

We can never lose by choosing God's will. And we can never gain by selecting what seems "good" if it is not in God's plan and purpose for us.

Are you confronted by a *good thing* that attracts you? Then find freedom in following Jesus' example. Like Jesus, determine to do the *right thing*, determining that in every situation you will worship God, and Him only you will serve.

The third temptation (Luke 4:9-13). The third temptation is particularly subtle and difficult to understand. Perched on the pinnacle of the temple with Jesus, Satan challenged Him to leap off, reminding Jesus that "if You are the Son of God" angels would appear to save Him from even dashing His feet against the stones below.

"If You are the Son of God." The key to understanding this test is found in realizing that the *if* in Satan's challenge of verse 9 is not the *since* of verse 3—and in remembering that Jesus faced each temptation as a human being. As a human being, the 40 days of hunger, capped by the appearance of Satan to test Him, must have struck Jesus with wonder. And perhaps even with doubt!

Picture a similar situation. Suppose you feel led by God to go to the nearest airport, and buy a ticket to Arizona. You get off in Tucson, and the Lord seems to lead you to a taxi. You get in, and head out of town. Finally you feel led to get out, and you walk down a deserted lane. There, surrounded by scrub and sand and cactus, you sit down. Expectantly. This has been the most unusual experience of your life! How often does God lead a person the way He has just led you? He must have something exciting in mind! And so you wait.

And you wait.

Night comes.

Then another morning. And still you wait. Another night. And another day. Hungry, and alone. And nothing happens!

How long will you wait until you begin to wonder. "Now, did God *really* lead me here, or was it my imagination?" How long before you yearn for some proof that God has been directing you and is still with you?

It was at just such a moment that Satan addressed Jesus. "If [and here we have the *if* of doubt] You [really] are the Son of God, throw Yourself down."

What the passage implies is the question, "Why not settle it?" God won't let His Son come to harm. Prove to Yourself the relationship You claim, once and for all.

"It is written." It's difficult to even suggest this interpretation of the third temptation. One hesitates to believe that, even in His

human nature, Jesus might have had doubts. But look at the passage the Saviour then quoted. He turned back again to the Old Testament, to Deuteronomy, and said, "You shall not put the Lord your God to the test" (Deut. 6:16, NASB).

But the Deuteronomy passage also has a reference. It looks back to an even earlier day when God's people, led out of Egypt and given demonstration after demonstration of God's power, ran out of water. At that moment of pressure they forgot all God's goodness, and cried, "Is the Lord among us or not?" (Ex. 17:7) In questioning God's presence and His love, they "put God to the test."

It was this very thing that Satan urged Jesus to do. Make God prove Himself! But Jesus would not. "Do not put the Lord your God to the test" (Luke 4:12). *Relationship with God must always rest on faith, and on confidence in God's trustworthiness.*

How subject you and I are to this avenue of temptation. How quickly, when troubles or pressures come, we begin to doubt God and to question His love. How quickly, when we've made a decision and things don't seem to be working out, we cry, "Is God still here? Did I make a mistake?"

When you and I are under pressures like this we need to remember the principle that Jesus Himself applied. We do not need proof. We can trust God. We are not to test Him. In our relationship with God too, faith is demanded.

Avenue of Testing	Problems in This Area	How Can I Apply Victory Principles?
The Physical physical instincts, desires, needs		
The "Good" letting something besides an appeal to God's will determine our choices		
Doubt failure to trust God when when things are difficult		

Temptations Study Sheet

♥ ***Link to Life: Youth / Adult***
Cover the temptations in a minilecture, so your group members will understand each one. Then put the chart (col. 1) on a chalkboard or overhead. Work together with the whole group to list a number of typical temptations that come through each of these avenues.

The temptations of Jesus were now over, for a little while. Yet throughout Christ's life on earth, Satan would attack Him. But our Lord had demonstrated, and would continue to demonstrate, that while He felt the same pressures from testing situations that you and I feel, Jesus never fell under their sway.

The power of a unique life was His. And that same power can be ours as well. For new life is exactly what Jesus offers to all who choose to follow Him.

Rejection: Luke 4:14-44

As Jesus moved out to teach and minister in the power of the Holy Spirit, there was initially great enthusiasm (vv. 14-15). People across the tiny country began to talk about Jesus with great admiration.

Nazareth (Luke 4:14-30). We don't know how long it was before Jesus made a visit to Nazareth, His hometown. But certainly all there had heard about His successes. As a mark of courtesy, the ruler of the synagogue even asked the young Man to read the Scripture.

Jesus unrolled the heavy scroll, and read from a place in Isaiah which His listeners knew described the Messiah.

"The Spirit of the Lord is on Me," Jesus read. "He has anointed Me to preach good news to the poor . . . to proclaim the year of the Lord's favor" (Luke 4:18-19). Then Jesus told them, "Today this Scripture is fulfilled in your hearing." *This was the clearest possible claim that the Carpenter who had been their neighbor was in fact the long-*

promised Messiah, the Son of God.

This claim seemed to stun the listeners. They were drawn to Jesus' "gracious words" (v. 22), but over and over they kept saying, "Isn't this Joseph's Son? We've known Him as a Child, a Youth, a young Man moving among us. Are we now to suddenly see Him as Israel's Deliverer?"

People today are faced with this same dilemma. Many have thought of Jesus as a teacher, as a good man, or a tragic historical figure who was killed because He was too far ahead of His time. But when we meet Jesus in Scripture, and hear His claims, we realize that Jesus calls on us to see Him as the living Son of God.

Jesus' neighbors were confronted with a decision they did not wish to make, and a claim they did not want to hear. The Bible says they "were furious" (v. 28), and that they tried to kill Jesus (v. 29).

In this reaction, this choice, we see a cameo portrait of Jesus' whole ministry. The scene in Nazareth was reenacted over and over during the next three years. In the end the furious anger Jesus aroused expressed itself in implacable hatred, and led to the Cross.

How important that our reaction to Jesus never parallel theirs. When we see Jesus, when we come to recognize Him as Son of God, we must reject either ourselves—or Him.

We may choose ourselves, and surrender to every temptation we feel. But if we do we will never experience the new life Jesus came to bring. Or, we may choose Jesus. And if we do choose Jesus, then we must also choose to respond to our temptations just as Jesus responded to His. We must take our stand on the Word of God, determine to practice that Word, and do it all in the confidence that Jesus, the Son of God, will bring us the victories for which we yearn.

The promise of power (Luke 4:31-41). Where will you and I find the strength to overcome our temptations, and to validate our choice of Jesus by obedience to His Word? Luke now tells us a series of stories. He shows us Jesus, casting out evil spirits (vv. 31-37). And he shows us Jesus, reaching out to heal and to strengthen the sick.

Surely the One who personally overcame temptation, and who used His power to bring health and wholeness to the sick of His day, will heal our hearts and give us the power to live new, and better lives.

♥ ***Link to Life: Children***

How do we know Jesus will help us when we need Him? Use the same chart suggested for adults (p. 653) but help the boys and girls fill in their temptations. Talk about how Jesus overcame by choosing to do God's Word.

Ask: "What makes it hard to do the right thing when we are tempted?"

Encourage the children to talk. Then read aloud Luke 4:38-41, while the children listen for proof that Jesus can help them win over their temptations. (He is able to heal sick people, cast out evil spirits; He is the Son of God.)

TEACHING GUIDE

Prepare

What are your greatest temptations? From which avenue do they come? How are you dealing with them? Are you able to overcome them?

Explore

1. Go around the group and ask each person to complete the sentence: "Temptations are. . . ."
2. Give a minilecture in which you explain the nature of the temptations which Jesus met and overcame. Use illustrations provided in the commentary of this study guide.

Expand

1. Put the "temptations" chart on the chalkboard or overhead. You may want to duplicate a full-page chart to give to your group members.

Begin by asking pairs to list as many temptations as they can think of that trouble Christians and others in our day.

Make a master list of temptations. Then analyze them, seeing how each relates to the sources of the three temptations with which Satan tried to defeat Jesus.

Make this study one in which you explore not only temptations, but also how they might be overcome through living God's Word.

Apply
Ask each person to identify *one* temptation which he or she faces regularly. Each is to privately determine its source, and a principle to live by to overcome it.

Then, without sharing the specific temptation, ask pairs to pray with each other, for each other, that Christ's strength may enable the other to win a spiritual victory.

STUDY GUIDE 102

Luke 5:1–7:17

THE CHOICE

Overview

These chapters cover what is often called Jesus' early Galilean ministry. Galilee was Jesus' home province. It was not technically Jewish, as was Judea, but contained a large Jewish population. Most of Jesus' ministry was focused near the Sea of Galilee, where Peter and James and John had labored as fishermen.

Strikingly, the Sermon on the Mount, the Transfiguration, and 25 of Jesus' 35 recorded miracles took place in Galilee.

The Jews of Judea, however, looked on Galileans with some contempt. They had a rude accent, and were not considered sophisticated in matters of religion.

This early Galilean ministry took place when Jesus was introducing His teaching and Himself. The later Galilean ministry is associated with hardening opposition.

▶ ***Judging.*** Luke, Paul, and James each dealt with "judging." They called on us to critically evaluate ourselves, but not others. According to James, passing judgment on others is playing God: "There is only one Lawgiver and Judge, the One who is able to save and destroy. But you—who are you to judge your neighbor?" (James 4:12) Yes, the church is to discipline those who openly and habitually sin. But there is no room in our faith for a critical attitude or judging of others' beliefs, motives, and convictions. We are to give each other the freedom to be responsible to God.

Commentary

Germs

For years the medical world laughed at the germ theory, the notion that infection and diseases are caused by tiny organisms no one can see. They questioned the need for special cleanliness and antiseptics in hospitals, and derided Pasteur and other early proponents of the germ theory.

It was so hard, later, to come to the man they had rejected and to admit, "You were right. We were wrong."

It's always hard to face a person who has been right when we've been wrong, and honestly to admit it—especially if what he has been right about is something really important. Oh, I can admit to one of my children, "You were right; I should have turned two blocks earlier." This doesn't hurt: it doesn't strike at my identity. But how much harder to admit, "Son, you were right. I didn't have any good reason to ground you. I was just feeling angry, and took it out on you. I'm sorry."

This kind of admission is much harder. It hits at something important to me; my desire to be a loving and fair dad, and to be viewed this way by my children.

But it was just this kind—the most difficult of admissions—the admission of being *wrong* about something important to His hearers' identity as Israelites—that Jesus now set out to call from the hearts of His fellow Jews. As Jesus entered the first phase of His public ministry, He presented Himself to Israel as the Lifegiver. To accept Him, people would have to admit that what they had known was not really life. Jesus would in His preaching present a bold picture of life as it is to be lived in God. To accept *this,* people would have to admit that what they were now living was not God's way of life.

These admissions were hard for Israel. They are hard for you and me. But we are faced with the same choice. Will we really follow Jesus, totally, and find in Him the way of life?

Jesus Is Lord: Luke 5:1–6:19

Commitment (Luke 5:1-11). All had been amazed at Jesus' teaching and His power. Yet most still hesitated, waiting for more evidence or for some sign before they committed themselves to Him. But some did not hesitate. They made the choice immediately—and with that choice made the confession commitment must involve.

One day as Jesus was teaching near the shore of Lake Gennesaret (a name for the Sea of Galilee), He was pressured by the crowds that thronged around Him. He got in the boat of a fisherman, and continued His teaching from it. When Jesus was done, He told the owner, Simon (who was later called Peter), to push out into deep water and let down his nets.

By all odds this would be a futile action. The fishermen of Palestine worked at night, when the schools of fish worked in toward shore to feed on the swarms of minnows in the shallower, warmer waters. But Simon did as Jesus told him. And an enormous shoal of fish swarmed into the nets! The nets even began to break with the weight. When a second boat joined them, both were so filled with fish they nearly sank.

This was evidence enough for Peter. He fell on his knees before Jesus, and instead of thanking Christ he begged, "Keep away from me, Lord, for I'm only a sinful man" (v. 8, PH).

Staggered by the haul of fish, Simon had been jolted into recognizing Jesus as Lord. There were no questions left in the mind of this simple fisherman.

It may seem strange that reports of the greater miracles of healing and expelling demons had not moved Simon earlier. Sometimes it is the simplest things that bring a person to realize that Jesus Christ is Lord. But by whatever agency, how vital it is that each of us realizes, as Peter did, just who Jesus is.

Seeing Jesus as Lord raised in Simon's mind a vivid picture of himself. Beside Jesus, Peter was revealed as "only a sinful man." Perhaps if you and I were to compare ourselves with other people, we might have some cause to boast. But when we compare ourselves to Jesus, we see our sin revealed in the light of His perfect purity. Simon, knowing himself, confessed his lack of life and goodness, and his need.

This confession of sin and failure seems so hard to make, until we have made it. Then we discover that, once we have admitted we are sinners, we are freed. For once we see ourselves as sinners we become more ready to hear the healing words of Jesus Christ.

Jesus said, "Don't be afraid; from now on you will catch men" (v. 10).

We who are sinners need not fear God. He forgives us, and transforms us as well. What Jesus told Peter is something He says to each of us who come to Him acknowledging our sin: *from now on, life will be different!*

Peter and his two companions left everything there on the beach—including the great catch of fish—and followed Jesus. All that had been important to them before was now willingly set aside. In the fulfillment found in relationship with Jesus Christ, all of life truly was becoming new.

♥ ***Link to Life: Youth / Adult***
Go around the circle and ask each person to compare and contrast his or her own conversion with Simon Peter's. What stimulated it? What was the role of a sense of sin? What image of Jesus played a part? What have been some of the changes in your life that can be traced back to your conversion?

Healing the inner man (Luke 5:12-32). Not all who saw Jesus' works and heard His teaching responded as Simon Peter and his friends. So Jesus moved on, to show graphically that His authority extended to the healing of the inner man as well as the outer.

In verses 12-16 we have a touching story that focuses attention on the inner needs of human beings, and shows us Jesus' concern for these needs.

A leper came to Jesus and fell down in front of Him, saying, "Lord, if You are willing, You can make me clean." The leper recognized Jesus' power, but was uncertain of Jesus' love.

We're all so prone to using others. Some give generously . . . to buy a reputation as generous. Some show up for church visitation, to be known as "soul winners." So it was a fair question. Was Jesus *using* the people He healed, just to build a reputation as a healer?

Jesus answered the implied doubt fully. He said, "I am willing." And then as Jesus spoke the healing word, our Lord reached out His hand *and touched the leper* (v. 13).

Lepers in Jesus' day, as in ours, were

untouchable. They had to cry out in the streets, to warn others away from them. They lived outside cities, separated from their loved ones and families. They were alone . . . and destined not to know the loving caress or gentle pressure of another's hand. But Jesus reached out and touched the leper!

If you've ever been lonely, ever felt rejected or unloved, you know what that touch must have meant. If you've ever been convinced that no one could possibly care for you, then you understand how that leper must have felt. Jesus' touch was not needed to heal the leprosy, but it was necessary to meet this man's deep, inner need for love.

Later, the leper would follow the Law. He would go, and show his body to the priests, and they would pronounce him cleansed from his disease. Then he would make the thank offerings the Law prescribed.

But what the leper would not show the priests was his heart. They had nothing to do with the heart. But Jesus does. And the touch of love had healed the heart even as the word of power had cleansed the external disease.

If any of your group members have hesitated to trust Jesus, or if they have been convinced of His power but uncertain about God's concern, direct their attention to the leper.

Jesus touched him.

As He yearns to touch all.

♥ ***Link to Life: Youth / Adult***

Ask your group members to put themselves in the place of the leper. If each was to come to Jesus today, what would be his or her greatest outer *need? (Perhaps for a job, or extra money, etc.) What would be his or her greatest* inner *need? (Perhaps for control of temper, for healing of a marriage relationship, etc.)*

Ask each to write out a paragraph: From the incident of Jesus and the leper, how do you think Jesus will respond to you when you bring Him your needs?

Ask several volunteers to read their paragraphs to the group.

In dealing with the inner man, it was not enough for Christ to communicate love. He had to provide forgiveness. So verses 17-26 report an incident that develops this theme.

Many were gathered to hear Jesus teach, including the religious leaders who were to become His implacable enemies. When a paralyzed man was ingeniously brought to Jesus over the dense crowd, Jesus recognized faith. He said to the man, "Friend, your sins are forgiven" (v. 20).

The religious leaders, the scribes, and Pharisees, immediately grasped the implication of this statement. Jesus was acting as if He were God! "Who can forgive sins but God alone?" (v. 21) But Jesus responded to their unspoken thoughts. Jesus asked them bluntly which was harder to say: Your sins are forgiven, or get up and walk? Clearly it is harder to tell a paralyzed man to walk, for then everyone will know immediately if a person speaking has authority to do what he says. But who can tell about authority to forgive sins? Forgiveness doesn't seem to carry the same visible impact.

So, Jesus said to the paralytic, "I tell you, get up, take your mat and go home" (v. 24). And immediately the man did!

What a lesson there is for us here. Jesus was touched by the physical need expressed in the paralysis. But His first concern was for spiritual needs. For the forgiveness of sins. Jesus' acts of healing were truly acts of compassion, but they were performed "that you may know that the Son of man has authority on earth to forgive sins" (v. 24).

There are times when we think that our greatest needs are for healing, for friendship, for more money. Jesus helps us focus on the real issues of life: and our first need is the need for forgiveness and for transformed hearts.

Jesus had asked the Pharisees, "Which is easier to say, 'Your sins are forgiven,' or to say, 'Get up and walk'?" It is clear that there, in that crowded room, it was harder to say, "Your sins are forgiven." A person who says, "You are healed," will be immediately shown to have authority, or shown up as a charlatan. But Luke reminded us that forgiveness too is expressed in a person's behavior!

Levi had been a taxgatherer (vv. 27-32). He was hated, because in those days men paid the government for the right to collect taxes, and then collected far more than was really due. Taxgatherers in Jesus' time were swindlers, money-hungry, and despised as collaboraters with a foreign occupying force. Levi was one of these men, and undoubtedly deserved his reputation as a "sinner."

Then one day Jesus came up to Levi and said, "Follow Me." And Levi followed!

Later Levi gave a party to introduce Jesus to his friends, who were outcasts like himself. When the Pharisees and scribes saw Jesus was associating with such people, they muttered indignantly. No doubt they were secretly delighted to have some apparent cause for criticizing Him.

Jesus answered sharply. Who needs a doctor? The well, or the sick? Jesus wasn't there to sit around with those who thought they were well, but to heal those who realized they were sick!

And what happens when Jesus touches the life of a sinner like Levi? What happens when a sinner accepts forgiveness, and chooses to follow Christ? Scripture gives us an exciting answer. It's found in the first book of the New Testament, a book that bears the name of Matthew, the disciple who was once known as Levi, the tax collector!

If we had known Matthew in his days as Levi, you and I would probably have despised him too. But what a great God we have! We have a God who cares about the despised. A God who can touch the hardest hearts with His forgiveness, and can transform the most warped personality. Through Jesus, the sinner can become a new person.

And this is our destiny too. If we come to Jesus, confess our sin, and receive His forgiveness, Christ will begin a change in us that ends in personal transformation. In Jesus, our life too can become new.

♥ ***Link to Life: Children***

Lead your boys and girls to "play doctor." Act out the story of Jesus and the paralytic. You can have observers, and several children helping the "paralyzed" person who is unable to move until Jesus speaks to him or her.

Remind the boys and girls that Jesus heals us inside *as well as out by forgiving our sins and helping us do what is good. On a chalkboard list sins that the boys and girls suggest—the kind Dr. Jesus forgives. Next to each sin list its opposite: the good things the person will do after being healed inside by Dr. Jesus.*

Conclude by helping each child make a "doctor's book." Have each draw on one side of a piece of paper a sin he sometimes commits—and on the other what Jesus wants him to do. The picture can be put up in each child's room at home, to first remind him to ask Dr. Jesus for forgiveness, and then to remind him of what Jesus will help him do if asked.

Jesus as Lord (Luke 5:33–6:11). Jesus had demonstrated clearly who He is. How did those around Him respond?

Many hesitated. Jesus recognized the natural hesitation of men to try the new. In the illustration of the new wine (5:33-39), He noted that one who has been drinking an old wine will hesitate to turn to the new. That person will say, "The old is good." But after a time old wine turns sour. When it is time for the new, even the wineskins (which in Jesus' time served as bottles) must be fresh and new.

Jesus had come to bring in the new. Men must choose Him, or would find the old turning sour and worthless.

Others criticized. The leaders particularly tried to find fault with Jesus. When Christ's disciples plucked grain to eat on the Sabbath, these religious men felt it was a violation of Sabbath law. It was not, for their interpretation of Old Testament Law on this point was wrong.

As Lord of the Sabbath Jesus, the Son of God, who had ordained this day of rest, would Himself determine what was right to do on it.

Some hated. On another Sabbath the leaders set a trap. They placed a man with a shriveled hand in the synagogue, and watched to see if Jesus would heal (to them, "work") on the Sabbath. Jesus had the man stand up "in front of everyone" and healed him. The Lord of the Sabbath announced that it was "lawful" to do good, and to save life, on God's special day.

These actions revealed just how sour the old wine of Judaism had become. The religious leaders had no concern for the man they tried to use against Jesus. He was nothing but a pawn to them. In His response Jesus revealed to all the total hypocrisy and emptiness of all their claims to religious superiority. These were nothing but empty men, who loved only their own place and price, and who were untouched by the hurts of those around them. Jesus' words and actions revealed their hearts to others, and they hated Him for it. "They were filled with insane fury and kept discussing with each other what they could do to Jesus" (6:11, PH).

Followers or observers? (Luke 6:12-19) The lines were being drawn. The crowds still hesitated. The leaders were becoming hardened in their hatred and rejection.

Jesus, after a night of prayer, selected 12 men to be His special disciples: men who had chosen to follow Him.

These men had few qualifications. They had little education. No important family connections. Some had dark pasts. They were fishermen; a tax collector; men of quick temper. But Jesus chose them to be with Him. These were men who had believed in Him, and been moved to confess and trust Him. Jesus is the Son of God—and these men believed.

How different the groups we have seen in these chapters. There were the crowds, who gathered around but hesitated to commit themselves to Jesus. There were the leaders, whose pride moved them to hatred. And there were the disciples, who in simple faith stepped out on the pathway toward transformed lives.

How important that we take our place as sinners at the feet of Jesus, accept His forgiveness, and rise to follow Him.

♥ ***Link to Life: Children***

Start a 12 + 1 *club. The 12 refers to the first disciples who chose to follow Jesus. The 1 is each child, who like the disciples decides to follow the Lord. The 1 also stands for a simple commitment that even a child can keep. That commitment is to do just one thing each day to please Jesus, because we are His disciples.*

Why not let your boys and girls design a club membership card (perhaps a 3 x 5 card) on which a child's name can be recorded. You may also want to include spaces for the children to record their daily deeds of obedience as well.

Discipleship Described: Luke 6:20-38

Jesus was surrounded by crowds who were eager to touch Him. He was a celebrity, and His touch was healing. But when Jesus began to teach what we know as the "Beatitudes," many must have had second thoughts.

The blessed (Luke 6:20-26). The words Jesus uttered seem stark and inexplicable when one first reads them. "Blessed are you who are poor. Blessed are you who hunger now. Blessed are you who weep now. Blessed are you when men hate you." And, "Woe to you who are rich. Woe to you who are well fed now. Woe to you who laugh now. Woe too when all men speak well of you."

The words seem stark, because they seem at first to contradict common sense. Who would willingly choose the "blessed" circumstances of poverty, hunger, weeping, and hatred?

To understand Jesus here, we need to realize that His contrast is not between two sets of circumstances, but between ways people react to life in this world. The contrast is between *Jesus' people* and *other people,* and what gives meaning to each group.

We can state the two principles that Jesus communicates quite simply:

> *Jesus' people are dissatisfied with what this world has to offer but are happy anyway. Other people are satisfied with what this world has to offer but are miserable.*

We know, for example, that there is nothing wrong with riches (1 Tim. 6:17-19). So Jesus was not condemning wealth when He pronounced woe on the rich. It is a love of money which is a root of every evil, not money itself (see v. 10). In desiring wealth, in fixing one's heart on money, a person opens himself up to woes.

Don was 40 when I met him, a middle management executive who, from college days, had determined to work his way to the top of his company and make millions. The week before I spoke in his church, Don had made a discovery that jolted him to the depths of his personality. *He* wasn't going to make it! All that he had worked and planned for, all he'd built his life around, was destined to elude him. He was not the "successful and rich" businessman he had pictured himself to be—and he never would be!

At first Don hadn't known what to do. His whole image of himself was shaken. And then, as I was sharing from this very passage, Don made a great discovery. The agony he was going through was really God's blessing. God had rescued Don from the misery of becoming the success he had planned to be . . . and, in the process, from seeking to build his life on empty and transient things.

Jesus knows that there is more to life than success; that the meaning of life can't be summed up on a balance sheet or in a bank account. How blessed for Don to weep now, and through his trauma to turn from what this world offers to seek his satisfaction in God. How blessed for Don to be turned, even through pain, toward God's way of living.

It is the same with the other things we set our hearts on. Have you built your life around being accepted by others; on being looked on as one of the "in" people? Are you a person who simply has to have everyone say nice things about you—your looks, your clothes, your personality? Jesus said, "How miserable for you when everybody says nice things about you" (Luke 6:28, PH).

How miserable you must be, to be satisfied with popularity. For you have missed the real meaning of life!

Jesus' Beatitudes pierce to the heart of human values, and force us to ask the basic questions we find so easy to ignore. What is life all about for me? What moves me? What determines my choices? What makes me glad or sad? Am I controlled by my needs, struggling as the pagans do to make sure I have enough? (Matt. 6:25-32) Am I controlled by pleasure, satisfied with the laughter and distraction I can find in amusements? Am I controlled by a desire for wealth, satisfied to see my cash and credit grow? (Luke 6:24) Am I controlled by a need to be liked and admired? (v. 26)

Jesus said, *"How miserable for you!* You might better be hungry, poor, weeping, and hated. For then at least you might turn from these empty things to Me, to find out what life is really all about."

Jesus' words jolted the men of His day, and they ought to jolt you and me too.

What is your life all about, and the life of your group members? Are they satisfied that they have found life's meaning? Or are they ready to hear what Jesus says about life, and where human beings can find meaning and purpose. For Jesus, the Lifegiver knows the meaning of life. And He tells us plainly.

♥ ***Link to Life: Youth / Adult***

Read or tell the story of Don as an illustration of one of the Beatitudes. Then have pairs work together to select one other beatitude, and to explain and illustrate it with a real or imaginary story like Don's.

By love (Luke 6:27-38). Jesus went on to tell His listeners, "Love your enemies, do good to those who hate you, bless those who curse you, pray for those who mistreat you" (vv. 27-28). In this Jesus tells us that *the meaning of life for the believer is found in love.* People, not things, are central in the new life that Jesus calls us to live. Giving, not getting, is what life is all about.

In this section's teaching we realize that there is something truly unique about Jesus' kind of love.

Sociologists have labeled one kind of human behavior "reciprocity." They have noted that in every culture this norm, or standard, seems to operate. It's expressed in our saying, "You scratch my back, and I'll scratch yours." This is what reciprocity means: you do something for me, and I'll pay you back. And reciprocity also dictates, you do something bad *to* me, and I'll pay you back for that too.

Most of us are bound by this norm. The Jones family sent you a Christmas card last year? Somehow you feel you *have* to send one to them this year. The Carlsons invited you over to their house? You know it's your turn to have them for dinner.

This norm of reciprocity operates even in the intimacy of family life. You bought me a present? I'll be warm and loving this evening. Your teenager mowed the lawn without being asked? Well, sure, he can have the car tonight.

The simple notion that we ought to be nice to those who are nice to us, and are under no obligation to be nice to those who aren't, seems to permeate every human relationship.

There is much to be said for the norm of reciprocity. It helps hold society together. If we couldn't depend on people responding in kind, there would be a terrible uncertainty in all our relationships.

It's just that *the Christian's behavior isn't to be governed by the norm of reciprocity!* Another norm, another standard, is to replace it.

The other norm is something we may call *initiating love.* We are to take the lead in initiating love. This is what Jesus meant when He said, "Love your enemies." We are not to love because we expect to be repayed. We are to love, even to lend, without expecting anything back. And we are to love this way because it is the kind of life to which Jesus calls us.

It seems frightening. How can I love, knowing I may be hurt by an enemy who does not respond as he should? How can I do good, uncertain about how others will see and respond to my actions? It *is* frightening. But Jesus lived this way. Even though others did hurt and hate Him.

When we decide to live a life of *initiating love*, we will have two consolations. First, we will be living as Jesus has commanded us; as He Himself lived. And second, we will discover in a love like God's what it means to have a truly abundant life.

♥ ***Link to Life: Youth / Adult***
Ask each group member to think of two friends or acquaintances toward whom he or she feels some hostility or awkwardness. Then have each jot down specifically *how he or she plans to reach out with initiating love.*

Without sharing the names of those involved, ask each group member to share how he or she plans to initiate love, and so be like our Heavenly Father.

We shouldn't get the impression that the life of love Jesus calls for is a totally negative experience, with our enemies taking endless advantage of us. Jesus explains. "The measure you use, it will be measured to you" (v. 38). In rejecting the norm of reciprocity for the norm of initiating love, you and I *set a new standard for those around us!* In becoming a model of Jesus' love, we will find that others do respond to us—and to Him.

Power for Our New Lives: Luke 6:39-49
The power of example (Luke 6:39-49). How does a person learn to live this kind of life? Jesus points out that we learn to live by following a person who knows how to live. And that, "Everyone, after he has been fully trained, will be like his teacher" (v. 40, NASB).

This observation strikes at the heart of all of us who are parents. How will our children learn to live Jesus' way? Will they see His life in us?

Because Christianity is a way of life that is learned from Christian models, Christ calls on us to engage in self-examination (v. 42). We have no right to criticize or instruct another about how to live until we are sure that our own lives are in harmony with Christ. If we are blind to God's way of living, and attempt to lead others, both we and they will "fall into a pit" (v. 39).

Again in this passage Jesus reminds us that the issues of life are settled in the heart. To be a good example, we do not need to know everything. We do not need to be perfect. All we need is a heart truly dedicated to Jesus. Out of a sincere heart godly actions will grow. As Jesus said, "The good man brings good things out of the good stored up in his heart" (v. 45).

A final illustration closes this chapter. How do we grow as Jesus' disciples, and in our capacity to model His life? Jesus said that we are to be people who hear Jesus' words, and do them. Only by full obedience to the teachings and words of our Lord will we be able to express the love in our hearts, and come to reflect His likeness in our world.

Resources for the New Life: Luke 7:1-17
Jesus' picture of the believer's way of life in Luke 6 portrays a counterculture. All that Jesus teaches goes against the grain of the ways men live in our world, and the values most men hold.

Where do we find the resources to enable us to move upstream; to be different in a world that demands conformity?

Jesus was done with His public teaching. As He entered Capernaum, the next two recorded events provide the divine answer to our questions about sources of strength.

A soldier's faith (Luke 7:2-10). The first incident involved a stranger, a Roman army officer on occupation duty in Palestine. While stationed in Palestine this man had come to know and love the God of Israel and God's people (vv. 4-6). He had also heard of Jesus. So when a favorite servant fell deathly ill, the centurion requested some of the Jewish elders to appeal to Jesus to heal his slave.

Jesus listened, and turned to follow His fellow Jews to the Roman's home. But in the meantime, the soldier had second thoughts. He, the conqueror, realized he was unworthy to have Jesus in his home. So he sent another message, addressing Jesus as "Lord." He begged Jesus simply to say the word. "I myself am a man under authority," the soldier said. As an officer, he derived his authority from the Roman government which had commissioned him. Because he spoke with Rome's authority, he could command soldiers and they would obey. He recognized the fact that Jesus spoke with the full and complete authority of divine power! Whatever Jesus commanded would be done.

Jesus "marveled at him" and told the crowds, "Not even in Israel have I found such great faith" (v. 9, NASB).

This is our resource too.

Faith.

But a particular faith.

Do we realize that the Jesus we know as Saviour *has all power?* Are we aware that He can command, and that His will will be done? We need not fear to live a completely committed Christian life, for we too can have faith in Jesus. His power is unlimited, and He will live out His life in us.

♥ ***Link to Life: Children***

Children are quick to include boys and girls like *them, and to exclude those who are not like them. But "outsiders" need to be treated with a special warmth if we are to introduce them to Jesus.*

From your curriculum cut pictures of the Roman soldier and a Jewish person of Jesus' day. Then ask your children to think of everything they can that makes the soldier different. *Talk about how most Jews felt about Romans in Jesus' time. Why didn't they like the Romans?*

Then ask each child to draw a picture of someone he knows who is very different from him and his other friends. Let each child explain his or her drawing, and talk about the person drawn.

Jesus was kind to the Roman soldier. How can we show love and be kind to the people your boys and girls drew?

New life (Luke 7:11-17). How great is Jesus' power? Soon after this Jesus met a funeral procession. On the bier was the body of a widow's only son. Jesus saw her tears, and said: "Young man, I say to you, get up."

And the dead awoke.

What a message for us. Have we been dead to Jesus' kind of life? Have we lived the world's way, with thoughts and desires tangled by the cries that distract others? No matter how dead we may have been spiritually, Jesus is capable of awakening us to new life. First comes faith. And then we too hear Jesus' words: Arise!

Arise, and live My new life of love.

TEACHING GUIDE

Prepare

Read through Luke 5:1–7:17. Which of these stories and incidents seems to you to focus on the known needs of your group members?

Explore

Select any one of the incidents in these chapters and give a 10-minute minilecture or minisermon on it. Be sure to apply as well as to explain the selected incident.

Expand

1. Select any or several of the "link-to-life" study activities suggested in this study guide. Work on it or them as an entire class, or in teams.

2. Or ask each member of your group to skim these chapters, and select *one* story or incident. Each then has about 20 minutes to prepare a mini-message like the one with which you launched the session. Ask for volunteers to then share insights with the rest of the group.

Apply

Ask any who did not share in the group to share their passage with another person this week.

STUDY GUIDE 103

Luke 7:18–10:24

DECISION TIME

Overview

There are two decisions that are critical in every human life. The first decision is to accept Jesus, the Son of God, as personal Saviour. In the first part of this study we meet some who made that decision.

The second decision has to do with discipleship. Will we follow Jesus completely? In the second part of this study we find the essence of discipleship, and survey the true disciple's life.

Depending on the makeup of your study group, you may want to emphasize the salvation section, or those passages which deepen understanding of discipleship.

What are some of the characteristics of the disciple's lifestyle that your group will find in Luke 9 and 10? Trust. Suffering. Humility. Purpose. Commitment. Involvement. And prayer.

▶ ***The Seventy-two.*** The other Gospels focus on 12 disciples. But Luke introduces us to a larger corps of close followers. Luke 10 tells us that Jesus appointed 72 that He sent out two-by-two to preach in Israelite towns. We know the names of the Twelve. But the 72 remain anonymous. Yet Jesus knew them and their ministries well. How good that today too we need not be well known by others to be effective disciples of Jesus Christ.

■ For a verse-by-verse exposition of this passage see the *Bible Knowledge Commentary,* pages 222-233.

Commentary

There are some decisions I hate to make.

I particularly dislike deciding what to order from a menu. I'll sit and stare at the listed foods, be the last one to order, and still try frantically to get out of saying to the waitress, "I'll take this."

I had a hard time deciding to buy our last car. I wasn't sure whether it was God's will or my desires that motivated me. And I was very frustrated.

Other decisions—often bigger ones—seem to come easily. It was easy to leave my Wheaton teaching position to move to Arizona, where I had no job or income except through writing. It was clearly the right thing to do.

What can we say about decisions? Some are easy. Some hard. But all of us face decisions that *have* to be made.

This was the situation in Jesus' day as we come to the events described in Luke 7:18–9:20. Jesus had presented Himself as Lifegiver, and had demonstrated His authority. Jesus had openly explained the principles on which the new life He offered is to be built. The counterculture of love had been clearly defined.

And now people had to choose. They had to decide to trust Jesus and commit themselves to Him, or to reject Him.

What were the reactions of people under the pressure of imminent decision? Why did those who hesitated hold back? Looking at them, we can perhaps understand our own reactions to Jesus' claims. And perhaps we too can see why today we *have* to make the choice they tried to avoid.

Why Wait? Luke 7:18–8:3

John the Baptist (Luke 7:18-23). One of those who seemed to hesitate now was John the Baptist! What a shock to see him waver, for the whole focus of his life had been to prepare the way for Jesus. Still, as we look at the circumstances, we can understand.

John was now in prison (Matt. 11:2), about to be executed by King Herod. The personal pressure John faced must have had something to do with the growth of doubt. But even more serious must have been the fact that Jesus' ministry was not taking the direction John had foreseen. John, like the other godly Jews of his day, was entranced with an Old Testament picture: a vision of a messianic King who would throw off the pagan yoke and bring in Israel's promised glory days. But John could see no evidence that Jesus was using His miraculous power to strike a blow for freedom. John did not expect the Messiah simply to go around teaching people to love!

So John sent two of his followers to Jesus to question Him: "Are You the One?" (Luke 7:19, NASB) "At that very time Jesus cured many who had diseases, sicknesses and evil spirits, and gave sight to many who were blind" (v. 21). Turning to John's followers, who had witnessed the healings, Jesus told them to report to John what they had seen.

What had they seen? Miracles? Yes. But *what kind of miracles?* The Old Testament had said the Messiah was to "open blind eyes, to bring out prisoners from the dungeon" (Isa. 42:7, NASB). Messiah would care for those in need. *His ministry would focus on people.* So Jesus sent the followers of John back to him to report. Then He turned to the crowds and He said, "Blessed is the man who does not fall away on account of Me."

John hesitated, because Jesus hadn't done what he expected.

What have you expected of the Christian faith? Have you seen it as a way to become better than others? As a basis from which to criticize sinners? To reject the youth who aches for drugs, or the adult who curses and tries to hide the emptiness of his life behind irreverence or pride.

Jesus told John, *Look at Me! See what I do!* Jesus did not come to judge. He did not come to build religious walls. He came to reach out to people, to heal, to save, to bring hope. To care. And happy are we if we never take our eyes from Him.

If we look at Jesus, we see *love* at the center of the life that He offers and demands. For people who expect something different, something less, no wonder there is hesitancy. But look again at Jesus. And choose.

♥ ***Link to Life: Children***
Work with your older children to create a giant maze. A paper tablecloth can be used. As you draw the maze, have false trails lead to ways that people try to gain heaven, but cannot. You can include things like "being good," and also false religions. If you want to use humor, include balloons, rockets, etc. The one path that leads to heaven is to be marked by Jesus. Jesus is our only way to God.

The crowd (Luke 7:24-35). The crowds around Jesus hesitated for much the same reason John had. While those who knew themselves to be sinners came to John for baptism, the religious leaders held back. And others, aware of their leaders' doubts, held back too.

But Jesus ridiculed these leaders now. John had come, and they all said, "He's too rough. And look at his clothes. What a fanatic." When Jesus came, they said, "He's too smooth! He parties, you know. And goes around with sinners."

Jesus labeled these reactions childish: like sulky children the leaders wanted to play "wedding" when it was time to play "funeral," and when it was time to play "funeral" wanted to play "wedding."

Whoever God sent them, they wanted someone else. And whatever the messenger's message, they wanted another.

We have to watch out for this attitude too. We're too prone to say, "God, I'll let you direct my life—if You give me a wife, a good job, nice children, retirement, etc." We hold back, because we want to retain control over our lives, just as the religious of Jesus' time did. But commitment to Christ involves acknowledging Him as *God!* And to confess this means that we give Him control of our lives.

Christian faith isn't something played by human rules. When we join ourselves to Jesus, we determine to let Him rule.

Rejection (Luke 7:36-50). The final person seen in this section does not hesitate. He simply rejects all that Jesus is because he feels, "I have no need."

The person is a Pharisee, a very religious man. Pharisees were conservatives, not liberals. They believed in God, in angels, in resurrection—in all the tenets of biblical faith.

But the Pharisees were *self-righteous.* They made distinctions between themselves and others, saying in effect, "I'm different." They believed that, even in God's sight, they were good.

As Jesus visited in a Pharisee's home, a

prostitute (cf. vv. 37-38) slipped in and began to weep, washing Jesus' feet with her tears. Immediately the self-righteousness of the Pharisee was revealed. He thought, "If this Man were a prophet, He would know who is touching Him and what kind of woman she is—that she is a sinner." And, the implication is clear, a true prophet would pull back from her in horror!

These two propositions express the basic foundation on which the Pharisee's religion was based. *Others* may need cleansing, or punishment. But I'm different. I have no need.

But look at the woman for a moment. The woman, who tradition tells us was Mary Magdalene, knew very well that she was a sinner. She came in tears, and humbly bowed down to kiss Jesus' feet.

How did she have the confidence to come? She surely knew the attitude of the Pharisee; an attitude of contempt, of hatred. But she also must have known the attitude of Jesus. Clearly she had faith that Jesus would not reject her, even in the home of a Pharisee.

Jesus looked into the heart of each of these people. He saw the woman's love and faith. And He saw the Pharisee's criticism and unconcern.

Jesus asked the Pharisee, "Who loves more? One who is forgiven much, or little?" (paraphrase) The answer showed that even the Pharisee supposed that forgiveness and love were linked. The one who is forgiven much loves much.

But the one who will not accept forgiveness will never learn to love!

Of all the figures in the New Testament, the Pharisee is the most tragic. He alone was totally cut off from Jesus' love. He alone *refused* to respond. And why? Because he kept on insisting, "I have no need."

There are things inside each of us that we're ashamed to even think of; that we cringe to imagine another person knowing. Yet Jesus knows. In every detail. And Jesus loves us still. He loves and reaches out to forgive.

Forgiveness unlocked a new life for the woman who recognized her need and came to Jesus. But refusal to admit need, hesitation to take our places before Jesus as sinners, cuts us off from Him as surely as it cut off the Pharisee.

So men hesitated, and found it hard to decide about Jesus for three reasons that Luke unveiled.

- This Jesus isn't what I expected from God.
- Jesus doesn't play by my rules.
- I have no need: I want no forgiveness.

What reasons do we give today? Are they as poor as these three? These were poor, you know, for each fails to reckon with the reality that Jesus Christ is God; that He makes the rules, and that each one of us *does* need the forgiveness that ushers in new life.

Respond: Luke 8:4-56

Christian decision is essentially response to Jesus Christ and to the Good News about Him. There will always be varied response to Jesus from any group of people. But, whatever the response, there are important things to remember.

The sower (Luke 8:4-15). The Parable of the Sower teaches that the Good News of Jesus falls like seed on men's hearts. The seed falls on different kinds of ground. Some hear, but quickly are distracted and forget. Some hear with delight, but fall away. Some let the cares or delights of this world choke out the good seed.

But why did Jesus speak a parable? He explained: "The knowledge of the secrets of the kingdom of God has been given to you, but to others I speak in parables, so that 'though seeing, they may not see; though hearing, they may not understand' " (v. 10).

Jesus had presented Himself and His message in the plainest of words. The seed had been sown. Those who had responded to Jesus would understand what He said now. Those who refused to respond would soon be unable even to hear.

It seems hard for some to grasp, but it is true. To hear Jesus' message and to hesitate is to reject Him. "Not now" is just as much a "no" as "never"!

And there comes a time when seeds of truth which have not been allowed to take root are snatched away.

This time had arrived in Jesus' ministry. Men who had seen Him, who had heard His plain words, must now choose. For those who hesitated, and thus implicitly refused to recognize the One they were unwilling to publicly disclaim, it would soon be too late.

Encouraging response (Luke 8:16-21). Jesus had not yet given up on His generation. He gave further exhortations and examples to help men respond with faith.

Jesus Himself had stood out like a lamp, shining clearly where all men could see. He had spoken clearly, so all could hear. Then came the warning. "Consider how you listen. Whoever has will be given more; whoever does not have, even what he thinks he has will be taken from him" (v. 18). The planted seed, the light of truth, both will be removed if not used.

How are we to use the seed and the light? When Jesus' family approached, Christ said, "My mother and brothers are those who hear God's Word and put it into practice" (v. 21). Response brings *relationship,* and our relationship hinges on whether or not we are willing to accept God's message about Jesus Christ. If we hear and believe, we become members of God's family. If we reject, we stay forever outside.

Invitation to trust (Luke 8:22-55). Perhaps the most important thing to remember as we ponder response to Jesus is *who it is* that we are invited to trust and to obey. Jesus' subsequent actions reinforced the awareness of all around Him of who He is.

Jesus stilled the storm (vv. 22-25). Jesus again demonstrated His power over nature, miraculously dispersing a storm and bringing a sudden calm to a raging sea. The creation obeys its Creator; it knows its God.

♥ ***Link to Life: Children***

This is a favorite children's Bible story, often used to encourage boys and girls to trust Jesus when they are afraid. Make a fun booklet to emphasize just who Jesus is, and why it is so wise to ask Him for help.

Give the children starter ideas for various "I'll never ask . . ." *pages. On the cover print WHOM WILL I ASK TO HELP ME WHEN I AM AFRAID? Inside pages may start with "I'll never ask a baby. . . ." or "I'll never ask my goldfish. . . ." Color or paste a picture of a baby, a goldfish, etc. on the appropriate pages. Make up about 10 "I'll never ask" statements for 10 pages of the booklet. Then let your class suggest "because " conclusions to the statements. For instance, "I'll never ask a baby because all he can do is cry." Be sure to let your boys and girls suggest their own "because" conclusions.*

Then, on the last page of the booklet, have a picture of Jesus stilling the storm. Print "I will ask Jesus . . ." and have your boys and girls suggest several "because" answers which you can print on the page.

He freed the possessed (Luke 8:26-39). In Gadara, Jesus met a man possessed by a legion (at least 6,000) demons, whose bondage was revealed in his filthy nakedness and ferocious strength (vv. 26-27). Jesus ordered the demons to leave, and freed the man from their supernatural oppression. Even demons bow before Jesus; Satan knows Him as Lord of all.

He raised the dead (Luke 8:40-56). Shortly afterward Jesus was called urgently to attend a dying 12-year-old. Hurrying to her side, Jesus was touched by a woman in the crowd. The woman had been hemorrhaging for a dozen years; yet at Jesus' touch she was instantly healed. Jesus paused, sought her out, commended her faith, and hurried on.

Arriving at the home of Jairus, the girl's father, Jesus found the women wailing and crying in the traditional Hebrew lament for the dead. Jesus turned them all out of the house, and took the hand of the dead child. Then He commanded her to awake, and presented her alive and well to her joyous parents.

The weeping women had seen her dead. They would now see her alive, and spread the word across Galilee. There was no need for anyone to know just how Jesus had raised the dead in that closed room. It was enough that all would know the girl lived.

Even death gave way before Jesus. He is the Lifegiver, and the Lord of life.

And so, as we think about our response to Jesus, we must remember just who He is. When we see His acts, as witnessed by the men and women of Jesus' day, we know. Jesus is Lord, and our Almighty God.

Climax: Luke 9:1-22

The climax of the first phase of Jesus' ministry followed immediately. Jesus had presented Himself to men as the Son of God. How would they respond? Would they trust Him? Or, because Jesus wasn't what they expected, would they refuse to admit their need and so reject Him and His forgiveness?

In a flurry of activity, Jesus sent His disciples out again to go from house to house and village to village to proclaim the Gospel and to heal (vv. 1-6). Even Herod, who had beheaded John the Baptist, was perplexed as the reports about Jesus continued to filter in. Could this be John, back from the dead to haunt him? (vv. 7-9)

When the disciples returned from their mission, crowds followed Jesus to a plain outside Bethsaida. He welcomed them, spoke more on the kingdom of God, and cured those who needed healing. Late that afternoon Jesus even met their need for food, performing the familiar miracle of the loaves and fishes (vv. 11-17). These men and women had now heard His words, seen His miracles, and fed on the bread He provided.

It was then that Jesus asked His disciples, "Who do the crowds say I am?"

They answered.

"Some say John."

But they do not say, "Our God."

"Some say Elijah."

But they do not say, "Our God."

"Some say one of the old prophets."

But they do not say, "Our God."

"But what about you?" Jesus asked. "Who do you say I am?" And Peter answered for them all. "The Christ of God."

And this is what it comes down to for all of us. Who do we say Jesus is? A good man? A religious leader? A spokesman for goodness and for truth? Only one answer will do. Only one answer will open the door to forgiveness and new life.

Jesus is the Christ. He is the Son of God.

♥ ***Link to Life: Youth / Adult***

Luke 9:18 presents the *critical question for the individual; a question to which there can be only two answers. Either Jesus is the Christ, the Son of God. Or, Jesus is somebody else.*

Have each group member select from Luke 7:17–9:20 a list of all the evidence that Jesus is, or is not, God's Son. If you wish, have them work in pairs. Take reports, and write a master list on the chalkboard.

The Meaning of Discipleship: Luke 9:23-26

Now the Gospel of Luke shifts its focus. Christ came, and offered new life to a world that, even after conclusive demonstration of who He is, rejected Him. But some believed. This little band of men who said, "You are the Christ, the Son of God," launched out on new life. From now on, while Christ would still speak to the crowds and their leaders, His message was primarily for those who had trusted in Him.

Jesus talked now about discipleship: about how we who are His followers can grow to experience the abundant new life that may be ours in Him.

Life saved or lost (Luke 9:23-25). Many puzzle over Jesus' warning, "Whoever wants to save his life will lose it, but whoever loses his life for Me will save it." We're helped when we remember the focus of Luke. As a Christian, with new life from God, you and I have the potential to be new and different persons. We saw it earlier. Jesus said, "Be like your Heavenly Father." God's intention for believers is that we might bear the family resemblance of His Son. You and I are to develop into persons whose character expresses the very stamp of God's own heredity. *This is our destiny.* We are to be like God throughout eternity, and, in this world, to become more and more like Him all the time.

But the potential self (v. 25) can be lost. We can choose to live the old way, by the values and motives that move men in this world. We can live the *old* life, and let the new remain unnourished, buried deep within us. If we do so choose, what we lose is ourselves, our experience on this earth of the person we could have been.

Earlier we saw a great choice each person must make: Will I accept Jesus' offer of life? Now we see a second choice: Will I become a disciple, put the old behind me, and become new?

This is a question you have to answer. Will you lose your old life, or are you determined to hold tightly to it, to try and save your "self"? Or will you let go, turn away from the old for Jesus' sake, and in so doing become the new, the true, you?

**Let him deny himself (v. 23).* Jesus gives a profound three-part prescription to anyone who wants to come after Him (v. 23). The first is: deny yourself.

Self-denial doesn't mean self-rejection. It doesn't mean wallowing in self-loathing, or turning away from everything you enjoy because, "If you like it, it must be bad." God "richly provides us with everything for our enjoyment" (1 Tim. 6:17). We know that, far from being worthless, you and I are of infinite value. Jesus thought enough of you to die for you. If He loved you so, how can you hate or reject yourself?

But denying self is important in discipleship—as long as we understand that it means *deny everything rooted in the old life.* Deny and reject "the lust of the flesh and the lust of the eyes, and the . . . pride of life" (1 John 2:16, NASB).

Carla had been angry. She struck out at her dad with biting words, then ran to her room. After the flood of tears she felt better. But she knew too that for her to follow Jesus would now mean going to apologize. How she fought making that apology! She told herself it had been his fault—and in some ways it was. She told herself she *couldn't* go and say, "I'm sorry." Not when *he* should by rights apologize to her first! Everything in her struggled against the self-humbling that an apology would mean. And for a long time she stayed in her room, as the tension within her grew.

Finally, Carla got up off her bed and, denying the fears and pride of her old nature, went to do what she knew Jesus wanted.

This is self-denial. Growth in the Christian life demands just this: the brutal setting aside of pride and fear and of all the "rights" that the old self demands as its due, to live instead a Jesus kind of life.

♥ ***Link to Life: Youth / Adult***
After explaining what "deny yourself" means, and how one is to lose his old life to gain the new, tell the true story of Carla. Then have each person write *anonymously about a true (or made up) event like that in the story of Carla.*
Collect the stories, and read about half a dozen.
Then, from the stories that illustrate this principle, see if your group can come up with guidelines to help them recognize a situation in which they need to deny themselves.

**Take up his cross (v. 23).* Please note. Jesus did not say, "Take up *My* cross." Instead He says to each of us, "Take up *your* cross."

But what is our cross? Some have thought of the cross as suffering, a reflection of Jesus' agony that fateful Crucifixion day. But that was *Jesus'* cross; that was God's unique will for *Him.* More central than the fact of suffering is the fact that the cross was both God's will for Jesus, and the symbol of Christ's full commitment to do the Father's will.

What is God's unique will for *you?* This is what taking up the cross means: to choose, as Jesus did, to do whatever God wills. This understanding is supported by a little word: "Take up his cross *daily*" (v. 23). Each day, you and I are to decide to do God's will. In this choice we will live as Jesus did, and will be His disciples.

**Follow Me (v. 23). The Living Bible* renders this beautifully and well: "Keep close to Me."

How can you and I ever find the strength to reject the old in us, and decide daily to do God's will? By ourselves, we can't. But we have Jesus' invitation, "Keep close to Me."

Jesus does not invite us to a "by-rule" way of life. Jesus invites us to personal relationship. As we do keep close to Christ, He encourages us and enables us. Jesus provides the power we need to live triumphantly, and to grow in that new life which, ultimately, is His.

This, then, is both the way and the necessity of discipleship. To be or not to be disciples is the choice we face: on it hinges the finding or losing of our new selves. We can be disciples as we deny the old in us, choose God's will daily, and follow close to Christ.

And how do we follow Christ? The rest of Luke shows us the way.

A Survey of the Discipled Life: Luke 9:37–10:24

We now move on to Luke's description of another flurry of activity. Yet in each incident, we see a little more of what it means to be a disciple. Later in Luke we will see some of these themes developed in great detail. Now we see the critical issues in a quick survey.

Trust (Luke 9:37-43). The very next day an incident occurred which showed the danger of misplaced faith. A man brought his only son to the disciples for healing. And why not? They were associated with Jesus. They had recently been sent by Christ on a healing mission. And yet, when the disciples attempted to cast out the spirit that was the cause of the sickness, they could not.

When Jesus came the man asked Him to look at his son (v. 38). The man had earlier asked the disciples to heal. Now, doubting, he asked Jesus. The failure of the disciples had undermined the confidence of this father in the Master!

Jesus responded almost bitterly. "O unbelieving and perverse generation," Jesus exclaimed. But nevertheless He added, "Bring your son here!"

Do we ask from men what we ought to be asking from God? Is our faith weakened because we have looked too much to Jesus' followers, and not enough to Jesus? A disciple is not a person who acts on his own. A disciple is a person whose trust is fixed in Jesus, and whose response to every need must be to bring that need to Him. Jesus has the mighty power of God. We can trust Jesus.

Suffering (Luke 9:44-45). Immediately after this demonstration of power, Jesus told His disciples that He would be handed over to men for suffering and death. This involved no buffeting by a cruel fate. This was by Jesus' own choice.

Sometimes we suffer too. How good to realize that, as Christ's disciples, we are not being tossed on waves of circumstance. Even as Jesus' suffering was purposive, so is all that we experience in following Him. God will use our experiences for the blessing of others and ultimately for His—and our—glory.

Humility (Luke 9:46-50). The Twelve were eager for the glory that discipleship would bring. They were so eager that each one wanted to be greater than the other! Jesus knew what they were thinking, and that it was rooted in the old self, not the new. He took a child, and told them that, at heart, greatness was to care about the little ones, the seemingly unimportant, the individual.

John quickly changed the subject. He was far more at home struggling with a knotty theological problem. He didn't want to talk about caring for a single child. But Jesus' words stood—and still stand. The great among His disciples are those who, like Him, welcome the least, and humbly stoop to care.

Purpose (Luke 9:51-56). One day on a trip through Samaria, Jesus was refused entrance to one village because He journeyed toward Jerusalem. James and John were incensed. In hot anger they asked the Lord to destroy the town with fire from heaven.

Jesus sharply rebuked them. How far they were from His spirit (v. 55). "The Son of man is not come to destroy men's lives, but to save them" (v. 56, KJV). And so too the disciple who would follow his Lord. We have a goal in life, a purpose that gives us meaning. Like Jesus, our heart's desire is to heal and to save.

♥ ***Link to Life: Children***

Children often like to mimic and act things out. In this application of Luke 9:51-56, let them choose to "be like John" or "be like Jesus" in responding to situations like the following: • Mom says to pick up toys but some of the toys belong to a younger brother/sister. • Brother bumps you and knocks you into a door. • A person you thought was a friend calls you names. Etc.

The "like John" actor(s) is to show an angry, hurtful response. The "like Jesus" actor(s) is to show a loving, caring response.

Let your boys and girls describe other situations where they have "like John" and "like Jesus" choices to make.

After running through the situations and acting out "like Jesus" responses, talk more about what Jesus would say and do. Have the children plan what they will do and say to be more like Jesus the next time they start to feel angry, like John.

Commitment (Luke 9:57-62). Many in Jesus' day volunteered or were called to discipleship. But many fell short of commitment.

There was the *eager disciple* (v. 57) who volunteered to follow Jesus anywhere—till Jesus warned that discipleship might be uncomfortable. There was the *reluctant disciple* (v. 59) who, when commanded to follow, wanted to wait until his father had died and been buried! Jesus rejected the excuse. "Go and proclaim the kingdom of God." There is no evidence that this reluctant disciple obeyed.

There was also the *someday disciple* (v. 61), who wanted only a little time. Just to say good-bye to the home folks. Then, someday soon, he would follow. This too was unsatisfactory.

You see, what Jesus seeks is the *now* disciple (v. 62). Jesus wants the person who will put his or her hand to the plow and, without looking back, move straight out to do God's will.

The figure of the plowman is succinct. As a teen, I plowed with an old one-horse hand plow, settling the reins around my shoulders, grasping the handles firmly, struggling to hold the blade level and steady, to make an even furrow. As the first furrow was cut into the virgin ground, I picked out a pair of marks at the far end of the field to line up carefully. If I looked back, the plow wandered, and the furrow snaked off across the field. Only by looking ahead, with eyes fixed on my guiding marks, could I do my job.

This is what Jesus asks of us. To fix our eyes ahead, on Him, and not to look back. We are to take the plow, *now,* and commit ourselves to His task.

Involvement (Luke 10:1-20). Then Jesus sent His disciples out again: 72 sent by twos across the land. Discipleship means involvement in the work of Jesus.

And what involvement! We're involved in what Jesus cares about. He is the Lord of the harvest (v. 2). We are involved in Jesus' method of ministering. We go out as sheep among wolves, depending neither on wealth nor status to win a hearing (vv. 3-7). We're involved with Jesus' success: God's power operates through us as we do His will, whether to heal or to bring judgment on those who reject (vv. 9-16). And yes, we're involved in Jesus' joy: we have a sure relationship with God, and we call men to share our fellowship with Him (vv. 17-20).

Prayer (Luke 10:21-24). This last sign of discipleship was one of Jesus' most notable marks. Christ acted in dependence on the Father. Jesus shared His joys with the Father too. In this prayer, Jesus said, "All things have been committed to Me by My Father."

Do you see it?

Do you hear?

Jesus has all power; it is all in His hands. We can come to Jesus, and in full dependence commit ourselves and our needs—in fact our very lives—into His keeping. Then we can step out with confidence, and live!

How good to be a disciple.

How good to learn to really live!

TEACHING GUIDE

Prepare

Decide to focus in class on salvation or on discipleship.

Explore

1. Go around the group asking each to tell how he or she goes about making a decision, and what kinds of decisions are hard for him or her.

Go around again, and have each tell if and how his pattern of decision-making affected acceptance of Christ.

2. Or give a minilecture on Jesus' call to discipleship (Luke 9:23-25). Tell the story of Carla to illustrate, using the approach explained in "link-to-life," page 669.

Expand

1. Brainstorm reasons why some people hesitate to decide to trust Jesus. Then set your group members the task of deciding what evidence compels a decision that Jesus *is* God's Son (see "link-to-life," page 668). Discuss: "How would you use this evidence to help a person make his or her decision, now?"

2. List the seven characteristics of the discipled life (pp. 669-671) on the chalkboard. Ask each person to select *one* of the seven that he or she finds "most difficult." Break into teams, based on the characteristics, with each person working with the team focusing on his "most difficult" area.

Each team is to study the relevant passage of Scripture carefully. Each should make a list of what it observes or learns, and also how this may help each step out as a disciple.

Apply

Ask each group member to meditate quietly on this question: "What does Jesus want of me, now." And then respond in silent prayer.

STUDY GUIDE 104

Luke 10:25–12:3

SPIRITUAL DETOURS

Overview

Luke emphasized the humanity of Jesus. It is only appropriate that many of the teachings of Jesus which Luke recorded show us how to live a human life in union with God.

This portion of Luke contains some of the best-known stories about Jesus' life. Here find the story of the Good Samaritan, the conflict between the sisters Mary and Martha, and the Lord's Prayer. As you show how each of them is linked with Christian spirituality, you will be communicating a vital message to the members of your class or group.

Here your group members can learn to recognize the false trails down which some believers are led, and to recognize spiritual reality from spiritual illusion.

▶ ***Spirituality.*** In the New Testament the adjective "spiritual" (*pneumatikos*) is contrasted with "soulish" (*psychikos*). The word "spiritual" is used to describe gifts, the law, the resurrection body, understanding, and the believing community, as well as a person. Thus a "spiritual" person or thing belongs to the realm of the Spirit. A spiritual person is, in essence, one who is not only indwelt by the Holy Spirit, but who also lives in obedience to the Spirit's promptings.

Christians have historically been uncertain about the nature of the truly "spiritual" life. Is it a life without sin? A life of prayer, or fasting? A life of withdrawal? In these paragraphs of Luke we begin to understand more of what spirituality is not—and how to live our lives in union with our God.

Commentary

When I was 19, after two years of college, I joined the Navy. At Great Lakes Naval Training Station, I sat in a barber chair and became a "skinhead," was issued my uniforms, and was introduced to Navy life.

There I received the traditional misdirection given newcomers in any special group. Left-handed wrenches and lost firing lines, and toothbrushes to scrub cracks in the barracks floor, were just some of the things I was told to fetch. And, because at first I really didn't know what was expected in this strange new life, I was often confused enough to follow false trails. It was all so new. And I wanted to do the right thing.

In many ways it's the same for us as Christians. To become a believer is to launch out toward a unique destiny: to become more and more like God the Father as the new life He has planted in us grows and matures. We are to learn to think and feel and *be* like Him.

This godly way of life we're to learn is distinctly different from the ways we have known. It's far more than mere morality; it's transformation. So it is easy to become confused about the road to personal spiritual renewal. It's easy to wander away from God's pathway, onto sidetracks that look promising but are really only dead ends.

Luke 10 shows how Jesus began to train His followers in discipleship. He began to show them how to live a new life. His words and actions drew contrasts between the way men of the world live and the way His followers are to live. All that is reported in this section of Luke reveals both the straight and narrow path of discipleship, and the dangerous detours and illusions that keep us from our new life's goal.

What are the false trails down which Christians wander? Perhaps members of your group have been disappointed because they have wandered down one or more of them, and missed true spirituality.

Activism: Luke 10:25–11:13

One of the most deeply ingrained human notions is that a person must do something to merit God's favor. We accept gifts from other people. But we seem to want to say of what we receive from God, "I earned it!"

The Good Samaritan (Luke 10:25-37). The activist's approach to life is implicit in a question put to Jesus by an "expert in the Law" (e.g., Scriptures).

But first, it's instructive to note that the man who portrayed the activist attitude put an insincere question to Jesus. He asked, "What must I do to inherit eternal life?" (v. 25) But the man was not really concerned about Jesus' answer. He was not motivated to ask his question by a personal sense of need: he was trying to trap Jesus. If he had been motivated by honest desire, the answer Jesus gave might have been more direct. As it is, the answer came all too clear. It was so clear that the questioner soon realized that *he,* not Jesus, was trapped!

"What must I do to inherit eternal life?" The query contains a contradiction. What does anyone *do* to *inherit?* Why, nothing! An inheritance is something someone else has earned. An inheritance comes as a gift. If your father is a millionaire and makes out a will leaving all to you, what did you do to inherit? Why, you were born into his family. The inheritance is based on relationship, not on performance. You do not *do* something to *inherit.*

Jesus turned the question back on the asker. How did this expert in Scripture "read" the Word? The man answered correctly. The heart of the Old Testament Law, and of all that God seeks to do in the human heart, is expressed in the command to love God fully and to love one's neighbor as oneself (v. 27). All the specific commands in the Law can be summed up by "love," for a person who loves fully and rightly will do what God's Word reveals to be the right thing (see Rom. 13:8-10). This, then, is at once the simplest and most profound demand in the Word of God. Love God completely. And love your neighbor as you love yourself.

Phillips translates Jesus' reply: "Quite right. Do that and you will live" (Luke 10:27).

But this of course is the problem. *Do all that!* Put all self behind; love God purely and perfectly. Love others as you love yourself. *Do all that* and you will live.

These words sounded doom to the questioner. He had been convicted from his own lips. For he, as every person who has ever lived, had fallen short of doing "all that." We have all had selfish thoughts. We have all neglected to put God first. We have all hurt our neighbors. Rather than bring hope, Jesus' demand that a person "do all that" brought dismay.

The expert in the Law now attempted self-justification. This is characteristic of the activist. He wants to earn what he gets. But he wants to use a balance scale to determine value. He wants to weigh his "good" against his "bad," hoping there will be more on the "good" side. Jesus' reply said in effect, "All right. Use your scales. But remember: your 'good' acts are not weighed against your 'bad' actions. Your acts are weighed against the standard of *perfection!* Your acts are to be weighed against *all* that love demands!"

When the expert realized that he had condemned himself, he quickly attempted self-justification. "Who is my neighbor?" (v. 29) How quickly we tend to do this. When we feel condemned, we try to modify the standards, whittling a little off here and shifting something there in a vain attempt to better measure up.

I recently visited a 21-year-old in the hospital. He had shot himself with a rifle. He went to church as a child, but left as a young teen. He said the thing that earned him an invitation to leave the church was a question he asked. "Why, when you're so proud of sending money overseas for missionaries, won't you have anything to do with the poor people across the street?"

Now, I don't blame the church for my young friend's drift to drugs at 13, or for his choice of bad company. But I do wonder. How many of the things we are proud of—our missionary budgets, our separation, our doings and duties—may at heart be expressions of an attempt to whittle God's standard of perfect love down to lists of things we can *do,* and in the attempt feel some pride?

At any rate, the expert in Scripture asked Jesus, "Who is my neighbor?" He didn't want to think he must love everybody!

We all know the story. We know how an injured Israelite lay, beaten and robbed and in pain, along the road between Jerusalem and Jericho. We know how a priest and a Levite (both men who knew and were to teach the Law) hurried on by. And we know that a Samaritan, a foreigner and a hereditary enemy of the Jews, risked stopping to help the injured man. He carried him to an inn and there paid the full cost of his care.

And we know what Jesus said to the expert who had questioned Him. "You go, and do likewise."

The expert in the Law had come in pride, trying to trap Jesus. Now he went away, and we can hope he went away feeling a personal sense of need. For Jesus challenged this activist on his own field of honor: "Go and *do*." You go, and *try*. *And when you realize that you cannot possibly do all things that are required by the divine law of love, then perhaps you will realize that relationship with God can never be based on human works or accomplishments!*

Go and do. Then, perhaps, this man would recall the message that Jesus so often taught. Life with God begins with confession and forgiveness. Life with God begins when we abandon our works, and throw ourselves on the overflowing mercies of our God.

♥ ***Link to Life: Youth / Adult***

The story of the Good Samaritan has often been used, appropriately, to help Christians realize that the "neighbor" Christians are called on to help is anyone we know who is in need. It is need, the human condition itself, that makes all *of us neighbors.*

But in telling this story we too often miss the fact that this incident is intended to display the futility of trying to win eternal life through human effort.

Help your group discover this emphasis by listing key phrases on the chalkboard. Have group members work in pairs to answer questions about each designed to help them understand this passage.

phrase	question
do to inherit	*What does anyone* do *to* inherit?
love . . . with all heart, etc.	*Who can achieve the standard described there?*
do all that	*Why did Jesus say this?*
who is my neighbor	*Why did the expert ask this?*
go and do	*What would the expert discover if he tried?*

Use the commentary to help shape your answers to these questions.

♥ ***Link to Life: Children***

Our neighbor is *anyone in need. But how do children become sensitive to other's needs.*

On one level, you can help them be sensitive to those with obvious needs in many ways. Create a class "get well" sign for a sick member. Visit and sing for an older, house-ridden individual. Collect food for the hungry, and bring it to a mission or a soup kitchen, etc. Even young children are not too young to be exposed to needs—or shown how to care.

Mary and Martha (Luke 10:38-42). The expert in the Law illustrated an activist attitude distorting the idea of salvation. But is this attitude found only in the unsaved? Tragically, we find it in those who are sincere Christians. The sisters and Lazarus were very close to Jesus. When Jesus and His disciples visited Bethany where the three lived, Martha rushed and bustled about, preparing a special meal for Jesus. Her sister Mary kept slipping away, to sit down and listen to the Lord. Martha, hot and frustrated that Mary wasn't helping, asked Jesus to tell Mary to help! Jesus had to rebuke Martha. Mary, who was staying close to Jesus, had "chosen what [was] better" and that would not be taken away from her. It was not what Martha was *doing for* Jesus that counted: it was that Mary had paused to listen to Him.

The Lord's Prayer (Luke 11:1-4). Activism is an attitude, an approach to life and to relationship with God. The activist wants to put his relationship with God on a "pay-as-you-go" basis. He feels a tremendous need to do something to earn whatever he receives from the Lord.

In unbelievers this attitude is focused on salvation. "Salvation can't be a gift!" they argue. "Let me do something to win God's approval. Let me earn my way to heaven." Like the expert in the Law to whom Jesus spoke, such people have not realized that they truly are lost.

Activism also characterizes the life of

many Christians. They too want to live on a pay-as-you-go basis. They feel that they have to work to keep God's favor. But we believers are children of the Heavenly Father! Helpless children, infants, unable in ourselves to love or to do anything well (see John 15:5). Activism, working to earn spiritual growth and gifts—leads only to the frustration that Martha felt as she bustled and hurried—and saw that her sister was closer to Jesus than she!

Then what is God's alternative? If we aren't to grow by self-effort, how *do* we grow? Jesus' answer comes as we see Him help the disciples develop an attitude, not of activism, but of *dependence.*

Consider the implications of the prayer that Jesus taught His disciples, and its relationship to Luke's present theme.

> Father in heaven, Holy is Your name. Your kingdom come, Your will be done on earth just as it is being done in heaven. Give us our daily bread. Forgive our sins, as we also live forgiveness with others. And lead us, Father . . . not into temptation, but deliver us from evil.
>
> Luke 11:1-4, author's paraphrase

In this simple prayer, Jesus taught all disciples to come to God as Father, not employer. We are to honor Him, not repay Him. We are to make requests of Him, not to demand earnings. We are to realize our need for constant forgiveness, not to shout in pride, "See how great I'm doing!" We are to request deliverance, not to promise, "I'll try harder."

The activist attitude is based on the idea that we can do something *for* God. The disciples' attitude is based on the awareness that *God can do something* in us!

♥ *Link to Life: Children*

It's not too early for boys and girls to memorize the Lord's Prayer, and think about its meaning. Just as children depend on their earthly parents, we can help them learn to depend on their Heavenly Father and express that dependence in prayer.

Select a simplified version of the prayer to memorize—perhaps the NIV *or Sweet Publications,* International Children's Version.

Make memorizing a game. Read the prayer with the class. Then let a child select one word *to erase. Read the prayer again, and let another child erase another word. By the time all words are erased, your children will have learned this prayer by heart.*

♥ *Link to Life: Youth / Adult*

The Lord's Prayer is too familiar to most adults. Like other familiar things, we tend to say or read them so quickly we miss the meaning.

Help your group focus in on the meaning of the familiar prayer by listing the following words on the chalkboard: relationship, will, dependence, godliness, activism. Ask pairs to take different words, and to study Luke 11:1-4 to answer the question: What does this prayer teach about "relationship," etc.

The prayer applied (Luke 11:5-13). The next few teachings of our Lord recorded by Luke reinforce all that the disciples' prayer implies.

**Persistence (vv. 5-10).* The first story teaches by contrast. If you have a friend who is at first unwilling to help you, keep after him. He'll finally come down and help just to be rid of you! And Jesus says in application, "Ask, and it shall be given. . . . Everyone who asks receives (vv. 9-10, NASB). *God is not like an irritable acquaintance!* You can depend on Him, because God cares. Ask Him, and He will give.

**Fatherhood (vv. 11-13).* The second illustration explains God's eagerness to meet our every need, and to grant our requests. God is our Father. The key to understanding our relationship with the Lord and His attitude toward us goes back to this fact.

The disciple of Jesus comes to His Heavenly Father. And the Father works in his life, even as the Father worked in the life of Jesus.

This short section in Luke 10 and 11, then, says something basic to each of us. It shows us how we can move on in discipleship and grow to be like our Lord. We cannot grow by attempting to earn. Prayer, not performance, is at the heart of our new life. Spirituality is found in depending, not in doing!

God the Father is eager to see us grow as His sons and daughters. When you and I come to Him, depending on Him to work in our lives and through our actions, asking Him for strength, forgiveness, leading, enablement—*then* God works His sweeping change in our personalities.

Have you grasped the meaning of your relationship with God? To a doer, God is at best a Friend, whose help seems to him to depend on persistent self-effort. To the Christian who has learned to depend, God is a Father, who can be relied on completely. How important then that we be followers of God, "as dearly loved children" (Eph. 5:1).

Do you depend on God? Have you come to Him, listened to His Word, and simply asked, "Father, make this real in me"? The road of the activist is a tragic dead end. The highway to spiritual transformation is the path of total dependence.

♥ ***Link to Life: Youth / Adult***

Put in the center of a chalkboard a column of words that describe Christian behavior. You can include whatever your group members suggest: churchgoing, prayer, helping others, whatever.

Leave these on the board as you give a minilecture explaining the activist approach to faith and life explored in Luke 10:25–11:13.

Then place checkmarks *to the left of each word that your group thinks describes something a person with an activist attitude might* do. *Go through the list again, and place checkmarks to the right of each word that your group thinks a dependent disciple might do. (Nearly every word will be checked twice!)*

Discuss: "What is the basic difference between a spiritual activist and a disciple? How can we tell one from the other? How can we tell if we *are activists in our faith, or dependent disciples? What are the key reasons that dependence is a pathway to spiritual growth, while activism is not?"*

Indecision: Luke 11:14-32

The people around saw all that Jesus Himself did in dependence on His Father. But they still hesitated. And they lost the opportunity for new life.

Power over the demonic (Luke 11:14-23). When Jesus cast out demons, people tried to explain it. It could be by the power of God. But might there be some other explanation? Jesus' enemies said His power over demons came from the prince of demons: it was just a trick to fool people into trusting Jesus. Christ's answers (11:17-18, 20) were unable to move them. Finally Jesus confronted them: "He who is not with Me is against Me" (v. 23). The time for indecision was past. People had to choose.

Indecision can spoil the Christian's life too. Coming to Christ as Saviour is only the beginning. One must own Him as Lord and decide for discipleship. But so many of us hold back! And only later discover that we have wandered into an empty way of life.

Vulnerability (Luke 11:24-26). Jesus illustrated the vulnerability of the man who is forgiven, but will not go on to full commitment. Jesus spoke of an unclean spirit cast out of a man. The man was cleansed, freed from the old dominion. But his personality, though put in order, was not occupied! He was like an empty room. What would happen to him? Unless he filled up the emptiness, other spirits even worse than the one cast out would come in.

Even the believer has no defense against evil as long as his or her life is empty. We need the positive, dynamic presence of Jesus Christ filling our lives. We must invite Him to possess us totally if our lives are going to change. Initial faith not followed by total commitment is another spiritual dead end for Christians.

Filled (Luke 11:27-28). How do we go about filling our lives with Jesus? Christ explained. "Blessed rather are those who hear the Word of God and obey it" (v. 28). *This* "doing" is not to be confused with the activist's self-effort. Instead it is an opening up of our lives to God, a dependence on Christ for enablement which frees us to respond to God's revealed will. This doing is a response, made simply because we want to follow Jesus, and depend on Him to enable us as we keep His Word.

Judgment ahead (Luke 11:29-32). This section closes with a warning of judgment. The people of Jesus' time had heard Him. Except for a small band, they had hesitated far too long. Now the time of invitation was almost past. The next great public evidence of who Jesus is would come in His resurrection (vv. 29-30).

Then Jesus reviewed how great a sin their failure to decide was. When Jonah came to

Nineveh, the people of that pagan city responded with faith. Sheba came to Solomon because she had believed the stories of his wisdom. Yet Jesus—far greater than any and all the Old Testament figures—had come to His people. Had they heard? Had they listened? No, they had hesitated, undecided. And they hesitated still, as the last opportunity of the nation to receive Jesus as King slipped away.

What a lesson for us today. Have our group members hesitated too long? Or drawn back from full commitment to Christ as Lord?

How important for us all to remember that Jesus, the One with all power, has said to us, "Follow Me." We cannot afford to hesitate. Hesitation has such a terrible cost. We might lose ourselves, and never know in this world all that it means to be transformed.

How good it is to know that we need not hesitate. Discipleship is not a "try harder" life, that we're afraid to try because we are sure that we'll fail. Discipleship is simply depending on God, our Father, confident in that intimate relationship that God will enable us to do His will, and transform us as He has said.

Illusions: Luke 11:33–12:3

I once spoke at a youth conference on evangelism held at Disneyland Hotel in California.

I had some free time, and visited the Circlevision theater in Tomorrowland. By linking nine cameras, the Disney photographers had provided a 360° vision of historic and scenic America, shown on giant screens that encircled the watcher. I was particularly jolted when the photographers took us inside a car careening down a twisting San Francisco street—and actually *felt* the bodily sensations of tipping and turning. It was as if we were in the car instead of standing on solid, carpeted floor inside the theater. Our eyes literally fooled our bodies; we felt what our eyes saw, what seemed to be happening, and not what was actually happening.

The Bible points to a similar phenomenon: "As [a man] thinketh in his heart, so is he" (Prov. 23:7, KJV). What a person perceives, what he sees as real, affects his whole personality and his behavior.

As Luke moves on in his record of Jesus' training of the disciples, the writer now shows us two particular illusions that can block our spiritual progress. The disciples of Jesus must see life and its meaning as does their Lord. To see as Jesus sees is vital as we seek to *be* as He is.

The lamp and the eye (Luke 11:33-36). Jesus makes this point in Luke with the illustration of the lamp. "[A person] puts it on a stand, so that those who come in may see the light" (v. 33).

Picture the lamp of Jesus' day. It was, in all but the wealthiest of homes, a shallow dish of olive oil in which floated a wick of flax. The wick was lit, and gave off a flickering light. The lamp was never bright. Today, coming into a brightly lit home, we're hardly conscious of the lamps at all. They shed so much light that what we *see* is the room they illuminate. But in Jesus' day men saw the lamp first: they came to the light, and as their eyes became accustomed to the semidarkness, they saw dimly the room that the lamp so imperfectly revealed.

The lamp of Jesus' day, then, was both a focus of attention and an illuminator of all that could be seen, however dimly. The lamp would enable a person to pick out the furnishings of a room, and to pick his way through without stumbling.

Jesus then pointed out to His listeners that the eye performs a similar function for the body. The eye too is a focal point: on it depends our perception of what surrounds us, and so too the choices that we make. We find our way through this life by evaluating what we see. We make our decisions by what appears to us to be the safest and best way. "When your eye is clear," Jesus then noted, "your whole body also is full of light" (v. 34, NASB). But what if the eye is faulty? What if you don't evaluate correctly? Then you are in darkness! Then you will be unable to move without stumbling. And so Jesus warns us, *Watch out that what you mistake as light isn't really darkness! (v. 35)*

With this simple illustration, Jesus had stated a profound truth. If we make a mistake in values, if what we see as important in life is really an illusion, how great is the darkness in which we walk! We will certainly lose our way. We will certainly stumble off the road of the disciple.

What is important? (Luke 11:37-54). After each key teaching, Luke reported events which illustrated his meaning. While Jesus was talking about illusory values, a Pharisee (one of those men whose values were completely distorted) invited Jesus to supper. At that table, Jesus showed a few of the false values against which His disciples must guard.

The conflict in values appeared as they were seated at the Pharisee's table. The Pharisee noted with surprise that Jesus didn't "wash" before the meal.

The washing spoken of here was not for cleansing. It was a religious ritual. Over the centuries the Pharisees had embellished God's Law with many human traditions and interpretations. In Jesus' day, these men were careful about every detail of their lives. In fact, their sense of religious superiority and their claim to spirituality was rooted in this care. So before each meal they would carefully wash, dipping their hands into a bowl of water, raising their arms to let the waters run down their elbows. One who had not gone through this ritual washing would not be considered "clean" enough to eat!

Jesus didn't follow this tradition. And, noting His host's reaction, Jesus launched into a scathing critique of the Pharisee's approach to spirituality, and of the values which lay at its root.

What were some of the externals that seemed important to the Pharisees? Ritual washing. Ceremonial cleansing of every dish from which they ate. Such careful tithing that a Pharisee would count the leaves of household herbs to make sure 1 of every 10 was taken to the temple (v. 42). It was on such compulsive concern for externals that the Pharisees had built their reputation for holiness! And, in their pride, they loved the front seats of the synagogue and to have men bow to them in public recognition of their spiritual superiority (v. 43). And the Pharisees accepted all this deference as their due. They actually thought they were spiritually superior, because they were so careful in keeping the minutiae of what they saw in God's Law.

How easy for us to fall into a pharisaic way of life. We too have our traditions, our own criteria of spiritual superiority. But are such things really measures of spirituality?

Yes, there are lesser duties that we as Christians should perform (v. 42). But we should not be *primarily* concerned with such externals.

As Jesus spoke to the Pharisee He defined the areas of prime concern: justice and the love of God (v. 42).

True spirituality is a matter of the heart. It is a matter of caring about the things that God cares about. And what God cares about is justice and love and doing good to others. Only when our hearts are so tuned will our eyes be cleared of illusion, and we will see reality as Jesus knows it to be.

Jesus was interrupted by an expert in the Law. But later He returned to His theme. "Be on your guard against the yeast of the Pharisees, which is hypocrisy" (see 12:1).

I used to think that hypocrisy was doing something you knew was wrong, to fool others. It can be: one meaning of the original word is "playacting." But there is another emphasis here. Hypocrisy is "outward show." The Pharisees were not pretending. *They actually thought that the outward show, the ritual, the attention to minutiae, was the real thing!* They had mistaken externals for the heart of faith.

Because they mistook outward show for reality, their inner eye was blind. What they thought was light, was darkness! With their values wrong, all that they might do could only lead them deeper into the dark night of the soul.

Warning (Luke 12:1-3). It was later that Jesus warned His disciples, and us, against viewing spiritual life as did the religious people of His day. Outward show had become more important to them than the heart; the external had become reality. Yet, there is a day coming when no one will be able to hide behind his illusions! "There is nothing concealed that will not be disclosed, *or* hidden that will not be made known" (v. 2).

When God reveals reality, how vital that neither you nor I nor our group members be found to have wandered into the cold, dark, empty world of outward show.

♥ ***Link to Life: Youth / Adult***

One helpful way to enable people to get at the meaning of a biblical passage is to paraphrase. In a paraphrase a person attempts to express meaning *without using the* words *of the original.*

So why not have your group members individually paraphrase Luke 11:37-44—imagining that Jesus is speaking to present-day Pharisees in the church.

When each has completed his para-

phrase, work together to do a group paraphrase. Talk through each suggestion made by group members, constantly referring back to the text to make sure the paraphrase expresses the intended meaning.

When the group paraphrase is completed, list together "the important points that Jesus made."

TEACHING GUIDE

Prepare
Before the group meets make your own list of "Christian activities" and do the paraphrase of Luke 11:37-44.

Explore
1. As group members come in, ask each to complete this sentence: "A spiritual Christian will. . . ." Each is to write down but not share his completion.
2. If there are non-Christians or new believers in your group, you may want to focus on the dialogue Jesus had with the man to whom He told the familiar story of the Good Samaritan. Use the "link-to-life" idea on page 674 to help all see the futility of attempting to gain acceptance by God through good works.
3. If your group is composed of more mature Christians, give a minilecture on the Good Samaritan story and its lesson, and move on to analyze the Lord's Prayer. Linking that prayer to key words, as suggested in "link-to-life," page 675, will help your group members discover its vital message of dependence as the key to spiritual growth.

Expand
1. To help your group members see that activism and dependence are basic *attitudes* toward the spiritual life, make a list of things that good Christians do—and then discover which might be done by the activist, and which by the dependent believer. See "link-to-life," page 676.
2. Or have individuals paraphrase Jesus' criticism of phariseeism, in Luke 11:37-44. Then work toward a group paraphrase that will give special insight into illusions which distort spiritual living (see "link-to-life," pp. 678-679).

Apply
Conclude by asking each person to complete again the sentence with which the group session was begun: "A spiritual Christian will. . . ."

Ask volunteers to share their first completion, and then the second.

How have impressions of spirituality changed through this shared Bible study?

STUDY GUIDE 105

Luke 12:4–16:31

LIFE'S ILLUSIONS

Overview
Some of the most familiar of Jesus' stories are found in these chapters of Luke. Among them are:

- the Parable of the Rich Fool.
- exhortation not to worry, but to remember the lilies of the field.
- the illustration of the narrow door.
- the Parable of the Great Banquet.
- the Parable of the Lost Sheep.
- the Parable of the Prodigal Son.
- the Parable of the Shrewd Manager.
- the story of the rich man and Lazarus.

Many of the stories involve money, and illustrate the tension that comes as we live in two worlds—the physical and spiritual. Jesus teaches us how to resolve that tension by giving priority to the spiritual, confident that our Heavenly Father will meet our needs.

But the stories also have another theme: they expose the games played by people who want to *appear* spiritual, but who have not really made God's priorities their own.

There is plenty of material in these chapters for several group sessions: many of the parables could each be given an hour or more of time. But there is profit too in seeing how these stories and events fit together, and apply to the issues that we face today while seeking to live as Jesus' disciples in the world of here and now.

■ For a verse-by-verse commentary on these chapters, see the *Bible Knowledge Commentary*, pages 237-247.

Commentary
It is easy for us to fall victim to illusions. Part of the reason is that a disciple does live in two worlds: the material-social world around him, and the invisible, spiritual world operating within and through the visible. Conflicts between these two worlds often occur. A choice that seems wise according to appearances is often not wise at all.

So we seem caught between what we see around us and something that God says is far more real. Standing between the two, the disciple needs to come to the place where he commits himself to one world only. He needs to recognize appearances as mere illusion, and grasp the tremendous fact that what is not apparent to us is far more real.

Carol's mother insisted she work toward a teaching certificate in college, rather than take the training Carol felt she wanted for missions. Carol's mother was moved by a concern for her daughter's security; certainly education was the safest course. So it might appear! But appearances can be misleading.

Between Two Worlds: Luke 12:4-48
Misleading (Luke 12:4-12). Jesus began to teach that appearances are misleading with a simple warning. He told His disciples not to fear (that is, stand in awe of) powers that can kill the physical body. Instead, stand in awe of God, who can give life to or can destroy the living personality (see vv. 4-5).

This instruction might well frighten us were it not for Jesus' next words. Not a sparrow falls, or a hair of our head is lost, but that God knows. So, Jesus said, "Are not five sparrows sold for two pennies? Yet not one of them is forgotten by God. Indeed, the very hairs of your head are all numbered. Don't be afraid; you are worth more than many sparrows." God's power is used *for* us, not against us. We stand in awe of God not because He will destroy us, but because He who has all power cares! We are important to Him!

How important is this realization? Jesus went on to show that when a person acknowledges Christ, that person is acknowledged *by* Christ in the presence of the angels.

What happens on earth is important in heaven! *The two worlds which seem so separated are actually linked . . . and God is in control of both!* How wonderful to realize that God, who does control, values us and will use His power on our behalf.

The rich fool (Luke 12:13-21). It is so easy to think of what is happening here on earth as the important thing. But what a spiritual disaster that is. One man who heard Jesus speak of God's control over the material shouted out, asking Christ to make his brother divide an inheritance. This man had completely misunderstood Jesus' teaching. *This world is not the important one!* So Jesus warned, "Watch out! Be on your guard against all kinds of greed; a man's life does not consist in the abundance of his possessions."

How easily we come to think of this world as the important one, and imagine that life is summed up in what we possess. Jesus told of a "rich fool" who finally felt that he had more than plenty.

He had so much that he tore down his barns to build larger ones. He was comforted to think that he had all he would ever need, and told himself, "You have plenty" (v. 19).

Older versions translate this, "Soul, you have." In the original, the word so translated means the man himself: his living personality. What this man had done was to confuse his life in this world, his bodily needs, with *himself.*

But a human being is more than an animal. He is more than a body and bodily awareness. A human being, formed in the image of God by God's own hand, is a deathless being who will exist in self-conscious awareness throughout eternity—either with God, or separated from Him.

The rich man thought that this world was all; that life consisted of luxury and plenty. How blind! What a tragic mistake! That very night, Jesus said, the man's personality was separated from his body, to leave this world and to answer to God. And all his *things* were left behind.

When we see reality clearly, we come to realize both that the physical universe is under God's control, and that the material is ultimately irrelevant to the real meaning of human life.

♥ ***Link to Life: Children***

It is often hard to help boys and girls realize that things are not necessary for happiness. This is especially so in a society like ours, where TV constantly creates desire for new toys and possessions.

Tell the story of Sarah (or Matt, if you teach a boy's class). "Sarah had a mommy who loved her, a daddy who loved her, a brother who loved her (usually), friends to play with, and a happy teacher at school. Sarah felt very happy and safe, because God had given her so many people to love and to love her."

Then list many things that Sarah ordered from a catalog, or bought at a toy store. Let your boys and girls take turns adding one item to the list each turn. But each time, name the item and repeat the quote above about the people God had given Sarah to love and to be loved by.

When the children have listed all the popular toys Sarah (or Matt) has received, then begin to work through the list, naming things that happened to the toys. This one was lost. Another was broken. A friend took this one home. Etc. But again, after each item is rubbed off the list, repeat the quote.

Finally Sarah (or Matt) will be left with what she had in the beginning; people who are God's gifts to her. The things on the toy list were nice, but they were not the things that were really important.

Finally ask each child to write a story like Sarah's about herself, and read it to parents when she goes home.

Lilies of the field (Luke 12:22-34). Jesus warned the crowds not to assume that abundance and luxury are keys to the meaning of life. Now Jesus spoke to the disciples about their attitudes toward life's *necessities!* The disciple is not to be concerned about food and clothing. His attitude is to be one of trust in God, who knows his needs, and who is in control of all things.

There are two things that Jesus' words bring to our attention.

(1) Disciples need not live in a state of anxiety. We can trust God for our physical needs as for all else. Because we need not be worried about such things, when we make decisions we're free to choose God's will, even if it may seem to involve loss of all we possess (v. 33).

(2) Our use of material resources will reflect our commitment to God, and the extent to which our hearts are set on His kingdom and righteousness (v. 31). Jesus said, "Where your treasure is, there your heart will be also" (v. 34). If we treasure things, possessions, or wealth, then our hearts will be drawn away from God. Like the rich fool, we will seek meaning in things. And with our vision clouded, we'll lose our way as disciples.

♥ ***Link to Life: Youth / Adult***
Divide by couples; have singles work individually. Ask each to quickly outline the major categories in the family budget, and estimate amounts spent on each.
Then ask each couple: "If you felt truly free of all concern for necessities, and free of all desire for luxuries, how would your life be different than it is now?"
Have two couples, or four singles, discuss this question against the background of their budget review.

Watch! (Luke 12:35-48) Jesus closed His discussion of the disciples' attitudes toward the material world with a warning. Be alert!

Christ's coming seems to many to stretch farther and farther into the future. How easy to settle down in this world. How quickly we, as servants of God, can come to enjoy what He has left in our charge while He is away. It is not wrong to enjoy. But we do know the Master's plan. This present world will be dissolved in fire (2 Peter 3:7-13). Thus all that we do here and now should be done in view of the fact of our Lord's appearance. How happy for us if we never let the world around us close our eyes to God. How happy if we resist the constant temptation to build our lives on things rather than on His coming.

♥ ***Link to Life: Youth / Adult***
Tell your group members the true story of Carla, a college student of the mid-sixties, and her mom. What entered into the decision-making of each? What does Luke 12:4-48 say about their process? How should each have gone about evaluating the situation, and making the decision?

Closing Doors: Luke 12:51–13:9
Christ's ministry was now focused on instruction of His disciples. Yet the door to life while swinging shut, was not yet closed to the crowds. And so Jesus warned them: the time is *now*. You must decide.

Christ asked how people who could judge the weather with a glance toward the sky could fail to interpret the meaning of the times in which they live (12:54-59). The signs had been given: the earth is on its way to court, to appear before the Judge of all. The time to settle is now, out of court, before sentence is passed.

But still Jesus' listeners tried to avoid the issue, and to speak of curiosities. Jesus warned them plainly. Several people killed in a recent disaster were no more guilty than they! "Unless you repent, you too will all perish" (13:5).

The Parable of the Fig Tree (vv. 6-9) is another warning. The tree represented Israel. It had been planted and cared for, but was barren. Now, it was given one last chance. If the tree did not respond, it would be rooted out.

The door is closing.
The Master of the house draws near.
Judgment, or joy, awaits.

Are People Pawns? Luke 13:10–14:35
When my oldest son was 12 we got a game called Jarts, which consists of big outdoor darts that one tosses at a circle marked out on the ground. We enjoyed the game until it became clear that my son was taking the competition too seriously, and was frustrated when I scored more points than he did. Finally I got smart, and changed the rules. Instead of seeing who got to 21 first, we began to see how many tosses it would take us to reach that amount adding our scores together. And then we began to enjoy the game.

There's something about any win/lose game that can make for frustration and even humiliation. Eric Berne, in *Games People Play* (Dell), suggests that we all play games with each other; we all try to win. We manipulate other people to make them serve our ends. The desire to "win," to feel ourselves better than others, or to gain a benefit at someone else's expense is all a part of the distortion that sin has stamped on the human personality. It's *natural* to play such interpersonal games, even for the believer. But it is totally contrary to the way of life of the disciple.

Luke illustrated, in the experiences and

conversations of Jesus, some of the strategies that people use to gain advantage. And he showed why these are contradictory to the life of discipleship. In probing the inner motives of men, Jesus probes our lives too. He helps us discover hidden patterns in our lives that might hold us back from full experience of the disciple's abundant life.

Formalism (Luke 13:10-21). Teaching in the synagogue on the Sabbath, Jesus saw a woman who had been oppressed for 18 years, bent almost double and unable to straighten up. Jesus called out to her and laid hands on her. Immediately freed, the woman stood upright and praised God. And the president of the synagogue was *annoyed!*

In fact, he was so upset that he announced: "There are six days for work. So come and be healed on those days, not on the Sabbath."

Immediately, Jesus labeled his response hypocrisy: "Outward show." This man was so caught up in the forms and traditions that he lost sight of people! But the same man would think nothing of untying an ox on the Sabbath, and leading it to drink (v. 15).

Jesus' illustration pierced through all the pretense to reveal the utter emptiness of formalism. His words "humiliated" the leaders, and then Jesus went on to warn. In the kingdom of God, many birds will come roost on the tree that faith produces. Don't mistake them for fruit! In the kingdom formalism, the notion that outward show and form is the reality, can, like yeast in flour, too quickly permeate the whole.

Name-droppers (Luke 13:22-30). Jesus warned against people who associate with Him without commitment. The day would come, Jesus warned, when such people would find themselves outside! Then they will cry out, "Sir, open the door for us." When the door is not opened they will protest, "We ate and drank with You, and You taught in our streets" (v. 26). Jesus will reject them: "I don't know you or where you come from." *It is origin, not association, that counts!* Spend all the time in church you want. Association with believers won't make you a Christian. You must have the life that comes from God.

Weaknesses (Luke 13:31-35). The Pharisees, who hated Jesus and were plotting to kill Him, now hurried up to warn Christ of impending danger from Herod. The name of this game is, "find the weakness."

The Pharisees would have been delighted if Herod *had* killed Jesus. But even the rumor might help them. Rumors make people worry. A lie here or there might upset a person you don't like. It might produce uncertainty, or even fear. If a weakness shows up in a person's character, you have something to use against him. You have a prop for your own pride; ammunition for belittling remarks. "Did you hear how Jesus just fell apart when He heard that. . . ?"

But Jesus was not afraid. He knew far more than His enemies about His suffering, and He never flinched or drew back. But Jesus took no special pride in His courage. Instead, His heart was touched with compassion for the very men who hated Him and tried to break His spirit. Jesus mourned over the Jerusalem that had rejected, and would soon crucify Him—and in turn would itself be destroyed (vv. 34-35).

Entrapment (Luke 14:1-6). We have a concept in our legal code called *entrapment*. It protects a person from being solicited by law enforcement officers to commit a crime, for which he can then be arrested. Crimes must be committed on the initiation of the criminal, not the police.

But entrapment is one of the games human beings often play with one another. We set up a trap, into which we hope they will fall.

The Pharisees, knowing Jesus had healed on the Sabbath, had Him to the home of one of their most respected members (v. 1). Right across the table from Him they seated a man afflicted with dropsy. And they watched.

Jesus brought the issue into the open. "Is it lawful to heal on the Sabbath or not?" Then, when the Pharisees would not answer, Jesus healed the man and let him go. Again Christ shamed His critics, pointing out that even a cow fallen into a pit would be lifted out on the Sabbath.

This is a bad game to play. Like "find the weakness," it is designed to embarrass another person. It is far worse when we bring in an innocent third party to use against our foe. How had the dropsied man felt? Had the Pharisees cared whether he were helped or not? Hardly! The man was merely a pawn, a way to get at Jesus. It is true. When we see others as pawns, and try to use them for our own advantage, we soon begin to treat others as unfeelingly as did the Pharisees.

Upstage (Luke 14:7-14). Jesus observed behavior at a feast which illustrates another game, one motivated by pride and selfishness. The point in this game is to make sure that everyone sees and admires you. Jesus noted men competing for better seats at a banquet, for seating in those days was ordered, with the most important guests ranked nearest the head of the table.

After pointing out the danger of pushing yourself into a high seat (you might be embarrassed if your host then reseated you lower down!), Jesus noted that anyone constantly trying to gain the spotlight and exalt himself will ultimately be humbled.

How empty when we act from motives of "what will others think?" How meaningless the approval of men, when only God can accurately evaluate, and only His approval counts in the long run.

Jesus suggested to His host that he might better invite the poor and the homeless to his banquet—not friends who would repay in kind. How much better to reach out in love to those who no one knows but God. It is not the spotlight, but the knowledge that God will more than repay acts of love, that should motivate us (v. 14).

Choice (Luke 14:15-33). Then Jesus told a story to those who were too busy with their games and personal concerns to respond to the feast of life God has prepared. In Jesus' story the invitation had been extended (v. 16). Many had been invited, even the game players, whose emptiness Jesus has exposed. Jesus came to save us all, even the most sinful. Yet in Jesus' story the invited guests began to make excuses. Each was simply too busy with profit and pleasures.

Whatever the excuse, saying no to the divine invitation remains rejection. A person who fails to respond to Jesus' invitation to life has rejected Him. Salvation is a yes or no issue, with no room for maybe.

Tragically, people of every age judge themselves too busy or too involved in their games to respond. But this will not keep God's house from being filled. The Gospel invitation goes out to the whole world, and all who will receive it will be welcomed. For those who will not, the doors will remain closed and they will be excluded from Christ's great welcoming feast.

Jesus then turned to the crowd (vv. 25-33). They too *had* to choose.

Even the closest of human ties that might sway a person against a decisive choice must be set aside. The word "hate" in verse 26 uses an idiom that men of Christ's time would have understood. To "hate" a person in a legal sense was to decisively reject any claim he might have to a portion of an estate given to another heir.

For us, Jesus' words and actions speak clearly. We must reject every little game people play for personal advantage. Formalism? Let us reject empty show, and care about others whom Jesus loves. Let's no longer be concerned with appearance, and value instead our commitment to the Lord.

♥ ***Link to Life: Youth / Adult***

Jesus exposed several games that people play to gain personal advantage over others. Briefly explain the games and passages to your group members. Then let each select one game, and after studying with a team of others the passage in which it is described, try to establish "rules" for that game. For example, the rules for the game of formalism might include:

(1) set standards higher than most people can keep.

(2) be sure to sneer a little when someone else falls short.

(3) remember that people's needs are less important than "doing things the right way." Etc.

After defining the rules, let each team try to come up with contemporary examples both within the church and secular world.

People, the Prize: Luke 15–16

What ways of living with others does Jesus commend to His disciples? He decisively rejected playing games that treat others as pawns. Instead, Jesus taught that His disciples are to treat people as the prize!

Valuing the sinner (Luke 15:1-10). The Pharisees, whose coldhearted formalism never made them hesitate to use others, began to criticize Jesus for His interpersonal relationships. "This Man welcomes sinners and eats with them" (v. 2). In response, Jesus told a story which establishes the theme of these two chapters in Luke's Gospel, and which clearly reveals the principles that are to guide us as we live with others.

If a man with a hundred sheep loses one (vv. 4-7), he will search for it, and rejoice when he finds it. If a woman loses one coin of her dowry (vv. 8-9), she'll sweep and hunt through the whole house. When she finds it, she will rejoice. It is the same for God, but with people. There is "rejoicing in the presence of angels over one sinner who repents" (v. 10). *To God, people are a prize!* We are important and valued, and the transformation of a single sinner brings joy, not only to God, but also to all who share His heart of love.

Have we grasped what this means? God won't manipulate us or play games with us. We're not pawns, even in God's ages-long battle with Satan. No, each of us is a shepherd's lost lamb, a woman's lost dowry coin. God the Father *loves* us, every one. And all that He does with us will be for our benefit and good.

What a wonderful confidence this is. I am not being used by God to gain some mysterious end of His. I *am* the end, the goal, that in me all His love might be expressed, and that I might thus share His glory.

The Prodigal (Luke 15:11-32). How appropriate that the story of the Prodigal Son follows Jesus' assertion of God's love. Does God really love us? We've rejected Him, wandered in far countries, spent the good gifts He has given us in selfish and often sinful pursuits. What is His attitude toward us now? God, like the father in the Prodigal story, is watching for us. When we turn to God, He comes to greet us. Stilling our confession, He assures us of His changeless love. And He prepares abundant life for us: the fatted calf of transformation.

But there was an older son, who represents the Pharisees, standing by. This son was unmoved by his brother's return. He was angry, and he criticized his father (vv. 25-30). In his anger the elder brother refused the love the father offered *him*—even though the father went out to entreat the angry son to attend the feast.

The story raises a vital question. Whose character do we bear? The father's, whose love overcame and made a way for the dead to live again? Or the elder son's, whose anger at love and at forgiveness so blinded him that he could not even see that *he* needed forgiveness too?

How exciting that when we have experienced the Father's love, we are invited to be like Him, freed forever from the cold self-centeredness that cuts people off from one another and from God.

♥ ***Link to Life: Children***

Boys and girls will be able to identify with the experiences of the younger brother. Draw a map on the board of his journey, showing him home, on the road away from home, in a far country at parties, in a far country with the pigs, on the road back home, and home again. Sketch in appropriate scenes.

Then show the boys and girls a series of circles, on which happy, sad, surprised, and worried faces have been drawn. Put a circle of tape on the back of each so it can be stuck on the chalkboard.

Ask the boys and girls to tell which circle/face shows how the young man felt—at home, leaving home, etc. Then explain that the Prodigal's journey is like any time we sin. We leave our Father's house (rebellion), we seem to be having a good time at first, but then we discover we feel terrible. When we decide to come back to God and admit we have done wrong, we may worry a bit at first. But God welcomes us and forgives us, and we can be happy again.

Encourage the children if they do wrong not to stay miserable, but to confess their sin quickly so they can be forgiven and restored.

The shrewd manager (Luke 16:1-14). The Pharisees had turned life upside down. They used people to gain things. Now Jesus set the values right, and pointed to the worth of individuals to a loving God. Jesus showed that the servant of God the Father must use things to gain the good of men and women.

This is the point of the story of the shrewd manager, called in some versions the "unjust steward." Jesus commended him because he was wise enough to use things to gain other ends. What he did was not right. But at least it put *things* in perspective as means, not ends.

We too are to determine what is to be used, and what is to be gained. We must then remain faithful in our commitment to the truth that people are of greater value. No man, Jesus taught, can serve two masters. You and I and our group members will either be mastered by our love for others, and give of what we own to meet their needs, or we will be mastered by our love for things, and in the end will use people to gain them (see v. 13).

The Pharisees heard what Jesus said. And they ridiculed Him, because at heart they were lovers of money (v. 14).

The Law and the heart (Luke 16:15-18). Jesus again attacked the Pharisees. "You advertise your goodness before men. But God knows your heart. And all that you hold splendid is utterly detestable to Him" (v. 15, author's paraphrase).

It was then Jesus turned to speak of the Law. Why the Law? Because these proud Pharisees actually rooted their pride in the Law of God! Yet no one can read passages like the first chapters of Deuteronomy, or the Prophet Isaiah, without being impressed by the fact that God is concerned with human beings. His every Word is spoken in love.

The Law, an expression of the way that men might love one another and show love to the Lord, will not pass away. The Law, in which the Pharisees sourced their pride, condemned them, for they had not responded to its central message: Love God. Love your neighbor.

An eternal issue (Luke 16:19-31). This segment of Luke closes with the story of a rich man and Lazarus. It is probably a true story, about real people. Scripture nearly always marks off Jesus' parables and illustrations, and no parable uses an individual's name.

The story draws attention to two men. One was rich, yet love for his fellowman didn't move him to use even a little for the beggar Lazarus.

When death came, the man left his riches behind. With all illusions and false appearances stripped away, he entered the torments of an eternity for which he had not prepared. But Lazarus, who must have sought the meaning of life in God rather than goods, found death a blessing.

Jesus now told of a conversation in the afterworld. The rich man gazed across the gulf fixed between blessedness and woe, and saw Abraham (the father of those who believe) with Lazarus. He called for help. But it was too late.

Then came an unusual request. If only Lazarus could be sent to the earthly home of the man now in torment, to warn his five brothers who were still living. Certainly they would listen if a familiar man returned from the dead to speak with them. Certainly then they would repent and change the direction of their lives.

Abraham's answer must have jolted him. "They have Moses and the Prophets; let them listen to them" (v. 29). They possessed the Word of God, the Word in which even Law breathed love. If they would not listen to God's Word, "They will not be convinced even if someone rises from the dead" (v. 31).

We know how true this is from history. Resurrection did *not* move the Pharisees. The Man who spoke these words was soon to die, and then to be proved victor over death, raised by the Father's power. And still many would not believe.

How important that we open our hearts to the Word of God. Let us listen to His call to discipleship, reject games that use others, and instead view others as God does: as the prize and focus of our new life in Christ.

TEACHING GUIDE

Prepare

Read through these chapters, making a list of each story or incident, and of its lesson for us. You may want to select one or more to concentrate on, based on the needs of your group members.

Explore

Discuss: "Have you ever felt that someone was *using* you?" Talk about why, how, and how it made you feel.

Give a brief minilecture tying together the stories and incidents in these chapters.

Expand

1. Use one or more of the "link-to-life" ideas on pages 682 (to sense impact of release from financial anxiety), 682 (to check decision-making processes), or 684 (to learn the "rules" for the games that people play with others, so the attitudes involved can be recognized and rejected).

2. Explore what it is like after death. Does a person become "nothing," or a "spirit," or what? From Luke 16:19-31 develop together a description of life after death.
3. Select any of the other passages which might be significant to your group members, and ask them to do a scenario for a modern TV special based on this story. Who would each of the central characters of the modern drama be? What would they do? How would they interact? How would the point be made and applied?

Apply
Have each person identify a person to whom he or she is close, and suggest one way he can communicate to that person that he or she is a prize rather than a pawn.

STUDY GUIDE 106

Luke 17:1–19:40

ONLY BELIEVE?

Overview
Some object to the Gospel's offer of forgiveness on the grounds that it is too easy. "Only believe?" a Navy buddy once objected. "Why, then you could go out and rob or rape or do anything you wanted to do!"

I tried to explain that a person who trusts Jesus as Saviour doesn't "want to" sin. That faith makes us different inside, and love for God, not fear of Him, motivates holiness. But somehow he just couldn't see it.

We Christians sometimes have just as much trouble seeing that "faith" as belief is *not* enough. Those who truly believe are called on to put faith into practice, and obey the One they have acknowledged as Lord.

In the words and incidents that Luke reports in these crucial chapters of his book, we Christians are helped to see discipleship's link between true faith, and necessary obedience.

▶ ***Faith and Works.*** Christians have often debated the relationship. But we can agree on certain basic statements. Salvation comes through faith and faith alone, for the death of Jesus purchased our forgiveness and new life. When a person has new life from God, that life will be expressed. Just as a living infant cries and moves, so a person with new life from Christ will express that life—in works. It is not that works bring life, but that those who are alive in Christ will work.

Commentary
We've all seen a child seated in complete concentration, taking apart a new toy. Somehow it seems so important to find out just how something new works.

We may feel the same way about "faith." What does it mean to "believe"? Does it mean sitting back and waiting for God to do something? Or does it mean acting? And how can I tell if my actions are just self-effort, that *activism* which is to have no role in discipleship?

Questions like these plague many Christians, and many who set out to be disciples hesitate at times, uncertain how to proceed.

Jesus' first disciples were uncertain too. Then the Lord taught them the functions of faith. Just as God teaches us the functions of faith through these vital chapters of Luke's Gospel.

Discipleship and Obedience: Luke 17:1-10
One day the question of faith crept unexpectedly into a conversation between Jesus and the Twelve. Christ was speaking a word of woe about those who put temptation to sin in another's way, to cause him to stumble (vv. 1-2). This was not a word for outsiders only: it was a word needed by disciples. Too often our ways of living with others harm rather than help!

Jesus then became very specific. "If your brother sins, rebuke him, and if he repents, forgive him" (v. 3). This is doubly hard. It's much easier to keep still when someone sins against us, and to try to hide the pain. We sometimes even think we're being "spiritual" by trying to ignore the wrong. But failure to be honest, trying to give the "outward show" of nothing wrong when there *is* something wrong, isn't God's way. "[Speak] the truth in love" (Eph. 4:15). Real love speaks out to remove the barrier that even inadvertent sins erect.

The loving thing to do is to rebuke the person who sins against you, for he needs the cleansing that forgiveness can bring as much as you need the barrier of hurt removed. So Jesus said, "Rebuke him."

And if he repents? Forgive! And this is difficult too. For our old self dwells on slights and hurts and takes a perverse pleasure in self-pity and in "righteous indignation."

But then Jesus made it even more difficult. "If he sins against you seven times in a day, and seven times comes back to you and says, 'I repent,' forgive him." The disciples were upset at this. "Lord," they cried, "increase our faith!" (Luke 17:5)

I can understand their feelings. When we were first married my wife and I lived in a house trailer 35′ by 8′. Our living room was only about 6 feet wide. And I had a problem. Ever since my teen years, I've been driven up the wall by mouth noises—especially gum, chewed with open-mouthed vigor. And my wife was a gum chewer! As I'd sit at the table, way across our 6-foot living room, I'd become aware of a growing, echoing sound: ker-chump, ker-chump, KER-chump, KER-CHUMP!

Finally, in desperation, I'd mention the gum noise, and be given a quick, full-hearted apology. And there'd be silence, as gum and mouth were clamped carefully shut. For a while. But soon, engrossed in reading, she'd forget. And then the sound would reach me again. And grow. Until I just couldn't stand it any longer, and in desperation would speak again. She was always quick to say, "I'm sorry." But after several recurrences, I'd begin to wonder, and to feel upset. "She *couldn't* care! Not and do it *again!*"

No wonder the disciples cried out to Jesus. "Help! If we have to live like *that* with people, then, Lord, increase our faith!"

But how can we understand Jesus' answer? He hardly seemed to sympathize. Instead of promising needed faith, He seems to dismiss their concern. "If you have faith as small as a mustard seed, you can say to this mulberry tree, 'Be uprooted and planted in the sea,' and it will obey you" (v. 6). Now, the important thing to note here is that Jesus was not speaking to Pharisees, who had no faith. He was speaking to the Twelve, who *did* believe in Him, and who *did have faith!*

Jesus' next words explain His reaction. Jesus asked them about a servant—literally, a bond slave. Doesn't his master have him work and do the tasks assigned? Don't both master and slave expect the servant to put his master's needs before his own? (v. 8) And, when the servant has done what he has been commanded, does he deserve any special commendation? Obviously not. *A servant's role is to obey his master: obedience is nothing out of the ordinary for a slave.*

And so Jesus applied the analogy. "So you also, when you have done everything you were told to do, should say, 'We are unworthy servants; we have only done our duty' " (v. 10).

What did Jesus mean? Simply this. Jesus had given His disciples a *command.* When a person sins, he is to be rebuked and forgiven. This is no optional activity, just for persons with exceptional faith! This is the way every disciple is to live with others—this is a matter of obedience to the Lord the disciple has determined to follow! In essence, Jesus said, "Faith is fine for moving mulberry trees, but faith has nothing to do with this!" When it comes to living by Jesus' commands, the issue is not one of faith but of obedience!

How this strikes at our excuses! We're so prone to complain, "Oh, if only I were a better Christian," or, "If I only had more, then, *then* I would do this, or that. Then I'd reach out to love, or pray for my enemy." To such thinking, Jesus has once and for all cried, STOP! You don't need extra faith to obey! What you need to do is to *remember that Jesus is Lord, and we who are Jesus' servants are called to do as He commands!*

This incident revealed the disciple's confusion about the function of faith in the life of a follower of Jesus. It is a confusion that many believers share today. While this incident does not give direct teaching about the nature of faith, Jesus does settle one thing. We can never draw back from doing God's revealed will because we feel we have inadequate faith. Or for *any* other reason. As servants of Jesus Christ, we are to obey when He speaks.

But then Luke showed how Jesus moved on to illustrate and to teach about the role of faith in the disciples' lives.

♥ ***Link to Life: Youth / Adult***
Launch class by putting the following phrase on the board, and go around the circle asking each person to complete it: "I wish I could have more faith so. . . ." You might want to record group members' answers on the chalkboard.

Then give a minilecture on Luke 17:1-10, drawing from the commentary and illustrations above.

You can then go back and look at the completed sentences and discuss which are really matters of obedience rather than faith. Or you can move on immediately, explaining that in these Luke chapters you will explore the real function of faith in the disciple's life.

The Functions of Faith: Luke 17:11–18:17

Faith stimulates obedience (Luke 17:11-19). Jesus heard 10 lepers calling to Him from a hill some distance from the road. They stood away, as society decreed they must. Still, they cried out for mercy (v. 13). In response Jesus told them to "go, show yourselves to the priests." The implication was clear to the lepers. A person who had been healed of an infectious skin disease was told in the Law to show himself to a priest so that he might be certified well. He was then to offer the prescribed offering to God (Lev. 13:2). They hurried away to do just this, and Luke says that *"as they* went, they were cleansed" (Luke 17:14). Because they trusted Jesus, they had not waited for the overt evidence of the disease to disappear. They went, confident that their need had been met, and that healing was theirs.

Faith is like this. It impels us to obey before we see the full evidence of God's work within us. Do you feel inadequate to rebuke, or even to forgive? Then remember who it is that spoke to you. Remember Jesus' power and His love. Let that confidence encourage you to act, and *as you obey* His victory will come.

Only 1 of the 10, when he saw that his healing was a reality, paused. He turned back, praising God in loud shouts, and thanked Jesus. Only 1 found time to return. And he was a foreigner (v. 16).

Do we take time to thank Jesus for our salvation, and our new life? Do we praise God that we have been healed within?

No, our salvation does not depend on gratitude. Jesus said to the leper as He sent him on his way again, "Your faith has made you well" (v. 19). Our salvation does not depend on what we do *after* Christ has spoken forgiveness to us. But how appropriate it is to come back joyfully to Him, with thanks and praise, to offer our whole selves as His willing disciples (cf. Rom. 12:1-2).

♥ ***Link to Life: Children***

We want to help boys and girls be thankful, and be thankful every day. One of the best ways is to teach them a "thank You, God" chorus or song. Nearly every book of choruses has one or more.

Teach the chorus and try to associate it with the children's happy feelings. Ask: "When do you feel happiest at home?" "When do you feel happiest at school?" "What do friends do that makes you feel happy?" Etc. When the children have suggested a number of things, let each suggest one happy time he or she wants to sing the thank-You song for.

As you repeat this activity you will associate their happy times with the "thank-You" song, and make it more likely that when something happens during the day that makes your boys and girls happy, they will remember to thank God.

Faith provides certainty (Luke 17:20-37). We live in a world where things are not always as they seem—where, in fact, reality is often hidden by illusion. It is faith that frees us to see through appearances, and know things as they really are.

The Pharisees were men without faith. They insisted on testing reality by sight and senses. What they could see and feel and understand—only that—would they take as real. So they plagued Jesus: "When will the kingdom of God come?" (see v. 20)

They were thinking, of course, of the promised messianic glory, the outward pomp and show. The Lord knew this all too well. "The kingdom of God is not coming with signs to be observed," Jesus responded (v. 20, NASB). Instead, "The kingdom of God is in your midst." Other versions offer various translations. The kingdom of God is "among" you. The old *King James* even says "within" you.

What Jesus meant, of course, was that God's kingdom was *already present in the person of the King!* The kingdom was *there,* then!

The Pharisees just couldn't see it. All they saw was a Carpenter from Galilee; a dusty fanatic who had attacked them and their position. All they saw was a hated enemy whose miracles of healing roused their enmity and fear, instead of their wonder and compassion. *The King was there!* But there were no outward signs of glory then. Only faith's eye could recognize Him, and believe.

Sadly, Jesus turned to His disciples. He

spoke of a coming time of trouble, when they too would long to see Christ's visible coming (v. 22). But instead, they would see Jesus suffer, and be irrevocably rejected by their generation. No, there would be no outward signs of His return, even later. Life would go on as it had in Noah's day (v. 26). People would be wrapped up in their own affairs; eating, drinking, marrying, going about the business of living in this world. Men would be unaware that, just beyond the curtain of heaven, Jesus stands poised. He stands, waiting for the day when He is to be revealed to all as King; the day when He steps into history, to judge.

If only the people before the Flood had had faith to see in Noah's warning the reality; to envision the coming waters of destruction. If only the people of Sodom had had faith to heed Lot's warning before fire rained down. And, if only *we* could understand that everything we take as solid reality today is destined to be destroyed when Jesus comes.

It is this, the reality of God and of His purposes, that faith's eye sees, and that unbelief is blind to. Faith provides certainty, for it looks beyond the visible to acknowledge the unseen.

How does faith help us, then? Seeing reality, the man or woman of faith acts. We flee the city of destruction, leaving all behind us (v. 31).

As in every apocalyptic passage, there is in verses 22-37 a concrete description of a real day to come. But of chief importance for us now is not to grasp each detail and try to fit it into the overall prophetic picture. What we need to do is to sense the impact of the whole. We realize that faith, the confidence that God's Word is *true,* enables us to escape entrapment by the appearance of things now. It is the certainty of faith that enables us to commit ourselves to God's values, and it is life by His standards that gives even our present life its meaning and its joy.

Faith motivates perseverance (Luke 18:1-8). Jesus often taught by contrast. He exposed the attitude of others, and against that background His own love and compassion stood out. It could hardly have been otherwise. He is who He is; they were who they were. The vast chasm between the character of human beings and that of God could hardly have remained hidden.

But now Jesus used contrast in a parable about prayer. He told of a judge, cold and unconcerned about God's opinion and uninterested in others' needs (v. 2). A widow appealed to him to right a wrong. The judge had the power and the responsibility, but he would not act.

She kept coming. Everywhere he turned, she seemed to be there. Finally, in exasperation, the judge decided to settle the widow's case. He still didn't *care.* It was only because she *bothered* him that he finally acted.

Sometimes we pray, and when no quick answer comes we may get the impression that God isn't listening. Perhaps we've prayed for a long time about something important to us with no apparent response. How easy it is then to wonder. Has God heard? Doesn't He care? Why doesn't He act? Discouraged, we may simply stop praying, feeling that He doesn't hear or care. Or we may frantically wonder what we've done to prevent an answer: has sin cut us off from God?

Jesus' illustration forces our attention in prayer away from *us,* to *God.* What is God like, really? Is He like the unjust judge? No, God is a Father, who loves us. Like the judge, God has the power and responsibility of righting wrongs, but unlike him God would never delay for lack of concern.

When faith shows us the person of God, we find quietness and confidence in prayer. We cry to God. He hears. And He *is* acting. We may not see just now what He is doing and what He will do, but we can trust the Lord.

Faith, then, is a central element in prayer. Faith moves us to persevere, not desperately, but with confidence. For faith lets us look beyond our circumstances and fixes our eyes on the Father who cares.

Faith frees us to kneel (Luke 18:9-17). Jesus' next parable speaks of the self-righteous, the person who prays with misplaced confidence. The Pharisee (vv. 11-12) did pray. He came to God. But he only saw himself. His vision was cluttered with the outward show, with the things he did and did not do. Self-satisfied and self-righteous, he saw neither God nor his own heart clearly.

There was also a tax collector there, too ashamed to even raise his eyes to heaven. Humbling himself before God, this man found forgiveness (vv. 13-14). And Jesus said, "Everyone who exalts himself will be humbled, and he who humbles himself will be exalted" (v. 14).

The man who cannot believe that God loves and forgives will always turn to self-righteousness or to despair. Only faith, a faith that lets us see God, frees us to discover our real selves.

Have we been hiding secret sin, even from ourselves? Then let faith's vision of God's love free us, to fall on our knees.

The next incident provides a climax. Jesus said, "Let the little children come" (vv. 15-17). Like children we too must receive God's kingdom. We must each take our place before God and, looking up, see a Father's face of love. And then, in a timeless portrait of what it means to trust, we may reach out, to take the Father's offered hand.

♥ ***Link to Life: Youth / Adult***
List on a chalkboard the "functions of faith" identified in Luke 17:11–18:17. Work in pairs or teams on each function, first discovering how it works in the passage, and then listing ways that each function or principle might apply to Christian experience today.

Faith's Object: Luke 18:18–19:10

Faith is a fine thing. But "faith" is not just a subjective phenomenon: it is not something simply inside us, whose reality is measured by how "strongly" we believe. Faith must have an object. And faith is only as solid as that object; only as valid as the thing we put our confidence in.

The rich young ruler (Luke 18:18-34). A wealthy ruler in Israel had listened to Jesus. Convinced that here was a good Man, the ruler posed a question: "What must I do to inherit eternal life?" (v. 18) Jesus probed to reveal the source of the blindness of this ruler, who saw Jesus as good but would not see Him as God, and who wanted to *do* in order to *inherit*.

Jesus listed the commandments that govern relationships between men (v. 20), and heard the ruler claim to have "carefully observed" them from youth. Then, with a single stroke, Jesus revealed the block that kept this man from faith. "Sell all that you possess . . . and come follow Me" (v. 22, NASB).

This was no condemnation of riches, nor was it a general command to all disciples. It was a skilled surgeon's deft stroke revealing a cancer. God spoke to the man: "Sell all; follow Me." And the man went away!

He went away sad, for he was rich.
He chose his wealth over his God!

Here we find echoes of the first and great commandment in the Law: "Love the Lord your God with all your heart" (10:27). Love of wealth had crowded out love for God as the central value in this man's life. And Jesus' command had revealed the flaw.

As the man went sadly away, Jesus remarked to His disciples that it is hard for a man with riches to enter the kingdom (18:24). Why? Because such men tend to misplace their hearts—and their faith.

With God set aside in one's life, a person seeks something else to have confidence in—good works, morality, respectability, even adherence to orthodoxy. Yet so many of our lives are empty today of Jesus' new life because we fail to admit that God is not *first* with us. That our ground of confidence has drifted, and shifted to become something other than Him.

The disciples were amazed (v. 26). They looked on wealth as a sign of God's blessing and approval. Who then could be saved? Only those who look to God for what they themselves can never do. Salvation, impossible with men, is like all things, possible for God (v. 27).

We must fix our faith in God.
He alone can do the impossible.

The disciples didn't understand. Still intrigued by the notion that the rich have difficulties, Peter said excitedly, "We have left all to follow You." Jesus answered them sympathetically. There would be far more in this world than they would otherwise have—and in the world to come, eternal life.

Jesus went on to speak of the great cost to Him of what we so freely receive (vv. 31-34). For God to do the "impossible," and give us new life, Jesus had to die. But "the third day, He will rise again" (v. 33, NASB).

Faith's power (Luke 18:35–19:10). What can faith do? Faith rested in Jesus, and anchored in God's love? The blind beggar whom Jesus passed cried out and was given sight. How can we doubt that faith in this same Jesus can give us sight, to see and grasp reality? (18:35-43)

What can faith do? Faith placed in Jesus and anchored in God's love? Zaccheus was a chief tax collector, who rushed to see Jesus out of curiosity. Jesus pointed to him, and told him, "Come down. . . . I must stay at your house today" (19:5). As the Saviour sat at Zaccheus' home, this tax collector found faith in Jesus. And he changed. Zaccheus showed the reality of the change in his life by repaying fourfold those he had defrauded, and giving half of all he possessed to the poor (vv. 1-8).

What a contrast!

The moral, rich ruler sadly turned away.

The scorned sinner volunteered to give away what had once been the center of his life. And Jesus said, "Today salvation has come to this house." Jesus had found another lost man, and he was saved.

What can faith do?

Faith in Jesus, a full-hearted confidence that frees from every chain and motivates obedience, can transform our lives.

♥ ***Link to Life: Youth / Adult***

Ask your group members to scan Luke 18:18–19:10 and identify the major individuals *described there. Let each person select one of these individuals. With others who made the same selection, discuss: "What is the object of this person's faith? How does it affect his life and choices?"*

Share discoveries with the whole group, and together discuss: "How has the fact that the object of my faith is Jesus affected my life choices?"

The Cost of Decision: Luke 19:1-40

It's something we need to consider. Salvation is free. But discipleship is costly. Zaccheus (vv. 1-10) not only illustrated the power of faith in Jesus to bring new life, but also introduced the cost of discipleship. What did the disciple decision cost Zaccheus? *Everything!* His life had been built on money. His goals, his purposes, his very identity as a person were built on the importance to him of wealth and material success. But suddenly Jesus came and brought life. And Zaccheus responded; he *chose.* He gave away half of all that he had to the poor, and repaid four times over any he had defrauded. The core of his personality, the values that had given him direction in life, had suddenly shifted. Shockingly, *people* became more important than dollars. *Honesty* became more important than gain. Zaccheus had become a different, new man!

This is what discipleship will cost you and me.

What are your values? What is your life built on? What is your identity? "Successful businessman?" "Social leader?" "Popular personality?" To the extent that what is important to you is not important to God, to just that extent discipleship will cost you. You will give up what is important to *you* in exchange for what is important to *Him.*

This doesn't mean, by the way, that you will necessarily stop being successful, or pretty, or popular. All it means is that these things will stop being so important. *You* will be different.

Discipleship does cost. This section of Luke raises the question of *how much.* What an important topic to explore with our class or group members as we conclude this exploration of the meaning of our faith.

Zaccheus (Luke 19:1-10). For this man, decision meant rejection of the old values on which his life had been based, and a commitment to the values of Jesus.

Never make the mistake of thinking that we are disciples simply because we agree with what the Bible says. Or go to church. A disciple is a person who has stepped beyond mere agreement to definite action. He has committed himself to *do.*

Actually, our actions always express our true values. Do we *say* that we have a heart for missions? Then how do we spend our money? Our actions express the values to which we are committed. We can lie even to ourselves about what we believe our values to be. But what is truly important to us will always show up in our behavior.

Being a disciple means we choose that which is important to Christ to become important to us too.

The Parable of the Tenants (the 10 minas) (Luke 19:11-28). Immediately after the Zaccheus incident, "as the crowd still listened attentively" (v. 11, PH), Jesus told a parable. The story involves three classes of people: working servants, nonworking servants, and enemies.

**Working servants.* One group singled out in the story might be called the working servants. They identified themselves as the master's servants, and accepted the responsibility. He gave each a gift, a certain amount of money, and instructed them to *use* this gift until the master returned.

The cost to these servants was simply

obedience: they went out and went to work. Yes, discipleship is costly. We are to use our gifts and talents until Jesus comes.

When the master returned, the working servants discovered that this cost was insignificant. The faithfulness of each was commended, and each was given opportunities beyond his dreams. Each received far more than he had ever been able to gain for his master.

**Nonworking servant.* This person is also identified as a servant of the master. The *relationship* is not in doubt. But this person failed to act as a servant should. He decided not to use the gift he'd been given; not to obey the master's command to work. Being a servant cost him nothing while the master was away, except perhaps the uneasiness of knowing he had disobeyed. But when the master returned, his choice not to obey cost him his reward.

In the end it costs us much more to choose not to live as disciples than any present cost might appear to be.

**Enemies.* Jesus mentioned some in the parable who have no relationship with the master. They have refused to be identified as servants; they are enemies. And at what a cost to them! When the master returns, they are assigned to destruction and to death (v. 27).

What then is the cost of deciding to be Jesus' disciples? Christ's parable points up the real issue. What will it cost us *not* to decide for discipleship? Only when Jesus returns, and reality is fully revealed, will we know how tragic a price those of us who call Christ Lord, and *do not the things He commands,* will have paid.

Glory ahead (Luke 19:29-40). The final scene shows Jesus entering Jerusalem, riding on a young donkey, fulfilling the promise of prophecy (Zech. 9:9). And the Bible tells us the whole crowd of His disciples shouted joyful praises to God for what they had seen *Him* do.

Certainly this passage has great theological significance. Here, in Jesus Christ, God's promise of Messiah's entrance into Jerusalem came true. But look for a moment at the disciples. See them shouting for joy. See them, thrilled by all they had seen *Him* do.

And with that vision put forever out of your mind the dismal image of discipleship as a drab and dreary existence, or as mere endurance in the desperate hope of something better later on. Realize that discipleship leads to joy. For as we live close to Jesus, He will act in our lives, and we will know the joy that comes from all that we see *Him* do.

Costly?

Not really. Discipleship is gain!

TEACHING GUIDE

Prepare

Meditate for a time on the life of Zaccheus. What do you suppose he became 10 years after his conversion? How will you be different 10 years from now?

Explore

1. List on the chalkboard the following sentence to complete: "I wish I could have more faith so. . . ."
2. After hearing completions and listing them on the chalkboard, give a minilecture on Luke 17:1-10, and follow the teaching idea developed in "link-to-life," pages 689-690.

Expand

1. Focus on the role of faith in the Christian life. List its functions as these are developed in the commentary, and let group members form teams to explore each aspect of how faith in Christ does affect our daily lives. See "link-to-life," page 692.
2. Or focus on the fact that faith is only as valid as its object. Use the idea in "link-to-life," page 693, to study Luke 18:18–19:10.

Apply

What is the cost of discipleship? Give a brief devotional based on Luke 19:11-28. Conclude by asking each to privately determine which class of person in the story he falls in—working servant, nonworking servant, enemy. How important to choose to become a working servant of Jesus: a disciple whose obedience wins a far greater weight of reward.

STUDY GUIDE 107

Luke 19:41–24:53

THE PRICE

Overview
Luke has marshaled his evidence and argued his case. He has demonstrated the right of the Man Jesus to our allegiance as Son of God. And he has carefully shown how those who choose to believe must make another choice as well: the choice of commitment to be disciples. Luke has shown us how to be disciples, and the many benefits of discipleship.

Finally, Luke is about to look at price. No, not the cost of discipleship, but at two other terrible costs. First there is the cost of rejecting Jesus. Luke wants us to understand the nature, motive, and the futility of a rejection which will cost human beings everything (Luke 19:42–21:4).

Second, there is the cost *to* Jesus of the new life He came to bring you and me. In the final chapters of his Gospel Luke told the story of the Cross. What Luke emphasized is the fact that Jesus remained in full control as event followed event, leading directly to His death. We need to grasp the fact that while rejecting Jesus will cost *us* everything, our salvation cost *Jesus* everything (Luke 22–23).

But the story does not end with the price. It ends, in Luke's report of the third day, with the prize! (Luke 24) Resurrection. Resurrection for Jesus. And resurrection for you and me!

■ See the verse-by-verse commentary in the *Bible Knowledge Commentary*, pages 253-264, for a detailed exposition of the NIV text.

Commentary
Why do people reject Jesus? Why do believers hold back, and refuse to commit themselves to Him as Lord? As we probe these next chapters of Luke, we begin to better understand the tragedy.

Whatever the motive an individual may have, the decision to reject Jesus is a terrible tragedy. Jesus wept over Jerusalem and the destruction that would inevitably come to the city (Luke 19:41-47). But those tears were no sign of weakness. Immediately Jesus entered the temple, and there expelled again those who defiled God's house. Jesus cared, and pitied the sinner. But Jesus, the Judge of all the earth, is also committed to do right.

The cost of rejection is judgment, and destruction is sure.

Rejection: Luke 19:41–20:44
The nature of rejection (Luke 19:47–20:8). In the temple, day after day, Jesus confronted the chief priests, the scribes (experts in the Law), and the other rulers of His nation (19:47). These were men who claimed divine authority to govern and to rule. So they challenged Jesus' authority. "By what right do *You* act?" (See 20:1-2.)

Jesus responded with a question about John the Baptist. Was he from God, or was his ministry merely human? Those who claimed such authority were silenced. They feared the people, and finally said, "We don't know" (v. 7).

What a picture! Men who pretended to speak with divine authority, forced by fear of the people they led to deny their own claim. With grand contempt, Jesus turned from them. "Then I *will not* answer your question" (see v. 8).

What had happened here? The authority of Jesus (who had clearly demonstrated His power through miracles and had openly claimed to be the Son of God) *was being challenged*. It is this very thing, the questioning of God's authority and the attempt to set up our own authorities (each of which is ultimately forced to make the chief priest's disclaimer) that is at the root of rejection.

When we own Christ as Lord, when we willingly subject ourselves to His will, we have found the only possible antidote to rejection. We can admit no other authority than God, and must respond to rather than question His Word.

Rejection's motive (Luke 20:9-18). But why should people try to set up their own authorities rather than submit to God? The Parable of the Tenant Farmers explains. They killed the heir to the vineyard, thinking, "Then it will be ours." The motive for rejecting Christ is the desire to play, and be our own, God.

Lucifer became Satan when he rejected the authority of God and determined to raise his own throne above the throne of God (Isa. 14:13). Sin in us constantly throbs out the same message: I, not God, must control.

Yet how empty such usurped authority is. We may claim it by rejecting God's authority over us, but when we try to reach any of our life goals, we will be forced to admit, just as the chief priests were, "I can't." How empty it is to insist on our own way, and then discover that apart from Jesus Christ's enablement we can do nothing!

And how dangerous it is to challenge God's authority. Portraying Himself as the Cornerstone, Jesus warned, "Everyone who falls on that stone will be broken to pieces; but on whomever it falls, it will scatter him like dust" (Luke 20:18, NASB).

Humanity may rush to challenge God. But such men will be broken or utterly crushed. Whatever they may *claim* in their rebellion, Jesus is still Lord and God.

The futility of rejection (Luke 20:19-44). It's fully human to believe that somehow we are still able to make it on our own, that we really are strong enough even to challenge God's authority.

Men from two groups that opposed Jesus came to challenge Him. Each relied on his group's strengths. And in each case, the strength proved a weakness.

The chief priests and scribes (vv. 19-26) prided themselves on their ability to adapt to changing political and social conditions. They had survived various foreign occupations; now they prospered under Roman occupation as well. Their watchword was compromise. These men had noted Christ's unwillingness to compromise. And so they felt that their strength (their "flexibility") might be used to trap this Man of principle.

Now, the people of Judea were totally antagonistic to Roman rule, and particularly resented the taxes they paid to these Gentile oppressors. If Jesus spoke against taxes, the leaders could report Him to the government and be sure of quick action. If Jesus spoke for taxes, He would surely lose influence with the people. So when these men raised the question of paying taxes they were sure they could not lose!

It did not go as they expected. Jesus asked for a coin (He didn't even have one in His own purse!). He looked at it, asked whose features were stamped on the coin, and told them bluntly, "Then give to Caesar what is Caesar's, and to God what is God's."

Jesus had not compromised.

Instead He had shown His questioners that their supposed strength was really their weakness. In *their* willingness to be "flexible" they had surrendered what was rightfully God's—their total dedication—in exchange for Caesar's gift of their position, and for monetary gain.

The Sadducees tried next. These "liberals" prided themselves on their freedom from dead literalism. So they challenged Jesus, who had shown such respect for the Scriptures, to show up His "unenlightened" position. They asked Him about resurrection—something they themselves did not believe in.

Jesus responded, arguing from the tense of verb (God *is* rather than God *was* the God of Abraham, Isaac, and Jacob) that these men are alive, and not dead.

Then, when Jesus asked *them* a question in return (vv. 41-44), these men hurried away. Jesus could answer His challengers, but they could not answer Him.

How we need to realize that, whatever the strength we rely on spiritually, it will be *our* weakness too. Are we intelligent? Do we rely on our intelligence to guide us through life, rather than seeking God's guidance and direction? This is rejection of God—and our strength when exalted above God will surely be our downfall.

Are we naturally warm and loving? Do we rely on our capacity to love, rather than on asking God to shed His love through our lives? Then we can be sure that our natural emotional responsiveness to people will betray us. We will love unwisely, sentimentally, and make choices that will harm both us and others.

You see, we human beings are not really

strong in anything! Only as we submit totally to God's authority; only as we surrender as disciples to His control, can we become the new people we should be.

Rejection, then, is at heart questioning God's authority, motivated by a desire to have what should be His—control of our own lives.

And this rejection, this claim of our right to control, is utterly futile. It is futile, for apart from Christ even our strengths become weaknesses, and life proves over and over again that apart from Him we can do nothing.

Now, Jesus Christ must have control over our lives. We must give Him control or, in that area in which we demand the right to run our own lives, we will not be disciples.

And we will not be transformed.

Results of Unsurrendered Will: Luke 20:45–21:5

If we do not surrender to God's authority, what will become of us? We will become like the scribes that Jesus now described. We will walk around, pretending to be religious and dedicated, while all the time we are simply trying to win the approval of others (20:46-47).

How much better to be like the poor widow Jesus then described, and honored above the wealthy who were throwing thousands of dollars into the temple treasury. She was honored for the few cents she contributed, because what she gave was her *all.*

This is really what God wants from us. Whatever we have. Whatever we are. Surrendered to Him, it will be enough.

♥ ***Link to Life: Youth / Adult***

Read aloud Luke 20:9-15. Ask each group member to jot down a phrase or sentence that explains why Christ was rejected by the leaders of His people. Read the parable several times if need be.

When the members have seen that Jesus was rejected because people wanted to be *or* play *God rather than surrender control, give a minilecture summing up the major teachings of Luke 19:41–21:4.*

NOTE: If you wish to consider the "signs of the end of the age" section (Luke 21:5-38), see the discussion and teaching ideas on Matthew 24–25 and Mark 13.

The Price Jesus Paid: Luke 22:1–23:56

Several themes are developed in these two chapters. There is the theme of suffering: of Jesus' agony expecting, and then experiencing the cross. And there is the theme of control. The Man dragged before the courts has the situation fully in His own hands! It is those around Jesus who prove to be weak, mere leaves swept by winds of circumstance. And, we see the theme of finality: "It is finished." Jesus' work is done. Salvation is won.

Judas (Luke 22:1-6). The desperate hatred of the Jewish rulers in these last moments of Jesus' life takes form in a plan to kill Him, put into Judas' mind by Satan. The experience of being close to Jesus had not changed Judas' heart. He had held back—now he made his decision to betray. Watch out when we hold back. "Close" doesn't count. The longer a person puts off the decision for Christ, the more likely the choice will be no.

The Last Supper preparations (Luke 22:7-18). As Judas negotiated Jesus' betrayal, Christ made preparation for the Last Supper, the traditional Passover feast. Jerusalem was packed with visitors, yet no room had been reserved. So Jesus sent two disciples to watch for a man carrying a water jug (normally a woman's work). They followed him home, and asked for room there.

Jesus was about to die. But even the smallest details show that He was still in complete control of every circumstance. And at the dinner, He spoke of His suffering.

The Last Supper (Luke 22:19-22). At the meal Jesus spoke of the purpose of His suffering. "My body *given for you."* "My blood . . . *poured out for you"* (vv. 19-20, italics added).

Jesus' destiny had been determined. He was committed to follow that destiny to the very end. And He made this choice "for you."

♥ ***Link to Life: Children***

Use a series of illustrations to help your boys and girls sense two aspects of sin: error, and rebellion.

Ask which is worse: to drop three cups while carrying them to the kitchen to be washed, or to get mad and throw a cup and break it?

To stumble and bump into a brother or sister and hurt them, or to hit them on purpose and hurt them?

To be late coming home because you don't know what time it is, or to be late on purpose after your mom has called you to come to supper?

Let the children talk about the situations. Then point out that Jesus died to take the punishment for our sin, even when we are most to blame. How much Jesus must love us!

Who is the greatest? (Luke 22:23-30) Jesus' disciples were insensitive. They did not understand what Christ was saying, nor were they aware of His sorrow. Instead they fell to arguing about who would be greatest in the glory days to come.

Jesus remembered how these men had stood by Him through His years on earth. "Yes," He assured them, "you will sit on thrones and rule" (see vv. 29-30). But *now* they were to be servants, as Jesus had been a servant.

Peter's denial predicted (Luke 22:31-34). Then Jesus spoke to Simon. If he only knew how Satan had desired to have him. But Jesus had prayed. *The Lord is still in control.*

Peter was so sure of himself; so proud and confident in his commitment. "Why, Lord, I'll never leave You." Peter was sure nothing could touch his loyalty. He felt self-sufficient and able. But soon he would deny the Lord. Only Jesus was truly confident with a cause.

Prayer (Luke 22:35-46). Jesus continued to warn His followers about the change to expect when He was gone (vv. 35-36). Then He led them out of Jerusalem to a garden, where He prayed. Jesus was in utter agony at the prospect of that next day. It wasn't the physical pain, but the fact that the Son of God would, as He bore the curse of sin, be cut off from the Father. *But He never lost control!* "Your will be done," was Jesus' decision.

And, after prayer, Christ moved steadfastly, ready to meet His destiny—and doom.

Arrest (Luke 22:47-53). Judas arrived with an armed mob and stepped forward to identify the Master with a kiss. Suddenly the disciples recognized the danger: Peter drew a sword and slashed at a servant of the high priest, severing his ear.

Jesus stopped him. With a touch, Christ restored the ear, and then submitted to these picked representatives of satanic power. *Jesus was not forced.* He chose to submit. He was in control.

Peter's denial (Luke 22:54-66). Now the scene momentarily shifted to Peter, who in naive confidence had proclaimed his readiness to follow Jesus even to death. Peter *had* followed. When the others ran, Peter even trailed behind the Lord, and slipped into the courtyard of a house where Jesus was being interrogated.

But Peter's bravery could only carry him so far. Accused of being one of Jesus' people, Peter denied it. Three times. And then as the cock crowed, Jesus, at that moment passing through the courtyard, turned a steady gaze into Peter's face.

With a sickening jolt, Peter realized what he had done. And he went outside, and wept bitterly.

How sickening for us when we realize our inadequacy. How desperately we need to look always to Jesus—for Jesus is always in control.

Trial before chief priests (Luke 22:66-71). Jesus now stood before the rulers of Israel after a night of brutal interrogation. "Tell us," they demanded, "are You the Christ?" Jesus answered, "You are right in saying I am" (v. 70).

Having heard the claim from His own lips, and disbelieving, for them the case was closed. Jesus had to die.

Trials before Pilate and Herod (Luke 23:1-12). Because the Jews, under Roman occupation, had no authority to execute, the leaders took Jesus to the Roman governor.

Pilate, unhappy about the request because he recognized the Jews' motives and found nothing criminal in Jesus' behavior, sent the Lord to Herod, who then ruled an area which included Galilee. How weak Pilate, this man with the power of life and death, was. He lacked the courage to act on his own convictions. He was a prisoner of circumstances; the ruler was ruled. Only Jesus stood tall.

Before Pilate (Luke 23:13-25). Herod's return of Jesus to Pilate is even more revealing. The Roman ruler was actually governed by the threats of his subjects! Against his own sense of justice, Pilate bowed to the mob's cry of "Crucify Him!" Pilate ordered the death of a Man he knew was innocent.

How clearly we see it here. You and I, whoever we are, are not strangers to weakness. We are not stronger than Peter or

Pilate. Jesus *had* to die for us. He alone had strength, and strength to spare. Jesus alone was and is in control.

Carrying the cross (Luke 23:26-31). On the way to His crucifixion, staggering under the weight and pain, Jesus was both jeered at and wept for. He turned to the women who cried. "Do not weep for Me; weep for yourselves and for your children" (v. 28).

The city of Jerusalem, which rejected and murdered her Lord, would soon be razed. Within decades, Titus and a Roman army would totally destroy the Holy City, plundering and killing the citizens that disease and starvation would leave alive.

"Weep not for Me."

The burdened Saviour's physical strength seemed to fail, but He remained in control.

Crucifixion (Luke 23:32-43). They came to the hill. The spikes were driven through hands and feet. The pole on which Jesus hung swung skyward, and fell with a sickening, flesh-tearing jolt into its hole. Unable to breathe when His weight hung on His arms, Jesus put His weight on the nail piercing His feet, and endured the searing pain, to lift up His body to gasp a breath again.

Crucifixion.

Life, death, each breath now a blaze of agony. *A blaze of agony which even now, Jesus chose!* He could have called angels to free Him.

Yes, Jesus was still in control.

And He chose to die.

Why?

At first the two thieves hanging beside Jesus both ridiculed, but then one turned, asking Christ to remember him when He came into His kingdom. Jesus' answer was clear: "Today you shall be with Me in paradise" (v. 43, NASB). In these two thieves we see our whole world, and the reason for Jesus' sufferings. For those who take the step of faith, and call on Jesus as did the dying thief, seeing in the crucified Jesus the coming King, there is the promise of paradise. Today.

New life forever.

And new life, now.

Death (Luke 23:44-49). All nature now put on mourning, and as darkness flowed over the scene, the great work of redemption was complete. The veil in the temple that had signified separation from God was torn from top to bottom. Jesus gave a great cry, and *He released His spirit!*

Even in death, Jesus remained in full control.

Burial (Luke 23:50-56). They took His lifeless body and laid it in a rich man's tomb. The body was wrapped in linen; the tomb door was sealed. And on the Sabbath all rested.

For the disciples it seemed the end. Jesus, their hope, had died. Though they planned to minister to the body, packing it in funeral spices, their great dream of God invading history seemed forever gone.

All of life now stretched out ahead, in empty years, meaningless years, years of living by habit, long after the sense of purpose and meaning was gone.

The Prize: Luke 24

Jesus' death must have left His followers with a deep sense of despair and an aching awareness of the emptiness of life. If history's record had closed with the cross and tomb, life for us too would be empty. Life would be nothing but a brief experience of sorrows, swallowed up by endless nothingness and night. But the tomb was not the end. The Resurrection that followed blazes for the power of God, and demonstrates the amazing vitality that transforms death to life—the same vitality that can and will transform our death to new life, even now.

Resurrection (Luke 24:1-11). At dawn on what we now call the Lord's Day, the women started toward the tomb with the burial spices. Their mood was broken when they found the stone that sealed the entrance removed, and two angels standing by the slab where the body had been laid.

♥ ***Link to Life: Children***

How long is forever? Let boys and girls make an illustrated book: We Will Live Forever. *Help them think of images, such as "longer than it takes a million million birds to fly" (illustrated by a line of birds flying across the sky); "longer than it takes to hitchhike to the farthest star"; "longer than it would take me to wash a world full of pans"; etc. Illustrate the last page with a cross and empty tomb, and the line, "I will live forever, because Jesus died and rose again for me."*

Frightened, the women fell, hiding their faces from the angels. But the angels asked, "Why do you look for the living One among the dead?" (v. 5)

It was a good question. Jesus had told them often that He would die and rise again. Christ had been as good as His word. He had risen!

Have we realized yet that it is Jesus' resurrection power that God pours into Christ's followers? Let's not lie among the dead, going through the empty motions that they do, trapped by the same frustrations, the same inadequacies. Let's take Jesus at His word today. He has come to give us abundant life. Let's trust Him, rise up, and live!

When the women reported the angels' words to the 11 disciples (vv. 9-11), they were too disheartened to believe. Sometimes past tragedy or failure so colors our view that we can't even believe eyewitness reports of resurrection. But, whatever our past experiences, *Jesus lives.* And because He lives, we too can live.

Road to Emmaus (Luke 24:13-27). That day, the living Jesus met two discouraged disciples traveling home from Jerusalem to Emmaus. He chose to go unrecognized at first, as they talked of the recent events and the death of all these disciples' hopes (vv. 19-21).

Walking along, Jesus began to show them all that the Scriptures had foretold of the necessity of His suffering and His entry into glory (vv. 26-27).

Today, Jesus offers us a present experience of new life. But everything we experience is rooted in a reality and a truth recorded in God's Word. *New life* is no mere feeling or hope. *New life* is a reality, rooted in the historic resurrection of Jesus and the proof that resurrection provides God's ability and willingness to transform you and me.

Recognition (Luke 24:28-35). The two disciples on the Emmaus Road must have been amazed and deeply touched as that third Man explained the Word. Eagerly they urged Him to enter into their home (v. 29). As He sat at table with them, praying over the breaking of the bread, they recognized Him.

At that moment, everything changed.

It's the same for us today.

We may hear others tell of their new lives. We may read of new life in the Bible. We have been reading of it in Luke's Gospel. *But new life begins when we see Jesus and come to know Him.* Our new life is found only in a personal relationship with Jesus Christ, the Son of God, who died for us, and who rose again.

Appearance and Ascension (Luke 24:36-53). The two disciples rushed to Jerusalem to share their joy. Even as they told the unbelieving disciples of their encounter with the risen Lord, He suddenly stood among them.

Jesus showed His hands and feet: death had truly been defeated by life. And then Jesus opened the Scriptures and helped them to understand.

Finally, Jesus promised His disciples power (v. 49). For the disciples themselves, a new life had just begun.

All the New Testament, all history, bears solid witness to the fact that these men and women were marked by a joy and power that turned their world upside down.

Luke can be closed the same way for you and me, with power . . . Jesus' power . . . available now as we accept Christ and choose to live as His disciples, and with praise—praise to God from each of us who knows by personal experience that Jesus truly does transform.

TEACHING GUIDE

Prepare

Read through Luke 22–24 at a sitting, letting Luke help you share the experience of Jesus' suffering—and resurrection.

Explore

1. Ask each group member to share the most important thing he or she has gained from your study of Luke's Gospel.
2. Or read Luke 20:9-15 together. Why do people reject Jesus? As your group members discover the answer, cover in a minilecture the nature, motives for, and results of rejecting Christ revealed in Luke 19–21. See "link-to-life," page 697.

Expand/Apply

Conclude your study with a worship experience. Point out Luke's emphasis, in describing Jesus' sufferings, on the fact that Christ remained in complete control. You may want to read some of the verses that demonstrate this theme.

Then ask your group members to meditate as they hear Luke's description of Christ's last days and His resurrection read aloud.

After the reading, and a few moments of silence, encourage each to pray as he or she wishes, to thank Jesus for the new life He has given us at the cost of His own.

STUDY GUIDE 108

Introduction

JOHN'S GOSPEL

Overview

The Gospel of John is distinctively different from the other three. They tell the story; John interprets through lengthy reports of Jesus' discourses. Only John focuses on distinct theological themes, contrasting throughout his writing such terms as life and death, light and darkness, belief and unbelief, truth and falsehood, love and hate.

While each Gospel presents Jesus as the Son of God, John carefully explains that by this description Jesus was "making Himself equal with God" (John 5:18). A number of times Jesus stated His deity in an unequivocable way (8:58; 9:35-37; 10:36; 14:9; 17:5).

Outline

The Word becomes flesh	1
Testimony about Jesus	1–2
Jesus on the new birth	3
Jesus and the Samaritan woman	4
Jesus' discourse on life	5
Jesus' discourse on the Bread of Life	6
Jesus faces opposition	7
Jesus claims to be God	8
Jesus heals a man born blind	9
Jesus as the Good Shepherd	10
Jesus raises Lazarus	11
Jesus predicts His death	12
Jesus washes His disciples' feet	13
Jesus' Last Supper discourse	14–16
Jesus' High Priestly prayer	17
Jesus' crucifixion	18–19
Jesus' resurrection	20–21

Commentary

The Gospel of John is a family Gospel. While the others were written to tell the story of Jesus, Matthew to the Jews, and Mark and Luke to the Gentiles, John was written for Christ's church. In this Gospel we have the deepest spiritual and theological teachings of our Lord. Some have noted that the Last Supper discourse (John 14–16) is the "seed bed" of the Epistles. The major emphases of the apostles' instructions to the church developed in the later New Testament all have roots in Christ's final instructions to the disciples.

In this introductory survey we'll see just a few of the things which make the Gospel of John so special, and suggest ways that your group members can sample this Gospel in preparation for a more careful, multiple study exploration of its chapters.

John, the Author

The Gospel does not name its author. But there is no real doubt that this book was written by John, the disciple and later apostle of Jesus.

John is named by the early church writers as the author of the book. Irenaeus, who knew Polycarp and others who were John's contemporaries, wrote that "John, the disciple of the Lord who also leaned upon His breast, did himself write a Gospel during his residence at Ephesus in Asia."

John also is the author of three New Testament epistles, whose use of key terms, such as light and darkness, life and death, link those letters to the Gospel that bears John's name.

We know most of John, of course, from the other Gospels. He was from a family that operated a fishing business in Galilee that employed others beside the sons. John's sentence structure and thought patterns show that he was very familiar with rabbinic methods of biblical interpretation. This suggests that he had gone beyond the basic studies expected of all Jewish men. There is nothing incompatible in Judaism with scholarship and carrying on a trade, so the fact that John was a fisherman in no way suggests ignorance or commonness.

It is clear from reading the Gospels that John, with Peter and his own brother

James, was in the inner circle of disciples. These three alone were invited to witness the Transfiguration. These three went on farther into the Garden at Gethsemane, to provide companionship at Jesus' lowest hour.

But the picture of John found in the Gospels is not always complimentary. He and James had a nickname, "Sons of Thunder," which suggests a wicked temper. That temper was displayed one evening when the two were eager to "call down fire from heaven" on a village of Samaritans who were unwilling to provide lodging because Christ's party was going to Jerusalem, the place where the Jews worshiped (Luke 9:51-55).

John and his brother were also ambitious. It was these two who got their mother to approach Jesus to ask Him for the highest positions in His coming kingdom (Matt. 20:20-28). Jockeying for position, and infighting for advancement, isn't something peculiar to modern corporate life!

Yet it is clear that John, an essentially competitive and achievement-oriented person, was deeply affected by his relationship with Jesus. In his old age he became the apostle of love, and this term, love, dominates his letters and infuses his Gospel with a special warmth. When John wrote this Gospel as an old man, possibly as late as A.D. 90, he had become a truly loving and sensitive person, whose own character reflected the most beautiful qualities of his Lord.

♥ ***Link to Life: Youth / Adult***
What kind of person was John? Help your group members to develop a "personality sketch" from one of John's late writings, 3 John (John's third epistle). From the things that concern John in this letter, and the words he uses, have your group brainstorm images of the kind of person John became as he grew in Christ.

Jesus in John's Gospel

John's Gospel emphasizes Christ's deity to a greater extent than the others. John began not with Jesus' birth, but with a statement of Christ's preexistence as God. John also reported a number of occasions on which Jesus declared Himself to be the "I AM" (John 4:26; 8:28, 58; 13:19; 18:5-6, 8).

This phrase is rooted in events reported in Exodus 3:14. Moses had been told by God to return to Egypt and wrestle God's people from the Egyptians, to lead them to freedom and the Promised Land. Moses hesitated, and among the questions he asked was, "Suppose I go to the Israelites and say to them, 'The God of your fathers has sent me to you,' and they ask me, 'What is His name?' " (Ex. 3:13) It was then that God announced His name, telling Moses to say, "I AM has sent you," and going on to tell Moses that "this is My name forever, the name by which I am to be remembered from generation to generation" (v. 15).

In fact, the term I AM (a form of the verb "to be") is the root of the Hebrew personal name for God, Yahweh, which is expressed in our English versions as the capitalized LORD. Thus "I AM" is *the* unique name of the God of the Old Testament as He revealed Himself to Moses, and acted in power to redeem Israel from Egyptian slavery! For Jesus to identify Himself as the I AM was to make an unmistakable claim to *be* Yahweh Himself, the one all Israel worshiped as God.

It is no surprise then that the Jewish leaders responded to this claim, as John reported in John 8:59, by picking up stones in an attempt to kill Jesus for blasphemy.

But there is more in John's Gospel than even this powerful claim to full identity with Israel's God. Jesus used seven symbols, linked with the phrase "I am," to show what He is *for humankind.* Jesus is God. But what does the fact of Jesus' deity mean for you and for me? This is what is expressed in the seven symbolic images that Christ used to describe Himself.

The seven are:

1. I am the Bread of Life	6:35
2. I am the Light of the World	8:12
3. I am the Gate for the sheep	10:7
4. I am the Good Shepherd	10:11,14
5. I am the Resurrection and the Life	11:25
6. I am the Way, the Truth, and the Life	14:6
7. I am the True Vine.	15:1

Each of these images, as noted, not only continues to affirm the full deity of Jesus, but tells us what it means for us that Jesus, the Son of God, chose to become man and live among us. Jesus is our bread, who sustains us daily. Jesus is our light, cutting through the shadows and illusions that darken this sin-cursed world. Jesus is the gate, the one door through whom we can go and find safety. Jesus is the Good Shepherd, who cares so much for the sheep that He was willing to give His life for us. Jesus is the resurrection and life; His vivifying power is so great that He is able to bring life even to our mortal bodies, and one day will raise us to total renewal. Jesus is the Way, the Truth, and the Life; no one can approach the Father except through Him. Jesus is the Vine, and as we remain in fellowship with Jesus His life flows into us as branches, enabling us to bear spiritual fruit.

Only because Jesus truly is God can we derive so much from personal relationship with Him.

♥ ***Link to Life: Youth / Adult***
In a minilecture explain the significance of Jesus' claim to be the "I AM." Then list the seven "I am" symbolic statements on a chalkboard, without explaining the symbolism. Let each of your group members select one *symbol to look into. Form teams of those who select the same symbol. Each team should look at the context of the statement, and from the symbol itself and the context try to define what this "I am" of Jesus means to believers today.*

The Dialogues of Jesus

One of the distinctive features of John's Gospel is its structure. This Gospel alone emphasizes Christ's discourses, while the others emphasize the acts of Jesus.

John's Gospel was written many years after Christ lived. Some believe it was written in the A.D. 90s, some 60 years after Christ spoke the words reported here. Yet we should not be surprised that John reported the words of the Lord so confidently. Undoubtedly John in his teaching had for years told and retold the discourses. We can be confident that his summaries of what were undoubtedly much longer sermons are accurate. Even more important, we can be sure that the Holy Spirit guided John to record just what God intended us to have.

What then are the discourses? Here are key talks that make up the bulk of this powerful Gospel.

1.	On the new birth	3:1-21
2.	On the water of life	4:4-26
3.	On resurrection and life	5:19-47
4.	On the bread of life	6:26-59
5.	On the deity of Jesus	8:12-59
6.	On the shepherd and flock	10:1-21
7.	More on the deity of Jesus	10:22-38
8.	On redemption	12:20-50
9.	On life while Jesus is gone	13:31–14:31
10.	On union with Jesus	15:1–16:33

A number of these discourses display a similar form or pattern. They are launched with a question from a disciple or onlooker. Jesus made a brief, enigmatic reply. And then Jesus went on to give a wide-ranging explanation.

♥ ***Link to Life: Youth / Adult***
Select any one of the discourses listed. First have your group mark the launching question, the initial reply, and the extended discussion. Have each read the discourse and in a single sentence sum up, "What is Jesus teaching here?" Discuss insights.

Chronology

The Gospel of John seems to hold closely to the chronological sequence of events of Christ's life, though some events are not reported. The list on page 705, adapted from Graham Scroggie's *Guide to the Gospels* (Fleming H. Revell), places events in sequence and suggests the traditional dating of each. You may wish to duplicate the list for your group members to have as you study John's Gospel.

Theology in John

John's Gospel is the most theological of the four Gospels. John had a distinctive way of expressing theological concepts. In the Gospel and in his letters, John taught by contrast. He set one concept against its opposite. While this is not done with some theological terms, such as "know," "word," "world," and "glory," most of John's key theological words are explored through contrast.

Among the paired terms that John used often are Life/Death, Light/Darkness, Belief/Unbelief, Truth/Falsehood, and Love/Hate.

If we are to understand John's Gospel we need to have some insight into how he used

Events of Jesus' Life

B.C.	
5	Birth of Jesus.
4	Circumcision and Presentation of Jesus. Coming of the Magi.
	Flight into Egypt. Massacre of the Innocents.
	Death of Herod the Great.
	Return of the Family to Nazareth.
A.D.	
8	Jesus' First Passover.
27	The Baptism and the Temptation of Jesus.
	First Passover of Jesus' Ministry (John 2:13, 23)
	Cleansing of the Temple.
28	John the Baptist Imprisoned.
	A Passover, some think, but more probably Purim (5:1).
	Jesus Begins His Ministry in Galilee.
	The Call of Four Disciples at Capernaum.
	Jesus' First Circuit in Galilee.
	The Choice of Twelve Apostles.
	The Sermon on the Mount.
	The Parables of the Kingdom.
29	Commission of the Twelve.
	Death of John the Baptist.
	Feeding of the Multitude. The Discourse on the Bread of Life.
	Peter's Confession that Jesus Is the Christ.
	The Transfiguration.
	Final Departure from Galilee.
	Jesus at the Feast of Tabernacles (7:2).
	Commission of the Seventy.
	Jesus Attends the Feast of Dedication (10:22).
30	Ministry in Perea.
	Lazarus Raised from the Dead.
	Jesus Passes through Jericho on the Way to Jerusalem.
	Public Entry into Jerusalem.
	Second Cleansing of the Temple.
	Jesus' Conflict with the Authorities.
	The Prophetic Discourses on Olivet.
	The Supper at Bethany.
	Jesus' Last Passover (11:55; 12:1).
	The Upper Room Discourse.
	Gethsemane.
	The Arrest and Trials.
	The Crucifixion.
	The Resurrection.
	The Appearances.
	The Ascension.

these terms, not only in his Gospel but also in the letters, 1, 2, and 3 John.

Each of the key terms are defined briefly here. Again, you may wish to duplicate the definitions chart and distribute it to your group members as an aid they can refer to while studying the Gospel or Epistles of John.

For a thorough discussion of each term as it is used by John, see the author's *Expository Dictionary of Bible Words* (Zondervan).

Definitions in Brief
John's use of:

KNOW — "Know" is a relational term. We come to know God by acknowledging Jesus as God's Son and our Saviour. "Know" also speaks of continuing fellowship with God as we live a life of obedience and love. See John 8:19, 31-47; 10:4, 14-15; 1 John 4:15-16.

WORLD — "World" (*kosmos*) as a theological term portrays human society as a system warped by sin and influenced by Satan. The world is energized by the sin nature. See 1 John 3:1, 13; 5:19.

WORD — John affirmed Jesus as the "Word" which existed with and as God from eternity. Jesus is the One through whom God expressed Himself. As the Word, Jesus is the creative power that brought the universe into existence, and the prophetic power that reveals and controls the future. Through faith we can have fellowship with the eternal Word of God. See John 1:1-14; 1 John 1:1-2.

GLORY — "Glory" speaks of God's splendor as seen in His self-revelation. It is an expression in this world of the beauty, power, and greatness of our God. See John 1:14; 17:4-5.

LIFE — "Life" can refer to biological life, but more important it speaks of the vitalizing power of God. We are given God's life when we believe in Jesus. This divine life-force makes it possible for us to live righteously now despite our mortality, and will find expression in our future bodily resurrection. See John 3:15-36; 5:21-26; 1 John 2–3.

DEATH — "Death" too is more than a biological concept. Death speaks of the spiritual state of human beings as separated from God, and morally warped. The spiritually dead lie under God's condemnation and have no way to win His favor. Only the gift of life through Jesus Christ can counteract the death which holds humankind in a firm grip. See John 5:16-26.

LIGHT — "Light" implies holiness, but its primary emphasis is on illumination. Jesus is *the* Light of the world, showing us the way to God. We are to live as His Word shows us how, and so be "children of the light." See John 1:4-9; 3:19-21; 8:12; 1 John 1:5-7.

DARKNESS — Morally, "darkness" describes sinful acts and a sin-filled lifestyle. Theologically spiritual darkness is the dominant evil power which holds the unsaved in bondage. Sinners choose to embrace the dark; only the light provided by Jesus turns us to a God in whom there is "no darkness at all." See John 3:19; 8:12; 1 John 1:5-7.

BELIEF — John often spoke of a superficial kind of belief in Jesus stimulated in observers by His miracles. But the belief John seeks to evoke through his Gospel is an active, continuing trust in Jesus that brings eternal life. The one who truly believes receives Jesus as Saviour, and expresses this faith in obedience and love for others. See John 3; 5; 8:31-32.

UNBELIEF Unbelief is not "doubt," but rather a failure to respond to Christ with belief. Unbelief thus is a moral, not intellectual concept which implies rejection of God. See John 3:16-21.

TRUTH Over half of the New Testament's uses of "truth" (*aletheia*) are found in John. John's focus is on the link of truth and reality. A thing is true because it is in harmony with reality as God knows reality. We can know (experience) reality only by choosing to keep Jesus' words, which show us life as God intends His children to live it. See John 17:17; 1 John 1:6-8.

FALSEHOOD "Falsehood" is not so much a matter of lying in John as it is a matter of deceit and illusion. All the world's notions of reality are at heart illusory. Only God's Word unveils the truth. Only by adopting and living by God's perspective can a person break away from falsehood and know the truth.

LOVE This is one of the most important concepts in the Bible. Scripture reveals God's love for us, and how we can respond to that love. In both Testaments we are taught to show love for God both by obedience and by loving others. John makes it clear that love is not something that flows naturally from the human heart, but must be awakened by God's initiating act of love in Jesus Christ. See John 3:16; 1 John 4:7-21.

HATE As a theological term "hate" speaks of the deep antagonism of the unsaved world to Jesus and His own. See John 3:20; 15:18-25.

Keeping in mind the way each of these terms is used by John will help you and your group members as you study this rich Gospel.

♥ ***Link to Life: Youth / Adult***
Pass out the word/definition list, so it will be available to your group during your study of John. You may wish to look up, read, and talk about the verses suggested with each term to illustrate John's use of it.

TEACHING GUIDE

Prepare
Read through John's Gospel rapidly at a single sitting. What are your main impressions?

Explore
Give a brief minilecture summarizing some of the distinctives of this Gospel and its special contributions to our understanding of Jesus and our faith. Supplement introductory material here with research in a verse-by-verse commentary, such as Victor's *Bible Knowledge Commentary,* pages 267-270.

Expand
Select one or more of the "link-to-life" activities suggested for a general introduction of some of the major themes in John's Gospel.

Choose from: developing an impression of the writer, the Apostle John (p. 703); exploring Jesus' seven "I am" statements (p. 704 [col. 1]); examination of one of Jesus' discourses (p. 704 [col. 2]); sampling John's use of key theological terms (p. 707).

Apply
Go around the circle, having each say, from initial impressions of John's Gospel, what he or she expects to find that will be particularly helpful to him or her.

STUDY GUIDE 109

John 1:1-18

THE DEITY OF JESUS

Overview

The Gospel of John speaks more clearly than any other of the deity of Christ. There can be no doubt: the Bible *does* teach that Jesus of Nazareth was fully God as well as truly man.

This teaching does not, of course, rest only on what we find in John's Gospel. There are many other passages that affirm Jesus' deity. Among the most powerful are:

Colossians 1:15-20. Jesus who expresses the invisible God was Himself the Creator of all things, and has priority over all.

Hebrews 1:1-13. Jesus is the "exact representation" of God's being, and sustains all things by His own powerful word. He is, as God, above all created beings, including the angels who are so superior to mortal man.

Philippians 2:5-11. Jesus, though "in very nature God" voluntarily surrendered the prerogatives of Deity to become a true human being. Now that He has been resurrected He has been exalted again, and in the future every tongue will confess that Jesus Christ is Lord.

It is this Jesus, God from before the beginning, whom John wants to show us in his Gospel. And from this Gospel John wants to teach us how to respond, from the heart, to Him as Saviour and Lord.

▶ ***Grace.*** "Grace" reveals both God and man. It shows human beings as helpless, trapped in sin. And it shows God willing and able to meet our deepest needs.

Commentary

The last of the apostles laid down his pen. His fingers brushed away one of the tears that still came so easily when he thought about the death and resurrection of his beloved Jesus. Even after all these years, he could still feel the same sorrow and joy he had felt so intently then.

John had been bewildered when Jesus died, and amazed by His resurrection. It had taken John and the others so long to understand, so long to really know who Jesus was . . . no, *is.*

John remembered those days just after the Resurrection when Jesus again walked with and taught His disciples. Taking up his pen again, the apostle bent over his manuscript to add: "Jesus did many other miraculous signs in the presence of His disciples, which are not recorded in this book. But these are written that you might believe that Jesus is the Christ, the Son of God, and that by believing you may have life in His name" (John 20:30-31).

John, the last of the apostles to die, gave us in his Gospel one of four portraits of Jesus written in the decades after Christ's death and resurrection. John's Gospel is unique in a number of ways. It was written long after the others, possibly some 40 years after the end of Jesus' life on earth. Unlike the other Gospels, which were written to present Jesus to different cultural groups, John was written as a universal Gospel. It is to all people of all times, and particularly to the church. John's purpose is to unveil the Man, Jesus, and to reveal Him as God.

Of course, the other Gospels present the deity of Jesus, but the central message and focus of John's Gospel is Jesus' deity. John's many years of ministry had taught him the importance of believers coming to know Jesus as God. John wrote his book for this purpose: "that *you* may believe that Jesus is the Christ, the Son of God" (italics added).

But why is this so important? And why is the present tense so important: that Jesus *is* the Christ. Not *was. Is!*

It's important because when we recognize Jesus as the God who lives *now,* we also discover that we "may have life" *now* through His name.

John was making no retreat from the facts of the Christian faith. John's failure to speak of Christ's birth does not deny the historic events that actually took place in space and time. It does not imply that these are unimportant. It is simply that John's goal was to help you and me see, through the historic Person, the living Christ who is present with us even now. John wanted us to understand not only who Jesus was, but who Jesus *is*. John wanted us to grasp the fact that in our personal relationship with the living Jesus we can experience new life as a present reality.

So, in the Gospel of John, the writer selected and organized historical events in order to unveil the living Jesus of today. As we see His glory, we will find in Him the vital source of a new life of our own.

Why is it so important that Jesus be unveiled? Recently I talked with a girl in her junior year in college, who wondered about her future. Should she continue in her church ministry major? Or take a course in some specialty that will prepare her for a job? How can she look ahead and know what is best for her to do?

Yesterday I spoke with a friend whose wife has asked him to move out. He knows that much of the pain both feel right now has been his fault: they are each struggling with deep hurts and even deeper uncertainties about their futures. Whatever choices they make now will shape the future for their children as well as for themselves.

From your own life, or the lives of members of your class or group, you can add other illustrations. You can point to incident after incident which bring home the fact that we must live in the constant company of uncertainty, and with the possibility of loss. For each of us, the future is hidden behind a veil. We are forced to make our choices blindly, hoping but never sure that what we do will turn out for the best, and hoping as well that the things we fear will never happen.

No wonder it was so important for John to unveil Jesus. We cannot know our personal futures. But we can be free to live with joy when we strip away the veil of history, and see there a Jesus who is the Son of God, and who brings us new life, *now*.

♥ ***Link to Life: Youth / Adult***

Have your group members work in pairs to list "things I can't control." Then combine to write a group list on the chalkboard. Let members add new things as they think of them. And be sure that, along with the weather, terrorism, and other international or universal things, your group members include what happens to them tomorrow, the outcome of their choices, etc.

Discuss: "Which of these areas make you most uncomfortable or anxious?"

Lead into the study of John's Gospel by pointing out that John presented a Jesus who is God—living today, and able to bring us a new life as well as to exercise His own control over those things which are beyond ours.

Eternity Unveiled: John 1:1-5

With the first words of the Gospel of John we see that John's task *is* to unveil. The other Gospels begin with the birth of Jesus or with an account of His human ancestry. Matthew and Luke emphasized that a man, a human being, was actually born in the normal way to a young woman named Mary in the ancient land of Judea at the time Herod the Great was living out his last days. John, on the other hand, tells us immediately the Child born then was the eternal God! His origin was not at His physical conception, but, as Micah said, his "origins are from of old, from ancient times" (Micah 5:2). And Isaiah called Him "Mighty God, Everlasting Father" (Isa. 9:6).

John's way of taking us back to eternity was to identify Jesus as "the Word" who was "in the beginning." Moreover, this Word "was with God, and the Word was God." Finally John said plainly that "the Word became flesh and lived for a while among us" (John 1:14).

The Word. The Bible gives many titles or names to Jesus. When He is called "the Word," we are reminded of His role in the Godhead from the very beginning. Human speech has the capacity to unveil thoughts, feelings, and emotions; to reveal the person behind the words. Jesus is God expressing Himself through Jesus.

When Philip asked Jesus to show the disciples the Father, Christ answered in gentle rebuke. "Anyone who has seen Me has seen the Father" (14:9). Another time Jesus explained to His disciples, "No one knows who the Father is except the Son and those to whom the Son chooses to reveal Him" (Luke 10:22).

This title, "the Word," teaches that Jesus is now, and always has been, the One through whom God expresses Himself. But how did God express Himself in history past, even before the Incarnation? Obviously God was known before Jesus' birth.

In Creation (John 1:3). Paul wrote that "what may be known about God is plain to them, because God has made it plain to them. For since the Creation of the world God's invisible qualities . . . have been clearly seen" (Rom. 1:19-20). The material universe itself speaks of a Maker, loudly shouting His handiwork:

> Day after day they pour forth speech; night after night they display knowledge. There is no speech or language where their voice is not heard. Their voice goes out into all the earth, their words to the ends of the world.
>
> Psalm 19:2-4

This Word of Creation is the word of Jesus before the Incarnation. "Through Him all things were made," John said. "Without Him nothing was made that has been made." From the very beginning Jesus has expressed God to humankind.

In life (John 1:4). But it was not just in the creation of inanimate matter that Jesus communicated God. On the spinning sphere hung in the emptiness of space, the Creator placed living creatures. These living creatures are different from dead matter; they moved, ate, responded to stimuli, and reproduced themselves. The creation of life was a voice testifying to God.

Only One who was a living Being Himself could be the source of other life. Dead matter does not generate life now, nor has it ever.

And then, among all the living things, the Creator planted another kind of life that was made "in Our image, in Our likeness" (Gen. 1:26). Not just life, but *self-conscious* life, came into being. This life that came from Jesus the Creator remains deeply rooted in Him. Our very awareness that we are different from all other living creatures is another wordless testimony to the existence of the God whose likeness we bear. Jesus gave us life itself, and by that life He expressed God to us.

In light (John 1:5). This final term introduces one other way in which God has expressed Himself through the preincarnate work of Jesus. In John's writings the terms *light* and *darkness* are often moral terms. Light represents moral purity, holiness, righteousness, good. In contrast, *darkness* as a moral term represents evil, all those warped and twisted ways in which sin had perverted the good in man, and brought pain to individuals and society. "The light shines in the darkness, but the darkness has not understood [or, extinguished] it."

The moral light is one of the most powerful and pervasive evidences of God's existence. Paul described pagans who have never known God's Old Testament revelation of morality, yet they "show that the requirements of the law are written on their hearts, their consciences also bearing witness, and their thoughts now accusing, now even defending them" (Rom. 2:15). There is a moral awareness planted deep in the personality of every person. Different societies may develop different rules to govern, for instance, sexual behavior. These rules may be glaringly different from the pattern set in Scripture. Still, *in every culture, there is the awareness that sexual behavior is a moral issue,* and that no individual can simply have any other person he or she wants, at any time or in any way.

The deep-seated conviction that there is a moral order to things is present in every human society. But society is in darkness; even though some sense of moral order and rightness exists, people in every society choose to do what they themselves believe is wrong. So conscience struggles, and individuals accuse themselves (or perhaps try to excuse as "adult" behavior they know is wrong).

Moral awareness in a world running madly after darkness is another testimony to us that light comes from the preexistent Word. Light, like creation and life itself, shouts out the presence of God behind the world we see.

Then, finally, the Word took unique expression in space and time. "The Word became flesh and lived for a while among us. We have seen His glory, the glory of the one and only Son, who came from the Father, full of grace and truth" (John 1:14).

♥ ***Link to Life: Children***
Boys and girls, like adults, have difficulty understanding how one *God can exist in*

three Persons, Father, Son, and Holy Spirit. Many analogies have been suggested, none of which can capture the reality of the Trinity. Simply put, this as other things concerning the nature of God, are simply beyond human understanding.

Still, it's helpful for children to use analogies. They are inadequate, but they do at least help. What are some of the better analogies? An egg, while it has shell, white, and yoke, is one egg. A poorer analogy notes that water, a single chemical substance, can be found as liquid, water vapor, and ice. Another poorer analogy notes that one person can be a husband, a father, and an employee.

We will never penetrate the mystery, for nothing in our universe partakes of the triune nature of God. How wonderful that we can trust the Word, which unveils reality even though we cannot yet grasp the reality revealed.

♥ ***Link to Life: Youth / Adult***
What does the Bible say about Jesus, who existed as the Word long before Creation? Take one or two approaches:

(1) Have your group members explore the passages summarized in the overview (Col. 1:15-20; Heb. 1:1-13; and Phil. 2:5-11).

(2) Or the Bible shows that the three Persons of the Trinity (Father, Son, and Holy Spirit) have different roles or tasks. One passage which speaks of this is Ephesians 1:3-14. Work together as a group with this passage, identifying the works of each Person.

Then discuss: "In what ways were the tasks assigned to Jesus an unveiling, or revealing, of the grace of God?"

Grace and Truth: John 1:6-18

A totally new level of communication begins with the Incarnation. We catch a glimpse of this fact in the ministry of John the Baptist. John, the Bible says, was sent "to testify concerning that light."

What a strange expression. John was sent to *identify* the light! Why? What was there about Jesus as the Light that demanded identification? When we examine the Baptist's message in the other Gospels, we see that John focused his preaching on twin ideas: (1) the promised King of Old Testament prophecy was about to appear, and (2) His coming demanded a moral renewal.

John rebuked sin in ruler and common man alike. His tongue lashed the religious. "You brood of vipers!" he cried scornfully. "Produce fruit in keeping with repentance" (Luke 3:7-8).

The Baptist's prescriptions were clear, simple reflections of Old Testament Law. "The man with two tunics should share with him who has none, and the one who has food should do the same," John told the people. "Don't collect . . . more [taxes] than you are required to," John told the tax collectors. "Don't extort money and don't accuse people falsely—be content with your pay," John told the soldiers (vv. 11-14).

The moral light shed in the Old Testament shone through the Baptist's message. His words pointing to the Person about to appear promised a kingdom in which moral light would not be lost in the darkness, but instead, darkness would be exiled by light. "The true Light," the Gospel writer said, "was coming into the world." And John the Baptist's mission was to make it clear to all that that Man *is* the Light.

But still, why? Why must John announce Jesus? Why did a people who already had the light of the written Law need to have light—an expression of true morality and reality—identified for them? The Gospel writer explained it to us with another term: *grace*. When the Word became flesh, we were given new light—a revelation that the divine morality is "grace and truth."

Law. It is important to understand that all revelations of God before Jesus came were true, but incomplete. Creation spoke of God's existence and power, but not of His essential character. Life testified to God's personhood, but told nothing of His deepest emotions or plans. Light, as awareness of morality, reflected God's holiness, but somehow His heart remained hidden. Even the Law of the Old Testament, which defined holiness and morality more fully and gave a glimpse of God as One who cares about people, still did not communicate God's heart.

There were still some questions left unanswered. What does God truly want with us? How does He react when we fail to meet His standards? "In the past God spoke to our forefathers through the prophets at many times and in various ways, but in these last days He has spoken to us by His

Son." It is the Son who is "the radiance of God's glory and the exact representation of His being" (Heb. 1:1-3). In Jesus, the Word is spoken! And what do we hear when the final revelation comes? "Law was given through Moses; grace and truth came through Jesus Christ" (John 1:17). In Jesus we see a morality that goes beyond law and can only be identified as grace.

How is grace portrayed in verses 9-13 of this chapter? The Creator entered the world He had made. He came to His own people, to whom He had given life. But His own people would not receive Him. He was rejected, scorned, and ultimately crucified. In spite of this, He reached out to individuals who would receive Him, and He gave them the right to become the children of God.

The human race did not seek out a family relationship with God. The reaching out was God's, and His alone. In spite of mankind's failure, God drew men and women to Himself and lifted them up, adopting them as His children and heirs. In this act of pure grace, a glorious light bursts into history. In Jesus Christ, the eternal Word, we discover that God's ultimate morality is one of love and of grace.

At first it is hard to realize that the God who spoke in the past is the same God unveiled in Jesus. We had never grasped the full extent of His glory. But John the Baptist was a witness to that light, and testified that He *is* the same. The splendor of God seen in the Son goes so far beyond the glimpses of glory that shine through the Law. Now, we must learn to live in grace's new relationship with the Lord, so that we can share His glory.

And so the theme of Jesus, the Living Word, unveiling God, dominates the Gospel of John. Jesus, full of grace and truth, unveiled now the relationship which God the Father had always yearned to have with humankind. And we, as His sons and daughters, must learn a way of life guided by the splendor of grace rather than by the flickering candle of Law.

For this, we must know Jesus. We must see Jesus as He is, God's ultimate Word of revelation. We must hear His Word, come to understand, and believe in Him. When we trust ourselves to Jesus, forever, and daily, we will learn what it means to "have eternal life in Him."

TEACHING GUIDE

Prepare
Look at a verse-by-verse commentary, such as the *Bible Knowledge Commentary,* pages 271-273.

Explore
1. Jesus was the "Word" (that is, the revealer of God) even before the Incarnation. Three concepts in John's introduction to his Gospel express how.

Give a minilecture on Jesus' roles in Creation, as life, and as light, and how each of these unveil God to human beings. Afterward discuss: "How much do we know about God from each source? What important knowledge is still lacking?"
2. The author suggested that John wanted us to realize fully that Jesus *is* God, and that this is vitally important to our Christian experience.

Use the launching activity found in "link-to-life," page 709, to help your group members sense how important it is for us, who can control so little in our lives, to trust the living Jesus who controls *all.*

Expand
1. John was called to "bear witness to" (identify!) Jesus as the Light. This was linked to the fact that Israel thought of God's revelation in terms of the Law that came through Moses, while "grace and truth" came (were unveiled) through Jesus.

Discuss: "How did people who received all their moral light from the Law pictured God? How might Jesus, who emphasized God's grace, have changed that image?"
2. Or look at parallel passages that deal with the full deity of Jesus, as outlined in "link-to-life," page 711.

Apply
Have each person share: "What is one evidence of God's grace through Jesus that you have experienced since becoming a believer?"

STUDY GUIDE 110

John 1:19–4:42

THE NEW HAS COME

Overview

We meet four people in these opening chapters of John's Gospel. They are John the Baptist, Nathanael, Nicodemus, and the unnamed "woman at the well."

John was Jesus' forerunner, sent to prepare Israel for His coming. Nathanael represented the godly Israelite who responded at the very first evidence that Jesus is the Christ, the Son of God. Nicodemus represented the religious leaders who realized from Christ's miracles that Jesus is "a Teacher . . . come from God," but whose spiritual blindness kept them from understanding the true message of the Old Testament, and whose spiritual deadness made them antagonistic to the Son of God. The woman at the well represents the myriad of human beings outside the chosen people who, when they meet Jesus, put their confidence in Israel's Saviour.

The theme of these chapters is salvation—and the way three individuals who typify all humanity respond to the One who alone can bring life to a lost humankind.

▶ ***Born Again.*** John often used the imagery of being "born of God" (see John 1:13; 1 John 2:29; 3:9; 4:7; 5:1, 4, 18). Spiritual rebirth is supernatural, not natural, and God Himself is the One who acts to give the believer new life (see John 1:12-13). New birth makes us God's children (v. 13), and leads to our moral transformation. One born of God will do what is right (1 John 2:29).

Commentary

Kurt had an uncomfortable feeling about God. As a boy he seldom went to church or Sunday School, but when he did, he was aware that he was with people who had moral standards much higher than his own.

When Kurt learned the Ten Commandments and heard the words of Jesus from the Sermon on the Mount, he was more uncomfortable than ever. The more he learned, the more aware he became of the gap in his own life between what he knew was right, and what he desired and did.

Kurt had all the "light" he wanted! Talk of God only produced flashes of guilt and shame. More light? A brighter light? No thanks! It was much easier to turn away from talk of God and from his own sense of sin.

So John the Baptist's first words about Jesus would surprise people like Kurt if they could understand them. Twice John said that the light of Jesus helps us see that God is "full of grace and truth." What is unveiled in the Son of God is not some higher, more burdensome standard of morality. Instead, Jesus revealed that God wants to relate to us as a Father relates to his children; through *grace,* not *law.*

For everyone who has ever felt like Kurt—that contact with God is painful or condemning—John now had a surprising message.

The Openhearted: John 1:19–2:11

Not everyone is fearful or unable to believe God loves him, as Kurt was. Some have always sensed God's love. It was the same in Jesus' day; some people were very close to God, and immediately responded to Jesus. We are introduced to two of these openhearted men in John 1. We also discover in this chapter a pattern which the writer followed in the rest of his Gospel.

The pattern. Jesus' unveiling of God typically took place *in miracle followed by discourse.*

In the other Gospels, miracles are generally treated as authenticating or teaching signs. For instance, Matthew concentrated reports of miracles in chapters 8 and 9. This section immediately followed the Sermon on the Mount and demonstrated the authority of the King over nature, evil spirits, disease, and even death. But John presented the miracles of Jesus as first steps in each fresh unveiling of the Father and His grace. In general, each reported miracle or group of miracles leads to a teaching discourse. The miracle thus does more than serve as the divine seal of approval on Jesus; it usually illustrates what He is about to teach as well.

So in studying the Gospel of John, we'll find this pattern over and over. New units of thought are introduced by miracles, and concluded with extended explanations by Jesus of some new aspect of God's grace.

John the Baptist (John 1:19-34). John was probably Jesus' cousin, and certainly a childhood friend. John had been sent by God to announce that the promised Saviour of Israel was about to appear. John was called to "testify concerning that Light," a Light much different from Jewish expectations. Even though John had known Jesus from childhood, he never recognized his Cousin as the Son of God. John too was looking for a different revelation than one of grace and goodness.

But when Jesus came to be baptized by John, John, in a private miracle, saw "the Spirit come down from heaven as a dove and remain on Him." John immediately believed.

Nathanael (John 1:35-51). John gave witness to Jesus and pointed Him out as the Son of God. Soon some of John's followers began to trail after Jesus, and Christ began to select men who would join His most intimate circle of followers. One of these, Philip, hurried to Nathanael and told him that they had found the Christ, and that He was Jesus of Nazareth.

Nathanael was skeptical. The prophets said nothing of anyone great coming from the Galilean town, Nazareth. But Nathanael went with Philip to see for himself. And he was stunned by Jesus' greeting: "Here is a true Israelite, in whom there is nothing false."

When Jesus went on to describe the place where Philip had found Nathanael, far out of Jesus' sight, Nathanael was convinced: "Rabbi, You are the Son of God; You are the King of Israel" (v. 49).

What do we learn from these two incidents? First, we note that each of these men had a preconceived idea of what God was like and how He would act. John described the stern judgments the coming Messiah would execute. Nathanael knew that the Deliverer would come from some place other than Nazareth.

Second, we note that Jesus did not completely fit the preconceived ideas of either. John never dreamed that his gentle, godly Cousin could be the mighty Deliverer that his preaching described (v. 33). Nathanael would find out only later that the Man from Nazareth was actually born in Bethlehem, the place the prophets foretold the coming King would be born. While both John and Nathanael believed deeply in God, both had concepts about His Son that were not fully correct.

Third, each received and responded to a small, personal miracle. Later Jesus would perform many public miracles, and some of these would be absolutely spectacular. It might seem insignificant to us for Jesus to describe the place where Nathanael was when Philip found him (v. 48). But each of these men, John and Nathanael, immediately recognized the hand of God. And *each immediately set aside his preconceived notions, to submit to the authority of Jesus*. Each accepted the fact that Jesus is the Son of God, the Only Begotten of the Father, the revealer of truth as well as of grace (vv. 34, 49).

These insights are important to us at the beginning of our study of John's Gospel. As we explore the written Word, you can expect God to be at work in your own and your group members' lives. God will perform private miracles for you. These probably will not be spectacular, nor will they be public. But, in little ways, God lets us know that He is speaking personally to *us*. And, like John and Nathanael, we each have our own ideas about what God is like and how He will act. But it is vital that you and I, like John and Nathanael, be willing to put aside our incomplete understandings of God and His grace when we discover, in Jesus the Son of God, some fresh unveiling of truth or fresh evidence of grace.

The disciples (John 2:1-11). At a wedding in Cana, Jesus sustained the joy of the occasion by turning water into wine when the supply of drink ran out. Few besides the disciples saw the miracle, but, actually, the miracle was for them. In that miracle Jesus began to unveil His glory, and "His disciples put their faith in Him" (v. 11).

♥ ***Link to Life: Youth / Adult***
Ask your group members to form pairs to do a "before and after" analysis of the ideas of John the Baptist and Nathanael about the Son of God. What did each look for before he discovered that Jesus was the One? How was Jesus different from what he had expected?

Discuss these questions in the group. Then share: "What ideas about God did you have before you became a Christian? How did these ideas later change? What would you be like today if you refused to change your views when you learned more of God's truth and of His grace?"

Light in the Darkness: John 2:12-25
In the next verses we sense the beginning of Jesus' public, and controversial, action. He and His disciples left Galilee and came up to Jerusalem. There they visited the temple and saw the money changers at work. These were businessmen who exchanged other currencies for coins minted at the temple, because the religious leaders had decreed that only temple money was acceptable to God. Smiling, the money changers inflated the rate of exchange—and probably gave the leading priests their cut. Other temple businessmen sold livestock for the sacrifices. A lamb brought by a worshiper might be rejected because of some blemish when inspected by a priest: it had to be traded then for an animal that was "acceptable." Jesus angrily drove the traders from His Father's house.

♥ ***Link to Life: Children***
What Jesus did in condemning the wrong is hard for boys and girls, and for adults! How can we help them protest what is wrongdoing today, and choose personal obedience to Jesus?

Set up typical case history situations, identify some options, and get your boys and girls talking about what to do in each case.

Let them suggest wrongdoing situations, or supply cases that reflect problems in your area. For instance: a child in class is cheating on a test; friends want you to throw hard snowballs at passing cars; you know where older children are selling or buying drugs; someone asks you to help take things from a store; etc.

List possible responses: just say no; tell an adult; tell your parents; threaten to tell if the children don't stop; etc.

Don't expect your boys and girls to come up with quick and easy answers. The point of this activity is to help them realize that it is hard to protest others' wrongdoing, and keep on doing right. How good to remember that Jesus made the hard choices, and that He can help us do what is right today too.

Suddenly Jesus was a public figure. He was popular with the crowds, because He challenged the corrupt leaders. In the spotlight more, Jesus began to perform a number of miracles. These signs were so spectacular and compelling that "many . . . believed in His name" (v. 23). But the belief of the people was shallow; so shallow that "Jesus would not entrust [or commit] Himself" to the crowds as He had to the Twelve.

What is a shallow faith? Perhaps it is best to think of it as *a faith that exists only as long as its object fits our expectations.* These people, who "believed" in Jesus superficially, turned away from Him when He did not speak and act as they expected (see 6:60-66). They "believed," but not enough to abandon their own notions and submit themselves fully to Jesus' fresh revelation of God.

May God protect you and me and those we teach from shallow faith as we study John's Gospel. May He help us be willing to abandon our old ideas when He calls us to submit fully to His Son, Jesus, so that we might find life now.

John now turns from a description of the reaction of the crowds to describe in detail the reaction of two individuals. Nicodemus, a ruler of the Jews, and a Samaritan woman, an outcast of the outcasts.

Nicodemus: John 3:1-21
Nicodemus was identified by John as a "member of the Jewish ruling council" (v. 1). It's important to realize that He was a religious as well as a political leader.

In Israel, civil and religious law were the same: the code of the Old Testament, as interpreted by the rabbis over the generations, guided the life of the Jew in the Holy Land, and anywhere a Jewish community existed. Nicodemus was one of the men who interpreted and applied God's instructions to Israelite life. These rulers represented divine authority to the Jews: they "sat in

Moses' seat" as interpreters of his Law.

Yet the land of Palestine was under Roman rule as well. Rome was the final authority; only the Roman procurator (governor) could pronounce the death penalty. Still, aside from the taxes Rome collected and the army garrison Rome maintained, day-to-day affairs were administered by the Jewish rulers rather than the Roman overlords. It was much simpler, and some "self-government" did help make subject people less troublesome.

Thus Nicodemus was a significant man: he held a civil power that would be backed by Rome, and he was a recognized interpreter of the Law of God as that Law was expressed in the written Word.

Nicodemus' first words revealed a growing conviction shared among the rulers that Jesus must be "a Teacher . . . come from God. For no one could perform the miraculous signs You are doing if God were not with him" (v. 2). Yet in spite of this belief, the rulers did not make their conclusion public. It's possible that Nicodemus' night visit was made in secret to avoid any impression of public support, and possibly to find out what this new Prophet was going to proclaim.

Jesus immediately jolted Nicodemus with the announcement that to even catch a glimpse of God's kingdom, a person must be *born again*. Nicodemus struggled with this strange idea, and then blurted out: "You can't mean 'reenter the womb and be born'! What do You mean by 'born again'?" (see v. 4) Even Jesus' explanation of the new birth as a work of God the Holy Spirit, and not a physical experience (vv. 5-8) brought the same response: "How can this be?" (v. 9)

Jesus' answer helps us see that His revelation of grace and truth is not foreign to the Old Testament! Grace and truth are imbedded in the very foundations of the Old: they simply had not been recognized. Thus Jesus exclaimed, "You are Israel's teacher, and do you not understand these things?"

To what was Jesus referring? Simply this: God's plan to give men and women a life and a relationship with Him not based on Law is clearly taught in the Old Testament!

For instance, Jeremiah promised a time when "I will make a New Covenant with the house of Israel." This new way of relating to God is specifically said to be unlike the older, Mosaic way. Under the New Covenant, God promised, "I will put My law in their minds and write it on their hearts" (Jer. 31:31, 33). When the new heart is created, new life comes; and one who is "born again" comes to know God in a totally different, deeply personal, family relationship. (See also Ezek. 11:19; 18:31; 36:26).

Through such passages as these, which Nicodemus as a recognized Bible authority should have known and understood, the "new birth" had long been taught. But Nicodemus did not know. And he did not understand. His concept of God was faulty. He knew about the Law, but he missed the promise of grace, which tells us that God loves us in spite of our failures and our sins.

Quietly Jesus went on to explain the grace of God and reveal underlying principles by which grace operates.

God's grace (John 3:16-21).

**God loves the world (v. 16).* It's easy to see in the Law a dispassionate, impersonal demand for justice and goodness. But God's involvement with us is *not* impersonal. To understand anything about His ways, we must realize that He is consumed with a passionate love for the world. The world may refuse to receive Him (1:12), but God continues to love.

**God gave His Son (v. 16).* God's love found ultimate expression in His gift of His Son, Jesus, who died in order to redeem the world that hated Him (see vv. 14-15).

**God gives eternal life (v. 16).* Through the death of His Son, God chose to give eternal life to His enemies. This life is called eternal not only because it will extend into eternity, but also because it is God's own life. He gives us His life; we become His children and have a new heredity (see 1 Peter 1:23).

**Apart from this life, all are perishing (vv. 18-21).* God had to act on mankind's behalf; apart from Him there was no hope. There is no use going through life thinking that our good and bad deeds are stacked on the weighing pans of some cosmic balance, and then hoping the good will outweigh the bad and earn salvation. There is no use in struggling to keep the Law in hopes that God might accept our righteousness (or at least our efforts). There is no hope for man in goodness, for we are already condemned: "All have sinned and fall short of the glory of God" (Rom. 3:23). To be born again is the only hope for mankind.

**Human response to light reveals our lost condition (vv. 19-21).* Man's response to moral light, in conscience or in God's Law, has been to choose darkness. This does not mean that every time we are faced with a moral choice each of us always chooses evil. It simply means that *no one* chooses the good every time. Often, even when we do the right thing, we do it from wrong motives or still feel an attraction to evil (v. 19).

How, then, will we respond to Jesus, the true Light who has come into the world? And what response is appropriate to this One who reveals God's ultimate morality of grace? There is only one appropriate response: to believe. To trust the God who offers us life as a free gift. To fully and thankfully commit ourselves to Jesus Christ.

The challenge. Jesus put quite a challenge to this man who had established his identity and his reputation as a religious leader. For all of Nicodemus' knowledge, Jesus told him, he had never even glimpsed the foundation of grace on which God's kingdom is built! How would Nicodemus respond? Would he, like John the Baptist, abandon his preconceived ideas and gladly submit to Jesus, whom he *knew* was "a Teacher who has come from God"?

How Nicodemus responded that night we do not know. Instead, we return to the Baptist (vv. 22-26). When Jesus began to teach, John's importance and popularity began to wane. John's followers became upset. But John told them, "He must become greater; I must become less" (v. 30). Jesus, not a human leader, must be given central place. John stood aside and welcomed Jesus to center stage.

We do know that Nicodemus continued as a ruling Pharisee, and at one point defended Jesus against hearsay accusations (7:50-51). And after Jesus' crucifixion, Nicodemus bought spices and helped to prepare the body of our Lord for burial (19:38-42).

♥ ***Link to Life: Children***

How can we help boys and girls understand being born again? Try a simple three-section pie-shaped chart on which you draw two circles and label them as illustrated.

The inner circle tells the story of being

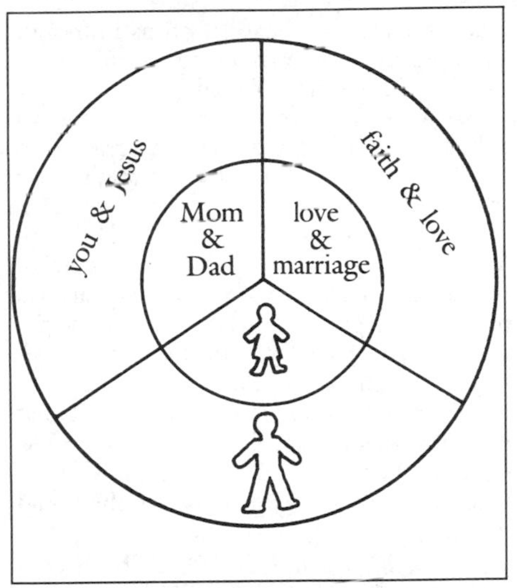

born once. It takes two people; your mom and dad. They fall in love and marry. You are born as a baby with physical life. The outer circle tells the story of being born again. It takes two people; you and Jesus. Jesus loves you and died for you, and you trust Him to forgive your sins. You are born again and given spiritual life so you will live forever.

Everyone who wants to go to heaven and live forever needs to get together with Jesus, to trust Him and accept forgiveness for all his sins.

♥ ***Link to Life: Youth / Adult***

Do your group members know that the new birth is taught in the Old Testament? Look up the Jeremiah and Ezekiel verses with them, to show that Nicodemus really should have understood Jesus' reference to being born again.

Then examine John 3:5-8 and 3:16-21 and as a group make a list of "statements about the new birth."

The Samaritan Woman: John 4:1-42

No one could have stood in greater contrast to Nicodemus than this woman. She was a Samaritan, a race that the Jews looked down on as having no claim on their God. Apparently the woman was an outcast in her own community as well; she came by herself to draw water from the community well. In biblical lands drawing water and chatting at the well was the social highpoint of a woman's day. In this woman's own village she was ostracized and marked off as immoral; an unmarried woman living openly with the fifth in a series of men.

As Jesus and this Samaritan woman talked, she tried to turn the conversation to theology (vv. 19-26). But Jesus focused on several other issues.

Gift (John 4:7-10). Jesus quickly established the fact, as He had with Nicodemus, that God's dealings with humanity are on the basis of grace. What we do is not the foundation of our relationship with God. Rather we must depend on what God is willing to do for us. Jesus pointed out that her sins made self-reliance foolish. How striking then to discover that the Son of God was willing to "give" what she could not earn.

Eternal life (John 4:11-15). In both conversations the gift Jesus promised was life; eternal life, welling up and supplying every need by its freshening springs.

Belief (John 4:39-42). Again Jesus looked for a specific response of trust, of faith, in Him. In this case that response came both from the woman at the well and from the Samaritan community.

At first many believed because the woman rushed back into her village with word that this Man, the Christ, "Told me everything I ever did." The villagers came out, heard Jesus, and even more responded because they heard Him for themselves.

Differences. In spite of the similarities we've seen in the two confrontations, there are differences in the way Jesus unveiled grace to these two people. To Nicodemus, Jesus stressed the fact that all stand condemned before God. Nicodemus, a religious man, took pride in his keeping of the Law and did not recognize his need for God's grace. But the woman at the well knew she was a sinner. Jesus did not mention man's lost condition to her; she knew! And she learned that Jesus knew too, and still was ready to offer her life as a gift. To this woman Jesus spoke of *worshipers.* He told her the good news that the Father seeks persons to worship Him in spirit and in truth (v. 23).

Why? Because while Nicodemus needed to see himself as a sinner in order to understand grace, the woman who knew she was a sinner needed to see herself as a person of worth and value. God finds us worthy of His concern in spite of our ruin. God values us enough to actively seek us, to welcome us to intimacy, and to rejoice in our worship.

Only a person like the Samaritan prostitute, an outcast from her own, could understand what this means. To be wanted, to be cared for when no one, not even herself, could see anything of value in her! This is grace indeed.

Summary

In these chapters, we've begun to see Jesus unveiling God, and we've begun to learn how to respond to that revelation of God.

John the Baptist and Nathanael were like people to whom faith comes easily. They needed little evidence to believe. They joyfully opened their hearts to learn from Jesus, even when what He showed them was different from what they had thought.

Nicodemus and the Samaritan woman were like those of us to whom faith comes hard. It was hard for Nicodemus, because his piety had earned him a reputation in the community. His image of himself as a good man was deeply ingrained. How hard it is for a person who has honestly tried to be good to realize that all those efforts provide no standing with God, that in spite of everything he stands already condemned and in desperate need of a new life, which can come only as a gift.

For the Samaritan woman, faith came hard because she *knew* she was a great sinner. Her sense of worth was worn away. How hard it was for her to realize that God valued her and wanted her to become a worshiper. How hard to believe that He was offering her eternal life as His love gift.

Yet this is the twin revelation of Light, the ultimate morality of God, which comes to us in John's Gospel. Grace says to each of us, "You count." God knows you as you are, and God still cares. He cares enough to send the Son, that you might have eternal life, become His child, and worship Him.

TEACHING GUIDE

Prepare
Read and mark any verses or phrases that may seem hard to understand. Check them in a good verse-by-verse commentary such as the *Bible Knowledge Commentary* (pages 273-288).

Explore
1. Put on the chalkboard the following quote from this text: "Shallow faith is a faith that exists only as long as its object fits our expectations." Ask: "When have you experienced or observed shallow faith?"
2. Do an analysis of the ideas of John and Nathanael about God, and their willingness to submit to Jesus even when He did not fit their expectations. See "link-to-life," page 715, for how to use this study to stimulate sharing about notions of God your group members held before their conversions.

Expand
1. Study the "new birth," looking into the Old Testament roots of this Christian teaching, and then developing a series of statements about it from John 3. See "link-to-life," page 717.
2. Divide into teams of four or five to work together completing a comparisons/contrast chart on the message of John 3 and 4, and the lessons to be drawn from Jesus' talks with first Nicodemus and then the Samaritan woman.

When each team has finished its studies, come together to compare results.

Apply
Have each share in a sentence or two: "What have you learned about the grace that came by Jesus from this study of John 1–4, and how is this important to you personally?"

	Nicodemus	**Woman at the Well**
THE LESSONS Feelings about self Feelings about God Idea of God's attitude toward him/her Idea of what God wants from people		
THE MESSAGE God's goal God's gift God's attitude toward people Man's response to God What grace is		

STUDY GUIDE 111

John 4:43–6:71

THE POWER OF THE NEW

Overview

This segment of John clearly illustrates the structure we've mentioned earlier. John 4:43–5:14 reports two miracles: one the restoration of a child near death, and the other the restoration of a long-term invalid to full health. These lead directly into one of Christ's sermons on the source of life.

John 6 tells first of the miracle of a few loaves and fishes multiplied to feed a great crowd. This miracle too leads directly to another major discourse: Jesus' sermon on the Bread of Life.

Yet the importance of this section isn't found in its structure, but in Jesus' teaching. How important to share with our group members the vision of that new life Jesus brings. And how important to unveil the wonderful truth that what Jesus gives, He Himself sustains.

▶ ***Bread.*** This was the primary food of people in Bible times. It was made from a variety of grains, often mixed with lentils or beans. The "loaves" were baked flat, about a half inch thick. In the Bible, bread is symbolic as the sustainer of physical life. Thus Jesus' quote: "Man does not live on bread alone" (Matt. 4:4) insists human beings are not mere animals. And the prayer: "Give us today our daily bread," is an expression of dependence on God to meet all our needs for life in this present world.

■ See the verse-by-verse commentary in the *Bible Knowledge Commentary*, pages 288-298.

Commentary

He was never sure when he began to change. At first he had fought against the paralysis. Shame had washed over him when his friends picked up his pallet and carried him to Bethesda pool. His mouth compressed tightly; his forehead was rigid with a frown. One could feel the determination, sense the voice inside him that demanded over and over, "I *will* walk again. I *will!*"

How he had watched that pool! He was so desperate to reach it when the waters were rippled, to win the healing people said would come to the first person to slip in them. He had dug his fingers into the pavement, frantically jerking his body across the stones.

But that was years ago. So many years. The friends were gone now, busy with their own affairs. His world was the tiny space occupied by his pallet on the pavement. He no longer struggled to reach the water. In 38 years he had learned to live with his paralysis; learned to accept his wasted, sticklike legs. All the old dreams were discarded. Now he was satisfied with an extra crust of bread in his begging bowl, or a little warmth when the wind brushed the clouds away from the sun. Thirty-eight years. Life had settled into routine, and he was . . . resigned.

Now, I don't *know* that this is what happened to the man described in John 5. We're told only that he had been ill for 38 years, and that he had no one. But it's easy to imagine what must have happened inside as the reality of his paralysis wore away his spirit. We can imagine his youthful plans; the success or the security he dreamed of, the family he'd have. And then came an illness that stripped him of everything: strength, companions, and finally, hope. No wonder when Jesus saw him, and "learned that he had been in this condition for a long time," His first words were, "Do you want to get well?" (John 5:6)

Do you want to be healed, or would the return of hope now be too painful to bear?

That question is more wise than it might seem. Lanny and Marie have been married over 20 years. For the past 5 years they've lived together, but apart. For a long time they had struggled, each wanting intimacy and oneness, but over and over again they had failed. The hurts grew deep and bitterness settled in. Finally Marie couldn't stand it any longer. She would stay with him, but not as a wife. And so life for each of them has now settled into polite loneliness. There is caring of a sort and, at times, fun. But always there is an emptiness that somehow hurts less than the pain they had when they were trying so hard.

Lanny and Marie still long for a deeper relationship and a oneness in their marriage. But neither can respond to the offer of a fresh change. The anguish of past failure has made them afraid to risk anymore.

Jesus' offer of new life comes to men and women who have often been in bondage to paralyzing defeat for untold years. For many of us, an invitation to take a fresh start would be heard with doubts and fear. To understand the grace Jesus unveils and see why it is safe to accept His offer, we need to see more clearly the life that Jesus holds out to us.

♥ ***Link to Life: Youth / Adult***
Tell your group members either the true story of Lanny and Marie, or the author's interpretation of the paralyzed man's experience. Then discuss: "Why might people with deep personal problems not *want to be healed? When is hope a threat that frightens rather than a blessing that excites? What in your life might feel threatening if you knew it could be healed?"*

The Miracle of New Life: John 4:43–5:18

The incidents in chapters 4–6 take place in different districts: Galilee, then Jerusalem, then Galilee again. But these incidents are linked by the logic of John's pattern of miracle and teaching. And common to each scene is Jesus' offer of eternal life; a life that can release us from our bondage to our past.

The first miracle (John 4:43-54). In Jesus' home district of Galilee, an official begged him to heal a terminally ill son. This was no appeal based on curiosity, or on some perverse insistence that Jesus prove Himself. When Jesus suggested such might be the case, the distraught official could only beg, "Sir, come down before my child dies!" The father was desperate, and he turned to Jesus as his only hope.

Christ sent the man away with the promise that the boy would live. The man believed. As he returned home, he was met by servants who excitedly told him that the boy's recovery had begun the same hour Jesus had said, "Your son will live."

The Word had reached out across the miles and brought life where there had been only the bitter prospect of death.

The second miracle (John 5:1-18). This is the miracle we've already noted. The paralyzed man had lived with death for 38 years. He had suffered the loss of all things and was so empty of hope that he had to be asked, "Do you *want* to get well?"

The man chose healing, and Jesus spoke the life-bringing word: "Get up! Pick up your mat and walk" (v. 9).

These two miracles focused attention on Jesus' claim to be able to bring and to restore life. Strangely, the miracles also created opposition. Jesus had healed the paralytic on the Sabbath, established in Scripture as a day of rest. The man was joyfully carrying his pallet out of the city (as Jesus had told him to do), when he was accused of breaking the Sabbath by "working" on the holy day. When the man explained what had happened, the leaders condemned Jesus because He had dared to heal (another "work") on God's Day. Jesus responded that He and His Father were both still at work (v. 17). This stimulated murderous anger from the Jews, who realized that with these words Jesus was "making Himself equal with God" (v. 18).

Against the background of these two miracles demonstrating Jesus' life-giving power and the fury of Israel's leaders, Jesus began to teach about God's grace.

♥ ***Link to Life: Children***
How long should we trust God and pray when we are sick? It took a long time for the paralyzed man in John 5 to be healed. But finally Jesus did act.

Work with your Junior-age boys and girls to make a list of the times they have been sick, and how long their sicknesses lasted. Then discuss: "Has God answered many of our prayers to be healed? Did it seem to take Him a long time to answer? Do you know people who have been sick a longer time?"

Usually God answers our prayers for healing quickly. But even if it takes a longer time, we can keep on praying and trusting God. Jesus is able to heal us, and to give us strength while we are waiting.

Sermon on the Source of Life: John 5:19-47

The Jews persecuted Jesus on the grounds that He was a Sabbath-breaker, and especially because He dared to claim He was equal with God. Jesus unhesitatingly told His angry critics that He and the Father are One. It is just this equality with God that enables Jesus to offer life to us.

One in action (John 5:19-21). The oneness of the Father and Son is seen in that "the Son can do nothing by Himself; He can only do what He sees His Father doing, because whatever the Father does the Son also does." Jesus' actions perfectly reflect the Father's will.

Two acts of Jesus have just expressed God the Father: restoring the official's son and healing the paralytic. Each shows God's desire to bring us life. But Jesus promised even "greater things" that will demonstrate *resurrection power.* God can take the physically and spiritually dead and give them life. In this task of giving life, Father and Son are One.

One in honor (John 5:22-24). Jesus perfectly reflects the Father, for They act as One. Now Christ went on to claim that He has authority to judge.

James warned us about speaking evil of or judging a brother. He pointed out that anyone who does judge steps out of his role as a subject of the Law and, in effect, claims authority over it. "There is only one Lawgiver and Judge, the One who is able to save and destroy" (James 4:12). So when Jesus stated that the Father "has entrusted all judgment to the Son," He was again claiming deity. Only God, who gave the Law, is above it. Jesus must be honored as God, and submitted to in all things. "He who does not honor the Son does not honor the Father who sent Him," is Jesus' inescapable conclusion.

The Jews had just criticized and persecuted Jesus because He healed on the Sabbath. By their definition, Jesus "worked" and so was a lawbreaker. By criticizing Jesus, they placed themselves beside God as judges, and yet they were outraged when Jesus made "Himself equal with God."

What is the judgment of Jesus to which we are to submit? It is that the one who hears Jesus and believes in God through Him has eternal life. Honor Jesus, and you pass beyond all condemnation, out of the realm of death into life.

♥ ***Link to Life: Children***
Play "how do we honor?" Mention different people and let the kids volunteer ideas of how we honor them. We honor the policeman by doing what he tells us. We honor mom and dad by obeying and showing them respect. We honor teachers by learning from them. We honor the flag by standing up and saying the pledge. We honor the President by standing up when he comes into the room. How do we honor Jesus? By believing in Him and accepting Him as Saviour.

The source of life (John 5:25-29). The life that Jesus brings us is resurrection life: life from death. We look forward to a resurrection day in the future; but today, by responding to the voice of Jesus, we can come out of the grave we are living in right now, and experience newness in Him.

Lanny and Marie are afraid to try to rebuild their marriage. Their relationship is wrapped in the graveclothes of the past, buried in the cold ground of old hurts and habits. They can never break out of their bondage to the dead past by themselves. But if they hear Jesus and honor Him, they can experience resurrection power through His gift of eternal life. Then there will be hope for them.

Witness of the Father (John 5:30-36). But how do we know that the Father and Son are One? How can we be sure Jesus is able to provide the eternal life He promises? Jesus pointed His critics to the evidence. It's not just that John the Baptist, a prophet, testified of Him. God the Father added His own unique seal in the life-bringing miracles that Christ's enemies had witnessed! Even the rulers recognized the validity of that testimony, as Nicodemus had admitted, "We know You are a Teacher who has come from God. For no one could do the miraculous signs You are doing if God were not with him" (3:2). The rulers could not deny the evidence. But they still would not commit themselves to Jesus, or honor Him as God.

Witness of Scripture (John 5:37-47). There

is yet another witness to Jesus. "You diligently study the Scriptures," Jesus said, "because you think that by them you possess eternal life." They were wrong; studying the Bible or knowing its contents backward and forward does not earn anyone eternal life. What the Scriptures do is point individuals to Jesus.

The Scriptures tell of sin and spiritual death. The message of the Word of God should have led these biblical scholars to do what the father of the dying boy did—recognize that his own efforts were futile, and look for God's grace to appear. These scholars should have recognized that they were no more able to earn God's favor than the paralytic was able to get himself into the pool. They should have been eagerly looking for the prophesied new life, and should have been ready to receive the gift from Jesus' hand.

By refusing to turn to Jesus, who is One with the Father, the men and women Jesus spoke to that day showed how far their hearts were from God. They would not believe; and because they would not believe, Jesus could not give them life.

♥ ***Link to Life: Youth / Adult***
Work through the John 5 teaching of Jesus as a group to be sure that your members understand its flow and the basic points Jesus was making. Then, in pairs or small groups of three or four, develop pithy sayings of not more than six words *that sum up some important point in the form of advice. For example: "Let Jesus judge." "Jesus works." "Rise and live."*

New Life Sustained: John 6:1-24
Again John described a miracle and then reported a teaching session growing out of it. This discourse deepens our understanding of the new life Jesus offers us through grace.

The public miracle (John 6:1-24). Great crowds had followed Jesus to see His signs and hear His teachings. They were with Him when mealtime came and passed, and they had had nothing to eat. Jesus took all the food that was available (five small barley loaves and two fish), prayed, and divided it among the people. The 5,000 men, plus women and children, all "had enough to eat," and the disciples collected 12 full baskets of leftovers.

The people recognized that a great miracle had been performed and cried, "Surely this is the Prophet who is to come into the world." Immediately they decided "to come and make Him King by force" (vv. 14-15).

We learn a lot from that phrase; they wanted to take Him by force and *make* Him King! A king is one who rules, not is ruled by others. But the men and women who participated in the miracle of the loaves and the fish were determined to *use* Jesus; they had no desire to obey Him. Jesus, knowing their motives, slipped away. By the next day the crowd had followed Him to the other side of the lake and began to ask Him many questions. He based His teaching on the miracle of the loaves, and presented Himself to the people as the "Bread of Life."

Sermon on the Bread of Life: John 6:25-59
The theme of the message is *life sustained.* Jesus told the crowd about food that "endures to eternal life" (v. 27). He said those who are sustained by it will never go hungry and never be thirsty (v. 35). Jesus promised to sustain a relationship with those who "remain in Me" so that life will be continuously experienced (vv. 56-57). It's not enough simply to have life; life must be sustained and developed. There must be provision for daily growth.

None of this concerned the crowd. They wanted a king who could validate himself by an acceptable sign. And what sign did they want? "Our forefathers ate the manna in the desert." They wanted to be fed, so they would not need to work.

Jesus rebuked them, and exhorted them to focus not on food that perishes but on that which endures to eternal life. They were to look for the true Bread from heaven, and put their trust in Him.

"I am the Bread of Life" (John 6:35-40). Each statement Jesus made stressed the continuing benefits of the life He brings. *You will never be hungry.* God will, in Jesus, keep on supplying that which sustains our new life. *You will never be thirsty.* A human being can go without food for weeks without dying, but he cannot go without water. Jesus promises to satisfy even that most intense of needs; He will see that we lack nothing we need. *I will never drive [him] away . . . I shall lose none of all that He has given me.* We can be sure Jesus will extend God's grace to us in a daily experience of eternal life as well as

in a permanent relationship with God.

"I am the Bread that came down from heaven" (John 6:41-51). The manna God provided for the Israelites during the Exodus is a picture of Jesus as the "living Bread." When God's people traveled through the wilderness, they had to depend on God to provide their food supernaturally. God provided the food in a way that would also teach the people something about their relationship with Him. Every day God gave enough food for that day. No one could gather more than a day's supply. There had to be a continual, constant dependence on God; He was the only source of sustenance.

The Jews murmured against Christ's claim to be "Bread that came down from heaven." They knew this Man and His family; how could He claim a heavenly origin? Jesus answered that it would be God who would draw men to Christ. And Jesus then went on to promise that anyone who believed in Him would have eternal life, and anyone who fed on the living Bread "will live forever."

"Eat the flesh of the Son of man" (John 6:52-59). Many see in those words a reference to the Communion service. "This is My body, given for you," Jesus would say as He instituted the memorial service. This is "My blood which is poured out for you." But to "eat" and "drink" the body and blood of Jesus means far more than to participate in a shared memorial, as the rest of our passage suggests. "Whoever eats My flesh and drinks My blood remains in Me" (v. 56). "He who feeds on this bread will live forever" (v. 58). "The words I have spoken to you are spirit," Jesus said (v. 63).

Jesus was using *body* and *blood* to represent everything needed to sustain and support life. Our lives will be supported so completely that we never will hunger or thirst. Our spiritual lives will be sustained so completely that they will endure until Jesus raises us up on the last day.

We are to go to Jesus and to Him alone, for all the resources and the strength we need to live our new lives. We can rely only on our Lord.

Rejection: John 6:60-71

The crowds that had been attracted by the prospect of free food now shook their heads. Not only did Jesus fail to produce the expected dinners, but He had begun to speak like some madman! Even a few of those who had been His disciples (in the sense of general adherents, not in the stronger sense of committed followers), "turned back and no longer followed Him" (v. 66).

But when Jesus asked the Twelve if they would leave too, Peter answered for them. "Lord, to whom shall we go? You have the words of eternal life. We believe and know that You are the Holy One of God" (vv. 68-69). Peter and the others understood no better than the crowds. But they were willing to trust Him.

You and I might not grasp the meaning of all of Jesus' words either. We can't yet tell just what "remaining" and "living" in Jesus, or "feeding" on Him, mean. But we do know that if we are to enjoy our new lives, we must keep on looking to Jesus daily to supply our needs, and to sustain us with His grace.

♥ ***Link to Life: Youth / Adult***

Lead your group in an analysis of the verbs in John 6:25-59. First list statements Jesus made about Himself: He is the "Bread from heaven," etc.). Continue the list with series of divine actions: Jesus will "raise up believers" at the last day.

Then try to match *the active verbs that suggest what persons are to do,* in view of *who Jesus is, with what God and Jesus do or will do.*

There may be differences of opinion as to which verbs fit where. Your discussion will help to clarify both the passage and the meaning of such terms as "eat" and "believe."

TEACHING GUIDE

Prepare
Examine motives of the crowds around Jesus as revealed in John 6:15, 25-27. Pray that God will guard your group members from similar motives in their relationships with Him.

Explore
1. Tell either the story of the paralyzed man or of Lanny and Marie. Follow the plan in "link-to-life," page 721.
2. Or tell about the paralyzed man, and his loss of hope as disappointing years passed. Explain the reason for Jesus' question: "Do you want to be well?" Then ask each group member to close his or her eyes, and imagine that Jesus is standing there, asking him or her that same question. Ask: "What in your life would Jesus be talking about? How does that question make you feel?"

Without having any identify the issue, do have each share about the feelings Jesus' question would arouse.

Expand
1. John 5 focuses on the theme of life itself. Use the method given in "link-to-life," page 723, to develop from this key chapter a number of "good-advice" sayings.
2. Or study John 6. Work for a content analysis as explained on page 724.

Apply
Ask each to pray silently, giving Jesus his or her answer: Do you really *want* to be healed?

STUDY GUIDE 112

John 7–9

LIGHT AND DARKNESS

Overview

Jesus said it in a dispute recorded in John 7:24. "Stop judging by mere appearances, and make a right judgment."

In a sense, this is the theme of this important section of John's Gospel, which focuses on "light."

Light and darkness are constant themes in John's New Testament writings. Those who live in darkness are confused, unable to see reality. Lost in a world of illusion they make judgments based on mere appearances, and are simply unable to grasp what is important and true.

Light, on the other hand, cuts through this darkness to unveil the right and the true. And Jesus is the Cornerstone of the kingdom of light; we begin to "see" when we acknowledge Him as the eternal Son of God.

But "light" also has a moral dimension. And it is this moral dimension that Jesus affirmed as He not only presented Himself to Israel as God, but also claimed the right to establish a *grace morality* which is far higher than the *legalistic morality* of the Jews, for it alone truly reflects the morality of God.

▶ ***The Jews.*** This designation is used often in the Gospel of John. John used it in a technical sense. He did *not* mean Israel, or the Jewish people as a whole. When John said "the Jews" he, unlike other Gospel writers, meant the religious leaders of the people who chose to oppose Jesus, and who represented a distortion of historic Old Testament faith.

Commentary

I hadn't been a Christian very long when I saw a stranger smoking a cigarette in the hall of our little church. I was shocked. I remember the pastor's son's reaction: "We don't smoke in church," Bruce announced in a chilly voice.

I also remember one of the men of that church, a police detective, who cupped his hand around his cigarette, trying to hide it, when he met some of our youth group on the street. I remember my own condemning attitude when one of the girls in our group said she hoped Jesus wouldn't return until she'd had time to enjoy life.

There were so many things that made me and other Christians I knew uncomfortable. There were so many things we considered wrong, in addition to the serious sins the Bible identified. And we felt compelled to judge all the ways in which another person seemed to miss our mark. Of course, if his ways were different enough, we'd have nothing to do with him.

To us, morality was summed up in doing "right" . . . and in cutting ourselves off from any relationship with those who did not do as we did.

We never realized that our attitude might distort true morality. We failed to see the light that Jesus brought into the world.

A World of Misunderstanding: John 7

We saw earlier that *light* and *darkness* are moral terms to John. They represent good and bad, righteousness and evil, as well as truth and falsity. Christ, the eternal Word (John 1) is the One through whom righteousness has always been communicated. Christ planted a moral awareness deep in every person, and revealed the nature of goodness back in the Old Testament. But John tells us that man's understanding and interpretation of light is faulty. Thus Paul can insist that the Law is "holy, righteous, and good," and still be convinced that Law had been an agent of death, stimulating sin rather than quieting it (Rom. 7:7-12).

We can see the distorted perception of the people of Jesus' day by looking at a series of incidents reported in John 7. Jewish thinking about morality was similar to my own in my early days of faith. Against the background of such attitudes, we will be able to see how Jesus displayed the glory of God, as He revealed a new morality, the morality of grace.

Hatred, uncertainty, and fear (John 7:1-13). Jesus' teachings and miracles had become widely known. His uncompromising presentation of Himself as God, and His offer of life to those who believed in Him, stirred up a number of reactions. Each reaction tells us something about the moral climate in Israel.

First, there was hatred (vv. 1, 7). The leaders of the people were charged with teaching God's Word to Israel. But they were so unlike God that they actually hated the Son of God who revealed Him. They in fact responded to Jesus with murderous rage.

Second, there was ridicule (vv. 3-5). Jesus' own brothers (in jealousy?) rejected the evidence of His works, and taunted Him.

Third, there was conflict. People argued with themselves and with each other. This Jesus. Is He a good Man, or a heretic? (vv. 12-13)

Fourth, there was fear. Even those who were convinced that Jesus was a Prophet and a good Man feared to take a stand. They knew they would be attacked, and probably persecuted by their religious leaders (referred to here and in other Johannine passages as "the Jews").

Looking at these reactions, we're forced to ask a question. What kind of results had Israel's interpretation of the divine Law produced? Had God's people become a community of love, caring, and closeness? Not at all! The people of God were angry, antagonistic, bitter, and fearful! There *must* be something wrong with an approach to faith that produces such a lifestyle! There must be a higher and better approach to morality and faith than *this!*

♥ ***Link to Life: Youth / Adult***

Set up the following paired qualities at opposite ends of continuum lines: love/antagonism, supportiveness/ridicule, harmony/conflict, acceptance/fear.

Either read the author's description of his first church's approach to faith and morality. Then ask each group member to mentally mark along each continuum line what kind of relationships this approach is likely to produce in the congregation. Divide the lines into quarters, and poll the group, recording how many mentally checked off each quarter. Then discuss: "What does the pattern shown here suggest? Why *did we expect what is shown here? What would it take to produce different expectations?"*

Or draw the same continuum lines, but ask each to mentally mark where they feel your own church *family falls along the lines. Then discuss: "What pattern is shown here?* What *led each person to mark as he or she did? If the pattern does not reveal an ideal situation, what might be done to move your congregation closer to the ideal?"*

You can then give a minilecture on John 7:1-13, and note that in these chapters your group will explore a grace morality which can *produce a truly loving faith community.*

God's authority rejected (John 7:14-24). At heart Israel had rejected God's authority. The leaders had made man's ideas supreme, and had missed the real meaning of the Law of Moses, which none kept (v. 19), even as they had rejected the evidence of the miracles that the Father empowered the Son to perform. If any of Jesus' critics had committed himself to do God's will, he would have recognized Jesus' teachings as the Word of God.

This is a critical point for us too. Moral and spiritual blindness are not rooted in our inability to understand. They are rooted in our unwillingness to submit completely to God. If anyone simply determines to do God's will, that person will be enlightened, and will first recognize Jesus as God's Son, and then acknowledge His teachings as God's Word.

Moral cowardice (John 7:25-36). When Jesus appeared at the Jerusalem festival, He taught openly. The rulers had determined to murder Christ, but they were afraid to oppose Him publicly! The crowds knew the leaders' antagonism toward Jesus; why wouldn't they act on their convictions? This led to much speculation. If Jesus were really leading the people astray, it was the responsibility of the leaders to arrest Him. Or "have the authorities really concluded that

He is the Christ?" (v. 26) Finally, stung by the criticism, the chief priests and Pharisees gave orders for Jesus to be arrested.

Increasing uncertainty (John 7:37-52). Jesus continued to offer the crowd words of eternal life, inviting them "to come to Me and drink." The guards sent to arrest Jesus returned to the leaders (who were conveniently absent when the arrest attempt was made!) and reported, "No one ever spoke the way this Man does!"

Furious, the leaders condemned Jesus, and in that act, broke the very code they claimed to uphold, for by Law no man could be judged without a hearing and examination of his behavior.

The authorities' quick condemnation was much like my reaction to the smoker in that church hallway. I felt anger and fear; I had rejected and condemned him without a hearing. I had had no real concern for him as a person.

When our "morality" produces responses that condemn and antagonize other human beings, then the "light" in us is darkness indeed! When we fear others and strike out at them, we are out of touch with the heart of God. And we have not understood the morality of grace that Jesus Himself revealed.

True Morality Revealed: John 8

We have just seen the moral climate of the community in which Jesus ministered; now we see the morality of Jesus Himself.

The woman (John 8:1-11). Unable to arrest Jesus, the Pharisees hoped to destroy His influence by forcing Him into a situation in which He would either directly violate the Law, or would insist on a drastic and unpopular penalty that was seldom enforced. The Pharisees and teachers of the Law brought a woman caught in the act of adultery to Jesus, and they challenged Him. "In the Law Moses commanded us to stone such women. Now what do You say?"

Jesus did not answer. Bending down, He began to write in the dust. Some have suggested Jesus was jotting down the details of sins committed by the accusers. As they continued to insist on a judgment, Jesus looked up. "If any one of you is without sin, let him be the first to throw a stone at her."

One by one the shamed rulers, condemned by their own consciences, slipped away.

Left alone with the woman, Jesus announced, "Neither do I condemn you. Go now and leave your life of sin."

As we analyze this incident, we begin to see the nature of a morality which flows from grace—in contrast to a legalistic morality. That legalistic morality is:

**Impersonal.* The Pharisees were quick to *use* the woman to strike at Jesus. She had no value in their eyes; they didn't care about her as a person.

But Jesus did care about her, individually. She was guilty, but in spite of her sin Jesus refused to condemn her. Grace salvages, rather than destroys, the individual.

**Selective.* The Pharisees brought the woman caught in the act of adultery. But where was the man? Their morality excused some while accusing others (see Rom. 2:11).

Jesus, however, raised the issue of universal guilt. "If any one of you is without sin, let him be the first to throw a stone at her," He announced. Every man there was forced to admit that he stood *beside* the woman, before the bar of justice.

The divine morality begins with the affirmation that all have sinned. But the Judge withholds condemnation in order to give life, and to encourage the sinner to "leave your life of sin."

**Punishment oriented.* The Law was a good and holy expression of righteousness. Adultery is wrong, and we are to care about doing right. But the Pharisees were not concerned with encouraging right action in Israel or with the reform of the woman. Their motives were not righteous, but vengeful.

On the other hand, everything Jesus did was righteous, and was designed to produce righteousness! Jesus affirmed the Law's penalty for sin, but demanded sinlessness from anyone who would execute it! Christ Himself judged the sin wrong, but rather than condemn the sinner, *Jesus withheld the penalty so that she might go and sin no more!*

Immediately after this incident, we are told that Jesus spoke to the people of Israel and said, "I am the Light of the world. Whoever follows Me will never walk in darkness, but will have the light of life" (John 8:12).

What is the light in which we are to walk? What is the moral pattern of grace we see in Jesus, in whose footsteps we are to walk also?

A grace morality cares first and foremost about those involved.

A grace morality humbly affirms solidarity with the sinner, not moral superiority.

A grace morality seeks not to condemn, but to lead others to a righteous life.

In each of these points, the morality of Jesus conflicted with the moral assumptions of the Pharisees, just as it conflicts with my own early self-righteous attitude toward others.

The character of grace morality (John 8:12-59). Now in discourses that follow the incident with the woman, Jesus defended and defined His right to serve as Light to the world. Jesus showed that He is the key, for in Jesus we have a:

**Divine standard (vv. 13-20).* The Pharisees who challenged Jesus were limited by a human perspective which was itself warped by sin. Thus they judged "by human standards." Jesus does not judge, for He came to bring life rather than condemnation. But were Jesus to judge (as one day He will!), His evaluation would penetrate to a reality that lies beyond human capacity to perceive. Jesus' standards are those of the Father Himself, whom the Pharisees did not even know.

**Divine origin (vv. 21-30).* The moral roots of Jesus' actions and teachings are from above, reflecting the heart of God. The moral roots of the Pharisees' approach were in this world, and reflect a sinful attitude. Unless the Pharisees abandon their own understanding and come in faith to Jesus, they would "indeed die in [their] sins" (v. 24).

**Divine experience (vv. 31-38).* True morality is to experience (to put into practice) Jesus' teachings. To know right but to do wrong (as the Pharisees had done) is to live in slavery to sin. But to practice Jesus' teachings is to experience a truth that brings total freedom.

John 8:31-32 combine several of John's key theological words in an illuminating way. To "know" the truth is not to intellectually comprehend, but to experience. To know the "truth" is not to focus on a body of knowledge, but to live in touch with reality as God knows reality. To "hold to" Jesus' teachings is not a reference to doctrinal purity, but to a commitment to put Jesus' teachings into daily practice. To be "free" is not to live selfishly, doing whatever one wants whenever one wants, but to live a disciplined and godly life which releases us from our bondage to sin so that the choices we make lead to what helps us rather than to what hurts. All this can be found if we are only willing to *really* be the disciples of Jesus.

**Divine response (vv. 39-47).* True morality loves those whom God loves. The Pharisees showed a family resemblance to Satan rather than to God, for they hated Jesus, who came from God. They also had contemptuously dismissed the adulteress, whom God also loved.

**Divine claim (vv. 48-59).* The Jewish leaders again attacked. This time they insisted that Jesus' teachings and miracles were demonic in origin. The power Jesus displayed was evil rather than good; from Satan rather than God. The dispute concluded with Jesus' affirmation that He existed long before Abraham. In fact, Abraham had believed in Him.

In Jesus' claim, "Before Abraham was born, I am," the Jews rightly recognized that Jesus was identifying Himself with the Yahweh of the Old Testament (see Ex. 3:14; *index* for I AM).

God Himself, in the person of Jesus Christ, has revealed His heart. Jesus has shown us the true nature of morality. And the roots of that morality are sunk deep in grace, and have no reflection of the distorted legalism of New Testament Judaism, or in a legalism of our own.

♥ ***Link to Life: Youth / Adult***

In a minilecture summarize the "grace morality" principles found in John 8. Then (1) ask your group members to work in teams to identify the opposite *moral ideas or attitudes. When this is done, each team is to seek illustrations in either John 7 or John 8 of these opposition attitudes in action. Or, (2) after identifying both the grace morality principles and their opposites, have teams draw on their own experiences to find situations (like the author's original illustration, or like the woman in John 8) where a moral dilemma existed. Discuss each case, defining how one would respond if he or she operated on grace morality, and how if he or she operated on a legalistic morality.*

The Final Illustration: John 9

Why hadn't the people of Israel responded

now that the Light of the world, Jesus, had come and so clearly illumined God's grace? John reported an event that clearly illustrated the reasons, and pointed out a danger that we each face in our own spiritual lives.

Who sinned? (John 9:1-12) The Jewish people knew God was a moral Person. But "morality" was translated into a simple formula: Those who do right will be rewarded; those who do wrong will be punished. It followed, from this formula, that any personal disasters were evidence of sin. Conversely, prosperity was a sign of God's approval.

This formula underlies the disciples' question about a man on the street who had been blind from birth. "Who sinned, this man or his parents?" That is, was the man's blindness a punishment from God for the future sins he would commit, or was his blindness a punishment for ancestral evil?

Jesus' answer was, "Neither." The blind man did not serve as a demonstration of the impact of sin, but rather as a demonstration of the power and love of God. His tragedy was a backdrop for blessing!

How often this is true for us. Sue experienced a painful divorce, deserted by her husband when she was three months pregnant and with a two-and-a-half-year-old son. The struggles of the next years were brutal. Yet out of them grew an understanding and sympathy for the needs of the divorced, an active personal ministry, and a book on how Christians individually and as congregations can minister to the suddenly single. The tragedy was a backdrop. It need not be explained by sin, but can be seen as God's avenue to blessing for her and for others.

Jesus healed the blind man. The neighbors were stunned. They brought the man to the Pharisees to see how they would interpret this latest spectacular work of Jesus.

He is a sinner (John 9:13-25). The Pharisees struggled against this new evidence of God's presence with Jesus. The healing had been performed on the Sabbath; here was an excuse to condemn it. Yet some of them hesitated. "How can a sinner do such miraculous signs?" (v. 16) Twice they questioned the man and interrogated his parents. Finally they pronounced their judgment: "Give glory to God. We know this Man is a sinner" (v. 24).

God listens to Him (John 9:26-34). The man who had been blind cut through the hypocrisy. When he was told the Pharisees "did not know where" Jesus came from (e.g., did not know His origins or the source of His powers), the man replied, "Now that is remarkable! . . . [God] listens to the godly man who does His will. Nobody has ever heard of opening the eyes of a man born blind. If this man were not from God, He could do nothing."

Furious, the Pharisees threw the man out on the streets. "You were steeped in sin at birth; how dare you lecture us!"

Your sin remains (John 9:35-41). Jesus found the man whose sight He had restored, and identified Himself as the Son of man (an Old Testament name of the Messiah). The man believed what Jesus said, and worshiped Him.

This blind man's inner vision, as well as his physical vision, had been restored. He recognized Jesus as the Light of the world. The judgment that comes on the world was not a judgment Jesus made, but one the world brought on itself. The blind saw . . . and those who claimed to see were shown to be blind.

Overhearing this remark, the Pharisees snarled, "What? Are we blind too?"

Jesus answered, "If you were blind, you would not be guilty of sin; but now that you claim you can see, your guilt remains."

The religious leaders of Jesus' day insisted that their moral ideas were right, and so they rejected Jesus and His teachings in spite of all the evidence. If only they would have admitted their moral blindness and turned to Jesus. He would have opened their eyes, even as He restored sight to the man born blind.

The people who cannot see the light are usually the ones who insist their moral concepts are right, and the ones who refuse to submit themselves to God's morality as revealed in Jesus.

♥ ***Link to Life: Youth / Adult***
Ask each group member to read through John 9 privately, and to underline *specific words or phrases that strike him or her as important.*

Then ask each to select three *of his or her underlined portions and make a summary statement from each about "A lesson I learn from John 9 is. . . ."*

Reassemble as a group and go around the circle and ask each to share the one *lesson he or she thinks is most important for him or her right now.*

In Summary

As the Light of the world, Jesus reveals the morality of God. In Him we see beyond all previous revelations of goodness. In His every action, Jesus gives a clear and unmistakable picture of grace. He shakes our old ideas of morality, and helps us to understand God's righteousness.

Jesus did not in any way condone sin. He even upheld the rightness of sin's ultimate penalty (John 8:7). But Jesus did demonstrate that God reacts to sinners in a far different way than we tend to. Man's legalistic interpretation of morality involves hatred and rejection of the sinner. It leads to judging others, and to the fear of being judged. It also leads to injustice, as some are excused for their failures while others are never accused. A legalistic morality blinds us to our own condition as sinners, and puts us beside those we have been so quick to condemn.

But God's morality, shown in Jesus, is a morality rooted in grace. It never compromises with sin, but it never rejects the sinner. It accords the sinner love and respect; it says that a person is of worth and value.

The goal of grace's treatment is to rescue the individual from slavery to sin, and to free him to sin no more. The person who lives in the light shed by Jesus is ever aware that he approaches others not as one who is exalted above them to judge, but as one who shares with them a common infirmity that prohibits anyone from casting the first stone.

How can we learn to live this new morality of grace? We are to learn from Jesus, by following Him out of the darkness and into His light (v. 12).

TEACHING GUIDE

Prepare

Jot down two or three moral dilemma situations in which a Christian might respond from either a legalistic morality or a grace morality.

Explore

1. Write on the chalkboard James 4:11-12. As group begins, ask: "How is this to be applied in our personal relationships?"

2. Construct continuum lines that contrast features of the Jewish community of faith revealed in John 7 with their opposites. Use these to evaluate either the author's opening illustration, or the interpersonal climate in your own church family. The "link-to-life" idea on page 727 shows how to use this activity to unlock the teaching of John 7.

Expand

1. Examine the basic elements in the grace morality that guided Jesus. Then divide your group into teams to see how a grace and legalistic morality contrast in practice. Your groups can apply them to the author's opening illustration, to data in John 7 and 9, to moral dilemmas you prepared, or to moral dilemmas they have had to deal with in their own experiences. See "link-to-life," page 729.

2. Or involve your group in direct Bible study of John 9, underlining key phrases and then sharing with the group, "A lesson I have learned. . . ." See pages 730-731.

Apply

Ask each of your members to write out a summary contrasting the *results* in the believing community of practicing a grace morality in contrast to the results of practicing a legalistic morality. Then compare with the author's summary (p. 731).

STUDY GUIDE 113

John 10–12

THE CHOICE

Overview
In these central chapters of John's Gospel we find clear evidence of the decisive rejection of Jesus by His people.

Christ presented Himself as the Good Shepherd who would die for His sheep (John 10:1-21). "The Jews" (John's term for the religious authorities) realized Jesus was claiming to be God, and tried to seize Him (vv. 22-42).

Christ demonstrated His power over death by raising Lazarus, who had been dead for four days (11:1-44). The Jews did not respond to the miracle, but were afraid their people would believe in Jesus and "take away both our place and our nation." They determined that Jesus must die (vv. 45-57).

Christ, acclaimed by the people on Palm Sunday, predicted His death (12:1-36), but the Jews continued in their fixed unbelief (v. 37).

Each of these chapters follows the same pattern. There is a clear presentation by Jesus of His claims, followed by a decisive rejection by the authorities, and a growing determination to kill Jesus to get Him out of the way.

Even so, Jesus did not condemn. But He did warn. "There is a Judge for the one who rejects Me and does not accept My words; that very word which I spoke will condemn him at the last day" (v. 48).

■ For a verse-by-verse commentary on each key phrase in this section see the *Bible Knowledge Commentary*, pages 309-319.

Commentary
Unlike the other Gospels, which trace the development of Jesus' ministry over three years, the Gospel of John focuses on the final months of Christ's life, when the issues had been clearly drawn.

Jesus, the Son of God, revealed over and over again the truth about life and light, and confronted His listeners with the necessity of choice.

John 10 through 12 depicts events that lead up to the Upper Room Discourse. In these chapters we see the final confrontation, and catch a glimpse of the ultimate evidence that will soon be offered to prove Jesus' claims.

The Shepherd and His Sheep: John 10
In the Old Testament, the picture of a shepherd and his sheep was often used to illustrate the relationship between God and His people. "The Lord is my Shepherd," one psalmist said. Another added, "We are the sheep of His pasture."

Shepherd was also a term applied to spiritual leaders in the Old Testament. Jeremiah chose harsh words to describe leaders who perverted their spiritual role: " 'Woe to the shepherds who are destroying and scattering the sheep of My pasture!' declares the Lord" (Jer. 23:1). The prophet declared that God would set His own Shepherd over His sheep when the promised Son of David (Jesus) reigns.

The people would have had these symbolic pictures of divine leadership in mind when Jesus announced, "I am the Good Shepherd" (John 10:11). Jesus then developed a contrast between Himself and the religious authorities of His day. Jesus was concerned for God's people, and exemplified the morality of grace. The Jewish rulers, on the other hand, ignored the welfare of their people. They, therefore, were false shepherds.

By this time, the leaders of Israel were firmly committed not only to rejecting Jesus' claim to divine authority but to destroying Him as well. So in this message Jesus did not speak to the rulers; He appealed directly to the individuals who made up the nation.

♥ ***Link to Life: Children***
Adults and children have been drawn to the shepherd imagery from faith's beginnings. Let older boys and girls look in their own Bibles and make discoveries from John 10:1-18. Guide their reading with questions: "What does a shepherd do for his sheep? How close are the sheep and shepherd?"

Study the passage yourself to be ready to point out verses or phrases they may miss.

List discoveries on the chalkboard. Then translate each observation into a statement about the relationship between Jesus and your boys and girls.

♥ ***Link to Life: Children***
Younger boys and girls can make model sheep. Cut cardboard in the shape of sheep. On one side glue cotton balls to make a wooly sheep. On the other side place a sticker that pictures Jesus. Jesus is always with His sheep, as close to us as anyone can be.

True Shepherd recognized (John 10:1-6). In Israel sheep were not herded with dogs or by men who walked behind them. The shepherd of the Middle East *led* his sheep. He knew each one by name, and the sheep recognized his voice. At night several herds of sheep might sleep in the same fold. In the morning, when the one door was unbarred, each shepherd could unerringly pick out his own flock. And each member of that flock would be able to distinguish his shepherd from the others because the sheep would know the shepherd's voice, just as God's people would recognize Jesus as the living Word of God.

The Pharisees who claimed to speak for Moses would be followed, but not by those who belonged to God. The true sheep would hear the voice of the Good Shepherd.

Good Shepherd identified (John 10:7-17). Now Jesus condemned the leaders of Israel, saying, "All who ever came before Me were thieves and robbers." Such men care "nothing for the sheep." Jesus, on the other hand, is the Good Shepherd. The Palestinian shepherd commonly slept in the single opening to the fold through which wild animals might attack. As "the door" Jesus protects His own, by placing His body between the sheep and their enemies. The Good Shepherd guides His sheep to pasture, concerned not only that they have life, but that they "have it to the full." How deep is the commitment of the Good Shepherd to His sheep? "The Good Shepherd lays down His life for the sheep."

How clearly this must have spoken to the men and women of Israel. Their rulers, like religious leaders of many times and many faiths, were quick to demand respect and obedience. They were quick to lord it over others; quick to judge, advise, condemn. But no one in Israel would imagine for a moment that one of the authorities would lay down his life for one of the common people. Those leaders might lay down their lives for truth. More than once the men of Israel had refused to fight on the Sabbath, and had been killed easily by pagans. More than one Israelite had offered his body to Roman swords rather than permit a statue of Caesar, or even the Legion Eagles, to enter Jerusalem. To die for a conviction was not that uncommon. But to die for love of the sheep? Never! Truth was important to the authorities; people were not.

But to Jesus, the sheep—sinners not worth the contempt of the righteous—were worth dying for!

One with the Father (John 10:18-30). Jesus could die for the sheep because He had the authority from God to lay down His life, and "authority to take it up again. This command," Jesus continued, "I received from My Father" (v. 18).

These words sent the Jews back to the old debate. "He is demon-possessed and raving mad," some said. But others answered, "Can a demon open the eyes of the blind?"

Again the Jews asked the central question: "How long will You keep us in suspense? If You are the Christ, tell us plainly" (v. 24).

Once again Jesus explained that His sheep hear and respond to His voice. To such He gives eternal life. He can bestow this gift because, "I and the Father are One" (v. 30).

♥ ***Link to Life: Youth / Adult***
The imagery of sheep and shepherds is as rich for adults as for children. Give your group members large sheets of paper and make crayons available. Each is to study John 10:1-18, and draw a picture *showing as many of the relationships as possible that Jesus represents between the sheep and the shepherd.*

When pictures are drawn, have each member show his or hers, and explain it. In the process your group will develop a much better picture of all that Jesus' presentation of Himself as the Good Shepherd means to us today.

Refusal to believe (John 10:31-42). Jesus' renewed claim to be God the Son was recognized by the people: "Again the Jews picked up stones to stone Him."

How strange. "Tell us if You are the Christ." And when Jesus told them, they tried to kill Him because they did not want to hear the truth!

The Jews accused Jesus of blasphemy "because You, a mere Man, claim to be God."

Jesus stunned them with a quote from the Psalms: "Is it not written in your Law, 'I have said you are gods'? If He called them 'gods' to whom the Word of God came—and the Scripture cannot be broken—what about the One whom the Father set apart as His very own and sent into the world?" (vv. 34-36) If those who receive the Word are exalted by the Lord Himself and called "gods," how much more deserving of that name is the One who *is* the Word?

The passage Jesus quoted is Psalm 82:6, "I say, 'You are "gods"; you are all sons of the Most High.' " The life Jesus offers us is eternal life, God's life. When we receive Jesus, we become the sons of God.

As Peter put it, "You are sons of God now; the live, permanent Word of the living God has given you His own indestructible heredity" (1 Peter 1:23, PH). Unable to grasp grace, the Pharisees and other leaders had no concept of what a personal relationship with God meant. They were no more able to understand the gift Jesus offered than they could imagine God could care enough for human beings to become a Man in order to bring us to Himself.

But while the leaders continued to try to arrest Jesus (John 10:39), many others heard in Jesus the voice of God, and began to believe.

The Resurrection, Now: John 11

Jesus now moved to a culminating miracle, a final demonstration of His ultimate authority as God's Son.

During Jesus' public ministry Christ had been very close to Mary and Martha and their brother, Lazarus. When Lazarus became seriously ill, the sisters sent a message to Jesus: "Lord, the one You love is sick." But to the amazement of the disciples, Jesus seemed to make no response. He stayed where He was for two more days before He set out with the Twelve for Bethany. When they arrived, Lazarus was dead and buried, just as Jesus had told His disciples he would be.

Martha rushed out to meet Jesus and, in tears, cried, "Lord, if You had been here, my brother would not have died."

Jesus consoled her. "Your brother will rise again."

Martha thought she understood what Jesus was saying. "I know he will rise again in the resurrection at the last day."

But Christ's words rearranged her thinking. "I am the Resurrection and the Life," Jesus said. "Do you believe this?"

Then Jesus went to Lazarus' grave. When He told the bystanders to roll away the great rock that sealed the cave, Martha objected. "But Lord, by this time there is a bad odor, for he has been there for four days."

Jesus demonstrated that His resurrection power was not limited to sometime in the future, but that His power to bring life knows no limits. "Lazarus, come out!" And, at Jesus' word, the man appeared in the cave doorway, still wrapped with the embalming linens. "Take off the graveclothes, and let him go," Jesus commanded.

This miracle stunned nearby Jerusalem. Many came to see Lazarus, and many believed. But the chief priests were still unmoved. They could not deny Jesus' signs. But what they could do was to act immediately on the high priest's pronouncement: "It is better for you that one man die for the people than that the whole nation perish" (v. 50). From that day on, the authorities plotted with renewed determination to execute Jesus.

Then Jesus withdrew and waited. Waited for the Passover, when He would go up to Jerusalem again and, as the Good Shepherd, would die for the sheep. Then Jesus would be restored on the third day, to an endless life.

What is the meaning of the resurrection of Lazarus for us? The same as it was for the disciples and other witnesses in Bethany. *This event is a demonstration of Jesus' ability to make His resurrection power available to His people—now!*

It is one thing to believe that Jesus has the power to raise us up on the last day. He does and He will. But it's something else to realize that Jesus' power is unlimited now; that Jesus can bring new life to the deadened areas of our own personalities; that because of Jesus' power, we can risk taking actions that we might otherwise never have the courage to take. We need never draw back from anything God asks, for the unlimited power of new life is ours in Him.

♥ ***Link to Life: Youth / Adult***
Draw a square "box" on the chalkboard. Write above it "Resurrection power." Have your group members study John 11, and in the box *write down Martha's concept of this power which she did believe Jesus had.*
Then outside the box *sketch Lazarus' tomb. Point out that Martha believed Jesus had power to bring life, but wrongly limited His exercise of lifegiving power to the future.*
Ask your group members to imagine something in their own lives that they have assumed lies outside the realm of Jesus' exercise of power. Then erase the box, *and read Romans 1:4, which says Jesus was "declared* with power *to be the Son of God by His resurrection from the dead." Even more than Lazarus' return to physical life, Jesus' own resurrection affirmed that He* now *has all power. Nothing in our lives is beyond His power to transform and to change.*
Give your group members time to meditate on this fact, and to praise Jesus that His power is available now.

The Hour Has Come: John 12

As this chapter opens, it is only six days until the Passover and Jesus' crucifixion. Jesus repeated the truths He had been stressing, and we are given a special insight into how Jesus Himself felt as the tension grew. We will also see in brief vignettes the reactions of those around Jesus.

Prepared for burial (John 12:1-8). At the home of Mary and Martha, Jesus was anointed with an expensive ointment as a sign of life. Mary did not know it, but the ointment (one used in embalming) expressed not only her love but the love of God, soon to be shared as Jesus gave up His life for us.

♥ ***Link to Life: Children***
The story of Mary's gift, and of Judas' reaction, contrasts two attitudes. "I love and give," and "I want it for myself."
Draw on the board a smiling face on the left, and then a mean, frowning face on the right.
Tell the story, with Mary represented by the smiling face and Judas by the frowning one. Then talk about these questions:
"Why is Mary smiling? (It makes us feel good to give, love makes us happy, etc.) Why is Judas frowning? (Selfishness makes us mean, etc.)" Also talk about which of these two people would have more friends, and why. Which would please God, and why?
Finally, let the boys and girls list under each fact things they do or might do that are like Mary, or like Judas.

Triumphal Entry (John 12:9-19). The next day Jesus entered Jerusalem to the cheers of the crowds. His entry fulfilled prophecy and seemed to the elders and priests evidence that "the whole world has gone after Him."

But Jesus' sudden popularity was rooted in the spectacular sign of the raising of Lazarus, not in true faith. A celebrity for a day in our society realizes how quickly such popularity disappears. The Triumphal Entry was an evidence of curiosity and enthusiasm, but not of faith.

Inner anguish (John 12:20-33). The pressure on Jesus in view of His approaching suffering was great. Still He remained firm in His commitment: "What shall I say? 'Father, save Me from this hour'? No, it was for this very reason I came to this hour. Father, glorify Your name."

There are several important spiritual principles in this brief section. It is through death that new life comes; a seed loses its individual identity to become the source from which many grains grow. In the holding onto one's life in this world, we will ultimately lose it. But the person who is willing to follow Jesus' example, turning away from those things that would only be for his own benefit and serving others as Jesus did, will find the true meaning of life. And will find fulfillment. So Jesus warned, "Whoever serves Me must follow Me." The example Jesus set in His death is one we are to follow in our lives.

What then will be the benefits of Jesus'

death? He will destroy the power of the ruler of this world (Satan), and will "draw all men to Myself."

In His death Jesus glorified God by bringing you and me into fellowship with Him.

They did not believe (John 12:34-43). Then the crowd that had just cheered Jesus as their King showed the shallowness of their allegiance. They rejected what Jesus said about Himself: "We have heard from the Law [the Old Testament] that the Christ will remain forever, so how can You say, 'The Son of man must be lifted up'?"

The people were still unwilling to submit themselves to Jesus as the Son of God. They insisted that their will, not God's, dominate. The passage says, "Even after Jesus had done all these miraculous signs in their presence, they still would not believe in Him." And those who *did* believe kept their faith secret because they feared the Pharisees and wanted human acceptance (vv. 42-43).

The final choice (John 12:44-50). Jesus said again what He had been teaching among them for months. But this was their last chance. Jesus would not speak to the crowds again.

What did Jesus say?

- I am the revealer of the Father.
- Belief in Me is belief in the Father.
- Whoever believes in Me will no longer live in darkness.
- If you reject Me, you reject the eternal life offered you by the Father.
- If you reject Me, you place yourself under sure judgment.

The living Word has spoken. Now is the time to respond, and to receive life through the Word.

In Summary

The repetition in John's Gospel is there for a purpose. No one must miss the central issues of life and death which Jesus raised. These are issues that you and I face today just as surely as the people of Israel had to face them.

Jesus, the Good Shepherd, revealed the loving heart of the Father. For the first time you and I realize how complete God's concern for us is: He will lay down His life for His sheep.

Jesus, in the incident at Bethany, also showed us the full extent of God's power. The eternal life Christ offers brings us a resurrection power that operates *now*. God is able to bring life even to the dead areas in our personalities today.

But we must respond with faith to the voice of God. Unlike the men and women of Jesus' day who held back, we need to hear in Jesus the voice of the Good Shepherd, and choose to follow Him.

TEACHING GUIDE

Prepare

Find in a concordance references to shepherds in Psalms, Isaiah, and Ezekiel. What do you discover there that helps you to better understand Jesus as your Shepherd?

Explore

1. Begin by concentrating on the imagery of the sheep and shepherd that has proven so powerful an image to God's people. Use the "link-to-life" idea on pages 733-734, which suggests direct study of the text of John 10 by group members.
2. Or provide your group members with a list of references to shepherds found in Psalms, Isaiah, and Ezekiel. Use a concordance to find the verses. Divide into teams, with each team looking at a different Old Testament book.

What do they learn about the relationship between God and His people through this image? What do they learn about their own relationship with Jesus?

Expand

1. You will probably want to take the rest of group time to look at the power incident reported in John 11. The resurrection of Lazarus reminds us, as it did Mary, that there are *no* limitations of time or space on the power of Jesus. Use the "link-to-life" idea on page 735 to help each group member remove any personal limits he or she may have unconsciously placed on the power of Jesus to touch deadened places in each life.

Apply

Read aloud John 12:44-50. Ask each to consider, and then share, what this last, powerful public statement of Jesus says to him or her personally.

STUDY GUIDE 114

John 13:1–15:17

JESUS' LAST WORDS

Overview
These chapters contain part of the extended private teaching that Jesus gave His disciples the evening before His crucifixion. It is commonly called the Last Supper Discourse. It is important, for here we find specific teaching on how Jesus' people are to relate to God and others during the Church Age.

Of particular importance is Jesus' emphasis on the Holy Spirit, and the role He is to play when Jesus has returned to the Father.

▶ ***Holy Spirit.*** The personality of the Spirit is taught in John 15:26. He is linked to both Father and Son, is the subject of a verb (testify) that implies personal action, and is given a name—Counselor. The Spirit's role in this age is so important that Jesus told His followers, "It is for your good that I am going away" for the Counselor could not come until after Christ's death, resurrection, and ascension. The Bible tells of a number of things that the Spirit does for and in believers. He is the Agent in our inner transformation toward Christlikeness (2 Cor. 3:17-18; Gal. 5:22-23). His presence provides the power we need to live a righteous life (Rom. 8:2-11; Gal. 5:5-6). He is the Source of our gifts and abilities to minister to others and enrich them spiritually (1 Cor. 12). How important that we learn to live in harmony with the Spirit, thus letting Him produce in us the fruit of love, joy, peace, and true goodness.

Commentary
Television's "60 Minutes" told the story of a nurse who works with the dying. She counsels the terminally ill patient, helps him or her face death, and plans with the family how to make the patient's last weeks or months most meaningful. Usually, as the end approaches, the patient wants to return home to spend the final days with family and friends.

As we reach these chapters in John's Gospel, we can sense a similar feeling. The mood changes. The sharp tone of conflict is muted. No Pharisee intrudes here. Instead we sense only tenderness and a strange sort of peace. Strange, because Jesus' life is now measured not by months or weeks but by hours. Jesus chose to spend the last hours on earth with His own. To His own—and to you and me—Jesus explains how to practice the presence of, and to know intimate fellowship with, God.

Prelude: John 13:1-30
The introduction to this most intimate scene in any of the Gospels features Judas. When he left the table, only those who loved Jesus remained. Only they would hear Jesus' words of comfort and triumph, spoken in a private room, shut away from doubting crowds and angry enemies.

Judas. Judas represented everyone to whom Jesus offers light and life, and who refuse to respond with faith.

Judas was one of the original Twelve. At the beginning, Jesus chose Judas to be with Him in His public ministry. Like the other disciples, Judas saw Jesus' miracles and heard His teaching. Judas drew close in those private times when Jesus explained His words to the Twelve alone. Judas, along with the other disciples, had often watched Jesus slip away before dawn to commune with the Father.

Yet Judas had failed to respond. Outwardly he looked like one of Jesus' followers. He acted like them. He talked like them. The other 11 did not suspect his inner core of sin and unbelief. But it was there, just as the greed and the uncaring attitude he shared with the Pharisees was always there.

Soon the hidden heart of Judas would be

revealed as he opened his personality to Satan's influence, and engaged in history's ultimate crime: he agreed with Jesus' enemies to betray the Lord to them for 30 pieces of silver—the price established in the Old Testament as payment for the death not of a freeman but of a slave!

Judas was later remorseful over the great betrayal. Filled with horror, Judas returned the money to the temple treasury and the priests. "I have betrayed innocent blood," he cried.

Under the Law, priests were charged with comforting and cleansing the sinner, but these priests responded with characteristic indifference. "What is that to us? That's your responsibility" (Matt. 27:4).

Frantic, Judas ran to the edge of one of the cliffs on which Jerusalem stands. With shaking hands he tied a piece of old rope around the limb of a tree . . . around his own neck . . . and threw himself out into space. The rope jerked, stretched . . . and broke. Judas fell to his death on the jagged rocks below (cf. Matt. 27:1-10 with Acts 1:18).

Even when he finally faced his own guilt, Judas still would not turn to Jesus for the forgiveness Christ had spoken of so often during the years they were together.

Judas proved he could wear a mask of piety. He could fit in outwardly even with the most sincere of Jesus' followers. But like the Pharisees, Judas' inner life was evil. He shared their lust for wealth, and he shared their lack of concern for other men and women. Finally, when Judas' betrayal of Jesus exposed his guilt even to himself, Judas still refused to respond to grace. Death seemed preferable to humbly bowing before Jesus, to beg forgiveness at His hands.

How good that Judas need not set the pattern for you and me! We can acknowledge our guilt freely, and trust ourselves to God's grace. We can come to the God each of us has betrayed, and find in Jesus Christ, God's Son, full and free forgiveness. And in Jesus we can find life; a life that fills our personality, remakes our attitudes and desires, and teaches us to reflect to others God's own love.

An example (John 13:1-20). Jesus "loved His own," the passage begins. It then goes on to describe a foot-washing. Clad only in a light robe, Jesus took a basin of water and began to wash His disciples' feet.

Peter was deeply upset. Jesus, his Lord, stooping to serve him like a common household slave! Never!

But Jesus insisted, and later explained. The simple ritual (1) reflected a great theological truth, (2) gave His followers an example, and (3) helped show how we today are to relate to the strangers who slip in among us.

(1) The theological truth. In the ancient world a person might bathe at home or in public baths. After such a thorough cleansing, he would strap on his sandals and walk the dusty streets. When a person entered a friend's house, a servant would wash the film of dust and dirt from his feet. The body was clean, but the feet, having been in contact with the world, needed constant cleansing.

In answer to Peter's objection, and then to his request that Jesus wash "not just my feet but my hands and my head as well," Jesus pointed out that Peter had already been cleansed (bathed). All that was required now was the continued washing away of the dust that might accumulate from traveling in the streets.

Many commentators take this exchange to suggest that in salvation, believers are completely cleansed. But in our daily life we may pick up contaminations that require Jesus' continual washings (forgiveness). "A person who has had a bath needs only to wash his feet; his whole body is clean. And you are clean," Jesus explained (v. 10).

(2) The example. Jesus went on to explain that His actions set an example—an object lesson in humility. If the disciples' Teacher and Lord stooped to wash their feet, they should have no hesitation to stoop and serve one another. "I tell you the truth, no servant is greater than his master, nor is a messenger greater than the one who sent him." Humbling ourselves to serve each other is Jesus' way to greatness.

♥ ***Link to Life: Children***
Children can learn early the joy of helping in little ways. Help your boys and girls make out "servant for a day" gift certificates for Mom. The certificates are to be good for one day that week. Talk about the little things they can do to help. Set the table. Not throw clothes or books on the floor when they come in from school. Fetch things Mom needs. Pick up their rooms—and

even a brother or sister's! The basic attitude of Jesus, His willingness to serve, can be encouraged in the young as well as the adult.

(3) The challenge. It's striking to realize that Judas was one of those whose feet Jesus washed. The betrayer was served in the same way as the faithful, and through it all, Jesus knew who was going to betray Him.

How is this an example and a challenge to us? You and I know there will be those in a fellowship of believers who have not yet responded to Jesus' message of forgiveness. Will they respond, or will they prove to be like Judas? Should we try to root them out or make distinctions in the way we treat the "true" brothers, and "false"? Never! Within the fellowship of faith we are to serve brother and Judas alike, even as Jesus stooped to wash all of their feet in that Upper Room.

The betrayer departs (John 13:21-30). Jesus identified the one who would betray Him by dipping a piece of bread in broth and handing it to Judas, saying, "What you are about to do, do quickly." The others didn't understand. They thought Jesus was sending Judas out to make a purchase for the festival. Instead, Jesus was releasing Judas to do what he had already determined to do. "As soon as Judas had taken the bread, he went out." The Bible adds, "And it was night."

♥ ***Link to Life: Youth / Adult***

Foot-washing is practiced by some Christian fellowships today. But most of us have never experienced the ritual. It has a powerful emotional impact on most, as one person takes the role of servant to another.

Holding a foot-washing can be a powerful way to open or conclude a group study or class. Have each person read the description of the event in John's Gospel, and meditate quietly on it. Then bring out a basin of warm water and towels, and begin to wash the feet of your group members, saying, "As Jesus washed the feet of the disciples, I am willing to serve you."

Or, as a variation, wash the feet of one, let him or her wash the feet of the person next to him, etc. Each should repeat the same formula.

Afterward debrief (talk about the experience). How did each person feel about having his or her feet washed? About washing another's feet? Why was this such a powerful example to the disciples? What can we learn from John's report of that first foot-washing?

The New Community: John 13:31–14:31

Within the Upper Room, the vision of a new community was being shaped. In the last few hours of His life on earth, Jesus sketched for His friends a picture of a future that they—and we—are to experience. It's important to realize that this revelation is for us. Here is a picture of your life and mine as Christians, a picture of our experience in Christ. The key to this experience is *relationship:* relationship with each other as members of a new community, and relationship with Jesus, the Enabler of the new community. Of all the words Jesus could have spoken in that last brief time with His own, these are the words He chose to share. How eagerly we, like the disciples, lean forward to hear each one.

The foundation (John 13:31-35). The foundation of Jesus' new community is a unique relationship. Here is how Christ explained it: "A new command I give you: Love one another. As I have loved you, so you must love one another. All men will know that you are My disciples if you love one another."

These are familiar words, yet strange ones. Love is nothing new; the Old Testament speaks often of love and reminds us to "love your neighbor as yourself."

But on closer examination, there are several things here that *are* new. The Old Testament spoke of loving our neighbors: Jesus focused on loving "one another." We who are Jesus' disciples are still to love our neighbors. But we have been welcomed in Christ into a new, intimate relationship with other believers! In Christ, we have become brothers and sisters, members of a single family (see Eph. 2:19; 3:6). In Christ, our relationship with each other is suddenly more intimate than any human relationship has ever been! In the closeness of our new relationship with God and with each other, love takes on a new savor—and a new necessity.

There is also a new standard by which to measure love. Love of neighbor was to be "as you love yourself." But here we are told to love each other "as I have loved you." Love as Jesus did? Love with a love that *gives* self? Yes, this is new. My brother becomes more important to me than I am!

Finally, there is a new outcome. The Christlike love that permeates the new community of Christian brothers and sisters is a witness to the world that Jesus is real. Only Jesus' living presence can explain such love for others.

This context of a loving community is vital in all that Jesus goes on to explain in these next chapters of John's Gospel. It is in the context of a new community marked off by love that all Jesus outlines can, and will, become a reality.

♥ ***Link to Life: Youth / Adult***

Work with your group to develop "love is" statements. Explain that love can be defined lexically (by words, as in a dictionary). But love can also be defined behaviorally (by describing love in action). God's love is often defined this latter way: we know the love of God through His act of sending His Son to die for us.

Give teams of four or five the task of completing at least 10 "love is" statements, making sure that each statement describes a specific act. For instance, "Love is helping" is not *acceptable; "Love is helping a neighbor clean a driveway on a cold, snowy morning" is. Your goal is to have the group stay away from abstractions, to give very specific descriptions of actions that communicate love.*

After five minutes or so list definitions on the chalkboard. Then explain the criteria of Christian love that Jesus outlined in John 13: it is a family love for "one another," it is a "like Jesus" kind of love, and it has the impact of witnessing to Jesus' reality in the faith community.

Then divide into pairs, and ask each person to share about one time when he or she has experienced this kind of love from another person, and what that experience of love meant to him or her. After sharing, a person can volunteer to tell his or her experience—or the partner's—to the whole group.

♥ ***Link to Life: Children***

Boys and girls can play "love is" too. Follow the instructions for adults. Boys and girls will come up with "love is" statements that reflect their own level of thinking.

After they come up with their definitions of love, ask if they know many people who are like that. Go on to describe other things those people do that show they are loving.

Formed while Jesus is away (John 13:36–14:31). The new community is rooted in relationship with Jesus, but not in the same kind of relationship that the disciples had experienced those past three or so years. Instead, Jesus would be away, physically, as the new community took shape.

But how could a community be formed around Jesus when He was not present? That issue nags at us today even as it troubled the early disciples. How are we to experience Jesus and God the Father when our Lord is not *here?*

**Trust (13:36–14:7).* Jesus' announcement that He was going and the disciples could not follow shook the 11. Peter promptly swore that he would follow Jesus even to death. Thomas puzzled over where Jesus might hide, and how they would ever find their way to that place. None caught the implications of death and resurrection that we can see so clearly now.

Even so, we can understand the fears that surged up at Jesus' announcement. Sometimes we too feel deserted and alone. When we do, Jesus' words can comfort us even as they comforted the 11. "Do not let your hearts be troubled," Jesus encouraged. He went on to explain two things: while He was absent, Jesus would be with the Father, preparing a place for each disciple and for the community. Then He would return and "take you to be with Me that you also may be where I am." Jesus' absence is temporary and purposive; while He is gone, we are to trust Him.

It's not necessary for us to know the location or to see the star charts that pinpoint the location of our Father's house. Knowing Jesus is enough. He is the Way, the Truth, and the Life.

Here, then, is our first instruction. Remember that knowing and trusting Jesus is enough.

♥ ***Link to Life: Children***

The idea of "going to heaven" is hard for children to grasp. But its effects are much like a person moving to another state: in each case the person is "alive" (in the sense of being a living, conscious person), and in each case we have no daily contact with him or her.

Use a real map or draw an outline of the United States. Ask your boys and girls to tell about friends or relatives who have moved away. Do they miss them? Do they ever write? Or visit?

After letting the children talk, ask: "Where do you think 'heaven' is?" (Let the boys and girls make suggestions.) "Do you know anyone who is in heaven?"

Again let the children share. Then explain that just as friends in another state haven't stopped existing because we don't see them anymore, so friends and loved ones who die still exist, even though we don't see them. One day we will die, and because we love Jesus we will be in heaven too, and meet all the friends and loved ones who have died before us.

**Prayer (14:8-14)*. In the Upper Room, Philip still was troubled. "Show us the Father," he begged.

Jesus answered that they had been shown the Father already, in Him! "Anyone who has seen Me has seen the Father." But then Jesus went on to note that even if Philip was unable to *see* God in Jesus' personality, the works God did through Jesus witnessed to the Father's presence. "Believe Me when I say that I am in the Father and the Father is in Me; or at least believe on the evidence of the miracles themselves."

What is important here is to note that while the Father was not present, He expressed Himself in the world through Jesus' actions, words, and character. So God does not need to be physically present to act in our world. Nor will Jesus need to be physically present in order to be a part of and act through the new community. In fact, Jesus promised, "Anyone who has faith in Me will do what I have been doing." Just as the Father acted in Jesus, so Jesus will act in believers.

It is in this context of complete confidence that Jesus tells us to pray. "And I will do whatever you ask in My name, so that the Son may bring glory to the Father. You may ask Me for anything in My name, and I will do it."

This is our second instruction for life in the new community. We are to expect Jesus to continue to act in this world and are invited to bring *everything* to Him in prayer, confident that He will answer.

**Following (14:15-31)*. The third instruction for life in the new community involves responsive obedience. Jesus promised He would send the Holy Spirit as a Counselor "to be with you forever." The Spirit is identified as the "Spirit of Truth," who will give insights to believers which are not available to people who do not belong to Jesus. As the Spirit teaches and brings to our minds the commandments of Christ, and as we obey, we will experience Jesus' presence in our lives. Jesus promised: "If anyone loves Me, he will obey My teaching. My Father will love him, and We will come to him and make Our home with him."

Finally, we are told that through the Spirit's presence we will find peace. This peace is not the kind of peace the world offers; it is a peace that frees us from anxiety and fear, in spite of anything that may happen.

Insights

There are many riches in these chapters that invite deep consideration; more consideration than we can give as we trace the teachings of John's Gospel in an overview. But here are a few for your meditation.

In Jesus' name (John 14:13). Asking "in Jesus' name" means more than simply tacking words on at the end of a prayer. To Old and New Testament people one's name was inextricably tied to his character and mission. Thus prayer is to be "according to His will and instruction, in order that the commission may be fulfilled" (Colin Brown, *New International Dictionary of New Testament Theology*, Zondervan). The "anything" we are invited to ask includes all things that can be identified with the kind of person Jesus is, and the grace He gives.

No wonder the Father will be glorified in answering prayers offered in Jesus' name. In the answers to such prayers the character of God Himself will continue to be revealed.

Jesus' presence (John 14:24). How can we experience Jesus' presence when He cannot be sensed, or seen by others? Where *will* we find Him now that He has gone? Jesus had already promised that He would be with His followers in the person of the Spirit. In this passage Christ explained that we will *know His presence experientially* when love finds expression as obedience.

There's a beautiful and delicate emphasis here. It is not outward conformity to rules that God seeks. God cares rather about a responsive inner attitude, a commitment to act on Jesus' words. We sense that "the" commandments are now "My" commandments, that the Spirit and Scripture's communication are deeply personal whisperings of our loving God. They are directions that lead us to joy and to fellowship.

What can so move us to see the personal nature of God's Word? Love. As we love Jesus, we respond to His commands. As we obey, we draw closer to Him. Step by step, as our love finds growing expression in obedience, we journey toward the Lord. And then, *we find Him*, and realize that He has been with us all the time! What a joy to experience the reality of God manifesting Himself within us.

If there is not love, there will be no inner response leading to obedience. And without the response of obedience, love will die. When love has died, then, like people of the world, we will see Him no more.

Power for the New Life: John 15:1-17
The new community of Jesus asks us to adopt a lifestyle far beyond our capacity. Knowing this, Jesus then explained how a life of fruitfulness is possible for human beings. The fruit Jesus promised here is, of course, the fruit of the Spirit, who will soon settle down into the disciples' lives. The "love, joy, peace, patience, kindness, goodness, faithfulness, gentleness, and self-control" Paul lists (Gal. 5:22-23) are promised in these chapters of John.

Where does the fruit grow? On a living vine, of course. Branches (and this is how we believers are pictured in Jesus' illustration) are unable to bear fruit by themselves. They must be connected to the vine. Roots and trunk support the life of the branch, and only the branch "remaining in" the vine has the potential for fruitfulness.

Several questions are asked about this passage in Scripture. They range from an eager, "What is *remaining in?*" to a fearful, "What does it mean to be thrown away and wither, especially with the reference to gathering branches and throwing them into the fire?" Let's look at these two typical concerns and then return to the great promise of fruitfulness.

Remain in Me (John 15:4). This often-repeated exhortation is explained here as well as in John 14. If we keep Jesus' commandments, we will remain in His love (15:10). As His words take shape and form in our personalities, as we experience for ourselves the goodness of God's will, we will live in the center of His love. Living close to Jesus is part of remaining in Him.

Thrown away (John 15:6). The simile of the vine and branches focuses on fruitfulness, and does not refer to salvation. This is why the text carefully says, "He is *like a branch* that is thrown away."

In any living vine the function of a branch is to bear fruit. But it cannot fulfill its purpose unless it remains in intimate connection with the vine. Without that intimate "remaining in Me" relationship, it will never accomplish what it was designed for. How empty will the life of a Christian who fails to remain in Jesus be? As empty as that of a branch torn from the vine; it has no potential for fruit bearing. Its only use would be to serve as fuel to provide momentary warmth; then it must disintegrate into ash.

The warning is clear. We cannot become what we are intended to be without having a close relationship with Jesus, with our love for Him expressed in obedience to Him. How tragic if you or I, branches now, fail to experience the joy that comes as we fulfill our potential for bearing fruit. How tragic if, after life is over, we can point to nothing but ashes.

The promise. But this paragraph is not meant to depress us. It's meant to excite us and to give us joy. *Because we are branches, we can draw life from Jesus the Vine!* What we cannot do by ourselves, Jesus can accomplish in us! The fruit of love, joy, peace, patience, kindness, goodness, faithfulness, gentleness, self-control—all these are possible now. As we live in Him, we will become fruitful. As we remain in Jesus, we will become the kind of people who can make the new community a reality here on earth.

How natural then that Jesus would return to this new-community theme. "This is My command," He repeated. "Love each other." We are Jesus' friends; we are enabled by His Spirit, empowered by His own life flowing through us; and we can fulfill His command to love one another.

♥ ***Link to Life: Youth / Adult***
Jesus chose a vine and branches to show us the way to a life of fruitfulness. Have your group members study John

15:1-17, and think of the nature of a vine and branches, to complete together the chart that lists and explains the analogies.

Jesus is like the vine in that . . .	I am like a branch of a vine in that . . .

TEACHING GUIDE

Prepare
Read through John 14 and 15, underlining any phrases that are particularly significant to you.

Explore
Begin with a foot-washing ceremony, as suggested in the "link-to-life" idea on page 740.

Expand
1. The key to life in the Christian community is love. So spend time working with your group members to deepen their understanding of the meaning of Jesus' "new commandment." The "link-to-life" suggestion on page 741 is designed to help your group members first define love, and then share ways in which they have experienced Christian love.
2. Or focus on Jesus' simile of the vine and branches as a way to express our relationship with Him. Use the approach outlined on pages 743-744. Then, if you have extra time, let your group members look for clues on how to "abide" in John 13 and 14.

Apply
Determine one way to love someone near you "as I have loved you," and so keep Christ's new commandment.

STUDY GUIDE 115

John 15:18–17:26

JESUS' LAST WORDS (CONTINUED)

Overview

These chapters, containing the last words of Jesus to His disciples and a lengthy prayer, are extremely significant, for they focus on the lifestyle of disciples, and on the church. Here we find out more of how we are to live with one another. And here, especially, we begin to see how we are to live as Christ's people in an often hostile world.

These chapters are so significant that literally hundreds of books have been written about them. I have one book of over 400 pages on John 17 alone. It has been suggested that every truth which has been developed by the apostles in the New Testament letters is here, in seed, in Jesus' Last Supper Discourse.

▶ ***Be One.*** John 17 stresses Christ's desire for believers to "be one as We are One." This has been taken as a prayer for Christian unity, and an argument for denomination unification.

A careful study of the chapter, however, makes it clear that what Jesus prays for is that we might experience our union with Him, even as He had experienced His own union with God the Father throughout His life on earth. Through faith we *are* united with Jesus, linked to Him in an unbreakable bond. But we must experience that union by living in responsive obedience, for the One to whom we are united is God.

■ See the *Bible Knowledge Commentary,* pages 326-334, for verse-by-verse commentary on this passage.

Commentary

Believers across the ages have yearned for the new community Jesus described to His disciples in the Upper Room. We long for the loving fellowship, the humility expressed in foot-washing, the deep experience of Jesus' presence, the sense of remaining in Him.

Some have found this ideal impossible to reach in society, and so they have formed separate communities. The monastery of the Middle Ages and the commune of the twentieth century often have been attempts to withdraw from carnal Christians or from the pollution of pagan culture.

But in these chapters (John 13–17) we do not hear Jesus advocate withdrawal. He calls us to involvement! The Christian does not experience Christ by removing himself from the world; we experience Christ *in* the world, though we are distinctly not *of* the world.

The World

John painted reality boldly, with vividly contrasting concepts. He showed us life versus death, grace versus law, light versus dark. Then he contrasted Jesus' followers (a fellowship of love) with the world (a society of mere men).

The Greek word used here for "world" is *kosmos.* According to the Arndt and Gingrich *Greek/English Lexicon of the New Testament* (Bagsters and Son), *kosmos* has several meanings. It can refer to "the sum total of everything here and now" (the universe as a whole). Or it can refer to "all beings above the level of animals." In this usage it includes both men and angels, or may focus specifically on mankind. In a moral sense, "the world" refers to "that which is at enmity with God," that is, every thought and action, every value and behavior, that is tainted by sin (pp. 202-203).

In this moral sense, the New Testament portrays the world as far more than tainted: it is lost in sin, ruined, and depraved. It is hostile to God and godliness. The principles on which the world operates stand in dark contrast to divine righteousness and a godly life.

To grasp the difference between the two approaches to life, we must be born again. We must be transformed by the renewing of our minds (literally, "perceptions," or "perspective") (Rom. 12:1-3). Because the "whole world is under the control of the evil one" (1 John 5:19), we are to keep ourselves "from being polluted by the world" (James 1:27).

What the world identifies as "adult," we recognize as perversion. What the world praises as "success," we often must label failure. What the world views as the highest of values—material success, popularity, and so on—we recognize as emptiness. There is a deep and abiding antagonism between the society of unredeemed man and the community of Jesus' own.

Because this antagonism always exists, there are two great dangers the Christian continually faces. The first danger is conformity: "Don't let the world around you squeeze you into its own mold" (Rom. 12:2, PH). And John added this warning in his first epistle: "Do not love the world or anything in the world. If anyone loves the world, the love of the Father is not in him. For everything in the world—the cravings of sinful man, the lust of his eyes and the boasting of what he has and does—comes not from the Father but from the world" (1 John 2:15-16). The world's basic approach to life is twisted and perverted. We are to love the people of the world but decisively reject (and fear) the attitudes and values of the world.

The second danger for the Christian is withdrawal. If we do not recognize the world system for what it is, we may unknowingly adopt its lifestyle. When we do recognize the world system for what it is, we may be so repelled that we seek to escape it. This, of course, is the route taken by early monastics; it is the way of the Essenes in Old Testament times, and the way of the Qumran community. It is also the way of a distorted kind of separatism practiced by believers in many churches today. When Christians attempt to protect themselves from the practices of others, they frequently build a wall that rejects people and refuses relationships with those "outside."

The New Testament picture of the world challenges us with important questions. How do we relate to the society in which we live? Should we withdraw? Are there any other options? How do we relate to non-Christians who have only seen worldly values? How can we construct the new community within the ruins of man's society . . . or are we even supposed to try?

♥ ***Link to Life: Youth / Adult***

Before your group meets ask four members to prepare for a short debate, with two on each side of the question. The question: RESOLVED, conformity to the world is a greater danger to modern Christians than unhealthy withdrawal from it.

You may want to meet with each team, perhaps for lunch or coffee. Be sure each understands the meaning of "world," and talk about the various problems related to conformity and to withdrawal.

Before the debate begins, give a brief explanation to the other group members of "world" in its moral sense.

Love in the World: John 15:18–16:33

The last paragraph we studied (15:12-17) restated Jesus' command to His disciples: "Love each other." In the context of loving each other, lasting fruit will be produced, intimate relationship with Jesus will be experienced, prayer will be answered. Together we will experience new life. But how will the world respond to this radical new community that is founded on principles so opposed to its own lifestyle and views?

With antagonism (John 15:18-27). Christ immediately warns that as we learn to live out the new community, the world will react with hatred. "Keep in mind that it hated Me first," Jesus reminded the disciples. "If you belonged to the world, it would love you as its own. As it is, you do not belong to the world, but I have chosen you out of the world. That is why the world hates you."

Antagonism develops because light shows up darkness, and grace morality reveals the perversion of sin. Jesus went on to remind His followers that men had seen Him do "what no one else did." They had been forced to recognize their own works as sin and, consequently, "They have hated both Me and My Father."

This witness of Jesus to the Father continues in and through the Christians in the new community (vv. 26-27). God has taken us out of the world. At one time, we were part of that sinful system, and our lifestyles reflected its values. But in Christ we have been "chosen *out of* the world" and have been called to live a new life *in* the world. Our lives and our relationships with others are to be a visible, continuing testimony to God in our godless, hostile world.

Our witness to God will produce hatred and persecution at times. But God the Spirit will shine through our lives, declaring that God is life and love and light.

With persecution (John 16:1-15). At times the world's antagonism has led to persecution, oppression, and death of those who follow Jesus. This would soon be the experience of the 11. Jesus warned, "They will put you out of the synagogue; in fact, a time is coming when anyone who kills you will think he is offering a service to God."

How are we to understand and to respond to persecution—often in small things, but sometimes the ultimate that Christ described, being killed because we love Jesus? Jesus helped us understand by speaking of the advantage to us of His return to the Father. By going away, Jesus made it possible for the Father to send the Holy Spirit to us. When the Spirit came, He would take the witness of the Christian under persecution and use it to prove the world wrong (or, convince, convict) about sin, about righteousness, and about judgment. The world will *see the truth* in Christians, and though the world as a whole will not respond with faith, individuals will believe.

The Holy Spirit will open our hearts and minds to understand the ways and the truth of God. He will make clear to us what Jesus has said in the written Word. He will give us the wisdom we need to apply that Word on a daily basis and to live in responsive obedience to our Lord.

A little earlier I noted two wrong reactions of Christians to the world. We can see more clearly now why they are wrong. If we adopt the values and lifestyle of the world, if we conform to the world system, God is left without a witness to truth and life and grace. But if we withdraw and cut ourselves off from the world's people in order to develop separated communities, God is also left without a witness. *Only by living in the world—by being involved daily with the men and women around us, by being involved in the issues of our own times and society—can we show the contrast between human ways and God's ways.*

The natural response to persecution, to antagonism, to pressure, is to withdraw or to conform. But you and I, like Jesus, are to live under pressure. We are to open ourselves to hurt. We are to resist protecting ourselves and, instead, to expose ourselves, for God yearns to reveal His glory in our lives. As we learn to love each other, we will have the strength to become involved in the world and to find joy in our suffering, even as Jesus found joy in His. We will begin to love all men, even as Jesus loved us and gave Himself for us.

Prayer is a resource (John 16:16-33). It is all too easy in reading Jesus' warnings to become fearful or depressed and to feel that the Christian life is a burden almost too heavy to bear. Jesus had already pointed to some resources He had given: the Holy Spirit, and Jesus' own continuing guidance. Then Christ spoke of the resource of prayer.

Jesus Himself was soon to leave the 11. At first the events of the Crucifixion would create despair, but soon the disciples would know joy. "I will see you again," Jesus promised, "and you will rejoice, *and no one will take away your joy.*" Life in the world, in spite of hostility and persecution, is a life of secure joy.

How is joy possible? It is possible because *we are not cut off from Jesus!* We are free to bring every need to Him in prayer, and can be confident that He hears us. "My Father will give you whatever you ask in My name," Jesus said. "Until now you have not asked for anything in My name. Ask and you will receive, and your joy will be complete."

Where can we find joy in times of pressure and uncertainty? First, by acknowledging that each of our ministries and everything we possess is God's. Jesus is Lord, and everything I have and do is committed totally into His hands. If Jesus in grace chooses to use it for His glory, I rejoice. And if He chooses not to use it, but to bring all I have planned and worked to achieve to an end, He can use disaster too to glorify Himself—and I rejoice.

To know that Jesus lives, that He hears, and that He responds as we speak to Him, brings abiding joy whatever the pressures may be.

And so Jesus concluded His words to His disciples. "The Father Himself loves you because you have loved Me and have believed that I came from God." With this assurance, what have we to fear? "I have told you these things so that in Me you may have peace. In this world you will have trouble. But take heart! I have overcome the world."

Jesus *is* Lord.
And God loves us.
No wonder we have peace and joy.

♥ ***Link to Life: Youth / Adult***
Divide the group in half. Each half is to study John 15:18–16:33. One group is to look specifically for troubles and pressures we may experience as we live Christian lives in the world. The other is to look for resources that help us live joyfully and confidently in the world. Each study should take at least 20 minutes.

When completed, ask members of each group to share impressions: "What is it like to live for Jesus in this world?"

Members of the first group may have a negative outlook, while those in the second may display a positive outlook. Talk about any differences that emerge. How important that we focus not on the trials we will face, but on the resources God has provided that guarantee inner peace and joy.

Jesus' Prayer for Us: John 17

The intimate Upper Room experience concludes with Jesus' prayer. This is a prayer for us, His people in the world. "I will remain in the world no longer," Jesus said, "but they are still in the world."

Jesus had described the world's hostility that we will face. Now what will He ask for us? What is His deepest desire?

Glory (John 17:1-5). Jesus first spoke to the Father about Himself, thus giving us a model. "I have brought You glory on earth by completing the work You gave Me to do." This work finished, God would lift Jesus to His presence again and give His Son the glory that "I had with You before the world began."

We live in the world now, but this world is not the end! The end for us, as for Jesus, is glory in the very presence of the Father. The word "glory" speaks literally of brightness, splendor, radiance. Expanded to denote the majesty and sublimity of God, it carries a sense of magnificence and splendor. In the verb form it means more than "to praise or honor"; it means to "clothe in splendor."

With Jesus' work on earth finished, He returned to the Father to be clothed again with the splendor that was His from eternity past. For Jesus, life in this world had a purpose. Christ lived to reveal and to glorify God. But life in this world was only a momentary experience for Christ.

How good to know that for us as well, life in this world is only a momentary experience. Like Jesus, we will be lifted by the Father when our work here is accomplished. Then we too will be clothed in a splendor like Jesus' own. While we are on earth we may never know the glory God intends for us, but one day we will see Jesus, and then, "we shall be like Him, for we shall see Him as He is" (1 John 3:2). Our destiny is to be clothed with our Lord in splendor.

Manifest Your name (John 17:6-10). What is the work God has for us on earth? To be "great"? To be noted evangelists? To be famous teachers? To be known and respected by all? Hardly. God wants a very simple thing, which every believer, no matter how humble, can share in fully. *God wants us to manifest (make known) His name.* We have received Jesus' words (v. 8) and believed in Him. Now we are to live out those words on earth. The quality of our lives is what will make plain to those around us the character of God. Each of us can brighten the world around us by reaching out to others with a grace and love that are like God's own.

Sanctified (John 17:11-19). Christ then prayed that God will guard us while we live in the world's hostile environment. "My prayer is not that You take them out of the world but that You protect them from the evil one." He asked that we be sanctified by God's truth, that is, that we will be set apart to a holy way of life, and then "sent into the world" (v. 18). We are to not only witness to, but are to personally experience Christ's joy as we become more and more like Him. And we have Jesus' added promise that He consecrates Himself to aid our growth in godliness.

Reproductive (John 17:20-26). Jesus then emphasized the fact that He was not praying just for the 11 disciples, but for "those who will believe in Me through their message." You and I, and our local fellowships, along with all believers throughout the centuries are included in this great commitment of Jesus and His Father to all who belong to Them.

The society of those who belong to Jesus is a community that grows in love and then multiplies. Jesus is still reaching out, through you and me, to rescue men and women lost in sin.

There is, of course, one source and one source only for the strength we need to live a God-glorifying life. This is our union with Jesus Christ. Jesus lived in union with the Father, drawing on Him for strength and power. As we are "brought to complete unity" with Jesus and the Father, then the world will know that Christ has sent us and that He loves us still.

♥ ***Link to Life: Youth / Adult***

Ask each group member to read through Jesus' prayer, and underline specific requests. Then each is to determine one way that he or she can be an answer to Christ's prayer this coming week.

Then as a group work through the verses and phrases each person has underlined, to develop a shared understanding of what Christ has prayed for.

Finally, go around the group and ask each to share how he or she can personally be an answer to Jesus' prayer this week.

TEACHING GUIDE

Prepare

Use Jesus' prayer as a model as you pray for your group.

Explore

1. Launch class with a debate on the greatest danger to a Christian from the world: is it conformity to the ways and attitudes of the world, or a withdrawal from the world (a separation or isolation), which keeps us from having an influence on people around us and on our society? See "link-to-life," page 746, for hints on how to set up and conduct the debate.

2. Or make a copy of the italicized sentence in the commentary, page 747. Do your group members agree or disagree with this strong statement of a need for Christians to be involved in the world? What do your members think the author is asking for? (Ask for illustrations of good and bad involvement.) And, how are your group members currently acting out this kind of positive involvement that Jesus called for?

Expand

1. Living in the world is a constant challenge. Divide your group in halves to study John 15:18–16:33. One group will look at the problems, the other at the resources God has provided. See how to guide this activity by looking at "link-to-life," page 748.

2. Or study Jesus' High Priestly Prayer. You may want to begin with a minilecture, emphasizing the importance of living in union with Jesus (see *overview*). But then involve your group in an inductive study of this prayer, as suggested in "link-to-life," page 749.

Apply

Ask each person to write a prayer for his or her children (present or future) reflecting one important thing learned in this study.

Then share the prayers, by offering them to God.

STUDY GUIDE 116

John 18–21

GRACE AND GLORY

Overview
John's themes of grace and life, and his emphasis on light versus darkness, find special expression in the final chapters of his Gospel.

John, like the other Gospel writers, reported in graphic detail the events that are associated with the crucifixion and the resurrection of Jesus. By comparing the treatment of each of the Gospels, we have a more complete picture of this three-day span than of any other period in ancient history!

John's emphasis is on triumph—the triumph of truth, the victory of life over the dark powers of death. How good to be able to share this sense of victory with those we teach. And how good to realize that for us as well, the resurrection of Jesus is the guarantee of life throughout eternity.

▶ ***Truth.*** Pilate demanded of Jesus, "What is truth?" The passage shows how captive this Roman ruler was to pressures, how controlled by the demands of others. Without a sense of absolutes, and a certainty that there is right and wrong to guide our decisions, we would be just as wavering and tormented. Thank God there *is* truth—that we know reality as unveiled in the Word of God. We need to choose to live by that truth, rather than the uncertainties of expediency.

■ If there are any specific phrases you do not understand, see the *Bible Knowledge Commentary*, pages 334-346 for verse-by-verse comment.

Commentary
The time for words had now passed. Jesus had spoken much about grace and life and light. And also of the darkness that grips those who are of this world. Now, if anyone had questions, those questions were about to be answered decisively.

How deeply is the world entrenched in darkness? How great is God's love for us, and His grace to us? How vital is the life that Jesus offers? How bright is the light by which we are invited to live? The answer to each of these questions is found in the events of the final night and day of Jesus' life on earth . . . and in His resurrection.

A World Entrenched: John 18:1–19:22
Earlier we saw that the context of the last long segment of John's Gospel has a distinctive setting: night. The flickering light of a fire may have lit the Upper Room as Jesus sketched the vision of a new community for His followers. But outside, the forces of darkness were gathering. The hatred of Satan and the antagonism of the world swirled in a dark storm cloud, ready to extinguish the Light of the world.

The context for all the events reported in the next chapters of John's Gospel is darkness. Even Mary's first encounter with the risen Lord takes place "while it was still dark" (20:1). When Jesus appeared to the disciples who were gathered behind locked doors for fear of the Jews, it was evening (v. 19). The mood does not change until John 21:4, when Jesus stood on the shore waiting for His disciples, "early in the morning."

But as Jesus and His friends left the Upper Room for a time of prayer, we see how deep the darkness truly is.

Betrayal (John 18:1-11). Judas, one of Christ's most intimate friends for the past three years, led temple guards and an antagonistic mob to drag Jesus to judgment. At first Peter tried to resist, striking out with a weapon. But Jesus would permit no resistance. Darkness must have its hour.

Desertion (John 18:12-18, 25-27). Peter's act of resistance was a rash yet brave act. But what else can we expect? Hadn't Peter promised to follow Jesus even to the death? Then Jesus was bound and dragged to the high priest (who had already, before the trial, condemned Jesus to death—see v. 14).

Peter followed the crowd, but in the darkness and among Jesus' enemies, His courage faded. When he was accused by servants of being one of Jesus' companions, Peter, shivering in the cold of the dark night, cursed angrily and denied his Lord.

Peter had the courage for an impulsive act, but as the darkness deepened and pressed in around him, that courage drained away.

Illegal trial (John 18:19-24). Called before an illegally convened court, Jesus was questioned behind closed doors, beaten, and then sent away to the Roman authorities, who alone had the power to condemn a person to death. The other Gospels described this scene in more detail than John did. He seemed to turn from the final revelation of the dark hearts of those religious leaders who were the keepers of the written Word, but now were struggling to suppress its light.

Pilate's weakness (John 18:28-38; 19:1-16). If the religious authority was perverted, what of the secular? Rome had no quarrel with Jesus, who at this time had never confronted or challenged its rule. This is the judgment of Pilate the Roman governor, who announced, "I find no basis for a charge against Him."

Yet, pressured and threatened by the Jews he supposedly governed, Pilate ultimately gave in to expediency and permitted Jesus' crucifixion.

Historic research has suggested some of the possible pressure on Pilate. Tiberius, a sick and violent emperor, ruled Rome. But much of his power had been exercised by Suetonius, the commander of his Praetorian Guard. At last this man was overthrown and killed, and the ever-suspicious Tiberius had many of those who had relied on Suetonius' influence executed. Some have thought that Pilate was aligned with Suetonius' party, and thus was particularly vulnerable. If so, the threat of the Jews to denounce Pilate as "no friend of Caesar" must have been particularly terrifying.

Pilate had no commitment to truth. Though there was no basis in law for the execution of Jesus, Pilate did the expedient thing and chose to compromise his conscience. Jesus would die.

How dark the world is with injustice and fear when there is no commitment to truth.

The crowd's preference (John 18:39-40). It was the habit in those days to release a prisoner (often a political prisoner) at the Passover festival. Looking for a way to save Jesus, Pilate offered the Jews a choice. Which prisoner would they like released: Jesus, or Barabbas, an insurrectionist, murderer, and robber?

The power of darkness was revealed in the swelling cry, "No, not Him! Give us Barabbas!"

The Crucifixion (John 19:17-22). And so the final stage had been set. The degree to which the darkness blinds man's eyes to grace and life and light is about to be revealed.

Because of darkness, a false friend had betrayed the Lord. Because of darkness, a true follower had denied his Master. Because of darkness, men charged with communicating God's truth had turned with murder in their hearts, against the God they claimed to serve. Because of darkness, a man convinced of Jesus' innocence permitted Him to be tormented and crucified. Because of darkness, the crowd that cheered Jesus' entrance into Jerusalem now demanded His death and begged the release of a murderer. In the last events of Jesus' life the nature of sin and the extent to which it had perverted mankind was finally revealed.

In the normal course of events, the depth of the moral darkness in which man lives is disguised with good works, kindness, generosity, caring. But under pressure, under the kind of pressure placed on every actor in Jerusalem that last tense day, the superficial is stripped away. The love that costs us nothing to give is shown to be flimsy cover for selfishness and fear. Only the love of God in Jesus, who remains committed to the ultimate sacrifice, burns steadily and bright.

♥ ***Link to Life: Youth / Adult***

As group members arrive, have on the chalkboard: "What kinds of things do most people prefer to do in the dark? Why?"

Make a list of the group's suggestions. Then focus on items that have moral dimensions, and ask why these are associated with darkness.

Point out that the context of these chapters in John is one of darkness (cf. 13:30). Ask group members to select one person or group of persons (Judas, Peter, the high priest, Pilate, the crowd) to study. What do his or their actions tell us about the dark nature of sin, so powerfully exposed in the events associated with Jesus' crucifixion?

Then share discoveries, and as a summary statement read the last paragraph before this "link-to-life" suggestion.

The Grace of God: John 19:23-42

John's attention was now drawn to Christ Himself. Jesus had suffered the brutal beatings and the mocking that prepared prisoners for crucifixion. His hands and feet had been nailed to the wooden pole. Now Jesus hanged on it, between heaven and earth, His weight resting alternately on the torn flesh of His feet, then on His hands. Around Him indifferent soldiers gambled for His clothing while His enemies smirked in satisfaction at His agony.

Even here, though, we see God's grace revealed, especially as we note incidents reported by the other Gospel writers. Even hanging on the cross, Jesus continued to think of others.

He prayed for His murderers (Luke 23:34). He welcomed the repentant thief with the promise of paradise (v. 43). And John tells of His gentle commending of His mother to the care of the "beloved disciple" (John himself, the writer of this Gospel).

Finally, His suffering complete, Jesus released His spirit and died.

The body was taken down from the cross. A secret disciple, Joseph of Arimathea, and Nicodemus buried the body in a new tomb that had been hewn out of a wall of rock. It was again night.

But the day was at hand.

The Life: John 20

Jesus had often spoken about life and death, light and darkness, grace and Law. He had also claimed to be the ultimate revelation of God.

In His last days, Jesus showed Himself the ultimate revealer of mankind as well. How darkness grips the human heart is evident in the way men responded to Jesus as the Crucifixion drew near. Yet even on the cross Jesus' forgiving, caring concern gives ultimate proof of God's great love for humanity. Only divine love and divine grace can explain Jesus' willingness to sacrifice Himself for those who hate Him. The cross *proves* grace.

But how can life be proven? How can Jesus' claim, "I am the Resurrection and the Life," be demonstrated?

The answer, of course, is the Resurrection! Paul, looking back, saw that Jesus was "declared with power to be the Son of God by His resurrection from the dead" (Rom. 1:4).

The first glimmerings of the ultimate revelation of Jesus as Life came before dawn. Mary slipped into the garden early. She saw that the stone sealing the tomb had been jolted out of its track. In tears she ran to Peter to report that the body of Jesus had been stolen. Peter and John came running to the tomb. John arrived first and, bending over, peered inside. There on a stone shelf were the linen wrappings. John fell back; he must have felt relief as well as disappointment. Jesus' body had not been stolen. He was still there.

But Peter stooped low and entered the tomb. He saw that though the burial wrappings were still there, the body was gone. It was impossible! But it had happened.

John then entered, and realized that Jesus truly was gone. But, "they still did not understand from Scripture that Jesus had to rise from the dead" (v. 9).

Then the puzzle began to come together. Mary, who was now standing in the garden outside the tomb, met Jesus and realized who He was. That evening, 10 of the disciples were gathered in a room with locked doors because they were afraid of the Jewish rulers. Suddenly Jesus was there, standing among them! Later, Thomas heard their report but refused to believe. "Unless I see the nail marks in His hands and put my finger where the nails were, and put my hands into His side, I will not believe it," Thomas said.

Eight days later Jesus stood before Thomas and invited him to take that test. Convinced at the sight of his Master, Thomas cried out, "My Lord and my God!"

The ultimate power of life was demonstrated in the resurrection of Jesus. Because Jesus is the Life now and forever, the power of death, and the fear of death, associated as they are with sin and darkness, lie shattered and broken at His feet. Because He lives, we too shall live.

1.

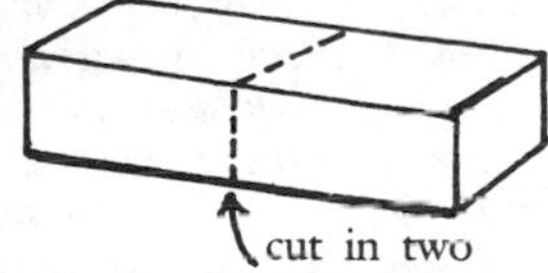

Cut shoebox and its top in two

2. Make construction paper "front" for tomb, cutting out "door" and "window," and folding up paper to make "track."

3. Cut out circle to represent the stone that rolled in the track.

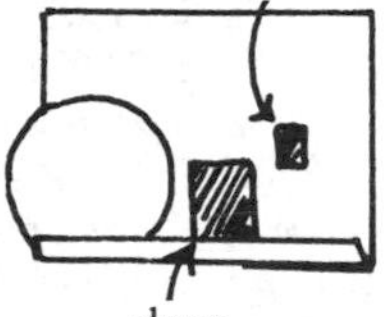

4. Use crayon to make tomb front and stone, and *also interior of shoebox,* seem stone-like (*tan* is the best color, with brown).

5. Attach to open front of shoebox, perhaps putting in cloth to represent empty grave clothes.

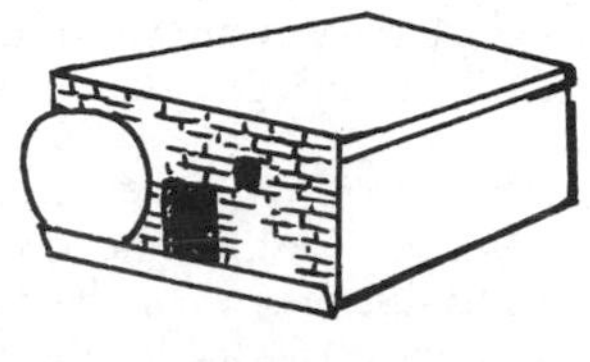

♥ ***Link to Life: Youth / Adult***
Thomas' resistance to faith is typical of the attitude held by many. Ask your group members to think back before their conversions and complete a statement like Thomas' that reflects their thinking then: "Unless _____, I will not believe."

Share the statements with each other. Then have each tell about his or her conversion. Did the "unless" happen? Or, as with Thomas, did something else awaken faith?

This should be a positive experience for any in your group who may not be Christians yet, who can be encouraged to express their "unless" and then be able to hear the others' conversion stories.

♥ ***Link to Life: Children***
Archeologists have learned much about the kind of tombs that were used in Jesus' time. The "new tomb" Jesus' body was placed in (19:41) was likely incomplete, with only the entry chamber and a room to its right finished. Many believe that the "Garden Tomb" in Jerusalem was the actual burial place of Jesus.

A major feature of New Testament tombs was the large stone disc, which rolled in a hewn track, to close the tomb. There was also a small opening which it covered, so small that John and Peter would have to "bend over" (20:5) to see inside.

You can help your boys and girls construct quite accurate paper models, or you can create a diorama to tell the story.

After telling the resurrection story, let your boys and girls "see" the empty diorama tomb, or play out the story with their paper model. Talk about how Jesus' friends had been so sad when He died. How did they feel when they discovered Jesus is alive? You may want to make up a class song about the Resurrection using words the boys and girls chose to describe the disciples' feelings in the lyrics. For instance, "Happy, happy, happy, Jesus is alive," can be one verse.

The Light: John 21
Even with Jesus' resurrection an established fact, the disciples were uncertain. What were they to do now? Confused, Peter and the others returned for a brief time to their old occupation of fishing, but with little success.

It is here John portrays the return of day. In the dawn's light, Jesus directed His disciples to cast their net on the right side of the boat. Suddenly the net filled with a shoal of fish, so many that the men were unable to haul them into their boat. When they returned to shore, the disciples found that Jesus had prepared fish and bread for their breakfast.

After the meal, Jesus spoke directly to Peter. Peter had denied his Lord three times. Now Jesus asked Peter three times, "Do you love Me?"

Three times Peter said, "Yes, Lord, You know that I love You."

And three times Jesus charged Peter,

"Feed My sheep," and, finally, "Follow Me."

Peter, ever impetuous, now asked what assignment the Lord had for John. Rebuking Peter gently, Jesus let him know that Christ alone will direct His disciples, and that disciples answer only to their Lord.

Think for a moment of what has been revealed in these few brief incidents. Jesus, the Light of the world, has again shown the disciples the path they are to walk, and that they are now to bring light into sin's dark realm.

In His resurrection glory, Jesus does continue to serve. He met the occupational needs of His disciples, even when the catch of fish was not necessary for their mission. Jesus stooped to prepare food for them. Jesus restored Peter to fellowship. Jesus helped Peter sense the completeness of his restoration, by telling him that he would be trusted with Jesus' own dearly loved sheep. Peter would now give his life to free, support, and care for other believers.

Jesus also taught that each individual's goal is personal responsiveness to the Lord. Christ will direct each believer into the avenue of service for which he or she has been equipped.

Finally, Jesus showed that in our concern for others we are not to judge them (21:22), but rather are to give each of our brothers and sisters the freedom, and encouragement to be responsive to Jesus as Lord.

For Jesus says, "Follow Me."

How gently Jesus' words echo across the centuries. Jesus, the Light of the world, began a great revelation of God. And Jesus *continues* that unveiling of the grace, the life, and the light in you and me.

♥ ***Link to Life: Children***
Boys and girls are able to make a heart response to Jesus as Saviour. We cannot "program" this response. And we should not manipulate children into a "profession of faith" that they do not understand. What can we do then? We can share the story of Jesus, His death, and resurrection for the forgiveness of sins. And then we can give each child a chance to pray, thanking God for forgiveness, saying thank You for the gift of eternal life. Let each child, in his own way, express appreciation for and trust in the Saviour.

A child's, "I love You, Jesus," may be far more an act of faith than raising a hand. So let's encourage the children we teach to thank Jesus, to express love to Jesus, and thus cooperate with God the Holy Spirit who is at work in the hearts of the boys and girls you and I tell the story of Jesus to.

♥ ***Link to Life: Youth / Adult***
The story of Peter's denial and Jesus' reinstatement is one of the most beautiful in the New Testament. Even after personal failures, God is able to use us in the service of others. The central issues in our relationship with Jesus remain do we love Him, and will we follow Him alone? (see v. 19)
The heart of serving Jesus is still caring for His sheep. And in it all we are to concentrate on our own commitment to Christ as Lord, not be distracted by worrying about others.

Break into teams of three to five. Each team is to identify as many personal applications of this passage to our Christian lives as they can.

Come together and work up a combined list of personal applications. Then, go around the circle. Ask each person to share which application is most important to him or to her, and share why.

TEACHING GUIDE

Prepare
Read John 18–21. What difference does Jesus' resurrection make in your life?

You can take several tacks in teaching this extended passage. Which of the study approaches would best meet the needs of your group, and should be emphasized?

Explore
1. As your group members enter, ask them to jot down their answer to the question: "What do people do in the dark that they don't want to do in the light?" List their answers.
2. Divide into teams to look at those associ-

ated with Jesus' death whose actions show the dark side of human nature. Each team is to look at one of these persons: Judas, Peter, the high priest, Pilate, or the crowd. Each is to sum up its insights by defining how sin had its impact on its person(s).

See "link-to-life," page 751.

Expand

1. Focus on conversion experiences of your group members. This activity is particularly helpful if some in your group are not yet Christians.

Give a minilecture covering the story of Thomas and his expressed doubt. Emphasize his insistence that "I will not believe" unless certain conditions were met.

Have your group members look back and complete "unless" statements of their own, then share their conversion stories. See "link-to-life," page 753.

2. Or divide your group into teams to seek applications of Jesus' restoration of Peter (John 21:15-23) to the life of Christians today. See "link-to-life," page 754.

Apply

Go around the circle and ask each to share briefly: "What is the major impression that the Gospel of John has made on you and your life?"

STUDY GUIDE 117

Introduction

ACTS AND THE EPISTLES

Overview

The story of Jesus is taken up after the Resurrection by Luke, whose Book of Acts gives a narrative insight into the spread of the Gospel. Acts is, in a real sense, the continuing story of Jesus who, through the Holy Spirit working in men and women of faith, actively continued Christ's own work in our world.

The first chapters of Acts deal with the church in Judea and its initial spilling over into Samaria. But then the focus shifts. Soon Luke's concern is the whole world, for while the Gospel came to the Jew first, it was also for the Gentile.

The shift is reflected particularly in a change of key characters. Peter is the leading figure at first. But soon Paul, the apostle to the Gentiles, takes center stage. We can hardly grasp the import of Acts or the New Testament epistles without paying close attention to this young Pharisee, who was transformed from an enemy of Christians to the most fervent of missionaries for Christ. Not only was Paul the most notable missionary in the history of Christianity, but as the writer of 13 of our 27 New Testament books, he continues to have the greatest impact on the church's faith and life.

In this study guide we'll examine the life of the Apostle Paul and see something of his significance in sacred history. Our time with the Apostle Paul will serve as an introduction both to Acts and to most of our New Testament epistles.

Commentary

The phrase, "New Testament times," is a common one. But its specific meaning is often unclear. It is probably best to think of these "times" as extending from the beginning of Jesus' ministry on earth (about A.D. 30) to the death of the last apostle, John, in the late 90s.

The period of the Gospels focuses, of course, on Jesus Himself. It is His story they tell. Then Acts takes up the tale, and for a decade or so Peter is Christianity's prime mover as the church begins and develops in Palestine. Soon, however, Acts reports the conversion of Samaritans and even Gentiles! The Gospel of Jesus is for everyone. Within a decade the focus of Acts shifts from the Holy Land to the entire Roman Empire. And the central figure becomes a passionate, committed man, the Apostle Paul.

Paul traveled the Roman Empire, proclaiming Christ, founding churches, and writing the letters to young churches which make up the bulk of the epistles in our New Testament.

Tradition tells us that Paul and Peter both were executed in the early 70s. The ministry of evangelism and teaching was taken on by another generation. Only the Apostle John lived on through the first century, to write his Gospel and letters very late in his life.

Yet there is no doubt that greatest impetus to the spread of the church came in the late 40s and extended into the 70s, as explosive expansion was spearheaded by the Apostle Paul who, with other missionaries, rushed out to share the message of Jesus with the whole world.

If we draw together passages from Acts and from Paul's letters, as well as material from other sources that tell us about life in the first century, we can develop a fascinating portrait of this man whom God used in such a powerful way.

Young Saul

"It's a boy!"

That announcement was always welcome in a Jewish home. Saul, who later became Paul, was born in the port city of Tarsus in Cilicia. It was a cosmopolitan town and important trading center, a strange home for pious Jews. Saul's family may have fled there during the terrible years when Roman

New Testament Times

A.D.*	Predominant Personality in Acts	Writings
35	Peter	
40		
45		
50	James	James, Galatians
55	Paul	Mark, 1 & 2 Thes.
60		1 & 2 Cor., Rom., Luke
65		Matt., Eph., Col., Phile., Phil., 1 Peter, Acts
70		Jude, 1 & 2 Tim., Titus, 2 Peter, Hebrews
75		
80		
85		
90		
95		John, 1, 2, & 3 John
100		Revelation

*Dates are approximate.

armies devastated Palestine. Financially successful, the family had won Roman citizenship. So Saul was born not only a Jew but a Roman, something in which he later took pride, and which was important for his mission (see Acts 22:25-29).

Saul was a product of two worlds. Committed to his Jewishness, he was still at home in the Gentile city. Throughout his life, Saul would seek out such cities, those centers of communication and culture, in his driving desire to communicate the Gospel.

Saul's life, however, centered in the history of his people and his God. As was the custom, by age 5 Saul was learning to read and write and study the Scriptures. By 10 he was taught the traditions which had grown out of generations of interpreting the Law. At 13 Saul entered the community of Israel as a responsible adult, and became a "son of the Law" (*bar mitzvah*). At that age some boys went on to deeper studies in Judaism under well-known teachers. It is a testimony both to Saul's promise and to the family wealth that he traveled to Jerusalem to study under the most famous of first-century rabbis, Gamaliel I. Already Saul had been trained both in the Scriptures and in the trade of tentmaking, for the Jews believed firmly that a scholar should labor, and that a laborer should be a scholar.

Saul talked about these days in the Book of Galatians, where he shared the deep commitment that infused his passionate young heart to the strictest interpretation of Judaistic faith and life, that of the Pharisee. This very passion for God became the motive that drove him to try at first to stamp out a hated heresy, "the Way," as Christianity was then known.

> For you have heard of my previous way of life in Judaism, how intensely I persecuted the church of God and tried to destroy it. I was advancing in Judaism beyond many Jews of my own age and was extremely zealous for the traditions of my fathers.
>
> Galatians 1:13-14

Young Saul was not a terribly attractive figure. Burning with passion, yet cold and untouched by people, this youth who had dedicated himself to the Law of Israel's God would one day, just outside Jerusalem, feel only a fierce joy as waves of hatred from a maddened crowd accompanied each stone that pounded the life from the church's first martyr, Stephen.

Saul's commitment was complete.

Conversion

And then came that day on the road to Damascus when Saul's whole world was jolted. The same Jesus whose followers Saul was planning to imprison confronted him in person! Stunned by the voice and blinded by the light that flashed around him, Saul crumpled to the ground.

At that moment, his world crumpled too. Everything that Saul had believed, and the strict way of life to which he had given his passionate allegiance, were suddenly revealed to be out of focus and off center. Rather than leading him to God, his training and his understanding of the Old Testament had led him to reject God's Son!

It would be a decade before Saul had all the pieces together again. But the next phase of his life would be committed completely to the one solid reality in which he could now believe. Jesus, whom Saul had persecuted, was Lord. Jesus was God's promised Christ, the Messiah. All of the energy of Paul's passionate nature was now focused on serving Him.

The 12 years following Saul's experience on the Damascus Road are hazy. He was probably converted in A.D. 34 when he was about 34 years old. We know that he immediately began to preach Jesus as the Son of God in Damascus (Acts 9:20). We know too that within a few months Saul escaped a Jewish plot to murder him, and returned to Jerusalem. We know that there Barnabas brought him to the apostles, where Saul shared his testimony and where the reality of his conversion was recognized (v. 27). But Saul's story was hardly more dramatic than that of many others in those days. He was certainly not invited to share the leadership of the Jerusalem church.

In Jerusalem Saul's zeal in proclaiming Christ again aroused anger. It is entirely possible that the old, driving, insensitive character of the Pharisee he had been was partly responsible for this reaction, even though the attitude of the Jewish community to Christians had long since hardened. Again Saul was forced to flee for his life, and the brothers took him (perhaps protesting) to the port city of Caesarea and "sent him off to Tarsus" (v. 30).

The next 10 years are obscure. In isolation the man who was God's choice to bridge two worlds, and through whom a clear formulation of the meaning of the Christian faith would be revealed, struggled to reconstruct his own picture of God and his understanding of God's Word. We can imagine Saul, poring over the Old Testament documents, seeking illumination. We can picture him, fasting and praying in the deserts of Arabia, where his final grasp of the Gospel was given him "by a revelation from Jesus Christ" (Gal. 1:12). We can see Saul slipping again into Judea, not this time as the flaming evangelist of his youth, but silently seeking out the apostles to discuss with them his vision of the Gospel. After some 15 days with Peter, and a brief meeting with James, the Lord's brother, Saul went on, visiting many churches incognito as he journeyed toward home. And we can picture Saul at home again in Tarsus—waiting.

How long did he wait? How long did he walk the streets of that great trade city, watching the ships of the Mediterranean world enter the port and slip away again? How long did Saul sit, working thoughtfully at his trade of tentmaking?

Why didn't Saul marry during those years

of waiting? He must have had the opportunity. But Ananias, the man sent by God to restore the sight he lost on the Damascus Road, had shared with the new convert the Lord's announcement of his destiny: "This man is My chosen instrument to carry My name before the Gentiles and their kings and before the people of Israel" (Acts 9:15). How deeply the sight of the crowded city streets, the swirling groups of men from different lands and backgrounds, must have moved him. As a Pharisee Saul had formerly viewed Gentiles as dogs, deserving only contempt and hatred. Now a Christian, the same man was beginning to see them in a new way—as individuals with worth and value, for whom Christ died.

And so Saul waited.

And then, finally, it was time for God's call.

On Mission

For most of the years of Saul's preparation the church continued to be a movement within Judaism. Then at Antioch came that mass conversion of Gentiles which led to Barnabas' dispatch by the apostles to investigate. It was clear to Barnabas that the spiritual response of the Gentiles was a work of God.

He stayed with the new believers for a time, but soon he recognized the need for help as more and more people were added to the church. "Then Barnabas went to Tarsus to look for Saul" (Acts 11:25).

God had begun that work among the Gentiles for which He had prepared the great apostle.

After a happy year during which Saul shared with Barnabas and others the leadership of the church at Antioch, the two were set aside by God for the first mission to the Gentiles. By the end of a two-year trip, Saul had emerged as the leader, and had taken a new name: Paul. This Romanized name was more appropriate for the Gentile mission than the Hebrew, Saul. The date was early in A.D. 48.

On the missionary journey, all of Paul's studies plus the truths which he had received by direct revelation seemed to come together with exciting clarity. In the crucible of his mission, in the conflict with the Jews who trailed his team and argued against him, in the questions raised by the converts, all that Paul had earlier worked out for his own peace and understanding was now applied to the church as a whole. The old revelation and the new were not only recognized to be a unified and consistent whole, but the relationship between seemingly conflicting elements was understood. The "Gospel to the Gentiles" and the very nature of New Testament faith had been worked through by this man, the church's greatest theologian and the first apostle to the world.

Again Paul returned to Jerusalem, this time by the Holy Spirit's clear direction, to share privately with the leaders of the Jerusalem church the Gospel which he had been preaching among the Gentiles. It was just 14 years after his conversion.

Paul discovered that the leaders in Jerusalem had nothing to add to his understanding. In fact, they affirmed Paul by recognizing his call as the apostle to the Gentiles, even as Peter was recognized as the apostle to the Jews (Gal. 2:1-10). Paul then returned to Antioch and, assured of the understanding and agreement of the other apostles and the leaders in Jerusalem, Paul began to consider writing a letter to the Galatians (those churches in that area which included the cities visited on the first missionary journey). The urgency of this work was highlighted by a striking incident. Peter came to visit Antioch, freely joining in fellowship with the Gentile converts. Then a party of "Judaizers" arrived. These men were believers, but believers who insisted that all Christians must adopt the Law and the Jewish lifestyle. When these men came, Peter refused to eat with the Gentile believers any longer!

Paul immediately saw that this was a vital issue. It raised the question of the Christian's relationship with Old Testament Law. So Paul "opposed . . . [Peter] to his face" (v. 11).

It is likely that this confrontation and the disturbing teaching of the Pharisee-Christian party led to the Jerusalem Council of A.D. 49, which is reported in Acts 15. Throughout the rest of Paul's life he would accept the burden of contending for the "pure" Gospel. Through his letters you and I too come to understand the uniqueness and joy of our own privilege, of being a part of Christ's church, and of joining with our brothers and sisters in a full experience of the Christian life's great adventure.

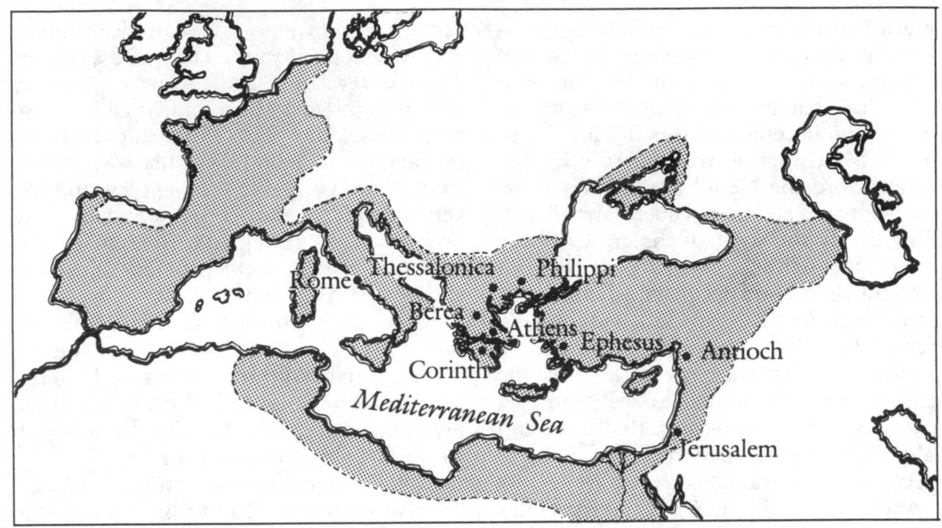

The Roman Empire

Paul, the Man

Eusebius records an interesting second-century description of Paul, perhaps passed on by a grandfather who had known the apostle. He was "a man in a good state of body, with eyebrows meeting and nose somewhat hooked, full of friendliness."

Today it's become popular to think of Paul as a bitter and joyless man, a distant intellectual, a distorter of what Jesus taught, and one who hated women. How far from the picture of Paul the early church drew. And how far from the portrait we have in Scripture! The austere Pharisee had undergone a complete transformation. The man who had cared for God in the abstract now cared for God in a deeply intimate way. And he loved people.

We can't help but realize the depth of this transformation as we look at Paul's words written to the Christians in Thessalonica, recalling his time with them. Paul's remembrance of love and intimate friendships was not written *about* a relationship, but to the very people who had experienced that relationship! What Paul wrote here must be the true portrait; the Thessalonians would have immediately perceived any deceit.

> We were gentle among you, like a mother caring for her little children. We loved you so much that we were delighted to share with you not only the Gospel of God but our lives as well, because you had become so dear to us.
>
> Surely you remember, brothers, our toil and hardship; we worked night and day in order not to be a burden to anyone while we preached the Gospel of God to you.
>
> You are witnesses, and so is God, of how holy, righteous and blameless we were among you who believed. For you know that we dealt with each of you as a father deals with his own children, encouraging, comforting and urging you to live lives worthy of God, who calls you into His kingdom and glory.
>
> 1 Thessalonians 2:7-12

The zealot had learned to love. The rigid Pharisee had become gentle. The man whose vision was the entire world yet found time for "each one of you."

There are many such cameo portraits of the apostle in the New Testament. And, because in teaching the New Yestament you will keep close company with him on his Acts journeys, and live with him in his letters, you'll want to help your group members come to see him as he was.

Seeing him in the intimacy of his sharing, you and your group will also discover the kind of person God uses in spiritual leadership—the kind of person each Christian is called to become.

TEACHING GUIDE

Prepare
What has been your past impression of the Apostle Paul as a person? Jot down a few words that describe it; then read the passages referred to in this teaching guide to meet him personally.

Explore
1. Give a minilecture overview of the decades of the first century, using the chart on page 757.
2. Ask your group members to jot down two or three words which describe the Apostle Paul, the dominant figure of these times, as each thinks of him. Write down the descriptive words on the chalkboard.

Expand
1. Give another minilecture, an overview of Paul's life, drawing from the commentary in this study guide. However, give only the facts. Avoid references to Paul's personality and character.
2. Divide into teams to look at New Testament passages which give insight into Paul's personality and character. Give each team a list of the guide questions under (1) and (2) below. Passages to be assigned to your groups are: Group 1: Galatians 1–2; Group 2: Philippians 3; Group 3: 1 Thessalonians 2; Group 4: 2 Corinthians 1.

From the passage(s) assigned, each group is to consider:

(1) Impressions of Paul as a person.
- (a) How did Paul relate to others?
- (b) What was Paul's attitude toward life?
- (c) What was important to Paul?
- (d) What was Paul's attitude toward himself?
- (e) How did Paul view his relationship with God?

(2) Reactions to Paul as a person.
- (a) What is the most attractive thing to you about Paul?
- (b) What do you think the people to whom Paul ministered felt about him?
- (c) What characteristics of Paul do you think are important for spiritual leaders today?
- (d) How do you think Paul's enemies viewed him?

When each team has studied its passage, come together and share impressions, and the basis for them.

Apply
Look back at the impressions of Paul revealed in the words initially chosen by group members. Discuss: "Which of these impressions were valid? Which should be changed? What new set of words would each person choose to describe the great apostle whom we meet in Acts, and in 13 of the New Testament epistles?"

STUDY GUIDE 118

Acts 1–4

THE ADVENTURE BEGINS

Overview

The "New Testament church" has fascinated Christians through the ages. The excitement, the vitality, the depth of fellowship portrayed in early Acts has attracted us. Many have sought to recapture those days: some by a reemphasis on the Spirit, others by restructuring the church as an institution.

No one can duplicate any moment in history. Yet as we study these first chapters of Acts we do discover principles which will vitalize Christian experience. We probably will not need to abandon our old. But we will need to make a fresh commitment to the God who worked so powerfully in the men and women of the early church. He lives today, and He is fully able to work just as powerfully in us.

▶ ***Filled.*** The events at Pentecost have been the focus of much theological debate. The text says the Holy Spirit filled the followers of Jesus. Specific signs were associated with that particular filling. There was a rushing, violent wind. Visible tongues of fire rested on each person. And when a crowd gathered each foreigner heard Jesus' followers "speaking in his own native language" (Acts 2:8). To understand the works of the Spirit it is important *not* to identify the Spirit's "filling," or the Spirit's "baptism," with any one of these signs. "Filling" is not itself tongues, or visible fire. For definition we have to go to key passages in the New Testament epistles (see *index*).

Commentary

I remember very clearly walking with five-year-old Paul the day he started kindergarten in Dallas, Texas. Paul was proud and excited—his first day at school! How grown-up he felt, and how grown-up and confident he looked. He was taking an important step into life's great adventure.

Each of us has times like this. For parent and child such moments are a strange mixture of excitement and loss. A whole phase of life is being left behind. We move on, sad, and yet somehow happy to meet the unknown.

It must have been very much like this for both Jesus and the disciples after Christ's resurrection. Their years together were past. The agony of the cross was history, swallowed up in the joy of Resurrection. During the 40 days after Christ rose, as Jesus still met with the disciples, both the Lord and the 11 must have been torn. Both knew the disciples would soon be launched on the greatest adventure the world has ever known, stepping out into the unknown to share Jesus with their whole world. They may have desperately wanted Jesus to remain with them. Yet, deep inside, the disciples must have known that they had been prepared for just this mission. They stood poised, hesitating, and yet eager to move on.

A New Focus

While the faith of Israel served as a foundation for the new faith about to break on a world unaware, what would happen during the months and years ahead was unknown to the disciples. This must have been hard for them. Usually we're most comfortable in familiar surroundings and situations.

We can see this in the disciples. For 40 days Jesus spoke with them about His Father's intention to build His own kingdom in man's world. Jesus also encouraged His disciples: "Wait for the gift My Father promised. . . . In a few days you will be baptized with the Holy Spirit" (1:4-5). Jesus did not push His followers unprepared into an adventure too great for them; He reminded them that He had promised them power. Even so, the disciples still looked longingly at the old patterns of thought and life. "Lord," they asked, "are You at this time going to restore the kingdom to Israel?" (v. 6)

This was a revealing and an important question. The Old Testament had foretold Jesus' coming, but the dominant impression the Jews had received was of His coming to be their King. They had visions of the Messiah rescuing them from Gentile dominion and giving them the exalted political and military position promised by the Old Testament prophets. Jesus' death had been doubly shocking to His followers. Not only had they loved Him, but they had also firmly expected Him to crush Rome's political and military power and to establish Israel as the dominant world power.

The believing Jews in Old Testament times knew that God rules over the whole world of men. Therefore, His sovereignty over history itself was recognized. But the Old Testament saint longed for the day when the hidden authority of Yahweh would be revealed to all, when the Lord's Messiah would rule *visibly* over the world of men. So even the Twelve who were closest to Jesus were disappointed as He continued to teach and preach and heal instead of confronting the Roman Empire.

Jesus had gently taught His followers that the Old Testament also spoke of the Messiah suffering and dying for men's sins. Christ's ministry was leading Him to a cross rather than a crown. But up to the very end, the disciples still had visions of their Camelot: a New Jerusalem, with Jesus (and themselves) ruling the world. The death of Jesus had crushed that hope momentarily. But when Jesus arose, the vision of power and glory again caught and held their imaginations. "Are You *at this time* going to restore the kingdom to Israel?" clearly reflects their longing for the life they had dreamed of so long.

Jesus' answer was gentle (vv. 7-8). First He pointed out that the prophesied kingdom would come, but that its coming was *distant* rather than "at this time." God will keep His promises, and this world will know Jesus' rule. But for now life is to have a different focus for Jesus' followers. That focus, stated in utmost simplicity, is this: "You will be My witnesses."

Jesus Himself is the focus, the center of the believer's life. The meaning of our lives, the reason that our time on earth can be a great adventure, is summed up in the fact that Jesus is real, and that our every action can be a clear demonstration of the vital impact of the living God on human experience.

This was something that the disciples had not yet grasped, but soon would. Jesus, living within them, would Himself transform their experience. Then everything they were as individuals and as a community would witness to His presence.

These words, "You will be My witnesses," were the last ones Jesus spoke to the 11. As a silent crowd of disciples watched, Jesus rose up, soaring away until the clouds hid Him from sight. Two angelic messengers completed Christ's answer to the earlier question.

"This same Jesus, who has been taken from you into heaven, will come back in the same way you have seen Him go into heaven" (v. 11). This present time, during which the focus of our lives and the heart of our adventure with God is summed up in Jesus, will come to an end. As Old Testament days came to an end in the cross, our age will come to an end when Jesus returns—to establish the kingdom promised in the Old.

Yes, that day will come. But for then the disciples had to turn away from the Mount of Ascension and return to Jerusalem to see what new thing God had in store. There they waited, gathering for prayer. Waiting for a challenge, and a joy, that they could not yet imagine!

♥ ***Link to Life: Youth / Adult***
As you deal with the disciples' question about Jesus' intention to restore the kingdom "now," you may wish to copy and distribute the chart (p. 764) which summarizes the basic relationships between the Old Testament and New.

♥ ***Link to Life: Children***
Jesus told the disciples what He wanted them to do. They were to be witnesses "in Jerusalem, and in all Judea and Samaria, and to the ends of the earth" (v. 8). Each Christian can witness to Jesus. To help boys and girls think about how they too can show love for Jesus, draw four concentric circles. Label the inner one Jerusalem, the next Judea, the next Samaria, and the last "Ends of the earth." Explain that Jeru-

Relationship Between the Old and New Testaments

Unity: in ultimate goal, the "glory of God."
Divergence: in emphasis

Old Testament —*theocratic purpose*	*New Testament* —*soteriological purpose*
1. God will rule the world through the Jewish Messiah's reign.	1. God will save individuals and society through the Jewish Messiah's work.
2. The nation Israel is emphasized.	2. The believing individual and community (the church) are emphasized.

Harmony: in teachings

The theocratic emphasis of the Old does not rule out concern for individuals (see Dan. 4; Ezek. 18; Nahum 1:6-7; Jonah 4).	The revelation of the fullness of God's salvation as it relates to individual transformation does not abrogate the emphasis of the Old (see Acts 1; Rom. 9–11).

Unification: in Christ

Jesus, the promised King of the Old Testament prophets, is also the Redeemer of the New Testament! In His person all of God's purposes will be fulfilled.

salem was home to the disciples (relabel the inner circle "home"). Relabel the next circles too: Judea is neighbors, Samaria strangers, and "Ends of the earth" other countries.

Help your boys and girls think how they can show Jesus' love in their homes, to neighbors, to strangers, and to people in foreign countries. List their ideas on the chalkboard.

You may want to have boys and girls make a "witnesses" booklet, with a "home" first page, on through "other countries." Each can draw a picture of himself or herself doing one thing from the list of ways to show others we love Jesus.

♥ ***Link to Life: Children***

A simple project can serve as a reminder to young children that Jesus who went to heaven will return. Give each a piece of construction paper. Punch and reinforce two holes, one at the top and the other at the bottom. Let the children decorate with a crayoned hillside at the bottom, and clouds at the top. Place a loop of yarn through the holes. Tape or staple a picture of Jesus to the yarn. By pulling on the back of the loop, the figure will move up from the hill to the clouds, or down from the clouds. Your children can print "Jesus will come back (Acts 1:11)" on their projects as a reminder of Christ's promised return.

The Day: Acts 2:1-21

The days of waiting passed (Acts 1:12-26). The little company of believers, numbering about 120, met daily. On one of these days, they chose Matthias to take the office which Judas had abandoned by his betrayal of Jesus. Judas, overcome with remorse and yet unwilling to turn to Jesus for pardon, had thrown the 30 pieces of silver for which he betrayed the Lord down on the temple floor and, rushing out, had hanged himself.

Now another must take his office as an apostle. Searching among those who had been with Jesus since the beginning of His ministry and who had also been witnesses to the Resurrection, the little company found two candidates. Following an Old Testament practice, they then let God choose between the two by casting lots (much like our drawing of straws).

The company of the Apostles was thus returned to its original number of 12.

Apostles. The word *apostle* means "one sent out." In secular Greek it often referred to a ship or naval force sent on an expedition, seldom to an individual. Yet the word was chosen by Jewish translators of the Old Testament to reflect a Hebrew word that referred to one acting as another's representative.

In the New Testament the word is found 10 times in the Gospels, 28 times in Acts, and 38 times in the epistles, usually referring to men appointed by Christ for a special function in the church. While these men are primarily the Twelve and Paul, others are also called apostles.

There is no doubt that the apostles were given special authority and power. Not only were they witnesses to the events of Jesus' life, but they were also authoritative interpreters of those events. As the body of apostolic teaching grew, it became clear that the church was being "built on the foundation of the apostles and prophets" (Eph. 2:20).

There is no indication in Scripture that the loyal apostles were replaced by others as they died (cf. Acts 12:2). As witnesses and interpreters of the purposes of God in the early days of the church, the apostles stand unique. But as witnesses to the reality of Jesus, the apostles were about to enter into an adventure which they share with all Jesus' followers of every age. And then the day arrived.

Pentecost (Acts 2:1). The Feast of Pentecost was one of the three annual Old Testament celebrations during which the men of Israel came to Jerusalem to worship at the temple. It was a time when Jews from around the world gathered in their ancient homeland and offered sacrifice to the God of Abraham and Isaac and Jacob.

Pentecost was a harvest festival, coming at the time of the grain harvest, just 50 days after Passover. Each year the firstfruits of the harvest were offered with joy and thanksgiving, accompanied by the recitation of Deuteronomy 26:3-10 by the worshiper.

Pentecost was clearly God's choice time for the initiation of Jesus' followers into their great adventure. Just 50 days before, Jesus Himself had been crucified—and raised again. Now, as an indication of the great harvest of everlasting life that Jesus' death had won, the 120 believers were about to be touched by the Spirit of God. They were to be the first of a vast multitude, the first of millions upon millions who would follow them into a unique relationship with God through Jesus Christ.

The choice of Pentecost was also an indication of the meaning of that new relationship for believers. The first words the Old Testament worshiper uttered at the Pentecost service were these:

> I declare today to the Lord your God that I have come to the land the Lord swore to our forefathers to give us.
>
> Deuteronomy 26:3

I declare that I have entered in! This is just what Pentecost meant to the first disciples, and what it should mean to us. Through Jesus, we have entered into everything the Promised Land foreshadowed; we are now free to experience the fullness of all the good things the Lord our God has chosen to give men.

And God's first gift was the gift of the Holy Spirit.

The Holy Spirit (Acts 2:2-21). The Bible speaks of the Holy Spirit as a Person, an individual distinct from and yet One with the Father and the Son. As God, the Holy Spirit had various relationships with men in Old Testament times. But the Old Testament also spoke of a coming day when God would enter into a new and special relationship with those who believe. Jesus had spoken often of this. Christ looked forward to a day when He would be back with the Father, and the Spirit "whom those who believed in Him were later to receive," would be given (John 7:39). The promised Spirit was to teach and guide believers (14:16) and, according to Jesus' final promise, to bring power for that new kind of life which bears witness to Jesus' reality (Acts 1:8). In that day, Jesus had said, the Spirit would not simply be "with" the disciples, but "in" them! (John 14:17)

And Pentecost was the promised day!

The Bible tells us that the Spirit's coming into believers was unmistakably marked. A mighty wind seemed to rush through the room where the 120 gathered; flames of fire flickered over each head; and as the Spirit filled them, individuals began to speak in languages they did not know.

This drew a great crowd of the men who had come to Jerusalem for the Pentecost festival. Each person heard the disciples speaking in the language of the land where he was presently living. "How is it," wondered the visitors, "that each of us hears them in his own native language? . . . We hear them declaring the wonders of God in our own tongues!" (Acts 2:8, 11) Perplexed and amazed, they asked each other, "What does this mean?" (v. 12)

All too often that same question is asked today—without listening to Peter's response to those first questioners. All too often the answer given is designed to argue for or against the existence of what has been called "the gift of tongues" in our day. Whatever our opinion might be as to whether God still gives believers this gift, the important point underlined by Pentecost is that now, at last, the Holy Spirit *is* given!

And this was Peter's response to those who demanded an explanation of the disciples: "This is what was spoken by the Prophet Joel:

> "In the last days," God says, "I will pour out My Spirit on all people."
>
> Acts 2:16-17

That great gift which God had reserved till the last days was being poured out freely now. All were to know the touch of the Spirit of God; both daughters and sons would be empowered by Him. Most significant of all, in that day on which the Spirit of God would flow out to touch and fill God's own, "everyone who calls on the name of the Lord will be saved" (v. 21).

God was moving out beyond the boundaries of Israel to offer to *all* people that relationship with Himself which is at the heart of eternal life.

The disciples themselves did not understand just then all that the Spirit's coming meant. They didn't see Pentecost as the beginning of the church, as it later came to be understood. They did not realize that the Holy Spirit, living in each believer, would Himself constitute a living link binding each individual to other believers, to form a vital, loving community.

But they did know that God's new day was *now!* They did know that the Holy Spirit had filled them with Jesus' promised power. And they did begin immediately to explain the striking witness that the rushing wind and the flames and the tongues had given to every observer of the reality of God's presence in these set-apart men.

♥ ***Link to Life: Youth / Adult***
In a minilecture explain the Old Testament Day of Pentecost, reading Deuteronomy 26:3-10. Then ask your group members to read Acts 2:1-21 to discover (1) how Peter explained the events of this particular Pentecost, and (2) the implications of the event that are spelled out by the Prophet Joel.

If you have questions about specific verses and phrases, see the Bible Knowledge Commentary, *pages 357-358.*

The Message: Acts 2:22–3:26

Jesus' last instructions had been to focus on Himself: "You will be My witnesses" (1:8). Acts 2 and 3 show how clearly the early disciples maintained that focus. The two sermons of Peter recorded here give us a clear picture of the apostolic message and the very heart of the Gospel.

What were the basic elements of the apostolic preaching?

1. *Jesus, the historical Person.* In each sermon Peter began by confronting his hearers with the Person who had lived among them; who was born, lived, performed His wonders, and taught in our space and time, "as you yourselves know" (2:22). This was no mythical person, no invention of disciples parlaying the ignorance of gullible crowds into the beginnings of a new religion. Everyone knew Jesus. He had been a public figure, a chief topic of conversation for at least three years. Just 50 days before, He had been executed at the insistence of the Jewish leaders, with crowds of the common people shouting for His blood. Peter's words, "As you yourselves know," made it very clear. The Gospel is firmly rooted in historical reality.

And all Peter's hearers knew perfectly well who the historical Jesus was.

2. *Crucified.* A second element of the apostolic preaching involved confronting the hearers with the crucifixion of Jesus, and even confronting them with their own guilt: "You . . . put Him to death by nailing Him to the cross" (v. 23).

3. *Raised.* A third element also involved the statement of historical fact: Jesus was loosed from death's bonds and raised up by God, and "we are all witnesses of the fact" (v. 32).

4. *Correspondence with Old Testament prophecy.* Peter then went on to point out that each of these historical events happened as God had foretold in the Old Testament. Rather than being a threat to the integrity of God's Word, Jesus and the events of His life and death and resurrection are foretold there. What Peter proclaimed was in fullest harmony with God's total revelation.

5. *The promised Messiah.* Peter then went on to interpret the facts he had laid out for his hearers. "Be assured of this: God has made this Jesus, whom you crucified, both Lord and Christ" (v. 36).

The conclusion is so clearly correct that his hearers were "cut to the heart" and begged the apostles, "Brothers, what shall we do?" (v. 37) This question led into the last element of the apostolic preaching.

6. *Repentance and faith.* The word *repent* is a military term meaning make an about-face. The men to whom Peter spoke had refused to accept Jesus as Lord and Messiah. They had hesitated, then passively participated in His execution. Now they were asked to make a clear-cut commitment and symbolize their response of faith by public baptism. And if they did? Then everything that Jesus' death and resurrection promised would become theirs: full forgiveness of sins and the gift of the Holy Spirit. The God they had scorned would welcome even them and, entering their lives, fill them with power to launch out new lives.

So, "Those who accepted his message were baptized, and about three thousand were added to their number that day" (v. 41).

How vital and contemporary these messages are even today. You and I have been invited by God to enter a living relationship with the historical Jesus. The Son of God lived and died and was raised again, all in accordance with the Scripture, that He might *today* bring forgiveness and power for a new life to all who respond to Him as Lord and Christ. He will be with us, as He was with the first disciples, charging us with the power we need to witness to Him.

♥ ***Link to Life: Youth / Adult***
The author lists six elements found in apostolic preaching of the Gospel. List the six elements on the chalkboard. Have pairs work with Acts 2 and 3 to record phrases from each sermon by element.

When completed, develop a group list. Then discuss: "Which element seems most important for contemporary presentations of the Gospel? Why? How can we best communicate it to others today?"

Community: Acts 4

When Frank accepted Christ as his Saviour, his parents saw his conversion as a denial of their family religion. At first they argued and ridiculed. Then, as they sensed the depth of their teen's experience with Jesus, they increased the pressure. They offered Frank that set of expensive drums he'd wanted, if only he'd give up this nonsense! Finally, the Leparises locked their son out of the house. If he would not remain true to the family faith, he would be cut off.

The first exciting days of the church saw many experiences similar to Frank's. There was change and growth. And there was opposition. The contagious enthusiasm of those who believed in Jesus threatened the secure foundations of many people's religious convictions, and uneasy tolerance gave way to hostility. It was then that the little company of believers began to realize that the church was a new community, a community of men and women who could be closer than any family, and who could provide the kind of loving support that believers then—and believers now, like Frank—would always need.

Opposition to the message of a living Christ formed quickly. Peter's sermon, stimulated by the healing of the lame man (Acts 3), was only one instance of the disciples "teaching the people and proclaiming in Jesus the resurrection of the dead" (4:2). Soon some 5,000 men had joined the company of the committed. An annoyed clique of rulers and elders acted. They arrested Peter and John.

The confrontation (Acts 4:5-22). Called before the ruling body of Judaism, the apostles were questioned about the miracle of healing which Peter had performed. Boldly, Peter responded. The miracle had been performed "by the name of Jesus Christ of Nazareth, whom you crucified but whom God raised from the dead" (v. 10). Only in Jesus, Peter went on to affirm, could salvation be found; there is no other name or way.

Such boldness from uneducated and common men stunned the elite group. Setting the apostles outside, the council conferred. There was no way to deny the public healing. Compromising, the rulers called Peter and John back and commanded them to stop all this talk about Jesus. Again speaking boldly, the two believers insisted that they would obey God rather than men. The frustrated rulers, unable to justify to the people any punishment of Peter and John, threatened them and let them go.

The fellowship of prayer (Acts 4:23-31). At this point in time we are introduced to one of the most significant dimensions of the new community's life. Peter and John immediately "went back to their own people and reported" (v. 23). In the brotherhood of the church, Peter and John found others who cared and with whom they could share. Immediately the whole company accepted the burden of the two as their own, and went to God in prayer.

Frank had many burdens to share with us too. There was tremendous pain for him, and often that pain brought tears. But he had Christian friends who cared—friends who would listen, who would encourage, and who joined with him in prayer. Frank discovered as a young Christian what the early church learned in its first adventurous days. *A Christian is never alone!* Not only has the risen Christ sent the Holy Spirit to be with us, but He has also knit us together in a community of fellowship and love.

This is one of the most important things we can learn as we begin our exploration of the New Testament. In the Scriptures we see portrayed a church in which those touched by Christ discover a new capacity to love and to care for one another. The church is more than a group of people who agree in their beliefs. The church is a family of brothers and sisters who experience the reality of Jesus' presence in and through their growing love for one another (cf. John 13:33-34). While some today have not tasted of that reality, this *is* a real and vital dimension of Christian experience. And God invites each one of us to reach out and know this touch of fellowship.

The text of Acts reports that as they prayed together "they were all filled with the Holy Spirit and spoke the Word of God boldly" (Acts 4:31). In the fellowship of prayer, God's power is poured again into our lives.

With one accord (Acts 4:32-37). This is a passage that has captured the imagination of Christians across the ages. "All the believers were one in heart and mind" (v. 32). Growing together, the early church experienced a unique unity. Possessions were sold by the rich, and the proceeds were distributed to the poor. The sense of oneness was so great that no selfish hesitation kept anyone from reaching out to meet another's need. Because concern for the brothers outweighed the value of material possessions, love's expression was both practical and free. "There were no needy persons among them" (v. 34).

This early evidence of the reality of Christian community is not necessarily a standard for the church today. But it is not as unusual as we may think. In our own local church just this kind of expression of love often takes place. Yet, the impact of the passage is not to promote some form of "Christian communism," but rather to highlight the truth of the writer's statement, "All the believers were one in heart and mind."

We are called to oneness in our shared faith. Oneness with our brothers and sisters frees us to share ourselves as well as each other, to support each other in prayer, and to express love in many vital and practical ways.

♥ ***Link to Life: Children***

How do people in your local church show love for others by helping meet their needs? Many churches have a food pantry stocked for the poor. Others have "deacon's funds" to meet emergency needs. Still others collect clothing or make up food baskets for special times of the year. Why not see if your boys and girls can take part in one of your congregation's projects. Perhaps they can help stack food in the pantry, go along to help deliver baskets, etc. It is never too early to give boys and girls the chance to experience what it means to reach out in practical love to others who have needs.

Homothumadon: One Accord. A unique Greek word, used 10 of its 11 New Testament occurrences in the Book of Acts, helps us understand the uniqueness of Christian community. *Homothumadon* is a compound of two words meaning to "rush along" and "in unison." The image is almost musical; a number of notes are sounded which, while different, harmonize in pitch and tone. As the instruments of a great orchestra blend under the direction of a concertmaster, so the Holy Spirit blends together the lives of members of Christ's church.

The first use of *homothumadon* is found in Acts 1:14. There, in the Upper Room, the 11 disciples and a few women were united in prayer. Earlier strife and jealousies that marred their relationships were gone; the disciples were one, waiting for the Spirit's promised coming. Then in Acts 2:1 we see 120 believers gathered, focusing together on the Lord as they sensed the Spirit's first dynamic touch. The next occurrence is verse 46, as the community (then some 3,000), "continuing daily with one accord [*homothumadon*] in the temple, and breaking bread from house to house, did eat their meat with gladness and singleness of heart" (KJV). Again in 4:24 we see the whole company, moved by Peter and John's report, as they "lifted up their voice to God with one accord" (KJV). As those who are Jesus' own make Him the common focus of their lives and seek to help each other find the Holy Spirit's freedom in their lives, *homothumadon* becomes the mark of Christian community.

Sometimes we look back on these early chapters of Acts as though they picture a church that has been lost—as though unity and love and the experience of Jesus' presence are things that cannot really be ours today. Let's not make this mistake. God's Spirit is still a present reality. *Homothumadon* is still possible in today's shattered and impersonal world. If we look for a reason for emptiness in our own experience, let's look first to our hesitancy to share ourselves with our brothers and sisters. Or look to our failure to let others pick up the burdens of our lives, and bring them in confident prayer to God.

The church, the new community Christ formed, *is* here today. *We are the church.* And God, the Spirit, is able to take our 11s, and our 120s and our 3,000s and, as we joyfully focus our shared life on Jesus, to orchestrate our lives to His wondrous "one accord."

TEACHING GUIDE

Prepare
What goals does the early Acts picture of the church suggest you should set, and pray about, for your group and your own congregation?

Explore
1. Brainstorm with your group: "What would we expect to find in an ideal church?"
2. Give a minilecture on *homothumadon*, and ask your group members to look at Acts 2:42-47 and 4:32-35 for evidences of the way "one accord" is expressed in the Christian congregation.

Compare what they suggest with the "ideal church" description the group has just brainstormed.

Then break into groups of five to discuss: "How do the two lists differ? How are they similar? What should we emphasize in our own relationships for our congregation to be as vital as that of the early church?"

Expand
1. Raise the question of how the early Jerusalem church became the kind of congregation described here. Divide into teams to explore the following themes and passages. Each team is to report to the group specific "to do" suggestions to strengthen the spiritual life of your group or congregation. The themes and passages are:

(1) The mission of the church (Acts 1).
(2) The power of the church (Acts 2:1-21).
(3) The foundational beliefs of the church (Acts 2:22–3:26).
(4) The resources of the church (Acts 4:1-31).

2. Or use any of the "link-to-life" teaching suggestions to focus on a theme of special concern to your own group. See pages 763, 766, and 767.

Apply
Have each person in your group share their completion of this sentence: "I am glad that our congregation is like the New Testament church in that it. . . ."

STUDY GUIDE 119

Acts 5:1–11:18

REACHING OUT

Overview

The early church was a dynamic fellowship. It was rooted in faith in Christ, and relationships between Christians were marked by *homothumadon*, that vital principle of "one accord."

But we would be mistaken to idealize the early church. It was a fellowship made up of mere human beings. There were tensions within the church, and pressures from those outside who opposed the Gospel message. All these forces sought to disrupt the oneness of the local body of believers, and to halt its growth. In these next chapters of Acts we look at some of the inner and outer pressures which, unless dealt with correctly, can distort our own churches too.

▶ ***Tongues.*** For a fuller discussion, see Study Guide 132. However, in these chapters note that "tongues" served a very special function. In Samaria they were an outward sign of union with the Jerusalem church, for they came only when the apostles laid hands on the new converts (Acts 8:14-17). The Spirit came on Gentiles at the house of Cornelius "while Peter was still speaking" the Gospel message. Later Peter argued that this was evidence that Gentiles received "the same gift" as Jewish believers (11:15-17). Thus in Acts speaking in tongues was an outward evidence of the unity of a church just discovering that it was to be composed not only of Jews but of Samaritans and Gentiles as well!

Commentary

"What's happened to us? We were so close before. And then we started growing . . . and. . . . " Carol's words reflect a common experience. A little group of believers comes together, grows close, and forms a local church. There's an exciting sense of closeness and warmth and enthusiasm.

As time passes, growth comes. We become busier and busier. New people come in whom we don't know, and before long the closeness we felt with earlier friends is lost. Soon decisions about buildings and parking lots and programs and staffing and so many other things crowd in on us.

It's easy then to look back at the earlier days and to long for the intimacy of that smaller group. It's also easy, if we've never experienced that kind of fellowship, to doubt whether it is even possible in this day and age.

All such longing is not only useless; it is also foolish. It is in the very nature of life to reproduce. It is in the very nature of Christian faith and life to reach out, to welcome more and more people into the family of God. It may be more difficult to maintain warmth and a sense of oneness in a church when growth comes. But the solution is never to push back to the past. The solution is in finding new ways to affirm and to experience our *homothumadon*.

It was no different in the early church. With growth and expansion came tensions. There were disagreements. There was sin. There were suspicion and misunderstanding. But through it all the early church expected that God the Holy Spirit would enable them to experience the unity that He Himself had fashioned in that bond which knits believers to Jesus and to one another.

Growing Tensions: Acts 5–7

These three chapters of Acts bring us back again to look at the Jerusalem church. There, with growth, came tensions from both within the believing community and from without.

♥ ***Link to Life: Youth / Adult***
The major focus of your study may well be on these tensions that had the potential of destroying the early church's unity and

Disruptive Tensions in the Early Church

Acts	Problem Described	Danger	Wrong Responses	Solution	Parallel Problems Today
5:1-11					
5:12-42			Permit sin Ignore sin		
6:1-7		Serious division within the church—destruction of *homothumadon*			
6:8–7:59	Jealousy, anger, and hatred against the church by outsiders				

spiritual power, yet were overcome. The chart can be used to help teams of group members study each incident, and explore ways to deal with parallel problems in congregations today.

Sin (Acts 5:1-11). The first tension emerged from within. A couple named Ananias and Sapphira wanted a reputation for benevolence like that of other believers who had sold their possessions for the benefit of the whole church. But Ananias and Sapphira didn't want to give all.

There was no demand by God or by the believing community that they should give all. As Peter asked, "After it was sold, wasn't the money at your disposal?" (v. 4) But rather than openly give a part, the two conspired to pretend that they had turned the full purchase price over to the church.

The sin was not in the choice they made for the use of their possessions; the sin was in their hypocrisy and in the lie they attempted to tell, not only to the brotherhood, but to the Holy Spirit.

God's judgment was swift. Both died. And the whole church was gripped with a deep sense of reverence and awe for God (called "fear" in the text).

Here is a remedy for our insensitivity as well. Let's regain awareness of just who this God is who has called us into relationship with Himself. When we are filled with awe because *God* is present with us, the little pretenses and games we play with one another are quickly set aside.

Official persecution (Acts 5:12-42). The aggressive preaching of the apostles, authenticated by "signs and wonders" (healing miracles), led to a revival. "More and more men and women believed in the Lord" (v. 14). This success filled the religious leaders with jealousy; they angrily imprisoned the apostles. But Peter and the others were released by an angel. By daybreak they were again speaking "the full message of this new life" (v. 20) to eager crowds.

The temple guards were ordered to rearrest the apostles. Afraid of the people's reaction, the guards "invited" the apostles to ne with them rather than attempting to ag them away. The Jewish leaders were urious at the disciples' continued charge that the Jesus they themselves had killed was now exalted by God to be Saviour and Lord. The leaders now wanted to murder the Twelve as well! Instead, they commanded the apostles not to tell others about Jesus, and they let them go.

The response of the Twelve sets the pattern for our response to similar pressures. "Day after day, in the temple courts and from house to house, they never stopped teaching and proclaiming the good news that Jesus is the Christ" (v. 42).

Suspicion within (Acts 6:1-7). As the number of disciples continued to increase, some of the Greek-speaking Jewish believers felt that their widows were being neglected when the resources of the church were distributed. This group of believers was made up of foreign-born Jews who had gathered for Pentecost from several different lands (see 2:8-10). They first heard the apostles' message in their own languages. Later, not knowing the Aramaic language of Palestine, they could communicate in Greek, the common second language of the Roman world.

Suspicious of the motives of the native-born stewards in charge of the distribution, these Hellenists raised a complaint that might well have hardened into a bitter split if it had not been handled wisely.

What happened was that the apostles called the church together and told them to "choose seven men from among you who are known to be full of the Spirit and wisdom" (6:3). These would be responsible for the distribution. The men they chose had names like Stephen and Philip—names that identify them as Hellenists! The misunderstanding was healed as men who those who had complained would trust were appointed to care for the distribution to all! And "so the Word of God spread. The number of disciples in Jerusalem increased rapidly" (v. 7).

The corporate witness of the church to the reality of Jesus' presence in their community brought its own sure response (see John 13:34).

♥ ***Link to Life: Children***

"That's not fair" debates often mark children's relationships. Junior boys and girls particularly are deeply concerned about fairness. "She got the bigger piece!" "He has more than I do."

Here's how to help your class members begin to deal with such conflicts in the spirit of the early church.

First, help them work out a fair approach. Set up problems: How will each get the same sized piece of cake? How can each get the same number of candies? How can each have a fair share of chores?

Possible solutions: One cut the cake evenly, another get first choice of pieces. Each take one candy alternately. Write chores on a slip of paper, draw one chore each day from a bowl.

Second, note the Acts 6 principle: trust the person who is worried about fairness so he or she will feel safer. Greek Christians thought the others were unfair, so the others trusted them to distribute the food fairly. We can trust the other person to go first when a fair way of dealing with the disputed issue has been worked out.

Hatred (Acts 6:8–7:59). The success of the church, and particularly its constant affirmation of Jesus, now brought a strong reaction. The preaching of the Gospel had polarized Jerusalem. Some responded to the message, while many others became just as hardened against it. These became opponents of the church, even as they had opposed Jesus during His earthly life.

The growing anger now broke out in a vicious mob attack on Stephen. Stephen's defense before the mob (Acts 7) traced the spiritual hardness of Israel from the days of Moses to the present. It was a bold challenge to these men, in which they were charged with faithlessness to the God they claimed to serve. Enraged, the listening crowd dragged Stephen outside the city gates and battered his body with stones until he died.

Thus the church offered up the blood of her first martyr, who prayed for his murderers as he died, "Lord, do not hold this sin against them" (v. 60).

♥ ***Link to Life: Children***

Dislike for Stephen was shown in an unmistakable way! But often boys and girls have "enemies" who show their dislike in other ways. Pushing at the bus stop. Telling stories to get them in trouble. Breaking their toys. And so on.

Ask your boys and girls to list "Ways you know someone doesn't like you."

Talk then about what to do when another child or adult doesn't like them. Tell the story of Stephen to show that even when people hated him enough to murder him, Stephen prayed for his enemies.

Work with your children to write a prayer they can pray for someone who does not like them. Give each child a copy of the class prayer, and encourage him or her to pray it when someone does something to him that shows he does not like him.

Expansion: Acts 8

Christ in His final charge to His disciples had told them to wait in Jerusalem until the Holy Spirit came to bring them power. Then they were to reach out beyond Jerusalem to share Jesus with the entire world. In 1:8 Jesus gave a pattern for that expansion: "You will be My witnesses in Jerusalem, and in all Judea and Samaria, and to the ends of the earth."

This pattern, in fact, gives us a way to outline the Book of Acts.

There are several ways to outline the Acts' history of the early church. One is to see this record as a report first of Peter's ministry to the Jews (Acts 1–12), and then as a report of Paul's mission to the Gentile world (Acts 13–28). Another is to see it as a history of the development of the Christian movement; its origins (Acts 1–5), its transition days (Acts 6–12), and its expansion to become a world religion (Acts 13–28). However, perhaps the best way to see Acts is in the framework suggested in 1:8, as the record of an expanding, dynamic life-force, reaching out to bring more and more of mankind into a vital relationship with Jesus Christ.

Judea and Samaria. The death of Stephen launched a great persecution against the church in Jerusalem. The believers, except for the apostles, were driven out and scattered throughout Judea and Jerusalem.

Everywhere the believers went they told others about Christ, and the message was received—even in Samaria.

The response of the Samaritans must have been something of a surprise. While the people of this district were viewed as mongrel Jews until excommunicated by Judaism in about A.D. 300, they were looked down on as a semiheretical and "foolish" sect.

The Progression of the Church

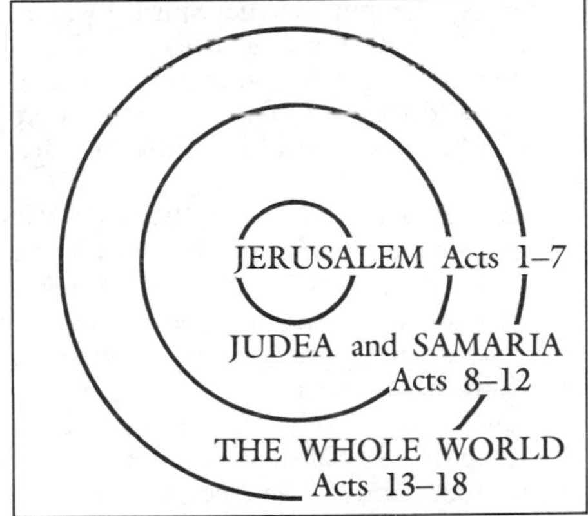

The origin of the Samaritans goes back to the deportation of the people of the Northern Kingdom of Israel in 722 B.C. Those Jews still left in the land mingled with other people imported by Assyria to form a loose culture that retained much of the Old Testament tradition, but developed its own theology and worship system. That the Samaritans had seriously distorted the revealed faith is clear from Jesus' conversation with a Samaritan woman, recorded in John 4, and also from Jesus' clear distinction between Israel and Samaria during His days on earth (cf. Matt. 10:5-7).

Now, however, the Samaritans not only heard the Gospel, but "the people with one accord gave heed" (Acts 8:6, KJV). Hearing reports of the mass conversion, the apostles sent Peter and John to investigate. Discovering that these men and women had truly believed, Peter prayed for them that they might also be given the gift of the Holy Spirit.

This significant incident in the life of the early church receives varying interpretations. What is important to observe here, however, is that the progression of the church outward from Jerusalem (Acts 1:8) proceeded in a series of steps that were given the seal of approval of God's Spirit. Here the Samaritans, later the Gentiles, were shown to be members of the one church of Jesus Christ, led by the apostles of our Lord (10:44-46; 19:1-6).

Since the 700-year-old antagonism between Samaritan and Jew had some of its roots in religious rivalry, it would have been easy for the Samaritans to accept the new faith, but to continue to affirm their identity as a group separate from Christian Jews. By mediating the gift of the Spirit through Peter, God not only affirmed the unity of the church as a single community, but also affirmed the authority of the apostles whom Jesus had chosen to lead it during the early years.

Simon. Acts 8 tells us that Peter's act in Samaria was misunderstood by at least one observer. Simon, a magician who had won a large following among the Samaritans, offered the apostles money if they would only give him such power.

Magicians were well known in the ancient world, and are spoken of in both Testaments. Our word is derived, through the Latin and ancient Greek, from *magi*, a priestly clan in Persia. From the first century A.D. on, the word was used of a variety of magicians, soothsayers, and astrologers. The usual guiding motive behind the life of such a person was acquisition of power to influence people and events through occult knowledge and arcane practice.

The Scripture makes it clear that this stands in direct conflict with God and His ways (see Deut. 18:10-14; Gal. 5:20). There *are* supernatural powers under the control of Satan; seeking knowledge or power through the occult and spirit world is unquestionably anti-God.

Acts 8 records Peter's stern rebuke of Simon. We hear nothing more of this magician in the biblical record. There is, however, early tradition telling of a heretical sect from the same era called the Simoniani. Whether or not this sect sprang from this Simon whom Peter confronted has never been confirmed.

The chapter closes with the report of the conversion of an Ethiopian government official. He was apparently a convert to Judaism, or at least a "God-fearer" who believed in Israel's God but who had not undergone the rites of conversion. The Holy Spirit led Philip away from Samaria and brought him to explain to the Ethiopian eunuch the way of salvation as expressed in the Old Testament passage, Isaiah 53.

Hebrew believers had begun to fan out across the ancient world. The Gospel message was carried with them. This seed would soon bring a rich harvest.

♥ ***Link to Life: Youth / Adult***

This chapter of Acts gives a special perspective on personal, one-on-one evangelism. Acts 8 tells us that persecution scattered the believers, who "preached (literally 'told the good news') wherever they went." The image is not of public preaching, but of talking about Jesus with everyone the believers met. The other incident concerns Philip, who was led away from a great revival he stimulated (vv. 12-13) to share the Gospel with a single individual (vv. 26-40).

To emphasize this lesson, why not ask group members to rank in terms of spiritual significance: evangelists, missionaries, TV preachers, pastors, individual believers. Then discuss criteria by which these should be ranked.

If the "numbers" criteria is used, examine Acts 8. Point out that if each present believer reached just one person, millions more would be won than by the most important single evangelist!

Encourage each group member to begin now praying for God's leading to a person who needs to hear the Good News of Christ.

Gentile Converts: Acts 10:1–11:18

Chapter 9 of Acts tells of the conversion of Paul, and events we looked at in Study Guide 117. And then the Acts history sketches one of the least-expected events in the Bible.

Gentile believers were suddenly welcomed into the church, with the same rights and privileges and blessings as the Jewish believers in Christ! And again at this turning point, the central figure is the Apostle Peter.

Peter. Peter and his brother Andrew were both members of the original Twelve. They were fishermen, perhaps in partnership with and certainly friends of James and John.

The Gospels show that Peter was leader of the Twelve. He is listed first in the four New Testament lists of the disciples. He is the most-frequently mentioned disciple. With James and John, Peter was a member of the inner circle of Jesus' intimates. In Acts, Peter clearly had the leading role, from his preaching of the first sermon on Pentecost, to mediating the Spirit to the Samaritans, and then to first proclaiming the Gospel to Gentiles.

While a leader, Peter remained a man of contrasts. He was bold, yet unstable. Quick to recognize Jesus as God's Christ, Peter was just as quick to object when Jesus spoke of the coming cross (Matt. 16). Ready to promise commitment to the death, Peter three times denied the Lord on the night of His trial (Mark 14).

In Acts the inconsistent Peter of the Gospels seems to have emerged as a man of firm and consistent leadership. Yet, later at Antioch, Peter would refuse to eat with Gentile converts for fear of the criticism of other Hebrew-Christians.

Peter stands as a reminder to us to rely on the stabilizing and strengthening power of the Holy Spirit. God can take our strengths and our natural gifts and use them, and He alone can protect us from our weaknesses. Because the Spirit *is* with us, we too can expect to live victoriously.

After these chapters, the focus of Acts shifts to the Apostle Paul. Tradition tells us that Peter continued his ministry among the Jewish people and traveled widely. Two of his last letters are found in the New Testament, the final one being written shortly before his own martyrdom. Early historians seem to agree that Peter died in Rome, executed during the violent persecution of Christians by the emperor Nero in A.D. 64.

The centurion. In the Gentile center of Caesarea, an officer of the Roman army who had come to believe in God was visited by an angel. The angel told the officer, Cornelius, to summon Peter, who would communicate God's message to him.

The next day, as the Roman's messengers were on the way to Joppa where Peter was staying, Peter had a vision. Three times a sheet filled with animals forbidden by Jewish Law as food (this is the meaning of "unclean" here) was lowered from heaven. Three times a voice commanded Peter to eat. And three times Peter protested against the divine command. Each time the lesson was driven home: "Do not call anything impure that God has made clean" (Acts 10:15).

While Peter was puzzling about the meaning of the vision, Cornelius' messengers knocked at the door.

Gentiles. To understand the need for Peter's preparation and the angry reaction of the Jewish believers when they heard later that Peter had actually entered a Gentile's home, we need to realize the attitude of the Jew toward all foreigners.

For hundreds of years the Jews, full of a sense of their own destiny as God's chosen people, had been politically subject to a series of foreign rulers. Vicious wars, filled with unspeakable atrocities, had been waged by and against the foreigners. Yet the Jews remained in bondage. The fact that this bondage was to men who had no standing or covenant relationship with God made the situation even more galling. Israel was forced to submit to a race they considered unholy and with whom they would never choose to associate. The Gentile was viewed with far greater loathing, and with less respect, than the slave of colonial days. In fact, no pious Jew would ever enter a Gentile's home. He would be contaminated if he did, unable to worship God until he had been ceremonially cleansed.

Thus in the earliest days of the church, the believers were astounded to find God extending His Spirit to the Gentiles! This called for a radical reorientation of their conception of God, and of themselves as the chosen people.

At Cornelius' home. Peter, taught by the vision of the unclean animals lowered from heaven, went with Cornelius' messengers. He entered the centurion's home and began to speak. "You are well aware that it is against our Law for a Jew to associate with a Gentile or visit him. But God has shown me that I should not call any man impure or unclean" (v. 28). Peter had responded quickly to God; he accepted a concept that, nevertheless, would keep on dividing the church for generations!

Cornelius told of the angel's visit. Now he and his family and friends were eager to hear what God would tell them through Peter.

So Peter began to speak about Jesus. He repeated again the basic apostolic Gospel we've seen in Acts 2 and 3, and again in chapter 4. And as Peter was speaking, the Holy Spirit fell on all who heard.

The Jewish contingent with Peter was amazed. They heard these Gentiles speaking in tongues just as they themselves had at Pentecost. It was clear that God had given these Gentiles the same gift that He had given them. Recognizing that God had revealed His will, Peter had the whole Gentile company baptized in the name of Jesus Christ.

Chapter 11 reports the reaction of some

in the Jerusalem church. They attacked Peter sharply. Peter went over the events step by step and shared this unanswerable conclusion: "So if God gave them the same gift as He gave us, who believed in the Lord Jesus Christ, who was I to think that I could oppose God!" (v. 17) And the passage reports, "They had no further objections and praised God, saying, 'So then, God has even granted the Gentiles repentance unto life' " (v. 18).

A new and exciting day had come for the early church. Soon the whole world would be invited to believe.

♥ ***Link to Life: Children***

Put on the board a series of concentric circles. In the bull's-eye draw stick figures representing the child and his parents. Explain that the circles closest to the center are for people who are "like you and your family." But the circles that are farthest away are for people who are "not like you and your family."

Let the boys and girls suggest people who fit in each circle.

Explain the lesson that Peter learned. That is one circle that includes everyone: the circle of God's love! Erase all the circles except the outer one. How good that God wants everyone to believe in Jesus, and become part of God's family. No matter how different from us people may seem, God loves them, and we are to love them too and help them know Jesus.

♥ ***Link to Life: Youth / Adult***

Lead your group to brainstorm and then discuss.

Considering their cultural viewpoint, the response of the majority in the early church to Gentile conversion was an amazing phenomenon. It was clear evidence of the reality of God's presence in these people's lives.

What parallels are there in our world of similar cultural conflicts? What groups are alienated from one another? What are the implications of the Gospel for such divisions? How might (or is*) Christ's presence in His church revealed in such relationships?*

TEACHING GUIDE

Prepare

What divisions are you aware of in your group or congregation? Pray that God will use this study to help in the healing.

Explore

In a minilecture briefly survey the content of each major division: Acts 5–7, Acts 8, and Acts 10–11. If you plan to concentrate on only one of these, give more time in your lecture coverage of the other two.

Expand

1. Look closely at the tensions that may tend to destroy unity in modern congregations even as they threatened the unity of the early church. Use the chart, and the approach suggested in "link-to-life," pages 770-771.
2. Or look at the role of personal evangelism in the expansion of the church. See "link-to-life," page 774.
3. In view of racial and religious tensions in so many parts of the world, it is valuable to remember that oneness in Christ is a reality which must be affirmed and lived! Ask each group member to read privately Acts 10 and 11, and *in a single sentence* sum up the message they convey.

Compare answers. The group members should recognize the message of a unity in Christ that supersedes cultural differences.

Then guide them to discuss local or national differences that exist today, and how to deal with them in a Christian way. See "link-to-life," above.

Apply

Discuss: "How do you and I find harmony with people with whom we differ in the church? Is the statement, 'I love him, but I don't like him,' a valid expression of Christian *homothumadon*? Why or why not?"

STUDY GUIDE 120

Acts 11:19–15:35

THE ERA OF EVANGELISM

Overview

What happens to a local church when the neighborhood changes, and "they" begin to outnumber "us" in a congregation? This is one of the issues dealt with in these chapters of Acts, as well as in significant New Testament letters. In each confrontation, a simple principle is affirmed, one we see developed here in its first form.

"They" don't have to be like "us" to be accepted and acceptable. As Paul wrote to the Ephesians, speaking of Jew and Gentile, whose differences were certainly as great as any that divide people today, "His purpose was to create in Himself [Jesus] one new man out of the two, thus making peace" (Eph. 2:15).

In these chapters of Acts we also read about Paul's first missionary journey, and learn about the evangelistic strategy the apostle developed.

Your group members will be able to gain many insights from these chapters about modern missions—overseas and in your own community.

So teaching this section of Acts can be an exciting adventure for you, and for those to whom you minister! These vital chapters can surely enrich your lives, and strengthen commitment to Christ's truth.

- A careful discussion of the restrictions placed by the Jerusalem Council on Gentile lifestyle, along with a discussion of each city Paul visited, is found in the *Bible Knowledge Commentary,* pages 382-396.

Commentary

As the number of Gentiles in the early church grew, some congregations developed that were predominantly Gentile. This was an issue the apostles and elders were forced to face, and with which they struggled. How *are* we to relate to those who are significantly "different" from us?

Persecution Increases: Acts 11:19–12:25

Outbreaks of persecution continued in Palestine. The believers were scattered beyond Judea and Samaria. They spread along the Mediterranean coast and crossed the waters to Cyprus. At first these Hebrew Christians shared Jesus only within the Jewish communities. But then some began to speak of Jesus to Gentiles as well. And at Antioch (see map, p. 779), a great number of Gentiles believed and turned to the Lord.

The Jerusalem church again sent an investigating committee, headed by Barnabas, a man we meet first in Acts 4:36-37. Barnabas was delighted by what he found. He encouraged and taught the Gentile converts, and then, led by the Holy Spirit, set out to find a man named Saul, who is known to history as Paul, the apostle to the Gentiles, the writer of the bulk of our New Testament.

Saul was probably then a man in his early 40s. He had been a Pharisee, one of that strict sect of Jews from which had come Christ's most vigorous enemies. A few years before, Saul had been a witness to Stephen's martyrdom. He had been filled with hatred for this heretical sect of "the Way" and had become one of the foremost persecutors in Judea. As the "heresy" spread, Saul had applied to the high priest for a commission to go to the Syrian city of Damascus and bring any followers of Jesus back to Jerusalem in chains.

On the road to Damascus, Paul had been thrown to the ground as a brilliant light flashed from heaven, and Jesus Himself spoke with him. Blinded, Saul stumbled into Damascus and waited in darkness, until the Lord sent a member of the church there to restore his sight.

Converted in this unique confrontation, Saul became an open and vigorous proponent of the faith he had earlier attacked. He'd been so bold that members of the

Jewish community in Damascus had finally determined to kill him. Escaping, Saul had returned to Jerusalem and sought out the brotherhood. But no one would associate with him. They were afraid that his "conversion" was a ruse to break into the Christian "underground."

Finally Barnabas had taken the risk. Convinced of Saul's sincerity, Barnabas had brought him to the apostles.

Saul had begun to boldly and publicly proclaim his new faith in Jerusalem. Again the Jews determined to kill him. Finally Saul was forced to flee from Jerusalem, and was returned by the brothers to Tarsus. Then, for a time, the Judean church knew a relaxation of persecution.

Then Barnabas went to Tarsus to look for Saul. They returned together to Antioch, and the two became part of a leadership team that ministered to the believers there. Later, when the Holy Spirit warned of a famine coming in Judea, Barnabas and Saul were selected to take the funds collected by this Gentile church to their Jewish brethren.

♥ ***Link to Life: Youth / Adult***

Barnabas is one of the most attractive people spoken of in the Bible. His name means "son of encouragement" or "consolation." A study of this man's life and ways of relating to others can be most helpful, as we see him model graces which can beautify every Christian person.

Give teams of five or six a list of the references to Barnabas in the New Testament. Each is to explore each verse and its context. But each team will try to answer a different question. Here are suggested questions for five teams:

(1) What five words best describe Barnabas' personality? (2) What were Barnabas' most important values? (3) Why would you like to have Barnabas for a friend today? (4) What impact did Barnabas have on the history of the church, and what about him enabled him to have that impact? (5) What qualities of Barnabas would you most like to see in your own life, and why?

The passages in which Barnabas is mentioned are: Acts 4:36-37; 9:27; 11:22-30; 12:25; 13:1-50; 14:1-23; 15:2, 12, 35-39; 1 Corinthians 9:6; Galatians 2:1, 9, 13; Colossians 4:10.

In the meantime, persecution had again intensified in Palestine. This time it came from an official source (Acts 12). James, one of the Twelve, was executed by King Herod Agrippa, who ruled as a puppet and vassal of Rome. This so pleased the Jewish community that Herod had Peter arrested as well, intending to execute him at the conclusion of the Passover feast. Peter was miraculously released by an angel and went into hiding. Herod himself now bore the brunt of God's judgment; he was suddenly stricken with an extremely painful disease and died.

Persecution slacked again. Barnabas, with Saul and a young man named John Mark (who later would write the Gospel of Mark), returned to Antioch.

♥ ***Link to Life: Children***

The story of the early church's prayer for Peter's release (Acts 12) is one of the most attractive in Scripture. It pictures the concern of the church for Peter, as that concern was expressed in prayer. And it reveals a surprise at God's quick answer to prayer that encourages you and me. Boys and girls like this story, which features a girl named Rhoda who is often pictured as about 12 years old. How good that we can show love by praying with and for others. And that we can believe in prayer!

On the chalkboard write problem, prayer, *and* answer. *After telling the story ask, and write the children's answers under each column: "Who had the problem, and what was it? Who prayed, and what did they ask? How did God answer the prayer?"*

Then move to the present. Do your boys and girls know any people who have a problem? Who will pray, and what will they ask?

Lead the boys and girls to share known needs, and to pray in class about them. You may want to leave the prayer record on the chalkboard, and see if next week there will be any answers to report.

Some teachers have found that a prayer notebook with each of these features adds an exciting dimension to Sunday School. Each week prayer requests are added, the boys and girls pray, and answers to prayer are recorded as well. How exciting it is to look at the end of a quarter at what the children have prayed for—and to see

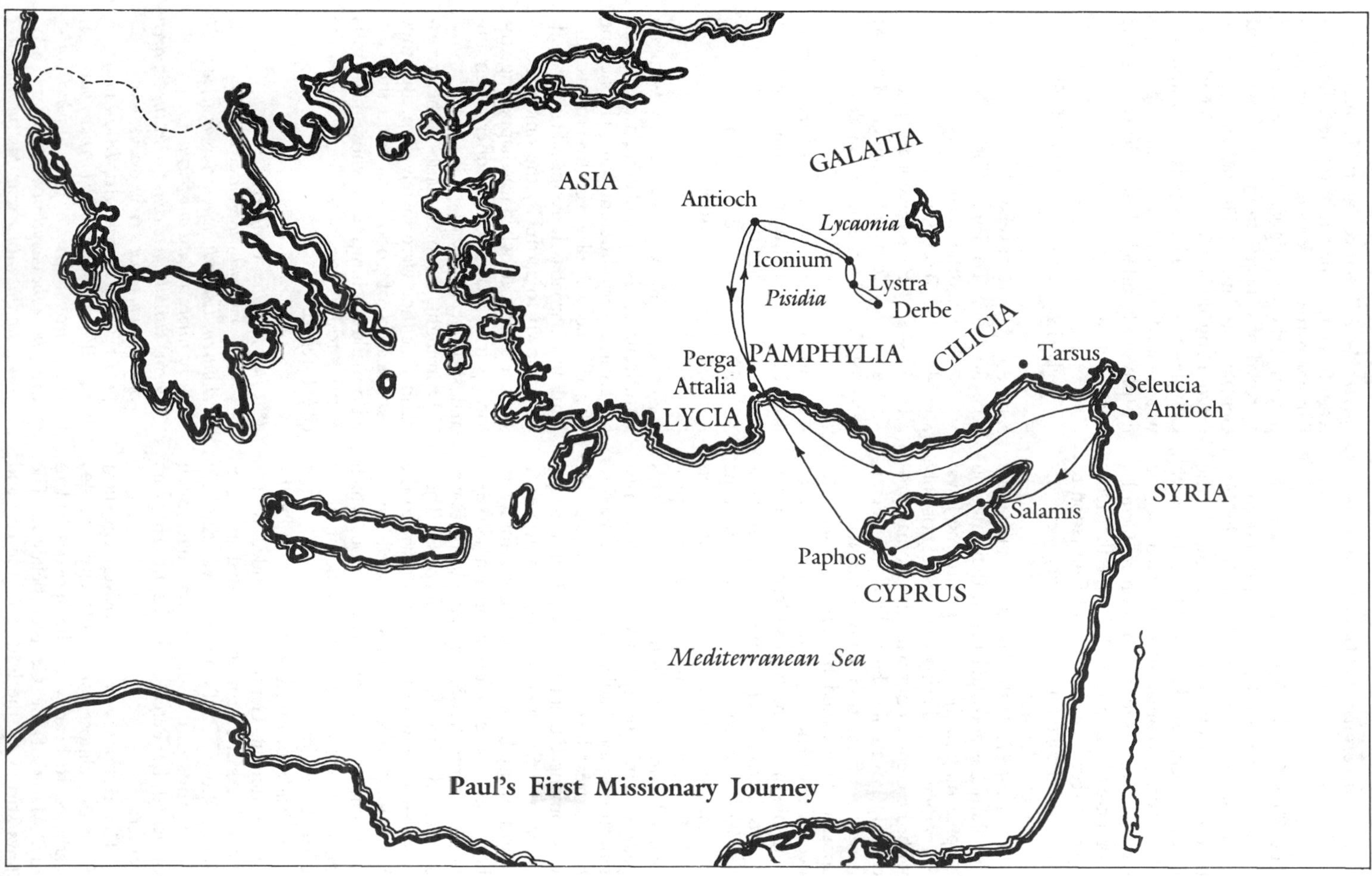

Paul's First Missionary Journey

the many prayers that God has answered for them.

The First Gentile Mission: Acts 13–14
Earlier, witness to the Gentiles had been an unplanned overflow of witness by the Hebrew Christians to other Jews. Now, for the first time, God spoke to the Gentile church of Antioch, commanding that two men be set aside for a specific mission to Gentiles (compare 13:2 and 9:15). As the Holy Spirit directed, Barnabas and Saul (soon to be called Paul in the Acts text) were ordained for the mission.

Acts 13:4-12. At the first stop on the journey Barnabas and Paul began their mission by preaching in the synagogue to the Jews. Soon they were sharing the Gospel not only with the Gentiles but with the Roman proconsul (governor). Here Paul, like Peter, had a confrontation with a magician, an apostate Jew named Bar-Jesus ("son of deliverance"). The evil sorcerer was stricken with blindness; the Roman leader believed.

Acts 13:13-52. Traveling on, the missionary team went to the city of Antioch in the province of Pisidia. Again, as Paul always did, he went first to the Jews and proclaimed Christ Jesus in the synagogue. This pattern in missionary work remained consistent throughout Paul's life. He continued to have a great love for his own people. He was convinced that they, the people through whom the Saviour had been given to the world, must have the first opportunity to hear the Gospel. This approach also had other benefits. In every synagogue there was a reserved place for "God-fearers." These were Gentiles who had been drawn to the high moral precepts and the exalted concept of a single, sovereign, Creator God, which then characterized Judaism alone of all the current religions.

In Pisidian Antioch, many Jews and many of the devout Gentiles responded to the Gospel. As the sermon recorded in verses 16-41 shows, Paul's message was the very same apostolic Gospel that had been preached by Peter some 12 or 15 years earlier.

The response was explosive. The next Sabbath "almost the whole city" (v. 44) gathered to hear what the apostles had to say. Many of the Gentiles believed. The Jews stirred up the leaders of the city and drove the missionary team away.

Acts 14:1-7. Traveling to Iconium, the team launched a new mission, and the now-familiar pattern was repeated. Beginning to preach at the synagogue, they soon gathered a crowd of converts from both Jewish and Gentile populations. The unbelieving Jews reacted angrily and stirred up a Jewish and Gentile reaction. The population of the city was divided. Finally the unbelieving majority physically attacked and drove out the missionaries.

EVENTS OF PAUL'S LIFE

A.D. 34	Conversion
A.D. 36	To Tarsus for "the silent years"
A.D. 46	To Antioch
A.D. 47–48	First missionary journey
A.D. 48	Jerusalem Council (Acts 15)
A.D. 49	Writes first epistle (Galatians)
A.D. 50–51	Second missionary journey
A.D. 53	Third missionary journey begins
A.D. 59	Journey to Rome
A.D. 64	Martyrdom

Acts 14:8-28. At Lystra, a city with no significant Jewish population, the mission began in a very different way. The healing of a cripple was observed by crowds, and Paul and Barnabas were mistaken for gods come down to earth. By the time the missionaries grasped what was happening, the local priests were about to offer up an animal sacrifice to them!

Distraught, the missionaries rushed to explain that they were merely men. But they *were* bearers of good news from the God who made all things, and whose many gifts testified to His goodness. The people of the city listened.

♥ ***Link to Life: Children***
Plan an evangelistic event with older children. Let each of your class or department invite at least one friend who doesn't usually go to church. Let the children help you make popcorn or cookies, and play a Bible story from Acts 13–14 to act out. We're familiar with birthday parties. A second-birthday party in which children share the Gospel in a simple way can be significant for your class members as well as for their unchurched friends.

At Lystra, another contingent of Jews from Antioch and Iconium arrived. These men had determined to follow the missionaries and try to undo their preaching. And they succeeded in arousing the city against Paul. He was attacked with cobblestones, dragged out of the city, and left for dead.

But the "dead" Paul got up, and returned to the city. The next day the missionary team began to retrace its steps, visiting again those groups of believers which had been formed in every place they had preached.

Several patterns established on this first missionary journey to Gentile lands continued to mark the evangelism of Paul and of other Christians throughout the days of the early church.

- They visited cities and lands where the Gospel had not been preached.
- They began their mission in the synagogues, first contacting the Jewish community and the Gentiles who had been drawn to Israel's God.
- The message was soon shared with the entire city, and the response was more positive from Gentiles than from Jews.
- Initial success led to persecution and opposition.
- After establishing a new group of believers by usually spending weeks or months with them to teach them, the missionary team moved on.
- Later the team returned. Those who had grown spiritually and had been marked off by the Holy Spirit were recognized and ordained as local leaders by the apostles.
- The missionary team, particularly Paul, remained in contact with the new churches. He sent letters of instruction and encouragement, and often sent representatives like Timothy and Titus to guide the new church for a time.
- Each church was, however, to depend on the leading of the Holy Spirit. As the independent congregation matured, that group of believers reached out to the nearby cities and towns to share the message of Jesus in their own local "Jerusalem and Judea" (1:8).

The explosive, multiplying dynamic of the church of Jesus Christ, infused with His Spirit and committed to live life's great adventure by focusing on its Lord, had begun the process by which the Roman world would be reached in a single generation.

♥ ***Link to Life: Youth / Adult***
List the basic elements of Paul's mission approach on the chalkboard. Work as a whole group to identify from Acts 13 and 14 each element described.

Then divide into teams to do one of these things: (1) Discuss how relevant this pattern is to today's missions. Does it give us any criteria for evaluating modern missions' strategy? (2) Discuss how the pattern shown here might be adopted by a local congregation's evangelism committee. How could we use New Testament principles in reaching our own city?

Acts 15

The missionary team returned to Antioch filled with joy, eager to report what God had done among the Gentiles (14:24-28).

But soon another kind of team appeared. These were men from Judea, who had been thinking seriously about the relationship between the Jewish church and the growing number of Gentile congregations. Their solution was to go back to a principle which had operated in Old Testament times. If a person who was not born a Jew wished to become a worshiper of God, he must first convert to Judaism. Identification with the people of the covenant was the only way to enter fully into relationship with the God of the covenant.

And so these Jewish believers traveled to the Gentile churches, teaching that "unless you are circumcised according to the custom [Law] taught by Moses, you cannot be saved" (15:1). To really be a Christian, they thought one had to first become a Jew, or at least surrender one's own culture and identity, and adopt the lifestyle of an Israelite.

This teaching stimulated a serious debate, particularly when it became clear that these teachers had not been sent by the apostles, and did not represent the official position of the Jerusalem congregation.

A delegation was sent from Antioch, led by Paul and Barnabas, to bring this issue to the apostles at Jerusalem. There, in about A.D. 48, the first council of the church was held.

Paul and Barnabas reported on the great moving of God among the Gentiles. Then they heard the demand made by some believers who were also Pharisees (the most strict of Judaism's sects when it came to stressing man's obligation to keep both the written Law of Moses and the oral traditions): "The Gentiles must be circumcised and required to obey the Law of Moses" (v. 5).

The Law. In studies of Romans and Galatians we'll discuss the Law in depth. For now, it's important to realize that the term "Law" is used in a number of ways, both in and out of Scripture.

At times "law" (*nomos* in Greek) is rendered "custom." At other times our word "principle" is more fitting. But even when *the Law of Moses* is specified, there may be different things on the writer's mind. At times *the Law* may be a way of referring to revelation itself, meaning God's total revelation of Himself and His will in Scripture. Finally, *the Law* spoke of the lifestyle of Israel, regulated as it was by biblical commands and traditions, which patterned the way the Jew spoke and thought and acted. The Pharisees surely believed that *the Law* indicated that distinctive way of life which set the Jews apart from all foreigners, and had for centuries marked them off as God's peculiar people.

In Acts it seems clear that the challengers were asking for more than moral and ethical purity from the Gentile converts. "It is necessary," they insisted, "to circumcise them, and to charge them to keep the Law of Moses." Circumcision was the sign of entry into covenant relationship with God; the visible mark of being a Jew. The Pharisees were demanding that Gentile converts reject their own culture and heritage, and adopt both the name and lifestyle of the Jew to be accepted as true Christians!

Acts 15 reports the struggle of the leaders with this issue, and the exciting outcome. The Law, Peter declared, was a burden no one had ever been able to bear successfully (v. 10). Since salvation is by the grace of God for Jew and Gentile alike, why burden the Gentile believers with the Jewish Law?

After further discussion, James summed up the council's conclusions. God clearly had acted to save the Gentiles, *as Gentiles!* In fact, the Old Testament prophets foretold a time when such a thing would happen, and even Gentiles would be called by God's name (v. 17). The Hebrew church then had to let the Gentiles keep on being Gentiles. They had to accept these Gentile brothers and sisters *as they were!*

There were, however, four specific warnings which related to aspects of the Gentile lifestyle which James felt should be brought to their attention. These warnings seem rooted in prohibitions which were stated by God before Law was given (see Gen. 9). The Christian converts were to have nothing to do with the idol worship which characterized their culture. They were to keep away from illicit sex (again, a common feature of the Gentile lifestyle). They were to give up unbutchered meat (something tremendously offensive to the Jew, which could have made it very hard for a Jew to have fellowship with a Gentile brother) (cf. Lev. 17:10-14; Deut. 12:16, 23-25), and they were to abstain from shedding blood (this probably means cruelty, murder, and even possibly service in the army). Later many Christians did take it this way: many in the early church refused to do military service, and were executed. Others did serve in the Roman army, but were persecuted for their refusal to enter into the official religious practices expected of soldiers.

The delegation returned joyfully to Antioch. The Jerusalem church had officially welcomed the Gentiles into the fellowship of the church. It had affirmed the fact that every culture has equal standing before God. From Jew and Gentile, God was about to form one new man. In Christ, the differences could be accepted and forgotten. Jesus, not our differences from one another, is to always be the focus of our shared life.

The problem would, of course, surface again and again. Paul, the leader of the Antioch delegation, would himself be the one to spell out in letters to the Galatians and the Romans just what the Law does mean to a Christian. But those days were still ahead.

For now, another great stride had been made. And the church knew a special sense of joy and peace.

■ For a discussion of Paul's split with Barnabas, see the *Bible Knowledge Commentary,* pages 396-398.

♥ ***Link to Life: Youth / Adult***
Divide your group into three factions. Give each faction a printed description of

its view. After each faction has read and talked about its role, have them come together to hold a "council" and try to reconcile their differences.

Faction 1: Jewish. You know that God chose your people, and gave you special promises as well as a Law to live by. God has sent you prophets, and His own Son came as a Jew to die for sins. You are convinced that your ways are right, and that they are also godly, in contrast to the ways of non-Jews. It is clear to you that if a person really wishes to please God he must live as you do, subject to the Law as a good Jewish Christian should be. And you are ready to contend for this truth.

Faction 2: Gentile. You have been saved through faith in Christ and are part of a vital Gentile congregation. You don't have anything against the Jews, but you certainly aren't one. You don't even feel comfortable with their strange customs, most of which have nothing to do with morality. You have been upset by these Jewish Christians who insist that you must give up your own culture and live as they do to be saved. You're concerned, and a little bit angry too.

Faction 3: You haven't thought much about the problem that bothers the other two factions. You've just been happy as a Christian, witnessing and praying. You don't know quite why the others are so upset, but you do care about both sets of brothers and sisters. And you also care about what is right in God's sight.

After about 20 minutes, debrief. How did members of each faction feel? Is it more important to be right, or to win? Is this a situation in which one side must win, and another lose? Or can there be compromise?

Then have your group members study Acts 15. In view of their own "council," what in Acts 15 seems particularly significant?

Finally, are there modern situations where similar attitudes and viewpoints exist? Identify them. How should they be dealt with?

TEACHING GUIDE

Prepare
Select the theme that you will emphasize in the development of this session.

Explore
Give a brief summary of the content of these chapters of Acts. You may wish to let your group members choose a study emphasis, as study methods suggested in this guide can easily be expanded to fill the time you have available.

Expand
1. For an enriching personal experience, lead your group members in a biographical study of Barnabas, one of our best biblical models of a loving Christian person. See "link-to-life," page 778.
2. Or to help your group members think more deeply about missions and evangelism, guide them to draw principles from Acts 13–14, which report Paul's first missionary journey. See "link-to-life," page 781.
3. Or look in depth at Acts 15, and the issue of whether a cultural group should be required to "live like" another to be acceptable as Christians. See "link-to-life," pages 782-783.

Apply
What would you have liked best about being a part of Paul's missionary team? What would you have liked least? Take a few moments at the end of your group meeting to share, and then pray together for missionaries who today are seeking to serve God in foreign lands.

STUDY GUIDE 121

Acts 16–19

THE GENTILE CHURCH

Overview

This portion of Acts contains the report of Paul's second missionary journey (see map), and a portion of the report of his third. During these years of journeying we find Paul moving from the provinces into the very cultural and trade centers of the Roman Empire.

A congregation founded in a central location, like Thessalonica, could become the hub from which the Gospel was spread throughout its area of influence. And this is, of course, exactly what happened. As Paul wrote in a later letter to the Thessalonicans, "The Lord's message rang out from you not only in Macedonia and Achaia—your faith in Christ has become known everywhere" (1 Thes. 1:8).

This was the true secret of the early spread of the Gospel: it did not rest on the shoulders of key men like Paul alone. Enthusiastic evangelism was a ministry shared by all.

But what made the first-century world so receptive to the Gospel message? In this study guide we look not only at the events reported in Acts 16 through 19, but also sketch the religious and moral climate of the first century. That world, like our own in so many ways, was ready to hear the Gospel message when it was appropriately shared. And it was ready to respond.

■ The Victor *Bible Knowledge Commentary,* pages 398-412, gives helpful information on the cities and people mentioned in these chapters.

Commentary

The world into which the church now advanced was very different from the provincial land of Palestine. Centuries earlier the conqueror, Alexander the Great, had begun a process which spread Greek culture and language across the Middle East. Asia Minor, Egypt, the Greek Isles, and the ancient Empire of Persia all fell to the conqueror and, after his early death, to the four generals who divided Alexander's spoils.

The spread of the Greek language and culture unified and linked the world of the New Testament. The vision of "one world" and of a "united nations" is no modern invention. It was Alexander's dream, hundreds of years before Christ. By the days of the early church, this dream had been realized to the extent that missionaries like Barnabas and Paul did not have the language barrier that missionaries face today. They could communicate everywhere they went in Greek, the second language of elite and commoner alike.

Greece conquered the world culturally. But it had taken the expansionist and brutal power of Rome to weld the world together politically. Under the first emperor, Augustus, the *Pax Romana* (Roman peace) had been imposed by force of arms. The empire which Rome held included not only Egypt and the Middle East, but extended even to the British Isles, encompassing France, Spain, and what is now West Germany (see Map of Roman Empire, p. 760). Roman government and Roman law brought an unprecedented stability to the world through which the missionaries traveled. There was no trouble with passports, no detours to avoid wars between bickering states. During the first years of Christianity's expansion, the new religion was considered a sect of Judaism by the government. As such the Christian faith was a "licit religion," with its freedom of practice guaranteed by the Romans!

The Roman world was far less unified religiously. The official religion of the empire was the cult of emperor worship. The classic religion of the period of the Roman republic (with its worship of a pantheon of interchangeable Greek and Roman gods and goddesses headed by Zeus [Jupiter]) now received only perfunctory attention. But existing alongside the official and the classic religions were a number of secret cults, generally referred to as "mystery religions." These originated in the East and became more and more popular, as the aberrations of succeeding emperors eroded confidence in the official faith. The austere and distant gods of Greece and Rome offered no personal relationship, and provided no personal religious experience. To fill this need, cults like the Eleusinian, the Dionyisian, the cult of the Great Mother (Cybele), and that of the Egyptian Isis and Osiris, spread through the empire.

These mystery religions featured initiation rituals, rites, and myths. The cults had little or no ethical content. Most stressed fertility in a female deity and had both sexual and social appeal. In the sense of belonging that came through initiation into the cult, and in the promise of a special relationship with a mythical deity, many looked for a meaning that life in the Roman Empire, for all its stability, did not provide.

The world, empty of promise or hope, was ready for the coming of the Saviour. And this world over which Rome ruled was uniquely shaped to permit the explosive spread of the one faith which actually does meet the deepest needs of man. A faith which rests not on myth, but on the historical fact of God's entrance into the world in the person of His own Son, Jesus Christ.

The Core

It is clear from our reading of Acts 16–19 that the Apostle Paul was sensitive to first-century culture. But it should also be clear that Paul was careful never to compromise the core issues of the Christian faith.

The distinction is often lost. It's so easy to take a practice sanctified by tradition and mistake it for a core issue.

For instance, for many years in the United States, Sunday evening was dedicated to evangelistic church services. Non-Christians could be brought to church, and an evangelistic message, with an invitation, became the expected thing. As American society changed and new recreational and entertainment patterns developed, Sunday evening no longer was a time when the unchurched slipped into the pew. Even the annual "revival meetings" were now attended primarily by believers. Yet, the approach to evangelism continued to be the Sunday evening or special revival service. A "Gospel message" was expected, even though the Gospel might be familiar to everyone present.

How different this picture is from Acts. There, Paul took the Gospel to people where they were, and he adapted the form of presentation to his listeners. We see Paul searching out a riverside place of worship, and sitting down to talk the Gospel over with Lydia and her friends. We see Paul moving into the synagogue and there debating in the classic way from the Old Testament Scriptures. When Paul stood before the philosophers in Athens, his presentation took the form of philosophic argument, using even pagan religious poetry and an Athenian altar to "An Unknown God" as points of contact. His presentation there never once referred to Scripture! And, in Ephesus we see Paul in the lecture hall of Tyrannus, holding "discussions daily" (Acts 19:9) like other itinerant teachers of his day.

As Paul moved to different settings and different cultures, he *adapted*. He easily shifted the location, and even the form of the Gospel presentation, to fit patterns his listeners were most likely to recognize and to understand.

Perhaps we too need to develop the cultural sensitivity of the early missionaries. Perhaps if we were more sensitive to our culture, and less rigid in our terminology, we too might be more effective in our modern evangelism.

Form and Content

It's important to realize that, while Paul clearly adapted the form of his Gospel presentation to fit the listener and the culture, Paul did *not* compromise the core itself. D.R. Jackson, in the *Zondervan Pictorial Encyclopedia* (5:725), noted that Paul spoke "in the way most appropriate to his hearers' circumstances and cultural background," but that certain basic themes are consistently present. The themes that Jackson suggests are: "(1) Christ's death, (2) Christ's resurrection, (3) witness testimony, (4) Scripture testimony, (5) power, and (6) forgiveness."

Wherever the Gospel message was preached, to Jews or others who had the background of the Old Testament, these elements were emphasized. But in the Acts

17 report of Paul's speech to the philosophers of Athens, the proclamation went further.

Paul began in Athens by affirming the existence of a "God who made the world and everything in it" (v. 24). This God is Himself the sole source of the material universe and animate life. The God who made the world has design and purpose woven into His Creation. History's ages are moving toward a divinely determined end; an end in which God "will judge the world with justice" (v. 31). The proof of God's reality and His concern for mankind lies in the fact that God Himself entered space and time in form, undergoing death and then experiencing a bodily Resurrection from the dead (see v. 31).

Here we have a true confrontation with the first-century world. Paul might have adapted the cultural forms for those to whom he spoke, but there was no compromise of the Gospel message. And that message went against the grain of the most basic beliefs and values of Paul's listeners, just as biblical Christianity contradicts the beliefs and values of modern man today!

A weary world view. Acts 17 mentions the two prevalent schools of philosophy in the time of the early church: Epicureanism and Stoicism. While differing from each other, both philosophies had the same practical purpose: each sought peace of mind. Stoics saw man as a rational being, felt that the world had a moral order, and emphasized a kind of universal law that pantheistically pervaded the universe. Epicureans saw man as a feeling being, emphasized the supremacy of the individual, and affirmed that the universe was but a random combination of atoms, mechanistically determined. They maintained that seeking pleasurable experience was the best way of life.

Neither philosophy had any place for a divine Creation. One viewed matter as eternal, while the other regarded matter as pervaded by, and essentially equivalent to, the Divine. Without a personal, supreme God who created for His own purposes, the universe had no known origin, and history had no direction or goal. An individual's relationship to either the universe or God (such a god as there was) had no meaning beyond its own existence; no purpose for life could be found outside the brief span of years allotted to an individual.

To someone seeking the meaning of human existence these ancient philosophies could only say, "Exist!" (Eat, drink, and be merry) or "Endure."

It is true that very few first-century men and women were philosophers, just as relatively few people of our own day consciously struggle with basic questions. But the emptiness of the then-current philosophies was reflected in the attitudes and ideas of the general population.

Even the old faith had no adequate explanations. The pantheons of ancient gods and goddesses were simply immortal men and women, freed to indulge in the sins and pettiness their worshipers yearned for themselves. These gods and goddesses had no real concern for humans. Oh, they might choose to favor a special hero, such as Achilles or Hercules, for a time. But they would capriciously turn away from him on a whim at any moment, or they might make him a pawn in a battle with some rival. What's more, the gods themselves were not all-powerful! Like men they were helpless before an impersonal fate. The average individual in the first century saw himself as caught under the crushing weight of chance, helpless to affect the course of his own life, and without any hope of establishing a relationship with a trustworthy supernatural power. Such people had only superstitious ritual or magic practices with which to ward off evil.

Even those mystery religions, which attracted many in the first century, offered at best some revival of life in the underworld, or the prospect of an escape from punishment, or escape from continued imprisonment in a succession of bodies (reincarnation). The concept of a conscious, bodily resurrection was unthinkable.

The view of reality in the ancient world was characterized then by these elements:

- an impersonal universe,
- an impersonal fate,
- an essential purposelessness,
- no hope for relationship with a faithful deity.

Within the framework of this common belief, man lived out his life. The lifestyle of the age had gradually lost the optimism of early Greek culture (ca. 400 B.C.) and was now burdened down with:

- pluralism (with many competing philosophies of life advanced),

- relativism (with each individual choosing his or her own thing, accepting the notion that what might be "right for me" may not be "right for you"),
- superstition (with a variety of straws grasped at in the hope of finding something to satisfy),
- syncretism (with religious and philosophical notions from many sources combined and recombined in an effort to find meaning).

Captured in a world they did not understand, men and women lived lives of quiet desperation or hopelessness. In the words of Paul, they existed "separate from Christ, excluded from citizenship in Israel and foreigners to the covenants of the promise, without hope and without God in the world" (Eph. 2:12). In the fullest meaning of the word, the first-century world was *lost,* wandering in meaningless illusion, never penetrating to the reality underlying the universe, and never knowing that a God exists who offers humanity a relationship through which we can recover both meaning and hope.

No wonder it was a weary world that the early missionaries invaded! And no wonder that, when we look beyond the surface—past the material peace and prosperity and the often unbridled sensuality—we discover a world of men and women desperately ready for the Gospel's Good News.

And today? How like the first century our day is! With all its material prosperity, our age is marked with a sense of weariness and hopelessness. Disillusioned by the unfulfilled vision of scientific conquests, as well as by the patriot's dream, more and more people turn to ancient avenues in search of hope. For most today the universe is as impersonal as it seemed in the first century. With sophistication we explain origins by an evolution that supposedly took place by random chance, bringing life from lifeless matter. From this empty, impersonal origin we seem to move toward a meaningless end. If that end doesn't come soon through a destructive atomic war, mindless depletion of earth's natural resources, overpopulation, or pollution of the environment, then the end will still come in some distant age when the universe itself runs down, the stars wink out, and an endless dark descends.

No wonder that within such an impersonal universe men and women increasingly turn to drugs, to hedonistic sensualism, to astrology or the occult, or to modern mystery faiths from the East, in a desperate search for meaning and for hope.

For perhaps the first time in centuries, the world view of modern man closely resembles the world view of New Testament times! The revolutionary truths so familiar to the Christian are truly revolutionary again. Returning again to the Gospel core, you and I are invited by a living Word to experience again the exciting days of the first century, when the church was vital, and the faith was young.

♥ ***Link to Life: Youth / Adult***

The author speaks of fitting the methods used to present the Gospel to the patterns of communication that are present in a society. Have your group members evaluate: which of the following approaches does not *"fit" today's world as an effective method in evangelizing?*

1. *Passing out tracts on a street.*
2. *Holding revival meetings in a church building.*
3. *Putting evangelistic sermons on TV.*
4. *Holding a debate on a college campus.*
5. *Busing children to Sunday School.*
6. *Sponsoring a Divorce Recovery Workshop in the community.*
7. *Holding Bible studies in homes.*
8. *Doing house-to-house visitation.*
9. *Plastering your car with "Jesus saves" bumper stickers.*
10. *Organizing a mayor's prayer breakfast.*

Discuss each, giving reasons why it does or does not fit contemporary culture. For each which does not *fit, ask your group members to suggest alternatives.*

Then share: "What was the most important influence in each group member's own conversion? How was the Gospel presented to him or her? What conclusions can be drawn, if any, about how to best communicate the Gospel in our modern world?"

Comments on the Text: Acts 16–19

Timothy (Acts 16:1-5). Immediately we are introduced to Timothy, a youth who typifies the first-century world. The son of a Jewish mother and a Greek father, Timothy reflected his century's melting-pot quality. Races and cultures united, retaining some-

ILLYRICUM
MOESIA
THRACE
Black Sea
Rome
Three Taverns
Forum of Appius
Adriatic Sea
MACEDONIA
Puteoli
ITALY
Tyrrhenian Sea
Philippi
Amphipolis
Neapolis
Thessalonica
Apollonia
Berea
BITHYNIA
GALATIA
PONTUS
MYSIA
ACHAIA
Troas
Assos
ASIA
Mitylene
Aegean Sea
Pergamum
PHRYGIA
Antioch
CAPPADOCIA
Thyatira
Messana
Rhegium
SICILY
Sardis
Philadelphia
Iconium
Lystra
Smyrna
PISIDIA
CILICIA
Corinth
Cenchrea
Athens
Laodicea
Colosse
Derbe
Syracuse
Ephesus
Miletus
PAMPHYLIA
Tarsus
LYCIA
Myra
Seleucia
Antioch
MALTA
Patara
CRETE
Lasea
Fair Havens
SYRIA
CYPRUS
Damascus
Paul's Second Missionary Journey
Sidon
Tyre
Ptolemais
The Great Sea
(Mediterranean)
LIBYA
Caesarea
Joppa
Jerusalem
EGYPT
ARABIA

thing of their heritage but also forming something democratic and new.

Conversion in Philippi (Acts 16:11-15). Luke, the author of Acts, who had joined the missionary company, identified Philippi as a "Roman colony and the leading city of that district of Macedonia" (v. 12). Originally Roman colonies were garrison settlements of Roman citizens in captured territories, often populated by army veterans and their families. They had such rights as autonomous government, freedom from taxation, and the legal privileges of those living in Italy. A crossroads for both sea and land trade routes, Philippi was an important center of business, government, communications, and culture. It was typical of the metropolitan centers that the missionaries chose for church-planting.

Lydia and the women with her were most likely Gentile proselytes (converts) to Judaism. While there was a state religion and mystery religions which featured myths and ritual, neither had any particular moral or ethical content. It was not surprising, in this complex religious climate, to find a group of women drawn to Judaism and gathering outside the city for worship. Nor was it surprising to see Paul sit down and informally share the Christian message.

Occultism (Acts 16:16-21). Inside the city we see another aspect of the religious climate of the Roman world. Paul and the others were followed by a slave girl who "had a spirit by which she predicted the future" (v. 16). As a fortune-teller, she earned a great deal of money for her owners—until Paul, in the name of Jesus, cast out the spirit.

Occultism was a feature of the first-century world just as it is a growing element in our own. Exorcism was well known (19:13-16); witchcraft and sorcery were practiced (vv. 17-20). Despite the many religions and philosophies, the average man sensed his hopelessness and knew uncertainty and fear. As Merrill Tenny pointed out, "The pagan world took for granted that men were under the influence of invisible forces of evil which continually sought their destruction. Only by obtaining ascendancy over these powers through magical arts could they retain their freedom" (*New Testament Times,* Eerdmans).

Roman citizens (Acts 16:35-40). Jailed in Philippi because of mob violence stimulated by the slave girl's owners, the missionaries were miraculously released. When the magistrates discovered that they had "publicly without a trial" (v. 37) beaten men who were Roman citizens, they quickly came to appease the missionary party. Such official misconduct might have cost them their positions, or even led to severe punishment! Roman justice, including the protection of the rights of the individual, was swift and fair. As today, federal justice superseded state and local systems.

♥ ***Link to Life: Children***

The story of Paul and Silas in Philippi has important lessons for boys and girls. One is illustrated by the reaction of the pagans when Paul cast an evil spirit out of a slave girl. Her owners were angry, and stirred up a violent mob. And Paul, not the wicked owners, was put in jail. Yet Paul and Silas sang in prison and praised God, for they knew what they had done pleased Him.

To illustrate draw a 4" circle, with one half a bright color (labeled "good") and the other half a dull color (labeled "evil"). Attach the circle to a piece of paper. Draw eyes and write "God" on one side of the paper and draw eyes and write "people" on the other. Rotate the circle and point out that people saw what Paul did as bad, but God saw it as good. See if your boys and girls can think of any time when they did something good that a teacher or parent thought was bad. How important it is to remember when that happens that God sees us. We always want to do what pleases God. Then, like Paul and Silas, we can sing and praise the Lord even if other people misunderstand. How important it is to know that we have done the right thing.

Thessalonica (Acts 17:1-4). Moving on to Thessalonica, Paul went first to the Jewish synagogue there. In the first-century world there were probably some 4 million Jews, and less than 20 percent lived in Palestine. Most major cities had colonies of Jewish citizens engaged in trade, banking, or manufacturing. In these Jewish centers the Old Testament faith had been maintained, and some of the Gentile population was attracted to Judaism. These Gentiles often became "God-fearers," adherents to the moral and theological teachings of Judaism but not full converts to its restrictive lifestyle.

Such Jewish centers were normally the place where Paul began his mission.

Athens (Acts 17:16-21). In Athens, Paul was confronted with a city full of idols and with philosophers constantly speculating on the nature and meaning of life. Luke noted, "All the Athenians and the foreigners who lived there spent their time doing nothing but talking about and listening to the latest ideas" (v. 21). This rather graphic description may remind us of today's intelligentsia.

Paul gave the residents of Athens a unique exposition of the Gospel, starting from the assumptions and ideas of his listeners and then leading them to a confrontation with revealed truth. His sermon here, so different from Peter's sermons recorded earlier in Acts, "recognizes the philosophical cast of mind of his audience and presents his message understandably to them in terms of the three great questions of philosophy: 'Whence,' 'What,' and 'Whither'; or otherwise stated, 'the origin,' 'the nature,' and 'the end of all things' " (Carter and Earle, *The Acts of the Apostles,* Zondervan). In his exposition Paul quoted, not from Scripture but from Greek religious poetry!

Corinth (Acts 18:1-5). Moving on from Athens, Paul came to Corinth, a city that typifies another dimension of the first-century world. *Corinth* was a byword for licentiousness and moral corruption, so much so that "to Corinthianize" was a common phrase meaning "to carry on immorally."

Here Paul lived for some time, teaching in the synagogue until he was expelled, and then teaching in the home of a believer next door to the synagogue.

Priscilla, Aquila, and Apollos (Acts 18:18-28). Two of Paul's well-known converts were Priscilla and Aquila, a couple who are also mentioned in Romans 16:3; 1 Corinthians 16:19; and 2 Timothy 4:19. Aquila and Priscilla went with Paul to Ephesus where they met Apollos who spoke powerfully of the coming Messiah. Apollos had known only about the ministry of John the Baptist, and had not yet heard the full Gospel. Rather than speaking up publicly, the quiet Priscilla and Aquila invited him home, and explained the Gospel "more adequately." This sensitive and loving instruction quickly won the open Apollos, who went on to become a powerful witness and evangelist.

How important that we do not correct others in a way that embarrasses or alienates them! How much we need the spirit of Priscilla and Aquila in the modern church.

Ephesus (Acts 19). Moving on to Ephesus, Paul found himself in one of the world's great religious centers. This city's life was dominated by the temple and cult worship of Diana (or Artemis). Here Paul again taught, first in the Jewish synagogue, then, when expelled, in the lecture hall of Tyrannus, who apparently was one of the many teachers of rhetoric or philosophy found in first-century cities. Paul rented his facilities for use when the owner was not teaching.

Within two years, the Gospel message had such an impact on the city that the business of the silversmiths and other craftsmen, which was based on selling religious items to tourists and pilgrims, had fallen off significantly. The leader of the tradesmen warned his fellow craftsmen not only of a loss of trade but "also that the temple of the great goddess Artemis will be discredited, and the goddess herself, who is worshiped throughout the province of Asia and the world, will be robbed of her divine majesty" (v. 27).

Again a riot ensued, but this time it was squelched by the city officials, who insisted that the swelling Christian movement "neither robbed temples nor blasphemed our goddess" (v. 37). Christianity did confront the culture and faith of the first century, but the confrontation was on the deepest levels of human experience, and not marked by disrespectful actions or language.

The church in mission is neither rebellious nor destructively radical. The Christian revolution takes place within the hearts of men. Confrontations that invariably follow the Gospel message are the outgrowth of personal transformation. With the Gospel comes a rediscovery of reality, and a recovery of hope. And *these* are the key to building the kingdom of God.

TEACHING GUIDE

Prepare
How do you believe that the modern world resembles first-century society?

Explore
1. As your group members assemble, brainstorm: "How do most people who are not believers view the universe? Where they came from? Where they are going?" List suggestions on the chalkboard.
2. Give a minilecture, describing the worldview of those who lived in the Roman Empire in the first century. Include an outline of the philosophical views then held, as discussed in the guide's commentary.

Expand
1. Have each person in your group read *quickly* through Acts 16–19, or assign a different chapter to different individuals. Each is to note the special qualities or traits of the people in the cities mentioned and how the apostle adjusted his presentations of the Gospel. After hearing reports, give a brief orientation to how the apostle sought to adjust the manner of presentation of the Gospel to cultural difference while retaining the Gospel's core.
2. Use the "link-to-life" suggestion on page 787 to think together about how to best share the Gospel in our own time.

Apply
Divide into pairs. Have each person think of one individual he or she knows. Describe that individual to the partner. Then think of how his or her differences can be used to tailor a sharing of the Gospel he or she can best hear.

STUDY GUIDE 122

Acts 19–28

PAUL'S IMPRISONMENT

Overview

These last chapters of Acts tell a tale of high adventure. Paul concluded a third missionary journey, undertaken to encourage churches already founded (20:2). The journey ended in Jerusalem.

There Paul was attacked by an angry Jewish mob. He was rescued and then held in prison by a Roman governor, till Paul exercised his right as a Roman citizen to be judged in the Emperor's court! After a stormy journey Paul arrived in Rome, where he awaited trial for two years in his own rented residence.

The Book of Acts ends here. But tradition suggests that Paul was acquitted. He traveled to Spain on another missionary venture, but was arrested again. During his second imprisonment Paul wrote his second Letter to Timothy. This time his imprisonment was ended by execution, and the great apostle joined the Lord whom he had loved and served so well.

While these Acts chapters are filled with adventure, they also suggest many lessons that we Christians need to learn. This study guide focuses on lessons that will be especially relevant to you and your group.

■ The chart analyzing reports in Acts of speaking in tongues (p. 794) is taken from the *Bible Knowledge Commentary*, page 408. This chart is typical of the helpful data contained in this excellent verse-by-verse resource, which should be referred to for answers to questions on details not dealt with in this *Teacher's Commentary* survey.

Commentary

There is only a brief report of Paul's third missionary journey in Acts (19:1–21:16). It's clear that this trip of encouragement was also a farewell journey: Paul felt the Spirit's compulsion leading him to Jerusalem, to terrible danger, and to a new phase of his ministry. Yet there is much we can learn from the brief report of that journey, and from the adventures of the apostle in the Holy Land and on his way to Rome.

The Power of the Gospel: Acts 19:1–21:15

These chapters highlight elements in Paul's ministry which we have seen earlier in Acts, but which raise questions that deserve our attention.

Is there a modern role for miracles in evangelism? (Acts 19:1-22) Luke's report of Paul's arrival in Ephesus makes several references to the supernatural.

First (vv. 1-7) he tells of Paul's meeting with "some disciples" whom Paul asked about receiving the Holy Spirit. These men had not even heard of the Holy Spirit. As Paul probed further, he discovered that they knew only of John's ministry announcing the Messiah was at hand. It was "John's baptism" (as a sign of repentance) rather than Christian baptism (as a sign of faith in and union with Christ) that they had received. Paul shared the Gospel message, and the men immediately responded. The Holy Spirit "came on them, and they spoke in tongues and prophesied."

If we analyze this and other incidents reported in Acts we note that not every reference to filling by the Spirit and not every reference to conversion tells of speaking in tongues. In the three cases which do speak of it, this experience seems to have served as a special sign to Jews (see chart).

This does not prove or disprove any modern view about speaking in tongues. But it does suggest that while that experience was real, it had a special purpose in New Testament times and was not always associated with evangelistic ministry.

But Luke went on immediately to tell of "extraordinary miracles" that God did

Paul's Third Missionary Journey

Speaking in Tongues in Acts

PASSAGE	TONGUES-SPEAKERS	AUDIENCE	RELATED TO SALVATION	PURPOSE
2:1-4	The 12 Apostles and others	Unsaved Jews	After salvation	To validate (for Jews) the fulfillment of Joel 2
10:44-47	Gentiles (Cornelius and his household)	Saved Jews (Peter and others) who doubted God's plan	The same time as salvation	To validate (for Jews) God's acceptance of Gentiles
19:1-7	About 12 Old Testament believers	Jews who needed confirmation of the message	The same time as salvation	To validate (for Jews) Paul's message

through Paul in Ephesus (vv. 8-22). Clearly in Ephesus miracles were associated with missions. But just as clearly this was "extraordinary" (v. 11) rather than the normal course of events. Acts mentions miracles in other missions settings (13:9-11; 14:3, 8-10; 16:18). Yet in other cities where the apostle spent varying amounts of time, such as Pisidian Antioch, Thessalonica, Berea, Athens, and Corinth, there is no mention of miracles. What conclusions are we to draw?

There are helpful hints here in Acts 19. The passage tells of seven sons of a Jewish priest who were apparently exorcists who tried to cast out an evil spirit using Jesus' name in a magical way. The demon-possessed man beat and stripped all seven! The demonic activity this suggests was very likely stimulated by the devotion of many in Ephesus to occult practices. Many who were now Christians had been involved in such evil, and those who had practiced sorcery publicly burned books of magic worth in our day some $2.5 million! *In a city where Satan had gained a foothold and the supernatural was a dominating theme, God's Spirit performed miracles that demonstrated Jesus' power over supernatural powers!* In cities like Athens, where the orientation was to the philosophical, there are no miracles reported, but Paul's presentation of the Gospel was tailored to the speculative bent of his listeners. This may provide us with our principle. The Gospel confronts human beings where they are. Where there is demonism and sorcery, the Holy Spirit may act to demonstrate the lordship of Jesus. Where there is moral and mental darkness, the Spirit may act through the holy lives of God's people and the simple message of the Gospel to demonstrate that in Jesus there is a better way.

♥ ***Link to Life: Youth / Adult***

Recently while teaching in a seminary in Indonesia, the author was told by missionaries and nationals that God did perform notable miracles in rural areas where the people practiced spiritism.

Ask your group to discuss: "Should this report be believed? Why, or why not?"

After discussion have half the group look at miracle reports in Acts. Have the other half of your group read the stories of Paul's ministry in the following passages (Acts 13:13-52; 17:1-9, 10-15, 16-34; 18:1-16).

Return to continue the discussion. What does the evidence each half found in Acts suggest?

Then study together *Acts 19:1-20. What do we learn about the kind of place where miracles did occur? How does this differ from places like Athens and Thessalonica? Either let your group members discover, or suggest to them, the principle that the author suggests (italicized in preceding commentary).*

How good that God need not prove Himself to us by miracles. But how good to know that He is a miracle-working God!

How are Christians to confront evils in society? (Acts 19:23-41) The temple of Artemis in Ephesus was one of the ancient world's wonders. It was the very center of the city's life, for the temple served not only as a worship center but as a bank, to which not only individuals but nations came for loans. The idol representing the goddess had been shaped from a meteorite (v. 35), and silver medals and miniatures sold there were critical to the area's economy.

When Paul brought the Gospel to this city and its surrounding area he did not attack Artemis directly. The city clerk testified that the Christians "neither robbed temples nor blasphemed our goddess" (v. 37).

What the missionaries did do was to confront the assumptions that lay at the root of idolatry. Paul presented no man-made god, but the God who made men. He told not of a lifeless lump of metal, but a living Person who came from heaven and who, resurrected after His death for our sins, returned there. The message and the power of the living Saviour themselves revealed the emptiness of idolatry. The result of the positive presentation of Christian truth was to discredit the false!

What an exciting concept. We *do* need to confront evils. But not by railing against them so much as by positive affirmation of Christian truth.

♥ ***Link to Life: Youth / Adult***
Idolatry was an evil. And the spread of the Gospel certainly threatened those who practiced it—to the extent that they tried to arouse the mob against Christians.

Our world too is not without its evils. For instance, abortion and pornography are both evils which are nevertheless practiced by many in our society.

Have your group members brainstorm: "How can we, without robbing or blaspheming these evils, confront them with Christian truth in such a way that they are discredited?" For instance, what is the difference between bombing an abortion clinic, and setting up a home for unwed mothers and a system that will enable unwanted babies to be adopted by childless parents?

Together list positive *and* negative *ways that Christians can lovingly confront abortion and pornography in our society.*

Was Paul right to go to Jerusalem? (Acts 20:13–21:15) Some have argued that Paul ignored divine warnings and went to Jerusalem against the Lord's will. It's clear that Paul was deeply aware of the danger he faced. Paul told the Ephesians he did not know what would happen, but that "in every city the Holy Spirit warns me that prison and hardships are facing me" (20:23).

These two chapters tell of several warnings Paul received. But the theory that Paul's insistence on going to Jerusalem in spite of them was disobedience cannot be sustained. Paul said his journey was "compelled by the Spirit" (v. 22). The warnings simply prepared Paul for what would happen, and strengthened his resolve. As Paul affirmed, "I am ready not only to be bound, but also to die in Jerusalem for the name of the Lord Jesus" (21:13).

The evidence of God's leading in our lives is *not* that everything we do turns out well. At times God leads us into hardship, just as He led Paul. What we need is Paul's resolve to do God's will, whatever that will involves, and the faith to believe with Paul that God's will is ultimately good.

Paul, the Jew: Acts 21:17–23:22
It would be wrong for us to idealize the Apostle Paul. He was a great man. And in most things he is a fine model for Christians. But Paul was human and had his faults. His unyielding nature was a strength when he confronted Peter in Antioch over Peter's refusal to eat with Christian Gentiles (see Gal. 2:11-16). Yet that unyielding nature was a weakness when he broke with Barnabas over his old friend and partner's desire to take John Mark on a second missionary journey (see Acts 15:36-41).

We can't sustain the charge of some that Paul went to Jerusalem against the expressed will of God (20:13–21:16). But a more significant question has been raised about Paul's conduct when he reached Jerusalem.

The charge. The charge some raise against Paul goes something like this. "Paul, you've always insisted that Christian faith has replaced Judaism. Yet when you came back to Jerusalem, you pretended to be a traditionalist. You took an Old Testament vow, and offered sacrifices at the temple, as though the old purification rites were still valid."

When Paul was later taken before the Sanhedrin (the Jewish religious and civil court), he claimed to be a Pharisee on trial because of his hope in the resurrection. While this might be partly true, it wasn't *really* truth, and Paul just said it to get the Pharisee and Sadducee parties in the Sanhedrin arguing.

It's true that Paul did speak out boldly about Jesus. But that was only when he had been accused of desecrating the temple. The problem is that Paul clearly compromised his convictions. He *knew* the Jewish ceremonies had no more meaning, but he went through them. He knew that his Christian faith was the real issue, but he tried to mislead the Sanhedrin. In Jerusalem at least, Paul was a *poor* example for Christians today, a man who compromised his convictions for convenience and safety.

The defense. Those who speak in Paul's defense note that the apostle had learned how to fit into different cultures to best present the Gospel in ways that were most likely to win a hearing. Earlier, in a letter to the Corinthians, Paul wrote, "To the Jews I became like a Jew, to win the Jews. To those under the Law I became like one under the Law (though I myself am not under the Law), so as to win those under the Law. To those not having the Law I became like one not having the Law (though I am not free from God's Law but am under Christ's law), so as to win those not having the Law" (1 Cor. 9:20-21).

Because Judaism's practices *were* irrelevant to relationship with Jesus, Paul felt free to adopt them if this would help him relate to the Jews he yearned to win to Jesus! In the same way, because Gentile lifestyle was irrelevant to relationship with Jesus, Paul was free to adopt it if that would help him relate to the Gentiles he yearned to win to Jesus!

A major theme in apostolic preaching was always the resurrection of Jesus. Paul wisely raised this issue, not to mislead, but to gain an opportunity to appeal to those Pharisees in the group who might be moved to defend—and thus be open to hearing—his resurrection message.

In fact Paul is an excellent example for modern Christians. He shows us how to adapt to the people we seek to minister to. He teaches us not to confuse irrelevant cultural issues with the core of the Gospel. And, as these chapters also demonstrate, Paul did not hesitate to proclaim the Gospel boldly when the opportunity came (cf. Acts 21:37–22:22).

♥ ***Link to Life: Youth / Adult***
The issue raised here is an important one. You might lead your group to explore it in one of two ways. Raise the question: "Did Paul compromise?" Have your group members read the Acts passage quickly, and vote yes or no. Divide into two teams. The yes to marshal their arguments, and the no to marshal theirs. Come together again to argue each side.

Or: read the "accusation" paragraphs from the commentary. Have your group take the role of defense attorneys. Members are to study the passage in teams of four or five to try and refute the charge.

Follow up either of these activities by reading the defense provided in the commentary. Then brainstorm at least 10 different modern situations in which Paul's principles can be applied. The principles again are: (1) Don't confuse irrelevant cultural issues with the Gospel core. (2) Be willing to adapt to relate to the people you want to reach. (3) Be bold in presenting the Gospel when the opportunity comes.

Paul, the Roman Citizen: Acts 23:23–26:32

The Roman Empire was a conglomerate of many peoples, bound together by the military power of Rome and a common second language, Greek. The Romans did not try to impose their own patterns of laws and customs on subject peoples. Instead each national group continued to govern itself to a large extent, using its historic institutions and laws. Thus a Jew in Rome was governed by Jewish law.

In fact, Roman law was superior to and superseded the laws of subject peoples. But a noncitizen could not bring a suit in a Roman court: he had to go to his national court for justice. Yet a Roman citizen could bring suit in a Roman court against a native of another nation. In such a case, it's obvious who would be favored!

Roman citizens also had special privileges. A noncitizen could be tortured in a judicial examination: a Roman citizen could not even be beaten before being condemned. And a citizen could never be put to death in some of the more brutal modes adopted in the empire.

Paul had used his citizenship in earlier situations. He had been beaten (illegally) and imprisoned (illegally) in Philippi (Acts 16). When the local officials learned that Paul was a Roman citizen, they were forced to come in person to apologize and to respectfully usher the missionary party out of their city.

In Jerusalem Paul was about to be "flogged and questioned" after the riot his preaching stimulated (22:1-25). When Paul revealed his citizenship, the "commander himself was alarmed when he realized that he had put Paul, a Roman citizen, in chains" (v. 29).

This position not only led the Roman military commander in Jerusalem to protect Paul, but also gave him an excuse to send him (protected by a detachment of nearly 500 soldiers!) to the provincial seat of government, Caesarea (a port city built by Herod the Great and a center of Greek and Roman culture).

Paul was kept there for two years, and had many opportunities to witness to the Roman governor and other royal personages (Acts 24:24-27).

When a new governor, Festus, was appointed, the Jewish leaders pressured him, as a favor, to return Paul to Jerusalem. Paul knew that in Jerusalem the Jewish leaders would find a way to take his life. And so he said, "I appeal to Caesar."

This was a legal expression, and the right of a Roman citizen. A citizen who appealed to Caesar was released from the jurisdiction of lower courts, and could take his case to Rome itself, and to the Emperor's court.

Within days King Agrippa, a grandson of Herod the Great and ruler of northeast Palestine, came to pay his respects to the Roman governor. Festus, confused over the issues raised by the Jews and by Paul's talk of resurrection, told the king about Paul and arranged for Agrippa's contingent to hear the apostle. Paul spoke respectfully to him, for the king was a practicing Jew who believed the prophets and was well-acquainted with Jewish faith. Agrippa advised Festus that Paul could simply have been released: there was no substance to the charges against him. But since Paul had appealed to Caesar, he must be sent to Rome!

Through the whole ordeal Paul never hesitated to use his citizenship to advantage. It is not wrong for a believer, who is a citizen of both this world and heaven, to use the tools this world provides.

♥ ***Link to Life: Youth / Adult***
Some Christians believe that reliance on God is expressed by refusing to use legal and other resources available to them. Give your group members the following poll, calling for True or False answers.

1. *I would never sue someone who defrauded me.*
2. *I believe buying insurance shows a failure to trust the Lord.*
3. *I give more money to missions than I save each year.*
4. *I would never run for political office because Christians should not be part of the world system.*
5. *I do not vote in local or national elections.*
6. *I would not call the police if I thought someone were about to break into my home.*
7. *I would not apply for food stamps even if I needed them.*
8. *I would not sign a petition to rid my corner store of pornographic magazines.*
9. *I would not write my congressman in an effort to affirm the right to life of the unborn.*
10. *I would not take part in a "neighborhood watch" against a rash of local burglaries.*

When the quiz is complete, have your group members indicate how many each person identified as True. Discuss any true answers. Why does the person feel that way? How is that item(s) different from ones he or she marked false?

Review Paul's willingness to use his Roman citizenship to advantage. Are we Christians all to use opportunities and advantages provided us by our place in society? If so, how are we to use them? Are there any principles that might guide our use? When are we not *to use them?*

To Rome and Beyond: Acts 27–28
Paul traveled to Rome by ship. In New Testament times many took passage on ships to travel the Mediterranean. These ships were not passenger vessels, but were coastal freighters who took on passengers in addition to their normal load. Wrecks of ships like the one Paul probably sailed on

have been located and studied by underwater archeologists.

The sailing vessels of that era were not particularly maneuverable, and generally ran before the winds. Against Paul's advice the Roman army officer escorting him to Rome set out to sea too late in the season. The boat was caught in a "wind of hurricane force" and tossed so violently for two weeks that, even with the cargo and ship's tackle heaved overboard, no one could eat and all were sure they would be lost.

The story of an angel's appearance to Paul promising him the lives of all aboard, and the subsequent shipwreck, has proven a favorite story for boys and girls as well as adults. How good to know that no matter how dark the future seems, God is able to deliver us.

♥ ***Link to Life: Children***

Let younger boys and girls tell about the most terrible storm they have ever been in. Where were they? What kind of storm was it? Were they afraid? Were their parents afraid? How bad must a storm be for all the grownups in it to be afraid?

Younger children will enjoy "making" a storm. They can shape small "boats" by folding and gluing paper into a "canoe" shape. Use a pin or needle for ballast. Put the little boats in a pan of water and let different children stir up the waters. See how easily the "boats" turn over and sink when the water is rough.

No wonder the people on the boat with Paul in the great ocean storm were terrified. Only Paul was not frightened, because God had promised him all would be well.

The small "boats" can be rescued from the pan, dried, and two small figures modeled from clay. Place them inside the boat, and mount it on a construction paper base. Print on the base, "God is with me." Like Paul, we can trust when others are afraid, for God is with us as He was with the great apostle.

In Rome Paul waited for his case to appear on the docket. He spent two years waiting, living in a rented house. But those days were not wasted. Paul met with Christian brothers, and spoke to the Jewish community's elders, some of whom believed, but many of whom rejected the Gospel message. Acts concludes with these words: "Boldly and without hindrance he preached the kingdom of God and taught about the Lord Jesus Christ." What an epitaph for the great apostle. Or for any one of Jesus' followers of any age.

Epilogue. Paul won release from this first imprisonment. During those two years he wrote four New Testament letters known as the "Prison Epistles," Ephesians, Philippians, Colossians, Philemon.

After his release Paul probably traveled to Spain to continue his ministry of church-planting. Later he was arrested again, and this time the verdict of the court was death. But during that second imprisonment Paul wrote what are known as the pastoral epistles, which include 1 and 2 Timothy and Titus.

The churches Paul founded did flourish, and the Gospel message continued to ring out. And, through the ages his letters have guided Christians and churches of every time and place.

TEACHING GUIDE

Prepare

Select the one or two issues raised in these chapters which you think may be most important to members of your own group.

Explore

1. Give a minilecture covering in no more than five minutes the events reported in Acts 19–28.
2. List on the chalkboard the four issues for which teaching suggestions are provided. Poll your group on which one or two they wish to explore. Or simply select the one(s) you believe relevant.
   - Are we to expect the miraculous today?
   - How can we best confront evils in our society?
   - What is the difference between "compromise" and "adapting to conditions" in presenting the Gospel?
   - Are we to use "worldly" resources to reach spiritual ends?

Expand

A teaching approach is developed in the commentary for each of the four issues defined in *explore*. Select, or let your group members select one or more of them for study. Then follow the "link-to-life" suggestions in teaching on each. These suggestions are found:

1. On the miraculous, page 794.
2. On confronting social evils, page 795.
3. On "compromising," page 796.
4. On use of "worldly" resources, page 797.

Apply

Read Acts 28:31 as Paul's epitaph. Then ask each group member to write a single sentence epitaph which he or she would be happy to have recorded at the end of his or her own life.

STUDY GUIDE 123

Introduction

ROMANS

Overview

Romans, perhaps more than any other New Testament letter, is a theological treatise. The letter explains carefully the nature of the righteousness that God demands from—and gives to—human beings.

The "by faith" kind of righteousness that Paul explains in Romans is distinctly different from the righteousness the Jews thought they would find in keeping the Law of Moses. In fact, Paul argued that one must not confuse righteousness and Law. The Christian is "not under Law, but under grace" (Rom. 6:14). Yet the Christian under grace is not free from righteousness: he or she is freed for the first time to truly *be* righteous!

The teachings of this New Testament letter are foundational to our understanding of our Christian faith. And truths revealed here are foundational to our experience of a victorious Christian life.

In this study guide we gain an overview of the Book of Romans, sum up the teachings of its major sections, and examine two concepts which must be understood to grasp Paul's teaching: the concept of righteousness, and the concept of Law.

It is well to remember that the conversion of Martin Luther, the great Lutheran reformer, and of John Wesley, who brought revival to Great Britain, came through study of passages in this great book. God still touches hearts and changes lives as He makes these truths real to men and women today.

Commentary

"But that means you can do anything you want to and still go to heaven!"

I heard that objection often from my Navy buddies. Faith alone the way to salvation? No careful keeping of the divine Law as an additional requirement? Then, what is to keep a person from going out and sinning as much as he pleases? Doesn't God care about righteousness anymore?

This is how my witness to Christ as a young Christian affected some of my friends, and how Paul's teaching affected many in New Testament times. How could faith be enough? There must be Law too. Or else God doesn't care anymore about righteousness. To most people now as then, Law and righteousness seem inseparably linked.

Some years into his ministry the great apostle wrote a letter to the church at Rome. In his letter Paul answered the objections of the people of his day, and he answers the doubting of our time. Paul's answer is found in Romans' careful explanation of how the Gospel is related to righteousness—both to God's righteousness and to our own.

♥ ***Link to Life: Youth / Adult***

At the beginning of your Romans study divide into teams of five or six to get the opinion of your group members on issues dealt with in Romans. Your goal is not *to find right answers, but simply to stimulate your group to puzzle over answers that will be developed during your study of this vital book. After teams have talked about the questions, come together and share ideas. Remember: do not correct wrong answers, but do promise that the questions will be answered in your study. You can profitably take as much as half your group time for this launching activity.*

Questions you might have the teams discuss include: "Do the Old and New Testaments disagree on how to be saved? What does the Bible mean when it says we are 'not under Law, but under grace'? Can a human being ever really be righteous? Why do I have so much trouble doing what is right—even when I want to? Are non-Christians really lost? What does it mean to live a 'righteous life'? Who is better off: a person who knows God's Law but doesn't keep it, or a person who doesn't know God's Law at all? What is the difference between 'sin' and 'sins'?"

Rome

As early as the second century B.C., a Jewish colony existed in Rome. After 63 B.C., when Judea became a part of the Roman Empire, this colony grew. By 59 B.C. Cicero wrote of it as powerful and influential.

At times the Jews suffered expulsion from Rome, and as in an A.D. 19 financial scandal. Yet, within a few years the Jews would drift back again to this center of finance, trade, and political power. In A.D. 49 Claudius expelled the Jews from Rome in an act mentioned in Acts 18:2. Strikingly, the historian Suetonius said that the cause of Claudius' action was the "constant indulgence of the Jews in riots at the instigation of one Chrestus." Apparently the message of Christ divided the Jewish community at Rome and, as it did in the cities to which Paul journeyed on his missions, provoked bitter and violent controversy! Priscilla and Aquila, whom we meet later in this letter and who are mentioned in Acts 18, were apparently converted at this time. They were already believers when Paul met them.

Claudius' expulsion edict, like the earlier ones, had no lasting effect. A few years later the Jewish colony again flourished and, as before, included Jewish believers in Christ. By the time Paul wrote this letter to the Romans, a large number of Gentile and Jewish Christians comprised a typical church.

Paul had longed to go to Rome, both to minister to the believers there and to be encouraged by them. But he was not able to go just then. So instead Paul sent a lengthy letter. In his letter we have our most careful, thorough, and detailed explanation of that Gospel which God called Paul to preach. In Galatians we catch glimpses of themes that Paul now fully develops. As we study Romans, we see that in Christ, God has truly taken a new and dynamic approach to the question of righteousness. The cage of the Law was designed to restrain *unrighteousness*. The freedom of the Gospel is *designed to produce in man the righteousness of God*. "In the Gospel a righteousness from God is revealed, a righteousness that is by faith from first to last" (Rom. 1:17).

Romans

Revealing Righteousness from God

- I. Introduction (1:1-17)
  - A. Salutation (1:7)
  - B. Personal items (1:8-13)
  - C. Theme (1:14-17)
- II. Deliverance: Righteous Standing a Gift (1:18–5:21)
  - A. Universal need of righteousness (1:18–3:21)
    - 1. Guilt of the Gentiles (1:18-32)
    - 2. Guilt of the Jews (2:1–3:8)
    - 3. Proof of universal guilt (3:9-20)
  - B. Provision of righteousness (3:21-26)
  - C. Harmonization: Justification and the Law (3:27-31)
  - D. Illustration: Justification in the Old Testament (4:1-25)
    - 1. Abraham, David, and justification (4:1-8)
    - 2. Circumcision and justification (4:9-12)
    - 3. Inheritance and justification (4:13-17)
    - 4. Faith and justification (4:18-25)
  - E. Exaltation: The certainty of justification (5:1-11)
  - F. Summation: The universality of justification (5:12-21)
- III. Victory: Righteous Living a Possibility (6–8)
  - A. The basis for victory: Union with Christ (6:1-14)
  - B. The principle: Enslaved to righteousness (6:15-23)
  - C. The relationship: Freed from the Law (7:1-25)
    - 1. Law and the believer (7:1-6)
    - 2. Law and sin (7:7-12)
    - 3. Indwelling sin and the believer (7:13-25)
  - D. The power: The Spirit within (8:1-17)
  - E. The end: Glorification (8:18-39)
- IV. History: Righteous Dealings a Certainty (9–11)
  - A. Israel's present rejection is just (9:1-33)
  - B. Israel's present rejection explained (10:1-21)
  - C. Rejection not complete (11:1-36)
    - 1. It is not total (11:1-10)
    - 2. It is not final (11:11-36)
- V. Community: A Righteous Reality (12–16)
  - A. Christ's impact (12–13)
    - 1. In the community (12:1-21)
    - 2. In society (13:1-14)
  - B. Christ's attitude incarnated (14:1–15:13)
    - 1. Uncondemning (14:1-13)
    - 2. Self-sacrificing (14:13–15:4)
    - 3. Purposive (15:5-13)
  - C. Paul's farewells (15:14–16:27)

This is God's gift to us too.

To live a truly righteous life. Not by the Law, but by faith.

Outline

Romans 1:17 is the verse that states the theme of Romans. Any adequate outline of the book must reflect the theme of righteousness.

As we trace through this outline, we discover that God has called us to lives of:

- Deliverance
- Victory
- Community

Romans in Brief

What will you and your group members find as you study Romans together? We can sum up the contribution of each major section of this towering New Testament book.

Deliverance (Rom. 1–5). Paul began by showing in his first three chapters that both Jew and Gentile desperately need righteousness, because each group stands guilty before God. The Jew had not lived by the Law God revealed, and the Gentile had not lived by the moral sense, experienced as conscience, which God has implanted in all human beings.

But God had acted in Christ to provide righteous standing before God to those who believe in Jesus. The death of Christ was a sacrifice of propitiation, on the basis of which God freely forgives sins past and future. That death is a demonstration not of our righteousness but of God's. The holy God must punish sin: the loving God was willing to take that punishment on Himself.

While the Jews object that this makes Law meaningless, Paul argued that the Gospel actually restores Law to its intended place. Law from the beginning was intended to serve as a mirror, to reveal sin. The Law was not a standard we must struggle to achieve, but a measure against which we might discover how far short we each fall.

As for faith, the Old Testament itself introduced the principle of a justification that comes by faith. Abraham and David are examples of men who were called righteous by God not on the basis of their good deeds, but because they trusted in His Word.

Paul can only conclude that we who have come to God by faith have sure and certain peace with God. We have been saved by the death of Jesus for sinners: our safety is guaranteed by His resurrection.

Yes, sin came into the world by one man's sin—Adam's. Because of that original sin death cast its pall over the whole human race. But now God has acted in one Man—Jesus Christ. And Jesus has brought humanity the promise of righteousness and life.

Victory (Rom. 6–8). The first chapters of Romans deal with the question of righteous standing before God. How can God pronounce sinners "not guilty"? Only because those sinners have trusted in Jesus, who died as their substitute, taking their punishment on Himself.

But when God pronounced such people righteous in His sight, His decree was no legal fiction. Christians are, by faith, actually united to Jesus Christ. That union is real: we were in union with Jesus when He died, so our death was real and not simply imputed. We were in union with Jesus when He was raised. Thus the power of God's Spirit, which raised Jesus from the dead, is also available to us in our mortality. The One who raised Jesus from the dead gives new life to us as well. Because of this new life, and because the Spirit's power energizes us, we can actually begin to live righteous lives here and now!

But *how* are we to live righteous lives? As a new Christian Paul tried to do right by struggling to obey the Law of God. He found that despite his struggles, he kept on falling short. At last Paul abandoned his efforts, and instead appealed directly to God the Spirit for power and leading.

This was the key. It is the Spirit within, and not the Law without, that the Christian looks to and depends on. One who lives in this way experiences his union with Jesus, and discovers that the Spirit is creating within a righteousness that the Law required but was never able to produce.

As we will see in our study of Romans 7 and 8, learning to relate *directly* to God the Spirit rather than seeking to relate to God indirectly through Law is a vital key to victorious Christian living.

History reviewed (Rom. 9–11). One of the questions Paul's exposition raises is, "Has God been fair? Was God Himself 'righteous' in His treatment of Israel?" Paul argued that God is the only judge of what is fair, and showed that Israel's present rejection is both justified and temporary. God has not abandoned His covenant people, nor has He gone back on His Old Testament commitments.

Community (Rom. 12–16). In his first two major sections Paul showed that God has given individuals who believe in Jesus a righteous standing, and has also acted to bring their state into harmony with righteousness. In this final section Paul looked at the righteous community, at the church which has been formed of those who believe. It is not only the individual Christian who is to live a victorious, righteous life. We Christians are a family, called to live together in a righteous, loving community.

Paul first explores acceptance, which makes it possible for those whose convictions differ to continue to live in community. He then shows us how the uncondemning, self-sacrificing attitude that marked Jesus' own personal relationships helps us create a loving, holy community of those who have faith.

What an exciting book you and your group members are about to study! What wonderful truths. Study of the Book of Romans can bring us assurance of salvation, can show us how to live a righteous, Spirit-filled life, and can help us be contributing members of a local congregation. What a privilege to study and to teach this great New Testament book.

Key Concepts

In our brief review of the Book of Romans, we've already touched on two concepts that must be understood to grasp the nature of our New Testament faith. Let's look at each of them more closely, as background for our study of this Book.

Righteousness. The Old Testament introduces the theme of righteousness, teaching that God's acts are "always righteous" (Jer. 12:1), for all God does is in harmony with His character. God, as the Creator and the moral Judge of the universe, is Himself the one valid standard of what is right.

God's righteousness is expressed in the Old Testament in the "righteous decrees and body of laws" God set out for Israel through Moses (see Deut. 4:8). In terms of God's own actions, two things display His commitment to righteousness. God will "judge the world in righteousness" (Ps. 9:8) and He will also "deliver [the sinner] in [His] righteousness" (31:1). Both God's acts of judgment and of salvation display His righteousness.

The Gospels, however, portray Jesus' teaching that those who seek relationship with God must find a righteousness that goes beyond the Law-based righteousness that engaged the attention of the scribes and Pharisees of His day (Matt. 5:20). Their view of righteousness was summed up in "lawful" behavior: Jesus called for a righteousness in which the very heart of the individual mirrors the heart of God (see vv. 21-48).

This emphasis of Jesus called for a dramatic shift of focus. Righteousness is not to be measured by what a person does or does not do. Righteousness is to be measured simply by whether or not a person truly is, in his heart, like God!

In Romans Paul demonstrated that this kind of righteousness simply is not possible for human beings. Our hearts are corrupted by sin. We reflect, not God's character, but the twisted motives and desires of Adam after his fall.

It is Romans that most clearly expresses God's solution. God fulfilled His commitment to judge sin by taking our sins on Himself as Christ died on Calvary in our place. And then through union with Jesus and by the gift of the Spirit, God set about the process of remaking us from within. His concern is not just that we act righteously, but that we truly *be* righteous. And to be righteous is to literally be like Him in our innermost character.

Thus Paul wrote that we will surely be "conformed to the likeness of [God's] Son" (Rom. 8:29).

To understand righteousness as a biblical concept, we must see that righteousness is at heart nothing more or less than God's essential moral character. God expresses His righteousness in judging sin, and in saving the believing sinner. The Law is at best a definition of how a human being who *is* righteous will behave, and in fact is God's revelation to humanity of how far we each fall short of being like God.

We must also see that the righteousness to which we are called cannot be defined by Law, which measures only behavior. If we are to be truly righteous, our character must be fully in harmony with God's own. And this is exactly why Jesus died and rose again.

In Christ, and through faith in Him, we are declared righteous by God, and through His Spirit made righteous by an inner transformation toward Christlikeness.

While we will be perfectly righteous only when we too are raised from the dead, we are even now growing toward Christlikeness, and through Christ we can live a righteous life now. As Paul wrote in 2 Corinthians 5:21, "God made [Jesus] who had no sin to be sin for us, so that in Him we might become the righteousness of God."

♥ ***Link to Life: Youth / Adult***

You may wish to sample key passages on righteousness to begin to build the biblical understanding which will grow out of your Romans study. Give individuals slips of paper on which one of the following verses has been written. After each individual reads a verse, give the rest of the group members an opportunity to volunteer a statement summarizing what it tells us about righteousness. Each statement should be in the form of a completion of a "Righteousness is . . ." statement.

The verses: Ps. 4:1; Deut. 4:8; 9:4-6; Matt. 5:20; Rom. 3:20; 4:23-25; 8:3-4; 2 Cor. 5:21. If you wish, add more verses by consulting a concordance.

Law. The theme of Law is one of the most significant in the Scriptures. It is also one which must be understood if the freedom we have in Christ, and the pathway God has marked out for us to live by are to be found.

The Hebrew word *torah* (translated "law" in the Old Testament) has complex meaning. Its basic meaning is "teaching" or "instruction." Depending on context, *torah* may have this general meaning, or may refer to the specific instructions given to Israel by Moses. In this later sense it may refer strictly to the Ten Commandments, to the whole set of ordinances established in the Mosaic writings, to the five books of Moses as a whole, or even to the whole Old Testament. The content of the *torah,* God's instructions to His people, thus includes not just moral but also ceremonial and civil matters.

This Law of Moses was, however, given to a special people for a special purpose. God had made covenant promises to the children of Abraham, Isaac, and Jacob. These people, known as Israel, were given the Law to teach them how to live in fellowship with God so that they might receive the benefits promised by the covenant.

While the moral aspect of the Law is universal in that it is an expression of the character of God and thus a divine definition of right and wrong for all, the Law itself was *not* given to Gentiles (see Deut. 4:32-40).

The true believer in Old Testament times loved the Law of God in all its aspects, for it was one of the primary means of God's self-revelation. The believer yearned to know God, and to be like Him, and thus found the Law (as God's revelation) precious (see Pss. 19:7-11; 119:12-16).

Jesus shared the appreciation of the Jew for the Law of God. He affirmed the whole of the Old Testament as God's sure Word (Matt. 5:18-48). But in the same context Jesus announced that He had the right to explain the Law's true meaning. In a series of "you have heard . . . but I say" teachings, Christ showed that the Law's external demands had always witnessed to the fact that God cares about the heart-attitude of human beings. Christ's statement that the whole Law can be summed up in the command to love God and to love one's neighbor underlines this fact. One who truly loves God and others will not do any of those things that Law marks out as a "thou shalt not" (see Matt. 7:12; 22:36-40).

While the Law, as an expression of God's character and of righteousness, was not done away with, its function as a guide to the believer has been done away with. Thus Jesus taught that "the Law and the Prophets were proclaimed until John. Since that time the Good News of the kingdom of God is being preached" (Luke 16:16).

The New Testament "law" is *nomos.* This Greek term functions in the New Testament with several different shades of meaning. On one hand, it captures and expresses the Old Testament's view summed up in *torah.* In other contexts Paul uses such phrases as "law of sin and death," meaning the "principle of sin and death" at work in every human being's life.

Paul, however, had one very special usage which helps us understand what to many seem contradictory viewpoints. In that use Paul viewed "Law" as an operating system, composed of the revealed moral code and human nature. If we take the moral law objectively, without considering any interaction when it is related to fallen man, then law is "holy, righteous and good" (Rom. 7:12). In pure beauty the moral law reveals the character of the God who gave it, and we are moved to worship and to praise.

But what happens when we bring law into contact with fallen men and women? Then Paul noted, "The very commandment that was intended to bring life actually brought death" (v. 10). Sinful human beings are not stimulated by the Law to do good, but are provoked to do wrong! Paul concluded that the problem with the moral Law was that it is "powerless" for it is "weakened by the sinful nature" (8:3).

We might use this simile. The sun that our planet circles is bright, beautiful, and beneficial. Without its heat and light our world would be dead, cold, and lifeless. But neither you nor I can look directly into the midday sun without going blind. The sun's rays will burn out our eyes.

Is this the fault of the sun? Does it change its character as a bright and beneficial thing? Not at all. The problem lies in the very structure of our eyes, which makes it impossible for us to look into the sun's fierce beauty without suffering our sight's destruction.

It is just this way with God's Law. It is beautiful and beneficial. But if human beings seek to relate to it the wrong way—if we link our moral efforts to Law and figuratively fix our gaze on it—we find only destruction. The fault is not in the Law nor in the sun. The fault is in the weakness of our physical and moral nature.

Whenever Paul spoke of God's Law in a negative way, it is this that he had in mind—not the Law in itself, but the way human beings and Law interact. Paul was urgently concerned that Christians did not make the mistake made by Israel, and seek righteousness by staring intently at God's Law.

It is not the task of Law to make men righteous. It is the task of the Law to show men how desperately they need a righteousness which comes from God rather than a righteousness based on their own futile, frustrated efforts.

♥ ***Link to Life: Youth / Adult***

Locate a number of passages in which Paul speaks negatively of God's Law. Pass out a sheet on which each of these references is written out. Ask your group members to read them, then discuss: "Is the Law of God good or bad?"

After discussion introduce the analogy the author makes between Law and the sun, and the impact of each on human beings. Be sure your group members see that when Paul spoke negatively about the Law he was invariably thinking of the effect Law produces in sinful human nature.

Verses you can use include: Romans 6:23; 7:5, 8-11; 8:3; 1 Corinthians 15:56; Galatians 2:21; 3:10-13; 1 Timothy 1:9-11.

The key to our understanding of both righteousness and the Law, as well as our understanding the secret of victorious Christian living, will be found as we examine further this great New Testament book.

TEACHING GUIDE

Prepare

For a detailed discussion of the Law and of righteousness, see the author's articles in the *Expository Dictionary of Bible Words* (Zondervan).

Explore

Take at least half your group time to talk over in teams your members' ideas about some of the key issues dealt with in Romans. See "link-to-life," page 800 for ideas on how to structure this study.

Expand

1. Give out copies of the outline of Romans found on page 801. Each member can use the outline to guide personal reading during your study.

You may want to give a minilecture summarizing the content of Romans, as outlined in the commentary, while your students follow on their outlines.

2. Or focus on one or both of the key concepts which Romans develops. For ideas on how to explore the subject of righteous-

ness, see "link-to-life," page 804. To explore the subject of Law, see "link-to-life," page 805.

Apply
If each group member were to learn just one thing from your study of Romans, what would he or she want to learn? Go around the circle letting each person share, saying why he or she made that choice.

STUDY GUIDE 124

Romans 1–3

THE QUEST FOR RIGHTEOUSNESS

Overview

The first three chapters of Romans carefully argue that all men are guilty before God. No one who relies on his observance of the Law will be declared righteous in the divine court. The Law, as a moral revelation of righteousness, offers no hope; it testifies against us so that "every mouth may be silenced and the whole world held accountable to God" (3:20).

Yet the devastating critique of our human condition ends on a note of hope. God has found a way to give us a righteousness that is apart from Law.

Romans' argument is interspersed with theological terms that we need to understand.

▶ ***Circumcision.*** The Old Testament rite was a physical sign and symbol of a person's participation in the covenant God made with Israel. Paul argued, however, that true circumcision is of the heart: a person *in* the covenant must live by the covenant's regulations. The true Jew is one inwardly, not just in the flesh.

▶ ***Conscience.*** Evidence that Gentiles have an implanted moral law is found in conscience. Every culture has standards of right and wrong, and every person fails to live up to what he himself believes is right. Conscience offers no hope, but is as condemning as the Law.

■ See the *Bible Knowledge Commentary,* pages 435-452, for verse-by-verse discussion of these chapters.

Commentary

I remember how guilty I felt.

As a young teenager, I had traced pictures of female underwear models from the Sears catalog, and hidden the "pinups" under my mattress. When Mom changed the sheets, she found them. And left them, exposed on the top of my bed.

Burning with shame, I'd tried to brazen it out. With attempted enthusiasm I hurried out to the back garden to offer Dad, who was trimming a peach tree, my help.

There were other times I felt guilty too. Like the time John Weimer and I picked the only plum on the new tree just before it ripened. Mom had been heartbroken; she'd looked forward so much to tasting that one plum. John and I hadn't even eaten it! We'd opened it and thrown the still-hard flesh of the fruit on our garage floor.

Guilt.

Sometimes it comes because of a willful choice of what is known to be wrong. Sometimes it overwhelms us for unwitting failures. Either way, to feel guilt is pure agony; a recognition of our failure and inadequacy.

Feelings of guilt are common in our society. Sometimes the feelings are rooted in specific acts. A spouse is unfaithful. A mother neglects a young child who is later injured. A teenager lies to his parents about where he is going. A businessman cheats on a government contract.

Sometimes our feelings of guilt are rooted in the growing awareness that we are unable to cope with life. We fall short over and over again. Somehow we must be to blame. The sense of guilt grows. Plagued by the awareness of our inadequacy, we may try any of several approaches to break free.

• One approach to handling guilt is to deny it. Our feelings of guilt, we say, come from hang-ups that society imposes on us. So we insist that everyone has the right to do his own thing, that there are no absolute moral standards that are binding on us.

• Another approach to handling guilt is to explain it away. We look back into our childhood and find reasons why we couldn't help ourselves; we made some of those bad choices because we had to. Often criminal behavior is explained away as being due to societal conditions rather than the individual's choice. Denying personal responsibility is a popular way to attempt to rid ourselves of guilt.

• A third approach to handling guilt is to punish ourselves. We feel "bad," and so we drink, or fail at our work or marriages to make ourselves suffer. Somehow we hope that if we suffer enough we won't feel guilty, even though failing actually will deepen our general sense of guilt and worthlessness.

• A fourth approach to handling guilt is to construct a system of do's and don'ts which we *can* live up to. Then we reassure ourselves of our goodness by meticulously keeping the rules we construct. If we still feel guilty, we compare ourselves with others who don't live up to our high standards, and remind ourselves how much better we are than others. This has historically been a favorite approach of the religious.

• Of course, there's a fifth approach. Just enjoy sin! The first pangs of conscience will recede if we throw ourselves into the pursuit of sinful pleasures. Perhaps we can sear our consciences enough so that we will no longer be troubled by guilt—except late at night when we wake up feeling empty and fearful and alone.

Guilt is such a big thing with us, and is felt so intensely by so many, that it is hard to grasp the fact that the Bible does not really speak about guilt feelings. Instead, Scripture speaks only of real guilt, of responsibility for acts of sin. Even here, guilt is hardly a dominant biblical theme. *Young's Analytical Concordance* lists only 6 New Testament references to guilt or guiltiness, and of the 17 Old Testament references, 8 are found in Leviticus 4–6 and refer to the sin offerings through which guilt was to be covered.

God seems far more interested in speaking to us of forgiveness than of guilt!

The most frequently used Old and New Testament words which speak of forgiveness have the same root meaning: to send away. In each case, what is sent away is not those feelings of guiltiness aroused by our sins or our inadequacy, but the sin itself. It is the *sin* that is forgiven and sent away.

The act of God in forgiving us through Jesus is the source of a new freedom for us. The New Testament quotes an Old Testament promise: "I will forgive their wickedness and will remember their sins no more" (Heb. 8:12). In another place this is repeated: "Their sins and lawless acts I will remember no more" (10:17). Because of Jesus, our sins have been dealt with fully and completely. As far as God is concerned, the issue is settled. Forgiveness is so complete that sins are no longer even remembered.

Then what of guilt?

Because our sins are dealt with and sent away, we are no longer guilty! We stand uncondemned before God! Justified by faith, we now "have peace with God through our Lord Jesus Christ" (Rom. 5:1). And in Jesus we can find inner peace as well.

Sometimes guilt feelings linger on after we have accepted Jesus and His forgiveness. This is one of the things we learn to overcome as we grow in our faith. A child frightened by a dog may grow up terrified of even the tiniest poodle. The fear remains, long after the reason for fear is gone. Often Christians feel guilt long after Christ has taken away their sins, and the real guilt is gone. How good to grow to the place where we can acknowledge the nature of sin, can accept Jesus' forgiveness, and can go on in our Christian lives freed from bondage to guilt feelings after the guilt is gone.

Yet before we can discover this freedom we must face the grim facts that Paul presents in the first three chapters of Romans. We must realize that we are guilty before God and utterly without hope in ourselves. Only when we face that fact are we likely to abandon our futile attempts to deal with guilt on our own, and come to Jesus for release.

♥ ***Link to Life: Youth / Adult***

Write the word "guilt" on the chalkboard. Ask your group members to write down one or two words that describe how guilt makes them feel. Then list their suggestions on the chalkboard under "guilt."

In a brief minilecture cover the ways suggested in the commentary that people try to deal with their feelings of guilt. Discuss: "Which of these approaches do you think most people would be likely to use? How have you in the past tried to deal with guilt feelings?"

After 10 or 15 minutes of discussion, move into Romans. Point out that while God's way of dealing with guilt is forgiveness, Romans 1–3 makes it clear that each of us must face the fact that we are guilty (not just "feel" guilty) before we are likely to turn to Jesus for salvation.

The Power of God: Romans 1:1-17

In his introduction Paul affirmed first that God has good news for humankind in Jesus Christ, His Son, who "was declared with power to be the Son of God by His resurrection from the dead" (v. 4). The Gospel, the Good News from God, is infused with this same life-giving vitality, for "it is the power of God for the salvation of everyone who believes: first for the Jew, then for the Gentile" (v. 16). And what does the Gospel message reveal? That there is a righteousness from God, which is available to human beings, and that it is "by faith from first to last."

Thus Paul's opening paragraphs are filled with promise. God has a message for us in Christ, a good word about a salvation which does not depend on what we do to earn it, but comes as a gift which can be received only by faith.

Later in Romans Paul examined each theme introduced here. He explained carefully the astounding nature of "salvation," and how it is that both life and righteousness are involved. Later too Paul helps us understand the nature of "faith." But first of all, Paul wanted to make sure that we fully understand why we need this salvation.

The reason is grim. Without salvation, we have no spiritual life. Without it, we have no righteousness. Without it, we stand guilty and condemned before the holy God. There is no hope for any person aside from the by-faith salvation that God offers us in Jesus!

No wonder Paul saw himself as "obligated both to Greeks and non-Greeks, both to the wise and the foolish" (v. 14). Paul had the Gospel, the message that can bring life to the lost. As a fellow human being like you and I, Paul was obligated to share the Good News of salvation with all.

The State of the Lost: Romans 1:18–3:20

As Paul penned these first chapters of Romans, one reality dominated his thoughts. That thought is stated in a critical verse in Romans 5: "By the trespass of the one man [Adam], death reigned" (v. 17). Our understanding of salvation must grow from our awareness of man's utter lostness.

All too often human beings begin their thinking about relationship with God with different assumptions. To some, a human being seems a person born with spiritual life who forfeits that life only when he personally chooses sin. Others believe that a person is born neutral. To them, the issue remains in doubt until the final judgment, when our acts will be weighed in a set of divine balances. If, at that time, there is more good than bad (so the thinking goes), eternal life will be the reward.

Paul had no such image of man. He took seriously the Old Testament picture of the Fall, and was convinced that all human beings are born spiritually dead and alienated from God. Both by nature and by choice, human beings willingly choose sin, even when they know the good. So the basic question is, "How do human beings receive spiritual life?"

This is a question that Paul himself never asked or even thought of in his early years. As a young Pharisee, the 30-year-old Saul assumed that life was his, and that he could please God by a rigorous keeping of the Law. Only later, jolted by the appearance of Jesus on the road to Damascus, did Saul go back to probe the untested assumptions on which his whole life had been based.

Now, writing to the Romans, Paul realized that there would be many others like himself who would not have traced the implications of the Gospel back to the basics. So in the first three chapters of this book Paul sought to demonstrate the deadness of humanity. He sought to prove our guilt, and utter lack of righteousness. Paul argued that we do not die spiritually because of sin; our sins demonstrate that we are spiritually dead.

Human beings never needed Law to show them how to live. Mankind's need has always been for life itself—something that is not communicated through God's Law.

Spiritual deadness (Rom. 1:18-32). Paul was familiar with the sinful lifestyle of the pagans, a lifestyle adopted and expressed in the stories of their gods and goddesses. The Gentiles had not come to this depraved state because they had no opportunity to know God. Paul pointed out that ever since Creation, God's invisible qualities have "been clearly seen" (v. 20). That which can be known about God through nature "is plain to them" (v. 19).

The question is, "How have human beings responded to God's revelation of Himself in Creation?" What has happened is that, when confronted by God, "they neither glorified Him as God nor gave thanks to Him" (v. 21). Instead they reacted *against* Him, exchanging "the glory of the immortal God" for dead images and idols.

An analogy helps. We've all seen two lovers walking side by side. We've seen their hands brush, then seen them grip. The love that exists between the two attracts: a touch stimulates a handclasp, and soon an embrace. We've also seen what happens when a hand brushes a hot iron or stove. There's a sudden jerk; the hand is pulled away. Instead of attraction there is repulsion.

This, Paul said, is what has happened between God and man. When God brushes against human beings, unveiling just a bit of Himself in creation, humanity jerks away! Humans desperately repress the truth, not thinking "it worthwhile to retain the knowledge of God" (v. 28).

To Paul and to us this reaction is evidence of the spiritual deadness of humanity. To contact God—the Bible's God of love and righteousness—and to be repelled! And then to choose all sorts of corruption and wickedness rather than Him! How plain it was to Paul as he went on to list the spiritual and moral wickedness that human societies have so clearly displayed. Such people must be both guilty and spiritually dead! If there were any life at all, they would respond as a lover to the God who loves each of us so.

♥ ***Link to Life: Youth / Adult***
Bring several copies of the day's newspaper to your session. Explain Paul's argument in Romans 1. Then ask your members to scan verses 26-32 and the newspapers to find modern-day evidence that mankind is spiritually dead and in rebellion against God.

God's judgment (Rom. 2:1-16). Paul then made it clear that God will surely judge the sins of humankind. No human being can lightly condemn others, for we too have sinned, and deserve judgment. What is called for is repentance. The Jew might be proud because he knew more of God than the Gentile. He had received God's Law. But what God is concerned with is not *knowing* good. It is *doing* good that counts (vv. 7-11).

Verses 14-15 are an interesting aside which have often been misunderstood. These verses read:

> Indeed, when Gentiles, who do not have the Law, do by nature things required by the Law, they are a law for themselves, even though they do not have the Law, since they show that the requirements of the Law are written on their hearts, their consciences also bearing witness, and their thoughts now accusing, now even defending them.

Paul here was pointing out that the Jews, recipients of the revealed Law, were not the only ones with moral standards! The Gentiles too had a moral nature, and a conscience that identified moral issues and led them to set up standards of right and wrong by which to judge themselves and each other. "By nature" they do what the concept of Law requires: they weigh, measure, and evaluate human behavior by moral criteria. They realize that moral failure calls for judgment, and they try to excuse and defend their failures. When God's Judgment Day comes, both Jew and Gentile will be shown to have fallen short of whatever standards each approves!

This is helpful for those who are honestly concerned about God's "unfairness" in failing to reveal His standards to everyone. God will not judge pagans by Scripture's standards of right and wrong. He will judge all men by their own standards.

But it makes no difference. For all fall short. The failure of individuals and of societies to live up to standards they themselves establish is additional evidence that men are both lost and dead. There is no help for us in ourselves.

♥ ***Link to Life: Youth / Adult***
You may want to lecture on the question "Are the heathen lost?" Key points are: God has *revealed Himself to* all *human beings (1:19-20; cf. Ps. 19:1-4).* All *have moral standards, and God's judgment will be based on the standards a person holds (Rom. 2:12-14). The sinful condition of*

[illegible] is demonstrated in the fact that individuals do not choose to respond to the truth they do possess, or live by the standards that they hold. Thus divine judgment is just: all do *have some knowledge of God and of morality. Anyone who is lost will be judged because of his or her own personal response to God Himself, and his or her own sins.*

Jews and the Law (Rom. 2:17–3:8). Paul then spoke directly to the Jew, who relied on the Law and "brags about your relationship to God." Simply knowing the Law does not make a person superior: one must *observe* the Law.

In essence, Paul was accusing Judaism of having become a religion of externals. It took pride in having the Law, but Jews "dishonor God by breaking the Law." Judaism took pride in physical circumcision, but ignored the inner circumcision of the heart accomplished only by God's Spirit. The Jews had many spiritual advantages (3:1-2). But their unfaithfulness (v. 3) had not shaken God from His commitments. God will still judge those who sin.

Righteousness (Rom. 3:9-20). Up to this point Paul had sought to demonstrate that all humanity is spiritually dead, and thus under God's judgment. Human beings are repelled by contact with God. They choose wicked acts, and even though Jew and Gentile alike have moral standards, they do not live up to them.

Then Paul moved from demonstration to proof! And for proof, he went back to the Old Testament, quoting various Psalms which tell us "there is no one righteous, not even one" (v. 10). This collage of Old Testament verses goes beyond argument. The evidence of history and personal experience Paul drew on is impressive. The statements of God in His Word are conclusive.

It is at this point that Paul returned to the Law. Whatever the Law has to say, it speaks to those who are under the Law (e.g., the Jewish people). And what it says is that all are guilty! Crushed by requirements that no one has ever perfectly met, the mouth of every human being under the Law is silenced, and "the whole world [is] held accountable to God" (v. 19). Since it is the function of the Law to condemn the sinner and demonstrate guilt, "no one will be declared righteous in [God's] sight by observing the Law." Instead "through the Law we become conscious of sin" (v. 20).

So humanity *is* lost. We are spiritually dead, and the very Law to which the Jews looked with such hope is actually an instrument of condemnation.

What Is the Gospel? Romans 3:21-31

Paul launched Romans by referring to the Gospel—Good News from God. What is that Good News? How is it possible for God to provide us with a "righteousness from God, apart from Law"?

Paul then said that "this righteousness from God comes through faith in Jesus Christ to all who believe" (v. 22), for there is no difference between Gentile and Jew, since all have sinned.

The basis on which God makes this offer is the blood of Christ, poured out as a "sacrifice of atonement" (v. 25). Our salvation rests on the work of God in Christ; there is no human contribution. God's grace, His free choice to *give* what we do not have and cannot earn, is at the root of salvation. All God asks from us is faith.

Paul also noted here that the Cross demonstrates not only grace but also God's justice. In the past too God offered believers forgiveness. But how could the holy God let sin go unpunished? The Cross shows the God who does not relax His standards. The penalty which justice demands—death for the sinner—was paid by God Himself. Ours is not cut-rate salvation. Ours is no cheap forgiveness. But it is God who paid the price in the blood of His Son.

The Gospel, then, is simply the message that God forgives guilty sinners, and does so righteously, on the basis of Christ's sacrificial death.

Law and faith (Rom. 3:27-31). To all who object that this robs the Law of honor, Paul responded, "Not at all!"

The principle of faith does exclude human boasting. And it makes salvation accessible to all. But this principle of faith actually *upholds* Law.

What Paul meant is, the Gospel finally puts Law in clear perspective, establishing in every eye the role that God has given the Law—not the role human beings mistakenly assigned to it. The Law's place as the revealer of our lostness is established. The Law's role is even exalted, for now we know. Law itself is a compelling call to look to Christ for a righteousness which can come only as God's gift, and only through faith.

♥ ***Link to Life: Youth / Adult***
Have each group member write a paraphrase of Romans 3:21-26, trying to explain the Gospel to a contemporary friend by expressing the concepts in these verses in modern terms. It may help them to know ahead of time that the word translated "sacrifice of atonement" is translated "propitiation" in older versions. Propitiation emphasizes averting God's wrath by satisfying the demands of righteousness, while "atonement" emphasizes forgiveness and removal of sins enabling establishment of a harmonious relationship with God.

TEACHING GUIDE

Prepare
Study carefully the flow of Paul's argument in these chapters so that you understand the main points. Check specific verses that raise questions in the *Bible Knowledge Commentary's* verse-by-verse exposition.

Explore
Launch class with an exploration of your group's ideas about, and experience with guilt. How does guilt "feel" to them, and how have they tried in the past to deal with guilt? See "link-to-life," pages 808-809.

Expand
1. Explain Paul's conviction that humanity is truly lost: without life, guilty and condemned. Sketch his first argument for this position (Rom. 1:18-32), and distribute newspapers so your group members can look for contemporary evidence of Paul's point. See "link-to-life," page 810.
2. In a minilecture sketch Paul's moral argument. In brief, this is that Jew and pagan both have standards of right and wrong, and that both violate those standards. The violation of one's own moral standards is the basis on which God will judge sin.

If you want to explore the question of "Are the heathen lost?" see the method suggested in "link-to-life," pages 810-811.
3. To help your group members clearly define the Gospel, have each paraphrase Romans 3:21-26. Work then on a group paraphrase that clearly expresses God's way of salvation.

Apply
Conclude with a minilecture that "puts together" what you have explored. Paul demonstrated that all are lost (1:18–3:8) and proved it from Scripture (3:9-18). Those guilt feelings talked about at the beginning are rooted in reality: we *are* guilty.

God's Law is not a solution to our problem, for Law is intended to make us aware of our spiritual death and lostness. "Through the Law we become conscious of sin." The solution is found in the death of Jesus, and the righteousness that God gives us through faith.

Invite any in the group who are troubled by guilt to talk with you later about how to receive and experience forgiveness.

STUDY GUIDE 125

Romans 4:1–6:14

BY FAITH

Overview

Paul had shown that all humanity lies, spiritually dead and without hope, under the judgment of God. The Law in which Israel had hoped was no aid to salvation, but rather a mirror set up to display the sinfulness of human beings.

Yet Paul did not abandon hope. Jesus Christ by His atoning sacrifice has made salvation possible. His blood released the flow of life and righteousness which comes to us as a gift.

But how is this gift received? In Romans 4 Paul reviewed sacred history, and highlighted a principle which has operated from the beginning, but which Israel had overlooked: faith. This towering chapter is one of the Bible's clearest and most powerful explanations of the nature of faith, and particularly of saving faith.

In Romans 5 Paul invited us to experience the peace that faith in Christ brings. We have been reconciled to God through Christ's death; we will be saved through His life.

Romans 5 then examines the theme of life. Adam's sin brought death into the world. This dark heritage has been the burden of every human being born of Adam's line. But Jesus, a new Adam, brings life and the gift of righteousness as well.

And then, in a pivotal section of this book, Paul taught that the key to our new lives is the union that faith forges with our resurrected Lord. Because we are now in Him, life and true goodness can and will be ours.

Commentary

Like other chapters in Romans these chapters are theological in character, and introduce theological terms. It is helpful to preview them, so that when we meet them in the text each passage's teaching will be clearer.

Justification. The Greek word translated "justify" or "justification" means "to acquit," "to vindicate," or "to pronounce righteous." These are important judicial terms, and the theological meaning is borrowed from the courtroom. In justification God clears those who have been charged with sins or failures. The Bible makes it clear that God will clear no one of the charge of sin on the basis of his or her efforts to keep the Law. One can be justified—declared righteous—only on the basis of faith.

The exciting revelation of Scripture is that with the *declaration* of righteousness God has also made possible the *experience* of righteousness. Thus in many contexts "justification" includes both God's "not guilty" verdict pronounced over the forgiven sinner, and the moral transformation of the sinner, which also is by faith.

Grace. God's gift of righteousness is received by faith, but is rooted in His grace. Grace is a dominant theme in the New Testament, but has Old Testament roots. Those roots are sunk deep in the compassionate and caring nature of God, who can be appealed to for mercy "according to Your unfailing love; according to Your great compassion" (Ps. 51:1).

In the New Testament "grace" (*charis*) has become a pivotal theological term. There grace affirms a radical view of relationship with God. It affirms God's attitude of love and acceptance. It affirms each person's helplessness. Grace is action of a caring God who stoops to lift us up, not because of any merit in ourselves, but simply because of His great self-sacrificial love.

Reconciled. This term is not a common one. But it is important. The word implies a restoration of relationship, a return of the harmony that once existed between God and human beings. The point is that conversion brings both a change of position, and a psychological and spiritual change, so our inner attitudes are brought into harmony with the divine reality. We who were once enemies of God now "rejoice in God through our Lord Jesus Christ" (Rom. 5:11).

Baptized. This term appears in Romans 6, which speaks of believers as those who are "baptized into Christ Jesus."

As do words in every language, "baptism" refers to different things. One reference is water baptism, which is a symbol of the spiritual reality spoken of in Romans 6. Another is the baptism by the Spirit spoken of in 1 Corinthians 12:13, which that passage defines as an act of the Spirit which unites us to Jesus and to other members of His body. In Romans 6, "baptism" is our union with Jesus itself: a bonding to Christ that is so real that we are considered both to have died with Jesus and to have been raised with Him. So "baptism" in Romans 6 does not speak of water baptism (the symbol) but of our union with Jesus (the reality that water baptism symbolizes).

For an in-depth discussion of each of these key terms, see the author's *Expository Dictionary of Bible Words* (Zondervan).

♥ ***Link to Life: Youth / Adult***
Write each of the four terms on the chalkboard. Ask your group members to jot down their own definitions of each word.
Then briefly share data provided in the commentary about each. After sharing, work with your group members to develop a single-sentence definition of each term as it is used *in this section of Romans.*

Faith: Romans 4

What is this "faith" that Paul proposed as the key to experiencing that salvation Christ has won for us?

Faith and justification (Rom. 4:1-8). "Faith" is what justified Abraham and David, representative Old Testament saints. "Abraham believed God, and it was credited to him as righteousness" (cf. Gen. 15:6).

It's not a question of what Abraham and David did or did not do to please God. The question is to whom does God *credit righteousness?*

In this argument Paul again asked us to be clear on the character of those involved in the transaction. Abraham and David, like you and me, were sinners. But God is the God "who justifies the wicked" (Rom. 4:5).

The term justification is central here, and its meaning is summed up well by Article 21 of the Augsburg Confession: it is "as when my friend pays the debt for a friend, the debtor is freed by the merit of another, as though it were his own. Thus the merits of Christ are bestowed upon us."

Paul's return to the Old Testament to demonstrate justification by faith is important. God is One, and Scripture is in full harmony with Scripture. The whole Word of God testifies to God's willingness to justify the ungodly, and in every context that justification is by faith.

Justification for all (Rom. 4:9-12). The Jewish reader was likely to object that this justification was for God's covenant people alone. Paul pointed out, however, that Abraham was counted righteous before he was circumcised! Thus he is the "father" of all those who believe, circumcised and uncircumcised alike. Faith is a universal principle that applies to all humanity's relationship with God.

Abraham's offspring (Rom. 4:13-17). The term "father" here is used as "founder of a line or family." That which makes a person one of Abraham's offspring is not physical descent, but rather faith in God. Those who are physically Abraham's descendants and those who are not must alike become members of his spiritual family. This is possible only by believing in the God in whom Abraham believed.

Resurrection (Rom. 4:18-24). Abraham's faith, portrayed so powerfully in the Old Testament, has a distinct New Testament flavor. When God told Abraham that he and Sarah would have a son, it was a promise that life would spring from the bodies of those who were "dead" as far as childbearing was concerned. Abraham faced this fact—"that his body was as good as dead—since he was about a hundred years old—and that Sarah's womb was also dead." But Abraham did not "waver through unbelief." He believed the promise God had given. And this faith was "credited to him" as that righteousness his actions showed he did not possess.

We too believe the message of life springing from death—the message of a resurrected Lord, who died for our sins and was raised for our justification. And for all of us who, like Abraham, commit ourselves to the God we are "fully persuaded . . . had power to do what He had promised" (v. 21), there is a righteousness we do not possess credited to our account.

♥ ***Link to Life: Youth / Adult***
Involve your group members in direct Bible study of Romans 4. Your goal is to help them develop a group definition *of saving faith.*

Begin by having pairs read the chapter together, underlining phrases that help them understand the nature of "faith." Then have each team try to write down 5 to 10 statements about faith *that sum up items they have underlined.*

Come together and put a combined list of statements on the chalkboard.

Then, referring to this list, work together to come up with your group's definition of saving faith.

New Life: Romans 5:1–6:14

A life of peace (Rom. 5:1-11). The result of our justification through faith is "peace with God through our Lord Jesus Christ."

This peace with God is objective and subjective. Objectively we have "gained access" to God, for the ground on which we stand is one of grace and not of works (v. 2). Subjectively, our new "at peace" relationship with God has multiple expressions. We "rejoice in the hope of the glory of God." "Hope" here and in the rest of the New Testament is a special term. It is *not* a word suggesting uncertainty (as, "Well, I *hope* I can make it.") It is instead a word of *confident expectation*. Christian hope is a sense of certainty that brings us joy, even if present circumstances are painful.

Paul specifies the basis of this joy producing hope. First, we know that present suffering is intended by God to produce the inner transformation of our character that God has always intended (vv. 3-4). Second, the Holy Spirit who has been given us pours out God's love in our hearts. There is the inner witness of the Spirit that God does love us as His own (v. 5). Third, there is the object evidence of God's love for us seen in the Cross. Christ died for us when we were still numbered among the ungodly. Surely the One who died for us when we were sinners and saved us from God's wrath will, now that we have been reconciled to God, save us "through His life" (vv. 6-11). The ever-living Jesus will keep us, and bring us through this life to the glory for which we hope (v. 2).

A life of righteousness (Rom. 5:12-21). We come now to one of the key passages in the Scripture—one which theologians pore over. Despite the questions the passage raises (for instance, as to the nature of imputed sin), the primary message of the passage is exciting—and clear.

Sin entered the world through Adam, and all descending from him have been sinners. Spiritual death, as God had clearly warned (Gen. 2:16-17), struck humankind. While no one was charged with "sin" (in the technical sense of a violation of divine law) until the Law was given, all *were* spiritually dead. Thus death reigned, bringing all humankind under necessary condemnation.

But then Jesus Christ came into the world, bringing a grace-gift to us. What flows from Jesus is not death, but life. What relationship with Adam meant was death; what relationship with Jesus means is eternal life—and righteousness.

For *just as sin is associated with and expresses spiritual death, so righteousness is associated with and expresses spiritual life!* Through Jesus, we come to life again and our new life will be marked by the reign of righteousness!

Union with Christ (Rom. 6:1-14). Paul here described a great reversal. We who were dead through Adam lived in sin. Now we who are alive through Jesus are dead to sin.

All this flows from the fact that our union with Jesus is in fact a *real* (not merely symbolic) union. We were bonded to Jesus so that His death was ours, and His resurrection ours as well. In this union our "old self" died to sin. A new self was created that is "alive to God in Christ Jesus." This new self is intended to live a righteous life.

Paul calls on us Christians to acknowledge by faith the reality of our death and new life, and to "not let" sin reign. As those who have been brought from death to life, we are to offer ourselves to God "as instruments of righteousness." We who relate to God through grace rather than Law will not be mastered by sin.

These few verses in Romans 6 are pivotal in the Book of Romans and in our lives. In Romans they serve to shift our gaze from what Jesus' death means for us in our standing with God, to consider what Jesus' death means for us in our present experience. And as pivotal verses, they deserve a closer look.

Romans 6 Revisited: Romans 6:1-14

In Romans 1–5 the Apostle Paul proclaimed the Good News of peace with God. Christ's redemption, received by faith, offers the forgiveness of sins.

Now, writing in the distinctive form of the diatribe, in which the writer inserts periodic objections which an imaginary opponent may make, and then answers them, Paul raised an important question. What shall we conclude from this promise of a salvation by faith, and an imputed righteousness? "Shall we go on sinning so that grace may increase?" (v. 1) That is, is the assurance of forgiveness a license to sin? Some might even go further. Since our sin seems to give God the chance to display His grace, shall we go on sinning so that even greater displays of grace might take place?

Paul responded to this idea with an exclamation: "By no means!" We might paraphrase it as an explosive, "Never!" And Paul says, "We died to sin; how can we live in it any longer?"

What happened to the sin nature? Paul's exclamation, and the verses which immediately follow, are the key to understanding the victory over sin which Christ has won for us.

Historically, there have been many different approaches to the "victorious Christian life." Each of them is related to a particular idea of what has happened to the Christian's sin nature.

**Eradication.* According to this theory, when a person becomes a Christian the sin nature itself dies. This means that the very capacity to sin is removed; whatever a Christian desires or chooses must flow from the new in him and not the old. Our common experience as well as the Bible's promise of *continued* forgiveness makes it plain that this theory does not fit the facts.

**Suppression.* According to this theory, when a person becomes a Christian he or she is given the power to control the sin nature. The capacity and the desire for sin are still present, but the Christian is responsible to hold down that desire.

In this approach a great deal of emphasis is placed on the Law as a tool for suppression. Guided by the Law's demands, and always aware of his own personal responsibility, the individual fights for mastery over his old self.

This grim struggle is something that Paul described in Romans 7. The apostle himself apparently once took this route—and failed.

**Self-crucifixion.* Noting that we were crucified with Christ (see 6:6; Gal. 2:20), this approach to the Christian life visualizes our sin nature as something that struggles to get off the cross again. It is the believer's responsibility, then, to live the "crucified life." Each temptation calls for renewed surrender to God.

At times this approach to Christian living has led individuals to see every human desire and pleasure as an indication of sin. When this happens, they have been led into a joyless life of denying themselves those very things which God gives us "richly . . . to enjoy" (1 Tim. 6:17, KJV).

**Penalism.* This approach views all temptations as attacks of Satan. The problem is never located within us; it's always the fault of Satan. The right response to Satan's attack is rejection. We are to resist Satan on the authority of Jesus, who at the cross won final victory over His enemy and ours, the devil.

But what Paul taught in Romans 6 is different from each of these four ideas. Paul's argument rested on a unique understanding of what did happen at the cross. And Paul taught us a unique way to respond when we sense sin's inner pull; a way that promises a freedom such as we have never known!

This way of release is based on the realization that through Christ's work on the cross our sin nature was *rendered powerless*. Oh, it still exists. And it still pulls us toward evil. But we do not *have* to respond. We are no longer slaves to sin!

Union (Rom. 6:1-4). Paul began here with the concept of identification, of our union with Christ. Paul's point was that this union with Jesus is not merely "legal" but is real. Because we who believe are now "in" Christ, His death was our death, and His resurrection was our resurrection.

Being "in Christ" is the very root and essence of the new life of the Christian. We have passed from death to life (the powers of death have no hold on us anymore). We are not "in the flesh," or "in sin" anymore. It is as if we were citizens of a new country—in Christ.

Romans 6:1-14

What Identification Means	How We Respond to Find Victory
I. Union with Christ in His death.	I. Understand what union with Jesus means.
Sin in our bodies is rendered inoperative, robbed of its lordship.	We were crucified with Christ that the dominance over the body of our sin nature might be rendered inoperative.
II. Union with Christ in His resurrection.	II. Believe (count what God says as true: "reckon").
We are made alive with Christ, free to serve God.	Stop turning yourself over to sin. Trust God's promise that you no longer must sin.
	III. Act on what you believe.
	Present yourselves to God rather than to sin and do His will.

This being the case, we have a share in Christ's triumph over the forces of death and hell. As they could not hold Him in their power, they no longer hold us in their power. The Cross, irradiated with the light of Easter morning, is the fundamental fact which will determine not only the history of the cosmos but our own personal history as well.

"Old self" (Rom. 6:5-10). This crucifixion of the "old self" (a term for the sin nature) did not eradicate the old desires or motives. They continue to betray our "place of origin," as a tell-tale accent marks our speech. The crucifixion of the "old self" did not remove the pull of temptation. Instead, what happened was that the "body of sin" (that whole package of old and warped responses) was rendered powerless or inoperative (v. 6). We will still feel the temptations, *but are not in their power*. Our days of slavery are ended. We are now free to choose the good.

Like Jesus, you and I are now alive to God, and we can choose to live for Him.

Response to sin (Rom. 6:11-14). How is the believer who feels a temptation to sin to respond? Paul's answer is, with faith. For salvation is a matter of "faith from first to last" (1:17).

We are to consider ourselves to be dead to sin (6:11). In other words, consider what God says about the "death" of your sin nature in respect to its power over you to be true. Realize you do not *have* to surrender to your temptations. Then, with full trust in the life that Jesus has given us, actively yield yourself to God, surrendering all to Him for acts of righteousness. In essence, we are to step out and *do* what is right, confident that as we obey the Lord, He will strengthen and enable us.

Donald Grey Barnhouse used to give this analogy to explain. He told of a crew whose captain went mad and was replaced in mid-voyage by the first mate. Now the old captain had no authority; the new captain was the one to be obeyed. Yet Barnhouse suggested that the crew might very well find itself jumping to obey when the old captain shouted out his orders. What the crew had to do was to constantly remember that the old captain need no longer be obeyed, and learn to respond to the voice of the new.

It's like this with us, Barnhouse suggested. Our old natures will keep on shouting out orders. But they have been stripped of all authority over us. We *can* obey them, but we *do not have to*. What we must do is to listen for the voice of our new Captain, Jesus, and choose to obey Him. He and He alone is to be obeyed, for the sin nature no longer can rule our lives.

The truths that Paul presented here in these early verses of Romans 6 do promise us a victory and freedom of which many have only dreamed. And the practical implications of this teaching are astonishing.

The past is now powerless. One of our greatest bondages has been to our past. In a very real way, our pasts determine our futures. The habits we've developed and the tastes we've cultivated have "programmed" our personalities. Each time we surrender to a temptation, we make it harder to resist the next time. Each sin in which we have indulged has paved the way for the next.

But that whole cluster of programmed responses was dealt with on the cross! We still feel the pull. But our future choices are no longer determined by those bad decisions we made in the past. "I can't help myself" is no longer true!

We have so many ways to talk about the bondage we experienced in the past. "I can't stop myself" is a cry that expresses hopelessness. So is, "The temptation is more than I can bear." No matter how true such statements may have been once, they are no longer true. Now, at last, there is release and hope.

On the solid basis of God's own Word I am assured that the power of the past over my present has been broken by Jesus. And I choose, by faith, to act upon that good word.

The next time inner conflict comes, I will present myself to God and let His righteousness find expression in me.

TEACHING GUIDE

Prepare

Study carefully Romans 6, looking especially at the *verbs* in verses 8-14. What do they tell you about our part in claiming the victory Christ won for us on the cross?

Explore

1. Put these statements on the chalkboard: "I can't help myself," and "The temptation is more than I can bear."

Ask each person to think of times when he or she has felt that way, and to identify what *most likely* stimulated those feelings in him or her.

Then promise that in this study you will together find a way to avoid such failures.

2. Use the "link-to-life" suggestion on page 815 to work together toward a definition of saving faith from Romans 4.

When that definition has been determined, explain that since the believer is to live a life of faith "from first to last," faith plays a key part in the victory Christ has promised over sin in our lives.

Expand

1. You may wish to define key theological terms found in this section of Romans. You can do this in a minilecture or as a participatory activity, outlined in "link-to-life," page 814.

2. Or go directly to Romans 6. In a minilecture cover the four concepts of "what happens to the sin nature" discussed in the commentary. Give out copies of the chart on page 817. Ask each person to *locate and underline* in verses 1-14 verses or phrases on which each item on the chart is based.

Form teams to discuss insights, and any questions individuals may have.

Conclude with a summary, using the "old captain" illustration the author includes. The main point is that we are no longer *bound* to sin: we are now free to choose to obey God. We *can* yield to temptation, but we no longer can say we "have to" or "can't help it."

Apply

Ask each person to remember the temptation each identified at the beginning of the group meeting. Ask each, without revealing the problem, to *write down* what he or she is going to do next time the temptation arises.

Then have several share these steps. Close in prayer, thanking God for victory and the freedom that now is ours to obey Him.

STUDY GUIDE 126

Romans 7–8

POWER

Overview

Romans 6:1-14 was a pivotal passage in Paul's argument. On the one hand it was the culmination of Paul's presentation that those who are spiritually dead can have life—through union with Jesus! It was also the launching pad for another presentation: an affirmation of freedom to live a righteous life. Here, in brief, is the line of thought we trace.

Not Under Law,
But Under Grace (Rom. 6:14)

(Digression: are we then
free to sin? [6:15-23])

How can we legally be freed
from the Law? (7:1-3)

Why must we be freed from
the Law? *(7:4-6)*

(Digression: if the Law is so closely
linked to sin, is Law evil? [7:7-12])

What happens to a believer who tries
to relate to God through Law? (7:13-25)

What happens to a believer who relates
to God through the Holy Spirit? (8:1-8)

What is the source of our victory
experience? (8:9-17)

Keeping this simple line of thought in mind can help us grasp the powerful teaching of this vital New Testament passage.

Commentary

We often picture Romans as a doctrinal book, full of deep and difficult truth. In fact, the Book of Romans is totally practical. In seeking to understand the human condition Paul did not turn to abstract theory. He simply looked around him, and saw in society and in each individual's experience a daily demonstration of the reality of sin.

In seeking to explain faith, Paul again resisted the philosophical approach. He simply went back to look at a flesh and blood man in a historical situation. He noted that, for Abraham, faith meant unwavering trust in God's promise. And in turn his unwavering trust led Abraham to respond to God's word.

Then, like the practical person he was, Paul turned his attention to how faith works in us to produce a righteous life. In particular, he explored how we find the freedom to be righteous. Oh, it is good to know that sin in his life had been "rendered inoperative." But we do still feel its pull! At times when we honestly want to respond to God, we may find ourselves actually choosing the opposite way. What does it take for us to live victoriously? How do we experience the flow of the divine power?

Paul's answer was simple, but surprising. "Sin shall not be your master, because you are not under Law, but under grace" (Rom. 6:14). Somehow release from the Law, to live a Christian life under grace is vital to our experience of freedom.

Chapters 7 and 8 in Romans hinge on this affirmation. In them Paul answered the questions his statement had raised, as outlined in this study guide's *overview.*

But before we look more at these chapters, we need further backgrounding.

Earlier in our study of Romans we noted that the concept of spiritual death lurked in the background of Paul's teaching in Romans 1–3. Another concept casts a shadow across the teaching in Romans 6–8. This is the concept that the believer has "two natures."

The Bible speaks very bluntly about human "sin nature." This is an inbred tendency to sin which warps and distorts the human

The Believer

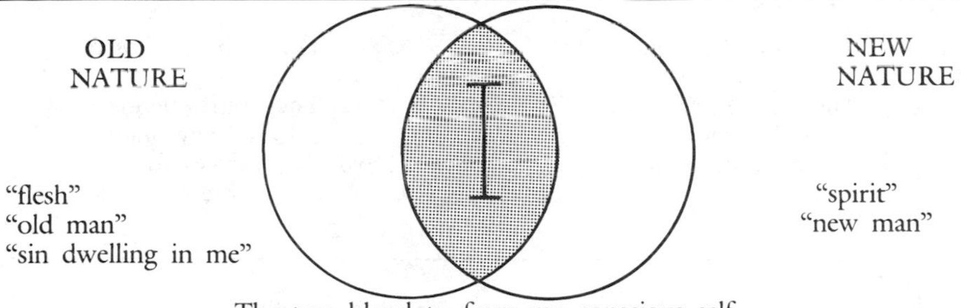

The two blend to form my conscious self, yet they are distinct.

Point:
The old and new natures are channels through which our lives are controlled, either by sin or by God.

Problem:
How are these two channels opened? What can we do to experience God's control?

personality. Human nature, which in the original Creation reflected the character of God Himself (Gen. 1:26-27), was twisted out of shape by the Fall. That fallen nature, warped and twisted, with its capacity and passion for every way but God's, remains with us. What God in Christ has done is to add a "new nature," or "new creation." Those who believe are "made alive" in Christ, with a new capacity for goodness which we did not possess before. Now at last we have both the desire and capacity to respond to God.

But these two natures, the old and the new, are at war within us. Christians are to "put to death" what belongs to the earthly nature, for the "old self with its practices" are to be put off and a "new self, which is being renewed in knowledge in the image of its Creator" put on (see Col. 3:5-11).

So now in one person there are two capacities. The one oriented to good and the other to evil. In each believer reactions, motives, desires, values, and behavior become channels through which God will express Himself in righteousness, or evil will express itself in sin.

The challenge of the Christian life is to learn to live as the new people we have become, and to increasingly reject the old we once were.

This distinctive understanding of the believer and our difference from other men and women is basic to Paul's prescription for victory. Understanding this background, we can move on to examine, in order, the answers to the questions raised by Paul, and answered in Romans 7 and 8.

Human Nature and the Law: Romans 7

How can we legally be free from the Law? (Rom. 7:1-3) Paul turned to marriage for an illustration. A married couple is bound to each other under the Law until one of them dies. The death of a partner frees *both,* so that the living partner is free to remarry. Our union with Jesus is a real union too, so when He died we were legally released from any obligation to the Law. God considers us to have "died to the Law through the body of Christ" (v. 4), and so to be free from any past obligation to live "under" it (6:14).

Why must we be freed from the Law? (Rom. 7:4-6) This is an extremely significant question. It is, in fact, central to the Bible's whole teaching on the Law and the believer. What Paul said here is that the old nature (our "sinful passions") is aroused (literally "stimulated," or "energized") by the Law! And the result of this stimulation is that we produce sin's deadly fruit.

But since we are "not under Law," we can relate to God in a new way. This new way is by the Spirit, who speaks to us directly from within. And, while Law energized the old nature, the Spirit energizes the new nature! The result of the Spirit's ministry is that we produce the fruit of righteousness.

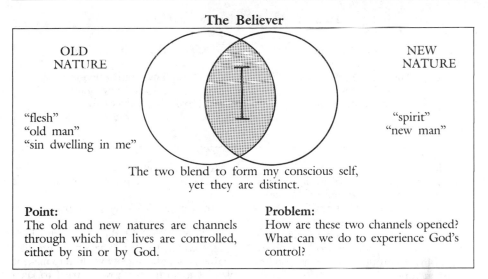

We see the energizing principle at work everywhere. The child who is told, "Don't touch the cookies, they're for company," finds his hunger for a cookie increased! The

Two Ways of Relating to God

Through the Law	Through the Spirit
The Law energizes the old nature which produces fruit to death	The Spirit energizes the new nature which produces fruit of righteousness

forbidden seems far more desirable.

When we approach life as interpreted through the Law, all marked off by "do's" and "don'ts," our old sinful nature is charged with energy. But when we approach life in God's new way, seeing each challenge as an opportunity to let God express Himself through us, we are on the way to victory.

What is the experience of the believer who places himself under the Law? (Rom. 7:13-25) Paul again showed his practical bent. He looked back to his own experience after his conversion when he tried to live the Christian life under the Law. And Paul shared the discouragement he felt then. No matter how hard Paul tried, sin kept on expressing itself in him.

You and I and our group members have had the same experience. We have wanted to do good. We've tried to keep what we saw as good laws or rules, and we've known the shame and agony of failure. Paul's deeply felt anguish, expressed in this rough paraphrase, reflects feelings that we have known only too well.

> I don't understand my own actions. I don't do what I want—I do the very thing I hate. Because I don't want to do the things I do, it's clear that I agree that what the Law says is good and right. I'm that much in harmony with God, anyway. But somehow I'm not in control of my own actions! Some sinful force within me takes over and acts through my body. I know that nothing good exists in the old me. The sin nature is so warped that even when I desire good I somehow can't do it. Sin, dwelling in me, is to blame for this situation. It all seems hopeless! The fact is that when I want to do right, evil lies close at hand. In my inmost self I delight in God's law. But another principle wars with the desire to obey, and brings me as a captive to my knees before the principle of indwelling sin.
>
> Romans 7:15-23 (author's paraphrase)

Paul's effort to keep the Law, with which he agreed, had failed. The sin nature had retained enough control over him to make it plain that no matter how he tried to keep the Law, he fell far short of the holiness and goodness it reveals.

Victory: Romans 8

Romans 7 ended with a cry: "What a wretched man that I am! Who will rescue me from this body of death?" (v. 24)

Romans 8:1-2 answered. "There is now no condemnation . . .because through Christ Jesus the law [principle] of the Spirit of life set me free from the law [principle] of sin and death." Sin within is overcome by a new and powerful principle, that of "the Spirit of life." Put simply, Paul found his answer in realizing that even as a believer he could not keep the Law . . . and was no longer trying! Paul no longer felt any *obligation* to try! Paul had finally accepted himself as really a sinner, with no hope of pleasing God. So Paul turned his gaze back to the Cross, and found joy in the thought of "no condemnation."

But then Paul made the great discovery! When he stopped *trying,* and instead relied on God to express His own divine life through Paul's personality, then "the righteous requirements of the Law" were "fully met" in him (v. 4). Sin lived in Paul. But Christ lived in Paul too. If Paul concentrated on keeping the Law rather than on trusting Jesus, his old nature was stimulated and he sinned. When Paul concentrated on trusting Jesus, the Spirit energized his new nature and he found himself living a righteous life.

Our obligation, then, is not to the Law,

but to respond to the leading of the Holy Spirit (vv. 12, 14). The Law has been replaced by an intimate, personal relationship with God.

Baseball provides an analogy. We want to get to first base. But to do so the batter does *not* look at first base. He watches the ball. He focuses all his energy in concentrating on hitting the ball as it is pitched.

In a sense the "righteous requirements" of the Law are first base to us. We yearn to get there. But too many believers focus their attention on first base—and constantly strike out! What Paul said was keep your eye on the ball—on Jesus Himself—and you will discover that you arrive on first base (a righteous life) without even trying.

How can relationship be the key to moral victory? How does relationship produce righteousness? Paul showed us that as we deepen our relationship with the Lord, the Spirit of God gains more and more control over our lives. Then the Spirit will "give life to your mortal bodies" (v. 11). Yes, in our mortality we are in the grip of sin. It has always taken resurrection, life from the dead, for God to express Himself in human beings. And resurrection is exactly what God provides for those who "live in accordance with the Spirit" and "have their minds set on what the Spirit desires" (v. 15).

Likeness of Jesus (Rom. 8:18-30). In Romans 5 Paul concluded his explanation of the Gospel by stating an underlying principle: all men are spiritually dead; they desperately need righteousness, and can only receive it as a gift.

Then, in Romans 8, as Paul concluded his explanation of how the Gospel produces righteousness in a believer, he again stated a principle which supported his argument. God had chosen to shape redeemed men in the likeness of His Son, Jesus Christ (v. 28). It is our destiny to be like Jesus. God is committed to produce in us all the love, all the joy, all the patience, all the long-suffering, all the goodness, and all the gentleness of Jesus.

This divine commitment means ultimate-

Comparison: Romans 7 and 8

Chapter 7	Chapter 8
I struggle to keep the Law.	I yield myself to Jesus.
Battlefield: self-effort	*Battlefield:* enablement
Combatants: law of sin in the flesh vs. law of the mind	*Combatants:* law of sin in the flesh vs. Spirit of life in Christ Jesus
Outcome: I serve sin.	*Outcome:* The requirements of the Law are fulfilled in us.
Summary: Romans 7:4-6	*Summary:* Romans 8:8-11
NOTE Relating to God through an impersonal code: "law"—20 times "I"—22 times "I do"—14 times	NOTE Relating to God personally through faith: "law"—4 times "Holy Spirit"—20 times

ly the renewal and transformation of the whole creation. It means that one day sin will be eradicated and that we will be "brought into the glorious freedom of the children of God" (v. 21). It also means that we *now* have hope. In another passage, Paul spoke of a progressive transformation, of a *growth* in Christlikeness which we can expect to take place. "We . . . are being transformed into His likeness," Paul wrote the Corinthians, "with ever-increasing glory, which comes from the Lord, who is the Spirit" (2 Cor. 3:18). As the Spirit of God shapes the likeness of Jesus within us, we need never concern ourselves with Law. The life of Jesus will overflow in spontaneous righteousness.

What the Law never was able to produce, the Spirit of God within us *is* producing, even now.

The New Testament on the Law
At this point, then, we need to review and summarize the New Testament teaching on Law.

The Law itself is, objectively, "holy, and the commandment is holy, righteous and good" (Rom. 7:12). As such, the Law has several important characteristics.

- Law establishes standards by which people can measure and evaluate their behavior.
- It provides a partial explanation of righteousness, illustrating righteous behavior and specifying what is unrighteous.

The Law (defined in this context as the moral and social commands given to Israel) is definitely *revelational;* it is designed to help us know more about both God and about what is good. The Law's revelation of the holy has several functions. These, strikingly, relate to the "old man" or the "sin nature."

- The Law is designed to bring the knowledge of sin (3:19-20). When a person looks at the Law's demands and then reflects on his own deeds, he becomes aware that he is a sinner.
- The Law is designed to stir up sin within us. This overlooked function is one often mentioned in the Bible. "The Law was added so that the trespass might increase" (5:20). It is because man *is* a rebel that God's commands stimulate his rebelliousness. Yet even this function has gracious intent: unless we recognize the sin within us we are unlikely to seek God's forgiveness in Christ.
- The Law is designed to demonstrate human need of redemption. Only a person who has given up, and ceased to rely on his own efforts to gain favor with God, is likely to turn to faith. It is our natural tendency to "try harder." If we look honestly at our lives, in the clear reflection provided by the Law, we see how futile our self-effort really is.

The Law and the believer. In theology it is common to distinguish "three functions" of the Law: (1) to reveal God, (2) to convict of sin, and (3) to guide the believer in his or her life with God. This third function is one over which there has been conflict. Some say that during the Old Testament era believers were guided by the Law to respond to God, but that the New Testament introduced a new way. Others believe that the Christian should be expected to keep the Law today, and that Law is still the means God uses to guide Christians to please Him. But neither of these notions seem to fit the New Testament facts.

The point made in Romans 7 is that Law *always* relates to the old nature (the capacity for sin in man). What's more, the Law always *energizes* that sin nature. This is true whether a person is spiritually dead (and possesses only one nature) or is spiritually alive (and possesses the two natures—the sin capacity and the new life capacity). The Law has *never* been the way that believers related to God (see 1 Tim. 1:8). Always the true believer, in Old and New Testament eras, responded to God directly and personally. Even when listening to Scripture's words, the true believer heard through the Law the loving voice of God, and was freed by faith to respond to Him.

The Old Testament principle of life by faith (presented by Paul in Rom. 4) was missed by historic Israel. They distorted the Law into something it had never been intended to be. They tried to make it a way of salvation. They tried to make it a ladder on which to climb, rung by rung, to claim a place beside God as good. In so doing, they lost sight of God Himself, ignored a personal relationship with Him, and thus fell from grace.

And so may we.

We too can read about righteousness in the Scriptures, and take the Bible's teachings as rules and laws to live by. We can make the mistake of seeing God as a rule maker, and the Bible as a rule book for the game of life. We can throw our energies into vigorous attempts to fulfill the "oughts" and "shoulds." But in so doing we will take our eyes off the Lord and our personal relationship with Him. For what we are called to in Christ is a growing closeness, a deepening love. What we are called to is the warm, loving guidance given by the Spirit, and the eager, "Yes, Lord," which moves us to respond.

If we try to live by Law, we miss the joy, and our inward battle wears away our hope.

How wonderful to know that God accepts us as we are: imperfect, falling short of goodness, and yet, because Christ *is* in us, we are growing toward His likeness. For our present sins and failures we have forgiveness. And for the rest of our lives we have the promise of progress toward God's goal—likeness to Jesus.

In another passage, Galatians 2:20, Paul summed it up this way, "The life I live in the body, I live by faith in the Son of God." As Jesus' life surges up within me, all the righteousness which the Law ever envisioned, and even more, will find its expression in me.

In Jesus we have peace.

And power.

TEACHING GUIDE

Prepare

Have you experienced in your own life the essential shift from Law to personal response in your relationship with God? How can you tell? It's as simple as, "All right, God, I'll try" versus "Lord Jesus, I trust You to do it through me and help me obey."

Explore

1. Give a minilecture introducing the two natures. Use the chart on page 821 on the chalkboard or overhead.
2. Also place on the board the "line of thought" outline from this study guide's *overview*. Divide into teams, each of which is to study one question and the passage which answers it. When each group has had 10 or 12 minutes to study, come together again for an interactive lecture.

Expand

1. Probably the best way to cover these two chapters is through an "interactive lecture." That is, ask the questions raised in the text in sequence. After asking each question, let the team that studied the relevant passage share their insights. Then sum up or correct what they have suggested in a brief lecture, using such aids as the charts on pages 822 and 823, and paraphrase of Romans 7 (p. 822).

Draw on material from the commentary only to supplement this interactive lecture, or to help answer questions your group members may raise.

2. Explain that the emphasis on relating to God directly by the Spirit does *not* rule out the objective Word of God which we have in Scripture. The issue is one of how we *perceive* Scripture.

The Bible as Law is perceived as saying, "You should," "You must," and "You ought," and is experienced as a demanding, nagging voice that calls on us to try our best.

The Bible as grace and the Spirit's voice, is perceived as invitation; a revelation of what God intends to do in and through us. Faith hears the Spirit's guiding voice and does not try, but surrenders, expecting Jesus to do in us what we are unable to do ourselves.

The difference between Law and Grace in the spiritual life is *not* that one uses the Bible while the other looks within to hear the Spirit. Both approaches use the Scripture. But only one turns completely from reliance on self to surrender with confidence to God, and in surrrender, steps out to actually obey.

Apply

Analogies and illustrations often make difficult ideas more clear. For instance, trying to live the spiritual life is like playing baseball—you have to keep your eye on the ball and not on first base.

There are other analogies. For instance: Law is like a magnet, which pulls at the sin nature within us. Law is not like a ladder, for it was not meant for us to climb on. Obedience is not like a "stop" sign along a highway, but like an escalator. Faith is expressed in the first step: the Spirit carries us along.

See how many such analogies your group members can come up with to express the truths which you have led them to study in this session.

STUDY GUIDE 127

Romans 9–11

RIGHTEOUS IN HISTORY?

Overview

These middle chapters of Romans have not been as popular as the rest. They shift from the meaning of Jesus' death and endless life for us to other issues. And they introduce concepts over which Christians still debate.

Many of Paul's readers in New Testament times were Jewish, and a Jew might well wonder if *God* was being righteous in justifying all by faith. After all, God had given Israel great covenant promises. And this Gospel of salvation by faith totally ignores the covenants. How could Paul dare to speak of as *righteous* the God who broke and ignored His ancient word?

Romans 9–11 contains Paul's answer to this major objection to the validity of the Gospel of salvation by faith. Part of that argument rests on two difficult theological concepts.

- ▶ ***Sovereignty.*** The word is not found in Scripture. But the concept—that God is free to act as He chooses, without any limits set by the actions of another—is deeply rooted in the biblical concept of God.

- ▶ ***Election.*** The New Testament often uses the term "the elect" or "God's elect" to identify believers (cf. 2 Tim. 2:10; Titus 1:1; 1 Peter 1:1). The Greek words indicate a "choice or selection." Some Christians believe that election implies God's choice of who *will* believe, while others say it implies His choice of those who *do* believe. See Ephesians 1:4, 11.

Commentary

"But I want to draw like Paul *now!*" Every so often my youngest, Tim, was filled with an awful sense of urgency. He felt such a terrible need at 13 to be able to do everything his 19-year-old brother did. And to do it just as well.

I heard it on the basketball court when Tim missed. *Now* was such a burden for Tim. He knew so many things he would be able to do only in the future.

I could understand my youngest son's feelings. You can too. Often you and I feel the same kind of urgency to see more evidence of Christ's presence in our lives. We want to be like Jesus *now.* The dimensions in which we still need to grow bother us deeply. We feel like the Apostle Paul when he placed himself under the Law and struggled to live up to the righteousness he saw expressed there. He tried. And when he failed, he felt condemned.

But then God taught him those truths which he shares with us in Romans.

God has taken us out from under the Law. Law did its work in making us aware of our sin and failure. The Law did its work in making us feel condemned. The Law did its work in forcing us to look away from ourselves to God—to find some other way.

And God had that other way prepared. Righteousness is imputed to men by faith. The death of Christ provided a basis on which forgiveness could be extended, freely, to all. What's more, the faith through which forgiveness comes also is the secret to actually becoming righteous. Through faith, in a deepening personal relationship with God, the new in us grows, and the Spirit's power is released to shape Christ Himself in our personalities.

The Law shouted out demands, telling us what we should be but are not. Grace invites us to accept ourselves as forgiven sinners—and to trust God to help us become new.

But *becoming* takes time. And becoming sometimes disturbs us. We fail to see that God seeks progress rather than perfection. When we step out from under the Law and realize that we have been given time enough to grow, the pressure is removed. What joy!

We can be ourselves—as immature and unskilled in God's ways as Tim was in his games—and yet we can rejoice in the fact that we still please God. We are growing, and it is growth He seeks.

God does not condemn.

Nothing can separate us from the love of Christ.

♥ ***Link to Life: Youth / Adult***
Tell briefly of Tim's frustration as he played with the author and his more mature brother. Have your group members list words: "How does that kind of frustration feel?"

Ask them to transfer these feelings to the personal and spiritual realms, and think of at least one area in which they now feel frustrated.

Then, against this background, ask each to read Romans 8:18-39 and look for one *message from God to them in their frustration.*

Let the group members share the message they find in this wonderful passage. Sum up by noting that we are assured of God's love as we keep on growing. Even in our times of frustration, we know *that nothing "will be able to separate us from the love of God that is in Christ Jesus our Lord."*

Paul's words of praise in Romans 8:18-39 culminate in a joyful shout. And we shout for joy along with the great apostle.

It's hard for us to grasp at first, but those words brought outraged objection from many Jews. Their thinking went something like this. "If God is so steadfast in His love, why has He abandoned Israel? Why have the promises to God's Old Testament people been so summarily set aside, to the benefit of Gentiles? Can Paul's God of righteousness justify His behavior toward the Jews?"

On the surface, the Israelites had a strong case. We cannot read the Old Testament without being struck by the fact that God outlined there a glorious future for the Jews. They, the descendants of Abraham, are promised the land of Palestine as a perpetual possession. They, the descendants of Abraham, are promised a special relationship with God in which He claims them as His own. They, the people of David, are promised that one day a Descendant of David will mount His throne and rule not only over Israel but over the entire earth.

When this promised King, the Messiah, comes, then Israel is to enter her days of glory. Israel's God will be recognized by all. The Gentiles will come to the Jews to learn about God, and will recognize the Lord as Lord of all. In those days of glory, peace will cover the whole earth, and the Messiah-King will enforce righteousness. Thus, the blessing of all humanity depends on the Jews. The proud, despising Gentile will recognize that Israel has been God's own all along.

This, the Jews firmly believed, was Israel's heritage. This was Israel's hope. And it was all rooted in what the Old Testament prophets proclaimed.

But when Jesus came, everything seemed to change! This Person, whom Christians proclaimed as Messiah and Lord, rejected the throne and chose a cross instead. And now Paul was preaching Jesus and faith to the Gentiles—and the Gentiles were believing in Him! Becoming like Jesus, not ruling with the King, was the focal point of the great missionary's concern. And those promises of a kingdom for Israel seemed to be set aside while Paul went on and on about "righteousness."

With all Israel's dreams of glory seemingly shattered, how could Paul speak of God as "righteous"? Hadn't God's Word and promises been broken? How dare Paul write with such confidence of God's enduring love?

These are challenging questions. Yet Paul in Romans 9–11, went about answering them. He began with history. And ended with a look ahead, into the future.

This same approach, looking back and looking ahead, is important for you and me in our own spiritual lives. When we—like Tim—sense the gap between what we are and what we yearn to be, we need to look back and see what God has done in our lives. And we need to look ahead, to see what God will do as He shapes Christ in us. We are *in the process* of moving toward that goal; we cannot truly know ourselves or God's grace until we see our lives from the perspective of the whole of God's great plan for us.

It's this way too in God's dealings with Israel. The Jewish objectors failed to see God's actions as righteous. They lacked perspective. They failed to understand history—and they failed to look far enough ahead.

Paul, looking back and looking ahead, shows us that God is righteous—and sovereign too.

Israel's Rejection: Romans 9:1-33

The true Israel (Rom. 9:1-6). Paul was proud of his Hebrew heritage, and was anguished over those of his race who had not responded with faith to Jesus, their Messiah. He fully acknowledged his Jewish critics' claim of a special relationship between Israel and God: "Theirs is the adoption as sons; theirs the divine glory, the covenants, the receiving of the Law, the temple worship and the promises" (v. 4).

Yet present events did not mean that God had gone back on His word (e.g., that "God's word had failed"). The failure was not God's but Israel's! The keystone of this first argument was Paul's statement, "For not all who are descended from Israel are Israel."

Descendancy (Rom. 9:7-13). Paul went back into sacred history and showed that, first of all, the promises *never* included *all* physical descendants of Abraham. Ishmael, though a child of Abraham, was not included in the covenant promises; only Isaac was (Gen. 21:12). Later Jacob and Esau were born as twin sons of Isaac and Rebekah. But God's purpose included one, and excluded the other! Before the boys were even born (and thus before they could have done either good or bad, so that their actions were no basis for God's choice), God announced that one was chosen and the other rejected as a participant in the covenant line.

Note here that "hated" (Rom. 9:13) is used in a legal rather than emotional sense. It reflects an ancient inheritance formula. God chose Jacob to be heir to the promise, and decisively rejected any claims of his brother, Esau.

So far, then, Paul had established from history that the idea of "Israel" has *never* meant simply the physical descendants of Abraham, Isaac, and Jacob.

Sovereignty of God (Rom. 9:14-23). At this point Paul's readers might make another objection. Paul had said that God *chose* Isaac and Jacob. Was it fair for God to choose some and reject others?

Here Paul took a definite stand. The God revealed in the Old Testament is a Sovereign God. He acted freely, without His actions being limited by what mere humans might do. And among His freedoms is the freedom to:

> Have mercy on whom I have mercy . . . and I will have compassion on whom I have compassion.
>
> Romans 9:15

Historically Pharaoh was given authority in Egypt by God—so that God might "display My power in you and that My name might be proclaimed in all the earth." So, Paul argued, God has mercy on those He chooses to, and He hardens those whom He wants to harden.

Paul reemphasized his position. A potter forms the clay into vessels that suit his own purpose. Who are men, mere lumps of clay, to argue with the God who shaped humanity?

This strong view of sovereignty has repelled some. Yet two things need to be considered. First, Paul in emphasizing sovereignty is *not* dealing with free will. If we go back into the Old Testament we find the Bible speaks both of God hardening Pharaoh's heart, and of Pharaoh hardening his own heart. God did not, in exercising His choice, violate the freedom of choice of His creatures. God did not *force* Pharaoh to do anything he would not have freely chosen to do.

Second, *all* humanity lies lost in sin, willingly and willfully alienated from God. The divine choice was made in eternity past that some be saved, even though all deserve condemnation. God was not and is not obligated to see to it that all are saved, even though the death of Christ is sufficient payment for all. While some see Paul's reference to two groups—"us," the "objects of His mercy," and the "objects of His wrath"— as evidence that God acted to choose each individual among "us," others see it only as evidence that God decided there would be two groups. In this second view, which group a person belongs to is strictly a matter of his or her own free choice.

Yet however we interpret its implication, it is clear that Paul argued from his conviction that God *is* sovereign. God is free to act, and has acted in history as He chose to act. And God as God has that right!

Gentile salvation (Rom. 9:24-33). Returning to his theme, that never in history has "Israel" included all the physical descendants of Abraham, Isaac, and Jacob, Paul quoted the Old Testament to make two points. First, the Old Testament has *always* taught that Gentiles would be saved (vv. 24-26). And second, the Old Testament has *always* taught that only a remnant (a part and not the whole nation) of Israel will be saved (vv. 27-29). So Paul's Gospel of salvation by faith is actually in complete harmony with the Old Testament, and does not suggest that God is unfaithful! It is just that "faith" has become the key to bringing in the Gentiles, and to separating the spiritual remnant from the merely physical descendants of Abraham.

Israel's Rejection Explained: Romans 10

Paul's desire (Rom. 10:1-4). Paul had dealt theologically with the issue the Jews had raised. Then he moved to an emotional level to express his deep passion for his own people.

Paul again shared his deep desire that the Jewish people come to know Christ. And he pinpointed Israel's problem: they have disregarded the "righteousness that comes from God and sought to establish their own," refusing to "submit to God's righteousness" (v. 3). It is this spiritual orientation, not God's unfaithfulness, which had led to the current rejection by the nation.

Hope (Rom. 10:5-13). Yet there is hope for the individual Jew, just as there is now hope for the individual Gentile. Christ has come down from heaven, died, and risen again. All that is left for a person to do is to believe. It is not a matter of "doing" the Law, but of confessing that Jesus is Lord, and believing in Him in one's heart. Everyone, each individual, who calls on the name of the Lord *will* be saved. Thus God *is* faithful still, and this Gospel message (as Paul's Old Testament quotes in this section prove) is in full harmony with the Word God spoke in the Old Testament to the Jews.

History (Rom. 10:14-21). One issue remained. Faith is stimulated by a hearing of the Good News, the Word of God. Had Israel had that opportunity? Of course! History demonstrates, in the prophets who cried out to Israel over the centuries as well as by the written Word Israel received, that God *had* spoken the Word to Israel that was to be received by faith. But those same prophets testified that Israel, though hearing, had not as a nation ever understood! In the words of Isaiah:

> All day long I have held out My hands to a disobedient and obstinate people.
>
> Romans 10:21

We can sum up Paul's argument to this point quite simply. History indicated that "Israel" had *never* meant every physical descendant of Abraham, Isaac, and Jacob. It has meant *some.*

On the one hand the fact that only some are involved reflects a clear choice by a Sovereign God. On the other hand, the fact that only some are involved reflects a clear choice by individuals. For Israel *had* heard the Word. Yet historically the nation had not heard or understood, but remained obstinate. It has always been *some* who have responded with faith to the message of God, but not all.

Thus the charge of the Jews that the God of the Gospel is unrighteous (for the principle of faith would mean that God had abandoned His Old Testament people), is shown to be totally wrong. There has *always* been a Gospel, a message from God that must be received by faith. And in history past as today, only some believe and are saved.

Israel's Rejection Incomplete: Romans 11

A remnant (Rom. 11:1-10). Paul then picked up the Old Testament concept of the remnant, and showed that Israel's present situation could hardly be described as "rejection by God." After all, Paul himself was a Jew, and he was a believer. For its first decade the church was a Hebrew church. Thousands of Jewish men and women in Paul's day were Christians—and thousands of Jewish men and women *today* are Christians as well! "So too," Paul argued, "at the present time there is a remnant chosen by grace" (v. 5). And even this has historical precedent: in Elijah's time God told His prophet that in all Israel there were some 7,000 God "reserved for Myself who have not bowed the knee to Baal."

Gentiles (Rom. 11:11-24). Here Paul introduced an aside to his Gentile readers, who might have been feeling superior to the Jews. The company of believers is like an olive tree, Paul suggested. Its roots are Jewish, sunk deeply in Old Testament history and God's ancient commitment to His chosen people. Gentiles are like branches that have been grafted into this tree. Recognizing this, the Gentile has no cause for pride. Rather we should consider how easy it will be for God to graft *back* the "natural branches" when the time for regathering comes at last.

All Israel saved (Rom. 11:25-36). With this said, Paul looked far into the future. He did not want his Gentile brothers and sisters to be conceited, or think that they had won Israel's promised place. The hardening of Israel is temporary, to last only until "the full number" of Gentiles has come into the church (v. 25). When the time comes, "all Israel will be saved" just as the Old Testament prophets promised (v. 26).

This was a new theme!

Paul had explained that God's present actions were in full harmony with the way God had acted in sacred history, so that the Jewish accusations of, "Unfair!" were groundless. But then Paul said that one day all the Old Testament promises to Israel will in fact be kept!

Today it is "everyone" who calls on the name of the Lord. In the future it will be "all Israel" (the nation) that experiences God's grace.

Why is this? It is because God *has* made Israel covenant promises and, Paul said, "God's gifts and His call are irrevocable" (v. 29).

In the future, history will demonstrate it. God's plans and purposes are far more complex and involved that we have supposed. Israel's vision of the future was not wrong, just incomplete. Our own vision of a heaven to be won and a hell avoided is also incomplete. God's glory will yet be displayed on earth as well as in eternity, as Jesus returns to take the throne as Israel's promised King. No wonder Paul concluded with a powerful doxology of praise:

> Oh, the depth of the riches of the wisdom and knowledge of God! How unsearchable His judgments, and His paths beyond tracing out! Who has known the mind of the Lord? Or who has been His counselor? Who has ever given to God, that God should repay him? For from Him and through Him and to Him are all things. To Him be the glory forever. Amen.

Conclusions

The Jews who accused God of unfaithfulness to His Word erred in underestimating the Lord. They had only a superficial grasp of God's plan and purposes. And, rather than submit to God, and seek out the whole, these men dared to condemn the Lord!

Tragically, you and I are sometimes found doing the same thing. We come to teachings that we do not understand, and rather than acknowledge our own limitations, we begin to lay charges against God.

For instance, we bridle at Paul's blunt statements about God's sovereignty and wonder that God should choose some to receive mercy (Rom. 9). We can't understand how this fits in with the revelation in Jesus of a God of love who is unwilling that *any* should perish (2 Peter 3:9). Instead of trusting in God's wisdom, righteousness, and love, we, like the unbelieving Jews of Paul's day, cry out, "Unfair!"

So what if we cannot understand? Is God accountable to us? Or can we, like Paul, see such things that are beyond our comprehension as fresh evidence of the depth of the wisdom and knowledge of God? We cannot fathom the wisdom and knowledge, but we *can* surrender in trust.

There are other things too. We complain and grumble about the slowness of our growth. Why the ups and downs? Why do some of our problems persist so long? "Am I really profiting from these years of bouts with depression? Why has God put off healing the hurts which divide my home?"

Yet Scripture demands that we see everything happening in our lives as an aspect of God's good plan for our growth and glorification. "In all things God works for the good of those who love Him," Paul affirmed (Rom. 8:28). We have been called "according to His purpose" (v. 28), and our lives are designed so that His purpose, of forming Christ within might proceed at God's carefully planned pace.

Looking at the pattern of my life, I must be willing to surrender my perspective to Him. He is Lord. I am not His adviser. His wisdom is beyond my own, and I surrender, praising, to that wisdom.

How tragic when we underestimate God. How tragic when we, like the ancient Jews, fail to read the lesson of history past and of history yet to come. God's wisdom *is* far beyond anything we can understand or grasp. *But what God says is true!* With complete confidence in the wisdom of God, I can bow before Him and surrender my wisdom to His.

From this day forward, I can live.
By faith.

And, in Jesus, I will experience the greatest adventure of all.

> For from Him and through Him and to Him are all things. To Him be the glory forever! Amen.
>
> Romans 11:36

TEACHING GUIDE

Prepare

Pray for those who may be troubled by the concepts of sovereignty and election, that God will help them trust His love and wisdom even if they cannot understand.

Explore

1. Begin with a brief study of Romans 8:18-39, guided by the "link-to-life" idea on page 828. This study links the normal frustration most of us feel about our growth with assurance that God loves us, and is at work in our lives.

This study leads naturally into Romans 9–11, by setting the Jewish reaction to the Gospel in stark contrast to Paul's expression of confidence and praise.

2. Or raise the troublesome concepts of election and sovereignty. Write the words on the board, and ask your group members to say what they believe these words mean, and how they feel about them.

Expand

1. It is not possible to deal positively with difficult concepts like election or sovereignty until we understand the biblical context in which they appear. So take the bulk of your group time for lecture coverage of Paul's argument in Romans 9–11.

Explain the objection that the Jews raised against the Gospel of salvation by faith (that God had not been faithful to His commitments to Israel). Then, using the material in the commentary, talk your group members through the text, paragraph by paragraph.

If you want more information as you prepare, consult the *Bible Knowledge Commentary*, pages 476-487.

2. Following the lecture, point out the fallacy in Israel's reaction. When the Jews had come to truth they could not understand, these opponents of Paul assumed that their knowledge was complete—and they charged God with being unfair!

Mention the two situations the author mentioned under "Conclusions" in which Christians are likely to do this same thing. Have your group members pair off to discuss one of the two, to suggest how we *should* respond when either troubled by a truth we do not understand, or when troubled by things God brings into our lives.

After the pairs have had three to five minutes, discuss these questions in the whole group.

Apply

Sum up the major thrust of these chapters: we need to trust God when we meet truths or experiences that seem unfair or which we do not understand. Conclude then by reading together, slowly and with personal commitment, Paul's great doxology in Romans 11:33-36.

STUDY GUIDE 128

Romans 12–16

A RIGHTEOUS, LOVING CHURCH

Overview

Paul had described God's gift of righteousness to humankind. He had shown that God's righteousness is both legal (providing a basis on which sinners can be acquitted before the divine court) and dynamic (providing an inner power which leads to the transformation of the believer from within).

Now Paul went on to make yet another vital point. Those individuals who have received the gift of God are to band together in community. In the community of those who believe, fresh aspects of God's goodness and His beauty will be expressed.

However, not every local church has experienced the joy of community. Why not? In these vital chapters of Romans, Paul described the attitudes and the actions which bond believers together in love, and which create a relational climate in which maximum personal spiritual growth can take place. How wonderful these chapters of Romans are! And how we need to take them to heart, making them our guidelines as we learn how to live together as God's holy, loving family of faith.

▶ ***Accept.*** This key term appears in Romans 14 and is used to describe our attitude toward all who are fellow-believers, even though they may differ from us in significant ways. The Greek word, *proslambano,* means literally "welcome," to actively draw another into one's society or circle of friends.

Commentary

I don't know why we picture righteous people as dull. But we do.

And we picture them as rather grim. As standing to one side, with a disapproving look on their faces while others frolic. Somehow the righteous person shows up dressed in black, while everyone else wears bright and colorful clothes. In the old movies we watch on TV, the scoundrel is the warm, engaging person who quickly makes friends.

How tragic when we let the world force our thinking into Satan's mold. Righteousness isn't like that at all! The righteousness that God gives us, and the righteousness that His Spirit is at work to shape in us, is a warm personal kind of thing. Rather than isolate us from others, for the first time we find it is possible to draw truly near. We find that the first fruit of the Spirit, love, warms and deepens our relationships with others who have become our brothers and sisters, one with us in the forever family of God. The second product, joy, makes the fellowship we share bright and colorful (see Gal. 5:22-23).

So let's exchange our old, mistaken picture of righteousness for the reality. Let's take off our imaginary suits of black. Let's put on our brightest party clothes. Let's reach out to others . . . stretch out our hands . . . touch . . . smile! Let's call for the music to play, the celebration to begin! Let's move out into the sunlight, feel its warmth, shout together, share our joy!

The righteousness of God finds its fullest expression in Christ's new, loving, and joyful community.

Homothumadon. In our study of Acts we introduced this Greek term which means, "with one accord." It was a word that God chose to describe the fellowship that existed within the earliest church. That word portrays the unique harmony and love that so impressed early observers. "See how they love one another," was the remark. These early Christians, so varied in background (there were both rich and poor, Judean and foreign Jew), found a unity and love that observers could hardly believe.

Jesus had spoken of this dimension of Christian community before His crucifixion. He told His followers, "Love one another as I have loved you. All men will know that you are My disciples, if you love one another" (John 13:34-35). God's plan for believers includes the demonstration of His righteousness in and through a loving community. Christ's church is to demonstrate to all the world that righteousness, correctly understood, means love and joy!

The church is also to be the context in which growth and transformation take place in believers. We are to be nourished in our growth toward Christ's likeness by one another. In the acceptance and love of our brothers and sisters, we're to sense God's own acceptance and love, and to grow in that freedom from Law which Paul explained so carefully. "Grow up into . . . Christ," Paul called it in Ephesians 4:15. Growing up, together, into Christ.

It is tragic that just as the Law has sometimes been distorted and misused by Christians, the church has too. Sometimes, rather than the joyful community of God's plan, the church has become a joyless assembly. Rather than loving and accepting one another as brothers on a common pilgrimage, some churches have become legalist assemblies where conformity and pretense are the price of admission. The vital dimension of growth in Christ as a way of life has been set aside, and agreement on our doctrines, or our convictions and customs has been imposed. No longer are imperfect people welcomed, loved, and accepted as they are, in the calm assurance that growth in Christ is all they need. Instead, the believer in such a church is forced to try to hide his imperfections, and struggle to live up to a new legalism, imposed not by God but by men.

No wonder then that Paul, all too familiar with this same tendency in his own day, turned in the closing chapters of Romans to outline for us the way to the righteous, loving community that God seeks to shape. Paul here gave us clear, simple guidance for shared experience of God's joy.

♥ ***Link to Life: Youth / Adult***

Ask your group members to rank on a scale of 1 to 10 the importance of the following:

1. *People accept me as I am.*
2. *I feel loved and wanted.*
3. *I can share with those close to me.*
4. *When I make mistakes, others don't condemn or reject me.*
5. *I don't have to be just like everyone else to be welcome.*
6. *I am valued and make a real contribution to others.*
7. *I don't have to compete but can cooperate with others.*

Discuss the rankings, encouraging your group members to share why *the high importance items are significant to them.*

Then move into the text, explaining that each item describes what the church of Christ is to be like—and these passages show us how to build just this kind of vital Christian fellowship.

Christ's Impact: Romans 12

Romans 12 begins with familiar and famous words. "I urge you . . . in view of God's mercy, to offer your bodies as living sacrifices, holy and pleasing to God—which is your spiritual worship." We can never have a truly Christian relationship with others until we are fully committed to God. Only when we are surrendered to Him will the world be powerless to squeeze us into its mold, and will we be transformed and able to live out God's good will.

This is important here, launching a section on interpersonal relationships. We can never substitute quality relationships with other Christians for quality relationship with the Lord. The real source of quality relationships with others is full commitment to the Lord. With this principle established, however, Paul does call us to look closely at the relationship we have with the brothers and sisters whom God has given us.

Mutual ministry (Rom. 12:3-8). The world's way is all too often to measure people *against* each other. How well we compete, and how much better we are than others, are ways we are measured.

This competitive dimension of society shows up in everything. School grades are a way of measuring people against others. Sports are designed to select winners, and to separate them from losers. Our economy and businesses are again expressions of a competitive approach to life. The way we view others and our opinion of them are all directly related to how they compare, in terms of skills, education, looks, talents, character, etc. In tremendously significant ways, measured against others, each individual stands or falls alone.

But when we come to the church, this

perspective changes. God views us as members of a body. In the body relationship we do not compete; we cooperate. "In Christ we who are many form one body, and each member belongs to all the others" (v. 5). Each of us has a different function, but our differences do not make anyone better or worse than another. The reason is that, whatever our gift (function), each of us contributes. Each of us is necessary!

How then are we to evaluate ourselves? We are each to focus on using our own gift to serve others. *We find fulfillment not in comparing ourselves with others, but in being ourselves and using whatever talent God has given in ministry!*

How exciting this is. No longer am I any more important than my brother, or he more important than I. We are each important, in and of ourselves.

It is impossible to overestimate the impact of this perspective on ourselves and on interpersonal relationships. When I develop the divine viewpoint:

- I am released from jealousy.
- I can find fulfillment in being who I am, rather than wanting to be like someone else.
- My friendships are not distorted by status—I am awed by none, and look down on none.
- I appreciate others for themselves, without feeling they must be different or must be like me.

Learning to take God's view of others as members with me in a body where cooperation, not competition, has value initiates a whole new way of relating to others that is unlike anything the world knows.

This is the first key to building a righteous, loving community. To see ourselves and others as God does, as valuable contributing persons in a family of faith.

Love's priority (Rom. 12:9-21). The key to life in the Christian community is love. Paul makes this very clear. "Love must be sincere. . . . Be devoted to one another in brotherly love. . . . Live in harmony with one another. . . . Overcome evil with good" (vv. 9-10, 16, 21).

The kind of love that Paul described is not a passive thing. Instead it involves an aggressive reaching out to care for others. "Share with God's people who are in need" (v. 13) is one practical expression of love. "Practice hospitality" (v. 13) is another. "Be willing to associate with people of low position [in society]" (v. 16) is yet another.

A climate of love is absolutely basic to the church of Jesus Christ. Without such caring, and reaching out to touch one another's lives, the church will fall tragically short of God's intended experience of His "good, pleasing and perfect will" (v. 2).

♥ ***Link to Life: Youth / Adult***
Let your group members engage in direct Bible study. Divide into teams of "church doctors" to study Romans 12:4-21 and prescribe for people who want the kind of church experience highlighted in the opening quiz (p. 834). How does this passage suggest we build the faith community?

Church and State: Romans 13

In one sense this is a digression. In another it is not. The church is a body, uniquely different from the secular society of which it is also a part. How are Christians to relate, not to each other, but to the state and to its secular citizens?

Human government (Rom. 13:1-7). Paul taught that God had instituted human government as a restraining power, an agent of justice to bring punishment to wrongdoers. This is no blanket endorsement of every and any form of human government. It is, however, an astute observation. Any state, for its own self-interest, must be concerned with morality and moral order! If citizens lied and stole and murdered one another, the state would fall to enemies from outside or to corruption from within. Thus human government, for its own sake and not out of respect for God, serves as God's agent in enforcing basic morality.

Christians are to recognize that the state (human government) has been ordained by God, and are to respect it as a divinely intended institution. Out of respect for God we are to pay taxes, show respect for those who govern, and in other ways be good citizens of the countries in which we live.

Personal corruption (Rom. 13:8-14). The citizen is to fulfill all his public obligations. Yet there is one debt which can never be paid: the debt we owe to all our fellowmen to love them (v. 8). Everything the commandments speak out against *harms* others (vv. 9-10). If we truly love them, we will do nothing to bring them harm, and thus love will lead us to fulfill the divine law as well as keep us from violations of human law.

We who are Christ's need to concentrate on love, rejecting all those sins that attract the lost. Love calls us to "clothe [ourselves] with the Lord Jesus Christ, and . . . not think about how to gratify the desires of the sinful nature" (v. 14).

♥ ***Link to Life: Youth / Adult***
Church/state issues concern many these days. Should Christians be allowed to educate their children in church schools? Should tax money be available to such schools? What right does the government have to legislate in moral areas, such as pornography and abortion? Should Christians in Communist countries be "good citizens," or revolt against oppression?

Not all of these questions are answered in Romans 13:1-7. But certain basic concepts about the nature and function of the state are defined here.

Set your group members to first, list all their church/state questions on the chalkboard, and then second, to study this passage to determine which can *and which* cannot *be answered from it. Finally, let your group members try to establish from the passage the principles which enable them to answer some of the questions, and to give these answers.*

Maintaining Harmony: Romans 14:1–15:13

Paul's primary concern in this section of Romans is not how the Christian is to conduct himself in society, but how we express our new life within the believing community.

This is not because society is unimportant. *It is because the Christian community as well as the individual is to witness to the reality of Jesus.* On the one hand, the Christian community is the context in which individual believers can grow to their full stature as Christ's people. On the other, the love which marks Christian relationships is itself a powerful testimony to Christ's presence. For each of these purposes to be achieved, the church must truly be the righteous, loving community which Scripture describes with *homothumadon.*

It's no wonder, then, that Paul described attitudes toward others which build community. Strikingly, each of the attitudes reflects Jesus' own attitude toward us.

Accepting (Rom. 14:1-13). Paul dealt with an issue which often creates conflict in churches: convictions. These are *not* matters which Scripture identifies as "sin." They are, however, issues which seem "wrong" to some believers, and "right" to others.

Actually, all of us differ from others in significant ways. We Christians have different opinions about what a believer should and shouldn't do. Some think women should be ordained; others violently disagree. Some, in Paul's day, thought it was "Christian" to be vegetarian, while others liked a good steak. Some then felt Christians should observe special "holy" days, and others felt all days are alike.

These differences tended then as now to divide believers into subgroups of "them" and "us." And all such antagonistic divisions are harmful to community! All distort the unity and ministry of Jesus' church.

How does Romans teach we are to deal with such differences?

**Positively.* Paul suggested several positive steps and attitudes we are to develop. First, we are to actively welcome even those with a weak faith (v. 1). Second, we are to recognize Jesus as Lord (vv. 6-12). Christ arose (and thus is alive) so that *He* might be Lord for His people. Each of us is responsible to Jesus as Lord; we are *not* responsible to each other. Third, we are to each explore the issues over which believers have convictions and "be fully convinced in his own mind" (v. 5).

**Negatively.* What we are *not* to do in our relationships with other Christians is clearly identified. We are *not* to condemn others whose convictions differ from ours (v. 3). We are *not* to look down on them for being "less spiritual" than we (v. 3). Bluntly put, *we are not to judge them at all* (v. 1). Jesus is Lord, and they are responsible to Him. If they have sinned, Jesus will judge them. We have no business intruding into this relationship of responsibility of a fellow believer to the Lord (v. 13).

We should look to Christ as our model. "Accept one another, then, just as Christ accepted you, in order to bring praise to God" (15:7). God does not condemn the brother we judge, but has accepted him (14:3). As far as his future is concerned, Jesus is able to make our brother or sister stand (v. 4).

How important then, that like Jesus, we love and accept each other, and try to build each other up rather than tear one another down because of the ways in which we differ.

Self-sacrifice (Rom. 14:13–15:13). Often the differences that do exist between us will trouble an entire fellowship. Some, who have the freedom to do what others question, may in the exercise of that freedom, cause the brother harm.

Paul is very clear here. Nothing (that is not identified in Scripture as sin) is unclean or wrong in itself. But neither is it more important than our brother or sister. So we Christians walk a fine line.

We affirm our freedom and responsibility to live by our own convictions. Yet we are careful not to flaunt them, so that others may follow our example despite personal doubts, or may condemn us for what we ourselves believe to be good and right.

In this area, Paul gives several practical suggestions:

"Whatever you believe about these things keep between yourself and God" (14:22).

"Make every effort to do what leads to peace and mutual edification" (v. 19).

"We who are strong ought to bear with the failings of the weak and not to please ourselves" (15:1).

The goal toward which we are to work, giving it priority rather than convictions, is "that with one heart and mouth you may [together] glorify the God and Father of our Lord Jesus Christ" (v. 6).

♥ ***Link to Life: Youth / Adult***
To help your group members explore this significant passage on Christian living, duplicate and give to teams of five or six members one of these two case histories. Each team is to study Romans 14:1–15:7, identify principles which might apply to its case, and then tell how they might be applied to help the people involved in the case history.

Case 1: Linda's children are in school now, and she wants to go back to work. Her husband Jim is opposed. He feels that it's a man's place to earn the family living, and that Linda should find fulfillment in her role as a wife and mother. Each feels very strongly about this situation, and each goes to the Bible to suggest he or she is right.

Case 2: Bob spoke in his class to express his doubts about drinking. Wine was drunk in Bible times. Drunkenness is wrong, but not a social drink now and then. Charlie Dobbs sees this as a vital moral issue, and drinking is absolutely wrong. He has angrily challenged Bob, and the class has begun to take sides.

Farewells: Romans 15:14–16:27

Paul's farewells are also revealing. He expressed confidence in the Spirit who was within the Romans. They did not need him, for they themselves had been fully equipped by God for a life of faith (15:14-16).

While Paul had long wished to visit Rome, God had not yet let him. Eagerly he looked forward to such a time, perhaps as a side visit on the way to Spain. What an adventure there: Spain! A land where the Gospel had not been heard.

Romans 16 is filled with personal greetings. If ever we wondered about the apostle and his relationships with others, these greetings are revealing. Paul had never visited Rome. He must have met these people elsewhere on his journeys. Yet, he had kept such close track of them that he knew the details of many of their lives.

What a warm and loving fellowship Paul must have experienced with his beloved brothers and sisters in the Lord. How real the community of which he wrote in these chapters must have been to him. Saul, the lonely Pharisee at 30, isolated from everyone in that distorted righteousness of works, had become Paul the apostle, a man of warmth and love, wrapped in the comforting cloak of Christian friends.

God's kind of righteousness has broken through the isolation of the lonely heart and, in the fellowship of those who love one Lord, brought celebration and joy.

With Paul	At Rome		
	Men		*Women*
Timothy	Aquila	Rufus	Priscilla
Lucius	Epenetus	Asyncritus	Mary
Jason	Adronicus	Phlegon	Tryphena
Sosipater	Ampliatus	Hermes	Tryphosa
Tertius	Urbanus	Patrobas	Persis
Gaius	Stachys	Hermas	Julia
Erastus	Herodion	Nereus	
Quartus	Olympas	Junias	
Phoebe	Apelles	Philologus	

In Christ, community is ours. Yet our names are known individually.

What a lesson. Our individuality is not surrendered, yet in the bonds of love in Christ's church each one can at last, severally and together, become all we were ever meant to be.

♥ ***Link to Life: Youth / Adult***
What was the role of women in the early church? This issue is examined in the study guides on 1 Corinthians 7 and 11.

Yet in this passage that emphasizes the cooperative nature of the body, it is interesting to note that Phoebe (Rom. 16:1) was called a deaconess (the same term used of men deacons in 1 Tim. 3). And that Paul mentioned so many women by name. You may want to point this out to your group, and ask whether convictions limiting women's roles in the modern church may not be among those issues to which Romans 14–15 relates.

TEACHING GUIDE

Prepare
What is the relational climate in your own group? Pray that God will build that warm fellowship which promotes mutual ministry and Christian love.

Explore
Launch this week's group session by asking your members to rank from 1-10 interpersonal factors which make for fellowship in the church. You'll find items to rank and how-to suggestions in "link-to-life," page 834.

Expand
1. Divide into teams to study Romans 12 for clues as to what believers might do to build the kind of local congregation which God has in mind ("link-to-life," page 834).
2. Romans 14–15 also lays down vital fellowship principles. Be sure to explore how we are to deal with differences in convictions. You can cover this material in a minilecture, or use the case-history approach explained on page 837.

Apply
Ask each person to examine his or her own attitude, and prayerfully ask God to purge him or her of judgmentalism, making room only for love.

STUDY GUIDE 129

1 Corinthians 1–4

A UNITED CHURCH FAMILY

Overview

First Corinthians is the New Testament's "problem epistle." In it Paul deals with a series of problems that existed in that young church, introducing each new issue with the phrase, *peri dei,* translated in our versions as "Now concerning," or simply, "Now. . . ."

The problems sound like a catalog of problems experienced by local churches today:

- Division in the church (1–4).
- Discipline (5–6).
- Marriage and divorce (7).
- Doctrinal disputes (8–10).
- Misunderstanding of spiritual (charismatic) gifts (12–14).

In addition, the letter touches on the role of women, the importance of the Lord's Supper, and on the centrality of the Resurrection in Christian teaching.

Within each section, Paul gives us a carefully reasoned discussion of the problem, and how to deal with it, making this letter one of the most practical and important for Christians today.

▶ ***Wise/wisdom.*** In 1 Corinthians 1–4 "wisdom" (Greek, *sophia*) is the perspective from which a person deals with the issues of life. Humans are "foolish" when they fail to realize that their notions must be subjected to divine evaluation. Only when a person abandons what seems wise by human standards to accept without hesitation the divine viewpoint as revealed in Scripture can he or she be truly wise.

Commentary

Near the end of his third missionary journey, Paul wrote a letter to a church in trouble. Some seven years before, he and his companions had founded the church in Corinth. Even though the members of the believing community were richly gifted, the process of transformation toward Christlikeness seemed constantly blocked.

Paul kept in touch with the Corinthian fellowship, as he did with all the churches. Finally, after a verbal report from the family of Chloe, and after a delegation arrived from Corinth asking for Paul's judgment on specific questions, this first letter to the Corinthians was written.

This is an important letter for us to read and to master. It is important because it helps us realize our own struggle for a real and vital faith may be a long one. And it is important because this letter presents principles that you and I and our group members can apply to help resolve problems that continue to plague modern Christian fellowships.

Corinth was an important city and had been from ancient days. It was situated on the isthmus bearing its name, and controlled land and sea trade routes. In New Testament times, it was not only an important commercial city but also the administrative center of the Province of Achaia.

Roberth H. Gundry's description of the city (*A Survey of the New Testament,* Zondervan) gives us an idea of the cosmopolitan character of Corinth.

> The athletic games at Corinth were second only to the Olympics. The outdoor theater accommodated twenty thousand people, the roofed theater three thousand. Temples, shrines, and altars dotted the city. A thousand sacred prostitutes made themselves available at the temple of the Greek goddess Aphrodite. The south side of the marketplace was lined with taverns equipped with underground cisterns for cooling the drinks.

Noted for its lax morals and scandalous lifestyle, Corinth was a completely pagan society—a society that created many difficulties for the believers who lived there.

Even though the Corinthian church was struggling, and is the only congregation that Paul called unspiritual in one of his letters, Paul began his letter with words of commendation and confidence. He was writing to people who had been "sanctified in Christ Jesus and called to be holy, together with all those everywhere who call on the name of our Lord Jesus Christ." Paul assured his readers that Christ "will keep you strong to the end, so that you will be blameless on the day of our Lord Jesus Christ. God, who has called you into fellowship with His Son Jesus Christ our Lord, is faithful" (1 Cor. 1:2, 8-9).

What a wonderful thing to remember always. No matter how much our own Christian experience may seem to involve struggle, how slow our growth, it is God who has called us into fellowship with Himself. And God is faithful. God *will* work in our lives, and will keep us strong.

But once Paul expressed his confidence, he plunged immediately into an analysis of the Corinthians' problems. And these problems were serious indeed.

A Method of Study

The Bible contains many different literary forms. There is narrative storytelling, as in Genesis and the Gospels. There is poetry, as in Job and the Psalms. There is the preaching of the prophets—and the carefully reasoned argument of many of the New Testament epistles. Each of the different literary forms are, in Scripture, a mode of the divine revelation. Yet each is to be studied in ways that are appropriate to its special character.

When we come to tightly reasoned passages of Scripture, the most appropriate Bible study method is to trace the writer's line of argument. That is, we must study carefully to follow his train of thought. This approach will guard us from taking a verse out of context, and interpreting it as if it stood alone. But most important, this method will enable us to truly understand what God is teaching us in a particular book or passage.

First Corinthians is one of the most closely reasoned of Paul's letters. In it Paul dealt with problems—and in it he carefully explained the principles, the very "thoughts of God," which we are to apply to resolve the problems.

It would be appropriate, then, to apply a particular type of Bible study *designed to trace an argument* to your group's study of 1 Corinthians. If you do, you will not only help your group members discover the deeper truths this great book teaches, but will also train them in an approach to Bible study which will enrich their own personal reading of God's Word.

In each of the 1 Corinthian study guides we'll apply this particular method, which you may choose to use in teaching. But we'll also discuss the key truths taught in each section, and provide alternative methods so you will not *have* to use this study approach if you feel it is not appropriate for your particular group.

How then do we trace the argument (the line of thought) of a closely reasoned passage of Scripture?

1. Read and reread a section to determine its subject.
2. Make a one-sentence summary of each paragraph within the section.
3. Rework sentences into a brief paraphrase of the section.
4. Go back and examine each paragraph in the text in more detail.
5. Determine and apply major teachings (principles).

If we apply this method to the first four chapters of 1 Corinthians, here's what may be discovered.

♥ ***Link to Life: Youth / Adult***
If you plan to use the direct Bible study method illustrated in this study guide, prepare your group by listing the five steps on the chalkboard. Step 1: Have each read the section through twice, and work together to give some "unity" title to the section. Step 2: In your meeting divide into teams of three or four and assign each team one *of the four chapters to summarize. Duplicate the summary sentence material from this study guide, and pass it out so each team can compare its summary sentences. Step 3: Duplicate and pass out the paraphrase developed from the summary sentences. Step 4: Skip. Step 5: Work as a group to determine principles, and discuss how they can be applied to our lives today.*

This first study is intended to familiarize your group members with this basic Bible study method. Ask each member of the group to study 1 Corinthians 5–6 before *your next meeting, using only Step 1 (title) and Step 2 (make sentence summaries of each paragraph).*

If you do not plan to teach this study method as you study 1 Corinthians, use the alternate teaching methods suggested at the end of this study guide.

The Subject: 1 Corinthians 1–4

When we read through these chapters quickly, several things are apparent. First, Paul talked here a great deal about *wisdom.* This word, and *wise,* appear no fewer than 27 times in this four-chapter section!

At the same time, it is clear that Paul is not concerned with an intellectual debate about the relationship between faith and philosophy. Paul immediately expressed his central concern: "I appeal to you . . . that there may be no divisions among you and that you may be perfectly united in mind and thought." The Corinthians had formed parties, or cliques, based on the supposed superiority of various Christian leaders. There was a "Paul party" and a "Peter party"; an "Apollos party" and a very spiritual type, "Jesus-only party." These divisions had shattered the unity of the local congregation, and created dissension. This whole section is basically about divisions, and how to maintain unity.

So we might give the section a title like this:

Maintaining Unity in the Church Family

As noted, wisdom is somehow critical here. But before we know just how, we need to trace the progression of Paul's thought, paragraph by paragraph. When we do, we will see that something called God's wisdom provides the solution to this very common, very human problem.

A Sentence Summary: 1 Corinthians 1–4

The goal here is to capture in a single sentence the main thrust of each paragraph.

For instance:

> I appeal to you, brothers, in the name of our Lord Jesus Christ, that all of you agree with one another so that there may be no divisions among you and that you may be perfectly united in mind and thought. My brothers, some from Chloe's household have informed me that there are quarrels among you. What I mean is this: One of you says, "I follow Paul"; another, "I follow Apollos"; another, "I follow Cephas"; still another, "I follow Christ."
>
> 1 Corinthians 1:10-12

Now, what is the subject of this paragraph? What is its focus? If we emphasize the problem, we might summarize this way: *The division in your church fellowship is wrong.*

If, however, we emphasize the goal, we'll pick up from Paul's first sentence: *I urge you to resolve your differences and restore unity in your church fellowship.*

Very often in translations of Paul's writings we'll find that the first sentence of a paragraph is a key to his subject. So let's choose the second summary (above) as the summary of this paragraph, though the first is not wrong. In developing summary sentences, there is always room for different ways of stating the same things.

If we work through the entire four-chapter passage, we may come up with summary sentences like those on the chart.

Paraphrasing: 1 Corinthians 1–4

When we have the summary sentences complete, we then read them over and see if the thought of each is closely linked to what precedes it and what follows. Can they be read aloud together, and so follow the apostle's thinking? Does the whole make sense?

In a paraphrase we do just this: we link the summary sentences and, if necessary, go back to any paragraph whose links to what goes before and comes after are unclear to us.

Paraphrasing in this way protects us against a common flaw in Bible study. We all tend to lose sight of the whole. As a result, we may misinterpret single verses or short paragraphs. A good paraphrase will bring the whole passage into clear view—and keep it in view—thus guarding us against "proof texting" or taking a thought out of context and misinterpreting it.

What might a paraphrase of 1 Corinthians 1–4 look like, and what will it tell us about Paul's line of thought? Here are the sentence summaries, reworked into a paragraph.

Paragraph	Verses	Summary Sentence
1	1:10-12	I urge you to resolve your differences and restore unity in your church fellowship.
2	1:13-17	The central fact is Christ, and that in Him we are one.
3	1:18-25	God's wisdom as shown in Christ is really at odds with man's "wise" approach to things.
4	1:26-31	In fact, it is Christ and not some superior wisdom who has brought you righteousness, holiness, and redemption!
5	2:1-5	I purposely kept my message simple when with you in order that your full reliance might be on the crucified Jesus.
6	2:6-10	Of course, there is a divine wisdom—but this comes through revelation, and its source is not in man's discoveries.
7	2:11-16	This wisdom involves a person coming to grasp God's thoughts, something that demands both hearing the revealed words and being enlightened by the Holy Spirit.
8	3:1-4	But you! Your jealousy and quarreling make it clear that you think and act on a merely human level.
9	3:5-9	Who do you think is important—we servants, or the God who works through us?
10	3:10-15	I'm thankful for the privilege of serving, but my foundation is Jesus, and what I build will be evaluated one day.
11	3:16-17	But don't you realize that the true construction is going on in your lives, that *you* are God's sacred temple, and that we all must build (not tear down!) the growing structure?
12	3:18-23	So don't fool yourselves with all those childish arguments about which leader is better; abandon that kind of thing, and focus on all that God has given you in Christ.
13	4:1-7	Grasp this principle: God Himself is the source of all that a man possesses, so how can anyone boast about having "superior" gifts or skills?
14	4:8-13	Rather than trying to build our own little empires, we apostles have abandoned all, having chosen humiliation, weakness, hunger, and persecution as our lot.
15	4:14-16	As your father, I warn you to imitate me in this and get your priorities back into harmony with reality.
16	4:18-21	And I warn you: unity in the family is so vital that in God's power I will discipline you when I come unless you abandon your worldly arrogance!

Unity in the Church Family
1 Corinthians 1–4

I urge you to resolve your differences and restore unity in the church family. Remember, Christ is the center of our lives and in Him we *are* one.

This may not sound like a very "wise" argument, but then the message of Christ and His cross has always been at odds with human wisdom.

And Christ, not some super "wisdom," brought you your righteousness, holiness, and redemption. That's why I kept my message simple when I was with you, that you might rely only on the crucified Lord.

Of course there is a divine wisdom, but it comes by revelation and not human discovery. This wisdom involves learning to think God's thoughts, something that requires both hearing the revealed words and being enlightened by the Holy Spirit.

But you! Why, your jealousy and quarreling make it very clear that you think and act like mere men. Who do you think is important: we servants, or God who works through us? I'm thankful I can serve, but my foundation is Jesus, and one day what I build will be evaluated. (Don't you even grasp the fact that the true construction is going on *in your lives* and that *you* are God's sacred temple? Building up people, not tearing them down, is doing God's work!)

So don't deceive yourselves with all those childish arguments over leaders. Abandon that foolish game and focus again on all that is yours in Jesus, you who are not on trial before any human jury! Can't you grasp the basic principle? God Himself is the source of all. How then can we boast about anyone's superior gifts or skills?

Why, rather than trying to build our own little kingdoms, we apostles have abandoned all that, and have chosen humiliation, weakness, hunger, and even persecution as our lot. So I warn you. Imitate me in this, and get your priorities back in order. And this *is* a warning. Unity in the family is so vital that, in God's own power, I will discipline you when I come unless you abandon your worldly arrogance!

What a powerful passage! And what a vital message for divided Christians today.

Reviewing the Text: 1 Corinthians 1–4
At this point, with the overview of the argument in mind, we can go back and look into each paragraph more closely. It is *now* that a verse-by-verse approach to Bible study can be helpful, for now our understanding of the thoughts and phrases will be guided by an overview of their context.

Often at this point we will make exciting discoveries, and see fresh meaning in verses that have become so familiar that we read over them, without thought. Often too we'll make a discovery that will lead us back to our paraphrase to make a change that brings the whole into clearer focus. In short, *a study of the details of the text is always more fruitful when we have first grasped the argument of the larger unit.*

This very point is one that Paul made in 1 Corinthians 1 and 2. He pointed out that man's ways of thinking (human "wisdom") and God's ways of thinking (His "foolishness") truly do *not* correspond. The Cross is given as an example. What human mind would have imagined that God would give us righteousness, holiness, and redemption by means of the execution of His Son as a criminal!

To the Greek mind the whole notion was idiotic: salvation, if there were such a thing, would have to come through some appeal to man's capacity to achieve. Furthermore, the Greek mind viewed God as immutable and unchangable. The Gospel presentation of Incarnation, the Cross, and Resurrection were simply ruled out; the Gospel contradicted one of the axioms of classical Greek philosophy.

To the Hebrew, the whole thing was foreign as well. Deliverance would come in another Exodus, with God breaking into history to perform miracles and punish Israel's enemies. A suffering Saviour? Never! Israel would settle for nothing less than a conquering king.

While the Greek and the Jew each clung to his own notion of how God must act, God had His own ideas. The Cross meant that each must surrender his own way of thinking, and submit to *a divine wisdom that operates on principles which are basically different from those that appeal to human thought!*

Man is impressed by human accomplishment: God chose to use things man despises.

Man is impressed by strength: God chose to use weakness.

Even in the church, the human tendency is to seek to build little kingdoms around differences—different leaders, different doctrines, different ways of baptizing, different likes and dislikes in music. It is *God's* way to reject that kind of thinking, and to build *unity* around the one thing that Christians have in common: Jesus!

Paul's whole argument is a warning to the church at Corinth—and to us—that we must learn to look at issues from the divine viewpoint. We must realize God doesn't think the same way we do. We must be willing to surrender our own way of thinking and earnestly search out His.

How? God has revealed His thoughts "in words taught by the Spirit" (1 Cor. 2:13). And God has given believers the Holy Spirit to interpret the written Word (vv. 9-15). In the Word and in the Spirit we have been given an astounding gift: "We have the mind of Christ" (v. 16). Searching the Word, guided by the Spirit, we are to learn God's way of thinking (His wisdom), and gradually learn to evaluate all things from His unique perspective.

This is why a tracing-the-argument approach to Bible study is so important. We're prone to grasp a single verse or teaching, and try to make it fit our way of thinking. We're apt to use the Bible to try to prove our point of view, or to disprove another's. But Paul here teaches us to study the Scripture so we can learn to *abandon* our own points of view, and submit ourselves instead to God's. By disciplining ourselves to trace the argument of a section of Scripture, we guard against our natural tendency to misuse, and we set ourselves to grasp the very thoughts of God.

Application: 1 Corinthians 1–4

When we have understood the flow of thought of a passage, and have gone back to understand details in the light of the whole, *then* we can discern principles and apply them. It is fascinating to see how all that Paul has said in these first chapters underlines two basic principles which are to guide you and me and our groups as well as they were to guide the Corinthians.

First, *Christ is One*. Unity in the church is vital, because unity alone can model this reality. A church that is splintered by disputes so that its members are at odds, dividing and competing, ignores Christ's call that we be "perfectly united in mind and thought."

Second, *Christ is the Source and focus of our faith*. The Corinthians had exalted mere human leaders to that position. "I'm a Paulite." "I'm a Peterite." In modern terms we might say, "I'm Methodist," or, "I'm Baptist," or even say, "I'm a Calvinist" or, "I'm a charismatic." Use of any such term to identify us makes that particular association or belief the defining difference—the focus of our identity. Paul argued that Jesus, and Jesus alone, is the basis for Christian self-identification.

To exalt leaders, or denominations, or doctrines, or experiences, to the level where they make us "different" from our brothers and sisters in Christ is to operate on that mere human wisdom which is nothing but foolishness in God's sight. As for leaders, they are merely servants of God. There is no place in the church for pride *in* a human leader, or *by* a human leader. If God blesses us through one of His servants, we are to address our praise to the Lord, and are to be loyal to God, not the leader.

There is one foundation and one only (3:11), and that foundation is Christ Jesus. Any person or group that tries to rest its faith, all or in part, on any other is foolish indeed.

How wonderful that Jesus *is* our foundation. And how wonderful that we can live by God's wisdom, refusing to let any of our "distinctives" separate us from heartfelt fellowship with brothers and sisters who, whatever our differences, still own Jesus as Saviour and Lord.

TEACHING GUIDE

Prepare
If you plan to use the study method suggested here, why not do your own sentence summaries of paragraphs and work out your own paraphrase? If you prefer it to the author's, use it in teaching your group. This teaching guide is primarily for those who do *not* choose to use the direct study method recommended.

Explore
1. List on the chalkboard: denomination, mode of baptism, view of spiritual gifts, separation, personality of leader. Ask: "What are some other issues that divide Christians?" Add suggestions to the list. Then ask your group members to express opinions: "Which, if any, are *valid* reasons for division?"
2. Or give a minilecture overview of Corinthians, listing the problems it covers (see *overview*). Assign teams *one* problem area, to develop a list of ways their problem shows up in the contemporary church. Record the lists on a chalkboard, and save.

Expand
1. Have your group work together to develop a "subject" statement from 1 Corinthians 1:1-12 that will sum up the issue dealt with in these chapters.

Then point out the principle in 1:13-17: Christ is One, so unity is essential.

2. List the following passage summaries on the chalkboard. Divide into teams, each of which is to look for insights in one of the assigned passages.

- 1 Corinthians 1:18-31: We must learn to think as God does, not as mere human beings do.
- 1 Corinthians 2:1-16: God's wisdom is given us in Scripture and understood through the Spirit.
- 1 Corinthians 3:1-22: Division over human leaders is worldly, ignoring God's wisdom.
- 1 Corinthians 4:1-21: Leaders are merely men who are servants of Christ, whose commitment merits imitation but not exaltation.

After about 15 minutes, come together and share insights gained.
3. Sum up the key principle which God's wisdom affirms: *Christ is the Source and focus of Christian faith.* We are never to exalt any person or doctrine or practice to the place where it, rather than Jesus, defines who we are, or sets us off as different from our brothers and sisters in Christ.

Apply
Return to the list of differences that your group evaluated at the beginning of the session. In view of 1 Corinthians 1–4, which differences now seem *valid* as a basis for division?

STUDY GUIDE 130

1 Corinthians 5–6

CHURCH FAMILY DISCIPLINE

Overview

"Church discipline" is an important, but often misunderstood and ignored, aspect of Christian congregational life. Dealing with a specific situation in Corinth, the Apostle Paul laid down principles which can help us deal with a variety of contemporary church situations—and can guard us from interfering in situations which are *not* subject to church discipline.

In brief, your group members will discover in this two-chapter passage that:

- professing Christians who practice immorality are to be expelled from fellowship;
- disputes between Christians should be settled within the church rather than by law;
- sexual immorality is *never* right, for we are to honor God with our bodies.

▶ ***Sexual Immorality.*** "Sexual immorality" encompasses all sexual intercourse outside of marriage. The serious nature of adultery and fornication (intercourse between *un*married persons) is seen in this powerful Corinthians passage as well as throughout the Scripture. There are two basic reasons: first, sex is sacramental, intended to bond two people together in the most intimate of human relationships. Second, marriage is a covenant, a commitment of mutual loyalty which is to reflect the commitment of God to His people. Within the context of covenant and sacrament, sex is beautiful and right. In any other, it is destructive and wrong.

Commentary

I recently talked with the pastor of a church I serve as an elder. One of the women in the local congregation, who for a time was growing rapidly in the faith, recently went through a painful divorce. At one point she had an affair with a neighbor, a situation about which we had confronted her, and had been assured it was over.

Just two days before the phone call, we discovered that she was living with her paramour. And as members of the family of God, we realized we were responsible to discipline her.

It wasn't an easy prospect.

We naturally drew back from this kind of confrontation. In the family of God, our deepest desire is to support and love, so discipline seems harsh and unloving. Can we really *care*—and at the same time deal decisively with sin in the fellowship, even passing judgment on sin and sinner as Paul did in 1 Corinthians 5? How, after Paul had spoken out in 1 Corinthians 4:1-5 against judging him and other leaders, can we judge a fellow Christian? Why, Paul had just written that he is not even competent to judge himself (v. 4).

Yet, in a society like first-century Corinth, there was a sure need for discipline. Immorality was an accepted part of the Corinthian lifestyle. The old passions and desires, the old way of looking at sexuality, were sure to crop up again and again in the church.

We have many parallels today, when the Playboy philosophy reflects the attitude of so many. Today in our individualism and relativism, many stress "freedom," and demand that each person be allowed to do his own thing without criticism. Today too many insist that what may not be right for you is not necessarily wrong for them. The modern label of the pornographic as "adult" and "mature" duplicates the mindset of the Corinthians and their culture. The sophisticated of Corinth were as adept as the sophisticates of today in pretending that evil is good and good evil.

In a world like ours and theirs, in which the "rights" of the individual are stressed, while old distinctions between right and wrong are blurred, there are sure to be times when immorality and other kinds of sin infect the church. The old ways of thought die hard. Transformation, while real, is gradual and progressive. On the journey to Christian maturity, both individuals and local congregations can falter.

That's what happened in my own congregation. And that's what happened in the Corinthian church. Facing the issue head-on, Paul helped the Corinthians—and us—to think through a number of difficult questions. In the process, Paul helped us learn more about God's mind and heart. And more about what it means to truly love one another.

Paraphrase

If your group members are studying this passage inductively, using the 5-step approach explained in Study Guide 129, let your group members compare their sentence summaries and paraphrases with each other. The paraphrase may look something like this one, which highlights central issues.

Discipline Is Essential
1 Corinthians 5—6

> Deal decisively with that case of sexual immorality you've been tolerating—put the man out of your fellowship! How can you have been proud of your toleration? Don't you realize such old taints can spoil the new person you are in Christ? Earlier, I told you not to associate with the sexually immoral, and I meant specifically those who call themselves brothers. I don't judge non-Christians; it's those within who are to be judged—and in this case expelled.
>
> Even such things as lawsuits and disputes are to be settled within the family. Why, the continued existence of such things is a tragic spiritual defeat. People practicing sin have no place in God's kingdom; you *were* like that, some of you, but after being washed and sanctified and justified in Jesus, all that is to be put behind. Don't misuse the, "Everything is permissible" principle. This is subordinate to the fact that Jesus is Lord. You can never take that body of yours, a member of Christ, and unite it with some prostitute! Utterly reject sexual immorality, for, as the temple of God's Holy Spirit, you belong to Him now.

At first glance, this summary does not seem to help much in answering the difficult questions about church discipline, and the necessary dimension of judgment. Yet as we examine this passage in our Bibles, we do find answers—and we learn what the right questions are!

♥ ***Link to Life: Youth / Adult***

Write the "right questions" on the chalkboard. Ask your group members to work in pairs, reading 1 Corinthians 5 and 6 and jotting down any answers they find. This activity should take up to 15 or 20 minutes.

The questions:

1. *How dare we judge others?*
2. *What kinds of things are to be disciplined?*
3. *Why must we discipline within the church family?*
4. *How do we discipline?*
5. *Doesn't discipline violate others' rights?*

Answers to Our Discipline Questions: 1 Corinthians 5

Let's deal with this passage first by looking at its answer to the five questions raised above about church discipline.

How dare we judge others? This is an important question, especially in view of Paul's statements in 1 Corinthians 4 about being judged by a human court (vv. 1-6). If we go outside this letter, we find more warnings. Jesus said, "Do not judge, or you too will be judged" (Matt. 7:1). And James asked, "Who are you to judge your neighbor?" after pointing out that God alone is "Lawgiver and Judge" (James 4:11-12).

Yet when we look at 1 Corinthians 5 we find that Paul had "already passed judgment" on one member of the Corinthian fellowship (v. 3). He commanded the church to assemble and "hand this man over to Satan" (v. 5). He told them "not to associate" with sexually immoral persons, which necessarily calls for an evaluation of who is and who is not immoral!

While on the surface this may seem contradictory, it is not when we make a simple distinction. *There are some things which we Christians have no right to judge. But there are other things which we must judge!*

This is really quite an obvious principle. I'm not a nuclear physicist, so I wouldn't be called in to judge the safety or danger of a new atomic power plant. I have no criteria or skill for making such an evaluation. On the other hand, I am a Christian educator. As such I'm often invited to churches or schools to evaluate their curriculums and programs. So in areas where I am not competent to judge, I refrain. In areas where I am competent, I should speak up.

We are not competent to judge another's motives or service (1 Cor. 4). Both Christ and James were speaking of critical evaluation of others who, while perhaps different from us, are not subject to us but to Jesus as Lord (see also Rom. 14–15). In 1 Corinthians 5, Paul was talking about *sin.*

And this, as we shall see, is one area in which we must accept our responsibility, and judge!

What kinds of things are valid causes for discipline? As we look at the Corinthian passage, it becomes even more clear. *God has made us responsible to judge those things that He Himself has declared to be sin!* We have not taken the judge's robes and declared "immorality is sin." Not at all. God has already spoken. When we act to discipline a brother who is practicing sin, all we are doing is agreeing with God in the judgment He has already pronounced!

It is understandable that the other things Paul mentioned in this chapter are things which Scripture also clearly identifies as sin: idolatry, adultery, homosexuality, thievery, drunkenness. God has announced His judgment on all of them. In these areas, the church must speak with God's voice. Our judgment must agree with His.

But note two things. First, the text speaks of "idolaters" rather than idolatry. It says "homosexual offenders" rather than homosexuality. This wording is important, not because it indicates a *person* rather than a sin, but because it indicates *a person who is habitually practicing the sin!* Paul is not saying that an individual is to be disciplined by the fellowship for a single act or failure. After all, transformation is not instantaneous; we need to give each other room to grow. But when a person habitually practices sexual immorality or thievery or homosexuality, *then* the family is to accept its responsibility and is to discipline.

Second, our judgment is limited to those who are professing Christians. Paul makes it very clear that his instruction not to associate with the immoral was given, "not at all meaning the people of this world who are immoral," for it is no business of the Christian to "judge those outside the church" (1 Cor. 5:10, 12). But those *inside* "must" be judged, and the "wicked man" must be expelled from the fellowship.

What church discipline involves, then, is judgment (1) of a practice which God's Word has unequivocably condemned as sin; (2) when that sin is habitually practiced; (3) by one who claims to be a member of the family of God.

Why must we discipline within the family? One answer is given in this passage. The family of God is to reflect the Lord's own purity. Permitting sin in Christ's body will taint the whole and will spread (vv. 6-8).

This point is particularly significant when we remember that the church is God's chosen agency for transformation. Within the fellowship of the family we find our examples, our support, our encouragement, our instruction, our admonition—all those influences God uses to help us enter into the great realities we are called to experience in Christ. A church family torn by disputes or soiled by the presence of those committed to habitual sins loses its power to transform. For the church to fulfill its purpose, holiness and discipline are necessities.

There's one other point, not made here but in 2 Corinthians. Discipline is also the *loving* way to deal with the sinner. The goal is not to cut him off, but to work for his restoration by helping him sense the seriousness of sin, and respond to God's call to holiness. When the Corinthian church obeyed Paul's demand, the result was restoration of the sexually immoral brother to fellowship with God and with the congregation (see 2 Cor. 2:5-11).

How do we discipline? In the case of habitual sin and continuing immorality, we know that Paul had earlier given them instruction in a now-lost letter (see 1 Cor. 5:9-11). We can assume that Paul's instruction included an explanation of the process which Jesus outlined in Matthew 18:15-17.

In that pattern, Jesus called for loving admonition from a Christian friend. If this failed, the leaders of the local congregation were to meet with the sinning believer. If he or she still refused to repent and give up the sin, then that person was to be cut off from fellowship. In Jesus' words, "Treat him as you would a pagan or a tax collector." In

Paul's restatement, which captures the meaning of those words exactly, he said, "With such a man do not even eat" (1 Cor. 5:11).

What about Paul's reference to delivering the sinner up to Satan? The thought is that the sinner who has not responded to the church must now suffer affliction and perhaps even physical death (cf. 10:10; 11:30, 32 with 1 Tim. 1:20 and 1 John 5:16).

Doesn't discipline violate others' rights? This question reflects an individualism characteristic both of Hellenistic times and of our own. Then, as now, people claimed personal freedom and privilege, insisting "everything is permissible" (1 Cor. 6:12). In our day this arrogant attitude has been expressed in law suits brought against churches which have expelled members for immorality.

But the argument from personal rights is an empty one. We Christians no longer belong to ourselves; our "rights" are no longer paramount. For we belong to the Lord. "You are not your own: you were bought at a price" (1 Cor. 6:19-20). Our bodies are now the temple of the Holy Spirit, who is in us (v. 19). Our bodies, as well as our hearts and minds, are God's. It is *His* right to be Lord, not our right to do as we please.

While we are free from external bondage, we are to exercise our Christian freedom within the limits imposed by God's purpose in our lives. When it comes to discipline in the church of Christ, we are not to hesitate to act because we feel we might violate a brother's rights. Instead we *must* act because God has charged us to uphold *His* rights.

And, of course, we discipline because we love the sinning brother or sister. He will only discover the meaning of his life, and we of ours, as we remain in full fellowship with our Lord. Because we love we discipline, and through discipline we invite our straying brother or sister to return.

Other Teachings: 1 Corinthians 6

Judging disputes (1 Cor. 6:1-8). Paul looked at one other case in which Christians are to judge. The word "judge" comes from a Greek root that means simply "to discern." In the case of church discipline, the word carries a legal connotation, and suggests passing judgment as on a criminal. In the "trivial cases" in 1 Corinthians 6, it should be understood to emphasize evaluation with a view to settling a matter in dispute as in a civil case.

The matters in dispute in the Corinthian church were the kind of things that today we might bring to small claims courts, or even make an issue in a civil suit. Christians who felt that another believer had cheated or defrauded them in some way angrily went to the civil courts to accuse one another.

Paul considered it shameful for believers to take a family dispute before secular courts, whose judges were not believers. He reminded them that one day God's saints will have a role in judging the world and angels; surely such comparatively trivial matters as those in dispute could be settled by a committee of Christians appointed to work out a fair resolution.

How much better to trust our differences to those we know love us and our opponent, rather than to an impersonal court of secular law.

Sexual purity (1 Cor. 6:12-20). Paul began by putting the principle: "Everything is permissible for me," into perspective. This principle is one that Paul himself taught, as seen in Romans 14:14. No doubt those who were sinning in Corinth remembered what Paul had taught them, and were using this Pauline principle to justify their behavior. This "permissible" principle is circumscribed by other principles. For instance, "Not everything is beneficial." A Christian *can* do things that do not particularly benefit him or others, but a wise believer will choose what is beneficial. Again, "I will not be mastered by anything." Some things a Christian *can* do may develop into habits that master him. For instance, some become slaves to their appetite for rich food. Yes, a Christian *can* overeat—but a wise believer will not develop such a habit.

But sexual immorality does not fall into either of these two limiting categories. The "all is permissible" principle does not apply at all, for "the body is not meant for sexual immorality, but for the Lord" (v. 13).

Sexual immorality is one of the worst of sins, for it violates the intimate relationship which a person has with Jesus Himself and the indwelling Holy Spirit. Jesus, who is Lord of the body, requires that we honor God in our bodies rather than sin against Him.

TEACHING GUIDE

Prepare
Look up all the verses on judging referred to in this study guide. Can you think of any cases where a church you were a member of exercised discipline? How would you evaluate it based on your study of this passage?

Explore
1. If you are using the 5-Step method suggested with your group, begin by forming teams to compare sentence summaries and paraphrases. You will also want to copy and pass out the paraphrase in this study guide. Then skip to activity 1, *expand*.
2. Briefly outline the situation in the author's church, shared at the beginning of this study guide. Ask: "What should the church leaders do, if anything?" And as answers are given, ask: "Why?"

Expand
1. Explain the situation in Corinth that Paul dealt with in this letter. Then list on the chalkboard the five questions to be answered from a study of this passage (see "link-to-life," page 847.

Set teams to studying the passage to answer the five questions from 1 Corinthians 5, with possible reference to 6:12-20. When the teams have finished, come together again to share answers.

Talk your group through their study, question by question, making sure that all the points raised in the commentary have been observed.
2. Tell about the situation the author describes of the woman in his local congregation. Ask the group to determine what the leaders and the congregation should do, step-by-step, to deal with this situation.

Or use another situation from your own experience as a case history.
3. Or hold a T/F quiz to see how well your group members have grasped the teaching of this passage. Include on your quiz such items as:

- Everyone is responsible for church discipline (T)
- Discipline is intended to maintain doctrinal purity (F)
- As soon as a person sins he or she is to be expelled from fellowship (F)
- Only those habitually practicing sin and refusing to attempt reform are subject to church discipline (T)
- The goal of church discipline is to punish (F)

Include additional T/F items if you wish. After all have answered, go over each item together as a review.

Apply
Pray together that God will guard members of your congregation from sins that call for discipline, but that any who are trapped by sin will respond to loving discipline by leaders and church.

STUDY GUIDE 131

1 Corinthians 8–10

CHURCH FAMILY DISPUTES

Overview

NOTE: 1 Corinthians 7 is discussed with 1 Corinthians 11, in Study Guide 133.

The Corinthian church was troubled by many problems. There were cliques and divisions, and there was immorality. Now we discover that the believers in Corinth were also divided over a doctrinal issue!

In 1 Corinthains 5 we saw that to maintain the unity and purity of the local congregation, God calls on us to discipline brothers and sisters who habitually sin. But what do we do to maintain unity when doctrinal differences emerge?

This passage gives us a surprising answer. We are to admit the fact that one side or the other will be more "right" in their belief. But who is "right" is not the most important issue! No matter who is "right" we are to maintain harmony by affirming love, and by refusing to let our disagreements force us into opposing camps. The "right" and the "wrong" are to continue to live together as members of a caring family!

How is this possible? The answer is found in these important Corinthian passages you are called to teach.

▶ ***Doctrine.*** The Greek word simply means "teaching." It is found 21 times in the New Testament, 15 in the Pastoral Epistles. Typically it means divinely communicated content, binding on the Christian community as God's truth.

Commentary

It seems peculiar. In a faith that claims to possess truth, Paul insisted on protecting the right of brothers and sisters to be wrong!

This is actually what we discover in this powerful section of 1 Corinthians. Among the issues raised by the folks at Corinth, and carried to Paul by Stephanus, Fortunatus, and Achaicus (1 Cor. 16:17) was a doctrinal dispute. The church appealed to Paul to settle the dispute, by telling them which side was right.

Paul settled it. But by explaining how such disputes are to be dealt with! Paul was careful not to give either side a club with which to bludgeon the other. Something else, Paul taught, was involved in the doctrinal conflict; something that takes priority because it is more important than being "right." When we grasp what Paul is teaching here, you and I and our group members will have a very necessary guide for us in modern times.

We need to remember that the New Testament church broke into the Hellenistic world with a Gospel of revolutionary truth *and* with a revolutionary relationship: love. The impact of the church was related to both truth and love, and to the fulfilled promise of personal transformation. It is to be the same in our century: the message of God is to be communicated, and the power of the Gospel is to be demonstrated in a loving community, peopled by transformed individuals.

Truth, love, and transformation are all essential.

But what happens then when there is a disagreement in Christ's body over truth? What happens when we are forced by our convictions to disagree, not over favorite leaders (as in 1 Cor. 1–4), but to disagree over truth itself? Is there any way to preserve love in such a dispute?

At most times in church history the answer has been, "Contend for the truth. Break with those who are not doctrinally 'pure.' " A few times the answer has been, "Emphasize love. Surrender truth for the sake of harmony." But each of these solutions is wrong! Each short-circuits the dynamic of the body of Christ. In New Testament times and in our own it is the *harmonious* testimony of truth, love, and transformation that has provided compelling evidence of the reality of Christ, and has overwhelmed the defenses of pagan cultures.

Our solution to the problem of doctrinal differences *must* affirm truth. But it must also maintain love, and facilitate personal transformation. And it is the pattern for just such a solution that Paul offered in 1 Corinthians 8–10.

Cultural Background

Before summarizing the thrust of this passage in a paraphrase, it's helpful to point out that the confusion in Corinth was compounded by the fact that there were *two* problems linked with this dispute over "food sacrificed to idols" (8:1).

Leon Morris, in *The First Epistle of Paul to the Corinthians* (Eerdmans), helps us understand why this issue was so important to the believers in the first century.

> First, it was an accepted social practice to have meals in a temple or in some place associated with an idol. "It was all part and parcel of the formal etiquette in society" (Moffatt). The kind of occasion, public or private, when people were likely to come together socially was the kind of occasion when a sacrifice was appropriate. To have nothing to do with such gatherings was to cut oneself off from most social intercourse with one's fellows. . . . Secondly, most of the meat sold in the shops had first been offered in sacrifice. Part of the victim was always offered on an altar to the god, part went to the priests, and usually part to the worshipers. The priests customarily sold what they could not use. It would be very difficult to know for sure whether meat in a given shop had been part of a sacrifice or not. Notice that there are two separate questions: taking part in idol feasts, and the eating of meat bought in shops, but previously part of a sacrifice.

What should the Corinthian Christians do? Not go to dinner at friends' homes because the food served there would have been offered previously to pagan gods or goddesses? (Actually, Paul had taught in 1 Cor. 5:9-12 that believers were *not* to cut themselves off from pagan contact—even with idolators.) As for the Christian's own homes, the temple meat markets were the normal places to shop. Should a Christian become a vegetarian?

In struggling with this issue, the Corinthians rightly went back to basic truths. They searched the truths revealed by God (Christian teaching, or doctrine) for guidelines. But different people came up with different answers! This truly became a doctrinal issue—not just a matter of personal conviction. It divided many in the church, and the dispute became so sharp that the parties appealed to Paul, asking him to tell them who was right.

Many commentators feel that Paul, in writing his answer, actually quoted from their own arguments. Here are phrases which seem to most to represent the doctrinal views that led one party to the conclusion that both the social practice and shopping at a temple meat market were acceptable.

- Doctrinal argument one:"An idol is nothing at all in the world" (8:4).
- Doctrinal argument two: "Food does not bring us near to God; we are no worse if we do not eat, and no better if we do" (v. 8).

In fact, these arguments are strong, and they reflect something of the spiritual growth of those who made them! God is *One!* All the gods and goddesses that the Corinthians had once feared and tried to appease, or had worshiped in the unlikely expectation of some kind of aid, did not even exist! These believers were freed from the emptiness of that whole system! They now laughed at the lumps of stone and metal that had once held them in bondage. When they attended social events, and idols were honored, the Corinthians felt only joy that they knew the true and living God, and dismissed the idolatry as empty and meaningless. Those who objected to their participation seemed to these men and women, so thrilled by the truth they now knew, to still be in bondage to false beliefs about pagan gods and goddesses that a Christian should discard.

As for food, this party also realized that all the rituals by which they once tried to please the gods were meaningless. Their relationship with Christ was a living reality, a vital, personal transaction. What a person eats or doesn't eat fails to delight God. It is what is in our hearts, not in our stomachs, that is Jesus' concern (see Matt. 15:17-20).

So this party in Corinth, basing their practices on what seemed to be sound doctrinal reasoning, participated in social idolatry without a qualm of conscience. They were right in their doctrine. And Paul gently agreed with their insights. But then Paul went on to show them how it is possible to be "right" and still be wrong!

♥ ***Link to Life: Youth / Adult***
Your group members need the background given above to help them understand these important chapters. So begin with a minilecture. Then, if you are using the 5-Step inductive study approach suggested in Study Guide 129, give your group members five minutes to read their paraphrases and make any changes the new data may suggest.

Then distribute a copy of the paraphrase in the text to each, and have group members pair off to (1) compare their paraphrases and the author's, and then (2) agree on at least two key points that Paul makes in dealing with this dispute.

Tracing the Argument
It is difficult to summarize paragraphs so packed with ideas as some are in this section of 1 Corinthians. But your group members' paraphrases may read something like this:

The Right to Be Wrong
1 Corinthians 8–10

Let's begin thinking about this idol question in terms of *love* rather than *knowledge*. Beginning from knowledge, we do conclude that idols are nothing. But this isn't the customary view. Someone might be led by your example at an idol feast to eat against his conscience. If you thus damage a brother for whom Christ died, *that* is a sin against the Lord Himself.

Look, you know I'm an apostle. As such, I too might claim certain rights, such as the right to be supported by you. But I gave up this right, and I work to earn my living. I freely surrender my rights and choose to live as a slave to everyone in order to reach them. It's like an athlete. He gives up many things while in training in order to win the prize. Well, my prize is people.

Now, as to your "knowledge," don't be ignorant of the fact that Israel's experience speaks to us Christians. Idolatry led Israel into all sorts of immorality, and brought on God's judgment. Are you to feel secure in your knowledge of the emptiness of idolatry? Watch out that you don't fall into the common temptations associated with it!

Really, flee idolatry. Our communion is with Christ, and our identity is with those who are one in Him. While idols are nothing, pagan sacrifices are offered to very real demons who are behind the pagan systems. So *don't* participate in idol feasts. Don't insist on your rights and your freedom. Choose what is beneficial to you and others.

But don't make a big issue of meat purchased at temple meat markets. If someone else makes an issue of it—like saying, "This is temple meat!"—then don't eat it, for his sake. God *doesn't* care what's in your stomach, but even eating and drinking can be done to God's glory. In this case, that means considering the impact of your actions on others—Jews, Greeks, and your brothers—and being guided in what you do by concern for their good rather than for the rightness of your position. This is what I do as I follow Jesus, so you follow my example.

What an exciting answer! But to understand it, we need to be sure we grasp several critical points.

Keys to Understanding Paul's Argument: 1 Corinthians 8–10
Limitations on knowledge (1 Cor. 8:1-3). In these chapters Paul was responding to the stance taken by the Corinthians. In the dispute there each side was concerned with only one issue: "Who is right?"

Each party based its conviction that *it* was right on an appeal to revealed truth, and on the belief that it had a better grasp of truth than the other party.

So Paul began with a warning. Approaching *any* issue from the viewpoint of superior knowledge alone is inadequate, and is dangerous. Why? Because each side in the argument will have at least *some* grasp of God's truth ("we all possess knowledge" [v. 1]). But if we put our emphasis only on knowledge of the truth, we are sure to develop a spiritual pride—pride that we know more and better than others ("knowledge puffs up" [v. 1]). But in fact any human being's grasp of truth is incomplete ("the man who thinks he knows something does not yet know as he ought to know" [v. 2]). Thus the attitude that we know the truth and that we are "right" is not only dangerous, but it is wrong.

In these opening verses Paul established an important fact. *The Corinthians had gone about dealing with the disputed issue in the wrong way!* In their focus on knowledge of God's truth they forgot love! They ignored the imperfection of human understanding, and, in effect, cut themselves off from growth in knowledge, for their pride about what they thought they knew cut them off from learning more!

Well, if the Corinthians' approach was wrong, how *do* we deal with doctrinal disagreements? *Be sure to begin by affirming love.* First, because love is the key to transformation. In the loving family of God, the Holy Spirit works to transform attitudes, values, behavior, understanding—our total personality. *Where there is love in the body, there will be openness to God.* As we open our lives to God, the Spirit guides us into "the knowledge of the truth" (Heb. 10:26).

We can visualize Paul's key concept here this way:

Dispute Handled through Knowledge

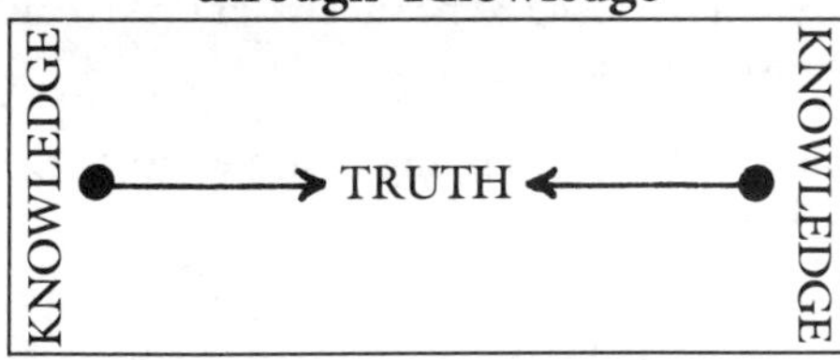

In the confrontational approach, each side claims to have a better grasp of the truth than the other. This leads to pride, and encourages a closed mind to aspects of truth not yet grasped. It does not help either side to open up to the Spirit of God for further teaching, and it causes divisions in the body of Christ.

In what we can call the commitment approach, each side affirms its love for and acceptance of the other. Side by side, without false pride, each humbly admits the limitations on human knowledge and concentrates on helping the other love God better. This leads to both sides remaining open to God, and to the teaching ministry of the Holy Spirit.

Dispute Handled through Love

When differences are approached in love, there is no retreat from our community to truth. Instead, there is a deep desire to know truth and to grasp it more fully—together.

Paul's rights (1 Cor. 9). At first it is a temptation to think that chapter 9 is unrelated to chapter 8. How did Paul move from talking about meat offered to idols, to the subject of apostolic rights?

The connection is this. Paul was highlighting something that the Corinthians had overlooked, an issue that was vitally important even though their dispute was essentially doctrinal. This issue is the *attitude* of those who knew an idol had no real existence, and who thus concluded: "I've got the truth, and according to truth I have a *right* to attend idol feasts and eat sacrificed meat." The attitude suggests that these people believed doctrinal correctness *in itself* justified their behavior.

Paul, however, confronted these believers with a factor they had not considered. Even if they were right about idols, and even if they were able to eat meat at idol feasts with a clear conscience, was their *insistence on exercising their rights* a truly Christian attitude? Which should have priority—our rights, or our brother's well-being? What do we care about most—a good steak dinner, or members of God's family who may not have our "mature" viewpoint?

In 1 Corinthians 8 Paul concluded that the Corinthians, rather than taking pride in their knowledge of the truth, really should have been ashamed of their lack of concern for others. First Corinthians 9 is a personal illustration: Paul was not just "preaching at" the Corinthians. Paul had himself chosen to give up *his* rights and privileges as an apostle, for their sake!

More truth (1 Cor. 10). Chapter 10 grows out of Paul's initial warning that our knowledge of truth is incomplete. He did commend the Corinthians for recognizing that an idol was "nothing at all in the world" (8:4). But now Paul pointed out the dangers of idolatry.

As far as participation in idol feasts was concerned, such things had always been associated with immorality. Did a person identified with Jesus think it was right, by participating, to link himself with all that the culture associates with idol feasts? In idolatry there are temptations common to all men: Christians are not exempt (10:13).

What's more, while the idols themselves are "nothing at all in the world," idolatry has always been used by demonic powers, which *are* real. Can a Christian, who shares in Communion and drinks "the cup of the Lord," go to an idolatrous feast and "drink . . . the cup of demons too?" (v. 21)

Clearly Paul had ruled that the "go to idol feasts" party was *wrong!* Their claim of a grasp of Christian doctrine was foolish, for they justified their actions on only part of the truth.

Finally Paul shifted focus to deal with the second issue: eating meat that may have been purchased at a temple meat market. Paul pointed out that this was not the same as participating in a festive and idolatrous party which had been dedicated to some pagan god or goddess. If the host at a private dinner party made an issue of the meat having been offered first to an idol, then, for the sake of *his* conscience, the Christian should not eat. But otherwise, Christians shouldn't make an issue of it. Just remember, Paul advised, that while the food in itself is morally neutral, in eating and in drinking, and in whatever we do, we are to seek God's glory, and to be sensitive to what will lead to the salvation of the lost, and to the benefit of our brothers and sisters.

Analysis

There are several vital lessons for us in Paul's handling of this early doctrinal dispute.

Begin with a commitment to love. Even if a brother or sister is wrong doctrinally, we are not released from the obligation to love.

Maintain a concern for truth. Paul kept a balance. He continued to love those on both sides of this issue, but he did not hesitate to make the truth clear, even when it revealed one position to be wrong.

Be sensitive to the relational implications of truth. One side in Corinth was so sure it was right—and sure that orthodoxy gave them the right to participate in idol feasts—that they disregarded *other* truths about relationships in the family. No single truth has priority, but must be held in balance with other truths. Our adherence to one doctrine does not justify ignoring other teachings in God's Word.

Don't treat one truth as the whole truth. We need to look beyond a doctrine that is being disputed, in order to see related truths in Scripture. By building their whole argument on the single truth that idols are nothing, the one faction in Corinth overlooked the reality of demons and the immoral cultural associations of idolatrous celebrations. By overlooking these other relevant truths the "I can eat" party in Corinth was "right," but reached a wrong conclusion.

Keeping these principles in mind can help us today when we have honest doctrinal differences within our congregations.

Paul's pattern. The way in which Paul dealt with error in Corinth was beautiful for its sensitivity and love. Paul even commended those who were wrong, for grasping those truths they had apprehended! Paul also commended them for their "strong" conscience. How wonderful that these men and women were able to cast off the attitude of a lifetime and, on the basis of God's Word as they understood it, find freedom from idolatrous bondage and fear. Anyone who is aware of the difficulties pagan peoples have with release from such bondage would commend these people too!

So, rather than beginning by saying to the "We can eat" party, "You're wrong," Paul began by commending and affirming them.

In the rest of the discussion Paul kept the focus on the relational, and encouraged all the Corinthians to act for the benefit of their brothers and sisters. Paul let them know he expected as much; that he really believed they cared. Paul did point out that because of two factors (two truths) the one party had overlooked, they were wrong. But at the same time Paul kept his appeal focused on *both* truth and love.

Paul's premise. How did Paul find the freedom to deal with error so gently? How was he able to commend those who were wrong, and to actually affirm their right to be wrong?

The answer comes when we realize that Paul operated with a basic premise—a premise that needs to be ours as we live with other Christians. You see, *Paul expected the Corinthians to grow.* He did not insist that everyone be doctrinally correct *now.* Paul knew that in the context of a loving family, in which even the erring brother is worthy of affirmation and concern, spiritual and personal growth *will* take place. As life is opened up to the Spirit of God, He will lead the people of God into all truth.

This premise helps you and me to relate to those who differ doctrinally today. our brothers—and we too!—are young. We have a long way to grow, and much more to learn. At best, our grasp of truth is incomplete. But if we keep on loving one another, God will bring us by His transforming power to a place where we both have a more complete knowledge of God's wonderful truth.

TEACHING GUIDE

Prepare
Because of the complex nature of the passage and its teachings, you will need to lecture more than usual. Think through the passage carefully, and make notes for your lecture presentation.

Explore
1. If you are using the 5-Step study plan, see "link-to-life," page 853 for a minilecture and group study plan to launch this group session.
2. Otherwise, begin with a 20- to 30-minute lecture containing these elements:
   a. Explanation of the cultural background of the dispute.
   b. Truths the "We can eat" party correctly understood.
   c. Paul's instructions in 1 Corinthians 8 and 9 on how to go about handling a dispute. Include the visuals on page 854 showing the difference between confrontational and commitment approaches.
   d. Explanation of the additional truths the "We can eat" party had overlooked, and why they were "wrong" even though "right" about idols being nothing.
   e. Summary of principles to be applied in dealing with modern doctrine disputes.

Expand
1. If using the 5-Step approach, follow up comparison of group members' paraphrases with a minilecture quickly covering points c, d, and e in *explore 2.*
2. Divide your group into teams to discuss either the following case history, or another more relevant to your own situation. Here are the instructions:

Imagine that you are a board member in a noncharismatic church, and that several in the fellowship have had a speaking in tongues experience, which they are attempting to share with others. A dispute quickly develops that threatens to split the church.

Determine:
- How might this dispute be handled if approached on the basis of knowledge?
- How might this dispute be handled if approached on the basis of love?
- What truths would you want to consider in addition to any teachings about spiritual gifts?
- What would you expect to be the outcome in your local fellowship? How long would you expect it to take to achieve this outcome?

3. Or assume you are the administrator of a Christian college. Would you invite a Christian with a significantly different doctrinal position to teach or lecture at your school? Why, or why not? How is this situation similar to or different from the local church situation with which Paul dealt?

Apply
Ask each member to identify Christians he or she has regular contact with whom he differs on some point of doctrine. Talk in pairs: "How have you tended to relate to them? How do you think you *should* relate to them? What can you do to put the teaching of these chapters into practice in this relationship?"

STUDY GUIDE 132

1 Corinthians 12–14

CHURCH FAMILY GIFTS

Overview

One of the problems in Corinth focused on spiritual gifts, and their relationship to spirituality. Today too similar questions surface, and similar confusion exists. Yet in this three-chapter section of 1 Corinthians Paul provided clear teaching. For instance, our study of 1 Corinthians 12–14 will tell us which of the following are true and which are false—and explain why!

- T or F? The more important the spiritual gift, the more mature and spiritual the person.
- T or F? The major evidence of the Holy Spirit in a person's life is his or her ability to speak in tongues.
- T or F? We must ask God for the spiritual gift we want.
- T or F? A person "under the influence" of the Spirit can't help shouting out.
- T or F? Some Christians have little to contribute to others.
- T or F? In church meetings, only the pastor should teach, because he's usually the only one with seminary training.
- T or F? There is no real test for "spirituality."
- T or F? Some people are more important than others in the church as in every other situation.

If your group members have ever had questions like these, or are uncertain about spiritual gifts and their relationship to Christian spirituality, this study is especially for them!

Commentary

It should be very clear by now in our study of 1 Corinthians. The New Testament church was not utopia!

Sometimes we imagine that it was. When we're plagued by problems in our local congregations, or unhappy about our personal spiritual progress, we long for those early days. We feel that somehow the church has lost its power; we wonder how to recapture those supposed days of constant victory.

Well, the New Testament church *was* dynamic. The truth, the love, the transformation that marked the Christian fellowship was distinctive in a world that was void of each. But that same trio is meant to characterize the family of God in every age, and in each we must struggle to maintain their balance. The way to victory now as in New Testament times was marked by struggle, setbacks, slow growth, and time. Maturity then as now comes only gradually, and often seems choked out by problems.

Actually, we need not be discouraged if at times our churches are marred by differences, problems, and disputes. Let's remember that Paul wrote 1 Corinthians when the church was young and vital and alive—and that even a vitally alive congregation will have problems. It is not the absence of problems, but *how we deal with them,* that determines our continued growth toward the full experience of blessing.

In Paul's letter, he guides us as well as the Corinthians to this understanding. Paul wanted us to know *how* to deal with issues that are likely to trouble any local church—including problems that may arise from confusion over tongues.

Background

Once again, some insight into the first-century world is helpful as we approach what seems to be a very contemporary issue.

Tongues. In the New Testament we first meet tongues in Acts 2, when on the Day of Pentecost the Holy Spirit welded the disciples into a new body, the church. Not only were there miraculous signs of fire and wind but, filled with the Holy Spirit, the disciples began to "speak in other tongues as the Spirit enabled them" (Acts 2:4).

"How is it," the observers asked in amazement, "that each of us hears them in his own native language?" (v. 8)

Later, when we meet tongues in Acts, they again seem to be foreign languages (see 10:44-46; 11:17).

Coming to 1 Corinthians, we learn that the tongues-speaker himself did not understand what he was saying unless a person with the gift of interpretation explained. Here interpretation of tongues is identified as a separate gift—a gift often possessed by a fellow believer in the congregation. Tongues, then, was not used evangelistically in the early church to reach outsiders, but was exercised within the family, and then only when an interpreter was present to make the message intelligible to others (1 Cor. 14:28).

Nothing in this passage ruled out tongues as a valid expression of the Holy Spirit's ministry through one of God's children. Instead, Paul was concerned in these chapters with putting this rather spectacular gift in perspective.

Cultural context. Perspective was especially important in a place like Corinth. It was universally accepted in the Hellenistic world that some were especially close to the gods. Usually this closeness was supposed to be manifested by trances, ecstatic speech, and other unusual or bizarre forms of behavior. All this was taken as evidence of special spiritual endowment. A person with epilepsy, for instance, was said to have the "divine disease." The oracles at religious centers were often given drugs to provoke their utterances. The oracle at Delphi, so prominent in the early days of Greece, breathed volcanic fumes from a cleft in the rock of the temple floor, and her unconscious mutterings were then interpreted by the priests.

It is not surprising, given this cultural perspective, that the Christians in Corinth were attracted to the gift of tongues. Nor is it surprising that they thought of such people as especially spiritual.

But their assumptions led to real problems in the Corinthian church. And Paul launched these chapters by challenging the assumptions carried over from paganism. Paul's very first words were: "Now about spiritual [gifts], brothers, I do not want you to be ignorant" (12:1).

The word "gifts" really should be placed, as I have, in brackets. It is not necessarily implied by the Greek word *pneumatikon.* As the alternate reading in the *Revised Standard Version* suggests, it might as well be rendered "spiritual *persons.*" This probably better reflects the issue that troubled the Corinthians. It was the issue of *spirituality itself,* and how spirituality is expressed in Christian experience.

We need to remember that the Corinthians were pagans just a short time ago, "somehow or other . . . influenced and led astray to dumb idols" (v. 2). It was dangerous for them to carry over into the Christian faith old notions about spirituality! But apparently they had been so influenced by the old assumptions that when someone in an ecstatic trance had pronounced an *anathema* ("be accursed") against Jesus Himself, a few of the Corinthians had actually been swayed! They had taken the state of the person making the utterance as evidence of divine inspiration!

Paul said firmly that no one could say, "Jesus be cursed," by the Spirit of God. Neither would anyone caught up in such an experience (as were the oracles of pagan faiths) ever announce, "Jesus is Lord," unless indwelt by the Holy Spirit. The state of the speaker was not to be taken as evidence of inspiration or of spirituality!

Paul dealt with this issue because there was then, as now, a great danger that in their ignorance some Christians would be led away from true spirituality by an unwarranted emphasis on this more spectacular manifestation of the Spirit. In his argument Paul did *not* attack the gift of tongues, or reject it. Rather he gave a lengthy explanation of how the Spirit does work in our lives, and in our churches.

Tracing the Argument: 1 Corinthians 12–14

Our insight into backgrounds helps us entitle this important section of 1 Corinthians, and also helps us trace the apostle's train of thought. A paraphrase condenses the argument, and makes it more clear.

True Spirituality
1 Corinthians 12–14

Brothers, don't view spirituality from your old pagan perspective. God is at work in all of us, but the Spirit's work is manifest in different ways. Yet, it *is* the Spirit who shows Himself behind each gift, and these expressions of His presence are dedicated to our common good. (Just how He works in each individual is *His* choice.)

Actually, we Christians are the body of Christ, many parts united in one. Like parts of the human body, we each have our own functions, as a "hand" or "foot" or "eye" or "ear." And we're each necessary; no one contribution should be singled out and exalted. So you're each in the body, and *this* is what's important. But if we were to rank gifts by their importance, tongues would hardly be at the top of the list.

Really, there's a better way to measure true spirituality: love. No gift profits a person exercising it unless he loves. You want to measure spirituality? Then look to kindness, patience, and those other practical expressions of real love. For it is love that lifts us out of childhood; love is the mark of spiritual maturity.

Focus on love, and realize that the gifts used for communicating God's Word should have priority when you meet. You see, intelligible speech builds up our brother, and it is such building-up gifts that we should value. So, in church don't burst out in a tongue unless an interpretation can be given. And don't misunderstand! I speak in tongues more than you all; I'm not rejecting this gift. But I'd rather speak 5 words that will help someone than 10,000 words in a tongue no one can understand.

So get over your childish preoccupation with tongues. Tongues are certainly *not* meant to be a sign of special spirituality within the body; as that kind of sign, their only appeal might be to pagans, as an indication of God's presence.

In church meetings let each one participate—but no more disorderly clamor! Take turns. God's work is marked by order, and you *can* control yourselves. As for the women who've been disrupting your meetings, they especially need to learn submissiveness. Tell them to be quiet in church and to discuss their questions with their husbands at home.

And if anyone there still wants to claim a "special spirituality," let him recognize the fact that I speak with God's own authority. So, brothers, don't forbid tongues, but do concentrate on communicating God's Word in your meetings.

Observations on the Text: 1 Corinthians 12–14

Several points within this extended passage have been disputed and discussed by Christians who differ doctrinally. Some are very important in tracing the apostle's thought and, in fact, interpretation of this passage may hinge on the grasp of the entire argument when more than one option is open to understanding individual verses. Here are observations that may be helpful.

To each one (1 Cor. 12:7) Each Christian has a spiritual gift, or "manifestation of the Spirit." The gifts differ, but have these common elements. (1) Each is a manifestation of the Holy Spirit's presence. (2) Each is "for the common good," that is, each is intended to build up the body of Christ. (3) Each is given "as He [the Spirit] determines." There is no true Christian in whom the Holy Spirit has not worked, providing a divine capacity enabling him or her to make a significant contribution to other believers.

Prophecy (1 Cor. 12:10). The emphasis on the ministry of prophets in Old and New Testaments is not on prediction, but on setting forth clearly what God has said. In the New Testament church *prophecy* can be (1) a gift, and/or (2) an office associated with authoritative expression of God's message.

It is best to always link prophecy with Scripture, either as an exposition of the Word, or as a message subject to the Word for authentication.

Desire the best gifts (1 Cor. 12:31). This is *not* an exhortation to individuals to ask the Spirit for any particular spiritual enablement. Instead it is an exhortation to the Corinthian congregation, needed because their attention had been drawn to "tongues" and they had actually ignored the more important ministries of the Holy Spirit.

The most excellent way (1 Cor. 12:31). The Corinthians had made two mistakes. First, they had taken a spectacular but less significant spiritual gift and given it priority in their meetings (see 1 Cor. 14). Second, they had carried over the pagan notion that such ecstatic utterances were a mark of spirituality—of special closeness to God. First Corinthians 13 dealt with this second issue. Here Paul answered the question, "How *do* we recognize special closeness to God in ourselves or in others?" All too often we yearn for a closer walk with the Lord. If we do not understand the closer walk, we're likely to grasp at an unusual experience such as tongues as the key. We're likely to listen to the person with the unusual experience, and take his gift or experience as the mark of divine favor.

Paul wanted the believers in Corinth to recognize the priority of the more important gifts in the ministry of the church, but he also wanted them to see that true spirituality is *completely unrelated* to the gifts a person may have from the Spirit. After all, Paul identified the Corinthian church as "still worldly" (3:3). Yet there was an exercise of *all* spiritual gifts in that body! (1:7)

The "most excellent way" Paul now introduced is the way to a deeper walk with God. *Love* is the key to our growth toward maturity, and love is the indication (a practical indication, according to 13:4-7) of true spirituality in others.

The church assembled (1 Cor. 14:1-19). With the principles explained in chapters 12 and 13, Paul moved on to apply them to church gatherings. Apparently these assemblies had become a bedlam. Brothers and sisters were shouting out in tongues at the same time; prophecy was discounted, and the prophet often interrupted; and apparently a group of women had become very aggressive about their gift of tongues. Paul told the church to correct these abuses. The principles he laid down are fascinating.

First, all believers could contribute—and tongues were not to be forbidden. After all, all are gifted, and these gifts are given "for the common good" (12:7). If participation is restricted, many will not contribute and their gifts will be lost, and the whole group suffer. (This is an interesting observation in terms of the contemporary church which tends to allow only one person to minister when the congregation gathers—the pastor.) Second, order must be maintained. There were rules to follow. Anyone claiming to have been "swept away" by the Spirit so he or she couldn't help interrupting was *not* acting by the Spirit. ("The spirits of the prophets are subject to the control of the prophets," 14:32). As for the women who had become so aggressive and dominating, they needed to learn to be quiet at church and to discuss things with their husbands at home. Submission was a principle these women needed to apply for their own personal spiritual growth—and for the sake of the congregation.

How like Paul! The most significant of Christian truths have the most practical application.

A sign to unbelievers? (1 Cor. 14:20-25) This is one of the most discussed passages in Scripture, and there are several explanations of why Paul seemed to say first that tongues are for, and then say they are not for, outsiders. One explanation is this.

In Greek culture, ecstatic utterances were taken as signs of the divine presence. Paul noted that unbelievers may view tongues as signs, even though believers were *not* to take them as a sign of spirituality (v. 22).

But such signs have limited impact on the unconverted. If an unbeliever should attend a Christian meeting and see everyone shouting out in tongues, his impression is likely to be, "What a madhouse!" (See v. 23.) But if he comes to a Christian meeting and hears the Word of God in plain talk, he'll be convicted by the Spirit and converted (vv. 24-25).

The point is, then, that while outsiders may *come* to a Christian meeting because they have heard about a miraculous sign, seeing the sign in action in the church will not lead to their conversion. That requires a presentation of the Gospel in words the visitor can understand.

Summary. Paul gave vital and clear teaching about an issue that divides believers today just as it troubled the early church. In this passage we find no license to reject the gift of tongues as a valid manifestation of the Holy Spirit. At the same time, we find a corrective to an overemphasis on this gift, which would attempt to make it *the* evidence of God's Spirit's presence, and *the* test of spirituality.

Once again Paul gently and delicately guided the Corinthians, and us, to affirm brothers who differ from us, and lifted up the vital role of love.

The Body: 1 Corinthians 12

In discussing spirituality and spiritual gifts, Paul introduced a powerful image of the church of Jesus Christ.

Two major images are given in the Bible: the church is a family, and the church is a body.

The concept of family is used often, and communicates the warmth of love and intimacy that is to mark the fellowship of believers. We are sons and daughters of God now through Jesus; as children of God we are also brothers and sisters. Learning to look at each other as brothers and sisters, and to think of ourselves as family, helps us realize why love truly is the mark of Christian fellowship.

Here, however, Paul asked us to see the faith community as a living body, and to visualize each believer as a functioning part of the body. While "family" speaks to us of relationships, "body" speaks to us of ministry.

These two images of Christ's church are never held up in contrast. Instead, they are two perspectives on a single reality. The *family relationship* is *context for ministry*. And *ministry* is the contribution that love leads each of us to make to our fellow family members.

The picture of a body also helps us see how Jesus continues to perform His work in our world. In Ephesians Paul tells us that Jesus is the "Head of the body" (Eph. 2:20-22). Jesus as living Head directs us—we who are His hands and feet and eyes and ears and mouth—to continue His own mission in our world. The compassion Jesus showed to the sick and weary and the sin-tormented, He still shows—through His body. When we as individuals and local groups of believers mature and become sensitive to the Lord's guidance, Christ ministers to us and through us.

Fellow members. Paul developed the analogy of the body in this passage to teach us about our relationship with each other. We are *dependent* on each other. No one person is fully equipped with all the spiritual gifts. Instead, each is given his own distinctive gift or gifts; each then makes his own unique contribution to "the common good" (1 Cor. 12:7).

It is through cooperation and coordination that each of us makes his or her contribution and, in turn, is helped and aided to grow. Individualism, with its emphasis on competition to discover the "best" and "greatest," is totally foreign to the body of Christ.

Yet the whole spirit of the Corinthian church was individualistic; they exalted favorite leaders, they competed doctrinally, they even competed to be given special individual "honor" because of the gift possessed. They were unable to see that each person needed the other and they were *interdependent,* not *independent.*

How much we need to rediscover the reality of the body of Christ today! For our age too is ruggedly individualistic. We too exalt competitiveness and individual achievement. We too find it hard to work with others in a team relationship. But we *are* a body. And it is as a body—honoring each part, ministering and being ministered to—that we must learn to live in God's family.

The more excellent way to experience life in Christ's body, and to find fulfillment in ministry, is to live the life of love that binds us together in harmonious unity.

♥ ***Link to Life: Youth / Adult***

To help your group members sense the fact that they are body members, outline a body on the chalkboard. Ask each person to think of how he or she contributes to others, and then select a part of the body that best represents him or her. Then go around the group, asking each to go to the board and put his or her name on the body part selected (remembering that only Christ is the Head). Each must then tell why he or she selected that part.

When all have finished, sit in a circle. Ask each to select one other in the group whom he or she particularly needs, and say to that person, "Susan, I'm glad you are a ____, because I need a _____ to. . . ."

This simple activity can help your group members sense the truth expressed in the body image: that we do need one another, and that we each have something to contribute to our brothers and sisters.

TEACHING GUIDE

Prepare
As you prepare this session, remember the teaching of 1 Corinthians 8–10. We can best deal with differences on the basis of love rather than on the basis of "I'm right."

Explore
1. Give your group the True/False quiz included in this study guide's *overview*. Talk over differing opinions before moving on into the session.
2. Or ask each group member to think about the congregation of which he or she is a member, and answer the following questions by writing down the first name or initials of those who come to mind:

- Who are the most gifted people in your church?
- Who are the most spiritual people in your church?

Form teams of those from the same congregation or if you attend the same church, the same age-group. Have each team discuss: "Are the same names on each of the two lists? What conclusion might you draw from this? How did you determine the most gifted? How did you determine the most spiritual?"

After about 10 minutes of discussion, move on to the next activity.

Expand
1. Give a brief minilecture covering the cultural and biblical background needed to understand the Corinthians' problem with the gift of tongues.
2. Then do a "reverse paraphrase" study. Pass out a copy of the author's paraphrase to each group member. Each is to go *from* the paraphrase to the text, to see how the author arrived at the summary.

Carefully work through the chapters together, using information in the study guide commentary to answer any questions that may arise.
3. Return to the launching activity and either review the True/False quiz, or discuss again the criteria by which the gifted and spiritual in the congregation were selected.
4. Or work from 1 Corinthians 14 and see if you can develop a "church bulletin" order of service for a meeting of the Corinthian congregation.

Apply
Ask your group members to sum up the session by each completing the following two statements: "Spirituality is not. . . ." and "Spirituality is. . . ." As time permits share the statements your members have written down.

STUDY GUIDE 133

1 Corinthians 7; 11

WOMEN IN THE CHURCH FAMILY

Overview

One of the problems faced by the early church was understanding the new role of women. It may be hard to grasp, but Paul's teaching stimulated one of the first "Women's Lib" movements! In Christ, possessing spiritual gifts, each woman could view herself as an individual of great personal worth and value.

The impact of this discovery, and the struggle to understand the implications of lifting women up to stand beside men, rather than crouching in their shadow, is reflected in questions posed for Paul to answer.

One of the questions had to do with divorce. In 1 Corinthians 7 Paul dealt with this issue, raised primarily by women who were seeking emancipation by questioning their traditional role as wives. In 1 Corinthians 11, Paul spoke to first-century Christian women who campaigned for the right to attend public worship with uncovered heads, to symbolize their equality with men. Some of these even disrupted the meetings by noisily challenging those who taught.

It is striking how many of the contemporary cries of women in our society are reflected in these passages.

In Paul's handling of these issues here, we are helped to see God's unique answer; an answer which affirms the full personhood and full participation of women in the body of Christ, and yet gently guides us away from drawing false conclusions about what full personhood means.

Commentary

It is important first to notice that the Bible takes a consistent stand in its basic attitude toward women. Genesis 1 affirmed the full personhood of Eve, and her full participation in God's image as that image is stamped on humankind. Eve also shared fully in the "dominion" which God intended mankind to exercise over creation.

> So God created man in His own image, in the image of God created He him; male and female He created them. God . . . said to them, "Be fruitful . . . and subdue."
>
> Genesis 1:27-28

With sin, a new necessity was imposed on the race. Woman was forced into a subordinate place, just as later the destructive nature of man's sinful impulses forced the imposition of government on society (cf. Gen. 3:16; 9:6 with Rom. 13:1-4). This subordination implies no demeaning of women. It made a wife no less important than her husband as a person—just as today a mayor, governor, or even President is no more important than a person who is an ordinary citizen. Romans 13 insists that the ruler's role is in fact to serve the citizen; and service rather than power is implied in Genesis 3's reference to a husband's authority.

But sin has a way of warping all things. Just as governments tend to become tyrannical, so "submission" became a denial of worth, and "authority" became the right to use and discard. The divine order, rather than upholding the worth of women, has actually been accused of denying it!

In Old Testament times, most cultures viewed women as chattels; they were denied rights commonly granted to men, and could be treated any way their husbands or owners pleased. It is probably difficult to grasp now, but the Old Testament's laws relating to women were significantly more liberal and supportive of women's rights than those in the rest of the world. Not that the Old Testament laws reflect the full restoration of women. Many Old Testament laws do *not* reflect God's ideal. They are accommodations to man's "hardness of heart," as Jesus pointed out in Matthew 19:8. Law itself does not present the standard of perfection, but represents an accommodation to the capacity of men to respond.

Yet, even in the Old Testament, there were indications that God would one day act to reaffirm woman's position *beside,* and not beneath, men.

With Christ, those promised days came! One of the most dramatic transformations was in men's attitude toward women, and in women's understanding of themselves. We see it so often throughout the Word.

> There is neither Jew nor Greek, slave nor free, male nor female, for you are all one in Christ Jesus.
>
> Galatians 3:28

The old ways of valuing and classifying people are no longer valid! In Christ, we are members of one body.

> I will pour out My Spirit on all people. Your sons and your daughters will prophesy.
>
> Acts 2:17

Since the Spirit's coming at Pentecost, *every* member of the body has been given a gift, and called to minister. Even the gift of prophecy, which Paul identified as very important (see 1 Cor. 12:27-30), is shared by women!

> I commend to you our sister Phoebe, a servant of the church at Cenchrea. . . . She has been a great help to many people, including me.
>
> Romans 16:1

Paul not only valued women, but he recognized them as eligible to hold office in the church. In the same context he called Priscilla and Aquila "my fellow workers in Christ" (v. 3).

It is difficult to see how some accuse Paul of a narrow, Pharisaic attitude toward women, or insist that the New Testament documents maintain a degrading, culture-bound view of the place of women in marriage and in the church. *It was exactly because the early church rejected society's view of women that the Corinthian problem arose!* Paul's guidelines here are not designed to put women "back in their place," but rather to help newly liberated women find their identity as persons of worth and value . . . and to help men, stunned by this sudden recognition of women as God's ministers in the body of Christ, to explore the implications of the new relationship.

♥ ***Link to Life: Youth / Adult***
Divide your group into two teams by sex, one with all men and the other with all women. Ask each team to vote first on whether the "women's lib" movement is a good or bad thing. Then ask each team to list answers to two questions: "What is valid about the movement? What is wrong about the movement?"

Do not *hear reports at this time, but ask the two teams to keep their lists for later discussion.*

Then give a minilecture covering some of the highlights on the Bible's view of women, as discussed in the commentary. It is against this background we must study the Corinthian and other New Testament passages relating to women.

Marriage Problems: 1 Corinthians 7

In every age there are twin tendencies to distort the search for a depth relationship with the divine. One of these is asceticism, the notion that by rigorous denial of bodily drives and desires one attains special holiness. The other is licentiousness, often rooted in the belief that the physical does not matter and that, therefore, full expression of any passion is acceptable.

Paul had devastated this second view while in Corinth, and he repeated his condemnation of immorality in this letter (1 Cor. 5). It's clear that some Corinthian Christians had carried over the playboy philosophy of Corinth into the church, and continued to regard women as men's playthings.

But others had taken the ascetic route. The affirmation of women as sisters in Christ, with full rights in the body of believers, tended to encourage this thinking. If women are to be regarded fully as persons now (and not just as *female*), doesn't it follow that marriage and the physical side of sexuality is ruled out? This notion gave rise to some of the questions the Corinthians raised, particularly as reflected in something Paul had taught: "It is good for a man not to marry" (7:1).

Looking over this passage, and outlining it, we can see the different kinds of marriage-related questions that troubled the

Corinthian church.

7:1-9	Does women's full equality rule out marriage?
7:10-11	What about divorce?
7:12-16	What about unbelieving spouses?
7:17-24	A basic principle stated.
7:25-38	What about our virgin daughters and engaged couples?
7:39-40	Any word for the widows?

Let's look at each of these segments in order.

Does women's full equality rule out marriage? (1 Cor. 7:1-9) As was his practice, Paul began by commending. It *is* "good for a man [person] not to marry." But immediately he corrected the misapplication of this saying, which he himself probably taught while with them (see v. 7). "Good" here does *not* imply "morally required," nor even imply "better." In fact, Paul went on to say that marriage is the normal state! And marriage means *marriage*—with its full sexual expression. The "holy marriage" of the celibate, which some in Corinth promoted, is not marriage at all.

Paul stated very clearly that life in this world means life in the body, and that human beings have bodily needs. One of the purposes of marriage is to help us satisfy those needs in a holy way; Christian couples are not allowed to deprive one another sexually (v. 5). Then Paul made a striking statement. In Christian marriage, it is not only the man who has marital rights, needs, and desires. The woman has them as well. She actually "owns" her husband's body just as much as she "owns" hers!

What a devastating break with the culture! Full sexual equality and partnership is an early Christian teaching which must have jolted Paul's readers thinking, as it does the thinking of some today.

What about divorce? (1 Cor. 7:10-11) To those Christians who for any reason were initiating divorce action, Paul passed on this blunt command: "No." Should this teaching, stated by Jesus, be rejected, the divorced person was to remain unmarried, or to be reconciled to his or her spouse.

The fact that Paul was thinking primarily of wives here suggests that some of the newly liberated women in Corinth felt that to "find themselves" they had to step out of the "bondage" of their marriages. Sometimes a sudden rediscovery of a woman's personhood does bring an individual to want to lead her own life, and build her own identity outside of the old relationships and "restrictions" of marriage. Paul made it clear that this is not the way to affirm individuality. But he also realized that some women in Corinth would divorce, despite his injunction. In that case, Paul insisted that such a woman either remain unmarried, or be reconciled to her husband.

Almost as an afterthought Paul added, "By the way, you men aren't to divorce your wives either." Clearly the divorce question was stimulated by actions taken by women, rather than men, and this leads us to suspect that the "women's lib" movement in the church was the cause.

What about unbelieving spouses? (1 Cor. 7:12-16) Even if a believer's spouse is not a Christian, the believer is not to initiate a divorce. Christ's presence in the believer reaches out to touch the unbelieving family members; spouse and children are "sanctified" (v. 14) in this way, in the sense of being privileged to experience the influence of Jesus through the believer.

At the same time, if the *unbeliever* initiates a divorce, the Christian partner need not feel guilty about it. In fact, when this happens, the believer is not "bound" (under obligation). The marriage is dissolved.

A basic principle (1 Cor. 7:17-24). Paul now spoke to a basic issue underlying these inquiries. In each case, the believers seem to be trying to "find themselves" or develop a new identity *by changing the conditions under which they lived.* A wife wanted to get a divorce so she could have a separate identity. A man wanted to make his marriage "spiritual" by eliminating sex. To these people, and to us, Paul replied, "Each one should retain the place in life that the Lord assigned to him and to which God has called him" (v. 17). What was Paul saying?

First, that God is sovereign.

God Himself has *assigned us* our roles in life. And God has *called us* to live in that role.

The newly liberated women in Corinth would not find themselves by seeking emancipation, or by trying to be like men. Instead, identity and fulfillment would be found in living out their calling as women, and as servants of the Lord. A slave's self-identity did not hinge on his being free. Possessing freedom doesn't make the free man any less Christ's slave. A Jew should not deny his cultural heritage, and a Gentile need not deny his (vv. 18-19). Instead, each believer is to make every effort to live for Christ *in the state in which he or she is called.*

It is by serving and loving God *as we are* that we discover our true selves, and find our fulfillment.

What about virgin daughters and engaged couples? (1 Cor. 7:25-38) Paul's advice to parents concerning arranging marriages for their unmarried daughters (which was the practice then), and to betrothed couples, was to put off marriage "because of the present crisis" (v. 26). In that particular crisis situation—about which we know little today—concern for a husband or a wife might threaten the believer's commitment to God. For instance, it is easier for most to face martyrdom and torture than to permit the torment of family members.

Still, Paul let the believer know that God will guide differently in some individual cases. Such persons will not sin if they marry. After Paul's defense of marriage in the opening paragraph of this chapter, it is clear that the apostle does *not* hold an ascetic or puritanical view!

A word to widows (1 Cor. 7:39-40). As for widows, of course they were free to remarry—but only to other Christians. And Paul said they might well be happier if they did not marry just now (contrast 1 Tim. 5:14).

And so Paul moved on, in 1 Corinthians 8–10, to another subject. But he returned to another problem that arose out of the restoration of women to full personhood in chapter 11. When he did return, his argument rested on the principle in 7:17.

We find fulfillment in being who and what we are.

God is sovereign.

God has assigned us our roles in life, and calls us to live in that place. It is by affirming the worth and the value of who we are, not in struggling to be something we are not, that we find fulfillment.

♥ ***Link to Life: Youth / Adult***
Interpreting 1 Corinthians 7 correctly calls for understanding the issues that Paul was addressing. So give a brief background on the problems in Corinth as discussed. Then pass out the following "Dear Paul" letters to teams of group members, each of which is to write a short answer to the letter based on the passage referred to.

#1

Dear Paul
Now that I am a Christian I realize I'm really "me," not just a wife and not just a mom. I've got to explore the new me your teaching helped me discover, so I'm divorcing my husband and starting out on my own! It's scary, but I sure appreciate the sense of worth Christianity has given me. Do you have any advice for me as I start my new life?
(see 1 Cor. 7:17-24)

#2

Dear Paul
I yearn to be spiritual. So I've told my wife the physical side of marriage is over for us, so I can devote myself to prayer and Bible study undistracted. She objects. Paul, isn't it wrong for a woman like her to want sex? I mean, isn't sex sort of morally depraved? Do you think I should get an exorcist, or just pray for her?
(see 1 Cor. 7:1-9)

#3

Dear Paul
What's your real view on marriage? Should we, or shouldn't we? I'm engaged, but I'm kind of uncertain. What are the pros and cons of getting married in the first place?
(see 1 Cor. 7:1-2, 7-9, 25-35)

When the teams have finished their study and written their letters, read and discuss them, supplementing their insights with information from the commentary.

Women in the Church: 1 Corinthians 11
The subjects taken up in this chapter of 1 Corinthians all have to do with public worship. The first subject focuses on several practices of the Christian women's liberation party. The second topic is the practice of the Lord's Supper. It is the first subject we want to concentrate on.

Paul began by praising the believers—including the women—for holding to his previous teachings (v. 2). Paul then went on to answer some who had challenged his teaching.

Again we need to understand the cultural background before looking at the passage itself. What really is at issue is the Corinthian women's desire to dispense with the veil (to go "uncovered") in public worship.

The veil covering. Sir William Anderson gives us some insight into the cultural implications of the veil:

> In Oriental lands the veil is the power and the honor and the dignity of the woman. With the veil on her head she can go anywhere in security and profound respect. She is not seen; it is a mark of thoroughly bad manners to observe a veiled woman on the streets. She is alone. The rest of the people around her are nonexistent to her, and she is to them. She is supreme in the crowd. . . . But without the veil the woman is a thing of nought, whom any man may insult. . . . A woman's authority and dignity vanish along with the all-covering veil that she discards (cited by Robertson and Plummer in *Corinthians One,* International Critical Commentary, p. 311).

Anderson's point is simple. The veil served *to affirm the woman's dignity as a woman.*

Why did the Corinthian ladies want to remove their veils in church meetings? Because they felt a need to symbolize their new status as full participants in the body of Christ. If they were equals of men, they wanted to be like men and to worship unveiled!

Paul's response is not a put-down. Instead, it is a reaffirmation of the fact that a woman can be valuable and worthwhile *as a woman.* No woman needs to seek liberation by struggling to become like man!

An inappropriate symbol. It is significant here that Paul does not argue, as he might have, from the cultural implications of going unveiled. In that society, the discreet matron would demonstrate her propriety in the way she dressed, while the *heterai* "available for hire") would advertise herself by her dress. Surely Paul could have taken the approach of shaming the Corinthian women for acting like harlots.

But Paul did not. Instead, he affirmed these women. He argued that there *are* differences between men and women, and that it is no disgrace to recognize the differences. Acting in ways appropriate for a woman to act in no way denies the Christian woman's worth and value, and it in no way threatens her participation in the body of Christ.

An unnecessary demand. In verses 2-16 Paul explained that there *are* differences between men and women that are to be acknowledged. But the differences are designed to make men and women *interdependent,* not to make one sex of lesser importance.

Paul's argument here is a theological one, finding its roots in the order of Creation. The man does have a certain priority; he was created first, and woman was shaped from his flesh. Eve was created to meet Adam's need for companionship rather than vice versa. This order in Creation is reflected in the relationship between a man and his wife. He is the "head" of the woman, even as Christ is the Head of man.

Usually it is at this point that the modern person rebels. "Head" to most of us means "power," and in our day that connotes suppression and oppression. But note that this is not the way Paul viewed it here. Man is the "image and glory" of God (v. 7). *Rather than indicating oppression by God, the Lord's headship over man implies an exaltation of man!*

So too with the woman. Man's headship over the woman does not imply subservience, but instead the lifting up of the woman. Headship does not proclaim the rights of men to enslave. Just the opposite. It insists that men should recognize the high value God places on woman not only as fully a person, but as man's "glory"! Thus, in wearing a veil (that "sign of authority"), the Corinthian women would be displaying for men and angels as well, the stunning fact that *in Christ it is no shame to be female!* Each time women participated *as women* in the ministry of the church, they would show again the value, worth, and glory of womankind.

In verses 11-16 Paul did make a cultural appeal. At that time long hair *was* womanly, and men would be ashamed to let their hair grow long. Would a woman ever think of shaving her head and appearing in public without her hair? Of course not! Why? She'd be ashamed. Somehow, without long hair, she would be denying her femininity.

So, Paul said, it really isn't proper to appear in church and pray unveiled either. For this too is a denial of feminity. A woman would be denying herself—not finding herself—by attempting to become like a man.

Echoes

It is here that we find echoes of the principle Paul stated in 1 Corinthians 7. We find fulfillment in being who and what we are.

God is sovereign.

He has assigned each of us our place. He has called us to live in that place. This is the message that echoes from those first-century days to our own. In tones of love, the great apostle reminded women who were breaking out of old, distorted images and shaking off feelings of worthlessness and unimportance that it was not necessary to deny their womanhood to find their new identities. Rather, they would find fulfillment in accepting themselves as women, and glorying in that fact. For a woman *is* important, not in spite of being a woman, but *as* one.

There are other passages in the New Testament relating to women in the church. Some of them are more difficult to understand than these two in Corinthians. But if we keep in mind the cultural background, and the argument developed by Paul in this particular chapter, we can understand better the point Paul makes.

In 14:33-36, on disorder in the congregational meeting, Paul is not telling women to "stifle yourselves." He is warning some of the more aggressive of the women's libbers to stop shouting and interrupting with their argumentative questions. They should instead talk things over with their husbands at home, and in the process learn a submission that is appropriate for them as wives.

First Timothy 2:11-15 does not teach that women cannot exercise their spiritual gifts when the body meets. We know that women can, and are to (Acts 2:17; 1 Cor. 12:7; 14:26). Instead the passage has a more narrow focus, on the role of a ruling elder. To "teach" (1 Tim. 2:12), as defined "with authority" is an elder's function. This particular function in the body of Christ—and only this function!—is reserved for men.

How important that today, we like Paul affirm believing women, and lift them up to become full participants as partners in our homes, and as ministering persons in Christ's church.

TEACHING GUIDE

Prepare

How are women affirmed as ministering people in your own local congregation? Is this an area in which your group members need to grow?

Explore

1. Begin with a minilecture overview of biblical and cultural background to Paul's teaching on women in 1 Corinthians.
2. Or break into male and female teams to discuss the pros and cons of modern women's lib. See "link-to-life," page 864. Follow this up with biblical and cultural background.

Expand

1. Study 1 Corinthians 7, using the "letters to Paul" approach suggested in "link-to-life," page 866. Have teams respond to typical Corinthians whose questions the apostle dealt with in this important New Testament chapter.
2. In a minilecture explain the issue behind Paul's instruction in 1 Corinthians 11, and show how he answered it. You may wish to comment also on 1 Corinthians 14:33-36 and 1 Timothy 2:11-15.

Apply

1. You may want to now hear reports from the teams of men and women who listed pros and cons of modern women's lib. In view of what your group has discovered in these Corinthian passages, how might items on the lists be reevaluated?
2. Ask the women in your group to serve as a panel, and discuss: "Is our church affirming us and our importance as full members of the body of Christ?"

STUDY GUIDE 134

1 Corinthians 15–16

RESURRECTION: THIS FAMILY IS FOREVER

Overview

The belief in a personal, bodily resurrection is basic to biblical faith. While one of the Jewish theological traditions (the Sadducees) rejected the concept, it *is* taught in the Old Testament (see Job 19:25; Pss. 17:15; 49:7-12; 73:23-26; Isa. 26:19; Dan. 12:2).

Jesus affirmed the resurrection in His teaching (see Matt. 22:29-32), and demonstrated His personal power over death by raising Lazarus (see John 11). Yet the raising of Lazarus and others by Jesus (see also Matt. 9:18-26) was merely a restoration of earthly life. It was not the total transformation exhibited in Jesus' own resurrection—and promised believers when Christ returns. What we do know is that when Christ returns the believing "dead will be raised imperishable, and we [who live then] will be changed" (1 Cor. 15:52).

Then, the limitations of our present nature will be lifted, and we who are now perishable will be imperishable; we who are weak will be filled with power; we who are mortal will be immortal. Forever and ever, Amen.

▶ ***Resurrection.*** Because the idea of resurrection was foreign to Greek thought, there existed no technical words in Greek to describe it. The Bible uses two common words, one meaning "to raise, to arouse" and the other "to awaken."

■ See discussion of difficult verses in 1 Corinthians 15 in the Victor *Bible Knowledge Commentary*, pages 542-547.

Commentary

Christ promised the believer an inner transformation. And there *was* transformation.

Believers found striking changes were taking place—within themselves, and in one another. The attitudes and ideas and ways of paganism died hard. Yet, there was clear evidence of God's work within the Corinthian body.

In spite of differences and divisions, and in spite of lax discipline, people were being delivered from superstition and fear. The bondage of idolatry was shattered; an exciting new freedom was experienced. God's presence in Corinth was abundantly demonstrated; all the spiritual gifts were operating in the body, and the church was excited about each new experience of the Spirit. The Corinthian's attitudes and values were changing too. They took very seriously Paul's teaching on marriage—and even went beyond what he intended in some cases.

The believers appealed to Scripture and to God's Word for guidance (through the apostolic teachings), and were praised for holding to the practices which Paul taught them. Women were breaking out of their servitude, rejoicing in their liberation, and asserting themselves in bold (if sometimes misdirected) ways. In general, the Corinthians seemed very responsive to truth; Paul always expected that they would respond obediently to his instruction.

Each of these facts give witness that transformation had begun. These believers *were* changing and growing, becoming new and different persons.

At the same time, their growth was retarded, apparently because of a lack of that vital quality Paul spoke of so often in his letters to the Thessalonians. To the church at Thessalonica Paul could say, "About brotherly love we do not need to write to you, for you yourselves have been taught by God to love each other" (1 Thes. 4:9). But to the Corinthians, Paul had to say, "knowledge puffs up, but love builds up" (1 Cor. 8:1), and then go on to show them how to handle their differences lovingly. It was to the Corinthians that the great exposition of love in chapter 13 was addressed, and one of Paul's last reminders to them was, "Do everything in love" (16:14).

A process. All this helps us realize again that growing toward Christian maturity is a process. God does work His transformation in our personalities, but that work takes place over time, and sometimes over more time than we desire!

Sometimes growth seems slow as we face problems like those that plagued the church at Corinth. We need to keep three things in mind here. First, as newness comes, there will be tension between the old and the new. Transition times are sure to bring problems.

Second, building the climate of love in the body will ease tensions. Love, like truth, is essential. By affirming our love for each other in spite of differences and strains, and by affirming together our commitment to truth, we *will* grow. We are being freed from the world's mold—that old way of thinking, of valuing, and of perceiving ourselves and others. We are being transformed in a process to which God has committed Himself. Words Paul would later pen to encourage the Philippians hold as well a promise for the Corinthians—and for us! "He who began a good work in you will carry it on to completion until the day of Christ Jesus" (Phil. 1:6).

And this brings us to the third thing. A day of completion is coming! In the day that Christ Jesus returns, our transformation will be complete.

♥ ***Link to Life: Youth / Adult***
Review Corinthians with your group. Brainstorm together: "What evidences do we have of spiritual immaturity in Corinth?" Then: "What evidences do we have of spiritual growth and personal transformation?"

To help your group in this review, you may wish to duplicate and distribute the "theme" chart.

Resurrection: 1 Corinthians 15

The culminating experience in our personal transformation is to be resurrection. Yet, some in Corinth denied this completion. They carried over into their new faith the typical Greek attitude toward life after death; they could not accept the idea of a bodily resurrection. Christian faith might have meaning for the here and now. It might even offer some astral form for their personalities after death. But, a *literal* resurrection? No.

Paul vigorously corrected them. If our hope is limited to this life, then we Christians are "of all men most miserable" (v. 19, KJV). Transformation begins in the present, but completion will come in the day of Jesus Christ. Then we will actually "bear the likeness of the man from heaven" (v. 49). What God does in our earthly lives not only excites us, it holds the glittering prospect of perfection to come. The transformation process finds its ultimate meaning in attaining this goal.

It *is* our destiny to *be like* Jesus. What is more, the Good News of Jesus rests on the fact of our Lord's own resurrection. Christ was raised bodily from the dead. His resurrection both demonstrates the power of God, and is the ultimate proof of His ability to provide forgiveness. Jesus' resurrection and our own are so intimately intertwined that to doubt either constitutes a denial of the Gospel message itself!

Eager to explain this vital truth, Paul, in 1 Corinthians 15, gives the classic and definitive New Testament explanation of resurrection.

Christ's resurrection (1 Cor. 15:1-11). Paul began by reminding the Corinthians of the content of the "Gospel I preached to you." In that original presentation, the Resurrection was given a central role.

> For what I received I passed on to you as of first importance: that Christ died for our sins according to the Scriptures, that He was buried, that He was raised on the third day according to the Scriptures, and that He appeared to Peter, and then to the Twelve.
>
> After that, He appeared to more than 500 of the brothers at the same time, most of whom are still living, though some have fallen asleep. Then He appeared to James, then to all the apostles, and last of all He appeared to me also.
>
> 1 Corinthians 15:3-7

In this summary we note two things: the events the Gospel affirms actually happened in the real world, and were neither mystical nor mythic in character. And the events took place "according to the Scriptures"; as predicted and in full harmony with earlier revelation. The fact is that both these ele-

Theme of 1 Corinthians

Passage	Theme	Principles
1 Cor. 1–4	Overcoming Barriers to Divisions	Reject pagan approaches, seeking to understand God's patterns of thought. Regard human leaders as servants; reserve glory for God.
1 Cor. 5–6	Discipline	Deal firmly with sin in the family. Act to resolve disputes equitably.
1 Cor. 8–10	Doctrinal Disputes	Love and truth are both required for resolution. Being "right" does not remove love's obligation to build up our brothers.
1 Cor. 12–14	True Spirituality	Possession of certain gifts is not evidence of spiritual achievement. Love is the key indicator of spiritual maturity. As a body, family members are interdependent; each gift is important, and each person's ministry is needed.
1 Cor. 7;11	Women's Identity	Affirm the worth and value of women. Equality as persons does not mean "sameness." Each person finds fulfillment in the role God has sovereignly chosen for him or her—and is *called* to that place. Because women are affirmed as equally valued persons in the body of Christ, no woman needs to deny her womanhood.
1 Cor. 15	Resurrection	Ultimate transformation is assured.

ments—the historical nature and scriptural roots—were *always* emphasized in apostolic preaching of the Gospel (see Acts 2:14-41; 3:11–4:12; 10:34-43).

The Gospel is simply not the Gospel if the element of Resurrection is removed. So Paul reminded his readers, "This is what we preach, and this is what you believed."

Believer's resurrection (1 Cor. 15:12-19). Paul then linked the resurrection of the believer to the resurrection of Jesus. If Jesus was raised, how can some say, "There is no resurrection of the dead"? If there is no resurrection, then Christ could not have been raised, and in that case "your faith is futile; you are still in your sins."

In the bluntest possible way Paul said that the doctrine of resurrection—the resurrection of Jesus and of the believer—is essential to Christian faith. Robbed of the resurrection, Christian faith would be an empty and futile thing indeed.

Resurrection: past and future (1 Cor. 15:20-28). But Christianity is *not* like one of the empty religions or mystery faiths that the first-century world practiced. "Christ has indeed been raised from the dead."

The resurrection is the key to our understanding of the past, and the doorway of hope for the future. Death came into the world through Adam's sin; life comes to humanity through Jesus' resurrection. The future will now unfold according to the plan of God: Christ is raised first; when Jesus comes, those who belong to Him will be raised, and then at the end—Jesus takes His kingdom and ultimately hands it over to God the Father. The ultimate enemy, death, will be put away forever as part of the "everything" Scripture promises will be put under the Messiah's feet (e.g., totally defeated and destroyed) (see Ps. 8:6).

Baptism for the dead (1 Cor. 15:29-34). In this aside, Paul noted the practice of some in Corinth of being "baptized for the dead." Between 30 and 40 explanations have been given for this phrase. The simple meaning of the words seems to suggest that some at Corinth were undergoing baptism on behalf of friends who died without that sacrament. In referring to the practice, Paul did not endorse it. In fact, he disassociated himself from it by referring to "those" people, and saying "they" rather than "we."

It's clear that in the cases mentioned in this paragraph, Paul was reasoning from experience rather than from revelation. Why bother, he said, to undergo such a baptism if your friends are simply dead and gone, and there is no resurrection? Why should the missionary team with Paul keep on endangering their lives if death is really the end? If this life is all, why not live by that contemporary maxim, "Eat and drink, for tomorrow we die"? (v. 32)

No, it is the prospect of the final transformation that leads the Corinthians to this peculiar practice, and to Paul's own commitment to his mission.

Paul's point was simply this: wandering from the truth about resurrection will certainly have an impact on daily life. What the Corinthians and Paul have been doing makes sense only if there *is* a resurrection coming. Once this conviction is abandoned, both practices and commitments which reflect the belief are sure to change.

The paragraph raises an important question for you and me. What do we do because we too believe in resurrection? How would our lives be different if we were to abandon this hope?

Resurrection body (1 Cor. 15:35-49). It was only natural that in the debate over resurrection some should inquire, "Well, what will this resurrection body be like, anyway?" Others challenged, "How can men rise when their bodies have decayed?" Paul replied that the objection is foolish. A dead-looking seed is planted in the ground, and a vital, living plant appears. Just as God gives the planted seed a form appropriate for its new life, so the resurrected saint will have a glorious body appropriate to full transformation.

No, the resurrection body will not be the same body we have now; natural life will be replaced by spiritual. The likeness we bear then will not be Adam's but, instead, we shall "bear the likeness of the Man from heaven" (v. 49).

This last phrase may be the key to our best approach to visualizing the resurrection state. The *Expository Dictionary of Bible Words* (Richards, Zondervan) notes:

> Many have found it fascinating to observe the capabilities of the resurrected Jesus and speculate on what being "like Him" might mean. For instance, the resurrected Jesus had "flesh and bones" (Luke 24:39). Why not flesh and blood?

Is it because "the life of a creature is in the blood" (Lev. 17:11) and a resurrected person is infused with a different kind of life? Others have noted Jesus' sudden appearance among His disciples in a locked room (John 20:26). Is this teleportation? Or can a resurrected person move between the atoms of the physical universe?

While such speculation has a fascination, we do best to let the issue rest with God, as John and Paul did. We do not yet know what we will be, but we will be like Him. The limitations of our physical nature will be gone, and, whereas we are now perishable, we will then be imperishable. Power will replace weakness; immortality will end mortality.

Conclusion (1 Cor. 15:50-58). Paul was now caught up in the glory of what lies ahead. Paul saw the dead being raised, the living caught up—all transformed! He saw the bright splendor shine as the perishable fades, and mortality is clothed with immortality. And then—then comes the triumphant shout: "Death has been swallowed up in victory" (v. 54).

Paul's conclusion is important: in view of the coming resurrection we are to stand firm, and let nothing move us. Since we see beyond this world, and beyond death, to realities others cannot see, we can follow Paul's admonition to "always give yourselves fully to the work of the Lord, because you know that your labor in the Lord is not in vain."

♥ ***Link to Life: Youth / Adult***
This chapter basically deals with two issues: "Is resurrection for real?" and, "What difference does resurrection make?"

Cover the first in a minilecture, pointing up Paul's evidence for a historic Resurrection in the past and a resurrection coming for the believer.

Then break into teams that are to determine from the text what practical difference belief in the resurrection means to believers. Have each team study 1 Corinthians 15:12-19, 29-34, 50-58.

Concluding Remarks: 1 Corinthians 16
This letter concludes with a note about a collection for needy brothers, a topic that is amplified in 2 Corinthians.

Paul shared a number of requests, added notes to friends, and also shared an exhortation:

> Be on your guard; stand firm in the faith; be men of courage; be strong. Do everything in love.
>
> 1 Corinthians 16:13

What a good word for the Corinthians and for us. We too may have problems, and we may not be growing as quickly as we would like. But as we remain committed to Jesus and to each other, we will experience more of the Spirit's transforming touch, as we move on with our brothers and sisters to God's glorious resurrection day.

TEACHING GUIDE

Prepare
What does Resurrection mean to you?

Explore
1. Begin with a review of 1 Corinthians. Use the chart found on page 871 as a review tool, and ask your group members to first list: "What evidences do we have in 1 Corinthians of spiritual immaturity? Of spiritual transformation?"
2. Give a minilecture summary of the Bible's teaching on resurrection. Draw from passages in the *overview* and commentary.

Expand
Have teams work with key paragraphs of 1 Corinthians 15 to determine the impact of the teaching of the coming resurrection on Paul and others in the first century.

Apply
Ask each group member to list three ways that belief in resurrection makes a difference to him or her personally.

STUDY GUIDE 135

2 Corinthians 1–3

THE INADEQUATE MAN

Overview
Second Corinthians is an intensely personal letter. In it the Apostle Paul shares his inner feelings in an attempt to help his readers understand principles on which ministry must be based. For you and me and those we teach, this is an important letter. Seeing the heart of one of the most effective ministers of all time helps us establish a firm foundation for our personal ministries.

Outline

I.	Personal Items	1–2
II.	New Covenant Ministry Principles	3–5
	1. Transparency	3
	2. Confidence	4
	3. Motivation	5
III.	New Covenant Ministry Exemplified	6–7
IV.	Giving under the New Covenant	8–9
V.	Authority and the New Covenant	10–13

▶ ***New Covenant.*** The "New Covenant" is a key New Testament term, with roots in the Old Testament. The "Old" Covenant with which it is contrasted is the Mosaic, or Law Covenant. The Law defined righteous *behavior,* and God's people were promised blessing if they lived by its regulations. But the Old Testament promised a New Covenant would be given, "not like" the older one (Jer. 31:33-34). Under the New Covenant, initiated by the death of Christ, God makes believers righteous by inner transformation. This letter helps us understand how to live under God's New Covenant, and to truly *be* righteous through and through.

Overview
Paul's earlier letter to the Corinthians had a mixed reception. For instance, the brother living immorally was turned around. Yet others bridled at Paul's teaching. It is clear from 2 Corinthians that some challenged Paul's authority and apostleship. They charged him with unwarranted pride and overconfidence, and with saying one thing one time and something else another. The recriminations of this segment of the Corinthian church were furious and bitter—so serious that Paul had to respond, to express his deep love for and continuing confidence in the immature congregation.

While Paul intended to deal with several specific questions (such as giving), the main thrust of his letter was to reassure the Corinthians. In spite of what Paul's enemies were saying, he did trust them completely. And he did care for them. Paul's motives and feelings, as well as his teachings, had been twisted by his critics. For the Corinthians' own benefit, Paul now opened his heart in complete self-revelation.

Earlier Paul had written to the Thessalonians and referred to his motives. "You know how we lived among you for your sake," he said (1 Thes. 1:5; see also 2:5). Paul's whole approach to ministry was to live among the members of a new body as a completely transparent man. He freely and openly expressed his motives, his feelings, his values—everything. Paul so loved his converts that he was ready to share with them not only the Gospel but his own self as well.

Certainly Paul had been this kind of man among the Corinthians. There could be no reasonable basis for doubting him, or for questioning his motives. Yet a group in Corinth did question. Their backbiting and innuendos were troubling the whole body of believers. Perhaps these were people converted after Paul left Corinth, people who never knew him. Or perhaps they were simply proud and bitter people whose pretensions of superiority—whether based on a claim of superior "knowledge" or on the supposed superiority of the gift of tongues—had been gently destroyed in Paul's earlier letter. At any rate, these people did attack Paul—bitterly. They could not refute his teaching, so they attacked him personally, seeking to undermine Paul's influence by making him appear to be a weak, plastic, venial man.

It should not have been necessary for Paul to defend himself against this kind of attack. Many in Corinth had been converted under Paul's ministry. But apparently even their confidence in Paul had been shaken. The weakness and failures which Paul identified in that first letter must have devastated the faithful; even they began to doubt that Paul could love and continue to respect them.

And so Paul wrote 2 Corinthians—which should have been an unnecessary letter. Yet in this letter Paul ministers to us in unique ways. We find answers to some of the most basic questions about spiritual leadership that face the church today. And we find, in the self-revelation of the apostle, a picture of the kind of person God is calling each of us to become.

Special Contributions of 2 Corinthians

What are some of the specific values your group will receive as you teach this great New Testament book?

Gain insight into transformation. Several times in the Corinthian letters Paul urged young believers to "follow my example, as I follow the example of Christ" (1 Cor. 11:1). "Transformation" sounds like such an abstract thing. Even when we say that transformation involves growth in Christlikeness, it is hard for us to grasp the meaning. But in the person of Paul (a living, breathing, real human being whom the body could watch and observe and listen to), Christlikeness took on fresh reality. In the close, personal relationship that Paul developed with his converts, they could learn the lifestyle of one who had traveled further than they down transformation's road.

The invitation of Paul to believers to "imitate me" or to "let me be your example in this" was not rooted in pride. It was rooted in the apostle's awareness that a living example is essential in the communication of Christian truth. As we see in other New Testament passages, the bridge between knowing God's truth intellectually, and building it into one's life, is often the modeling of truth in another's life.

This is one reason why 2 Corinthians is so important to us today. We don't know Paul as a person. We don't live in his first-century world. But in this letter, we not only meet Paul face-to-face, we meet him heart-to-heart. In this most intimate biblical portrayal of Paul as a person, we discover in him the kind of person God is calling us to become.

Learn how to motivate. In a nationwide survey of 5,000 pastors I conducted through Renewal Research Associates, a Phoenix foundation, *every respondent,* when asked to identify the greatest need he saw for strengthening the life and ministry of his church, gave "getting my lay people more involved as ministering people" a first- or second-priority ranking. The problem these pastors faced was one of motivation. How could they move others to follow Jesus? What is the *motivational key* to making disciples?

All too often we hear a presentation of the Scriptures that is encased in an "ought" framework. We're made to feel guilt or shame for what we haven't done; we're urged to try harder. Such guilt-producing approaches, however, create a sense of hopelessness, and actually retard transformation. At best, they force us into a flurry of activity which we call "ministry."

God has a far better way; a far more freeing way! In 2 Corinthians, we'll come to know Paul the motivator, and will discover a different avenue to making disciples.

Discover how to exercise spiritual authority. A final focus in our exploration of this intimate letter will be authority. This too is a question troubling the church today. What is the nature of spiritual authority? How is it expressed and exercised? How can we have authority that isn't oppressive, impersonal, restrictive—even degrading?

In observing Paul gently exercise his authority with the Corinthian church, we gain new insights into how Christian authority operates. In the process, we'll find guidance for our own lives, in our homes, and in the church of God.

This New Testament letter truly is a rich and exciting one. Once again God's Word will speak to each of us. In listening, and taking what Scripture teaches to heart, we will find new and open doors leading to faster personal spiritual growth.

Biographical Study

Because this letter is such a personal one, one effective way to study it is by using the biographical method. As noted in an earlier study, the basic method for exploring the New Testament Epistles is what is called the *synthetic* method. That is, we try to trace the thought of the writer over extended passages, and then put it all together, often by using paraphrase. In this study I'll continue to trace the flow of the apostle's thought so your group members will be able to master content. But you may also wish to help your group members come to know Paul, the man better. For his words, "Let me be your example," are written not only for the Corinthians but for Christians throughout the ages. In exploring Paul's motives, values, and attitudes; in sensing his feelings and emotions, and discovering the basic convictions that shaped him, we will learn much about what it means for us to be truly Christian men and women.

There is another reason for use of the biographical method of Bible study. It helps us understand truth in ways we might not if we remained strictly "logical" in our approach. Truth in Scripture is *not* divorced from life. When seen in and through life, we often discover dimensions of truth we might not otherwise glimpse.

Truth in life. Yet, it's important to remember that what we see in Scripture through the filter of life is rooted in revealed truth. The living example of men like Paul does not have validity in itself; instead, the lifestyle is valid only when it expresses truth.

For instance, in this letter we'll meet Paul as vulnerable and inadequate. We'll see that Paul, under attack from the Corinthians, did not respond from a position of strength. Instead, he responded by revealing his weakness! At the very beginning of this letter Paul wrote, "We do not want you to be uninformed, brothers, about the hardships we suffered in the province of Asia. We were under great pressure, far beyond our ability to endure, so that we despaired even of life. Indeed, in our hearts we felt the sentence of death" (2 Cor. 1:8-9). How striking! Paul immediately exposed himself to his enemies.

How they might have used that against him! Can't you hear Paul's critics now? "Paul's not so great. Look, he gets depressed just like some new believer! Why, what does he know of victorious Christian living? He even admits feeling despair."

Or, "How can you ever respect a weak person like that! Paul needs help!"

Why did Paul give his enemies this kind of edge? Why didn't he simply exercise his great power as an apostle and strike out against his critics? Why didn't he at least begin by recounting his strengths, rather than by revealing his weaknesses?

Paul's underlying motive for this approach was his desire to minister to the Corinthians. Paul knew that, to minister effectively, he would have to identify with them in their humanity before he could show them a way to rise beyond themselves. Paul also grasped a basic truth—and realized its full implications. In order to truly minister to others, you must be completely honest and real with them.

♥ ***Link to Life: Youth / Adult***

Have your group members use the biographical study method, without taking time to explain it to them.

Begin by having each person read silently 2 Corinthians 1:1–2:4 and then jot down impressions of Paul as a person. Say: "If you could choose one word to characterize Paul, what would it be? Why?"

Then in pairs reread this passage, pausing after each verse to discuss: "What insights do you get into Paul's motives? His values? His feelings, attitudes, and thoughts?"

As a whole group, go one step further: "What do you think was Paul's image of himself? How did he view others? How did he view God?"

Finally, ask each individual to write a paragraph of no more than 200 words on what Paul would say if he were asked to "tell us everything we need to know to understand you as a person."

God's Comfort: 1 Corinthians 1:1–2:4

Paul was concerned first of all in laying a basis for continuing ministry to the Corinthians—and especially to his critics. He knew that a basis for ministry to others calls for sharing, not preaching. That is, we are most effective in helping others when those others see us as like them. If we are truly like others, then there is hope, for those who are overwhelmed by a sense of weakness cannot learn from people they view as strong—and therefore not like them.

Paul *could* have begun his letter with an appeal to his unique authority as an apostle. However, Paul wanted all the brothers and sisters in Corinth to identify with him as a mere human being, so that they would see the divine power which was expressed in his life as something they could draw on too.

This is the significance of Paul's statement that God "comforts us in all our troubles, so that we can comfort those in any trouble with the comfort we ourselves have received from God." It is because I have known troubles, and experienced God's enablement, that I can understand and come alongside those who have troubles like mine. If a brother or sister realizes that I am speaking about God from personal experiences that are like their own, they will be able to receive God's comfort from me.

Because of this conviction Paul was willing to share his weakness, even revealing his times of despair, to build a foundation for a solid continuing ministry to that church.

♥ ***Link to Life: Youth / Adult***

When your group has completed its initial biographical work from 2 Corinthians 1:1–2:4, point out that Paul was strikingly open and revealing in these verses. In view of Paul's example, how would they evaluate possible objections to an exhortation to also "be real"?

- *"But, people will lose respect for me."*
- *"Exposing weakness like that must undermine authority."*
- *"It's all right, but it can be carried too far."*
- *"If you share weaknesses, won't young Christians become discouraged and feel that Christ doesn't come through as promised?"*
- *"People today feel uncomfortable with all this 'personal' and 'self-revelation' stuff."*

After letting your group respond to these objections, move immediately to a direct study of 2 Corinthians 2 and 3.

The Case for Openness: 2 Corinthians 2:12–3:18

The context makes it clear that Paul was speaking about something he called a "New Covenant" ministry. As a result of that ministry, the Corinthians themselves were a letter of recommendation, for Christ through Paul had engraved His own person on their hearts. They were living letters, "written not with ink but with the Spirit of the living God, not on tablets of stone but on tablets of human hearts" (v. 3). It is this unique ministry of inner transformation that Paul spoke of when he said that God has "made us competent as ministers of the New Covenant" (v. 6).

Paul contrasted his ministry with the ministry of Moses. That Old Covenant ministry had a certain fading glory, but is not to be compared with the splendor of the present ministry of the New Covenant.

Paul brings the issue into focus:

> Therefore, since we have such a hope [that is, the hope of inner transformation], we are very bold. We are not like Moses, who would put a veil over his face to keep the Israelites from gazing at it while the radiance was fading away.
>
> 2 Corinthians 3:12-13

What Paul was referring to was the Old Testament description of Moses, entering the tabernacle of God and returning to speak with the Israelites, transfused with a radiance and splendor.

Remember that Moses was leading a group of people much like some of the Corinthians. The Israelites were constantly challenging Moses' leadership. They murmured, complained, plotted against him, and at times were on the verge of stoning Moses to death! But when Moses came away from the Presence of God, with that visible splendor shining on his face, the people must have been stunned into temporary silence. We can even imagine Moses taking daily walks through the camp, pleased by the quiet that fell.

But then Moses noticed that the splendor faded. The glow went away! And "Moses . . . put a veil over his face to keep the Israelites from gazing at it while the radiance was fading away" (v. 13). *A process of deterioration was taking place, and Moses could not bear to have others see it.*

But ah, the contrast! Paul said, "We are not like Moses"; instead, "We are very bold." And Paul explained:

> Where the Spirit of the Lord is, there is freedom. And we, who with unveiled faces all reflect the Lord's glory, are being transformed into His likeness with ever-increasing glory, which comes from the Lord, who is the Spirit.
>
> 2 Corinthians 3:17-18

What did Paul mean? Simply this: I unveil and reveal myself in order that you might see Jesus in me. Jesus is not revealed in some supposed human "perfection," but rather in our progressive transformation. It is not, "See how good I am," that witnesses to the reality of Jesus, but, "See what God is doing in such a sinner."

So Paul revealed his weaknesses. And in doing so, he also revealed the reality and the power of Jesus. Paul *was* weak, but the Spirit of God was constantly at work in him, working His transformation, overcoming his weaknesses, and infusing him with new strength. By taking off the veil that hid the real Paul from others, Paul knew that his critics would discover a weak and needy person. But Paul also knew that these people *would also see Jesus!*

Core truths. How stunningly clear. In Paul's explanation of his openness and vulnerability, we see reflections of basic truths testified to by the Word of God.

- We are sinners, warped and twisted out of shape, far from being the persons we want to be, or that God intends us to be.
- Jesus Himself enters the life of the believer; once born again, we receive "His own indestructible heredity" (1 Peter 1:23, PH).
- God is *in the process* of working His transformation in us believers; we "are being transformed into His likeness with ever-increasing glory" (2 Cor. 3:18).

To Paul, the implications of these truths were compelling. As a leader, called to be an example, Paul *had* to take the veil off his life and personality, and let others see him as he really was. Of course, Paul realized that the Corinthians would discover he had weaknesses; his transformation, like our own, was incomplete. But Paul also knew that since Jesus was in his life, his brothers and sisters would also be beholding the Lord's glory (2 Cor. 3:18). As others saw Jesus at work in Paul, they would find the confidence to hope for their own transformations.

It costs to be this kind of Christian. Some will misunderstand and try to use our weaknesses against us. Others will tend to look down on us. But once again, Paul has opened for us God's way of thinking—a way so very different from man's. Not pride or self-protection, but humility and self-revelation. Paul's understanding of this truth led to his commitment: "We have renounced secret and shameful ways; we do not use deception, nor do we distort the Word of God. On the contrary, by setting forth the truth plainly, we commend ourselves to every man's conscience in the sight of God" (2 Cor. 4:2).

May the Lord use Paul's example to free us and our group members to live, and to minister, in this same open, powerful way.

♥ ***Link to Life: Youth / Adult***

Give a minilecture explaining Paul's argument in 3:12-18. As the illustration shows, Moses veiled his face when he left *the presence of God because a process of* deterioration *was taking place; the radiance on his face faded.*

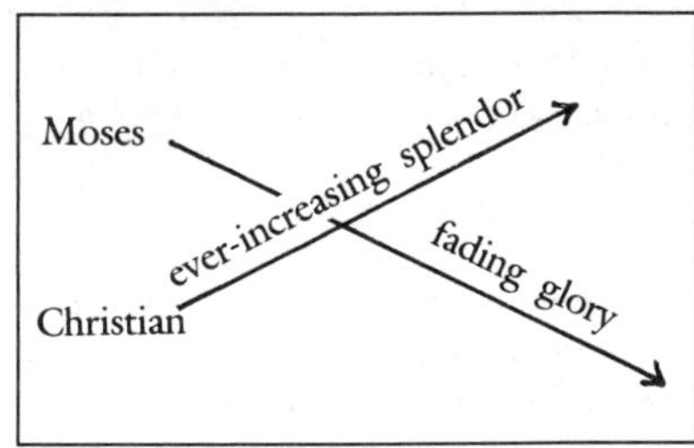

Now Paul said, believers are bold and remove veils, because God is present within, and the Holy Spirit has undertaken a process of transformation. *The radiance of our lives shines with "ever-increasing glory." Only when our veils are removed can people see that Jesus is within, making us better people, and lifting us beyond our own innate weaknesses to bear the very likeness of our Lord.*

TEACHING GUIDE

Prepare
What evidences of transformation can you see in the lives of those you teach? Be prepared to encourage individuals with feedback just before or after your group meets.

Explore
Launch with the biographical study of Paul through 2 Corinthians 1:1–2:4 as explained in "link-to-life," page 876. This study should take at least half of your allotted time.

Expand
1. Raise objections to self-revealing in Christian interpersonal relationships. Let your group members try to answer them, as outlined in "link-to-life," page 877.
2. Give a minilecture on 2 Corinthians 3, using the illustration included on page 878. It is important to see that while self-revelation, as Paul practiced it in this book, *does* establish a common bond with others, it is the fact that Jesus has been at work within to gradually transform that finally frees us to share. We share so that others can see the reality of Christ's work in our lives, even though honesty in sharing will reveal personal weaknesses and needs.

Apply
How have members of your group seen Jesus in the lives of one another? Go around the circle and share, so each can sense how his or her life is having an impact on the brothers and sisters with whom he or she shares.

STUDY GUIDE 136

2 Corinthians 4–7

THE MINISTRY OF RECONCILIATION

Overview

Paul's vision of his New Covenant ministry was rich in the promise of a progressive transformation for believers. "We . . . are being transformed into His [Jesus'] likeness with ever-increasing glory, which comes from the Lord, who is the Spirit" (2 Cor. 3:18).

Yet the Corinthians displayed less evidence of transformation than did other congregations! We know from Paul's first letter to them that their fellowship was marked by divisions, by doctrinal disputes, by confusion over spiritual gifts, even by immorality that was winked at by the local body.

How could Paul maintain his confidence in this unspiritual church, despite all the evidence that existed to the contrary? The answer is given in 2 Corinthians 4–5; an answer that gives us hope as parents, as members or leaders of modern congregations which, like that in Corinth, fall short of God's ideal.

▶ ***Reconciliation.*** This theological term means "to bring into harmony." In this passage Paul argued that the death of Jesus brought humanity to a place of harmony with God; where forgiveness can flow. But there is also an experiential dimension to reconciliation. We are to *live* in harmony with God, reflecting in ourselves the righteousness of God. It is to this end that Paul ministered—and in this passage he shows us the key to a ministry of reconciliation of our own.

Commentary

Paul was not only a great evangelist and teacher. He was a master motivator. In 2 Corinthians we see Paul at his best, and discover how first of all the apostle maintained his own optimism, as well as the way he motivated others to full commitment to Jesus Christ.

Actually, we are given hints in the first three chapters. These hints are found in phrases like:

- "Our hope for you is firm" (1:7).
- "You help us by your prayers" (v. 11).
- "We will boast of you in the day of the Lord Jesus" (v. 14).
- "I was confident of this" (v. 15).
- "I had confidence in all of you" (2:3).
- "Reaffirm your love for him" (v. 8).

The same encouraging optimism is expressed in a phrase from chapter 4: "Life is at work in you" (v. 12).

How are these phrases related to Paul's own optimism, and to spiritual motivation of others?

The football coach who chews out his players is doing it to motivate them. The parent who demands, "Sit down and do your homework *before* you go out," is seeking to motivate. The pastor who preaches a fiery sermon on coming judgment is seeking to use fear to motivate his congregation to action.

We have so many ways of attempting to move people. We set goals for them, and urge them to achieve. We make rules, and insist that others keep them. We shame, urge, condemn, and plan competitions in the hope that *something* will move others to respond. The unhappy wife nags her husband, the disappointed parent belittles his child, and even the proud parent withholds praise in an effort to stimulate still higher achievement. And all of them, at times, wonder, "Why?"

"Why doesn't my husband improve?"

"Why doesn't my child *try*?"

"Why don't members of our congregation get involved?"

The answer to all these questions is the same. It's because we're trying to use man's approach to move others. And as Paul taught in 1 Corinthians 1 and 2, human wisdom is not God's kind of wisdom. God has His own unique and vital way of doing His work in our lives.

The Role of the Leader

One of the basic elements in God's approach to moving believers to follow Jesus is a theme repeated over and over in the Corinthian epistles. It is the theme of the leader's *example*. Paul could, and often did, say to his readers "Imitate me in this," or, "Follow me as I follow Jesus."

In these chapters we see revealed two factors in Paul's own attitude which are critical if we as parents or leaders are to create a climate which will free others to respond and to grow.

Unconditional love. This is the first characteristic of the effective parent or leader. How often we see it stressed in this book.

Apparently Paul's first letter was taken by some in Corinth as rejection; an indication that Paul no longer loved them. They took his gentle explanation as "cold and unfeeling" reasoning. So over and over in this letter Paul reassured them. "We are not withholding our affection from you" (2 Cor. 6:12).

Sometimes we hear psychologists suggest that to withdraw love is an effective way for parents to discipline children. Far from it! In fact, it is the awareness of unconditional love—that sense of certainty that we are supported by a love that will never let us go—that creates the context for growth. Where there is uncertainty about love, there is also uncertainty about our personal worth and value. There is also fear of failure, and an unwillingness to take a risk. It seems safer not to try; safer never to fail, safer never to risk the possible withdrawal of love.

Whatever we can say about human approaches to motivating others—about nagging, shaming, expressing anger, chewing out, or demanding achievement, one thing is sure. These do *not* communicate unconditional love.

Expectant confidence. This was the second key to Paul's approach to motivation. Paul let the Corinthians know that he was confident they would grow. "I have great confidence in you," Paul said. "I take great pride in you. I am greatly encouraged; in all our troubles my joy knows no bounds" (7:4).

Here, remember, Paul was not writing to the Thessalonians, whose work of faith and labor of love and endurance inspired by hope were so abundantly plain. No, Paul was writing to the Corinthians, the church marked by division and marred by troublesome disputes.

It is easy to see how Paul might have expressed confidence in believers like those in Thessalonica. But the Corinthians? Yet, over and over, Paul assured the recipients of this letter that he had confidence in them. And his confidence was not because of the Corinthians' achievements, but in spite of their lack of achievement!

While the Corinthians had begun to lose confidence in themselves, Paul strongly affirmed that his confidence had not been shaken. Paul would believe in these men and women—until they were finally able to believe in themselves.

This is the key. For growth, there must be the assurance of love, and the prospect of hope. For a person to be motivated, there must be a confident expectation of success. That expectation cannot be based on performance alone. For no matter how we may try, our efforts are bound to fall short at times.

As parents or as leaders, we need to not only extend others our unconditional love, but we need a basis on which we can honestly and confidently express our own confidence that even the most hopeless will succeed.

♥ ***Link to Life: Youth / Adult***

Ask your group members to look back into their own childhoods. How did their parents seek to motivate them? What impact did this approach have on their personalities? (For instance, do they feel confident? Do they act decisively? Do they take risks? Do they have a good image of themselves, and a sense of personal worth?)

Let your group members discuss their experiences for 10 to 15 minutes. Then briefly contrast methods some use in trying to motivate with Paul's own affirmation of unconditional love, and his expressions of confidence in the Corinthians.

Break into teams to locate such expressions, and look at their context in chapters 1–6.

A Basis for Confidence: 2 Corinthians 4–5

Paul's confident reassurance of the Corinthians was not an attempt to manipulate them. It was not just a motivational technique. Instead, what Paul was doing was sharing with these uncertain and ashamed believers what he really felt about them.

Expressions of confidence, if honest, do motivate. But such expressions cannot initially be based on others' past performance. If our hope for ourselves and for others is based on performance, there is bound to be a growing sense of discouragement and ultimately, the loss of hope.

This is a trap that parents often fall into with their children. Time after time they instruct or encourage or request. And time after time the child fails to respond, or "forgets," or simply ignores. He doesn't do his homework. She forgets to make her bed. He neglects his chores. She keeps on resisting correction. He won't confess misdeeds, no matter how gently or firmly you deal with him. She won't clean up her room.

Before long, a parent's confidence is worn away. Before long, the parent *expects* the child to disappoint. And the child, sensing the parent's attitude, begins to expect himself or herself to fail.

The child learns to live by the expectations of failure that we have communicated.

It is so important for us to learn Paul's secret. The secret of maintaining one's own confidence, and thus being able to build confidence and hope—and motivation to change—into others' lives. What is that secret? Paul explained.

"We do not lose heart" (2 Cor. 4). Paul was deeply aware that he had been entrusted with his ministry by God. As to the Gospel message, God is able to make its light shine in dark hearts. Ultimately, God is the source of all change in human hearts (vv. 1-6).

As for Paul himself, he was deeply aware that he was a mere "jar of clay." Despite the terrible pressures under which he must have lived (vv. 7-12), Paul spoke out with faith and confidence. He knew that "the One who raised the Lord Jesus from the dead will also raise us with Jesus and present us with you in His presence" (v. 14). The message of Christ glows with a vitalizing power: the very power that raised Jesus from the dead, at work in human beings.

"Therefore," Paul said, "we do not lose heart" (v. 16). The foundation for Paul's confidence in the Corinthians was his bedrock belief in Jesus, and the Resurrection power that the message of Jesus unleashes.

At this point Paul laid down an important principle which was at the core of his confidence. Outwardly Paul admitted deterioration: we are "wasting away." But inwardly Paul experienced a daily renewal. As a result Paul said, "We fix our eyes not on what is seen, but on what is unseen. For what is seen is temporary, but what is unseen is eternal" (v. 18).

This concept deserves exploration. What Paul said is that *anything* that exists in this world of time and space is subject to change. Children grow up. Job descriptions change. Buildings decay. Civilizations fall. Even cliffs are eroded by wind and rain. Anything that we can see is by its very nature subject to change!

This is true of those children of ours who can't remember to make their beds—and of the Corinthians, who could not seem to get beyond disputes and arguments. If what troubles us is a behavior that we can see, then we need to remember that it is temporary. It will change, by the very nature of things in this world of change! How foolish then to become discouraged and give up, even if behavior that bothers us persists for months or years. We need to remember, with Paul, that what we see can change. And it will change.

But Paul did more than remind us that things in this world are temporary. He affirmed realities which are *not* subject to change. "We fix our eyes . . . on what is unseen. For what is . . . unseen is eternal."

There are realities which God knows, and has revealed, that are utterly stable and on which we can count. In our ministry with others, we must not only remember that some things are temporary. We must fix our hope on unseen things which are eternal.

Heaven ahead (2 Cor. 5:1-10). In a brief aside Paul looked at some of those unseen things which are utterly real. There is an "eternal house in the heaven" that will replace our mortal body. Aware of this reality, we look beyond our earthly life and yearn to be present with the Lord. Because we believe completely in this unseen reality, we "make it our goal to please Him," aware that our deeds on earth will be evaluated, and we will "receive what is due" based on how we live our present lives.

It is important here to note that the "Judgment Seat of Christ" (a *bema*) has nothing to do with salvation. The believer's acts are judged, with a view to rewarding him or her (see 1 Cor. 3:15; 4:5).

A ministry of reconciliation (2 Cor. 5:11-12). To understand this passage, we must realize first that Paul was not talking about evangelism when he spoke of his "ministry of reconciliation" (v. 18). "Reconciliation" literally means to "bring into harmony." When we set our watch by the electric clock in the kitchen, we are "reconciling" our watch to the clock. We change the one so that it keeps time set by the standard of the other. This is what Paul wanted for the Corinthians; to bring their lives into harmony with the pattern set by God.

Paul pointed out that it's only appropriate that we live by the heartbeat of God's life rather than by the old heartbeat of humankind. Since Jesus loved and died for believers, they should "no longer live for themselves but for Him who died for them and was raised again" (v. 15). As they do this, they will "become the righteousness of God" in Him (v. 21).

It is this goal of leading believers to life in full harmony with God's righteousness that Paul had in mind when he said, "We implore you on Christ's behalf: Be reconciled to God" (v. 20).

With this understood, we can go back and look at Paul's explanation of how he could express such amazing confidence even in the Corinthians.

Paul began the paragraph assuring the Corinthians that his expressions of confidence were no insincere attempt at flattery (vv. 11-12). Yet how could Paul be totally honest and, while criticizing the Corinthians' behavior still speak of his joy and confidence in their future progress? Paul explained that this is because his approach was so different from "those who take pride in what is seen rather than what is in the heart" (v. 12).

This statement takes us back to the core concept expressed earlier. Some base their pride on what can be seen and measured. "Aren't the folks in my congregation spiritual! Fifty percent of them show up on prayer-meeting night." And, "My Johnny is an ideal Christian boy. Why, he reads his Bible every day."

This is *not* to say we shouldn't be pleased by evidence of spiritual progress or commitment. But pride in the 50 percent who come means shame on the 50 percent who don't! And, neither coming nor not coming provides a basis for judgment of individual spiritual progress. Indeed, because anything that can be seen is temporary and subject to change, those who boast in externals set themselves up for a fall when the percentage drops off, or Johnny forsakes his Bible reading.

What then *are* we to take pride in? Paul said, "What is in the heart." We can't *see* what is in the heart, of course. We can't measure it. But the Christian knows that Jesus Himself is resident in the heart of believers. And Jesus is eternal. He will not change no matter what.

Paul told the Corinthians his view wasn't madness (v. 13). It was utter sanity. Because, Paul said, "Christ's love compels us" (v. 14).

Paul's point was this. There is only one thing that will really bring about change in a believer's life, and move him or her toward Christlikeness. That is the love that Christ Himself pours into the heart in which He dwells. Mere human forms of motivation—the attempts to coerce, to shame, to move by guilt—may bring conformity of action. *But they will never change the heart, and it is the heart—the unseen world within—with which Christian ministry is concerned.*

Paul now stated a powerful theological argument. Christ died for all. He died for us in order that we who live should stop living for ourselves, and begin to live for Him. *That is, God's purpose in the Cross was to change us, and change the focus of our lives.* Paul was confident that Jesus, who now lives in the hearts of believers, will bring about the change that He died to gain! It is inconceivable to Paul that the purpose of Jesus' death on the cross could be thwarted. God *would* change the Corinthians. Paul had hope and confidence, not because of what he saw in the Corinthian's actions, but because he looked beyond appearances and saw Jesus living in these believers' hearts.

The next paragraph is important, because it shows us how to live with others to encourage this change Jesus has come into their lives to make. Paul said that from now on "we regard no one from a worldly point of view" (v. 16). That is, we simply do not judge them by what we see. If we looked at Jesus in this way, we would see only an idealistic Carpenter, murdered by wicked and selfish men. But we look at Jesus through the eyes of faith! In the Cross we do not see defeat, but victory! Though we do not see Jesus with our physical eyes, we recognize Him as the living God, our Saviour and our Lord.

In the same way, we must learn to look at our brothers and sisters with the eyes of faith. We must affirm, with Paul, that "in Christ" they are "new creations." The old *has* gone, the new has come within. And because the new has come, in time, behavior too will change and our loved ones or friends *will* learn to love the One who died for them.

How do we help them come to this commitment? Paul said that Jesus' ministry of reconciliation was accomplished by "not counting men's sins against them." God doesn't count our sins. He doesn't say, "You've failed 32 times. Oh, my, there's 33." And He doesn't hold our sins against us. He keeps on loving, keeps on holding out hope.

This is just how we are to treat others—our children, our spouses, our brothers and sisters in the Lord. We don't say, "That's the thirty-second day you forgot to make your bed, and tomorrow will be 33." And we don't hold failures against them.

Instead we remember that, in Christ, there is a newness rooted deep within. We keep on expressing love. And we keep on expressing confidence and hope. And through it all we make God's appeal. Bring your life into harmony with who God is, that "in Him [you] might become the righteousness of God."

A Life of Love: 2 Corinthians 6–7

Paul had revealed the convictions which enabled him to maintain confidence in the Corinthians. Now he shared more of what love means.

Love means urging (2 Cor. 6:1-2). Unconditional love does not rule out exhorting. Paul called on his readers not to receive God's grace in vain.

Love means self-sacrifice (2 Cor. 6:3-13). Paul reviewed the hardships he had suffered in ministry. He had endured everything as a servant of God, out of love. Paul had been completely open and caring—it was time for the Corinthians to open wide their hearts to Him as well.

Love means separation (2 Cor. 6:14–7:1). The Christian will refuse to be linked with evil. Commitment to Christ calls for purification "from everything that contaminates body and spirit."

Love means joy even in pain (2 Cor. 7:2-16). Paul's relationship with the Corinthians had brought both of them great pain. Paul felt great anxiety over the Corinthians, as well as deep hurt. And Paul's letter caused the Corinthians sorrow. Yet that sorrow was beneficial—the godly repented and changed. And the change in them was complete (v. 11). As a result the sorrow each experienced was one of those temporary things Paul had been speaking of in these chapters.

And the pain even produced joy. Paul felt joy when Titus came and told the apostle "about your longing for me, your deep sorrow, your ardent concern for me so that my joy was greater than ever" (v. 7). Titus too felt joy as he learned the sincerity of the Corinthians' faith, and saw their responsiveness to instruction.

And so a great danger was avoided in Corinth, and the church there was set back on the path to righteousness. And through it all, Paul in total honesty was able to encourage his friends, and to say with a full heart, "I have great confidence in you; I take great pride in you. I am greatly encouraged; in all our troubles my joy knows no bounds."

How wonderful when we have learned Paul's secrets of motivation, and have taken them to heart, so that we say to others who are struggling, "I am glad I can have complete confidence in you" (v. 16).

Because we believe in Jesus, and hold the unseen far more real than what is visible to the eye, we can reach out with unconditional love and confident hope, and by our example help others to grow.

TEACHING GUIDE

Prepare
Ask God to help your group members adopt Paul's attitude toward their children and others in the family of God.

Explore
1. Have your group think together about how their parents tried to motivate them when they lived at home. What methods were used? How did this affect their development? See "link-to-life," page 881.
2. Or divide into teams to seek evidence in 2 Corinthians 4–7 (1) that Paul loved the Corinthians unconditionally, and (2) that he had complete confidence in their growth toward holiness.

After teams report, discuss: "What would it have been like to have Paul for a parent? What would he have done differently from your parents? What the same? How is your own parenting like or unlike what we would expect from Paul?"

Expand
Give a careful lecture exposition of 2 Corinthians 4–5. Be sure that your group members understand (1) the principle of not looking to the seen but to the unseen, (2) the inner motivation that alone can move Christians to follow Jesus, (3) the purpose in the Cross which Jesus is sure to achieve in believers, (4) how to regard others who are Christians despite weaknesses or failures, and (5) what we *do* to encourage growth (e.g., "not count trespasses" and not "count *against* them").

Apply
Divide into teams, keeping any married couples together. Have each team respond to the teaching on 2 Cor. 4–5 by telling (1) what we are most likely to "count against" our kids; (2) what we can do at home to put the teaching of this passage into practice.

Or if your group members do not have children, ask each person to think of a relationship with someone to whom he or she is close, and whom he or she seeks to influence.

STUDY GUIDE 137

2 Corinthians 8–9

NEW TESTAMENT PRINCIPLES OF GIVING

Overview

John wrote in the introduction to his Gospel, "the Law was given by Moses; grace and truth came through Jesus Christ" (John 1:17). In a sense, the rest of the New Testament is an exposition of the grace and the truth which came through Jesus.

Here, in 2 Corinthians 8 and 9, the Apostle Paul outlined the grace principles governing a New Testament pattern of giving which supplants the Old Testament principle of the tithe.

The way Paul developed this topic also illustrates his approach to New Covenant ministry. In the preceding chapters Paul had expressed a confidence in Christians based on the reality of Christ in their hearts. Now, rather than command or coerce, Paul simply taught and encouraged his readers to give as a free and personal response to Christ.

These chapters also are an illustration of Paul's use of spiritual authority, which we explore in the next study guide. Rather than demand, the apostle carefully guarded the freedom of individuals to be personally responsible to God, and reminded us all that response to God must not be made "reluctantly or under compulsion, for God loves a cheerful giver" (2 Cor. 9:7).

What a privilege to be able to affirm the grace of God as we teach, and to encourage in our group members a free, spontaneous and loving response to Jesus which the Lord Himself loves to see in you and me.

Commentary

It's said most Sundays in most of our churches. As the collection plate is passed, the congregation is encouraged to give God "tithes and offerings."

There's nothing particularly wrong with this familiar phrase. Unless we make the mistake of reading into it a theology of giving that has its roots in Old Testament Law rather than in the vital new principles of grace-giving that the New Testament establishes for God's people. It is significant that the Epistles mention no tithes, and the offering which God seeks is that of the person himself as a "living sacrifice . . . which is your spiritual worship" (Rom. 12:1).

Background

The tithe in the Old Testament. The Law established a concept of tithing which, at first glance, seems simple. Leviticus 27:30-33 says that a "tithe of everything from the land" was to be set aside for use as God might command. Other passages expand this initial instruction. According to Numbers 18:21-32 tithes were to be used for the support of those dedicated to serve God. According to Deuteronomy 12:5-14 and 14:22-26, the 10 percent was to be brought to a central sanctuary, later established by David at Jerusalem, for distribution.

However, 14:27-29 and 26:12-15 introduce *another* tithe, this one to be collected every third year and distributed locally to the needy! Some students of Scripture believe that as many as three separate tithes can be identified. But surely there are two: the yearly 10 percent taken to support those who led Israel in worship, and a tri-annual 10 percent used to support widows and orphans.

In Old Testament times this giving posed no threat to the believer, and Scripture does not see it as a burden. God is able to make the land produce abundantly, so His people will have all they need and more. Giving is a way of worship; a way to express confidence in God (see Mal. 3:10).

In addition to the tithes which the Israelite *owed* to God, the Law established a principle of voluntary contributions. These contributions, called "freewill offerings," were given spontaneously, out of love. They were not a duty, and they were not considered "bribes" to buy divine favor.

Thus in the Old as well as the New love flowed: beyond duty there was the privilege of expressing devotion through one's giving to God, and of expressing concern for God's people by lending to the needy.

As we move into the New Testament era, however, we note several important contrasts. The Epistles never call for a tithe. There is no single worship center and no priesthood to be supported by the old, annual temple tithe. While giving to support individuals who minister full time is mentioned in the New Testament, no letter suggests this be done through a local tithe. The New Testament emphasizes a deep concern for the poor and needy, especially within the family of faith. Paul and others did organize offerings to be taken up for those in hunger-ridden foreign lands. But the guidelines for giving that Paul laid down nowhere mention or imply that the tithe is to be used to measure a Christian's obligation.

So we need to look carefully in our study of 2 Corinthians 8–9 to see if new principles of measure are introduced.

The New Testament view of possessions. The principles of giving which we find in 2 Corinthians reflect an attitude toward possessions which is consistent throughout the New Testament.

Jesus taught that the believer is not to trust in possessions, nor consider material things treasures (Matt. 6:19-33). The manager in one of Jesus' parables was considered shrewd because he *used* worldly wealth to prepare for his future (Luke 16:9). Jesus went on to show that no one can serve two masters: we will either love God and reject money as the focus of our lives, or we will love money and God will take second place. "You cannot serve both God and money" (v. 13). The believer, then, will give God first place and use money in God's service.

The New Testament Epistles reflect this teaching. The love of God will be reflected in sharing what we have. "If anyone has material possessions and sees his brother in need but has no pity on him, how can the love of God be in him? Dear children, let us not love with words or tongue but with actions and in truth" (1 John 3:17-18).

Paul told Timothy to "command those who are rich in this present world not to be arrogant nor to put their hope in wealth, which is so uncertain, but to put their hope in God, who richly provides us with everything for our enjoyment. Command them to do good, to be rich in good deeds, and to be generous and willing to share. In this way they will lay up treasure for themselves as a firm foundation for the coming age" (1 Tim. 6:17-19).

While it is not wrong to be wealthy, and while material riches can be used to help others, the love of money *is* a problem, a "root of all kinds of evil" (v. 10).

The composite we draw suggests that worldly riches are not in themselves evil. The issue is one of how they affect our values and choices. If we put God first, and respond lovingly to the needs of others, we can use our possessions to prepare for eternity. But if we put money first, we will fall short of full commitment to God and fall short in our obligation to love others.

Our use of our resources then becomes one means of measuring our dedication to God and our commitment to eternal values.

♥ ***Link to Life: Youth / Adult***
Open with a T/F quiz and a "quick check" review of key Bible verses. Have each person take the quiz first, then together look up the verses that give the answer. As you check references, discuss how the verse suggests we should answer the item.

Quiz

T F 1. *Ten percent of what we make belongs to God (1 Cor. 16:2).*
T F 2. *Having riches is in conflict with commitment to God (Luke 16:13).*
T F 3. *Money is the root of all evil (1 Tim. 6:18).*
T F 4. *The rich have a special opportunity to do good (1 Tim. 6:18).*
T F 5. *The rich trust their wealth rather than God (1 Tim. 6:17).*
T F 6. *Most of my problems would be solved if I had a million dollars (Luke 12:14).*

After discussing, point out that our attitude toward God and possessions will be reflected in our giving. Give an overview of giving in the Old Testament, then ask: "How do you *determine how much to give, and what to give toward?" If your group will discuss, let them, before moving on to study 2 Corinthians 8–9.*

♥ ***Link to Life: Youth / Adult***
Or put this list of questions on the chalkboard. Each person is to jot down his or her answer. Then form teams to look into 1 Corinthians 8–9 and discover what answers Paul would give.

- *What is the "right amount" for a Christian to give?*
- *Is "giving" the best name for making our contributions?*
- *What are valid motives for giving: why do we give?*
- *What are some of the results of generous giving?*
- *What are we to look to as the ideal example of Christian giving?*

Grace Giving: 2 Corinthians 8–9
Several things help us put this passage's teaching on giving in perspective. In the early New Testament church there were no buildings to finance, no curriculums or programs to support. Yet there were needs within the body. Funds were given to the apostles and to others who traveled as missionaries. Often local elders would be supported to free them for a full-time ministry. Paul wrote to Timothy about needy widows who were also supported by the congregation. However the first obligation for their support fell on children and grandchildren. The great collections of which the New Testament speaks here and in other passages (cf. Acts 11:27-30; etc.) were, however, intended for the support of Christian brothers and sisters in lands struck by famine or some other natural disaster. Essentially then "giving" in the New Testament was focused on meeting "people needs." Its goal was to enable others to simply survive, or to carry on ministries recognized as important by the church.

It is not surprising then to discover that the term used for "giving" in this New Testament context is not the typical Greek word for making a gift. Instead the New Testament adopts the Greek word *koinonia*, which means "sharing." As Christians shared life in Christ, their family relationship was expressed by a sharing of financial and material resources.

In these chapters of 2 Corinthians then Paul wrote to encourage members of this congregation to share their material possessions with needy brothers. His whole approach and argument was a demonstration of the revolutionary approach to motivation explored in our last study guide. Paul held no rallies and called for no pledges. He sent no letters filled with underlined appeals. Paul set up no "buy a brick" campaigns; he put no red ribbon threaded through a giant thermometer to creep upward toward Paul's campaign goal. There was not even an every-member canvass. In fact, Paul seems to have found an entirely different way.

If we keep in mind these two factors, that "giving" is really sharing to meet needs in the body of Christ, and that New Testament giving focuses on people needs, we will be able to better understand what Paul teaches us here.

Two examples (1 Cor. 8:1-9). Paul began by telling about the way the churches of Macedonia had shared generously despite extreme poverty. Their act of service was viewed as a privilege, and their example provided a standard against which the Corinthians could measure their own earnestness.

But the Macedonians were not the prime example of the grace of giving: Jesus is. Jesus demonstrated this grace in that though He was rich, He gave all ("became poor") that through His poverty we might become rich.

There is no appeal here to the tithe as a standard against which to measure our giving. Instead Paul pointed to other believers and to Jesus, whose love moved them to give, first themselves and then money.

Willingness (2 Cor. 8:10-12). Paul was pleased that the Corinthians had earlier expressed a strong desire to help. But the Corinthians needed to carry their intentions through to completion, "according to your means." This is an important factor in grace giving. Paul said it again. "If the willingness is there, the gift is acceptable according to what one has, not according to what he does not have."

On the one hand, one need not be a millionaire for his or her contribution to be significant. Even the gifts of those who have little and can give little are acceptable. What God is concerned with is the willingness: the love that motivates the believer to share (cf. Luke 21:1-4).

The principle of "equality" (2 Cor. 8:13-15). Here Paul laid down an important principle. The goal in grace giving is "that there might be equality." This is *not* Christian communism, in any sense. Paul's vision is of a worldwide church, an international body. In the first-century world, as in our own, there were at times famines or other natural disasters, which left whole populations on the verge of starvation. The collections which Paul spoke of here were for the relief of Christians in such areas. What Paul pointed out is that, at present, the plenty enjoyed by the Corinthians could supply others' needs. In their turn those others might one day supply the Corinthians when they had needs.

The body image is appropriate here. Just as the food we take in is digested and distributed to all parts of the body, in order that every bodily part can function, so the funds God supplies to believers are to be shared with those in need so they can live and function as God intends.

Action encouraged (2 Cor. 8:16–9:5). Paul told the Corinthians that Titus and another brother were coming to take and distribute their liberal gift, and urged them to "show these men the proof of your love and the reason for our pride in you" by having it ready.

Giving as sowing (2 Cor. 9:6-11). Paul turned to another image that had its roots in the Old Testament. Sharing with others is like sowing seed: the more generously one sows the more he or she will reap.

This is *not* a promise that one who sends in $7 will get $77 in return. Instead it is an affirmation of God's ability to outgive His people. "God is able to make all grace abound to you, so that in all things at all times, having all that you need, you will abound in every good work." *The conviction that God is able to supply our needs is intended to free us to give generously, without fear that we will deprive ourselves or our family by responding to meet the needs of others.*

In this context Paul said that "each man should give what he has decided in his heart to give, not reluctantly or under compulsion, for God loves a cheerful giver." Again, Paul was careful not to place believers under any obligation to give, and not to specify any percentage as appropriate. Each is to give "what he has decided in his heart," and that decision is not to be made reluctantly or under compulsion.

The outcome of grace giving (2 Cor. 9:12-15). Paul now summed up the results of generous giving. It supplies the needs of God's people. It overflows in expressions of thanks to God, and stimulates praise. It demonstrates the obedience (commitment) that is appropriate to our profession of faith. It generates prayers for the giver by the one who receives.

And, as Paul had shown earlier, it permits us to experience the faithfulness of God who is able, and does supply our needs as we use our material possessions to help our brothers and sisters.

Implications

In an earlier study we saw that the Apostle Paul abandoned typical approaches to motivating others. He did not demand. He did not try to produce guilt. He did not manipulate. Rather Paul put great trust in the fact that Christ does live in the believer, and he based both his confidence and his appeal to others on this reality.

What kind of pattern might we see in our local churches if we were to build our stewardship programs on the gracious principles Paul presents in 2 Corinthians 8 and 9?

In seems that such a program would feature these elements:

We would present needs. Paul did not hesitate to share with the churches the needs of those for whom he planned to take up a collection. The needs emphasized were human needs. It is not *wrong* to give today to support the local church as an institution, or to support denominational programs. But the strongest and best motivation for giving is to respond to brothers or sisters whose needs are real and basic.

We would encourage our people to evaluate our own needs in view of the resources and against the needs of their brothers. Wealth is comparative. In some situations a person with a thousand dollars is rich; in others a person with that amount is poor. In some societies all our needs can be met with the expenditure of a few thousand dollars a year. In other situations our most basic needs may require the expenditure of many thousands of dollars. God does not set a fixed amount that Christians are to give, but He does call on us to evaluate what we have (and need) and to look honestly at what others have (and need).

We are then to give what we can and what we wish to, but not what we cannot spare or are unwilling to share.

We would reject manipulation. Like Paul

we would protect the freedom of our brothers and sisters to respond to God as they themselves choose, and do nothing to force or manipulate giving.

We would teach freeing truths. While Paul did not manipulate, he did not hesitate to teach truths which release Christians from fear and from bondage to the material. Like Paul we might remind others of God's great gift in Christ. We might emphasize God's commitment to us, and affirm that we cannot outgive a God who is able to make all grace abound to us. We might also teach that the person who gives sparingly will reap sparingly, and that giving generates many spiritual benefits.

These are principles we need to implement in our churches. But before we apply them to stewardship in the church, we can apply them in our own lives. As we take to heart the truths Paul taught here, we experience both freedom and release. We are freed from compulsion in our Christian lives. And, through growing trust in God, we are released from our bondage to possessions and enabled to respond freely, and generously, to meet others' needs.

♥ ***Link to Life: Youth / Adult***
Divide into teams to take the role of a church stewardship committee. Ask each team to develop a stewardship program for the congregation that puts principles from 2 Corinthians 8–9 into practice. After 10 or 20 minutes, reassemble and compare programs.

Then check the programs against the principles mentioned above.

TEACHING GUIDE

Prepare

Evaluate your own giving by the teaching of 2 Corinthians 8–9.

Explore

1. Begin with the T/F "quick check" quiz on giving on page 887. Use it to lead into a minilecture giving background on both the Old Testament tithe and the New Testament's attitude toward riches and material possessions.
2. Or distribute the list of questions suggested in "link-to-life," page 888. Break into teams to discuss. Then have the teams check their ideas by trying to find answers to each question by studying 2 Corinthians 8–9 together.

Expand

1. In a minilecture cover the main points Paul makes in these chapters, guided by the commentary in this study guide.
2. Ask the study teams to take the role of a church stewardship committee, and determine steps they might take to establish a "grace giving" stewardship program in your church. See "link-to-life," page 890.

Apply

Encourage each group member to write down a list of factors he or she will use to reevaluate his or her own giving.

Or ask each to pick a key verse from these chapters that expresses something he or she needs to apply in thinking about personal giving. Share the verses, and share why each made the choice he or she did.

STUDY GUIDE 138

2 Corinthians 10–13

SPIRITUAL AUTHORITY

Overview
In 2 Corinthians Paul shared principles of his New Covenant ministry. That ministry leads to the inner transformation of believers, as promised in Jeremiah's ancient prophecy (31:33-34).

The New Covenant ministry is one of openness and transparency, for God the Spirit is at work within and we see Christ in each others' lives as the process of transformation is revealed (2 Cor. 1–3). New Covenant ministry relies on the reality of Christ in the heart to motivate change, and is not discouraged by apparent lack of progress. The New Covenant minister expresses confidence in others, "not counting their trespasses," sure that Christ will move believers to live a righteous life (2 Cor. 4–7). New Covenant ministry, as illustrated by grace giving, guards the freedom of each individual to respond personally to God, while teaching truths that release us to respond generously (2 Cor. 8–9). Now, in the last chapters of this most personal of Paul's books, we see how the apostle exercises spiritual authority in such a way that it builds others up rather than tears them down.

▶ ***Authority.*** The Greek word is *exousia,* and its basic meaning indicates "freedom of choice." A person with great authority has maximum freedom of choice; one under authority has his or her freedom limited. The secret of spiritual authority is that it creates rather than limits others' freedom of choice.

Commentary
"Authority" is such a difficult word. We use it in so many ways.

- An encyclopedia is cited when someone asks, "What's your authority for that statement?"
- Professor so-and-so is introduced as an "authority on cybernetics."
- "Where's your search warrant?" is a demand for evidence of authority.
- "By the authority vested in me, I now pronounce you man and wife."

Yet, in our society, the idea of authority has had many negative connotations. To many it tends to imply control, restriction, coercion, and impersonal command. "Authority" and "authoritarian" can seem almost synonymous, and it's hard for most of us to imagine how we might exercise authority without somehow asserting a right to control or command.

It's no wonder that spiritual leadership and authority are misunderstood. And it's no wonder that a parent's authority over a child can be distorted. No wonder those called to lead the church of God, and given His authority for that task, are often troubled and uncertain. No wonder we often resort to a worldly approach to the exercise of authority—and stimulate rebellion rather than response.

Paul's Approach to Authority: 2 Corinthians 10–13
We may not be aware of it as we read 2 Corinthians, but it is true that in this letter the apostle was exercising spiritual authority.

We're not likely to realize it, because Paul did not even mention authority until chapter 10. His second and final mention of authority came near the end of this letter, in chapter 13. In each of these two contexts Paul gave a definition of the purpose of authority in the body of Christ. Authority was given to Paul by the Lord "for building you up rather than pulling you down" (10:8; see also 12:10). How much Paul hoped, as he closed this letter, that when he visited he would not be forced to be "harsh in my use of authority" (13:10).

We tend to think of authority as something essentially harsh. But in the body of

Christ, the use of authority is marked by a distinct gentleness. Even the Corinthians missed the authority in the apostle's approach. Deceived again by their reliance on their old ways of understanding, they could not understand why the apostle did not simply insist and command and demand. "Why," they must have wondered, "doesn't this leader *lead*?" They mistook Paul's wisdom for weakness. We know that, from Paul's "defense" in the opening of chapter 10.

> By the meekness and gentleness of Christ, I appeal to you—I, Paul, who am "timid" when face to face with you, but "bold" when away! I beg you that when I come I may not have to be as bold as I expect to be toward some people who think that we live by the standards of this world. For though we live in the world, we do not wage war as the world does. The weapons we fight with are not the weapons of the world. On the contrary, they have divine power to tear down strongholds. We demolish arguments and every pretension that sets itself up against the knowledge of God, and we take captive every thought to make it obedient to Christ.
>
> 2 Corinthians 10:1-5

God's approach to authority operates on divine power. Through God's methods, Paul would be successful in taking "captive every thought" and making it "obedient to Christ."

What are some of those methods? Listen, as Paul's letter itself unveils them:

- "Not that we lord it over your faith, but we work with you for your joy" (1:24).
- "I urge you, therefore to reaffirm your love for Him" (2:8).
- "Dear friends, let us purify ourselves from everything that contaminates body and spirit, perfecting holiness out of reverence for God" (7:1).
- "I am not commanding you, but I want to test the sincerity of your love" (8:8).
- "Here is my advice about what is best for you" (v. 10).
- "Was it a sin for me to lower myself in order to elevate you?" (11:7)

And the freedom that Paul found to exercise his authority in such gentle ways was rooted both in his knowledge that this *is* God's way to use spiritual authority, and in the knowledge that it is *God* who exercised authority through him.

In 2 Corinthians 13 Paul gave a warning: he would not "spare" those who failed to respond to his letters. Yet even here Paul himself would not act. What Paul would do was expect *God* to act, because Christ truly was speaking through him. The Lord would enforce the spiritual authority of His servant—Paul would not rely on worldly ways to punish those who did not respond.

> On my return I will not spare those who sinned earlier or any of the others, since you are demanding proof that Christ is speaking through me. He is not weak in dealing with you, but is powerful among you.
>
> 2 Corinthians 13:2-3

♥ ***Link to Life: Youth / Adult***

Put the word "authority" on the chalkboard. Divide into teams, and ask each team to come up with five things that might be said by a person with authority to those under him or her. These should be in the form of quotes: of words spoken by the one with authority.

After a few minutes, come together and list the authority statements. Then distribute a sheet of paper on which you have copied Paul's authority statements, quoted in the commentary.

Ask your group members to compare the two sets of statements. "How are they alike? How do they differ?" Discuss: "How would hearing each set of statements from an authority figure make you feel? Which authority figure seems strong? Weak? Which would you prefer in a spiritual leader? Why?"

Finally, ask: "Can you develop a tentative definition of spiritual authority from Paul's words to the Corinthians?"

Authority Principles

The issue of spiritual authority is complex and important enough to warrant an entire book, not just part of a chapter in this *Teacher's Commentary*. But we can sketch basic characteristics of spiritual authority as demonstrated by Paul, which will give us perspective and help to sensitize us to what is behind the last, most intimate chapters in this very personal epistle.

Source. Spiritual authority, unlike secular authority, is not rooted in position. An officer in the army or the president of a corporation has authority by virtue of his or her office. Spiritual authority, however (even though it may be associated with an office in the church, or one's position as a parent), is actually rooted in one's *gift*. Paul relied on "the authority the Lord gave me" (13:10) in his dealings with the Corinthians.

This is important to grasp. If our authority is truly given us by the Lord, then He will be responsible for authenticating it! This is why Paul could say to those who demanded proof that Christ was speaking through him, "*He* [Christ] is not weak in dealing with you" (v. 3, italics added). Jesus will vindicate the authority He has given.

Goal. Paul made it very clear that the purpose or goal of spiritual authority is to "build up." His authority was exercised purposefully and wisely: he used the spiritual weapons in God's arsenal to "take captive every thought to make it obedient to Christ" (10:5).

A very important concept is expressed here. It is *Jesus* who is the Head of the church. And He is the Head of every man. The spiritual leader does not use authority to bring believers to obey the leader. Instead, spiritual authority is always exercised to lead the local body and individual believer to obey Christ. The spiritual leader is not to attempt to exercise control over others; instead, he seeks to free them to be responsive to Jesus.

There are a number of reasons why this concept is vital. Authority that seeks to *control* focuses on externals. A person can "exercise authority" to manipulate or control another's behavior through all the secular motivation methods looked at in the last study guide. One reason why these methods are so often adopted by Christian leaders is that they are successful! But this is true only if we measure success by conformity. It is true that many leadership methods are adapted to produce different kinds of achievement. Using them, we can raise money, build bigger buildings, increase attendance in Sunday Schools. But the one thing that such methods cannot do is to produce *commitment*. Commitment is a change within the human personality, an aspect of transformation. Commitment comes when a person freely chooses to respond to God.

All this underlies Paul's statement that authority has been given him to "build up." Rather than gain control over others' behavior, *Paul's exercise of authority was designed to free them to choose God's way willingly*. This thought also finds expression in Paul's confident assertion that "Christ's love compels us" (5:14). It was the reality of Christ within, not external pressures, that Paul relied on to motivate believers to respond to the Lord.

Relationships. Paul had also, in relinquishing any claim to a supposed right of authority to control, helped us to see more clearly the relationships appropriate to spiritual leadership. Paul did more than hint when he spoke of meekness and gentleness and insisted to the Corinthians that he would not "lord it over your faith" (1:24) but rather would "lower myself in order to elevate you" (11:7).

Rather than be relationally *over* others, the person with spiritual authority takes his or her place alongside the other and thus lifts them up. We can illustrate the distorted and appropriate concepts of authority with simple diagrams like those on page 894.

The "chain of command" diagram represents the leader as *between* God and the person under his or her authority. This is the kind of structure used to chart military or business (and too often church) organizations. It indicates lines of control and responsibility. But this concept significantly distorts the biblical concept of authority.

An approach charting authority actually requires two diagrams. The first represents the *fact* of authority. While the leader *is* "above," and the led "under," *the leader is not between the individual and God*. Instead, both the leader and the follower recognize Christ's lordship over each of them, and over both of them together.

The fact of authority does admit the right of the leader to lead, but it denies the right of the leader to control. Instead, the leader's *influence flows from his or her gift* (the fact that Christ *is* speaking through this person), and it flows from the example the leader gives as a person who has experienced significant growth and transformation.

But even this chart is inadequate to represent how the leader *exercises* spiritual authority. We need another diagram for this;

one that shows the leader choosing to humble himself, even to "lower myself in order to elevate you." How did Paul lower himself?

♥ ***Link to Life: Youth / Adult***
Use the charts in a minilecture summary of the implications of Paul's view of spiritual authority. Then break into teams, divided by sex, to attempt to diagram the appropriate relationship between a husband and wife and God.

After about five minutes, have each team draw its diagram on the chalkboard and explain why they chose their particular representation.

Discuss as a group: "What are the implications for husband/wife relationships of the traditional chain of command diagram? What are the implications of the alternative diagrams drawn on the board? How might spiritual authority be best exercised in the home by husbands? By husbands and wives as parents?"

Finally, pair off by couples. Ask each husband and wife to first agree on a diagram which represents the present situation *in their own relationship. Then ask them to agree on a diagram which represents the* ideal situation *in their relationship. Each spouse can then share with the other what he or she thinks they need to do to work toward the ideal, or to strengthen the ideal which is being realized.*

Paul requested rather than ordered. He gave advice rather than commands. Paul shared his weaknesses, and thus took a stand beside men and women who knew themselves to be weak. Paul refused to "lord it over your faith," even when the Corinthians' worldliness made them critical of Paul's shameful lack of "boldness"!

The characteristics which the Corinthians associated with leadership were as foreign to true spiritual leadership as are the traits that we associate with it today!

What Paul had done was to take to heart, and to put into practice a servant leadership demonstrated by Jesus, and commanded by Jesus for those who would minister in His church.

> You know that the rulers of the Gentiles lord it over them, and their high officials exercise authority over them. Not so with you. Instead, whoever wants to become great among you must be your servant, and whoever wants to be first must be your slave—just as the Son of man did not come to be served, but to serve, and to give His life as a ransom for many.
>
> Matthew 20:25-27

Attitude. What is the appropriate attitude of the leader? A servant attitude. A servant who sees others, not himself or herself, as important. A servant who humbles himself, concerned only with doing his master's will. A servant who willingly sets aside every outward symbol of power and relies completely on the power of God within the men and women he or she leads to stimulate response.

It almost seems embarrassing to read the

Authority Concepts

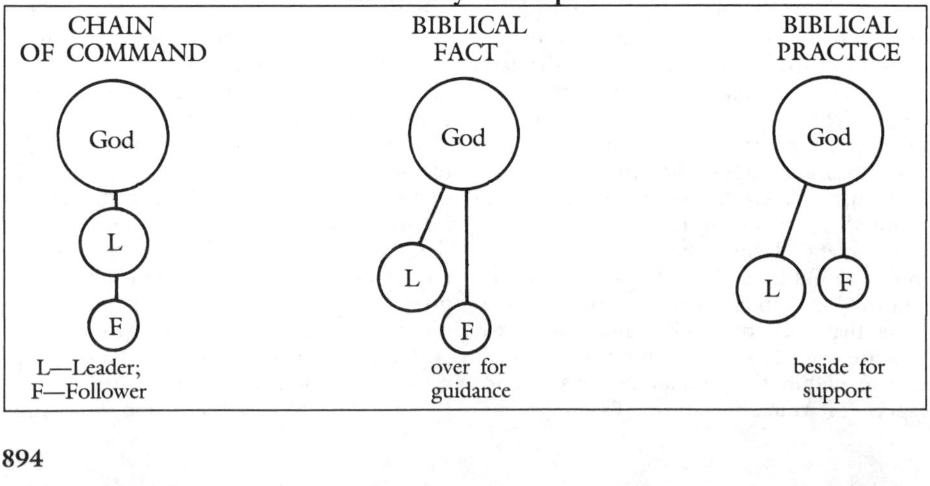

words Paul writes in these last chapters of this letter. We're almost ashamed for him as he speaks out of the intensity of his love and pain. He seems almost, well . . . weak.

And yet Paul was strong. Strong in God's way. "For Christ's sake, I delight in weaknesses, in insults, in hardships, in persecutions, in difficulties. For when I am weak, then I am strong" (2 Cor. 12:10). This was Paul's perspective. And it should become ours.

God's ways are not our ways, and His thoughts are not our thoughts. And so our greatest need is to learn His ways.

♥ ***Link to Life: Youth / Adult***

A seminary has officially adopted the concepts of spiritual leadership sketched here, and seeks to train its students to become servant leaders. But now that many graduates have found their way into the denomination's churches, the seminary is experiencing a grassroots backlash. The people in the churches are complaining that this seminary's graduates are "weak" leaders!

Have your group members discuss as if they were on the board of this seminary: "Why are our grads considered weak leaders? What can we do to correct this situation?"

Comments on the Text

The marks of leaders (2 Cor. 11). The Corinthians, still superficial and still evaluating by worldly criteria, were attracted to "strong" leaders. These were persons who as "trained speakers" (v. 6) seemed very impressive. They claimed the right of support, and like most of us the Corinthians seemed more impressed by that for which they paid than that which came at little cost (v. 7). But they presented a distorted Gospel (v. 4), and Paul called them "false apostles" who were masquerading as Christian leaders.

What are the marks that we see in Paul of one who is a true Christian leader? Paul first of all cared deeply about the Corinthians' spiritual welfare (vv. 1-3). He refused to burden anyone financially in order to demonstrate that he was no spiritual profiteer (vv. 7-11). Paul's commitment has led to deep suffering—floggings, hunger, thirst, danger after danger (vv. 16-27). Paul felt deeply with the weakness of the weak; was in anguish when he heard of a believer's sin (vv. 28-30). In short, Paul not only identified with those to whom he ministered, he cared enough for them to accept personal hardship in order to benefit them.

What an example the apostle left for you and me. Ministry to others is *not* just a matter of sharing our knowledge of the Word. It is a matter of sharing ourselves: of being the caring, self-sacrificing kind of person whose spiritual authority is matched by his or her commitment to others out of full commitment to Christ.

Overcoming weakness (2 Cor. 12:1-10). Bible students agree that Paul suffered from some unidentified disease. How did it happen that Paul, whom Acts tells us did miracles of healing (see Acts 14:8), was not himself healed? Despite Paul's prayer God chose this physical disability as the apostle's lot. Finally God revealed to Paul, "My grace is sufficient for you, for My power is made perfect in weakness" (2 Cor. 12:9). God's grace worked through Paul despite his weaknesses: the Gospel's power did not rely on human strengths or abilites.

What a wonderful lesson to us, not only in our times of sickness, but also as we contemplate spiritual leadership. God does not rely on the strengths that our society exalts. God's power can and will flow through even those who are "weak" in the qualities secular leaders count on to make them effective.

Christ is speaking though me (1 Cor. 13:1-10). This is the ultimate secret of the Christian leader's authority, and of his or her power. Christ does speak through leaders, and Christ is "powerful among" His people. Christian leaders do not need to rely on merely human means to motivate or to discipline. God Himself authenticates the Christian leader, moving believers to respond, and acting in those who will not respond to discipline and to change.

TEACHING GUIDE

Prepare
Read these chapters carefully, and check a good verse-by-verse commentary like the *Bible Knowledge Commentary,* pages 576-585, if you have specific questions.

Explore
1. Begin by having your group members work in teams to develop five typical things that a person in authority might say to someone "under" him or her. Then have your group compare these statements with statements by Paul in 2 Corinthians. See "link-to-life," page 892.
2. Follow up with a minilecture on the characteristics of Christian spiritual authority drawn from the commentary.

Expand
1. Divide into teams by sex, for group members to apply the biblical concept of spiritual authority to the husband/wife relationship. See "link-to-life," page 894.
2. Or divide into teams that take the role of the board of a seminary that taught its students a biblical concept of spiritual authority—and found people in the churches perceived its graduates as "weak leaders." What should the seminary board do? See "link-to-life," page 895.

Apply
Pair husbands and wives to agree on a diagram that represents how their relationship does, or should, function. Or if group members are unmarried, have them diagram the relationship that existed between their parents. See "link-to-life," page 894 for ideas.

STUDY GUIDE 139

Galatians 1–2

THE GOSPEL

Overview
Paul's brief letter to the Galatians is one of the New Testament's earliest, probably written around A.D. 49. Like Romans, it explores the relationship of the Mosaic Law to the Gospel of Jesus Christ and, like Romans, concludes that Law was temporary. It has now been replaced by a better, more effective way of relating to God through the Spirit.

Also like Romans, Galatians is concerned with the experience of holiness, and how God's people can live a righteous life. Paul shows us here that, though it may initially seem frightening to remove the strictures of Law, God's better way produces a righteousness which the Mosaic Code could never produce. Christ has set us free for freedom—not freedom *from* righteousness, but freedom to be truly good (Gal. 5:1). This little book has proven exciting to generation after generation of Christians, who through it have realized that they are saved by faith—and that the Christian life is *lived* by faith as well!

▶ *Gospel.* The "Gospel" is mentioned a number of times in the first chapter of this letter. The Greek word simply means "good news." But Paul intended us to understand a specific content: there is an unmixed "Gospel of grace" which Paul preached, and an "other gospel" which is a mixture of faith and works, grace and law. In this little book we and our students are helped to understand the real Gospel, the Gospel of grace.

Commentary
It was early when the apostle rolled over on his pallet and saw the shafts of morning sunlight sifting through the shutters.

The confrontation over Peter's sudden unwillingness to eat with Gentile converts (Gal. 2:12) had heightened Paul's awareness of the dangers facing the young church. Then messengers had come, reporting that delegations of Christian Pharisees had visited the cities where churches had been planted. They taught that the Gentile Christians must place themselves under the Law of Israel, and many were obeying them.

Deeply burdened, Paul had called a number of the brothers together and prayed with them through most of the night.

Now, fully awake, Paul decided to act. Filled with a deep sense of urgency, he found a pen and papyrus sheets and attacked the task he had set himself. His pen raced; passionate phrases appeared. All the churches in southern Galatia must receive a copy of this, his first letter of instruction and his first attempt to set down a theology for the new Christian movement.

"Paul, an apostle—sent not from men nor by man, but by Jesus Christ" (1:1). These Judaizers claimed to be authorized by the Jerusalem church. As if man's authorization counted!

"I am astonished that you are so quickly deserting the One who called you by the grace of Christ and are turning to a different gospel" (v. 6). Yes, God knows it *is* a different gospel! The Gospel rests solely on the grace of God. These Judaizers would make it a gospel of works-plus-faith. But works-plus-faith is not the Gospel; it is a distortion that robs the Good News of its grace. It is a different, perverted gospel!

"Am I now trying to win the approval of men, or of God? Or am I trying to please men? (v. 10) The gall of those Judaizers! "Paul just tried to make it easy for you," they had suggested. "He was trying to please you, afraid of your response if he didn't make the Gospel easy. But," they had continued, "there's no such thing as 'easy believism' to the Gospel. God insists that your faith cost you something!"

Paul's pen raced on. *"The Gospel I preached*

is not something that man made up. . . . I received it by revelation from Jesus Christ" (vv. 11-12). On and on, the words filled sheet after sheet. How exciting now to put down on paper all the deep understanding and struggles that the one-time Pharisee had spent years working through in his own life. How exciting to share with the brothers—the little children he himself had midwifed into God's kingdom—the full glory of what the Gospel is, and the glorious fulfillment that is offered to all who believe in Christ!

The scene just sketched is imaginary. But it must have been much like this. It's easy to visualize Paul pouring out his love and concern in those passionate words to the Galatians which we read in our New Testament.

And even today, Paul's words are needed. Today too questions arise and Christians feel concern about the true nature of the Christian Gospel. Isn't it a little too easy to just "accept Christ"? Can we really say that salvation is through faith and by grace, plus *nothing*? Shouldn't a Christian at least be expected to live a certain holy life after he has come to know Jesus? Shouldn't God have a right to reject a person who believes in Jesus, but shows no respect for God by continuing to sin?

In a later letter to the Romans (which we'll study with the last chapters of this book) Paul goes on to define the relationship of the Gospel to righteousness. He shows just how the Gospel produces a holy life. But in Galatians the focal point of Paul's instruction is different. The relationship between Law and God's grace is at issue. The question is, "What lies at the heart of the pure Gospel?"

♥ ***Link to Life: Youth / Adult***
Set your group members to work in teams. Each team is to develop three distorted *statements of the Gospel. That is, the Gospel is to be stated in such a way that it is different than the Gospel as presented in the Scriptures. The more subtle the distortions the better.*

When each team is finished, write their statements on a chalkboard or overhead. Then work as a group to eliminate the distortions *from each statement.*

This process may well lead to disagreement. Do not force a conclusion in that case, but rather work together to develop questions about the Gospel your group members may have, which you can promise will be answered during your study of the Book of Galatians.

Paul's Defense of His Gospel: Galatians 1:1–2:10
After Paul and Barnabas returned to Antioch from their first missionary journey, they found men who had come from Judea and were teaching that "unless you are circumcised, according to the custom taught by Moses, you cannot be saved" (Acts 15:1). This teaching implied far more than simply accepting circumcision.

In the Old Testament, circumcision was a key element in the covenant God had made with Abraham. A Hebrew boy, on the eighth day of his life, was to have the fold of skin covering the end of his penis cut off. God said to Abraham, "Any uncircumcised male, who has not been circumcised in the flesh, will be cut off from his people; he has broken My covenant" (Gen. 17:14). To the Judaizers this act symbolized, as it does in Scripture, becoming a true Jew. In other words, this teaching implied that to be a Christian, one must first become a Jew. And the Bible makes it clear that the Judaizers intended exactly this: "the Gentiles must be circumcised and required to obey the Law of Moses," just as every Jew was required to do! (Acts 15:5)

The Judaizers were apparently aggressive, visiting not only Antioch but also going to other Gentile churches. And these men, who apparently did believe in Jesus, claimed a special authority for their teaching: "We are from *Jerusalem*! We're members of the first (and thus the true?) church!"

Paul and Barnabas vigorously opposed the men who taught this in Antioch (v. 2). So Paul and Barnabas, along with some others, were appointed to go to Jerusalem and see what the apostles and elders there had to say about this question.

The Judaizers had *not* been commissioned by the Jerusalem church. Nonetheless, once this issue was raised, this first council of the church held "much discussion" (v. 7) on the matter. The result was that the church recognized the fact that God showed He had accepted the Gentiles "by giving the Holy Spirit to them, just as He did to us. He made no distinction between us and them for He purified their hearts by faith." It would thus be wrong for the Judaizers to "try to test God by putting on the necks of the disciples a yoke [the Law] that neither we nor our fathers were able to bear." The Judaizers insistence on circumcision and Law was rejected, for "we believe it is through the grace of our Lord Jesus that we are saved" (vv. 8-11).

All this seems to have happened after Paul wrote his letter to the Galatians, though this is debated. Surely Paul made no mention of the determination of the Jerusalem Council, which it seems likely he would have if its determination had been made before he wrote.

All in all, we can credit both Paul and Barnabas with recognizing the threat to the Gospel posed by those who would mix it with Law. Even Peter, as we'll see later, did not "act in line with the truth of the Gospel" in this matter (Gal. 2:14).

In his letter to the Galatian churches, then, Paul could not defend his position by referring to the determination of the gathered leaders of the Christian church. Instead, Paul had to develop a different line of defense.

Another Gospel (Gal. 1:6-10). The Greek language makes a clear distinction between "others." There is another of the same kind (*allos*), and another of a different kind (*heteros*). Paul, after a few words of greeting, launched immediately into a confrontation with the Judaizers. What the latecomers preached was *not* the Gospel Paul had shared: it was a "different gospel" which because of the difference was "no gospel at all."

With no equivocation, Paul condemned that perverted gospel, and also those who preached it: let such a person "be eternally condemned" (v. 9).

The Judaizers had accused Paul of weakening the Gospel to "please men" and to "win the approval of men." That is, they claimed that Paul shaded the truth because he didn't want conflict, and instead wanted an "easy" message. Paul's confrontation with those who preach the "different gospel" would now show just how willing the apostle was to fight for the truth of the Gospel he had been charged by God with delivering (v. 10).

Received by direct revelation (Gal. 1:11-17). Paul had been a persecutor of the church when he was converted. He "went immediately" into Arabia, and there struggled to understand the Old Testament in light of his experience with Jesus. Paul stressed, "I did not consult any man, nor did I go up to Jerusalem to see those who were apostles before I was."

This was important to Paul. The Judaizers claimed an authority they said was derived from Jerusalem. Paul claimed an apostleship equal to that of the Twelve, and a revelation which came to him directly by God.

Confirmed by the other apostles (Gal. 1:18–2:5). Paul spoke of twice going to Jerusalem to "get acquainted with" the leaders there.

His second trip was directed by God, to "set before them the Gospel that I preach among the Gentiles" (2:2). The leaders confirmed Paul's Gospel, and affirmed that he had been right in confronting the "false brothers" who sought to introduce legalism. On that trip the Jerusalem leaders had accepted Titus, a Greek, as a brother and had not even suggested he should be circumcised.

Paul's experience with the other apostles, then, suggests that there was no conflict with the Gospel he preached and the Gospel as it was understood by leaders in Jerusalem.

Paul's commission affirmed (Gal. 2:6-10). The leaders in Jerusalem "added nothing to my message." Instead they recognized Paul's calling, to take the Gospel to the Gentiles, even as Peter's calling was to bring the Gospel to the Jews in the Holy Land and throughout the world.

The only concern the leaders in Jerusalem expressed was that the Gentile churches should "continue to remember the poor," which Paul was eager to do.

Paul thus has buttressed the claim which he made when he began this argument:

> The Gospel I preached is not something that man made up. I did not receive it from any man, nor was I taught it; rather, I received it by revelation from Jesus Christ.
>
> Galatians 1:11-12

Paul stood for the Gospel because he was convinced that the Good News he presented is true, and that he held a commission from God Himself to proclaim it in Gentile lands (see vv. 15-16).

Confrontation: Galatians 2:11-21
It's clear from both Galatians and Acts that the confrontation that occurred between Peter and Paul in Antioch dealt with a basic issue. And at that point, only Paul realized what this issue was.

Peter had come to visit the church in Antioch, and at first had gladly participated fully in the body's life. But when some of the Judaizer party arrived as well, Peter drew back from the Gentile believers. And other Jewish believers in Antioch followed Peter's example!

This action, which divided the church into two camps, was not "acting in line with the truth of the Gospel."

There's no doubt that Peter's action and that of the Jewish minority must have hurt the Antioch believers personally. It implied that Gentile believers were second-class citizens in God's kingdom.

But Paul saw more than the momentary hurt, and more than the hypocrisy. Paul saw the deadly intrusion of Law into the Gospel message. Paul reacted. He confronted Peter publicly, and charged him with hypocrisy.

> We who are Jews by birth and not "Gentile sinners" know that a man is not justified by observing the Law, but by faith in Jesus Christ.
>
> Galatians 2:15-16

Those who put their faith in Christ ought not to mix Gospel and Law, but affirm a justification that comes from faith alone. "A man is not justified by observing the Law, but by faith in Jesus Christ. . . . Because by observing the Law no one will be justified" (v. 16). God's verdict, declaring a person forgiven and free from the guilt and penalty his sins deserve—and God's power, breaking the bondage of sin to free an individual to become truly good, have nothing to do with the Law. Justification is a gift of grace, freely extended to all who put their faith in Jesus Christ.

"I do not set aside the grace of God," Paul insisted, "for if righteousness could be gained through the Law, Christ died for nothing" (v. 21).

Life and Law. It is still a little difficult to grasp what Paul was saying. That is, until we see the key place of Galatians 2:20:

> I have been crucified with Christ and I no longer live, but Christ lives in me. The life I live in the body, I live by faith in the Son of God, who loved me and gave Himself for me.
>
> Galatians 2:20-21

Jesus' mission on earth was not to utter some new call for redoubled effort to keep the Law. Jesus' mission, and the heart of the Gospel—was to issue an invitation to life. It is tremendously dangerous to let our own focus shift from *life* to the *Law.*

Righteousness can never come through the Law. Only new life can bring us that justification from God which means both (1) entrance into a new relationship with God and (2) the dynamic of God's power within to make possible the love, goodness, and holiness which all religions hold out as an ideal, but only the Christian faith is able to produce.

This issue is clarified in Paul's climactic statement to Peter. And with this said in the letter, Paul moved on immediately to an explosive statement that analyzes the differences between the two approaches to the Gospel. Is the believer to work out his relationship with God through the Law, or is he to do it by recognizing the nature and dynamic of life?

As we move on in this letter, we will discover *why* the legalistic approach to Christian experience is doomed to fail. And we will catch the New Testament's first glimpse of the life principle which brings us freedom.

For any who have ever felt burdened in his or her Christian life, or felt weighed down by "oughts" and "shoulds," these next chapters contain the charter deed to personal freedom and to joy.

♥ ***Link to Life: Youth / Adult***
Analyze Paul's confrontation with Peter, Galatians 2:11-21. What does it suggest about the influence of legalism? About Paul's character and commitment?

Then work in teams to define: Exactly how was Peter "not acting in line with the truth of the Gospel"? Also in teams, try to paraphrase Galatians 2:14-21, the words Paul spoke to Peter.

In the Victor *Bible Knowledge Commentary* Dr. Donald K. Campbell has this helpful explanation of Galatians 2:20:

In Galatians 2:20 Paul enlarged on the meaning of verse 19. He "died to the Law" because "he [Paul] was crucified with Christ"; he was able to "live for God" because Christ lived in him. Basic to an understanding of this verse is the meaning of union with Christ. This doctrine is based on such passages as Romans 6:1-6 and 1 Corinthians 12:13, which explain that believers have been baptized by the Holy Spirit into Christ and into the church, the body of all true believers. Having been thus united to Christ, believers share in His death, burial, and resurrection. Paul could therefore write, "I have been crucified with Christ" (lit., "I have been and am now crucified with Christ"). This brought death to the Law. It also brought a change in regard to one's self: "And I no longer live." The self-righteous, self-centered Saul died. Further, death with Christ ended Paul's enthronement of self; he yielded the throne of his life to Another, to Christ. But it was not in his own strength that Paul was able to live the Christian life; the living Christ Himself took up His abode in Paul's heart: Christ "lives in me." Yet Christ does not operate automatically in a believer's life; it is a matter of living the new life "by faith in the Son of God." It is then faith and not works or legal obedience that releases divine power to live a Christian life.

What a wonderful affirmation we have here of the core of the Gospel. It is by faith from first to last, for faith releases the power of God to be at work within our personalities, to express Jesus through our lives.

TEACHING GUIDE

Prepare
You may wish to supplement group activities from material on Paul's life (see Study Guide 117), or from material on the Jerusalem Council (see Study Guide 121).

Explore
1. Divide into teams to formulate statements of the Gospel which will be subtly "different" from the Gospel as it is presented in Scripture. Your group will then work together to get rid of the distortions. In the process your members will become aware of any problem in their own understanding of the Gospel and will be motivated for study of the rest of this great New Testament book. See "link-to-life," page 898 for how-to ideas.

Expand
1. In a minilecture review the approach of the Judaizers, as it is discussed in the commentary on Acts 15 and on Galatians 1.
2. Work together or in teams to first explain, then to paraphrase what Paul was saying in his confrontation with Peter as reported in Acts 2:11-21. See "link-to-life," page 900.
3. Write Galatians 2:20-21 on the chalkboard. Ask each group member to pick a single phrase, and share what the truth represented means to him or her. Or a group member may choose a phrase he or she does not understand, and ask a question about it.

Apply
One paraphrase of Galatians 2:20 suggests, "If He loved me enough to give Himself for me, then He loves me enough to live out His life in me." Share this paraphrase, and ask each group member to meditate on it as a closing prayer.

STUDY GUIDE 140

Galatians 3:1–5:12

GOOD NEWS OF FAITH

Overview
In Galatians we have Paul's first powerful defense of the Gospel. Some from the Pharisee party in Judea who had trusted Christ apparently retained their zeal for the Mosaic Law. They traveled to the churches Paul had founded, and taught that the Gentile Christians they must be circumcised and must keep the Law of Moses to be saved. In essence, they said that to be a true Christian a Gentile must become Jewish in lifestyle, and live by the Old Testament's code.

Paul confronted this view, insisting that what these men taught was different gospel from the Gospel of God's grace in Jesus Christ. Paul insisted that there can be no mixture of Law and grace in the Gospel of Christ without robbing the Gospel of its power.

Now, in the extended and carefully argued bulk of Galatians, Paul explained *why* the Law is not for Christians now. Paul's argument emphasized three points: The Law is opposed to life (3:1-18). The role given Law in Scripture is a limited one (3:19–4:7). And, the Law is an inferior path which leads to spiritual disasters (4:8–5:12).

For further background on the New Testament's view of Law as it relates to the Christian life, see Study Guide 126.

■ It will be helpful as you prepare to teach this important passage to read through a good verse-by-verse commentary like the *Bible Knowledge Commentary,* pages 596-606.

Commentary
In Paul's initial defense of his Gospel he reported a conflict which he had with Peter in Antioch. When even Peter was influenced by members of the Pharisee party, and separated himself from Gentile Christians, Paul confronted him.

"We who are Jews by birth," Paul said, "know that a man is not justified by observing the Law, but by faith in Jesus Christ" (Gal. 2:15-16). Paul then pointed out that all the Law was able to do was to demonstrate that the one under it was a lawbreaker. There was no power in the Law to create holiness.

But the Christian is not under Law, because "through the Law I died to the Law so that I might live for God" (v. 19). That is, because of the Christian's union with Christ the believer is legally released from the Law. How? By dying with the Saviour. For a person who is "dead" is not responsible to keep the Old Testament code, but is released from its hold.

Thus the Christian, as the old man who was crucified with Christ, no longer lives. But our union with Jesus was not just union in His death (Rom. 6:1-6). It was also union with Jesus in His resurrection. Now "Christ lives in me." In fact, the daily life of the believer is the Christ life, lived "by faith in the Son of God, who loved me and gave Himself for me" (Gal. 2:20).

This is the key to understanding the Gospel. What the Gospel offers is not just forgiveness, but new life! And that new life is lived by faith, *not* by a return to the Law. And so, Paul concluded, "I do not set aside the grace of God, for if righteousness could be gained through the Law, Christ died for nothing" (v. 21).

This powerful and wonderful affirmation of life in Christ, and of faith as the key to our experience of that life, is the background against which Paul now analyzed Law. The Law, while an expression of the holiness of God and good in itself, could never produce life, and indeed has nothing to do with life. If we think of the Gospel of God's grace in terms of the new life it provides, and then understand the faith principle which enables us to experience the new

Life Versus Law

GALATIANS 3–5

Why isn't the Law for us now?

I. The Law is opposed to life (3:1-18). This is demonstrated by:
   A. Experience: How did you first receive and live your spiritual life? (3:1-5)
   B. Example: How did Old Testament saints receive spiritual life? (3:6-9)
   C. Exposition: What does the Scripture teach about how life is to be received? (3:10-18).

II. The Law's role (3:19–4:7) is shown in Scripture to be severely limited:
   A. In extent: It is temporary (3:19-20).
   B. In ability: It cannot make alive (3:21-22).
   C. In function: It was a custodian (3:23-24).
   D. In force: It is nullified today (3:25–4:8).
      1. Because we are "in Christ"
      2. Because we are now sons

III. The Law is an inferior way that now leads to tragic results for the believer (4:8–5:12). Law leads to:
   A. Dissatisfaction: It robs us of joy (4:8-19).
   B. Bondage: It robs us of freedom (4:20–5:1).
   C. Powerlessness: It turns us from expectant faith to hopeless effort (5:2-12).

life, we will see why legalism is futile.

In Galatians 3:1–5:12 we look at the first part of this spiritual equation: the futility of trying to link Law with life. Then, in Galatians 5:13–6:16, we see the second part: the secret of how to live our new life in Christ by faith.

♥ ***Link to Life: Youth / Adult***

Begin this session with sharing. Ask simply: "What has been the greatest help to you in learning to live a Christian life?"

Encourage each person to share.

When the sharing is complete, introduce the session with a brief review of Galatians 2:11-21.

Paul in Galatians rejected the "different gospel" of the Judaizers who would bring Law back into the believer's relationship with God. The contrast that Paul drew between life and Law is the key that helps us trace his argument and outline this great book.

Why Not Law? Galatians 3:1–5:12

The major portion of Galatians, as reflected in the outline, is a devastating critique of looking to the Law for help in living the Christian life. Before we trace through each passage, let's take a look at some of the particularly significant points Paul made.

Importance of faith (Gal. 3:10). Paul spoke in this passage to "all who *rely* on observing the Law." He did not suggest that the Law itself is somehow bad or wrong. What he did insist was that the Law had never had anything to do with faith, and therefore that reliance on the Law, either as a way of salvation, or as a way to work out one's salvation, was inappropriate.

Paul made an interesting point in verses 15-18. If the Law was so important, how did people ever get along without it? The Law wasn't even introduced until some 430 years after Abraham's day. Certainly Abraham and the other patriarchs had meaningful relationships with God!

Most important, however, is the fact that the principle of faith in God's promise (v. 16) which was introduced in Abraham was never set aside by the subsequent introduction of Law. Faith has *always* been the way to God; God's promise has never depended on keeping that latecomer, the Law.

Law for restraint (Gal. 3:19-29). The Law was introduced because of sin, and thus it relates to sin, not holiness. The Law was to be a *temporary* expedient, to function only until Christ came.

Picture, if you will, a raging tiger trapped behind bars. The bars were introduced because the tiger's wild impulses make him dangerous to all. Would anyone expect the *bars* to tame the tiger? Of course not! That is not the purpose of bars; they are to *restrain*. What happens, then, if someone does succeed in taming the tiger, using a different principle than putting him in a cage? The bars can be removed! There is no longer any use for them.

This, essentially, is Paul's argument. Now that faith has come and believers have been "clothed . . . with Christ" (v. 27), we have been truly tamed! How foolish, then, to insist that the tamed beast continue to live behind bars! Especially when all along God had affirmed His intention of removing the bars as soon as the new and living Way came (see Jer. 31:31-34).

Law as teacher (Gal. 4:1-7). Paul used another illustration to make the same point. It was common in the Greek culture of his day to place a young child under the supervision of a family slave, called a *pedagogue* (a word sometimes translated in Gal. 4:2 as "guardian," "trustee," "manager," etc.). The pedagogue made sure that the child obeyed the parent, whether the child wanted to obey, or not. Until the children would "receive the full rights of sons" (v. 5) they were, in fact, no more than the slaves of a slave! They had to obey a slave who obeyed their father.

But then the great day came when a child was accepted as an adult. Now the father spoke directly to him. Now the son responded directly to his father. The pedagogue had no more place in their relationship.

The Law, Paul said, was a pedagogue. Jesus' redemption act is that great event in history marking the transition from childhood to sonship. The Law, which up until Jesus had a pedagogue's purpose, now had nothing to do with our relationship with God! "So you are no longer a slave, but a son; and since you are a son, God has made you also an heir" (v. 7).

It is striking to see what happens when people, still fearing the tiger in them and unable to grasp the fact that Christ really does tame, seek to hide behind the bars of legalism. Such legalism seems at first to promise a certain kind of security. Its bars not only keep us in; they keep others out.

But Christ's people are not made to cower in barred caves and cages! We have been shaped by God to live on the plains and in the mountains and, yes, in the jungles of the whole wide world. Jesus Himself set us the example. He stepped boldly from the security of heaven and was caught up in the rush and swirl, the joys and agonies of human experience. He entered the homes of publicans and sinners, enjoyed the wedding parties, reached out to touch and heal the hurting, and confronted the hardened Pharisees. Jesus was totally involved—yet uncontaminated. He rubbed shoulders with sinners—and remained pure. He lived with and like other men—and revealed God. His whole life was an adventure.

It is to just this kind of adventurous life that you and I are called today. Jesus did not come

Law, the Pedagogue—*Until* Christ

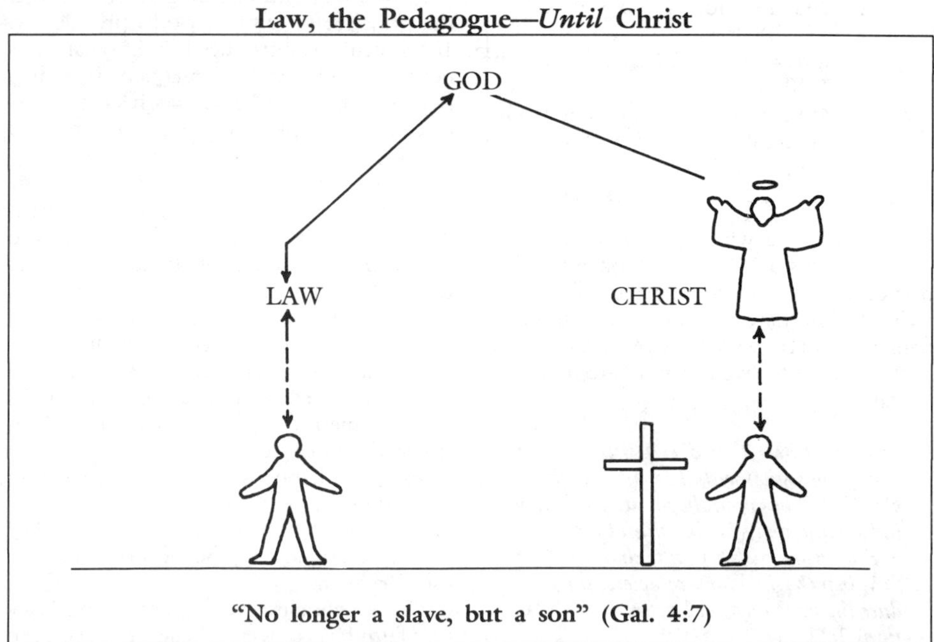

"No longer a slave, but a son" (Gal. 4:7)

to bring a new set of bars for our cages. He came to tame the tiger in us and to release us, to live as He Himself lived in the world of men.

The meaning of our lives, the adventure of it, isn't to be found in the cages that Christians make for themselves and decorate so attractively. No, meaning and joy for us are to be found in stepping outside the old cages, dismissing the no-longer-needed pedagogues, and setting out into the future to live as *sons*.

All too often, Christians draw back.

We fear.

We don't realize that as God's sons we now have His life. Like the Judaizers of Paul's day, we hurriedly try to shape new bars as fast as God tears them down. In deepest agony Paul cried out to the cage-builders of his day, "How is it that you are turning back to those weak and miserable principles? Do you wish to be enslaved by them all over again?" (v. 9)

You will lose your joy there (v. 15).

You will lose your freedom (5:1).

You will lose your power (v. 3). You will lose all that Jesus died to make available to you as you live your new life in Him.

Falling away (Gal. 5:4). This verse has troubled many. It reads, "You who are trying to be justified by Law have been alienated from Christ; you have fallen away from grace." What was Paul saying?

It's important to realize that here Paul was focusing on present-tense salvation, not on past-tense. What Paul meant when he warned against falling away from grace must be grasped from the context of the passage.

Paul had shown that the Law was a pedagogue. Once, Law was the avenue through which a believer experienced his relationship with God. But now that relationship is direct and personal, as with a child who at last receives the "full rights" of sonship (4:5). What, then, if a son keeps going back to his old pedagogue for directions? Clearly, he has alienated himself from the personal relationship. Such a fall from grace back into old practices and ways means simply that the individual *is no better off than he was before*! All the freedom, all the joy, all the adventure of the life a child of God is to live by faith, has been drained away—traded for something that is worse than nothing. "Christ will be of no value to you at all" means simply that being a Christian will not make the *difference* in daily life He intends it to. A person will be no better off than he was before being a Christian, as far as living the Christian life is concerned.

This seems a hard thing to say. No better off? Why, heaven has been won, at least.

Yes, but the Christian faith is not solely concerned with eternity. The Christian faith includes God's affirmation that life *now* is important too—important to God, important to others, and important to you.

The wonderful life that God offers you and me in Christ is one which provides a solid hope for meaning, joy, and fulfillment today. And that life is appropriated by faith, not by trying to keep the Law.

♥ ***Link to Life: Youth / Adult***

Draw on the chalkboard the best tiger you can. Explain, as in the author's analogy, that the tiger's nature makes him dangerous. So we put bars around him to make a cage. Then set your group the task of coming up with predictions *and* guidelines. *Predict: "What will happen if the bars are removed?" Guidelines: "Under what condition(s) will it be safe to remove the bars?"*

After discussion explain that we are the tigers, the Law the bars of the cage, and that if our tiger-nature is changed, there is no need for bars.

Or use the illustration on page 904, and explain the "pedagogue" role in biblical times, and the implications of Paul's argument.

Then give each group member the outline on page 903, and ask pairs to read through Galatians 3:1–5:12, guided by it. Each pair is to (1) note every reason given why the believer is freed from Law, and (2) to put a check mark beside verses or phrases he or she does not understand.

Come back together after 15 to 20 minutes to compare observations and ask questions.

Observations on the Text: Galatians 3:1–5:12

The Law is opposed to life (Gal. 3:1-18). Paul launched his argument against the "different gospel" of the Judaizers by expressing amazement. Their own experience with God was rooted in faith, not Law (vv. 1-5). "Did you receive the Spirit by observing the

Law, or by believing what you heard?" It was not Law that brought them life; the key in their conversion was faith. "Are you so foolish?" Paul asked, that "after beginning with the Spirit, are you now trying to attain your goal by human effort?" (v. 3) The Spirit actually had operated among these churches and worked miracles not through observing Law, but "because you believe what you heard."

It is clear, then, from the experience of modern Christians that life in Christ is a matter of faith from first to last. If life is received and lived by faith, why then turn to the Law as an aid to spiritual attainment?

Not only has faith proven to be the key to modern Christian experience, but it was also the key to the experience of Old Testament saints (vv. 6-9). Abraham "believed God" and it was his faith that was credited to him as righteousness.

But *why* hadn't the Law functioned in the spiritual experience of Abraham and all those generations after him whose relationship with God was rooted in faith? Because the Law and faith are contrary principles. Law condemns, bringing under its curse all who do not "do everything" written in it (v. 10). Christ died to release us from the "curse of the Law" so that we might relate to God through faith.

The Law, according to the Scriptures, is severely limited (Gal. 3:19–4:7). First, Law was not only added long after faith was introduced as the principle by which we relate to God (3:17-18), but was always intended to be *temporary,* in effect only until Christ (the Seed) came (vv. 19-20).

Second, Law never had the function of bringing life; that was the role given to faith (vv. 21-22).

Third, Law was merely a pedagogue, a family slave intended to watch over young children until "faith should be revealed." Its goal was to "lead us to Christ that we might be justified by faith" (vv. 23-24).

Finally, the Law is no longer in force as far as we are concerned (we are "no longer under the supervision of the Law"). In Christ we are now "sons" and as such not subject to a pedagogue. We all—male and female, slave and free—have received the "full rights of sons."

The phrase, "full rights of sons," reflects Roman law rather than Jewish traditions. In Roman law the father had authority over every member of his family. He was also considered to own his children's property, and had the right to control their behavior, including the right to discipline. But the father was also committed to help his child, and as an heir, what the father possessed was considered to belong to the child as well. All the resources of God become ours as heirs of God, and we are able to draw directly on them to live our new lives.

This relationship is an immediate and personal one, and is not mediated through some go-between who, like Law, has no more standing than a family slave.

Attempts to live by the Law lead only to spiritual disaster (Gal. 4:8–5:12). What happens within when a believer tries to live as if under the Law rather than as a son with a direct, immediate relationship with God?

The person who tries to relate to God by rigorous legalism will, as the Galatians, lose his or her joy (see 4:15).

That individual will find himself or herself in bondage, living as a slave rather than a freeman (4:21–5:1). Paul considered a historical event a figurative expression of a basic principle (see. Gen. 21:8-21). Sarah, childless, had urged Abraham to follow contemporary custom and father a child with her slave, Hagar. The child of this "surrogate mother" would legally be Abraham's and Sarah's. Abraham had finally given in, and Hagar bore a son, Ishmael. But rather than joy, the child brought Sarah only pain. Hagar looked down on her mistress, for it was now clear that her childlessness was not due to Abraham's inability to father a child. Ishmael thus became a constant reminder to Sarah of her own failure as a wife.

Later, when Sarah did have the child God promised Abraham, Isaac, Sarah's resentment increased. By custom Ishmael would receive a major share in Abraham's estate. Sarah wanted it all for her son, Isaac. She demanded that Abraham send Ishmael away.

At first Abraham refused. He not only cared for Ishmael, but in those days to reject Ishmael would be a crime against the boy.

But God intervened.

God told Abraham to expel Ishmael and Hagar, and God promised that He would Himself take care of Ishmael and bless him. Reassured but reluctant, Abraham did as his wife urged, but only at God's command.

Looking back, Paul realized why God

told Abraham to do something so foreign to his character. Sarah had been right, but not for her selfish reason when she said, "Get rid of the slave woman and her son, for the slave woman's son will never share in the inheritance with the free woman's son" (Gen. 21:10; Gal. 4:30). The principle of promise and of Law simply do not and cannot mix. Only the one who is a son on the basis of God's promise can inherit God's blessing. There is no hope for one who seeks relationship on the basis of Law.

Paul concluded his argument with a powerful statement. Anyone who lets himself be circumcised (that is, places himself under Law) finds that "Christ will be of no value to you at all" (5:2). What did Paul mean?

It's as if you stood at a fork in the road, with one path leading to the north and the other to the south. You must choose one path or the other. You cannot choose both, for they lead in opposite directions.

The Galatian Christians, like you and I, stand always at just such a fork. We must either take the path of relating to God through Law, or of relating to God through the faith. *We cannot have it both ways.* If we are trying to relate to God through the Law, we are not living by faith. And if we are living by faith, we turn our backs on all that Law implied. Being a Christian will make no practical difference in our lives ("Christ will be of no value to you"). We who are called to live in the sphere of God's grace will fall from that grace. Our hope for transformation now will be replaced by futile self-effort, for "the only thing that counts is faith expressing itself through love" (v. 6).

As we go on in Galatians we will discover more about what it means to live by faith. But for now, we know one thing for sure. Focusing our attention on trying to keep God's Law is not the answer, either for salvation or for the abundant Christian life.

There is something, something linked with faith, that provides a far better way.

TEACHING GUIDE

Prepare

If you are unclear about any of the concepts introduced in this study guide, check the *index* for references to the Law and to faith.

Explore

Ask each person in your group to list three things that have been most helpful to him or her in growing in the Christian life.

Then list on the chalkboard, and discuss. Note particularly whether or not anyone lists the Law or the Ten Commandments as an aid to his or her spiritual growth. If no one does, ask why not. If someone does, ask how it has helped.

Expand

1. Tell the story of the tiger whose wild nature led him to be placed behind bars. Have your group both predict what would happen if the bars were removed, and define conditions under which the bars might be safely removed. See "link-to-life," page 905.
2. Explain the image of the Law as pedagogue, which Paul used. See illustration on page 904.
3. Distribute a copy of the outline of chapters 3–5 to each group member. Let them work through the passage in pairs, jotting down any questions, and recording Paul's reasons why the Law has no relevance to the Christian's life. See "link-to-life" on page 905.

Apply

Share: "What does it mean to you to hear Paul say: 'It is for freedom that Christ has set us free'? What *is* freedom, and how do we stand fast in it?" (Gal. 5:1)

STUDY GUIDE 141

Galatians 5:13–6:18

THE GOOD NEWS OF FREEDOM

Overview

In Galatians Paul was deeply concerned with contrasting his Gospel with a counterfeit taught by Judaizers—men who insisted that to be a Christian one must keep the Mosaic Law.

Paul first characterized his Gospel. It is a Gospel of life; life that is ours through faith in Christ. The Law could never produce life, nor enrich it. Law was a temporary expedient, a household slave charged with directing the immature till Christ appeared. Now that Jesus has come and reaffirmed the ancient place of faith, Law is no longer relevant. Now there is an exciting freedom: freedom found in a new, direct relationship with God; freedom to live a truly good life.

Now, in the final section of the Book of Galatians Paul explained how the dynamic of faith operates in the believer to produce a righteousness that Law was never able to generate. As we read it, we need to be aware of several key terms, and how each of these terms is used in Paul's argument. The key words are:

- freedom • sinful nature
- the Spirit • new creation
- fruit

There are also key phrases. Among them are "live by the Spirit" (5:16), "led by the Spirit" (v. 18), and "keep in step with the Spirit" (v. 25).

As we study this passage we will realize in a fresh way the wonder of the Good News of Jesus, and its promise for each life.

Commentary

For the first time in his life, Jim found himself wildly cursing. The vicious words poured out, fed by a rage that both frightened and exhilarated him. His face twisted with anger, Jim shouted out words that he had been too ashamed even to think.

"Good! Good!" encouraged the young professor when Jim's rage finally collapsed in sudden exhaustion. "Jim, you're really learning to express your feelings. The real you is finally surfacing."

The scene is imaginary, but it has been repeated many times. The young professor represents one particular school of psychological therapy. "We're only allowed to talk about the here and now. And we're going to learn to express what we really feel. So whatever you feel—about yourself, about anyone else here—I want you to express it openly and honestly."

Such instructions are designed to break through the barriers of convention that cause people to repress their feelings, and to help them find a kind of release. The notion seems to be that by bringing negative feelings out into the open, the person will rid himself of them. Somehow this process is supposed to give a new freedom to individuals to find themselves, and to grow.

This is *not* a picture of Christian freedom. Such excesses can turn us away from the whole idea of freedom. Some of us are frightened to discover that God has now taken away the bars of the Law and has left us uncaged. No wonder that we, like the Galatians, rush to build new cages! We not only seek safety from a hostile world, but we just as desperately try to place restraints on our hostile selves. We know only too well the hidden thoughts and motives, the secret desires, that we struggle to keep buried. If the bars of the Law are taken away, won't something terrible in us be released?

♥ ***Link to Life: Youth / Adult***

What does "freedom" mean to most people, and how does their notion of freedom affect their lives? Divide your group into teams. Each team is to take one of three people and on the basis of his or her view of "freedom," predict how he or she is likely to behave: on the job, at home, in friendship. The people are:

- Jack. *Jack is a libertarian. To Jack, freedom means, "I do what I want to do when I want."*
- Jenny. *Jenny is a legalist. To Jenny any thought of freedom is frightening. She looks to a long list of do's and don'ts to protect her from herself and others.*
- Jan. *Jan is a Christian whose idea of freedom is freedom to love Jesus and others.*

After each group has developed a profile of each individual, have them share with the rest. Discuss: "What is *freedom to the Christian? How have members of your group experienced freedom? Do they feel free now?"*

Freedom

The Bible insists, "It is for freedom that Christ has set us free" (Gal. 5:1). Scripture is not speaking of the kind of freedom the young professor was encouraging. For the Bible says, "Do not use your freedom to indulge the sinful nature; rather, serve one another in love" (v. 13). Christian freedom is designed to help us grow in goodness.

Let's be sure of one thing. In affirming freedom, the Christian is not expressing a desire to release sinful passions. In affirming freedom, the Christian responds to God's own call to shake off old bonds and to find Christ's pathway to goodness. The Law, throughout its long history, never succeeded in producing righteousness. We are to look beyond Law now—to a better way.

The group therapy offered Jim a counterfeit freedom. Encouragement to express anger and other negative feelings (in order to "get rid of" them or to "get in touch" with oneself) has been shown to produce just the opposite of the desired effect. The more a person expresses hostility, the more deeply he seems to feel it. And the more quickly he interprets others' actions as a cause for anger. For a person without Christ in a society of people who do not respond to God, the Law's restraints are both wise and necessary. Unchecked, the tiger within man does quickly take control.

But there is a basic difference between the believer who has established a personal relationship with God through faith and the unbeliever who has not. The Christian is no longer under the Law because, unlike other men, he can now "live by the Spirit" (v. 16). An entirely new principle of life governs and guides the believer and provides a basis for Christian freedom.

Made alive. One of the most exciting themes in Scripture is that of life. In Genesis we see God giving life to all His Creation. We see Him breathing a special life into Adam and Eve: physical life, and more! They were spiritually alive, aware of God, capable of fellowship with Him.

When Adam and Eve chose sin, they died spiritually (Gen. 2:17). This spiritual death was passed on to their children and became the one great devastating flaw in humankind. Dimly aware of God and goodness, man's spiritual deadness leads him to respond to the self-centered drives of his sin-warped nature rather than to God. "As for you, you were dead in your transgressions and sins," Paul wrote later in Ephesians 2:1. "All of us also lived among them at one time, gratifying the cravings of our sinful nature and following its desires and thoughts. Like the rest, we were by nature objects of wrath" (v. 3).

Man needs both human law and divine Law. Without restraint, with each individual given license to express his cravings, society would fall and individuals would prey on those weaker than they and, in turn, be a prey to the stronger.

If we think this picture is exaggerated, we are ignorant of history. The wars, the rapes, the murders, the systematic crimes of economic oppression, the private brutalities—all fill in the details of man's Fall. The very fear which so many feel when one speaks of freedom from the Law's restraint is adequate testimony that, deep down, each of us is already aware of man's depravity—by each being aware of our own.

But the Bible story does not stop at death. The Bible goes on to share the Good News of *life.* God "made us alive with Christ even when we were dead in transgressions" (v. 5). When we come by faith into a relationship with Jesus Christ, God plants His own new life within our personalities. All the New Testament writers speak of it. Peter, the other apostle on whom the Book of Acts focuses, put it this way: "For you are sons of God now; the live, permanent Word of the living God has given you His own indestructible heredity" (1 Peter 1:23, PH). There is a new kind of life swelling up within the Christian. It is God's kind of life, and our possession of God's life changes everything.

We wisely are afraid to remove the restraints from our old selves. But who feels a need to restrain God?

The Spirit. Now we will begin to penetrate to the root of our freedom. Six times in the next few verses of Galatians (5:16-25) Paul spoke of the Holy Spirit.

"Live by the Spirit" (v. 16).

"The Spirit . . . is contrary to the sinful nature" (v. 17).

"Led by the Spirit . . . not under law" (v. 18).

"The fruit of the Spirit" (v. 22).

"We live by the Spirit" (v. 25).

"Keep in step with the Spirit" (v. 25).

The dynamic of Christian freedom is found not only in the possession of new life but also in the person of the Holy Spirit. God Himself has entered us with His gift of power.

In affirming freedom, Paul was not telling us to let the old nature go on an orgy of selfish self-expression. Instead Paul was asking us to trust ourselves to God the Holy Spirit, and to look to Him alone to express through us that quality of life which is both new, and His own.

Only if the tiger in me is truly tamed do I dare take the bars away. With new life and through the Holy Spirit's power, I can at last find the courage to be free.

Observations on the Text: Galatians 5:13–6:18

This vital and exciting passage contains Paul's explanation of what he meant when he wrote in Galatians 2:20, "I no longer live, but Christ lives in me. The life I live in the body, I live by faith in the Son of God, who loved me and gave Himself for me." Paul found freedom not to be "himself," but to be his *new* self. And Paul realized that new life as God's own.

Christian freedom (Gal. 5:13-15). We are never to mistake Christian freedom for the kind of liberty the therapy group tried to force on Jim. Christian freedom is always in harmony with the Law, though it does not rely on the Law.

Christian freedom is not freedom "to indulge the sinful nature" but rather freedom to "serve one another in love." Here Paul argued, as he did in Romans 13:8-10, that the entire Law can be "summed up in this one rule: 'Love your neighbor as yourself.' " Thus the person who expresses the new life within him or her by loving others will find his actions actually fulfill the Law of God (see 8:3-4).

The problem with the Law has always been that while it warns us if we misuse freedom, it can never produce love. But now, with a new life from God and with the Holy Spirit granted to us, love *can* be produced in our hearts, and expressed in loving acts.

New nature and Holy Spirit (Gal. 5:16-18). The Holy Spirit is not motivated by the cravings of a sinful nature, for He does not possess one. We do possess a sin nature, which Law has never been able to change. So the real issue in the Christian life is whether we will live according to the old nature, or the new that has been given us in Jesus.

Paul argued that Law is linked with the old nature, for it speaks out against its sins. On the other hand, the Holy Spirit is associated with the new nature. If we surrender ourselves to the Spirit, to let Him guide or control us, then the Spirit will see to it that we do not "gratify the desires of [our] sinful nature" (v. 16).

The who issue of Christian life and freedom *has nothing to do* with the Law.

Acts of the sinful nature (Gal. 5:19-21). All those things which the Law speaks out against and is designed to protect society from are listed here. And they flow from the old, sinful human nature. As long as our sinful nature is in control, and its desires expressed in our actions, Paul's list of evils will appear in our lives.

Fruit of the Spirit (Gal. 5:22-26). As the sin nature produces its fruit in an individual's life, so the Holy Spirit also produces fruit. That fruit, love, joy, peace—all those things we yearn for—stand in stark contrast to the fruit produced by man's sinful nature. And that fruit appears as we walk by, and keep in step with, the Spirit of God.

And against this fruit no law has ever been passed.

Christian freedom must be understood in the context of man's two natures. Freedom is a release from the domination of the old and warped within us, and a release which gives the Spirit full reign to produce good fruit. Christian freedom is the capacity, and the strength, to act in love, to know and share joy, to experience and promote peace, and all those other blessings that come only through the Spirit of our God.

Freedom to Live

GALATIANS 5

"sinful nature" (death)	**"Spirit" (new life)**
Characteristics	
* not responsive to God * in conflict with the Spirit * ruled by its cravings	* responsive to God * in conflict with the sinful nature * ruled by God
Products	
immorality impurity debauchery idolatry and witchcraft hatred discord jealousy fits of rage selfish ambition dissensions factions envy drunkenness orgies	love joy peace patience kindness goodness faithfulness gentleness self-control
Relationship to the Law	
The Law is "against such things" (5:23) and was added "because of transgressions" (3:19).	NONE "Against such there is no law" (5:22).

Greetings and injunctions (Gal. 6:1-18). The last chapter of this early New Testament letter contains several injunctions and personal greetings. The brothers are encouraged not to deal harshly with those who are learning to walk the new life (vv. 1-2). One who falls should be restored gently. Each brother should seek to help others along the way and fulfill Christ's new commandment to love (John 13:33-34). Recognizing the divine source of the new life, each man can rejoice in his own gifts and actions without the kind of pride that comes from feeling better than someone else (Gal. 6:3-5).

In all of life's adventures, we can live in total honesty with ourselves and with God. We will never deceive ourselves into believing that Christian freedom is a license to sin (vv.7-10). We can always commit ourselves to doing good, sure that "at the proper time we will reap a harvest" (v. 9) of joy.

Summing up (vv. 12-18), Paul again pointed us to the cross of Jesus Christ, where He (and each believer too!) was crucified. Jesus died—but He rose again. In Him, you and I have risen as well to a new life in a new world. It is a world not ruled by the old Law but one filled with the vital presence of God Himself. In this new world "neither circumcision or uncircumcision means anything" (v. 15). Jew and Gentile meet at the cross, and at the cross each abandons his old lifestyle and culture, to find, as Christ's new creation, a new and better way.

♥ ***Link to Life: Youth / Adult***

Ask your group members to explore the implications of the image of "fruit" in this passage.

Draw a tree with roots and branches, on which fruit labeled love, joy, peace, etc., are found. The fruit are specifically said to be the "fruit of the Spirit."

What does that suggest about the Spirit's role? About our own? See how many different implications your group can draw in six minutes.

TEACHING GUIDE

Prepare
Be prepared to talk through these chapters, verse-by-verse, with your group members. The *Bible Knowledge Commentary's* verse-by-verse approach can supplement the material here.

Explore
1. Tell the story of Jim and his therapy group. Discuss: "If you were Jim, would this experience help you feel more free? Why, or why not? What would it make you feel? What in Jim's case would constitute freedom?"
2. Divide into teams, each of which is to take a different person's concept of freedom and from it develop a profile that suggests how that person will tend to act. See "link-to-life," pages 908-909.

Expand
1. Give a minilecture on the roots of Christian freedom, drawing on material in the commentary.
2. Then work with the whole group through these chapters, summing up paragraph by paragraph.

When you come to Galatians 5:19-23, distribute the Galatians 5 chart.

Apply
Go around the circle, giving each person a word or phrase from Galatians. Ask each to try explaining its meaning briefly, and then let others add to or refine the definition.

Appropriate words and phrases are: • freedom • the sinful nature • live by the Spirit • led by the Spirit • fruit of the Spirit • against such things there is no law.

STUDY GUIDE 142

Ephesians 1–2

ONE PEOPLE

Overview

Ephesians was written by Paul to a congregation established on one of Paul's later missionary journeys (Acts 19). It was written from Rome, probably in A.D. 62 or 63.

The theme of Ephesians is the church as a living organism, the actual body of the living Christ. It is a key book for understanding our personal relationship with Jesus, and how to live with our fellow Christians in a nurturing, ministering relationship.

Ephesus was "the" religious center of the province of Asia. The great temple of Artemis there drew tourists and worshipers, and served as a giant bank from which cities and nations as well as individuals applied for loans. This highly successful institutionalized religion is the backdrop against which Paul gives us a vision of the church of Jesus Christ. This church is no institution: it is a body, a family, a holy but living temple. It reveals a glory in the living personalities of its members which far outshines the glory of the stone temple of Ephesus, even though that temple was four times the size of the Parthenon of Athens.

This book is an important one for Christians to study today. It helps us not to think of our own churches in institutional terms —as buildings and programs and activities alone. It helps us to see ourselves, and one another, as living expressions of a Christ who still expresses His glory in human lives.

Commentary

When we skim the first two chapters of Ephesians, one brief paragraph stands out. In it, Paul expressed a prayer for the assembled believers in Ephesus. When we read that prayer today, we see again the theme of knowing Christ personally, and the desire for a daily experience of the divine power. We become aware that Paul included *us* in his sweeping request that all God's people might experience Him as present, filling "everything in every way" (Eph. 1:23). Look at that prayer now, and visualize Paul praying for you and those you teach.

> I keep asking that the God of our Lord Jesus Christ, the glorious Father, may give you the Spirit of wisdom and revelation, so that you may know Him better. I pray also that the eyes of your heart may be enlightened in order that you may know the hope to which He has called you, the riches of His glorious inheritance in the saints, and His incomparably great power for us who believe. That power is like the working of His mighty strength, which He exerted in Christ, when He raised Him from the dead and seated Him at His right hand in the heavenly realms, far above all rule and authority, power and dominion, and every title that can be given, not only in the present age but also in the one to come. And God placed all things under His feet and appointed Him to be Head over everything for the church, which is His body, the fullness of Him who fills everything in every way.
>
> Ephesians 1:17-23

♥ ***Link to Life: Youth / Adult***

Ephesians contains two powerful prayers that Paul prayed for young believers. This is one; the other is in 3:14-21.

Ask each group member to silently read one or both of these prayers. Say: "Imagine that Paul, or a parent or spouse or close friend is praying that prayer for you now. Which part of the prayer is most important to you, personally?"

After group members have read the prayer and marked the most important parts, share. Which part seemed most important to each person, and why?

Then point out that during the study of Ephesians each will learn truths that will help that prayer be answered in his or her life.

Grasping the Hope

Helen hung up the telephone. "O Lord," she whispered, "give me strength."

Lucille, an older friend from her Thursday evening Bible study, had asked for Helen's help. "You're the only person I know who cares," Lucille had said. "I can talk to you."

Last week their study group had met at Lucille's home, and Helen had stayed after the others left. She'd listened as Lucille, a divorced woman with two grown sons, told of her husband's unfaithfulness and desertion. She shared how her sons blamed her; she described her loneliness and her struggle to get in touch with God. In tears, Lucille said how grateful she was for Helen. Helen really seemed to care.

But caring wasn't easy. Helen had grown up believing she was inadequate and unable to love. Her sense of inadequacy had led to a series of choices that turned her away from others. Now, at 37, it was almost impossible for Helen to reach out.

It had been easier that night after the Bible study. She was already at Lucille's house. No choices had to be made. There was no time to think about a coming confrontation; no time to worry about what she'd say or do. No time to feel the tension grow and the perspiration come cold and clammy. But to choose to visit Lucille, to get into the car and drive the dozen miles across town to where she lived, that would take time. As the days passed, as fear gripped her each time she thought of Lucille, the strength never seemed to come.

How different Helen's hesitation is from Paul's prayer. Helen asked for strength. Paul asked that you and I might *grasp the power that is ours.* Helen was asking for something she already possessed! Having failed to grasp the hope of Christ's calling, she was living in unnecessary defeat.

Paul's vision of the present power of Jesus is one of the most striking emphases of this Christological epistle. Even the word "hope" takes on special meaning in the New Testament. We say, "I hope," and mean "I would like, but am uncertain about." New Testament hope has no note of uncertainty. It is a term of *expectancy.* "Hope in God" (Ps. 42:11) is a call to an active faith which *expects God to act.* Paul's prayer is that you and I might grasp all that we confidently expect, as God's new people. For we are a people in whom God's own incomparably great power is even now at work!

If the "working of His mighty strength" is available to us now, how inappropriate are the desperate, hopeless prayers we so often utter. How tragic Helen's cry, begging for a power to act that has been her heritage ever since she was "included in Christ."

And how important these first chapters of Ephesians, for they help Helen—and us—realize just who we are as a people of God through Jesus Christ.

An Overview: Ephesians 1–2

There is nothing more influential in shaping our actions than our self-image. That is, how we see ourselves, how we feel about ourselves. A person who sees himself as capable will act confidently. A person who sees himself as weak, and unable, is all too likely to refuse to try.

In our spiritual experience too our image of who we are plays a significant role. And it is to just this issue that the first two chapters of Ephesians are addressed. They help us to develop a vital, correct sense of our identity in Christ. They help us understand who we really are as Jesus' people, and thus help free us from our bondage to old frustrations and inabilities.

The Godhead (Eph. 1:3-14). In these powerful verses Paul drew past, present, and future together. He looked at the work of each of the Persons of the Godhead as it relates to you and me. God the Father, in eternity past, chose us in Christ to be holy and blameless. He predestined us to be adopted as sons, pouring out His grace on us in Christ. God the Son, in history past, redeemed us through His blood, bringing us forgiveness and lavishing on us gifts of wisdom and understanding. Even now we are "included in Christ," and looking forward to the complete fulfillment of God's plan and the glory that fulfillment holds for us. Now too we have been sealed by God's gift of the Holy Spirit, the living guarantee of our inheritance to come.

What stunning truths! Somehow you and I, with all God's people, have been the focus of His concern from before the Creation of the universe! Each person of the Godhead—

Father, Son, and Holy Spiirt—has been involved in bringing us the grace in which we now stand. In view of all this, there is *no way* that a Christian can see himself or herself as insignificant, unimportant, or ineffectual. The focused energies of God have been spent on our redemption because in Christ we are significant to Him. We are important. And, with God's Spirit present in us, we have the power to live "to the praise of His glory" (v. 14).

Prayer (Eph. 1:15-23). Paul desired, then, that we might enjoy a full experience of our position in Christ. We have a new identity now—we are "saints" and we experience "His incomparably great power for us who believe." And it is *His* power: the power of a Jesus who is now raised from the dead, seated at the Father's "right hand" (the ancient place of authority), far above every competing natural or supernatural authority. Perhaps most significantly, Jesus is Head "over everything for the church, which is His body." This theme, that we are members of a living organism over which Christ is the living Head, is a theme Paul picked up in later chapters of this powerful little book.

Alive in Christ (Eph. 2:1-10). God is fully aware of who we *were*. We were "dead in . . . transgressions and sins" and we used to follow "the ways of this world." We were dedicated to "gratifying the cravings of our sinful nature." So in affirming our new identity in Christ, there is no question of misunderstanding. God knew full well what we were.

But it is *were*. We are no longer what we were! Now we have been "made . . . alive" in Christ. His grace has been poured out on us and we were "raised . . . up with Christ," recipients not of a reward but of a gift. Who are we now? "We are God's workmanship, created in Christ Jesus to do good works, which God prepared in advance for us to do."

God knows who we were: it is up to you and me to take Him at His word about who we now are! We can no longer think of ourselves in the old way, or burden ourselves down with past guilts. In Jesus we are renewed: we are His own fresh creations, shaped by the divine hand for the good works He calls us to do.

One in Christ (Eph. 2:11-18). Another aspect of our new identity has a direct impact on our relationship with other Christians. We once defined our relationships with others on the basis of the things that made us different, even as Jew and Gentile were aware of the cultural and religious gap that not only separated them, but also made them enemies. But now in Christ the gap has been closed, and Jesus has made peace. From even such hostile elements God has made "one body." By being reconciled to God, we are at the same time reconciled to one another.

Family of believers (Eph. 2:19-22). The "one body" theme is important, for the new identity we are urged to grasp is not found in isolation. We are to see ourselves as "fellow citizens with God's people" (v. 19). As members of God's household, we are "being built *together* [italics mine] to become a dwelling in which God lives."

This last theme is one that Paul developed carefully in both Ephesians and Colossians. We have been given new life, and have been given power to live it. But we do not live isolated lives. We grow to full stature in Christ as members of a household. It is in the fellowship of other believers that individuals are formed into a living, growing organism that "rises to become a holy temple in the Lord" (v. 21).

This focus on the community of faith gives us a new perspective on personal growth and identity. It also gives us a new perspective on Christ. In Ephesians we no longer see Jesus primarily in relationship to the believing individual. We see Jesus as Head of a living body. We see God's intention to:

- "bring all things in heaven and on earth together under one Head, even Christ" (1:10);
- place "all things under His feet" and appoint "Him to be Head over everything for the church, which is His body" (vv. 22-23); and
- set Christ Jesus Himself as the chief Cornerstone. "In Him the whole building is joined together" (2:21).

As we read on in Ephesians we will see Christ pictured more and more as Head of the body. In the first two chapters, however, Paul focused on *our* identity. What does it mean for us to be "in Christ"? What does it mean to have been snatched from death and given life? Just why was Paul so sure that our daily lives will be transformed if we

My New Identity

Portrayed in Ephesians 1 and 2

What God has done	What we now have
1:5 ______	1:6 ______
1:8 ______	1:7 ______
1:13 ______	1:7 ______
1:13 ______	1:9 ______
2:5 ______	1:13 ______
2:6 ______	1:18 ______
2:8 ______	1:19 ______
2:13 ______	1:23 ______
2:19 ______	1:23 ______
2:22 ______	2:4 ______
	2:5 ______
	2:13, 18 ______
	2:14 ______
	2:16 ______
	2:19 ______
	2:20 ______
	2:22 ______

Record above your own discoveries of your identity in Christ. After your research, write below which of your findings seems most significant to you and why:

______

______

______

grasp the hope of our calling, if we know what we can expect as members of Christ's body?

One way to help our group members build a picture of our new identity is to read and reread these first chapters of Ephesians, noting what Paul says we have in Christ, and what God has done for us. How rich to realize that, now, what we do have in Christ includes redemption. Power. Life. Peace. Membership in the family. Christ Himself to guide us.

And how wonderful to realize what God has done for us in Christ. That He has chosen us to praise Him. That He has adopted us as sons, and reshaped us. That our personalities now bear the mark of His workmanship.

As we explore these chapters, the wonder grows. In Christ we truly are a new people! We have a new identity now, individually and together. With the newness that being in Christ brings, we shrug off forever the bondage of past hopelessness.

♥ ***Link to Life: Youth / Adult***
Divide into pairs. Give each member a NEW IDENTITY chart. Each pair is to find in Ephesians 1 and 2 evidence of what God has done, and of what we now have and are in Christ. When the passages have been studied, each should individually write out which of the findings seem most significant to him or her and why.

In the Spirit of Worship

We would miss the tone of these early chapters if we failed to note that Paul's great affirmation of our hope is framed in liturgy. Many commentators see major blocks of these two chapters as early church hymns; credal confessions used regularly in the worship of the first century.

These liturgical elements are found in chapter 1:3-12, 20-23 and in chapter 2:4-10, 14-18. Each lifts our hearts to the person of Christ, to appreciate all God has done for us and for His own glory.

Worship was important in the life of the early church, and it is important now. Not only is worship vital because God merits our praise; it is important to the worshiper. Only when we shift our gaze from ourselves and our inadequacies to God and His power of endless life can we believe that we too have been "raised up with Christ and seated . . . in the heavenly realms" (v. 6). Worship is not selfish; we do not worship God because of the benefits we receive. Yet in losing ourselves in praise and adoration, we discover more of who God is. And an adequate view of God will free us from the bondage of our own inadequacies.

This emphasis on worship helps us remember something else. In the early church, gatherings of the church body were not just to hear a sermon.

The life of the church was focused on reaffirming community by a liturgy of Communion and the Word. Justin Martyr, writing his *First Apology* about A.D. 150, gave two accounts of worship in the early church.

> On finishing the prayer, we greet each other with a kiss. Then bread and a cup of water mixed with wine are brought to the president of the brethren, and he, taking them, sends up praise and glory to the Father of the universe. . . . When the president has given thanks and the whole congregation has assented, those whom we call deacons give to each of those present a portion of the consecrated bread and wine and water. And on the day called Sunday there is a reading of the Apostles, or the writings of the Prophets are read as long as time permits. When the reader has finished, the president in a discourse urges and invites us to the imitation of these noble things. Then we all stand up together and offer prayers. And, as said before, when we have finished the prayer, bread is brought and wine and water, and the president similarly sends up prayers and thanksgivings to the best of his ability, and the congregation assents, saying the "Amen"; the distribution and reception of the consecrated elements by each one takes place and they are sent to the absent by the deacons. Those who prosper, and who so wish, contribute, each one as he chooses to. What is collected is deposited with the president, and he takes care of orphans and widows, and those who are in want on account of sickness or any other cause, and those who are in bonds, and the strangers who are sojourners among us, and briefly, he is the protector of all those in need.

Robert Webber, a professor at Wheaton College and author of a number of books on worship, notes that early church worship services had this general form:

Liturgy of the Word
Lessons from Old and New Testaments
Sermon
Prayers
Hymns

Liturgy of the Eucharist
Kiss of peace
Offering of bread, wine, water
Prayers over elements
Remembrance of Christ's death
Amen, said by all
Communion
Sharing of material possessions

In this structure, worship—focused on Christ through Word and Communion—marked the gathering of the local congregation. In the reading, the prayers, the responses, and the sharing with one another, the body of Christ came together to focus shared praise on her Lord. Paul reflects this same kind of service briefly in Colossians 3:16.

As we read Ephesians, we again sense that worship was the heartbeat of the early church. We find hope by grasping who we are in Christ. But hope becomes a reality when we confess Christ with other believers.

The better we come to know God through worship, the more clearly our astounding new identity becomes real to us. For Christ is the source of our reality. Apart from Him, we are nothing. In Him, we experience the fullness of the one Person able to fill us in every way.

♥ ***Link to Life: Youth / Adult***
Reproduce the liturgical elements in Ephesians 1 and 2 on a single sheet or overhead. Distribute to teams. Each team is first to make a list of "what we learn about worship."

Then half the teams should focus on how to apply what is learned to personal worship. The other half should seek to apply them to church worship services. The goal of each is to come up with realistic suggestions for strengthening private or public worship.

TEACHING GUIDE

Prepare
Pray Paul's prayer in Ephesians 1 for your group members daily as you prepare and teach Ephesians.

Explore
1. Ask each person to imagine Paul is praying his Ephesians 1 prayer for him or her, and to determine which request would be most important. See "link-to-life," pages 913-914.
2. Or tell the true story of Helen (p. 914). Ask your group members to predict. Will she go see her friend, or won't she. Each must explain *why* he or she made the prediction.

Expand
1. Do the chart study of Ephesians 1 and 2 in class, to help your group members develop a sense of their new identity in Christ. See "link-to-life," page 916.
2. Or do the liturgical study suggested in "link-to-life," page 918.

Apply
1. In fact, Helen did *not* go see Lucille. Ask your group members to select *one* of the truths from Ephesians 1 and 2 that might have freed her to respond. Go around the circle and let each express the truth chosen, and share why he or she sees it as a freeing truth.
2. Or ask for volunteers to plan a worship time for your next social gathering that will use group suggestions to enrich corporate worship.

STUDY GUIDE 143

Ephesians 3:1–5:2

ONE BODY, ONE FAMILY

Overview
Ephesians gives us three images which help us think about the church. Two of these images are brought into focus in the midsection of Ephesians.

The three images that are intended to give us a vision of who we are as Christ's church are those of a *body,* a *family,* and a *holy temple.*

The three images share a common emphasis. Each reminds us again and again that we are one with our brothers and sisters, even as we are one with Christ. But each of the images also has its own distinctive emphasis.

The biblical picture of the church as a body reminds us that we are called to a life of good works. Even as our own bodies act to carry out the intentions of our minds, so the body of Christ acts on earth to carry out the intentions of Jesus, our living Head.

The biblical picture of the church as a family reminds us that we are called to a life of love. As the human family is the context for growth and intimacy, so the family of God is a context in which God's love is expressed to welcome each other and to help each other grow.

The biblical picture of the church as a temple reminds us that we are called to a life of holiness. As a temple reminds us of the worship of God, our calling as a holy temple is to bring God praise and honor and glory.

■ See the *Bible Knowledge Commentary,* pages 628-637 for a verse-by-verse discussion of these chapters.

Commentary
The New Testament gives us three vivid pictures of what the church is. Each is found in Ephesians. Each differs from other biblical illustrations that describe the church. These show us not what the church is *like,* but what the church *is.*

Of course, we know that the church is people. Not organizations or buildings or programs, but people. The Greek word *ecclesia* means "congregation," and more specifically a "called-out congregation." Those who have responded to God's invitation in Christ are called out from humanity to fulfill all of mankind's ancient dreams in a vital, new community. Each of us responds to that invitation individually, but once we respond, we are part of a great company. We are suddenly members of a new community, linked intimately to other men and women who have joined their lives to Jesus. It is important for us to realize that now our identity is to be found not in isolation but in and through the community of Christ's church. We grow in our capacity to live as God's persons within this fellowship.

So it is vital to learn what the church is. Discovering the nature of the church and learning to live as its members is critical to our personal growth and fulfillment.

The body of Christ. All believers are "members together of one body, and sharers together in the promise of Christ Jesus" (3:6). Stress here is laid on the church's unity. Each of us is linked to Christ and one another. This oneness is a truth we must accept.

Also implicit in this portrait is the notion that the church lives only as she responds to her Head. Christ alone is Head of the church. We look to Him for direction and guidance. What is His goal? Scripture tells us that Christ continues His work in our world. He is absent in one sense, seated at the right hand of God (1:20). Yet in another, He is physically here, alive and active in our century. Christ is in heaven, but His body lives and moves on earth. We who have been "created in Christ Jesus to do good works" (2:10) carry out God's hidden plans. You and I, together with all believers, are called to be a contemporary incarnation of the living God. Christ reveals Himself in human flesh, the human flesh of His living church.

The family. This second portrait of the church in Ephesians is that we are all "members of God's household" (v. 19). The "whole family of believers . . . derives its name" (3:14) from God the Father. That name is "family," and from God's name as Father we learn that we are children together. We are brothers and sisters now in the loving, intimate context of a home.

It was in our parents' home that we first learned to love. Now, in God's family, we learn of His love, and to love one another.

A holy temple. The third picture of the church is found in 2:20-21. Here we see a building being raised. We see the Foundation and Cornerstone clearly—Jesus Christ. And we see the process—stone is joined to stone by the Master Builder. As the building grows, we discover that it is a temple. A holy temple, Scripture says, "in the Lord" (v. 21).

This too is the church. Fallen humanity, re-created by God, and now in Christ, a fitting expression of the holiness of God.

Each of these three pictures highlights aspects of who and what we Christians are. Each helps us to understand ourselves as individuals, and to understand the importance of developing an appropriate lifestyle together as God's new community.

♥ ***Link to Life: Youth / Adult***
Put the Word Picture chart on the chalkboard. Ask your group members to brainstorm in threes. How are the images similar to each other? What are the implications of each image?

After hearing from the threesomes, sketch the main implications. As members of the body we are to see ourselves, responsive to our living Head, as expressions of Jesus on earth. As family, we are to see each other as brothers and sisters, called to love and be loved. As parts of a temple we are to see ourselves as growing, increasingly expressing the holiness of God.

Comments on the Text: Ephesians 3:1–4:6

The argument (flow of thought) in this section emerges from Ephesians 2. Verses 11-18 teaches that Christ's great act of reconciliation brought sinners to God, and welded them together in a new creation. "One new man" (v. 15) was formed from individuals of different cultures and backgrounds. Differences, even those which had caused hostility, were made irrelevant, as interpersonal peace came with a shared access to our common Father.

Paul concluded (vv. 19-22) that both household and temple rest on a single foundation, Jesus Christ. And oneness is characteristic of both.

A mystery revealed (Eph. 3:1-6). Paul now called the church a "mystery." The word (*mysterion*) is used in the New Testament primarily by Paul (20 of 27 occurrences) and is always associated with a verb of revelation. What is a "mystery"? It is an insight made available to Christians which was not made clear in the Old Testament.

The "mystery" here is the fact that the

Word Pictures of the Church

Ephesians 1:15 through 2:22

	Similarities	Implications
Body		
Family		
Building (Temple)		

In what ways is the church a body, a family, and a temple? What are the implications of these realities for us as members of Christ's church?

Gentiles would be "heirs together with Israel, members together of one body, and sharers together in the promise of Christ Jesus" (v. 6). While Isaiah and others had foretold that Gentiles would one day be saved, all thought theirs would be a subordinate position. No wonder Paul repeats and repeats in Ephesians the doctrine that the church is *one.*

God's wisdom revealed (Eph. 3:7-13). Paul, as the Apostle to the Gentiles, had been called by God to reveal this unexpected aspect of God's eternal plan. Paul reminded us that that plan expressed the "manifold" (that is, complex or multifaceted) plan of God. God is at work in the church, doing far more than we may imagine. What is important for us however is to realize that "in Him [Christ] and through faith in Him we may approach God with freedom and confidence" (v. 12).

Another prayer (Eph. 3:14-21). In this prayer Paul again expressed his desire for believers. To understand it we must note the context: it comes in a section in which Paul had been affirming the unity of a church made up of many differing individuals. Here Paul prayed that "being rooted and established in love" we believers might experience the love of God and be filled with His fullness. What "love" are we to be established in? In context it is not the love *of* God, or even love *for* God. It is *love for one another as members of the family of God!* It is in the context of loving relationships within the church that we experience, through one another, the depths of God's love. It is in this context that we grow to the fullness of Christ.

All this is possible only because God is "able to do immeasurably more than all we ask or imagine, according to His power that is at work within us."

Living in love and unity (Eph. 4:1-6). Paul's exhortation and prayer for an experience of unity closes with an exhortation. Live in love. Maintain unity. We, Christ's church, *are* one. We know—as no mere association of men can—"one body and one Spirit . . . one hope when you were called—one Lord, one faith, one baptism; one God and Father of all, who is over all and through all and in all" (vv. 4-6).

Implications of Oneness

Paul's stress on oneness troubles many. There have always been differences within the church. Presbyterians have their distinctives, Baptists theirs. Calvinists disagree with Arminians. Some appreciate formal worship; some ask only for a small room where a few can sit in silence and listen to the voice within. Today some hesitate to links hands with anyone who fails to speak in tongues, while others draw back from any who do. More recently, some have insisted that we view the doctrine of inerrancy—that the Bible as originally written contained no errors—as the criteria to divide the "true evangelical" from the false. And yet we hear Paul say, the church is one. And we wonder. If we are one, why does division mark us instead of unity?

A number of answers have been suggested. Here are a few.

- *Unity is only spiritual.* "The invisible church is one, but the visible church, made up of human beings, will always fall short of unity."
- *Organism vs. organization.* "A true bond exists (and can be affirmed, among believers) but this bond need not be expressed in any kind of organizational union."
- *Local unity.* "The only true expression of the church on earth is found in local congregations. Thus the oneness of the local body is all that was ever intended."
- *True church.* "All others outside our group who claim to be Christians are deceived. Since we define all who are unlike us as out of the body, it's easy to claim that unity exists—right here among us."

Each of these, and other formulations, are honest attempts to deal with a difficult question. Yet each falls short of Scripture's affirmation of our oneness as body, family, and temple of God. Looking at Ephesians carefully, we can see errors in each view.

In Ephesians 2:11-18, Paul dealt with deeply rooted cultural and social differences. Jew and Gentile had lifestyles and world views which were incompatible. These led to hostility. When the Gospel message was first shared in Judea, only Hebrews responded. Then, as the word of the Good News spread, Gentiles began to believe too!

One faction in the early church insisted that, to come to Christ, Gentiles must give up their heritage and become Jews. A council was called in Jerusalem to decide that issue. Relationship with Jesus, not culture, made a Christian. The right of Gentile and Jew to their own cultural heritage was affirmed.

Not everyone could stand the tensions such differences caused. Some in the early church still insisted that unity could come only from sameness. But again Paul affirmed the right to be different. God made one new man from *two*. He did not bring harmony by removing differences, but by destroying barriers. He attacked "the dividing wall of hostility" (v. 14), and made its foundation, the Law, irrelevant. In Christ *life* is the only issue. Have we been made alive in Christ? Then we *are* one body, one family, one temple being constructed by the Lord.

In the early church, the Jewish believer continued to live the Hebrew way. The Gentile continued in his way. Each turned from sin, but cultural distinctions were retained. And yet, they still affirmed their identity as one. In Gentile lands Paul took up collections for poor believers in Jerusalem. The family reached out to help. When the Greek-speaking minority in the earliest church in Jerusalem, felt their widows were being treated unfairly in the daily distribution, they complained. Seven deacons were selected to supervise the funds. And every one of the seven bore a Greek name! (Acts 6) Not only in daily fellowship but also in organization, the early church affirmed God's Word. There were differences, but the church was one.

We need to be very careful here. Do I as a dispensationalist draw back from the covenant theologian? As a noncharismatic do I reject the brother who praises God in tongues? Do I let differences cut me off from fellowship with my brothers, or from organizational expressions of our unity? In Christ my brother and I *are* one. My life with him must affirm, not deny, a unity that God says *is*.

In Ephesians 4:1-6, Paul spoke of several aspects of our oneness: one hope, one Lord, one faith. I can accept and ignore many differences. But what about differences in doctrine? What about the person who claims to have the divine life, but whose beliefs differ from mine?

There were doctrinal differences in the early church. Neither Scripture nor early church history suggest that oneness is possible with those outside the body. But here again, life is the issue. One who has Christ's life is to be acknowledged and affirmed no matter how he may differ from us in ideas about Scripture, gifts, separation, predestination, or whatever. Paul's expression of one faith, one baptism, and one Lord is not meant to be exclusive, as a test of purity. Rather it is inclusive, demonstrating the broad-based reality believers know and affirm.

This same approach was taken in the early church. Irenaeus, writing about A.D. 190, offered evidence that the substance of Christian faith received from the apostles was confessed by the church everywhere. This can be our confession too: the confession of a company of men and women who share a common life and know a common Lord. In this confession, we affirm our unity with the church visible and invisible, the church past, future, and present everywhere today. Listen to the ring of the ancient words:

> Now the church, although scattered over the whole civilized world to the ends of the earth, received from the apostles and their disciples its faith in one God, the Father Almighty, who made the heaven, and the earth, and the seas, and all that is in them, and in one Christ Jesus, the Son of God, who was made flesh for our salvation, and in the Holy Spirit, who through the prophets proclaimed the dispensations of God—the comings, the birth of a virgin, the suffering, the Resurrection from the dead, and the bodily reception into the heavens of the beloved, Christ Jesus our Lord, and His coming from the heavens in the glory of the Father to restore all things, and to raise up all flesh, that is, the whole human race, so that every knee may bow, of things in heaven and on earth and under the earth, to Christ Jesus our Lord and God and Saviour and King, according to the pleasure of the invisible Father, and every tongue may confess Him, and that He may execute righteous judgment on all. The spiritual powers of wickedness, and the angels who transgressed and fell into apostasy, and the godless and wicked and lawless and blasphemers among men He will send into the eternal fire. But to the righteous and holy, and those who have kept His commandments and have remained in His love, some from

> the beginning of life and some since their repentance, He will by His grace give life incorrupt, and will clothe them with eternal glory.
>
> Having received this preaching and this faith, as I have said, the church, although scattered in the whole world, carefully preserves it, as if living in one house. She believes these things everywhere alike, as if she had but one heart and one soul, and preaches them harmoniously, teaches them, and hands them down as if she had but one mouth. For the languages of the world are different, but the meaning of the tradition is one and the same.

Living a life worthy of this calling—a humble, patient, loving life—we will maintain the unity of that body which *is* one in Christ.

♥ ***Link to Life: Youth / Adult***

List on the chalkboard the quotes on page 921 that express differing views of unity. Ask each person to write a statement that expresses his or her view. Read them and add any sentences that express significantly different ideas to those on the chalkboard.

Then cover quickly Ephesians 3:1–4:5 in a minilecture, and distribute the quote from Irenaeus.

Let pairs study the quote, and try to come up with a brief statement about Christian unity as Irenaeus might have framed it.

Comments on the Text: Ephesians 4:7–5:2

Paul now developed implications of the church's life as the body of Christ. The risen Christ is pictured as giving gifted persons to the church "to prepare God's people for works of service, so that the body of Christ may be built up" (4:12). Several aspects of this statement may seem strange to us.

Gifted persons (Eph. 4:11). Other passages on gifts focus on various talents or abilities. We recall gifts such as teaching, faith, and showing mercy, and we tend to define gifts as heightened capacities to serve God and others. Usually when we speak of spiritual gifts, we wonder, "What can I do to contribute? What special ability has God given me?"

This is no error. While each of us has faith and exercises that faith in prayer, some have a heightened capacity to believe. While each of us has a capacity to communicate, to teach, some of us have that ability in a special degree. *This* is the gift of teaching. While each of us can reach out in love to care for those in need, some are gifted to a special degree with the capacity to show mercy. And each believer has one or more of such supernatural endowments.

But in this passage, Paul was not talking about spiritual gifts! Some people have *become* gifts! Some are given to the body for special purposes. Who are these gift-persons? Apostles. Prophets. Evangelists. Pastor-teachers. And what is their calling?

Leadership's task. Gift-people are "to prepare God's people for works of service" (v. 12). Leaders are not to *do* the work of the ministry; leaders are to prepare the laity to minister.

It is here that we have often missed the implications of the body portrait, and developed congregational patterns that deny rather than express what the church *is*. All too often leaders are hired by a congregation to do the "work of the ministry." The pastor is expected to teach. To evangelize. To counsel. To visit the sick. To pray with the discouraged. If the church grows in size and new members are added, it is taken as an indication that their local congregation is healthy and the minister is doing his job. If the church fails to grow or the budget is not met, the one to blame is the minister. After all, he was hired by the church to minister.

How different is this view from the Bible's portrait of a living body! In a living organism, *every cell contributes*. The body's health depends on each member fulfilling its special function. No one person can carry out the functions of the living organism the Scripture describes. No one person or team of paid professionals was ever intended to. The role of leaders within the church has always been to help the members of the body grow in capacity to minister; to help each individual find and use his or her spiritual gifts. The role of leaders has always been to lead all believers into a fulfilling life of service.

When we miss this, and put the ministry of the church onto the professional, we have lost sight of who we are. The local congregation becomes weak, unable to respond as a healthy body to the directions of its Head.

Becoming mature (Eph. 4:12-16). Paul here set an initial goal for our works of service. We are to build up the body, "until we all reach unity in the faith . . . and become mature" (v. 13). *The first ministry of believers is to other believers.*

It is vital that we "grow up into Him" if we are to be a valid expression of Jesus in this world. The whole body "grows and builds itself up in love, as each part does its work" (v. 16).

This is sometimes hard to accept. We look at the world and are burdened by the need for evangelism. We look at the poor and are burdened by the need to establish justice. We look at the suffering and are impelled to comfort and to care. So sometimes we slip into the trap of organizing the local church to undertake one or more of these tasks. We program evangelistic efforts and buy more buses. We commit ourselves to an active social welfare involvement. All too often we lose sight of the fact that the first function of the body is to build *itself.*

When my oldest son was about five, he wanted to mow our lawn. We had a push mower then. The kind in which the blades moved only when the wheels moved, and the wheels were moved by people power. Well, Paul pushed and strained—and finally found an answer. He leaned on the handle, lifted the wheels off the ground, and easily moved the mower on just the back roller! How busy he looked, chugging up and down across our lawn. And how little grass he cut!

After a while, I would explain. "Soon, Paul, you'll grow, and then you'll be able to make those blades turn. Then you can help a lot."

How often in the church we concentrate on organizing spiritual five-year-olds to push better lawn mowers, and wonder why so little of God's grass gets cut! The church is called to "grow up into Him who is the Head, that is, Christ" (v. 15). Maturing within the body, growing more and more like Jesus, is the believer's first calling. To equip the church for service, believers must minister to one another and to the world.

Don't misunderstand: this focus on building one another up is not "selfish." It is essential. Only as we grow toward maturity together can we respond fully to Jesus as He directs us to serve in the world. Only a strong and healthy body can carry out the tasks assigned to it. Our effectiveness in communicating the Gospel and the love of God to the world around us depends on our growth toward maturity. This kind of growth takes place as we—members together of one body—build each other up in love, each part doing its own ministering work (v. 16).

♥ ***Link to Life: Youth / Adult***
Outline the church as a body on the chalkboard, and set your group members to discuss in teams of five the following three questions:

Sharing (Eph. 4:17 5:2). At times we make living in and as a body more difficult than it is. We think of ministering relationships, and we wonder, "How do we develop them?" "What are we to *do*?" And, uncer-

The Church Is a Body

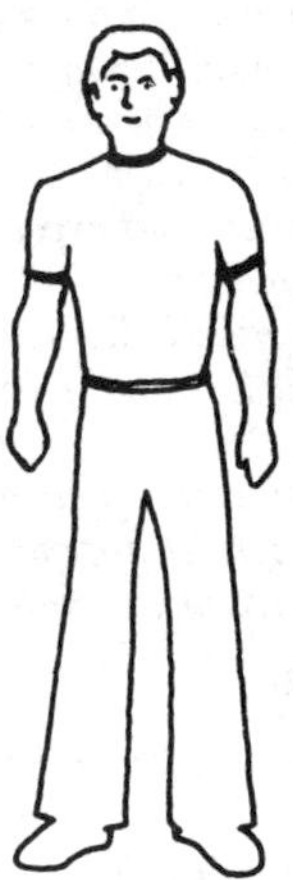

Visualizing the church as a body, do the following:

1. What part of the body are leaders (remembering that Christ alone is the Head)?
2. What part of the body would you most like to be?
3. What spiritual gifts (see Rom. 12 and 1 Cor. 12 for typical gifts) seem most closely associated with the part you selected?

tain, its all too easy to draw back. We forget that living in Christ's church is like living in a family.

The apostle brings us back to the concept of simple sharing by pointing out in 4:16 that the body builds itself up *in love*. Paul then exhorted us to "live a life of love, just as Christ loved us and gave Himself up for us" (5:2). Over and over Paul brought into focus the personal relationships that are to be developed by members of the body. In the context of these natural relationships, our giftedness grows.

As members of the body, we must no longer live as the Gentiles do (4:17-19), but become a loving family in which growth can take place. How do the Gentiles live? Without sensitivity, indulging themselves in sensuality. This is a picture of men and women who see others as something to use. Love never degrades others or places things above human values. "I tell you this, and insist on it in the Lord, that you must no longer live as the Gentiles" (v. 17).

How are we taught to live together in Christ? Putting off the former way of life (vv. 20-32), we are to live with a totally new attitude: a new self that is like God in true righteousness and holiness. How does righteousness find expression in human relationships?

• *By putting off falsehood and speaking truthfully*. This involves more than not lying. It involves an open sharing of ourselves with one another, rejecting deceit.

• *By rejecting the sinful actions anger drives us toward*. Anger is not given a place. Before evening comes, we are to move toward reconciliation.

• *By rejecting gossip and unwholesome talk*. In our conversation we seek to build others up, not tear them down.

• *By ridding ourselves of bitterness, rage, slander, and every form of malice*. In their place, we are to express kindness and compassion, forgiving each other as God has forgiven us.

"Be imitators of God, therefore, as dearly loved children and live a life of love" (vv. 1-2). In every New Testament passage that teaches that the church is a body, we also find an emphasis on the loving relationships that are to develop between believers. It is through living with one another in love that ministry opportunities are created, and ministry takes place.

This is the simplicity we sometimes miss. The love that grows between family members and draws us closer to each other, moves us to care. As we care, we reach out to bear one another's burdens, to encourage and support—we minister. It is in loving that our spiritual gifts come into play.

Local churches. The Ephesians' description of a life of love helps us define the characteristics of a healthy local church today. We have already seen that a local congregation must have a biblical understanding of ministry. The church that has a biblical understanding:

- Sees leaders as equippers.
- Sees each member as a minister.
- Pays close attention to maturing and building believers up in Christ.
- Seeks to help individuals and groups within the church serve as Christ leads.

Through such ministry, the maturing congregation has the greatest impact on the world around.

Now we see another critical aspect of local church life. Relationships within the church are to be marked by love. Jesus spoke of that at His Last Supper. "Love each other," He told His disciples, "as I have loved you" (John 15:12). This new commandment also contained a promise. "All men will know that you are My disciples if you love one another" (13:35). Christ placed His highest priority on love within the body, for He knew we could only become one through ever-deepening personal relationships. Only through love can we build each other to maturity. Only through love can the church bear compelling witness to Jesus as Lord. When others see Jesus' love lived out in the brotherhood of faith, there is no explanation but one: God is real.

If our local congregation wants to be the church, we need to:

- *Come to know each other well*. We cannot love a person we do not know.
- *Learn to share our lives with each other*. Love involves bearing each other's burdens. We need to trust others enough to reveal our burdens to them.
- *Reach out in caring to meet others' needs*. As burdens are shared, we want to respond.

These are very practical guidelines. They let us look at a congregation's lifestyle and see ways to encourage growth. Do people know each other well? If not, we need to plan time to be together. Do we share? If not, we need to grow used to opening our lives to one another. Do we reach out? If not, we need to concentrate on ways to minister to people. In short, we need to see what the New Testament reveals: that the heart of ministry is not to run a program or fill an organizational slot, but to focus on people and their needs.

"Live a life of love," Scripture says (Eph. 5:2). *Be* the church—the family of God—that you *are.*

TEACHING GUIDE

Prepare

Select one or more themes found in these chapters to emphasize, depending on your evaluation of your group's needs.

Explore

1. Divide into teams to suggest implications of the Bible's statements that the church is a body, a family, and a holy temple. See "link-to-life," page 920.
2. Or begin with a minilecture, tracing the teaching of Ephesians 3:1–4:5 on unity.

Expand

1. List views of unity on the chalkboard, and ask for others. See the "link-to-life" process explained on page 923 that suggests ways to look at this important issue in view of church history as well as Scripture.
2. Or place a body diagram on the board, and have your group work to answer the three questions raised in "link-to-life," page 924.

Apply

Briefly survey Ephesians 4:17–5:2, and list the practical implications the author draws. Evaluate. Which of these are you experiencing in your group or congregation? What might you do together to deepen your relationships and expressions of family love?

STUDY GUIDE 144

Ephesians 5:3–6:20

ONE IN LOVE

Overview

Ephesians affirms the oneness of Christians, bonded together in Christ. We've looked at that oneness as expressed in the images of a body and of a family.

Each of these is an image not of what the church *is like,* but of what the church *is.* Each is an image of what we are called to experience, together, as God's people.

In this study we look at the third image, that of the holy temple. We also examine a basic attitude which is vital to adopt if we are to truly *be* Christ's church: the attitude of submission. Finally, we look at those schemes of the devil which are focused on distorting our life together—and at the armor God has provided for us to enable us to withstand.

How good to look into this, one of the deepest and most important of Paul's letters, and learn with our students how to build oneness through a truly practical love.

▶ ***Submission.*** The New Testament emphasizes a voluntary (James 4:7) rather than a forced (Luke 10:17) submission. Submission is appropriate in social roles (as citizen or slave, see Rom. 13:1; Titus 2:9). It is also appropriate in Christian interpersonal relationships. Here the image is one of responsiveness and willingness to yield to one another out of love.

Commentary

Each section of Ephesians adds to our understanding of our identity together as the church. Each shows how we can help each other know Christ better. Looking back over these sections, we can sense the wonder of it all—and see practical guidelines for a vital new lifestyle.

Ephesians 1–2. Here we see Jesus, raised from the dead to the Father's side as Head of the church. And we see our new identity in Him. We, who were cut off from God by sin, are forgiven and provided with spiritual life. The power that raised Jesus from the dead fills us, lifting us out of our inadequacy and empowering us for something new. We now live in hope, because we are in constant touch with a God who has committed Himself to us.

All this is ours because of Jesus Christ. Seeing Him as the Source of our life moves Paul to expression after expression of praise.

Ephesians 2–3. In these chapters we learn that power for the new life God has given us is channeled through the community of the church. We are not to live isolated lives; we are to live in intimate relationship with other believers. To illustrate this, Paul portrayed the church as a body, a family, and a holy temple. Each of these images stressed the fact that the church is one. We are to seek, and maintain unity in order to experience together the divine power.

Living together as a body, we build one another up and grow toward maturity. As family, we find our attitudes and values changed as love becomes the touchstone of our lives. As God's temple we find our lives taking on a holiness which exposes evil for what it is. *Learning to live together as the church is the key to individual growth, love, and holiness. As we live in true fellowship with others we discover the living presence of God.* The relationship between Christ and the individual is experienced in the fellowship of the saints.

Ephesians 4–5. The practical meaning of living together as a body, family, and temple is amplified in these chapters. Living in the body means each person ministers to other members, using the spiritual gifts supplied by God and developed by gifted leaders. Living as members of the family means coming to know and care for one another deeply, expressing that care in openness, compassion, forgiveness, and a deep involvement in each others' lives. And, as we'll

Ephesian Emphases

Chapters	Doctrine	Emphasis
1–2	Christ is exalted as Head over all.	We have life and power in Him.
2–3	The church is one body, one family, and one holy temple.	Unity is to be maintained.
4–5	The church is to learn to live as body, family, and holy temple.	We love and minister to each other and live together righteously.

see, living together as a holy temple means rejecting dark things and building our commitment to goodness, righteousness, and truth. All of these are learned within the context of the new community, created and led by Christ.

Again we see it clearly. To know the living presence of Jesus, we are called to experience the fellowship of the church. In the church, the new creation of God, we each will find renewal.

Renewal as a Holy Temple: Ephesians 5:3-20

The church is a holy temple. Therefore, we are to live as God's holy people.

Here the contrast is that of night and day, darkness and light. It's as though we've passed through a pitch-black tunnel—stumbling, mired in dirt and filth—and then suddenly broken into the light. At first we're blinded by the brilliance. Then, as our eyes adjust to the shimmering glow, we realize where we are. We're in a new and different world, a world without impurity or greed or idolatry. A world of goodness, righteousness, truth, and purity. And this is how we are to live—with eyes opened to holiness, making the most of every opportunity to do God's will. What is it like, this holy life? This too is found in relationships—in the way we live with others inside and outside the church. What are the marks of holiness in contrast to the ways of darkness?

As we live in love, caring for others rather than using them, we reveal the righteousness of God and we expose evil for what it is.

How does the church expose evil? By mounting a crusade, or picketing? Hardly. *Evil is exposed by providing an example of righteousness.*

Paul put it this way: "Everything exposed by the light becomes visible, for it is light that makes everything visible" (5:13-14). As children of light, we reveal darkness for what it is. In the light shed by the holiness of God's people, evil is revealed as evil.

And so we again see the church: a body, a family, a holy temple. A *people* of God, not just individual Christians.

Individualism

In reviewing what Ephesians teaches, we see a major difference between the church and our culture. *Competitiveness* is valued by our society. We are a nation of individualists; we approach life's issues *alone*.

In school we work individually for grades, and compare with others to see whose score is highest. In sports we sometimes compete by teams, but always we keep individual statistics. In business the company that grows makes the best product, or promotes it most effectively. Each salesman works to make his quota, to be in the top for the month or year. We measure ourselves against others by our educations, our incomes, our cars, our vacations, and even by our roles in church organizations. Our society appreciates rugged individualism. The exaltation of one person above others is reflected in our ways of living together, and in our idea of what leadership involves. To win, compete, excel—all these things a person does *against* the crowd.

Darkness	Light
sexual immorality	goodness
impurity	righteousness
greed	truth
obscenity	thanksgiving
coarse joking	
idolatry	
drunkenness	

And then we come to the church of Christ, and enter another world. Here we see a living body that "grows and builds itself up . . . as each part does its work" (4:16). Every person ministering to others is the sign of a healthy body. Not competition but cooperation is the heart of the Christian lifestyle. Even leaders are not exalted as "the" ministers, but are subordinated to the members, whom they are to serve by equipping them for *their* ministering work!

Like a family, the church is more concerned with brothers' and sisters' needs than their accomplishments. It is more committed to love than victory. Love is what Jesus showed when He gave Himself for us. "As dearly loved children," we are to "live a life of love" (5:1-2) that is just like Christ's! We are invited to surrender personal ambitions and subordinate our needs to the needs of others, being wiling to give ourselves up for those who have become so dear.

Here too we see a holy temple, in which the struggle to lift ourselves above the others—to use them for our gain—is rejected in favor of goodness, righteousness, and truth.

The lifestyle of the church decisively rejects the individualism of society, and values cooperation over competition. This lifestyle does not exalt the leader over the led, but sees serving others as the highest calling. Unity leads us to abandon pride of place or position and accept each other as fully equal in the community we share. Paul portrays this new attitude in Philippians 2:

> If you have any encouragement from being united with Christ, if any comfort from His love, if any fellowship with the Spirit, if any tenderness and compassion, then make my joy complete by being like-minded, having the same love, being one in spirit and purpose. Do nothing out of selfish ambition or vain conceit, but in humility consider others better than yourselves. Each of you should look not only to your own interests, but also to the interests of others.
>
> Your attitude should be the same as that of Christ Jesus: Who, being in the very nature of God, did not consider equality with God something to be grasped, but made Himself nothing, taking the very nature of a servant, being made in human likeness.
>
> And being found in appearance as a man, He humbled Himself and became obedient to death—even death on a cross!
>
> Philippians 2:1-8

This is the new world of relationships, so dramatically different from the world of individualism we have known.

But this new world raises many questions. What about the differences in station and position that exist in society? What about the great distinctions between slaves and free, parent and child, husband and wife? How do we live our new lives in our roles in society? Do we reject social order, to affirm the unity Christ has formed within the church? Paul turns to these questions in Ephesians 5.

Submission: Ephesians 5:21

It seems strange to find Paul speaking of submission in view of his emphasis on unity. Accept a subordinate position? We who are lifted up in Christ, made so completely equal that Paul himself insisted, "There is neither Jew nor Greek, slave nor free, male nor female, for you are all one in Christ Jesus" (Gal. 3:28).

This idea of superior/subordinate positions—of submitting within the framework of societal roles and relationships—must have troubled the early church as it does us today. In three of the New Testament letters this same issue is explored. We hear the same message from each: "Wives, submit to your husbands" (Eph. 5:22; Col. 3:18; see 1 Peter 3:1). "Children, obey your parents" (see Eph. 6:1; Col. 3:20). "Slaves, obey your earthly masters with respect and fear" (Eph. 6:5; see Col. 3:22; 1 Peter 2:18). And for all, "Submit yourselves for the Lord's sake to every authority instituted among men" (v. 13). It is in the framework of the real world of human differences and inequalities that the church's oneness is to be expressed.

How can this be? How can we experience oneness while recognizing and respecting the rights of those placed "over" us?

Mutual submission. Whenever we move into this area of authority, we tend to emphasize the "rights" of the superior to control or influence the person below. Paul immediately showed that control is not the frame of reference from which to begin. His discussion began with the command, "Submit to one another out of reverence for Christ" (Eph. 5:21). We are to maintain a humbleness that considers others—whatever their place in life—as "better than yourselves. Each of you should look not only to your own interests, but also to the interests of others" (Phil. 2:3-4). Maintaining an attitude of loving concern for one another strips authority of its "rights" and also strips submission of its humiliation. Whatever role we have been given provides an opportunity to serve our brothers and sisters in the Lord.

Mutual responsibilities. Reading through the passages in Ephesians, Colossians, and 1 Peter that deal with human relationships and societal roles, we find that *the scales are not weighted in either direction!* The child obeys parents in the Lord, but parents are not to exasperate or embitter their children. Discipline is to be distinctively Christian. The slave is to serve wholeheartedly. But masters are to treat the slave with consideration and concern, doing what is right and fair.

Within the context of whatever role, the Christian's deep concern for others as persons is to guide and control.

Occasion to serve. The underlying thought is that authority and submission are not to be viewed as humiliation, but as *providing different opportunities to serve.* If I am a master, I serve my slaves by treating them with fairness and respect. If I am a slave, I serve my master with wholehearted loyalty.

The Christian attitude toward authority and submission is drastically opposed to the perceptions of the world, which see the one in authority as exalted, and the other as debased. There, each person's value is determined by the position he holds. But in Christ's church that whole pattern is rejected. Each persons' value exists *apart from his role.* The slave is just as important to God as the master, the child as the parent, the woman as the man. It is simply that one who is a slave has a different kind of opportunity to serve than does the master. The Christian view of authority and submission shifts the focus completely from power, to service.

♥ ***Link to Life: Youth / Adult***
In a minilecture explain the concept of societal roles not as power structures *but as roles that give Christians differing opportunities to serve. Then divide into teams, to study parallel passages on submission, and to answer the questions. Come back together to share insights.*

Husband/Wife Relationships: Ephesians 5:22-33

Nowhere is this concept seen more clearly than in marriage.

The pagan view. In Paul's time, pagans saw women as inferior beings, playthings for the dominant male. To be "head of the house" was to accept the common notion that authority was the male's rightful providence. Children and wives were only responsible to obey. The wife was not equal to her husband as a person, or in any other way. His needs and concerns dominated the household, and the wife existed to fulfill those needs and to serve him.

Contemporary interpretations of Ephesians 5 that describe the wife as finding total fulfillment in her relationship with her husband and household reflect the pagan, not the Christian view. So does the notion that

Parallel Passages on Submission

Relationship	Eph.	Col.	1 Peter*
Husband/wife	5:22-23	3:18-19	3:1-7
Parent/child	6:1-4	3:20-21	
Master/slave	6:5-9	3:22–4:1	2:18-21

*Note that Peter speaks of relationships with persons who are *not* within the church. Ephesians and Colossians speak of relationships within it.

Questions to explore

- How does each "superior" relationship provide an opportunity to serve?
- How does each "subordinate" relationship provide this opportunity?
- How might each person's attitude toward authority affect the relationship between them?

the wife is so "under" the authority umbrella of her husband that she is not to speak or act except at his direction.

The Christian view. The Christian view is quite different. Women are seen as persons of equal worth and value. In the structure of society, men are given the role of head of the house, a role affirmed by God in this passage. But their headship is modeled on the way Christ loved the church, not on human systems of authority. This headship focuses attention on the way a "superior" is called to serve the "subordinate"! Specifically, Ephesians 5:27 portrays Christ as giving Himself up for the church "to present her to Himself as a radiant church, without stain or wrinkle or any other blemish, but holy and blameless." In pursuit of this ministry, Christ nourishes and cares for the church. In the same way, husbands are to nurture their wives, seeking always to help the wife grow as a person and as a Christian.

What a contrast with the pagan view! Suddenly things are reversed. The wife is transformed from an unimportant adjunct, who exists only to meet her husband's needs, to a person of intrinsic worth and value, becoming the focus of her husband's concern. Instead of demanding that she live for him, he begins to live for her! Rather than keeping her under, he seeks to lift her up. Christian headship lifts the wife up as the rightful object of a husband's loving concern.

In this context, the husband serves by being a Christlike head; the wife serves in responsive submission to one who lifts her up and holds her beside him.

♥ ***Link to Life: Youth / Adult***

Again use a minilecture to sum up the difference in pagan and Christian views of headship, as expressed in Ephesians 5:22-33. Then divide into teams, asking half the teams to suggest how the couple in the case history will go about solving the problem if they adopt the "pagan" view of headship in the home. The other half is to say how they will deal with it if they adopt the Christian view, taking Christ as the model who chose to serve His bride and build her up.

Each set of teams is to determine what this couple will do. Then hear reports from all.

Case History

Leona wants to go back to school for premedical training. Her goal is to become a doctor, so she can help others as well as support herself and their six-month-old daughter should something happen to Ben. This notion upsets Ben. A woman's place is in the home, he says, especially since they have a baby. Besides, in his family the husband always takes care of the wife and children. To hear Leona talk about a career makes Ben feel uneasy.

But it's tough for Leona too. Ben's been out of work two times in the last six years—for long periods of time. She doesn't like being a housewife and wants to use her God-given intelligence for something other than washing dishes. Besides, deep down she is not confident Ben will always take care of them. And she does not want her daughter to grow up on welfare if she can help it.

In summary. What both Paul and Peter do in their letters is to help us realize that our place in society is irrelevant to the oneness that is to exist in the church. For the Christian, who lives to serve others, the role in which that service is offered is unimportant. Slave and master are one in Christ, lifted up and seated with Him. How foolish then to define a brother first of all as "master," and feel the alienation that "authority" often creates. How foolish to think of ourselves as unimportant if our role is that of "slave." How useless to bridle against being a woman, as though it were better to be a man! How foolish, when we are all members of one body, one family, living stones in that holy temple constructed by the Lord. How freeing it is to realize that my worth and value as a person rests on who I am in Christ, and that my position in the world simply defines my opportunities to serve.

The Devils' Schemes: Ephesians 6:10-20
Paul concludes this letter with a warning. Satan is actively struggling against God. All his energies are focused on shattering the unity of the church. The enemy will attempt to cripple the body, to introduce dissension into the family, and to corrupt the holy temple. Against the enemy's attacks God has equipped us with His own armor: "The full armor of God so that you can take your stand against the devil's schemes" (v. 11).

Many different interpretations of the armor have been given, and its equivalents in the panoply of the Roman soldier of Paul's day have been discussed. But what is most important has often been overlooked: Paul here describes *the armor which enables us to stand against attacks on our life together as Christ's new community.* Viewed from this perspective, what are the divine resources we have been given?

The belt of truth. Put off falsehood and speak truthfully to your neighbor, Paul has warned, for we are all members of one body (4:25). Openness and honesty gird us together; misunderstanding and hidden motives divide.

The breastplate of righteousness. "There must not be even a hint of sexual immorality, or of any kind of impurity, or of greed" (5:3) among God's holy people. Righteous living is essential, guarding the very heart of our shared lives.

Feet fitted with the Gospel of peace. More than once in this letter Paul has stressed how the Gospel brings peace, reconciling us to God and making us one. In Ephesians, peace is the bond that holds the unity created by the Spirit. When unity is maintained, Christ's church is enabled to move in full responsiveness to its Head.

The shield of faith. We maintain a confident hope in the reality and power of God. This trust extinguishes doubt. We are inadequate in ourselves, yes. But our trust is in God, who "is able to do immeasurably more than all we ask or imagine, according to His power that is at work in us" (3:20).

The helmet of salvation. Salvation has brought us a new life and identity. By keeping our identity as Christ's living church constantly before us, our perception of life is transformed. Satan's dreams of distorted relationships cannot cloud the mind of a person who grasps the full meaning of the salvation we enjoy in Christ.

The Spirit's sword. Why does Paul explain here that the sword is "the Word of God"? (6:17) It is because, in all of Ephesians, Paul has not discussed Scripture as he has the other elements of our armor. This vital tool is needed for us to wage our spiritual warfare.

And, in it all, on all occasions, we need prayer.

TEACHING GUIDE

Prepare
Ask God to help each of your group members grasp the powerful concept that societal roles do not make people more or less important, but are God's way of giving each of us differing opportunities to serve one another in love.

Explore
1. Ask pairs to sum up in three statements the major teachings of Ephesians 1–4.
2. Focus on the critical concept that societal roles do not define a person's importance, but rather define his or her opportunities to serve others. Use the "link-to-life" idea on page 930

This study should take more than half your group time, and is vital preparation for a study of husband/wife relationships in Ephesians 5:22-33.

Expand
Work in teams on the case history involving differing needs in a marriage relationship. How will the couple go about solving their conflict if they adopt the pagan notion of headship, and if they accept the Christian concept as modeled by Jesus? See "link-to-life," pages 931-932.

Apply
Briefly survey the armor of God, as explained in Ephesians, by which we are able to recognize the devil's schemes for disrupting the unity of the church. Then ask each group member to share which piece of armor seems most important to him or her, and why.

STUDY GUIDE 145

Philippians

CALLED TO JOY

Overview

This brief, warm letter was written to Philippi from Rome in early A.D. 63. Paul was especially close to the church in this, the leading city in Macedonia. His letter, rather than a reasoned exposition or corrective of a local error, is simply an expression of friendship and of shared joy in a common faith.

Three things seem particularly special about this short letter. First, its key word is "joy." "Joy" and "rejoice" occur again and again, and suggest a helpful strategy for the book's study.

Second, Philippians contains one of the most powerful New Testament affirmations of Christ's deity and lordship. Jesus who was God from eternity emptied Himself to become a man and, after suffering death, was raised again to His original glory and given a name above every name: Lord.

Third, Paul shared his own personal goal in life—his yearning for a present experience of that transformation which will be his at the resurrection.

How great an opportunity we have, to teach this short, but warm and powerful review of what we Christians have in Christ.

▶ ***Joy.*** Old Testament terms cast joy in terms of the worshiping community's response to God. Relationship with Him is the key to joy. The key New Testament term (*chairo*) indicates both a state of joy, and that which brings us joy.

Commentary

The New Testament makes it abundantly plain. It is relationship with Jesus that is a vital source of our joy. Jesus Himself spoke of two ways that we might find joy in Him. He said, "If you obey My commands, you will remain in My love, just as I have obeyed My Father's commands and remain in His love. I have told you this so that My joy may be in you and that your joy may be complete" (John 15:10-11). And, "Until now you have not asked for anything in My name. Ask and you will receive, and your joy will be complete" (16:24).

As we go on we make other discoveries about joy. We see that it is produced in us by the Holy Spirit, and is a fruit of His presence (see Luke 10:21; Gal. 5:22; 1 Thes. 1:6). It is not linked with material possessions but rather is an overflow of salvation (Acts 8:8; 16:34).

Even persecution could not dampen the joy that glowed in early Christians, for their joy was not dependent on external circumstances (see Acts 13:52; 2 Cor. 7:4; James 1:2). Peter even said that "in this [salvation] you greatly rejoice, though now for a little while you may have had to suffer grief in all kinds of trials. These have come so that your faith—of greater worth than gold, which perishes even though refined by fire—may be proved genuine and may result in praise, glory, and honor when Jesus Christ is revealed" (1 Peter 1:6-7).

It is true that even pagans can know joy, as they find it in the good things that God has given to all human beings so liberally. But the Christian knows a heightened joy; a joy that is rooted in the bond that exists between the believer and the Lord, and the bond that exists with other believers whom we have come to love (see Rom. 16:19; Phil. 1:4, 25-26; 2:2, 29; 4:1; Heb. 13:17; 1 John 1:4). The deeper our relationship with Jesus and with His people, the greater the joy that awaits us, and the less that joy is dependent on external circumstances.

Who is Jesus? Philippians 2:1-13

To understand why Jesus is the key to joy, we must grasp who Jesus is. Paul, in a great and powerful affirmation of faith, made Christ's true identity perfectly clear. Many believe that the words in Philippians 2:5-11 are from an early Christian liturgy, used as a confession of faith in the churches which Paul founded.

Jesus is our example (Phil. 2:1-5). Paul looked with awe at Jesus' willing surrender of the prerogatives of Deity to become a human being, and to die for us on a cross. But the self-sacrifice of Jesus is also a powerful call to the believer. Those of us who look to Jesus as our Saviour are also to look to Him as our example! In fact, our "attitude should be the same as that of Christ Jesus."

When we adopt His attitude, there will be a dramatic impact on our relationships with others. We will be "like-minded." What Paul envisions here is a *community* of believers who model their personal relationships with each other on Jesus. Such a community will be united, having "the same love," and being one in spirit and purpose (v. 2). Our unity will not be based on having the same convictions (see Rom. 14–15), or even on holding exactly the same doctrines (see 1 Corinthians 8–10). Ours will be a unity that grows out of love; out of a Christlike attitude.

Paul then looked at how that attitude is expressed in individuals. It is expressed by doing "nothing out of selfish ambition or vain conceit, but in humility consider others better than yourselves. Each of you should look not only to your own interests, but also to the interests of others" (Phil. 2:3-4). It is this total unselfishness that we see exhibited so powerfully by Jesus. He did not "grasp at" His equality with God. He "made Himself nothing" to come to earth as a human being— a Servant. Here He even humbled Himself to the extent that He willingly died a criminal's death. And all for us.

If you and I have this attitude toward our brothers and sisters in Jesus, there *will* be Christian unity. And we will truly be one, in spirit and purpose. We, like Jesus, will live to serve. And in serving we, like Jesus, will find the way of exaltation.

This, of course, was part of Paul's total vision. Because Jesus humbled Himself, God the Father exalted Him—"to the highest place" (v. 9). For us as well as for Jesus, the way *up* is down. For us, as for Jesus, God exalts us when we humble ourselves in service of others.

Jesus is God (Phil. 2:6-11). This is the foundational truth in Christianity. In this confession the early church affirmed the pre-existence of Jesus as God, affirmed His incarnation as a true human being, affirmed His death on the cross, His resurrection and His coming again to be revealed as Lord of all.

We should note that the phrase stating Jesus was "found in appearance as a man" does *not* imply that Christ only *seemed* to be a human being. The Greek word here is *schema,* which lays stress on what was visible to the beholder. The Son of God was seen by men to be a man, and He truly was what He appeared to be: one of us.

What a passage for meditation today as we remember our Lord, and focus our thoughts on who He is—and how much He has done for us. For this is One:

> Who, being in very nature God, did not consider equality with God something to be grasped, but made Himself nothing, taking the very nature of a servant, being made in human likeness. And being found in appearance as a man, He humbled Himself and became obedient to death—even death on a cross! Therefore God exalted Him to the highest place and gave Him a name that is above every name, that at the name of Jesus every knee should bow, in heaven and on earth and under the earth, and every tongue confess that Jesus Christ is Lord, to the glory of God the Father.

♥ ***Link to Life: Youth / Adult***
Give each group member a sheet of paper on which this passage has been duplicated. Ask each to meditate on it, considering just what it tells him or her about Jesus.

If any have questions, take time to answer them. (For a verse-by-verse exposition, see the Bible Knowledge Commentary, *pages 653-655.)*

Point out that all we have and are as Christians is rooted in the truth Jesus affirmed in this great confession of faith.

Then ask each to compose a two-or three-line prayer, picking up one of these themes. It should be a prayer of praise or thanks that focuses clearly on who Jesus is, or what He has done for us.

Jesus is the source of our salvation (Phil. 2:12-13). Paul concluded with an exhortation to the Philippians to continue obeying his instructions, as they had. In this way they were to "work out your salvation with fear and trembling, for it is God who works in you to will and to act according to His good purpose."

This call to "work out your ['own,' as some versions have it] salvation" has troubled some. They have seen it as a demand to perform, or perhaps salvation will be lost. But this is not what Paul is suggesting here.

The word commonly translated "salvation" does look at personal salvation, in the Christian sense of salvation from sin. But that salvation has several aspects. There is the initial forgiveness won through faith in Jesus. There is present deliverance from the dominating power of sin in our lives. And there is ultimate salvation; deliverance from even the presence of sin when resurrection day arrives.

Here the word "therefore" links Paul's words with what had been said before. And Paul had been speaking to the Philippians about a unity to be found by adopting the attitude of Jesus—a unity which 4:2-3 tells us was at least strained in the local body.

What Paul was saying, then, is that the church is to work out (to express) in their lives together the deliverance which Jesus has won for them, and is to do this with a proper sense of awe, realizing that God Himself was at work within them, present to will and act according to His good purpose.

As the Christians at Philippi modeled on Christ, and adopted His attitude, they would find deliverance from the things that divided them and would in fact give visible expression, together, to the salvation that was theirs in Jesus Christ.

Yes, the Jesus we worship truly is God. And, as the God-Man, Jesus set us an example, showing us the attitude which is the key to Christian unity, and is also the key to expressing in our fellowships the salvation which is ours in Him.

Paul's Personal Goal: Philippians 3

If there was ever a man who was deeply aware of his need to experience the present-tense salvation referred to in 2:12-13, it was the Apostle Paul.

Paul's later ministry, expressed in this book and in Colossians and Ephesians, increasingly focused on the present impact of Jesus on His church. Toward the end of Paul's life, arrests grew more frequent. He spent an increasing amount of time in prison. With less and less personal contact with the congregations he founded, Paul kept in touch through correspondence, friends, and disciples such as Timothy and Titus. Paul watched as the early flush of excitement and expectancy was tempered by the sober necessity of living in a hostile world. Challenges to the faith were raised. Some wanted to blend the philosophies of paganism or the ritualism of Judaism with the new Way. Clearly the church needed a better understanding of its uniqueness. The Good News of God's action in the past and His promise for the future must not obscure the fact that God *is,* and that "the present time is of the utmost importance" (Rom. 13:11, PH).

So Paul's prison letters turned the attention of believers to Christ Himself and to an exploration of what it means to live as members of Christ's body.

In Philippians Paul shared a very personal testimony. Centering his own attention on Jesus, Paul spoke of his own present experience—and his daily goal in life. He is one of those who:

> Glory in Christ Jesus, and who put no confidence in the flesh—though I myself have reasons for such confidence.
>
> If anyone else thinks he has reasons to put confidence in the flesh, I have more: circumcised on the eighth day, of the people of Israel, of the tribe of Benjamin, a Hebrew of Hebrews; in regard to the Law, a Pharisee; as for zeal, persecuting the church; as for legalistic righteousness, faultless.
>
> But whatever was to my profit, I now consider loss for the sake of Christ. What is more, I consider everything a loss compared to the surpassing greatness of knowing Christ Jesus my Lord, for whose sake I have lost all things. I consider them rubbish, that I may gain Christ and be found in Him, not having a righteousness of my own that comes from the Law; but that which is through faith in Christ—the righteousness that comes from God and is by faith. I want to know Christ and the power of His resurrection and the fellowship of sharing in His sufferings, becoming like Him in His death, and so, somehow, to attain to the resurrection from the dead.
>
> Philippians 3:3-11

Paul's deeply personal desire, expressed here, is not a yearning for some distant future. Paul concentrates instead on his *ongoing daily experience with God,* an experience that can lift the endless repetition of emptiness, and give life vitality and meaning. To understand, we need to note several of Paul's themes here.

Knowing Christ (Phil. 3:8). Paul focused here on relationship; on a personal experience of Jesus Christ that deepens as the days pass. This is Paul's first goal.

Having righteousness (Phil. 3:9). Again Paul was not looking ahead. Paul was concerned about moral transformation *now.* We Christians are to experience a holiness, rooted not in the do's and don'ts approach of Law, but in a dynamic goodness that only divine power can bring.

Resurrection power (Phil. 3:10). It is easy to misread these words. Paul was not referring to the future resurrection promised to believers. Paul spoke later of that time (vv. 20-21). Here Paul expressed his deep yearning to experience God's resurrection power.

Paul had expressed this earlier, in Romans. "He who raised Christ from the dead will also give life to your mortal bodies through His Spirit, who lives in you" (Rom. 8:11). But Paul had not yet arrived at a full experience of that power (Phil. 3:12). The daily goal that Paul set for himself was a fuller experience of Christ's resurrection life, bringing vitality and power to his present.

Reading Paul's words, we become aware that life does have meaning. In Christ we too are called heavenward (v. 14). We are invited to know the touch of a God who is always present. We are invited to a deepening personal relationship with Jesus; to a growing and dynamic righteousness; and to an experience of power that can transform us and our lives. What a goal for you and me—and our group members—to adopt. What examples we have, first in Jesus, and now in Paul.

The Search for Joy: Philippians

As noted at the beginning of this commentary, the theme of "joy" is woven throughout this small New Testament book. This theme probably should guide us in our teaching, as we help our group members examine what it is that can bring believer's inner joy.

♥ ***Link to Life: Youth / Adult***
Write the word "happy" on the left side of the chalkboard. Ask your group members to list "what most people *believe makes them happy." When the list is complete, write on the right "joy." Discuss: "Is there a difference between happiness and joy? If so, what is it?" Then point out that in your study today you will all discover what it is that can bring Christians joy—even if they lack those things most people believe are necessary to make them happy.*

Sources of joy in Philippians 1. Paul was in prison, his chains restricting him to a small rented house in Rome. The apostle, whose life had been dedicated to establishing churches by traveling to the key cities in the Roman Empire, had been set aside.

Yet as Paul wrote to the Philippians we sense the warmth of his love, and we also sense a confidence and joy. Paul reached the most distant lands by prayer, and was reassured about his converts by his conviction that "He who began a good work in you will carry it on to completion until the day of Christ Jesus" (v. 6). But there were other sources of confidence as well. Though in chains, Paul had the opportunity of witnessing to the Praetorian guards assigned to watch him. And Paul heard that others, stimulated by his imprisonment, had become more zealous in preaching the Gospel.

In verses 4-5 Paul speaks of praying "with joy" for the Philippians "because of your partnership in the Gospel from the first day until now." This was not a sharing in salvation, but rather partnership in spreading the Gospel. Paul and the Philippians had a common concern for communicating the Gospel to the lost.

In fact, this theme is expressed again and again in the first chapter. Even Paul's imprisonment should have been gladly accepted by his friends because "what has happened to me has really served to advance the Gospel" (v. 12).

Paul's chains stimulated some to speak out more courageously. But others, who saw Paul as a rival, had increased their own missionary effort out of "selfish ambition." Paul was glad, for from whatever motives "Christ is preached" (v. 8), and "because of this I rejoice."

In this first chapter, then, Paul presented

sharing the Gospel as a basic source of Christian joy. As we reach out to others with the Good News of Jesus we too will discover, with Paul and the Philippians, an overflow of Spirit-produced inner joy.

Sources of joy in Philippians 2. Paul now looked to other believers and viewed them as a source of joy. Paul's joy would be complete when the Philippians adopted Christ's attitude and were "like-minded, having the same love, being one in spirit" (v. 2).

Paul next used an Old Testament image. He saw himself and his own likely execution as a "drink offering" poured out on a sacrifice. This drink offering was voluntary, and intended to add its own rich savor to the basic sacrifice. Paul viewed his coming death not as loss, but as a joyful service he willingly offered on behalf of all who had come to Christ through him. And Paul urged the Philippians not to be upset, but rather to rejoice with him that he has been privileged to give himself for their sake.

Finally, Paul spoke of being "glad" (rejoicing) in the recovery of a messenger from Philippi, who had been extremely ill.

Throughout this chapter, the focus is not so much on the Gospel itself as on those who have responded to the Gospel. And the joy Paul spoke of wells up from being able to serve others, and from seeing God at work in others' lives.

Sources of joy in Philippians 4. Finally Paul spoke of a joy that is ours in the Lord Himself. He told us to "rejoice in the Lord always. I will say it again: Rejoice!"

And Paul went on to tell us how we can experience joy in knowing Jesus. We are to remember that the Lord is near, and rather than being anxious are to present every need to Him with thanksgiving. As we do, God's own peace will fill us. And, to keep our hearts and minds fixed on the Lord we are to focus on whatever is true and noble, putting our faith in Jesus into practice, and thus experience God with us.

TEACHING GUIDE

Prepare

How have your group members caused you joy? How closely can you identify with Paul as he speaks of his affection for the Philippians?

Explore

1. Have your group explore the difference between happiness and joy. See "link-to-life," page 937.
2. Or give a lecture on "joy," drawing from passages other than Philippians.

Expand

1. Divide into teams, one of which is to look at Philippians 1–2 and 4. Each team should first locate occurrences of "joy" and "rejoice." Then by a study of the context determine the *specific source* of joy.

Have the teams report. Then, working with the chart below, have your group members list every way they can think of that Christians today can find joy by sharing the Gospel, serving others, or deepening personal relationship with the Lord.

Happiness vs. Joy

Happy	Joy	What We Can *Do*
Money Security Nice home Success Health Love Friends Leisure Travel Family etc.	chap. 1 sharing in Gospel Christ preached chap. 2 other believers sacrifice self for others chap. 4 Lord Himself	

2. Or, give a minilecture on Paul's vision of Christ, and how that vision affects Christians. See commentary themes, "Who Is Jesus?" and Paul's Personal Goal."

Apply

1. Have each group member select one thing the group suggested from the "what we can do" section of the study chart that each has been doing or intends to do. Each should then share his or her experience or plans. Then close in prayer thanking God for the sources of continuing joy that He has made available to us through Jesus.

2. Or, use the "link-to-life" idea on page 935 to respond to Philippians 2's great affirmation of who Jesus is.

STUDY GUIDE 146

Colossians 1–2

A NEW HUMANITY

Overview

This brief but significant letter reflects a challenge raised by false philosophical systems that attempted to infiltrate and distort Christianity in its early centuries. This system, known as Gnosticism, is known in its developed form from second-century writings. Its basic tenets are confronted here by the Apostle Paul.

The Gnostics claimed a special, hidden knowledge not available to ordinary Christians. But their beliefs in fact contradicted basic Bible truths!

In responding to the challenge Paul powerfully affirmed basic tenets of the biblical faith. He made it clear just what God is like, who Jesus is, how we come to know God, and how we can experience a vital spiritual life through relationship with the Lord. The book can be outlined quite simply.

Paul wrote this letter while in Rome in prison, and sent it in A.D. 62 or 63.

Outline

I.	Introduction	1:1-2
II.	Christ, God in the Flesh	1:3-29
III.	Christ, the Way to God	2:1-23
IV.	Christ, Key to Spirituality	3:1–4:1
V.	Personal Notes	4:2-18

■ For a discussion of background and a verse-by-verse commentary on key concepts developed in Colossians, see the Victor *Bible Knowledge Commentary,* pages 667-686.

Commentary

Two of the most powerful words in advertising, I've been told, are *new* and *free.*

When the Gospel message echoed across the first-century world, both these elements were emphasized. "It is by grace you have been saved, through faith—and this not from yourselves, it is the gift of God—not by works" (Eph. 2:8-9). The Gospel is free! And, God created one "new man out of the two" [Jew and Gentile], thus making peace" (v. 15). The Gospel brings that which is refreshingly new!

Suddenly all the old categories men used to define themselves, and the old ways they attempted to understand the world and their relationship to the divine, were shattered. The new had come. Commenting on Colossians 3:11, Ralph Martin (in *Colossians: The Church's Lord and the Christian's Liberty* [Zondervan]) observes:

> In the society of Christians a new type of humanity is being formed. Christ's life flows out to His people and is reproduced in their midst. One proof of this new life was seen in the canceling of restrictions and inhibitions which made the ancient world so socially stratified and class-conscious. Paul had shown how in the church barriers of race, social distinction, and sex were being broken down as Christians acted on their baptismal profession of initiation into the body.

But many in the ancient world struggled against the idea of "new." They were attracted to the church but tried to adjust Christ to fit their old categories. They tried to define Christianity in terms of their human philosophies rather than letting Christ define them as a new humanity.

We have the same problem. We have seen that the church is a living organism. Yet today we still persist in diagramming its structure as a business rather than a body. The leadership is called to equip members of the body. Yet all too many Christians view the pastoral staff as men hired to do the teaching and evangelism that is the body's ministry.

We see in the New Testament that a dynamic holiness is to mark the character of believers, and the believing community. And yet we persist in trying to define our righteousness by lists of things we do and things we don't. Constantly the temptation is to push and squeeze the totally new into the old and familiar ways. In Christ, the *new* has come, and in the church—God's new humanity—we find a life that calls us to a fulfillment that can be found only in Christ's completely different way!

Understanding this, it is not too surprising to discover that in the once-important center of Colossae, the church was being drained of power by a group of men who claimed advanced knowledge (*gnosis*) but were attempting to fit Christianity into an old and empty philosophic system: the Gnostic way.

Not until the middle of the second century did the church fathers combat a developed form of Gnosticism. Yet most scholars see the terms Paul uses in Colossians and the concerns he deals with as indicating the presence of this heresy in Colossae. These Gnostics were concerned about issues explored by people of all ages:

- What is God like and what is His relationship to the world?
- How does a human being gain access to God's true presence?
- How does the human being find fullness of spiritual life?

Gnosticism not only posed these questions, but claimed to answer them. When a local congregation formed at Colossae, early Gnostics hurried in to redefine Christ and the Gospel in their own terms.

♥ ***Link to Life: Youth / Adult***

Here are a number of statements that Christians today might or might not make. Ask your group members to determine which, if any, they agree with. Then tell them that some of these statements reflect an ancient heresy called Gnosticism. At the end of class time, you will return to these statements and reevaluate them in light of what you find in Colossians 1 and 2.

- *I feel closest to God alone.*
- *Wearing lipstick is not spiritual.*
- *I know she's spiritual; she can quote over 2,000 Bible verses.*
- *I'm suspicious of things I enjoy. God doesn't want me to get entangled in the world.*
- *The really spiritual people in our church are the ones who teach Sunday School and come to every meeting.*
- *I just won't associate with people who curse and smoke.*
- *I always look to the Ten Commandments to tell me how to live.*

What is God like? The Gnostics were dualists. They saw all things in terms of two contrasting principles. On the one side was good, which was associated with the spiritual and the immaterial. On the other side was evil, which was associated with the material universe. God Himself was perfectly good, spiritual, and totally disassociated from the material. He would not pollute Himself by any such contact! The material universe was an accident or, at worst, the error of the last of a long series of supernatural beings—intermediaries—ranked between God and matter. To God, the pure Spirit, the world was alien and despicable.

To the Gnostics how jolting was the idea of an Incarnation! God become man? God take on human flesh? Never! Christ must be a lower intermediary or an "appearance"—a shadow of God cast on a screen. But God in human flesh? Unthinkable!

It was also unthinkable that God might wish to enter believers' lives. Instead the Gnostics saw the human being as trapped; a spark of the divine held captive in a fleshly prison. Salvation meant release from bondage to all that was material, including our own bodies! Resurrection? God's life, lived out in a corporate body shaped of loving men and women, in whom Christ now walks this world? Ugly! Horrible!

How does a human being gain access to God? The Gnostic saw God as remote and inaccessible. God might be approached through the long chain of intermediaries that stretched between Him and matter. Jesus Christ might even be one of these intermediaries. But since Jesus had contact with this world, Christ's rank within the chain must be low. Here is a partial explanation of Paul's reference to the worship of angels (Col. 2:18): people were striving to gain the attention and support of beings who form a chain leading to God. These powerful spirits should be placated, the Gnostics taught, for human destiny lay in their hands, not in God's.

How does a human being find fullness of life?

Gnostic Way Versus God's Way

Gnostic Way	God's Way in Colossians
dualistic "good" — "evil" spiritual — material divine — nondivine to know — to do There is no contact between these two systems.	
Christ—a lower intermediary or an appearance.	
Man—a divine spark imprisoned in an evil, material body.	
Salvation—freedom from the evil, material prison.	
Way of salvation—found through special knowledge, asceticism, and honoring angelic intermediaries.	
Individual morality—ascetic self-denial of needs, drives, desires, and appetites.	
True religion—subjective, speculative. Escape to a realm in which the material plays no part.	
Angels—powers between God and men who must be honored and used as access to the fullness.	

The Gnostics said, by practicing the way of life they propounded. That way of life stressed asceticism and rigid regulations, abstinence and self-punishment. For liberation from the evil, fleshly body must be good. The angelic intermediaries were honored by ritual and self-discipline. In this way, the fullness might be found.

So some at Colossae were imposing this approach to spirituality on the church there. And Paul wrote this letter to refute the false teaching that warped both faith and Christian experience.

♥ ***Link to Life: Youth / Adult***
Give a lecture covering the main tenets of the Gnostic way. Use the left side of the comparison chart to sum up their teachings. If you wish, duplicate the chart and distribute it as a study guide.

God's Way: Colossians 1–2
The Gospel of Christ simply did not fit the Gnostic's categories, which were drawn from well-known philosophies of that time. Only a drastic reordering of these old categories enables the believer to grasp the fantastic new hope held out to man. The body of Christ—the new and living organism of which you and I are a part—is at the heart of that newness. Christ living in His body forms the new humanity, and transforms us as well as all our old ideas about life. So the Book of Colossians not only challenged the people to whom it was addressed; it challenges us now. Am I able to set aside my old ways of thinking about spirituality and to enter joyfully into the new?

Commendation (Col. 1:1-8). As always, Paul began with a commendation. The Colossians' lives were marked by love for all the saints. God's Gospel had taken root among them, and was growing and producing fruit.

Concern (Col. 1:9-14). At the same time, Paul had a deep concern for this church, a concern he expressed in his prayer. Paul was eager that God would fill the Colossians "with the knowledge of His will through all spiritual wisdom and understanding" (v. 9), that through knowing God's will their lives might be worthy of Him.

Paul was eager that growth, good works, and empowerment might be theirs. He was eager that they experience fully what it meant to live *now* in the kingdom of God's Son.

Who Jesus is (Col. 1:15-23). The kingdom is Christ's. Clearly then, we must grasp who Jesus is. In this passage, which was possibly adapted from early liturgy, Paul contradicts every Gnostic category!

- Jesus is the express "image of the invisible God" (v. 15). He is not some distant, inferior reflection.
- Jesus is the direct Creator of all things in the material and spiritual universe—even of the angelic hosts. By Him and for Him everything was made (vv. 16-17). Clearly God and the material universe are not at odds!
- Jesus is Head of the body, and He is supreme in everything (v. 18). The fullness of God resides in Him alone (v. 19).
- In a real Incarnation—in Christ's physical body through death—God *has* reconciled us, bringing us into His very presence. In Christ we are "holy in His sight, without blemish and free from accusation" (vv. 20-22). In fact *spiritual effects are accomplished in the physical body*. Again, our life in this world and our life with God are not at odds, but harmonize.

Paul concluded that the Colossians should continue in their faith, "established and firm, not moved from the hope held out in the Gospel" (v. 23). In this way they would experience the reality of being new men and women in Christ. Christ is the sole focus, the center, and to understand newness, we must keep our lives centered in Him.

Mystery (Col. 1:24-29). Paul now showed that his ministry was to help the saints grasp this great mystery. No knowledge is hidden, as the Gnostics claim. All has been revealed, even the great secret that "Christ is *in you,* bringing with Him the hope of all the glorious things to come" (v. 27, PH).

In Christ (Col. 2:1-15). Here Paul appealed to the Colossians to realize that Christianity calls us to live our present life "in Christ." This involves not only reliance on the Head, but also participation in the body (vv. 6-7). In being joined to Christ by the Spirit's baptizing work (v. 12, see also 1 Cor. 12:13), we were so completely united to Him that we experienced not only His death but also His resurrection. Having thus been made alive with Christ (Col. 2:13), we are freed to live a resurrection kind of life *now*. Christ's death canceled and made irrelevant all the old things that once cluttered life and opposed us (v. 15). Life is now the issue; our sole goal is to live Jesus' life in this world.

God's new humanity (Col. 2:16-23). How empty the rigorous life the Gnostics proposed! Keep regulations. Worship higher powers. Eat this. Don't eat that. Strictly observe rituals and taboos. In Paul's judgment, "Such regulations indeed have an appearance of wisdom, with their self-imposed worship, their false humility and their harsh treatment of the body, but they lack any value in restraining sensual indulgence" (vv. 22-23).

Paul's point is that while such self-discipline may limit expression of certain kinds of sins, the sin nature will still find occasion to express itself—as in spiritual pride.

The person groping for a touch of God loses connection with Christ when he or she focuses on the shadows of human effort. That taste of true spirituality, for which we all yearn, is found in relationship with Jesus Christ as Head of a living body. It is from the Head that "the whole body, supported and held together by its ligaments and sinews, grows as God causes it to grow" (v. 19).

And so both Colossians and Ephesians emphasize that the church as Christ's living body is the key to understanding—and becoming—God's new humanity.

What is God like, and what is His relationship to the world? God *is* Jesus, Creator and Sustainer of all things visible and invisible. And God walks the world today in that body of which Christ is living Head.

How does a human being gain access to

God's true presence? By the reconciliation won through Christ's blood and death and by intimate relationship with others who have life through Jesus.

How does a human being find fullness of life? That question will be answered as we finish our study of Colossians by examining chapter 3.

The Threat

Gnosticism in the early church was no harmless alternative to faith. It challenged the very core of living faith by attempting to set Jesus aside, and make Him something less than the center of our lives. Gnosticism also attempted to set the body of Christ aside, by raising many objections to oneness. Love and caring became less important than fulfilling rituals. Unity was displaced in favor of hierarchy, not only in the spirit world but also in the church. Those with "special hidden knowledge"—the Gnostics—were at the top. Next were those whose rigid adherence to rituals and other religious duties made them "more spiritual" than the herd. The attitude that calls us to "consider others better than ourselves" (Phil. 2:3) gave way to rank and pride. Living with other believers in harmony and peace was set aside as unimportant.

Gnosticism also rejected the concept that the Christian's calling *is* to live in this world. The kingdom was viewed as far-off, and spiritual. Good works were ridiculed. After all, the world is the corrupt dwelling place of sin. Only by withdrawing could one find a touch of the divine. The kind of commitment Jesus knew—to walk and talk and love a band of sweaty men as the perspiration poured down His own back—was unknown to the Gnostics. The idea that Jesus, through His body on earth, might desire to touch the filthy among sin-warped humanity was foreign to their thought. (Sometimes it is foreign to us as well!)

Yet a study of the Gnostics against whom Paul wrote is helpful to us. It raises questions that each of us need to face.

Where do we center our faith? In Jesus, or in the practice of religion?

Where do we place our priorities? On knowing and loving each other as members of one body? Or have other things intruded and led us to build our own hierarchies and establish our own little rules: rules that enable us to keep our brothers at arm's length and to feel better than they?

And, where do we see our calling? Are we simply to worship, in some cloister set apart from the world? Or are we to *be* God's kingdom now, and reach out to touch the poor and the lost?

"He has rescued us," Paul wrote to the Colossians (1:13). Rescued, we are the new humanity. Old categories no longer fit, and we cannot define ourselves by them. To discover who we are, we must submit all thoughts to Christ.

TEACHING GUIDE

Prepare

Read the text of Colossians 1 and 2 carefully, against the background of Gnostic beliefs as discussed in this study guide.

Explore

1. Give your group members a series of statements with which to agree or disagree. Some of these reflect contemporary expressions of Gnostic attitudes. See "link-to-life," page 941.
2. Distribute the chart on page 942 which lists Gnostic beliefs. Explain each, supplementing with information in the commentary. It is important that your group members understand the Gnostic system as background for their study of the text.

Expand

Divide into teams of five to study Colossians 1 and 2 directly. Each team should find verses/concepts in Colossians that confront Gnostic ideas expressed in the chart.

When teams have studied the text, come together and discuss what they have found. The commentary on specific passages will help you make sure your group members have noted all important points.

Apply

Review the statements used in the opening study activity. How would the group now evaluate each? Discuss: "What is the key to Christian spirituality and experience?"

STUDY GUIDE 147

Colossians 3–4

A NEW LIFE TO LIVE

Overview

In the first two chapters of this Bible book, Paul set out truths which contradict the notions of those later known as Gnostics. This heresy taught that the material was evil, and the immaterial good. God, good and spiritual, was isolated from the universe in which we live by His own moral character and nature. Jesus, in this system, was either an unreal shadow or a lower-order of angelic being.

Paul directly confronted this view. Jesus is God in the flesh. And it was in His real human body through death in that body that Jesus accomplished the greatest of all spiritual tasks: our redemption. What is more, Jesus Himself is the Creator of both material and immaterial worlds, and holds authority over each. We Christians find our fulfillment in Jesus and in relationship with Him. There is no "higher knowledge" than knowing Jesus, and no spiritual secrets that are not unveiled in Him.

Now, in Colossians 3, Paul applied these basic truths to our Christian lives. Spirituality is not withdrawal from this world, but is living Jesus' life *in* the world. What a privilege to help our group members discover the characteristics of true spirituality, and to help each see how he or she can live in intimate union with Jesus.

▶ ***Holiness.*** New Testament holiness involves joyful commitment to God and to good, expressed in all we say and do.

Commentary

A famous preacher of an earlier day wrote a book about his early search for a full life in Christ. He told of his struggle for holiness—hours of prayer for purification from selfishness and wrong desires. He told how he guarded his every word and action, struggling to bring them into conformity with God's will.

Finally exhausted by the pursuit, he contracted TB and spent a year in a sanitarium. There he met a young woman of his denomination who was recuperating from the same disease. She seemed so tranquil and pure. He watched her for weeks and became convinced that she had found the secret that eluded him. One night as he struggled in prayer, he felt he could wait no longer. He rose to find her, determined to ask for the way to peace.

Before he could leave, there was a knock on his door. There she stood, her face contorted as her body shook with sobs. "Brother Harry," she gasped. "I've watched you all these weeks. If anyone has found the secret of holiness, it's you. I've *got to know!*"

Spiritual Reality

This true story illustrates the deep frustration many have felt in their search for an answer to the Gnostics' third question: How does a human being find fullness of life? How do we experience the reality of Christ and know the meaning of a Spirit-filled life?

Many suggestions have been made. Many different descriptions of true spirituality and how to find it have been given. Often the prescription promises a shortcut: immediate attainment of a higher kind of life. Among these ways are:

The special experience. As the result of one dramatic moment, the Holy Spirit's power will flow unimpeded for the rest of your life, eradicating sin and lifting you to fullness.

This is an attractive view. The change is sudden. It is clearly supernatural; God's work alone. And it promises freedom from the nagging tensions that have been our lot. No more struggle! Just surrender and be lifted to a higher plane.

We must be careful not to dismiss special experiences altogether. God sometimes brings us to crisis confrontations with Himself, and these result in valid spiritual breakthroughs. But we deceive ourselves if we expect any such experience to confer instant sainthood.

Special knowledge. This also seems attractive, appealing to our feeling that there must be something more to the simple message of Christ than meets the eye. Sometimes we expect special knowledge from learning to read the Hebrew and Greek of the original biblical documents. Sometimes it is a special key to interpreting the Bible, a key not given to the ignorant masses who take Scripture in its plain sense. Sometimes it is theosophy or some modern cult that imposes a system so like Gnosticism on Scripture that they are almost indistinguishable.

And how attractive it is to believe that once I know the hidden thing, I will have fullness. How attractive to feel that knowledge sets me above others and brings me closer to God.

Ritual observance. Here fullness is attained by careful keeping of prescribed rituals and taboos. We refrain from eating meat, keep Sunday or the Sabbath, guard our behavior, and keep everything within prescribed rules. Soon we have developed lists and traditions defining every situation and telling us what pleases God.

This is probably the least satisfactory approach. Our attention to details leads us further and further from relationships with others. Even fellowship with Christ is set aside in our commitment to rules. But the feeling that life is empty will always intrude.

Self-denial. This approach will always tempt those who are ascetically inclined. Pushing down desires, controlling the body by severe fasting or punishment, and being suspicious of anything associated with the material world has a strange appeal. It seems so spiritual! Escape from life to an ethereal plane!

The Gnostics chose to do so. Spirituality had to be found beyond the world of things and persons. And so the body and desires associated with this world had to be denied.

It is true that Paul told the Colossians to "put to death, therefore, what belongs to your earthly nature" (3:5). The Christian life has always been a walk of discipline. But it is not discipline for discipline's sake; we deny ourselves certain things because Christ has called us to something so much better.

Licentiousness. This obviously is not a way to find spiritual fullness—but some have reasoned that since our bodies are part of the evil material universe, it doesn't matter what they do. They can indulge every fleshly desire, for whatever is done cannot contaminate the spiritual element within. Spiritual reality is found through special knowledge, subjective experience, or the ritual observations totally divorced from daily life.

We have something of this same notion today—the idea that what we do on weekdays, in business, or other relationships has nothing to do with Sunday faith. Spirituality is pressed into a single compartment and never integrated into our total experience.

♥ ***Link to Life: Youth / Adult***

Tell the true story of the minister with which the chapter opens. Discuss: "What do you think his idea of holiness and spirituality was?"

Then survey the various approaches that many have taken in a search for spiritual vitality discussed earlier. Encourage sharing. Have any in your group tried one or more of these approaches? What happened to them?

Allow plenty of time for this sharing. It is important to prepare the group for shared study of Colossians 3.

Our Hidden Life

In contrast to these shortcuts, Paul encouraged us to think in terms of gradual renewal and growth.

"All over the world this Gospel is producing fruit and growing" (1:6). Paul's prayer for the Colossians was that they might also be "bearing fruit in every good work, growing in the knowledge of God" (v. 10). Live in Christ "rooted and built up in Him" (2:6).

The Colossian prayer provides important background for our understanding of Paul's pathway to spiritual fullness. That prayer reveals something that I have called in another book, the "Colossians cycle" (p. 947).

The prayer that explains the cycle is found in Colossians 1:9-11. Here Paul asks God to:

> Fill you with the knowledge of His will through all spiritual wisdom and understanding. And we pray this in order that you may live a life worthy of the Lord

The Colossian Cycle*

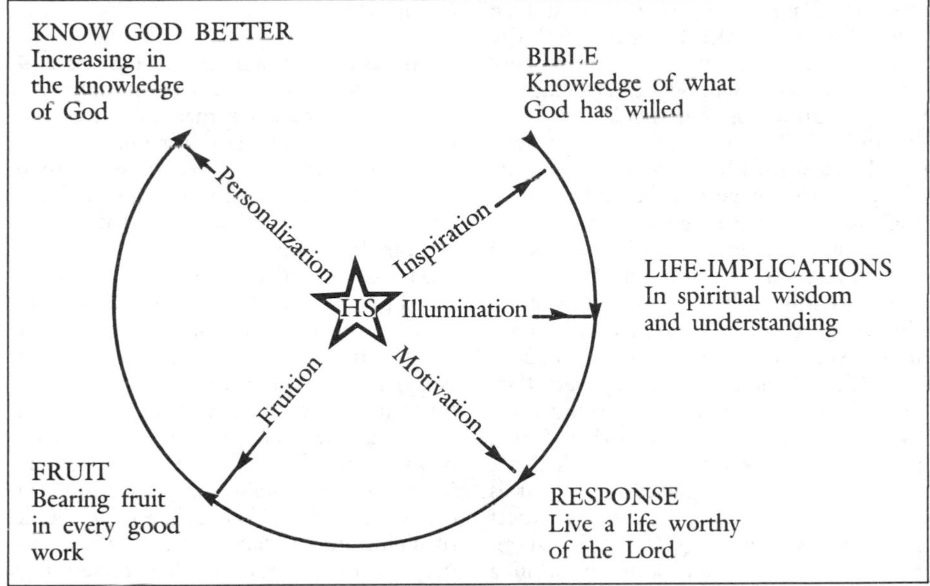

*from *Creative Bible Teaching*, Richards, Moody Press

> and may please Him in every way; bearing fruit in every good work, growing in the knowledge of God.

The first element, a "knowledge of God's will," is literally a knowledge of "what God has willed." That is, the apostle has not looked to personal experiences of leading, but to revelation. God has made Himself and His will known to us in the Word. Personal experience of God begins with this revelation of Himself through the Prophets and Apostles.

But we are to hold this knowledge with "all spiritual wisdom and understanding." Each of the terms here focuses our attention not on intellectual knowledge or information. Each speaks of practical knowledge: of ability to apply what is known to daily life, and see its implications for our choices and actions.

As we apply what God has willed to our everyday lives, wisely letting God's Word guide our choices, we will live lives that are truly worthy of the Lord.

In this process God Himself will be actively at work within and through us, producing the Holy Spirit's fruit in our personalities even as we are active in every good work.

Finally, we will be "growing in the knowledge of God." This culminating thought is not of growth in knowledge *about* God, but growth in knowing Him personally. We will experience God in our lives, and find personal spiritual fulfillment, only in this way.

What a corrective to many of our own practices and assumptions. Knowing the Bible is not the key—applying what God has revealed in our daily lives is what counts. Knowing what we should do is not enough—it is putting what we know into practice to live a life worthy of God. As we, encouraged by the Holy Spirit, fulfill these responsibilities God Himself produces His good fruit in our lives, and makes Himself real to us.

It is against this background that Paul in Colossians 3 now shows us how to grow in a spiritual—and holy—life here on earth.

It is only natural for Paul to emphasize this. He thinks of Christianity in terms of *life*. And all living things grow. Growth is a natural, gradual process. There is direction to growth, but the change is often imperceptible day to day.

Paul's call is to "continue to live in Him [Christ], rooted and built up in Him" (2:6). This exhortation helps us resist those tempting promises of instant spiritual maturity. We are to be satisfied with Christ, to accept the growing processes of life in Him, and to resist the glamorous promises of hidden knowledge or special experiences that offer us shortcuts to glory. No wonder Paul spoke of a "new self, which is being renewed in knowledge in the image of its Creator" (3:10). Renewal is a process; growth is a way of life. Keeping our hearts fixed on Christ, we are to be satisfied with progress—not to demand perfection now.

Paul also focused on the hiddenness of spiritual life. Experiencing fullness may not be the exciting, obvious, or supernatural thing we dream of! Paul pointed out, "Your life is now hidden with Christ in God. When Christ, who is your life, appears, then you also will appear with Him in glory" (vv. 3-4). The glory will be seen when Christ appears. Don't look for it until then!

Our perception of fullness in Christ is much of our problem. What do we expect fullness to be like? Some aesthetic experience? No wonder some look for it in a sudden endowment. Some visible mark of piety? No wonder some look to ritual and observances.

In fact, we should not expect spiritual fullness to be marked off by its striking difference from ordinary living! Remember Jesus' incarnation? What set Him apart during the early years? He was a Man among men. He laughed. He enjoyed companionship. He ate and drank like other men. He was so much a man that His own people did not recognize Him. His claim to be the Son of God was heard with amazed disbelief, for He did not fit their image of the Divine. And yet, God walked the earth in the Man Jesus. In His life, we see God unveiled. We discover holiness in the love and compassion of One whose company was sought out by prostitute and sinner. His glory? That we will see when He returns in power.

Godliness in human flesh lives a Jesus-kind of life. And this is exactly what the apostle wanted us to realize. Holiness is not being "different." Holiness is not being "strange." It is being the same kind of loving person Jesus was. True holiness is hidden in daily life, expressed in the ordinary, and revealed in our living relationships with other people.

With this background, we can understand how jolting the teaching of Colossians 3 and 4 really was. Holy living, the fullness of living our relationship in Christ, is to be sought in the context of our ordinary lives in this world.

Comments on the Text: Colossians 3–4

Raised with Christ (Col. 3:1-4). Paul began by stressing the fact that we have been raised with Christ. Earthly regulations and concepts of spirituality are to be set aside. Our attention is to be fixed on things above, on Jesus, for it is only in Him that our real life can be found.

Two ways of life (Col. 3:5-11). Paul compared two ways of life. One way flows from what is called the "earthly" nature. This is not the *material nature* (e.g., the physical body) but the sin nature shared by all of humanity. The evil things that flow from the human heart are to be rejected by God's people. There is no place in the spiritual life for "sexual immorality, impurity, lust, evil desires and greed." The believer is to be rid of such things as "anger, rage, malice, slander, and filthy language." It is these things which pollute us and block our experience of Christ, not the fact that we exist as material beings in a material universe.

Evidences of holiness (Col. 3:12-17). But the truly spiritual life is not an empty life. That is, it is not so much characterized by what is absent from it as by what is present. So Paul tells us that as God's chosen people we are to cultivate such virtues as "compassion, kindness, humility, gentleness and patience." In our relationships with others we are to "bear with [put up with] each other and forgive whatever grievances you may have against one another." Love, which motivates all these expressions of our new life, is to characterize all our personal relationships.

All this may fall short of our dreams and images about spirituality. But these common things are the material from which spirituality is forged. These are the evidences of true holiness.

Opportunities to serve (Col. 3:18–4:1). Different stations in life become irrelevant when holiness and spirituality are in view. In every relationship—as children, spouses, citizen, and/or slave—we have full opportunity to live a holy and truly spiritual life.

Prayer (Col. 4:2-6). The way of life that Paul sketched is supernatural. Thus Paul emphasized the role of prayer. We are to depend on the Lord ourselves, and encourage others to focus their lives on God.

Greetings (Col. 4:7-18). Paul concluded with greetings to his Colossian friends, and by claiming a runaway slave, Onesimus, as his "faithful and dear brother" (v. 9). For the touching story of this young slave, see the Book of Philemon.

Summary

The Gnostics, whose influence was shaking the Colossian believers, had a notion of spirituality that drastically distorted the Christian way. It was rooted in a doctrine that robbed Jesus of His central place. Rather than seeing Jesus as the focus of all God's acts, the Gnostic pushed Him aside as one of a series of intermediaries. Thus Jesus would no longer be the touchstone by which the believer measured his life, or the source of power and daily guidance we all so desperately need. Jesus would also no longer be the pattern for the truly spiritual life. The "compassion, kindness, humility, gentleness and patience" (3:12) that marked Jesus' days on earth were far too ordinary to be viewed by the Gnostics as "spirituality"! Though Jesus lived the truly spiritual life, His incarnation was not seen as the model of the Christian's calling. Instead, an individual under the Gnostic influence wandered off in a futile search for some experience or hidden knowledge that would transform the mundane.

How important that Jesus truly be the center of your life and mine—and the center of the life of those we teach. He and He alone is the hope of glorious things to come in this life as well as in eternity (1:27). And it is Jesus who calls us to live the same life on earth that He lived; a life of holiness, as holiness is expressed in the ordinary events of each succeeding day.

TEACHING GUIDE

Prepare

In what ways is your own spiritual life and experience satisfying?

Explore

1. Tell the true story of the minister that launches this study. Ask your group members to try to define his concept of holiness. Is that concept accurate? Why, or why not?
2. Explain the various approaches to seeking holiness discussed in the commentary. Encourage your members to share their own experiences if any have approached the spiritual life from one of these avenues. See "link-to-life," page 946.

Expand

1. Give a minilecture on the Colossians cycle explained in the text. If this shaped a Christian's understanding of his or her spiritual life, how would such a person define spirituality? How would he or she define holiness?
2. Point out that Jesus was Himself the one truly holy and spiritual Person that this world has ever known. Discuss: "If we built our idea of holiness and spirituality on what we know of Jesus' life on earth, what would characterize our ideas?"

After your group has tried to define spirituality by reference to Jesus, break into pairs to study Colossians 3. What in this chapter would reinforce or modify the definition of holiness/spirituality just arrived at?

Apply

Go back and write a short note to the minister whose story opens this study, sharing how he can find peace and know true holiness.

STUDY GUIDE 148

1 Thessalonians

THE WORD: HEARD AND LIVED

Overview

Many believe that the Thessalonian letters are the earliest written by Paul. Though the apostle and his team had little time in Thessalonica (cf. Acts 17:2), the church he founded there grew rapidly, and reached out to promote the Gospel in the surrounding province. Paul's letter is one of warm encouragement, a restatement of many truths which he had already taught them.

The book can be outlined simply, using the theme of the Word of God and response to it.

Outline

I. The Word Heard	1:1-10
II. The Word Shared	2:1–3:13
III. The Word Lived	4:1–5:28

Two characteristics of this letter suggest a special study approach. First, it is rich in a variety of *repeated themes.* This suggests that a thematic study, rather than a verse-by-verse or paragraph-by-paragraph exploration can be helpful. Second, the book is personal, expressing beautifully how the Apostle Paul himself went about sharing God's Word with his converts. This suggests a special exploration of relationships in ministry.

Each of these approaches is taken in our present study of this small, but exciting, New Testament letter. And each will prove especially enriching to those you teach, seeking as Paul to help them live lives worthy of our Lord.

Commentary

We know from Acts that Paul did not stay long in Thessalonica. The disturbance described in Acts 17 forced the missionaries out of the city; later attempts by Paul to return were blocked (see 1 Thes. 2:17-18). Yet, looking at this early missionary letter, we see how quickly Paul communicated core truth to new converts, and the impact the truth had. "You became imitators of us and of the Lord," Paul reminded his Thessalonian readers. "The Lord's message rang out from you . . . your faith in God has become known everywhere. . . . How you turned to God from idols to serve the living and true God, and to wait for His Son from heaven, whom He raised from the dead—Jesus, who rescues us from the coming wrath" (1 Thes. 1:6-10).

Paul here pointed out the complete reorientation that came when people of the first century grasped the meaning of the Gospel's core.

- A personal God lives.
- The God of the universe calls us to know and serve Him.
- This God invaded history in the person of His Son, and through His Son's death and resurrection God rescues us from coming judgment.
- Jesus' return testifies to the promise that the universe has an end as well as a beginning.

Within the framework of the Gospel's glowing revelation of reality, individuals could once again find meaning, purpose, and joy. The underlying reality is God Himself. The life-transforming fact is that this God calls us into personal relationship with Himself!

We get a clearer impression of Paul's exposition of core truth through Charles Horne's discussion (in the *Zondervan Pictorial Encyclopedia*) of the doctrines referred to in the two Thessalonian letters:

> First, as respects the doctrine of God, Paul indicates that there is one true God (1 Thes. 1:9). From this one true and living God the Gospel is derived (1 Thes. 2:2). To Him they submit themselves for approval of their labor (1 Thes. 2:4, 10).

He providentially directs their lives (1 Thes. 3:11), and He is the one who will perfect the Thessalonians at the coming of Christ (1 Thes. 5:23). He has both chosen them (1 Thes. 2:4) and is even now calling them unto His own kingdom and glory (1 Thes. 2:12). And this God is faithful; He will accomplish the work which He has begun (1 Thes. 5:24).

Second, as respects the doctrine of Christ, the apostle so unites the Son with the Father that their essential unity is indicated (1 Thes. 1:1). He is described as "the Lord," the common term for God among the Jews of this time.

Third, as respects the doctrine of the Holy Spirit, the apostle teaches that it is the Spirit who makes the message effective in the hearts of the hearers (1 Thes. 1:5). The Spirit gives joy in affliction (1 Thes. 1:6); the Spirit calls believers to a holiness like His own (1 Thes. 1:7). . . .

Fourth, as respects the doctrine of eschatology, the apostle has considerable to set forth. From the futuristic perspective the "obtaining of salvation" is principally conceived in the Thessalonian epistles (1 Thes. 5:9; 2 Thes. 2:14). The basic emphasis theologically in the Thessalonian epistles is eschatological. The definite announcement of the Second Coming rounds off each step in the apostolic argument.

The new converts had been firmly grounded in core truth. A new view of reality, penetrating beyond the mists of illusion and empty human reasoning to the Person who made the universe for His own good and loving purposes, literally revolutionized the lives of first-century people.

♥ ***Link to Life: Youth / Adult***
Ask your group to take the role of first-century pagans. Most believe in no gods, but think all is ruled by fate. Nearly all try to placate or manipulate whatever spiritual powers there may be by making offerings nevertheless. Some have turned to mystery faiths, which feature entry rituals much like the rituals of contemporary lodges. All view the material world as permanent; none foresees a resurrection; most fear a dark and empty half-life after death.

Divide into teams, each of which is to read at least two chapters of 1 Thessalonians and to make a list of everything they learn about this God the apostle preaches. What is He like? What does He do? What are His concerns? What changes in one's view of life and its meaning would He make?

Come together again to hear reports, and to begin to sense through each team's discovery just how revolutionary Christian truth we take for grated today was in the first-century world.

The Power of Love

It would be a mistake to believe that the New Testament church captured the first-century world on the power of a "better idea" alone.

Paul did not preach a new philosophy. The response of new converts was, at heart, a response to a personal God who, in Jesus, offers forgiveness and an endless relationship with Himself. This is the Gospel's real power.

The revelation of God as a Person who loves came as a jolting surprise in the first century. W.W. Tarn, in *Hellenistic Civilization* (London, Edward Arnold), notes that two vital elements in the new religion, quite apart from the figure of the Founder, had no counterpart in Hellenistic thought. The first was the revelation of personal immortality and resurrection. The second was the fact that:

> Of all the Hellenistic creeds, none was based on love of humanity; none had any message for the poor and the wretched, the publican and the sinner. Those who labored and were heavy laden were to welcome a different hope from any which Hellenism could offer.

The mystery cults offered initiates a mystical association. Help was given in case of illness and with burial costs. But cult members were not family. Their god or goddess did not love them, nor were the initiate's fellows brothers and sisters bound together in a mutual commitment of love.

And then the Gospel message came.

God loved them. Christ died for them, according to the Scriptures. God invited them to receive forgiveness of sins and to become a member of His family, *forever.*

The message of the Gospel was then, as now, the stunning word that *God seeks to establish a permanent personal relationship with you!*

It was the personal dimension of the Gospel message, even more than its core truth, that captured hearts. When Paul addressed the Thessalonians and wrote, "Brothers loved by God, we know that He has chosen you," he was striking a totally new chord (1 Thes. 1:4)

Essentially Paul's mission was to communicate not only the truth about God, but also the love of God.

So, how did He communicate the love of God? And how does the New Testament indicate that we are to communicate today the wonder of personal relationship?

Paul's time in Thessalonica. Paul and his companions had gone to Thessalonica early in his second missionary journey (about A.D. 49). Acts 17 tells us that he first approached the Jewish community and for three Sabbaths presented the Gospel. It's likely that he stayed in this Greek city for up to six months, until finally the Jews marshaled opposition and expelled him. Thus the Christian church there was largely composed of Gentiles (1 Thes. 1:9; 2:14; Acts 17:4).

Thessalonica, as was typical of the cities in which Paul chose to found new churches, was located on the main highway from east to west, had a good harbor, and was a trade center. It was also the largest and most important city in Macedonia, and its capital.

The church founded there was a vigorous one; it grew rapidly, both in size and commitment.

"You became a model to all the believers in Macedonia and Achaia. The Lord's message rang out from you not only in Macedonia and Achaia—your faith in God has become known everywhere" (1 Thes. 1:7-8). Since this letter was written in A.D. 50 or 51, it is clear that the Gospel not only took root quickly but also that within a very short time this new church moved out aggressively to plant more churches throughout the province of Macedonia.

Paul had not only succeeded in communicating God's love and the reality of a personal relationship with Jesus. He had somehow equipped the new believers to communicate that same relationship to others. Perhaps this is what Paul meant in chapter 1 when he wrote, "You became imitators of us and of the Lord" (v. 6). Turning from their empty idols, they joyfully committed themselves to know and to serve the "living and true God" and were willing to "wait for His Son from heaven" (vv. 9-10). These new believers embraced both the relationship and the content of the Gospel.

Reality. Looking at 1 Thessalonians 2, we begin to sense how Paul and others in the first century communicated the reality of this Gospel relationship. The means is so simple and so obvious that we might tend to overlook it when we read this epistle. Yet, it rests on a profound and basic principle.

The Scriptures claim to reveal the truth about life and its meaning. We're told in its core truths about a God who created the universe in which we live. We're told that He created man in His own image, and that even though man sinned, God determined to redeem him. We're told that one day Jesus, who was born into the real world, who lived and died here and was resurrected bodily and ascended into heaven, where He now is with the Father, will one day return in triumph. The great questions about the origin, the meaning, and the goal of the universe are given a distinctive and positive answer. We're told that this is an accurate description of reality; that one day we will be present when God's Son returns from heaven. Then we will *know,* because we will participate in that great final denouement.

But we must take all these affirmations on faith. We cannot test these realities personally. We cannot experience them directly now. The core truths of the Gospel *are* true. We believe them. But we cannot test them experientially.

However, the Gospel also presents relational truth! The Bible affirms that God loves us and that, to Him, each person is a precious and valuable individual, worth even the ultimate sacrifice. The Bible claims that when you and I respond to Jesus, God draws us into His family; we become His sons and daughters, and we become brothers and sisters in a new and loving community.

This Gospel truth is also presented as reality. And this reality we can experience now! We *can* test it experientially! *We can know the love of God as He loves us through His family.*

This theme occurs so often in Scripture

that it is hard to see how we sometimes miss it. "Christ's love compels us" (2 Cor. 5:14). "You are a letter from Christ," he explained, "written not with ink but with the Spirit of the living God, not on tablets of stone but on tablets of human hearts" (3:3). The living personality of the Christian becomes the message as God writes His own character and personality on us.

No wonder Jesus gave us the new commandment to "love one another as I have loved you" (John 13:34). *The reality of the love of God is communicated in our love,* both for one another, and for the lost for whom Christ died.

The Gospel claims about relationship are testable. And the test of that reality is love.

The pattern. 1 Thessalonians 2, and particularly verses 7-12, give us a picture of the intimate relationships which characterized Paul's own ministry in this new church. The picture is all the more striking when we realize how short a time Paul had with them. It is a picture of a person who validates his message of love by loving.

> We were gentle among you, like a mother caring for her little children. We loved you so much that we were delighted to share with you not only the Gospel of God but our lives as well because you had become so dear to us.
>
> Surely you remember, brothers, our toil and hardship; we worked night and day in order not to be a burden to anyone while we preached the Gospel of God to you.
>
> You are witnesess, and so is God, of how holy, righteous and blameless we were among you who believed. For you know that we dealt with each of you as a father deals with his own children, encouraging, comforting, and urging you to live lives worthy of God, who calls you into His kingdom and glory.
>
> 1 Thessalonians 2:7-12

A stranger might come to town and propound new doctrines in order to gain a following. In the New Testament world, it was expected that such an itinerant teacher *would* come, and that he would make a living on the fees he charged his disciples before he moved on. But no passing philosopher or proselytizer would ever arrive, undergo hardships to support himself, and actually *love* those he taught! No one had ever before shared *himself* as well as his philosophy. No one had ever spoken of a father-child relationship with a loving God, and then gone on to actually treat his disciples with that same tender family love he insisted that God offers.

Paul's communication of the Gospel characteristically involved building a personal relationship with new believers, in which the reality of God's love would be experienced, now.

♥ ***Link to Life: Youth / Adult***

In a minilecture, briefly sketch the role of love in validating the Gospel message in the first century. Then have your group members break into teams. Each should study 1 Thessalonians 2:7-12, and answer the first—plus one of the next two—questions.

- *If you were a new believer in Thessalonica, how would you know that Paul loved* you?
- *How might you demonstrate love to a non-Christian friend, and thus communicate the relational dimension of the Gospel?*
- *Or, how, in a modern local church, might this kind of love find expression? List at least 20 practical ways in which members might "love one another."*

The dynamic church of the New Testament—as well as the dynamic church of every age—is a church in which the twin thrusts of truth and love are understood and kept in balance. Just as there is a place in evangelism for the presentation of core truths, so there must be a place in evangelism for communicating the love of God, through building personal, loving relationships with others.

Transformation

Hellenistic religions and philosophies did have moral content. Some were highly ethical and proposed strict standards, while others seemed actually to foster immorality. But none gave the adherent any real hope.

Then the message of Jesus broke out on the world with the promise that not only would believers have a new relationship with God, but they would also become new and different people as well! Christianity promised the power to *become* righteous.

True to this promise, believers in Thessalonica began to experience a progressive transformation that touched every aspect of their personalities. "Your faith is growing more and more, and the love every one of you has for each other is increasing," Paul wrote in his second letter (2 Thes. 1:3). The capacity to trust and the freedom to love were increasingly characteristic of these young believers. God was working an inner transformation.

Looking yet again through the Thessalonian epistles, we gain a clear impression of the extent of the transformation that Christianity provides.

Anxiety and fear marred many lives, then as now. Increasingly the Thessalonians were able to act in faith, trusting not only God but one another (see 1 Thes. 1:3, 10; also 2 Thes. 1:3-4). Even when suffering affliction, these men and women were able to retain their confidence (1 Thes. 3:4).

Isolation was as much a fact of first-century life as of our own. Individualism created the lonely crowd then as now. But when Christ entered a person's life, this changed. Increasingly the new believers developed the capacity to care. As a result, they reached out in love to others, and others drew close to them as well. Barriers between people of differing cultures were breached as Christ's transforming power brought a new freedom to love (1 Thes. 1:3; 2:7-11; 3:6-10, 12; 4:9-10; 5:13). Love for God and man became a reality.

Moral compromise was replaced by steadfastness and commitment. The courage to live by inner convictions, unswayed by circumstance, developed naturally with growth in the new faith (1:3; 2:14; 3:4, 8).

Motivations also underwent an increasingly dramatic change. The self-interest, materialism, natural drives, and passions that once controlled thoughts and actions were replaced by new values and desires (1:6; 2:4-6, 14; 3:3; 4:3-6, 11-12; 5:8, 12). The very core of the personality underwent a gradual transformation as believers experienced more and more of the power of Jesus Christ.

Personal failures, an inability to be what they wanted to be, must have nagged first-century men and women even as it does us today. But disappointment and shame were gradually replaced too as believers discovered a new power for holiness. God's transformation worked within to make these growing believers more and more like the Lord (3:12; 4:1, 3, 7; 5:23).

Lack of goals and meaning plagued many lives. With Christ, even this changed. The letters to Thessalonica show us that a new sense of purpose and meaning, which could be expressed practically in daily life, now gripped the believers. A commitment to good deeds, to honest work, and to right behavior took on fresh and deeper meaning as Christians recognized that every action could reflect credit on their Lord (4:1, 11-12; 5:14-15). Daily duties as well as the privilege of serving others began to bring new satisfaction.

The newness of this life did not come from improved circumstances or from sudden prosperity. The newness of these Christians' lives was deeply rooted within the believers' own personalities. The fulfilled promise of transformation is part of the secret of the early church's power. "Do not conform any longer to the pattern of this world, but be transformed" (Rom. 12:2) lost all tinge of mockery, and brought a living hope.

This transformation is not automatic. It wasn't in New Testament times, and it's not today. But transformation is uniquely provided in the Holy Spirit's working, through distinctive resources closely associated with God's Word.

We saw in 1 Thessalonians 2 that God communicates His love through human beings. His truth about relationships is validated by love within the body of Christ.

It is important to remember that *church* in the New Testament has an uncluttered meaning. Today we commonly associate the term with a building, Sunday morning services, or an organization with membership, officers, programs, and planned activities. None of these ideas was characteristic of the church of New Testament times. At that time, *church* meant something basic and clear, namely, *community.* The church was an assembly of people, called out of the world into the closest of all possible relationships. The church was and is the family of God.

Thus *church* in the Scripture is a *relational* term. Always in view are the people, who share a common relationship with one Father and with one another as brothers and sisters. In the intimate context of family relationships, God chooses to work His transformation in human lives.

It shouldn't be too surprising, then, to find that when a person is born again as a child of God, the Lord chooses to put him in this family. Here growth toward Christian maturity takes place. "Therefore, encourage one another and build each other up, just as in fact you are doing," Paul urged the Thessalonians. "Live in peace with each other. . . . Warn those who are idle, encourage the timid, help the weak, be patient with everyone" (1 Thes. 5:11, 13-14).

The Thessalonian letter helps us see the quality of relationships appropriate to the family of God. As believers strive together to be responsive to the Word, they provide continual examples for each other (1:7; 2:14). Within the family is an intense love, a love that reaches out and seeks to draw others close. "You yourselves have been taught by God to love each other. And in fact, you do love all the brothers," Paul praised the Thessalonians (4:9-10). In the closeness of the family, we verbally exhort and instruct each other (2:11; 4:1). In our concern for each other, we comfort and encourage (4:18; 5:14). The love is so real, the belonging so sure, that we don't hesitate even to admonish or to discipline (v. 14).

How wonderful to view the world in a fresh, new way shaped by the core truths communicated in the Word of God. How wonderful to experience even now the reality of God's love. And how wonderful to experience personal transformation, aided and encouraged by others in the loving family of our God.

TEACHING GUIDE

Prepare
Read through 1 Thessalonians, marking both core and relational truths.

Explore
Assign roles to your group members as first-century pagans. Then have teams examine 1 Thessalonians, to identify core truths that will change their view of God and the universe. See "link-to-life," page 951.

Expand
1. Give a minilecture on the role of relationships in communication of the Gospel.
2. Still in their role as first-century persons, ask your group members to study 1 Thessalonians 2:7-11. How would they know that Paul loved them? How can we demonstrate the relational dimension of the Gospel in our own evangelism or church fellowships? See "link-to-life," page 953.
3. Conclude with a minilecture on transformation, as illustrated in 1 Thessalonians. Stress the importance of Christian love as a context for this kind of growth.

Apply
Thessalonians emphasizes the importance of core truth, of love, and of transformation. Ask each group member to share which of these has been most important in his or her spiritual journey, and tell how.

STUDY GUIDE 149

2 Thessalonians

THE DAY OF THE LORD

Overview

This brief note is closely linked to Paul's first Epistle to the Thessalonians. It was written within three or four months of the other, and intended to clear up confusion about the future.

Growing persecution had led some in the city to believe that the "Day of the Lord" of which Paul had taught had arrived. Paul wrote to explain, and to teach them how to live under persecution.

The letter can be outlined simply.

Outline

I.	Greetings	1:1-2
II.	Persecution and Judgment	1:3-12
III.	The Day of the Lord	2:1–3:5
IV.	A Request and a Warning	3:6-15
V.	Final Words	3:16-18

As we approach this study of a book that emphasizes prophecy, it is important to remember that in Scripture prophetic teaching is *practical*. That is, the Christian vision of the future is intended to have application to the believer's present experience. Prophetic teaching is not focused on constructing prophetic systems, which link future events in any particular sequence. We are able to fit prophesied events together, to some extent. But the major emphasis of the Bible itself is on seeing the relevance of yet-future things to our lives today.

■ For a verse-by-verse commentary, see the *Bible Knowledge Commentary*, pages 713-725.

Commentary

Paul's first letter was full of references to the future. In fact, the new faith the Thessalonians had adopted so enthusiastically had captured their own imaginations, and created a vital new hope. The Thessalonians were eagerly waiting "for His Son from heaven, whom He raised from the dead—Jesus, who rescues us from the coming wrath" (1 Thes. 1:10). They had caught something of Paul's own attitude, for the apostle had fixed his hope, and joy, and gloried in the crown which would be his "in the presence of our Lord Jesus when He comes" (2:19). How motivated these new believers were to "be blameless and holy in the presence of our God and Father when our Lord Jesus comes with all His holy ones [angels]" (3:13).

While the Thessalonians looked forward with Paul to Christ's coming, there were still confusions and uncertainties. Paul had only had a few brief months in their city. It's not surprising that some had misunderstood his teachings.

Some there were very upset about believers who had died. They apparently viewed the return of Christ as imminent, and assumed that the Second Coming would take place in their own lifetimes. They were uncertain about what would happen to those who died before this event took place.

Paul did not correct their assumption that Christ's coming was imminent. Like them, Paul believed the Lord could return at any time. But Paul did not know *when* that "anytime" would be. So in his first letter the apostle described the Rapture, in which believers are caught up in the air to be with the Lord. He did not fit this event into any prophetic scheme. He simply wanted the believers to realize that death had not cut their loved ones off from the hope of glory to come. Both those who live at Christ's return, and those who have died, will be caught up together!

> Brothers, we do not want you to be ignorant about those who fall asleep, or to grieve like the rest of men, who have no hope. We believe that Jesus died and rose again and so we believe that God

will bring with Jesus those who have fallen asleep in Him. According to the Lord's own word, we tell you that we who are still alive, who are left till the coming of the Lord, will certainly not precede those who have fallen asleep. For the Lord Himself will come down from heaven, with a loud command, with the voice of the archangel and with the trumpet call of God, and the dead in Christ will rise first. After that, we who are still alive and are left will be caught up with them in the clouds to meet the Lord in the air. And so we will be with the Lord forever. Therefore encourage each other with these words.

1 Thessalonians 4:13-18

Paul emphasized that "about times and dates we do not need to write you" for "the Day of the Lord will come like a thief." But in view of its certainty, the believers are told to "encourage one another and build each other up, just as in fact you are doing" (5:1-2, 11).

In view of all these references in Paul's first letter, it is clear that eschatology—teaching about the future—had a significant place in the instruction of those congregations the great apostle and missionary founded throughout the Roman Empire.

While eschatology had a central place in early Christian teaching, as we have noted, misunderstandings did arise. And this was particularly true in Thessalonica, where Paul had so little time to ground the new believers before he was forced to travel on. Paul's first letter emphasized the Christian's hope, and answered one question they had about those who had died. But more questions arose. And so a second letter was sent. This letter centered on the future—and on the impact our vision of the future is to have on Christian life.

♥ ***Link to Life: Youth / Adult***

Divide your group into five sections. Assign each section one chapter of 1 Thessalonians. Each is to read his or her chapter individually, and locate references to the future God has planned for believers, and to see what impact that future is to have on believers now.

Have your group members report their findings chapter by chapter.

Discuss: "Why was teaching about prophecy given such a high priority when Paul had so little time with the Thessalonians? What role should prophetic teaching have in our own faith? Why?"

Do not discuss at length, but use this preliminary study to stimulate awareness of prophecy's significance as a stimulant to Christian living.

When Paul wrote his second Letter to the Thessalonians, it dealt with three specific issues that had surfaced in Thessalonica. Each was directly related to prophecy.

Persecution: 2 Thessalonians 1

Paul had been driven from Thessalonica by persecution organized by jealous Jews (Acts 17:5). A mob attacked several of the brothers, and a riot ensued. Paul was forced to leave that very night. Despite the fact that a number of Greeks and a few prominent women were members of the new congregation, the mob actions had apparently stirred up considerable opposition. In this second letter Paul wrote movingly about "all the persecutions and trials you are enduring" (v. 4). There were a number of enemies who actively "troubled" them. The Greek word, *thlipsis,* is a strong one, and suggests great emotional and spiritual stress caused by external or internal pressures.

Here the context suggests both kinds of pressure. The external pressures are suggested by the riots and physical mistreatment described in Acts, and undoubtedly continued after Paul left the city. The internal pressures came as the Thessalonians wondered: how could this God who loved them permit them to experience such suffering? How does this relate to Jesus' deliverance of believers "from the coming wrath"? (1 Thes. 1:10) Aren't troubles here an evidence of divine judgment?

To answer, Paul turned to Scripture's vision of the future. He commended them for their perseverance and faith despite the persecutions they endured. And then explained just what will take place when Jesus returns.

God is just: He will pay back trouble to those who trouble you and give relief to you who are troubled, and to us as well. This will happen when the Lord Jesus is revealed from heaven in blazing fire with His powerful angels. He will punish

> those who do not know God and do not obey the Gospel of our Lord Jesus. They will be punished with everlasting destruction and shut out from the presence of the Lord and from the majesty of His power, on the day He comes to be glorified in His holy people and to be marveled at among all those who have believed.
>
> 2 Thessalonians 1:6-10

The justice of God might well be questioned if only what happens in this life is considered. But when we realize that God has set a future time to fulfill His role as Judge, then our inner pressures are relieved. The stress that is natural under external persecution is quieted when we look ahead, and realize that God has created a truly moral universe. God will both "pay back trouble to those who trouble you and give relief to those who are troubled." When Jesus returns all will be set right.

Paul said that it was "with this in mind" that he shaped his prayers for the Thessalonians. He did not pray that they might have relief *now* from their troubles. Instead Paul prayed that God would continue to work among them, "so that the name of our Lord Jesus may be glorified in you, and you in Him, according to the grace of our God and the Lord Jesus Christ" (vv. 11-12).

♥ ***Link to Life: Youth / Adult***
Sketch the background of this church as it relates to persecution. Then give your group members the following series of statements to try to answer from 2 Thessalonians 1:

- *Christians should be immune from persecution and suffering.*
- *God's love is shown by delivering His people from troubles.*
- *Christians who suffer have reason to doubt God's love.*
- *We should always pray that suffering believers will be delivered from their troubles.*
- *If God was both good and all powerful, He would not let His people suffer. Therefore He must either not be good or not be all powerful.*

Anxiety: 2 Thessalonians 2:1–3:5
The troubles experienced by the Thessalonians led to another, very specific worry. Paul had taught them that Jesus would return, to catch the believers up into the clouds. The dead would be raised and the living taken with Him.

Paul had also taught them about "the Day of the Lord." This is a technical theological phrase in both the Old and New Testaments. It always identifies a span of time during which God directly or indirectly, but personally, intervenes in history to accomplish some specific aspect of His plan. In most cases the phrase draws our eyes toward the culmination of history, when great acts of terrible judgment will shake our earth. The prophets describe this coming day in graphic, powerful language.

> Woe to you who long for the Day of the Lord! Why do you long for the Day of the Lord? That day will be darkness, not light.
>
> Amos 5:18

> The great Day of the Lord is near—near and coming quickly. Listen! The cry on the Day of the Lord will be bitter, the shouting of the warrior there. That day will be a day of wrath, a day of distress and anguish, a day of trouble and ruin, a day of darkness and gloom, a day of clouds and blackness.
>
> Zephaniah 1:14-15

The believers in the Thessalonian congregation, who were first recruited from "God fearers" who were Gentile adherents of Judaism (Acts 17:4), were familiar with this apocalyptic vision. They had understood Paul's own teaching about the coming Day of the Lord. But now, under intensifying persecution, the rumor had spread that they were already *in* that "day"!

This disturbed them intensely, because they expected "the coming of our Lord Jesus Christ and our being gathered to Him" to take place *before* the great time of troubles (2 Thes. 2:1). Had they missed the Rapture? What was happening?

Paul answered by a reference to other familiar Old Testament prophecy: prophecy he must himself have touched on when he taught the young church. They were to disregard rumors that "the Day of the Lord has already come" (v. 2). This will not happen "until the rebellion occurs and the man of lawlessness is revealed" (v. 3).

This individual, identified in Daniel's prophecy, and also spoken of by Jesus, is the person we know as the Antichrist. (For background, see Study Guides 67 and 90.)

Note that Paul was *not* saying the rebellion must precede Christ's appearing. He simply said the "Day of the Lord" will be ushered in by the Antichrist's rebellion.

How then do we explain present persecution? Paul said the "secret power of lawlessness is already at work." The forces of evil are presently active in our world. But they are currently restrained (most believe by the Holy Spirit) (v. 7).

Paul made it clear that the appearance of this Satan-empowered person will be unmistakable. He will come "in all kinds of counterfeit miracles, signs and wonders." And he will delude the mass of humanity.

Again, Paul's concern in this teaching on prophecy was practical. Paul wrote to reassure the Thessalonians that the trouble they experienced, while inspired by active evil at work in the world, were *not* the troubles Scripture speaks of when describing the end times.

Paul concluded his instruction. He exhorted the Thessalonians to stand firm, and hold to the teachings he had given them. Understanding how painful their persecution was, Paul asked that the Lord "who loved us and by His grace gave us eternal encouragement and good hope, [would] encourage your hearts and strengthen you in every good deed and word" (vv. 16-17).

And finally Paul asked for prayer for him, that the message of Christ might spread rapidly and be honored, and that he might be delivered from evil men so he could continue his ministry. As for the Thessalonians themselves, "We have confidence in the Lord that you are doing and will continue to do the things we command. May the Lord direct your hearts into God's love and Christ's perseverance" (3:4-5).

♥ ***Link to Life: Youth / Adult***
In a minilecture help your group understand the main elements of the Old Testament prophetic teaching which underlines this chapter. Emphasize again that here Paul is not building systems, but is seeking to reassure fearful believers that the "Day of the Lord" had not yet occurred, and that they could still look forward to the coming of the Lord from heaven.

Idleness: 2 Thessalonians 3:6-18

So far we've seen that two of the concerns of the Thessalonians were resolved by a reference to prophetic truth. The doubts caused by present persecution were resolved as Paul made it clear that God's judgment on the persecutors is reserved until the time of Jesus' return. For now, believers are to persevere in spite of troubles, sure that God will make all things right in His own time.

Confusion about the "Day of the Lord" was also rooted in present persecution. The Thessalonians' troubles seemed so intense that some thought the time of the end had come. But if this were so, why hadn't the Lord come to deliver them? Paul simply pointed out that the time of ultimate trouble indicated by "the Day of the Lord' will not come until the Antichrist—the "lawless one"—appears. And as his appearance will be marked by apparent miracles and wonders, that appearance will be well marked.

The last issue Paul raised in chapter 3 also is linked with his teaching on the Second Coming. But this is a very practical rather than theological kind of concern. It seems that some in Thessalonica reasoned that, since the Lord might come at any moment, it made little sense to plan ahead. Why even work, if Jesus might come before evening? Why plan, or prepare for the future, if Jesus' arrival might make any preparations moot?

So those who reasoned this way simply sat back, idle, and refused to work! They let other Christians feed them, and sat around gossiping their lives away.

This was a total misunderstanding of the meaning of imminence. The fact that Jesus *may* come at any moment does not mean that He *will* come during our lifetimes! God calls us, not to sit and wait, but to be actively and responsibly involved in the affairs of this life. Paul wrote very bluntly:

> You yourselves know how you ought to follow our example. We were not idle when we were with you, nor did we eat anyone's food without paying for it. On the contrary, we worked night and day, laboring and toiling so that we would not be a burden to any of you. We did this, not because we do not have the right to such help, but in order to make ourselves a model for you to follow.
>
> For even when we were with you, we gave you this rule: "If a man will not

work, he shall not eat."
We hear that some among you are idle. They are not busy; they are busybodies. Such people we command and urge in the Lord Jesus Christ to settle down and earn the bread they eat. And as for you, brothers, never tire of doing what is right.

2 Thessalonians 3:7-13

It is true that all God's plans focus on a grand, future culmination linked with the second coming of Jesus. But what we know about those plans is intended to motivate us to godly living now. And they are intended to resolve doubts and uncertainty caused by painful experiences in this present life. When we realize that the universe is moving toward God's intended end, and that in history's great culmination all of His good purposes will be fully realized, we are strengthened to live for Jesus now—to live with perseverance, to stand firm, and to actively do the will of God.

♥ ***Link to Life: Youth / Adult***
Paul emphasized two themes in this book: one, in chapter 3, is that of responsibility. *Each believer is to live responsibly in this world, working to meet his or her own needs. The other theme is that of* purposefulness. *The Christian understanding of the future provides us with a sense of goal and purpose—of the meaningfulness of life—that others lack.*

The theme of purpose is expressed particularly in Paul's prayers or reference to prayer (1:11-12; 2:13-16; 3:1-5). Discuss briefly the responsibility theme, and then set pairs to study the prayers. In view of the future God has planned, what can give our lives meaning and purpose? What can we do *that our lives will not be wasted?*

TEACHING GUIDE

Prepare
Research the teaching of Daniel and of Jesus on prophecy, as background for teaching chapter 2 of 2 Thessalonians.

Explore
Set your group members to work on chapters of 1 Thessalonians to discover how significant the future God has planned seems to Paul. See the approach laid out in "link-to-life," page 957.

Expand
1. List statements that express the beliefs of some about God, believers, and trials here on earth. Then set teams to work studying 2 Thessalonians 1 to identify truths which enable us to evaluate the validity of the statements. See "link-to-life," page 958.
2. Or give a minilecture on the prophecies of Daniel and of Jesus which are reflected in chapter 2. Try not to focus dogmatically on any particular prophetic system, but show the practical impact of understanding the "Day of the Lord" on the persecuted Thessalonians. See "link-to-life," page 959.
3. Or challenge your group members to discover in Paul's 2 Thessalonians' prayers purpose and meaning for the Christian life, which will stand the test of Christ's return.

Apply
Let each group member draw from his or her personal knowledge of Scripture. What else lies ahead? As each shares, he or she should also tell how this yet-future event might shape the believer's way of life today.

STUDY GUIDE 150

Introduction to 1, 2 Timothy; Titus

THE PASTORAL LETTERS

Overview

Paul wrote three brief letters to two young men he had trained for ministry. These letters, 1 and 2 Timothy, and Titus, are called the "Pastoral Epistles." Each was written between A.D. 64–67, near the end of Paul's life. Second Timothy dates during Paul's second imprisonment in Rome, just months before his execution.

Neither Timothy nor Titus were what we today would call "pastors." Each was, however, a young leader who traveled to churches in various cities of provinces when problems emerged, or special guidance was needed. We can sense a number of the problems they had to deal with by reading Paul's instructions to them; problems ranging from selection of local leaders, to order in the churches, to confronting heresy, to maintaining a stress on godliness and good works.

Each of the three letters has a somewhat different focus. Yet the content of the three overlaps significantly. For this reason, it's helpful when teaching the pastorals to look at major themes occurring in each, and draw together the teaching in these books to gain a comprehensive picture. In our studies in the pastorals we will do just this, looking at what these epistles contribute to our understanding of Christian teaching, of the qualifications of leaders, and of the way leaders are to function in the church.

■ For a verse-by-verse study of each individual book, see the *Bible Knowledge Commentary,* pages 727-767.

Commentary

I like to read the last words of famous men, even when I suspect someone else may have put those words in the celebrity's mouth. Examples of questionable but famous last words, include those of the Emperor Julian, vigorous opponent of Christianity in the A.D. 360s, who supposedly said, "Thou has conquered, O pale Galilean." And there was the millionaire whose last word to his gathered sons was reported to be "Remember—buy low and sell high."

But last words do give us insight into the values, concerns, and focus of a life. If I could record not just a saying, but a solid core of guidance for future generations, what would I say?

Pretentious. It would be pretentious for you or me to presume to look ahead and give words of wisdom to guide future generations of our families. We are so limited in our understanding that we cannot see what next year holds, much less the coming decades. But as we come to Paul's final letters in the New Testament, and to other late writings, we realize that we are reading "last words" which *do* apply to us today. These letters contain guidelines for living as God's family in a world that is all too often an enemy of Christian values.

These letters of Paul are more than words of wisdom from a gifted leader; they are words written under the inspiration of the Holy Spirit.

The first 30 years of the New Testament era had passed now. Jesus had entered history. The church had grown and developed after His death and resurrection. The power of the Gospel had brought hope and new life to millions of first-century pagans. The church had met opposition and attack, and had affirmed Jesus Christ as the center of its life. The church had come to understand itself as Jesus' body, and God's family and holy temple. The men and women who were the driving force in these early years—Paul, Peter, Barnabas, John, Apollos, Priscilla, and the others—were now old.

There had been other changes. Christianity was no longer a novelty. The church knew second-and-third-generation believers. Once each Christian was a convert from paganism or Judaism, but now young men and women had grown up knowing the truths of the faith from childhood. Soon the Roman government would take an official position against Christianity. Within the faith, false teachers intruded, infiltrating twisted doctrine and warped lifestyles.

A clear form of organization with definite offices and roles had developed within the church. How that organization was to function, without taking on the unhealthy characteristics of bureaucracy, was another challenge the church had to face.

During the decades of the 60s through the 90s, Paul and the others looked ahead to foresee these emerging problems and needs. They knew that they must commit their ministry to others who would faithfully carry on the work of God. Thus they were led to leave us, in books like 1 and 2 Timothy, Titus, 2 Peter, Jude, and the three letters of John, their last words. These letters speak to us today with a living authority and a wisdom that is part of our heritage from the Apostolic Age.

Paul, Timothy, and Titus

Paul. The Book of Acts closes with Paul imprisoned in Rome. Most commentators feel that he arrived there (Acts 28) about A.D. 59. Paul was kept under very lenient restraint. He had his own rented home, and welcomed many visitors. It was during this time that he wrote the Prison Epistles—Colossians, Ephesians, Philippians, and Philemon. The apostle eventually gained his opportunity to appeal to the emperor, and won his release.

Paul then very probably made his intended visit to Spain. An early church father, Clement of Rome, reports that Paul went "to the extreme limit of the west" before he suffered martyrdom. We can gather that he also had time to visit Ephesus in Macedonia (1 Tim. 1:3) as well as Crete (Titus 1:5). Paul planned to spend the winter in Nicopolis on the west coast of Epirus (3:12). Certainly the apostle was again free, totally immersed in his ministries as a missionary and church supervisor.

But when Paul wrote 2 Timothy, he was imprisoned a second time, and this time under no gentle restraint: he was in chains (2 Tim. 1:16). He lacked warm clothing and books (4:13). The prospect was so grim that Paul wrote, "I am already being poured out like a drink offering, and the time has come for my departure" (v. 6).

What had happened?

Paul's release from his first imprisonment probably took place around A.D. 60 or 61. His journey to Spain may have taken two years, say till 63. On his return Paul revisited many churches and wrote supportive letters to young Timothy and Titus (early 64). Then came a series of events that unleashed opposition to Christianity throughout the empire!

Nero Claudius Caesar was Emperor of Rome from A.D. 54 to 67. Though a vicious and unbalanced man, his first five years were marked by sound administration, because he was content to let two supporters, Seneca and Burrus, run the empire. By 62, however, the young emperor grasped the full power of his position, having put to death those who had previously restrained him (including his mother). The situation rapidly deteriorated. In July of 64 a fire broke out in a slum and destroyed half of Rome, and the rumor circulated that Nero had put his capital to the torch in order to have more space for one of his grandiose building schemes.

The increasingly unpopular emperor looked for a scapegoat upon whom he could turn the wrath of the people. Christians, already hated by the Roman mob, were chosen. During the next five years suppression of Christianity became the official policy of the Roman state, and persecution was intensified.

Paul was rearrested, tumbled into a maximum security prison in Rome, and, within months after writing his second letter to Timothy, was executed. Deserted and alone during his last days (see v. 16), the aged apostle's final thoughts were for the harassed church, and the youthful leaders who must now accept the burden of guiding its course.

Timothy. Our impressions of Timothy come from Acts and from the letters he received from Paul. Timothy was a youth of good reputation, probably a resident of Lystra (Acts 16:2). His father was a Greek and his mother a devout Jewess who, with his grandmother Lois, instructed Timothy in the Old Testament Scriptures (Acts 16:1; 2 Tim. 1:5, 14). Timothy was probably a teen when he first joined Paul; fifteen years later Paul could write, "Don't let anyone look down on you because you are young"

(1 Tim. 4:12).

It's uncertain how heavily Timothy was involved in missionary work during the intervening years; however, his name keeps appearing in association with Paul and Silas. Certainly Paul had known this young man intimately. And Paul now committed to Timothy much of his own ministry, and gave him his last words of advice. Certainly, Paul was aware not only of the difficulties facing the church but of Timothy's own weaknesses. Bastien Van Elderen, New Testament scholar and archeologist, sums up the impression of Timothy conveyed in Paul's writings in the *Zondervan Pictorial Encyclopedia:*

> He was a fairly young man who was somewhat retiring, perhaps even a bit shy. He appears to be sincere and devoted, but at times perhaps frightened by his opponents and their teachings. This perhaps is also reflected in his apparent inability to cope with the problems in the Corinthian church.

How encouraging it is to see the mission of the church being committed to ordinary people. Retiring. Perhaps a bit shy. Sincere, but uncomfortable with opposition, and all too often unable to cope. Just ordinary people, like you and me. Yet Christ's church has endured and, from generation to generation, communicated the life that is our Saviour's enduring gift to those who choose to make Him their own. How important then Paul's last words to Timothy would be. They comfort us ordinary people, and give us guidelines for maintaining the church of Jesus Christ as His living, growing family.

Titus. We know even less of Titus than of Timothy, yet the infrequent reference in the epistles to this young leader is consistently favorable. He shows genuine devotion and concern (2 Cor. 8:16-17); he is committed to those he serves (12:18). And Titus was apparently effective even in areas in which Timothy proved indecisive. Van Elderen reflects on the impact of Titus' visit to Corinth as Paul's emissary during a time of antagonism against the apostle.

> When Paul arrived in Troas, he did not find Titus (2 Cor. 2:13). Although there were promising opportunities for mission work in Troas, Paul's concern about Corinth and Titus led him to proceed to Macedonia. . . . In Macedonia Titus brings to Paul a comforting report about the Corinthians, which gives him much joy and peace of mind (2 Cor. 7:6-14). Titus seems to have established a good rapport with the Corinthians and Paul exuberantly expresses his gratitude for the happy turn of events.

Aside from this portrait of an effective and promising young leader, we know only that Titus was a Gentile who remained uncircumcised. He, like Timothy, accompanied Paul and later Barnabas on missionary journeys. Now, like Timothy, Titus must provide leadership in place of the apostle, and like Timothy, would profit from Paul's final advice.

Issues and Answers

The emphasis in each of these three letters is different. We might suggest that in 1 Timothy Paul's focus is the life to which the church is called. In 2 Timothy Paul's focus is on the work to which leaders are committed. The letter to Titus, on the other hand, emphasizes the way in which the church is to accomplish God's purposes in this world.

Yet despite different emphases, there is constant overlap of content, and there are recurring themes which find parallel expression in each book. The chart shows the areas of overlap, and helps us to see how certain critical issues grasped the apostle's attention during his final days. We can best understand the teaching of these last letters, not by studying each separately, but by examining them together, looking for Paul's answers to the common and recurring problems he dealt with.

What a heritage these letters are. Christ's church was designed to endure. Though at times our grasp of spiritual realities has seemed weak, and our life flame dimmed, the church *has* endured.

Yet, enduring is not God's sole goal for His family on earth. God yearns for us to live fully. The gift of His life is ours in Christ: the great desire of God's heart for us is that we might experience that life to the full.

Our problem of how to experience real, vital life in an enduring institution—the ongoing, structured church—has been an-

Common Content in the Pastoral Epistles

The Life of the Church 1 Timothy		The Work of Leaders 2 Timothy		The Way of the Body Titus	
1:3-7	Goal of ministry: love from pure heart	1:3-12	Called to holy life, fervent love	1:1-4	Concern for "knowledge of the truth that leads to godliness"
1:8-11	Lifestyle *contrary* to *sound doctrine* described	1:13-14	Must guard *sound doctrine*		
1:12-17	Paul an example of a saved sinner; "eternal" life	1:15-18	Onesiphorus an example		
1:18-20	Timothy's goal to be a minister of the faith	2:1-7	Timothy to entrust truth to faithful men who will minister		
2:1-7	Pray and live to bring salvation to others	2:8-13	Paul's endurance for the salvation of elect		
2:8-10	Examples of godly life	2:14-19	Leaders must live godly lives		
2:11-15	Special limits placed on women's role	2:20-21	Limits placed by individual's response		
3:1-15	Leader's qualifications	2:22-26	How a leader lives, teaches, and corrects	1:5-9 1:10-16	Leader's example Leader's duties
4:1-5	False lifestyle	3:1-9	False leaders		
4:6-10	Danger of distraction from godliness				
4:11-16	Need to set example in faith, speech, life, etc.	3:10-17	Need to continue in godly life and teaching		
5:1-8	Respect toward others in the family: "put religion into practice"	4:1-5	Need to preach and live true doctrine	2:1-15	Godly life and doctrine applied
5:9-16	Widows' role				
5:17-20	Elders' responsibility				
5:21-25	Various injunctions				
6:1-2	Slaves' attitudes				
6:3-10	False doctrine; wrong motives				
6:11-21	Charge to pursue godliness, truth, love, etc., keep faith in Christ central	4:6-18	Paul an example of persevering workman, athlete	3:1-11	Practical results of our common salvation

swered in the providence and purpose of God. The answer is one we will come to understand to an even fuller degree as we meet ourselves in the issues raised by these final letters of the Apostle Paul.

TEACHING GUIDE

Prepare
Read through the three Pastoral Epistles at a sitting. Jot down your major impressions. What do you see as their greatest contribution to your church and the group you teach?

Explore
1. Ask your group members to write down the "famous last words" they would like to pass on to others at their deaths.
2. Explain the background of the Pastoral Letters in a minilecture, sketching just why these "last words" of Paul can be so important to the modern church.

Expand
1. Distribute copies of the "Common content in the pastorals" chart to each group member. Ask each person to select *one* of the topics dealt with in at least two of these letters, and read about them in the biblical text. Each should take notes and sum up briefly what is taught. Or you may wish to assign topics to individuals or pairs so all can be covered.
2. Hear reports from the individual research. Each individual or pair should share what his or her passages said, and then briefly comment on how it is relevant to the church or to Christians today.

This process will enable your group to get a quick overview of these letters, and also to begin to apply their truths to each others' lives.

Apply
Ask each to sum up in a single, pithy "last words" saying the main thrust of Paul's advice in the section he or she studied.

STUDY GUIDE 151

1, 2 Timothy; Titus

CALLED TO TEACH

Overview
The church of Jesus Christ is called to endure. But it is also called to experience fully the life that God shares with us in Christ.

One of the most challenging tasks faced by Christians in any age is to maintain the vitality of Christ's life in what is at the same time a family—and an institution. And too often our approach to teaching and learning is institutionalized, as we model on the public school rather than on what is unique in the nature of our faith.

Teaching and learning is one of the major themes of these "last word" letters of Paul. New generations must have faith's life communicated to them. New converts too must be taught. And so 1 and 2 Timothy and Titus each contain instructions from the apostle on the communication not just of Bible truths, but of life in Christ.

What a thrill to learn from the apostle how you and I can better teach God's Word. And how we can have an even greater impact on the spiritual lives of those God has called us to instruct.

▶ ***Teach.*** There are a number of Hebrew and Greek words that can be translated as "teach," and a number translated as "learn." Yet both agree that *what* we teach is the Word of God that comes from outside the realm of human experience. Our challenge is to communicate this Word from "outside" in such a way that it is woven into each believer's life.

Commentary
Over and over again in Paul's last words to Timothy and Titus he returned to the theme of teaching. His concern seems obvious. Certainly the continuation of the church across the ages demanded transmission of Bible truths. Probably one of the most quoted verses from the Pastoral Epistles is 2 Timothy 2:2: "And the things you have heard me say in the presence of many witnesses entrust to reliable men who will also be qualified to teach others."

This verse appears on the seal of the seminary I attended. It's a common theme at seminary commencements. Much of our education in Sunday School as well as in special training and discipleship classes hopes to do just this: entrust the task of teaching so that truth may be passed on to the next generation.

But we are so confident we know what "teaching" means that we may fail to ask what it meant to Paul when he wrote to Timothy and Titus.

Education
The *Random House Dictionary* defines *education* as "the act or process of imparting or acquiring general knowledge, developing the powers of reasoning and judgment, and generally of preparing oneself or others intellectually for mature life." In our society *education* implies *school,* and to us the key phrases in this dictionary definition are "imparting or acquiring knowledge" and "preparing oneself intellectually." To teach or to learn, education focuses on knowledge and on the intellect.

This is, of course, an accurate definition for our society. School systems teach reading and writing, history and science, business and law, so learners will be "prepared intellectually for the mature life."

In our society teaching is imparting knowledge and processing information; learning is acquiring knowledge and using information. It's hard for us to realize that teaching did not have the same meaning for Paul or Timothy or the other early readers of these letters.

William Barclay, in *Educational Ideals in the Ancient World* (Baker), suggests that Jewish education was very different from our notions of teaching and learning.

> The very basis of Judaism is to be found in the conception of holiness. "You shall be holy for I the Lord your God am holy." "And ye shall be holy unto Me: for I the Lord am holy, and have severed you from other people that ye might be Mine." That is to say, *it was the destiny of the Jewish people to be different*. Holiness means difference. And their whole educational system was directed to that end. It has been precisely that educational system which has kept the Jewish race in existence. The Jew is no longer a racial type; he is a person who follows a certain way of life, and who belongs to a certain faith. If Jewish religion had faltered, or altered, the Jews would have ceased to exist. First and foremost, the Jewish ideal of education is the ideal of holiness, of difference, of separation from all other peoples in order to belong to God. Their educational system was nothing less than the instrument by which their existence as a nation, and their fulfillment of their destiny, was ensured.

See what Barclay is saying? The Hebrew concept of education was *not* "to impart knowledge" or to "prepare oneself intellectually." It was to produce holiness and to impart a distinctive lifestyle. When Paul wrote to Timothy and Titus about the importance of teaching in the church, his concept of education was Hebrew, not twentieth century.

What does this mean for us? First, it illustrates why we must guard against reading a twentieth-century meaning into Bible words. Secondly, it encourages us to explore Scripture in order to determine from the Bible itself the meaning of such terms as *teach* and *instruct*.

We need to carefully examine these letters to find out what kind of teaching and learning Paul was so concerned about. Do we have this kind of teaching in our churches today? Are there better ways to communicate our faith to coming generations than we have found? How do we pass on our living relationship with Jesus Christ to others?

Goals of Education

In each of his three last letters Paul seems to plunge immediately into statements about the goal of Christian teaching. In 1 Timothy he warned against false doctrine and urged commitment to the truth. Paul stated succinctly his goal in teaching the truth: that goal is "love, which comes from a pure heart and a good conscience and a sincere faith" (1 Tim. 1:5). In 2 Timothy, Paul brought up the same issue. "What you have heard from me, keep as the pattern of sound teaching, with faith and love in Christ Jesus" (2 Tim. 1:13). And in the opening of Titus, Paul spoke immediately of "the knowledge of the truth that leads to godliness" (Titus 1:1). The goals that Paul had in mind for teaching in the church aren't limited to gaining intellectual knowledge. In fact, Bible knowledge is never an end in itself! It is to produce love, faith, and godliness in our lives.

Measuring learning. Paul was not so much concerned that believers *knew* the truth as he was that the truth produced a distinctive way of life in them. The measure of effective teaching is not how much a person knows, but how well he or she lives.

Schools evaluate learning by testing and measuring knowledge. How many books has the student read? What was his final grade? Were the answers on the exam correct? Even in the church there's a tendency to think that the "educated" Christian is the one who has gone to Bible school, a Christian college, or seminary. The individual who has memorized the most Bible verses, who always has the right answer to a doctrinal quiz, or who can authoritatively chart a premillennial picture of the future, may be viewed as the model of a well-taught Christian.

But if we take our stance with the Apostle Paul, we realize that evidence of Christian learning is not found in what is known. It is instead found in the love, faith, and godliness that are to mark the believer's life. Paul urged Timothy and Titus to be engaged in the kind of teaching that links truth with life; the kind of teaching that has as its product loving, trusting, and godly men and women. Paul would say that character is a better indicator of a well-taught Christian than knowledge.

♥ ***Link to Life: Youth / Adult***
Divide into teams to study 1 Timothy 1:3-7; 2 Timothy 1:13-14; and Titus 1:1-4. From these verses each team is to develop a definition of education.

Compare the definitions. Then give a minilecture on the view of teaching and learning implicit in the Bible, as contrasted to the modern view reflected in the Random House Dictionary.

Truth . . . and Life

One of my old friends, a coprofessor at a school where I taught, is a dichotomous thinker. That is, he tends to think in opposites, in either/or fashion. At one time the faculty senate began to talk of redesigning our curriculum, to better equip young people for the practical demands of the ministry. My friend was visibly upset. If our curriculum were to be "practical," we would have to sacrifice "academic respectability." Education must be either "academic" (concentrating on truth) or "practical" (concentrating on methodology), and *he* was going to stand firmly on the side of truth! He could never see education involving *both* the academic *and* the practical. For him it had to be either one or the other.

Yet nothing could be further from the Apostle Paul's thought in these letters. To him, teaching's goal is knowledge expressed in love, faith, and godliness. Truth and life—the "academic" and the "practical" must be intimately linked.

- Paul said sinful acts are "contrary to sound doctrine" and do not conform to the "glorious Gospel of the blessed God" (1 Tim. 1:9-11).
- Paul expressed concern about "how people ought to conduct themselves in God's household, which is the church of the living God, the pillar and foundation of the truth" (3:15).
- Paul's goal was "knowledge of the truth that leads to godliness" (Titus 1:1).
- Paul taught that temperance, self-control, faith, love, endurance, and reverence are "in accord with sound doctrine" (2:1-3).
- Paul encouraged Titus to stress basic doctrinal truths "so that those who have trusted in God may be careful to devote themselves to doing what is good" (3:8).

Looking over these statements, we can see several things. (1) Knowing the truth, being committed to sound doctrine, must lead to godliness, love, self-control, reverence, etc. (2) Not only is truth expected to have an impact on life, but life is to be in harmony with truth. Our good works will reflect our beliefs. (3) Truth produces the godly lifestyle, not vice versa. Being a "good person" does not bring one to the truth. But truth, accepted and applied, does produce godliness in us.

The kind of teaching that Paul urged links truth and life and communicates both content and lifestyle. Teaching that attempts to communicate the faith simply as a good way of life is woefully inadequate; but teaching that attempts to communicate the faith merely as a system of beliefs is just as wrong.

Our twentieth-century emphasis on teaching as the transmission of information is *not* an adequate model for teaching God's Word.

What then *is* the teaching that Paul so urgently demands?

Teaching

In Paul's First Letter to Timothy, he gave him quite a list of subjects to teach, including: exposure of false doctrines, myths and genealogies; law; sound doctrine; the glorious Gospel; mercy; truth; dedication; prayer; harmony; women's dress and appearance; marriage and dietary practices; qualifications for leaders; conduct; sayings, truths of the faith; the practice of religion; relationships with fellow Christians; treatment of widows; ways to select elders; contentment; righteousness; faith; love; endurance; hope in God; and doing good.

In looking over even this incomplete list, someone may argue, "But this isn't about *teaching!*" That argument, of course, presupposes the narrow view that teaching involves only the verbal communication of beliefs and concepts.

But this is the whole point. Paul was concerned with communicating doctrine, mercy, commitment, conduct–truths *plus* a whole new way of life. *Christian communication is to touch the entire person;* to shape beliefs, attitudes, values, and behavior.

To teach the whole person, instruction must go beyond processing information. Even true information. As we look at 1 Timothy we realize that biblical teaching *does* involve verbal instruction. But it also involves urging, pointing out, commanding, setting an example, giving instructions.

Titus 2

You must teach what is in accord with sound doctrine. 2 Teach the older men to be temperate,
worthy of respect, self-controlled, and sound in faith, in love and in endurance.
3 Likewise, teach the older women to be reverent in the way they live, not to be slanderers or
addicted to much wine, but to teach what is good. 4 Then they can train the younger women to love
their husbands and children, 5 to be self-controlled and pure, to be busy at home, to be kind, and to
be subject to their husbands, so that no one will malign the Word of God.
6 Similarly, encourage the young men to be self-controlled. 7 In everything set them an example by
doing what is good. In your teaching show integrity, seriousness 8 and soundness of speech that
cannot be condemned, so that those who oppose you may be ashamed because they have nothing
bad to say about us.
9 Teach slaves to be subject to their masters in everything, to try to please them, not to talk back to
them, 10 and not to steal from them, but to show that they can be fully trusted, so that in every way
they will make the teaching about God our Saviour attractive.
11 For the grace of God that brings salvation has appeared to all men. 12 It teaches us to say "no" to
ungodliness and worldly passions, and to live self-controlled, upright and godly lives in this present
age, 13 while we wait for the blessed hope—the glorious appearing of our great God and Saviour,
Jesus Christ, 14 who gave Himself for us to redeem us from all wickedness and to purify for Himself
a people that are His very own, eager to do what is good.
15 These, then, are the things you should teach. Encourage and rebuke with all authority. Do not
let anyone despise you.

Christian teaching calls for a personal involvement that touches every aspect of the learner's life.

If we study the Pastoral Epistles carefully, we see that Paul's stress on instruction typically focused more on shaping lifestyle than passing on truth! These second-generation Christians knew and accepted the basic doctrines of our faith. What they needed most was to learn how to live lives that were in harmony with the truths they knew! We might summarize Paul's view of teaching by using his own words: teaching is helping the people of God learn how to "conduct themselves in God's household" (1 Tim. 3:15).

A key chapter. Titus 2 can help us understand what is involved in this kind of teaching.

Let's look at each of the boxed words and see what they mean. "Teach" sound doctrine is *laleo,* "to speak, assert, proclaim." What is to be the subject of this vocal instruction? Not "sound doctrine" itself, but a lifestyle that is in harmony with the revealed truths that shape our understanding of God, and of the meaning of life in this world.

"Teach" (v. 2) is not in the original. The Greek, however, does have a common grammatical construction that implies an imperative, urgent communication. What is to be given such urgent attention? Why, a way of life which is "temperate, worthy of respect, self-controlled, and sound in faith, in love, and in endurance."

"Teach what is good" is *kalodidaskalous,* used only here in the New Testament. The older women are responsible themselves to be admirable persons, and then to instruct the younger women.

"Train" here is *sophrontizo.* It means "to encourage, advise, urge." In New Testament times the word focused on teaching morality and good judgment. In essence the older women were to show concern for the moral development and improvement of the younger women.

"Encourage" is *parakaleo,* which means to "encourage or exhort." It suggests a close relationship; a closeness allowing the individual to correct a younger man.

"Example" is *typon.* This word means more than a "visible impression." It suggests "a pattern or example to follow." We teach others God's ways by *showing them by our way of life what those ways are.*

"Teaching" in verse 7 is *didaskalia,* "the act of [typically verbal] instruction."

"Teaches" (v. 12) is *paideuousa.* The word suggests giving parentlike guidance and daily correction, as to a child.

"Teach" is again *laleo,* "to speak."

"Encourage" is again *parakaleo.* Finally, "reprove" in verse 15 is *elencho,* which means "to bring to light, expose." In context it means to convince, to reprove if necessary in order to convict.

When we integrate all these terms and concepts into our notion of teaching, what do we discover? First, the teaching ministry is one of shaping lives, not simply one of passing on even true information. Second,

Christian teaching deals with every aspect of our lives. The tensions of daily life, relationships with others—all these are the concerns on which Christian teaching is focused. Third, we would conclude that "teaching" is a very broad term. It simply means bringing the insights of Scripture to bear on the daily lives of learners by modeling, instructing, encouraging, advising, urging, exhorting, guiding, exposing, and convicting.

♥ ***Link to Life: Youth / Adult***
Duplicate and distribute to each person Titus 2, with the key words and phrases boxed. Talk through the meaning of these words, as explained above, so your group members thoroughly understand them.

Divide into teams of five to six to (1) list together what *is to be taught. Then (2) ask the teams to compare or contrast the teaching process implied in Titus to our own "schooling," characterized by the following elements.*

a. concentration on content
b. takes place in formal classroom
c. has defined, logical curriculum
d. teacher, student have defined roles
e. formal atmosphere
f. tends to focus on lecture
g. has gaining knowledge as goal

On Guard
Paul's balanced approach to teaching was intended to help the early church, and you and me today, avoid tragic errors. On the one hand, Christians cannot neglect doctrine if we are to know reality. On the other hand, if believers think that only orthodox doctrine is important, we can end up with debates, antagonisms, and finally sterility of life. We can take pride in being right—but cut ourselves off from others who may differ from us. And with all our knowledge we can fail to experience the warmth and vitality of a growing relationship with God, and with our brothers and sisters in Christ.

The kind of teaching that stresses *only* knowledge is all too likely to produce sterile Christian experience. When we teach our children by stressing mastery of stories, of information, of doctrines, we may produce youth who have the right answers but who do not know the loving touch of Jesus. Paul urged us to guard against this pitfall by communicating the full Gospel: the Good News that "faith" involves both adherence to truth, and commitment to a truly Christian lifestyle.

TEACHING GUIDE

Prepare
Think about each individual in your group. What would Paul suggest you "teach" him or her if he were guiding you today?

Explore
1. As group members come in, ask each to write a one-sentence definition of "education."
2. Divide into teams to study 1 Timothy 1:3-7, 2 Timothy 1:13-14, and Titus 1:1-4, and develop a biblical definition of education. See "link-to-life," pages 967-968.
3. Give a minilecture on the view of teaching and learning implicit in the Bible, as contrasted to the modern view reflected in the *Random House Dictionary*.

Expand
Distribute copies of Titus 2, with the key educational terms boxed. See "link-to-life," page 970 for methodology and follow-up activities.

Apply
1. Discuss: "Think back on your own Christian education. What kind of teaching have you had? What have you learned? Who were your primary teachers? What do you feel are the strengths and weaknesses of your experience? How might you improve on it?"
2. Or, ask your group to imagine they have been given the task of designing a Christian education program for eighth-graders in your own church. "What kind of teaching program do you feel Paul might approve of? What would you want to avoid?"

STUDY GUIDE 152

1, 2 Timothy; Titus

CHRISTIAN LEADERSHIP

Overview

The process and content of teaching are both important in Christianity. But so is the *person* of the teacher or leader. Paul, about to die, now emphasized to his young successors the importance of selecting reliable local church leaders.

First Timothy 3 and Titus 1 are the key New Testament passages which describe the qualifications for spiritual leaders. There are many other passages in the New Testament that help us understand Christian spirituality. First Corinthians 13 looks at it from the perspective of love. Galatians 5 looks within, and describes the fruit that the Spirit produces in the person who walks in step with the Lord. Other passages describe the quality relationships that mark the church as God's family (as Eph. 4 and Col. 3). But the pastoral passages are unique. *They describe the spiritual person in terms of observable behavior!*

You and I cannot look into the heart of another person and measure his peace and joy. But we can observe an individual's way of life, and see by what he or she does the extent of that person's progress toward Christian maturity.

Strikingly, it is spiritual maturity that is to be considered when we choose leaders. It is not how much a person knows, not how many degrees a person may hold, not a person's status in society. What Christians are to consider in choosing leaders is the extent to which a person's life demonstrates the transforming touch of Jesus Christ.

Commentary

Not long ago the headlines carried news of two 747s that collided on the ground in a fog, killing hundreds. The verdict of the investigators? "Human error." The safety system was foolproof, but one of the pilots had not followed procedures.

Today there's a great debate about the use of nuclear power to supplement power generated by coal, oil, and water. "Unsafe!" the environmentalists cry. "Foolproof," the electric companies reply. Yet there is the nagging fear that no matter how foolproof the system, there may be room for human error.

Our systems may be perfect, but people are not. We must always consider the human element.

A communication system. In our last study we noted Paul's deep concern with effective communication of the faith to succeeding generations. Sound doctrine and the distinctive Christian way of life must be taught. The Pastoral Epistles even describe a system of teaching that is divinely designed to transmit both truth and life.

Dr. Merrill Tenney pointed out that the topics touched on in Titus alone constitute a fair digest of New Testament theology, and goes on to list the following:

- The personality of God (2:11; 3:6)
- The qualities of His love and grace (2:11; 3:4)
- His title as Saviour (2:10; 3:4)
- The saviourhood of Christ (2:13; 3:6)
- The Holy Spirit (3:5)
- The implication of the Triune Being of God (3:5-6)
- The essential deity of Christ (2:13)
- The vicarious atonement of Christ (2:14)
- The universality of salvation (2:11)
- Salvation by grace, not works (3:5)
- The incoming of the Holy Spirit (3:5)
- Justification by faith (3:7)
- Sanctification (purification) of His own people (2:14)
- Separation from evil (2:12)
- Inheritance of eternal life (3:7)
- The return of Christ (2:13)

These truths are to be affirmed and maintained. But if we read Titus again, we find that this brief book also gives a fair summary of Christian lifestyle! Here we read about:

- Godliness (1:1)
- Faith (1:2; 2:2)
- Qualities of leaders (1:5-9)
- Ministry of leaders (1:8-9)
- Temperance (2:2)
- Love (2:2, 4)
- Self-control (2:2, 5-6)
- Endurance (2:2)
- Dedication to doing good (2:7; 3:1, 8, 14)
- Personal integrity (2:7, 10)
- Seriousness (2:7)
- Subjection to authority (2:9; 3:1)
- Trustworthiness (2:10)
- Rejection of sin (2:12)
- Humility (3:2)
- Considerateness (3:2)
- Peaceableness (3:2)
- Harmony (3:10)

It is both doctrine and a way of life that Paul yearned to pass on to the next generation through the system of teaching and communication that the pastorals describe.

Yet the apostle was deeply aware that no system is foolproof; we must pay the closest attention to the human element. So over and over Paul focused attention on the "reliable men" (2 Tim. 2:2) to whom the transmission of the faith is to be entrusted. Men who will be "qualified to teach others."

Selection of Leaders: 1 Timothy 3, Titus 1
In both 1 Timothy and Titus, Paul described the qualifications and responsibilities of church leaders.

They are to manage (take care of) the church (1 Tim. 3:5).

They are to be entrusted with God's work (Titus 1:7).

They are to both encourage sound doctrine and to refute those opposing it (v. 9).

In essence, leaders are responsible for both the beliefs and the lifestyle of the local Christian community. Whether our leaders are called pastors or elders or deacons, they are responsible for the communication of the faith.

What sounds foreign to us about Paul's guidelines for selecting these leaders is that he did not stress academic or intellectual equipment. True, leaders must "keep hold of the deep truths of the faith with a clear conscience" (1 Tim. 3:9), and "hold firmly to the trustworthy message as it has been taught" (Titus 1:9). But apart from this commitment to sound doctrine, and a grasp of truth that enables the leader to encourage, rebuke, and explain (2 Tim. 4:2), little is said about knowledge. What the apostle did stress was character, or quality of life. The person recognized as a leader and given responsibility for teaching in the church is to be above reproach, married to but one wife, temperate, self-controlled, respectable and upright, hospitable, not an alcoholic, not violent but gentle, not quarrelsome or quick-tempered, not a money lover, a good manager of his family, not a recent convert (who might be susceptible to conceit), well respected by non-Christians, not overbearing, a lover of good, holy and disciplined. Qualities such as these, rather than verbal skills or success in business, or the capacity to preach a good sermon, are to be given first consideration in selecting local church leaders.

A chart found in my *Theology of Church Leadership* (Zondervan) lists 28 such characteristics, and gives a brief explanation of each.

We should ask, "Why?" Why not give first consideration to a seminary transcript, or capacity to preach, or previous success, talent, or spiritual giftedness? Yet on such qualities Paul was silent when giving directions on the choice of leaders!

"Paul, what spiritual gifts should a leader have?" No answer.

"Paul, what kind of training should a leader have?" No answer.

"Paul, should we select a successful businessperson or a community leader?" Only silence.

"But Paul, isn't it important for a leader to be able to preach an interesting sermon?" Again, except for his remark that a leader should be adept at teaching, there is no response. Instead, Paul points us away from such considerations and says over and over again to look first to the *quality* of the life.

But *why*?

It is because Christian leaders must *live* God's truth.

If teaching in the church involved only *knowing*, then those whose knowledge was superior should be leaders. But for Chris-

Qualifications for Leadership

Scripture	Qualification	Explanation
Titus 1:5-9	1. Above reproach	Not open to censure; having unimpeachable integrity.
	2. Husband of one wife	A one-wife kind of man, not a philanderer (doesn't necessarily rule out widowers or divorced men).
	3. Having believing children	Children are Christians, not incorrigible or unruly.
	4. Not self-willed	Not arrogantly self-satisfied.
	5. Not quick-tempered	Not prone to anger or irascible.
	6. Not addicted to wine	Not fond of wine, or drunk.
	7. Not pugnacious	Not contentious or quarrelsome.
	8. Not a money-lover	Not greedy for money.
	9. Hospitable	A stranger-lover, generous to guests.
	10. Lover of good	Loving goodness.
	11. Sensible	Self-controlled, sane, temperate.
	12. Just	Righteous, upright, aligned with right.
	13. Devout	Responsible in fulfilling moral obligations to God and man.
	14. Self-controlled	Restrained, under control
	15. Holding fast the Word	Committed to God's Word as authoritative.
	16. Able to teach sound doctrine	Calling others to wholeness through teaching God's Word.
	17. Able to refute objections	Convincing those who speak against the truth.
Additional from 1 Timothy 3:1-7	18. Temperate	Calm and collected in spirit; sober.
	19. Gentle	Fair, equitable, not insisting on his own rights.
	20. Able to manage household	A good leader in his own family.
	21. Not a new convert	Not a new Christian.
	22. Well thought of	Good representative of Christ.
Additional from 1 Peter 5:1-4	23. Willingly, not under compulsion	Not serving against his will.
	24. According to God (in some Greek texts)	By God's appointment.
	25. Not for shameful gain	Not money-motivated.
	26. Not lording it over the flock	Not dominating in his area of ministry (a shepherd is to lead, not *drive* the flock).
	27. As an example	A pleasure to follow because of his Christian example.
	28. As accountable to the Chief Shepherd	Motivated by the crown to be gained—authority to reign with Christ.

tians, truth and life are both vital. Using biblical knowledge to form sound doctrine means knowing by experience; it leads invariably to the distinctive lifestyle Paul highlighted in these letters. The goal of teaching sound doctrine is to produce love (1 Tim. 1:5) and godliness (Titus 1:1).

Isn't it obvious, then, that we should choose as leaders those who are approaching this goal, rather than those who may simply be starting on the way? Isn't it clear that the conceptual, schooled knowledge of the Bible, while it may be a step toward truly understanding Christian truth, does *not* indicate achieving that goal? Anyone who is short of the goal, who relies on his or her intellectual knowledge alone, should never be considered for spiritual leadership.

This is the underlying reason that Paul repeated his list of qualifications for leaders in the church. A person recognized as a teacher in the community of faith must himself or herself have *learned.* And we recognize such a person by character, not transcript.

How Leaders Teach

So far we've seen that teaching, in the biblical sense, is not "teaching" as we know it in secular education. For the distinctive task of transmitting both true doctrine and a godly lifestyle, we are to choose leaders whose qualifications are a demonstrated Christian life—evidence that they themselves have *learned.* Those who are spiritually mature will be able to guide and teach the church. The immature, no matter how much they know, will not be able to maintain or build God's family.

These final letters of Paul are full of insights into *how* leaders can build and maintain the church family.

How Paul taught Timothy. "Pursue righteousness, faith, love and peace," Paul urged (2 Tim. 2:22). "Continue in what you have learned and have become convinced of" (3:14). Timothy is not only to command and teach truth; he is to "set an example for the believers in speech, in life, in love, in faith and in purity" (1 Tim. 4:12). He is to give himself wholly to his ministry and to "watch your life and doctrine closely" (v. 16), "so that everyone may see your progress" (v. 12). The process of communication does involve instruction, but it also requires that the teacher be willing to *live out* his teaching. The person whose life is an illustration of the faith is essential in God's plan for Christian teaching and leadership.

What is striking is to note that the Christian lifestyle which Paul urges, and qualifications for Christian leaders, show striking correlations.

Looking at the two side by side makes it clear. It takes a person like the one described on the right to teach the way of life described on the left!

Think how foolish it would be to expect a violent or competitive person to help others become peaceable and humble. How foolish it would be to ask a money-hungry or morally loose person to teach others godliness. How impossible to ask an intemperate or impulsive person to guide others into a life of self-control and integrity!

Ability to communicate may not depend on character. A individual may express information brilliantly. But only a person who *lives* the Christian life can lead others into the lifestyle that truth produces.

Christian Lifestyle and Leaders

Christian lifestyle includes	*Christian leaders are*
• godliness	• above reproach
• faith	• temperate
• temperance	• self-controlled
• love	• respectable and upright
• self-control	• hospitable
• endurance	• not alcoholics
• dedication to good	• not violent but gentle
• integrity	• not quarrelsome or quick-tempered
• seriousness	• not money-lovers
• subjection to authority	• well-respected by nonbelievers
• trustworthiness	• lovers of good
• humility	
• considerateness	
• peaceableness	

The Bible's approach to teaching by word and example has several implications. The first is that the classroom or lecture hall, in which individuals gather infrequently for impersonal contact with an instructor, is inadequate for the kind of total communication the Bible portrays. Somehow the learner needs to see the teacher in real life if lifestyle is to be caught.

A second implication grows immediately from the first. It's important that a personal relationship between the Christian leader and the learner be developed. How can we learn faith, patience, temperance, love, and self-control from a stranger? We need a Paul/Timothy closeness, which enables us to say too, "You . . . know all about my teaching, my way of life, my purpose, faith, patience, love, endurance, persecutions, sufferings" (2 Tim. 3:10-11). We can know these things only if leader and learner are close, sharing friends.

Each of these considerations implies a kind of fellowship and closeness that is uniquely a part of the body of Christ. As we come to know and love one another, we have opportunity to learn from each other and especially from leaders to whom God has entrusted the health of the church and the communication of the faith.

Leaders Alone?

Scripture teaches that leaders bear the responsibility for the community: they are entrusted with the task of building and maintaining both soundness of doctrine and depth of Christian experience. In this context they are portrayed as the overseers and managers of the local congregation. Peter exhorts those recognized as leaders (elders) to "be shepherds of God's flock that is under your care, serving as overseers . . . not lording it over those entrusted to you, but being examples to the flock" (1 Peter 5:2-3).

But is this kind of communication the sole preserve of leaders? Or is it open to all of us? The Bible says that *each of us is to communicate our faith in exactly the same way—by Word and by life.*

In the Old Testament, Scripture commands parents to communicate the reality of God. "These commandments that I give you today are to be upon your hearts. Impress them on your children. Talk about them when you sit at home and when you walk along the road, when you lie down and when you get up" (Deut. 6:6-7). The teacher is qualified by having the "Word in the heart," having an intimate relationship, and being a daily example—observable and available for sharing. We who are parents communicate our faith by instruction as example, as God helps us reach our heart's desire, bringing up our children in the Lord.

It's the same in communicating our faith to unbelievers. Peter encouraged us to "always be prepared to give an answer to anyone who asks you to give the reason for the hope you have," speaking "with gentleness and respect"(1 Peter 3:15). In the context it is clear that Peter expected the Christian's unusual way of life to be observed and to raise questions. Example leads to explanation, and together the spoken Word and demonstrated life portray to those outside the faith the reality of Jesus Christ.

It's clear, then, that the system of communicating Christian faith described by Paul is

Principles of Communication

Principle	Passage from Deuteronomy
The Word is lived out by the model, who is its teacher.	These commandments that I give you today are to be upon your hearts.
A close, "among" (= family) relationship exists between the teacher and the learner.	Impress them on your children.
The context of teaching is a daily life shared by teacher and learner alike.	Talk about them when you sit at home and when you walk along the road, when you lie down and when you get up (Deut. 6:6-7).

not limited to leaders alone. And that the character of any person who seeks to teach is of utmost importance. All who want to share Jesus' love have the powerful and inseparable resources of the Word and their life example to enable them to reach others with the good news that new life is ours through Christ.

TEACHING GUIDE

Prepare
How have you been able to share not only your grasp of Scripture but also your example with those you teach?

Explore
1. Ask your group members to write down the names of three people in their church that they consider to be spiritual leaders.
Divide into teams of six to compare names. Then *develop a list of criteria* used by team members to decide who to name as leaders.
2. Distribute the chart listing and explaining the 28 qualifications of leaders given in 1 Timothy, Titus, and 1 Peter. Have the same teams work to determine: What principle(s) seems to underlie Paul's selection of criteria for choosing leaders? After the discussion, have the group reassemble and hear team reports.

Expand
1. Give a minilecture, illustrated by the comparison of leader qualities and Christian lifestyle to be taught. Help your group members understand that as Christian teaching involves *both* communication of doctrine and lifestyle, an effective Christian teacher must both know and model (be an example) of that which he or she communicates.
2. Return to the original teams, and again make a list of "spiritual leaders" in your church, this time using the criteria Paul and Peter provided. Share the names now on the lists. If any of the lists differ, talk about why.

Apply
1. If your group members have families, have two couples work together to determine effective ways to teach "forgiveness" in the home, using the basic principles Paul has laid down in the pastorals.
2. Or, have teams work together to determine how they might best communicate the Christian doctrine of forgiveness to non-Christian friends, neighbors, or coworkers.

STUDY GUIDE 153

1, 2 Timothy; Titus

CHURCH LEADERSHIP

Overview

The Pastoral Epistles are Paul's last words to leaders of the young church. These brief letters to Timothy and to Titus have their own unique value. They show us how we are to communicate our faith (Study Guide 151). They teach us how to recognize and select spiritual leaders (Study Guide 152). And they give us insight into different categories of leaders, and how our local church leaders are to function.

In these brief letters we meet apostles, overseers (bishops), elders, and deacons. What do we know about the role of each, and how each functioned?

In addition, the pastorals raise a question linked with a sensitive modern issue. Paul told Timothy to commit what he had been taught to "reliable men." And he said that he did "not permit a woman to teach or to have authority over a man" (1 Tim. 2:12). Does this mean that women cannot function as leaders in the church? And, if so, what specific leadership roles are they not to take?

The structure of modern churches is not the same as that of the first-century church, even though we use some of the same identifying terms. Even so, there is much we need to learn about leadership from the pastorals and to apply today if we too are to maintain healthy, vital congregations.

For a complete discussion of this subject see the author's *Theology of Church Leadership* (Zondervan).

Commentary

When Paul and the other early missionaries established a new church, they characteristically stayed for a time, teaching and instructing. They would make another visit to the young church at a later time to complete what was unfinished "and appoint elders in every town" (Titus 1:5). From this practice, referred to in the Book of Acts and several New Testament Epistles, we draw both principles and some questions.

- Paul (with Timothy and Titus) did not function as local church leaders. What were they?
- Elders (plural) were to be established in every town. Nothing is said about ordaining a "pastor" of a local church. What was the task of elders? What about pastors?
- Elders were appointed on the missionaries' *return* visit. Why not on the first?
- New Testament letters dealing with leadership seem to assume (or to explicitly teach) male leadership. What about women in the local church? Can they be leaders?

Exploring questions like these does not necessarily lead us to challenge our own forms of church government. But it does help us think more clearly about spiritual leadership and its function in the local church.

♥ ***Link to Life: Youth / Adult***

Divide by sexes. Ask the women to discuss their feelings about being women in your church. Do they feel accepted and valued? If not, why not? How is either acceptance or nonacceptance communicated to them?

Ask the men to discuss their feelings about women in your church. Do they feel the women are accepted or valued as persons? How do they communicate either acceptance or nonacceptance?

Leadership Terms

Several different words identify church leaders in the New Testament.

Apostle. This word, which in the New Testament can mean "ambassador," "delegate," or "messenger" (e.g., "missionary") is used predominantly of the original 12 disciples and of Paul. These, whom we might call "the Apostles" had unique authority in all the churches. But there were also others called "apostles," such as Barnabas (Acts 14:14), and even the little-known Andronicus and Junias (Rom. 16:7). These apostles were itinerants, who traveled widely founding and then guiding a number of local congregations, much as do modern missionaries.

Whether or not there are modern apostles is often debated. But if so, they surely fall into the category of "apostle" and not "Apostle."

And if there are apostolic ministries, they will surely, as in New Testament times, extend beyond ministry in a single local church.

Bishops. The Greek word we translate "bishop" in some versions means "overseer," or "one who takes care of." Jesus is called "Bishop of your souls' (1 Peter 2:25, KJV). The word suggests a special responsibility to superintend, or to watch out for.

The parallel descriptions of qualifications for the bishop (or *overseer*) in 1 Timothy 3 and for the *elder* in Titus 1 suggest that these two terms, along with "shepherd," "presbyter," and "pastor," are synonyms. Titus especially seems to use "bishop" and "elder" interchangeably. And Paul's letter to the Philippian church is addressed to three groups in the congregation: "all the saints . . . with the overseers and deacons" (Phil. 1:1).

Though we do not know the specific duties of the overseer, it's clear that the overseer worked within a functioning, local congregation.

Elder. This Greek word, like our own, refers first to age: "older one." The Romans had a similar term in Latin: *senatus,* or "senator." The Jews used "elder" as a title for members of local councils and for the inner group of the Sanhedrin.

In early Christianity, teams of elders were responsible for overseeing local congregations (see Acts 14:23). The *Expository Dictionary of Bible Words* (Zondervan) discusses the appointment and tasks of elders.

> The appointment of elders is mentioned in both Acts and Titus. The term "appoint" need not imply apostolic selection of elders; but it does indicate official apostolic recognition and installation. Apparently elders were appointed only on subsequent visits of the missionaries to congregations they had established (Acts 14:21-23; Titus 1:5). It was necessary for a congregation to exist for some time before those whose growth toward maturity and whose gifts would be recognized by the local community could be appointed as elders. The religious con man might temporarily deceive with smooth words. But within a community that shared life intimately, time would reveal true character and motivations.
>
> Scripture gives no well-defined job description for elders. We do know that elders functioned within local congregations and assembled with other elders to consider matters that affected Christians. The word "elder" probably suggests age, and certainly indicates spiritual maturity.
>
> The role of elder requires distinctive spiritual gifts, as well as developed Christian character. After all, every one of God's people is called to spiritual maturity. But not every mature believer is called to serve as an elder.
>
> One critical ministry of elders is mentioned in 1 Timothy 5:17: "The elders who direct the affairs of the church." A hint about the directing role is found in the concept of overseer (*episkopos*). By the way it was used in the secular society, this word, often translated "bishop," suggests both administrative and judicial functions. The same meaning seems applicable to the church, particularly when the concept is linked by Peter with the image of shepherding (1 Peter 2:25).
>
> Although we have no detailed description of the tasks of an elder, the hints found in the New Testament are suggestive. The church is a body, with its own unique organic kind of life. Gifts of overseeing are needed to understand and guard those processes and relationships which permit the local community to function in an organized way. Thus, being an elder calls for insight into the nature of the church and an understanding of how the body functions and the way the gift of administration operates.

Deacons. The Greek word means "to serve" or "to wait on." A deacon literally is the servant of someone. A deacon in the New Testament church was a helper, or agent, of the governing authorities.

In Acts 6 the apostles appointed deacons to supervise food distribution to needy Christian widows. There were high spiritual qualifications for this service; yet it was recognized as a subordinate ministry established to free the apostles for teaching and prayer.

What is important to note is that on both the local and "national" levels there were those who accepted responsibility for maintaining sound doctrine and the holy lifestyle in the church.

Multiple Local Leadership

Some see the Pastoral Epistles and other New Testament books as challenging our contemporary practice of hiring a single pastor. It is clear from 1 Timothy 5:17-18 that some local church leaders in Paul's day gave their full time to ministry and were supported by the congregation, "especially those whose work is preaching and teaching" (v. 17). So the problem does not seem to be whether or not local leaders should include paid professionals.

Where we are more seriously challenged by the New Testament is in our typical local church structure which sets a lone pastor as the "man at the top." We often see this structure as a pyramid with the pastor (or "senior pastor") at the peak, and all others (associate pastors, board members, committee members and ordinary laymen) as under.

But Paul speaks explicitly of "the elders who direct the affairs of the church" (v. 17; Titus 1:5). From these and other references it's clear that the New Testament concept of local church leadership is that of a *team,* rather than of individual "superstar" leadership.

Why multiple leadership? There may be several reasons. (1) No individual can expect to have *all* the spiritual gifts needed to adequately oversee the life of a congregation. We need a blend of gifts. (2) Leaders need to be close to individuals in the congregation and to be aware of doctrinal and practical needs. No one individual can develop close enough relationships with all members of a typical congregation. (3) We are all human and fallible. Team leadership permits discipline, correction, and instruction of leaders by other leaders. (4) Leaders give leadership by *example.* While an individual may provide a good example of individual qualities, no individual can model a functioning body. A leadership team can be an example of the loving, caring community the whole church is to become.

What can we learn about how local church leaders are selected? I noted earlier that elders were "appointed" by the apostles or men like Titus when they made *return* visits to churches. Why? Because elder qualifications focus on personal growth and spiritual maturity, evidenced both by life and by grasp of sound doctrine. Men needed time to mature before their qualifications could be distinguished.

But who then selected them? In the New Testament, the apostles or their representatives seem to have made the official appointment. The word "appoint" is *epitithame,* which has the meaning of "ordain" or "give official recognition to" rather than that of "select." The process seems to involve growing congregational trust in certain members and acknowledgment of their maturity. It was only then, when leadership qualities had developed and been recognized in the local congregation, that leaders were given official recognition by apostolic "appointment."

♥ ***Link to Life: Youth / Adult***

Give a minilecture on local church leadership roles, emphasizing the need for leadership teams rather than "one-man rule."

Then either: (1) ask your group to assume that it is establishing a local congregation. How would they diagram an "ideal" structure? What would they want to write into their constitution to reflect New Testament patterns? Or: (2) distribute copies of your own church's organizational chart and constitution. In what ways does it reflect New Testament patterns? In what ways might it be modified to better reflect New Testament concepts of church leadership?

Reliable Men?

Of all the questions raised about church leadership, one is particularly important and deeply felt these days: "Must leaders always be *men*? May women be elders? May women be pastors? And if not, why not?" The discussion is often blurred by a semantic problem: what we in the twentieth century have defined as the elder role is usually not what Paul was talking about. Hence, is it even relevant to apply his qualifications to a job that sometimes more resembles a business manager than a spiritual leader?

Nevertheless, each of us, in whatever ecclesiastical arrangement we find ourselves, must face the general question of women's role in church leadership.

To respond to this issue, we need first of all to review how the New Testament affirms the equality of women with men in the body of Christ. In a day and culture that typically counted only men, the emphasis on women is surprising. Women were with the original disciples after Jesus' ascension; and "they all joined together constantly in prayer" (Acts 1:14). The conversions of individual women are noted (Lydia in 16:14-15; Damaris in 17:34). In other cases, Scripture records that "not a few prominent women" and "a number of prominent Greek women" believed (vv. 4, 12). Paul ended his letter to the Romans with a list of notes to special people in the church there; a third of these are women!

There are women whom Paul called his "fellow workers" who "have contended at my side in the cause of the Gospel" (Phil. 4:3). Paul used the word *fellow worker* to describe Timothy (Rom. 16:21), Titus (2 Cor. 8:23), Demas and Luke (Phile. 24), Priscilla (Rom. 16:3), and Euodia and Syntyche (Phil. 4:3), the last three being women.

Phoebe was a deaconess (Rom. 16:2), and many commentators feel that 1 Timothy 3:11 refers not to deacons' wives but to deaconesses. In the practical, ongoing work of the church for which the deacons were responsible, there would be certain tasks clearly more suited to women (such as assisting another woman at baptism, counseling women on relating to husbands and children, etc.).

In this Age of the Spirit, even the gift of prophecy (which many feel includes proclamation or preaching) is for daughters as well as for sons (Acts 2:18; 1 Cor. 11:5). In the church, each person is a priest, and each has spiritual gifts through which he or she can contribute to the health and ministry of the whole. It is completely out of harmony with the Bible to make artificial distinctions between men and women in the church, relegating women to a second-class position. Each woman and each man in the church is free to find fulfillment as a ministering person. "There is neither Jew nor Greek, slave nor free, male nor female, for you are all one in Christ Jesus" (Gal. 3:28).

Women leaders? Why then in the pastorals does the same writer, Paul, "not permit a woman to teach or have authority over a man"? (1 Tim. 2:12) Why are they to "learn in quietness and full submission"? (v. 11) Why are bishops and deacons referred to as "husbands" and "men" (1 Tim. 3:2, 8, 12; Titus 1:6) without exception?

In the whole context of Scripture (where women *do* prophesy!) it is clear that Paul is not suggesting a woman may not open her mouth when men are present. Church leadership is the topic of the pastorals, and since leaders oversee the purity of the Christian community's doctrine and lifestyle, it is clear that the particular "teaching" Paul refers to is the "teaching with authority" that Paul urges on Timothy and Titus as their ministry. It was Timothy's role to "command and teach" (1 Tim. 4:11) the things of God as an apostolic representative. Apparently Paul did not permit a woman to be ordained to such an office of responsibility.

As to the "quietness and full submission," the *Bible Knowledge Commentary* (Victor) notes (p. 735),

> The word *hesychia,* translated "quietness" in 1 Timothy 2:11 and "silent" in verse 12, does not mean complete silence or no talking. It is clearly used elsewhere (Acts 22:2; 2 Thes. 3:12) to mean "settled down, undisturbed, not unruly."

Today? What about today? Well, there are many who would disagree with this instruction of Paul's.

- Some suppose that Paul was simply a male chauvinist. He spoke from the context of his own time, and thus shared a common prejudice against women. "For our enlightened day," they suggest, "such a limit does not apply."
- Some, less eager to discount Scripture, still suggest that the restriction was peculiar to first-century culture. In that society, a woman leader would not have had the same respect as a man. In today's world, the situation has changed, so we are free to suppose the restriction no longer applies.
- Others suggest that it is all right for

women to serve on the church board "at the invitation of" (and thus under the authority of) the men of the congregation.

Among those who take Paul's restriction at face value are the following:

- Some say that his ruling is based not on culture but on creation. God ordained male headship as long ago as Genesis 2, not because of any superior intelligence or strength, but simply because headship had to be tested somewhere to prevent anarchy. In everyday society, we may rearrange roles and responsibilities to our hearts' content, but in the home and the church—divinely ordained institutions—we are bound to follow the order demonstrated in Scripture.
- Some extremists make this teaching the foundation of an attack on women as persons, declaring that the disqualification for church leadership demonstrates female inferiority.
- Still others simply say that, whatever the reasons behind this teaching, it is better to follow it than to debate it.

What strikes me as being of most concern here is not so much whether women are or are not to be affirmed as pastors or as elders. On this issue each of us is responsible to examine the Word for guidance, and to follow what we believe to be God's will. I feel free to hold my own convictions, and to permit others to hold theirs.

What most concerns me is that the debate about women *leaders* may cause us to lose sight of the fact that women *are* full and equal members of the body: gifted, valued, ministering members.

Another concern is that women may be tempted to make the issue of ordination a symbol of their acceptance as persons.

Either of these is tragic. On the one hand, the whole church in our day needs desperately to affirm women as people and open itself in every way to the ministry God intends to offer the whole body through them. On the other hand, women and men both need to learn to live comfortably and affirmatively within whatever limitations God has placed on them. Each of us needs to develop a healthy self-esteem based not on position but on recognition of who we are in Christ. We each have God-given gifts with which to serve others.

If a women *should* be disqualified from an office in the church, such a disqualification would in no way make her less significant as a sister, a person, or a unique and utterly vital member of the body of Christ.

♥ ***Link to Life: Youth / Adult***

Read 1 Timothy 2 to the group. Ask each individual to write a brief summary statement of his or her impression of the limitations on women which it implies.

Have group members read their statements. Then explain the various ways Christians have tried to deal with such passages. Discuss: "Do any of these seem to resolve the questions raised?"

Then in a minilecture describe the broader view of women in the church taken in Scripture and discussed in this guide's commentary.

You might wish to use the illustration to point out that however we interpret such limiting passages, the areas of limitation are very small.

The Well-being of the Body

God's church is to glorify Him. It is meant to praise and worship its Lord and Head, Jesus Christ. It is also meant to build up and to encourage its individual members. God desires that we be whole persons, and one of the reasons He has given us the church is to help our individual growth.

Not every member of a congregation will

Roles of Men & Women

Men	*Men & Women*	*Women*
father children serve as elders, deacons	• in image of God • given spiritual gifts • ministering people ("fellow workers") • "prophesy"	bear children, mother serve as deaconesss

hold an office, but every member ought to be ministering to others and exercising the gifts he or she has been given.

On what basis do we choose leadership in the church? First, we look at the qualifications for leaders that Scripture sets out. We look for those who are mature, and who are ministering now in ways that leaders are to serve the people of God. We rid ourselves of the notion that church leadership is some sort of reward system or status symbol. Instead, we seek to affirm those whose gifts and calling demonstrate that they are God's choice for building up the church of God. And the more we mature, the more clearly we realize that we need one another and the contribution each of us makes to all.

TEACHING GUIDE

Prepare
Determine before you teach whether you will emphasize the question of women's role or other leadership issues.

Explore
1. Have men and women in separate groups explore their impressions of whether the women in your congregation are valued and accepted or discounted. See "link-to-life," page 977.
2. Or raise the questions posed at the opening of this study guide about leadership. What ideas about answers do your group members have?

Expand
1. Read 1 Timothy 2 to your group, and then use the teaching process suggested in "link-to-life," page 981. Be sure to emphasize in your minilecture the total context of Scripture, in which women are seen as valued and gifted members of the body. The illustration on that page may help group members see that if there is a limitation placed on the role women can have in leadership, it is a very small matter indeed compared to the common identity, giftedness, and ministry shared by men and women.
2. Or focus on the different titles given leaders in New Testament times, and the function of these leaders. To apply what is learned, let your group members either try to develop a constitution as if they were beginning a church, or evaluate your own church's organization and constitution. See "link-to-life," page 979.

Apply
Affirm the contribution of each member in your group, men and women, to one another's spiritual growth. Start with any individual, who is to name another and tell him or her how that person has contributed to his or her life. The person named is to then choose another, moving from person to person until all have had a chance to share.

Not everyone, of whatever sex, can be an elder or deacon. But every believer can exercise spiritual gifts which enrich the lives of others.

STUDY GUIDE 154

Philemon

NOTE TO A FELLOW WORKER

Overview

This short letter, just 335 words in Greek, was written by Paul while he was in prison in Rome, about A.D. 62 or 63. It is a personal note, written to a well-to-do Christian named Philemon about a runaway slave, Onesimus.

The slave had apparently stolen funds from his master and planned to lose himself among the masses in Rome. There he met Paul, was converted, and under the apostle's gentle teaching, determined to return to his master.

The letter is important in two respects. First, it shows the "moral suasion" approach to spiritual leadership that Paul adopted. This approach is explained in 2 Corinthians, in which the apostle explained the basic principles which guided his relationships with his converts.

Second, the letter gives us insight into how early Christianity dealt with an evil institution. Slavery then as at any time in history was repugnant—a denial of the dignity and worth of human beings. Yet Christians launched no crusade against slavery. Rather, as Paul shows us here, Christ introduced love into the heart of master and slave. As a slave Onesimus sought to be profitable to his master (v. 11); as master Philemon would learn to see Onesimus also "as a man and as a brother in the Lord" (v. 16). It is Christ's power to transform relationships that has, in history, motivated movements which have led to emancipation.

Commentary

Slavery was an important institution in the Roman Empire. Most slaves were laborers, the machines of their day. Yet a number of slaves were educators, physicians, skilled artists, and administrators. Materially slaves were often better off than the poor freedmen, who had to work for a daily wage. Their food and clothing was comparable, and slaves were often better housed.

Yet slaves were not people in a legal sense, though the law did provide a minimum of protection for them. A slave with marketable skills might also earn enough money on his own time to one day purchase his freedom, a thing alluded to in 1 Corinthians 7:21.

Yet, as the *Expository Dictionary of Bible Words* (Zondervan) notes, slavery was still slavery:

> However much the bondage of slavery might be mitigated by the comparatively good conditions in which a slave lived, the central fact of slavery remained. A slave was not his own person. He was required to do his master's will, not his own. He was bound to serve, not his own interests, but the interests of his master. This reality underlies many sayings in the Gospels. The Roman soldier said to Jesus, "I say to my servant [*doulos,* "slave"], 'Do this,' and he does it" (Matt. 8:9). Jesus spoke (Luke 17:7-10) of the *doulos* who worked in the fields and then prepared his master's supper: only afterward did he sit down to eat. "Would he thank the servant because he did what he was told to do?" Jesus asked (v. 9). The answer, of course, is no. In obeying, the *doulos* only did his duty.

There were three sources of slaves in the first century. First was capture in war. Second was being born of a slave mother. Third was through sale. A parent might sell a child, or an adult might sell himself to pay debts. Release from slavery might also come through different avenues. It was not uncommon for a slave to be freed by his master. Or a slave might purchase his own freedom with funds he earned and saved. And, of course, a slave might die. Yet, while a person lived as a slave, he or she was morally and legally perceived as one who owed loyalty to his or her master.

Despite the wrong deeply imbedded in this institution, and its violation of the most basic of human rights, slavery was one of the foundations of first-century economy and society. Giving wholesale freedom to slaves would have meant starvation to great segments of the population. In that age there simply were no available alternatives which might have provided the slave population with employment and housing. It is against this background that the New Testament instructs both slaves and masters (Eph. 6:5-9; Col. 3:22; 1 Tim. 6:1-2; Titus 2:9-10; 1 Peter 2:18). Slaves are to serve their masters faithfully, while masters are to be considerate of their slaves and treat them with respect. A believer need not be free to live a truly Christian life; a believer need not even free his slaves to treat them in a Christian way.

Yet, while Christianity posed no immediate threat to this accepted institution, Christ brought a new perception of human beings and a new relationship between master and slave which ultimately led to emancipation. Only, as in the early years of this country, by somehow defining a slave as less than human could the institution persist.

♥ ***Link to Life: Youth / Adult***
Give a minilecture on slavery in the first century, and on the Bible's expressed instructions to slaves and to masters. Then discuss: "What modern institutions or practices violate basic rights of human beings created in the image of God? If we take a New Testament approach, how will we deal with these institutions or practices?"

Philemon

This brief letter contains several clearly defined sections.

Greetings (Phile. 1-3). Paul expressed his appreciation and love for Philemon, a "dear friend and fellow worker." It seems possible that Philemon lived in Colosse. Paul, in that letter, noted that the letter carrier, Tychicus, "is coming with Onesimus, our faithful and dear brother, who is one of you" (Col. 4:9). Paul very probably included this brief personal note to Philemon with the letter sent to the Colossian congregation.

Thanksgiving and prayer (Phile. 4-7). The form here is typical of first-century letters. Secular letters from the first century also express thanks to the gods and assure of prayers. But Paul filled this form greeting with unique content: he thanked God for Philemon's faith and love, and prayed that Philemon might continue to be active in sharing his faith. Paul also expressed personal appreciation: "Your love has given me great joy and encouragement, because you, brother, have refreshed the hearts of the saints."

Paul's plea (Phile. 8-22). It is in this, the major section of the letter, that we see Paul's "moral suasion" approach. The apostle did not use his authority to command Philemon to accept Onesimus back (and, implicitly, not to charge or punish him for his earlier theft). But Paul did not hesitate to state his case strongly.

On the one hand this is an "appeal," and Paul wanted Philemon's response to be "spontaneous and not forced." Philemon could refuse to respond.

On the other hand, Paul pressed his appeal. He reminded Philemon of their mutual love. He expressed his own love for Onesimus. He spoke of Onesimus' conversion. He pointed out that the runaway slave was now a brother, and will be "useful" to him once again. He reminded Philemon of all that individual owed Paul, and asked that Onesimus' debt be charged to his own account. In view of all this, Paul made his request with confidence that Onesimus would obey.

Final greetings (Phile. 23-25). Again using a pattern common to first-century letters, Paul closed by sending greetings from mutual acquaintances and friends.

♥ ***Link to Life: Youth / Adult***
Distribute copies of the Book of Philemon, which can be photocopied on a single sheet. Point out that Paul was able to use moral suasion because of the relationship he had established with Philemon. Have group members work in pairs to discover from the text characteristics of the relationship which permitted Paul to persuade rather than command.

Each pair should make a list of characteristics of the relationship between these two men. Come together and develop a group list. Then discuss: "How critical is re-

lationship to influence? With whom do group members have this kind of relationship? How have any of these people been able to influence them? How have your group members influenced the others?"

TEACHING GUIDE

Prepare
You may wish to research slavery in the Roman Empire as background to this letter.

Explore
1. Give a minilecture on slavery in the Roman Empire, and on the New Testament instructions for slaves and masters.
2. Have your groups brainstorm. What modern institutions or practices may be like slavery in that they deny basic human rights? If we were to approach such practices as Paul and other New Testament writers do, how would we seek to respond to the practices the group members have identified?

Expand
1. Give a minilecture reviewing Paul's style of leadership, which relies on moral suasion rather than on command. Review principles he presents in 2 Corinthians, and determine which should be identified.
2. Distribute copies of Philemon to each member. Have them work in pairs to identify characteristics of the relationship which Paul had with Philemon, on which he based his appeal and persuasion. See "link-to-life," page 984, column two.

Apply
Write a letter to a son or daughter or a close friend, attempting to use the same kind of appeal that Paul used. Then form groups of three to hear and comment on each other's letters. Is the tone of your letters of appeal the same as we see in Philemon? How will the person who receives your letter probably feel about it? Will they want to respond? Why or why not?

STUDY GUIDE 155

Introduction

HEBREWS

Overview

This letter was written to Hebrew Christians who apparently were disturbed by legalistic Jews who traveled to young churches, arguing that an Old Testament lifestyle must be maintained by believers in Jesus. The letter shows that Christ is the reality which Old Testament institutions only foreshadowed. Believers need not go back, but must go forward to experience a new life in Christ which does not depend on the old ways.

Outline

I. Jesus, the Living Word	1:1–4:13
A. The deity of Jesus	1:1-14
B. Warning to listen	2:1-4
C. The humanity of Jesus	2:5-18
D. Hearing Jesus' voice	3:1–4:13
II. Jesus, Our High Priest	4:14–8:13
A. Jesus' priesthood	4:14–5:10
B. Warning to persist	5:11–6:20
C. More on priesthood	7:1-28
D. Nature of New Covenant	8:1-13
III. Jesus, the Perfect Sacrifice	9:1–10:39
A. Cleansing provided	9:1-28
B. Removal of sin	10:1-18
C. Warning to persevere	10:19-39
IV. Jesus, Our Sanctification	11:1–13:25
A. The role of faith	11:1-40
B. Nature of discipline	12:1-12
C. Warning to respond	12:13-28
D. Exhortation to love	13:1-25

■ For a technical introduction to the Book of Hebrews and a verse-by-verse commentary see the *Bible Knowledge Commentary,* pages 777-813.

Commentary

The authorship, date, and addressees of Hebrews are uncertain. One early tradition identifies Paul as author. Another mentions Barnabas. But the letter itself does not say, and the literary style is quite unlike that of the great apostle.

It seems likely that the book was written in A.D. 68 or 69, primarily because the writer speaks of the Old Testament sacrifices as if they were still being offered. These sacrifices were made only at the temple in Jerusalem, and that temple was destroyed with the city itself in A.D. 70 by the Romans.

While the letter seemed to have been written to a particular congregation (see Heb. 13:23)—perhaps in Palestine—its destination is not specified. But it is clear that the intended readers were Christians of Jewish background. The writer not only spoke constantly of Old Testament events and institutions, he also contrasted Jesus, and His position and His ministry to them. Clearly the Book of Hebrews is intended to demonstrate the superiority of Christ and the way of life built on faith in Him to the way of life expressed in Old Testament Law and custom.

As we read Hebrews we can sense something of the desperation that its readers may have felt. They seem, like many Christians today, to have been people who yearned desperately for a satisfying spiritual life—and felt uncertain of achieving it. So members of this Hebrew-Christian congregation were wondering about what they had given up—and what they had gained. They were looking back longingly at the old ways of Judaism, at the traditional pattern of life that had seemed so stable and secure. They were wondering if the way of life they had left wasn't perhaps better than the new one they had adopted.

We can sympathize with their uncertainty and their unhappiness. The Old Testament faith bore the stamp of divine revelation. God had spoken through the prophets, through angels, through history itself, and through acts that were clearly miraculous.

He had spoken by means of the seven annual festivals of worship that marked the Hebrew year, and in the sacrifices that dealt with sin and gave the worshiper a way to express praise. God had spoken in the closely regulated way of life of the committed Jew, and in the divine Law, which expressed the highest moral tone. A man who was born a Jew and whose heart was warm toward God found in the total pattern of life under the Old Testament a great sense of fulfillment and identity.

But then Jesus came—the Messiah the prophets had foretold—promising a salvation that included, but went beyond, the glimpses given in the Old Testament. These Hebrew men and women had believed in Jesus. They turned from what they had known all their lives, and ventured out to discover a new way of life, and a new identity. And then, somehow, the venture threatened to turn sour. They had tried, but had somehow missed the promised maturity. They had missed the wholeness.

The Book of Hebrews points out that in Christ there *is* far more than an Old Testament faith offered. There is a maturity, an experience with God, a full and complete salvation that through history had awaited Jesus' coming. And it is this *full* salvation that the Book of Hebrews explains.

In this introductory session you can sample some of the exciting truths in Hebrews—and raise questions that will be answered in a study of each section of this vital book.

What might you sample? The superiority of Jesus as revealer of God (Heb. 1:1 3). A key concepts chart that pinpoints life-changing truths in each chapter. And a preliminary study of three warnings that are given in the course of this book's argument.

The Superiority of Jesus: Hebrews 1:1-3

The Book of Hebrews begins with Jesus. Total confidence in Him must be the basis of our new life, and of our identity as Christians.

It was particularly important to begin with Jesus in writing to these Hebrew Christians. The Hebrew Scriptures had given glimpses of the truth that the "God of Abraham, Isaac, and Jacob," as the Jews often identified Him, was really one God in three Persons. However, the doctrine of the Trinity was never explicitly taught in the Old Testament. It could be glimpsed in the plurals of Genesis 1, as God said "Let *Us* make man in *Our* image" (1:26, italics added). It could be detected in the very term by which the unity of God was affirmed each Sabbath in the synagogue: "Hear, O Israel! The Lord is our God, the Lord is One" (Deut. 6:4, NASB). That "One" in the original permits a compound unity, such as that of a single bunch of grapes which is composed of numerous units. Glimpses of the Trinity could also be seen in the many Old Testament references to the Spirit of God as distinct from God Himself.

Yet, only when Jesus came and taught, "I and the Father are One" (John 10:30) was truth about God as three Persons fully disclosed. When it was disclosed, and Jesus began to explain that "no one comes to the Father except through Me" (14:6), it became vitally important that believers learn to rest their full confidence in Him.

It also became important to realize that *all there is* of salvation for us is to be found in Jesus. There is nothing higher or greater than knowing Jesus. There is nothing beyond knowing Jesus that is key to a supposedly "higher" spiritual experience. The Bible says of the Holy Spirit, "He will bring glory to Me [Jesus]" (16:14). In everything in our Christian lives, God has determined that the focus should be on Jesus. We can come to know Jesus better . . . but we can never find anything better than knowing Jesus.

So it is important for us to begin with an accurate impression of Jesus—just as it was vital that the Hebrews to whom this letter was written grasp just who He is. Our vision must leave no doubts that Jesus is God.

How powerfully these first verses of Hebrews portray His glory:

> In the past God spoke to our forefathers through the prophets at many times and in various ways, but in these last days He has spoken to us by His Son, whom He appointed Heir of all things, and through whom He made the universe. The Son is the radiance of God's glory and the exact representation of His being, sustaining all things by His powerful word. After He had provided purification for sins, He sat down at the right hand of the Majesty in heaven.
>
> Hebrews 1:1-3

Sonship belongs to Jesus (Heb. 1:2). This term has been used by some to question the full deity of Jesus. But the term "son" is designed to emphasize relationships between the Persons of the Godhead, not to suggest that Jesus is a created being. Even the term *firstborn* (v. 6), according to Arndt and Gingrich's *Greek Lexicon,* "is admirably suited to describe Jesus as the One coming forth from God to found the new community of saints" (p. 734). He is "Firstborn" in that He is the Founder, the Model, the One with the Father's full authority to act (see Rom. 8:29; Rev. 1:5).

The clearest evidence of Jesus' position as a full Member of the Godhead is given in these early verses, as we see who Jesus is, all He accomplished, and all that will be His.

The coming kingdom belongs to Jesus (Heb. 1:2). Jesus has been appointed "Heir of all things." He will inherit and purify this world at His coming, and then create a new heaven and a new earth. He is Heir to all, and this constitutes a promise that one day all will be fully God's.

Creative power belongs to Jesus (Heb. 1:2). Jesus is the One who spoke, and in speaking caused our whole vast universe to appear. Jesus is the One who billions of years ago acted to shape stars so distant that astronomers can only guess at their existence.

The original glory of God belongs to Jesus (Heb. 1:3). The phrases "radiance of God's glory" and "the exact representation of His being" are both strong assertions. *Radiance,* the light shining forth from a luminary, is all that the human eye can see. Similarly, all that we can see of God shines through Jesus! *Exact representation* assures us that there is a total and complete correspondence between the eternal God and the Man, Jesus. If you and I look at Jesus, we see exactly what God is like, for Jesus is God, and reveals Him exactly.

Sustaining power belongs to Jesus (Heb. 1:3). Even today the entire universe would flicker out of existence if it were not for the power of Jesus, energizing the so-called "natural laws" that govern our physical universe.

Redemptive work belongs to Jesus (Heb. 1:3). As a Man, Jesus walked our earth and knew our nature and weaknesses. But now, once again, He has returned to "the right hand of the Majesty in heaven." His work has been fully accomplished. He rests now, knowing that He has provided a salvation able to make us whole. Now, seeing Jesus, the focus of our praise and worship, restored to glory, we need to learn to rest in the fact that Jesus *is* God.

♥ ***Link to Life: Youth / Adult***

Give a minilecture on the reason the Book of Hebrews was written. Then ask teams of four to five to examine Hebrews 1:1-3. What helps you feel most confidence in Jesus? Why? What might have been most important to an early Hebrew Christian? Why?

You'll want to be available to answer any questions group members have concerning the meaning of any terms.

Let each group report. Then point out that the basis of our Christian life, like the basis to which the recipients of this New Testament letter must return, is total confidence in Jesus and a willingness to seek fulfillment in Him.

Key Concepts in Hebrews

The writer of the Book of Hebrews constantly returned to the basics of our faith. His first words direct our attention to Jesus, for He is the foundation and the core. In nearly every chapter the writer continued his perceptive, direct approach, and continued to highlight truth which, when appropriated, will bring us to wholeness in our Christian experience.

The key concepts chart (p. 989) summarizes the truths your group will discover in Hebrews—and the meaning of those truths for every life.

♥ ***Link to Life: Youth / Adult***

Duplicate and distribute to each group member the key concept chart. Ask each to identify one truth they want to better understand or apply. If you wish to take the time, go around the group and ask each to share the area which seems most important to him or her.

Warnings in Hebrews

There are three extensive warning sections in the Book of Hebrews. They are understood by some to be warnings against the loss of salvation. As we examine them in context, however, we can see that actually they are warnings to Christians against missing out on the full experience of that

Key Concepts Chart

Hebrews		Theme	Concept	Key Verses	Key Words	Meaning
Foundation Truths . . .	Chap. 1	Jesus' identity	Jesus is God	Heb. 1:1-2	whole, complete	Jesus is enough . . . there is nothing more I need.
	2	Our identity	We are Jesus' brothers	Heb. 2:11	mastery, dominion	I need to see myself raised to mastery of life in Jesus.
	3 & 4	Life-principle	Experience our position	Heb. 4:10	rest, faith, response	When I trust and obey God I enter His rest.
	5	High Priest	Jesus links us with God	Heb. 4:16	weakness, link	When weak, I can come confidently to Jesus for forgiveness and aid.
	6	Maturity	Security stimulates growth	Heb. 6:18	insecure, foundation	I can forget myself and launch out in reckless trust that the Atonement is complete.
Deeper Truths . . . Identity	7	Priesthood	Relationship is assured	Heb. 7:25	guaranteed relationship	I can have assurance of salvation: Jesus is my Guarantee!
	8 & 9	Law	Righteousness is necessary	Heb. 8:10	commandment law, inner law	I can trust Jesus to make me progressively more righteous as I trust and obey Him.
	9 & 10	Sacrifice	Holiness is ours	Heb. 10:14	guilt, cleansed	I can see myself in Jesus as a holy, not a guilty person.
Deeper Truths . . . Lifestyle	10	Warning	Maturing takes time	Heb. 10:35-36	process, persevere	I can know that daily commitment to God's will will produce maturity.
	11	Faith	Faith enables	Heb. 11:6	enablement, obedience	I can meet any challenge enabled by faith in God.
	12	Discipline	Faith becomes commitments	Heb. 12:10	patience, holiness	I can discipline myself to full commitment to faith's life.
	13	Love	Faith produces love	Heb. 13:20-21	externals, grace	I can find life's real meaning in others and in Christ.

salvation Jesus provides. They are warnings to a people who are almost ready to abandon the only process that can produce maturity.

You may want to use some of this introductory session to look quickly at these warnings.

Hebrews 3–4. The first of these warning passages is found in Hebrews 3 and 4. Looking back we can see several significant features of the warning that sets a pattern repeated in the other warning sections as well.

In the warning, two directions or courses of action are examined. One is for believers to obey when they hear the voice of God. The other possible response is to disobey; to hear what God is saying, but to harden our hearts against Him and doubt that His direction is best. When this happens we will rebel.

Each of these two courses of action has an outcome. If we disobey, we will never experience God's rest. Entry into a Sabbath-rest (a peace despite troubles) which Christ has made available to us simply cannot be experienced by those who refuse to trust and obey. But if our daily life *is* marked by obedience, then we will experience His rest. As the Scripture says, "Today, if you hear His voice, do not harden your hearts" (3:15).

Thus the first danger that can rob us of the full experience of salvation is presented. We are warned against *unbelief* and *disobedience*. We are reminded that for progress in the life of faith we need to keep a firm trust in Jesus and respond in obedience to whatever He says to us.

This is hardly an exhilarating or startling insight. It doesn't appeal to our eagerness for instant maturity. Instead it sets before us a disciplined pattern of daily life. It describes a process that is to be lifelong, yet a process which both satisfies our hearts with present rest and promises constant progress toward beginning to reach maturity.

Hebrews 6. This chapter contains the second great warning. Note that the pattern set in the earlier warning is repeated here, and that the issue is basically the same.

The warning is addressed to believers. It examines two courses which the believer can take. One course is that which leads to maturity. The other is to "become lazy" (v. 12), and lay faith-foundations over and over.

Each of these courses also has an outcome. We're told that if we fail to go on, our lives will be marked by unfruitfulness (vv. 7-8), and that we will fail to possess all that being in Christ provides. We're also encouraged. If our approach to life in Christ is one of building on the foundation already laid, we will fully grasp the hope within. How exciting that phrase is! Our hope is that Jesus, who is eternity-now for you and me, will reshape us into His likeness.

This too is a significant warning for people who were becoming discouraged with their Christian lives. They looked back and wondered if they were "really" saved. Over and over again they tried to lay a foundation that Jesus had laid once for all in His death. They were so preoccupied with these foundational matters, which were actually settled already, that they had grown slack about daily obedience and daily growth.

This is common too. One of Satan's attacks on God's children is focused in just this area. You're discouraged about sin cropping up in your life? You're unhappy about your lack of progress in the faith? Satan is sure to suggest, "Well, maybe you're not saved. Maybe you need to run to Jesus again. Maybe you need to keep going back until it 'takes' and your sin problem is settled, and perfection comes in a flash."

Don't let Satan deceive! The sin question has been settled. In Jesus' death for you, you stand holy and forgiven in God's sight. But perfection does not come in a flash. Perfection and maturity are things you grow toward, with the benefits of Jesus' death being progressively applied as you trust and obey God. Through that process you *grow toward* what will ultimately be the full experience of that costly, blood-won salvation which is yours in Him.

Hebrews 10:26-39. When we come to the third great warning passage in chapter 10, we find the same themes repeated. God is again warning a people eager to hurry up the process and to find instant maturity. God is saying, "When the growing gets rough, My way for you is not to turn back, but to tough it through."

This warning also follows the pattern set in the others. First, it is addressed to believers: "We" are the subjects" (v. 26ff).

Also, two courses are contrasted. The one involves throwing away our confidence in the completeness of Jesus' work (v. 35), and

Warnings in Hebrews

Question	Heb. 3–4	Heb. 6	Heb. 10:26-39
Who is being warned?			
What are they told to do?			
What are they told *not* to do?			
What consequences follow the wrong response?			
What benefits grow from the right response?			
What is the danger against which we are being warned?			

shrinking back (v. 39). The other course of action is, as in early days, to stand fast (v. 32) and "to persevere so that when you have done the will of God, you will receive what He has promised" (v. 36). Again a commitment to disciplined doing of the will of God stands contrasted with giving up on Jesus, and striking out to find some other way to live.

The critical issue here then is clear. If, understanding what Jesus has done, the Hebrews now shrink back and turn away from Him, they can *never* find the fulfillment for which they yearn. There is only one way to experience salvation fully. The product of maturity never comes apart from the process.

♥ ***Link to Life: Youth / Adult***
Briefly outline the pattern seen in the warnings. Then give each person a warnings chart, and let teams of three or four work to fill out each cell. Or, you may set each team to work on a different passage, and then have your group members complete their personal charts as other teams report.

In one sense, these warnings are frightening. They are given in all seriousness, and should be listened to seriously as well. Yet the fright that Christians have felt has often been misplaced: we have feared the wrong thing!

This will be clear as we go on to teach Hebrews 3–4 and Hebrews 6 in future sessions. But the reason for the fears, and the reasons why many are unfounded, both become clear as we continue to look at Hebrews 10.

> If we deliberately keep on sinning after we have received the knowledge of the truth, no sacrifice for sins is left, but only a fearful expectation of judgment and of raging fire that will consume the enemies of God. Anyone who rejected the Law of Moses died without mercy on the testimony of two or three witnesses. How much more severely do you think a man deserves to be punished who has trampled the Son of God underfoot, who has treated as an unholy thing the blood of the covenant that sanctified him, and who has insulted the Spirit of grace? For we know Him who said, "It is Mine to avenge; I will repay," and again, "The Lord will judge His people." It is a dreadful thing to fall into the hands of the living God.
>
> Hebrews 10:26-31

To understand these verses, we must remember where they come in this book. They come *after* the writer has explained the full meaning of Jesus' death. They follow his clear presentation of the fact that Jesus' sacrifice "has made perfect forever those who are being made holy" (v. 14).

At this point in the book the readers *know* that perfection is promised, and that they can draw closer to it daily as they "spur one another on toward love and good deeds" (v. 24). But what happens if they refuse to count on these things as true? What happens if they still turn back—to Judaism or to any of the other routes that are seen as possible shortcuts to maturity? According to Scripture, this would be to "deliberately keep on sinning after we have received the knowledge of the truth" (v. 26). According to this same verse, if we make this choice and turn away, "no sacrifice for sins is left, but only a fearful expectation of judgment."

This terrible portrait immediately conjures up visions of the loss of our salvation. Yet it seems that from chapter 6 on the writer of Hebrews has tried to show us that salvation *can't* be lost! Jesus' death is the perfect sacrifice that makes us holy.

What then is meant? Simply this. The phrase "no sacrifice (or "offering") for sins is left" lets us know that God cannot apply the benefits of salvation until we deal with our own sin by confession. It's not that Jesus' blood is inadequate to cleanse from willful sin after conversion. It is simply that even God's perfect provision cannot benefit us in our present experience if we persist in rejecting God's truth about how to go on to maturity.

And not only this. The temptation to seek shortcuts also opens us up to judgment and punishment. People who rejected the Old Testament Law given by Moses were punished severely—even by death (10:28). How much more worthy of punishment is a person who looks at Jesus' blood and its meaning and then turns away to look for fulfillment in Judaism—or in tongues, or in "groups," or in witnessing, or in pet doctrines? God says that it is the "blood of the covenant" that sanctifies (v. 29). It is the power of the blood of Jesus that makes us holy, and it is our constant reliance on Jesus, expressed in daily trust and obedience, that applies that blood to our experience and makes us grow.

Trampling the Son of God underfoot (v. 29) by seeing Him as *insufficient* is one of the grossest rejections of God's grace. Believers who do so will taste the discipline of the God who accepts responsibility to judge His own people as well as men of this world (v. 30).

And so the writer urged, "Do not throw away your confidence" (v. 35). Persevere. Do the will of God, and you *will* receive what He has promised.

TEACHING GUIDE

Prepare
Preview Study Guides 156 and 157 for more background on the warnings in Hebrews discussed there.

Explore
1. Brainstorm with your group. What do Christians look to beside or other than Jesus as ways to spiritual fulfillment? List their insights. Then discuss: "What experiences might lead Christians to look to such things for fulfillment? In what ways, if any, has our own Christian experience been disappointing?"
2. Introduce the Book of Hebrews and why it was written as a lead in to group study of Hebrews 1:1-3. See "link-to-life" suggestion on page 988.

Expand
1. Distribute the key concepts chart, and let your group members look through it for a truth that seems particularly relevant to them. See page 989.
2. Or use the chart provided with "link-to-life," page 991 to guide teams in direct study of the three major warning passages in Hebrews.

Apply
Simply point out that the Book of Hebrews is intended to encourage, not discourage believers. Ask your group members to pray that God will help them see His pathway to maturity, and to realize more fully all that Jesus has provided for His own.

STUDY GUIDE 156

Hebrews 1:1–4:13

JESUS, THE LIVING WORD

Overview
In Ephesians, Paul described the armor that equips believers to live in one body. Only one piece of this armor is explained—the sword of the Spirit, which is "the Word of God." In Hebrews, God's Word is again a sword (Heb. 4:12-13). It is "living and active. Sharper than any double-edged sword, it penetrates even to dividing soul and spirit, joints and marrow; it judges the thoughts and attitudes of the heart."

Yet there are questions about the Word. When we want guidance and help, how do we experience it as "living and active"? When we are uncertain, how do we tap its "penetrating" power?

And, does God speak to us only through His written Word? Or may Christ speak to us with another voice? Often when we want to know God's will we become confused.

In Old Testament times it seemed so simple. God had given laws and rules through Moses that regulated every aspect of life. When special guidance was needed God sent a prophet, authenticated by miracles. Now, however, as the Hebrew Christians apparently felt, though we too have a written Word, the voice of God is less certainly heard.

The writer of Hebrews understood. And he moved immediately to make one thing clear to his readers. In Christ we have an even greater revelation than that from Moses. And, through relationship with Jesus, we have access to the very voice of the living God.

Commentary
In Israel's past God communicated to His people in many ways. The writer identifies some in the first verses of this book—and then goes on to say that *now* God "has spoken to us by His Son" (1:12). A person who wishes to hear God's voice must now look to the Son, who is the "exact representation" of God's very being.

The writer then went on to show the superiority of Jesus *as One who reveals God* to first angels, and then to Moses.

Jesus' Superiority as a Revealer of God: Hebrews 1:4–3:6
Jesus' superiority to angels (Heb. 1:4-14). The writer now began an extended argument to prove that Jesus is superior to angels. Why is this important? The answer is seen in 2:2. There the writer referred to "the message spoken by angels," which was binding on Israel. The Jews believed that their Old Testament had been mediated through angelic messengers. The Word of God was deeply respected in part because of this supernatural mediation. But now, the writer said, *the Spokesman is greater than the angels!* The Messenger is God Himself, exalted above the ancient messengers, for He is the very Father of eternity.

The Hebrew Christians, aware of the Bible's teaching about angels and aware that angels had been intermediaries in the past, found it difficult to fully accept the fact that, in Jesus, God had established direct communication. There was the temptation in the early church to think of Jesus as a "high" angel. To counter this, the writer of Hebrews made it clear at the outset that Jesus is superior to all angels.

**Superior relationship (1:5)*. Jesus stands *beside* God the Father as His Son, not *below* Him as a creature.

**Superior as Deity (1:6-9)*. None of the angels is called God, and no angel is worshiped by his fellows. Yet Jesus is given the name of God, and the angelic hosts worship Him.

**Superior as Creator (1:10-12)*. Like the angels (who are immortal, not knowing birth or death as we do) Jesus will outlast the universe. Unlike angels, however, He was there "in the beginning" when He laid the foundations of Creation. Angels change and grow in knowledge as the centuries unfold God's plan, but Jesus remains the same; as God He knows all.

**Superior in destiny (1:13)*. No angel was ever invited to share the rule of the universe as God's equal. But for God to picture Jesus "at My right hand" indicates that Jesus shares God's rule even now.

In every way Jesus is superior—and thus it must be that the revelation He brings, and the salvation He offers is superior to the fragments offered in the Old Testament. There is no need to look elsewhere.

In Jesus we have the whole truth—and in Jesus the best possibility of being made whole.

An application (Heb. 2:1-4). It was this writer's habit to apply what he said as he moved along. In Colossians and Ephesians Paul spent several chapters developing doctrine. Then, toward the end of the books, he focused on the practical meaning of his earlier teaching. Not so in Hebrews. This writer was always ready to interrupt the flow of his thoughts to make application, which in turn stimulates more teaching.

What is the application of this initial presentation of Jesus as the ultimate spokesman? "We must pay more careful attention, therefore, to what we have heard" (v. 1). We dare not ignore the message of a great salvation, which has been announced by the Lord Himself and confirmed by Spirit-given signs.

The great salvation (Heb. 2:5-18). What is the "great salvation" that the writer described? Hebrews views salvation as nothing less than the exaltation of humanity (vv. 5-13), and as an escape to freedom (vv. 14-18). And what the writer said will sound strange to us if we persist in identifying human beings primarily as "sinners."

Of course, we have all sinned. All humankind, apart from Jesus, lies dead and deadened underneath the curse. But still, beauty lies within the sleeping corpse.

Before the poisoned fruit, beauty lived. Then beauty died but somehow remained within, awaiting the kiss of life. Christ, stooping to claim His bride, quickens us to life and restores the beauty.

Quoting the Old Testament, the writer recaptures the wonder of the psalmist who has discovered man's lost identity:

> What is man that You are mindful of him, or the Son of man that you care for him? You made him a little lower than the angels; You crowned him with glory and honor and put everything under his feet.
>
> Hebrews 2:6-8, quoting Psalm 8:4-6

God made man in original glory, "in His own image" (Gen. 1:27) and God gave him "dominion" (v. 28, KJV). That dominion was lost in the Fall, shattering God's glorious intention. But the Fall did not shake God's love. Man was still God's concern, still cared for. And so Jesus stepped down to become Man, suffering death that He might bring "many sons to glory" (Heb. 2:10). *This is the exaltation of humankind!* In Christ, we have been lifted up to share the Son's glory, becoming in Him so fully "of the same family" that we are called by Jesus Himself, "My brothers" (vv. 1-12).

This exaltation, vaulting us far above the angels to be Christ's brothers in God's family, is also our deed to freedom. Satan, who held the power of death, was destroyed by Christ's self-sacrifice. Now we are freed. There will still be temptations to fall back into the way of death. But now Christ lives as our faithful High Priest to help us when we are tempted. We who have been dead are now alive—and now we can hear and respond to the voice of God calling us back to beauty.

♥ ***Link to Life: Youth / Adult***

Involve your group members in direct Bible study. Have pairs work for 10 to 15 minutes with Hebrews 1–2 to seek answers to the following questions:

- *What does this passage teach about angels?*
- *What is the relationship of Jesus to angels? What is our relationship to angels?*
- *How is our relationship to God different from His relationship with angels?*

After each pair has finished, come together to compare answers. Then use the visual to sum up the important teaching of this exciting passage.

Jesus' superiority to Moses (Heb. 3:1-6). Moses stands as an example of faithfulness to God in the Old Testament and in history. Not only was the written Word of the Pentateuch given through Moses, but God

Hebrews 1 and 2 describe our relationship with angels and Jesus. He "was made a little lower than the angels" for a time (2:9), that He might bring *us* to glory. We can chart it like this:

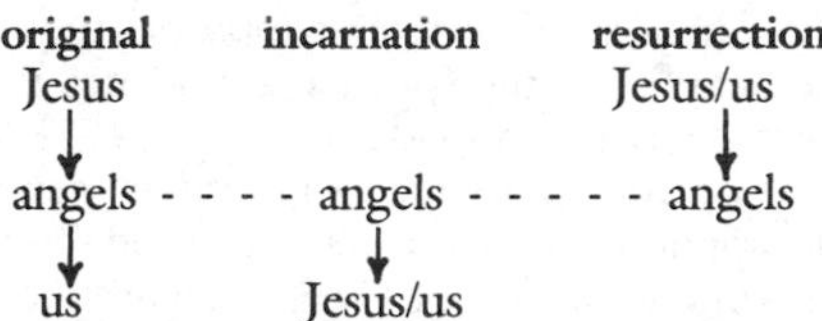

Jesus is not only exalted above the angels, He has lifted us up to share this destiny with Him! To experience the full meaning of salvation we must never drift from the amazing truth that, in Christ, we *now* have the capacity for mastery and dominion.

commended this faithful man. Yet Jesus surpasses Moses, for Jesus is the Builder of the house in which Moses was a servant! We, who are the "house" that Jesus is now building, are to fix our eyes on Jesus, not on Moses, and to give Jesus honor.

Hearing God's Voice: Hebrews 3:7–4:13
It is important to keep in mind when we read the Old and New Testaments that the relationship between them is that of fragments to the whole. Visualize a picture puzzle, half completed on the table, with many parts spread, unconnected, beside it. That is like the Old Testament. The outline, the basic themes and colors, may be clear. But still the whole is not seen. Come back later, when the puzzle is complete, and suddenly it all fits. Things you saw in part are now clear. The real shape and form of that bit of green is different than you imagined; it's far more beautiful and complex than you'd dreamed. Yet, when you see it together, it is clear that even the fragment suggests the whole.

Throughout the Book of Hebrews the writer referred back to the fragments of truth given in the Old Testament, and reinterpreted them in light of the whole. He spoke of them as "shadows," which dimly outline the reality and yet are not reality. Through it all, the writer showed that the reality which has now been fully revealed in Christ truly was there all along.

When we begin to think then about the Christian's new "way of life," we are not suggesting that it *contradicts* the Old Testament way of life under Law. Instead, we're saying that shadowy truth about spiritual truth which was contained in the Law has been brought into fresh focus. *Now, at last, the basic, heart issue of the believer's lifestyle has been isolated and revealed.* From the complicated details of Old Testament regulatory laws, the Book of Hebrews isolates the critical principle. This principle now is to guide us, in Christ, into a life of rest.

The example drawn (Heb. 3:7-11). Quoting Psalm 95:7-11, the writer focused our attention on an *attitude* that characterized the relationship to God of a particular Old Testament generation. It is the generation of those freed by God's power from slavery in Egypt, and led by Moses toward the Promised Land. These men and women heard God's voice at Kadesh Barnea telling them to enter the land, but they hardened their hearts and refused to respond. As a result, God was forced to declare, "They shall never enter My rest" (Heb. 3:11). In this context, *rest* clearly refers to the land of Canaan, promised to Israel by God, toward which God had led His people after releasing them from slavery (see Ex. 3–11).

An application made (Heb. 3:12-15). The writer immediately made his point. We have been raised to take a position in Christ. Our share in Him makes us the new men and women we are, and opens up the possibility of a victorious life. But our share in Christ will be of no practical value to us if we permit the same attitude to develop in us as was displayed by Israel of old. This attitude, characterized here as sinful and untrusting (v. 12), can harden us and keep us from responding to God's voice when He speaks to us.

The focus in our life with Jesus today is not to be on lists of do's or don'ts, or even on the Bible's revelation of right and wrong behavior. The primary issue and the focus of our concern as believers is to be this: Is my heart open to God? Am I eager to learn what God wants me to do, and am I willing to do it?

A tragic end (Heb. 3:16-19). The writer now returned to that Old Testament generation, to identify them clearly, and to mark off sharply the tragic results of hardening hearts and lives to the Lord. Who were the rebels? They were actually men and women who had experienced the mighty acts of God by which He freed them from slavery in Egypt! With whom was God angry? These very people who sinned—and whose bodies ultimately fell in the wilderness, never to know the rest of entering the Promised Land. And who does God declare can never experience His rest? No one who disobeys God can ever enter His rest!

A "rest" remains (Heb. 4:1-11). This section of Hebrews is complicated by a multiple use of the word "rest" and by a complex argument. We can best follow the thought if we sort out some of the elements, rather than attempt to analyze the passage verse by verse.

**The promise stands.* This is the thought with which the chapter begins (v. 1). Even though a later, obedient generation did enter the Promised Land, that entry did not completely fulfill the promise of a "rest" for God's people. In fact, much later, in the time of David, the promise and the warning were repeated: "Today, if you hear His voice" (v. 7). If God's full blessing for His people had been granted when Joshua led Israel into Palestine, then the promise of a rest would not have been repeated much later to the people of David's day, or by the writer of Hebrews to Christians then and now.

**The nature of rest.* The word "rest" is used in Hebrews 3 and 4 in three distinct senses. First is the usage we've seen. Entry into the Promised Land, so large a feature of Old Testament history, is a portrait—a tangible example—of the idea of rest.

It was an appropriate picture. God had promised the land to Abraham and his descendants. During the years of Israel's slavery in Egypt, pagan peoples had populated and improved the land. They had built houses, planted vineyards and orchards, and tamed the wilderness. Yet their lifestyle more and more evidenced the grossest of sins. The time of their judgment by God corresponded with Israel's release from slavery. In coming into Canaan, Israel would be God's instrument of judgment on sin—and would inherit riches for which she had not labored. The people would sit under trees they had not planted and drink wine made from grapes of vines they had not cultivated. They would come into a land where the work had been done—and they would rest.

Like Israel of old, you and I in Jesus have been delivered from slavery. Sin's power in our lives has been broken, and we are called by God to enter a "Promised Land" experience, in which we will rest. We are to enjoy the benefits of the work Jesus has done for us. The Christian life is not one of struggle to carve out a bare living in the wilderness. The Christian life is one of appropriating all the benefits of the spiritual abundance that Jesus so richly provides.

A second connotation of "rest" is seen in the application of the term to God's own rest on completion of Creation. The Jewish teachers had noted a fascinating feature of the Genesis account. For each of the first six days, the text speaks of "evening and morning." The beginning and the end were clearly marked off. But the seventh day has no such demarcation. The rabbis took this to mean that God's rest has no end. With the creative work complete, God is not *inactive,* but He no longer creates, for that work is done.

Strikingly, it is *His* rest (4:5) that believers are invited to enter! We are to come to the place where we appropriate fully what God has done, and while never becoming inactive, we do stop *laboring.* The load of a Christian life that some experience as a struggle is lifted. The pressure of trying harder is gone.

**Entering rest.* The analysis of the early generation that failed is a specific application to the believer's experience. "There remains, then, a Sabbath-rest for the people of God" (v. 9). The Bible tells us that we are to rest from our own work, just as God did from His (v. 10). The lifestyle of the person who is raised to mastery of life in Christ is not to be the ceaseless struggle some know. There is to be an experience of rest.

In chapter 3's analysis of the early generation that failed to experience the promised rest, we saw that the critical problem involved their attitude toward God. This people heard what God said. But they hardened their hearts, and would not respond. Unwilling to trust God, they were unable to obey.

Modern psychology thinks of an "attitude" as a disposition or tendency to respond. Attitudes are always linked to behavior. To say that a person has a critical attitude implies that in many situations he will tend to criticize (rather than appreciate) others.

The rebellious attitude exhibited by the men and women Moses led out of slavery also had clear consequences. When God spoke to them, their tendency was, first of all, to fail to trust Him. And, second, to disobey.

In the Bible these two characteristics, trust and obedience, are always linked. Trust in God (believing what He says to us is prompted by love, and actually does mark out the very best pathway for us) is critical to the kind of obedience God desires. A person who does not trust, but rather fears, might produce an *outward conformity* to the orders of a tyrant. But only trust and love enable us to make a willing, inner commitment to follow the instructions of our Heavenly Father. When we trust God, we are freed to obey from the heart.

What then contrasts with the rebellious attitude of the disobedient generation? A *responsive* attitude. When we hear God's voice today, what is important to God and to us is simply that we trust ourselves to Him and obey.

Faith in God, expressed in obedient response to His voice, is the critical principle which sums up the lifestyle expected of God's children. What you and I are to concentrate on in our Christian lives is entering God's rest by making faith's response whenever we hear His voice.

How can we sum it up? Let's realize the implications of God's own rest. Since Creation itself, there has been no contingency for which God has not planned; no problem for which He hasn't a solution. God has been active while at rest, for all has been cared for. For us to enter God's rest means simply to learn to be responsive to God's written and contemporary voice, and let His living Word guide us to the solutions He has already prepared for our every difficulty. Like God, we remain active. But amid all our work, we are at rest. We are not troubled, burdened, or loaded down. We know that God will lead us through His living Word, and that we will find His prepared and Promised Land by listening to Him.

Some have interpreted the next words in Hebrews 4 as a threat:

> The Word of God is living and active. Sharper than any double-edged sword, it penetrates even to dividing soul and spirit, joints and marrow; it judges the thoughts and attitudes of the heart. Nothing in all creation is hidden from God's sight. Everything is uncovered and laid bare before the eyes of Him to whom we must give account.
>
> Hebrews 4:12-13

To those who fail to see themselves as Jesus' brothers, and to understand the thought of Hebrews 3 and 4, it may seem frightening. Such people might cringe as they imagine these verses describe God examining *them,* to highlight each hidden fault. But this is not the point at all! The writer has just explained rest. That rest goes beyond the promise of Palestine to Israel. God's rest is a rest of soul and spirit, a rest of thought and attitude. The inner person is to be at rest as well. And we can rest, for nothing is hidden from God's gaze. He knows our deepest, most secret needs, and with His Word lays bare that need—and guides us into rest.

♥ ***Link to Life: Youth / Adult***

Ask each person to read Hebrews 4:12-13, and jot down two words that describe how these verses make him or her feel.

List the feelings on the chalkboard, and then ask what your group members think the verses mean.

Then in a minilecture explain carefully the teaching of Hebrews 3:7–4:11. When we understand the "rest" God promises those of us who will maintain a trusting and obedient attitude, we discover that verses 12-13 are a promise, and not a threat.

God's Living Voice

Today too Jesus is the voice of freedom for you and me. As the ever-living Word, He calls us today to enter His Promised Land of rest.

But we still wonder. How do we hear Christ's "today" voice? In a verse torn from context? In circumstances? In a friend's advice? As far as Scripture is concerned, it is clear that God's voice is heard *in the flow of the Bible message*. But that flow is not itself God's voice. God's voice speaks to us through the understanding we gain from grasping what the Scriptures teach.

What I mean is this. Note how carefully the writer of Hebrews develops his argument. Step by step he has helped his readers see the superiority of Christ, and realize their own release through Him. Such careful development tells us that God does not depend on shedding light in snatches! God works carefully to help us understand a whole new way of thought. *It is in the understanding—in the context of the message—that the living voice is heard.* Yet God's voice is itself subjective and personal. The Holy Spirit speaks through the Word to you with His answer for your problem—for your most pressing present need. And He speaks through the same word with His answer for my problem, though my needs may be different. The Holy Spirit within us actively applies God's truth to our individual situations, and He Himself is the voice of our living Lord.

It is true that the Spirit may speak to us through circumstances. And God may use a Christian friend. But always, the voice is heard within the flow of the message given us in Scripture's written Word, as God the Holy Spirit looks deep within our souls and spirits and applies His truth to you and to me.

And when we hear this living voice, telling us God's way, then we hurry to obey in joyful trust and faith. By obeying, we enter the land of rest and freedom that Jesus has proclaimed.

TEACHING GUIDE

Prepare
Be sure you understand the difficult yet important Hebrews 3:7–4:13 passage on God's rest and His living voice.

Explore
1. Encourage your group members to share. When was the last time each was aware that God was speaking to him or her? What was God saying, and what did each do?
2. Or begin with the study of angels suggested in "link-to-life," on page 994, which emphasizes the importance of listening to Jesus who is the true revealer of God.

Expand
1. Ask your group members to read and jot down the feelings generated by Hebrews 4:12-13. See "link-to-life," page 997.
2. Give a minilecture carefully working through the argument of Hebrews 3–4. Be sure that your group members understand (a) the meaning of rest, (b) the attitude which motivates response to God's voice, and (c) the meaning of Hebrews 4:12-13 as a promise in that context.

Apply
Ask your group members to share. What most helps each to be responsive to God when the Holy Spirit (God's living voice) guides or directs?

STUDY GUIDE 157

Hebrews 4:14–8:13

JESUS, OUR HIGH PRIEST

Overview
In the Old Testament the high priest was the man appointed to represent the people before God. He was the man who dealt with sins and weaknesses by offering the necessary sacrifices for sins (Heb. 5:3). But as a link between God and man, the Old Testament priest was never enough. He was a shadow representing the coming perfect intermediary.

Hebrews 4:14 affirms that in Jesus "we have a great High Priest." As a human being He is able to sympathize with us in our weaknesses. Yet He is also God: the Son has "gone into heaven" to take His stand in the very presence of the Father.

Because Jesus is both God and Man, He is an adequate link between us and the Father. So the Scripture says, "Let us then approach the throne of grace with confidence, so that we may receive mercy and find grace to help us in our time of need" (v. 16). When we fail and are ashamed, or when we are overwhelmed and need help desperately, we need never draw back. Jesus, human like us, will understand. And Jesus, God as is the Father, is able to aid.

It is important, when we have heard the voice of God calling us to act, and still feel inadequate, that we turn to Jesus as High Priest and realize all that He is able to do for us.

In this important study, then, you will guide your group members to see Jesus as their High Priest, and rely on Him.

Commentary
For the Hebrew Christians to whom this letter was written, the ministry and qualifications of a priest were well known. For the modern reader, without any intimate experience of the Old Testament priestly concept, these may seem strange. Yet what these chapters teach is important, for they speak not only of the shadow pictures of the old economy but of realities vital to Christian experience.

The Priestly Ministry: Hebrews 5:1-10
This passage begins by making three statements about the priesthood . . . and then by commenting on two.

Its function and qualifications (Heb. 5:1-3). The priest represented other men "in matters related to God" and offered "gifts and sacrifices for sins." Jesus of course offered Himself, and by that one sacrifice, opened the door to permanent relationship with God. Anyone who desires to come to God can come through Jesus. Thus Jesus fulfills everything that the Old Testament hinted at concerning relationship with God.

The high priest of the Old Testament had to be "selected among men" and be "able to deal gently with those who are ignorant and are going astray, since he himself is subject to weakness." Jesus was surely chosen from among men, for He became a Man. But what about "subject to weakness"?

Hebrews 4:15 says that Jesus is able "to sympathize with our weaknesses" because as a Man He was "tempted in every way just as we are—yet without sin."

This verse is often misunderstood, in part because of misunderstanding of weakness. Weakness does not refer to our human tendency to give in to temptation, but to our capacity to feel it! Our weakness is human frailty itself: the hungers, the desires, the pains to which we are subject and which push and pull against our wills. Jesus, in taking on human nature, took on our *weaknesses* as well. At every point in every way, Jesus was tested as we are. In fact, He was tempted *beyond the point at which we give in!*

Imagine two prisoners of war being tortured to make them do a propaganda radio broadcast. One, after two months, can stand it no longer and yields. The other resists beyond the two months for years, even though the pressures increase. Both learned something of their weakness as the pressures grew. But only the one who continued to resist *really* knew how weak he was, as he daily had to cope with and overcome his human frailty. Only the one who continued to resist understood the full weight of pain that being a human being involves.

And this is what the Bible says about Jesus. He knows more about human frailty than we do. He really understands how terrible it is to be *weak*. And because He understands, He is able to sympathize with us when we find ourselves tempted.

In Hebrews 5 the writer says more about Jesus' humanity and its relationship to His present high priestly ministry. First, in Gethsemane Jesus knew a desperate extremity which drove Him to pray "with loud cries and tears" (v. 7). Note that Jesus prayed to One who could "save Him from *death,*" not "save Him from *dying.*" And God did, taking Jesus from the very grip of death in Resurrection. Yet Jesus' suffering extended through the ultimate—dying itself. Jesus surely *does* understand human weakness: He experienced all that it means.

This full and total identification with us enables Jesus to "deal gently" with us when we go astray. The Greek word, *metriopatheia,* suggests a balanced involvement. We've seen mothers so upset at a child's accident that they are unable to help. *Metriopatheia* suggests both feeling with the injured, yet being detached enough to react and to act for the other's good.

Second, the writer says that Jesus met His dying with "reverent submission." Thus He was able to "learn obedience" from the things He suffered (vv. 7-8). We never benefit from our trials or sufferings when we react rebelliously or in panic. God seeks to strengthen us through every experience of life. Meeting life with reverent submission frees us from being overwhelmed, and helps us grow in our own ability to feel with those who are hurt or needed without becoming so "sympathetic" that we are unable to help.

Finally the writer notes that these experiences and His suffering "made [Jesus] perfect" (v. 9). The phrase does *not* suggest that Jesus fell short, as God or as a human being. The Greek word, *teleios,* speaks of *a perfection that is related to the purpose or function for which a thing or person is designed.* If Jesus were to be fitted for the task of High Priest. He "learned," in the sense of personally experiencing, the pain of being human and the cost of obedience when suffering is involved.

And thus, as a truly qualified Person, Jesus was appointed by God, who alone has the right to determine who will be High Priest to His people (vv. 4-6), to His priestly ministry.

♥ ***Link to Life: Youth / Adult***

List the following phrases on the chalkboard, and ask your group members (1) to vote on agreement or disagreement, and then (2) to explain why *each voted as he or she did by saying what he or she thinks the phrase means.*

- *Jesus was tempted just as we are.*
- *Jesus was subject to weakness.*
- *Jesus learned obedience through suffering.*
- *Jesus was made perfect by His suffering.*

Your goal is not to "show up" those who answer wrongly, but rather to help your group members grasp each of these themes as it is related to Jesus' priesthood. So after hearing opinions go over the passage carefully, helping your members see that each of these truths encourages us to come freely to Jesus rather than hold back in shame when we are aware of our own weakness and human frailties.

On to Maturity: Hebrews 5:11–6:8

The writer was discouraged. If only these Jewish believers could grasp the import of Christ's High Priesthood! If only they would grasp these basic truths, apply them, and by "constant use [application]" go on to maturity! But these Christians are immature, and "slow to learn," not having grasped even the elementary truths of the Gospel.

Deep controversy has raged over what the writer is about to say in Hebrews 6. There are few passages that have stimulated more debate. Over the years, four main interpretations of Hebrews 6 have been suggested:

(1) These verses speak of Jews who had *professed* Christ but stopped short of true faith.

(2) These verses refer to believers who have fallen into sin, and will lose their reward.

(3) These verses refer to believers who have slipped back into unbelief, and have lost their salvation.

(4) These verses give a hypothetical case, used to demonstrate the foolishness of a panic which insists "hold on" when Christians should instead "go on."

Before we select one of these, let's look carefully at what verses 1-4 call elementary teaching, or if you will, foundation truths.

Foundation truths. It is important to see these truths for what they are—truly foundational. Remember that a foundation is a solid and secure base on which one can build. Once the foundation has been laid, we can trust ourselves to it and get on with the business of construction. What the writer identified for these panicky Jewish believers who look back to the Old Testament faith and lifestyle are foundational truths that should provide security. Grasping them, feeling secure, these believers should have gone on to maturity.

What are the foundation truths on which we can rely?

- Repentance from dead works. Coming to Christ we realize that our works had nothing to do with salvation or the life Jesus offers. We turn away from a "works righteousness" in the Christian life as well.
- Faith in God. Trust in God is the key to salvation. That transaction of saving faith is complete.
- Instruction about baptisms. In the early church, careful instruction preceded baptism. It is likely this refers to the basic doctrines taught and accepted before baptism took place.
- Laying on of hands. This may refer to church discipline (leaders were appointed with the laying on of hands) or perhaps to teaching about the Holy Spirit (whose entry into the believer was so symbolized).
- Resurrection of the dead and eternal judgment. These doctrines summarize the believer's hope.

The writer, then, is asking us to believe so fully that when Christ came into our lives *all these things were settled* that we no longer worry about our relationship with the Lord. We *know* that He loves us. We *know* that we are saved.

The emphasis on an already laid foundation, and the Hebrews' tendency to look away, leads us to conclude that the fourth suggestion best explains the teaching of verses 4-10. The writer is posing a hypothetical case to demonstrate just how foolish the Hebrews' panic and uncertainty are. The writer says, "Let's not go back again as if there were no foundation to rest on." The fact is that *the basic issues of death, faith, and resurrection have been settled by the finished work of Christ.* So the writer asks:

> What would you want to do? View your failure as a falling away of God, so access is now lost? How then would you ever be restored—you who have been enlightened, tasted the heavenly gift, shared in the Holy Spirit, and known the flow of resurrection power? Do you want to crucify Jesus all over again, and through a new sacrifice be brought back to repentance? How impossible! What a disgrace, this hint that Jesus' work for you was not enough.
>
> Hebrews 6:4-6, author's paraphrase

The point here is simple. God wants us to know that Jesus' death is enough. There is no more need for sacrifices for sin. By His one sacrifice Jesus made "perfect forever those who are being made holy" (10:14). *You and I, like the Hebrews, are free to get on with the business of living for Jesus because He has resolved forever the question of our relationship with God.*

Two brief paragraphs that follow reinforce this understanding. From 6:7-8 we learn that the issue is one of fruitfulness. God is (and we are to be) concerned with the products of maturity.

Verses 9-12 are words of encouragement. Calling the readers, "dear friends," the writer looks at the fruit they have already produced. Their work, their love for God, and love for God's people, show that they have taken first steps, and are making progress. But how we each need, not hesitant progress, but a full commitment to that obedience which brings us maturity.

♥ ***Link to Life: Youth / Adult***
Ask your group members to each write a paraphrase of Hebrews 6:4-6. When completed, share the four historic views of this passage sketched in the commentary. Which of the views did each member assume when he or she did the paraphrase?

Then discuss the passage in its context, sharing the author's paraphrase or one of your own.

Because Jesus is our High Priest, we are freed from doubts and uncertainties, and can go on in our Christian lives, confident of our salvation.

Our anchor. Just to make sure that his readers had not misunderstood, the writer spoke of the confidence we can have in the full access won for us by Jesus. Our access is guaranteed by God's oath, so that "we who have fled to take hold of the hope offered to us may be greatly encouraged. We have this hope as an anchor for the soul, firm and secure. It enters the inner sanctuary behind the curtain, where Jesus, who went before us, has entered on our behalf" (vv. 18-20).

More on Priesthood: Hebrews 7:1–8:13

The writer's previous references to Melchizedek are now explained. This mysterious figure, who was king of Jeruslaem in Abraham's day, was offered tithes (the tenth part of one's goods, set apart by the Old Testament Law for the priesthood) by the patriarch himself! To the writer, this demonstrated the superiority of the Melchizedekian priesthood, for the unborn Levi, head of the tribe from which Old Testament priests were drawn, might be said to have paid tithes to Melchizedek through his great-grandfather, Abraham (7:1-10).

The writer now contrasted Christ's priesthood with that of the Old Testament order (vv. 11-28).

- The new Priest's ministry does not rest on family line but on "the power of an indestructible life" (v. 16).
- The former priesthood was set aside because it was unable to provide perfect access. In Jesus, we have "a better hope . . . by which we draw near to God" (v. 19).
- The former priests died. Jesus continues forever as a permanent Priest. "Therefore He is able to save completely those who come to God through Him, because He always lives to intercede for them" (v. 25).

This, the writer exults, is the High Priest we need. You and I, living in a culture in which the priesthood principle is relatively unknown, may dismiss these arguments as irrelevant. But our High Priest is a present reality, a reality we need to grasp and know. Because Jesus lives as our High Priest, we too have guaranteed access to God. In failure, we can claim the promised mercy. Under the daily pressures of our lives, we can claim the help of a Man who knows our every need, and who knows as well the path of victory.

The writer now made an important observation. The change in priesthood indicated a change in other elements of the Old Testament system. And one of those changes was a change in covenant—that is, a change in the nature of the promises God has made to us that define how He relates to us as His people.

The Old Testament itself promised that one day the Old Covenant of Mosaic Law would be replaced, because it was inadequate. Thus the Hebrews' yearning for the old ways was doubly unwise. But where does the superiority of the new lie? Why is it so much better for us? In part because, in Jesus, we have a better High Priest. But also because of *the impact of the New Covenant on our very personalities.* God had said that when the new comes:

> I will put My laws in their minds and write them on their hearts. I will be their God, and they will be My people. No longer will a man teach his neighbor, or a man his brother, saying, "Know the Lord," because they will all know Me, from the least of them to the greatest. For I will forgive their wickedness and will remember their sins no more."
>
> Hebrews 8:10-12

God's change in the system is a simple one. He takes the laws which express righteousness and puts them, not in external commandments, but on inner tablets of mind and heart. Notice that two things are necessary. We must know *what* God's righteous standards are and *how* to translate them into personal experience. The Law can tell us what the standards are. But only a changed heart will enable us to live by those standards.

This is what is so exciting here. God now puts His laws in our minds and writes them in our hearts.

It is through the Bible that we come to understand the will of God. And it is here we find the principles that show us how to live a righteous life. But it is only the transformed heart, which spontaneously responds to God and His Word, that will move us to righteousness.

We can summarize then what Hebrews here reveals. Mosaic Law does deal with righteousness. The shadow it cast across the Old Testament showed that God, its Giver, is righteous. The shadow shows us something of what righteous behavior is. The shadow shows us that God really cares about seeing righteousness in us. But commandment law was only a shadow; it could not *produce* righteousness. It dealt with externals, but did not touch the heart.

Then Jesus came. In Jesus' human personality, the full righteousness of Commandment Law was expressed as living truth. Then Jesus died. And in His death and resurrection, Jesus snatched us up and, calling us "brothers," brought us into the divine family. In making us sons, God planted deep within us something of Jesus' own personality. "Christ in you," Paul says, is "the hope of glory" (Col. 1:27). When Jesus entered our lives He brought righteousness with Him. That which had been expressed in external commands now is expressed in our hearts and minds. That very element of the old system which broke down (the human element) has now been changed.

The outer Commandment Law of the old has become an inner law through the new.

And all this is enhanced as we see Jesus as our High Priest. When we see Jesus as High Priest, we realize that the shame of failures that once drove us from God no longer matters. Jesus understands, He sympathizes, and He can help us overcome our weaknesses. Because of Jesus we run *to* God, not from Him.

And Jesus as High Priest promises not only access but also renewal. He is constantly at work within us, writing His law and very personality in our inner selves. This too is ours through Jesus, our High Priest.

Because of Jesus, the door to God is always open, and so we always have hope. The old doorkeepers, the Aaronic priests, are gone. Their struggle to keep open the crack that the Old Testament opened in relationship to God is ended. Jesus has come, and He has not only thrown open the door, but He stands in it to welcome us personally when we turn to Him.

TEACHING GUIDE

Prepare

Read through Hebrews 4–8 several times to familiarize yourself with the writer's argument.

Explore

1. Share briefly: "How do you tend to feel about yourself when you sin or fall short? How do you tend to think God feels about you?"

2. Or list phrases from Hebrews that speak of Jesus' humanity, and of His "weakness," "learning," and being "made perfect." After seeing how your group members under-

As our High Priest, Jesus is the link between us and God. As High Priest, He holds us. Our safety does not depend on *our* grip, but on His.

stand these phrases, show how they relate to the high priesthood of Jesus and His capacity to sympathize with us and to help us. See "link-to-life," page 1000.

Expand

1. Work on a paraphrase of Hebrews 6 to help your group members sense that the foundation of salvation has been laid. Our challenge now is, secure in our faith in Jesus, to build on that foundation, going on to maturity. See "link-to-life," pages 1001-1002.
2. Or work as a class to make a one-sentence summary of each paragraph in Hebrews 7 and 8, showing the superiority of Jesus' priesthood and the New Covenant He made with humankind.

Apply

Sketch on a chalkboard the two drawings on page 1003 that represent aspects of Jesus' high priestly ministry. Ask each person to draw his own sketch representing one thing he has learned about his relationship with God through this session.

Ask each person to show and explain his or her drawings.

Close in prayer, thanking God for all Jesus means to us.

STUDY GUIDE 158

Hebrews 9–10

JESUS, THE PERFECT SACRIFICE

Overview

The sacrificial system was a vital element in Old Testament faith. The Mosaic Law code established standards which, while shaping the lifestyle of Israel, no individual could live up to. And anyone who fell short, in even one point (James 2:10-11), was guilty of sin.

Yet God made provision for sinners. With the Law, God gave Moses the pattern for building a tabernacle, and established a sacrificial system. A sinner could bring a required blood sacrifice, have his sins covered, and so approach God. The one way into the tabernacle—the only door to the courtyard of the place of meeting with God—opened onto the altar of sacrifice. There was no other way for a sinner to approach God. Only blood on the altar could cover human sin.

The writer of the Book of Hebrews argued that the Old Testament sacrifices spoke of Jesus, the perfect Sacrifice, who has done what animal sacrifices could never accomplish. Jesus has actually *perfected* the sinner washed in His blood, and made the sinner holy in God's sight! There is no need for repeated sacrifices, for by His one sacrifice on Calvary Jesus has fully met our need, freeing us completely from sin, guilt, and shame.

Why is this teaching so important to believers today? Because, when we understand just what Jesus has done for us, we find our conscience cleansed and experience release from our bondage to past failures. And we have hope that we will live a new and holy life.

Commentary

There's something almost soft (too soft?) in the tone of the previous four chapters of Hebrews. It's almost as if, in emphasizing the compassion of Jesus our High Priest, the writer is saying, "Don't let sin bother you. It's all right with God."

After all, the promise of sympathy, the guarantee of access, the assurance of mercy—all these seem to indicate indifference to something we are sure the holy God must care about deeply. How can God deal so gently with those of His family who resist His voice and rebel against Him?

In fact, God is *not* being soft. Or indifferent. But to see what He is saying, and to grasp its impact, we need to understand the difference between shame and guilt.

Shame and Guilt

Let's suppose a person cheats on his income tax returns by misrepresenting income and expenses. Let's further suppose the fraud is discovered, and we're listening in on an interview between the individual and an Internal Revenue agent:

"OK, I guess you've got me."

"Yes, Mr. Anderson. I'm afraid it's all pretty clear."

"Well, you can't blame me for trying. I suppose everybody gives themselves the benefit of the doubt."

"I think you've gone beyond that. This is a pretty clear case of fraud, and we're thinking of prosecuting you."

"Now wait a minute! I'll pay the tax you say I owe, and the penalty too. But you can't prove I didn't just make an honest mistake."

"I think we can prove fraud, Mr. Anderson. And it's very possible that we'll try."

"Please. I won't try to talk you out of it. But—well, will my children have to know?"

Notice the three different evaluations of the same act. And the three possible responses.

- *Guilt*. Mr. Anderson committed fraud. He was guilty of breaking the law. No matter how he felt about himself or his actions, the objective guilt remained.
- *Guilt feelings*. This is the personal sense

of guilt Mr. Anderson might well feel, but apparently did not. Instead, he justified his actions: "Everybody gives themselves the benefit of the doubt."

- *Shame.* No matter how Mr. Anderson may justify his action, the question, "Will my children have to know?" shows more was involved than guilt and guilt feelings. There was also shame, that agonizing worry about what other people would think.

We need to distinguish between each of these. Guilt speaks of the objective blame that has accrued through a specific act, and that merits punishment. Guilt feelings focus on how a person feels about himself. Shame springs from fear of others' disgust, disappointment, or ridicule once they know.

In our society we concentrate almost entirely on guilt feelings. Strikingly, the Bible seldom speaks of them. The focus in Scripture is on guilt as an objective reality. But today much Gospel preaching promises release from *felt* guilt through faith in Christ.

Sometimes missionaries, moving into another culture, begin by proclaiming freedom from guilt feelings and are stunned that no one seems concerned. As they learn more about the culture, they discover that the deep-felt need there relates to shame. To be exposed in the eyes of others—there is the terror.

In shame cultures the Gospel presentation may well shift from the emphasis given in guilt cultures. And if it does, we find that Scripture presents Jesus as the answer for shame as well as guilt.

> See, I lay a stone in Zion, a chosen and precious Cornerstone, and the one who trusts in Him will never be put to shame.
> Isaiah 28:16, author's paraphrase

The Hebrew culture was distinct in that both guilt and shame were understood. And in Jesus, God promises to these believing Hebrews the one remedy that speaks to *all* our needs. In Jesus, God provides release from guilt, guilt feelings, and from shame as well!

This is the answer to the uncomfortable feeling that perhaps our compassionate High Priest, revealed in Hebrews 5–8, shows too little concern for holiness. The picture of Jesus holding open the door, and inviting us to come to God relates specifically to shame. Our failure to respond to God's voice drives us to hide ourselves from Him. We cannot face God, knowing that He knows. But in the High Priest, we discover that God does not condemn or ridicule. In His eyes, we remain precious and respected. Jesus knows the weakness of our flesh: He understands, and His response is one of sympathy.

This is how God deals with our shame. But how does He deal with our guilt and with our guilt feelings? The answer to this question is found in Hebrews 9 and 10.

♥ ***Link to Life: Youth / Adult***
Help your group distinguish between guilt, guilt feelings, and shame.

Tape the dialogue between the tax examiner and Mr. Anderson to play to your group. Ask them to analyze Anderson's responses and tell how he feels about his tax fraud.

Lead the discussion into a comparison between guilt and guilt feelings and shame. How are these related? How do they differ?

Ask your group to come up with several specific illustrations *of each.*

Finally, put the chart (p. 1007) on the chalkboard to clarify the thrust of the chapters you will study this session.

Observations on the Text: Hebrews 9–10

The earthly tabernacle (Heb. 9:1-10). The writer immediately launched his readers into the argument. The Old Testament system included a sanctuary carefully designed by God. The inner sanctuary, representing the very presence of God, was entered only by the high priest. Even then, he entered only once a year and always carried the blood of a sacrifice he had offered "for himself and for the sins the people had committed" (v. 7). The veil, which covered the inner sanctuary at all times and was pulled aside only briefly for the animal sacrifice, was God's visual aid, a reminder that the door to God was not yet thrown open. In the same way, it was clear that the repeated sacrifices, which never succeeded in removing the veil, "were not able to clear the conscience of the worshiper" (v. 9). Sins were merely "covered." This is the meaning of the Hebrew word *kaphar*—"atonement." But sin had not been removed, and so the guilt remained.

I read in the newspaper about a woman

Jesus Deals with Sin

An act of sin . . .	generates	Jesus deals with sin as	providing
	Shame	High Priest (compassionate)	Access (Heb. 5–8)
	Guilt	High Priest and blood sacrifice	Forgiveness (Heb. 9–10)
	Guilt feelings	High Priest and blood sacrifice	Cleansing (Heb. 9–10)

who lost both kidneys to disease. For eight months she had lived on a dialysis machine. Pumped through the machine, her blood was kept clean of impurities. The machine took the place of kidneys temporarily. The article went on to tell how she had been disappointed three times as donor kidneys were thought available for transplants, then refused. The transplant was her real hope. She only used the machine until real kidneys became available.

It was like this with the Old Testament saints. The sacrifices, like the dialysis machine, kept them going. But the real hope for life was that someday a *cure* could be found. Someday transplanted life might deal with the sickness from within. And until then, the repeated sacrifices only reminded Israel of how sick with sin they really were.

Then Jesus came to effect the cure. He came to deal with the poison of sin from within, not to cover it but to cleanse from it. Jesus, the true Sacrifice to which all the animal sacrifices had pointed, in one unique act, *perfected forever* those of us set apart to God by His death.

An interesting phrase in Hebrews 10 helps us get a better glimpse of what God is trying to communicate to us. "In practice, however, the sacrifices amounted to an annual reminder of sins" (10:3, PH). Rather than removing the sense of being sinners and guilty in God's sight, the Old Testament sacrifices reminded men of their helpless and guilty state. How? In the same way that every time that kidney patient came to a dialysis machine to take another treatment she was reminded that she was *ill*. The machine that saved her life was a constant reminder of how near death was!

Jesus has come. The cure has been effected! And you and I are to be overwhelmed with a joyous sense of being *well!*

Christ's blood (Heb. 9:11-15). Then the writer contrasted the old system with Christ. As High Priest, Jesus:

• Entered	not the earthly sanctuary	but heaven.
• Offered	not the blood of animals	but His own blood.
• Obtained	not temporary covering	but eternal redmption for us.

As a result, Jesus has succeeded in cleansing our consciences from those acts that led to death "so that we may serve the living God" (v. 14). Jesus' death was to set us free from sin and guilt—totally free!

One sacrifice (Heb. 9:16-28). Now the writer turned to one of those typically Jewish arguments understood by the Hebrew Christians. Why death? Because inheritance (see v. 15) comes only after the death of a benefactor. So our inheritance in Christ came after—and through—His death. But more than that, death has always been associated with cleansing. The Old Testament in fact "requires that nearly everything be cleansed with blood, and without the shedding of blood there is no forgiveness" (v. 22). It was sufficient that the earthly sanctuary, which copied heavenly realities, be cleansed with animal sacrifices. But heaven itself demanded a higher sacrifice. And so the writer concluded that "now He [Christ] has appeared once for all at the end of the ages to do away with sin by the sacrifice of Himself" (v. 26).

By a single, sufficient sacrifice, Jesus has done what all the old repeated sacrifices could never accomplish. Sacrificed once, He took away the sins of His people.

Once for all (Heb. 10:1-10). This is a theme the writer wished to stress. Endlessly repeated sacrifices could never take away sins. In fact, their repetition was a reminder of guilt! If guilt were truly gone, there would have been no need for an annual sacrifice. But now Jesus has offered a single sacrifice, and "we have been made holy through the sacrifice of the body of Jesus Christ once for all" (v. 10).

Completeness (Heb. 10:11-18). In summing up, the writer made perfectly clear how completely Jesus has dealt with sin and guilt. By that one sacrifice "He has made perfect forever those who are being made holy" (v. 14). Sins are remembered no more. With forgiveness extended, "there is no longer any sacrifice for sin" (v. 18). *We have been cleansed.*

Hope of forgiveness (Heb. 10:19-25). Now comes another of those familiar digressions. Let us draw near to God, realizing that shame and guilt have been taken away by our great High Priest. Cleansed from a guilty conscience, we hold on to the hope forgiveness brings. Indeed, we now concentrate on "how we may spur one another on toward love and good deeds" (v. 24). With this cleansing, we are free to concentrate on living together for God.

God's dealings with His people (Heb. 10:26-39). A reaction almost always follows such a definite proclamation of forgiveness. Will the promise of forgiveness stimulate a believer to live carelessly? After all—if we're forgiven anyway. . . .

This reaction misunderstands many dynamics of the Christian life. Fear will not motivate us to respond to God. It is love and an awareness of who we are in Christ that frees us to hope. And it is God's power within our new lives that enables us to respond. But there are always some who misunderstand. Even some believers. And so the writer pens a warning. If there is deliberate, continuous sin, we do not benefit from Christ's sacrifice. Instead of freedom we find judgment—and that judgment is severe. The blood of Christ is not to be trampled underfoot, as though it were associated with unholiness. God "will judge His people" (v. 30), and under that judgment, we will know the terror roused by an angry Father.

But note—God is still dealing with His people. He acts, because the proclamation of full forgiveness is not meant as a license for sin. The message of forgiveness is intended to lead us into a life of holiness!

We are to keep on living God's way and find the same kind of holiness Paul described in Ephesians and Colossians. "You stood side by side" with those who were persecuted. "You sympathized with those in prison and joyfully accepted the confiscation of your property" (vv. 33-34). Confidence in God must not be thrown away because of difficulties in our lives. Holding fast to God and doing His will, "you will receive what He has promised" (v. 36). The holiness the writer speaks of is ours in Christ, something each of us will experience in our own daily lives.

♥ ***Link to Life: Youth / Adult***

Ask each group member to read through Hebrews 9–10 quickly and underline any teachings that relate to shame, guilt, or guilt feelings.

Compare findings and share any questions or insights group members may have. Then focus on the five critical issues discussed next.

Holiness Now?

Looking back over these two chapters, we find some amazing statements.

- Jesus "obtained eternal redemption" for us (9:12).
- Jesus cleansed "our consciences from acts that lead to death, so that we may serve the living God" (v. 14).
- God has made us "holy through the sacrifice of the body of Jesus Christ once for all" (10:10).
- Jesus by His one sacrifice "has made perfect forever those who are being made holy" (v. 14).
- "Their sins and lawless acts I will remember no more" (v. 12).

All of this, argues the writer, cleanses us from a guilty conscience (v. 22) and frees us to draw near to God and live in hope.

There is no equivocation in these statements. No "ifs." No carrot-and-stick approach to life, holding out promises for performance of God's will and threatening condemnation should we fail to heed His voice. Instead there is a promise and the firm conviction that with our consciences cleansed we *will* "serve the living God."

What are the "acts that lead to death," and how do they affect our consciences so that we cannot serve God?

Guilt and forgiveness. In our day the meaning of the word "guilt" has shifted in the minds of most people from a biblical to a nonbiblical sense. We tend to use the word in the sense of "guilt feelings." The sense of being guilty or unclean is generally what we mean when "guilt" is used in print or conversation. But this sense of guilt feelings is *never found* in the Bible. There the word "guilt" means actual guilt incurred by acts of sin.

Actually, the word "guilt" appears seldom in the Scripture. There are only 6 occurrences in the New Testament and 16 in the Old. Instead the emphasis in Scripture is on forgiveness: 60 times the New Testament speaks of forgiveness, and the Old Testament many times more.

Forgiveness in the Bible is never seen as "passing over" guilt. The root meaning of both Hebrew and Greek words for forgiveness is "send away." God deals with guilt by *sending off* sin, not by overlooking it. With forgiveness, the source and cause of "guilt feelings" is removed, for the sin and guilt are gone.

Holiness. When we realize that our sins are truly gone, and will not be remembered against us, God's Spirit works in our consciences to cleanse and free us.

Conscience is that faculty which not only evaluates acts morally, but which *looks backward* and evaluates *past* actions. The Greeks saw conscience in a very negative light, as the accuser of mankind. In reminding of past failures it tormented men and women. The memory of the acts stored there lead to death in that they are chains: they bind us to an awareness of our inadequacies and weaknesses. They remind us of patterns of failure that have become part of our personalities. In this way, by shaping our sense of who we are, conscience robs us of our freedom to risk obeying God, by robbing us of our faith in His ability to change us.

And then Christ's good word comes to us, affirming forgiveness. The acts stored up in our consciences, the past failures and sins that bind us, are sent away. God remembers them no more—and we too are to forget our past! Instead of looking *backward* we are to look *ahead*! Rather than heeding conscience's message that we are sinners, we are to heed Jesus' message that we are now holy! And, convinced that Jesus truly has changed us, we have faith enough to step out and to obey, acting as a holy people would act.

It is this that the writer of Hebrews teaches. As long as our consciences were archives of failure, its reminder of our sin programmed us for death. Cleansed, our minds and hearts filled with a sense of holiness, we are now filled by God with that confidence and faith which lead us to actively serve Him.

God wants us to respond to Him, stepping out in joyful obedience. But He knows that a sense of guilt and shame will block responsiveness, not encourage it! Feelings of guilt and shame focus our attention on ourselves and not on God, from whom our strength must come. Feelings of guilt and shame make us hesitate; we dare not risk the burden of still more. A sense of guilt and shame blocks the flow of love which is the key motivation in the Christian's life. God does not seek to *make* us respond to Him. Instead He sets us free and invites us to shake off our past failures, and step out to experience liberty.

As a basis for this freedom—to assure us of our acceptance even if we should fail—God clearly announces the great realities. Jesus has once and for all dealt with sin. With sin forgiven, both guilt and shame loose their grip.

- God is not ashamed of you.
- God does not condemn you as guilty.

Because of what Jesus has done as our High Priest, God views you and me as perfect forever. In God's eyes, we are holy. And in proclaiming freedom God undertakes to make our experience of holiness coincide with who we are in Jesus, His Son.

TEACHING GUIDE

Prepare
You may wish to check some of the references to Old Testament practices in a good verse-by-verse commentary like Victor's *Bible Knowledge Commentary,* pages 801-809.

Explore
Play a tape recording of the imaginary conversation between a tax payer and tax collector. Move on to discuss your group members' experiences with guilt, guilt feelings, and shame. See "link-to-life," page 1006.

Expand
1. Have your group members in pairs read quickly through Hebrews 9 and 10 to answer the following questions:

(a) Hebrews 10:1-4 shows that the Old Testament system for dealing with guilt was *inadequate* and *frustrating*. How?

(b) Verses 5-10 explain the purpose Jesus came to accomplish. What was it?

(c) Verses 11-18 explain the implication of *repeating* the Old Testament sacrifices. What was it? What is the meaning of Jesus' *one* sacrifice?

(d) In view of Jesus' one sacrifice, how are we to see ourselves? (vv. 19-22) How are we to respond to others? (vv. 23-25)

2. Or develop a chart which you all work on together. In one column list "what Jesus has done." In the other "what it means for us." Then work through chapters 9 and 10 filling in the chart, and supplementing members' insights from the commentary.

Apply
Ask your group members to visualize every past sin and failure totally forgotten, by God and by themselves and by others. Then share: "How does this vision affect your feelings about God? About yourselves? About your future? About your past?"

After sharing, affirm to your group members that, on the authority of Scripture, their sins are forgiven and forgotten by God. Now each can step out to live as a totally new person in Christ.

STUDY GUIDE 159

Hebrews 11–13

JESUS, OUR SANCTIFICATION

Overview

The author of Hebrews demonstrated the superiority of Jesus over the Old Testament system, which foreshadowed His ministry. Jesus is superior as a revealer of God. Jesus' priesthood is far superior to the priesthood of the Old Testament, just as the covenant He makes is superior to the old Law Covenant which came through Moses. And Jesus has offered a superior sacrifice—Himself—which purifies the worshiper and deals once for all with sin.

On the basis of what Jesus has done for us, we are now made holy—and are enabled to live a holy life! Thus Jesus produces a righteousness which the old system was never able to do.

In the last chapters of Hebrews the writer went into just *how* we appropriate the sanctification that Christ provides. In chapter 11, we see the role of faith, not only for our own lives but in the lives of believers of every age. In chapter 12 we see the importance of making every effort to move toward the goal of holiness—and learn how to respond to the loving discipline of the God who is committed to bring His children to a godly maturity. Finally, in chapter 13, we are given a final warning and shown how the practical holiness is demonstrated in Christian behavior.

In these, as in other chapters of Hebrews, we and our students are invited to a fresh, exciting vision of how great our privileges are as God's own.

Commentary

The last thought of Hebrews 10 launches into a new major section of this book. We are not people who cower back and are ruined, but who fasten on faith, and so preserve and enrich ourselves.

With this thought the writer launches us on an adventurous exploration of how the believer, secure in his new identity as one of God's holy ones, is to live. With the "deeper truths" about who we are in Christ explained, the writer moves on to explore in-depth truth about our new way of life.

Fasten on Faith: Hebrews 11

Often when we think of "faith" our image is one of subjective experience. But the validity of Christian faith does not rest on either our sincerity or our fervency. Christian faith stands or falls on the *truth* that the Word of God reveals. Thus the writer began Hebrews 11 by helping us realize that it is confidence in the reality of things we cannot see that lies at the root of faith. It is only "by faith we understand that the universe was formed at God's command, so that what is seen was not made out of what was visible" (v. 3).

Much of what the writer has told us about our new selves is invisible too. We can't see Jesus, standing as the link between us and heaven. We can't see ourselves as God does, holy and cleansed by the one great sacrifice of Christ. But when our minds accept these as fact, and we become certain of them even though we cannot yet see their full reality revealed, *then* we are ready to begin to live by faith.

But faith is more than conviction of the reality of the facts that God has unveiled. Faith also exists as response to those facts. The Scripture makes it clear: "Without faith it is impossible to please God, because anyone who comes to Him must believe that He exists and that He rewards those who earnestly seek Him" (v. 6). Faith is focused confidence in a person who not only exists, but who seeks a personal relationship with us. God loves us. He is *not* uninvolved. Instead, He is a rewarder of those who diligently seek Him.

When we are willing to accept as fact what God's Word says, and in response reach out to seek and to experience relationship with Him, then we have begun to live by faith. And then we will be rewarded.

This living by faith—accepting as fact the truths that we cannot touch or feel or see, and then acting on them—seems such a simple prescription for life. Lest we make the mistake of equating simplicity with ineffectiveness, the chapter moves on to detail the accomplishments of faith.

Enablement (Heb. 11:4-31). In this extended passage the writer invites us to look into the lives of a host of heroes of the faith, and to see how faith expressed itself in their experiences. We see as the writer analyzes each life that, essentially, faith *enables.*

**Faith enabled Abel (11:4).* Aware that God required blood sacrifice (see Gen. 3:21; 4:7), Abel offered a sheep rather than fruit and vegetables. Faith found for Abel the way of acceptance, and "by faith he was commended as a righteous man."

Faith's first enabling step for us is the same. Pleading Jesus' one unique sacrifice, we receive the same testimony of imputed righteousness.

**Faith enabled Enoch (11:5-6).* The four verses devoted to Enoch in the Old Testament say twice that he "walked with God" (Gen. 5:21-24). One verse affirms that he walked with God for 300 years. His relationship was consistent.

For each of us too faith promises the possibility of a daily, consistent walk with the Lord, for faith enables us to please Him.

**Faith enabled Noah (11:7).* Noah lived in a time when all had turned their backs on God. He alone remained faithful. When warned of a coming flood, Noah devoted 120 years to the building of a great boat miles from any sea. Faith enabled Noah to cut through the contrary views of his contemporaries and to accept the warning of impending disaster as fact. And faith enables us to withstand social pressures and respond with reverence, obeying the command to build.

Faith can enable us to be different as well. We can build our lives on a revelation of the future that men who do not know God count foolish.

**Faith enabled Abraham (11:8-10).* The life of faith is a life of risk, of stepping out into the unknown with nothing more solid before us than God's command. Faith enabled Abraham to take an uncertain journey, not knowing where he was going, but only that God had summoned him.

Faith can enable you and me to take risks as well. We can even stand long periods of uncertainty (v. 9), for faith assures us that God's summons rests on His eternal purposes. What a solid foundation for our lives!

**Faith enabled Sarah (11:11-12).* Here is a most encouraging example. When Sarah first heard the promise, she doubted and laughed (Gen. 18:12-15). But first doubts were overcome. Faith swept in to enable her dead womb to gain the vitality needed for childbearing.

Often we're overcome by first doubts. Parts of our personalities seem deadened and withered. But faith can be restored. Even such "second-chance" faith can enable us to experience vitality in areas of our lives we saw as being dead.

**Faith enabled all (11:13-16).* Sometimes we have a difficult time identifying with great men of faith like Abraham. How good then to know that countless *unnamed* men and women looked ahead, lived, and died, assured that the promises would yet be theirs. These may remain unknown to us—but not to God.

It isn't our greatness in the eyes of others or even in our own eyes that's important. Faith enables unknown people as well. Faith enables each of us to count on God's promises—and because of faith "God is not ashamed to be called their God" (v. 16).

**Faith enabled Abraham (11:17-19).* Faith was of constant importance in Abraham's life, as it is in ours. The first steps of faith led to further steps, until finally the ultimate test came. Abraham was commanded by God to sacrifice his only son on an altar. Faith enabled Abraham to take even this jolting command in stride, and never lose confidence in God. He was even ready to believe that God could raise his son up, even if he were dead, for God had promised that Isaac was the key to his descendants (v. 19).

We too can trust God even this much. When we view Him as totally trustworthy, even the most difficult steps of obedience are made possible.

**Faith enabled the patriarchs (11:20-22).* Each father mentioned here looked ahead to a future that was unknown, but yet was guaranteed by God. Counting God's picture of tomorrow as sure, each ordered the life of his children as if that future were present.

Sometimes it's easier to let God have control of our lives than to guide our families into full commitment to Him. The sacrifice we'd willingly make ourselves we hesitate to impose on our boys and girls, wishing instead for their "happiness." Faith gives us a clearer view. We look across the generations and commit ourselves and our loved ones to the realities He says will be.

**Faith enabled Moses (11:23-29).* The many ways faith changed the life of Moses are stamped vividly on the pages of the Old Testament. Here we're reminded that at every critical stage in his life, faith shaped him for his ultimate ministry. His parents' initial faith saved his life (v. 23). Growing up, faith led him to throw in his lot with the slave people of Israel rather than his adoptive royal family (vv. 24-26). Faith enabled him to defy rather than give into Pharaoh, remaining obedient to the heavenly King (vv. 26-27). Faith led Moses to command the people to keep the first Passover, and to walk boldly into the Red Sea (vv. 28-29).

Almost every difficulty, every challenging experience, every danger, every decision in Moses' life was faced on the basis of faith's obedient response. Faith enabled each obedient act, and the pattern of faithful obedience that emerged made Moses the man he finally became.

It's the same with us. In everything in life we need to be guided and enabled by faith. As we live by faith, we will progressively become the persons God wants us to be.

**Faith enabled Rahab (11:30-31).* Faith took the godly Moses and made him even more a man of God. But Rahab was a prostitute! Did faith enable her?

Yes. This inhabitant of Jericho, a city marked for destruction, believed God. She acted in faith to save the Jewish scouts, and instead of sharing the fate of the disobedient, she became a member of the people of God.

Whatever your past, and whatever your old associations, faith can produce a great transformation. Through faith you can lose your old identity as sinner—and become a child of the living God.

Faith enables you and me. This is, of course, the point the writer of Hebrews made. As example after example is given, we are shown that *faith works!* Faith does enable.

A promise of success? (Heb. 11:32-40) The pathway of faith that Hebrews commended is the answer to our search for meaning and progress in the Christian life. But it is no guarantee of good times.

Here the writer gave examples of victories won by faith's obedience (vv. 33-34), but he also presented the record of those whose lives of faith led to suffering (vv. 35-38). He told of those tortured to death, of others mocked and flogged and bound in prison, and still others killed by stoning or murdered by the sword. Some lost everything and fled naked into the desert, to live like animals in caves or holes.

No, taking the path of faith and committing ourselves to obey God no matter what, in no way promises that the circumstances of our lives will be pleasant.

Yet how comforting. Hebrews speaks to us in our difficult situations and in our failures, and it reassures us. Faith doesn't guarantee good times. Faith guarantees our realization of the hope we have for transformation *within.* Through faith, we are enabled to catch from day to day a growing hint of what we will be at Jesus' return, when the complete experience of perfection will be fully known.

♥ ***Link to Life: Youth / Adult***
List each person Hebrews 11 mentions by name on the chalkboard. Together examine each one, defining (1) just what faith enabled, and (2) just why the responses described were difficult.

Then divide into teams of 5 or 6 for sharing. Which tests seem more difficult? Which have your group members experienced? How has their faith in Christ helped?

Discipline's Way: Hebrews 12

In Hebrews 11, the writer concluded that God has provided us with something the ancients waited for. His "something better" (v. 40) is to be made perfect in a maturity marked by the present experience of God's holiness. But how will God accomplish this promise now that the foundation for holiness has been laid by Christ?

Follow God's way (Heb. 12:1-4). The writer just listed a great group of men and women who witness to the value of a life of faith. In addition, the reader can fix his eyes on Jesus and see him walk God's pathway—and receive the crown! Yes, Jesus' path led to a cross. But His suffering was not the end. Holding fast to God's will by faith, Jesus chose to endure far more than such a choice could ever entail for these Hebrew Christians. Jesus' obedience cost Him life itself. The Hebrews, like you and me, had not yet resisted sin to the point of bloodshed.

The testimony given by people of faith and by Jesus Himself urges us to set aside everything that hinders and follow God's way.

Encouragement (Heb. 12:5-13). Now comes a word of encouragement. God will help! God commits Himself as a good Father to discipline and even to punish those He loves.

Several important characteristics of God's discipline are given:

**Discipline is a family thing.* If suffering (one aspect of discipline) comes, some may fear God is angry or rejecting them. Not so. Even hardship is part of God's guidance for His sons (v. 7).

**Discipline's purpose is our good.* Whatever motive human parents may have in discipline, God's sole concern is our good. He is motivated only by love (vv. 6, 10).

**Discipline has a clear goal in view.* Through discipline, God helps us to share His holiness (v. 10).

**Discipline's product is assured.* Though an extended time may be involved, and our experience during this time may be painful, we can rest assured. God's discipline does produce "a harvest of righteousness and peace for those who have been trained by it" (v. 11).

When we understand God's attitude and purpose for disciplining care, strength replaces feebleness. Discouragement gives way to hope.

Toward holiness (Heb. 12:14-28). Again, the writer turned to application and exhortation. Progress toward the goal of holiness is vital. We are to concentrate on working out holiness in our relationships with everyone (v. 14).

One danger is that we might miss God's grace in the discomfort of discipline. If we do, bitterness may grow up. Another is immorality—that focus on the sensual that led Esau to exchange God's promise for a cup of soup.

What is to protect us from such misunderstandings? Our vision of God. In the Old Testament, this vision brought terror. He was revealed in a mountain of burning fire, associated with darkness, gloom, and storm. Even Moses was terrified and reacted, "I am trembling with fear" (vv. 18-21). But what is *our* vision of God? In Christ, He has been revealed with "thousands upon thousands of angels in joyful assembly" (v. 22). Looking beyond shadow to see the reality, we greet the God who speaks as a Judge—yet His judgment has been executed in Jesus, and He now counts us "righteous men made perfect" (v. 23).

Yet, we can never forget that it is *God* who speaks (vv. 25-29). We reach out to touch the hand of a God who "is a consuming fire" (v. 29). But we are warmed, not burned! Yet still the fire consumes! The universe itself is shaken at His word; created things flee away. Only that which cannot be shaken will remain. What is that? The kingdom we are called to share. "We are receiving a kingdom that cannot be shaken," the writer concluded. "Let us be thankful [note, not fearful!], and so worship God acceptably with reverence and awe" (v. 28).

And so the writer promises us that God *will* guide us into an experience of His holiness. At times our way may seem difficult. But so was Jesus' way. Through it all, we are assured of the Father's changeless love. The fire that sears the universe merely warms God's sons and daughters. With this confidence, we can endure hardships and move on to holiness.

♥ ***Link to Life: Youth / Adult***

Ask each person to write a brief description of a childhood incident that he or she associates with discipline.

Share and discuss these experiences.

Then together analyze Hebrews 12:5-13. How were the remembered experiences like or unlike what Hebrews tells us of God's approach to discipline?

Then together try to answer the following questions:

- *What do I learn about God?*
- *What do I learn about myself as God's child?*
- *What do I learn about my role as a parent?*
- *What do I learn about my own children?*

The Holy Life: Hebrews 13

In the closing exhortation, Hebrews almost sounds familiar. Here are many echoes of Ephesians and Colossians. And why not?

Living holiness is the same for the believing Hebrew as for the Gentile Christian. The common element is, "Keep on loving each other as brothers" (v. 1). Love is holiness lived out in the body of Christ.

Caring (Heb. 13:1-3). Caring for others is described briefly. A concern for those in prison or the mistreated is a common theme.

Value people (Heb. 13:4-6). Placing value on people rather than on things, and being willing to use things but not people, is also a reflection of Old Testament and New Testament teaching.

We will never find contentment in possessing things. Our contentment will be found in God, and in the good news that He has promised never to leave us. We are His.

Authorities (Heb. 13:7-8, 17-18). The theme of respecting authorities is also a common one. This time the emphasis is on relationships with leaders in the church. We are to remain responsive to them, and to imitate their faith.

Jesus is superior (Heb. 13:9-14). The ritualistic approach—in Jewish rather than Gnostic systems—is set aside. Our hearts are strengthened by grace; the altar we serve is supplied with the living Bread.

What is the reference to going "outside the camp"? (v. 13) In the Old Testament system, the offerings for sin were made on an altar, but the animal carcasses were eventually burned outside the camp, away from populated areas. Similarly, the writer notes, Christ died on Golgotha, outside the city walls.

Nothing in Hebrews suggests that the old way was wrong. As a system instituted by God, it was good. But the old was temporary. It foreshadowed only. When the new that it mirrored came, reality replaced shadows. The old priesthood faded away as a single High Priest took His stand in the heavens. A single sacrifice replaced the endless repetition. And the promise of perfection became a present possibility.

This is the call Hebrews makes to these believing Jews. Recognize the superiority of Jesus. Make Him the center of your life. Leave the walls of the old city—the old system—and going outside it find everything you need in Jesus Christ.

Benediction (Heb. 13:20-21). The book closes with a great benediction.

> May the God of peace, who through the blood of the eternal covenant brought back from the dead our Lord Jesus, that great Shepherd of the sheep, equip you with everything good for doing His will, and may He work in us what is pleasing to Him, through Jesus Christ, to whom be glory forever and ever. Amen.
>
> Hebrews 13:20-21

TEACHING GUIDE

Prepare

You may wish to focus on just one of the two major themes in this passage.

Explore

1. Give a brief minilecture on faith, as that confidence in the objective truths revealed by God which enables us to act on them.
2. Study Hebrews 11, noting each of those who were enabled by faith for special accomplishments. See "link-to-life," page 1013 for a method to use in this study, and suggestions for personal application.

Expand

1. Let your group members share a personal experience from their childhood—one they associate with discipline. Evaluate these, and then compare them with the discipline principles explained in Hebrews 12. See "link-to-life," page 1014.
2. Then examine the active verbs in Hebrews 12 that indicate how we are to respond to God's discipline to benefit from it. Note, "Don't make light" (v. 5), "Do not lose heart" (v. 5), "Endure" (v. 7), "Submit" (v. 9), and "Strengthen your feeble arms and weak knees" (v. 12).

As we respond appropriately to God's discipline, His good purposes will be achieved in our lives.

Apply

Read the benediction. How many book themes are reflected? Which has meant most to individuals in your group, and why?

STUDY GUIDE 160

James 1:1–2:13

FAITH'S LIFESTYLE

Overview

James is thought to be the earliest of the New Testament's letters. It was written when there was a company of Jewish believers, probably between A.D. 45–48. The author is James "the Lord's brother," not James the Apostle (see Acts 12:17; 15:13; 21:18; 1 Cor. 15:7; Gal. 1:19; 2:9). James the Apostle, the brother of John, was martyred about A.D. 44 (Acts 12:1-3).

Like the other brothers of Jesus, James did not believe in Him at first (John 7:2-5). But after the Resurrection this brother was not only converted but became a key leader in Jerusalem and at the Jerusalem Council (Acts 15). One tradition nicknames James "camel knees," because of the calluses he was supposed to have developed from long hours spent in prayer.

James' theme is "faith." But here faith is not saving faith, or justifying faith. James' theme is practical: he looked at the *lifestyle which is to be produced by faith in Jesus*. James knew, with Paul, that true faith generates obedience, and so he gently encouraged the early Jewish church to live a life that was worthy of their profession of Jesus as the Christ.

In structure, James is much like Proverbs. He gave a series of short, pithy exhortations, touching on a variety of subjects important in the Christian life. What a wonderful book to teach if we, like James, want to help our people learn to live for the Lord.

Commentary

The church we see portrayed in the early chapters of Acts was both typical of what the church is to be, and yet different. At first the Jewish people viewed Christianity as a sect, as much an expression of Judaism as Sadduceeism, Phariseeism, or the withdrawn Essenes. Recognized and named "the Way," the Christian community took part in the life and culture of Judea, worshiped at the temple as did the others, and maintained the lifelong patterns of obedience to the Law.

It is in this context that the first of our New Testament letters was penned. Later sharp distinctions would occur between Christians and Jewish doctrine and practice. Later would come the exploration of the meaning of a faith that reaches out to encompass the Gentile as well as the Jews. But none of this is found in the Book of James. Instead of emphasizing salvation by faith, James presupposed the apostolic teaching we see in Acts 2 and 3. What James emphasized is the life of faith, which followers of "the Way" are encouraged to live.

By Faith

One of the striking features of the Book of James is its frequent references to faith. In spite of this, though, James had not always been well received. Martin Luther, that great advocate of faith from the time of the Protestant Reformation, looked on James with suspicion and called it an "epistle of straw," certainly not a letter with the weight or importance of his favorites, Galatians and Romans.

Why did Luther hold such a dim view of the Book of James? The reason is not hard to find once we set Luther's position against the backdrop of his cultural context and personal religious odyssey.

In Luther's day, the church was enduring one of its periodic cycles of corruption where the pattern of biblical truth was perverted. A playboy pope, Leo X of the house of Medici, had succeeded to the papal chair and was selling the offices of the church to whomever could pay well for the privilege. The archbishop of Mainz, the primate of Germany, having borrowed the money to buy his office, was allowed to issue indulgences to recoup his expenses. These indulgences promised the complete and perfect remission of all sins to those (or their dead relatives or friends) who subscribed to the building of Saint Peter's Cathedral in Rome (though only one half the money went for this purpose, the rest repaying the archbishop's loan). A popular jingle of the time phrased the promise well:

> As soon as the coin in the coffer rings,
> The soul from purgatory springs.

Luther had recently discovered for himself the tremendous truth that salvation, a person's entrance into a personal relationship with God, is a free gift received through faith in Jesus Christ. He realized that the Gospel then consists of what God, in Christ, has done for human beings. No one could ever buy salvation!

Thus Luther and the other Reformers were drawn to those books of the Bible which stress the meaning of Christ's cross for all who trust Him. James, with its ethical and practical emphasis on man's response to God's initiative, found little favor. In their situation, James even seemed at times to support the other side!

Interpreting Scripture

Luther's suspicion and others' misunderstanding of the Book of James point out an important feature of good biblical interpretation. *We must be careful to read Scripture in the context of its own time—not of our time.*

Viewed from the perspective of the Protestant Reformation, James even seemed to contradict what is taught in the Books of Galatians and Romans. All of James' talk of being "justified by works" seemed to deny Paul's affirmation that justification is by faith alone. With "salvation" viewed as the *entrance into* relationship with God, James' approach (in which salvation is viewed as the continual outworking of the meaning of Christ's presence in the believer's life) is easy to misunderstand.

Today too if we approach the New Testament with neat definitions of Bible terms fixed in our minds, remaining unaware of possible other meanings, we are liable to misunderstand some of the interplay of great Bible truths.

One of the best ways to avoid misunderstanding the Bible then is to take a look at the circumstances in which a book was written. Then we go on to define the author's purpose. An important corollary is to look at the range of possible meanings of each significant Bible term and then decide which, in the context of the author's purpose and time, is intended.

We will want to keep the following two principles of interpretation in mind as we read the Book of James: (1) understand the settings, and (2) look at all the possible meaning of terms. These two principles will help us discover not only the message of James, but the message of many other passages in God's Word.

The setting. What then was the setting in which James wrote? What was his purpose? And how do these differ from the setting of a book such as Galatians?

James wrote to the earliest church. He wrote in the days when the church was Hebrew-Christian, made up of men and women who had known the God of the Old Testament and who, under the dynamic preaching of the Apostles, now recognized Jesus of Nazareth as their resurrected Lord and Saviour. The Book of James is *not* an evangelistic book written to people in a culture where faith is foreign. The Book of James is a book of guidelines for living, which was written to the family who had a full knowledge of who Jesus is, and who had chosen to make Him the center of their lives.

Essentially then James was concerned with how the new faith in Jesus is to find expression in the lives of members of that early community. James and Paul were, in fact, exploring different aspects of a common salvation. Paul, the obstetrician, was explaining what happens at birth. James, the practical nurse, was changing diapers and holding the hands of toddlers as they learned to walk. Because the setting and the purpose of the two writers differed, a difference in emphasis naturally followed. As John Calvin pointed out in Luther's day, "It is not required that all handle the same arguments."

It is helpful to note several contrasts between the setting of James and the setting and purpose of Paul's letters.

JAMES	PAUL
stresses the *work of the believer* in relation to faith	*stresses the work of Christ* in relation to faith

is concerned that the *outcome of faith* be fruit (2:14), so that no one be able to confuse creeds with Christianity	is concerned that the *object of faith* be Christ, unmixed with self-reliance or self-righteousness
writes shortly after the Resurrection, when the church is Jewish and the Old Testament well known	writes later, when the conversion of Gentiles raised questions never asked or thought of earlier

These are important contrasts which help us see that we must study James in James' own terms, not in view of later developments in the early church or in church history.

Key terms. We've already noted that "faith" is a key term in the Book of James. And we have suggested that faith has more than one kind of impact in a believer's life. It is by faith we enter into relationship with God. But it is also by faith that we continue to live the Christian life (see Rom. 1:17; Gal. 2:20). What we must avoid when we read the Bible then is reading *either* the "saving" or the "lifestyle" meaning of faith into a particular verse until we have considered which meaning is intended by the author. Studying God's Word demands that we read to discover the writer's meaning, not to read our own impressions and theological biases into the text.

Another word that is often *read into* rather than read, occurs not only in James but also throughout the New Testament. It is "saved." To many people, whenever this word is found, it is automatically read as though the passage deals with entrance into a personal relationship with God. With some passages this creates no problem: "Everyone who calls on the name of the Lord will be saved" (Rom. 10:13), or, "There is no other name under heaven given to men by which we must be saved" (Acts 4:12). Clearly these verses are dealing with that invitation to enter into eternal life through faith in Jesus.

But some other passages trouble those who have only a narrow view of the meaning of "saved." James asks in chapter 2, "Can such faith save?" (v. 14) He seems to answer that human works are somehow necessary. Is he denying Paul's teaching of salvation by grace through faith, apart from works? (Eph. 2:8-9)

Paul himself wrote in Philippians 2:12, "Continue to work out your salvation with fear and trembling." Was Paul contradicting here what he had written elsewhere? Is the Bible inconsistent? Is its teaching about salvation unclear?

The answer comes when we go back into the Old Testament and note that the root meaning of "salvation" is *deliverance*. In most cases the deliverance the Old Testament speaks of is from present dangers and enemies. Only infrequently does "salvation" in the Old Testament context look beyond this life to focus on an individual's eternal destiny. The underlying theme is that God is a real Person who does intervene in human affairs on behalf of those who trust Him.

In the New Testament it is more clearly defined just how God intervenes. Strikingly, God's intervention is pictured as something with past, present, and future implications. In the past, God acted in Jesus Christ to provide us with forgiveness of sins and a new life. By a simple act of faith, we enter into all that Christ has done for us in history, and at that point we "are saved."

But God's intervention for us is not finished yet! In the person of the Holy Spirit, Jesus Himself has come into our lives. He has linked us to Himself with an unbreakable commitment; and because He is present in us, we are also "being saved." This is clearly what Paul spoke of in Philippians: "Work out your salvation with fear and trembling," he wrote, "for it is God who works in you to will and to act according to His good purpose" (Phil. 2:12-13). We approach life seriously, but with confidence. Christ's *present-tense deliverance* is being worked out in our lives even as we continue to trust and rely on Him, and as we demonstrate that trust by meeting life boldly, head-on.

There is a future dimension of salvation as well. The Bible tells us that Jesus will return, and then we will be *fully* saved. We will be fully delivered from all that sin has done to twist our personalities and to warp us away from God (see Rom. 8:18-24).

It is important then when we come on the word "saved" in the Bible not to impose a single or narrow meaning on it. What "salvation" is in view here? Past tense? Present tense? Future? If we make this simple distinction and realize that each aspect of salvation affirms God as One who acts in the lives of those who trust Him, we are freed both from misinterpreting our Bible and from many an agonizing doubt about our personal standing with God.

James

Let's return then to the Book of James, and view it as God's guidance concerning *present-tense* salvation. Let us see it as guidelines for living our faith; for a lifestyle that emerges from a vital, intimate relationship with the Living God.

Outline

I.	Practicing Faith's Lifestyle	1:1–2:13
	A. Personal implications	1:2-18
	B. Interpersonal implications	1:19–2:13
II.	Principles of Faith's Lifestyle	2:14-25
III.	Problems for Faith's Lifestyle	3:1–4:17
	A. Taming the tongue	3:1-12
	B. Subduing the self	3:13–4:10
	C. Judging the judge	4:11-12
	D. Humbling the haughty	4:13-17
IV.	Prospects and Promises for Faith	5:1-19
	A. Future redress	5:1-6
	B. Present resources	5:7-19

♥ ***Link to Life: Youth / Adult***

Give a minilecture as an introduction to this book. Contrast the concerns of Paul and James, and discuss the importance of knowing which of several meanings a word has in its context.

Then distribute outlines of James to each group member.

You may need to take up to 20 minutes for this overview, and even longer if your group raises questions.

Faith's Personal Impact: James 1:2-18

After a very brief introduction, James immediately confronted his readers with a number of practical, personal implications of a living faith. Each of these looks within, and asks the individual to probe his own reactions, values, and perceptions.

Our attitude toward trials (James 1:2-4). James called on us to actually welcome trials and difficulties. These are to produce unmixed joy, not because the trials themselves are pleasurable, but because we look beyond the immediate experience to foresee the result. God permits such experiences as a test (intended to show the validity, not weakness) of our faith. Such trials call for perseverance, which in turn produces maturity and spiritual wholeness. If we are able to look beyond the present and see the product God intends to produce through our suffering, we will experience joy.

This perspective is impossible for most men. But those who have confidence in God value character above pleasure, and eternity above the present moment.

Our expectation of God's aid (James 1:5-8). Trials are likely to panic us. When a person doesn't know which way to turn, he or she may fear to make decisions or may constantly change his or her mind. James reminded us that ours is a giving God, and one of His gifts is wisdom.

This "wisdom" is practical: it is the capacity to apply spiritual truth to daily decisions.

James promised that God will show the person who asks the way to go. "Belief" here suggests a willingness to respond and act on God's guidance. The wavering individual, who hesitates to respond obediently, will be unable to receive what the Lord is eager to give.

Our awareness of our identity (James 1:9-11). Human beings tend to evaluate themselves by various standards. One of the most common has to do with status and income. James called on those who are poor and once angry about their poverty, to throw off the old attitude and realize that, in this new relationship with God, they have been raised to riches. And the wealthy, once confident in their pride, are to remember their spiritual poverty. The old symbols of status, like this present life itself, are as perishable as grass.

Our acceptance of responsibility (James 1:12-15). Faith brings the believer a new sense of personal responsibility. It's common for human beings to excuse sins by blaming God or Satan ("The devil made me do it" is for some more than a saying). James knew that many different circumstances may stimulate our desire to turn from God's way.

But James analyzed the situation carefully. It is not the external thing itself that tempts us; it is our reaction to it. An alcoholic may be tempted overwhelmingly by the smells wafting from a brewery, while a teetotaler is repelled. The odor is the same in each case. What differs is the reaction the odor causes. Candy is a terrible temptation to a fat person on a diet, but another who dislikes sweets won't even notice it.

James showed us that God brings no experience into our lives in order to drag us down. His gifts are always and only good. If we feel temptation, the problem is in our own inner desires. Unless we deal with our temptations on this basis, our initial desire will grow into sinful acts, and this to a sinful lifestyle.

If we recognize temptations as flowing from our own nature, we can deal with them by rejecting sin and responding as the new in us directs.

Our expectation from God (James 1:16-18). James reminds us that we are to expect only good gifts from God. And there is a good gift which counters the tendency to sin that makes us susceptible to temptations.

God has chosen to "give us birth through the word of truth." The old nature which responds wrongly is balanced now by a new nature, which responds to God, for it has been created as a "kind of firstfruits" of all He created. The promise of complete righteousness in the resurrection is guaranteed as we see God creating righteousness within our hearts now.

Faith's lifestyle then calls for us to adopt various personal perspectives on life. We are to see the long-term purpose in trials, and rejoice in that purpose. We are to expect to receive wisdom from God, and to ask for and act on His guidance. We are to see our identity as rooted in relationship with God, to accept responsibility for our temptations, and to expect God's good gift of a new nature to enable us to overcome.

♥ ***Link to Life: Youth / Adult***
List the topic paragraphs on the chalkboard (James 1:2-4, 5-8, 9-11, 12-15, 16-18). Work in pairs to (1) title each paragraph, (2) identify the attitude *that faith engenders, and (3) contrast it with the attitude which might be seen in those who do not maintain a living trust in God.*

Hear reports and list insights on the board. Then discuss: "Which of these attitudes that faith calls for seems most important? Why? Most difficult? Why? What experiences may have helped to develop that (those) attitude(s) in you?"

Faith's Interpersonal Impact: James 1:19–2:13
James then moved on to explore another aspect of faith's life. Men and women in relationship with Jesus find that that faith also transforms their relationships with others.

Our responses to others (James 1:19-21). Human nature is charged with selfishness and pride. These show up not only in immorality (the use, rather than the valuing of others), but also in anger and antagonism. James told us that the quick, hostile reactions of men to one another are changed by faith. Patience and meekness replace anger and pride.

Our standards of behavior (James 1:22-25). At the heart of the believer's new way of living with others is the realization that God's Word is to be acted on, not just heard. The doer of God's Word is "blessed" *in his doing* (v. 25).

Our view of religion (James 1:26-27). Christian faith gives us new perspective on religion. It no longer is a ritual kind of thing, but now is seen to be a response to others that mirrors the concern of the God who is Father to humankind. Pure religion is now understood to "look after orphans and widows in their distress and to keep oneself from being polluted by the world."

Our welcome to others (James 2:1-7). The unity found in Christ has its source in the fact that in His church, all are family. Rich and poor stand side by side in Him. Thus, in the church, believers are to reject all artificial distinctions and to affirm unity in every way. Rich and poor are to be treated with equal respect and appreciation as persons; anything else is to blaspheme the name by which we are called.

Our calling of love (James 2:8-13). As persons of faith, responsive to the royal law (the command to love one another was uttered by King Jesus [John 13:33-34]), we are to love our neighbors without partiality. Making distinctions between rich and poor and thus showing favoritism, is as much a violation of the divine intent as the more obvious sins identified in the Law.

It's important to understand James' point

when he said "whoever keeps the whole Law and yet stumbles at just one point is guilty of breaking it all." The Law of the Old Testament is a unity. As a whole balloon is broken by just one pin prick, so a person becomes a "lawbreaker" by violating just one requirement of the Mosaic Law.

♥ ***Link to Life: Youth / Adult***
Use the same procedure to explore this passage as was used to study James 1:1-18.

The paragraphs that pairs should title and study are: James 1:19-21, 22-25, 26-27; 2:1-7, 8-13.

James, as a leader of the Jerusalem congregation, was showing a pastor's heart in this brief letter. He knew that faith in Jesus can and will change our lives. And he encouraged his congregation by showing them the new attitudes and relationships which faith will produce.

TEACHING GUIDE

Prepare
As a "pastor" to your group, what evidences do you see of faith's impact on their lives?

Explore
Begin with a minilecture on the Book of James, and the distinctive view of "faith" which shapes this short letter. See "link-to-life," page 1019 for ideas.

Expand
1. Set pairs to work on each of the brief paragraphs in James 1:1-18. Each is to carefully analyze the lifestyle James linked with a living faith in Jesus as a prelude to group discussion. See "link-to-life," page 1020.
2. Or set half the pairs to work on James 1:1-18 and the other half on 1:19–2:13. Again, use the approach suggested on page 1020.

Apply
Go around the circle asking each person to share one way in which he or she has seen his or her lifestyle changed by faith in Jesus.

STUDY GUIDE 161

James 2:14–5:20

FAITH'S CHALLENGES

Overview

The Book of James is about faith. But it is *not* about "saving faith." It is about the role faith plays in the life of a person who is already a believer.

In our last study we saw James' insights into personal and interpersonal aspects of the life of faith. A believer's character (1:2-4), attitudes (vv. 5-8), emotional responses (vv. 19-21), behavior (vv. 22-27) and priorities (2:1-13) are all reshaped by faith. Thus participation in the community of those who take Jesus as the focus of their lives brings a total reorientation of the individual, and of all that he or she is. Christian faith is not merely assent to a set of propositions about Jesus: it is a living trust in the Lord which leads to a whole new way of life.

In this study you will help your group grasp a basic principle that underlies this faith-lifestyle (vv. 14-25), and examine problems to be faced by the man or woman of faith (chaps. 3–4). Finally you will look together at the prospects for the person of faith—redress of wrongs when Jesus returns, and until then all the resources we need to overcome.

▶ ***Justify.*** The Greek word means "to vindicate" as well as "to pronounce righteous." Depending on the context, *justify* can mean "found innocent" or "vindicated in a particular course of action." It is important to keep each meaning in view as we study James 2.

Commentary

James was a man deeply concerned that those who have faith in Jesus express that faith in an appropriate lifestyle. Knowing God means a total reorientation for human beings who were before blinded and lost. It is against this background of concern that those who claim Jesus live a life of faith that James, in chapter 2, penned a paragraph which greatly troubled Martin Luther and others who thought that James suggested a salvation that is won through human effort rather than by the work of Christ on Calvary.

Principles of Faith: James 2:14-26

Here is what the troublesome passage says:

> What good is it, my brothers, if a man claims to have faith but has no deeds? Can such faith save him? Suppose a brother or sister is without clothes and daily food. If one of you says to him, "Go, I wish you well; keep warm and well fed," but does nothing about his physical needs, what good is it? In the same way, faith by itself, if it is not accompanied by action, is dead.
>
> But someone will say, "You have faith; I have deeds."
>
> Show me your faith without deeds, and I will show you my faith by what I do. You believe that there is one God. Good! Even the demons believe that—and shudder.
>
> You foolish man, do you want evidence that faith without deeds is useless? Was not our ancestor Abraham considered righteous for what he did when he offered his son Isaac on the altar? You see that his faith and his actions were working together, and his faith was made complete by what he did. And the Scripture was fulfilled that says, "Abraham believed God, and it was credited to him as righteousness," and he was called God's friend. You see that a person is justified by what he does and not by faith alone.
>
> In the same way, was not even Rahab the prostitute considered righteous for what she did when she gave lodging to the spies and sent them off in a different

> direction? As the body without the spirit is dead, so faith without deeds is dead.

We can avoid misunderstanding if we only look at the thesis James stated so clearly. He was speaking of an individual who claims to have "faith," but whose "faith" has not produced any change of life. He asked, "Can *such faith* save him?" (v. 14, italics added)

James thus was looking at a particular *kind* of "faith," that actually stands in contrast with what Paul and other New Testament writers call "faith." While the kind of "faith" James examines does exist as intellectual acknowledgment of God (e.g., "God exists"), it does *not* exist as a trust in God that generates response. In this it is like that of demons, who know full well that God exists, but who rather than trust and love Him "shudder" (v. 19).

This kind of faith is seen in human beings who, despite their claims to "believe" in God are unresponsive to the needs of their brothers and sisters. *It is not linked with response*—either to God or to God's children.

James then contrasts dead faith with a real and vital faith in God. As seen in both Abraham and Rahab, true faith produces fruit. Abraham's "faith and his actions were working together, and his faith was made complete by what he did. And the Scripture was fulfilled that says 'Abraham believed God, and it was credited to him as righteousness' " (vv. 22-23). That is, God's recorded statement that "Abraham believed God" was demonstrated to be true by Abraham's subsequent obedience to the Lord! Where there is true faith in God, that faith will never exist apart from works, but will find expression in the believer's way of life.

But what about the statement that "a person is justified by what he does and not by faith alone"? (v. 24) Doesn't this conflict with the teaching that salvation is by faith, apart from works?

Here we turn to the second meaning of *justify* as "vindicate." The *Expository Dictionary of Bible Words* (Zondervan) says:

> It is not beyond our efforts to resolve the apparent conflict between Romans and James. Consider the following: James does not teach that Abraham was pronounced righteous on the basis of his actions. James teaches that Scripture's announcement that Abraham *was* righteous is vindicated on the basis of Abraham's subsequent obedience. He did right because God's action actually worked within him to make him righteous! James is speaking of two kinds of faith, only one of which is saving faith. He teaches that saving faith will be vindicated by the actions that flow from it and in this sense complete it.
>
> What is particularly significant to us here is that James joins Paul in suggesting that justification is something more than a judicial declaration. True, in response to faith, God does declare sinners acquitted and righteous before Him; but He does more than that. God acts within the believer to make righteousness a reality. Thus the Gospel offer of salvation by faith includes more than a pardon: it also includes a transformation. God will declare the sinner righteous, and then God will act to *make* the sinner what God has declared him to be.

The kind of faith which saves also transforms, and that transformation will show up in the lifestyle of the true believer.

♥ ***Link to Life: Youth / Adult***
In a minilecture work carefully through this critical passage. Then have group members individually write a paraphrase of these verses. This process will help each see if he or she has grasped the verses' teaching.

Read several paraphrases to the group, or work together to develop a group paraphrase that takes the best insights and combines them.

And so James calls us today to look at our Christian faith not only as *what* we believe, but also as *how* we believe. Has our response to God been a dry, intellectual kind of thing? Have we simply accepted as true the historical facts about Jesus' life and death and resurrection? Or have we gone beyond recognition to a wholehearted trust in Jesus? A trust that involves not only the confidence that He has forgiven us, but also involves the commitment of our whole person into His loving hands. A commitment of all that we are and have to Jesus now. When we make this commitment, "This kind of faith" not only will save us but will also transform our lives.

Problems for Faith: James 3–4
After his sweeping assertion of the principle that faith must find expression in our lifestyle as well as in our beliefs, James focused on problems that each of us must deal with. These are, in essence, challenges to the way of life that faith promotes.

What is so surprising is that these are such common, ordinary problems. There is no demand here that our faith move mountains, produce miracles, or at the very least lead us to venture overseas without support, to carry the Gospel to distant tribes. Rather than the extraordinary feats we sometimes associate with great faith, James directs our attention to the unspectacular business of the common man's ordinary daily life.

Taming the tongue (James 3:1-12). The tongue is the first challenge for faith. It's so easy for us to slip and to criticize or say something cutting about our brother. It's so tempting to gossip. The person who has his or her tongue under control has definitely matured in the life of faith.

Subduing the self (James 3:13–4:10). Each of us has natural desires and passions that constitute another challenge to faith. We can recognize the influence of the old passions when we see "bitter envy and selfish ambition" in our hearts.

On the other hand we can recognize the divine wisdom by its traits. It is "pure . . . peace loving, considerate, submissive, full of mercy and good fruit, impartial and sincere" (3:17).

What is so serious about our desires? If we act out of the old passions our relationships with others will be marked by conflict. There will be "quarreling and fighting" (4:1-2). What is more, the *things we desire* will be wrong. We will not obtain them, first because we have not associated them to our lives with God (v. 2), and second because when we *do* ask God, we "ask with wrong motives" (v. 3).

James went on to further emphasize the seriousness of the materialistic and selfish viewpoint that is linked with our old lives. "Friendship with the world is hatred toward God" (v. 4). Here "world" is used in its theological sense as the world system: the whole set of values, attitudes, desires, and passions that characterize sinful human society.

The challenge for faith, then, is to submit oneself totally to God. We are to adopt His viewpoint and His values, even at the cost of personal pain and humbling ourselves before Him (vv. 8-10). The reorientation of life which comes when we make full commitment to God will transform our desires, and by making us those who love rather than those who desire, will change our relationships with others as well.

Judging the judge (James 4:11-12). Another common problem faced by all of us is our tendency to judge and evaluate each other in a negative, condemning way. James pointed out that God alone, who makes the law, is competent to judge. Faith struggles against this tendency to judge and criticize a neighbor.

Humbling the haughty (James 4:13-17). Finally, faith comes into direct conflict with pride and the human tendency to rely on one's own self. Arrogance, boasting, and approaching life as though our lives were under our control rather than in God's hands is likely to grow with success and accomplishments. Faith maintains the awareness that we are each dependent on God, and faith frees us to relax in the assurance of His loving guidance for our lives.

♥ ***Link to Life: Youth / Adult***
Go around the circle and ask each person in the group to complete the following sentence: "I would like more faith so I could. . . ."

List each completion on the chalkboard. Then discuss: "How do we tend to see faith? What do we expect our faith in God to accomplish?"

Then list the "problems for faith" headings in James 3—4. Divide into teams, each of which is to examine one or two of these areas, to define just what problem we human beings have, and how faith leads us to approach it.

Prospects and Promises: James 5:1-20
The men and women to whom James wrote lived, as we do, in a time when injustice was common and suffering the all-too-often lot of believer and unbeliever alike. What does a life of faith promise to Jesus' followers? What are the rewards of joining with others on faith's great adventure?

The prospect (James 5:1-6). James wanted to recognize immediately that there is no promise in Christianity of utopia now. Instead James spoke out for the oppressed, warning the wealthy who defraud the poor laborer while they live "in luxury and self-indulgence" (v. 5). Earthly treasures will rust away, and the very rust will be evidence against the oppressors in the coming judgment.

The impact of this message is not to call the poor believer to vindictive joy at the prospect. Instead, James sought to call rich and poor alike to realize that a day *is* coming when God will show His justice as well as His love. To the rich this is a call to repent. To the poor it is a message of hope. This world is not the sum and substance of reality. When Jesus comes, the world as well as individuals will be renewed.

Present promises (James 5:7-20). What about now, as we wait patiently for Jesus to return? James tells us that the person of faith has many resources.

There is patience (vv. 7-12). Job waited, trusting God's timing. And the end of Job's life demonstrated the compassion and the mercy of God (Job 42). Like Job, the suffering believer today can commit himself and his suffering to the Lord.

There is prayer (James 5:13-18). We have the privilege of joining with our brothers to bring both illness and sin to God for healing. James insisted that we not underestimate the importance of prayer. "The prayer of a righteous man is powerful and effective" (v. 16).

Note that many see the promise of healing here as linked with confession, and the sickness as a divine judgment. In any case, we are to bring all our needs to Jesus, confident that He does hear and answer prayer.

There is caring (vv. 19-20). This last resource is seen in the final words of James, "My brothers, if one of you should wander from the truth" (v. 19). The response of the believing community is not to condemn but to seek to restore. The family is a community of life. Whatever life may hold, within the family there is the certainty of caring and concern.

TEACHING GUIDE

Prepare

Work through James 2:14-25 carefully, and be ready to answer any questions on this "problem" passage.

Explore

Review briefly James' concern with faith's lifestyle. Then give a minilecture, working carefully through James 2:14-25. Ask each group member to paraphrase this passage, and then work together to develop a group paraphrase.

Expand

1. Have your group members complete a statement about "faith" and how each wants faith to enrich his or her life. See "link-to-life," page 1024.
2. Divide into teams. Give each team one or two of the topics in James 3–4 to analyze. What is the nature of these ordinary problems of life that faith deals with? How does faith affect our attitudes and behaviors in this problem area?

Apply

Sum up the prospects and the resources we have as faith in Christ shapes us and our lifestyles.

STUDY GUIDE 162

1 Peter 1:1–4:6

THE CALL TO SUBMISSION

Overview

Peter's first letter was written in a time when the church was beginning to feel the flames of persecution. Written to the "scattered" by Peter, this letter was probably directed to clusters of believers in various cities of the empire.

Peter's letter is a call to holiness in troubled times, and a recognition that even suffering can be a gift from God. No fewer than seven different Greek words for suffering in this letter suggest the intensity of the persecution.

Perhaps the most striking feature of the letter is Peter's emphasis on submission as the Christian's response under pressure. Despite suffering, discrimination, and ridicule, the path of holiness involves acceptance of our pain and an awareness that even suffering can be a gift from God.

In this first session on this striking New Testament book, you will help your group members explore this path that we find so difficult to travel.

▶ ***Submission.*** The Greek terms are *hypotasso* or *hypotage*. The words indicate a subjection or subordination. While this may be forced (as the demons who submit to God, Luke 10:17), Christian submission is voluntary. We submit to secular authority (Rom. 13:1), to one another (Eph. 5:21), and Christian slaves even choose submission to harsh masters (1 Peter 2:18). Here Peter called on us to submit when persecuted, and keep on trusting God.

Commentary

The first-century church was divided by two cultural traditions—Jewish and Gentile—from which people were drawn to become one in Christ.

At first, the church was Jewish. The community of faith grew immediately after Jesus' resurrection as a sect of Judaism. These first believers were surprised that God would accept pagan outsiders just as He accepted the chosen people—by faith in Christ. Still, for its first two decades, the new community was primarily Jewish.

Then came the explosive days of missionary expansion. Spearheaded by Paul and others, the Gospel was carried throughout the Roman world. And thousands responded. The makeup of the church changed: Gentiles predominated. Teachers began to explore the new faith's relationship to Hellenistic philosophies and ways.

Looking back at Ephesians and Colossians, it is clear that Paul wrote to men and women of Hellenistic orientation. It is equally clear that the Book of Hebrews was written to Jewish believers, for it deals with Christian faith in the traditional categories of Old Testament theology. Despite their differing audiences, all three books consider the very same issues. They help readers grasp the superiority of Christ. They each affirm Jesus as the center of our faith, the heartbeat of our new lives.

Christ is superior to the cosmology of the pagans and to the revealed shadow-truths of the Jews. New life in Jesus cannot be found through the ascetic self-denial of Gnosticism or the ritual observances of Judaism. Identity is found in our resurrection life, portrayed in Ephesians and affirmed in the Hebrews' pronouncement that we have been lifted to glory as the sons of God. Theme after theme in these books compares, though each is adapted to the history and to the Gentile or Jew to whom it is addressed.

One implication of this is clear. As the church continued to mature, its identification with either tradition was gradually being lost! Believers shook off the tendency to identify themselves as Gentile-Christians or Jewish-Christians, and found a new, common identity in Christ alone. Shaking off old identities to understand who they were in Christ became a vital issue for a worldwide church, composed of such diverse elements.

And, as Christians began to view themselves as a separate and distinct people in themselves, so the world around began to realize that Christianity was not just a sect of Judaism. It was a religion in its own right—and it was not a "licit," or governmentally approved religion either!

There is much controversy over 1 Peter. Most theologians agree that it was written near the end of Peter's life. Probably he wrote from Rome, just before his martyrdom under Nero around A.D. 64.

The debate focuses on whom Peter wrote to. He addressed his letter to the "scattered," to *diaspora* (1:1). This word identified Jews who lived in major Gentile cities throughout the world. Along with Peter's identification as an "apostle to the Jews" (see Gal. 2:7), this seems to prove that the letter was meant for Christian Hebrews.

On the other hand, the book speaks of "the empty way of life handed down to you from your forefathers" (1 Peter 1:18) and gives a catalog of distinctly Gentile vices (4:3-4). These references and others make it hard to limit Peter's readers to Hebrew Christians. It is possible that Peter addressed this letter to mixed communities, composed of both Hebrew and Gentile Christians. But it is certain that Peter, like Paul and the writer of Hebrews, addressed common issues, and emphasized those themes which soon made the Christian church distinct.

Foundation Truths: 1 Peter 1:1–2:12
Looking at the introductory section of Peter's letter, we are struck by the familiarity of the truths he developed. These are the very same truths portrayed throughout this study as the foundation for a life of holiness.

For instance, Peter began with praise to God, who has in His great mercy "given us new birth into a living hope" (1:3). How familiar this is! Paul emphasized that the dead have been raised to a resurrection kind of life in Ephesians 2. And again in Colossians, he said, "God made you alive with Christ" (2:13). This belief was shared by the writer to the Hebrews. In Christ, we have been lifted up, freed from our fear of death, and made members of God's family (Heb. 12:7-10) and called to *keep* on loving one another as brothers (13:1). Our hope of holiness rests on this foundation.

♥ ***Link to Life: Youth / Adult***
Briefly review the historical setting in which Peter wrote, as the church began to develop its own separate identity. Then use the chart below to examine themes common to 1 Peter, Ephesians, Colossians, and Hebrews, which are foundational to the Christian's new identity, and which lay the basis for Christian holiness. You may want to work together to identify topics in 1 Peter, then assign different books to teams who will search for parallels.

Common Foundation Themes
A basis for holiness

	Summary	Parallels		
1 Peter		Eph.	Col.	Heb.
1:3, 23	New, resurrection birth			
1:4	Inheritance			
1:9-12	Present experience of salvation benefits			
1:14				
1:15-16				
1:17				
1:19-20				
1:22				
2:5, 9				
2:10				
2:11				
2:12				

What is Peter's concern for this church we belong to, and which in Christ has a unique identity? Reading through the book quickly, we note a number of repeated themes, including a constant emphasis on suffering.

Peter warned that life in this world may involve suffering grief in all sorts of trials (1:6). Suffering as Jesus suffered is not unexpected (2:18-23).

In fact, we may even suffer for doing what is right! (3:14) Christ suffered, we are reminded. So we should arm ourselves with His attitude (4:1) and not be surprised at painful trials (v. 12).

Another repeated theme is submission. Peter seemed to place great emphasis on living appropriately under human government (2:13), within the framework of society's other institutions (v. 18; 3:1), and within the church (5:5).

While these themes are often repeated, neither seems to sum up Peter's major concern. Instead, Peter seemed most concerned with holiness. We have been called in Christ, Peter said, to be holy (1:14-15). After all, we "are being built into a spiritual house to be a holy priesthood" (2:5). We are, he insisted, a "chosen people, a royal priesthood, a holy nation, a people belonging to God, that you may declare the praises of Him who called you out of darkness into His wonderful light" (v. 9).

Peter called Christ's people to "live such good lives among the pagans that, though they accuse you of doing wrong, they may see your good deeds and glorify God on the day He visits us" (v. 12).

Peter, writing to the church of God—not the Jewish church or the Gentile church but the church that finds life in Jesus alone—called us to *a life of practical holiness*. While that life involves, as we expect, a commitment to "abstain from sinful desires" and to "live such good lives" that our "good deeds" are evident, one of its major features is submissiveness! A holy life is a life of Christian submission.

Submission's Path: 1 Peter 2:13–3:9

In the Bible holiness is associated both with an active love for others and a decisive rejection of every kind of evil. These themes are found in Peter too. "Now that you have purified yourselves by obeying the truth so that you have sincere love for your brothers, love one another deeply, from the heart" (1:22). And, "Rid yourselves of all malice and all deceit, hypocrisy, envy, and slander of every kind" (2:1). A life of practical holiness will always be marked by these two qualities.

But Peter went on to develop in great detail an aspect of a holy life that Paul only mentioned: living in willing submission within the framework of authorities that exist in society. At first, it seems peculiar to relate this to holiness. But, as we trace Peter's argument, we see that the relationship does exist in God's eyes, and we understand why.

Man's authority (1 Peter 2:13-17). We Christians submit to authorities "instituted among men" (v. 13) for the Lord's sake. Doing good is always within the framework of our society. Our freedom in Christ is not an excuse to flaunt human laws or to withhold respect.

Unjust authorities (1 Peter 2:18-25). What if people in authority treat us unjustly?

Selecting the critical area of potential mistreatment in his own society, Peter looked at the relationship between slave and master. The slave is to submit, Peter wrote, and to maintain due respect "not only to those who are good and considerate, but also to those who are harsh" (v. 18). This is not an endorsement of slavery. Nor is it suggesting that a person should not seek relief, if society makes it possible. Peter simply focused on an extreme case to provide a clear illustration of the principle of submission. In Peter's world, a slave had no right to demand considerate treatment. It was perfectly legal, though morally wrong, for a master to treat his slave harshly.

Did harsh treatment release the Christian slave from his obligation to submit with respect? No, Peter said firmly. The Christian's call to a life of submission is *not conditional*. Another person's failure to live God's way does not release us from our responsibility to so submit.

To show us that God does not ask of us any more than He was Himself willing to do, Peter invites us to look at Jesus. Christ suffered, for doing only good! Even though He might have, Jesus did not retaliate. In His submission Jesus gives us an example of how we are to live. After all, if the body is incarnate Christ in the world today, we would expect Jesus to want us to live the way He did.

♥ ***Link to Life: Youth / Adult***
*Play "I've got a right to . . ." with your group. Give them this series of open-ended statements, and ask each to write down how a person (*not *how he or she) might finish them. The statements:*

- *My boss doesn't pay me enough, so I've got a right to. . . .*
- *My parents don't listen to me, so I've got a right to. . . .*
- *My spouse cheats on me, so I've got a right to. . . .*
- *The tax law is unfair so I've got a right to. . . .*
- *My church doesn't view women as real persons, so I've got a right to. . . .*

Let your group members share responses, and explain why people might respond that way.

Then look together at 1 Peter 2:18-25 and discuss it. Emphasize the fact that our responsibility to others is not conditional *on how they treat us. Then together try to decide how the Apostle Peter might complete the open-ended statements above.*

Husbands and wives (1 Peter 3:1-7). In the husband/wife relationship, submission is again enjoined. Here Peter was addressing a problem that exists today, when Christan wives are married to men who "do not believe the Word" (v. 1). Peter did not suggest aggressive evangelism. Instead, the wife is to adopt a course of *aggressive submission.* Quietly demonstrating the inner beauty Jesus brings, wives are to communicate the Lord through the holy way of submission.

Of course, believing husbands are to be considerate (v. 7). But, as the slave is not released from the holy way if he has a harsh master, neither is the wife with an inconsiderate spouse.

♥ ***Link to Life: Youth / Adult***
Break into "counseling teams" to determine from 3:1-7 how to advise a woman with the following problem:

My husband is upset with me for being a Christian. He doesn't want me to go to church or pray around the house. Some friends told me to take a stand for Christ: to pray openly at meals, to keep tracts around for him to read, and to pin up Bible verses on sin and salvation where he'll be sure to see them. So far, it just makes him mad. He's even started ridiculing me for being so "holy." I don't mind suffering for Christ, especially if it will help win my husband. What should I do?

Attitude toward suffering for good (1 Peter 3:8-12). In it all, our goal is to "live in harmony with one another" (v. 8). And how? "Be sympathetic, love as brothers, be compassionate and humble. Do not repay evil with evil or insult with insult, but with blessing, because to this you were called" (vv. 8-9).

It is so natural to strike back when we are treated unjustly, to focus our energy on anger and rebellion, and to rage against injustice and find ways to overthrow the person or system under which we live. But Peter called us to a different kind of life. Rather than exploding, we focus our energy on love.

Every human society has its share of evil. Each of us who are hurt or mistreated by the system might easily be drawn into endless crusades. It is not that we are to compromise with evil or fail to work for social change. However, *we are never to be drawn away from the first calling of holiness: to live God's love.* So Peter's concern is that unjust treatment never tempt us to return evil for evil, and forsake our commitment to good.

Compromise: 1 Peter 3:10–4:6

It is hard to grasp what Peter's teaching implies. Was he compromising with evil? Should we simply *adjust* to sin? Are we to be unmoved by injustice? To ignore society's festering sores?

To some who have read the prophets' ringing calls for justice—because God is committed to justice—Peter's stress on submission seems to contradict the Lord.

Romans 13. Yet Paul deals with the issue of submission, and in the same way. "Everyone must submit himself to the governing authorities" (v. 1), Paul said. Because human government is instituted by God for a good purpose, one who rebels against this authority is rebelling against what God has created.

Note that only rebellion is at issue here. Paul did not speak of changing governments or obtaining redress within existing law. Both he and Peter instructed believers not to *rebel,* even when they receive unfair treatment. The issue is not abstract. It is how we respond when someone in authority treats us unjustly.

Sovereignty. Peter's exhortation was grounded in theology. He went far beyond Jesus' example here. Peter's approach was rooted in the concept of a sovereign God—a God who permits injustice in our world and works His good purpose despite them. The conviction that God is sovereign underlies both of Peter's references to Jesus as our example of living with injustice. Now, tracing his argument, we are led to a totally new understanding of submission and suffering.

Christ, the Suffering Servant (1 Peter 2:18-25). In thinking of harsh treatment given a servant, Peter naturally thought of Jesus. Christ often spoke of Himself as a Servant (see Matt. 20). Like the harshly treated slaves of Peter's example, Jesus was persecuted by those He served—and for doing good. In this experience, Jesus never retaliated or threatened. He bore the insults and pain, even to Calvary. How did Jesus find the grace to respond righteously? The Bible says, "He entrusted Himself to Him who judges justly" (1 Peter 2:23). Jesus looked beyond the immediate circumstances and saw the sure, steady hand of God!

Christ acknowledged as Lord (1 Peter 3:10–4:6). In a carefully developed argument, Peter helped us understand his earlier reference to Jesus' committing Himself to God.

Peter began by explaining how a Christian is enabled to react with love rather than in anger. A quote from the Old Testament explains that "the eyes of the Lord are on the righteous, and His ears are attentive to their prayer" (3:12). God is carefully superintending the lives of His children.

This is especially important to remember in the unlikely circumstance that one suffers for doing what is good (vv. 13-14). Peter explained carefully how we are to respond in such a circumstance.

- First, don't be frightened.
- Second, remember and acknowledge in your heart that Christ is Lord.
- Third, be ready to explain why you are able to maintain a hopeful attitude despite the injustice.
- Fourth, maintain gentleness and respect in your response, keeping a clear conscience.
- Fifth, your behavior will shame those who have spoken evil of you.

Peter then comforted us. How much better it is to suffer for doing right than for doing wrong! This kind of suffering is truly Christlike. Jesus too suffered for sins that were not His (v. 10). In fact, Christ's death was the ultimate injustice: He was executed, instead of His persecutors who deserved to die. But God used this miscarriage of justice in a wonderful way! Through His death Jesus brought us to God. From tragedy and injustice, God brought good.

And this is the point! *When we do right and suffer for it, we can be sure that God intends to use our experience for good.* Whatever happens to members of God's family, we can be sure that our loving Father is at work for good.

The next passage, which seems obscure, should be understood as an analogy. Peter showed us the far-reaching extent of Jesus' work by going back to the great Genesis Flood, when an ark carried eight people through the waters of raging judgment. Jesus is our ark. In our union with Him—for this is the impact of "baptism"; (see 1 Cor. 12:13; Col. 2:12)—we have been lifted *beyond* fact, we have been delivered to a new life! *And we are to live this new life now.* Freed by Jesus from bondage to "evil human desires," we are to live our new lives by "the will of God" (1 Peter 4:2).

The analogy is a powerful one. Noah and his family were snatched from an old world that was destined for destruction. Carried safely through judgment's storms, their ark landed in a new world. Here great changes were made. The waters once suspended in the atmosphere had fallen to earth. Ecology had changed. Now, human government was instituted and man given meat to eat (see Gen. 9). Noah's family had to develop an entirely new way of life.

This is exactly the case with you and me. We have been snatched from an evil world dominated by Satan. As members of Christ's kingdom who now walk in light (1 Peter 2:9), we must learn to live in His new creation. Old things are to be put aside. Now our lives are to be according to the will of our God (4:6).

Submission? As Peter explained it, submission is not compromise. It is an expression of the Christian's confidence that Jesus is Lord. It is also an expression of our commitment to live by God's will rather than by the drives and passions of a lost humanity.

God's will may lead us into experiences of injustice. It did for Jesus. Yet, in Jesus' submission we find not only an example but also hope. Jesus' death and resurrection—accomplishing our salvation—made it plain that God worked His good through His Son's suffering. And He can work good through the suffering of His other children as well.

By committing ourselves to God when we suffer injustice, we let Him work in and through our lives.

And so submission *is* an aspect of holiness. Yes, holiness is love, and holiness is goodness. But holiness is also submission to the will of God when that will leads to the suffering of injustice. Love, goodness, and submission each demonstrate the fact that we are separated to God, and to Him alone.

TEACHING GUIDE

Prepare
How do you respond to the injustices you suffer in your own life?

Explore
1. Give a minilecture on the background of 1 Peter, and the teachings which he, Paul, and the writer of Hebrews all affirm, which set Christianity apart from both Gentile and Jewish culture. Use the study chart on page 1027.
2. Play "I've got a right to . . ." by having your group members predict how people might complete a number of sentences indicating a response to unjust treatment. See "link-to-life," page 1029.

Expand
1. Together study 1 Peter 2:18-25 and determine how Peter might complete the statements used in *explore* (2). Then divide into teams to determine how to counsel a woman with a difficult marriage on the basis of 1 Peter 3:1-7. See "link-to-life," page 1029.
2. Finally, work through 1 Peter 3:10–4:6 carefully. On the chalkboard make a list of "what to do when I suffer unjustly."

Apply
Ask God for grace to submit.

STUDY GUIDE 163

1 Peter 4:7–5:14

THE CALL TO SUFFER

Overview

Peter's first letter focused on the themes of submission and suffering. Yet the book is vibrant with optimism. We sense this tone in the opening chapter. Peter praised God

- for new birth
- for a living hope
- for an inheritance that can never perish
- for shielding by God's power.

In view of these great blessings we have joy, even though "now for a little while you may have had to suffer grief in all kinds of trials" (1:6).

Such trials are precious, for they are intended not to trip us up, but to demonstrate the genuineness of our faith, that when Jesus Christ comes He—and we—might receive praise, glory, and honor for our faithfulness.

So salvation does *not* promise an easy life here. Instead we can expect difficulties and trials. After all, Jesus Himself was not immune to suffering. And we are called to walk in His steps.

The subject of suffering is not a popular one. But it is an important one. For none of us is immune to the pain associated with our human frailties. How important to help those we teach come to see suffering in God's perspective, and so strengthen both their faith, and their hope.

■ For a verse-by-verse commentary on each reference to suffering in this Bible book, see the *Bible Knowledge Commentary,* pages 837-857.

Commentary

Throughout the later letters of our New Testament, hope predominates. We Christians have hope because of our participation in Christ. Even suffering changes when viewed as the continuation of Jesus' life on earth, and as the life He continues to live through members of the body.

And so Peter called us to "rejoice that you participate in the sufferings of Christ" (4:13). A Christian's suffering is no cause for shame. It is to be seen as God's hand at work in our lives, shaping and equipping us in wise discipline.

In thinking about our own suffering, it is instructive to remember what we read about Jesus in Hebrews. "Although He was a Son, He learned obedience from what He suffered and, once made perfect, He became the source of eternal salvation for all" (Heb. 5:8). Suffering was necessary to perfect Jesus for His role as sympathetic High Priest. Of course, Jesus was already perfect as God. But to become our High Priest, Christ had to experience human weakness.

We often misunderstand the nature of weakness. All too often we think of it as sin or as giving in to temptation. Not so. Our *weakness* is feeling the pressures life places on us. Our *flaw* is choosing to surrender to sin. Jesus did not choose sin. He was without flaw. But Jesus did know hunger and exhaustion. He knew the pain of rejection, and the hurt of ridicule. Jesus knew feelings of abandonment and felt the anger of those whose hearts fed on hate. In all this, Jesus suffered. And in all of it, He experienced what it means to be human. Having learned, He became our salvation.

It's very possible that suffering is necessary to perfect us in the same way. Jesus is the High Priest, but you and I are a royal and holy priesthood (1 Peter 2:5, 9). We not only participate in Christ's experiences, we participate in His ministry. And for us to sympathize, we need to know what it means to hurt.

This is an important thought. Our calling does not pull us *away* from the world. Instead, it leads us *to live Jesus' life in the world*! Jesus' ministry was to seek and to save. He never forgot the lost; instead He lifted them up to become sons.

Perhaps one good that God brings through our suffering is to remind us of our fellowmen—of the pains they know and the suffering they experience, without any source of joy. If we remember who we are, we may be moved to reach out as Jesus reached out. Instead of drawing away from those who sin, we reach out with a firm and loving grip and draw them to Jesus, who holds the door open wide.

♥ ***Link to Life: Youth / Adult***
Ask each person to jot down a word or two reminding them of at least three personal experiences of suffering. This can be physical suffering, emotional pain, whatever.

Then in groups of three, ask each person to share at least one of these experiences. How did it affect your life? How long did the experience last?

After each has shared, draw the whole group together again. Looking back, can your members see any good *which has come from the experience he or she talked about?*

From your group members' experiences, try to construct a list of different positive results that may come from suffering.

Pain and Suffering in Scripture
The ancient Stoic philosophers saw suffering as man's fate in an impersonal universe. Even the wisest have, throughout history, been forced to shrug off the question as unanswerable. And those who are antagonistic to God have argued that the very existence of suffering in a universe supposedly created by a good God proves that "God" either does not exist, or that He is not good.

Yet the Bible affirms God, and teaches both His power and goodness. And, in the context of a personal universe, the Bible speaks directly about human pain and suffering.

Pain and suffering in the Old Testament. The Hebrew language has many different words that communicate the ideas of pain and suffering. Here are some of the more frequently used:

*Ka'ab *emphasizes pain.* While physical pain is involved, words derived from *ka'ab* are most concerned with the mental anguish associated with hurt.

*'Asab *and its derivatives.* These words are translated as grief, sorrow, and wound. Here too both physical and mental pain are in view.

**Use of* hil. This is a graphic word that is very strong: it suggests writhing in agony, and is used of terror at disaster and extreme mental anguish.

A study of the use of these words in the Old Testament draws attention not to painful events themselves, but to how human beings are affected by life's tragedies. If it were only the bout with illness, or the loss of a job, or an unjust lawsuit, in itself, but the real suffering is in how such events affect us within—the doubts, the uncertainties, the fears, as the future we looked forward to seems dashed and all ahead black,

The Book of Job reminds us that while the Old Testament is sensitive to human suffering, it offers no easy answer. God permitted Satan to assault Job, a truly good man. Despite the most intense suffering Job maintained his trust in God—until three friends tried to explain *why.* Then Job too was catapulted into an attempt to explain his experience.

Job and his friends had an image of God as righteous Judge. So the friends concluded that Job's suffering must be a punishment from God. Job had not knowingly sinned, and so would not admit fault. Yet Job himself had no other explanation. Overwhelmed by what seemed betrayal by the God he trusted, Job began to challenge the beliefs of his friends about how the Lord works in human affairs.

Job's inability to explain his suffering, and the accusations of his "friends," brought the sufferer close to despair. How clearly we see in Job, stripped of hope and fearful in a universe he suddenly did not understand at all, reflections of our own feelings during times of intense personal suffering.

At the end of the Book of Job God did intervene. He restored Job, and corrected his friends. *But God did not explain.* Job was left without answers, to simply trust a God whose motives and purposes no human being can fully know.

There are, however, fascinating insights in the Old Testament. First, as Job illustrated, the reasons for the suffering of the good man are often hidden. We must simply trust God to bring good in the end, even as He restored and blessed Job.

Second, Job's friends were right in that *sometimes* suffering is associated with sin. God "does not leave the guilty unpunished" (Num. 14:18). Yet suffering can also be instruction: it can be a means of grace by which God shows the sinner his need for repentance. It was suffering which often led people to call on the Lord for relief (Isa. 14:3).

Third, several of the words for suffering in the Old Testament are associated with childbirth. The *Expository Dictionary of Bible Words* suggests that in Hebrew terms, "Pain's essence is summed up in the writhing body and straining muscles of the woman in the pain of childbirth. The image is theologically significant. It offers hope, in that the outcome of the pain is the emergence of fresh life into the world." God intends that our suffering will in some mysterious way give birth to good!

One other theme in the Old Testament is important. Isaiah looked ahead to the appearance of a "Suffering Servant." This Individual would come to do God's will, even though that will brought Him intense pain. If ever good was given birth in suffering, it was so in the death of Jesus. As Isaiah said:

> Surely He took up our infirmities and carried our sorrows, yet we considered Him stricken by God, smitten by Him, and afflicted. But He was pierced for our transgressions, He was crushed for our iniquities; the punishment that brought us peace was upon Him, and by His wounds we are healed. We all, like sheep, have gone astray, each of us has turned to his own way; and the Lord has laid on Him the iniquity of us all.
>
> Isaiah 53:4-6

Pain and suffering in the New Testament. There are many Greek words for pain and suffering in the New Testament, most with broad meanings that parallel those of the Old Testament.

But most New Testament references to suffering use the Greek word *pascho* and its derivatives. Strikingly, these words constantly are linked with the events associated with Jesus' crucifixion. He is the primary example of suffering, and in a study of Jesus' suffering we learn much about its nature.

Many of the special insights come from our Book of 1 Peter.

**Suffering and sin.* The Bible definitely links suffering and sin. In the Fall Adam and Eve, and all the human race, became subject to suffering. At times suffering is *directly* related to our own sin, in that suffering comes as a consequence or punishment of our own acts. A person who is imprisoned for a crime obviously is suffering both as a consequence of and as a punishment for his or her sins.

On the other hand, suffering is often *indirectly* related to sin. A person shot or injured by a criminal suffers not because he did something wrong, but because of the sin of another.

In our sin-cursed world we are subject to much suffering that is "unjust" in the sense that we suffer because of others' actions rather than our own. But, whomever's the fault, it is sin in our universe which is the cause.

Peter gives us the ultimate example of unjust suffering. He points out that Jesus suffered "the righteous for [*hyper,* lit. "on account of"] the unrighteous" (1 Peter 3:18). The sins for which Jesus suffered on the cross were not His own. In the immediate situation, it was the sins of Jesus' enemies among the Jews that brought about His pain. In the grand context of eternity, however, Jesus suffered because of your sins and mine. It was the sin of all humanity which brought Christ to the Cross.

So the Bible never suggests that our experience of pain and suffering will be "fair." Like Jesus, we will often suffer not for what we do but for what others have done, or simply because sin has warped society itself out of God's intended shape.

**Suffering and God.* While the Bible associates suffering with sin and sees sin as the basic cause, Scripture affirms that our Sovereign God is also involved.

We Christians are told, when overtaken by unexpected and unjust suffering, to "set apart Christ as Lord" (v. 15). We are to remember that God is Sovereign, and nothing is permitted to happen except by His will.

In looking again at Jesus we realize that His own suffering was "by God's set purpose and foreknowledge" (Acts 2:23).

**Suffering and purpose.* Again, the suffering of Jesus demonstrates that though an injustice, Jesus' suffering had a purpose. Through it God intended to bring us to

Him through the death of Christ (1 Peter 3:18).

So the suffering of Jesus teaches us important truths. Sin can be the indirect as well as direct cause of suffering. And when we suffer unjustly, God not only is sovereignly involved but also is at work through the experience, to bring about some good purpose of His own.

**Suffering and the Christian.* The New Testament does speak directly to the issue of the suffering saint.

First Peter 1:3-9 points out that the suffering we experience now demonstrates the genuineness of our faith and will bring glory when Jesus comes. Romans 5:3-4 adds that "suffering produces perseverance; perseverance, character; and character, hope." So suffering is intended to make a contribution to the inner transformation of the Christian.

First Peter 2:13-25 encourages us to bear up under unjust suffering, and commit ourselves to live good lives, "conscious of God" (v. 19). We are to remain aware that by living godly lives under pressure we follow Jesus' example and walk in His steps.

Paul even spoke of such suffering as fellowship (lit., "participation") in Christ. Christian suffering is associated with God's plan to complete the mission of Jesus in our world (see Phil. 3:10).

A Theology of Suffering?
Human suffering is and will remain largely a mystery. Yet from 1 Peter, which draws together so many themes seen in both Old and New Testaments, it is possible to develop a practical theology of suffering, which links God's view, purposes, and role in human suffering in a positive, redemptive view. The chart below identifies key verses in 1 Peter, from which a study group can work.

♥ ***Link to Life: Youth / Adult***
Give each person in your group a copy of the "Practical Theology of Suffering" chart. Divide into teams to first of all sum up Peter's teachings, and then to construct a series of 10 statements that express a Christian view of suffering.

Together: 1 Peter 4:7–5:11
Use of gifts (1 Peter 4:7-11). Peter reminded us that we can see in the very sins of our

A Practical Theology of Suffering

1 Peter passage	Teaching
1:3-6	
1:7-9	
2:18-20	
2:21-25	
3:10-18	
4:1-2	
4:12-19	
5:6-7	
5:10-11	

A Christian view of suffering

1.
2.
3.
4.
5.
6.
7.
8.
9.
10.

society which causes human sufferings the end of all things. God will judge. Until then, we believers must be deeply committed to each other, to help and encourage each other to keep on serving God.

Suffering (1 Peter 4:12-19). How much we need encouragement. Especially when we suffer as Christians, experiencing pain unjustly. Then the encouragement we receive, will help us commit ourselves to our "faithful Creator and continue to do good."

Authority in church (1 Peter 5:1-4). We have seen many exhortations in Peter about living under authority. Peter now advised those in authority in the church. Leaders are to provide an example to the flock. Autocracy, selfish motives—none of these are appropriate for those who walk in Jesus' way.

Submission and humility (1 Peter 5:5-6). Submission within the church and humility in all relationships is fitting for Christians. We live under authority in every aspect of our lives.

God's care (1 Peter 5:7). Is submission surrender? Not at all. As we have seen, submission is an expression of trust in a sovereign God. Knowing that God is *God,* we can cast all our anxieties on Him, because He does care for us.

The devil (1 Peter 5:8-9). Satan will attack the church's ways of life. But we are equipped to resist.

Finally, Peter gave his benediction. It's a reminder of the glory and power that suffuses and transforms all the suffering we might know.

> The God of all grace, who called you to His eternal glory in Christ, after you have suffered a little while, will Himself restore you and make you strong, firm and steadfast. To Him be the power forever and ever. Amen.
>
> 1 Peter 5:10-11

TEACHING GUIDE

Prepare

Study 1 Peter and fill in the chart to be used in your group session.

Explore

Divide your group into teams to share experiences they have had with suffering, and to see what good may have come from their pain. See "link-to-life," page 1033 for a process.

This activity can have many benefits in relationship-building as well as in gaining insights into God's way of working through suffering.

Expand

1. Engage your group in direct Bible study, designed to help them develop from 1 Peter a distinctively Christian view of suffering. Use the chart provided on page 1035.
2. After hearing from the study teams, work together to develop 10 statements that sum up the Christian perspective on suffering. Be ready to supplement with insights from other passages, discussed in this study guide's commentary.

Apply

Pray together, thanking God specifically for the way He has used suffering in your lives.

STUDY GUIDE 164

2 Peter; Jude

DANGER!

Overview

The later letters from the New Testament era show a growing awareness of dangers facing the young church. In 2 Timothy, the last letter Paul wrote before his death, we find grim warnings about false teachers and a growing pollution of the church. Now, in two other late letters, one written by Peter and one by Jude, we discover the same strong note of warning.

Because 2 Peter and Jude are so closely linked, not only in theme but also in specific content, it is helpful to teach and study them together.

Most believe 2 Peter was written just before the apostle's death, in A.D. 67 or 68. Jude may have been written as many as 10 or 15 years later.

While 1 Peter deals with dangers from outsiders hostile to the Christian community, 2 Peter and Jude examine dangers that emerge from within. Each book warns us about the same two problems: the emergence of false teachers, and of false teaching.

For anyone concerned today with heresy, or with recognizing false teachers and cults, these two books are extremely valuable. They are also helpful to the average Christian, for they call us back to the simplicity of a godly life, and teach us to commit ourselves to loving God and doing good.

■ For a verse-by-verse commentary on each of these short New Testament books, see the *Bible Knowledge Commentary,* pages 859-879 and 917-924.

Commentary

One of my family's favorite TV series used to be "Lost in Space." The Robinsons, two passengers, and a friendly robot moved through the galaxy facing new threats each week. When the robot sensed some dark, mysterious force approaching, he would shout out, "Danger! Danger! Danger!"

In the last half the first century, a threat far more sinister than those dreamed up by TV scriptwriters assailed the churches. The two short books of 2 Peter and Jude were written to sound an urgent alarm. As we move on in time (rather than in space), we too need to be alerted to spiritual dangers and be prepared to meet them.

Peter and Jude

Who were these two men, and what was the historical context in which they wrote?

Peter. The writer is, of course, the most prominent of the Twelve in the Gospels and the dominant figure in the early chapters of Acts. This is the second of two letters Peter wrote to the early church. It too is a "last days" letter, written at the end of the apostle's career.

According to the early church historian, Eusebius, Peter was martyred during Nero's persecutions (about A.D. 67–68). The letter was most likely written one of these years.

Heresy was clearly threatening the church, a heresy that challenged both doctrine and lifestyle. The books of 2 Peter, Jude, and 2 Timothy all contain clear teaching that combats this danger.

Jude. The writer's identification of himself in verse 1 and in early church tradition have led to the conviction that Jude was a younger brother of the James who led the Jerusalem church, and thus was a younger half-brother of Jesus. It is very difficult to establish a date for Jude's short letter; suggested dates range from the late 60s to the 80s. The similarity with 2 Peter does not indicate that one copies the other. Instead it suggests how widespread the threat within the church had become, and that there was a common body of teaching to help congregations deal with such dangers.

Paul's Concern

Actually, early words of warning come from

Paul in 2 Timothy, as well as from Jude and Peter. Paul warned Timothy of the teachers who have "wandered away from the truth" (2:18). He spoke of "terrible times" when "people will be lovers of themselves, lovers of money, boastful, proud, abusive, disobedient to their parents, ungrateful, unholy, without love, unforgiving, slanderous, without self-control, brutal, not lovers of the good, treacherous, rash, conceited, lovers of pleasure rather than lovers of God." Worst of all, these people will retain "a form of godliness but denying its power" (3:1-5). While Timothy was to teach, correct, rebuke, and encourage with "great patience and careful instruction," he was also to realize that "the time will come when men will not put up with sound doctrine." They will instead shape doctrine to "suit their own desires" (4:2-3).

Times of stress are coming. Christians must recognize the signs of danger and be prepared to protect the purity of the church.

Persecution. When Paul, Peter, and Jude were writing these letters, danger signs were all around. Gentile nations had recognized Christianity as a faith distinct from Judaism, and the Jews had also become hateful and envious.

Other sources of opposition existed. In 2 Timothy Paul mentioned Alexander the metalworker, who did him "a great deal of harm" (4:14). He was probably one of those whose living came from selling images of the gods. His livelihood was threatened by the growing Christian movement. Later even the butchers who sold meat for pagan sacrifices lost income because the people were forsaking the temples. The Emperor Nero would soon formally accuse Christians of "hatred of mankind" and put many of them to horrible deaths.

The Roman world was used to multiple faiths, all tolerated and existing side by side. Just as in the modern East a person may be both a Buddhist and Shintoist, the Roman world saw no problem with one person worshiping many gods or having several religions. Christianity challenged this ethos. The Christians refused to worship the emperor, which left them open to the charge of treason. They disturbed families with their insistence on total allegiance to one God. Many refused to serve in the military and to worship the legion eagles. All in all, Christians were becoming a disruptive force in society. Often in the next decades local magistrates would initiate persecutions against these strange and unpopular people.

By the time of Trajan (about A.D. 100), problems caused for the empire by the spread of Christianity were serious. Pliny the Younger, governor of Bithynia around A.D. 112, executed a number of Christians. Then he wrote to the emperor asking for advice and instruction. Trajan instructed Pliny that those who admitted they were Christians and refused to give up their belief were to be executed. But the governor should not hunt Christians down or accept anonymous accusations. And, of course, any Christian willing to give up his or her faith and offer sacrifice to the emperor was to be released.

Within 30 years after Jude's and Peter's letters, Christians would face a world in which their faith was itself adequate cause for execution! Yet, as we read these "last letters" of the Bible, we note a strange thing. *The danger that most concerned the apostles is not the danger from without!* They were confident that, when believers were called before judges, God would stand beside them and give them the words for their defense (see Matt. 5:11, 44; 10:17-20; Luke 21:12-19; John 15:20-21; Acts 4:1-31). Throughout history, persecution has tended to strengthen rather than weaken the church. We see in fact that the great danger to Christians does not live in the antagonism of outsiders at all!

Perversion. The great danger to the early church, as to us today, is that what is central in the life of the corporate body might be perverted. Outsiders can never prevail against the body of Christ. But if the church is to remain strong and vital, it must be strong *within.* And inner strength depends on sustaining sound doctrine *and* a godly lifestyle.

Paul warned Timothy that opposition will come from "men of depraved minds" (2 Tim. 3:8).

"There will be false teachers among you," Peter then warned. These "will secretly introduce destructive heresies. . . . Many will follow their shameful ways and bring the way of truth into disrepute" (2 Peter 2:1-2).

Jude appealed to the church to contend for the faith, "For certain men . . . have secretly slipped in among you. They are godless men, who change the grace of our God into a license for immorality and deny Jesus Christ our only Sovereign and Lord" (v. 4).

Each of these letters warns against the twin threats of false teaching and ungodly living *within* the church.

Twin Threats

It helps us, in reading 2 Peter and Jude, to have an overview of the nature of the dangers with which they are concerned. Let's look at each threat separately.

False teaching. There was a body of teaching or doctrine, entrusted by God to the prophets and apostles and recorded in the Scriptures (2 Peter 3:2). A number of false teachings are mentioned in these letters and in 2 Timothy. Paul pointed out the mistaken belief that the resurrection of believers had already occurred. Peter warned against those who question Jesus' second coming and the certainty of the final judgment (2 Peter 3:6-10). However, both Peter and Jude made it clear that the critical heresy that threatened the church had to do with who Jesus is. The godless men who secretly slipped into the fellowship change God's grace and "deny Jesus Christ our only Sovereign and Lord" (Jude 4). Peter insisted,"We did not follow cleverly invented stories when we told you about the power and coming of our Lord Jesus Christ" (2 Peter 1:16). The false teachers who secretly introduced destructive heresies were actually "denying the Sovereign Lord who bought them" (2:1).

The crucial doctrinal danger is to deny Jesus as Sovereign Lord.

We can understand why. The New Testament teaches that Jesus is the center of our faith, our life, and hope. Continuing in a personal relationship with Jesus is the only means we have to break the hold of sin or to give us freedom from tension, fear, or guilt. Christians have no power in themselves to produce a life of wholeness.

Any teaching or doctrine that denies Jesus Christ His primacy or reduces Him to less than God robs Him of His glory, and us of our hope. Such a system of belief is what Paul calls a counterfeit faith.

An ungodly life. While the necessity for sound doctrine is much in the minds of Peter and Jude in these warning letters, it's clear that they warn against moral decline even more. Just as Paul insisted that leaders be chosen for their spiritual maturity, so Jude and Peter warned against leaders whose lifestyles mark them off as perverters.

A number of terms and concepts here need explanation, lest we think an ungodly way of life is simply a life of gross and open sin. For instance, what is the "depraved mind" Paul speaks of? (2 Tim. 3:8) And what are the "passions" or "evil desires" that find such frequent mention in these letters?

The Greek word translated "mind" here is *nous,* and is much more than intelligence, or the organ of thought. Greek scholars point out that this term refers to the sum total of the mental and moral outlook or state of being. We might call the biblical "mind" an attitude, a perspective, a way of thinking about and approaching life.

Is there a distinctively Christian life perspective? Of course there is. We are to find worth and importance in people rather than things. We are to love, not to use or abuse others. The Christian perspective measures material against eternal values, and finds the unseen more real than the visible. The Christian outlook on life enjoys holiness and finds sin uncomfortable; it rejects instinctual responses in favor of self-control. By loving God and others, a Christian finds fulfillment that no other focus for life could possibly provide.

Anything that draws us from this distinctive Christian perspective on life is a dangerous threat to the church. Only by building our lives on God's values can we find the holiness that gives the Christian fellowship its vitality and its power.

What may draw us into the world of illusion that is secular society's "mind"? Jude and Peter spoke often of passions and instinctual desires. It would be a mistake to understand these as merely sexual terms. The word translated "passions" or "desires" is a Greek word *epithumia.* In classical Greek the term is morally neutral; it simply means "desire." It could mean having a longing for something worthwhile, or it could imply desiring a forbidden object.

When a person enters into a friendship with Jesus, he gets a new life in which the old desires, thoughts, and choices are to be transformed. The "desires" (*epithumia*) that concerned Paul, Peter, and Jude are leftover drives and stirring passions of our old way of life. Peter identifies them as "the evil desires you had when you lived in ignorance" (1 Peter 1:14). We are not to conform to them or be "enslaved" by all kinds of passions and pleasures (Titus 3:3).

It's not wrong for a Christian to have feelings and wants. After all, God Himself promises that He will give us "the desires of our heart" (Ps. 37:4). We are free to move toward that which we want deeply; and as we live with God, He Himself will cause us to desire His best (see 103:5).

One difficult lesson for an astronaut to learn is that his old physical reactions, adapted to earth's gravity pull, are inappropriate in weightlessness. He takes a normal step, and bounds off the floor, He needs to learn to shuffle his feet to keep contact between magnetic shoes and the metal spacecraft. He grasps a wrench to turn a bolt, and finds himself, not the bolt, turned by the force he exerts. In his new environment the astronaut's old instinctive reactions are wrong!

The Christian too lives in a new environment: a kingdom ruled over by God's dear Son. The desires that shaped our perspective before we knew Christ produce the wrong responses now. Thus Peter and Jude warned us against men who claim to be spiritual leaders but whose lifestyles indicate that they "follow the corrupt desire of the sinful natures" (2 Peter 2:10) and react "like brute beasts, creatures of instinct" (v. 12), their personalities shaped by the *epithumia* of fallen humanity.

The real threat to the church is not persecution from without but corruption from within. How can we recognize this danger? Corruption from within involves a desertion of sound doctrine. When we "reinterpret" or reject the apostolic teaching recorded in Scripture, and especially when we deny the central teaching of Scripture about the person and work of Jesus, we wander from the truth and place our generation in jeopardy.

But corruption from within also involves a retreat from a holy life. When we begin to respond to life situations as instinct tells us, motivated by the old *epithumia* that gripped us before we knew Jesus, our whole perspective becomes warped. The Bible says it: "Do not conform any longer to the pattern of this world, but be transformed by the renewing of your mind [*nous*]" (Rom. 12:2). We must understand that a commitment to both sound doctrine and a godly life is essential, not only for church leaders, but for all believers. Any retreat from either, and we hear, through Peter and Jude, God's own danger alarm.

♥ ***Link to Life: Youth / Adult***
Give a minilecture summarizing the concerns of these later New Testament letter writers. Quote from 2 Timothy to illustrate themes. Then ask each person in your group to quickly *read through one of these books (Jude or 2 Peter) and to* circle the number *of the verses which speak about either the teaching or the ways of false teachers.*

If you wish you may want to divide the tasks: give different members single chapters, or have half look for false teachers' doctrines and half for false teachers' ways.

When each has finished this task, ask for first impressions of the books. How might their message be described in a single sentence?

Your goal in this introductory activity is to simply familiarize your group members with the books as a whole, as a prelude to closer examination of specific themes.

A Positive Christian Life

In our next study we will look carefully at these books' descriptions of false teachers and false teaching. For now it is important to note that we have protection against the influence of evil within. *In a sense, there are certain commitments of the Christian which immunize him or her from the threats of false teaching!*

Productive lives (2 Peter 1:1-11). God has given Jesus' people great promises and gifts. These provide "everything we need for life and godliness through our knowledge of Him" (v. 3). Through God's provision we partake of the divine nature and thus "escape the corruption in the world caused by evil desires" (v. 4).

Our first protection against corrupting influences from within is a commitment to that godliness which God's work in Christ has made possible for us. Peter calls on us to "make every effort" to develop qualities that reflect God's nature. These qualities are (vv. 5-7):

- faith — as full commitment to Christian teaching.
- goodness — literally, "virtue," or moral excellence.

• knowledge	as understanding drawn from God's revelation.
• self-control	as the ability to "hold yourself in."
• perseverance	as steadfastness in the face of opposition.
• godliness	as conduct that shows we are aware of God's presence.
• brotherly kindness	as a real affection for our fellow Christians.
• love	as a real commitment to do good to others.

Such qualities will "keep you from being ineffective and unproductive in your knowledge of our Lord Jesus Christ" (v. 8).

The person who is fully committed to living for Jesus is unlikely to be drawn away to follow false teachers or false teaching. It is rather the lukewarm and indifferent Christian who is susceptible.

God's sure Word (2 Peter 1:12-21). A parallel line of defense is full confidence in "the truth you now have" (v. 12). Peter reminded us how great a confidence we can have in the Scriptures, whose prophetic words about Jesus have proven true, thus demonstrating that the Spirit truly "carried along" Scripture's writers so that the Word has its origin in the will of God.

A vision of reality (2 Peter 3:1-13). Unlike those who scoff, we know that this present world will be destroyed. Looking forward to that great cataclysm we fix our hope not on anything in this material universe but on the new heaven and earth God will create. Our vision of the future, and values shaped by the expectation of Christ's return, motivate us to live "holy and godly lives."

Persevering in the faith (Jude 20-22). Jude closed his letter with a description of the life to which we are to commit ourselves. As we focus on these things, we will be immune to the appeal of false teachers and false teaching.

What are we to concentrate on? Praying. Keeping ourselves in God's love (which 1 John 5:1-4 defines as loving one another and obeying the Lord). Looking expectantly toward Jesus' coming. Being merciful to those who waver, and seeking to snatch them from judgment even while keeping clear of all that corrupts them.

If we lead lives like this, we and the church itself will be safe from all influences that would corrupt.

TEACHING GUIDE

Prepare

Study 2 Timothy as well as Jude and 2 Peter, and prepare a 15- to 20-minute lecture on the background of these "warning" letters.

Explore

Have your group members read quickly through 2 Peter and Jude to identify verses that deal with false teachings and false teacher's lifestyles. See "link-to-life," page 1040.

Expand

1. Promise that next session you will look in depth at false teachers and false teaching. Give your group members an assignment, to be completed before the next session. Each should reread these short books and try to determine:

- characteristics of false teachers
- the appeal of false teaching
- false doctrines that were taught
- a correct response to false teaching.

2. Work through the four passages discussed in the commentary which teach how we can protect ourselves against false teachers and false teaching.

Apply

Share: "What do you feel is your best defense personally against false teachers or false teaching? Why did you select this particular one?"

STUDY GUIDE 165

2 Peter; Jude

HERESY

Overview

Throughout church history, many who have been labeled heretics have been tortured and put to death, or driven from their homes. Even Luther called on the princes to repress a peasants' movement for equality in his day. And Calvin did not hesitate to affirm the death penalty for an early unitarian in Geneva.

But often those called heretics by the majority were the true believers! The followers of Huss were brutally repressed by the church, and the Huguenots (French Protestants) were mercilessly massacred. Wars on the continent and even in England were often motivated, or at least justified, by religion.

This raises a question. What is heresy, and who is the heretic? How is the church to guard against heresy? And how is the heretic to be treated?

These may seem irrelevant questions in our society. We value tolerance so much that taking a stand for truth, or for righteousness, is foreign to us. Yet the early church did take a stand, in a society much like our own. The early Christians insisted that Jesus is the only way to God.

Certainly we do not execute heretics today, and we do not persecute those who differ from us. We don't want to. But we should be able to recognize heresy. And we should know how to respond to false teachers, like those against whom Jude and Peter warned, who creep into the church today, to introduce their still "destructive heresies" (2 Peter 2:1).

Commentary

The *Random House Unabridged Dictionary* defines *heresy* as an "opinion or doctrine at variance with the orthodox or accepted doctrine." In Roman Catholic tradition, the reference continues, a heretic is "a baptized Roman Catholic who willfully and persistently rejects any article of faith." Both these definitions focus attention on doctrine, but in Scripture the word has a wider application.

The Greek word from which *heretic* derives is *hairesis,* and means "sect, party, or school" (as of a school of philosophy). It was used of the "party of the Pharisees" in Acts 15:5, which Paul called "the strictest sect of our religion" (26:5). In the Christian movement heresy came to refer to a dissenting faction or group holding some opinion or dogma that marked them off from the rest of the body (1 Cor. 11:18-19; Gal. 5:20). In essence, heretics seem to be individuals within the church who hold to some way of thinking or living that sets them off from scriptural doctrine, lifestyle, and fellowship.

As we saw in our last study, factions may develop over various teachings such as the Resurrection or the Second Coming, but the truly critical element in "destructive heresies" has to do with the person of Christ. No doctrine that fails to give Jesus preeminence as God and Sovereign Lord can be considered "Christian."

But heresy also involves variation in lifestyle. God's people are called to holiness. When we desert Christian attitudes and values, turning to a licentious following of old impulses and desires, we have also fallen into heresy. We have become a faction, dividing the body.

An Overview of Jude: Jude 1-2

Even a cursory reading of Jude helps us sense how serious heresy is.

Godless men (Jude 3-4). Jude intended to write an encouraging letter, but felt compelled to urge his readers to resist "godless men" who had "slipped in among you" and who both denied Jesus and twisted grace into a license for immorality.

Judgment (Jude 5-7). Jude reviewed God's

acts of judgment, and warned against modern outbreaks of immorality.

False teachers (Jude 8-10). Jude portrayed the false teachers as ignorant of spiritual realities, reacting as "unreasoning animals" in that they were driven by instincts rather than higher faculties. This failing was reflected in their contempt for authority. The reference to a dispute about the "body of Moses" in verse 9 is to a book called the *Assumption of Moses*. Jude did *not* suggest this book is Scripture: his point was that even in devotional literature a powerful angel like Michael does not show contempt for an angel of higher rank, Satan, but waits for the Lord to rebuke him.

History of rebellion (Jude 11-13). Like Cain, these leaders harmed their brothers. Like Balaam they were moved by a passion for money. Like Korah they wanted to be leaders though God did not call them for leadership. Each of these suffered judgment—and so were the false teachers who troubled the church.

Enoch's prophecy (Jude 14-16). Jude again referred to well-known devotional literature. Even here God is known as One who will judge the ungodly.

Perseverance (Jude 17-23). The writer closed with a call to the true believers to persevere, faithful to and contending for the truth of the Gospel.

Analysis of Heresy: 2 Peter; Jude

When we study the details of the Book of Jude, and compare them with 2 Peter, we gain a clear picture of false teachers and false teaching.

Characteristics of false teachers. Paul instructed Timothy and Titus to officially recognize those in the churches who had matured in the faith and who demonstrated their reliability by adhering to sound doctrine, and by living exemplary Christian lives. Now Peter and Jude identified false teachers by the opposite characteristics.

False teachers claim a special knowledge or interpretation that differs from the common core of belief in the Christian community. They charge that the doctrine recorded in Scripture is "cleverly invented stories" (2 Peter 1:16). They also reject the authority of Scripture, and of the present leaders of the Christian community (2:10; Jude 8, 10). False teachers can be recognized by their insistence that they alone have the truth. Sooner or later in their denial of apostolic teaching they attack the person of Jesus, and seek to rob Him of His centrality.

False teachers also claim freedom to live a life moved by the old passions. They are competitive. Rather than serve, they use and exploit others. They rationalize their immorality and "are grumblers and faultfinders; they follow their own evil desires; they boast about themselves and flatter others for their own advantage" (v. 16). At every point their characters lack the qualities Paul said are to be found in spiritual leaders.

Jude warned that some "have secretly slipped in among you" (v. 4), which implied that neither the false teaching nor the sinful lifestyle may be evident initially. No wonder Paul warned that those considered for leadership "must first be tested" and then serve an apprenticeship as deacons "if there is nothing against them" (1 Tim. 3:10). He pointed out that while "the sins of some men are obvious," the "sins of others trail behind them" (5:24). Because flaws of character are not always readily apparent, selecting church leaders should never be a hasty or careless process.

Appeal of false teachers. How does it happen that those who introduce heresies all too often find followers within the church?

First, it's clear that their appeal is to the immature: those who are not deeply grounded in sound doctrine or the fellowship of the church. No wonder Peter began his letter with the exhortation to "make every effort to add to your faith goodness; and to goodness, knowledge; and to knowledge, self-control; and to self-control, perseverance; and to perseverance, godliness; and to godliness, brotherly kindness; and to brotherly kindness, love. For if you possess these qualities in increasing measure, they will keep you from being ineffective and unproductive in your knowledge of our Lord Jesus Christ" (2 Peter 1:5-8) Growth in the disciplines of the Christian life must follow our initial step of faith if we are to resist the lure of false teachers.

But what *is* their appeal? In part it is an appeal to pride in a superior and special knowledge that sets some apart from others. "They may believe that, but *we* know better!" Yet the main thrust of heresy's appeal seems to lie in its promise of freedom to indulge our instinctual desires. "They mouth empty, boastful words," Peter said, "and, by appealing to the lustful desires of sinful human nature, they entice people who are just escaping from those who live in error. They promise them freedom, while they themselves are slaves of depravity—for a man is a slave to whatever has mastered him" (2 Peter 2:18-19). Certainly it is inviting to "follow mere natural instincts" (Jude 19). It's hard to surrender our desires to God for reshaping and to deny ourselves the sensations our old way of life has led us to crave. The false teacher justifies any and all behavior by corrupting God's grace into a "license for immorality" (v. 4).

Some time ago on a talk show, a young challenger insisted to Billy Graham that sexual intercourse was the same as a ham sandwich. Sex and hunger are both "natural" desires, he argued: when you feel a desire, you satisfy it. After all, if God has made an experience pleasurable, then it must be good.

The false teacher seeks to encourage within the church a passion for pleasure that draws people away from the life of holiness and self-control to which the Christian is called. Some will become "lovers of pleasure rather than lovers of God," Paul warned (2 Tim. 3:4)

Yet the Christian life is not a miserable withdrawal or a dreary denial of every pleasant thing. But we are to find our pleasure in what God calls holy, not in distorted passions and desires. Scripture promises, "At Thy right hand there are pleasures forevermore" (Ps. 16:11, KJV).

Any invitation to share a special revelation that the rest of the church does not possess, or any promise of freedom to indulge our every "natural" desire with God's blessing, should be a warning to us. We may have met a false teacher who seeks to shatter the oneness of the body in which God has placed us.

♥ ***Link to Life: Youth / Adult***
Each group member was asked to read these two short epistles in preparation for this session. Each was to identify characteristics of the false teacher and false teaching.

Divide into teams to compare findings. Each team should be sure to include characteristics of doctrine, personality characteristics (2 Peter 2:10, 15; Jude 4, 12, 16, 19), and characteristics of their ministry (2 Peter 2:17; Jude 16).

If your group did not *prepare beforehand, assign 2 Peter and Jude to teams for study at the beginning of your session.*

Our Response to False Teachers
Jude tells us that we are to "contend" for the faith. To some in history, contending for the faith has meant to attack those who deviate from sound doctrine. Such an approach led to men and women burned at the stake, to wars, and inquisitions fashioned in order to enforce conformity. Yet there is no hint in the Bible of a crusade to exclude the deviate. How then do we "contend"? Here are several principles from these letters to help us.

Stand on unshakable foundations. Paul reminded Timothy that in spite of doctrinal challenges from Hymenaeus and Philetus, who have wandered away from the truth. . . . God's solid foundation stands firm, sealed with this inscription: "The Lord knows those who are His," and, "Everyone who confesses the name of the Lord must turn away from wickedness" (2 Tim. 2:17-19).

We may proceed with the firm conviction that, while we may be uncertain who belongs to the Lord, He does know. But at the same time, one who confesses the name of the Lord "must turn away from wickedness." *Open sin* calls for judgment and discipline in the Christian community.

Give gentle instruction. Rather than trying to silence the false teacher with shouting, Paul instructed, "Don't have anything to do with foolish and stupid arguments" (v. 23). Debate may be exciting, but it is not productive. Instead, the leaders of the Christian community are to "gently instruct" those who oppose (v. 25). We prayerfully communicate sound doctrine "in the hope that God will grant them repentance leading them to a knowledge of the truth, and that they will come to their senses and escape from the trap of the devil, who has taken them captive to do his will" (vv. 25-26).

The fleshly approach of the false teacher is to attack, challenge authority, ridicule, strike out, and abuse. The Christian must respond with love, recognizing that he is not battling against an enemy but *for* a fellow human being. In this spiritual confrontation, the warfare is between God and Satan. As for us, we are to simply "be merciful to those who doubt, snatch others from the fire and save them; to others show mercy mixed with fear—hating even the clothing stained by corrupted flesh" (Jude 22-23).

Depend on divine judgment. Our response to heretical challenges to the Christian community should not be confused with compromise. There can be no retreat from truth, *or* withdrawal of love. God "knows how to rescue godly men from trials and to hold the unrighteous for the day of judgment" (2 Peter 2:9). Both in this life and the life to come, the Lord involves Himself directly in the judgment of those who persistently rebel against Him. We can trust the false teacher to God and be free to concentrate on building ourselves up in the faith.

These letters then not only warn of dangers from within the church but also describe safeguards. If we as individuals and fellowships are firmly committed to these principles, we can be confident that we will be immune to any heresy which might appear. So let's:

- Be aware of the characteristic of false teachers and false teaching, so we can recognize and reject each.
- Follow only leaders who meet the qualifications given by Paul in his letters to Timothy and Titus.
- Study to understand the apostolic doctrine preserved for us in Scripture.
- And commit ourselves to the holy way of life and the unique values to which God calls us in His Word.

♥ ***Link to Life: Youth / Adult***
Give a minilecture summing up how we are to respond to false teachers and false teaching, and the safeguards God has provided for us. Draw on 2 Timothy as well as Jude and 2 Peter, as in the commentary.

2 Peter

To see even more fully God's plan of protection for His own, we'll trace the thought of 2 Peter.

Peter began by reminding us that God "has given us everything we need for life and godliness through our knowledge of Him who called us by His own glory and goodness" (1:3). Jesus is sufficient; we don't need to look for something beyond a relationship with Him. Chapter 2 is devoted to a description of false teachers and their end. Chapters 1 and 3 encourage and exhort believers, showing us how to avoid the growing dangers from within.

Growth vital (2 Peter 1:5-11). The faith that brings us into relationship with God marks only the beginning of our life with Him. We are to concentrate on maturing in character so that we are no longer attracted by the false teacher's alluring promise of liberty. If you do these things," Peter said, "you will never fall" (v. 10).

Apostolic teaching trustworthy (2 Peter 1:12-21). Peter reminded the readers that the sound doctrine of the church is rooted in reality. The apostles did not relate "cleverly invented stories" but communicated historical facts to which they were eyewitnesses. All they reported is in harmony with the prophetic Word of the Old Testament. The two Testaments stand as one, giving sure witness to the foundational truths of the church.

In this passage one phrase of verse 20 has been puzzling. The *New International Version* translates it "no prophecy of Scripture came about by the prophet's own interpretation," while the *King James Version* renders it "no prophecy of the Scripture is of any private interpretation." The original Greek supports either of these renderings, and both have suggestive implications. In the first case, we are reminded that it is God who spoke through His prophets and apostles. The Word is trustworthy because it is His own. In the second we are reminded that a false teacher may quote Scripture but give his own interpretation, which will differ from what the whole Bible teaches and from what the church has historically taught. When a sect, such as Jehovah's Witnesses, presents its own distinctive interpretation of Bible passages to deny the deity of Christ, we can look to the Word itself to refute the heresy. We can also look to the church as a whole, past and present, to see the voice of faith universally affirm that these verses teach that Jesus *is* God, fully human, and yet one with the Father from all eternity.

While there have been, and are, differences in interpretation of minor details of doctrine, the core of apostolic faith, as represented in the Apostle's Creed, has been the joyful affirmation of the church universal.

Judgment coming (2 Peter 3). This chapter is a striking affirmation of the trustworthiness of God's Word. Looking across the coming generations, Peter warned scoffers who will doubt Christ's return and question the certainty of judgment. They will insist that "since our fathers died, everything goes on as it has since the beginning of Creation" (v. 4). Yet God *did* intervene in the past to destroy the world in judgment, and this same God will intervene again, to destroy the works of human society (vv. 10-13).

We are not to let scoffers shake us from our certainty that Jesus will keep His promises. Because this universe will pass out of existence, we are to concentrate on that which is eternal. "So then, dear friends," Peter urged, "since you are looking forward to this, make every effort to be found spotless, blameless, and at peace with Him" (v. 14).

As we concentrate every effort on pleasing Him who has delivered us into the kingdom of Jesus Christ, we will be untouched by the lure of false teachers. They offer only the fleeting pleasures of a world that will someday flare up, and then burn out.

♥ ***Link to Life: Youth / Adult***
Help your group sense the meaning of the coming destruction of this universe.

Have teams of five brainstorm for five minutes to generate a "complete list" of things we value. Give a few launching suggestions—our homes, a favorite vacation spot, a close friendship, etc.

Write a combined list on the chalkboard for later analysis.

Then work through 2 Peter 3 together, answering the following questions:

- *What is the basic attitude of "scoffers" to this world? Their attitude toward God? What might we suppose their values might be?*
- *What according to Scripture is the destiny of this world?*
- *What is to be the basic attitude of believers toward this world? Toward God?*

When your group members have come up with their answers to these questions, look at the list of "things we value." Work down the list, item by item. In view of what Peter wrote, what does your group think of each "valuable" thing?

Some valid conclusions that your group members may draw include: • It is not wrong to appreciate any of God's good gifts, the temporary as well as the eternal. • It is best to concentrate our efforts on those things which have eternal value. • Most important of all is concentrating every effort "to be found spotless, blameless, and at peace with" God.

TEACHING GUIDE

Prepare
You may wish to give a brief report on any cults active in your area, and their teachings.

Explore
1. Encourage any group members who may have once been influenced by false teaching to tell about the experience. What were the false teachers like? What did they teach? How and why were you influenced? What led you back to sound teaching and fellowship?
2. Hear reports from those who prepared for class, or divide into teams for direct Bible study of false teachers and teaching in Jude and 2 Peter 2. See "link-to-life," page 1044.

Expand
1. Give a minilecture on how we are to respond to false teachers and false teaching, and how God guards us against it.
2. Or give a minilecture on cults that are active in your area. Focus on the key heresy—their view of Jesus.
3. Or look together at 2 Peter 3, and help your group members evaluate the impact on their own lives of "sound doctrine" concerning the Second Coming.

Apply
Discuss together: "What can we do to guard our family, friends, and church against false teaching?"

STUDY GUIDE 166

1 John 1:1–2:2

WALKING WITH GOD

Overview

John's letters are probably the last written of our New Testament. Despite the persecution of the last part of the first century, John's warm, pastoral letters call Christians to live a life of simple love and obedience. It is the inner life of the man and woman of God that concerned John, for the deepest issues of life lie within.

John's letters are not closely reasoned or marked by step-by-step arguments. Instead, John stated and then returned again and again to the themes that concerned him—themes like light, love, and truth. In simple, powerful prose John reminded us of the basic truths that shape our lives and relationship with the Lord.

Outline

I. Invitation to Joy	1:1-4
II. Walking in the Light	1:5–2:29
A. Being honest	1:5–2:2
B. Being loving	2:3-11
C. Being separate	2:12-17
D. Being alert	2:18-29
III. Walking in Love	3:1–4:19
A. Children of God	3:1-10
B. Caring for others	3:11-20
C. Confidence	3:21-24
D. Allegiance	4:1-6
E. God's love	4:7-21
IV. Walking by Faith	5:1-21
A. We have eternal life	5:1-2
B. We know God hears us	5:13-15
C. We are freed	5:16-21

Commentary

It's quite easy to sense the personalities of Peter and Paul from material in the New Testament. In the Gospels bombastic Peter blurted out his first thoughts; in Acts a matured and Spirit-filled Peter dominated early-church history. And Paul spoke so openly of his feelings and motives that sometimes we're embarrassed by his totally honest revelations.

But it's hard for us to visualize John, so humble that in his Gospel he cannot bear to name himself. With quiet joy he refers obliquely to "the disciple whom Jesus loved" (John 21:7). We know that John was one of the inner circle along with his brother James, and with Peter. We know that at the Last Supper John found a place as close to Jesus as possible. But what else do we know about this quiet apostle? And what do we know about his writings?

John and His Writings

The man. When John and his brother James, the sons of Zebedee, began to follow Jesus, they were apparently quite young and passionate. Once the disciples were passing through Samaria on the way to Jerusalem. James and John went on ahead to find lodging in a village. When the Samaritans, who hated the Jews as much as they were hated, learned the party was traveling to Jerusalem, they refused them shelter. Furious, James and John confronted Jesus. "Lord," they asked, "do You want us to call fire down from heaven to destroy them?" (Luke 9:54) Their nickname was appropriate: "Thunderers."

Another time the disciples saw a man driving out demons in Jesus' name, but the man was not one of their company. "We told him to stop," John reported, "because he was not one of us" (Mark 9:38). John was again corrected by Jesus because his zeal had missed the spirit of his Master.

A final Gospel incident (Matt. 20:20-28) completes John's portrait. He and his brother whisper privately to their mother. Shortly she approaches Jesus. Could the places of authority at Jesus' right and left hand be reserved for her sons when the Lord takes power in His kingdom? Jesus explained to the mother and to the two sons that He did not have the authority to grant such a request. Later the other disciples heard of the pair's attempt to gain advantage, and reacted with understandable anger. Then Jesus explained to the Twelve that greatness in His kingdom is not found in authority but in servanthood: a servanthood far removed from the self-concerned attitude of James and John.

We can understand John; we've all known (and possibly been) such firebrands. We understand his quickness to take offense and the anger that urged him to strike back. We understand the pride that held others at arm's length. We understand the drive to succeed, the hunger to be somebody and gain a high place even at the expense of friends. We understand all this because these are the motivating passions (*epithumia*) in our world. These are the desires that the New Testament encourages us to replace with a set of values summed up in the concept of holiness. Yes, we understand young John only too well. He is so much like us!

But when we come to John's writings, we meet a different man. We meet a man whose favorite word was *love,* a man who was gentle, so selfless that he hardly mentioned himself or his feelings, except as they related to the needs of the men and women to whom he ministered. We meet a man who *was* transformed, who demonstrated in his own personality the Bible promise that we can be changed by beholding Jesus (2 Cor. 3:12).

John emphasized the love Jesus had for him even in the days before he matured; thus he calls himself, "The disciple whom Jesus loved." What a message for you and me. Jesus loves and accepts us, no matter what our stage of growth. Jesus' new life *will* grow within us and, as John, we will become more and more like our Lord.

John's writings. John's epistles were probably written from Ephesus and circulated in the churches in Asia. They were immediately accepted by the whole church: we even have evidence of an exegesis (study and explanation) of John's Gospel from as early as A.D. 150.

Like Peter and Jude, John counseled the church about dangers from within. He warned against antichrists who were trying to lead believers astray. Like the others, John identified the spirit of antichrist with the denial that "Jesus Christ has come in the flesh" (1 John 4:2). The person of Jesus is the central doctrinal truth, and a relationship with Him, who *is* God, is the irreplaceable essence of our Christian experience. He also reminds us that sin by any name is the devil's work: we are not to be moved by appeals to our passions.

Invitation to Joy: 1 John 1:1-4

The heresy emerging in the days of Peter and Jude was an even greater danger during John's last years. As competing teachers introduced conflicting doctrines, many Christians became confused about who was the false teacher, and who was the true. Confusion also arose as the drive for holiness brought an unexpected reaction: those who slipped into sin began to wonder if they still had a personal relationship with God.

John focused on the doubts, fears, and uncertainties that well up in believers of every era who try to follow Jesus, yet who often find themselves stumbling and unsure.

John immediately shared with us his deep personal concern. He wrote in order "that you also may have fellowship with us. And our fellowship is with the Father and with His Son, Jesus Christ" (v. 3). "Fellowship" is the Greek word *koinonia.* It's a word of intimacy and means "communion; close relationship; participation; sharing." John's desire for us is what we ourselves yearn for: a warm, comfortable relationship with God in which we are aware of being close to Him in heart and mind.

John has seen in the historical Jesus (vv. 1-2) the reality of *life.* In Jesus eternal life entered time, and through Jesus John personally experienced that fellowship he desired for all of us. We can almost picture the old man deeply aware of how close he now stands beside his Lord, beckoning you and me to come closer and share with him that intimate relationship with the Father and Son that makes joy complete.

Walking in the Light: 1 John 1:5–2:2

How can we have fellowship with God? In this familiar yet vital New Testament passage, John unlocked truths that can transform us—and our attitude toward ourselves as well as toward God.

Light (1 John 1:5-7). John's first answer to the question of how believers can have fellowship with God was simple. God is Light.

If we walk in the light, we will have fellowship.

Often when John spoke of light (and he used the term 30 times in his writings), he was quoting Jesus: "I am the Light of the world. Whoever follows Me will never walk in darkness, but will have the light of life" (John 8:12; see 9:5; 12:46). The essential nature of God as light sets God apart from man. Man's sinful condition has made the world lie in darkness. Even worse, "Men loved darkness instead of light because their deeds were evil" (3:19). Confronted with the nature of God, men twist and struggle to turn away from such holiness. "Light" and "darkness" are *moral* terms in John's writings. The character of God is expressed as light; the character of sinful man is expressed as darkness.

So in this first letter, John confronted us with a disconcerting reality. If we are to be comfortable with God and live in intimate fellowship with Him, we must "walk in the light, as He is in the light" (1 John 1:7). Our values, our behavior, our attitudes, our commitments must be in harmony with God's character rather than with the natural passions of fallen humanity.

But this seems to raise a terrible barrier. If we must walk in light to have fellowship, how can we, who feel sin's pull and all too often give in to temptations, ever be comfortable with God? Isn't each sin a retreat to darkness? If sinlessness is the avenue to fellowship, who then can stand in the presence of God?

But John was *not* talking of sinlessness. "If we walk in the light," he said, "the blood of Jesus, His Son, purifies us from all sin" (v. 7). Even those walking in the light need forgiveness, and cleansing from sins they commit. While it is possible for us in Christ not to sin, we can never claim that it is impossible to sin.

John's primary target here seems to be those who "claim to have fellowship with Him yet walk in the darkness" (v. 6). These men and women speak glowingly of their closeness to God and the fellowship they enjoy—and yet make a practice of sin! Their lifestyle is not godly; it is patterned after the ways of the false teachers described by Jude and Peter. No one who makes a practice of sin can claim fellowship with God. God's nature is light, not darkness. Those who walk in light as He is in the light may fall, but they will quickly turn away from that old lifestyle to find forgiveness in Jesus.

We might sum up John's teaching this way; if the direction of your life is toward the Source of light, you will find forgiveness for your failures and inadequacies. But if the direction of your life is toward the darkness, then you may be sure you have nothing in common with God.

Confession (1 John 1:8-10). John's readers were confused by two false teachings. The first was the claim that those who choose sin's lifestyle can maintain fellowship with God. This John labeled as a lie (v. 6). The second claim was by those who said they were without sin (v. 8). They based their claim to fellowship with God on the belief that they matched God in His moral perfection! John called this claim self-deceit: "We deceive ourselves and the truth is not in us" (v. 8).

Truth and falsehood are not related so much to the trustworthiness of the teller as they are to correspondence with reality. The problem with the claim of sinlessness is not that the motives of the claimant are unpure. His or her report may be made with honest conviction. But the report of sinlessness is mistaken: it does not correspond to reality. "We deceive ourselves and the truth is not in us."

What is the reality of sin for the Christian? The simple fact is that while in His death Jesus dealt fully with sin, the sin nature within us is not eradicated. The ingrained responses still tug. We still experience pride, lust, anger, hatred, and fear. The capacity to sin remains ours and will be an ever-present burden until we find our full release in resurrection.

But the capacity to sin, and even the temptation to sin, are not really the issue in the Christian life. What is at issue are our *choices.* While we can feel the old passions stirring, we also have a new appreciation for godliness. We *want* to be like Jesus! Now two sets of desires war within us, and we have been given the freedom to choose. We can walk in the light and live in the radiance shed by the Living Word. Or we can turn our backs and chase off into the darkness after the illusive pleasures of sin. The choices we make, not the temptations we experience, are what move us into darkness or into light.

But again John is sensitive. Men and

women who turn toward the light, and begin that hesitant journey toward holiness, find that their sinful "deeds will be exposed" (John 2:20). In the radiance of the light of Jesus, we become aware of pools of darkness in ourselves. Things we did that before seemed natural and proper become tawdry and shameful. Motives we suppressed come to light. The action we justified we see to be a petty release of antagonism. Our drive to succeed is recognized as a materialism that has pushed aside the needs of family and replaced the value of persons with the love of money.

The more we live in the light Jesus sheds, the more aware we become of how unlike God we are. Rather than feeling comfortable in His presence, we pull back in shame and hopelessness, deciding we are forever separated from Him. Or, unable to face the reality, we deceive ourselves and deny the blemishes that surface. "My sin is gone," we insist. And since pettiness and antagonism are wrong, we rechristen our reactions "righteous indignation." We dare not acknowledge our materialism and distorted values, so we justify our drive to succeed by the money we can give to missions. Closing our eyes to reality, we wander through life, insisting on our sinlessness and yet wondering why we have only an aching void inside rather than fellowship's joy.

But what's the alternative? How can a sinful and sinning human being maintain a joyful and comfortable relationship with a holy God? John says, "If we confess our sins, He is faithful and just and will forgive us our sins and purify us from all unrighteousness" (1 John 1:9). *The basis of our fellowship with God is not our sinlessness, but His forgiveness.*

Let's remember the development of John's explanation before going on. You and I are invited to live our lives in intimate relationship with the Lord, in comfortable closeness and joy. The key to experiencing this kind of fellowship is to walk in light, not darkness. Some may claim fellowship while obviously choosing sin. They lie. Others may claim fellowship on the basis of a supposed sinlessness. They deceive themselves. The reality is that we are imperfect—and yet can have fellowship!

To have fellowship involves choosing a basic direction *toward* godliness; walking *into* the light, we can see God and reality. But we also become aware of our sins and failures. We will become aware of all that God still has to do within us to make us truly godly.

We cannot live in fellowship with God if we live a lie: to walk in the light means we must face and deal with the reality of our sin.

How do we deal with sin? We confess (lit., "acknowledge") sins. Instead of pretending or hiding our sins, we acknowledge them to God. And God "will forgive us our sins and purify us from all unrighteousness." God's forgiving grace will remove every barrier between the believer and God, even that of remembered guilt, so that we can be comfortable in the very presence of our Lord.

One last important promise is given us by John. God will not only forgive us as we acknowledge the sins we discover, but He will also purify us. God will touch our motives and desires, and He will gradually reshape us. Like John himself, as we walk into the light of Jesus, we will gradually lose the old anger and drive for prestige, and will become men and women who love.

A dangerous promise? (1 John 2:1-2) Some, reading John's letter, were sure to object to his teaching. "If we know we can be forgiven," they say "then why not sin? If that's all there is to fellowship, why make the effort to follow Jesus?" The objectors of course misunderstand. Only the person who *wants* to live in darkness will pervert the promise of forgiveness into a license for sin.

John was writing to help us avoid sin. "But if anybody does sin, we have One who speaks to the Father in our defense—Jesus Christ, the Righteous One. He is the atoning Sacrifice for our sins, and not only for ours but also for the sins of the whole world" (vv. 1-2).

How completely sufficient is the blood of Jesus Christ! Enough for the whole world, it surely is enough for you and me. Let us then go on boldly, with full confidence in Him, and walk in the light. We are moving toward holiness. But on the journey, we do not need to hide our sins. We need to acknowledge them, and receive not only forgiveness but the purifying power of our God.

♥ ***Link to Life: Youth / Adult***
Work carefully through 1 John 1:5–2:2, making sure that your group members un-

derstand each key term.

Then sketch these three persons, and ask each person in your group to select the one he or she is "most like."

*Myra. *You always felt like a failure. Never did well in school. Boys stayed away from you in droves. You have the feeling no one really likes you. You thought that becoming a Christian was the answer. But now you've failed so many times to be a "good Christian" that you're close to despair.*

*Jana. *You've never failed. Always got top grades. Popular. You graduated third in your law school class, and are moving up in your firm. As a new Christian, you're as determined not to fail in your faith as you have been in your other efforts. In fact, you won't even* admit *the possibility of failure.*

*Sally. *You're just an average person. Win a few, lose a few. Of course, now you've got a really important goal: to live close to God. And that's what's bothering you a little bit. You're so, well—average. How can you be special enough to come close to Him?*

Divide into teams based on the individual your group members felt most like. Take a few minutes to share why each chose that person.

Then explore: "How does John's teaching in 1 John 1:5–2:2 meet the special needs of this type person?"

TEACHING GUIDE

Prepare

John's teaching on walking in the light, and the role of confession in the Christian life, is so important that you will want to spend an entire session on it. Pray that your group members will experience what you teach, and find the joy of walking in the light.

Explore

1. Ask your group members for impressions: What kind of person do they think John was? What do they remember about him from the Gospels? Introduce the three incidents mentioned in the text that reveal his impetuous character. Close the discussion by pointing out that even with his imperfections, John is called the disciple "whom Jesus loved."

2. Examine 1 John 1:1-4. Ask each member to write down in 10 words or less the purpose of this letter. Hear different statements. Then discuss: "What makes this goal important to you?"

Expand

In a minilecture lead your group through 1 John 1:5–2:2, making sure they understand just what John taught. Then use the "link-to-life" suggestion on pages 1050-1051 to help each apply these truths to his or her life.

Apply

Have the teams share with each other how 1 John 1 applies to them.

STUDY GUIDE 167

1 John 2:3–4:21

WALK IN LOVE

Overview

When John called us to fellowship, he called us to "know" Jesus. Paul uttered the same call: "I want to know Christ and the power of His resurrection and the fellowship of sharing in His sufferings, becoming like Him in His death, and so, somehow, to attain to the resurrection from the dead" (Phil. 3:10). Knowing Jesus opens the door to a present experience of resurrection power.

But how can we tell if we "know" Him?

Part of our problem is that we can be confused by different meanings of the word "know." For instance:

- "I know *that*" means I have information.
- "I know all about bass" may be a claim that I can catch them.
- "I know Henry" may express friendship, acquaintance, or simply ability to identify a person in a crowd.
- "I know Plato" probably is a claim to understand his philosophy.
- "I know what you mean," can even be an expression of sympathy.

What then does it mean to "know" Jesus? *The Dictionary of New Testament Theology* (Zondervan) points out that the Greek word used here, *ginosko,* means basically "grasping the full reality and nature of an object under consideration. It is thus distinguished from mere opinion, which may grasp the object half-correctly, inadequately, or even falsely."

How important then, John's promise, 'We know that we . . . know Him" (1 John 2:3).

Commentary

Inner Evidence of Relationship: 1 John 2:3-17

John wrote to people who knew about Jesus, but who were not sure that they knew *Him.* We know about Jesus, but our grasp of truth may be incomplete, or we may have been misled by a false system of doctrine. How can we be sure that in spite of gaps in our understanding, we have a close personal relationship with the Lord?

John launched into an explanation of how we can be sure, not theoretically but experientially, that we know Jesus. He wants us to be free from nagging doubts and fears.

We respond to His commands (1 John 2:3-6). Jesus said, "My sheep listen to My voice; I know them, and they follow Me" (John 10:27). Those who belong to Jesus are responsive to His voice.

It's important not to misunderstand here. John does not suggest that relationship with God is *established* by obedience; rather, that relationship is *demonstrated* by obedience.

Sometimes people claim to know God but are unresponsive to His Word and His way of life. Such a person may possess accurate information about God and may be able to debate finer points of theology. Such a person may have memorized much of the Bible and regularly be in church. But unresponsiveness to God's voice shows the claim, "I know Him," to be false. Relationship is demonstrated by walking "as Jesus did" (1 John 2:6).

The central command (1 John 2:7-11). This idea of responsiveness can be distorted into a legalism in which the list of do's and don'ts grows longer. We try to measure our relationship with God as we do the temperature—by degrees.

To avoid this error, John quickly noted a central command from which all else flows. That command has been known and revealed through both the Testaments, but has been given fresh meaning in Jesus' coming. Jesus calls us to "love one another. As I have loved you, so you must love one another" (John 13:34). John said that the one who hates his brother cannot be walking in the light (1 John 2:11).

If you or I wonder if we're really responsive to Jesus' voice, we don't have to measure ourselves against a list of things we do or don't do to please Him. All we have to do is look within to see if we are reaching out, to care for our fellow Christians.

The listeners (1 John 2:12-14). John seemed to have more confidence in the people he wrote to than they did themselves. He didn't question their relationship with Jesus. He was sure that they did know Him and that they could live in fellowship with God.

John had reasons for his confidence:

- These little children had made an initial commitment to Jesus, and their sins had been forgiven.
- These fathers had lived in relationship with a God who had demonstrated Himself to be stable and trustworthy from the beginning of the universe.
- These young men had been challenged in their faith by the evil one, and God's strength and His Word in them had enabled them to overcome the threat.

These people could take the test John suggested. They could examine themselves and discover that they were responsive to Jesus' voice; they had begun to love. These inner drawings toward Jesus help us to be sure that we do know Him.

Divided hearts (1 John 2:15-17). John helps us look within to discover evidence of the reality of our relationship with Jesus. Now John warned that in order to love and respond to God, we must stop acting from the motives that reflect the world's value system.

Again John gave a common word a distinctive moral slant. *Kosmos* ("world") in Greek can mean the universe itself, the planet on which we live, or mankind. In a moral sense, however, "world" refers to the created universe and to mankind *as fallen.* This world, John says later (5:19) "is under the control of the evil one." The values and the attitudes that characterize the world—"cravings of sinful man, the lust of his eyes and the boasting of what he has" (2:16) do not come from God.

A Christian cannot live with a divided heart, responding one moment out of love for God and at the next turning to the world for pleasure. If we want to demonstrate (to ourselves, as well as to God) that we know Him, we need to make a clear-cut commitment to do the will of God rather than respond to the world's passions.

♥ ***Link to Life: Youth / Adult***

Copy "know" entries from several dictionaries to distribute to the group. Have teams list as many kinds *of "knowing" as they can find or think of, and how might each be measured.*

Then ask each team to read 1 John 2:3-17. What kind of "knowing" seems important to John? How can that kind of knowing be measured?

What can we do to enrich our "knowledge" of God?

Warning Against Antichrist: 1 John 2:18-27

John helps us see inner, subjective evidence that we know Jesus. You and you alone know if you are responsive to God's voice. A new Christian might be responsive, but as yet show little change in lifestyle. And you and you alone know if you are beginning to love. If you find the stirrings of obedience and love within yourself, then you can have confidence that you know Jesus.

But what are the objective criteria? How about those who claim to be Christians, and even to be teachers, but who are instead antichrists? How can we recognize false teachers and false prophets?

John gave several principles to guide us. First, they "went out from us" (v. 19). The false teacher comes into a local fellowship, begins to teach his lies and, when he cannot influence the whole group to follow him, takes the little band he has deceived and starts his own sect or movement. Watch out for those who would divide and separate Christ's people. They go out because "they did not really belong to us" (v. 19).

Second, they deny Jesus is the Christ. Rejecting the Son, they reject the Father also. Jude and Peter as well have stressed that the false teacher sooner or later distorts the Bible's teaching on who Jesus is.

Finally, there is a subjective element in discerning false teachers. God the Holy Spirit has taken up residence in every true Christian. Our resident Teacher is a sound interpreter of the written Word and of the teachings of men. "You do not need anyone to teach you," John boldly declared (v. 27); the Holy Spirit will "guide you into all truth" (John 16:13).

This whole passage is a great corrective for our own day. Are we afraid to fellowship with those who have differences from us, yet are brothers and sisters in Christ? Are we worried when small groups of believers get together in homes to pray and study the Bible, afraid that they may go astray without the pastor there to answer every question and correct every misunderstanding? If so, we have fallen far short of a biblical confidence in the Holy Spirit's ability to teach and guard His own.

So, there *are* objective criteria by which to test relationships with Christ. There is also the prompting and loving guidance given by that Person who has taken up permanent residence in our lives.

The Sin Question: 1 John 2:28–3:10

The emphasis on looking within to find a subjective basis for confidence that we know Jesus does raise a serious question. Paul insisted that leaders be chosen whose lives demonstrated holiness. Jude identified false teachers by their actions. Why then did John seem to retreat from a clear-cut call for active holiness? Why did he first assure us of forgiveness when we fall, and then go on to reassure us that we can be sure we know Jesus by looking within to sense responsiveness and love? Doesn't what we *do* matter anymore?

John was writing to ordinary people like you and me who became Christians, looked forward to a new kind of life, then perhaps were crushed to discover that everything wasn't different after all. The promised freedom from old habits and sins didn't come.

Experiences like these are common, because the Christian life involves growth. We are born again into a new world through faith in Christ.

Yet the old *kosmos* that we knew so well has patterned our personalities. The gift of new life does *not* include spiritual amnesia, or wipe away old thought patterns, emotions, and responses. All these are still there; still deeply ingrained. The old *will be* replaced, but gradually—through growth and grace.

It is the "gradually" that so troubles us. We want to be rid of the old immediately. We want to be all new, *now*. When we stumble and fall and then fall again, it's only natural to wonder if we've made a mistake about our relationship with God. Perhaps we are *not* born again. Perhaps our failures and stumbling into sin indicate that we only *thought* we believed!

John wrote to release us from this torment. If you want to be sure you know Jesus, first look within. If you are responsive, even in a stumbling way—if you find love in your heart—you can be confident.

But what about our failures and sins? "Dear children," John wrote, "*continue* in Him" (2:28).

How comforting! Take your place as a child. Don't expect to be mature yet. But do continue in Him. Do keep on growing. And as you mature, you *will* come to the place of victory over sins.

John said several important things about sin in this short passage:

- Through faith we are now God's children. When Jesus appears we will be completely like Him. As we keep His promise of transformation in view, and fix our desire on the goal of perfection, we will grow in purity here and now (3:1-3).
- There is no compromise with the sinfulness of sin. Violating God's standard of righteousness is sin. There is no sin in God. No one living in Him keeps on sinning (vv. 4-6).
- Objectively we can say that one whose life is committed to habitual sin is "of the devil" rather than of God. No one "born of God will continue in sin" (vv. 7-10).

Reading these verses we become aware that John was talking about the pattern of a person's life. He was not talking about isolated acts of sin, but about the direction of one's journey. The question is not, "Does he sin?" but, "Does he make sin a habit?" When God's life takes root in the human personality, that "seed remains in him" (v. 9), the life of God within struggles against sin, and the Spirit nudges us in a new direction.

So, over time, there *is* objective evidence of a righteous life to match the inner witness of love and responsiveness to God. Over time. Not necessarily immediately. But the objective evidence *will* come.

John promised, "No one who is born of God will continue to sin" (v. 9). It is not possible for sin to keep us in bondage, because the life of God within us will overcome the evil.

♥ ***Link to Life: Youth / Adult***
Have each group member read 1 John 2:28–3:10 carefully, and see if he or she can make a list of fifteen (15) statements about sin.

When each is finished, first answer questions. Many will need to note that John is talking not about being sinless, but about choosing a sinful way *of life.*

When questions are answered, begin to list the statements of your group members on the chalkboard.

When all have been listed, try together to write a paragraph on "sin and the Christian."

Love's Way: 1 John 3:11-24
From the beginning God's message to man has been "love one another" (v. 11). Yet somehow the attitude of Cain has intruded. The Old Testament commanded, You shall "love your neighbor as yourself" (Lev. 19:18). *The Dictionary of New Testament Theology*, (Zondervan) comments, "Love in this context means devotion toward one's neighbor for his sake, accepting him as a brother and letting him come into his own."

Yet among the passions that move us, a spontaneous love for others is missing. We can respond affectionately and even unselfishly to those with whom we have a special tie. But even family relationships may degenerate into the anger of Cain. Hurts, frustrations, real and imagined slights, all build up. The exploding divorce rate and the deep canyons of alienation that mar so many families today are vivid evidence that the way of Cain is still with us.

The contrast is especially glaring when we see how John used the word "love" (*agape*). Love is a central reality of God's nature. "God is love," John reminded us (1 John 4:8). God expresses love in the gift of Jesus; we receive that gift by a response of love. Knowing that we are loved and loving in return drives out the fear that destroys trust (v. 18). One who is God's and who walks in His light will necessarily live in love. Such love will not only change the character of an individual's relationship with God but also the nature of his relationship with other people. If we truly live in God, then we will live in love, for God is love.

God promises us who know Jesus that the reactions and responses of Cain will be replaced by the reactions and responses of Christ. John immediately confronts us with this contrast: "Do not be like Cain, who belonged to the evil one and and murdered his brother" (3:12). Did the murder drive Cain into Satan's hands? Not at all. In fact, the murder demonstrated how deep Cain already was in the evil one's grip.

Why did Cain murder Abel? Was it due to slights or parental unfairness? No, it was "because his own actions were evil and his brother's were righteous" (v. 12). Abel's good revealed Cain's sinfulness. Rather than acknowledging his sins, Cain tried to hide them from himself. He turned his shame into anger at Abel; antagonism welled up in his heart; he murdered in hatred. The entire process makes it plain that Cain did not know God.

And so we return to the theme of John's letter. How can we be confident that we know God? As we love our brothers, we can be reassured that we walk not in Cain's darkness but in Christ's light.

Contrast (1 John 3:11-15). John held up Cain and Christ for us to compare. Cain reacted with hatred to a brother who was good. Christ responds with love to sinners who reject God. Each expresses his feelings in action. Cain took another's life. Christ gave His own life for others. Cain's actions revealed him to be evil. Christ shows Himself to be good, a God of love.

Earlier John contrasted light and darkness to help us understand the Christian life. Now he contrasted love and hatred. No one who hates lives in God. But one who lives in God will love.

Love's expression (1 John 3:16-20). John is quick to note that love is not a feeling or an intention. Love is a choice that binds us to a distinctive course of action. "We ought to lay down our lives for our brothers," John said. "If anyone has material possessions and sees his brother in need but has no pity on him, how can the love of God be in him?" (vv. 16-17) Love is not a matter of words but of acts.

Then John added, "This then is how we know we belong to the truth, and how we set our hearts at rest in His presence whenever our hearts condemn us" (vv. 19-20). John noted earlier that we may become discouraged when we find ourselves slipping, unwillingly, into sins. He encouraged us to look within and see love awakening in our responsive hearts. When you and I sense

Dealing with Uncertainty about Relationship with God

UNCERTAIN	CONFIDENT	UNCERTAIN
Because we see ourselves slip into acts of sin.	Because our hearts are responsive and we feel loving.	Because we feel ourselves drawn to sin and antagonistic to our brothers.
Then . . . examine heart, and sense the desire to be responsive.	*Then* . . . we choose to be obedient and practice love.	*Then* . . . examine actions and see obedience and love practiced.
This is evidence we know Him.	This is evidence we know Him.	This is evidence we know Him.

responsiveness within, we can be sure we know Him.

But *what if our hearts condemn us*? What if, looking within, we become aware of feelings of antagonism toward a brother? What if bitterness blocks us off from giving or receiving forgiveness? If our hearts condemn rather than justify us, then it would seem logical that we do *not* know Him.

All too often you and I are aware of failure within us that others may not see. Depression may come, and with depression everything looks black. We feel guilty and helpless. John, with his deep sensitivity to our human experience, understands and answers. When it is your heart that causes you uncertainty about your relationship with God, then look for another evidence of relationship. What evidence? Love. Not as a feeling or emotion, but love expressed "with actions and in truth" (v. 18). When we choose love's way in spite of our feelings, we have evidence that we know Him.

God's desire is for each of us to find rest. But if we find ourselves troubled by a nagging uncertainty because of either our actions or our hearts, God wants us to continue to trust. As we live in Him, His Spirit *will* purify and transform us.

False Teachers: 1 John 4:1-6

John returned briefly to the theme of many late New Testament letters. How can we test for counterfeits and false prophets? First, doctrinally. Jesus, God's Son, has come in the flesh. This confession will never be made by false teachers. And second, by lifestyle. The world, with its "cravings of sinful man, the lust of his eyes and the boasting of what he has" (2:16), is put away by the mature believer. When a teacher speaks from the viewpoint of the world, we know he is not from God.

The true believer will also recognize John's writings as God's truth. The Holy Spirit will confirm it. When teaching is out of harmony with the written Word, the Spirit Himself will bring disquiet within the believer.

Dimensions of Love: 1 John 4:7-21

In these next verses John helps us see the way of love in the Christian community. He wanted us to experience close fellowship with Jesus and the Father, and live in intimate community with fellow-believers. John was not exhorting us to pump up the emotion we call "love." He was explaining why love is valuable to the church, and how we can *choose* to live love.

In these verses there is no threat to make us feel guilty if we have fallen short of love. John did not lay a burden of obligation to make us struggle harder to do something we cannot do. Instead he simply pointed out that God is love, and to live in fellowship with Him is to live in love. If in our association with other Christians we fall into the world's way of antagonism and selfishness, then we are not experiencing God's presence.

These words of John bring hope. If we have failed to love, we acknowledge our sin to God and experience His forgiveness and cleansing. Only if we deny the importance of love in our relationships within the church, and let barriers arise between people have we lost our way. What do believers need to understand about love in order to experience fellowship with God? Let's trace the thought of the passage.

Love is central (1 John 4:7-8). Because God *is* love, the person who shares God's love *will* love. This is simply a fact; a reflection of the reality that where there is no will to love, God is absent.

Love initiates (1 John 4:9-12). John made abstract love personal when he explained that God loved us and "sent His Son as an atoning sacrifice for our sins" (v. 10). God's action is especially striking since *we did not love God* when He gave Himself. Loving meant initiating action without immediate return (and, in the case of many whom God loves, without *any* return). Here is a model for love in the Christian community. Since God loved us in this same way, we ought to love one another in the same manner.

Relationships in society are usually governed by reciprocity. I am nice to those who are nice to me. Jim invites me to lunch; I invite him in return. I borrow tools from Stan; he borrows tools from me. Even sinners, Jesus once commented, love those who love them (Matt. 5:46). But love in the Christian community is not to depend on repayment. We are to take the initiative in loving, even when the ones we reach out to do not respond.

At first this seems like a strange instruction. Won't such lovers be taken advantage of? Won't the unresponsive drain the people who do care? John's answer is twofold. First, the capacity to love in this way exists in every person who is born of God. Thus, it is not a few loving the rest, but *it is all of us loving one another*! Each of us has the opportunity to reach out and initiate actions that meet the deepest needs of our brothers and sisters.

Second, as we take up the joyful burden of loving others, God, who no one has seen, becomes strangely *visible* in the church. We see God Himself as He "lives in us and His love is made complete in us" (v. 12). As God becomes more real among us, even those who have not responded will be touched by His love.

God does live in us (1 John 4:13-16). Is such love possible? Of course! We don't rely on any capacity of our own to love our brothers. In the person of the Holy Spirit God lives in us and will love through us. We learn to share God's love for us.

Love frees us from fear (1 John 4:17-18). John has an exciting prospect for the fearful and doubting. As we see God's love taking visible shape in the community of faith, we become more confident and more like God. "In this world," John said of the believing community, "we are like Him" (v. 17). Love transforms us. We realize that God is not angry or eager to punish; love has driven out fear.

The way love drives out fear is beautiful. When Stan became a Christian, he was antagonistic, bitter, and quick to take offense at others whom he thought slighted him. Burdened by a poor self-image, Stan could not believe that God accepted him with all of his faults. Every time something went wrong, Stan was sure God was punishing him and he cringed. Even when everything seemed to go smoothly, there was always an aching fear that kept Stan from feeling peace or satisfaction.

Then Stan became a member of a truly loving church whose members accepted him as he was. They understood his behavior, overlooked his insults, and returned only love. They invited this unpleasant young man into their homes.

Gradually Stan began to realize that these people loved him in spite of himself. He could be real with them, and they still cared. For a time Stan became worse, testing their acceptance to see if it were real. Finally he was convinced. *He was loved*! With this discovery came a great release. Through the love of his brothers and sisters in Christ, Stan experienced the reality of God's love. The message of Calvary he had accepted intellectually now released the knots of guilt and fear deep within. When Stan found a community of people who were like God in this world, he was freed to grow into a loving person himself.

Love is our proper response to God (1 John 4:19-21). Stan was freed to love only by being loved. John pointed out that it is the same with all of us. We did not love God; God loved us. God reached out first. But in being loved by God, we are freed to love in return. Then we can reach out to others.

Who do we love when God's love frees us? Yes, we do love God. But we also love our brothers. In fact, love of God and love of His family are so inseparably linked that John flatly stated, "If anyone says, 'I love God,' yet hates his brother, he is a liar" (v. 20). Love wears no blinders that cut off some while focusing on others. When love touches us, our whole personality is affected. We see God and sensing His love, are drawn to Him. We see people for the first time. We reach out to touch and to care.

Love has transformed us.

In Christ, and in His community of faith, we *will* learn to walk in love.

♥ ***Link to Life: Youth / Adult***

What makes a church a loving community? Brainstorm together for qualities and actions which are characteristic of a loving Christian community.

Then read or tell Stan's true story. What were the qualities of the church of which he was a member? What qualities beside those already listed does his story suggest?

In what ways is your *congregation a loving church? What might your group members do to show love within your fellowship?*

TEACHING GUIDE

Prepare

Select from the exciting truths in this passage those which will be most important to those in your group.

Explore

1. Distribute some definitions of "know" for your group to look at, and determine how "knowledge" can be demonstrated. Have the group members read 1 John 2:3-17 to determine what John meant by "know" and how that knowledge is demonstrated. See "link-to-life," page 1053.

2. Or have your group members individually read 1 John 2:28–3:10 to develop statements about "sin." Your goal is to help your members see that God's presence in our lives means that we will not sin *habitually:* the Holy Spirit will work a gradual transformation and release us as we continue to grow in our relationship with the Lord. See "link-to-life," page 1055.

Expand

1. Use the chart on page 1056 to give a minilecture, explaining how God helps us to know (subjectively) that we truly do know Him.

2. Focus on the primary *objective* evidence that an individual or congregation truly does know Jesus in an experiential sense—the expressions of love that God works within.

Either have your group members read 1 John 2–4 and list ways that love is demonstrated by Christians, or use the "link-to-life" idea on page 1058.

Apply

Ask each person to examine himself or herself, using the criteria demonstrated during the study. How does each know that he or she truly "knows" Jesus?

Invite any who are still uncertain to stay late and talk with you or to call later in the week.

STUDY GUIDE 168

1 John 5; 2, 3 John

WALK BY FAITH

Overview

"Life" and "death" are key words in John's Gospel as well as in his epistles. They are not, however, just words about our future. They are terms describing the present experience of human beings.

A person who has a personal relationship with Jesus Christ has experienced a new birth, and *has* eternal life now. A person without that very personal relationship which is established by faith is spiritually and eternally dead, even while physical life persists.

In this last chapter of John's pastoral first letter, he wrote about life, eager that believers should *know* that they have life now.

The very brief letters of 2 and 3 John reflect themes seen in all John's writings. There are love, obedience, truth, warnings, and notes of joy.

How clearly the pastoral concerns of John shine through—giving you and me an example as we too share God's living Word.

- First John 5 contains three passages over which theologians debate. This study guide discusses each, but you may wish to check further in a verse-by-verse commentary like the *Bible Knowledge Commentary,* pages 900-904. The three disputed passages are:
  - 1 John 5:6-7: Jesus came "by water and by blood."
  - 1 John 5:14: We are to pray and ask "according to His will."
  - 1 John 5:16-17: There is a sin that "leads to death."

Commentary

"I can hardly wait to die so I can live."

This rather strange statement actually reflects the attitude of some misinformed Christians, who suppose that eternal life is something we inherit only after death. Such people, who look at their present lives with despair, and think that only eternity holds hope, need to hear John's concluding thoughts. "God *has given* us eternal life, and this life is in His Son. He who has the Son *has* life" (5:11-12, italics mine). Eternal life is ours, and we are to enjoy it *now*.

Faith: 1 John 5:1-12

The core meaning of "faith" (*pistis* in Greek) is a personal relationship established by trust and trustworthiness. For a Christian to say, "I believe in Jesus," is not so much a statement affirming certain beliefs *about* Jesus as it is an affirmation of trust. It is a confession that the Person, Jesus Christ, about whom I learn in the Bible, has become more than a historical figure to me. I have recognized Him as a real and living Person, and I have not drawn back in fear. Instead, I have confidently placed all I am and all I hope to be in His hands. Faith is abandoning ourselves and our efforts and resting in Jesus' promise of forgiveness and transformation.

John's special emphasis within this core of meaning is this: Jesus' claim to be true and trustworthy has been authenticated by God.

Only faith will receive the testimony about Jesus. John wants us to know that faith brings life. As we respond in faith to Jesus, we become one of a great company who *have* eternal life, now.

Faith's focus (1 John 5:1-5). John makes it clear that new birth, through which we receive life from God, comes through faith in Jesus Christ alone. This first verse says literally, "Everyone believing 'Jesus is the Christ' is born of God." John went on to point out that believing is a trust response and that there can be no relationship with God except through Jesus.

Faith's initial act of trust ushers us into a new world in which we love God and demonstrate that love by obedience. The presence of eternal life now means that we will be able to overcome problems that trouble us. We will be strengthened by the eternal life that has taken root within our personalities. The things that are impossible for us today will become possible tomorrow.

Faith's testimony (1 John 5:6-12). The meaning of verse 6 is obscure, and is the subject of much debate. The verse identifies Jesus as "the One who came by water and blood"—not by water only. Did John mean "came into the world"? Or "came into our lives"? Or perhaps he simply meant "presented Himself to us." Does the water speak of the bag of waters in the mother, that breaks just before the child is born? If so, John referred here to the Incarnation, and affirmed the fact that Jesus, God's Son, entered the world as a Human Being to live in space and time and history. His presence was verified by men, and recorded for all generations to come.

Or does the water refer to Jesus' baptism by John in the Jordan River, the initiation of His public ministry?

Does the blood refer to the sacrificial death through which Jesus freed us? Certainly this is the central New Testament usage of the term.

Or did John use both terms in a very specific way, to echo what he wrote in his Gospel—that on Golgotha "one of the soldiers pierced Jesus' side with a spear, bringing a sudden flow of blood and water"? (John 19:34)

Whatever John may have in mind for the first two sources of testimony, he added a third that is very clear. God the Holy Spirit gives a testimony to each believer that is in harmony with the other two. History tells us of Jesus' birth as a Man. Scripture records His death and resurrection and explains the meaning of those events. As we hear the Gospel story, God's own Holy Spirit confirms its truth within us. These three witnesses provide a unified testimony to Jesus that we can accept, for God's testimony is sure. When we hear and believe, we *know*; God the Spirit confirms the truth within our hearts (1 John 5:10).

What of those who hear the Gospel promise of life and prefer to seek God in someone or something other than Jesus? John's answer was clear and unequivocal. Such a person has made God out "to be a liar, because he has not believed the testimony God has given about His Son" (v. 10). Since eternal life is only in the Son, "He who has the Son has life; he who does not have the Son of God does not have life" (v. 12).

The claim that Jesus is the only way to God angered the people of the first century. They wanted to search for God in their own ways. They wanted their philosophies, their gods and goddesses who embodied human passions and reflected the image of man. Today too people demand the right to do their own thing in morals and religion. They reject the idea of an absolute.

But John was not concerned with what people *want* to believe about God. John was concerned with *reality*. The fact is that God has spoken. *He* has said that only in Jesus can life be found. You or I may reject what He says, but our rejection will not change reality.

It's important for us to grasp the implications of the unchangeable nature of God's Word. Conferences and councils may meet and announce changes in doctrine and practice. Those who claim to represent the church may announce that homosexuality is now acceptable, but that will not change the fact that God condemns that lifestyle. Some who claim to represent the church can announce that as we evangelize, we must respect the good in other religions, and never suggest that their traditional faith might not lead to God. But God says that life can be found only in Jesus.

Today, as in John's day, we need to communicate to a hopeless world not the acceptable illusion people desire, but the reality they need. Jesus, God's Son, is the promise of victory—and the only way to God.

♥ ***Link to Life: Youth / Adult***

Write 1 John 5:12 on the chalkboard: "He who has the Son has life; he who does not have the Son of God does not have life."

Divide into teams of four or five. Each team is to come up with at least 10 questions *that this verse might answer. For instance, "Are the heathen really lost?" "Can I know I'm saved?"*

Then call the group together, list the questions on the board, and discuss: "Which of these is most important to you, personally? Why?"

This activity can be very important for any who are unsure of their salvation. If we have believed God's testimony about Jesus (vv. 9-11), then on the basis of God's own Word we can know *that we have eternal life.*

Concluding Remarks: 1 John 5:13-21

John's concluding remarks summarize and apply his teaching. John helps us to realize how great a gift we have received in Jesus, and in each other.

Prayer (1 John 5:13-15). Our whole attitude toward prayer is changed when we know we possess eternal life now. We are not probationers, waiting uncertainly just outside the door until death ushers into life. No, John wrote so that we who believe "may know that you have eternal life" (v. 13). How does such knowledge affect our prayers? John explained that it gives us "assurance . . . in approaching God" (v. 14).

Will God accept us? Have our failures made Him angry? Will God turn His back on us because of some inner attitudes that lurk, still unchanged, in our personalities? Or will He ignore us because of some habits we are not yet able to break? Such fears keep us from praying with confidence.

But John's letter has quieted these fears. There have been failures, but the blood of Christ cleanses. Sin, confessed, forgiven, and forgotten is no barrier to fellowship with God. Is an inner attitude still warped? Are aspects of my lifestyle still unchanged? John told us we *have* eternal life through faith in Jesus. We will see His life in us overcome our shortcomings.

With such concerns laid to rest, what should be our major prayer concern? Only that what we ask—what we desire—be what God wants too. Whatever we ask that fits His will, we can be sure we will *have*.

The word for God's will here is *thelema*. It does not usually refer to God's decree or unalterable plan, but what God desires to happen. We might say that praying in God's will means harmonizing our wishes and desires with God's.

How is such a harmony possible? First, God reveals His values, attitudes, plans, purposes, and intentions to us. We know, for instance, that the pride of possessions that motivates people of the world is rejected by God. He values persons, not things. It follows then that a request to God expressing a prideful desire for possessions is not according to His will. We can expect such a request to be refused. But we can expect a request that *is* in harmony with God's own deep concern for persons to be heard and granted. So understanding and adopting God's values helps us pray in His will.

It is also possible for us to pray according to God's will because the Holy Spirit lives within us. His voice is heard by believers. He can lead us to desire and pray for those things God wants for us.

It's important to realize that John is *not* stating a "condition" we must meet before we can expect God to answer prayer. Just the opposite! With our relationship to God established in Christ, we can approach God with confidence. As God the Spirit works within us, our prayers will more and more harmonize with God's will. We can look forward to answered prayer as a daily experience in our Christian lives.

♥ ***Link to Life: Youth / Adult***

In a minilecture stress the confidence we can have in our relationship with God, and the expression of that confidence in God. Then help your group members sense this reality by alternate images.

That is, ask your members to suggest alternate images *that contrast with a negative image that misunderstands the promise about praying in God's will. For instance: "Prayer in God's will isn't an obstacle course we have to run, but. . . ."*

Have each group member complete the sentence with another image that contradicts the "condition" image suggested by the obstacle course. Other starter images might include: "Prayer in God's will isn't:

- *A race you have to run without knocking over any hurdles, but. . . .*
- *A mountain you have to climb to get God to listen, but. . . .*
- *A price you have to pay to buy God's interest, but. . . ."*

After doing a few of these together, let your group members come up with both alternate images, the is not *and the* is.

Sin in the fellowship (1 John 5:16-17). When we acknowledge our sins to God, He forgives and cleanses us. But what if we see a fellow Christian slip? John encouraged us to pray for the brother or sister. God will answer our prayers, and bring our brother back.

John does note, however, that there "is a sin that leads to death" (v. 16). Was John teaching that those who have eternal life can lose it?

In the Bible, "death" has several meanings. Biological death comes to all the living. Spiritual death, the legacy of sin, grips each of us until its hold is broken by Christ. And there is the realm of death, which is that experience of alienation from God, of captivity to the world's ways, from which the believer is rescued.

John tended to overlook biological death. To him, the glorious present possession of eternal life was so vital and real that the moment of transfer from this world to the world beyond was hardly of concern.

Yet even for the believer, sin can lead us back to experience death. What sin? Sin denied or unconfessed. Sin justified by excuse and argument. Sin not brought under the covering of Jesus' blood because we choose to turn from the light to wander in darkness. What John seemed to be saying here is that there is sin that opens directly into this realm of death. Not every sin catapults us into the world of illusion from which we have been delivered, but some do.

If we see a brother or sister whose angry spirit leads him to strike out at others, or whose desires are still captivated at times by greed, we are to pray for him. Such wrongdoing is sin, but it does not necessarily blind our brother to the light.

But some sins are so dark that choosing them returns a person to the deepest darkness of this world. What are these sins? John didn't say.

What he did say is that the one born of God *will not continue to sin.* The life of God within will struggle against sin and bring the believer again to the light. The whole world may be under the control of the evil one, but the one who has new life from God is kept safe: "the evil one does not touch him" (v. 18).

While John did not define the sin that leads directly to the realms of death, it is possible to speculate. All the later New Testament letters are concerned with heresy, with false teaching about doctrine, and lifestyle. John himself said that false teachers wormed their way into the fellowship of the church, but later "went out from us, but they did not really belong to us" (2:19). It seems likely that the sin of which John was speaking is that of apostasy: of turning away from both Christian truth and Christian lifestyle.

Wait, John was saying. If you see a brother turn away from Christ, pray. And if the person has been born of God, he will not continue in his sin. God will protect him from Satan's grasp, and bring him back. But if he continues, departure indicates he is a false brother, cease your prayers. Let him settle down in the world of death and darkness, which is his home and his destiny.

How delicately John put it all. For you and me, there is no question about our personal relationship with Christ. We each know our own hearts; we receive God's testimony and his assurance of eternal life. But we do not judge another who claims to be a brother. We pray when we see one brother troubled by sin's remaining taint. And, if another turns dramatically away from Christ, we wait. If he is one of God's own, he will be kept safe, and will return.

About others—we withhold judgment.

About ourselves—ah, about ourselves we can be sure!

2, 3 John

These two brief letters to individuals show how completely the themes seen in John's first letter dominate his later thinking. Joy is found by walking in the truth. We are called and commanded to "walk in love" (2 John 6). As we continue in the teaching of Christ, we are protected from deceivers, who snap and tear at Christ's body on earth.

While each of the letters might be studied in its own right, the letters can also be looked at as a summation of John's thoughts. It is this way that you can best use these two pastoral notes to sum up the major teachings of the apostle of love.

♥ ***Link to Life: Youth / Adult***
Divide into teams of five. Assign half the teams 2 John and the other half 3 John to study. Each team is to first underline words *that reflect common themes in John's writings.*

In 2 John these are: love, truth, joy, obedience, and deceiver antichrist.

In 3 John these are: love, truth, joy.

After each team has identified theme words, members are to (1) develop a definition *of the term, and (2) to illustrate its significance for Christian life and experience from their letter and 1 John.*

You may wish to make a concordance available for each team.

Come together after 20 minutes or so and share discoveries.

TEACHING GUIDE

Prepare
Read through 1 John to review the significance of the key words: truth, love, joy, obedience, and deceiver antichrist.

Explore
Begin by dividing into teams, half of which are to look at 2 John and half at 3 John. Finding key words used by John, defining them, and showing their importance by reference to 1 John will launch your study with a good review. See "link-to-life," pages 1062-1063.

Expand
1. If those in your group lack assurance of salvation, focus on 1 John 5:12. By listing questions which this powerful verse answers, you can help each develop confidence in God and the Gospel's promise. See "link-to-life," pages 1060-1061.
2. Or focus on the need of your group for greater confidence in prayer. First John 5:14 has confused many with its call to pray "according to God's will." Give a minilecture to help group members understand that this is a promise rather than a condition for answered prayer. Then work together to develop contrasting images that will emphasize God's eagerness to hear us and the assurance we can have in bringing all our needs to Him.

Apply
Express your own joy in personal progress you have seen in the lives of those you teach (see 3 John 4). Let your group members know you love them, even as John loved those to whom he ministered in the first century.

STUDY GUIDE 169

Introduction

REVELATION

Overview

The Book of Revelation was written by John the apostle, apparently in exile on the Isle of Patmos. Even though it is an unveiling, or "revelation," it is without doubt the most difficult book to understand. At the same time, its basic outline is clear.

Outline

I.	Introduction	1
II.	Letters to Seven Churches	2–3
III.	Things to Come	4–22
A.	The heavenly throne	4
B.	The seven-sealed scroll	5
C.	Opening six seals	6
D.	The Great Tribulation	7
E.	Opening the seventh seal	8
F.	The fifth and sixth trumpets	9
G.	Mighty angel and a scroll	10
H.	The two witnesses	11
I.	The seventh trumpet	11
J.	Seven key persons	12–15
K.	Bowls of God's wrath	16
L.	Fall of Babylon	17–18
M.	Jesus' second coming	19
N.	Jesus' reign	20
O.	Great white throne judgment	20
P.	New heavens and earth	21

While we can outline the content of this great book, saying just what each event portrayed means is something else again. And yet study of this book contains a unique promise of divine blessing: "Blessed is the one who reads the words of this prophecy, and blessed are those who hear it and take to heart what is written in it, because the time is near" (Rev. 1:3).

Commentary

There are a number of reasons why it's so hard to be "sure" about our interpretation of Revelation. We can illustrate two of the most significant.

Symbolic words. Look at this paragraph from Revelation 1, in which John describes Jesus as He appeared in John's vision:

> Among the lampstands was Someone "like a Son of man," dressed in a robe reaching down to His feet and with a golden sash around His chest. His head and hair were white like wool, as white as snow, and His eyes were like blazing fire. His feet were like bronze glowing in a furnace, and His voice was like the sound of rushing waters. In His right hand He held seven stars, and out of His mouth came a sharp double-edged sword. His face was like the sun shining in all its brilliance.
>
> Revelation 1:13-16

It is clear from the repetition of "like" that this vision of Jesus has special significance. Each element has some meaning beyond its mere appearance. Each has *symbolic* meaning, affirming a reality beyond itself.

If we look through the rest of Scripture we gain impressions of what various elements suggest. John Walvoord, writing in the Victor *Bible Knowledge Commentary,* suggests several possible references:

- *White hair* — Purity and eternity of Jesus as God (cf. Dan. 7:13).
- *Fiery eyes* — Judgment of sin (cf. Rev. 2:18).
- *Bronze feet* — Material of altar of Old Testament sacrifice, suggests judgment (see also v. 18).
- *Seven stars* — Held in right hand,

	they symbolize Jesus' sovereign power of the churches.
• *Sword*	A type of sword *(rhomphaia)* used to kill, refers also to judgment.

Note that several kinds of clues are used in an attempt to understand the symbolism. First, there is a search of other biblical material to find similar references (as the white hair), or specific use of the material (as the bronze). There is also a search of context (the seven stars) and a general reference to culture (the significance of holding them in the right hand, and the particular use put to the type of sword mentioned in the text).

But we also need to note that several of the elements of this vision simply cannot be explained by looking to any of these sources. And we must also remember that there is no guarantee that our explanations are correct.

Strikingly, Scripture often does explain the significance of symbols and acts. For instance, the New Testament explains the veil that hung in the Old Testament temple between the holy of holies and the outer room as signifying that the way to God was not yet open. When Jesus died, that veil was miraculously torn from top to bottom (see Matt. 27:51; Heb. 9:8).

Likewise, the miracles God did in bringing Israel out of Egypt were explained. They were performed as a judgment on the gods of Egypt, and to let both Israel and the Egyptians know that the Lord truly is God.

So we have a long biblical tradition of explanation of symbols, as well as the appearance of some symbols which are not explained. When the text of Scripture does not itself explain symbols, it is not wise to be dogmatic about their meaning.

This is one thing which makes the Book of Revelation hard for us to understand. It often uses symbolic language which is not explained in the text. For this reason, there are some things reported about which we must remain unsure.

Apocalyptic vision. There is another thing that makes it unwise for us to be too dogmatic about Revelation. John described what he saw in his vision of the end times. In giving us this description, he *was limited to the language and images of his own time.*

For instance, imagine that one of our great great grandfathers, who lived 150 years ago, was suddenly transported to our time. He witnesses a traffic jam, sees a TV football game (replete with replays), is taken in a 747, and goes to an air-conditioned movie. Then he is returned to his own age, and given the task of explaining it all to his contemporaries.

He lacks all the terms and images we use to describe what are to us commonplace events. He has experienced something that no one else in his day can even imagine. How terribly difficult it must be for him to struggle for words to communicate what he has seen.

Well, this was exactly John's situation. What he saw are real events. And John reported what he witnessed. But he had to struggle with an inadequate vocabulary, and use imagery that may communicate something of his vision to the people of his day—even though his imagery did not exactly describe what he saw.

Look, for instance, at this passage. What, really, was John describing? The events are real, surely. And they will happen. But just *what* is he talking about?

> The first angel sounded his trumpet, and there came hail and fire mixed with blood, and it was hurled down upon the earth. A third of the earth was burned up, a third of the trees were burned up, and all the green grass was burned up.
>
> The second angel sounded his trumpet, and something like a huge mountain, all ablaze, was thrown into the sea. A third of the sea turned into blood. A third of the living creatures in the sea died, and a third of the ships were destroyed.
>
> The third angel sounded his trumpet, and a great star, blazing like a torch, fell from the sky on a third of the rivers and on the springs of water—the name of the star is Wormwood. A third of the waters turned bitter, and many people died from the waters that had become bitter.
>
> Revelation 8:7-11

It is clear from this description that John described terrible cataclysms that will strike our earth. Some imagine that what he saw and tried to describe was a terrible atomic war, or perhaps a space war. But the fact is, we can't *tell* just what it was John saw.

We know that it was terrible, and associated with worldwide divine judgment. We can also be sure that when it does happen, we'll recognize the events. But till then there is much uncertainty.

These are two of the reasons why it is not easy to understand the prophetic visions relayed to us in the Book of Revelation. We sense the power and terror of the last days that John described. But we dare not be dogmatic in our interpretation of them.

♥ ***Link to Life: Youth / Adult***

Help your group members sense why you will not be dogmatic in your study of Revelation, but instead try to sense the main thrust of chapters and passages.

First, let your group members try to describe, as a great great grandparent might have, one or more of these commonplace events. Remind them that they cannot use words or images that did not exist in earlier times. Each can try to describe one of the following:

- *A trip in a jet plane.*
- *A superhighway after rush hour.*
- *A televised football game.*
- *A space shot.*
- *A computer.*

If you wish, you might let your group members select anything they wish to describe, and see if others in the group guess what they wrote about.

Then read from Revelation 9, and ask: "What do you think John was describing here? What can we know about it from the description? What can't we be sure about?"

Conclude with a minilecture on symbolism as illustrated in Revelation 1.

Do not suggest that we are unable to make any *sense of Revelation. We* can! *But do help your group members see why we cannot be dogmatic in our interpretations, and must remain skeptical of those who claim to "know" just what this book teaches in every detail.*

The History of Interpretation

Across the centuries of church history there have been various interpretations of Revelation and of prophecy in general.

My *Word Bible Handbook* (Word) sums up the history succinctly:

The Early Church. The *Didache* was probably written about A.D. 100. It gives this picture of the future as understood in the post-apostolic church: "Watch for your life's sake. Let not your lamps be quenched, nor your loins unloosed; but be ye ready, for ye know not the hour in which our Lord cometh. When lawlessness increaseth, they shall hate and betray and persecute one another, and then shall appear the 'world-deceiver' as Son of God, and shall do signs and wonders, and the earth will be delivered into his hands, and he shall do iniquitous things which have never yet come to pass since the beginning. Then shall the creation of men come into the fire of trial, and many shall be made to stumble and shall perish, but they that endure in their faith shall be saved from under the curse itself. And then shall appear the sign of an opening in heaven, the outspreading of the heaven; (b) then the sign of the sound of the trumpet; and the (c) third, the resurrection of the dead, yet not of all, but as it is said: The Lord shall come and all His saints with Him. Then shall the world see the Lord coming upon the clouds of heaven" (Ante-Nicene Fathers, Vol. VII, 382).

In A.D. 140–160 Justin Martyr wrote, "I, and as many as are orthodox Christians, do acknowledge that there shall be a resurrection of the body, and a residence of a thousand years in Jerusalem, adorned and enlarged, as the Prophets Ezekiel, Isaiah, and others do unanimously attest" (Fathers, Vol. 1:239).

Irenaeus, a great missionary and church father, who died in A.D. 202, summed up the picture of the future taught in his day. "When the Antichrist shall have devastated all things in this world, he will reign for three years and six months, and sit in the temple at Jerusalem; and then shall the Lord come from heaven in clouds, in the glory of the Father, sending this man, and those who follow him, into the lake of fire; but bringing for the righteous the times of the kingdom, that is, the rest, the hallowed seventh day; and restoring to Abraham the promised inheritance, in which the kingdom of the Lord declared that 'many coming from the east and from the west should sit down with Abraham, and Isaac, and Jacob'" (Fathers, Vol. 1:560).

It is clear from these early fathers, as well as from the writings of Tertullian, Cyprian, Lactantius and others, that for some 300 years the church did integrate Old Testament and New Testament prophetic pictures and took them in their literal sense. They expected Christ's return to precede a time of blessing, promised in the Old Testament, before the world would end.

To the Reformation. A review of commentaries on the Book of Revelation shows a shift in understanding prophecy occurred after the early centuries. A leader of the African church, Tyconius, wrote a commentary around A.D. 390 in which the events Revelation describes were spiritualized. His allegorical approach was adopted, and later used to justify the development of the papacy as a political power. The allegorical method of interpreting Revelation was followed by Pirimasius (ca. A.D. 550), Alcuin (A.D. 735–804), Maurus (A.D. 775–836), and Strabo (A.D. 807–859).

Joachim of Fiore (ca. A.D. 1130-1202) challenged the dominant allegorical interpretation by introducing a chronological division. He divided all of history into three ages: the Age of the Father (Creation to Christ), the Age of the Son (Christ to his own day), and the Age of the Spirit (his time, until final judgment). When the Reformation came, this chronological approach was fastened on by Luther, Calvin, and others. The Antichrist-beast of Revelation 13 and the harlot of Revelation 17–18 were interpreted as the papacy, and as Rome. Events in the history of western Europe were linked to the various seals and trumpets of the book.

The Catholics responded with a commentary on Revelation in which Francisco Ribera (A.D. 1537–1591) argued that the Antichrist was an individual who would come in some future time, not the pope. Other Catholic writers argued that Revelation applied only to events before the fall of Rome, in A.D. 476.

The medieval scholars, the Reformers, or the later Catholic theologians attempted to relate Revelation to the prophetic picture found in the Old Testament and build a unified picture of the future.

♥ ***Link to Life: Youth / Adult***
Give a minilecture summarizing the history of prophetic interpretation through the Reformation. Note especially that in the early church Revelation was interpreted in the light of Old Testament prophecy. *Only later were spiritual interpretations (which assumed that prophecy in Old Testament and New Testament was symbolic, speaking in general ways of the blessings of the saved and God's judgments on the sinner). It was later still that Revelation was interpreted by linking its events with past history—either the history of western Europe or of the Roman Empire.*

In modern times three different views of the future have been expressed in prophetic systems. Each system tends to take a different view of Revelation.

Premillennialism is the view of the early church, revived in the nineteenth century by the Plymouth Brethren.

The premillennialist believes that there is a literal Antichrist who will appear. He will bond Europe into a single power, make a treaty with Israel as foretold by Daniel, and then break that treaty and try to set himself up as god. The Old Testament prophecies of invasion of the Holy Land and destruction of a Northern (Russian) army by God will then be fulfilled. After seven years of intense Tribulation, Jesus will return and crush the Antichrist's forces, and chain Satan. He will establish a redeemed Israel as this world's premier nation, and rule from Jerusalem for a thousand years. Afterward Satan will be released and lead a final rebellion. This universe will then be destroyed, final judgment be pronounced, and God will create a new heaven and earth.

This vision of history ahead, all agree, is one that fits the *literal sense* of the words of both Old and New Testament prophecy.

But not all agree that the literal sense is the intended sense in prophecy.

Postmillennial. This view, which had gained in popularity before the First World War, sees a gradual conversion of humanity through the spread of the Gospel. When the world has been converted, an era of peace

Modern Prophetic Systems

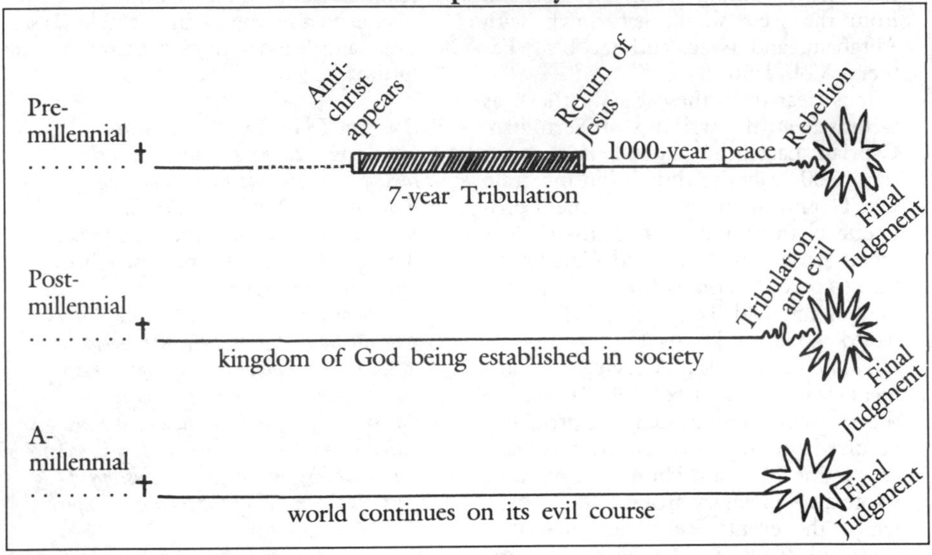

Pre-millennial
Anti-christ appears
Return of Jesus
1000-year peace
Rebellion
7-year Tribulation
Final Judgment

Post-millennial
kingdom of God being established in society
Tribulation and evil
Final Judgment

A-millennial
world continues on its evil course
Final Judgment

will be known, and society purified by the Christian majority. This era of peace is what is foretold in the Old Testament and suggested in the image of the thousand years ("the Millennium"). Some postmillennials do expect an outburst of evil before Jesus returns.

Amillennial. This group rejects the idea of a time of blessing on this earth. The Old Testament prophecies like the images of Revelation are thought to be symbolic, and to symbolize the spiritual blessings Christians experience through relationship with God. Thus this school does not believe prophecy should be taken in its literal sense.

Within these traditions there are currently two major approaches to the interpretation of Revelation. The *futurist* has a premillennial orientation, and tries to understand the events John describes by reference to Old Testament and New Testament prophecy. The modern *historist* sees Revelation as a panorama of history itself, but does not try to link it to specific events in the history of Rome or of western Europe. The modern historist generally believes that the seven major visions of Revelation simply look from different perspectives, at all of history between First and Second Comings.

The chart sums up the interpretations of these two schools of Revelation's major segments.

♥ ***Link to Life: Youth / Adult***
Continue lecturing using the chart that compares the three prophetic systems, and then pass out the comparison sheet that outlines the futurist and modern historist positions.

Summary
The Book of Revelation will continue to cause debate. However, whatever our approach to interpretation we cannot help but be stunned as we read John's sweeping descriptions of judgment. God *is* in control. Judgment day *will* come. And nothing human beings can do can thwart or change the sure purposes of our God.

TEACHING GUIDE

Prepare
Make notes for your lectures during this introductory session. Prepare the charts and other materials for distribution.

Explore
1. Ask your group members to give their impressions of Revelation. Have they read the book? Was it easy to understand? What

Interpretations of Revelation

Chapter	Futurist	Modern historist
4	Suggests the Rapture of the church.	Suggests awe-filled worship by church of all ages.
5	Relates scroll to Daniel 7:13-14 as deed to the Old Testament's promised Davidic Kingdom.	Scroll speaks of redemption and believer's rule in Christ today.
6	Initiates events that Jesus described in Matthew 24:5-8, leading into the Great Tribulation.	Shows impact of the Gospel on the earth, as Christ conquers through the message of His cross.
7	Sees the 144,000 as Jewish missionaries active in Tribulation.	Sees 144,000 as symbolic "perfect number" of the saved.
8	Initial judgments of Tribulation.	Natural disasters are a warning to the unsaved.
9	Demonic enemies are released to torment man.	An invasion of anti-Christian forces operating in the spiritual realm.
10	An interlude.	A message that God will not abandon believers.
11	The two witnesses are Moses and Elijah (Matt. 17:10-11), who preach for 3½ years in Jerusalem and are killed near end of first half of the Tribulation.	The period of 3½ years is symbolic. Witnesses are the true church speaking against false faith.
12	The Jewish people are preserved by God from Satan during Antichrist's rule.	War in heaven is a picture of Jesus' victory on Calvary preserving the church from persecution.
13	The Antichrist and false prophet appear and form European state.	Symbolic expression of Satan's attack on church by anti-Christian governments and false religion.
14	An overview of the final judgment of God on human society, represented by "Babylon."	An image of final judgment.
15–16	Literal descriptions of events on earth at the end of the Tribulation.	Symbolic descriptions of final judgment.
17	"Mystery Babylon" represents false religion of Antichrist.	The woman is pseudo-religious influences in the world today.
18	Civil, secular, and military power of the Antichrist.	Represents all past, present, and future materialistic centers.
19	Jesus returns as foretold by Old Testament prophets to battle enemies.	Symbolizes the complete victory of Jesus over all enemies.
20	Jesus sets up 1,000-year kingdom, then destroys Satan in last great battle.	Satan was "bound" at birth of Jesus. 1,000 years is symbolic of believer's present exaltation of Christ.
21	The vision is of eternity.	The vision is of the triumphant church, not of a literal city or new earth.
22	Jesus is coming again, soon!	

do they think of its value and purpose?
2. Help your group members realize why we should not be dogmatic about our interpretation of Revelation. Let them attempt to describe modern scenes to folks who lived long ago. See "link-to-life," page 1066.

Expand
In a lecture format give your group members background on different prophetic systems and explain the modern historist and futurist approaches to understanding this book.

You may want to distribute copies of the chart contrasting the views of those with these two approaches of Revelation's key chapters.

Apply
Divide into teams. Let each team select one or more of the chapters of Revelation. Guided by the chart, read the chapter and see which approach seems to best fit the content: the futurist or the modern historist.

STUDY GUIDE 170

Revelation 1–3

LETTERS TO SEVEN CHURCHES

Overview
Many believe that Revelation 1:19 is the key to understanding the book. That verse records words spoken by Jesus to John telling him to write "what you have seen, what is now and what will take place later."

According to this division the vision of Jesus recorded in Revelation 1 is "what you have seen."

"What is now" is reflected in the message to seven existing churches found in Revelation 2–3.

"What will take place later" is in the bulk of the book, chapters 4–21.

In this study we look at both "what you have seen," John's vision of Jesus, and at "what is now," his letters to seven churches.

Many commentators see these churches as representative of churches in every age. Their strengths and weaknesses are typical, and we are to gain insight into our own congregations by studying them. Others see the churches as representative of the ages of church history, with the first, Ephesus, representing the apostolic church and the last, Laodicea, representing the church of our own day. Whatever one's view, there are many insights we can gain as we learn how Jesus Himself evaluates His people—and there are many warnings we can heed.

What a privilege for you and me to lead others in a study of this book which uniquely unveils Jesus, not in His humanity, but in the glory we shall see when He returns.

Commentary
There's no more puzzling book in the Bible. The vivid images and the sketches of terror on earth and cataclysmic disaster in the universe beyond are hard to grasp. And even harder to interpret.

Are these outlines of future history . . . of events that will actually happen in space and time? Are they pictures of past history, using vivid imagery to describe persecutions under pagan emperors? Or are these symbolic presentations of experiences believers may undergo now and that will finally be seen to be elements in God's final judgment?

It is easy to become involved in debate about interpretation as we explore this final book of the New Testament. It is easy to become caught up in constructing systems, debating how a detail fits into our prophetic program, or arguing against another person's system. The problem is that we can develop a prophetic system with some confidence, and still miss the point of this great book! For this final, culminating book of the Bible begins with a statement and a promise to which we need to pay the closest attention. The statement is:

> The revelation of Jesus Christ, which God gave Him to show His servants what must soon take place.
>
> Revelation 1:1

And the promise is:

> Blessed is the one who reads the words of this prophecy, and blessed are those who hear it and take to heart what is written in it, because the time is near.
>
> Revelation 1:3

Concerning the statement, Dr. John Walvoord says, "It is a revelation of truth *and* Christ Himself, a disclosure of future events, that is, His second coming when Christ will be revealed" (in *The Revelation of Jesus Christ,* Moody). Walvoord's point is simple. *The central focus of this book is Jesus!* Everything we read must be interpreted and understood in relation to what the events disclose about Him.

For instance, Revelation 6 describes four horsemen who bring war, anarchy, famine, plague, and death to earth. If we focus on a prophetic system we will ask, "Is this a literal event to come? Does it describe the first or second part of the Tribulation? What are corollaries with Old Testament prophecy? How can we fit this in the time sequence of past, or future history?

Yet if we focus on such questions and debate these issues, we miss the dominant and jolting impact of John's picture. It is the Lamb of God (v. 1)—the gentle Jesus who allowed Himself to be led away and crucified—who has opened the seals in order to loose these awesome judgments on the earth! God's love has been firmly established; now we see a new quality expressed. The judgment so long and patiently withheld begins, and we are introduced to the wrath of the Lamb.

The "things that must soon take place" are related to this new and final unveiling of God. As we read Revelation we will gain a new awareness of who God is and how His character as righteous Judge will find expression at history's end.

And the promise? "Blessed is the one who reads . . . and takes to heart what is written." As we experience this book, we want to catch a clearer vision of Jesus—and take what we discover of Him to heart and into our lives.

Revelation: Revelation 1

The word "revelation" comes from the Greek *apokolupsis*. It means to reveal, bring to light, or disclose. It is often used of God's communication to us of supernatural secrets—of information we could never discover if God did not tell us. The secrets are about His plans, intentions, motives, or interpretations of events, and we could only guess about these without a divine word.

But "revelation" is also God's *self-disclosure*. He wants us to know *Him,* and as He presents information, God also communicates Himself.

To John this revelation of the person of God is always a central concern. In his Gospel, John showed that Jesus came in the flesh to show us the Father (John 14:9-11). The Incarnation, through which God entered history to share our humanity, was an unveiling that is recognized by faith. Now, in the Bible's last book, John describes another coming—one still future—in which Jesus' unveiling of God will be recognized by all humanity. Then "every eye will see Him" (Rev. 1:7). All those who have rejected Jesus as the One "who loves us and has freed us from our sins by His blood" (v. 5) will see His glory, and "all the peoples of the earth will mourn because of Him" (v. 7).

Comparisons (Rev. 1:4-11). We can see a number of comparisons between the way John unveiled God's person in his Gospel and what he revealed of God in the Book of Revelation. This is summed up in the chart. As we look at it, we begin to realize that in this New Testament book we will meet our Lord not in His role as Servant, but as the One who is high and lifted up, the Sovereign God.

To know Jesus now as "Him who loves us and has freed us from our sins by His

The Revelation of Jesus

Features	John's Gospel	Revelation
Who is unveiled	Jesus	Jesus
What is unveiled	Life, Light Grace, Truth	Wrath of the Lamb (Rev. 6:16)
For whom is the unveiling	Those who believe believe (John 20:21)	Every eye will see Him (Rev. 1:7)
Quality of God emphasized	Love (John 3:16)	Holiness (Rev. 4:8)
Expression of that quality	Washed us from our sins in His blood (John 3:16; Rev. 1:5)	Wrath (Rev. 6:16-17)
Man's response	Believe in Him (John 6:69; 10:41) Praise (Rev. 1:6)	Fear, anger (Rev. 9:20-21)

blood, and has made us to be a kingdom and priests to serve His God and Father" (vv. 5-6) brings believers joy and leads to praise. To be confronted by the Jesus we meet in Revelation will bring terror to unbelievers and stimulate them to intensified rebellion (9:20-21).

Yet God wants *us* to see Jesus as the wrathful Lamb as well. You and I are to look at history's end and through John's vision realize more fully who He is who loves us. We need to see the ultimate impact He will have on the created universe and on all the world's people.

As we see the Lamb finally releasing His wrath, you and I will be better equipped to make daily choices and evaluate our present view of eternity. And we will gain a far greater sense of what it means to live with a Jesus who is the *holy* God.

♥ ***Link to Life: Youth / Adult***
Ask your group members to write down one or two words only that sum up their impressions of Jesus.
Jot down their words on the chalkboard. The chances are the words will focus on Jesus' love, forgiveness, mercy, etc. Point out that these impressions are not wrong, but are *incomplete.*
Then in a minilecture help your group see that the main value of this study will be in what you learn of Jesus, rather than in what you learn about prophecy. Use the chart comparing the revelation of Jesus in John's Gospel with His image unveiled in Revelation.

First glimpse (Rev. 1:12-20). Now John plunges us into his own unsettling experience.

John the apostle was now a very old man, in his eighties or nineties. The year was A.D. 95 or 96, over 60 years after the death and resurrection of Jesus. Under a wave of persecution stimulated by the Emperor Domitian, John had been exiled to the little island of Patmos, a forbidding and craggy spot in the Aegean Sea. While he was cut off from fellowship with the church he loved, and deeply concerned about the persecutions his "little children" were undergoing, John was given a great vision. He was taught that Jesus is the center of history to come, and a mighty voice commanded him to "write what you see." And so the Book of Revelation is, in essence, a report by an eyewitness.

The first sight John saw was Jesus Himself, in a startling and unexpected form:

> Someone "like a Son of man," dressed in a robe reaching down to His feet and with a golden sash around His chest. His head and hair were white like wool, as white as snow, and His eyes were like blazing fire. His feet were like bronze glowing in a furnace, and His voice was like the sound of rushing waters. In His right hand He held seven stars, and out of His mouth came a sharp double-edged sword. His face was like the sun shining in all its brilliance.
>
> Revelation 1:13-16

John's reaction to this vision was to fall in terror at the figure's feet. But then the man reached out a hand and touched John, saying, "Do not be afraid."

What is most striking about this brief vignette is that it is *John* who falls stunned and terrified before Jesus! Remember, John is the "disciple whom Jesus loved." John is the one who was always closest to Jesus, reaching out to touch Him, straining to hear every word, catching and focusing for all of us the glorious love of God communicated in the Son. John, the apostle of love these 60 years, meets again the object of his love . . . and his first reaction is fear!

We, like John, will meet in the Book of Revelation an aspect of God's character that, while we have always known it is there, might not seem to fit the personality of the One we've come to love. But Jesus' words calm us as they did John. Whatever terrible visions may unfold in this revelation of Jesus, we will not fear. Jesus places His hand on us, and says, "Do not be afraid." Then we remember that we are His.

But what about this strange description of Jesus? What is the significance of the white hair and feet like molten bronze? And why seven stars?

Symbolism. The Book of Revelation is filled with symbols and symbolism. There has been much debate about the reason for, as well as the meaning of, particular symbols. Yet throughout Scripture, and especially in prophetic literature, similar imagery can be found. It is particularly helpful in trying to understand Revelation to look in the book itself for an explanation, or to look for Old Testament corollaries.

For instance, the "seven golden lampstands" (v. 12) are identified almost immediately (in v. 20) as representing seven churches to whom John is told to write. Because when the number seven is used in the Bible it often suggests wholeness or completion, many conclude that the seven churches represent all churches. Our own congregation may well be reflected in one of these pictures.

The white hair and brazen feet are not explained in the text. But the hair reminds us of Daniel 7:9, where God is described as "the Ancient of Days. . . . His clothing was as white as snow; the hair of His head was white like wool."

The feet of burning brass might suggest the altar of sacrifice and the life that had to be offered for sin (see Ex. 38:2). The altar and the other articles used in the sacrifice were always of bronze.

But, however we understand the elements of this description, the overall impact of this revelation of Jesus is clear. There is glory. There is holiness. There is awesome majesty. And there is terror.

John even felt terror at the vision, until Jesus' touch removed fear. That touch reminds us that the overpowering Person we are about to see in action is also the God we love—and who loves us.

♥ ***Link to Life: Youth / Adult***
You may wish to let your group members work a bit on the symbolism in Revelation. If so, here are verses which contain a symbol—matched with verses which help us understand or interpret it.

Revelation	*Parallel*
1:3	Rev. 1:20
1:16	Rev. 1:20
2:17	Ex. 16:33-34
3:7	Isa. 22:22
9:1	Rev. 9:11
12:1-2	Rev. 12:5-6
12:4	Rev. 12:9
13:1	Rev. 17:3, 7-8
13:11-17	Rev. 19:20
17:1	Rev. 17:15

Letters to the Churches: Revelation 2–3
The majestic figure now instructed John to write what he had seen, and then dictated to John letters to seven churches.

These are historic churches that existed in John's day., Each was marked by the characteristics the letter describes. Yet in these churches we see pictures of our congregations of today. Some commentators have also felt they found a portrait of church history—with each of the seven churches representing a different development in the Christian era, from New Testament times to the present.

What is more important for our understanding of these two chapters is to keep in mind again that the Book of Revelation *is primarily a revelation of Jesus Christ*. The most important question we can ask is, "What does this passage tell of Him and my relationship with Him?"

If we ask this question we're struck by the fact that John's vision of Christ as Judge places Him among the lampstands, and the lampstands are the seven churches. Jesus may not be *visible* in our congregations in all His glory. But *He is among us*! We sense Jesus' presence in these letters, and we also see something of the way we are to respond in view of His presence. If we can catch a glimpse of Jesus *among us* in all His glory, we will respond to the pressures of wealth, poverty, or persecution in the way these early churches were exhorted to respond.

As we see through faith what John saw, our confidence in the power of God and our freedom to live committed lives will grow.

The church in Smyrna. Let's look at one of the seven churches in more detail and see how we can receive help or guidance from these letters.

The city of Smyrna lies about 35 miles north of Ephesus. In New Testament times it was a port city, and very wealthy, one of the finest in Asia. Under the Emperor Diocletian pagan and Jew alike focused intense persecution on the believers in Smyrna. This oppression led to extreme poverty among the Christians—not simply "being poor" but being destitute, possibly because they had been robbed of all their goods by their persecutors.

Tragically, the persecution Jesus speaks of was to increase. Yet Christ said that as the intensity of persecution grew, the Smyrnan believers were to "not be afraid of what you are about to suffer" (2:10). They were to remain faithful, even though faithfulness might bring them death.

Church	Characteristic	Description of Jesus	Desired Response
Ephesus, the steadfast church (2:1-7)			
Smyrna, the persecuted church (2:8-11)	undergoing suffering, poverty, persecution	the One who died but is alive again	remain faithful
Pergamum, the morally compromising church (2:12-17)			
Thyatira, the doctrinally compromising church (2:18-29)			
Sardis, the counterfeit church (3:1-6)			
Philadelphia, the obedient church (3:7-13)			
Laodicea the materialistic church (3:14-22)			

The Seven Churches

It would be easy to be overwhelmed by such a message. We are to remember that Jesus, in all His power and glory, is *among us*. And we are to remember Him as "the First and the Last, who died and came to life again" (v. 8). Jesus too has undergone suffering and death . . . and Jesus has been raised to new life. He understands, for He has experienced what they are experiencing. He is fully aware of their afflictions and poverty (v. 9).

How then was the church in Smyrna guided by this letter, and what can we learn about our own experiences of suffering?

First, Jesus *is* there, aware of His people's needs. He Himself has experienced suffering like theirs. Yet now He is alive; the end of His suffering came, and glory followed.

Second, aware of His glorious power, the believers are to fear none of the things they will suffer. There will be persecution. Some will even die. Yet the persecution will result in Jesus' gift to them of a crown of life. They will have eternal life, and will be untouched by the *second death* . . . the ultimate judgment of God on those who do not know Jesus, or respond to Him.

Jesus understands our suffering because of what He has suffered. Knowing we will share in His ultimate victory over sin and death gives us courage to live fearlessly in times of pressure.

You and I and our congregation may not be a Smyrna church just now. But we do experience our own pressures, suffering, and afflictions. And whenever we do, the vision of Jesus standing among us in all His glory, and the words of promise He speaks, will sustain and guide us.

♥ ***Link to Life: Youth / Adult***
Draw on the chalkboard or duplicate and distribute the "Seven Churches" chart above. Together work through the letter to fill in the three columns of the chart, and then talk about the meaning of Jesus "among us" in His nature as "the One who died but is alive again" when we experience suffering.

Then divide into teams, each of which is to take one or two of the remaining churches. Each team should study its church(es), and complete the chart. Then together discuss how our present experiences *may parallel those of the church, and how the particular revelation of Jesus is relevant to us at such times.*

Revelation is *the unveiling not so*

much of a prophetic system or even of the future but of Jesus Himself. As you and your group study this wonderful book, keep your eyes fixed on Him. As you do, all the benefits promised those who read and heed John's last words will be yours.

TEACHING GUIDE

Prepare
You may want to check a verse-by-verse commentary like the Victor *Bible Knowledge Commentary* for background information on the other churches before your group meets.

Explore
Ask your group to jot down one or two words that sum up their impression of Jesus. Record these impressions.

Then in a minilecture point out John's striking reaction Jesus' appearance, and use the chart to contrast Jesus as seen in the Gospel with Jesus as seen in Revelation. See "link-to-life," page 1073.

Expand
1. You may wish to let your group check out a few of the symbols in Revelation, and see how comparing them with other biblical passages can enrich our understanding. See page 1074.

2. Or focus the rest of your study time on the letters to the seven churches which Jesus dictated to John. Study one of them together as a group project. Then divide into teams, each of which is to examine one or two of the others.

Use the chart and process outlined in "link-to-life," pages 1075-1076.

Apply
Ask your group to repeat the process of jotting down one or two words that sum up their impression of Jesus. But now do so in view of the vision seen thus far in your study of Revelation.

List the words each suggests on the board. Then discuss: "How is this vision of Jesus intended to make believers feel? How might it affect unbelievers?"

STUDY GUIDE 171

Revelation 4–18

PRELIMINARY JUDGMENTS

Overview
With chapter 4 of Revelation, the scene shifts. Here is how John describes it:

> After this I looked, and there before me was a door standing open in heaven. And the voice I had first heard speaking to me like a trumpet said, "Come up here, and I will show you what must take place after this." At once I was in the Spirit, and there before me was a throne in heaven with Someone sitting on it.
> Revelation 4:1-2

In these two verses we have moved from earth to heaven, and from the then present to what is to come. We have moved from Christ standing among the candlesticks (churches), to the Father on His eternal throne.

From this point on in the Book of Revelation, we are thrown ahead in time.

The question most Bible students ask is, "How *far* ahead?" Do we see in Revelation an unfolding of church history, as some have argued. Or are we seeing events associated with history's end?

Whichever position we take, the powerful images and terrible descriptions continue to remind us that our God is a flaming fire; a God whose righteousness and whose justice will surely strike terror in the hearts of those who reject Him.

Commentary
I have suggested that our most fruitful approach to the study of Revelation is to avoid majoring on the details of this or that interpretive system. Even so, we need to review how believers have approached this book before looking into its major section.

We can distinguish four major systems of interpretation taken by those who have a high view of Scripture as God's Word to man.

Allegorical. This approach, with its roots in early church history (Clement of Alexandria and Origin) regards Revelation as a writing of encouragement. It was intended to assure the first-century reader of the ultimate triumph of Christianity, not to predict the future. As the Book of Revelation shows us vision after vision, we are convinced of God's "sure triumph, glorious over and amid them all" (R.C.H. Lenski, *Interpretation of St. John's Revelation,* Luthern Book Concern).

Preterist. This approach views Revelation as a record of conflicts between the early church and paganism/Judaism. The final chapters are thought to portray a contemporary triumph of the church. In this view, the focus of Revelation is the first century itself. The book's value is in revealing principles of God's action, not in delineating specific time periods or events.

Historical. This approach has traditionally suggested that Revelation is a symbolic overview of church history, culminating in Jesus' second coming. During Reformation times this was the most popular interpretation, with the beasts of Revelation 13 identified as the pope and the papacy. The major problem with this approach is its great flexibility; over 50 different interpretations of history have emerged, and each has identified the events and characters of Revelation to fit a particular historical point of view.

Modern historists tend to see the book not as images of specific events but rather as seven parallel pictures of how God is at work within history.

Futurist. This approach looks at Revelation as prophetic, and suggests that with the beginning of chapter 4 the book describes events that are still to come, not only for John but for us as well. This system of interpretation suggests the events describe a time period just preceding the return of Christ, the Tribulation time mentioned in

Matthew and in the Old Testament.

The Old Testament prophetic passages are expected to be fulfilled literally, and Jesus is to rule on earth as glorious King. Thus Revelation is correlated with pictures of the future given by Daniel, Isaiah, Ezekiel, and other Old Testament prophets.

Which one? It's clear from a quick glance at these different systems that the approach we take to Revelation will affect our understanding of it, and may even distract us from its chief value! If we take a historical view, we may try to correlate events with councils, persecutions, and movements in church history. If we take the allegorical, we may look for meaning, but deny that the events described could ever happen. If we take the futurist view, we might easily become involved in speculation about how a specific future event correlates with others described in this book or in the Old Testament.

To me, the futurist view seems most in harmony with the whole of Scripture. But I do not want to argue for the futurist position. Nor do I think we should try to build a detailed picture of history to come from the teachings of this majestic book. What I want, for myself and those I teach, is a fresh vision of Jesus, standing as an awesome figure at history's end.

When we do study Revelation to meet Jesus, and our vision is drawn beyond time to an eternity in which He is Lord, our lives and our faith will be enriched.

The Framework: Revelation 4–5

The general framework for a futurist interpretation is provided in Revelation 1:19. There John is told to write "what you have seen, what is now" (chaps. 2–3) and "what will take place later" (chaps. 4–21).

But beyond noting that we will treat the rest of Revelation as describing events at history's end, we need spend no more time on systems. We can instead take John's viewpoint, and see these events from the perspective of heaven. We will stand beside the Lord in heaven and keep our eyes fixed on God.

Lord God Almighty. Seated on a throne, in a blinding riot of color, is a figure. Lightning plays around Him, flashing on four angelic beings who praise Him day and night, saying:

> Holy, holy, holy
> is the Lord God Almighty, who was, and is, and is to come.
>
> Revelation 4:8

Just beyond this inner circle are 24 elders, who also worship. They joyfully lay their crowns before the throne and say:

> You are worthy, our Lord and God, to receive glory and honor and power, for You created all things, and by Your will they were created and have their being.
>
> Revelation 4:11

This first vision of God immediately focuses our attention on His holiness. He, the Eternal, the Creator, the Source of all being, is holy, holy, holy. *What we are about to see in the events of history to come is a revelation of the holiness of God.*

That revelation of holiness does not repel those who know Him. Instead, it stimulates those who live in His presence to worship Him and give Him "glory, and honor and thanks" (v. 9). A revelation of God's holiness will always lead those who know Him to praise and to purity. But soon we will see an entirely different reaction from those who stand in rebellion against Him.

The Lamb. The figure on the throne is holding a book, a scroll that is sealed (locked) and cannot be opened. With John, we are heartbroken that no one can be found to open the book. Somehow we sense that the scroll *must* be opened and read.

Then one of the elders announces that there is One who "has triumphed" and can open the scroll and its seals. "Then," John records, "I saw a Lamb, looking as if it had been slain, standing in the center of the throne, encircled by the four living creatures and the elders" (5:6). The elders and four living creatures give the Lamb the same worship they offered to the Father (a clear identification of Jesus as God). They break into a song of praise:

> You are worthy to take the scroll and to open its seals, because You were slain, and with Your blood You purchased men for God from every tribe and language and people and nation. You have made them to be a kingdom and priests to serve our God, and they will reign on the earth.
>
> Revelation 5:9-10

The singers are now joined by millions of angels who praise the Lamb, saying:

> Worthy is the Lamb, who was slain, to receive power and wealth and wisdom and strength and honor and glory and praise!
>
> Revelation 5:12

Finally, in antiphonal response, "Every creature in heaven and on earth and under the earth and on the sea" joins the choir:

> To Him who sits on the throne and to the Lamb be praise and honor and glory and power, forever and ever!
>
> Revelation 5:13

And those around the throne echo: "Amen."

God who is God. These two chapters of worship and praise are a necessary introduction to John's description of things to come. They are as necessary for us as they were for him.

Perhaps we have been so filled with wonder at a God who loves us and gave Himself for us that we tend to miss an important reality. Though God in Jesus gave Himself for us, *He remains the center of the universe.* It is God, not man, for whom all things were and are created. It is His glory, not our glorification, that is important. As the Westminster Catechism states, "The chief end of man is to glorify God and enjoy Him forever." We must never neglect this reality or come to feel that somehow the chief end of God is to glorify man! We must never measure what happens or what is described in the Book of Revelation from a human viewpoint. All that occurs must be measured against who God is.

Judgment Begins: Revelation 6–9

We must realize God is the ultimate measure of every event before we come (in chapter 6) to the breaking of seals on the scroll God holds. For as each seal is opened, new terrors are unleashed on earth. If we see only the impact of those judgments on mankind, we are likely to criticize God's holy actions. But it is only after century upon century of grace that God unleashes the punishment required for sin.

Looking at man's unwillingness to respond to God's grace, Paul asked, "Do you think you will escape God's judgment? Or do you show contempt for the riches of His kindness, tolerance and patience, not realizing that God's kindness leads you toward repentance?" (Rom. 2:3-4)

Now, after humanity has rejected God's kindness for millennia, and only now, the dam of God's patience breaks, and judgment floods the earth. Paul's warning is fulfilled: "Because of your stubbornness and your unrepentant heart, you are storing up wrath against yourself for the day of God's wrath, when His righteous judgment will be revealed" (v. 5). The wrath that comes only underlines the grace of God, for now we see what human sin and unwillingness to repent has always deserved.

The seals (Rev. 6). As the seals are opened, war and famine and disease invade the earth, and millions are killed. A fourth of earth's population dies under this first wave of judgment. Then comes a second wave, with cataclysmic earthquakes and jolting changes even in the stellar universe. These events are so obviously supernatural that even unbelievers are convinced of God's intervention in the world. "They called to the mountains and the rocks, 'Fall on us and hide us from the face of Him who sits on the throne and from the wrath of the Lamb! For the great day of Their wrath has come, and who can stand?' " (vv. 16-17)

As this terrified howl issues from earth, we hear other voices as well. Those who were hated by the world and have been martyred because they responded to God's call: "How long, Sovereign Lord, holy and true, until You judge the inhabitants of the earth and avenge our blood?" (v. 10)

God's judgments on mankind are not unjustified. They are in fact required by man's own injustice to man, and by humanity's hatred of those who have responded to God's love.

The multitude (Rev. 7). In chapter 7, we see a group of men and women "that no one could count, from every nation, tribe, people and language" (v. 9), who stand before God redeemed. We are told who they are. "These are they who have come out of the Great Tribulation; they have washed their robes and made them white in the blood of the Lamb" (v. 14). Seeing them, we realize that even in the time of wrath God has remembered mercy!

The chapter opens with the calling of

144,000 people, 12,000 from each of the 12 tribes of Israel. At the beginning of the time of wrath these are set aside to serve God. (Many Bible students believe they are evangelists who will go throughout the world calling people to faith in God during the Great Tribulation.) Whoever they may be; one thing is clear from the chapter: *God's love will operate to call men to Himself even in the time of wrath!* God's tender love has reached down amid the terrors with continuing promise of personal relationship and caring:

> Never again will they hunger; never again will they thirst. The sun will not beat upon them, nor any scorching heat. For the Lamb at the center of the throne will be their Shepherd; He will lead them to springs of living water. And God will wipe away every tear from their eyes.
>
> Revelation 7:16-17

Even in the days of wrath, only a person's hardness of heart can keep God's love out.

The seventh seal (Rev. 8). The book now continues with descriptions of more judgment on earth. Again these pictures are cataclysmic, so immense they seem unreal.

> The second angel sounded his trumpet, and something like a huge mountain, all ablaze, was thrown into the sea. A third of the sea turned into blood, a third of the living creatures in the sea died, and a third of the ships were destroyed.
>
> Revelation 8:8-9

John is clearly struggling to find words. It's helpful as we read these chapters to remember that what we have here is a *description* of events beyond imagination, events impossible to portray in words. It is as though someone from colonial days were suddenly dropped into our century and asked to explain to one of his contemporaries such sights as spaceships and jet planes, television and skyscrapers. He would have had no words to adequately convey such a vision out of the future.

So we should not find it hard to see why John has to struggle for words. "Something like a huge mountain, all ablaze" is the closest he can come to describing the sight he sees. Many reading these words see visions of atomic warfare. That may be. Whatever it is John describes, it is destruction beyond our wildest dreams, beyond our greatest fears.

Demonic invasion (Rev. 9). In this new plague (apparently demonic) beings from the Abyss torment, but do not at first kill, the people remaining on the earth. After five months, more supernatural beings are released, and they destroy a third of the human beings who have survived the earlier judgments.

Yet, in spite of all these supernatural judgments:

> The rest of mankind that were not killed by these plagues still did not repent of the work of their hands; they did not stop worshiping demons, and idols of gold, silver, bronze, stone, and wood—idols that cannot see or hear or walk. Nor did they repent of their murders, their magic arts, their sexual immorality or their thefts.
>
> Revelation 9:20-21

They had rejected the love of God. Now not even the wrath of God could persuade their hard hearts to repent.

Interlude: Revelation 10

As we move on into Revelation 10, it is apparent that all that has gone before is preliminary! Now John hears an angel announce, "There will be no more delay! But in the days when the seventh angel is about to sound his trumpet, the mystery of God will be accomplished, just as He announced to His servants the prophets" (vv. 6-7)

John is told to take a scroll from an angel and then to speak out "about many peoples, nations, languages and kings" (v. 11). In these next chapters, we will meet the individuals, the forces, and the institutions that emerge to struggle in deadly conflict with each other and with God Himself, as history draws to a close.

Two Witnesses: Revelation 11

In this chapter a specific period of time is mentioned. During these 42 months, Gentiles will "trample on the Holy City." Daniel 12 mentions this same period of time, as well as many of the individuals and forces we meet in Revelation.

Now John introduces us to two individuals identified as "witnesses." In spite of the victory of Gentile powers over the Holy City, these witnesses are given supernatural powers that protect them and enable them to strike back against God's enemies. Finally, after 42 months of testifying, the two are killed by a supernatural being who comes from the Abyss. Their bodies lie in the open, and the whole world rejoices at the death of the two prophets who used truth to torment those who lived on earth.

But after three and a half days, we see the witnesses restored to life! Their enemies watch in anger and terror as the two ascend to heaven in a cloud. At that very hour an earthquake strikes the city, destroying a tenth of it.

Many have debated the identity of the two witnesses. Often they are said to be Elijah and Moses. Whatever their identity, their ministry during the time leading up to the end is clear. They will testify to the power of God. After they ascend into heaven, we hear again the praise of those before the throne:

> We give thanks to You, Lord God Almighty, who is and who was, because You have taken Your great power and have begun to reign. The nations were angry; and Your wrath has come. The time has come for judging the dead, and for rewarding Your servants the prophets and Your saints and those who reverence Your name, both small and great—and for destroying those who destroy the earth.
>
> Revelation 11:17-19

Those Who Destroy: Revelation 12–14
The first figure John describes is a pregnant woman who is under attack by a great red dragon. The dragon is identified as Satan (12:9). We are told that he is the leader of a group of angels who rebelled against God.

While some see this as a description of Satan being cast from heaven originally, the passage clearly relates these events to the 42 months of Tribulation on earth. The woman, probably representing Israel, is taken to a place of safety in the desert while the war in heaven is fought.

When the enemy loses the battle in heaven and is cast down to earth, he pursues the woman. When he is unable to reach the woman, he goes off "to make war against the rest of her offspring—those who obey God's commandments and hold to the testimony of Jesus" (v. 17).

Now the dragon is joined by a beast who rises out of the sea. Satan (the dragon) gives "the beast his power and his throne and great authority" (13:2). The symbolism here parallels again the prophetic picture in Daniel 7. Given supernatural powers, this world ruler exercises "authority over every tribe, people, language and nation" (Rev. 13:7). He receives worship from all who do not belong to God (v. 8). Satan, who has always yearned for the worship and the place belonging to God alone, now seems to achieve that goal through the counterfeit Christ who rules in his name.

Finally, to these two is added "another beast, coming out of the earth" (v. 11). The unholy trinity is now complete. The second beast acts as spokesman for the first, using miraculous powers to force men to worship Satan and the Antichrist. He kills all who refuse to worship and forces "everyone, small and great . . . to receive a mark on his right hand or on his forehead, so that no one could buy or sell unless he had the mark, which is the name of the beast or the number of his name" (vv. 16-17).

These are the destroyers. Satan's heart is revealed at last. God acts in love, giving people freedom to choose to follow Him; but Satan acts in hatred, *forcing* people to surrender their freedom to Him.

But we are encouraged as the voice from heaven says that Satan "is filled with fury, because he knows that his time is short" (12:12).

He knows his time is short, because the Lamb stands beside the throne of heaven. There is anguish and antagonism on earth, but the glorious figure who dominates Revelation is about to do battle with His enemies.

He will act on behalf of His saints
To finally,
utterly,
completely,
ultimately,
destroy the destroyers.

And so chapter 14 returns us to the side of the Lamb. We watch as an angel proclaims the message of the "eternal Gospel . . . to every nation, tribe, language and people" (v. 6). Believers who are being persecuted are encouraged to have "patient endurance" and "obey God's commandments and remain faithful to Jesus" (v. 12).

But as for anyone who worships the beast and his image, another angel delivers a message of judgment. "He, too, will drink of the wine of God's fury, which has been poured full strength into the cup of His wrath. . . . There is no rest day or night for those who worship the beast and his image, or for anyone who receives the mark of his name" (vv. 10-11).

Further Judgments on Earth: Revelation 15–18

Now more judgments are released on earth, and "with them God's wrath is completed" (15:1).

Before these judgments begin, those who belong to God and were victorious over the beast praise God in song. Against the background of human sin and Satan's rebellion, the righteous judgments of God call forth our praise.

> Great and marvelous are Your deeds, Lord God Almighty. Just and true are Your ways, King of the ages. Who will not fear You, O Lord, and bring glory to Your name? For You alone are holy. All nations will come and worship before You, for Your righteous acts have been revealed.
>
> Revelation 15:3-4

It is important to remember that the judgments are righteous as we read of ugly and painful sores, of scorching heat, and of waters turning to blood. We must remember the figure of Christ as we read of people who gnaw their tongues in agony and curse God because of their pains. We must keep the perspective of the angel who declared:

> You are just in these judgments, You who are and who were, the Holy One, because You have so judged; for they have shed the blood of Your saints and your prophets, and You have given them blood to drink as they deserve.
>
> Revelation 16:4

The persecutors of God's people, in all their pain, "refused to repent and glorify Him" (v. 9); in all their agony "they refused to repent of what they had done" (v. 11). Even in the final judgment, with earthquake and lightning and volcanic holocaust, "they cursed God on account of the plague of hail, because the plague was so terrible" (v. 21).

Another woman (Rev. 17). From Reformation times, commentators have identified the woman of chapter 17, portrayed as the "great prostitute," and named "Babylon the Great," with apostate religion. The Reformers saw her as papal Rome. We can broaden their interpretation by seeing that when Scripture speaks of Babylon as a religious system, it points to a counterfeit faith—sometimes pseudo-Christian, often pagan in nature.

During the end times apostate religion apparently will form a relationship with the secular power that is Satan's emissary. Raised to world power, false religion will join eagerly in this persecution of those who remain faithful to Jesus.

Finally, the secular power, consolidated from at least 10 national entities into a single state, acts to destroy even the apostate church and permit only the worship of Satan and his beast (see vv. 12, 16-17).

There is much detail and much symbolism in Revelation 17. Here again we are reminded of Daniel's prophecy of the development of the final world rule of the Antichrist (Dan. 12). Certainly the detail is significant, and to examine the passage would provide a clearer picture of the future; but what is important to us is to see God revealed against the final patterns of history.

By this criteria, what is important here is to see that *religion may be the enemy of God*. It is not belief that is important; *what is important is the one in whom we believe*. A counterfeit faith, no matter how much it may seem in harmony with our culture, is an enemy of God. One day Satan will no longer need to hide behind these attractive counterfeits, and he will sweep away the facade and demand that all people worship him.

The city of Babylon (Rev. 18). From the beginning of Scripture, "Babylon" has been significant. Genesis 11 describes people building a tower at Babel to reestablish a political basis for unity. In the Old Testament, "Babylon" was a symbol of godless political and economic power. God's people have always been warned to flee from Babylon (see Jer. 50:8-9; 51:6, 44-45).

Revelation 18 makes it plain that Babylon here represents not only political power but also material wealth and luxury. As God's judgment consumes the city of Babylon, her merchants and kings and sea captains and sailors will weep and mourn for their lost riches:

> Because no one buys their cargoes anymore—cargoes of gold, silver, precious stones and pearls; fine linen, purple, silk and scarlet cloth; every sort of citron wood . . . and bodies and souls of men.
>
> Revelation 18:11-13

But earth's weeping and mourning over Babylon's destruction is matched by heaven's joy!

> Rejoice over her, O heaven! Rejoice, saints and apostles and prophets! God has judged her for the way she treated you.
>
> Revelation 18:20

When the state and its leaders trample the individual; when *things* have more value than *persons*; when all is bent to the warped pattern set by Satan . . . then the fall of Babylon will bring joy to the godly.

Characters in the Drama

In Revelation 10–18 we see personalities against whom Jesus, the Lamb, stands in sharp contrast. As we look at each element in the drama, we can see why God's wrath is just. We can also better understand His character as we see what He hates.

The witnesses. These men reveal unregenerate mankind's deep-seated antagonism to God's spokesmen. These prophets draw vicious anger from the world, in spite of divine protection and authenticating miracles. Just as Jesus was slain by men who angrily rejected Him, so the witnesses are constantly under attack. Finally, the world gladly takes sides with the devil himself and rejoices at the apparent destruction of these men of God.

Only when this concentrated hatred for God and His people fully manifests itself does Jesus take up His great power and begin to reign.

The evil trinity. This trio is made up of Satan, the first beast (the Antichrist), and the second beast (a false prophet), and is a counterfeit of God the Father, Jesus, and the Holy Spirit. Satan is the key figure here. He empowers the other two (who are apparently human beings) to deceive and coerce the world into a willing worship of Satan. This is a trinity dedicated to destruction, not redemption. They do not serve men, but instead demand that men serve them. They do not die for humanity, but rather take lives when people will not obey their unholy commands.

At every point Revelation's portrait shows us a stark contrast between the motives, values, and character of Satan and those of God. In the final confrontation, Satan knows his time is short. He is eager to bring all those he can snare with him, to destruction. Most of humanity eagerly joins this rush toward disaster, angrily rejecting repentance even under the most severe of warning judgments.

Counterfeit religion. Humanity has always been religious. No culture is without some faith, some ritual practice of religion. But religion, while on the surface a good thing, has never been a friend of God. At the time of the end a "world church" joins the beast (secular power) in a systematic assault on believers, seeking their deaths.

It's all too easy in our pluralistic society to be tolerant of false religions or even to attempt to compromise Scripture's teaching in order to make room for their adherents in the family of faith. In Revelation we see the unveiling of reality. These faiths at heart are enemies of God and His people. Against them, totally committed to care for His own, stands the Lamb in all the glory of His power.

We are not to attack adherents of false faiths now. But we are to recognize the essential anti-God character of religion. We are to hold even more firmly, not to religion but to our relationship with the One who is Lord of lords and King of kings.

Political Babylon. Here we see the final culmination of world government. It leads to unparalleled prosperity but also to unparalleled regimentation. The mark of the beast is needed before a person can buy or sell anything; there is total control over the individual. The luxuries, the power, the seeming security convince people that they have no need to depend on God. Pride and self-reliance mark the rise of the world state; mourning and anguish over lost wealth mark her destruction.

In Revelation 18 we see this Babylon being destroyed. The treasures people lay up for themselves are subject to rust and theft, and to the destroying fire. No political system can unify the world or bring the blessings God alone can provide for His people. The Babylon system has to be destroyed, for it is a political system that feeds on injustice and pride and that encourages rejection of God. It is a political system that leads persons and nations astray (v. 23). It has no room for either saint or prophet, and kills those willing to witness of the reality of God (v. 24).

And what do we see of God through political Babylon? Against the transitory glimmer of human achievement, we see the glow of God's changeless glory. Against the background of the wealth destroyed in Babylon's fall, we see the treasures stored up for us in the presence of Christ Himself. Our destiny is to worship Him, not wealth or power. Man's Babylon will fall. But the city of God will stand forever and ever.

TEACHING GUIDE

Prepare
Read through these chapters to gain a panoramic view of events. It is the panorama rather than the details you want to help your group members focus on.

Explore
Prepare a reading, using verses like those quoted in the commentary. Give a one- or two-sentence summary of the contents of a chapter—then have your group members join you in a responsive reading of the refrain.

Expand
Select any of these focused studies to do together, or in teams.
1. Compare the vision of God's holiness seen in Revelation 4–5 with the vision of Isaiah in 6:1-8. Meditate on each passage. Then discuss: "How do these teach us to praise God?"
2. Or read Revelation 6–9 with Romans 2:4-10. Note particularly Rev. 6:15-17 and 9:20-21. What do we learn about the nature of God's judgments?
3. Or examine poetic praise songs found in Rev. 10–18 (11:15, 17-18; 12:10-12; 15:3-4; 16:5-7). In each context, what leads to praise? What in these chapters can *you* praise God for? What in these chapters seems hard for you to bring to God in praise?
4. Or, select one of the characters or institutions that is prominent at history's end. How does Jesus stand in contrast to that person or institution? What does God's judgment on this person or institution tell us about Jesus?

Apply
What is the single most important thing you learn about Jesus in these powerful chapters of Revelation?

STUDY GUIDE 172

Revelation 19–22

ENTRANCE TO ETERNITY

Overview

These final chapters of the Bible give us Scripture's clearest portraits of eternity. In them we see the destiny of saved and unsaved alike.

One stereotype of Christianity that is found in literature and the media is the "hellfire evangelist." He is usually portrayed as an Elmer Gantry: someone so twisted by his own sins that he finds release only by laying a burden of guilt on his listeners. He frightens them with visions of a God who seeks any excuse to drag people away to endless torment.

Often Christians, captivated by the vision of God's love in Jesus, turn away from the picture of a lake of fire and the idea of eternal damnation. A few theologians have also looked for other ways to describe the destiny of those who resist God's grace to the end. Some have suggested annihilation—the idea that for the lost, death is simply the end. The evil people of this world slip into death as into some endless and dreamless sleep; they simply cease to exist. Others have supposed a final reconciliation of all with God. Colossians 1:20 is taken to mean that the Hitlers of this world will find a place in glory with those they massacred.

But the Bible affirms the existence of a real heaven—and a real hell. And the Bible also answers the question, "How could a loving God condemn anyone to a lake of eternal fire?"

Yet we do not need to fear hell. In Jesus, our destiny is heaven.

Commentary

As background to understanding these last chapters of Revelation, where we are confronted with a lake of burning sulfur as well as a renewed and holy earth, we need to think about the nature of human beings. To see who humanity is, we must go back before the Fall (Gen. 3) to the story of Adam and Eve, told in Genesis 1–2.

"Let Us make man in Our image, in Our likeness. . . . So God created man in His own image, in the image of God He created Him" (1:26-27).

There are many other statements in Scripture that speak of man's identity and destiny. "You made him [man] a little lower than the heavenly beings," the psalmist exults (Ps. 8:5). Short-lived though we are (144:4), yet only we in all creation have a share in the image and likeness of God. Only we have been chosen to be lifted to glory (Heb. 2:10) and to be called "brethren" by the God who stooped to take on human nature (v. 17). God has always intended an unimaginable exaltation for His people.

The fact that sin broke into human experience and tainted the race has not changed God's commitment to us. In fact, our sin became the occasion for the fullest expression of God's love: He came as a Man to bear sin's punishment so that we might become righteousness in Him (2 Cor. 5:21).

At the same time, God's act of rescue, and Scripture itself, tells us that human beings are not mere sparks that glow in the dark and then are gone. God's gift of life to man, investing in us His own likeness and image, made us more than the animals. We are persons in the same way God is a Person. *Because we share this with Him, we are too significant to disappear as though we had never been. The very nature of human beings as bearers of the divine likeness demands that even after the body has returned to dust, the personality, the "living being" of Genesis 2:7, must remain.* Unlike God in that we have a beginning, we are like God in that once we are born we have no end!

To suppose that even the lost can suffer annihilation is to deny a significance to the individual that the Bible and the death of

Jesus for us constantly affirms.

Who Is God?

To see each human being as a person of eternal significance tells us something about God as well. He is a Person who loves *eternally*. You and I know what it means to suffer the loss of a loved one. Even a child suffers when a pet dies. But what a difference between the two. We know that our loved one still lives, while the pet is gone. The human being has eternal significance; the pet lives for a brief moment and then exists only as a memory. But God could not create a race to be the focus of His love whose members would lose their being and live only in His memory. He gave us something of His own nature in Creation so that He might love us and know our love forever.

When we ask the question, "Who is God?" we can only reply that He is a Person who, in love and perfect holiness, chose to create beings with whom He would share Himself, whatever the cost. And the cost was one *He,* not we, had to pay!

- It was the price of anguish, as over and over His loved ones rejected His love.
- It was the price of crucifixion-death, as His loved ones nailed Him to the cross.
- It was the price of seeing many of His loved ones reject forgiveness, selecting instead an endless death.

If we were to be truly like Him, truly free beings with choice and personal responsibility, then God could not demand that we accept His love against our will. He could not program us so that we did not have the possibility of real choice. He chose to suffer His own deep pain over each one who refuses to turn to Him. He allowed people the freedom to be endlessly separated from Him.

All this may sound speculative or philosophical. But several things are clear. He does not want "anyone to perish, but everyone to come to repentance" (2 Peter 3:9). Certainly God's choosing to suffer in order to rescue beings who turned against Him demonstrates once and for all that God takes no delight in our punishment. God is not the kind of person who would enjoy condemning anyone to a lake of fire.

It is because there is no other way to deal with the results of sin in beings whose nature grants them endless existence that the lake of fire of Revelation will exist. But for man to be truly human, and for God to share Himself with man, some such way to deal with sin had to be. It is not desirable. But it is necessary.

Hallelujah: Revelation 19

In spite of the pain, there is joy in heaven as history's end comes. As the glorified figure of the Lamb prepares to battle His enemies on earth, we hear the multitude shouting:

> Hallelujah! For our Lord God Almighty reigns. Let us rejoice and be glad and give Him glory!
>
> Revelation 19:6-7

Heaven open (Rev. 19:11-21). Immediately Christ Himself enters the battle. "He is dressed in a robe dipped in blood," and "He treads the winepress of the fury of the wrath of God Almighty" (vv. 13, 15).

The armies of the beast are gathered on earth to make war against Christ. . . . But their efforts are futile. The two human members of the evil triumvirate are "thrown alive into the fiery lake of burning sulfur" (v. 20). As for the rest of their army, all are killed in the battle, and "all the birds gorged themselves on their flesh" (v. 21).

The irresistible power of the Lamb who is also King of kings and Lord of lords ends the battle almost before it begins!

Interlude: Revelation 20:1-10

The thousand years. Now we find, somewhat surprisingly, that the battle described in Revelation 19 is followed by a period of a thousand years (20:3-4, 6-7).

During this period several things happen. First, Satan is "locked and sealed" in the Abyss, to "keep him from deceiving the nations anymore" until the thousand years end (v. 3).

Second, there is a "first resurrection" at which believers killed during the time of terror and the Antichrist's rule are given new life. "They will be priests of God and of Christ and will reign with Him for a thousand years" (v. 6). The text specifically says that the rest of the dead will not come to life until this thousand-year period is over.

Then, after the thousand years of Christ's rule on earth, Satan is released from his prison, and the final battle is fought (vv. 7-10).

Why a thousand-year interlude? Many suggestions have been made. Certainly the Old Testament prophecies of a glorious kingdom on earth can be fulfilled during this time span. But even more may be involved.

One suggestion is that during this time sin's true nature will again be demonstrated. Sin has found expression throughout the ages in the characters of both individuals and societies. Often today society itself is blamed for individual failure: the environment, some argue, programs people into actions which, in a just and moral society, they would never voluntarily choose. The rule of Jesus and the resurrected saints will provide a truly just, moral society, and thus an ideal environment. Individuals will be released from those social pressures that now stimulate them toward wrong choices. Will human beings be "good" under ideal conditions?

Revelation suggests that once Satan is freed (v. 8), he will succeed in deceiving the nations. Millions will choose, *against their environmental setting,* to follow Satan and rebel against God.

As we look at Revelation's terrible picture of final judgment, we can never forget that those who have taken sides against God have done so by their own free choice. The character of sin is again revealed in the final rebellion, and the judgment of God is shown to be just. Fire flares from heaven to destroy the rebellious host. The devil is "thrown into the lake of burning sulfur, where the beast and the false prophet had been thrown." And Scripture adds, "They will be tormented day and night forever and ever" (v. 10).

The Great White Throne: Revelation 20:11-15

Now suddenly earth and the heavens are gone. We're shown an empty universe . . . empty except for the throne of God and for humanity, gathered before Him. *Of all that God has created, only human beings, whose personalities are indestructible, remain.* All the dead not raised in the first resurrection are here, and each person is judged according to what he has done. All whose names are not written in the Book of Life are judged by their works. Since this judgment is based on the criteria of their own actions rather than on their faith in Christ, all fall short (Rom. 6:23). Then the Scripture states clearly and simply, all are "thrown into the lake of fire."

Two resurrections. This is one of the concepts taught in Revelation that is only hinted at in the Old Testament. Daniel spoke of a resurrection in which those who "sleep in the dust of the earth shall awake: some to everlasting life, others to shame and everlasting contempt" (Dan. 12:2). But dividing the resurrection into two widely separated events is a distinctive contribution of the Book of Revelation.

Forever and ever. The second resurrection, a prelude to official condemnation, is a resurrection to death rather than to life. When the believer is resurrected, he is transformed, changed to the image of Christ (Rom. 8:29; 1 John 3:2). In the resurrection of the unsaved, the individual is *unchanged.* He is conscious, aware, but his character and his attitude toward God retains sin's twist. The man consumed with anger is an angry man still. The jealous person is still jealous. The lustful still lust. In the lake of fire, the old desires burn, but are forever unsatisfied. This is one reason why the lake of fire is called the second death (Rev. 20:14). It is an endless captivity to what one is when he dies. There is no hope for change, no hope for growth, no hope for transformation. Fixed forever, unchangeable, the personality of the lost burns as much from inner torment as from the cauldron John can only liken to burning sulfur.

In this picture you and I can find no pleasure. And neither can God. But because the human personality does have endless conscious existence, and because people were made free to choose so that they might freely choose to love God, those who will not respond to God condemn themselves.

Now we can understand a little more of God. Against His own desires that all might be saved, God

- *did* create man like Himself, and so give the gift of endless life to all.
- *did* create man like Himself, and so give each of us the freedom to choose.
- *did* come in Incarnation to take on Himself the suffering that brings us forgiveness.
- *did* offer that forgiveness as a grace/gift to all who will receive it by faith, and
- *did* withhold the punishment sin deserves, extending the day of grace and postponing judgment. But ultimately God

- *will* bring all mankind before Him to face the final judgment that holiness demands.

God's desire is to bring all to everlasting life. But Scripture says that "the cowardly, the unbelieving, the vile, the murderers, the sexually immoral, those who practice magic arts, the idolaters and all liars—their place will be in the fiery lake of burning sulfur. This is the second death" (21:8).

Another View: Revelation 21:1–22:6
The description of the final judgment has been somber and sparse. There are no psalms of praise here, no sounds of joy and gladness. There is only a grim description of what must come.

But in the last two chapters of Revelation there is an obvious change of tone. We are given another view of eternity. With the task of judgment past, now the family gathers to share the joy of God's presence and the rich gifts He has prepared for those who love Him.

In these chapters we have a hint of what we call "heaven." It is a different picture from the stereotype of the dead becoming "angels," and then relaxing on the clouds with harps.

Instead we see a scene in which we each keep our individual identity—yet a world where everything is truly new.

The New Jerusalem. The first vision is of a sky city, coming down from heaven over a newly created earth. This is the Holy City, the New Jerusalem, and is identified as the dwelling place of God. From now on He will be "with men, and He will live with them" (21:3). God's presence will bring perfect peace and joy; "He will wipe away every tear from their eyes. There will be no more death or mourning or crying or pain, for the old order of things has passed away" (v. 4).

This magnificent city is described as a cube some 1,500 miles long and wide and high. Its walls are of pure gold; its foundations are of precious stones; its streets are transparent. Most importantly, the city has no temple. Nor does the city need sun or moon; God's presence within it gives light: "The nations will walk by its light, and the kings of the earth will bring their splendor into it" (v. 24).

John then goes on to picture the river of the water of life. Its clear water flows from the throne of God right through the middle of the city. The trees by its banks yield fruit; its leaves are for the "healing of the nations." In this new universe there is no curse; there is personal access to God; there is no night. God's presence provides light, and the people "will reign forever and ever" (22:5).

New cosmology. Other passages of Scripture tell us that the present heavens will "disappear with a roar; the elements will be destroyed by fire, and the earth and everything in it will be laid bare" (2 Peter 3:10). So, Peter continued, the Christian is one who looks forward to a "new heaven and a new earth, the home of righteousness" (v. 13). Peter echoed Isaiah, who prophesied:

> Behold, I will create new heavens and a new earth. The former things will not be remembered, nor will they come to mind.
>
> Isaiah 5:17

New humanity. Little is said here about the future of mankind, aside from the implication that kings and nations still exist. Men are still men, not angels. And none who enjoy this new and endless existence are tainted by sin.

To see more of what the future holds for us, we need to look at other New Testament passages. We find that when we stand in God's presence, we will be transformed into Jesus' likeness. "We shall be like Him, for we shall see Him as He is" (1 John 3:2). And Paul said that God has predestined us "to be conformed to the likeness of His Son" (Rom. 8:29). All that mankind potentially is . . . all that Jesus was as a Man . . . we will be.

Paul told the Corinthians that the believer's resurrection body will be imperishable in contrast to our present perishable body. It will be marked by power rather than weakness. It will be controlled by the spiritual, rather than subject to the physical. Yes, the dead "will be raised imperishable, and we shall be changed" (1 Cor. 15:52, see vv. 35-54). When the mortal becomes immortal, then death itself will be swallowed up in our great victory.

In these words of Scripture we see a glorious promise. But the scene is so far removed from our present situation that it is hard to get any clear picture. We can perhaps see more in the Gospel's description of Christ after His resurrection. He was able to eat with His disciples; He had flesh and bones (Luke 24; John 21). Yet He also could "appear" among them in a locked room (20:19). He was recognizable: the same individual, yet different.

Jesus' new capacities will undoubtedly be ours as well in resurrection. The greatest wonder of all is that we shall be like Him, freed from every stain of sin. To be perfected and yet retain our individual self—this is our glorious destiny. "He who overcomes," God promises, "will inherit all this, and I will be his God and he will be My son" (Rev. 21:7).

New dreams? Many have asked, "What will we *do* then?" God has given every believer gifts for ministry; each one of us participates in the great work God is doing in our world. One of His first gifts was the gift of work to Adam and Eve, so they could share in the Creation act (Gen. 2:15). He made people able to have dominion and capable of taking an active role in the supervision of God's universe. Would our creative and active God shape eternity for a *passive* existence?

Against this background, some have made fascinating suggestions about our ministry in eternity. One great Bible teacher, Dr. Donald Grey Barnhouse, used to tell of his expectation that one day God would say to him, "Donald, go create a world, people it, and govern it for Me." The endless universe itself seemed to Dr. Barnhouse a stage for the fulfillment of God's plan for man. We, who have been made in His image and likeness, and given a destiny of dominion, must (it seemed to Barnhouse) fulfill that destiny in some universal way.

But all such ideas are speculation. We are not told in Scripture just what our role or ministry in eternity will be. Yet we do know that God shaped us uniquely for Himself and for His glory. We can be sure that eternity will be full, and fulfilling, to each one of us.

Coming Soon: Revelation 22:7-21

Three times in these closing paragraphs the promise is made, "Behold, I am coming soon." Eternity may seem far off. Yet for each of us the return of Jesus and the events foretold in Revelation have an immediacy. "Soon" may be tomorrow! *There is nothing that must happen before the events we have read of in Revelation may begin.*

These paragraphs also make it clear that we are to learn to live with this sense of immediacy. Thus John reports, "Blessed is he who keeps the words of the prophecy of this book" (v. 7).

But how can we keep the words of the prophecy? We have been shown what God Himself will do at history's end. What is there for *us* to keep? The next verses explain.

The vision of a glorified Christ, stepping into history to judge, will have an impact on every reader. It is *not* an evangelistic impact: no one can be frightened into heaven. The good news that brings salvation is the story of the love and forgiveness God offers human beings in Jesus.

And so the voice of John warns, "Let him who does wrong continue to do wrong; let him who is vile continue to be vile; let him who does right continue to do right; and let him who is holy continue to be holy" (v. 11). *The words of this book will move each reader in the life direction he or she has chosen to go!*

If we have taken to heart God's call to holiness, seeing the future in Revelation will stimulate us to a holy life. If we have taken to heart God's call to do right, then seeing Jesus at history's end will deepen our desire to do right.

Illusion is always the enemy of holiness. We delude ourselves into thinking that what we do now is unimportant, that we need not make choices, that we need not act responsibly. We may feel that we only need settle down and wait for Christ to come, and all our problems will be over. But we are ministers, members of the body of Christ! As such, we are His voice and arms and legs and hands and feet in this time of grace. And the present time *is* of utmost importance. The present time is the Age of Grace, the time of God's kindness and tolerance and patience, meant to lead all persons to repentance (Rom. 2:4). In this age of God's extended kindness, you and I, as agents of His reconciliation, are called to grow more like Him and to communicate by our own love His love for others.

The unveiling of the righteous Judge in Revelation is not meant to overpower us with guilt because of what we may not have done in the past. It is rather to help us look ahead and motivate us to live for Christ and for others. He *is* coming soon; the judgment will then begin. While we yearn for that coming for our sakes, we also yearn to share the love of God with others *now* . . . for their sakes.

Revelation, then, is a book for believers. The Spirit and the Bride say, "Come." And because we are convinced that He will come soon, we dedicate ourselves to do right and to be holy. but for the others, the message of judgment will not melt the heart like the message of God's love. For them the Good News of Jesus' life and death, unveiled in John's Gospel as the coming of grace and love, is the message we have to share.

TEACHING GUIDE

Prepare
Read these Revelation chapters several times, to sense the tone of each.

Explore
1. Have your group members brainstorm everything they can think of that convinces them God is a loving Person.
2. Luke 16:19-31 reports the story of a rich man and a beggar named Lazarus. What in the story suggests that the dead are not only conscious, but also retain their capacity to sense and feel?
3. Have your group members read Revelation 3:19-20, and then answer these questions:
- What is the tone of the chapters?
- Is there any hint of vindictiveness?
- How do these chapters help you understand the character of sin?

4. Finally, brainstorm together: "Can you think of any alternatives to the final judgment described here?" List your group members' suggestions. Then in a mini-lecture speak about the nature of man and the nature of God. In view of these truths, evaluate the alternative. Can your members see why God did not choose any of them?

Expand
Have your group read individually the picture of "heaven" given in Revelation 21–22. Afterward, ask each to share: "What one thing in this picture is most attractive to you?"

Apply
Suggest that we cannot "frighten" anyone into heaven (see Rev. 22:11). But encourage each group member, in view of the reality of both hell and heaven, to pray for and witness to neighbors and friends.

STUDY GUIDE 173

New Testament Truths

WHO IS GOD?

Overview

Looking back over Scripture we can see and summarize truths that have been uniquely revealed in the New Testament.

There are a number of obvious contrasts between the Testaments. The Old Testament revelation came over a span of a thousand years; the new in a burst of unveiling initiated by Jesus' incarnation.

The Old Testament affirms a special relationship between God and Israel; the New Testament proclaims a New Covenant extended to all humankind. The Old Testament looks forward to the coming of the Messiah; the New Testament looks back, and finds in the Cross and Resurrection a Suffering Saviour.

There are other contrasts. Law, as a guide to response to God, has been replaced by the Spirit who rewrites righteousness within. In the intimacy of a spiritual family, with immediate access to God, we know the realities only symbolized by the Old Testament system of sacrifices and priesthood.

Yet, despite the differences, the unity of the Old and New Testaments stands out. While Law was set aside, the righteousness it represented was not. The Old Testament sacrifices were discontinued, but only because the perfect Sacrifice had been offered.

In looking at New Testament theology we are *not* looking for a different God or a different faith. Instead, we look to see unveilings that make the New Testament a completion, rather than a replacement, of the Old. Nowhere do we see this more clearly than in our view of God, and of humankind.

Commentary

The New Testament brings our destiny in Christ into focus. The realities of God's dealings with people are fully exposed now; what was hinted at is given full attention. Something similar happens in relation to God Himself. We know much about God through His words and works reported in the Old Testament. Yet the deepest revelation of God as a Person awaited the coming of Jesus, in whom we truly come to know the God of love.

His Personhood: Ephesians 1:1-14; John 17

The Old Testament begins with God. The underlying reality in Genesis 1 is not the material universe but God. He is always viewed as a Person, never a mindless force. He is a Person who plans, chooses, acts, and enjoys His labors.

But the person of God seems remote in much of the Old Testament. The warmth of intimate relationship, while known by many (such as the psalmists) was not central in each believer's experience of God. God was faithful, yes. He loved His people; acted for them when they were in need; disciplined them when they strayed; guided them spiritually, morally, and socially through the Law. But still there was hesitancy. The Israelites did not easily call God "Father." Abraham and Isaac and Jacob were fathers to the race.

The New Testament reveals God not only as a Person but as a Person desiring intimacy. The dominant image of God in the New Testament is that of Father. He has all the attributes of personhood and a warmth in His every act that, while present in the old days, was not fully realized. Paul expressed it amazingly: We cry, "*Abba*, Father" (Rom. 8:15). We feel the impact of this cry when we realize that *Abba* is one of the first words an Aramaic child uttered as he reached up toward a father who bent down to cuddle him: *Abba* is "Daddy"!

God a Person? Yes. And such a Person. The Sovereign Lord, the Creator, the Redeemer, the King of Hosts, the Mighty God . . . all this . . . and to us, "Daddy."

Trinity: John 5:16-47; Ephesians 1:3-14
There are numerous indications in the Old Testament that the one God of Israel is a unity of Persons. "Let *Us* make God in *Our* image," God said (Gen. 1:26). Even that great statement of affirmation given Israel in Deuteronomy 6:4, "Hear, O Israel: The Lord our God the Lord is One," selects as the word for "One" a term used for "a cluster of, or composed of, many grapes."

The New Testament expands the hint of plurality by revealing the three Persons who make up the Trinity. There is the Father. There is the Son. And there is the Holy Spirit. Each distinct, yet together One.

Neither the Old nor New Testament attempts to explain how three can be one. Instead they simply insist that Father and Son are One (John 1:1; 10:30); that the Spirit proceeds from Father and Son (John 15:26); that Each is a personality distinct from the other, while one with the others (Mark 1:10-11; John 14:26; 16:12-15).

This is a great mystery that no analogy can explain. No definition that leans toward modalism (the idea that the One simply expresses Himself in three aspects or modes) nor a definition that robs the Son and Spirit of their full deity will do. Trinity is an unavoidable truth in the New Testament. Understanding of that mystery awaits our resurrection.

Incarnation: John 1:1-5; Philippians 2:1-11
Old Testament history provides many evidences of God's concern for His people. But the ultimate evidence of God's willingness to become involved in our human condition is the Incarnation. In wonder Paul repeated a confession of faith of the early church:

> He appeared in a body, was vindicated by the Spirit, was seen by angels, was preached among the nations, was believed on in the world, was taken up in glory.
>
> 1 Timothy 3:16

Jesus often spoke of His coming from the Father and returning to the Father. The clear teaching of the New Testament is that the Son existed as God from all eternity with the Father. In an inconceivable act of self-emptying, the eternal Son set aside His prerogatives as God, and entered the world He had created—as a Baby. "He too shared in their humanity so that by His death He might destroy him who holds the power of death" (Heb. 2:14). To accomplish His redemptive work, God became truly Man, blending into one the divine and human natures.

It's clear from Scripture that there is distinctive purpose behind the Incarnation. The central goal was to accomplish redemption; Jesus lived a sinless life and died a sacrificial death in atonement for our sins. Yet there were other purposes as well. For the first time, God was *seen* in our world. Jesus' life and actions express the person of God in ways no words could have. His life defines holiness. His compassion explains love. His patience opens our eyes to God's heart attitude toward you and me. Most of all the Incarnation tells us that God cares enough to become involved. He does not stand back, urging us on from a safe vantage point. He strips Himself of His glory and, accepting the form of a Man, humbles Himself even to death.

Once and for all the Incarnation decides the unsettling question, "What does God really think about me?" Is God a policeman, looking for crimes to punish? Or a nagging parent, always finding fault? Is He an impersonal force, oblivious to insignificant humans as He crushes mankind beneath the steamroller of history? Is God an idealist, who in His concern to restructure society ignores the individual? Or is He so caught up in Himself that He demands we cringe before Him, caring only that we offer fearful praise? What *does* God think of us?

To God we are not criminals, not naughty children, not ants, not pawns in some grand game, not "nothings." To God we are special, the objects of His love and concern. Rather than demanding service from us, God sets aside His robes of glory and becomes our Servant. Rather than demand full payment from us for sin, He gives His own life in our place. God became Man to tell us—and show us—how much He loves us.

Sacrifice: Hebrews 10; Romans 3:12-26
The death of the incarnate Christ on Calvary was the climax of His life on earth. It was an event exceeded in significance only by the Resurrection. The New Testament explains that death as an atoning sacrifice.

In the Old Testament, sacrifice played a

central role in Israel's spiritual experience. Immediately after God gave the Law, He instituted the sacrificial system. The blood of the sacrificial animal, offered on the altar, made atonement, or covering, for sin. Sin was not removed, but it was covered. God was then free to act in grace toward those He loved even though their characters and actions cried out for judgment.

The question, "How can a holy God deal kindly with sinful man?" is answered in the Old Testament by sacrifice. "I have given [the blood] . . . on the altar . . . that makes atonement for one's life" (Lev. 17:11).

But the blood of sacrificial animals was not able to remove sin, only to cover it. Death is the necessary and essential outcome of sin. Paul explained, "The wages of sin is death" (Rom. 6:23). Even God could not set aside this necessity: between darkness and light, holiness and sin, death and life, there can be no compromise. The issue must be faced and resolved.

The New Testament reveals the divine solution. Sin brings death, but God sent His own Son to die as a Substitute for the sinner.

God presented Jesus, the Bible says:

> As a sacrifice of atonement, through faith in His blood. He did this to demonstrate His justice, because in His forbearance He had left the sins committed beforehand unpunished—He did it to demonstrate His justice at the present time, so as to be just and the One who justifies the man who has faith in Jesus.
>
> Romans 3:25-26

Jesus, by His death, entered the presence of God "once for all by His own blood, having obtained eternal redemption" for us (Heb. 9:12).

The Old Testament sacrifices were, in effect, a dramatization of Calvary. The repeated lessons, teaching that only death could provide a remedy for sin, looked forward to that once-for-all death of God's Son.

And so our understanding of God grows. Who is He? A Person. One in three.

One who through human birth became totally involved in our condition. One who ultimately sacrificed His own life that through His death you and I might be made alive.

Indwelling: John 14:16-27; Romans 8:1-17

God's involvement in our lives is not limited to history. Jesus entered time and space to break the power of sin and make eternal life available to us. But the New Testament reveals that God continues to be involved; the Holy Spirit lives in the renewed personality of the one who chooses to trust Jesus.

This is one of the great contrasts between the Old and New Testaments. God has always yearned for an intimate relationship with His straying creatures. Through the Law He pointed out the way of holiness, and He held the door open through sacrifice. Yet the relationship was never as close as it might have been. Those who believed, trusted, accepted, and responded to the mediating Word of the Law. But there was not the *immediate* relationship, the intimacy of children with a father.

In the guidance pattern of the Old Testament, the Law was an *external* guide to holy living. It was outside the person, pointing the way for faith and standing as a testimony against unbelief. Where there was failure, sacrifice was available to restore fellowship. Yet in Old Testament times there was a veil hung between the holy of holies, that place in the temple where God's presence dwelt, and the worshipers were outside.

When Jesus died, the veil was torn from top to bottom to signify that the way into the holiest is now open. Both the Law and worship revealed God's desire to have fellowship with man. Yet both also spoke of a barrier that held God back from the depth of intimacy He desired. After Jesus' resurrection, God acted to initiate a close relationship. God the Holy Spirit came to take up residence within the personality of the believer.

The presence of the Holy Spirit within us is the basis for a change both in the Law and in worship. Paul said that the Law was in force "until faith should be revealed" (Gal. 3:23). Now that Christ has died, responsiveness to the Spirit within replaces the external rule of Law. The Old Testament foretold this change. Looking forward to a time when the New Covenant would replace the Mosaic, Jeremiah spoke God's promise: "I will put My law in their minds and write it on their hearts" (Jer. 31:33). The pathway of righteousness that the Law described is now, in the person of the Holy

Spirit, engraved *within* us. God's own love of righteousness grows within us as we come to know Him better and learn to follow the leading of His Spirit within.

There is a similar change in access to God. "Let us then approach the throne of grace with confidence" (Heb. 4:16). In another passage Paul explained. We have now received full rights as sons, through faith in Jesus. "Because you are sons, God sent the Spirit of His Son into our hearts" (Gal. 4:6). As a member of the family, we have immediate access, guaranteed by the presence of the Holy Spirit in our lives.

God's involvement with individuals, even the unthinkably *total* involvement of God in each believer's daily life, is hinted at in the Old Testament. But the fullness of that reality is revealed only in the New.

Many Christians fail to grasp God's total involvement with us. But what a vital reality to see! *We are never alone; never cut off from God's presence.* In every time of need, whether for mercy (because we have failed) or for grace to help (when we are challenged beyond our abilities), we have the fullness of God Himself within. In the person of the Holy Spirit, God continues to reach gently into our lives. Paul, caught by the wonder of it all, praised God:

> Now to Him who is able to do immeasurably more than all we ask or imagine, according to His power that is at work within us, to Him be glory in the church and in Christ Jesus throughout all generations, forever and ever! Amen.
>
> Ephesians 3:20-21

Who Is God?

OT	NT passages	NT insights
GOD is a Person	John 17 Romans 8:15 Ephesians 1:1-14	
GOD is Three in One	John 5:16-47 Ephesians 1:3-14	
God is known indirectly through Word and act	John 1:1-5 Hebrews 1:1-3 Philippians 2:1-11	
Animal sacrifice maintained relationship with God	Hebrews 10 Romans 3:21-26	
God was present with Israel in the temple	John 14:16-27 Romans 8:1-17	

TEACHING GUIDE

Prepare
Read through each of the major passages referenced in the commentary, and jot down your answer to the study questions on the chart (above).

Explore
Introduce the chart which sums up Old Testament revelation about God, and the questions that were incompletely answered. Let each group member choose one area to focus on; then form teams of those who made the same choice. Each team is to study the key New Testament passages, answer the questions, and determine how the fuller revelation of the New Testament adds to our present relationship with God.

Expand
After each team has studied its New Testa-

ment passages, determined its answers, and summarized what the New Testament revelation adds to our present relationship with the Lord, come together again to share.

Share in the whole group, which will permit you to add insights a team may have missed. Or, for variety, form new small groups of one or two members from each team. This alternative will give everyone a chance to share and talk about what they have discovered.

Apply

Complete the chart together. Then ask each person to write a brief paragraph of praise. Spend the last five minutes letting each person lead in praising God by reading his or her praise paragraphs.

STUDY GUIDE 174

New Testament Truths

WHO IS MAN?

Overview

New Testament theology is not just about God. It is also about human beings. The Scriptures not only tell us who God is, but they define human nature and human destiny as well.

Philosophers of all the ages have searched for the meaning and purpose of human life. Yet the answers are here, in the Bible. Those answers are not just for the philosopher who wishes to speculate. They are answers to the basic and practical questions that shape the lives of every man.

The Bible helps us understand why we do things we hate. It helps us learn how to experience a new birth that brings a change within. The Bible shows us how to live our present life in intimate fellowship with God. And it teaches us how to develop the relationships with others that not only help us to grow, but also express the love of Christ in our world.

Here the New Testament throws open the door to understanding truths only hinted at in the Old. If we are to truly live a human life in intimate fellowship with God, we need to understand what Scripture says about who we are, about sin, death, life, faith, new birth, family, transformation, incarnation, and resurrection as well.

What a privilege it is to help those we teach grasp something of the wonder we find in the Word of God. And to help them shape their new lives in accord with God's truth.

Commentary

The New Testament brings our destiny in Christ into focus. The realities of God's dealings with people are fully exposed now; what was just hinted at is now given great attention. In it all we learn about that wonderful relationship God invites us to have with Himself, and with His other people on earth.

Man: Romans 8:15-31; Hebrews 2

The Old Testament presents the human race as the apex of God's creation. Only we share the image of God; only we participate in dominion over creation (Gen. 1; Ps. 8). The New Testament reveals that God did not intend for us to remain creatures forever. God means to lift us to glory as sons, acknowledging us as Jesus' brothers.

Hebrews 2 establishes that we are God's special concern. We are so important to God that He chose to share our humanity and, by dying free us from our bondage to death. The evolutionary theory encouraged us to search for our roots in the heavings of some primeval sea, and to see ourselves as the product of random matchings and mutations. But the Bible affirms man's uniqueness. Our roots are in God's act of Creation. We are the product of His conscious, loving plan. Each human being has worth and dignity because God affirms our identity and importance.

Sin: Romans 1:18-21; 5:12-21

While we are the focus of God's creation and the objects of God's love, we are also sinners. Genesis tells us of the entrance of sin into human history. The rest of the Old Testament traces the impact of sin on individuals and society.

In spite of clear guidelines from God outlining the way of holiness, Israel constantly turned from the Law to sin and idolatry. Some terrible moral fault seems to warp and twist individuals and society.

In the New Testament Paul explained that sin makes us unresponsive to God. Rather than choosing to reach out to Him, we jerk away. We desire darkness rather than light, and willingly commit ourselves to selfishness and sins. Sin is more than lawless acts: it is woven into our fallen nature. We commit acts of sin because we are sinners: the moral distortion that brings tragedy to the race is deeply imbedded in each individual's personality.

Why do people reject a God who loves them and wants only their best? Sin. For sin alienates us and expresses itself in antagonism to the true God.

Why do men and women who know what is right persist in choosing to do wrong? Sin. For sin motivates us to unreasonable passions for evil.

Why are we who share a common humanity divided into warring camps by hurts and hatreds? Sin. For sin demands that selfish passions be satisfied. Sin angrily rejects others who seem to threaten satisfaction of our selfish needs.

Why do societies develop in ways that institutionalize injustice, create poverty, and dehumanize the poor? Sin. All the alienation, all the antagonism and selfishness of individuals, is multiplied in society. Injustice is the social expression of a fault rooted deeply within the personality of every person born into our world.

Sin has not changed the fact that God loves me or that he sees I have worth and value. But sin has cut me off from the experience of God's love and has kept me from enjoying God's kind of love in human relationships.

Death: Romans 5:1-14; Ephesians 2

When I turn from God to sin, I cut myself off from the source of life and become subject to death. The Genesis story records how God warned Adam that the day he ate from the forbidden tree, he would die. And death came: immediate death as alienation from God and God's life, followed all too soon by a physical death that separates us from the material universe as well. *The Dictionary of New Testament Theology* (Colin Brown, [ed.], Zondervan) comments that this immediate death is the basic condition of the sinner's life. "He lives as a sinner *in* death. Death is thus the power dominating his life, and to that extent a *present* reality. 'Spiritual' death and 'physical' death, inextricably bound up together, constitute the reality of a life in sin."

The fact of our death in sin explains our helplessness. Where there is no life, there can be no hope. Physical death cuts us off completely from the material universe. There is no response to sights or sounds or touch; the capacity to respond to such stimuli is gone. Just so, spiritual death cuts us off completely from God. There is no response to His words or acts or touch: the capacity to respond to Him is completely extinguished.

Our only hope lies not in any efforts we might make to reestablish relationship with God, but in the possibility that He may act. The only act of God that can help is if He would give a gift of life. Only an inner resurrection, bringing life where there is death, can meet our need.

Life: John 3:16-21; Ephesians 2:1-10

The Bible says God "gives . . . life to the dead and calls things that are not as though they were" (Rom. 4:17). What we could not earn or merit, God provided as a free gift. "When we were dead," the Bible says, He "made us alive with Christ" (Eph. 2:5).

As we have seen in 1 John, the life God gives us is *eternal* life. It is eternal because of its endless extent. It is eternal because it is God's own life. Peter called the gift of life an implanting within the believer's personality of God's own imperishable seed (1 Peter 1:23).

In the New Testament the great dividing line between people is not religious, sociological, or racial. It does not matter whether we are born into a Christian, Buddhist, or Communist culture. It does not matter whether we are rich or poor, ignorant or educated, oppressed or oppressor. The great issue is simply: do we have the life of God within, or are we still in the realm of death?

Many of our debates and differences recede to insignificance in the face of this basic question. Are your practices like mine? Do you believe the same way about prophecy? Do your ideas on holiness match mine? Does your experience of the Holy Spirit duplicate my own? Such issues divide Christians today. But in God's sight the dividing line is: Have you received new life from Christ? Then you belong to Him . . . along with all the rest of His forever family. Do you lack the new life? Then you stumble in the realm of death, cut off from the life of God, out of fellowship with Him and His people.

Faith: Romans 4; Galatians 3

In the Old Testament, God's relationship with His people was regulated by a covenant, a commitment or promise. The Psalms are full of expressions of confidence in God's faithfulness to His covenant promises. "I trust in Your unfailing love; my heart rejoices in Your salvation" (Ps. 13:5).

Such expressions focus attention on the trust relationship that developed between God and His people. Faith is not a discovery of the New Testament writers. It is the eternal bridge of relationship spanning the gulf caused by sin. What the New Testament does is to put that faith relationship in sharp focus, and calls for individual response to God.

The New Testament points out that each individual has an opportunity to receive God's offer of salvation as a free gift. Each of us must choose to make a commitment to Jesus as Saviour and Lord or to hold back. Opportunity and decision both hinge on trust. Life and death depend on our responding in faith to God's presentation of Himself in Christ as trustworthy.

In Old Testament times the individual seems almost submerged in the nation. It is Israel as a whole that is disobedient and undisciplined, or responsive and victorious. It is Israel that has a destiny. . . . Messiah is to come to deliver the chosen people. Individuals were noticed and cared for by God, but the nation was the focus of the prophets' concern.

In the New Testament, however, the faith-invitation is directed to individuals, not to a nation. It is not the historic destiny of each man and woman. When the New Testament speaks of faith, the doorway of invitation is opened wide and each person may choose to step across—or not.

New Birth: John 3

Entering into a new spiritual life is like being born again. The analogy has many implications. Each is closely associated with growth. A newborn child has the potential for maturity; yet the fulfillment of that promise comes only after a long process of growth and learning. The Christian too is urged to keep on growing in Christ, and is reminded that we "are being built together" to become a dwelling in which God lives by His Spirit (Eph. 2:22).

There is another implication that is sometimes overlooked. Birth catapults the newborn into a different world, in which a totally different lifestyle must be learned. Understandings, attitudes, values, and behaviors must be developed.

Spiritual birth may come after understandings, attitudes, values, and behaviors that contradict the Christian lifestyle have become deeply ingrained. Colossians says that God has "rescued us from the dominion of darkness and brought us into the kingdom of the Son He loves" (1:13). A citizen of God's kingdom has to reject the old ways of darkness while learning how to live a new life.

This kind of learning involves far more than gaining new information: a personality is being rebuilt. To understand how spiritual growth takes place, we need only to look at the process of an infant growing. How does a maturing child learn to function in society? Essentially, lifestyle is learned and personality shaped in the family. In the context of intimate and loving relationships provided by the family, a way of life is both taught and caught, explained and modeled. The family relationship provides the essential context for the growth of an infant. In the same way, every born-again Christian needs a family in which to grow.

The exciting announcement of the New Testament is that God has provided just such a family for us, in one another.

One Family: Romans 12; Ephesians 2:11–3:20

Three New Testament figures portray the community of those who have been given life in Christ. One is family. This is reflected in the New Testament's many uses of the terms "brother" and "sister" and in multiple references to our new position as children of God.

The second figure is that of a body. We are pictured in such intimate relationship with Jesus and one another that only the organic relationship of cell linked to cell, interdependent organs, and a head in loving control, can portray the reality. The third picture is of a temple into which both individuals and the church as a whole are built as a fitting home for God's Holy Spirit.

In each of these figures, intimate relationship, oneness, and unity are stressed. We are linked to one another as brothers and sisters, fitted together as parts of the body, joined by the Master Builder so that no cracks appear between the building blocks. The family analogy stresses the quality of relationship, the body highlights the division of labor, and the temple portrays essential holiness.

But why was the family chosen to epitomize a quality relationship? And what characteristics of family relationships are most significant?

If it is going to be normal and healthy, a family needs to express love and acceptance. The family expresses attitudes and values in daily behavior and explores these in conversation. So a healthy family life is marked by open communication, by honest sharing of what is happening within each person. The family is a shared life, with example and instruction, correction and encouragement. There lifestyle and character develop.

How striking then to see these same characteristics in the New Testament church. "Be devoted to one another in brotherly love" (Rom. 12:10). Christians are called to long-term commitment, shared lives, and open communication. We are to live comfortably with others and look to our leaders for an example of the kind of persons we are to become.

God has provided believers with a family in which He means us to live and grow.

At times we lose this vision of the church as a family, and we think of it as an organization. We think of it as buildings and programs and activities, rather than as a network of relationships. We involve ourselves with tasks, committees, and service at the expense of love for one another. We neglect getting to know and supporting each other. It's then that our growth in Christ is stunted or warped. Just as poor family relationships cause personality problems for growing children, poor relationships within the family of God cause problems for growing Christians. But poor relationships are not necessary! We can recover the New Testament emphasis on the church as family . . . and love one another as Christ commands.

Transformation: Romans 8:28-29; 1 Corinthians 13; 2 Corinthians 3

What kind of growth can be expected in the newborn Christian? The Bible says that we shall take on Jesus' likeness. "We shall be like Him," John promises, "for we shall see Him as He is" (1 John 3:2).

This transformation does not imply loss of individual personality or identity. It does mean, however, a change in values and perspectives, a new love for light, and a rejection of darkness. It means we will love God and will want to take on His motivations and desires.

As we are transformed, we will grow to love "as I have loved you" (John 13:34). "Love your enemies," Jesus instructed His disciples (Matt. 5:43). He went on to demonstrate that kind of love by dying for those who were so eager to kill Him.

It's helpful to think of transformation as becoming loving. "Your attitude should be the same as that of Christ Jesus" (Phil. 2:5). Then Paul went on to portray the love expressed by Jesus as He became a Servant and then died for us. What's more, the New Testament gives an interesting equation linking love and law. "He who loves his fellowman has fulfilled the law." All the commandments are "summed up in this one rule: 'Love your neighbor as yourself.' Love does no harm to its neighbor. Therefore love is the fulfillment of law" (Rom. 13:8-10).

Incarnation: Ephesians 4:17–5:20; Colossians 2:6-15; 3:1-17

When John wrote, "Whoever claims to live in Him must walk as Jesus did" (1 John 2:6), he introduced an amazing truth. *The Incarnation has not ended!*

Jesus perfectly expressed the reality of God in a human personality. We can never enflesh God as Jesus did, in fullness. But we *do* express God in this world. God has taken up residence in us and through the Word and the Spirit and the family is reshaping us to be like Jesus. Paul bluntly says that we "reflect the Lord's glory," for we "are being transformed into His likeness with ever-increasing glory, which comes from the Lord, who is the Spirit" (2 Cor. 3:18). God still walks the earth in the person of the believer. He still expresses His love through incarnation.

We can see why the family is so vital in God's plan and why the church as a family received so much New Testament attention. It is in the family that the newborn is nurtured. It is in the family that transformation takes place. If we are to represent God in our world today, we must be like Jesus. If we are to become like Jesus, the church must be the family God designed . . . not an impersonal organization.

What happens as we incarnate God? First, as we live a life of love, we help everyone see

God as the loving Father He is. Secondly, as we live a holy life, we turn our backs on the sins that destroy individuals and society. Our full commitment to God's values and priorities is a vivid testimony to God. Jesus, the Light of the world, is reflected in our faces. In that reflection both evil and good are made known to all people.

A third aspect of Incarnation is seen in the direction of our love. It is intense for those who are our brothers and sisters, but it is also warm for those who are as yet outside the family. We can express our love in concern for physical and social as well as spiritual needs of those around us. Jesus fed the hungry crowds and healed the paralytic as well as forgave him.

At the same time, the Christian's concern must be for people's deepest need, for release from sin's grip. Jesus sought out sinners, explaining that the sick, not the healthy, need a doctor (Matt. 9:12).

Incarnation means that as we experience the new life, we will love our brothers and sisters, grow in holiness, and reach out to those yet living in the realm of spiritual death. Our relationships with other Christians as well as with non-Christians around us will be transformed.

And so we are again confronted with the fact that the New Testament emphasizes relationships. In the New Testament focus on persons, we are called to new ways of life, to new kinds of relationships.

- With God, we are to joyfully cast off our fears and relax in the reality of a Father's love. We need never question His commitment to us.
- With fellow Christians, we are to draw closer in love and service. We are never again alone because we are members of a family that is one in Christ.
- With non-Christians, we are also to build bridges of love. We may reject their lifestyles, but we are to care for the persons themselves with a respect and compassion that reflects Christ's self-sacrificial love.

The transformation we seek will reorder our priorities. The world, with its cravings of the flesh, its lust of eye, and pride of possession will no longer appeal. People, not things, will become of ultimate concern. And we will experience this transformation as we live close to others in the family of God.

Resurrection: 1 Corinthians 15; 1 Thessalonians 4:13-18

In speaking of eternal life, the New Testament gives a new emphasis to resurrection. Jesus presented Himself as "the Resurrection and the Life" (John 11:25). Individuals can look forward to an endless life in a place prepared for them (John 14:2). What's more, the ancient and terrible grip of sin will at last be broken. In the resurrection "we shall be like Him, for we shall see Him as He is" (1 John 3:2).

The Old Testament does speak of resurrection (Isa. 26:19; Dan. 12:2). But this focus is on God's purpose for humankind on earth, not on the eternal destiny of the individual. When the promised Messiah comes, the Old Testament affirms, God will redeem His people. He will establish justice on the earth, bring the Gentiles into the covenant of God, and reign over a kingdom that supplants all the competing kingdoms of man. The shattering impact of war, the degradation of poverty, the pain of sickness and early death—all these will be abolished when the Messiah comes to reign.

Then came the unfolding of the New Covenant in Christ's blood. Not only will Jesus the Messiah bring in the kingdom; Jesus the Messiah will bring individuals eternal life, now! He will call out men and women to live God's life in the sin-warped world. Then they will know a personal resurrection, in which the transformation begun is complete, to forever reflect Jesus in their restored personalities.

The kingdom promises will be kept. Jesus speaks of them (Matt. 24). The early church expected them (Acts 1:6-7). The whole New Testament strains forward toward a second, visible coming of its Lord in glory (1 Cor. 1:7; 2 Thes. 1:3-10). But the visible kingdom of Jesus on earth is now understood as only one part of God's complex and wonderful plan. Individuals can look forward to resurrection and to eternal life.

The New Testament even reveals a resurrection for all creation. This universe will be dissolved in a fervent heat and put away, like a worn-out garment. Then God will shape a new heaven and a new earth to be the home of righteousness (Rom. 8:18-21; 2 Peter 3:13).

But what of those who pass from this world without faith or life? What of those who fight any response to God, and choose the darkness rather than the light? There is resurrection for them too, but not to life and fellowship with God. Their resurrection is to death and endless separation, which the Bible graphically calls a "lake of fire" (Rev. 20:14). God, unwilling that any should perish, offers the free gift to all. But not all will accept it.

Through both Testaments the underlying reality remains the same. God seeks personal relationship with us, whom He created in His image. God's deep personal concern for us is revealed through the whole of Scripture.

The teachings about man's nature, about sin, about death and life, about faith and resurrection, are to be found in the Old as well as in the New Testaments. But in the New Testament the focus is sharpened. In the New, the wonder is fully revealed.

Now we can know the destiny that is ours in Jesus Christ.

Who Are We?

Questions	Scripture	Answers
How special are human beings?	Hebrews 2 Romans 8:15-31	
What impact does "sin" have on us?	Romans 1:18-21 Romans 5:12-21	
What is the nature of "death"?	Romans 5:1-14 Ephesians 2	
What is "life" and how is it received?	John 3:16-21 Ephesians 2:1-10	
What role does "faith" play in relationship with God?	Romans 4 Galatians 3	
What does "new birth" imply?	John 3	
Why did God make us "family"?	Romans 12 Ephesians 2:11–3:20	
What does God seek to do in us now?	Romans 8:28-29 1 Corinthians 13 2 Corinthians 3	
How can we represent Jesus here?	Ephesians 4:17–5:20 Colossians 2:6-15 Colossians 3:1-17	

TEACHING GUIDE

Prepare
Read through each of the major passages referenced in the commentary, and jot down your answers to the study questions on the chart.

Explore
Introduce the chart which raises basic questions about our relationship with God and others. Let each group member choose an area of interest, and form teams of those who select the same area. Each is to examine the passages referred to and come up with answers to the question(s).

Expand
After teams have explored the passages suggested with their question(s), come

together again. Work through the chart on the chalkboard, filling in answers from each team and adding your insights from the text or your personal study.

Apply

Go around the circle, asking each person to share what truth explored suggests God's personal will for his or her life just now.

INDEX